ENCYCLOPEDIA OF
WORLD BIOGRAPHY
SUPPLEMENT

30

ENCYCLOPEDIA OF WORLD BIOGRAPHY

SUPPLEMENT

$\dfrac{\text{A}}{\text{Z}}$ **30**

GALE
CENGAGE Learning

Detroit • New York • San Francisco • New Haven. Conn • Waterville. Maine • London

Encyclopedia of World Biography Supplement, Volume 30

Project Editor: James Craddock

Editorial: Tracie Moy, Jeffrey Muhr

Image Research and Acquisition: Leitha Ehteridge-Sims

Rights Acquisition and Management: Mollika Basu, Jermaine Bobbitt, Jackie Jones

Imaging and Multimedia: Lezlie Light

Manufacturing: Drew Kalasky

For product information and technology assistance, contact us at
Gale Customer Support, 1-800-877-4253.
For permission to use material from this text or product,
submit all requests online at **www.cengage.com/permissions.**
Further permissions questions can be emailed to
permissionrequest@cengage.com

Gale
27500 Drake Rd.
Farmington Hills, MI, 48331-3535

ISBN-13: 978-1-4144-5905-9
ISBN-10: 1-4144-5905-X
ISSN 1099-7326

This title is also available as an e-book.
ISBN-13: 978-1-4144-6278-3 ISBN-10: 1-4144-6278-6
Contact your Gale sales representative for ordering information.

Printed in the United States of America
1 2 3 4 5 6 7 12 11 10 09 08

CONTENTS

INTRODUCTION

The study of biography has always held an important, if not explicitly stated, place in school curricula. The absence in schools of a class specifically devoted to studying the lives of the giants of human history belies the focus most courses have always had on people. From ancient times to the present, the world has been shaped by the decisions, philosophies, inventions, discoveries, artistic creations, medical breakthroughs, and written works of its myriad personalities. Librarians, teachers, and students alike recognize that our lives are immensely enriched when we learn about those individuals who have made their mark on the world we live in today.

Encyclopedia of World Biography Supplement, Volume 30, provides biographical information on 175 individuals not covered in the 17-volume second edition of *Encyclopedia of World Biography (EWB)* and its supplements, Volumes 18, 19, 20, 21, 22, 23, 24, 25, 26, 27, 28, and 29. Like other volumes in the *EWB* series, this supplement represents a unique, comprehensive source for biographical information on those people who, for their contributions to human culture and society, have reputations that stand the test of time. Each original article ends with a bibliographic section. There is also an index to names and subjects, which cumulates all persons appearing as main entries in the *EWB* second edition, the Volume 18, 19, 20, 21, 22, 23, 24, 25, 26, 27, 28, and 29 supplements, and this supplement—more than 8,000 people!

Articles. Arranged alphabetically following the letter-by-letter convention (spaces and hyphens have been ignored), articles begin with the full name of the person profiled in large, bold type. Next is a boldfaced, descriptive paragraph that includes birth and death years in parentheses. It provides a capsule identification and a statement of the person's significance. The essay that follows is approximately 2,000 words in length and offers a substantial treatment of the person's life. Some of the essays proceed chronologically while others confine biographical data to a paragraph or two and move on to a consideration and evaluation of the subject's work. Where very few biographical facts are known, the article is necessarily devoted to an analysis of the subject's contribution.

Following the essay is a bibliographic section arranged by source type. Citations include books, periodicals, and online Internet addresses for World Wide Web pages, where current information can be found.

Portraits accompany many of the articles and provide either an authentic likeness, contemporaneous with the subject, or a later representation of artistic merit. For artists, occasionally self-portraits have been included. Of the ancient figures, there are depictions from coins, engravings, and sculptures; of the moderns, there are many portrait photographs.

Index. The *EWB Supplement* index is a useful key to the encyclopedia. Persons, places, battles, treaties, institutions, buildings, inventions, books, works of art, ideas, philosophies, styles, movements—All are indexed for quick reference just as in a general encyclopedia. The index entry for a person includes a brief identification with birth and death dates *and* is cumulative so that any person for whom an article was written who appears in the second edition of *EWB* (volumes 1-16) and its supplements (volumes 18-30) can be located. The subject terms within the index, however, apply only to volume 30. Every index reference includes the title of the article to which the reader is being directed as well as the volume and page numbers.

Because *EWB Supplement,* Volume 30, is an encyclopedia of biography, its index differs in important ways from the indexes to other encyclopedias. Basically, this is an index of people, and that fact has several interesting consequences. First, the information to which the index refers the reader on a particular topic is always about people associated with that topic. Thus the entry "Quantum theory (physics)" lists articles on people associated with quantum theory. Each article may discuss a person's contribution to quantum theory, but no single article or group of articles is intended to provide a comprehensive treatment of quantum theory as such. Second, the index is rich in classified entries. All persons who are subjects of articles in the encyclopedia, for example, are listed in one or more classifications in the index—abolitionists, astronomers, engineers, philosophers, zoologists, etc.

The index, together with the biographical articles, make *EWB Supplement* an enduring and valuable source for biographical information. As school course work changes to reflect advances in technology and further revelations about the universe, the life stories of the people who have risen above the ordinary and earned a place in the annals of human history will continue to fascinate students of all ages.

We Welcome Your Suggestions. Mail your comments and suggestions for enhancing and improving the *Encyclopedia of World Biography Supplement* to:

The Editors
Encyclopedia of World Biography Supplement
Gale, a Cengage Learning company
27500 Drake Road
Farmington Hills, MI 48331-3535
Phone: (800) 347-4253

ADVISORY BOARD

ACKNOWLEDGMENTS

Grateful acknowledgment is made to those publishers, photographers, and artists whose works appear in this volume. Following is a list of the copyright holders who have granted us permission to reproduce material in this volume of *EWB*. Every effort has been made to trace copyright, but if omissions have been made, please let us know.

PHOTOGRAPHS AND ILLUSTRATIONS APPEARING IN EWB, VOLUME 30, WERE RECEIVED FROM THE FOLLOWING SOURCES:

AKG-IMAGES LONDON: Henrietta Howland "Hetty" Green, Karl Richard Lepsius, Pier Paolo Pasolini, Winfried Georg Sebald.

ALAMY IMAGES: Esther Williams, Dmitri Medvedev, Francis Walsingham, James Stuart, Marcantonio Raimondi, Natalie Wood, Jerry Lewis.

AP/WIDE WORLD PHOTOS: Nell Jackson, Arlene Blum, Augusto Boal, Cornelia Funke, Cornell Capa, Diana Vreeland, Emil Jannings, Gladys Madalie Heldman, Horton Foote, Osamu Tezuka, Stieg Larsson, Susan Butcher, Vladislav Tretiak, Walter Wellesley "Red" Smith.

ART RESOURCE: Hallie Quinn Brown.

BRIDGEMAN ART LIBRARY: Gustave Gaspard Coriolis, Jose Maria Eca de Queiros.

CENTRAL CHINMAYA MISSION TRUST: Swami Chinmayananda.

CORBIS: Josef Breuer, Marie Adelaide Belloc Lowndes, Eleonora Duse, Henry Gwyn Jeffreys Moseley, Isabelle Autissier, Jim Bowie, Scott Nearing, George G Stokes, James Bailey.

EVERETT COLLECTION: Carl Laemmle, Sr.

GETTY IMAGES: John T Scopes, Allen Dulles, Donna De Varona, Jake Ehrlich, James Wong Howe, Marvin Miller, Ned Buntline, Steffi Graf, Jim Corbett, Ahmet Ertegun, Anne Bracegirdle, Annika Sorenstam, Arrigo Boito, Bill Veeck, Carlo Lorenzini (Collodi), Carlotta Grisi, Conchita Cintron, Cristobal Balenciaga, Curtis Mayfield, Dr Fiedrich Karl Rudolph Bergius, Ernest Ansermet, Ernie Harwell, Ferguson (Fergie) Jenkins, Francois Arago, Georg Solti, Girolamo Fabrici (Hieronymus Fabricius), Jacques Barzun, James Jamerson, JG Ballard, John Ogilby, Johnnie Johnson, Larry Doby, Leonard Chess, Mia Hamm, Michaelle Jean, Nancy Lopez, Oscar Stanton De Priest, Pat Garrett, Pat Summitt, R Crumb, Ray Kurzweil, Richard D'Oyly Carte, Robert Bolt, Rosalynn Carter, Rosemary Casals, Shigetaro Shimada, Stan Lee, Stefan Zweig, Thelma Schoonmaker, Thomas West De La Warr, Tito Puente, Victor Gruen, Vincent Auriol, Walter O'Malley, William A Hulbert, William Joyce, Willie Dixon, Doris Day, Herb Brooks, Adolf Bastian, Elizabeth Barry, Hughings Jackson, Paulina Kellogg Wright Davis.

IMAGE WORKS, INC.: Georges Auric, Thomas Brisbane.

LANDOV: Frank A Wilczek, Lars von Trier, Ryotaro Shiba.

LIBRARY AND ARCHIVES CANADA: Edward Blake, Mary Ann Shadd Cary.

LIBRARY OF CONGRESS: Caroline Harrison.

NEW YORK PUBLIC LIBRARY: Regina M Anderson (Andrews).

NEWSCOM: Giorgio Bassani, Aime Cesaire, Jack Kirby, Pedro Eugenio Aramburu, W Mark Felt Walter Baade.

OGDEN UNION STATION FOUNDATION: John M Browning.

PICTURE DESK INC.: Delores Del Rio.

SMITHSONIAN INSTITUTION-ARCHIVES CENTER OF THE NATIONAL MUSEUM OF AMERICAN HISTORY: Mary Streichen Calderone.

OBITUARIES

The following people, appearing in volumes 1-29 of the *Encyclopedia of World Biography,* have died since the publication of the second edition and its supplements. Each entry lists the volume where the full biography can be found.

ALFONSIN, RAUL (born 1927), Argentinian politician and President, died of lung cancer on March 31, 2009 (Vol. 1).

AQUINO, CORAZON (born 1933), Philippina politician and President, died of complications from colon cancer, in the Philippines on August 1, 2009 (Vol. 1).

BAUSCH, PINA (born 1940), German dancer and choreographer, died of cancer in Wuppertal, Germany on June 30, 2009 (Vol. 2).

BEHRENS, HILDEGARD (born 1937), German soprano, died in Tokyo, Japan on August 18, 2009 (Vol. 2).

BLANCHARD, FELIX "DOC" (born 1924), American football player and military pilot, died of pneumonia in Bulverde, Texas on April 19, 2009 (Vol. 21).

BOHR, AAGE (born 1922), Danish physicist, died on September 8, 2009

BORLAUG, NORMAN (born 1914), American biochemist, died of complications from cancer in Dallas, Texas on September 12, 2009 (Vol. 2).

BRUTUS, DENNIS (born 1924), South African poet and political activist, died of prostate cancer in Cape Town, South Africa on December 26, 2009 (Vol.3).

BUCKLEY, WILLIAM F., JR. (born 1925), American conservative author, editor, and political activist, died in Stamford, Connecticut on February 27, 2008 (Vol. 3).

CALDERA, RAFAEL (born 1916), Venezuelan politician and President, died in Caracas, Venezuela on December 24, 2009 (Vol. 3).

CLARKE, ARTHUR C. (born 1917), English author, died in Colombo, Sri Lanka on March 19, 2009 (Vol.18).

CRONKITE, WALTER (born 1916), American journalist and television news broadcaster, died of complications from dementia in New York on July 17, 2009 (Vol. 4).

CUNNINGHAM, MERCE (born 1919), American dancer and choreographer, died in Manhattan, New York on July 26, 2009 (Vol. 4).

DALY, MARY (born 1928), American feminist theoretician and philosopher, died in Gardner, Massachusetts on January 3, 2010 (Vol. 4).

DIDDLEY, BO (born 1928), American musician, died of heart failure in Archer, Florida on June 2, 2008 (Vol. 29).

ERICKSON, ARTHUR (born 1924), Canadian architect and landscape architect, died in Vancouver, British Columbia, Canada on May 20, 2009 (Vol. 5).

FISCHER, ROBERT JAMES (born 1943), American chess player, died in Reykjavik, Iceland on January 28, 2008 (Vol. 5).

FOLKMAN, M. JUDAH (born 1933), American physician and medical researcher, died of a heart attack in Denver, Colorado on January 14, 2008 (Vol. 22).

FOOT, MICHAEL (born 1913), British left-wing journalist and Labor Party member of Parliament, died in Hampstead, London, England, on March 3, 2010 (Vol. 5).

FRANKLIN, JOHN HOPE (born 1915), African-American historian, died in Durham, North Carolina, on March 25, 2009 (Vol. 6).

GARBER, MARY ELLEN (born 1916), American sportswriter, died in Winston-Salem, North Carolina on September 21, 2008 (Vol. 29).

HABASH, GEORGE (born 1926), Palestinian leader of the Arab Nationalist Movement and the Popular Front for the Liberation of Palestine, died of a heart attack in Amman, Jordan on January 26, 2008 (Vol. 7).

HAIG, ALEXANDER M., JR. (born 1924), American military leader, diplomat, secretary of state, and presidential adviser, died in Baltimore, Maryland on February 20, 2010 (Vol. 7).

HILLARY, EDMUND (born 1919), New Zealander explorer and mountaineer, died in New Zealand on January 11, 2009 (Vol. 7).

ICHIKAWA, KON (born 1915), Japanese film director, died of pneumonia in Tokyo, Japan on February 13, 2008 (Vol. 29).

JACKSON, MICHAEL (born 1958), African-American singer, died in Los Angeles, California on June 29, 2009 (Vol. 8).

JORDAN, HAMILTON (born 1944), American presidential adviser, died of cancer in Atlanta, Georgia on May 20, 2008 (Vol. 29).

KEMP, JACK (born 1935), American football player, congressman and secretary of housing and urban development, died of cancer in Bethesda, Maryland on May 2, 2009 (Vol.8).

KENNEDY, EDWARD M. (born 1932), American senator, died of brain cancer in Hyannis Port, Massachusetts on August 25, 2009 (Vol. 8).

KHAN, ALI AKBAR (born 1922), Indian musician, died of kidney failure in San Anselmo, California on June 18, 2009 (Vol. 24).

KIM, DAE JUNG (born 1925), South Korean human rights activist, died of pneumonia in Seoul, South Korea on August 18, 2009(Vol.).

KOLAKOWSKI, LESZEK (born 1927), Polish philosopher, died in Oxford, England on July 17, 2009 (Vol. 9).

LAMBSDORFF, OTTO (born 1926), German minister of economics, died in Bonn, Germany on December 7, 2009 (Vol. 9).

LARROCHA, ALICIA DE (born 1923), Spanish pianist, died in Barcelona, Spain on September 25, 2009 (Vol. 27).

LEDERBERG, JOSHUA (born 1925), American Nobel Prize-winning geneticist, died of pneumonia in New York City, New York on February 2, 2009 (Vol. 9).

LEVI-STRAUSS, CLAUDE (born 1908), French social anthropologist, died of cardiac arrest in Paris, France on October 3, 2009 (Vol. 9).

LOPEZ, ISREAL "CACHAO" (born 1918), Cuban musician, died of kidney failure im Coral Gables, Florida on March 22, 2008 (Vol. 29).

MAHARISHI MAHESH YOGI (born c. 1911), Indian guru and founder of Transcendental Meditation movement, died in Vlodrop, Netherlands on Fenruary 5, 2008 (Vol. 10).

MCNAMARA, ROBERT S. (born 1916), American secretary of defense and president of the World Bank, died in Washington, D.C. on July 6, 2009 (Vol.10).

NIRENBERG, MARSHALL (born 1927), American biochemist, died of cancer in New York City, New York on January 15, 2010 (Vol. 11).

NOLAND, KENNETH (born 1924), American color-field painter, died of cancer in Port Clyde, Maine on January 5, 2010 (Vol. 11).

O'FAOLAIN, NUALA (born 1940), Irish author, died of lung cancer in Dublin, Ireland on May 9, 2008 (Vol. 29).

PAUL, LES (born 1915), American guitarist, inventor, and producer, died of pneumonia in White Plains, New York on August 13, 2009 (Vol.28).

POKORNY, JAN HIRD (born 1914), Czech-American architect, died in New York City, New York on May 20, 2008 (Vol. 29).

PYM, FRANCIS (born 1922), British statesman, died in Sandy, Bedfordshire, United Kingdom on March 7, 2008 (Vol. 12).

ROBBE-GRILLET, ALAIN (born 1922), French novelist and filmmaker, died of heart failure in Caen, France February 18, 2008 (Vol. 13).

ROBERTS, ORAL (born 1918), American evangelist, died of pneumonia in Newport Beach, California on December 15, 2009 (Vol. 28).

SAFIRE, WILLIAM (born 1929), American journalist, died of pancreatic cancer in Rockville, Maryland on September 27, 2009 (Vol. 13).

SALINGER, J.D. (born 1919), American writer, died in Cornish, New Hampshire on January 27, 2010 (Vol. 13).

SAMUELSON, PAUL A. (born 1915), American economist, died in Belmont, Massachusetts on December 13, 2009 (Vol. 13).

SCHILLEBEECKX, EDWARD (born 1914), Belgian Roman Catholic theologian, died in Nijmegen, Netherlands on December 23, 2009 (Vol.14).

STUHLINGER, ERNST (born 1913), German rocket scientist, died in Huntsville, Alabama on May 25, 2008 (Vol. 29).

SUHARTO (born 1921), Indonesian president, died in Jakarta, Indonesia on January 27, 2008 (Vol. 15).

TILLION, GERMAINE MARIE ROSINE (born 1907), French anthropologist and author, died in St. Mande, France on April 19, 2008 (Vol. 29).

TOULIN, STEPHEN EDELSTON (born 1922), British-American ethical philosopher, died of heart failure in Los Angeles, California on December 4, 2009 (Vol. 15).

UPDIKE, JOHN (born 1932), American writer, died of cancer in Danvers, Massachusetts on January 27, 2009 (Vol. 15).

WILSON, CHARLIE (born 1933), American politican, died of a heart attack in Lufkin, Texas on February 10, 2010 (Vol. 29).

WYETH, ANDREW (born 1917), American painter, died in Chadds Ford, Pennsylvania on January 16, 2009 (Vol. 16).

ZINN, HOWARD (born 1922), American political scientist and historian, died of a heart attack in Santa Monica, California on January 27, 2010 (Vol. 16).

St. Alphonsa of the Immaculate Conception

St. Alphonsa of the Immaculate Conception (1910–1946) was the first female saint canonized from India. She spent most of her life in religious service, often suffering with grave illnesses. After her death, various religious sources reported that those who asked for her help were grante d miraculous intercession, and she had many devoted followers. She was canonized as a saint by the Roman Catholic Church in 2008.

Born Anna Muttathupandatu on August 19, 1910, in Kudamalur, India, Alphonsa quickly became known by the nickname Annakutti. She was born prematurely when her mother, Maria Puthakari, reportedly became frightened by a snake that wrapped itself around her while she slept. Eight days later Fr. Joseph Chanckalayil baptized Annakutti in the Syro-Malabar rite of the Roman Catholic Church. She was the youngest of five children. Her father was a doctor and a small farmer. Her mother died when Alphonsa was only three months old.

After her mother's death, the young Annakutti was first sent to her grandparents in Elumparambil. They were a devout family, and the youngster learned to lead the family's evening prayer by the time she was five. She had her First Communion on November 11, 1917. A story of her life published on the *Vatican News Services* web site described Alphonsa as saying of that experience, "Already from the age of seven I was no longer mine. I was totally dedicated to my divine Spouse." She began elementary school at the school of Thonnankuzhy at the same time.

When her first school cycle ended in 1920, Alphonsa transferred to Muttachira, and went to live with an aunt, Anna Murickal. Her aunt, who had originally been given guardianship of the girl upon Maria's death, was very demanding and expected obedience. Though her aunt was religious, Alphonsa became even more dedicated to her faith and began to spend time with the Carmelite nuns.

Attempted to Avoid Arranged Marriage

Alphonsa's aunt worked relentlessly to find the young girl a husband. Alphonsa tried to avoid marriage, already feeling a call to enter religious life. She reportedly had a dream during which someone, possibly a young Carmelite nun, invited her to become a religious sister. Her aunt did not relent, though, continuing to dress Alphonsa in the finest clothes and jewels. Even her friends nicknamed her the "little bride" because of the way she was dressed.

Even before she was a teen, Alphonsa's aunt had chosen a suitor for her, a young man from a good family. Once the young girl discovered the planned arrangement, she appealed to her uncle to forbid the marriage, to no avail. In imitation of other saints and in an attempt to avoid going to the church for the marriage, the young girl went to a nearby fire pit, where people burned chaffs and husks. Her intent was to burn one foot so that she would not be able to walk to the church. While sitting on the edge of the pit, however, she slipped in, burning her feet and legs as well as her skirt and the ends of her hair. She managed to get back home to change her clothes so that her aunt would not find out, but subsequently she fainted, and a goldsmith had to be called to remove the metal bangles from her burned ankles. It took her more than three months to recover and regain her ability to walk. In spite of the fervor of her desire, Alphonsa's aunt still wanted her to marry, but her uncle intervened and gave her permission to enter a convent.

Joined Clarist Sisters

Though she had a close relationship with the local Carmelite sisters, Alphonsa joined the Poor Clares, the Clarist Sisters of Malabar. These Poor Clares were Franciscan tertiaries who lived according to religious vows in a community, but who were not affiliated with the Poor Clares elsewhere in the world. In 1927 she went to live with this community, becoming a postulant in 1928. She was given the name Alphonsa, in honor of St. Alphonsus Liguori.

During her postulancy, Alphonsa was still allowed to visit home. Her aunt was still set on marriage for her niece. When Alphonsa first arrived home, there was a goldsmith on the porch making ornaments for her. Her aunt told Alphonsa that she was already promised in marriage and that it would be impossible to back down. Her uncle, though, stepped forward and forbid any further marriage plans on the part of Alphonsa's aunt.

Healed During Prayer

Alphonsa took the habit of her order, but she was constantly suffering from ailments. In 1932 she taught at the convent school, where she and the children shared a mutual love. When Alphonsa became ill, the students visited and assisted her, and continued to ask for her prayers and her advice. It was said that those who came to her found her advice profound and her prayers on their behalf quickly answered. Because of her illness she was removed from the school shortly thereafter, and became an assistant teacher, catechist, and secretary.

The sisters delayed Alphonsa's entrance into the novitiate until August 12, 1935, because of her frequent illnesses, though her novitiate should have begun in 1934. Only a week into her novitiate, she deteriorated into illness, hemorrhaging from her nose and eyes and with wounds on her legs. During her prayers to a priest, Fr. Kuriakose Elia Chavara, she was reportedly cured. In fact, they would both be beatified in the same celebration almost 50 years later.

On August 12, 1936, Alphonsa made her perpetual vows with the Clarist Sisters of Malabar. While she continued to be ill, she believed that she was meant to suffer joyfully with Christ. According to her biography on the *Vatican New Services* web site, she declared, "No matter what my sufferings may be, I will never complain and if I have to undergo any humiliation, I will seek refuge in the Sacred Heart of Jesus."

Miracles During Her Lifetime

Even while ill, she was said to make miraculous predictions. An example of this was a political matter between the Bishop and the government. The Bishop had issued a letter defending the Church's right to run schools, though the educational minister disagreed. The Bishop went to Alphonsa to ask for advice, and she responded that it was

the minister who would be imprisoned, not the Bishop. Soon afterwards, the minister had to relinquish his post, having never imprisoned the Bishop.

Another alleged miraculous occurrence included much suffering for St. Alphonsa. According to the story, on October 18, 1940, she surprised a thief, scaring him away, but also suffered psychological trauma herself. She lost her memory and her ability to read for almost a year. When she finally recovered, it was discovered that she could unexpectedly read and translate unfamiliar foreign words and dialects.

It was also said that Alphonsa had the gift of prophecy. In a reported vision of St. Therese, the Little Flower, Alphonsa was told that she would no longer suffer from contagious diseases, but that she would continue to suffer throughout the remainder of her life. According to the story, she took on the suffering of a Bishop and a teaching sister with malaria, who were cured when she took on their symptoms.

Death and Funeral

In July of 1946, after much physical suffering, Alphonsa finally received permission from her spiritual director to pray for her own death. She was granted her request with the caveat that she must add the words "If it be Thy Will" to the end of her prayer. She died on July 28, 1946, at the age of 36, in Bharananganam. Her last words, to her superior, were that she was at peace.

Alphonsa's body lay in state that afternoon and evening. Her funeral was small, and her spiritual director, who gave the homily, compared her holiness to that of St. Therese.

After her death, Alphonsa's former students often went to visit her grave and pray. According to the stories they told of their experiences, their requests were often granted. Soon, their elders were praying for her intercession as well. People began to travel to her grave from across the country, though there had been no confirmation of her sanctity from Church authorities. People who asked for her intercession reportedly began to see cures for everything from blindness and deafness to clubfeet. There were no caste or class distinctions in the people who were healed. Her tomb in Bharanamganam is known as the Liseux of India, after the birthplace of St. Therese of Liseux.

Beatification and Canonization

Within six years, thousands had visited Alphonsa's grave from all over India. The Cardinal Secretary of the Sacred Oriental Congregation, who attended to the Malabar rite, sent a letter to the Bishop of Palai to start a diocesan investigation into her canonization. That investigation began less than seven years after her death. It was then referred to the Congregation of the Causes of Saints (CCS) at the Vatican. The CCS did a thorough investigation of her life and writings. Her writings were approved in 1970 and she was granted her first step on the way to sainthood by then-Pope John Paul II on February 8, 1986, along with Fr. Chavara, who had interceded on her behalf in her novitiate at Nahru Stadium of Kottayam.

According to the laws of the Roman Catholic Church, Alphonsa then needed another miracle in order to be declared a saint, and it came in the reported cure of a ten-year-old boy named Jinil. Jinil was born with twisted legs, and the doctors had declared that he would forever be disabled. In 1999 his parents took him to the shrine of Blessed Alphonsa, where it was claimed that his legs became straight and he was cured.

St. Alphonsa of the Immaculate Conception was authorized for Canonization on June 1, 2007, by Pope Benedict XVI. The canonization took place in Rome on October 12, 2008, but there were also celebrations in Bharananganam, India, with the center of celebrations being in the Alphonsa Chapel on the campus of St. Mary's Forane Church. St. Alphonsa became the second Indian saint after the martyr St. Gonsalo Garcis. She was the first female Indian to be declared a saint.

Books

Ball, Ann, *Modern Saints: Their Lives and Faces,* Tan Books and Publishers, 1983.

Bunson, Matthew, Margaret Bunson and Stephen Bunson, *John Paul II's Book of Saints,* Our Sunday Visitor, 1999.

Holböck, Ferdinand, *New Saints and Blesseds of the Catholic Church: 1984-1987,* Volume 2, Ignatius Press, 2003.

New Catholic Encyclopedia, Jubilee Volume, 2nd Edition, Gale, 2000.

Periodicals

Associated Foreign Press, October 8, 2008.

Economic Times, October 12, 2008.

The Hindu, September 2, 2007; October 13, 2008.

Online

"Alphonsa of the Immaculate Conception (1910-1946)," *Vatican News Services,* http://www.vatican.va/news_ services/liturgy/saints/2008/ns_lit_doc_20081012_alfonsa_en.html (September 12, 2009).

"Beatification of Father Kuriakose Elias Chavara and Sister Alfonsa Muttathupandathu," *Vatican News Services,* http://www.vatican.va/holy_father/john_paul_ii/homilies/1986/documents/hf_jp-ii_hom_19860208_stadio-kattayam_en.html (September 12, 2009).□

Bartolomeo Ammanati

Italian artist and architect Bartolomeo Ammanati (1511–1592) created several treasures of the Italian Renaissance in Florence, Rome, and other cultural centers of the period. His best known work may be the Ponte Santa Trinità, one of the famous bridges that span the Arno River in Florence. It was completed in 1570, destroyed in World War II, and rebuilt in the 1950s. "The heart of the bridge was its three arches," wrote R. L. Duffus in the *New York Times,* about the efforts to reconstruct the cherished

Florentine landmark. "These arches were surpassingly lovely, even though thousands who looked upon them could not have told why they were so."

Ammanati was born on June 18, 1511, in Settignano, a hillside town northeast of Florence that had been a marble quarrying center for centuries. He came of age at the tail end of the Italian Renaissance, which had flourished for much of the previous century on the peninsula before spreading to northern Europe. At the onset of the Renaissance in the early 1300s, Italian artists, painters, and architects rediscovered some of the principles of visual perspective, naturalistic human forms, and harmonious building design that had been lost since the end of the Classical period of ancient Rome and ancient Greece. In Italy, Renaissance multi-discipline masters like Michelangelo and Filippo Brunelleschi became as famous as their wealthy patrons.

Trained by Sansovino

As a young man, Ammanati studied under Bartolommeo "Baccio" Bandinelli, a lesser known talent of the Renaissance whose surviving works include several sculptures for the wealthy Medici clan. Ammanati then moved on to Venice, where he trained as an architect under Jacopo Sansovino, who designed that city's famed Biblioteca Marciana, or Library of St. Mark's. Ammanati was an assistant to Sansovino during the first stage of the library's construction, which began in 1537. Between 1544 and 1546 he was in Padua completing his first commissions for the palace of the Benavides family. These commissions included a triumphal archway and family crypt.

Giorgio Vasari was the great chronicler of the Renaissance period, publishing the first volume of his magnum opus, *Lives of the Most Excellent Italian Painters, Sculptors, and Architects, from Cimabue to Our Times,* in 1550. Vasari issued a separate volume on Jacopo Sansovino that contained details about Ammanati's early career, stating that he moved to Rome in 1550, the year he turned 39. Vasari was the same age as Ammanati, and worked as an artist and architect, too. Vasari managed large-scale projects for the Medicis and other art patrons of the era, and in this capacity worked closely with Ammanati for a number of years.

In Rome, Ammanati joined with Vasari and Giacomo da Vignola (sometimes called Giacomo Barozzi) to design the Villa Giulia, a residence commissioned by Pope Julius III, the reigning head of the Roman Catholic Church. The Pope's villa later became the National Etruscan Museum. A wealthy Florentine official, Ugolini Griffoni, then commissioned Ammanati to design the Palazzo Griffoni, completed in 1563 on the Piazza della Santissima Annunziata in the Tuscan capital.

Commissioned by Medici Rulers

With Leonardo da Vinci, Michelangelo reigns as the most prolific and famous artist of the Italian Renaissance. One of his masterworks, the Laurentian Library attached to the Medici family church of Florence's Basilica of San Lorenzo, was unfinished when he died in 1564. Vasari assigned Ammanati to complete Michelangelo's design for the vestibule staircase for the library. By this point Ammanati was also busy with another Medici family project, a rear extension of the great Pitti Palace.

The Palazzo Pitti was more than a century old by that point and had recently been acquired by the wealthy Medici heirs. It had been designed by Brunelleschi, the architect who built the greatest among Florence's trove of landmarks, the immense Duomo of the church of Santa Maria del Fiore. Ammanati was commissioned by Eleanor of Toledo, wife of Grand Duke Cosimo I de' Medici, to expand the Pitti Palace. Eleanor was a wealthy Spanish aristocrat who in 1539 wed Cosimo, the duke of Florence and grand duke of Tuscany. Cosimo's Medici ancestors had been wealthy bankers and underwrote some of the early and middle Renaissance period's greatest works of art. Cosimo's primary achievement was to forge an alliance with the Holy Roman Emperor, Charles V, in a war against France, whereby he was granted ruling status of Florence and Tuscany by the emperor. This elevated the Medicis from banker-philanthropists to powerful hereditary rulers.

Working with Cosimo, Eleanor, and Vasari, Ammanati planned an expansion of the Pitti Palace that nearly doubled its size and connected it with Cosimo and Eleanor's primary residence, the Palazzo Vecchio. At the rear of the Pitti Palace, the couple wanted a spectacular park and sculpture garden, and Ammanati fulfilled their wishes by excavating the nearby Boboli Hill. This cleared the land for a palace wing, gardens, and even an amphitheater. The project was linked by what is undoubtedly Ammanati's second best-known project, the internal courtyard (*cortile*) that connected the palace to the gardens. For this he created black marble arches that provided a dramatic contrast to the white marble statues they were designed to showcase. The cortile also featured a novel but widely copied rusticated façade, meaning that the masonry surface was deliberately left rough but geometrically beveled. "Ammanati succeeded in fusing the town palace and the country villa," noted an essay in the *International Dictionary of Architects and Architecture,* "as the cortile facade faces the expanse of the lower Boboli Gardens, looking directly to the open-air theater which forms the closure of the vista across the formal lawn-beds which continue the outer lines of the projecting wings."

Built Ponte Santa Trinità

The excavation of the hill at Boboli provided the building materials for Ammanati's next major project, the Ponte Santa Trinità bridge. Florence was bisected by the Arno River, and the waterway had been an essential but problematic part of the city's history for centuries. It linked it to other important city-states of northern Italy, like Pisa, but was prone to devastating seasonal floods. One major breach of its banks occurred in 1557, when the waters swept away a five-arch stone bridge built by architect Taddeo Gaddi, who also designed another famous span in the city, the Ponte Vecchio, before he died in 1366.

Ammanati was commissioned to design the replacement bridge. He planned a sturdier span with three arches

constructed from the stones excavated at Boboli. Completed in 1570, the Ponte Santa Trinità bridge was named for a nearby church. In the early 1600s, four statues were added representing the embodiment of the four seasons of the year. The Ponte Santa Trinità's picturesque trio of flattened elliptical arches became a favorite of artists, tourists, and finally photographers, and a vista capturing it and the immense red brick Duomo remained a signature image for the city for centuries.

After supervising the Ponte Santa Trinità project, Ammanati built a church in the Tuscan town of Foiano della Chiana, the Tempio (Temple) di Santo Stefano della Vittoria. Back in Florence, he built houses for the Arte della Lana, or Wool Guild, before heading east again to Lucca, a city near Tuscany's Ligurian Sea coast. He designed its Palazzo Provinciale in the late 1570s, which later became the main museum of the city. It featured Serlian arches, named after Sebastiano Serlio, an architect who codified many of the classical principles discovered anew in the Renaissance period.

Regretted Exuberant Style

Ammanati's last major architectural project was the Jesuit College of Rome and Church of San Giovannino, built by Pope Gregory XIII and completed in the first half of the 1580s. By then, Ammanati had witnessed dramatic changes in the political and religious landscape of Italy in his lifetime. Rome was famously sacked in 1527 by rebellious troops of the aforementioned Charles V, the Holy Roman Emperor, and the Protestant Reformation was underway across much of Europe. Rome was home to the spiritual and administrative center of the Roman Catholic Church at a complex known as the Vatican, and following the shattering developments of the Reformation, the Church began attempting to rein in some of its excesses while rooting out future dissent. The Church's new policies served as historical place markers for the end of the Italian Renaissance.

In 1545 the Roman Catholic Church enacted doctrinal reforms that became known as the Counter-Reformation. Church leaders began to disdain the late Renaissance style known as Mannerism, whose hallmarks were elongated forms, vivid colors, and a great deal of nudity. Protestants viewed this art as symbolic of a corrupt church, and favored austere houses of worship designed to provide little distraction for those seeking spiritual elevation. The Catholic Church followed suit and issued strict guidelines about religious art, especially anything that could be construed as lascivious or inspiring lustful thoughts.

The Inquisition was the second prong of the Church's new era of restraint. This was a network of tribunals and ecclesiastical judges who sought to purify the Church of various heretical strains and improper interpretations of the Gospels and doctrine. Not even artists were immune from its summonses, and one of the Venetian Renaissance's most famous painters, Paolo Veronese, was rebuked for his massive work *The Feast in the House of Levi,* that was commissioned as another version of *The Last Supper,* depicting Christ's final meal with his apostles. Later in life, Ammanati grew more religious and was mortified by the nude statues he had created for the Medicis and other patrons. He even asserted that if he were permitted to destroy them he would do so.

The embarrassing works included a full-sized bronze Venus, a nude with a somewhat coy pose. Another was Florence's *Fountain of Neptune,* which depicted the famous Roman god of the sea with Cosimo I de' Medici's face and surrounded by playful naked water nymphs and satyrs. Neptune was made from an immense block of marble, and the rest was fashioned from bronze. The octagon-shaped fountain was created for the Piazza della Signoria in the 1560s. Soon after it was erected, Florentines derided it, vandalized it, and began to wash their laundry in it.

Married to Literary Icon

In 1550 Ammanati wed the poet Laura Battiferri, a 26-year-old widow and one of the most learned and accomplished women in Renaissance Italy. Agnolo Bronzino, one of the foremost Mannerist painters, depicted her in profile in one of the style's best-known portraits. She died in 1589. Ammanati died three years later, on April 13, 1592, and left his estate to the Society of Jesus, or Jesuits. This was the religious order founded by St. Ignatius of Loyola in 1534 that played a key role in the Counter-Reformation.

The two works which Ammanati regretted both survived the ages, despite his repentance. The nude *Venus* is part of the stellar collection of Spain's Museo del Prado in Madrid, while the marble *Neptune* was eventually removed to a museum for safekeeping and replaced with a replica at the Piazza della Signoria.

The fate of the Ponte Santa Trinità is perhaps the most stirring epitaph to Ammanati's artistry. It stood until August of 1944, when retreating troops of Nazi Germany bombed it along with Florence's other famous bridges. The stones were recovered from the Arno, along with the shattered statues of the four seasons, and used in the rebuilding, which was completed in 1958.

Books

"Bartolomeo Ammannati," *International Dictionary of Architects and Architecture,* St. James Press, 1993.

Paoletti, John T., and Gary M. Radke, *Art in Renaissance Italy,* third edition, Laurence King Publishing, 2005, p. 460.

Vasari, Giorgio, *Le vite de' piu' eccellenti pittori, scultori e architettori,* nine volumes, Istituto Geografico De Agostini, 1967.

Periodicals

New York Times, July 17, 1949; March 17, 1958.

Times (London, England), April 6, 1945. □

Regina M. Anderson

Regina M. Anderson (1901–1993) was a librarian, playwright, and patron of the arts. She was the first black branch supervisor in the New York Public Library system. Additionally, she is credited with being an instrumental supporter and organizer of the Harlem Renaissance movement.

Regina M. Anderson was born on May 21, 1901, in Chicago, Illinois. Her father, William Grant Anderson, was a prominent criminal defense attorney. Her mother, Margaret Simons Anderson, was a homemaker. As a child she attended Normal Training School and Hyde Park High School. Upon graduation she studied at Wilberforce University in Ohio, where she worked as a library assistant. She later transferred to the University of Chicago. While there, she worked in the Chicago Public Library system.

Anderson found her upper middle class social circle in Chicago to be rather oppressive. In 1923 she traveled on vacation to New York City. She was immediately drawn to the city's free-spirited atmosphere, and never returned to her hometown. That same year she applied for a job in the New York Public Library system. She was hired despite a dispute at her initial interview regarding her race. According to an article by Etheline Whitmire in *Libraries & the Cultural Record,* Anderson replied that she was "American" when asked to identify her race. The interviewer quickly responded, "You are not an American. You're not white." Anderson's heritage was diverse. Her paternal grandparents were Swedish and American Indian. Her maternal lineage included a Confederate general of unknown descent and a Jew who was the offspring of a Madagascar mother and an East Indian father. Anderson felt "American" was the most accurate reply to the question posed. Whitmire added that upon her hire, Anderson was told that because of the color of her skin, "We'll have to send you to Harlem." She was named the junior clerk of New York Public Library's 135th Street Branch under Ernestine Rose, a prominent advocate for the African-Americans served by that particular branch.

New York State of Mind

Anderson arrived in New York at the beginning of what was then considered the "New Negro Movement." Today that time period is known as the Harlem Renaissance. She soon moved into an apartment in the Sugar Hill neighborhood of Harlem with Ethel Nance and Louella Tucker, both of whom were actively involved in supporting the Negro arts movement. Nathan Huggins, in his book *Harlem Renaissance,* described Anderson as part of the new scene: "Harlem was filled with young Negro men and women who were writing and singing and dancing and painting and acting, and she was in the midst of it all." Anderson indeed soon found herself an integral part of the scene around her.

Anderson and her roommates soon became well known for welcoming Negro artists of the time into their home, or "580," as the apartment on Nicholas Avenue became known among Harlem residents. It was a place where young black writers, painters, actors, and musicians could find a warm meal, a couch to sleep on, and a sympathetic ear. According to *Notable Black American Women,* "Regina Anderson... would convince her employer and the director of the library, Ernestine Rose, that a new artist had joined the community and deserved a chance to present his or her works at the 135th Street Branch. Gatherings or time spent at 580 could thus launch an artist's or writer's career." The apartment became such an integral part of the Harlem Renaissance that Carl Van Vechten included it in his 1926 novel *Nigger Heaven,* which was about the New Negro Movement of the time.

Anderson's influence was not confined to helping artists perform at the library's 135th Street Branch. She also helped inspire the now-famous Civic Club dinner. In March of 1924, Charles Johnson, the executive director of research and publicity at the National Urban League, planned a small dinner party to celebrate a soon-to-be released novel by well-known black author Jessie Fauset. Anderson and her friends encouraged him to expand the party to include both well-established Negro artists and fresh faces on the Harlem arts scene. Eventually 110 guests attended the soiree on March 21. Alain Locke served as master of ceremonies, and W.E.B. Du Bois gave a speech. Jean Toomer, Countee Cullen, and Langston Hughes presented their work. In addition to the Negro artists, the audience also included white publishers and editors. According to *Notable Black American Women,* "Not only did the literary symposium and dinner result in the establishment of a patron/advisor relationship for several writers, but [white editor] Paul Kellog was so impressed by the talent demonstrated that he offered an entire issue of *Survey Graphic* for the publication of black writing. This special issue was published in March 1925... and later in 1925, it was combined with drawings by Winold Reiss to form the definitive volume of the Harlem Renaissance, *The New Negro.*"

Began to Write Plays

In 1926 Anderson married William Trent Andrews Jr., an attorney and New York City assemblyman, and the two had a daughter, also named Regina. Marriage and motherhood did not lessen her activities in support of black artists, and she continued to be involved in the Harlem arts scene. At the end of the 1920s, she became one of four organizers of W.E.B. Du Bois's theater group, the Crigwa Players. The name stood for Crisis Guild of Writers and Artists, and stemmed from *Crisis Magazine,* at the time the official publication of the National Association for the Advancement of Colored People, or NAACP. The name soon evolved to Krigwa for reasons unknown. For the first several years of its existence, the group was housed in the basement of the 135th Street Branch. Later it evolved into the Negro Experimental Theater, and today it is known worldwide as the Harlem Experimental Theater.

As a member of the group, Anderson began writing her own plays under the pseudonym Ursula Trelling, and several of her plays were highly successful. Her first, a drama titled *Climbing Jacob's Ladder,* was described by Du Bois as "thrilling." This was high praise from someone known to be an unusually harsh critic.

While Anderson's contributions to the Harlem Renaissance are lengthy, it is important to remember that she was also working as a librarian in the nation's largest public library system at the same time. In this post she was equally, if not more, accomplished. In the book *Harlem Renaissance and Beyond,* authors Lorraine Elena Roses and Ruth Elizabeth Randolph wrote, "For forty-four years, Regina M. Andrews diligently safeguarded black culture in her dual capacities as professional librarian and dramatist, combining them when possible. She thought that professional librarians could play a crucial role in human relations by stimulating intellectual growth and thereby promoting cultural tolerance. Anderson sought to use her position as a librarian and playwright to preserve African and Afro-American history and culture."

Continued Her Education

Between 1926 and 1929, Anderson took additional college courses at the City College of New York and Columbia University School of Library Service, including reference, cataloging, literature, and library economics. During this time, she was often transferred to different branches within the city's library system. She soon realized that she was not receiving the promotions and pay raises being given to other employees in similar positions, and asked W.E.B. Du Bois, on behalf of the NAACP, to intercede on her behalf. This resulted in a lengthy dispute between Anderson and the library system.

Du Bois remained committed to her cause and eventually, in June of 1930, she received a promotion from Grade 2 to Grade 3 library assistant. Eight years later, she was again promoted, this time to acting supervising librarian of the 115th Street Branch. Whitmire noted the importance of the occasion by quoting a local paper that wrote, "To Mrs. Regina Andrews of New York City goes the distinction of being the first Negro to be placed in full charge of a public library branch in the city of New York. Mrs. Andrews was appointed to head the branch at 201 West 115th Street . . . [which] is used by Columbia University students and by Negro and Spanish residents who make up the bulk of the population of the neighborhood." The distinction earned Anderson the honor of being one of ten black women honored at the 1939 New York World's Fair for their professional accomplishments.

In 1940 Anderson was transferred to the Washington Heights Branch of the library system, where she would remain until her retirement. Eventually the word "acting" would be dropped from her title and she became the supervising librarian. During her tenure at the Washington Heights branch, she instituted a program known as Family Night. Whitmire quoted Anderson describing the event as a "library-sponsored community forum organized primarily for adults [that] invites audience participation from all adults—young and old. A variety of themes, presented through speakers, panel discussions, and books, have been concerned mainly with the political, social, and cultural life of countries in South East Asia, Latin America, and Africa. These evenings also function as a meeting place for the many diverse elements of the community engaged in cultural exploration and exchange." This was a modest description indeed for a gathering where exceptional speakers regularly participated in the lecture series. People such as Eleanor Roosevelt, Langston Hughes, and Marcus Garvey led lively discussions of current events and their implications.

While working as a supervising librarian, Anderson was named to the National Council of Women of the United States and selected as the National Urban League representative to the United States Commission for UNESCO. In these roles she was given the opportunity to travel overseas on multiple occasions. She was awarded the National Council of Women Musical Arts Group Award and the Asia Foundation Award which allowed her to visit eight German states or cities, six African countries, South Korea, Japan, India, Pakistan, Afghanistan, Thailand and Iran. Many of these trips provided inspiration for Family Night topics and speakers.

In 1967 Anderson retired. She made a request to continue Family Night on a volunteer basis, but her request was denied, and the Family Night program ended, much to the dismay of the community. In 1971 Anderson again teamed up with former roommate Ethel Nance to co-edit *Chronology of African-Americans in New York, 1621–1966*. Anderson died in upstate New York on February 5, 1993, of unspecified causes. She was 91 years old.

Books

Huggins, Nathan, *Harlem Renaissance,* Oxford University Press, 1971

Notable Black American Women, edited by Jessie Carney Smith, Gale Research Inc., 1992.

Roses, Lorraine Elena, and Ruth Elizabeth Randolph, *Harlem Renaissance and Beyond,* G.K. Hall & Co., 1990.

Women in World History, edited by Anne Commire and Deborah Klezmer, Yorkin Publications, 1999.

Periodicals

Libraries & the Cultural Record, Vol. 42, no.4, 2007

Online

"Regina Anderson," *African American Registry,* http://www.aaregistry.com (November 4, 2009). ☐

Andronikos II Palaiologos, Emperor of Byzantium

Andronikos II Palaiologos (1259–1332) endured a turbulent 46-year reign as Byzantine emperor. This scion of a Greek dynastic kingdom struggled to resolve a set of inherited problems both internal and external that threatened a newly revived Empire in the East. Much of his tenure was blighted by military blunders that resulted in major territorial losses to the Turks, Bulgarians, and Italians. "It was as clear to contemporaries as it is to us today that under Andronikos II the Empire, which had been on the offensive since the [1220s]," wrote Mark C. Bartusis in *The Late Byzantine Army: Arms and Society, 1204–1453,* "had entered a period of retrenchment, a period from which it would never really emerge."

Andronikos II was born in 1259 to Theodora Doukaina Vatatzina, whose grandfather's brother was John III Doukas Vatatzes. It was under this ruler that the aforementioned era of renewal had begun back in the 1220s. On her mother's side, Theodora was related to another aristocratic family, the Komnenos. Andronikos II's father was Michael VIII Palaiologus, the founder of the Palaiologian dynasty. All of these families—Vatatzes, Komnenos, and Palaiologos—rose to power during a period of crushing setbacks for the Byzantine Empire earlier in the thirteenth century. The problems began with the Fourth Crusade to retake Christianity's holy city of Jerusalem from the Muslim Ayyubid rulers. Instead, the Crusade, launched in 1202, turned into a full-scale war against the Byzantine Empire—another Christian realm but one which practiced the Orthodox, or Eastern rite. The Byzantines had been long sundered from their Latin counterpart, the Western Church in Rome that was headed by the pope.

Driven Out of Constantinople

The largely French peasant Crusader army sailed from Venice and other Mediterranean ports, but a series of score-settling acts took over from the original goal of capturing Jerusalem. The Crusaders first besieged Constantinople from the sea and then broke through its heavy fortifications in April of 1204. They sacked the city and set up the new

Latin Empire, centered in Constantinople. The remnants of Byzantium also fell prey to Muslim invaders from the East, who established an enduring authority throughout that part of Asia and the Middle East.

Andronikos II was born in Nicaea on the shores of Lake İznik. Now called İznik, Nicaea had been the site of two important ecumenical councils early in Christian church history, and was the locus of a new Empire of Nicaea founded by Greek noble families. The leaders of Nicaea and two other Greek states were determined to retake Constantinople and reestablish the Byzantine Empire and their version of Orthodox Christianity. Andronikos II's father was one of these leaders, and in 1261, two years after Andronikos II's birth, an army led by Michael VIII Palaiologus retook the important city.

The Byzantine Empire was reestablished, and the heirs of Michael VIII would lead it for the next two centuries. Andronikos II was proclaimed co-emperor in 1261, though he was just two years old. His father undertook a great rebuilding effort in the city during his childhood, and in 1274 sent ambassadors to Lyon, France, for the Second Council of Lyon. This was an attempt by Pope Gregory X to unite the Greek and Latin branches of Christianity once again. A union was agreed upon, but was vehemently opposed by top leaders inside the Orthodox branch in Constantinople. Andronikos II's father supported the union and dealt harshly with its opponents, including the holy men, called patriarchs, who led the Eastern branch of Christianity.

Crowned Co-Emperor

In 1272, at the age of 13, Andronikos II was crowned co-emperor with his father. Over the next decade his father engaged in various military campaigns to win back lost territories of the Byzantine Empire, but the planned union with Rome was dissolved by a new pope in 1282. Andronikos II's father died that same year and Andronikos II became the sole emperor. He was 23 years old, and for the past eight years had been married to Anna, the fourth daughter of King Stephen V of Hungary. Anna's paternal grandmother was Maria Laskarina, who was the sister of the Greek noblewoman who wed John III Doukas Vatatzes. Anna's maternal grandmother, by contrast, was the daughter of a chief of the Cuman, one of the last nomadic pagan tribes in Western Europe.

The couple's first child was Michael IX, born in 1277. A second son, Constantine Palaiologos, was thought to have been born a year later. Anna died around 1281, when she was around 21 years old. In 1284, the widowed Andronikos II married his second wife, Yolanda of Montferrat, who took the Greek name Eirene upon becoming empress. Her father was William VII, the Marquess of Montferrat, a border region in northern Italy that had a claim on the Kingdom of Thessalonica. Thessalonica was a so-called Crusader State in northern Greece, seized from Byzantium during the Fourth Crusade but retaken by Epirus in 1224. It was another of the Greek states forced out of the Latin Empire in the events following 1204. Andronikos II's marriage to Eirene effectively abolished Montferrat's claim to Thessalonica.

Andronikos II would have four more children by Eirene. His first-born son, Michael IX, was proclaimed co-emperor in 1281 and ruled jointly after around 1295. Father and son faced multiple threats in the years of their joint rule. One of their goals was to retake the administrative division known as Thessaly that had come under the control of the Komnenos family. They were also still rebuilding Constantinople and fortifying other sites at the edges of the Empire, so a new 10 percent tax was levied on the *pronoia*. The pronoia were all those within the Empire who had been granted a source of revenue by imperial decree. Because it was the poorest who were forced to give part of their income or crops to the local pronoia, the financial burden fell hardest on the peasantry.

Dismantled Byzantine Navy

Andronikos II tried to cut expenses from the imperial budget. One major financial drain was the Byzantine navy, which had been active since the fourth century C.E. as a military force and played a vital role in several past triumphs in the Byzantine imperial timeline. Andronikos II followed his advisors' suggestion to scuttle the fleet, and though he later tried to revive it—as did his successors on the throne—the once-dominant naval power in the Eastern Mediterranean never regained any capacity. This loss of naval power was also linked to the rise of the republics of Venice and Genoa, both of which sought lucrative footholds in the east for trade purposes with Asia. In 1285 Andronikos II concluded a war that his father had started with Venice over trade routes, religious doctrine, and other insoluble issues. By making peace with Venice, Andronikos II thought he could rely on the ardently seagoing Venetians for maritime help, but in the late 1290s the Byzantines were drawn into Venice's war with its other major rival at the top of the Italian peninsula, the Republic of Genoa. The end result was that both Venice and Genoa were able to either gain or firmly secure lucrative properties in the east—Venice in the Aegean Sea's island of Crete, and the Genoese with a Black Sea port called Caffa, located in present-day Ukraine.

One reason for Andronikos II's decision to dismantle the Byzantine navy was the fact that ships of this era relied entirely on manpower, and this necessitated the enslavement and feeding of hundreds of galley slaves. The Byzantine army faced similar personnel shortages. To staff his military campaigns, Andronikos II was forced to rely on outsiders. Some were Cretans who had fled Venetian rule. Andronikos II granted them lands and revenue status, but they rebelled and became a threat to internal stability. Another group was the Alans, a Turkic people who had, in previous centuries, been pushed from Central Asia westward into Europe. During Andronikos II's rule they were fleeing an expanding Mongol empire, and formally asked him for permission to enter Byzantium. He granted it on the grounds that they lend soldiers to a campaign against the actual Turks, who had been pushing into the edges of the Byzantine empire since the 1260s.

The Turks and the Bulgarians were two major enemies at Andronikos II's doorstep. The Bulgarians also practiced an Eastern Rite form of Christianity, but had long resisted

Greek and Byzantine domination. The Second Bulgarian Kingdom controlled large parts of the Balkans but also faced a threat from the Mongol warriors of the Golden Horde. The Ottoman Turks were the more serious threat to the Palaiologus rule, however. This was the successor state to the Seljuk Sultanate of Rûm in Anatolia, which itself was a remnant of a major Persian Sunni-Islam empire of the eleventh and twelfth centuries.

Sought New Allies

The agreement Andronikos II struck with the Alans requested their service against the Turks in battles led by his son and co-emperor, Michael IX. They did this for a time, but then began to desert in large numbers after meeting up with a genuine mercenary force hired by Andronikos II: the Catalan Company of Almogavars. This was a professional force led by Roger de Flor, a former Knight Templar and occasional pirate. There were several clashes between the Alans and the largely Spanish and Italian Catalan force, especially when the Alans learned the Europeans were being paid an enormous sum for their services. Both had been engaged to rid the Turks from Asia Minor under Michael IX's command, but the son of an Alan leader was killed in one camp fight, and then de Flor was slain when he visited Michael IX's compound in Adrianople in 1305. That incident led to an all-out melee, with scores of Catalans slain; they fled to northern Greece, as did the Alans.

The Ottoman Turks achieved major territorial victories during Andronikos II's era, including the former ancient Roman province known as Bithynia on the Black Sea. Osman I, the founder of the Ottoman Empire, was Andronikos II's own age and would create a dynasty that dominated this region until the end of World War I. In response, Andronikos II turned to the west for new allies. At one point, he attempted to arrange a marriage for Michael IX with Catherine I of Courtenay, the daughter of the Emperor of Constantinople who had once ruled the Latin Empire in Constantinople before Andronikos II's father ejected the Western Europeans from the city. That plan fell apart, and Michael IX instead married a princess of Armenia. Four years later, in 1298, Andronikos II negotiated a marital contract involving his youngest daughter by Eirene, the five-year-old Simonis, to the Serbian king, Stefan Milutin, in exchange for military assistance.

Michael IX spent years at war against the Byzantine Empire's enemies. He died in Greece at the age of 43, leaving his father as sole emperor once again. Andronikos II was opposed to the next Palaiologus in the line of succession, his grandson Andronikos III—Michael IX's son with Rita of Armenia. This purported heir's sister was Theodora, who had been matched with Theodore Svetoslav, the tsar of Bulgaria, in yet another strategically arranged marriage. When Andronikos II attempted to remove his grandson from the line of succession, it provoked a civil war that drew in Bulgaria, for Svetoslav had by then died and Theodora married Michael Asen III, another Bulgarian king. This civil war lasted nearly eight years, until 1328, and included an attempted kidnapping of the aged emperor by Michael Asen III, his grandson-in-law. Finally, the

armies of Andronikos III prevailed and took Constantinople in 1328. Andronikos II was deposed on May 24, 1328, and lived his remaining years in a monastery. He died in 1332. The Palaiologos descendants ruled Byzantium from Constantinople until the city was seized by the Ottoman Turks in 1453.

Books

Bartusis, Mark C., *The Late Byzantine Army: Arms and Society, 1204–1453,* University of Pennsylvania Press, 1997, pp. 67–84.

Laiou, Angeliki, "Andronikos II Palaeologos," in *Dictionary of the Middle Ages,* 13 volumes, American Council of Learned Societies/Charles Scribner's Sons, 1989. □

Ernest Ansermet

Ernest Ansermet (1883–1969) was among the most prolific and progressive orchestral conductors of the twentieth century, making important creative contributions to some of the groundbreaking musical innovations of the 1910s and 1920s.

Ansermet (An-sair-MAY, with the first syllable ending in a nasal sound) served as conductor of the orchestra for the Ballets Russes, the Russo-French dance company whose productions accompanied several of the pioneering scores of composer Igor Stravinsky, and he led the world premieres of scores by Stravinsky and other key twentieth-century composers. Taking the Ballets Russes on tour in the then-musically conservative United States, Ansermet was exposed to early jazz and other forms of African-American music, and he became one of the first European musicians to champion African-American traditions and to write about them. Ansermet remains best known, however, for his creation and leadership of the Orchestre de la Suisse Romande, the Swiss symphony orchestra that he conducted from 1918 until well into his ninth decade. Although the orchestra was not among the absolute top rank of European ensembles, and although Ansermet disdained the lifestyle of the jet-setting star conductors who emerged after World War II, recordings by the orchestra were everywhere in music shops for decades. "There was probably not an LP collection anywhere across the globe that didn't include at least one by Ansermet and the Suisse Romande," noted Geoffrey Norris of the London *Daily Telegraph.*

Studied Mathematics

Ernest Alexandre Ansermet was born in Vevey, Switzerland, on Lake Geneva, on November 11, 1883. Ansermet's father was a teacher who encouraged his talent for mathematics, and his mother had an aptitude for music and gave him some lessons at home. At first, Ansermet seemed destined for a career as a math teacher. He attended Switzerland's University of Lausanne, majored in math and physical sciences, and was ready for a job when he graduated in

1903. For several years he taught math at a high school in Lausanne.

Perhaps with musical interests already on his mind, Ansermet enrolled in classes at the Sorbonne university in Paris. While there, he took the chance to enroll in conducting and composition classes at the Paris Conservatory with the Portuguese conductor and pianist Francesco de Lacerda and with the French pedagogue André Gedalge. He met the creator of the French Impressionist style in music, Claude Debussy, and wrote an orchestral arrangement of a Debussy piano work, "Les Epigraphes Antiques." Ansermet also became acquainted with the fast-emerging stars of the next compositional generation: Maurice Ravel and the Spain-to-Paris transplant Manuel de Falla.

Much the same pattern continued when Ansermet returned to Switzerland, where he decided definitively to pursue a musical career. He continued his studies in Geneva, with composer Ernest Bloch among others, and Lacerda lined up a job for him conducting the orchestra at the Montreux Casino in 1912. That led in 1915 to another conducting job, with the Subscription Concert Orchestra of Geneva, and it was in that year that Ansermet made the acquaintance of a still more influential composer: Igor Stravinsky, who was living at the time in a small town on Lake Geneva. Two years earlier, Stravinsky had set the musical world on its ear with the intense, quasi-primitive music for the ballet *The Rite of Spring,* which featured the dancers of the Ballets Russes.

Benefited from Stravinsky Friendship

The two got along well, and Stravinsky introduced Ansermet to Serge Diaghilev, the director of the Ballets Russes and a key player in putting together the controversial but tremendously buzzworthy Paris premiere of *The Rite of Spring.* Diaghilev invited Ansermet to conduct the company's resident orchestra, and in late 1915 Ansermet stepped to the podium to lead a performance of *Soleil de nuit* (Sun of the Night), a ballet score by Nikolai Rimsky-Korsakov. In 1916 Ansermet led the orchestra on a tour of the United States, where the avant-garde music of Stravinsky and Ravel was as yet little known.

In addition to introducing Americans to new musical experiences, Ansermet soaked up the music of his host country, showing special interest in the sounds that were just beginning to acquire the name of jazz. He admired the New Orleans clarinetist Sidney Bechet, whom he considered a genius, and he spoke appreciatively of the New York dance band the Southern Syncopated Orchestra, led by composer and songwriter Will Marion Cook. At the time, it was rare for classically trained musicians in the United States to express anything other than disdain for African-American ragtime and jazz.

Ansermet later heard Bechet, the Southern Syncopated Orchestra, and other African-American musicians who visited Europe during the World War I years. In 1919 he wrote an article in a Swiss literary journal *Le Revue Romande,* arguing that the melodic origins of African-American spirituals had little to do with their musical and cultural essence, "because it is not the material that makes Negro music, it is the spirit." Ansermet went on to make observations, quoted in the anthology *Reading Jazz,* about African-American rhythm, and he praised "the astonishing perfection, the superb taste, and the fervor" of the playing of the Southern Syncopated Orchestra. His 1919 essay was among the first European writings on jazz, and its insights came well in advance of those of many American critics.

Meanwhile, Ansermet's European conducting career had taken off. As conductor of the Ballets Russes orchestra he was on the podium for the first performances of some of the greatest classical works of the twentieth century: Erik Satie's *Parade* (1917), Stravinsky's *L'histoire du soldat* (The Soldier's Tale, 1918), and Falla's *El Sombrero de Tres Picos* (The Three-Cornered Hat, 1919). His work in the Western hemisphere led to an invitation to form a National Orchestra of Argentina, and by the end of the 1910s decade he was clearly a young conductor on the rise and in demand internationally.

Ansermet, however, cared little for fame. His focus returned to the area where he had been raised. It was known as the Suisse Romande, a name denoting the French-speaking portion of trilingual Switzerland. Ansermet's goal was to create a world class orchestra in the area, and in 1918 he founded the Orchestre Romande, with himself as music director, conductor, and chief administrator. He would remain at the helm of the orchestra for nearly 50 years, stepping down only two years before his death.

Hosted Musician Refugees from Nazis

In the 1920s, Ansermet turned down offers from several internationally known orchestras in favor of remaining in Geneva and conducting his new ensemble. He shepherded the orchestra through a series of financial problems during the Great Depression. By 1940 the group had taken on the name under which it became widely known due to Ansermet's enormous discography: the Orchestre de la Suisse Romande. The orchestra's seasons in those days were enriched by the appearances of artists who had fled the growing control over classical music by the National Socialist cultural apparatus in Germany, Austria, and Italy; among Ansermet's guest conductors were Arturo Toscanini and Bruno Walter. A low point for Ansermet in the late 1930s was the end of his long friendship with Stravinsky after the two quarreled over cuts to Stravinsky's piece *Jeu de cartes* (Card Game). The disagreement was later patched up, but the two never again became really close.

After the end of World War II, Ansermet remained in the forefront of contemporary music, conducting the premiere of Benjamin Britten's opera *The Rape of Lucretia* at the Glyndebourne Festival in England in 1946. The dawn of the LP era saw a period of strong growth in Ansermet's recorded legacy, although his recording career stretched back to his tour as conductor of the Ballets Russes orchestra in 1916. Ansermet's discography with the Orchestre de la Suisse Romande covered the works of some 75 composers, and many of his albums have been reissued as compact discs and even digital tracks. The iTunes digital download service as of 2009 listed 68 albums containing Ansermet performances. "For 50 years," noted James Reel of the *All Music Guide,* "he directed an orchestra that was second-rate in tone and technique, yet Ernest Ansermet drew performances from it that cut right to the heart of the music," resulting in albums that "retain strong interest for collectors who value nuance over tonal sheen."

Ansermet's discography focused heavily on the French, Swiss, and Eastern European music he had championed from the start; among his specialties were the compositions of Claude Debussy, Béla Bartóok, his countrymen Frank Martin and Arthur Honegger, and of course Stravinsky. Despite his affinity for twentieth-century music, he disliked the systematic 12-tone method of composition that was reaching its peak of intellectual fashion during the later part of his career, and he wrote an entire book, *Fondements de la musique dans la conscience humaine* (Foundations of Music in the Human Conscience, 1961) aimed at discrediting it. Ansermet also frequently conducted the works of Classical-era composers Haydn, Mozart, and Beethoven, although this aspect of his work was underrepresented in his recorded output. He composed a number of pieces himself, including the full-length orchestral work *Feuilles de printemps* (Leaves of Spring). His shorter prose essays were collected in a 1983 volume titled *Ecrits sur la musique* (Writings on Music). Many volumes of his prolific correspondence have appeared in their original French, but his writings remain untranslated.

Ansermet was apparently a memorable figure when holding the conductor's baton. A 1985 Ansermet tribute broadcast by Britain's Channel 4 television collected surviving film footage of the conductor, inspiring Nicholas Shakespeare of the London *Times* to describe him this way: "He stood, grave and remote above his orchestra, baton jabbing, almost as if he were miming the music of Stravinsky (to whom he was almost a brother) or Debussy, whom he once met, or any of the other romantics whom he interpreted hardly raising his arms. Certainly, when he listened, you could see the music inside his severe and haunted head." Ansermet's avoidance of the personality cult of the conductor manifested itself in a feeling of remoteness on the part of the man who, Shakespeare wrote, "bore a passing resemblance to Frankenstein." In 1967 Ansermet stepped down from the leadership of the Orchestre de la Suisse Romande, whose international prestige suffered considerably in the decades after his departure. He remained active, however, as a guest conductor and recording artist until shortly before his death, in Geneva, on February 20, 1969.

Books

Baker's Biographical Dictionary of Musicians, centennial ed., Nicolas Slonimsky, editor emeritus, Schirmer, 2001.

Reading Jazz, edited by Robert Gottlieb, Pantheon, 1996.

Periodicals

American Record Guide, January-February 1999.

Daily Telegraph (London, England), January 19, 2008.

Times (London, England), July 25, 1985.

Online

"Discografia Ernest Ansermet" (Ernest Ansermet Discography), http://www.scona.ch/ansermet/discografia.php?ishow=0/ (September 22, 2009).

"Ernest Ansermet," *All Music Guide,* http://www.allmusic.com (September 22, 2009).

"Ernest Ansermet," *Orchestre de la Suisse Romande,* http://www.osr.ch (September 22, 2009).

"Ernest Ansermet 1883–1969," *Diva International* (Switzerland), http://www.divainternational.ch/spip.php?article22 (September 22, 2009). □

François Arago

French scientist François Arago (1786–1853) was a mathematician, astronomer, physicist and, in the last 23 years of his life, director of the Paris Observatory. He also served briefly as prime minister of France during a period of political turmoil that preceded the Revolution of 1848. Embedded in the sidewalks and roads of Paris are the Arago Medallions, which are several dozen bronze markers that plot out the Paris Meridian; in Arago's era French scientists sought to have this declared the international standard for the 0-degree measurement for the Earth's lines of longitude.

A rago hailed from a family of French-Catalan origin in Estagel, a town in the Pyrénées-Orientales *département* of France. This administrative district is located on France's border with Spain, and many of its inhabitants are speakers of Catalan, one of modern Spain's official languages. Arago was born on February 26, 1786, the first of four sons in a family that would eventually number 11 children. His father served as a mayor of Estagel, but when Arago was still a child the family moved to Perpignan, the capital of Pyrénées-Orientales, where his father became an official at that city's branch of the Monnaie de Paris, or French Mint.

From an early age Arago demonstrated an impressive gift for mathematics. At the municipal college in Perpignan he sped through the preparatory courses for the entrance examinations to Paris's famed École Polytechnique, or Polytechnic School. Despite the prejudices of the examiners, who were suspicious of Arago's Catalan origins, he won a place and began classes in Paris in late 1803. At the same time he also served as a cadet in the artillery service, for his original intent was to become an officer in the French army.

Appointed to Paris Observatory

Arago spent just a year at the École, leaving when political dramas related to the increasing power of Napoléon I of France erupted. He was recommended for a position as an assistant at the Observatoire de Paris, or Paris Observatory. This center of astronomical study dated back to 1671 and

had been making important discoveries in planetary science and cosmography since then. At the time, its director was Pierre Méchain, the discoverer of several faraway galaxies and recurring comets. Méchain had also undertaken a scientific quest to plot out the exact cartographic coordinates of what was called the Paris Meridian. This was the north-south axis that bisected France, and passed through the actual Paris Observatory grounds. The mission to measure it exactly was part of King Louis XIV's plans to affirm and extend French power in the 1660s.

Méchain had undertaken the effort to extend the points of the Paris Meridian south into Spain before his death in 1804. Other high ranking government officials handed over these duties to Arago and his Observatory colleague, the French astronomer and mathematician Jean-Baptiste Biot. Arago and Biot set out from Paris in early 1806, double-checking the triangulations made by Méchain in the Pyrénées. The Meridian line passed through Barcelona, the capital of Catalonia, and down through the Mediterranean onto a spot on the Balearic Islands.

Thus began the most adventure-filled period of Arago's rather eventful life. He spent the better part of a year on several islands in the Balearics, including Ibiza, Majorca, and Formentera. He was stranded alone on Majorca at the outbreak of the Peninsular War in the spring of 1808. This was an uprising against the Spanish monarchy exploited by Napoléon that drew the kingdoms of Portugal and Great Britain to defend the Iberian peninsula, which Napoléon was determined to conquer. Incorrectly suspected of aiding the French invasion forces by the fires he lit on the peak of the Clop de Galazo, he was jailed at the Bellver Castle fortress in June of 1808, but managed to arrange an escape via a small fishing boat in late July. The vessel reached the port of Algiers, clear across the Mediterranean, a week later, and Arago sought shelter at the home of the French consul in the Ottoman-held pirate haven. The consul arranged for Arago to return to Marseille on board a ship that also contained two live lions that the Dey, or Muslim ruler, of Algiers was sending as a present to Napoléon. The ship was attacked by Spanish pirates, and the entire crew was taken to the ancient coastal Catalonian town of Rosas.

Family Believed Him Dead

Rosas was just across the border with France and was a heavily fortified site; during this period of the Peninsular War it was held by England's Royal Navy. Arago and his fellow detainees from the ship were imprisoned in the town's ironclad fortress in one of the casemates, or small gun chambers. They had only dry bread to eat, a "very unsubstantial food for one who could see from his casemate, at the door of his prison, a sutler selling grapes at two farthings a pound, and cooking, under the shelter of half a cask, bacon and herrings," Arago wrote in his autobiography, *The History of My Youth*. He and his fellows had no money for food, but Arago added that he "decided, though with very great regret, to sell a watch which my father had given me."

Finally, Rosas fell to the French army, and Arago was removed to Palamós, further south along the Catalonian coast. In November of 1808 he boarded another ship bound for Marseille, although the war was still raging. This time the vessel was blown off course to Béjaïa, another port on the North Africa coastline. Arago and his fellow travelers decided to trek to Algiers over land, a trip of about 80 miles, but through extremely inhospitable territory. The party arrived in Algiers on Christmas Day of 1808, and learned the Dey had been beheaded. There was a fresh set of diplomatic problems with the new Dey, but finally Arago and another French citizen were permitted to leave in the spring.

Arago finally reached Marseille's lazaretto, or quarantine area, on July 2, 1809. He still carried the cache of surveying records he had made for the Paris Meridian, which had been concealed in the front of his shirt during his 14-month odyssey to reach home. Before depositing them with the Bureau des Longitudes in Paris, he stopped in Perpignan to visit his family. His father had always asked for information about his whereabouts from captured Spanish soldiers who passed through the city, and was dismayed to see a Spanish officer wearing the watch that Arago had sold in Rosas for food. For months, his Roman Catholic family had had Masses said in his remembrance, believing he was dead.

Nominated to Academy of Sciences

Arago was hailed as a hero for his efforts and became instantly famous. His name was proposed as a candidate to the French Academy of Sciences, which elected him a member in September of 1809 at the age of just 23. He was made the astronomer of the Paris Observatory, and with the data he brought back, wrote Paul Murdin in *Full Meridian of Glory: Perilous Adventures in the Competition to Measure the Earth,* "He was able to confirm the shape of the Earth by tabulating the length of one degree of latitude across Europe, from London to Formentera. Even over the ten-degree latitude difference from the north to the south it was clear that the degree got longer towards the pole."

Arago reunited with Biot to survey the coasts of France, England, and Scotland for their Paris Meridian work a few years later. The Paris line competed to become the international standard, but finally an international scientific conference in 1884 declared the Greenwich Meridian to be the starting point for the Earth's lines of longitude. The Greenwich Meridian at 0 degrees passes through the Royal Observatory at Greenwich, England. It divides the world into Eastern and Western hemispheres on a scale of 360; the 180-degree line exactly halfway around the world, serves as the International Date Line.

Arago had a long and distinguished career in France until his death in 1853. In the realm of physics, he measured steam pressure at varying temperatures, and also conducted experiments on the velocity of sound and magnetism. Science credits him with the discovery of what is known as rotatory magnetism, which English chemist Michael Faraday explored further in the 1830s, and also worked closely with French optical engineer Augustin-Jean Fresnel for many years. Arago's work with Fresnel, who was a close friend, involved the polarization of light. Their efforts helped explain the phenomenon known as the aurora borealis.

Served as Prime Minister

Arago joined a long list of notable French scientists in 1830 when he became director of the Paris Observatory. He entered politics that same year when he was elected to the chamber of deputies, the lower chamber of France's parliament, from the Pyrénées-Orientales département. In 1838 the chemist Louis Daguerre demonstrated a new method of image production to him, and Arago used his position as perpetual secretary of the Academy of Sciences and in parliament to champion the invention; the Academy bought the rights to the daguerreotype in 1839, and with that the era of photographic reproduction began.

In February of 1848, King Louis-Philippe, the last Bourbon monarch ever to rule France, abdicated after 18 years on the throne when his liberal constitutional monarchy ultimately failed to prevent widespread economic difficulties for France's poor. Arago joined the new provisional government and was named to the cabinet as minister for marine and colonial affairs on February 24, 1848. On April 5, he took over the ministry of war, too. This was a period of tremendous social upheaval for France, which on March 2 had declared universal male suffrage. Arago fell in with the spirit of the times, ordering better food rations for the French navy and issuing a decree that formally ended capital punishment by flogging for sailors. He also abolished the enslavement of Africans in all of France's colonies.

On May 10, 1848, Arago was elected to the Executive Power Commission, a five-member body that ruled as co-heads of state. He was named president of the Commission, which in effect made him France's 25th prime minister. His tenure was brief, however: after riots in June, the Commission government was overthrown after it voted to close the national workshops established a few months earlier to alleviate high unemployment.

Napoléon's nephew, Louis-Napoléon, was elected president of France, but seized dictatorial powers in December of 1851 and demanded an oath of allegiance from all civil servants. Arago resigned his post as astronomer with the Bureau des Longitudes in protest, but the new emperor refused to accept the resignation. Arago was already in poor health by this point, and after a trip to his native northern Catalonia he returned to Paris, where he died on October 2, 1853, at the age of 67.

The Da Vinci Code Conspiracy

Arago's work on the Paris Meridian was commemorated in 1994 by the installation of an "invisible art" project by Dutch conceptual artist Jan Dibbets. The round bronze Arago Medallions begin at the Paris Observatory and measure out the north-south axis as Méchain, Biot, and Arago had plotted it. Several of the markers pass through the Louvre Museum and its courtyard, and author Dan Brown wrote about this location in his 2003 novel *The Da Vinci Code,* describing the markers instead as clandestine indicators to the Paris tomb of Mary Magdalene. The popular novel's plot hinged upon the claim that Christ was said to have escaped death by crucifixion and instead fled to

France with Mary Magdalene, a secret fanatically guarded by the founders of Christianity in Brown's fictional account.

Books

Arago, Francis, "The History of My Youth," in *Lives of Distinguished Scientific Men,* translated by W. H. Smyth et al., Volume 1, Ticknor and Fields, 1859, pp. 51, 59.

Murdin, Paul, *Full Meridian of Glory: Perilous Adventures in the Competition to Measure the Earth,* Springer, 2009, pp. 122, 152.

Ten, Antonio E., "Arago, Dominique-François-Jean," in *Biographical Encyclopedia of Astronomers,* edited by Thomas Hockey, Volume 1, Springer, 2007, pp. 54–55.

Periodicals

New York Times, August 15, 1854.□

Pedro Eugenio Aramburu

Argentine military officer and politician Pedro Eugenio Aramburu (1903-1970) belonged to the military junta that overthrew President Juan Perón in 1955. He served as Argentina's president from 1955 to 1958. In 1970 he was kidnapped by terrorists and later executed.

Pedro Eugenio Aramburu was a major figure in the 1955 military overthrow of Argentina's Juan Perón, the Argentine general and politician who rose to power during a particularly turbulent period in his country's history.

Following the junta, Aramburu became Argentina's president. During his subsequent three-year administration (1955-1958), Aramburu replaced Perón's installed constitution with Argentina's previously implemented democratic constitution. The development, however, accomplished little in stabilizing the South American nation. Power continued changing hands and, ultimately, Aramburu was kidnapped and executed by a terrorist group that sought to restore Perón to power.

Received Military Education

Pedro Eugenio Aramburu was born on May 21, 1903, in Rio Cuarto, a city located in the Cordoba province of Argentina. He later attended the country's National Military College. Located in El Palomar, Buenos Aires, Argentina, the institution provided undergraduate education for officers later placed in the Argentine armed forces.

Following graduation, Aramburu climbed through the military ranks. In 1922, he became a sub-lieutenant in the Argentine army. By 1939, he became a major. In 1943, he secured a position as instructor in the Escuela de Guerra (the "School of War"). Later he became the institution's director. By 1955, he had risen to the rank of general and became the commander in chief of the Argentine army.

Ascended Amid National Strife

Aramburu's thirty-year military ascension occurred in the midst of ever-present national strife. Argentina rarely experienced political peace in its turbulent history. Societal discord plagued the nation as far back as the late nineteenth century, a period that witnessed a growing separation between its wealthy and its poor.

The country moved into the twentieth century under the rule of the National Party, an elitist coalition supported by the military and prosperous landowners. A radical force emerged from the country's middle class, however. This group embraced democracy and sought to wrest power from the privileged wealthy. While revolutionary in nature, the radical group accomplished change through ballots instead of bullets. In 1916, it helped elect Hipólito Yrigoyen to a six-year term as president.

Still, disaffection prevailed: the changing of the ruling guard accomplished little that would positively impact the Argentine working class. As such, Yrigoyen declined a second term, but he was re-elected in 1928. His new term was cut short. The global economic depression exacerbated the country's existing problems, which led to a 1930 military coup.

Until 1943, a conservative oligarchy, a concentrated cabal of wealthy and politically empowered elitists supported by the military, exploited the country by engineering governmental policy that best served its own interests. While this military-landowner alliance could reasonably claim that it engendered economic recovery, it also fostered corruption that only aggravated existing social problems and class tensions. Further, the power elite adopted a foreign relations policy that essentially surrendered Argentina's neutrality and economic interests to the increasingly powerful Axis power arising in Europe (spearheaded by Germany's Nazi leader Adolf Hitler). Within this climate of external (global) and internal (national) problems, Colonel Juan Domingo Perón rose to power.

World War II sparked industrial expansion in Argentina. In turn, this expansion led to the formation of a large blue-collar workforce. Perón, the military head of the Labor Department, became its recognized leader. From this constituency arose a new group called the Peronistas, which supplied Perón a power base that led to his election in 1946 as president.

Perón supporters gained majorities in both of Argentina's houses of Congress, and Perón ushered in an era of political, social and economic change. He solidified his popularity with the masses when he married an attractive former actress named Eva Duarte, the famous and much beloved "Evita." A champion of the poor, the First Lady handled labor relations and social services until her untimely death in 1952. Meanwhile, her husband developed a five-year plan to expand Argentina's economy and improve relations with the United States, which had become strained during World War II. Perón also installed a new constitution that allowed a president to succeed himself in office, which led to his second term.

Plotted Overthrow of Perón

Bolstered by its congressional majorities, the Peronista Party re-nominated Perón as its presidential candidate in the 1952 elections. It also had passed legislation that would enable it to imprison the government's harshest critics. The congress also began suppressing Argentina's free press. As a result, the government endured increased criticism from opposition parties and the news media.

Perón was re-elected president by a large majority but, by this time, the seeds of his subsequent downfall had already been planted. Argentina had been suffering an economic and political downswing. In 1950, Aramburu, then a colonel in the Argentine Army, plotted with three other army officers to overthrow Perón. It would take several years for the plot to reach fruition.

Meanwhile, the Perón administration came under increasing critical fire, as the president continued harassing the free press, legalized divorce and prostitution, and became hostile toward organized religion. In November 1954, Perón leveled accusations of sedition against members of the Roman Catholic clergy. He also abolished religious education in public schools and incited violence against churches. As hostilities heated up, Peronista thugs set fire to major churches in Buenos Aires. The compounding unrest set the stage for Aramburu's rise to power.

Led Military Coup

Factions within the military and government sought to oust Perón. On June 16, 1955, an initial coup was thwarted. Dissidents in Argentine's naval and air forces staged a rebellion in Buenos Aires. Navy and air force planes bombed Casa Rosada, the city's presidential office building. Three hundred and sixty people were killed before the loyal army quickly quelled the uprising.

The second ouster attempt was successful, but only barely so. On September 16, dissidents from all three branches of the military, joined forces in rebellion. The coup was called "Revolución Libertadora", and Aramburu, now a general, was a leading participant. Heading a group of rebels, Major General Eduardo Lonardi attacked and held Cordoba. At the same time, Aramburu attacked Perón forces at Curuzu Cuatia, but he fled when overwhelmed by Perón reinforcements. Perón and loyal staff members were confident that they would crush the uprising. Admiral Isaac Rojas, a rebel officer, however, had captured a cruiser ship and headed for Buenos Aires. This development alarmed Perón, who was well aware of Rojas' reputation as a fighter. Perón sought refuge in the Paraguayan embassy. Later, he resigned and fled to the Buenos Aires Harbor, where a Paraguayan gunboat transported him away from the country. He eventually went into exile in Spain, where he remained until 1973, under the protection of Generalísimo Francisco Franco.

Perón's too hasty retreat proved pivotal to the rebels' success. "We never expected him to prove such a coward," Aramburu told *Time* magazine. "If he had taken the field against us, the revolution would have been crushed."

Became President

The civil war lasted three days. Four thousand people were killed. By September 20, Major General Lonardi was installed as the country's provisional president. He promised to restore Argentina's democratic government. He appeared reluctant to destroy Peronism, however, which continued thriving among workers and some members of the military. As a result, Aramburu engineered Lonardi's overthrow. The Lonardi government ended after only two months, following a non-violent coup.

Aramburu became president of Argentina on November 13, 1955. He remained in office until May 1, 1958. Admiral Rojas served as his vice president.

Replaced Dictatorship with Democracy

Once in office, Aramburu initiated an agenda of suppression against Peronists, forcing them out of the military, government and business. Also, Aramburu restored the democratic constitution, which had directed Argentina from 1853 until the Perón regime. With the restored constitution, a president couldn't succeed himself. In addition, Aramburu removed Perón's name from public display.

During his rule, Aramburu ceased suppression of the press and strived to eradicate governmental corruption. To avert potential dictatorships, he sought to rein presidential power while strengthening congress. "Ours was a revolution against the dictatorial state system," he was quoted by *Time* magazine. "We could not live in it. We were suffocating. We fought for the right to live."

Aramburu also instigated free elections and decreed that military officers would not be able to become presidential candidates. He applied this ruling to himself. His intent was to restore the Argentine government to the people. "It is not a new thing in our country, and it seems to be a Latin American evil, that military personalities seek to make themselves dictators through recourse to the arms that the people themselves pay for," he told *Time*. "We shall so conduct ourselves that the army, in a democratic spirit, as in such other countries as the U.S., England and France, may remain aloof from partisan political strife."

Meanwhile, Perón tried to continue influencing the country's direction from exile, as he would for the next two decades. In Argentina, Peronists tried to regain power. Aramburu's government crushed a June 1956 revolt. Thousands were arrested and imprisoned for treason, and alleged Peronistas were executed. Later, Perón sympathizers characterized the executions as slaughter.

Retired from the Military

After Aramburu stepped down as president, Arturo Fondizi was elected in February 1958. Aramburu also retired from the army to focus on politics. As his own directive prevented him from succeeding himself as president, he didn't launch another presidential bid until 1963. As part of his campaign, he formed the "Union del Pueblo Argentino" (Union of the Argentine People, or UDELPA). He campaigned with the slogan "Vote UDELPA and He won't return," which referred to Perón. But Aramburu's presidential bid was unsuccessful. He came in third in the election. Arturo Umberto Illia was the winner.

The new president's administration proved a troubled one, as it witnessed increasing national debt, inflation, worker dissatisfaction and a rise in political dissidence. Only three years later, Illia was ousted from office after a coup. Military leaders installed Juan Carlos Onganía, a retired general, as president. While Onganía sought to restore economic and social stability, his regime was oppressive. He eliminated Argentina's legislative bodies and suspended the democratic constitution, which exacerbated national unrest. In the wake of his measures, the number of terrorist groups increased, as did terrorist acts. Some of these groups were Peronists; others were Marxists.

Kidnapped and Executed by Terrorists

One of the most serious terrorist acts involved the kidnapping and subsequent execution of Aramburu, allegedly carried out by Perón sympathizers. On May 29, 1970, kidnappers posing as army officer entered Aramburu's Buenos Aires apartment and forcibly removed the former general and president. The group was either known as the Montoneros or the "Juan Jose Valle Command." Its members communicated to Onganía's government that a revolutionary court had sentenced Aramburu to death in retaliation for the firing-squad executions of twenty-seven Peronists in 1956, as well as for the execution of General Juan Jose Valle, who had led the attempted 1956 coup. As was later reported, however, it was Aramburu's vice president, Isaac Rojas who ordered the executions of the Peronists. But Aramburu had indeed

ordered Valle's execution, reportedly weeping as he signed the papers. (Valle had been Aramburu's friend and classmate at the National Military Academy.)

Peronists leaders immediately denied any involvement. Also, Perón, who was now seventy-four years old and still exiled in Madrid, Spain, denounced the actions, warning that Aramburu's execution could lead to civil war in Argentina. But Aramburu was executed three days after his kidnapping, on a farm in Timote, Carlos Tejedor, in the Buenos Aires Province.

In June 1973, Perón returned from exile to Argentina. In a special election in November of that year, he was elected president, garnering 61.9 percent of the nation's vote. By this time, he was married to former exotic dancer María Estela Martínez de Perón, his third wife (known as "Isabel"). She was his running mate in the presidential election. For remaining followers, the long wait proved unrewarding. The elderly Perón was no longer the charismatic leader that inspired so much loyalty, nor was his "Isabel" an "Evita." Further, and ironically, the re-empowered president began suppressing the kind of terrorist groups he had once supported. He died in 1974. His wife succeeded him a president.

Aramburu was sixty-eight years old when he died. Described as stern, uncompromising and shy, he never aligned himself with one political party. Rather, he viewed himself as a "man of the center." He was survived by his wife, Sara, and two children, Sara Elena and Eugenio Carlos.

Books

"Aramburu, Pedro Eugenio," *Almanac of Famous People, 9th Edition*, Thomson Gale, 2007.

"Pedro Eugenio Aramburu," *Merriam-Webster's Biographical Dictionary*, Merriam-Webster Incorporated, 1995.

Periodicals

Time, June 3, 1957; June 15, 1970.

Online

"Argentina-History," *Encyclopedia of the Nations*, http://www.nationsencyclopedia.com/Americas/Argentina-HISTORY.html (December 4, 2009).

"History of Argentina," *Emayzine.com*, www.emayzine.com/lectures/HISTOR~4.htm (December 4, 2009). □

Georges Auric

French composer Georges Auric (1899–1983) was internationally successful as a film composer, earning some renown as well for his works in the pure classical idiom in which he was initially trained.

Textbooks about classical music mention Auric as a member of a group of young French composers of the 1920s, known as Les Six (The Six). James Reel of the *All Music Guide* expressed a common attitude among

France apparently regarded him as a sort of phenomenon, and at one 1914 concert at the Independent Musical Society, composer Maurice Ravel served as his page-turner. By the beginning of World War I the teenager numbered some of France's most prominent intellectuals among his friends, and had weighed in as a music critic with an article on the nonconformist composer Erik Satie, published in the prestigious *Revue française de la musique.* The two composers were good friends until Auric later wrote another article criticizing Satie's work.

In 1914 Auric switched from the Paris Conservatory to an elite private music school, the Schola Cantorum, where he studied with composer Vincent d'Indy. When he turned 18 in 1917, he was drafted and initially sent toward the zone of France's grueling trench warfare against Germany, but friend pulled strings and had him assigned to a war ministry job in Paris. The war helped to turn Auric strongly against the German influence in music. After the war ended, Auric was ready to emerge at the forefront of the French avant-garde. He wrote several well regarded new pieces; one of them, *Huit poèmes de Jean Cocteau* (Eight Poems of Jean Cocteau), helped pave the way for an important future collaboration. *Adieu, New York!* (1920) anticipated a growing French infatuation with American jazz.

Wrote Ballet Scores

In the early 1920s, a group of young French composers—Auric, Poulenc, Milhaud, Honegger, Louis Durey, and Germaine Tailleferre—became known as Les Six. They did not have a single common style, but most tended to embrace the influence of popular music and to emphasize a close relationship between music, dance, and poetry. Auric maintained a relationship with Serge Diaghilev, founder of the famed Ballet Russes, and composed music for several new ballets staged by the Russian ballet impresario: *Les fâcheux* (The Insane, 1924), *Les matelots* (The Sailors, 1924), and *La pastorale* (The Pastoral, 1925). The first of these, noted Jeremy Drake in the *New Grove Dictionary of Music and Musicians,* "shows a facility for mood creation and a virtuosity in the manipulation of highly varied material that presages [Auric's] film music." Auric also composed comic operas and several instrumental works, culminating in the Russian-influenced "Piano Sonata in F" of 1930–1931.

That ambitious work did not command the attention that Auric hoped it would, but by then he had begun a new phase of his career. In 1930 he worked with Cocteau on the latter's surrealist film *Le sang d'un poète* (The Blood of a Poet), which was not released until the following year due to disputes over its controversial content. The year 1931 also saw Auric provide the score for *A nous la liberté* (Freedom for Us), a commentary on industrial society that is considered a classic of French cinema. Auric continued to compose concert music, such as the "Violin Sonata" of 1936, but in the late 1930s his growing success in the field of film music meant that that genre absorbed more and more of his energy. After having scored only one film in 1934 and one in 1935, Auric composed six full-length soundtracks in 1936, seven in 1937, and eight in 1938.

classical critics and historians when he wrote that Auric "never gained the popularity and respect of his three more famous compatriots" among Les Six—Francis Poulenc, Darius Milhaud, and Arthur Honegger. Yet Auric's music, through his film scores, may have been heard by more people than the work of those three composers combined. Auric's career in film soundtracks began in 1930 through an association with the French avant-garde filmmaker Jean Cocteau, but it expanded to include some of the classics of British and American cinema.

Family Moved to Nurture Son's Talent

Georges Auric (o-REEK) was born on February 15, 1899, in the town of Lodè in southeastern France. Auric's family moved to the larger city of Montpellier when he was young, and he began taking music lessons at the local conservatory. By the age of ten, Auric was writing music of his own. A Montpellier music writer noticed the youngster's talent and suggested that the family move to Paris, where Auric could study at the high school of the Paris Conservatory, France's national music academy. They arrived there in 1913, just as the musical world of Paris was thrown into controversy by the premiere of Russian composer Igor Stravinsky's radical ballet *The Rite of Spring.* Auric attended the premiere.

Something of a child prodigy, Auric was soon giving concerts of his own, featuring both his piano playing and music of his own composition. The top composers in

The outbreak of World War II in 1939 slowed the production of France's cinema industry, and after Paris fell to the Germans the following year, French filmmakers operated under strict censorship rules. Auric, who spent much of the war in rural southern France, joined a group of composers called the Front National de Musique and composed music for films that helped keep the French sense of national identity alive during German occupation. One of these films, written by Cocteau and directed by Jean Delannoy, was *L'éternel Retour* (The Eternal Return, 1943), a modern retelling of the medieval legend of the lovers Tristan and Yseult—an originally French story, but one that had been identified with Germany since the composition of Richard Wagner's opera *Tristan und Isolde.*

After the war's end, Auric reunited with both Delannoy and Cocteau and created scores for two widely acclaimed French films. Auric's 1946 score for Delannoy's *La symphonie pastorale* (Pastoral Symphony) earned him the Music Prize at the first Cannes Film Festival. Cocteau's romantic adaptation the same year of the fairy tale *La belle et la bête* (Beauty and the Beast) resulted in one of Auric's most distinctive scores. Impressionist in style, Auric's music at first seems unsynchronized with the action on the screen but instead forms a unique parallel narrative. Auric's score was lost until 1992, when it was rediscovered by the single-named Swiss conductor Adriano; he later led a new recording of the music that was released on the Naxos label.

Wrote British Comedy Soundtracks

Although he was strongly identified with French culture, Auric experienced considerable success abroad as a film composer in the late 1940s and 1950s. His British career began in 1945 when he stepped in as a substitute for a composer (named as Arthur Bliss or Frank Bridge in different sources) slated to write the soundtrack for a film of George Bernard Shaw's play *Caesar and Cleopatra.* That led to a series of assignments for the Ealing studio, including Ealing's most celebrated comic production, the 1951 Alec Guinness vehicle *The Lavender Hill Mob.* Auric's music, according to Mark Koldys of the *American Record Guide* in a review of a Chandos-label recording of Auric's film music from this period, "proves to be as British as steak and kidney pie, even if a slight French accent does trickle in now and then." Many of the scores are whimsically humorous in nature.

Auric also worked as a film composer in the United States. Although his American soundtracks were few in number, they were of consistently high quality. The 1951 film *Moulin Rouge,* directed by John Huston, gave Auric the chance to view France musically through American eyes. Auric's other major American film, *Roman Holiday* (1953), also had a European setting. Auric reunited with Huston for the 1956 film *Heaven Knows, Mr. Allison.* For his work on the 1963 documentary *The Kremlin,* Auric was nominated for an Emmy Award. Despite his forays abroad, most of Auric's film work took place in France; he composed several full-length soundtracks there in almost every year of the 1950s. Among them was the 1955 Max Ophuls classic *Lola Montès.* In 1960 Auric's collaboration with Cocteau continued with the latter's film *Le Testament d'Orphée* (The Testament of Orpheus).

Auric never stopped composing music for the concert hall. Among the most important works of his later years were the *Partita for two pianos* (1953–1955) and two series of short piano pieces called *Doubles-jeux* (Double Games, 1970–1971) and *Imaginées* (Imaginings, 1976). In 1962 he became the director of the venerable Paris Opera and its light-opera cousin, the Opéra-Comique. But he continued to write scores for films and television programs into the 1960s and 1970s. He was heavily honored toward the end of his life; among his laurels were induction into the French Legion of Honor and, in 1979, the American Academy of Arts and Letters.

Auric married artist Eleanore Vilter (also known as Nora Smith) in 1938; she later used the name Nora Auric. In 1979 Auric published a memoir, *Quand j'étais là* (When I Was There); two studies of Auric's music have appeared in French, but English-language writings about his life and music are sparse. In Drake's words, "Much has still to be discovered about Auric, a public figure, but a secretive man and an enigmatic composer who so often seemed to hide his feelings behind a curtain of rhetoric." Auric died in Paris on July 23, 1983, and was buried next to his wife in the city's Montparnasse cemetery.

Books

International Dictionary of Films and Filmmakers, Volume 4: Writers and Production Artists, 4th ed., St. James, 2000.

New Grove Dictionary of Music and Musicians, 2nd ed., edited by Stanley Sadie, Macmillan, 2001.

Periodicals

American Record Guide, September-October 1996, May 2000.

Online

"Auric, Georges," *Screenonline,* http://www.screenonline.org.uk/people/id/840536 (September 25, 2009).

"Auric: La Belle et La Bete," *Naxos Records,* http://www.naxosdirect.com/title/8557707 (September 25, 2009).

"Georges Auric," *All Music Guide,* http://www.allmusic.com (September 25, 2009).

"Georges Auric," *Find a Grave,* http://www.findagrave.com/ (September 25, 2009).

"Georges Auric," *Internet Movie Database,* http://www.imdb.com (September 25, 2009).

"Georges Auric (1899–1983)," *Lenin Imports,* http://www.leninimports.com/georges_auric.html (September 25, 2009).

"Goodbye Again," *Film Score Monthly,* □

Vincent Auriol

French politician Vincent Auriol (1884–1966) served as the first President of the nation's Fourth Republic during the politically tumultuous post-World War II era. A member of the Socialist Party, Auriol served in the French parliamentary assembly for over twenty-five years, acted as mayor of the southern French town of Muret, and participated in

the French Resistance during World War II. He won election to France's top executive office in 1947 and presided over a series of constantly shifting cabinets and numerous prime ministers, striving to maintain a fragile power structure. During his tenure, he spoke out against the growth of Soviet power and supported the establishment of NATO. He chose not to run for re-election, leaving the Presidency after just one term in 1954. In the years following his administration, Auriol remained active on the political scene, writing for a left-wing newspaper and helping maintain government stability in the midst of a military-political crisis at the end of the 1950s. After his death in 1966, Auriol's memoirs of his term of power were published as the multi-volume *Journal du Septennat.*

Born Jules Vincent Auriol on August 25, 1884, in Revel, Haute-Garonne, France, Auriol was the only son of baker Jacques Antoine ''Paul'' Auriol and his wife, Angélique Virginie (Durand) Auriol. When the future president was but three years old, he lost his left eye in an accident involving a toy pistol and wore a glass eye throughout the rest of his life. In 1889, however, he enrolled at the Saint-Vincent-de-Paul convent school in Revel, where he soon proved himself an apt student. Auriol completed his primary education with flying colors in 1896 and continued with his studies at a local secondary school. There, the young scholar had his first exposure to the tenets of socialism in a philosophy course and pursued an interest in music, studying both the violin and vocal performance. After Auriol earned a *baccalaureat*—the French equivalent of a high school diploma— in Latin and Greek in 1902, he enrolled at the University of Toulouse to study law and philosophy. He was active in student life and political activities, serving as President of the General Association of Students and Secretary of the socialist student group. Shortly after completing his law degree in 1905, Auriol joined France's socialist political party, Section Française de l'Internationale Ouvrière (French Section of the Workers' International, or SFIO).

By the end of 1905, Auriol had established himself in practice at Toulouse, where he concerned himself primarily with labor law. Over the next few years, he remained committed to the socialist cause, and began writing articles that were published in newspapers including *La Cité* (The City) and *La Dépêche du Midi* (The Dispatch of the South. In 1909, Auriol also helped establish the left-wing paper *Le Midi Socialiste* (The Socialist South) and served as its editor. Three years later, he wed a student at the University of Toulouse, Michelle Aucouturier, who came from a socialist family with connections to leftist French politician Jean Jaurès; the couple later had a son, Paul, and a daughter, Jacqueline, who became a famous aviator and broke the world's jet speed record in 1952.

Important to National Politics

Auriol's formal political career commenced with his election to the French parliament from the Haute-Garonne town of Muret in May of 1914, the first of what would be a series of continuous re-elections until World War II brought about the end of the Republic in 1940. While in the assembly, Auriol became an expert on economic affairs for the SFIO and joined the assembly's finance commission in 1916. The following year, Auriol met the influential socialist politician Léon Blum and became a supporter of his policies; in 1920, he was among the few socialist members of the assembly who joined Blum in refusing to participate in the Communist International (Comintern) movement. From 1924 to 1926, Auriol chaired the finance commission, during which time he was elected mayor of Muret. Like his parliamentary seat, Auriol retained this local position until 1940. Between 1936 and 1938 he served as finance minister, justice minister, and chief of staff under the alternating governments of Blum and Camille Chautemps. As finance minister, Auriol made a controversial decision to dramatically devalue the French currency.

In July of 1940, Auriol was one of a minority of members of the assembly who voted against granting absolute power to French military figure Phillippe Pétain; (also known as Marshal Pétain;) and his Vichy Regime. This vote proved prescient when the Vichy government worked with the occupying German Nazi government and further compounded the nation's wartime difficulties. Soon after the vote Auriol was arrested and imprisoned, first in the central district of Indre and later at his home in the south of France. He managed to escape this house arrest in October 1942 and joined the Resistance movement operating out of the nearby mountains in Aveyron. There, he was an active resistor and began work on a book, *Hier-Demain* (Yesterday-Tomorrow), which was published after the close of the war in 1945. In the fall of 1943, Auriol left France by way of London and soon joined the Free French forces led by General Charles de Gaulle in Algeria. He held key roles in the Resistance leadership in North Africa, and founded a weekly magazine, *Fraternité*, that was published in Algiers. Back in France in 1945, Auriol regained his political positions in both Muret and Haute-Garonne, and was re-elected to the national Constituent Assembly. From November of that year until January of 1945, he was a minister in the provisional government of de Gaulle.

Served as President of the Fourth Republic

Under the French constitution at the time, the nation's president was elected not by popular vote but by the Constituent Assembly. After de Gaulle resigned from his post as the provisional president of the assembly in early 1946, that body selected a succession of politicians to fill the seat. A number of changes then occurred rapidly as the assembly—led by the SFIO as the majority party—began to hammer out a revised constitution. Scholars widely acknowledge Auriol's vital role in this process, and the assembly approved the new constitution in October of that year. The following month, Auriol advanced to become the head of the assembly on the strength of the support of his own party and that of the Mouvement Républicain Populaire (Popular Republican Movement, or MRP). In January of 1947, Auriol carried the vote to become the first President of the Fourth Republic. (In France, the establishment of a new constitution ushers a new era of government.)

A believer in a weak presidency, the newly-elected leader chose to sublimate the power of his office to that of the assembly. Indeed, Auriol's entry in *A Dictionary of Political Biography* observed that "he relied less on the formal powers of the presidency (which were few) or on appeals to public opinion, than on his insider's knowledge of France's political class and on his remaining constitutional rights over the appointment of governments." The political climate of the Fourth Republic was an unstable one, with Auriol overseeing the dissolution and creation of new cabinets more than ten times during his presidency; he later joked about being awoken repeatedly in the middle of the night to accept the resignation of yet another prime minister. Perhaps Auriol's greatest achievement was his deft management of these highly fragile coalitions that allowed the nation to continue to function adequately—if not necessarily smoothly—under his leadership.

During his presidency, Auriol frequently spoke out against the rise of Soviet expansionism and expressed support for the North Atlantic Treaty Organization (NATO), which was formally instituted in 1949 to provide a unified military defense force. He gave a speech at the opening ceremony of the Supreme Headquarters Allied Powers Europe (SHAPE) at the town of Rocquencourt, located near Paris, in 1951. That same year, he made a visit to the United States which inspired *Time* to judge him "the sort of incumbent the French public wants (but has seldom had) in the presidential Elysee Palace, a genial approachable man who possesses enough native dignity to give his job as chief of state just a wisp of kingly bearing." During his term, Auriol also traveled through France's African colonies, then located primarily in the north and west of the continent; the *Historical Dictionary of France* observed that "although a supporter of an enlightened attitude to colonialism he was nonetheless reluctant to countenance the breakup of France's overseas empire." Indeed, the nation retained formal control over these territories until some years after the end of Auriol's administration. Auriol declined to stand for election to a second term, citing the high pressures of the office. He passed executive power to new President René Coty in January of 1954.

Continued Political Commentary

The former president remained active in public life for many years after his term expired, however, writing commentary for the newspaper *France-Soir* (France-Evening) and serving as honorary President of the United Nations Fédération Mondiale des Anciens Combattants (Worldwide Federation of Veterans, or FMAC). Auriol's work with FMAC took him around the world campaigning for peace until his retirement in 1963. Not shy about sharing his views about the present state of politics, in 1958 Auriol left retirement to open a public correspondence with General and fellow ex-President Charles de Gaulle regarding the increasingly weak government's inability to end a mutiny of French troops in North Africa—an action that some considered a grab for personal power by the general. "It is not possible that you would make the Republic capitulate before the violence of a faction and that you would draw out of compulsion a power that would be illegitimate," Auriol boldly stated in a letter. De Gaulle protested that his ambitions were to gain power only through legitimate means, which he won in June of 1958. Although Auriol initially threw his weight behind de Gaulle, in time he withdrew his support over such issues as the 1962 proposition to directly elect the president, believing it to clash with his long-held principles of democratic republicanism. Instead, he put his political might behind the failed socialist candidacy of François Mitterrand in 1965. His frustration with what he perceived as divisions within the socialist party led to his decision to give up his membership after over 50 years in 1958.

That same year, Auriol began work organizing his political memoirs, the *Journal du Septennat* (Journal of the Seven Years), although these were not published until some years after his death on January 1, 1966, after a long period of declining health. He was interred not far from his birthplace in Muret, France. The man and his legacy were largely well-regarded both during his lifetime and after his death; a 1951 *Time* magazine profile proclaimed Auriol "brave, attractive, fundamentally sound; but addicted to expediency and sterile compromise. To the U.S. he can well represent the best of 'third force' France." Only with the publication of his memoirs did Auriol's full effect in the maintenance of a stable government during one of France's most difficult modern political periods become widely known.

Books

Guilleminault, Gilbert, *La France de Vincent Auriol*, Éditions Denoël, 1970.
Historical Dictionary of France, Scarecrow Press, 2008.

Periodicals

New York Times, January 2, 1966.
Time, April 2, 1951.

Online

"Notice biographique de Vincent Auriol," CHAN Centre historique des Archives nationals, http://www.archivesnationales.culture.gouv.fr/chan/chan/notices/Vincent_Auriol.htm#bioauriol (January 11, 2010).
"Vincent Auriol," Assemblée Nationale, http://www.assembleenationale.fr/histoire/biographies/IVRepublique/Auriol-Vincent-Jules-27081884.asp (January 11, 2010).
"Vincent Auriol (1884–1966)," Chemins de mémoiré, http://www.cheminsdememoire.gouv.fr/ (January 11, 2010). □

Isabelle Autissier

Considered one of the most technically savvy and daring sailors of the modern era, French skipper Isabelle Autissier (born 1956) completed the first solo circumnavigation of the globe by a woman in 1991. She also set a New York-to-San Francisco speed record in 1994, sailing from coast-to-coast via a long loop around South America's Cape Horn. Autissier gained the most notoriety, however, for her participation in the Around Alone, a solo-around-the-world yacht race. In both 1994 and 1999, raging storms disabled her boat, prompting daring rescues that made headlines the world over.

The fourth of five daughters, Isabelle Autissier was born October 18, 1956, in Paris. She grew up in LaRochelle, a port town on the Atlantic coast of France. Her architect father, Jean, was crazy about sailing and taught Autissier to navigate the seas during summer vacations, which the family spent on the Brittany coast. As a child Autissier dreamed of one day sailing around the world alone. During the late 1970s, Autissier earned a college degree in nautical engineering. She worked as a marine scientist and marine science instructor before dedicating herself to sailing. As a young adult Autissier built a 32-foot steel sloop she dubbed *Parole*. She sailed the vessel around the Atlantic by herself, seeking to master the art of single-handed sailing.

Autissier entered her first big race, the Mini-Transat, in 1987. She was 30 years old. The Mini-Transat is a solo yacht race in which competitors sail the Atlantic Ocean from Brittany, in northwest France, to the French Antilles in the Caribbean. Autissier finished third and found herself hooked on solo racing. In the late 1980s she competed in the highly competitive La Solitaire du Figaro, a proving ground for future single-handed transatlantic racers. Twice, she finished among the top 12.

Completed Around-the-World Challenge

By 1990, Autissier had purchased a 60-foot cutter intent on entering the BOC Challenge—a solo, around-the-world race, later renamed the Around Alone. At 27,000 miles, it is the longest race for an individual in any sport. Autissier named her boat for her bank sponsor, dubbing it the *Ecureuil de Poitou-Charentes*. A typical BOC Challenge takes about 10 months, during which time the racers circle the globe in four separate stages while racing through the world's roughest oceans. The race, the longest sailing event for solo yacht racers, takes place every four years.

Autissier entered the 1990-91 race, which started in Charleston, South Carolina. The first leg consisted of a nearly 7,000-mile run to Cape Town, South Africa. Stage two took racers from Cape Town to New Zealand, which was about 7,000 miles away. From there, they sailed about 6,000 miles to Uruguay for stage 3. The final leg, at 5,700 miles, took racers from Uruguay back to Charleston, South

Carolina. For sailors, the race is fatiguing and high-risk. Typically during the race, they are lucky to get four hours of sleep each day. They eat freeze-dried and boiled food.

When the 1990-91 race commenced, Autissier got off to a fair start. Autissier, the only woman in the race, completed the first leg without incident. But during the second leg of the race, as she approached Australia, she lost her mast to the rough seas and whipping winds. Undaunted, she sewed several sails together, made a makeshift rig and slowly sailed the gimpy boat to Sydney, Australia. Though she only had to cover about 600 miles to reach port, the trek took three days. "In my mind, I never thought about asking for help," she told the *New York Times.* "My boat was safe and I was not injured, but I had to make it go as fast as I could."

Once repairs were made, she re-entered the race and finished seventh out of 18 racers. For Autissier, it was a moment of victory. No other woman had ever completed the grueling race and no other woman had ever circumnavigated the globe alone. Autissier, however, was always quick to downplay her accomplishments in terms of her gender. Speaking to *Women's Sports and Fitness,* Autissier put it this way: "I was an individual who just did things. Others said, 'Look, you are the first woman who sailed alone around the world!' Well, yes, but in the end is that what's really important? What's important is that I did something I wanted to do. I have always lived like this."

Autissier enjoyed the race so much she decided to do it again during the next running, in 1994-95. She began to study meteorology in earnest and acquired a new boat, dubbed the *Ecureuil Poitou-Charentes II.* In order to test out the vessel's capabilities and train for the race, Autissier hired a three-man crew to join her on a 14,000-mile trial run from New York to San Francisco, which required them to round Cape Horn, South America. They set off in the spring of 1994 and completed the voyage in a record-breaking time of 62 days. The previous New York-to-San Francisco speed record was 76 days, set in 1989 by Georgs Kolesnikovs, a sailor from Niagara Falls.

Rescued at Sea

The 1994-95 Around Alone race commenced in September 1994, with 19 solo sailors, including Autissier, who was feeling upbeat about her recent success on the seas. Following her gut instincts about the Atlantic and its weather patterns, Autissier left port sailing in an easterly and slightly north path. The rest of the skippers turned due south. While this path increased the number of miles Autissier had to sail in order to reach Cape Town, the weather turned out to be more favorable. She completed the first leg of the race in a record time of 35 days, sailing into Cape Town five days— and about 1,200 miles—ahead of the other sailors. Autissier bested by two days the passage record for that leg of the race. The *New York Times* reported that race director Mark Schrader was astounded by her lead. "Barring a gear failure, she has such a commanding lead now that it seems impossible for anyone to catch her in the remaining 16,000 miles of the race." One boat was lost at sea during the first leg, but the skipper was rescued by another racer.

The second leg, a 6,700-mile trek to Sydney, Australia, began in late November. This leg, which took racers through the Southern hemisphere, was known for being rough, requiring sailors to navigate their vessels through icebergs and storm systems. Five days into the second leg of the race, Autissier encountered a ravaging storm. The waves tipped her boat to the side, splitting her 83-foot mast. To save the boat, Autissier had to cut through the heavy rigging and ripped sails that kept the mast attached to the boat because the damaged mast, whipping around, posed a severe threat to the hull. According to *Sports Illustrated,* Autissier sent this message to race headquarters, "Thirty knots of wind, sea dark, sky crying. There is almost nothing left on the deck, nothing left of my dream." She created a makeshift mast, then headed for the Kerguelen Islands, which were 1,100 miles away. The repairs took several days.

Autissier re-entered the race and within days encountered another storm, this one with 40-foot waves and the worst to hit sailors in the history of the race. With winds whipping at nearly 60 miles per hour, the storm knocked her boat into a 360-degree roll and ripped off the mast, wrecking the steering system and leaving a massive hole in the deck. The boat flooded, knocking out her communications system. Ever hopeful, Autissier tried bailing with a bucket, then realized the situation was impossible. Within two hours of the rollover, she activated her emergency beacons. She was about 900 miles southeast of Adelaide. Autissier passed the next four days hunkered down in the front of the boat, in a compartment used for storage, hoping for a rescue.

The Australian Navy sent a boat—the *HMAS Darwin*— toward the area. Military planes went out scouring the seas for her boat. After it was located, a Seahawk rescue helicopter was sent to pluck Autissier from the wreckage via a winch and deliver her back to the *HMAS Darwin.* The cost of the rescue mission hit about $1.5 million, prompting much criticism for Autissier. The storm damaged several other boats, too, but Autissier's was the only one lost to the sea. A salvage crew was later dispatched but returned empty-handed.

Capsized in Storm

Obsessed with the seas, Autissier continued competing in the stressful, demanding sport of solo sailing. She got a new sponsor and had a new 60-foot sailing ship built, which she named the *PRB* in reference to the French building products company that sponsored her—Produits de Revêtement du Bâtiment. In 1996, she entered the *PRB* in the Vendee Globe competition, a solo, straight-through-no-stops-around-the-world race. Her boat, however, lost its rudder and she was disqualified while making repairs. She completed the race anyway, marking her second successful solo circumnavigation of the globe.

In 1998, Autissier entered the next running of the Around Alone. Just before the race commenced, Autissier told a reporter for the Columbia, South Carolina *State,* why she enjoyed participating in such solo odysseys. "You're out to sea for a very long time, and I do like that. It's wonderful to be just flying on these boats, to push them as fast as they can go. I like the balance between the long periods of being out to sea, and the speed of trying to get there first.''

After six months of sailing, she was halfway through the third leg of the race and feeling hopeful she would achieve her goal of winning the race. Autissier had won the first leg of the race and was leading in the third stage. Sailing the *PRB* and headed for Uruguay, she encountered a treacherous storm that capsized her boat. The mast and rigging broke apart. Autissier tried maneuvering the keel but was unable to right the boat, which was now upside-down in the water with the cabin windows below her. She had no electricity. The boat was filling with water. She had no choice but to activate her alarm beacon once more.

Italian racer Giovanni Soldini, who was 200 miles northeast of Autissier, took off in rescue. As he neared the area where he thought the *PRB* might be, he looked out and saw only chunks of ice bobbing on the water and wondered if he would even be able to spot her capsized vessel. Eventually, he spotted the upturned hull and pulled up alongside yelling for Autissier. When she failed to appear, he feared the worst. Next, Soldini got a hammer and threw it at the *PRB*. The loud whack got Autissier's attention and she popped out of the hatch. While waiting for rescue, she had straightened up the boat as best she could so it would go down with dignity. She left her personal belongings, boarding Soldini's boat with only her passport. She left the hatch open so the ship would fill and sink. Twenty-four hours had passed since she had set off the first beacon. The two sailed for Uruguay. Soldini was given a 24-hour race credit to make up for the time he spent rescuing Autissier and he went on to win the race.

Afterward, Autissier announced her retirement from solo yacht racing—but not sailing. She started competing in regattas and resumed work as a marine scientist. In 2010 Autissier sailed a boat to Antarctica to test a new device invented to identify ''growlers,'' floating ice chunks. The device was called an anti-UFO because it spotted unidentified floating objects.

Periodicals

Motor Boating & Sailing, March 1995.

New York Times, December 21, 1993; October 12, 1994; October 24, 1994; November 27, 1994; January 11, 1998.

Sports Illustrated, January 9, 1995.

State (Columbia, South Carolina), September 27, 1998.

Time, March 1, 1999,.

Women's Sports and Fitness, November 1999.

Online

''France: Isabelle Autissier Using Safran's anti-UFO System,'' *BYM Marine & Maritime News,* http://www.bymnews.com/news/newsDetails.php?id=64329 (December 29, 2009). □

B

Walter Baade

The German astronomer Walter Baade (1893–1960) made discoveries of fundamental importance to the evolving understanding of the cosmos in the twentieth century.

Baade (pronounced BAH-duh) was sometimes known as the scientist who doubled the size of the universe; his newly accurate measurements of the distances of stars in the Andromeda galaxy, made possible partly by wartime blackouts on the United States' west coast, resulted in a doubling of the estimated distance from Earth of those and other celestial bodies. That discovery sprang from Baade's groundbreaking identification of so-called stellar populations, types of stars differentiated by their stages of evolution. Although later observers have refined his ideas, Baade made profound contributions to the general modern conception of the life cycle of stars. He was the first to identify the supernova as a distinct phenomenon, and he may have helped to coin the word. Baade furthered the understanding of the nebulas and globular clusters that fascinate backyard astronomers, and he helped to develop the field of radio astronomy.

Pushed Toward Career in Ministry

Born Wilhelm Heinrich Walter Baade on March 24, 1893, in Schröttinghausen, in the western German region of Westphalia, Baade never used any first name other than Walter. The oldest of four children, he was the son of a schoolteacher, Konrad Baade, who made sure that he received a strong education in the classical German model. Konrad Baade received a promotion to principal, and the family moved to the more substantial town of Herford when Walter was ten.

He studied at the Gymnasium, or select high school, in Herford, and his parents hoped that he would become a Protestant minister. From the time he was in his mid-teens, however, Baade was fascinated by astronomy.

Baade matriculated at the University of Münster in 1912 but switched after a year to the University of Göttingen, which had for centuries boasted a reputation as a center for astronomical research. Thanks to a defective hip that eventually killed him, he was able to continue studying through World War I, doing national service at an aeronautical research institute in Göttingen rather than being drafted into the military. He completed a Ph.D., in 1919, and then took a job at the University of Hamburg Observatory in nearby Bergedorf. Even at this early stage of his career, Baade realized that the United States was emerging as a key center for astronomical research. He dreamed specifically of being able to work at the Mount Wilson Observatory in the San Gabriel Mountains outside Los Angeles, with its powerful 60- and 100-inch telescopes and what was then a perfectly clear and dark night sky, unlike the hazy, light-polluted skies of suburban Hamburg.

The rampant inflation that stressed German society in the 1920s made it difficult for Baade to travel to the United States. But he made a point of meeting American astronomers when they were visiting Europe, and he impressed his superiors at the observatory in Bergedorf, agreeing to travel as far afield as the Philippines when total eclipses of the sun, which provide once-in-a-lifetime experiences for astronomical photography, occurred in different parts of the world. He discovered an asteroid, 944 Hidalgo, that had the largest orbit of any asteroid known at the time, and a comet, designated 1922c. Baade met Mount Wilson astronomer Harlow Shapley in Cambridge, England, and was inspired to pursue Shapley's specialty of studying star clusters and variable stars (stars whose brightness varies), fields that seemed to offer

promising new insights into the dimensions of the visible universe. In 1926 Shapley paved the way for Baade to receive a Rockefeller Foundation fellowship that allowed him to come to the United States for a year, meet astronomers at various facilities, and conduct research of his own.

Worked with Edwin Hubble

Baade came prepared with a series of important papers on clusters and variable stars, and he added several more to his portfolio over the course of six months he spent living in Pasadena, California, and working at the Mount Wilson observatory. He was particularly inspired by the work of Edwin Hubble, later the namesake of the Hubble Space Telescope, who had done close studies of nearby stars using the observatory's unprecedentedly powerful telescopes. By the time he returned to Hamburg, Baade was recognized as one of the most important rising young astronomers in the field. The Hamburg observatory, hoping to keep him on staff, gave him promotions and raises, and the observatory at the University of Jena offered him its directorship. Baade married Johanna "Hanni" Bohlmann, one of his assistants, in January of 1929; the marriage lasted until Baade's death, and he later applied her nickname, Muschi, to an asteroid he discovered.

With the goal of returning to the United States firmly in mind, Baade turned down German teaching and research posts. To go with his growing body of discoveries, he made himself an expert in the fields of astronomical photography and photometry, the measurement of the light and radiation

emitted by astronomical bodies. When a staff position at Mount Wilson became available in 1930, Baade jumped at the chance and was hired, but had to apply for an advance on his $3,300-a-year salary in order to buy tickets for passage on the steamship *Los Angeles* for himself and his wife. After passing through the Panama Canal they arrived in California in October of 1931.

In his early years in southern California, Baade was the Mount Wilson staff resource for astronomical photography. But he soon began to focus on his own research and to make discoveries that reoriented the field of astronomy. One of them involved the supernova, a stellar explosion that may be triggered by a star's gravitational collapse into itself; a supernova may temporarily make a star into the brightest object in the night sky. Baade and Swiss-born physicist Franz Zwicky wrote a paper that identified the ways in which a supernova differed from an ordinary nova, which is caused by the explosion of hydrogen attached to a dwarf star. According to Baade biographer Donald E. Osterbrock, writing in the *Journal for the History of Astronomy,* Baade and Zwicky "apparently . . . coined the name 'supernova' in 1933."

Baade continued to visit Germany as Nazi ideology deepened in the 1930s, sometimes to visit his ailing mother and at other times to attend scientific conferences. A scholarly researcher to the core, he made the declarations necessary to stay in good standing with the German government, while at the same time assuring his supervisors in California that he was opposed to the Nazi regime. He found himself in France just before the outbreak of World War II on September 1, 1939, and barely managed to board a ship for the United States before the country's borders were closed. An Austrian colleague who taught at Stanford University was not so lucky; he was trapped in France and was eventually sent to a concentration camp.

Took Advantage of Wartime Blackouts

During the war Baade, who had applied for American citizenship but never completed the citizenship requirements, was classified as an enemy alien. Until strings were pulled, he was restricted to daytime activities—a fatal curfew for an astronomer. But the wartime environment ended up working to Baade's advantage. With lights in the Los Angeles area frequently subject to blackouts because of the fear of Japanese aerial attack, Baade deployed the observatory's 100-inch telescope in examinations of the Andromeda Galaxy, the nearest one to Earth's own Milky Way. He was able to make unprecedented observations and photographs of individual stars in the galaxy, and he noticed that its various areas, its core and spiral arms, tended to contain different kinds of stars. In the "arms" were hot, blue stars that were relatively new, while the core contained older, red stars. Baade called these types Population I and Population II, respectively, and the concept of stellar populations became important in future research into the large-scale workings of the cosmos.

As he refined his methods after the war, often working at the new 200-inch telescope at southern California's Mount Palomar Observatory, Baade was also able to identify more than 300 stars in Andromeda that were termed

Cepheid variable stars (named for a star called Delta Cephei). The brightness of these stars changed at a constant rate, making them useful in estimating their distances from Earth by means of a graphic calculation called a period-luminosity curve. Baade's observations proved that the period-luminosity curve as it existed at that time applied only to Population II stars, making the majority of accepted distance estimates incorrect. In the broad terms in which the discovery was reported in the press, it seemed that the universe had suddenly been revealed to be twice as large as astronomers had thought.

The publicity-shy Baade had to speak up for himself when Shapley, who had encouraged his career so many years earlier, tried via several conference papers and a Harvard press release, to claim credit for the discovery. Baade, according to Osterbrock, called a paper delivered by Shapley at a 1952 American Astronomical Society meeting "simply shameless," and complained that he had "lifted wholesale" parts of a paper Baade had earlier delivered in Rome, Italy, "without any acknowledgements." Other astronomers quietly made sure that Baade's name was properly attached to the news, and in time his new estimate of cosmic dimensions became the discovery for which he was perhaps most famous among amateur astronomers.

In the 1950s Baade frequently worked in the emerging field of radio astronomy and made important discoveries about the Crab nebula and other mysterious sources of radio signals. He retired in 1958 but was invited to give lectures at Harvard University, the Institute for Advanced Study at Princeton University, and other prestigious institutions. In June of that year he gave the Henry Norris Russell Lecture at a meeting of the American Astronomical Society in Madison, Wisconsin, which was considered the society's highest lifetime achievement award. After a sojourn in Australia that allowed him to observe the skies of the Southern Hemisphere, Baade returned to Germany, where he underwent an operation designed to correct his hip deformity. It was successful, but complications developed during his recuperation, and he died of respiratory failure in Göttingen, West Germany, on June 25, 1960. Baade always preferred hands-on research to writing academic papers, but many of his ideas were considered quite influential. The British astronomer Fred Hoyle, as quoted in the *Dictionary of Scientific Biography,* noted that "almost every one of Baade's papers turned out to have far-reaching consequences." A group of his writings were edited by the astronomer Cecilia Payne-Gaposchkin and released as a book, *Evolution of Stars and Galaxies,* in 1963.

Books

Dieke, Sally H., "Baade, Wilhelm Heinrich Walter," in *Dictionary of Scientific Biography,* edited by Charles Coulston Gillispie, Scribner's, 1970.

Osterbrock, Donald E., *Walter Baade: A Life in Astrophysics,* Princeton, 2001.

Periodicals

Journal for the History of Astronomy, 1995, 1996, p. 301; 1997, 1998.

Online

"The Bruce Medalists: Wilhelm Heinrich Walter Baade," *Sonoma State University Department of Physics & Astronomy,* http://www.phys-astro.sonoma.edu/index.shtml (October 1, 2009).

"Walter Baade: Master Observer," *Astronomical Society of the Pacific,* http://www.astrosociety.org/pubs/mercury/31_04/baade.html (October 1, 2009).

"Wilhelm Heinrich Walter Baade," *Notable Scientists: From 1900 to the Present,* Gale, 2008. Reproduced in Biography Resource Center. Farmington Hills, Mich.: Gale, 2009. http://www.net.galegroup.com/servlet/BioRC□

James Anthony Bailey

The American circus entrepreneur James A. Bailey (1847–1906), the "Bailey" in the durable Barnum & Bailey partnership, was the operational genius behind the giant touring circus that toward the end of the nineteenth century became known all over the world.

Bailey, in fact, was directly responsible for several of the major drawing cards of the famed circus. It was he who ordered the acquisition of Jumbo the elephant. He pioneered the concept of a circus with multiple rings, and his logistical solutions to the problems involved in moving loads of animals and equipment over land and sea were so sophisticated that they were studied by military officers. Bailey also was involved in another famous spectacle of nineteenth-century life, "Buffalo Bill" Cody's Wild West show. In the words of an 1891 *New York Times* profile, Bailey could, "without exaggeration, be called the creator of the modern circus."

Ran Away After Abuse

Unlike his business partner, the garrulous showman P.T. Barnum, Bailey shunned publicity and avoided newspaper reporters. Parts of his biography are obscure, and despite his importance in the history of American entertainment, he has never been the subject of a full-length biographical study. James Anthony Bailey was born in Detroit in 1847, perhaps on July 4, and his birth name has been variously given as McGuinness, McGinnis, and McGinness. He was the youngest of four brothers. Their father died when Bailey was about ten, leaving, according to the *New York Times* profile, an estate worth a then-sizable $20,000. But, for whatever reason, that was not enough to keep Bailey from a life of servitude and abuse on a farm near Pontiac, Michigan, that belonged to a sister or an appointed guardian (accounts conflict). After suffering repeated whippings on the slightest of pretexts, Bailey ran away from home at age 12.

"I remember well now that morning when I started down the country road, determined never to return except as my own master," Bailey told the *Times.* "I wore a big straw hat, a little brown jacket and trousers that buttoned to it, and I was barefoot. My only possession was a jackknife, with one broken blade." Bailey got work as a farm laborer for $3.25 a month, binding wheat in sheaves by hand. Deliverance from

cities. Bailey was undiscouraged by the loss, for he knew that he was gaining valuable operational knowledge. He went even further into debt when the Great London Circus went bankrupt during a U.S. tour and was seized by a printer who advanced Bailey the money to purchase and continue operating it.

In 1879 Bailey incorporated the new show into the existing Cooper and Bailey Circus, creating an entity with the elaborate name of Howes' Great London Circus and Sanger's Royal British Menagerie and Cooper & Bailey's International Allied Shows. Cooper retired from the business in 1881, and Bailey once again pursued a merger with an important rival: P.T. Barnum's Museum, Menagerie, and Circus, based in Brooklyn, New York, and already billing itself as "The Greatest Show on Earth." Its owner, Phineas T. Barnum, was one of nineteenth-century America's great showmen, with decades of experience as a promoter of not only circus acts but also novelty acts like Tom Thumb and even the triumphant tour of Swedish opera star Jenny Lind. When he joined forces with his rising young competitor in 1881, the new entity soon became the Barnum and London Circus.

From the start, Barnum was the public face of the partnership, but Bailey was its operational genius. His first and for many years most famous coup was the purchase, from England's Royal Zoological Society, of Jumbo the elephant, advertised as "The Towering Monarch of His Mighty Race, Whose Like the World Will Never See Again." The sale of the elephant was roundly condemned in Britain, but he became one of the new circus's leading attractions from 1882, when Barnum and Bailey walked him across the Brooklyn Bridge in his American debut, until he was killed in a collision with a train in St. Thomas, Ontario, in 1885. Barnum and Bailey split their operations in that year but reunited in 1888 and mounted a tour under the new name of the "Barnum & Bailey Greatest Show on Earth."

this work came when the Robinson & Lake Circus passed through Pontiac. Bailey, along with other boys, signed up to hang posters and distribute flyers advertising the show, and the circus owners took a liking to him and agreed to take him on as an employee. The advance agent who had initially hired the boy was named Bailey, and he took that last name in gratitude.

Bailey's last non-circus employment came during the Civil War, when he worked as clerk for a sutler, or military provisioner, attached to the 114th regiment of Ohio Volunteers. After the war's end Bailey looked once again for opportunities in the circus industry and was hired, around 1868, as an advance agent himself, by Hemmings and Cooper's Circus. In that year he married Ruth Louisa McCaddon of Zanesville, Ohio; her brother, Joseph T. McCaddon, became manager of the Forepaugh Circus. They had no children. Bailey worked industriously, and in 1873 owner James Cooper sold him a partnership in the enterprise. It was soon renamed the Cooper and Bailey Circus.

Took Circus on International Tour

From the beginning, Bailey had big plans for the company and for American circuses in general. Despite Cooper's objections he took the Cooper and Bailey Circus to Australia, where an American circus was a distinct novelty. He reaped large profits, losing all of them and going into debt when he returned via South America and incurred huge transportation expenses in reaching the mountainous continent's far-flung

Methods Impressed Military Leaders

While he was still in competition with Barnum, Bailey had begun to add a second ring to his circus shows, strengthening the impression of an action-packed spectacle. He envisioned the evolution of the circus to its later three-ring form, perhaps surrounded by a track with additional performers and animals. The Barnum & Bailey circus continued to grow, and Bailey undertook the considerable task of planning for a five-year European tour. "The work of putting the show on a steamer was a spectacle," a *New York Times* writer recalled much later in Bailey's obituary. "Freight cars and elephants were lifted by cranes and lowered into the holds of vessels. Every conceivable bit of circus paraphernalia was loaded between decks, and the show sailed." Bailey was defeated only by the transportation system in Russia, where railway tracks were laid a different distance apart from those in western Europe, but his logistical schemes were so elaborate that they were reportedly studied by European military commanders.

Bailey's operational accomplishments rested on a foundation of hands-on leadership. His employees, according to the *Times* profile, called him "a worker from Workville" and regarded him as a taskmaster who expected the same level of hard work from them that he himself delivered. He was, however, also considered highly approachable if an employee reported a problem, and he was known to quietly aid circus workers who had fallen into financial problems. Bailey was credited with helping to make the circus into a form of family entertainment, diminishing its carnival freak show aspect as he developed his giant spectacles with friendly clowns for diversion. According to the *Times,* he put on the payroll "three Pinkerton detectives, who have a very summary manner of disposing of all fakirs, sharps, crooks, and followers." Circus employees were salaried workers rather than transients hired for a season, and many of them worked for Bailey for years.

Bailey acquired another major competitor, the Fore-paugh Circus, in 1890, but continued to operate it separately from the Barnum & Bailey Circus. After Barnum's death in 1891 he was sole proprietor of Barnum & Bailey. He continued to add elaborate new entertainments to the giant spectacle, importing natives from far-flung lands to create an "Ethnological Congress," and mounting an historical pageant centered on the Roman Emperor Nero. In 1894 Bailey purchased a controlling interest in Buffalo Bill's Wild West, a cowboy-and-Indian spectacle that, like Bailey's own shows, drew crowds on both sides of the Atlantic Ocean. Several times, Bailey suffered breakdowns as a result of overwork, and in the early 1900s decade he constructed a substantial house called The Knolls in Mount Vernon, New York, mounting there some of the substantial art collection he had acquired in his European dealings.

During the foreign tours of the Barnum & Bailey circus, other troupes had the American field to themselves, and a comparatively new circus operated by the seven Ringling brothers of Baraboo, Wisconsin, grew quickly to fill the void. Bailey again pursued a partial merger with an important rival, selling the Ringlings part interest in the Forepaugh circus in 1905. The following year, Bailey fell ill with a condition diagnosed as erysipelas. He died at his home in Mount Vernon on April 11, 1906, leaving his estate, estimated at $8,000,000, to his wife. She sold the Barnum & Bailey Circus to the Ringling brothers the following year, creating the enduring Ringling Brothers and Barnum & Bailey Circus—"The Greatest Show on Earth."

Books

National Cyclopedia of American Biography, James T. White & Company, 1935.

Saxon, A.H., *P.T. Barnum: The Legend and the Man,* Columbia, 1989.

Periodicals

New York Times, April 19, 1891; April 12, 1906.

Online

"Bailey and the Ringlings," *Ringling Bros. & Barnum & Bailey Circus,* http://www.ringling.com/TopLanding.aspx?id=11610 (October 10, 2009).

"Biography of Joseph T. McCaddon," *Princeton University Library: McCaddon Collection of the Barnum and Bailey Circus, 1871–1907,* http://www.diglib.princeton.edu/ead/ (October 10, 2009). □

Cristóbal Balenciaga

Spanish fashion designer Cristóbal Balenciaga (1895– 1972) became one of the twentieth century's most respected and influential couturiers. After early success dressing royalty in his native Spain, Balenciaga relocated to Paris during the tumultuous years of the Spanish Civil War. There, the designer founded the fashion house Balenciaga, which helped define high-end looks from the late 1930s until the 1960s and propelled him to the heights of the profession. Worn by monarchs, actresses, and socialites alike, his apparel encapsulated the tasteful elegance of the upper echelons of mid-century European and American society. Although the designer closed his couture operation in 1968, his legacy—both through his work instructing young designer and his lasting influence on form—can be readily seen in the fashion world of the modern-day. Now part of the Gucci Group, the House of Balenciaga continues to produce men's and women's fashions, as well as accessories, shoes, and fragrances.

Born Cristóbal Balenciaga Eisaguirre on January 21, 1895, in the small town of Guetaria in the northern Basque province of Guipúzcoa, Spain, Balenciaga began his career with the fabric arts while still a child. His father, a seaman and local mayor, died when the future designer was quite young, and his mother worked as a seamstress to support Balenciaga and his two elder siblings. After completing three years of elementary education—a period so brief that Lesley Ellis Miller characterized it as "hardly time enough for the basics of reading, writing, arithmetic and catechism, let alone the luxury of art appreciation" in *Cristóbal Balenciaga*—the twelve-year-old Balenciaga entered an apprenticeship as a tailor. This early training in the art of precise garment construction and fitting informed the designer's later *haute couture* offerings, which were characterized by a strict attention to line and form. Additionally, throughout his career Balenciaga produced only couture garments—those made specially to order for a particular client, cut and fitted precisely to the customer's measurements and each one of a kind. Unlike some of his contemporaries who lacked the necessary construction skills to actually produce such a garment, Balenciaga drew on his early tailoring training to have direct involvement with the garment-making process long after he had risen to great fame.

By 1912, Balenciaga had won the patronage of the aristocratic Marquesa de Casa Torres, who sent him to Paris to develop his craft. There, the teenager became acquainted with such influential fashion designers as Paul Poiret and began collecting examples of Parisian fashion to reinterpret for the Spanish market as the head dressmaker for a Spanish tailor in San Sébastian, a resort town that was the summer residence of the Spanish royal court. By the middle part of the decade, he reputedly felt sufficiently confident in his

abilities to establish his own titular shop in San Sébastian with some 30 employees; records shows that in 1918, Balenciaga and financial backers Benita and Daniela Lizano Landa formally registered his design operation in the town. Writing in the *New Yorker,* Judith Thurman observed that Balenciaga's "business was built on the premise that a lady changed her clothes three times a day, disdained the familiarity of inferiors, flaunted her diamonds but never her indiscretions, and travelled with several steamer trunks and a maid." By all indications this outlook melded well with the practices of the era, and Balenciaga's business thrived in San Sébastian until the advent of the 1930s.

Set Up Shop in Paris

During the 1930s, Spain's political culture became increasingly turbulent in the wake of the collapse of the nation's monarchy, and ultimately exploded into the bloody Spanish Civil War toward of the end of the decade. These events most likely contributed to Balenciaga's decision to relocate both himself and the heart of his business to Paris, as his domestic customers—largely members of the Spanish royal family who had split their time between Madrid and San Sébastian—simply disappeared. Balenciaga had opened two additional outposts in Madrid and Barcelona in the mid-1930s that produced clothes under the Eisa label. Soon after the outbreak of the Spanish Civil War in 1936, however, the designer left Spain, spending time in London before continuing on to Paris. There, he established a

new House of Balenciaga at 10 Avenue George V that remained his center of operations until his retirement in the late 1960s. In August of the following year, he presented his first Parisian couture collection thanks to financial assistance from fellow Basque Nicolas Bizcarrondo and Frenchman Vladzio Zawrorowski d'Attainville. The partnership between Balenciaga and the latter man was personal as well as professional, with the two living together openly as a couple until d'Attainville's death in the late 1940s.

At its inception, Balenciaga's line was received somewhat cautiously by the French fashion press, but the support of *Harper's Bazaar* editor Carmel Snow helped propel the House of Balenciaga to the lofty heights of haute couture. Soon, Balenciaga began to build a Paris-based business that catered to a French, British, and American clientele while still maintaining a Spanish presence with his Madrid and Barcelona operations, although at least the Madrid location closed for a period during the height of the Spanish Civil War. When war came to the rest of the continent, Balenciaga continued to produce his high quality, high cost garments; in fact, the Spanish fashion icon was one of the few designers continuing to work in France during World War II. Although his precise reasons for primarily remaining in the country during the tumultuous fighting and German occupation of Paris are unknown, some have speculated that the turmoil still underway in his native country deterred him from returning to Spain for the duration. Reports indicate that Balenciaga showed a collection in Nice in 1942 at the height of the conflict. Despite the challenges of the period, the designer continued to produce innovative shapes, including a nipped waist silhouette that foreshadowed designer Christian Dior's landmark New Look silhouette at the end of the decade.

Committed to the spirit of haute couture throughout his lengthy career, Balenciaga resisted the move toward ready-to-wear that many of his contemporaries embraced in the years following World War II. Speaking to Thurman in 2006, fashion designer and former Balenciaga associate Hubert de Givenchy explained that "Balenciaga's couture was not only a style of dress but a code of conduct...He took the old-fashioned view that a woman should confide herself to a single couturier. When the New Look began turning heads, and some of his clients deserted him, he was profoundly grieved by their fickleness, and that of the press." Already an intensely private person who shunned the limelight that other designers craved, Balenciaga withdrew even further from public life as a result of this perceived blow, barring certain journalists from his fashion shows and, with rare exception, refusing to grant interviews from 1948 on. Entrance to the design house itself was strictly controlled, with only a privileged few winning access to the near-silent Balenciaga work environment.

Became Premier Couture Designer

This era of increased reticence arrived alongside a period of great influence for the designer, however. Beginning in the late 1940s, Balenciaga introduced increasingly unfitted silhouettes into his design presaging the loose sack dress of the following decade—a trend so distinctive that it even became the focus of an episode of the popular television comedy *I Love Lucy.* His stature as a "designer's designer" grew throughout the 1950s, and after the death of Dior in 1957, Balenciaga became the unquestioned king of haute couture. His structural forms drew at some times on his own Spanish national costume heritage, with flamenco-infused flounces and matador-styled jackets, and at others on forms in nature; Balenciaga's biography in *Contemporary Designers* noted that "these pure inventions in silk were likened by fashion writers to banked clouds, giant flowers, and gliding swans." Less fantastical but equally respected were the designer's cleanly and thoughtfully designed daywear, which combined figure-forgiving cuts with tastefully expensive fabrics and construction techniques. A line of fragrances rounded out the house's offerings from the mid-1950s onwards.

As the cultural shifts of the 1960s changed the landscape of fashion, Balenciaga combined new trends such as knee-high boots alongside his classics, although he never became an interpreter of the era's youth culture. In 1966, Balenciaga received an offer to design new uniforms for Air France's flight attendants, and he followed through with sharply modern skirt-and-jacket combinations in blue serge that appeared at the end of the decade. In a departure from his standard couture mold, Balenciaga's airline attire was not individually fitted, but instead designed and produced on a larger scale in what was arguably the designer's only venture in the ready-to-wear market. Despite this shift in production style, the uniforms retained much of Balenciaga's signature daywear look and have drawn comparisons to his couture suits of the decade. The uniforms also displayed the designer's failure to understand the needs of the job and the zeitgeist of the time, however: they focused strongly on form to the exclusion of allowing for necessary working movements and offered a more traditional take on fashion than the young women of the decade preferred. Writing in *Balenciaga,* Miller decried the flight attendants' ensuing complaints as "a sad finale to a long and rich career."

Ended Couture Operations

Indeed, by the late 1960s, Balenciaga had realized that the couture era had largely passed. His creations—among the most expensive items of clothing for sale in the world—appealed to an increasingly scarce client base dedicated to the art of apparel regardless of cost and had no connection to the growing youth culture. In response, he closed his couture houses in Paris and Barcelona in 1968 and his remaining house in Madrid the following year. Retreating yet further from public view into retirement at his Spanish country house, the designer made his final public appearance at the funeral of fellow fashion designer Coco Chanel in 1971. Balenciaga completed his final work—a commissioned wedding dress for Spanish dictator Franco's granddaughter, who later became the Marquesa de Cadiz—in early 1972. On March 24 of that same year, Balenciaga died in Javea, Spain, at the age of 77 as the result of a heart attack. He was interred soon thereafter in his hometown of Guetaria.

The story of the House of Balenciaga did not end with the designer's death, though. Perfume production continued even after the closure of the couture houses, and in 1978, Balenciaga's heirs sold the business to German firm Hoechst. The new corporate owner launched the ready-to-wear collection that Balenciaga had so stubbornly refused to do—despite making comments toward the end of his life that if only he were younger, he would have infused a special wit and style into the market—and Ramón Esparza came on board to design for the new label. Perfume launches continued apace throughout the next two decades while designers came and went, largely failing to ignite the kind of passion women had had for Balenciaga in its heyday. After the rise of French designer Nicolas Ghesquière to the house's top design slot in 1998, however, Balenciaga again began to attract attention for its distinctive fashions, which at times drew inspiration from its founder's archival collections. That founder himself remained alive not only in the minds of fashion lovers, but also in the hearts of fellow Basques. In 1999, Guetaria town officials launched an initiative to build a museum dedicated to the life and works of the fashion legend. Financial mismanagement impeded progress, however, and the institution was not expected to open until at least 2011.

Books

Contemporary Designers, 3rd ed., St. James Press, 1997.
Miller, Lesley Ellis, *Cristobal Balenciaga,* Holmes and Mier, 1993.
Miller, Lesley Ellis, *Balenciaga,* V&A Publications, 2007.
Steele, Valerie, ed., *Encyclopedia of Clothing and Fashion,* Charles Scribner's Sons, 2005.

Periodicals

New York Times, March 25, 1972; August 30, 2009.
New Yorker, July 3, 2006.

Online

"Biography," Official Balenciaga Web site, http://www.balenciaga.com/int/en/Default.aspx?nav=/the-house/biography/cristobal-balenciaga (January 2, 2010).□

J. G. Ballard

British author J.G. Ballard (1930–2009) wrote fiction that seemed prophetic in its dark, sometimes apocalyptic themes.

Often controversial when they first appeared, Ballard's novels and short stories gained a substantial readership as contemporary society came more and more to resemble his dystopian visions. When Ballard submitted *Crash,* a novel depicting individuals who are sexually excited by automobile accidents, to a publisher, one of the publisher's evaluators commented, according to the *Times* of London, that "this author is beyond psychiatric help." Ballard, for his part, considered the criticism "proof of complete artistic success," and he lived to see

Crash filmed by the celebrated Canadian director David Cronenberg in 1996. Ballard's novels to a greater or lesser degree anticipated rampant consumerism, the cult of celebrity, terrorism, and even global warming. Never comfortable with the science fiction label, he nevertheless used speculative and often surreal concepts as starting points for social critique in his 15 novels and various short story collections.

Pampered Upbringing in China

James Graham Ballard was born to British parents on November 15, 1930, in Shanghai, China. Ballard's father was a scientist employed by a textile firm, and Ballard spent his childhood isolated from the culture in whose midst the family lived. He did not speak Chinese, his only contact with Chinese people came when he interacted with family servants, and he ate a Chinese dinner for the first time only many years later in Britain. The Japanese invasion of China and the outbreak of World War II, however, insured that history caught up with Ballard's affluent family. In 1943 they were imprisoned in the Lunghua concentration camp by Japanese authorities.

Ballard was still in his early teens, and, according to the *Times,* he had "not happy, but not unpleasant memories of the camp." He lived with his family in a single room and ran through the camp's crowded public spaces with other young people. Still, the experience left its mark on the young man and contributed to the tense, unpleasant atmosphere of his

later fiction. The family was released in 1945 and returned to England the following year. They found their homeland devastated, an experience that further darkened Ballard's outlook. He attended the private Leys School in Cambridge, which he said reminded him of the Japanese concentration camp, and then enrolled at King's College at Cambridge University, taking courses in psychiatry. He was already beginning to write short stories.

According to the *Times,* Ballard complained that Cambridge was an "academic theme park," but perhaps the real source of his dissatisfaction was that he was becoming more interested in literature than in medicine. He left Cambridge to study English at the University of London, then joined Britain's Royal Air Force in 1953 and spent a stretch stationed in Moose Jaw, Saskatchewan, Canada. In 1954 he returned to England, and the following year he married Helen Matthews. Faced with the necessity of supporting a family that soon included one son and two daughters, Ballard took a job in 1957 as an editor at a business magazine called *Chemistry and Industry.* In 1961 he moved the family into a small house in the London suburb of Shepperton, where he remained for the rest of his life.

Wrote Speculative Disaster Novels

By that time, Ballard's formal literary career was already in full swing, and in 1962 he quit his editorial job and became a full-time writer. His first published short story, "Prima Belladonna," appeared in 1956 and featured a woman whose eyes were insects. His first novel, *The Wind from Nowhere,* appeared in 1962 and dealt with a society devastated by a giant storm. Another disaster novel, *The Drowned World,* was set in a flooded London in which humans were forced to live on the top floors of buildings. The book is sometimes regarded as one of the first to depict the effects of the rising sea levels that are predicted to result from global warming.

In 1964 Ballard took his family on a vacation in Spain. His wife died unexpectedly of pneumonia on the trip, leaving Ballard to return to London and raise his three children alone. His next novel, *The Crystal World,* extended the disaster themes of its predecessors, but after that his work took a new and disturbing direction that he later noted was in part his attempt to deal with the pain caused by his wife's death. Ballard's next book, *The Atrocity Exhibition,* had a unique narrative form: it consisted of a group of short, realistic or quasi-scientific fragments that, in the words of his *New York Times* obituary, "drew on events like the Vietnam War, the death of Marilyn Monroe, and the deaths of James Dean and Jayne Mansfield in automobile accidents to posit a connection among the mass media, violence and sexuality." Particularly notorious was a segment called "The Assassination of John F. Kennedy Considered as a Downhill Motor Race." Published in 1969 in Britain, *The Atrocity Exhibition* was at first censored in the United States by its own publisher, Doubleday, which destroyed all the copies it had printed. It finally appeared in the early 1970s as *Love & Napalm: U.S.A.,* published by Grove Press.

Reviews were widely divergent, with such intellectual heavyweights as critic Susan Sontag (pro) and novelist Paul Theroux (con) weighing in on opposite sides. Equally controversial, if not more so, was *Crash* (1973), which contained passages like this: "Vaughan unfolded for me all his obsessions with the mysterious eroticism of wounds: the perverse logic of blood-soaked instrument panels, seatbelts smeared with excrement, sun-visors lined with brain tissue. For Vaughan each crashed car set off a tremor of excitement, in the complex geometries of a dented fender, in the unexpected variations of crushed radiator grilles, in the grotesque overhang of an instrument panel forced on to a driver's crotch as if in some calibrated act of machine fellatio." Even negative evaluations conceded the skill in Ballard's prose, and the novel's outlandish concept seemed to gain relevance in a media environment increasingly focused on violence and gore. A new generation of readers came to *Crash* after the release of Cronenberg's 1996 film, which, like the novel itself, accumulated a cult audience.

Ballard's other major novels of the 1970s were less outrageous but no less intense in their implied critiques of contemporary society. *Concrete Island* (1974) featured a protagonist trapped on a highway median island, while *High Rise* (1975) dealt with a group of residents of an apartment tower who revert to tribal behavior. In the 1970s and 1980s collections of Ballard's short stories began to appear. Many of them had appeared in the innovative British science fiction magazine *New Worlds* under the editorship of Michael Moorcock, and some involved more conventional science fiction and fantasy themes. Ballard rarely dealt with technology in anything but a negative light, however, and he himself disliked the application of the science fiction classification to his work, preferring to say, according to the London *Times,* that his books "pictured the psychology of the future."

Wrote Novel Rooted in Wartime Experience

For his next major book, however, Ballard turned to his own past and forged one of his most successful creations. *Empire of the Sun,* depicting a preteen boy who survives a Japanese internment camp during World War II, contained fictionalized versions of Ballard's own experiences. The book was a bestseller and became even more famous after it was filmed by famed U.S. director Steven Spielberg and screenwriter Tom Stoppard in 1987. Although the book seemed to be a departure from Ballard's darkly surreal earlier novels, Moorcock, who was a close friend of Ballard's, argued in a London *Times* essay that "this book revealed, with its images of a Shanghai deserted by its former residents, its empty buildings and swimming pools, its crashed plane and wrecked machines, its solitary, introspective protagonist, the realities of his supposedly invented images," and seemed to confirm that many of the horrors of Ballard's fiction grew out of his early experiences of inhumanity and disaster.

The book brought Ballard a measure of financial security. He got his first credit card—up until that point he had simply withdrawn whatever cash was available from his bank on Monday morning and spread it out across the week. He continued, however, to live in his modest Shepperton home until just before his death. Ballard won the Guardian Fiction Prize in 1984 and took home other literary awards as well. When selected as Commander of the British Empire in 2003, however, he turned the honor down because of his antiroyalist views. Strongly libertarian in his political outlook,

Ballard had little use for either the left or right wings of British politics. He wrote a second fictionalized memoir, *The Kindness of Women* (1991), that dealt with life in England after World War II.

Ballard also continued to write fiction, with such books as *Millennium People* (2003) returning to his tendency to depict provocative themes. That book depicted terrorist bombings of the Royal Albert Hall and the Victoria and Albert Museum by a clique of disaffected wealthy Londoners, while *Kingdom Come* (2006) drew parallels between shopping mall culture and fascism. Diagnosed with prostate cancer, Ballard completed a nonfiction autobiography, *Miracles of Life: Shanghai to Shepperton,* before his death in London on April 19, 2009. "His fiction was perhaps too invariant for him to rank as the greatest literary figure of his generation," wrote the London *Independent* in its obituary, "but of all the writers of significance in the last decades of the 20th century, he was maybe the widest awake."

Books

Ballard, J.G., *Miracles of Life: Shanghai to Shepperton,* Fourth Estate, 2008.
St. James Guide to Science Fiction Writers, 4th ed., St. James, 1996.

Periodicals

Independent (London, England), April 21, 2009.
New York Times, April 21, 2009.
New Yorker, April 20, 2009.
Reason, July 2009.
Times (London, England), April 21, 2009; April 25, 2009.□

Ann Bancroft

American explorer Ann Bancroft (born 1955) tallied many polar firsts. In 1986, she reached the North Pole via dogsled, becoming the first woman to cross the ice and stand on the very top of the earth. In 1993, she led an all-female expedition to the South Pole, becoming the first woman to reach both the North and South poles. Bancroft completed another arctic first in 2000-01, when she crossed the Antarctic landmass on foot alongside Norwegian explorer Liv Arnesen, becoming the first to complete such an expedition.

Enjoyed Early Fascination with Ice

Bancroft was born September 29, 1955, in St. Paul, Minnesota, to Richard and Debbie Bancroft. She grew up alongside four brothers and sisters in the Twin Cities suburb of Mendota Heights. Frequently, Bancroft accompanied her father on excursions to northern Minnesota to camp and canoe. She also enjoyed backyard winter camping, although she had a hard time persuading her cousins to join her for a frosty night out. Bancroft's first overseas trip came during elementary school when her family spent two years in Kenya.

When Bancroft was 12 she stumbled across *Endurance,* a book that recounted polar explorer Ernest Shackleton's 1914 ill-fated Antarctic journey. After the ice froze and crushed Shackleton's boat, his team spent nearly 500 days trying to find a way home. This story of South Pole survival captivated Bancroft and she dreamed of following in Shackleton's footsteps. Just reading the book was a triumph for Bancroft, who was diagnosed with dyslexia in seventh grade. For Bancroft, the words and letters of the Shackleton saga were scrambled on the page, but the pictures drew her in to the story and kept her reading.

Later in life, after completing her North and South pole treks, Bancroft told the *St. Paul Pioneer Press* that having dyslexia prepared her for polar exploration. "My learning difference has been a gift," Bancroft said. "Obviously, it's been very painful and frustrating, but it's given me that linear, step-by-step attitude. On these polar trips, when it gets tough and ugly and you want to quit, the only way to do it is to put one foot in front of the other. It's a familiar feeling to maintain that focus on a goal."

As a child, Bancroft played tennis and focused on sports because she found she could excel there, unlike in the classroom. Bancroft attended the University of Oregon, earning a bachelor's degree in physical education in 1981. She started running in high school and played field hockey in college, then continued in sports by running 10Ks and marathons. After college, she taught physical education and special education in St. Paul, Minnesota, and in Minneapolis. Bancroft also continued her outdoor adventures through cross-country skiing and mountain climbing.

Tackled Mt. McKinley and North Pole

In 1983, Bancroft tackled Alaska's Mount McKinley. Standing more than 20,000 feet above sea level, Mount McKinley is North America's tallest peak. During the two-week ascension, her climbing partner struggled with hypothermia and began hallucinating at the summit. Bancroft calmly helped him down. Afterward, Bancroft was contacted by Will Steger, a science teacher turned expedition leader. Steger was friends with her climbing partner and after hearing about her strength and grit on the ice, he asked her to accompany him to the North Pole. In October 1985, she joined Steger's team to train. By mid-winter, they had relocated to the icy lands of northeast Canada, where they spent two months training and driving the dogsleds that would take them to the North Pole. The Steger International Polar Expedition included seven men, 49 male dogs and Bancroft. They began their journey across the Arctic Ocean in March 1986, setting out from the northern tip of North America where the land and sea meet. There was only 20 minutes of sunlight that first day and the team made it less than two miles pulling their sleds of food, fuel, and equipment over the craggy ice.

In an effort to replicate the experiences of the early explorers, the team decided to complete the journey without air drops of fresh food, dogs, or supplies. They set out with heavy sleds towing three tons of supplies. Bancroft described the trip in an essay for *True to Ourselves.* "As expected, the frozen ocean was very rough. Huge walls of ice buckled up to form what we called mountain ranges but are known as pressure ridges. Some were 30 feet tall and demanded that we go ahead of the sleds to chip and cut a path or road to get the sleds up and over these impasses." Some days, the temperature reached 75 degrees below zero. During the journey, two of the eight team members were airlifted out—one with broken ribs from a sled accident, the other with frostbite. The remaining six, including Bancroft, reached the North Pole on May 2, 1986, becoming the first group to arrive at the pole with no aerial help since 1909 when Robert E. Peary trekked there.

Organized South Pole Trip

When Bancroft returned home, she found she could not go back to teaching, though she retained a passion for educating children. Completing the mission revived a childhood dream—leading an all-female expedition to Antarctica, the windiest, southernmost edge of the earth. Bancroft gathered a team of mountain climbers and skiers. They included Sue Giller, Sunniva Sorby and Anne Dal Vera. They nicknamed the team AWE, calling themselves the American Women's Trans-Antarctic Expedition. They intended to cross Antarctica without dogsleds or any other motorized machine so as not to impact the environment.

Raising money to fund the $1 million expedition proved just as grueling as the training. "Because we did not plan to include men or dogs on this expedition, we had difficulty finding anyone who would believe that we could or should attempt to pull 240-pound sleds in the harshest environment of the globe," Bancroft recounted in *True to Ourselves.* For Bancroft, trip preparation also included creating a curriculum around the upcoming trip that touched on math, science, geography and women's issues. Once they started the journey, 200,000 schoolchildren followed along via e-mail and computer linkups. In this way, Bancroft merged her love for the arctic with her love of teaching.

After five years of preparation, the team members flew to the edge of Antarctica, to a place called Hercules Inlet, mounted their skis, hooked up their sleds and began their journey on November 9, 1992. The women skied in a line, each pulling a sled, for about 12 to 15 hours a day. At times, the winds reached 100 miles per hour and the temperature dipped to 50 degrees below zero. On January 14, 1993, they reached the South Pole, having covered 660 miles in 67 days. Initially, the team intended to trek 840 more miles to complete passage across the 1,500-mile continent. Sick with bronchitis and fatigue, two of the team members decided to bow out at the South Pole. In the end, Bancroft decided to end the quest, too, realizing there was no way they could afford two planes—one to pick up members at the South Pole, and another to pick up the finishers at the other end of the continent.

Despite the disappointment, Bancroft had achieved two firsts—she was the first woman to travel by foot to both poles and was among the first team of women to make it to the South Pole. Bancroft returned home $400,000 in debt and dreaming of her next trip. "The goal was not so much reaching the pole itself," she told *Runner's World.* "It was a bit more universal. Why do we all take on struggles? Why run a marathon? I think we're all striving to push ourselves, and in the process of overcoming struggles and challenges, we get to know ourselves better."

Trekked Across Antarctic Landmass

After Bancroft returned home, she was contacted by Liv Arnesen, a Norweigan explorer who was in the midst of planning a solo trip to the South Pole. The two corresponded and in 1994, Arnesen completed her trip. The two women finally met in 1998 and Bancroft asked Arnesen to join her on a journey across Antarctica. Bancroft wanted to hike to the South Pole again, then continue across Antarctica to the other side of the continent to complete her ocean-to-ocean goal. Together—and apart—the women spent two years training for the adventure by kayaking and running with backpacks full of kitty litter. They also strapped car tires onto harnesses and drug them down gravel roads to replicate the endless task of pulling their heavy sleds full of gear, food, and fuel.

In October 2000, Bancroft and Arnesen flew to Cape Town, South Africa, with 720 pounds of gear, ready to head to Antarctica. Due to unexpected delays with their transport company, they did not get a lift to their departure point— Queen Maud Land, Antarctica—until November 13. The flight took five hours. With no fuel supply in Antarctica, the crew had to carry the fuel on board in barrels, making the ice landing dangerous. After landing, the crew spent eight hours using hand pumps to refuel the plane before leaving. The flight alone cost them about $500,000.

On November 14, 2000, Bancroft and Arnesen set off on their journey across the ice. In *No Horizon Is So Far*, Bancroft discussed the trip. "My first day on the ice, I awoke to the thrilling contradictions of Antarctica: Simultaneously, my world seemed to have shrunk to the size of my sled, and yet expanded to the edges of the horizon. Life was reduced to its most elemental: staying warm, setting up shelter, eating, sleeping. These activities were the constant undercurrents running beneath the flow that was the daily task of gaining miles. . . ."

Each woman pulled a packed sled for about 12 hours a day across the chunky tundra. There was always the danger of falling into a crevasse. Some days, they were able to use the wind to sail, but that was hard work. "Windsailing across the ice is a little bit like waterskiing and windsurfing," Bancroft told *Sports Illustrated Women*. "The largest sail was 33 meters [about 108 feet]. Your knees are your shock absorbers, and when you're increasing your speed you've got to edge with your skis, so your legs get pretty beat up. In some ways it was harder on us than pulling our 250-pound sleds. It was like a marathon every day for 100 days."

Eating was tough, too. To have enough energy, they each needed about 5,000 calories a day so they ate a high-fat, high-calorie diet of oatmeal doused with cooking oil, chocolate, marzipan, and sports drinks. Other staples were rehydrated with water—soup, pasta, or fish. They also needed to consume a lot of salt, which they lost through sweating, so they ate crushed potato chips. It took about four hours a day to melt enough water to meet their drinking and cooking needs. During the adventure, Bancroft and Arnesen kept in contact with 3 million students in 146 countries through daily text messages, photos, and video. They also gave interviews by satellite phone, charging their batteries with solar panels.

Bancroft and Arnesen reached the South Pole on January 16, 2001, after covering about 1,300 miles in 64 days. They tarried on and reached the continent's other side

in February 2001. This was the leg of the journey Bancroft had been unable to complete in 1993 during the female-only expedition. By completing this leg, Bancroft and Arnesen became the first people to cross the Antarctic landmass on foot. But there was still more to go. There still remained the Ross Ice Shelf, a 400-mile-wide floating ice mass that extends from the edge of the continent to the sea. Technically, they had crossed only the Antarctic landmass. To conquer the entire continent, they would need to cross the ice shelf, too. Time, however, was not on their side. There was only a limited number of days left when a ship, following an ice-breaker, could even pick them up at the ocean's edge before the weather made passage impossible. A plane pickup at that stage would be too risky as well, with winter setting in. Due to lack of wind and delays in their start date, they realized they probably would not make it in time, so they had to end the trip. They called for a plane pickup and were plucked from the edge of the Ross Ice Shelf. The 94-day, 1,700-mile trip had cost about $1.5 million.

Bancroft returned home to life in Minnesota with her longtime partner, graphic artist Pam Arnold. She was already dreaming of her next trip. In 2011, Bancroft planned to trek Antarctica again, this time with a team of six women—one from each of the earth's habitable continents. In this way, she hoped the exploration would demonstrate global cooperation and encourage people from all over the globe to realize they could come together to solve problems.

Books

Arnesen, Liv and Ann Bancroft, *No Horizon Is So Far*, Da Capo Press, 2003.

Atkins, Jeannine, *How High Can We Climb?*, Farrar, Straus and Giroux, 2005.

Neuman, Nancy M., ed., *True to Ourselves: A Celebration of Women Making a Difference*, Jossey-Bass Publishers, 1998.

Periodicals

Runner's World, January 1994.

Sports Illustrated Women, October 1, 2001.

St. Paul Pioneer Press (MN), April 30, 2000; July 23, 2001; October 23, 2008.

Time, October 20, 2003.

WIN Magazine, November 2000.

Online

"About Ann," Ann Bancroft Foundation, http://www.annbancroft foundation.org/_root/index.php?content_id=5082 (December 31, 2009).□

Isabel Chapin Barrows

Isabel Chapin Barrows (1845–1913) was the first woman ever to work at the U.S. Department of State. She filled in for her ill husband as a stenographer to the U.S. Secretary of State, and later served as a secretary for congressional committees in the 1870s. Both of

these were brief episodes in an event-filled, adventurous life with several other notable firsts. Barrows was also a missionary in India and a graduate of the University of Vienna who became the first licensed woman doctor in the District of Columbia. She was also the first female ophthalmologist in the United States.

Barrows was born Katherine Isabel Hays in 1845 in Irasburg, Vermont. Her parents were immigrants from Scotland and she was one of seven children in the Presbyterian family. Her mother was a teacher, and her father a physician who moved the family to Hartland, Vermont, around 1857 to set up a medical practice there. As a teenager, Barrows assisted her father in his work, and then completed her formal schooling at the Adams Female Academy in Derry, New Hampshire. This was one of the first single-sex schools for New England women and offered a solid academic education at a time when few women were expected to have careers outside the home.

Widowed in India

Barrows married a Congregationalist minister, William Wilberforce Chapin, in Derry on September 26, 1863. Less than four months later, the couple set sail for India to serve as missionaries, which was a decade-long commitment. They landed in Bombay and settled in Ahmednagar, but her husband died from diphtheria in March of 1865, just ten months after their arrival. She stayed on, teaching at a girls' school, then decided to go back to America and earn a medical degree so that she might return to India better qualified to meet the urgent healthcare needs of its populace.

Those plans were set aside for a few years after her marriage to Samuel June Barrows, whom she had met while working at a sanatorium in Dansville, New York. Barrows's brother was the assistant superintendent at the facility, and she had come there to work as a bath assistant and trainee in hydropathy, or water therapy. Samuel Barrows was there for a restorative spell to escape the bustle of New York City. A printer and telegraph operator, Samuel was also a skilled stenographer, which he used in his career as a reporter for the New York *Tribune*. Stenography, also known as shorthand, is a method of speed-writing that relies on symbols or abbreviations to represent human speech on the page. They were wed on June 28, 1867, in Brooklyn, New York, by the Rev. Henry Ward Beecher, the prominent anti-slavery activist.

The couple lived in New York's Greenwich Village, where Barrows was continuing her medical studies as her husband returned to his *Tribune* duties. She also decided to learn shorthand to help her husband with his reporting chores. "The papers had begun to print abstracts of sermons, and a reporter was often assigned to two pulpits on a single Sunday," she recalled in her 1913 tribute to her husband, *A Sunny Life: The Biography of Samuel June Barrows.* "Mr. Barrows could get more credit because I could take one of his assignments."

Subbed at State Department

Upon their marriage, Barrows and her husband had resolved to follow a plan that was remarkably egalitarian for a mid-nineteenth-century marriage: they would give equal time to the other's educational and professional pursuits. This necessitated many major moves, and time apart, too. Initially, they agreed that Barrows would complete her medical studies and then support her husband while he trained to become a Unitarian minister. When Samuel Barrows received an offer to move to Washington, D.C., to serve as the private secretary to William H. Seward, the U.S. Secretary of State, she moved with him for the first few months, then substituted for her husband when he fell ill in the summer of 1868. This made her the first woman to work at the U.S. State Department.

Barrows left her husband in Washington and returned to New York City to resume her course work in medicine at the pioneering Women's Medical College of the New York Infirmary for Indigent Women and Children. There were few women doctors in the United States during this era, and they faced tremendous obstacles in gaining acceptance into regular medical colleges and qualifying for the licenses granted by state medical boards. In 1849, Elizabeth Blackwell had become the first woman to graduate from a U.S. medical school, and four years later opened the New York Dispensary for Poor Women and Children. It became the New York Infirmary for Indigent Women and Children when it moved to New York City's Lower East Side, and demand for its services forced it to move once again, to Stuyvesant Square in 1858, the same year that Blackwell and her sister Emily launched the Women's Medical College at the site.

Mary Safford, one of Barrows's fellow students at the Women's Medical College, wrote to the University of Vienna's medical school and asked permission for the two women to attend lectures in ophthalmology there. "The authorities were so dumbfounded at the suggestion, no women ever before having applied, that they did not know how to say no," Barrows recalled in *A Sunny Life.* "'You must go,' said my young husband, 'if I have to live on pea-soup and sleep in a coal box.'" He provided financial support for her year there by returning to his work as a journalist. "No better opportunities ever came to two women, and we worked hard and lived simply, as was eminently proper," she wrote. After a year of advanced study, which included training in eye surgery, Barrows sailed for America and joined her husband once more in Washington.

Opened Washington Practice

Barrows became the first practicing female ophthalmologist in the United States, where the prejudices of the era relegated her to a post as chief ophthalmologist at the Freedmen's Hospital in the District of Columbia, the pioneering healthcare institution founded during the Civil War for former slaves. It became the teaching hospital for Howard University's School of Medicine, where Barrows was hired as a professor of ophthalmology. She was also the first woman physician to have her own medical practice in the nation's capital. During this period she also worked as a stenographer for congressional committee sessions, and was once again the first woman ever to hold that job.

In the early years of their marriage, Barrows and her husband formally joined the Unitarian church. Founded during the upheavals of the Protestant Reformation in Europe, the Unitarians were independently run churches and required no creed from its adherents. In America, the Harvard Divinity School was the foremost training ground for ministers of this faith, and Samuel Barrows began his studies there in 1871. He spent the next three years at the school, supporting himself by working as private secretary for Louis Agassiz, the noted Swiss paleontologist.

Barrows eventually joined her husband in Cambridge with their young daughter, Mabel Hay Barrows, and from there all of them went to Leipzig, Germany, in the fall of 1875. "Her father was her devoted slave," Barrows wrote about her young daughter in *A Sunny Life,* "and when we were in public places in Europe he constantly attracted attention because, at the time when men usually allowed their wives to carry the baby, our baby rode aloft in his arms."

Edited Unitarian Newspaper

In previous years Barrows's husband had earned a small fortune as a correspondent for the *Tribune* out West, where he rode with General George A. Custer's forces and dispatched exciting reports from the heat of battle. When the couple and their daughter returned from Germany, the *Tribune* offered him another assignment with Custer, but he asked his wife for her thoughts first. "I telegraphed: 'Please do not go,'" she recalled in the biography of her husband. That he did not take the assignment was indeed fortunate. Barrows added in the biography, "Never was I so glad as on that sad May morning when I picked up the paper and saw that General Custer, his brothers, friends, and soldiers had been pitilessly slain by the Indians!"

In 1876 Barrows and her husband finally settled in Dorchester, Massachusetts, where he became the pastor of Meeting House Hill, but their globetrotting was far from over. While her husband served as a pastor and editor of the Unitarian national weekly newspaper, the *Christian Register,* she served as his assistant editor. This assignment had the longest tenure, lasting from 1880 to 1896, most of it spent in Boston, where Samuel Barrows was also pastor of Boston's First Unitarian Church. She never again practiced as an ophthalmologist, but instead poured her considerable energy into various social justice causes. She was active in the civil rights movement and in Native American causes, and then took up the cause of prison reform along with her husband. In 1886 Barrows was elected official reporter and editor of the National Conference of Charities and Corrections. She later wrote an important survey, *The Reformatory Treatment of Women in the United States,* that discussed incarceration and rehabilitation methods from state to state.

Barrows's husband was also an advocate for prison reform, and in 1896 ran for a seat in Congress. He was elected from Massachusetts's Tenth Congressional District as a Republican and served two years on Capitol Hill. In 1899 the family moved to New York's Staten Island when Samuel Barrows became director of the New York Prison Association. Their work in the prison reform movement had introduced them to scores of other progressive activists around the world, and in 1907 they made an extensive tour of prisons in Europe. They became close friends to two Russian reformers: Nikolai Tchaikovsky, who had spent time in America as the founder of a utopian commune in Kansas, and Catharine Breshkovsky, another Russian socialist. Both were jailed by tsarist authorities for their involvement in the Socialist-Revolutionary Party. The ailing Breshkovsky remained in the notorious prison of the Peter and Paul Fortress in St. Petersburg, but Barrows's husband and others successfully petitioned Russia's ambassador to the United States for Tchaikovsky's release.

Returned for Burial

In the spring of 1909 both Barrows and her husband planned another trip abroad for a meeting of the International Prison Commission and to pressure various European governments for Breshkovsky's release. The couple traveled separately, because Samuel Barrows's job as head of the New York Prison Association required meetings over a new state prison complex being planned to replace the dreaded Sing-Sing facility in Ossining, New York. In St. Petersburg, Barrows received word that her husband had died of pneumonia. She sailed back to bury his ashes at their favorite campsite in Quebec, then went back to Russia to plead with Russian officials to release the aged Breshkovsky. She also represented the United States at the International Prison Congress event in Paris.

Barrows was a prolific writer who authored newspaper articles, essays, speeches, and her husband's biography, and even a children's novel set in India. She died in Croton-on-Hudson, New York, on October 24, 1913.

Books

Barrows, Isabel Chapin, *A Sunny Life: The Biography of Samuel June Barrows,* Little, Brown, and Co., 1913, pp. 65, 67, 88, 91. □

Elizabeth Barry

English actor Elizabeth Barry (1658–1713) emerged as one of the first genuine female stars of the London stage. A versatile performer and key figure from the epic era of Restoration drama, she excelled in both comedic and tragic roles, and several significant playwrights of the period wrote works specifically tailored for her. Writing in *The First English Actresses: Women and Drama 1660–1700,* Elizabeth Howe called Barry "perhaps the most famous professional woman of her time in London."

B arry was thought to have been born in 1658. Her origins are obscure. There is one biography of her, but it was written nearly 70 years after her death, and the author, Edmund Curll, is considered an unreliable historical source. In his *Life of Barry,* Curll claimed that Barry was the daughter of a barrister who went bankrupt during the English Civil War of 1641–51 after raising a

regiment to aid King Charles I against Oliver Cromwell's Puritans. Charles was beheaded in 1660 in one of the more notorious episodes from English royal history, but the newly created form of republican rule failed, and the king's son returned from exile and was crowned as Charles II in May of 1660.

The 25-year reign of Charles became known as the English Restoration, and brought with it several significant cultural, religious, and political shifts in the British Isles. Under Cromwell, all public plays had been banned and the theaters shuttered, for the Puritans viewed them as dens of immorality and rightfully considered drama a way to criticize and even mock the regime in power. The more liberal Charles ordered the theaters reopened, and granted licenses to two new theater companies. One was the King's Company, which enjoyed the financial support of the king, and the other was the Duke's Company, whose patron was Charles's brother, the Duke of York.

Object of Wager

The Duke's Company was headed by Sir William Davenant, the poet laureate and renowned playwright. According to Curll, Davenant knew Barry's father and took her into his household when she was about 12 years old as a favor when the Barry family fortunes declined. This story may have circulated after Barry gained fame on the stage in order to give her a family of more reputable origins; there were also rumors that she had been a mere servant at an estate in

Norfolk. In any case, she was supposedly trained for the stage by Lady Mary Davenant, who took over the management of the Duke's Company after the death of her husband in 1668. Barry may have made her debut in *Alcibiades,* an early play by Thomas Otway, whose first performances were not recorded. Her performance as Draxilla was reportedly dreadful, and two other stage appearances also went badly.

Supposedly among the audience members on one of those nights was John Wilmot, an acclaimed poet and satirist who was the 2nd Earl of Rochester. Known simply as Rochester, he was a close confidante of Charles II but also a famous rake who personified the freewheeling atmosphere of the Restoration court and the London theater scene. Rochester and his clique of fellow playwrights were known as the Merry Gang, and their exploits achieved legendary status. They were prodigious drinkers, kept mistresses, patronized brothels, and on occasion were sent into exile because of their inflammatory writing. Rochester had married Elizabeth Mallet, a wealthy heiress from Somerset, in January of 1667.

Rochester was said to have made a bet with his friends that he could tutor Barry and turn her into the best actor on the London stage in a mere six months. She apparently agreed to the plan, and Rochester rehearsed her on the stage and in costume. Her appearance as Queen Isabella in revival of the Earl of Orrery's *Mustapha* in 1673 was considered a triumph and the start of an illustrious career. Her first major roles from this period included Elvira in *The Wrangling Lovers or, the Invisible Mistress* by Edward Ravenscroft, and Constanta in Thomas Durfey's *Madam Fickle or, the Witty False One.* On March 24, 1677, she originated the role of Hellena in *The Rover or, the Banish'd Cavaliers,* a play by Aphra Behn. Behn was an important playwright in Restoration comedies and one of the first women to achieve success in the field. Hellena was a so-called "breeches" role, requiring Barry to don male clothing as part of the plot, masquerading as a man to court a beautiful woman with whom Hellena's true love, Willmore, is smitten. Behn was said to have based the Willmore character on none other than Rochester.

Had Child by Rochester

Women players had come into vogue only during the liberal Restoration era; prior to this, the feminine roles had been played by men dressed in women's clothing. Mary Saunderson and Mary Lee were the best known of Barry's predecessors in London. Barry gained fame playing early "witty-heroine" roles like Hellena, and it was a period when typecasting was standard. An actor usually excelled in one type of character and stuck with that. Barry was one of the first to expand her repertoire, soon taking on adulterous female roles such as Emilia in *A Fond Husband,* another Durfey play.

The libidinous society portrayed on stage had its counterpart in real life. Barry became romantically involved with Rochester, which may have given her performance in *The Rover* some added authenticity. Rochester had also, at times, impersonated a physician, calling himself "Dr. Bendo." The doctor advertised himself as an infertility specialist, and for his more modest patients, the doctor's "wife" would make house calls. This was of course Rochester disguised as a matronly woman. His writings were somewhat scandalous, too, and earned the wrath of Charles II, but Rochester also penned a heartfelt poem to his wife, "Absent from Thee," that has endured over the centuries as a work of genuine romantic sentiment.

The romance between Barry and Rochester resulted in the birth of a daughter, named Elizabeth Clarke, in December of 1677. Rochester was away in the country at the time, which reportedly angered Barry, as did his congratulatory letter in which he told his mistress he was happy the baby was a girl, which he called the gender "I love—it was just as well for a bastard," according to Janet M. Todd's *The Secret Life of Aphra Behn.* Later, his letters to her took on a more caustic tone, possibly because of her relationships with other men. At one point Rochester even warned her that he was planning to remove the child from Barry's care, but their quarrel abated, and Rochester died in the summer of 1680 at the age of just 33, probably from syphilis.

Rose to Prominent Company Role

Over the next decade Barry went on to become one of the leading actors of the London stage. She starred in several notable works, including *The Orphan,* a 1680 work by Otway, with whom she was also romantically involved and who allegedly wrote the play with her in mind. The role of Belvidera in *Venice Preserved, or A Plot Discover'd,* a 1682 tragedy that became one of the more enduring works of the Restoration era, was also said to have been tailored for her by Otway. Her co-star in that production was Thomas Betterton, the leading male actor of the era and husband of Mary Saunderson. Barry and Betterton also appeared together in a well-received adaptation of Shakespeare's *King Lear* by the playwright Nahum Tate.

Betterton effectively ran the Duke's Company after the death of Davenant with the support of his widow. In 1682 the Duke's and King's Companies merged into the United Company, which dominated the London scene for the next dozen or so years as the only licensed theatrical company in the city. Barry was one of its central figures, and was regularly honored with an annual "benefit," a special performance in which all door proceeds went to the actor, and could net the beneficiaries a generous sum. Contracts show that when the United Company was booked for a royal performance, the actors' fees were paid through Barry. Christopher Rich took over the running of the company in 1693, and soon earned the enmity of the actors for his tyrannical style of management and financial misdeeds. This led Barry, Betterton, and other top actors to stage a walkout. They submitted a petition listing their grievances to the Lord Chamberlain, and requested permission from the monarch to form a new company.

Charles II had died in 1685, and was succeeded by James II, who granted the actors a license for a new theater company. This was a cooperative venture, with Barry and the other top actors as shareholders. It was known informally as Betterton's Company, and staged its first production, *Love for Love* by William Congreve, at Lincoln's Inn Fields, a large public square. Anne Bracegirdle was another shareholder, and equally as famed as Barry; the pair were a popular force on stage, with Barry taking the sober, tragic female roles while Bracegirdle excelled in the livelier, more comedic parts. As women they earned less than their male colleagues,

but were granted the right to wear "liveries," scarlet capes that marked them as servants of the king. With these, they could not be arrested without the permission of the Lord Chamberlain.

Criticized for Bluntness

Unlike the beloved Bracegirdle, Barry was derided in some quarters. As Howe noted, Barry had "a strong and combative personality," and she also had a second daughter out of wedlock, this one by the playwright George Etherege, a friend of the late Rochester. "Her combination of toughness and success made her the target for some of the most vicious and vituperative satire of the whole period," Howe wrote. "In lurid language Barry was pictured as a mercenary prostitute, unbounded in her lust for money, prepared to do anything for profit." Like another well-known woman on the London stage, Nell Gwyn, Barry occasionally delivered an epilogue as herself, as she did following the last scene in Durfey's 1697 play *The Intrigues at Versailles.* Here she stepped out of character and used verse to satirize her critics. "In this way the 'star system' was born," wrote Howe, "in which the scandalous, glamorous personal reputation of the performer, rather than the role she played, held people's attention."

Barry retired from the stage around her fiftieth birthday to her home in Acton, where she died of a fever on November 7, 1713. In the 2004 biopic of Rochester, in which Johnny Depp played *The Libertine,* Barry was played by Samantha Morton.

Books

Howe, Elizabeth, *The First English Actresses: Women and Drama 1660–1700,* Cambridge University Press, 1992, pp. 30, 98.

Todd, Janet M., *The Secret Life of Aphra Behn,* Rutgers University Press, 1997, p. 193.

Periodicals

Times (London, England), August 31, 1974; July 26, 1980. □

Gasparino Barzizza

The Italian educator and author Gasparino Barzizza (1360–c.1430) was an important transitional figure who laid the groundwork for the spread of humanist ideas in the early Renaissance period.

The Renaissance era is sometimes supposed by students to have marked a sharp break from the teachings and literature of the medieval era. Moreover, the Renaissance has been closely associated with the city of Florence and a few other large Italian cities that were home to powerful noble families who cultivated the arts. Barzizza did not really fit either of these models, however. He was a teacher, associated with the university in the small city of Padua, who taught the traditional subjects of grammar, rhetoric, and prosody, much as they had been taught to him and, indeed, had been handed down for centuries. But in his classes and writings, and especially in a series of informal lectures for which he charged admission, he helped to open up the possibility of reading ancient texts anew, a trend that stimulated the development of humanism in general. His hero among ancient writers was not the abstractly philosophical Aristotle but the Roman statesman and dramatist Seneca, whose works were closely concerned with secular affairs.

Trained as Notary

Barzizza has received less attention from scholars than have other early Renaissance figures such as Francesco Petrarca, known as Petrarch. He is thought to have born in 1360. Barzizza was not a family name but the name of his family's small estate, near the city of Bergamo; his name appears as Gasparino Barzizza, Gasparino da Barzizza (Gasparino of Barzizza), and Gasparinus de Bergamo. His family boasted that it could trace its ancestry back to the pre-Latin Lombard population of the area, but in reality he grew up as a member of the minor nobility. Like other literate and educated young people of modest means, he was probably trained initially as a notary. He, along with other northern Italian nobles, would have heard of Petrarch's groundbreaking writings, but there is no evidence that he was a close follower of the so-called Father of Humanism.

For reasons unknown, Barzizza apparently began to pursue higher education when he was in his late 20s, and had the wherewithal to do so. He studied grammar and rhetoric with Giovanni Travesi da Cremona at the University of Pavia and in 1392 he was presented for a *laurea*, a kind of graduation ceremony that certified his mastery of several subjects. He is known to have traveled to Padua, where he notarized a deed in 1393, but then returned home after his father's death as he and his brothers divided up their father's estate. Gasparino's brothers, Jacopo and Antonio, became involved in the factional struggles carried out by noble families around Bergamo, but he himself had different plans. He made contacts among the most powerful of the local families, the Viscontis, and began teaching at a grammar school associated with the Bergamo cathedral in 1396. Between 1400 and 1403 he married the noblewoman Lucrezia Agliardi.

In 1403 Barzizza joined the faculty at Pavia as an assistant to his former teacher Travesi. Apparently because no full professorship opened up there, he moved to Venice and became a tutor to the children of several noble families, including the nine-year-old future humanist and politician Francesco Barbaro. The following fall he was appointed to the faculty at the University of Padua, where he would remain until 1421. It was unusual, especially in a time when the bubonic plague constantly threatened to shorten the human lifespan, for a teaching career to begin so late; he was 47 at the time. But his vigorous teaching and writing career would have put an end to any doubts.

Barzizza exerted an impact on education and culture in Padua in several ways: as a university professor and as the operator of his own residential school. He became, as a result of all these activities, a figure of some renown in the area, and the children of the nobility, who played a major role in the transformation of Italian life over the next half century, flocked to his classes. Thus, although he did not seek out attention in purely literary circles, he became an important figure in the intellectual life of the early Renaissance in Italy.

Charged Admission to Lectures

R.G.G. Mercer, the author of the major scholarly study of Barzizza's life and work entitled *The Teaching of Gasparino Barzizza*, divides Barzizza's lectures into official and unofficial events. The official lectures, which followed the established curriculum of Latin grammar, rhetoric, and literature, with regular disputations or debates according to established rules. Barzizza's official lectures are less well documented than the other aspects of his university career, probably because they were not fundamentally out of the ordinary. Barzizza was in no way simply going through the motions, however; he wrote treatises on punctuation and etymology, among other subjects, perhaps as instructional aids for his students.

Barzizza's unofficial lectures, for which he had to obtain permission from the university rector, apparently aroused special interest, for they were an ongoing phenomenon, and Paduans had to pay to hear them. It was mostly through these lectures that humanistic ideas were introduced to Padua. Barzizza lectured on the moral philosophy and on the dramas of Seneca, very different fare from the parts of speech and rhetorical devices covered in his official classes. The extent to which Barzizza's lectures on Seneca's letters touched on live issues was shown by the fact that one lecture series was greeted with hostile criticism from rival humanists.

Barzizza's influence over the next generation of northern Italian leaders was cemented by the household school he operated over the entire period of his tenure in Padua, from 1407 to 1421. He used the Latin term *gymnasium* to describe it, and basic instruction in the Latin language, carried out largely through rote repetition, was a key part of the curriculum. The school had up to 20 students, living in a group of several apartment blocks acquired by Barzizza, at any one time, and these lessons apparently could be rather noisy affairs; teaching grammar and logic to boys was included along with hammering metal and forging iron in a list of activities outlawed around the same time in certain areas of the city of Bologna. Barzizza gave lectures at this school as well, asking students to reflect on questions of what constituted ethical behavior or good government—questions that went back to the ancients, but that under Barzizza's guidance were being asked and explored anew.

Owned Large Book Collection

Barzizza owned one of the largest libraries of classical texts in northeastern Italy, and his home and household school were important centers of learning for that reason alone. He acquired books and other texts by buying them, copying them out himself, or sometimes giving them to students to copy, for, in the days before the invention of the printing press, scribal skills were important in themselves. He also lent many of his books out to others, but in 1412 a period of financial hard times forced him to sell some his books, which would have been among his most valuable possessions. Barzizza's library, according to Mercer, was notable for "a striking absence of scriptural, patristic [relating to the church fathers], or other sacred works."

The list of students who passed through Barzizza's school or university classes reads like a who's who of intellectual and political life in mid-15th-century Italy. It included nobles from Padua and the Veneto (the province that included the city of Venice), physicians, the rhetorician Antonio Carabello (who carried Barzizza's work directly forward), lawyers and law professors, and churchmen who rose to the top of the Catholic hierarchy. In 1410 and 1411 Barzizza was head-hunted by the University of Bologna but was prevailed upon to remain in Padua by leading local citizens. He was apparently offered a teaching job in Siena in 1413 or 1414 as well.

Barzizza was finally tempted away from Padua not by a better job or higher salary, but by a major scholarly research project that interested him: a group of manuscripts by the Roman orator, politician, and political theorist Cicero was discovered and brought to Pavia (or possibly Milan) in 1421, and Barzizza went there to supervise their copying and investigate their contents. The last decade of his life is not well documented. He was apparently a venerated figure, and he gave lectures in Milan and perhaps other cities. The date of his death is uncertain; one manuscript refers to his burial on July 1, 1430, but an oration praising the departing governor of Bergamo, who did not leave office until the end of July or August, has also survived. It is possible that the speech was written by Barzizza before his death and delivered by someone else.

Books

Mercer, R.G.G., *The Teaching of Gasparino Barzizza,* Modern Humanities Research Association, 1979.

Oxford Companion to Italian Literature, Oxford, 2002.

Online

"Latin Scholarship: Giovanni di Conversino, Coluccio de' Salutati, Gasparino da Barzizza," in Jebb, Richard C., *The Classical Renaissance,* University of Mannheim, Germany, http://www.uni-mannheim.de/mateo/camenaref/cmh/cmh116.html#543 (February 2, 2010).□

Jacques Barzun

The French-born American writer and educator Jacques Barzun has been, in the words of David Gates of *Newsweek,* "a real-life Renaissance Man."

Over a career lasting more than 70 years, Barzun has put his encyclopedic knowledge of European and American culture to use in dozens of books, covering everything from literature and art to research methods, biography, crime fiction, and even naval history. A professor for many years at Columbia University and an influential figure in New York's publishing world, Barzun became one of the best-known public intellectuals in the

United States and a prominent defender of the Western cultural tradition against attacks originating from the politically leftist sectors of the academy. At the age of 92 he compiled a lifetime of knowledge into the vast general history *From Dawn to Decadence: Five Hundred Years of Western Cultural Life, 1500 to the Present.* The book became a bestseller and brought Barzun and his unusual erudition a new circle of admirers.

Taught Class at Age Nine

The son of literary scholar Henri Barzun and his wife, Anna-Rose, Jacques Martin Barzun was born on November 30, 1907, in an artists' colony called L'Abbaye de Créteil, in the town of Créteil near Paris, France. The colony was a place where the arts flourished, and such innovators as the poet Guillaume Apollinaire and the future surrealist painter Marcel Duchamp were frequent guests in the family home. Barzun went to school in Paris itself, at the Lycée Janson de Sailly. The outbreak of World War I caused a teacher shortage in France, and Barzun's school adopted an English system whereby older students took on teaching duties. Barzun stood up in front of a class for the first time at the age of nine. He has rejected the idea that his cultural ideas were shaped by early exposure to war. "Why must you find trauma where there is none?" he demanded of *New Yorker* writer Arthur Krystal. "I grew up a child of a bourgeois family, with emancipated parents who surrounded themselves with people who talked about ideas. My views were formed by my parents, by the lyceé, and by my reading. How else should I be?"

Barzun's father was part of a diplomatic mission to the United States during the war, and when Barzun finished high school he was given the option of studying in England or in America at Columbia University, which the elder Barzun considered the country's finest educational institution. Barzun, who had worked on his English by reading the novels of James Fenimore Cooper, chose the latter and enrolled at Columbia at age 15. A history major, he was class valedictorian when he graduated in 1927. But he found time for extracurricular activities such as writing a class musical called *Zuleika, or The Sultan Insulted.* He completed a master's degree in one year and was immediately hired as an instructor in the school's history department.

Barzun would remain as a history faculty member at Columbia until his retirement in 1975, winning promotions to assistant professor (1938), associate professor (1942), full professor (1945), Seth Low Professor of History (1960), and University Professor of History (1968). From 1955 to 1958 he was dean of graduate faculties, and during an increasingly tumultuous decade from 1958 until 1967 he served as the university's provost, winning high marks for his administration of the school's finances. Beyond Columbia, however, it was for his writing—densely detailed yet always elegant and appealing to a general readership—for which Barzun became best known.

Attacked Racist Ideas

In the latter part of his career, Barzun was sometimes classified as a defender of tradition, but some of his early books were quite innovative in their thinking. His first two books dealt skeptically with the concept of race at a time when quasi-scientific racism was still alive and well in university environments; *Race: A Study in Modern Superstition* (1937, reprinted 1956) was well ahead of its time in questioning the concept of race in general and its applicability to European peoples in particular, whose roots Barzun showed to be tangled in various soils of antiquity. With his books *Romanticism and the Modern Ego* (1943) and *Berlioz and the Romantic Century* (1950), Barzun played a key role in making the culture of the Romantic era an acceptable subject for academic study. The book about Hector Berlioz had an influence beyond the academy as well; it helped to rescue the *Symphonie Fantastique* and other Berlioz works from a general impression that they were bombastic and sensationalist. Barzun's traditionalist side first showed itself in *Darwin, Marx, Wagner: Critique of a Heritage* (1943), which took issue with the reduction of human experience to fixed principles and theories that Barzun found in the work of all three of those towering figures of the modern era.

Along with these academic tomes, Barzun wrote works directed at a more general readership. He showed the breadth of his knowledge during World War II when he had no trouble complying with a military request for an *Introduction to Naval History* (1944). Barzun, who had become a U.S. citizen in 1933, wrote enthusiastically about the culture of his adopted country, with special attention to its educational system. In such works as *The*

Teacher in America (1945), Barzun resisted the pragmatic approach of American educational reformer John Dewey. Barzun endeared himself to sports fans with one of his most-quoted maxims, "Whoever wants to know the heart and mind of America had better learn baseball"; the line appeared in the 1954 book *God's Country and Mine: A Declaration of Love Spiced with a Few Harsh Words.*

At Columbia, Barzun helped organize and taught courses in the school's famed Colloquium on Important Books curriculum. His most important collaborator, both as an educator and as an author (the two often showed each other manuscripts in progress), was Columbia English professor Lionel Trilling. Historian Fritz Stern, who took a Colloquium course taught jointly by Barzun and Trilling, recalled to Krystal: "There I was, listening to two men very different, yet brilliantly attuned to each other, spinning and refining their thoughts in front of us. And when they spoke about Wordsworth, or Balzac, or Burke, it was as if they'd known him. I couldn't imagine a better way to read the great masterpieces of modern European thought." Barzun essentially introduced the literature professor to the novels of Henry James, and thus played a part in creating the prestigious status James's novels enjoy today. Barzun's 1957 textbook *The Modern Researcher* remained a standard guide to academic research procedures for several decades.

The 1960s were not a congenial time for Barzun, who defended traditional curricula and traditional hierarchies of university life against the egalitarian ideals of the student counterculture. Barzun was suspicious of reducing history and literature to abstract historical forces. "It is Barzun's contention that history is fundamentally made by individuals, and that all forms of determinism are grievously mistaken and destructive," wrote M.D. Aeschliman in the conservative *National Review.* "Human liberty is an absolute datum of consciousness and reality: The human person's 'supreme pleasure and prerogative,' he writes, 'is to feel himself at once a moral being and a natural philosopher.'" Barzun tried to resist the incursion of psychoanalytic theory into literary and historical studies in *Clio and the Doctors* (1974). In 1975 he retired from Columbia's faculty and took an ongoing position as an adviser to the Scribner's publishing house.

Compiled Crime Fiction Reference Book

Part of the secret of Barzun's productivity as a writer was his ability to nurture a project over the course of years or even decades. With co-author Wendell Hertig Taylor he indulged his passion for mysteries and crime fiction with the reference book *A Catalogue of Crime;* published in 1971, the book was based on notes Barzun had kept going back to his days as a Columbia undergraduate. Barzun's magnum opus, *From Dawn to Decadence,* likewise had a long gestation. "I began thinking about this monster around about 1935," Barzun told the *Austin Chronicle.* "And I started it after retiring from Scribners. As usual I made a lot of plans, about scope, organization, features... but not with the idea that once I had decided on a plan, I would follow it to the last detail.... I spent about three years on that, including the ordering of the notes and books which I'd been accumulating from 1929. I still have all of those notes from graduate school. Then after two years of mulling, I began to write."

Work on the book was interrupted by Barzun's move from New York to San Antonio, the hometown of his second wife, Marguerite Davenport. Barzun's first marriage, to Marianna Lowell in 1936, produced three children, James, Roger, and Isabel. He met Davenport in San Antonio while giving a lecture at Trinity University there, and married her in 1980 after his first wife's death. Barzun donated 2,700 books to Columbia, but kept 2,500 and installed them in his spacious new house in a San Antonio gated community. Asked by various interviewers whether he missed New York's intellectual atmosphere, Barzun consistently defended his new home, pointing to its noted symphony orchestra among other attractions.

By the time the 877-page *From Dawn to Decadence* was published in 2000, Barzun was 92 years old. Despite Barzun's downbeat conclusion that the energies that had sustained Western culture since the Renaissance era were flagging, the book hit the top reaches of book sales charts. The sheer depth of knowledge at Barzun's command was perhaps its major selling point. Anne Dingus of the *Texas Monthly* called it "a do-it-yourself B.A. in book form," and Gates asserted that the book "will go down in history as one of the great one-man shows of Western letters, a triumph of maverick erudition like Johnson's *Dictionary* or Burton's *Anatomy of Melancholy*—assuming, as Barzun does not, that there'll be a history for it to go down in." Some reviewers took issue with Barzun's negative treatment of trends in contemporary thought, but his success in bringing an in-depth treatment of history to a general readership was undeniable.

Barzun continued to live in San Antonio, rising each morning at six, exercising for 40 minutes, and answering as much correspondence and as many requests for help and advice as he could. He suffered from some physical problems and used a cane for mobility, telling Krystal, "Old age is like learning a new profession. And not one of your own choosing." But Barzun was able to attend many of the ceremonies marking his 100th birthday in 2007, and as of this writing (late 2009) he remained active at the age of 102, often collaborating with an unidentified scholar who was at work on his biography.

Periodicals

Independent on Sunday (London, England), February 25, 2001.

National Review, November 19, 2007.

Newsweek, May 22, 2000.

New Yorker, October 22, 2007.

St. Petersburg Times (St. Petersburg, FL), July 28, 2002.

Texas Monthly, September 2000.

Online

"Jacques (Martin) Barzun," *Contemporary Authors Online*, Gale, 2009.

"The Man Who Knew Too Much: Jacques Barzun, Idea Man," *Austin Chronicle*, October 13, 2000, http://www.austinchronicle.com/gyrobase/Issue/story?oid=78886 (November 10, 2009). □

Giorgio Bassani

Giorgio Bassani (1916–2000) was one of the most accomplished Italian poets, editors, and novelists of the twentieth century. Writing largely against the travesties of Fascism in Italy as well as working as a part of the Resistance movement during World War II, Bassani explored the effects of Fascism on Italian Jews. His most noted work, *Il giardino dei Finzi-Contini* (The Garden of the Finzi-Continis), not only won the Viareggio prize in 1962, but was also adapted into an Academy Award-winning film in 1971.

Giorgio Bassani was born on March 4, 1916, in Bologna, Italy, to a Jewish surgeon and his wife. He had two siblings, Paolo and Jenny. He grew up in the city of Ferrara, Italy, a small walled city located in the Po Valley between Bologna and Venice. It would come to be the setting for almost all of Bassani's later works.

Bassani was only six years old when Benito Mussolini took over as Italy's dictator and Fascism became a way of life. Bassani's anti-fascist leanings, though, were not solidified until he was at the University of Bologna studying literature. Here he was introduced to the philosophical works of Benedetto Croce, an importance influence on Bassani's later work. He began his studies in 1934, but in 1938 the Racial Laws were enacted, as well as the *Manifesto del Razzismo* (the Declaration of Racism). These Racial Laws included a decree on September 5, 1938, that forbade those of Jewish birth from beginning the new academic year at any publicly funded educational or cultural institution. This enraged Bassani, who was luckily able to finish his studies and find a job in a newly formed school for Jews.

He published his first work in 1940, *Una città di pianura*. He had to publish this work under the pseudonym Giacomo Marchi, taking the name of his Catholic grandmother, Marchi, in order to bypass the racial laws that forbade a Jew to be published in Italy. This first work embodied a sense of Bassani's spiritual fatigue.

In 1940, at the height of World War II, Bassani became active in the anti-Fascist Resistance in Italy. He even helped to found the Action Party. Because of his involvement with the Resistance, he was imprisoned from May until July of 1943. In July of that year, Mussolini's Fascist regime fell to the Allies, and he was released. He married Valerina Sinigallia shortly afterwards, in August of 1943, and the couple had two children.

He moved his family, including his parents, to Florence, where they lived from 1943-1945. Civil War ensued in Italy and he was forced into hiding there under an assumed identity. While he was in hiding, many of his family members were sent from Ferrara to Buchenwald, a concentration camp, where they died.

Published Post-War Poetry

At the end of the war, Bassani and his family moved to Rome. In order to support them, he took on several different roles as

a literature teacher, a librarian, and a scriptwriter. In 1945 he published his first volume of poetry, *Storie di poveri amanti* (Stories of Poor Lovers). It was re-issued in 1946 with additional poems and renamed *Storie di poveri amanti e altri versi* (Stories of Poor Lovers and Other Poems). In 1947 he published a second volume, *Te lucis ante* (Before the Day Ends). Several of these poems spoke to the pain he felt during his time in prison.

In 1948 Bassani became the editor of the literary review *Botteghe oscure* (Obscure Shops). He published four of his short stories between 1949 and 1955. The first, in 1951, was *Un altra libertà* (Another Freedom). The second, published in 1952, was *Una lapide in Via Mazzini* (A Plaque on Via Mazzini), which told the story of Geo Josz, a holocaust survivor from Ferrara who comes home to find his own name on a plaque commemorating Jews lost during World War II. In 1953 he published *La passeggiata prima di cena* (A Stroll before Supper), which discussed the 1870 unification of Italy. It was later published as a book. Finally, in 1955, he published *Gli ultimi anni di Clelia Trotti* (The Last Years of Clelia Trotti). This work was also later published as a book and won the Charles Veillon prize in Italian Literature in 1955. He also co-edited the Milanese review *Paradone* from 1953-1955.

In 1956 he published *Cinque storie ferraresi* (Five Stories of Ferrara). It was republished in 1960 as *Le storie ferraresi*, revised as *Dentro le mura* (1973), translated by Isabel Quigley as *A Prospect of Ferrara* (1962), and also translated by William Weaver as *Five Stories of Ferrara* (1971). This volume included his four previously published works from

Botteghe oscure as well as a new work, *Una notte del '43*. Because all five stories took place in Ferrara, the characters and places interacted within different stories, giving the work cohesiveness. Several themes predominated: history, social consciousness, and Jewish identity. *Cinque storie ferraresi* won the Strega prize in 1956.

Continued Writing

From 1957 until 1967 Bassani went on to become a theater history teacher at the National Academy of Dramatic Arts in Rome. He found time, though, to write another novella, *Gli occhiali d'oro* (The Golden Spectacles), published in 1958 and translated into English in 1960. This work was an extension of the Ferrara stories, so much so that it was added to the revised version of *Le storie ferraresi* in 1960.

In *Gli occhiali d'oro,* Bassani used for the first time the device of a first-person narrator, as opposed to the third-person omniscient narrator he had used in the past. In this case, the narrator identifies with the main character, Dr. Athos Fadigati, a respected physician, who eventually discloses his homosexuality. He is tolerated at first until he falls in love with a university student. He eventually commits suicide. The narrator, a Jew, understands Dr. Fadigati's sense of exclusion, as the narrator was ostracized after the anti-Semitic laws of 1938.

In 1958 Bassani became an editor at the Feltrinelli publishing house. He is credited with the discovery of Sicilian writer Giuseppe Tomasi di Lampedusa (1896–1957), and with publishing di Lampedusa's greatest work, *Il Gattorpardo* (The Leopard), in 1958. He also collaborated on several periodicals: *La Fiera Letteraria* (Literary Fair), *Il Mondo* (The World), *Nuovi Argomenti* (New Arguments), *L'approdo* (Landing), and *Letteratura* (Literature).

In 1960 he also published *Una notte del '43*. This work symbolized a turning point where the town of Ferrara stopped being just a setting and became an entity all its own. Ferrara had begun its transformation to more than a place with the publication of *Gliocchiali d'oro* (The Golden Spectacles), which was an extension of the Ferrara stories, reaching its completion with *Una notte del '43*.

Il giardino dei Finzi-Contini

Bassani's most famous work, *Il giardino dei Finzi-Contini* (The Garden of the Finzi-Continis) was published in 1962 and translated into English in 1965. It is, first and foremost, a love story between the narrator, nicknamed Celestino, and the daughter of the Finzi-Continis, a wealthy Jewish family living on an estate outside of Ferrara. It covers the years 1929-1943, and the reader is warned from the outset that all of the Finzi-Continis will be deported with the other Jews of Ferrara in 1943, except for their son Alberto, who dies a year earlier.

It is a story of isolation and of not acting until it is too late. The Finzi-Continis, Ermano and Olga, the mother and father, Alberto the son, and Micol the daughter, isolate themselves from the Fascist laws of the city of Ferrara. When the anti-Semitic laws are passed, they gladly open their tennis courts and library to Jews who are no longer able to use those available to the public. They cling to what they have, showing no interest in the present state of life for Jews in Italy. A book review in *Time* stated: "Although the novel is about Jews, it is only incidentally about Jewishness; the Finzi-Continis' confrontation with Fascism is employed to expose a painful paradox: life can be understood only in the past, but only in the present can it be lived. The problem is how to do both." *Il giardino dei Finzi-Contini* won the prestigious Viareggio prize in 1962.

Continued Writings

In 1963 Bassani collected his poems from 1942 until 1950 in a volume called *L'alba ai vetri: Poesie 1942–50* (Dawn at the Windows: Poetry, 1942–1950). He became the vice president of Radiotelevisione Italian (RAI) in Rome from 1964–65. He published the novella *Dietro la porta* (Behind the Door) in 1964, and it was translated into English in 1972. It is the story of the effects of bullying on a young man whose friends demean his family and against whom he cannot fight back. The narrator, looking back, tries to come to terms with these events. Bassani published *Due novelle* in 1965 and *Le parole preparate, e altri scritti di letterature* (The Prepared Words) in 1966, which was revised and enlarged as *Di là dal cuore* in 1984.

He wrote his final book in 1968, *L'airone* (The Heron), and it was translated into English two years later. It is about a middle-aged man who is estranged from his life: his wife, possessions, and identity. The reader follows him for 24 hours throughout a hunting trip where he sees perfect animal bodies in the window of a taxidermist's shop and decides that the only way to be perfect in life is through death, and he commits suicide. He won the Campiello prize in 1969 for this work. He also won the Nelly Sachs prize in 1969 and was a recipient of the Premi Roma.

Later Life and Death

In 1971 Vittorio De Sica directed a film interpretation of Bassani's *The Garden of the Finzi-Continis*. This revitalized De Sica's career, winning an Academy Award in the United States for Best Foreign Film. De Sica said in an interview with the Toronto *Globe and Mail* that he "felt very strongly that such a very subtle and often poetic film . . . could interest and move a very, very large audience and confront them with what happened in the Second World War."

Bassani, meanwhile, traveled the United States from 1972–74. In 1972 he published a collection of stories called *L'odore del fieno* (The Smell of Hay), which was translated into English in 1975. He also published additional poetry in *Epitaffio* (Epitaph) in 1974. He was a visiting professor at the University of California at Berkeley in 1976. He published additional poems in *In gran segreto* (With Great Secrecy, 1978). He had his work compiled in several books over the next few years: *In rima e senza: 1939–1981* (Rhymed and Unrhymed, 1982), *Rolls Royce and Other Poems* (1982), and *Di là dal cuore* (Behind the Heart) and *Italian Stories* (1989).

In the last years of his life Bassani suffered from Alzheimer's and Parkinson's Disease. He died in San Camillo hospital in Rome on April 13, 2000 at the age of 84.

Books

Encyclopedia of World Literature in the 20th Century, Vol. 1: A-D, edited by Steven R. Serafin, St. James Press, 1999.

Holocaust Novelists, edited by Efraim Sicher, in *Dictionary of Literary Biography, Vol. 299,* Gale, 2004.

Italian Novelists Since World War II, 1945-1965, edited by Augustus Pallotta, in *Dictionary of Literary Biography, Vol. 177,* Gale Research, 1997.

Reference Guide to Holocaust Literature, edited by Thomas Riggs, St. James Press, 2002, p. 20-22, 443-444.

World Authors: 1950-1970, edited by John Wakeman, H. W. Wilson Company, 1975.

Periodicals

Globe & Mail (Toronto, Ontario, Canada), January 24, 1997.

New York Times, November 8, 1996; April 14, 2000.

Time, August 6, 1965.□

Adolf Bastian

German ethnologist Adolf Bastian (1826–1905) is best known for his "psychic unity of mankind" theory, which arose from his extensive world travels and exposure to various world cultures. He also strongly influenced later scientists with his ideas and his fieldwork methodology.

While Adolf Bastian is best known for advancing the concept of mankind's "psychic unity," he also made significant contributions toward the development of ethnography and anthropology.

Indeed, history assigns to Bastian the role of "founding father" of ethnography, a branch of anthropology that involves application of the scientific method to the study of different societies. Specifically, ethnography explores elements such as culturally distinctive behavior and traditions. Bastian's seminal contributions to the discipline evolved from numerous insights gathered through his extensive travel. By the end of his career, he had visited every populated continent. In the process, through his own example, he advanced the value of practical fieldwork.

Enjoyed Diverse Education

Bastian was born on June 26, 1826, in Bremen, Germany, into a family of thriving merchants. His parents' prosperity provided him substantial higher education opportunities, and the innately curious Bastian exploited this advantage by engaging in a self-directed and wide-ranging curriculum. Essentially, whatever intrigued him, he pursued with intellectual fervor at appropriate academic institutions. He studied law at the University of Heidelberg and studied natural sciences (including biology) at the Humboldt University of Berlin, the Friedrich Schiller University of Jena, and the University of Wurzburg.

But Bastian was particularly fascinated with ethnography. He was introduced to the discipline at Wurzburg, where he

would form the basis of his later ethnographic work. Here, he first advanced his hypothesis that human nature is both basic and universal—that is, its essential elements are tied together, but not by history nor geography. Stated plainly, different cultures separated by huge gulfs of space and time displayed striking similarities, in terms of religion and philosophies and even specific elements of their rituals.

Bastian, sensing that he was onto one of the great secrets of humankind, demonstrated almost obsessive interest. He expanded on his ideas in *Das Besdändige in den Menschenrassen und die Spielweite ihrer Veränderlichkeit*, another multi-volume effort. Published in 1868, the work advanced beyond Bastian's previous work by describing plentiful and powerful examples of analogous behaviors present in the existing societal foundations (behaviors and customs) of different cultures.

Developed "Psychic Unity" Theory

Bastian formalized his theories into the concepts of *Volkergedanken*, or folk ideas, and *Elementargedanken*, or elementary ideas. Both of these idea sets, he believed, developed differently in their details among societies (again, based on factors such as geography and history). The sets shared surprising commonalities at their core, however, and essentially, as he first perceived and then communicated, basic themes and motifs were universal and transcended culture, history, time, and geography. In different cultures, these ideas were apparent and recognizable in fables, myths, proverbs, and other cultural beliefs. Ultimately, all of his travels, research and contemplation led Bastian to develop the inclusive "psychic unity of mankind."

With this "psychic unity" theory, that advanced the notion that all human beings share the same mental framework, Bastian erected intellectual bridges that connected science, religion and philosophy. Bastian not only supported his theory by describing prevalent behavioral patterns; he also collected evidential artifacts from across the world. For example, he felt that the rug-weaving craft was particularly illustrative, as the practice was present in diverse nations such as Turkey and China—and while the craft was common to humankind, the artistic nature of the actual weaving proved quite different among various cultures.

All along, Bastian employed the "comparative method," an approach that was developed in the nineteenth century to determine the origin of languages. It was later deployed by pre-eminent anthropologists, who perceived its intrinsic value and applicability to their own scientific discipline.

Meanwhile, Bastian's theory gained acceptance. He pursued his ideas by further global explorations. In 1866, he embarked on a four-year sea voyage that took him to Asian countries. These travels resulted in yet another ambitious and extensive account, the six-volume *Die Völkerdes östlichen Asien* ("The People of East Asia"). Upon his return, Bastian settled in Germany and assumed the post of professor of ethnology at the University of Berlin.

Established Museums and Organizations

Bastian also helped establish several important ethnological institutions and organizations. In 1869, working with Virchow,

attended the lectures of Rudolf Virchow (1821–1902), a renowned German physician, biologist and anthropologist. He finally focused his attention on medicine, however, and in 1850, he earned his medical degree from Charles University in Prague, located in what is now the Czech Republic.

Embarked on First Global Voyage

After obtaining his medical degree, Bastian secured a position as a ship's doctor and embarked on an eight-year voyage across the world. The ship's course took him to Africa, Australia, China, India, Mexico, South America, and the West Indies. With his previous fascination with ethnography strongly reasserting itself, he noticed distinct similarities existing between cultures, even as these cultures were separated by thousands of miles. The perceptive Bastian concluded that parallel concepts formed the foundations of all civilizations.

In particular, he realized that similar themes resided at the core of various myths and ceremonial rituals embraced by diverse and geographically estranged cultures. How could this be, he wondered? It was an intellectually seductive mystery, and Bastian dedicated most of his career to finding the resolution.

Meanwhile, he chronicled his accounts. In 1859, he returned to Germany and sat down long enough to describe his travels (complete with his trenchant observations) in a three-volume worked entitled *Der Mensch in der Geschichte* ("Man in History"). Eventually published a year later, the comprehensive work delineated the main components that he founded the Berlin Society for Anthropology, Ethnology and Prehistory. The institution established a means of sharing new information arising from the research activities of its many notable members. That year, Bastian also began serving as the editor of the publication *Zeitschrift fur Ethnologic*, working with Virchow and Robert von Hartmann, a German philosopher whose popular book *The Philosophy of the Unconscious* was published the same year.

In addition, during this period, Bastian served as head of the Royal Geographical Society of Germany, and then in 1873, he founded the Berlin Ethnological Museum. Bastian served as its first director and, during his tenure, greatly enlarged the museum's important collection. In 1878, he helped establish the German Africa Society of Berlin, an organization that encouraged German colonization of Africa. Moreover, during his extensive travels, Bastian collected an enormous number of cultural artifacts. He gave many of these to the Royal Museum in Berlin. His contributions proved so plentiful that the museum needed to open a second building.

Mislabeled as an Evolutionist

Because of the nature of his work, Bastian was often identified as an evolutionist. This label was misleading, however, as he didn't believe in the concept of unilinear evolution, a theory of social evolution (now discredited) that maintained that all societies undergo the same stages of development. This idea was developed and embraced by scientists such as Auguste Comte, Lewis Henry Morgan, Edward Burnett Tylor and Herbert Spencer. Unlike his contemporaries, Bastian believed that many possible outcomes could arise from the same beginnings, with different cultures developing in their own unique environmental and historical contexts. Bastian clarified this position in 1868 in *Das Besdändige in den Menschenrassen und die Spielweite ihrer Veränderlichkeit*: "What we see in history is not a transformation, a passing of one race into another, but entirely new and perfect creations, which the ever-youthful productivity of nature sends forth from the invisible realm of Hades." Also, as his stance suggests, Bastian had a monogenetic view of human origins—that is, mankind arose from one geographic source. Other evolutionists believed that races evolved separately.

Influences and Impact

Bastian's ideas were influenced by concepts first related by Johann Gottfried Herder (1744–1803) and then by Theodor Waitz (1813–1866). Herder, a German philosopher, saw relationships existing between tradition and progress, and he described outward manifestations of historical events as driven by an "inner force." Waitz, a German anthropologist and psychologist, expanded Herder's ideas in his Volksgeist theory. In turn, Bastian's own work influenced others. For instance, his "elemental" and "folk" ideas preceded the "kulturkreis" (or cultural circle) theory developed by ethnologists Fritz Graebner and Wilhelm Schmidt. Also, Bastian proved a strong influence for German anthropologist Franz Boas (1858–1942) and Swiss psychiatrist Carl Gustav Jung (1875–1961).

Jung integrated Bastian's "psychic unity" theory into his own famous theory of the "collective unconscious," which states that part of the unconscious mind is shared by all humankind and, resulting from ancestral experience, strongly relates to religion and science.

Bastian's ideas also resonate in later theories developed by anthropologists such as Paul Radin and Claude Levi-Strauss. Further, Bastian's views of multilinear cultural development helped point the direction for future research, particularly as seen in the work of people like Boas, Alfred Radcliffe-Brown, and Bronislaw Malinowski.

Bastian even influenced how future research would be conducted: He championed the value of the scientific method, particularly as it applied to his own area of research, and he practiced what he preached. As such, he advanced usage of long-term studies and in-depth cultural analyses, especially related to dying cultures. In this way, Bastian helped promote the value of scientific fieldwork. At the time, most ethnographers were theorists who rarely conducted in-depth field study. Conversely, Bastian took time to learn the languages and rituals of the cultures he studied, and he never viewed the people he studied as merely subjects. Rather, he considered them to be his research partners and demonstrated respect for cultures' spiritual beliefs and religious customs, even though he did not belong to any religion.

Later Activities

Bastian continued to travel the world, even in his later years. In the 1880s, he left from Germany on voyages to Africa and the Americas. He also continued to publish. His other major works included *Sprachvergleichende Studien mit besonderer Berücksichtigung der indochinesischen Spracher* (1870), *Die Kulturldnder des alten Amerika* (1878), *Der Buddhismus in seiner Psychologie* (1881), *Der Fetisch an der Kiiste Guineas* (1885), *Die mikronesischen Kolonien* (1900), and *Die Lehre vom Denken zur Ergänzung der Naturwissenschaftlichen Psychologie, für Überleitung auf die Geistewissenschaften* (three volumes, 1902).

In 1886 he was honored for his extraordinary accomplishments by being elected as a Fellow of the American Philosophical Society.

Bastian traveled until he died. He passed away on February 2, 1905, in the Port of Spain in Trinidad, on a return voyage.

Books

"Adolph Bastian," *Merriam-Webster's Biographical Dictionary*, Merriam-Webster Incorporated, 1995.

Online

"Adolf Bastian," *Emuseum@Minnesota State University, Mankato*, http://www.mnsu.edu/emuseum/information/biography/abcde/bastian_adolf.html (November 1, 2009)

"Adolf Bastian," *Encyclopedia.com*, http://www.encyclopedia.com/doc/1E1-Bastian.html (November 1, 2009)

"Adolf Bastian," *New World Encyclopedia*, http://www.newworldencyclopedia.org/entry/Adolf_Bastian (November 1, 2009).

"Adolf Bastian," *Today in Science History*, http://www.todayinsci.com/B/Bastian_Adolf/Bastian_Adolf.htm (November 1, 2009)□

Eleanor Baum

In 1984 Polish-born, American-raised Eleanor Baum (born 1940) was appointed dean of the Pratt Institute's School of Engineering, becoming the first female to lead an engineering school in the United States. A trailblazer, Baum entered engineering in the 1950s, breaking down barriers as the lone female in most of her college classes. As a dean, Baum worked diligently to encourage women and minorities to enter the field.

Eleanor Baum—the only child of Anna and Sol Kushel—was born February 10, 1940, in Vilna, Poland, now known as Vilnius, Lithuania. She did not spend much time there, as her Jewish family escaped the country at the start of World War II. Sol Kushel owned a rubber factory and knew that he would be rounded up with other "capitalists" by invading Russian forces as soon as they reached his city. Trying to avert this fate, he created a phony visa stamp for Curaçao, figuring the border guards had not seen many visa stamps for that country and would not be able to quickly identify it as a fake.

Escaped Poland During WWII

In *Journeys of Women in Science and Engineering,* Baum recounted her family's exodus from their homeland. "We sneaked out of Poland in the middle of the night, crossing the border in a farmer's wagon covered with hay; they had me, an infant, drugged so I wouldn't cry. My father was wanted by the communists." The danger followed them even after they left Poland. By this time, Europe was teaming with soldiers from Nazi Germany who were busy rounding up Jewish people and sending them to concentration camps.

Baum's family finally escaped Europe—after passing through Russia and Japan—and chose to settle in Quebec, Canada, because Baum's father had attended college in France and was comfortable speaking French, Canada's official language. When Baum was three, the Kushels moved to Brooklyn, New York. As an only child of refugees who lost all of their relatives to the war, Baum grew up with overly protective parents who had high expectations for her. At times, though, Baum was embarrassed by her parents' accents. "It was a time in American history when people with accents weren't trusted," Baum told the *New York Times.* "They weren't 'American,' and it took a very, very long time for my parents to assimilate—so I always grew up thinking my parents were 'different.' And a little strange."

Rebelled, Became Engineer

At Brooklyn's Midwood High School, Baum enrolled in the advanced math and science classes because they sounded interesting. She did well in both subjects and was encouraged to become a teacher. Baum considered the option but realized all the male students who excelled in math and science were talking about becoming engineers, not teachers. Much to her parents' dismay, Baum started

entertaining the idea. This was during the 1950s, long before the women's movement helped broaden the opportunities available to women. In the 1950s, women were encouraged to become teachers, nurses, or secretaries if they wanted a career.

As graduation approached, Baum's mother continued to suggest she become a teacher. Her parents even went so far as to cut out newspaper articles trumpeting the joys of teaching because the career allowed mothers to be home in the afternoon to care for their children. "One day I rebelled and announced that I was going to be an engineer," Baum recalled in *Journeys of Women in Science and Engineering.* "My mother turned green and said, 'You can't do that; no one will marry you!'" Baum's guidance counselor also urged her to reconsider, suggesting no one would want to hire a female engineer. "I resolved at that moment that someone would hire me because I was going to be a very good engineer." Initially, pursuing engineering had more to do with rebellion than with the career itself.

Baum applied to several engineering schools and was met with rejection. One school denied her admission, saying there was no way she could enroll because the campus lacked women's restrooms. Eventually, Baum got accepted at City College of New York and found herself the only female in most of her electrical engineering classes. When Baum had trouble with a concept, her teachers did little to help, concluding that women were incapable of understanding some things. During laboratory classes, Baum's male colleagues asked her to record the data while they ran the experiments. Despite the challenges and hostile atmosphere, Baum graduated in 1959.

Encountered Sexism on Job, In School

Baum's first job was at the Sperry Gyroscope Co. in New York. Sperry manufactured navigation equipment. Baum, however, did not enjoy working at Sperry. Most of her co-workers assumed she was a secretary so she was forced to spend a lot of time and energy explaining her real position. In addition, no one was used to working with a female engineer. Speaking to the *New York Times,* Baum recounted her frustrations from that time. "When I had to consult with another engineer, the thought was that I was over there flirting with them. The supervisor had a talk with me: 'I don't want you going over there and flirting with the guys.'" Baum's supervisor did not believe her when she said she was getting information for the project she was working on.

In addition, Baum found the work she was assigned boring, so she decided to go back to school to learn more so she could get a different type of engineering job. She returned to City College intent on earning a master's degree, then received a fellowship to the Polytechnic Institute of Brooklyn. Initially, Baum did not realize the fellowship was aimed at students working toward doctorate degrees. She received the fellowship because the school had extra money through the National Defense Education Act. Naturally, this upset Baum's traditionalist mother who was sure she would become overeducated and never marry.

Baum went into engineering to avoid teaching. As a graduate student, however, she was forced to teach. Much to her surprise, she found she loved working with students.

Baum's time at Brooklyn Polytechnic was filled with ups and downs. She found some teachers very supportive, while others were hostile toward her, angry that she was taking up their time and filling a seat in their class that could have gone to a male student. Some of the unsupportive teachers figured Baum would get married and spend her time raising a family instead of using her degree. She found her biggest ally in physicist Paul Baum, however. They married in 1962 after he finished his doctorate in physics at the University of Illinois.

Named Engineering Dean

After earning her doctorate in 1964, Baum worked in the aerospace industry. During her brief employment in the world of commercial engineering, Baum worked on airplane navigation systems, electric vehicles, and electric power generation. Eventually, Baum and her husband decided to leave the industry behind and teach. With two young daughters, Baum wanted the flexibility of a university schedule. By 1967, Baum was an associate professor at the Pratt Institute in New York City while her husband taught at Queens College.

In 1971, Baum became the chair of the electrical engineering department at Pratt. In 1984, she was named dean of Pratt's engineering school, which at the time had about 850 students. The school offered undergraduate degrees in chemical, civil, mechanical, and electrical engineering. In taking the position, Baum became the first female to head an engineering school in the United States. After several successful years on the job, Baum was hired as the dean of Cooper Union's Nerken School of Engineering in 1987. Located in Manhattan, Cooper Union is a small, private school where students are admitted on merit and receive full-tuition scholarships paid for by endowments.

At Pratt and at Cooper Union, Baum worked to increase female and minority enrollment in engineering. As a dean at Cooper Union, Baum made herself highly visible to the public and worked hard to encourage young men and women to study engineering, fearing the United States was not putting out enough engineers to fill all of the positions available in the industry. Baum was frustrated that many qualified youngsters were choosing other career paths—such as business or law school—which they deemed more glamorous than engineering. Baum told the *New York Times* that, in her experience, many high school students were reluctant to study engineering. "I think part of it is that society still has a negative image of engineers. People think of engineers as not terribly educated, inarticulate, mad-scientist types, klutzes, nerds. They think of engineers as being involved with instruments of destruction and war; that's true for some engineers, but certainly not for most."

Welcomed Women into Engineering

One of Baum's biggest achievements was increasing the number of female engineering students at the college. When Baum started at Cooper Union in 1987, females accounted for just five percent of the student population.

After 12 years on the job, she had increased female enrollment to 38 percent, mostly through outreach projects. She also hired more female and minority faculty members and released teachers who were not supportive of women in engineering. Baum's work in this area was so visible that she was invited to Australia to advise universities there on ways to encourage more females to seek engineering and science degrees. Some of Baum's outreach projects included introducing girls to female engineers who worked in the field so they could explain their jobs and serve as role models.

At Cooper Union, Baum also worked to change the curriculum so engineering students were exposed to real-world applications early on in their college career. She began encouraging freshmen to get involved with engineering projects so they could witness firsthand how smart engineering can improve lives. Some projects students have worked on included designing low-tech ways for the people of Ghana to acquire clean water. Another group of Cooper Union students worked on urban harbor pollution control, while another project had students working with doctors to develop tests for artificial limbs.

Baum has also been active in several professional engineering organizations, including the American Society for Engineering Education, the Institute of Electrical and Electronics Engineers (IEEE) and the Society of Women Engineers. In addition, she has worked with engineering school accreditation boards.

As Baum looked to the future, she hoped to continue spreading the message that engineering is cool and can make a real difference in the world. "Most people equate engineering with work that involves a lot of tough math, but there's so much more to it," she told the *Institute,* a publication of IEEE. "Engineering is about working on interesting projects and making the world a better place. When that becomes the message, everyone can relate."

Books

Ambrose, S., Dunkle, K., Lazarus, B., Nair, I., Harkus, D., *Journeys of Women in Science and Engineering,* Temple University Press, 1997.

Periodicals

Courier-Mail (Brisbane, Queensland, Australia), June 30, 1987.

New York Times, December 16, 1984; June 4, 1989; June 22, 1999.

Online

"Eleanor Baum, Ph.D.," Embry-Riddle Aeronautical University, http://www.erau.edu/administration/trustees/tr-baum.html (December 19, 2009).

"Eleanor Baum: Rebel Engineer," *The Institute,* (December 19, 2009).

"Women In Engineering: Creating A Professional Workforce For the 21st Century," Gifts of Speech: Women's Speeches from Around the World, http://gos.sbc.edu/b/baum.html (December 19, 2009.□

Marie Adelaide Belloc Lowndes

Marie Adelaide Belloc Lowndes (1868–1947) was an Anglo-French writer whose suspense novels gained her a wide readership on both sides of the Atlantic in the early decades of the twentieth century. Her best known work is *The Lodger,* inspired by the real-life Jack the Ripper murders in Victorian London. The 1913 story has been adapted to film no less than four times.

Belloc Lowndes was born in 1868 in the Marylebone district of London, where her parents had a home. Her father, Louis Belloc, was a French lawyer and already in poor health; he died the year that Belloc Lowndes turned four. Her mother was Elizabeth "Bessie" Rayner Parkes, who was in her late thirties when she married. There were prominent persona on both sides of the family: her father's father was Jean-Hilaire Belloc, a French painter, and her maternal grandfather was Joseph Parkes, a leading Whig politician and British reformer before his death in 1865. Belloc Lowndes was also the great-granddaughter of Joseph Priestley, a respected theologian in the Unitarian faith and the first to publish scientific results on the discovery of oxygen.

Educated by Nuns

Belloc Lowndes's childhood was divided between England and France, where her paternal grandparents lived in a village called La Celle St. Cloud. Her younger brother, Joseph Hilaire Pierre Belloc, was born there and would go on to achieve fame as a poet, biographer, journalist, and Member of Parliament. Their mother was a distant figure during much of their childhood, and Belloc Lowndes was cared for by a nurse for whom she had little affection. Both children were raised in the Roman Catholic faith, and Belloc Lowndes received the bulk of her formal education at a convent school run by sisters of the Order of the Holy Child. An event from her youth may have provided some of the inspiration for her *Lodger* story: in 1877 her maternal grandmother passed away, and Bessie Parkes Belloc inherited a property on London's famed Wimpole Street along with a sizable sum. The house had lodgers, and Bessie was swayed by an investment pitch from one of them. She gave him her inheritance, and it vanished.

Belloc Lowndes married rather late in life for a woman of her era: she was 28 at her 1896 wedding to Frederic Sawrey Lowndes, a London journalist of the same age. He was the scion of a prominent landowning family in Buckinghamshire who were staunch Anglican Church supporters and not entirely keen on his marriage to a Roman Catholic. He was educated at Oxford and began a 45-year career with the *Times* of London in 1893. His line of work, with its access to details about the most salacious crimes and scandals of the day, would provide his wife with the inspiration for many of her novels.

Belloc Lowndes's first published works were royal biographies. Her first novel, *The Philosophy of the Marquise,* garnered little attention from reviewers. She fared better in 1904 with her second novel, *The Heart of Penelope,* a story of forbidden love and romantic intrigue. A review in the *Times Literary Supplement* praised its characterizations, noting that "Lowndes writes of them all with now and then an apt flash of wit, and a constant and gratifying security of style and phrase."

Focused on Middle Class Woes

Eight more titles of similar fare were to follow before Belloc Lowndes hit her stride with 1913's *The Lodger,* her first crime-centered work. Among her other works of that time were 1905's *Barbara Rebell,* a 1910 short story collection called *Studies in Wives,* and *The Chink in the Armor* from 1912. Her protagonists were usually well-born English-women comfortable both at home and on the Continent, like Belloc Lowndes herself, and the plots followed them through fairly typical romance- or inheritance-focused travails.

The Lodger originally began as a short story that appeared in the January 1911 issue of *Mc Clure's,* a popular magazine of the day that featured fiction from such contributors as Jack London, Mark Twain, and Sir Arthur Conan Doyle. Belloc Lowndes later said that the seed of the story was planted by a snippet of conversation. As she wrote in her journal in 1923, she "heard a man telling a woman at a dinner party that his mother had had a butler and a cook who married and kept lodgers," according to Mary Jean DeMarr in the *Dictionary of Literary Biography: British Mystery Writers, 1860–1919.* "They were convinced that Jack the Ripper had spend a night under their roof."

Even in 1913, when *The Lodger* was published, the gruesome Jack the Ripper slayings of seven prostitutes in London's East End more than two decades earlier still captivated the public. The murders took place in one of the most congested urban areas in the world over several months in late 1888 and incited a frenzy of detective work, newspaper headlines, and general panic. The name "Jack the Ripper" came from a letter the purported killer sent to newspapers and Scotland Yard detectives. Though theories about the possible identity of the killer abounded, the crimes went unsolved.

Crafted Subtle Portrait of Menace

In Belloc Lowndes's book, a mysterious renter she called "the Avenger" has rented a room from Robert and Ellen Bunting, former domestic servants who are married and struggling financially. Both are avid readers of the tabloid newspapers that have stoked public terror in London's East End over a recent spate of horrific slayings. Ellen begins to worry when the new tenant's comings and goings seem to coincide with the slayings, and then finds herself drawn into a maze of deceit. DeMarr wrote that Belloc Lowndes's novel "reveals many of the features that were to characterize much of her best work: her ability to depict a variety of sorts of people with sympathy, her skillful building of plots that create terror, her placing her characters in believable and wrenching situations, and her use of actual fact to undergird her fiction."

The Lodger earned a good review in the *Times Literary Supplement,* where Walter de la Mare called its author "mistress of 'the art of thrilling'" and recommended the story "because she has touched what might well have been the crudest of bloodcurdlers with a real human and kindly sympathy." The work was first adapted for the stage in a dark comedy titled *Who Is He?,* which tanked at London's Haymarket Theatre but did a little better in its New York City premiere in January of 1917. Nine years later *The Lodger* was adapted for the screen by a young, unknown writer-director named Alfred Hitchcock and became a box office smash. The silent film, which bore the subtitle *A Story of the London Fog,* was set in the present time, which permitted the director to modernize the media fascination with the murders via the new medium of radio. Hitchcock considered this to be his first real work as a filmmaker, and it featured many of the hallmarks that became commonplace in the rest of his movies: a plot relying on mistaken identity, a duplicitous female protagonist, and a cameo appearance from the portly director.

Belloc Lowndes's most famous novel would be remade several more times. There was a 1932 talking version from another director, and a 1944 update with Merle Oberon, one of Hollywood's biggest stars of the era. There was a campier horror-genre version in 1953 starring Jack Palance as *The Man in the Attic,* and Australian actor Simon Baker took on the title role for a 2009 retelling of *The Lodger* set in contemporary Los Angeles.

Drew Upon Sordid Criminal Acts

None of Belloc Lowndes's subsequent novels ever fared as well as *The Lodger.* She continued to focus primarily on crime stories, however, and produced about one new title every year until her death in 1947. In *The End of Her Honeymoon,* the novel that succeeded *The Lodger,* an English couple visits Paris on their honeymoon, and the husband mysteriously vanishes. *Good Old Anna* was a 1915 wartime drama reflecting English tensions about secret German agents on the British Isles during World War I. *Why They Married* was a collection of seven tales about marriage. A 1925 novel, *Bread of Deceit,* featured a young London debutante and her accidental acquaintance with one of the city's latest crimes of depravity. It was published in the United States as *Afterwards.*

The rights to Belloc Lowndes's 1931 novel *Letty Lynton* gave film star Joan Crawford one of the best roles of her career, but the movie was shelved by U.S. court order in 1936 after a copyright suit was filed against MGM studios by the authors of a successful play from 1930 bearing the title *Dishonored Lady.* The case eventually went all the way to the U.S. Supreme Court, which upheld the lower court's decision and forced the studio into an agreement preventing it from ever being shown again. Both Belloc Lowndes and the playwrights at the center of the case had based their story on a sensational Scottish case of the 1850s in which a Glasgow heiress was charged with poisoning her lover with arsenic when he threatened her with blackmail.

Belloc Lowndes visited the United States for the first time in 1925, and returned to New York City often. She also traveled frequently to France, staying at the La Celle St. Cloud property. In London, she and her husband entertained prominent figures at their home at 9 Barton Street near the Houses of Parliament. Among their circle of friends were some of the most acclaimed writers of the era, including her brother Hilaire Belloc, Henry James, Robert Browning, Oscar Wilde, and Émile Zola. Speaking at the 1936 *New York Times* National Book Fair, she ventured a guess at why the reading public seemed to have an insatiable appetite for murder mysteries. "I feel that almost every human being—with the exception of my three children—is a potential criminal," she said, according to the *New York Times.* "Opportunity makes the criminal. Anybody might commit murder if the occasion arose. Murder for money, of course, is the most common of all."

Belloc Lowndes died at the home of her daughter Elizabeth, the Countess Iddesleigh, in the Hampshire village of Eversley Cross on November 14, 1947. Elizabeth's sister Susan edited their mother's voluminous lifetime correspondence for a 1971 tome, *The Diaries and Letters of Marie Belloc Lowndes,* that provided a compelling glimpse into British letters and high society across several decades. There were also three volumes of memoirs, but as DeMarr noted, it was the writer's suspense-filled tales that really showcased her talents. Belloc Lowndes's "crime fiction is still readable, even absorbing," DeMarr asserted. "She was concerned with ordinary people facing extraordinary pressures and fears and was skilled in depicting complex human relationships. Her female characters are often assertive and competent."

Books

DeMarr, Mary Jean, "Marie Belloc Lowndes," in *Dictionary of Literary Biography,* Volume 70, *British Mystery Writers, 1860–1919,* edited by Bernard Benstock and Thomas F. Staley, Gale, 1988, pp. 199–204.

Periodicals

New York Times, June 7, 1925, p. BR8; November 17, 1936; March 26, 1940.

Times (London, England), November 15, 1947.

Times Literary Supplement, October 28, 1904; January 4, 1913; September 17, 1971. □

Friedrich Bergius

German chemist Friedrich Karl Rudolph Bergius (1884–1949) invented a process that produced synthetic fuel from coal. In addition, he developed methods that broke wood down into edible sugar. In 1931, he received a share of the Nobel Prize for Chemistry (with Carl Bosch) for developing these high-pressure processing methods that found practical use for industrial applications.

As a chemist who transitioned his research and knowledge into commercialized, practical application, Friedrich Karl Rudolph Bergius had an enormous impact on the world. Moving from the academic, laboratory setting and into the business sector, he developed hydrogenation processes applicable to industry. Specifically, he researched the effect of high pressures and temperatures on chemical actions. In this way, he developed a process that produced motor fuels via hydrogenation of coal. The Royal Swedish Academy of Sciences acknowledged his accomplishments and their implications by awarding him a share of the 1931 Nobel Prize in Chemistry.

The future Nobel laureate was born in Germany on October 11, 1884 to Heinrich and Marie Haase Bergius. His birthplace, Goldschmieden, which is near Breslau, was once part of the Prussian Province of Silesia, which became a part of Poland.

His family heritage included scientists, theologians, successful businessmen, and high-ranking military officers. As such, his parents placed great importance on education. Also, Bergius' father, who operated a chemical factory in Mulheim, cultivated his son's early interest in chemistry, allowing him to witness up close the chemical processes that took place within an industrial setting. This early experience provided the young Bergius with a grasp of both industry and science and the potential interrelation of the two fields.

Heinrich Bergius also sent his son to a factory in the heavily industrialized Ruhr valley in Germany. There, Bergius profited from a six-month study of the practical applications of metallurgy.

Taught by Renowned Chemists

Bergius' formal education began in 1903, when he entered the University of Breslau and studied chemistry under renowned German chemists Richard Wilhelm Heinrich Abegg (1869–1910), who pioneered the valence theory, Richard Herz (1867–1936), who discovered the Herz reaction, and Albert Ladenburg (1842–1911). Meanwhile, Bergius supplemented his education at his father's factory, studying various practical applications and increasing his knowledge about chemicotechnical processes.

His ongoing education was interrupted by a year of military service. Afterward, he enrolled at the University of Leipzig in Germany, where he conducted doctoral research under Arthur Rudolph Hantzsch. His thesis, *Uber absolute Schwefelsaure als Losungmittel,* involved absolute sulphuric acid applied as a solvent. Though started under Hantzch, the research was completed under Abegg. Subsequently, Bergius received his doctorate degree in chemistry in 1907.

Stimulated by the vibrant intellectual atmosphere of Hantzch and Abegg's laboratories, Bergius decided to devote future efforts to scientific research. This career choice steered him toward the Institute of Berlin, where he worked with Walther Herman Nernst (1864–1941), a German chemist and physicist. In 1909, he entered the University of Karlsruhe, also in Germany, where he worked with Fritz Haber, who would later receive the 1918 Nobel Prize in Chemistry for work related to the synthesis of ammonia from its elements. It was Haber who introduced Bergius to the principles of high-pressure reactions.

With Nernst and Haber, Bergius worked on developing a method of making ammonia from hydrogen and atmospheric nitrogen. In addition, working with Haber and Carl Bosch at Karlsruhe, he played a part in the development of the Haber-Bosch Process.

"[The laboratories of Nernst and Haber provided me the opportunity] to witness the use of the high-pressure methods in investigations into the ammonia equilibrium and ammonia synthesis," recalled Bergius, in the lecture that accompanied his 1931 Nobel Prize (as recorded by the Nobel Prize web site). "I tried my hand...at syntheses by high-pressure techniques, with the then imperfect apparatuses, and with little success."

He advanced to a higher level in 1909, however, when he accepted an invitation to conduct research at the University of Hannover, in Hannover, Germany, where he worked with Max Ernst Bodenstein (1871–1942), the German chemist who earned accolades for his research into chemical kinetics. In Bodenstein's lab, Bergius studied the breakdown of calcium peroxides, successfully developing a practical method and deploying pressure up to three hundred atmospheres (one atmosphere amounts to 14.7 pounds per square inch).

Established His Own Laboratory

During this period, Bergius developed a leak-proof, high-pressure apparatus that enabled him to extend his research into other areas. In order to further advance his research, however, he needed his own laboratory, as available lab equipment proved insufficient. He established his facility at Hannover, where he continued working with high-pressure techniques, investigating the effects of high pressure and high temperature on wood and peat on coal formation, as well as the transformation of heavy oils and oil residues into lighter oils.

He eventually realized that he could increase gasoline yield, and this awareness had significant impact: It increased gasoline output at a time when the automobile was gaining widespread acceptance as a primary mode of transportation.

Bergius' lab eventually grew to include workshops and plants staffed by fellow researchers. Subsequent research resulted in the hydrogenating effect of hydrogen on coal and heavy oils under high pressure.

Meanwhile, Bergius was also teaching physical and industrial chemistry at the Technische Hochschule at the University in Hannover. His lectures involved metallurgical science, technical gas reactions, and the equilibrium theory. These educational activities only lasted one year (1911), however, as other activities began to consume his time.

Recognized and Realized Commercial Applications

In 1913, Bergius received a patent for the manufacture of liquid hydrocarbons from coal. During the next two decades, Bergius and other scientists in Germany, Britain and Canada refined his processes for commercial usage. Essentially, the process worked in this way: Powdered coal was mixed with tar or a tar derivative, which turned it into paste. The mixture was then placed in a steel cylinder and subjected to high temperatures (840 degrees Fahrenheit) and high pressure (nearly 3,700 pounds per square inch). The resulting hydrogen gas then combined with the carbon or carbon compound in the coal. From there, light-molecule hydrocarbons like gasoline were distilled off. In 1935, Germany produced about 300,000 tons of motor fuel through this coal-hydrogenation process. The same year, an English company (Imperial Chemical Industries Limited) built a hydrogenation plant that boasted an annual capacity of 150,000 tons.

Entered the Commercial Sector

After receiving his patent in 1913, Bergius soon found it hard to sustain his laboratory and its research, as the size of experiments needed to be expanded to apply methods to industry. Thus, in 1914, Bergius accepted an offer from German businessman Karl Goldschmidt to move his lab to the firm of Th. Goldschmidt A.G., located in Essen, Germany. Bergius also assumed the position as the firm's research director, which he held until 1945. Because of his new role, he moved to Berlin, where he remained until 1921.

Also during this period, Bergius helped develop a large industrial plant at Rheinau, near Mannheim. He did this to assist development of coal-hydrogenation processes on a large scale. In 1921 he moved from Berlin to Heidelberg, so that he could be closer to the facility, as well as to foster his relationship with Heidelberg University.

While Bergius was able to significantly improve coal-hydrogenation, the process proved economically unfeasible after World War I, when demand for gasoline substantially decreased. In 1926, Bergius sold his related patents to a large German chemical firm (Badische Anilin-und Sodafabrik). This organization later merged with other German chemical companies to form I.G. Farbenindustrie Aktiengesellschaft. Subsequently, this new company continued the work in a large industrial scale, increasing hydrogenation research, improving Bergius' processes, and increasing the yield of gasoline from coal in economically effective fashion.

Awarded a Nobel Prize

In 1931, he received a share of the Nobel Prize in Chemistry. His co-recipient Carl Bosch (1874–1940) continued Bergius' work after Bergius sold his patents. The Royal Swedish Academy of Sciences extended the award "in recognition of their contributions to the invention and development of chemical high pressure methods," according to the Nobel Prize web site. Once a professor at the University of Heidelberg, Bosch became the Principal of I.G. Farbenindustrie in 1925. Ten years later, he was appointed the company's chairman of the board of directors.

During the presentation ceremony, an Academy representative described Bergius' high-pressure methods as an extraordinary improvement in the field of chemical technology. At the time he received his award, Bergius declared that his own work on high pressure had come to an end. "Many problems which stimulated the urge to research in the course of work on high-pressure reactions which lasted for almost two decades, must remain uninvestigated, because efforts are now devoted to another field. The need for concentration is an important result of many years of practical research," he explained in his Nobel ceremony lecture (as quoted on the Nobel Prize web site).

The award to Bergius and Bosch was a bit of a departure for the Royal Swedish Academy of Sciences. Typically, Nobel Prizes were awarded to individuals involved in pure, or non-commercial, research, but Bergius and Bosch's work involved the commercialization of scientific processes that were developed in laboratory research.

Bergius also received honorary doctorate degrees from the University of Heidelberg and the University of Hannover. He also was elected to the board of directors of many associations and companies involved in coal and oil. In addition, he was a member of the American Chemical Society and the Verein Deutscher Chemiker, and he published many articles in newspapers and scientific and technical journals.

Developed "Food from Wood" Method

During his career, Bergius also engaged in research to develop a method to produce sugar from the cellulose in wood and, in turn, convert it into alcohol, yeast and dextrose. To accomplish his aims, he combined concentrated hydrochloric acid and water. The mixture initiated the breakdown of wood cellulose. The method became known as "Food from Wood." He used the money he received with the Nobel Prize to continue his experiments (often, to further his research, he invested his own money).

Just as his previous research assisted Germany during World War I, this later research helped his country during World War II, as it created carbohydrate material that helped alleviate problems related to food shortages.

Earlier, Bergius dabbled with the process while in England. In the 1930s and 1940s, however, he increased his efforts in this area. During World War II, the plant that he earlier founded in Rheinau provided the products that Germany needed.

Left Germany

After World War II, Bergius left Germany and moved to Austria. Later, he settled in Madrid, Spain, where he founded an industrial company for the government. But he found it increasingly difficult to find work after the war, as his technical innovations had helped extend Germany's involvement in the global conflict.

In 1948, he left Europe and moved to Argentina. Until his death, he served as a technical research adviser for Argentina's Ministry of Industries. While in South America, he continued working on his "Food From Wood" process, developing fermentable sugars and cattle food.

Bergius died in Buenos Aires on March 30, 1949. He was married to Ottilie Krazert. The couple had two sons and one daughter.

Both of Bergius' focus areas, the hydrogenation of coal into gasoline and the hydrogenation of wood into food products, became widely used commercially and industrially.

Books

"Friedrich Bergius," *World of Chemistry*, Gale, 2009.

Periodicals

Time, November 23, 1931; September 21, 1936.

Online

"Bergius, Friedrich Karl Rudolf," *history.com,*, http://www.history.com. November 11, 2009).

"Chemical reactions under high pressure," *Nobelprize.org*, http://nobelprize.org/nobel_prizes/chemistry/laureates/1931/bergius-lecture.pdf (November 11, 2009).

"Friedrich Bergius," *NNDB.com*, http://www.nndb.com/people/408/000100108/ (November 11, 2009).

"Friedrich Bergius," *Nobelprize.org*, http://nobelprize.org/nobel_prizes/chemistry/laureates/1931/bergius-bio.html (November 11, 2009).

"The Nobel Prize in Chemistry 1931," *Nobelprize.org*, http://nobelprize.org/nobel_prizes/chemistry/laureates/1931/ (November 11, 2009).□

Hendrik Petrus Berlage

Dutch architect Hendrick Petrus Berlage (1856–1934) is widely acknowledged as the foremost Dutch figure in his field of the late nineteenth century and has been called the Father of Modern Architecture in the Netherlands. Drawing on the work of contemporaries including Frank Lloyd Wright and Louis Sullivan later in his career, Berlage trained in Switzerland and traveled to Europe before establishing his Dutch architectural practice. Berlage's pioneering architectural designs serve as predecessors to the full-blown twentieth century Modernist style perfected under such architects as Le Corbusier and Mies van der Rohe. While his most famous work is Amsterdam's Beurs, or Stock Exchange, designed in 1896 and completed in 1903, the architect also designed numerous other homes, offices, and public buildings, including the Berlage Bridge and the *Gemeentemuseum* (Municipal Museum) in The Hague.

Born on February 21, 1856, in Amsterdam, the Netherlands, Berlage was the eldest of the four children of civil servant Nicolaas Willem Berlage and his wife, Anna Catharina Bosscha. The Bosschas had an artistic heritage—Berlage's grandfather had been a writer and historian—and the young Berlage initially dreamt of becoming a painter. To that end, he enrolled at the Rijksacademie van Beeldende Kunsten (Royal Academy of the Fine Arts) after completing his secondary education at a *hogere burgerschool* in 1874. The following year, however, the young student forsook painting in favor of architecture before completing even a year at the school, leaving the Academy to travel to Zurich. There, he enrolled at the Eidgenössische Technische Hochscule (Institute of Technology), where he presumably studied under respected architect Gottfried Semper. Berlage's coursework in Zurich culminated with a design for an Italian Renaissance-style art school and museum in 1878. Writing in *H.P. Berlage,* Pieter Singelenberg argued that this "choice of subject is already characteristic, bespeaking Berlage's later designs for all branches of the minor arts and his solicitude for the artistic past." Equally, this design displayed the traditionalism that informed the first years of Berlage's artistic development.

Employed Traditional Styles in Early Career

In fact, art remained a primary force over the next three years of the young Berlage's life, as he traveled extensively through Europe sketching people, places, and objects. At the same time, he also began honing his architectural skills. During the fall of 1879, he assisted with the construction of Frankfort, Germany's *Panoptikum* (Wax Museum) and then worked for a short time at a Dutch architectural firm near Arnhem. By September of 1880, Berlage had set out for Italy and he spent the next several months touring the country. By 1882, Berlage had returned to Amsterdam, where he went into architectural practice with Theodorus Sanders. Among his first projects with Sanders was a *Panopticum* similar to the one on which he worked in Frankfort and the *De Hoop* coffeehouse. By 1884, Berlage had advanced to a full partnership and was producing the vast majority of the firm's designs, including a plan for a new Stock Exchange that was submitted into an international architectural competition sponsored by the city. Although the firm's Renaissance-influenced design took fourth place, continued delays in the execution of the project made the results of the competition moot. In 1886, Berlage won a silver medal from the Dutch professional association Maatschappij tot Bevordering der Bouwkunst (Society for the Promotion of Architecture) for his designs for potential additions to Amsterdam's historic Munt Tower.

By 1889, Berlage had left his partnership with Sanders to strike out on his own. He entered a well-received design for a massive mausoleum to the architecture exhibition at that year's World Fair in Paris—the same event which marked the unveiling of the Eiffel Tower—and won a commission to renovate the business offices of the Amsterdam brokerage firm Kerkhoven & Company. Despite the retention of essentially traditional architecture features in his works to this point, Berlage was already beginning to consider new design ideas; writing for *Grove Art Online,* Singelenberg pointed out that "Berlage voiced doubts in 1886 about the imitation of earlier styles, and in 1889 he protested strongly against both imitation and the falsification of materials." This shift away from replication of existing styles hastened, and between 1889 and 1893 his designs show an increasing movement from the old to the new. An 1892 design for a private residence in Bussum, The Netherlands, for example, draws on the standard English cottage architectural style but eliminates the purely decorative elements common to form.

From 1893 onward, this rejection of historical style hastened as Berlage channeled the general international shift away from highly derivative classical architecture. Critics generally identify Berlage's design for Amsterdam's De Algemeene Building, built on a commission from the insurance company of the same name, as the first of this second phase of his architectural career. The smooth façade and restrained decorative effects of the building set it apart from the standard of the day. "Through a sober and sparse interpretation of period architecture, Berlage achieved his goal and created an expressive and monumental effect, strengthened by the imposing scale of the building," observed Sergio Polano in *Hendrick Petrus Berlage: Complete Works.* The following year, Berlage wrote a treatise on architecture entitled *Bouwkunst en Impressionisme* (Architecture and Impressionism) in which he outlined his belief that structures should rely on simplicity and character of form rather than extensive use of stylistic detail to achieve the best visual effect. "Art does not, by any means, commence with the ornament, the presence of which is not a question of principle but one of more or less luxurious treatment . . . the artist has to see it that the useful becomes beautiful," the architect proclaimed in a 1911 lecture on the topic (as quoted in Polano's book). An added benefit of this focus on the practical over the purely decorative, in Berlage's mind, was the reduced cost of producing such a building.

Designed the Amsterdam Stock Exchange

In 1896, Berlage commenced work on what would become his most famous edifice: Amsterdam's Stock Exchange. The city had long hoped to erect such a building, and to that end had already conducted two major design competitions, including the one in which Berlage and Sanders had placed fourth some years previously. A professional relationship with city alderman M.W.F. Treub led to Berlage receiving the commission from the City Council outright, and the architect promptly began on the design for the extensive structure. Over the next two years, he produced not one but three total schemes in conjunction with friend and adviser Albert Verwey, a poet who suggested artistic themes to unify the building's spirit. Throughout these designs, the plan for the ground floor—which had to meet certain stipulations present in the commission—remained the same, while the upper two stories evolved to reflect Berlage's shifting architectural ideas. Polano argued that these versions "show a quest for a logical simplification and growing economy of means, an 'honest synthesis' of building and reasoning." Capped by a substantial tower, the completed design melded the simplicity and monumentality of form that Berlage admired with a series of varying angles and elevations that allowed the structure to blend with its neighbors in the city's main square. The Stock Exchange's interior contained massive halls for the sale of grain, stocks, and commodities; this latter space featured a glass and metalwork gabled roof supported by a series of stone columns that exemplified the unification of function and beauty. Construction on the Stock Exchange began in 1898 and lasted until 1903, and its erection is widely acknowledged as the beginning of a new architectural movement in the Netherlands.

More immediately, however, the Stock Exchange and its fame won Berlage a great deal of new commissions. Throughout the 1890s, he designed a great number of private residences, of which the best known is the Villa Henny in The Hague. Commissioned by Carel Henny, a longtime supporter of Berlage and his work, the home—termed a "mad house" and the "yellow peril" by contemporary critics for its unusual angular design and brilliant yellow roof tiles— represented a fully realized product of Berlage's desire to unify the exteriors of structures with their interior functions. These homes often reflected aspects of the Art Nouveau style that had begun to rise in international popularity during the decade. Aside from the groundbreaking Stock Exchange, Berlage's most significant commercial structure of the late nineteenth century was his design for the headquarters of the Algemeene Nederlandsche Diamantbewerkersbond (Dutch Diamond Workers Union), a starkly monumental structure built between 1897 and 1900.

Shifted Styles in Later Career

With the completion of the Stock Exchange in 1903 came a new phase of the architect's career. He designed a number of social housing projects under the auspices of the Netherlands' 1901 Public Housing Act, along with private residences, offices, and public buildings, but none of these achieved the artistic heights of his defining Stock Exchange plan. By 1911, Berlage had achieved a sufficient degree of international renown that he traveled to the United States to embark on a lecture tour. During this visit, the architect seems to have dedicated much of his spare time to the observation of the contemporary architectural styles dominating the American landscape. Scholars have noted that Berlage seems to have already been at least somewhat familiar with the designs of H.H. Richardson before his voyage, and the trip certainly also acquainted him with the styles of Louis Sullivan and Frank Lloyd Wright. After his return, he published the 1913 work *Amerikaansche Reisherinneringen* (American Travel Memories) and became one of the most vocal European supporters of Wright's architectural designs; Singelenberg noted in *Grove Art Online* that "Berlage particularly admired Wright for his spatial solutions and geometry and his refined use of materials."

In the latter years of his career, Berlage tried his hand at urban planning, producing schemes for the Dutch cities of Amsterdam, Utrecht, and Gronigen, along with the Indonesian city of Batavia. As Berlage's entry in the *International Dictionary of Architects and Architecture* argued, however, "it would be wrong ... to put too much emphasis on his importance as a town planner: for Berlage, towns existed above all only because of the architecture." Indeed, he continued to produce architectural designs throughout the 1920s. These often reflected his observations in the United States during the previous decade and channeled the rising school of Functionalism, and included Amsterdam's Berlage Bridge and The Hague's First Church of Christ the Scientist. The best known of the architect's later works, however, is The Hague's Municipal Museum, constructed from a second design reconceived in 1928. Centered on a courtyard, the museum relied on a series of increasing elevations and linked viewing chambers to create a space distinctly suited to its function as a museum.

Berlage died in The Hague on August 12, 1934, at the age of 78. The following year, the city's Municipal Museum—the last of his major works to be completed—opened. Considered shockingly bold early in his career and a remnant of the traditional at the end, during his decade-spanning career

Berlage helped pave the way for the international growth and subsequent predominance of such styles as De Stijl, Modernism, and the Bauhaus. His works remain a vital and respected part of the Dutch landscape, and many have hailed him as the father of that nation's architectural spirit.

Books

Goode, Patrick, ed., *The Oxford Companion to Architecture,* Oxford University Press, 2009.
International Dictionary of Architects and Architecture, St. James Press, 1993.
Polano, Sergio, *Hendrik Petrus Berlage: Complete Works,* Rizzoli International Publications, 1988.
Singelenberg, Pieter, *H.P. Berlage,* Meulenhoff, 1969.
Singelenberg, Pieter, *H. P. Berlage: Idea and Style,* Haentjens Dekker, 1972.

Online

"Berlage, H.P.," Grove Art Online, http://www.oxfordartonline.com (January 5, 2010).□

Hippolyte Bernheim

The French physician and educator Hippolyte Bernheim (1840–1919) made important contributions to the study and therapeutic application of hypnotism, laying the groundwork for the modern understanding of hypnosis.

Hypnosis-like procedures had been popularized in Europe by the German-French physician Franz Anton Mesmer in the late eighteenth century, and trance states bearing some degree of similarity to hypnosis exist in many cultures. In the 1840s the British physician James Braid had coined the term "hypnotism" and laid the foundations of hypnosis as a discipline. Yet, for most of the nineteenth century, hypnotism remained something of a mystical cure, relying on vague theories of animal magnetism rather than resting on a foundation of scientific investigation and theory. It was Bernheim, along with the Parisian neurologist Jean-Martin Charcot, who began to change this situation. Their ideas about the nature of hypnotism differed sharply, and the two emerged as rivals, but it was the ideas of Bernheim that gained acceptance over the long run.

Studied with Top Physician-Scientists

Of Jewish background, Hippolyte Bernheim was born in Mulhouse, in the Alsace region of eastern France. Several different birthdates appear for him in medical reference sources, but recent works give the date April 27, 1840. Bernheim studied medicine at the University of Strasbourg, went to Paris for further studies with the prominent pathologists Armand Trousseau and Victor Cornil, and then returned to Strasbourg to take the high-level French teaching exams known as the *agrégation*. He went to Berlin for postgraduate studies with Rudolf Virchow, the pioneering pathologist who investigated the role of social factors in medicine.

Thus trained by some of Europe's top medical thinkers, Bernheim was ready to embark on a career as a medical school professor. The outbreak of the Franco-Prussian War in 1870 temporarily sidelined his plans, however. Native to the Alsace region that was one of the primary sites of contention in the war, he was uprooted. He served as an intern in Strasbourg's hospitals, taking the chance to get further on-the-job training from two leading physicians there. But when the city fell to German forces, Bernheim had to make his way to Switzerland. There, he joined with French fighters as an ambulance driver. After the catastrophic defeat suffered by French forces under Napoleon III at Sedan in September of 1870, the Alsace region was annexed to Germany and remained part of that country until after World War I. The Strasbourg medical school was moved north to the city of Nancy, and it was there that Bernheim was finally elevated to a professorship in medicine in 1873.

Before he ever encountered hypnosis, Bernheim made important medical discoveries. His research centered on rheumatic fever, typhus, and cardiac disorders that affect breathing, one of which is still referred to as the Bernheim syndrome in some countries. He continued to teach at Nancy, and in 1879 he was offered the chair in ambulatory medicine (the equivalent of a full professorship in modern terms) there. In 1881 he was chosen as president of the Nancy Medical Society. These honors did not diminish his curiosity or his desire to improve his skills, and the following year, when working with a patient whose sciatica failed to respond to treatment, he sought the advice of a suburban Nancy physician named Liébault who, despite the thoroughly negative attitudes of colleagues, had treated patients with hypnosis.

Pursued Study of Hypnosis

Bernheim's patient improved under Liébeault's care, and Bernheim set out to learn the unorthodox physician's methods. The two founded a clinic together, and soon Bernheim had thrown himself wholeheartedly into the study of the still-novel phenomenon of hypnosis and its medical applications. The leading figure in the field at the time was Charcot, who worked at a Paris hospital called the Salpêtrière because it was housed in a former gunpowder factory. Charcot expanded on Mesmer's theories of a connection between hypnosis and magnetism, and suggested that hypnosis occurred in three distinct stages, those of lethargy, catalepsy (rigidity), and somnambulism.

Although he always spoke highly of Charcot's abilities, Bernheim soon became convinced that the Parisian was mistaken about the fundamental nature of hypnosis. In 1884, citing Liébeault as a primary inspiration, Bernheim wrote De la suggestion dans l'état hypnotique et dans l'état de veille (On Suggestion in the Hypnotic State and the State of Wakefulness), one of the first of a series of books in which he criticized Charcot's ideas and established his own theory of hypnosis. In Bernheim's view, hypnosis was related not to magnetism but to the power of suggestion, which operated similarly under hypnosis and under normal conditions. He

believed that hypnosis and sleep were closely related. Bernheim's view had the corollary that most people could be hypnotized, an idea that turned out to be correct.

The competing ideas of Bernheim and Charcot were soon grouped into so-called Nancy and Salpêtrière schools, respectively, with both groups aiming to take on patients to demonstrate the superior efficacy of their methods. Bernheim is estimated to have hypnotized some 10,000 patients over the course of his career at the Nancy clinic. Both physicians realized that cases of what would now be called neurosis had to be separated from those involving more serious mental disorders, and both are credited with helping to establish procedures for scientific investigation of hypnosis.

Visited by Freud

Among the foreign clinicians observing the Bernheim-Charcot debate with interest was the young Sigmund Freud, who visited Bernheim in Nancy and ended up spending several weeks there. "I witnessed the astonishing experiments performed by Bernheim on his hospital patients," Freud wrote, as quoted in the Dictionary of Scientific Biography, "and it is there that I experienced the strongest impressions relating to the possible use of powerful psychical processes which remained hidden from human consciousness." The germ of Freud's idea of free association was formed during his work with Bernheim during this period, and Freud arranged for the translation into German of two of Bernheim's books, De la suggestion et ses applications à la thérapeutique (On Suggestion and Its Applications to Therapy, 1886) and Hypnotisme, suggestion, psychothérapie (Hypnotism, Suggestion, Psychotherapy, 1891), for which he wrote a sizable preface. Bernheim's use of the French word for psychotherapy represented a very early usage of the term; the English word "psychotherapy" dates only to around 1890.

Despite Freud's enthusiasm for Bernheim's ideas, the young Austrian was a student of Charcot and remained largely loyal to Charcot's overall theory of hypnosis. Most of his colleagues initially held the same view, and Bernheim's innovative ideas took time to gain acceptance. A big step forward came in 1904, when Bernheim showed that disorders of the sort then known as hysteria (fear, often involving perceived physical symptoms that have no organic cause) could be cured by hypnotic suggestion, despite Charcot's contention that it was an illness marked by a series of physical stages.

Bernheim's clinic was popular, and he was a sympathetic and effective practitioner who could range from authoritarian approaches to subtle manipulation of a patient, depending on what he thought might be most effective in a given case. He continued to practice in Nancy and even had success in converting Charcot to some of his positions. Bernheim's later years, however, were less than fully happy. His clinic suffered a decline in business, partly because he supported fellow Alsatian Jew Alfred Dreyfus in the face of ongoing accusations, increasingly motivated by anti-Semitism, that Dreyfus had transmitted military secrets to German diplomatic personnel (a series of events known as the Dreyfus Affair). Bernheim left Nancy after retiring in 1910, settling in Paris. He continued to write and to see his ideas gain gradual acceptance.

Bernheim died on April 2, 1919, in Paris. Although Bernheim's importance in the history of hypnosis is widely recognized among practitioners in the English-speaking world, the only full-length survey of his life was published in French (Blum, *La vie d'Hippolyte Bernheim*). Although not the originator of hypnosis, he furthered the development of many of the ways the practice is used today.

Books

Dictionary of Scientific Biography, edited by Charles Coulston Gillispie, Scribner's, 1970.

International Dictionary of Psychoanalysis, edited by Alain deMijolla, Gale, 2008.

Roback, A.A., *Jewish Influence in Modern Thought,* Kessinger, 2005.

Zunse, Leonard, *Biographical Dictionary of Psychology,* Greenwood, 1984.□

Edward Blake

Canadian politician Edward Blake (1833–1912) was one of Canada's leading liberals during the nineteenth century. During his career, he served as the premier of Ontario, the Liberal Party leader, and as a member of Canada's federal House of Commons. He later moved to England and served in the British House of Commons.

E dward Blake was a historic Canadian political figure. A successful lawyer first, he became a politician and enjoyed a long career. Personal deficiencies prevented him from achieving full potential, however: He was the only Canadian liberal leader who never became the country's prime minister. Suffering from poor health, insecurity, inflated ego, and heightened sensitivity, he nevertheless made his mark by sheer force of will, intelligence, education, and natural ability.

Edward Blake was born on October 13, 1833 in Adelaide Township in Upper Canada. He was subsequently baptized as Dominick Edward Blake by parents William Hume and Catherine (Honoria) Blake. Blake grew up in a log cabin in a strict, even oppressive, religious family environment: His Anglican family members were intensely evangelical. In addition, the family kept close-knit ties. In keeping with their forebears' tradition, his father and mother were cousins. Blake's paternal grandfather married a Hume cousin, and the couple immigrated to Canada from Ireland, accompanied by friends and relatives.

As a child, Blake suffered health problems. As such, his early education was home based, with lessons provided by his father, mother, and a tutor. The curriculum proved random and loosely formalized. For instance, Blake received Latin instruction from his father as he dressed in the morning.

Blake spent his childhood in Toronto, where his father became a successful lawyer, politician, and judge. This instilled in Blake a drive to excel, which was further reinforced by his father's later financial difficulties, which arose around 1857. From that point, Blake strived to maintain a comfortable level of financial security for himself. All the while, the family remained close. After Blake married Margaret Cronyn in 1858, he moved in with his parents on their Humewood farm.

Studied Law in College

Blake's formal, higher education began when he entered Upper Canada College in 1846. He later enrolled in the University of Toronto. He received his Bachelor of Arts degree in 1854 and his Master of Arts in 1858. Specifically, he studied law and, in 1856, he was admitted to the bar. His mother described his academic approach as a bit arbitrary, however. Indeed, Blake was an autodidactic, or self-directed, student, a quality which later influenced his legal and political career. Even his teachers considered him a curious individual of strong intellect.

After he was admitted to the bar, Blake became a successful equity lawyer in Toronto. Business started slow, but between 1857 and 1867, he took on as many as two hundred and fifteen Court of Chancery cases. This was a remarkable number, as well as an indication of his ambition and energy. In comparison, if he had lived in the late twentieth century, Blake would probably have been diagnosed as an overachieving workaholic.

At first, he formed a partnership with Stephen M. Jarvis. His brother, Samuel Hume Blake, soon joined the firm, which became known as Blake and Blake. Eventually, the firm developed into Blake, Cassels, and Graydon LLP. In 1858, he strengthened the firm by bringing in his other brothers, as well as Rupert Mearse Wells and James Kirkpatrick Kerr.

Earlier that year, on January 6, he married Margaret Cronyn, the daughter of Benjamin Cronyn, the first bishop of the Anglican diocese of Huron County, Ontario. The couple wed in London, Upper Canada. They had three daughters, but two of them died in infancy. They also had four sons, one of whom also died in infancy.

Recruited into Politics

A professional with liberal sympathies, Blake entered politics in 1867. He was encouraged in this direction by George Brown (1818–1880), a journalist and newspaper editor who founded the *Toronto Globe*. Brown knew and respected Blake's talents as a lawyer, and he felt that Blake had great potential as a politician, despite some apparent weaknesses. "Not much of a politician," Brown judged, "but [he is] anxious to learn and as sharp as a needle," (as recorded by the Dictionary of Canadian Biography web site).

When he entered public service, Blake enjoyed the advantages of independent wealth. At the time, he was only thirty-three years old and was worth $100,000, which was a considerable sum for a young man of his period.

By entering politics, Blake enhanced his reputation in legal professional circles. In 1869, current Canadian Prime Minister Sir John A. Macdonald (1815–1891) tried unsuccessfully to persuade Blake to become a judge, with the intention of having him serve as the head of the Chancery to Queen's Bench. Blake realized that Macdonald was motivated by political considerations, however, so he turned down the position.

This choice appeared in keeping with Blake's demonstrated values. He brought into his political career the liberal, reformist, and religious ideals developed in his upbringing, but it was his law career that truly bolstered his liberalism. One case in particular underscored this personal development: In 1858, Blake challenged the constitutionality of the "double shuffle" in the conservative cabinet of Macdonald and George-Etienne Cartier. In this case, which was argued in the Court of Queen's Bench and specifically directed at crown lands commissioner Philip Michael Matthew Scott VanKoughnet, Blake persuasively reasoned with impressive conviction that "no man being a member should be placed in power without being sanctioned by the people," (as quoted by the Canadian Biography web site). At the time, the *Toronto Globe* editorialized that Blake displayed considerable oratorical skills.

Advanced Through the Political Ranks

Upon entrance into his new career direction, Blake focused on provincial politics, serving the South Bruce province from 1867 to 1872. In 1867, he gained a seat in the Federal House of Commons, which he held until 1891. A year later, Blake became the leader of the Ontario Liberal Party. In 1871, he became the second premier of Ontario, when he helped oust Macdonald (1815–1891), who had become involved in the Pacific Scandal, which involved bribes accepted by conservatives that were related to national rail contracts. Macdonald was compelled to resign as Canada's prime minister and, in the wake, governmental power changed hands from the conservative to the liberal government. Blake was also offered the role of prime minister, but was forced to turn it down because of ill health, something that plagued him throughout his life.

In 1872, Blake abandoned provincial politics to enter federal politics. That year, he participated in the federal election. He did this because the so-called "dual mandate" rule, which allowed politicians to simultaneously serve in provincial and federal capacities, had been abolished. Though he had been involved in provincial politics for a relatively brief period, Blake made a significant impact as Ontario's premier, establishing an enduring liberal political influence in his home country.

By 1873, Blake seemed the logical choice to head the federal Liberal party, but he refused this offer as well. When the Liberal government dominated the 1874 federal election, however, Blake agreed to become a member of the cabinet of liberal Prime Minister Alexander Mackenzie. Subsequently, Blake served as minister without portfolio for one year (1873–1874), minister of justice for two years (1875–1877), and he also became president of the Queen's Privy Council for Canada.

After the Liberals were defeated in the 1878 federal election, Blake succeeded Mackenzie as party leader in 1880. He failed to defeat Macdonald's conservatives in the 1882 and 1887 elections, however. Blake resigned as Liberal leader in 1887, recruiting Wilfrid Laurier as his successor.

During this period, he continued suffering health problems, which were exacerbated by pressures from workload and demanding expectations from the public and professional colleagues. In particular, he suffered excruciating headaches and, at times, verged on complete nervous exhaustion.

Moved to England

Blake finally resigned from Canadian politics in 1891, leaving the country's House of Commons to move to Britain. His political career didn't stop there, though. In 1892, Blake joined the British House of Commons as an Irish Member of Parliament, supporting the Ireland's Longford South constituency. Unfortunately, his health continued deteriorating. He served until 1907, when he suffered a stroke on May 24. As the stroke left him partially paralyzed on the left side of his body, he was forced to resign. Then in August, he applied for and was granted stewardship of the Chiltern Hundreds, a legal entity that allowed resignation from the House of Commons. With his British parliamentary career officially over, Blake returned to Canada to live out his retirement.

Promise Unfulfilled

During his career, Blake also served as a senator and chancellor at the University of Toronto from 1876 to 1900. Despite his long career, Blake never lived up to his true potential as a politician. Part of this was simply due to bad luck: In the 1882 and 1887 federal elections in Canada, he faced off against the Macdonald faction, which was then at the zenith of its popularity. Even more significantly, his personality engendered career-limiting problems. He was described as domineering, particularly in Liberal party matters and parliamentary activities. He was prone to giving long speeches, some often lasting as much as six hours. This left little room for even the most sympathetic colleagues to express their views, display their leadership, garner political experience and gain the trust of the electorate. Prominent Liberal party member Sir Richard Cartwright (1835–1912), wrote in his memoirs titled *Reminiscences* that Blake allowed "nothing for his supporters to say," a problem that Cartwright described as a nearly "positive disease." Cartwright did concede that Blake demonstrated substantial "general ability," but he added that he was "intensely ambitious" and "exceedingly sarcastic," as well as "absurdly sensitive to criticism," a trait that frequently made Blake behave "like a spoilt child."

Canadian historian John Charles Dent wrote (as quoted by the Canadian Encyclopedia web site) that Blake possessed "a manner as devoid of warmth as is a flake of December snow, and as devoid of magnetism as is a loaf of unleavened bread."

Blake's physical presence added to negative impressions. He has been described as a "commanding figure" that stood out from the crowd due to his broad-shouldered physique and a round face haloed by a coarse beard and festooned with round glasses. Further, despite being a verbose orator, Blake found informal, small talk discomforting, which made it difficult for him to establish close friendships.

Personality deficiencies even affected his family life. Even though he valued strong family ties, he could be aloof and even harsh, particularly toward his wife Margaret, who was described as a kind and intelligent woman. She often felt compelled to remain silent in his presence. Still, Blake depended on her for emotional support, which she unselfishly provided. She also offered him a peaceful haven from his high-pressure public life.

Died in Toronto

After retiring from the British House of Commons in 1907, Blake lived out the rest of his life at his home on Jarvis Street in Toronto, residing close to other family members. His later years were spent in near seclusion, except for occasional holiday visits. In 1906, aware that his remaining time was short, Blake began settling his estate and destroying much of his political correspondence.

He passed away on March 1, 1912. He was seventy-eight years old. Surviving Blake were his wife, a daughter (Sophia Hume) and two sons (Edward William Hume and Samuel Verschoyle Blake). Like their father, both sons were lawyers. Margaret Blake died in 1917.

While Blake possessed none of the innate personality traits that typically make for a successful politician, he compensated for his deficiencies through his large intellectual capacity and natural ability. Further, this allowed him to establish a strong reputation in liberal politics and gain the respect of colleagues and constituents.

Books

"Blake, Edward," *Merriam-Webster's Biographical Dictionary,* Merriam-Webster Incorporated, 1995.
Cartwright, Sir Richard, *Reminiscences,* Toronto, 1912.

Online

"Blake, Edward," *Dictionary of Canadian Biography,* http://www.biographi.ca/ (December 1, 2009).
"Blake, Edward," *TheCanadianEncyclopedia.com,* http://www.thecanadianencyclopedia.com/ (December 1, 2009).
"Mrs. Dominick Edward Blake," *CollectionsCanada.gc.ca,* http://www.portraits.gc.ca/ (December 1, 2009).
"The Honourable Dominick Edward Blake," *Spiritus-temporis.com,* http://www.spiritus-temporis.com/edward-blake/ (December 1, 2009).□

Vasily Konstantinovich Blücher

Vasily Konstantinovich Blücher (1889–1938) was one of the first military heroes of the newly created Soviet Union. During the six-year-long civil war that threatened to reverse the 1917 Bolshevik Revolution, Blücher masterfully commanded Red Army troops to deliver coordinated attacks on White Russian forces across a vast theater of war stretching across Eurasia. He later held a key military post in the Soviet Far East and worked to bring China into the Communist fold. In 1938 he was targeted by Soviet leader Josef Stalin in a bewildering purge of top military commanders, and died in custody.

Blücher came from a peasant family in the Yaroslavl Oblast region. He was born in 1889, just 28 years after a tsarist decree freed imperial Russia's vast population of serfs, the farmers who worked in the service of major landholders. "Blücher" was apparently not the actual family name, but was instead bestowed on the family by their landlord in honor of the great Prussian field marshal Gebhard Leberecht von Blücher, who had defeated the French forces of Napoleon I at the Battle of Waterloo in 1815.

Jailed for Union Organizing

Blücher learned the trade of metalworking as a young man and worked in a factory in Mytishchi, near Moscow, but was arrested around 1909 for organizing a workers' group at his job site. Four years earlier, a wide-ranging coalition of leftists opposed to the autocratic regime of Tsar Nicholas II had unsuccessfully attempted a political uprising known as the Russian Revolution of 1905. The Tsar's government dealt harshly with political opposition after that. For his 1909 transgression, Blücher was sentenced to a prison term of 32 months. When the tsar led Russia into the quagmire of World

War I in 1914, Blücher enlisted in the imperial army and became a noncommissioned officer. Badly wounded, he was discharged in 1915 and went to work at a shipyard on the Volga River in Nizhny Novgorod. He moved on to a factory job in Kazan, and joined the Russian Social Democratic Labor Party, or RSDLP.

The RSDLP had been officially outlawed almost since its inception in 1898. It was the party of Vladimir Ilyich Lenin, who would lead its hard-line faction, the Bolsheviks, to power at the end of 1917. When the March revolution erupted that year and forced Nicholas to abdicate, Blücher was in another Volga River city, Samara, and was a key member of the newly formed Samara Revolutionary Committee. He became a commissar of the Red Guards, the armed units of workers that formed the basis of the new Soviet Army.

In November of 1917, Blücher was dispatched to command a Red Guard force against an anticommunist uprising in the city of Orenburg on the Ural River. The revolt was engineered by the Cossacks, the legendary cadre of cavalry forces that enjoyed a relatively generous autonomy under the tsar for their wartime services and role as border guards. The Orenburg uprising was led by Alexander Dutov, and grew in strength when it allied with the Czechoslovak Legion, a large detachment of troops of the former Austro-Hungarian Empire left behind in Russia at the end of World War I that took up arms against the Bolsheviks. The Cossacks and Eastern European contingent allied with White Russians, or former imperial military leaders and elites seeking the restoration of the monarchy. These were the belligerents in the Russian Civil War of 1917–23.

The Bolsheviks struggled to hold power in the face of an array of well-funded foes. The Whites benefited from enormous foreign aid, including new detachments of foreign troops. The anti-Bolshevik side scored a major victory in June of 1918 at Chelyabinsk and soon seized a large section of the Trans-Siberian railroad.

Commanded Large Peasant Force

Blücher was put in charge of the South Urals Partisan Army, a 10,000-strong force, whose aim was to meet up with the regular Soviet Army and rout the Whites. Blücher and his units trekked over 900 miles in just six weeks, and assailed the Whites from the rear. "There he spread panic and disorder for many months," wrote Albert Parry in the *New York Times.* "The best regiments could not corner his detachment, which at times dwindled to a handful but always found new volunteers from among the peasants of the villages it passed through." Finally, in September of 1918 Blücher's forces linked with the Red Army and the Whites retreated. He became an instant war hero in the new Soviet state, and was honored with the first ever Order of the Red Banner from the government for heroism in combat.

Blücher's partisan army was incorporated into the regular Soviet army as the 51st Division of the Red Army and marched toward Siberia, where a naval commander, Admiral Aleksandr Kolchak, had declared his opposition to the Bolshevik Revolution and installed himself at the head of a military government in the area. Kolchak commanded a vast army of former Austro-Hungarian empire soldiers, who had been captured during World War I and sent to Siberian prisoner-of-war

camps. The British sent massive amounts of military aid to Kolchak's forces. Red Army victories in the territory held by Kolchak began in the spring of 1919, and Blücher's units took Siberia's historic capital, Tobolsk, on September 7, 1919. Blücher and his forces then moved on to Yalutorovsk and seized it, while sustaining heavy casualties.

Blücher's next mission was to take his forces westward to suppress a new rebellion in the Ukraine and Poland. A newly created Polish Republic had allied with anti-Soviet Ukrainian rebels to disrupt Soviet goals in the region. Blücher was sent to turn back advances by the forces of Polish General Jósef Piłsudski, but en route he learned that Piłsudski, had been defeated. At that point, Blücher was ordered by Lenin and other top Soviet officials to head south. There, his forces eliminated the threat posed in the Crimea by another White commander, Baron Pyotr Nikolayevich Wrangel. A former high-ranking officer in the tsar's army, who had seized Volgograd and key sites in southern Russia and the Caucasus. In the fall of 1920, Blücher's troops succeeded in retaking these cities and ports on the Black Sea, effectively ending all serious threats to the world's first Marxist state.

Set Up Chinese Military Academy

In 1921 Lenin placed Blücher as the military commander of the Far Eastern Republic. This was a buffer state, sometimes called the Chita Republic, that covered a large swath of territory in the east that included the crucial port city of Vladivostok. Japan had been a threat and continued to support the Whites even when pushed back. In 1924 Blücher was sent to Canton, China, as the Soviet military adviser, but initially arrived undercover using the name "General Galen." Canton was the headquarters of the Kuomintang (KMT), or Nationalist government, of Sun Yat-sen, whose forces had overthrown the Ch'ing dynasty in 1911. Since then China had been mired in civil war, and once the Soviets quelled the internal threat of the Whites, they turned to their neighbors to seek new allies. This Moscow-based "Communist International" movement was known by its shortened form, the Comintern.

The Comintern's envoy in Canton was Mikhail Markovich Gruzenberg, alias Michael Borodin (1884-1951). Borodin worked closely with Blücher to establish a pro-Soviet cadre among the KMT, and they brought Russian officers to teach at the Whampoa Military Academy, near Guangzhou, China. Sources note that the woman who became Blücher's second wife, Galina Kolchugina, came with him on this mission and taught courses on political propaganda and fomenting unrest at the Whampoa Academy. During his time in Canton, Blücher mapped out the KMT's Northern Expedition, which sought to wrest control of northern China from the local warlords and unify the frontier under the KMT banner between 1926 and 1928. The Sino-Soviet alliance, however, fell apart after the death of Sun Yat-sen in 1925. General Chiang Kai-shek became head of the KMT, and launched a purge of its Communist elements. The KMT made a formal break with the Soviets in April of 1927.

Blücher was appointed military commander of the Ukraine before returning east once again in 1929 as head of the Special Red Banner Eastern Army. This came at a time when the Japanese military had grown increasingly aggressive and Chinese officials had warned Western powers that the Soviets were covertly funding Communist Party activities elsewhere. Blücher moved aggressively against former White Russian troops who had been permitted to settle in the Chinese city of Harbin. He accused them of colluding with the Chinese to reverse Soviet gains in the area. In the Russo-Chinese Eastern Railroad War of 1929-30, Blücher won a decisive advantage for the Soviet state and was honored with another newly created medal, the Order of the Red Star.

Final Battle at Khasan Lake

After Lenin's death in 1924, the Russian Communist Party and Soviet Union came under the control of Josef Stalin, who grew increasingly autocratic. In 1932 Stalin favored Blücher with a seat on the Presidium of the Soviet Union. Three years later the hero of the Russian Civil War was made a Marshal of the Soviet Union. In July of 1938 Blücher was sent once again to the Far East, when Japan—whose army had occupied the Korean peninsula long before—began moving aggressively at the Soviet-Korean border. This was the Battle of Khasan Lake, and though the Soviet Union regained all positions, Blücher's army suffered heavy casualties. In the newly fearful climate of Stalin's regime, this put both his career and life in danger.

Stalin had launched several major economic initiatives since taking over, and eliminated opposition to his authority by targeting anyone whose loyalty to the Party and his goals he deemed suspect. He began purging top army officials in 1937, starting with General Mikhail Tukhachevsky who, like Blücher, was a much-decorated hero of the Russian Civil War. Initially, Blücher took part in some of the judicial panels in what became known as the Great Purge, including the one that condemned Tukhachevsky. One source claimed Blücher was even the commander of Tukhachevsky's firing squad. After the Khasan Lake event, however, he, too, was dismissed from his positions in an embarrassing downfall for one of the first five Marshals of the Soviet Union. On October 22 he was arrested and charged with spying for Japan.

Died in Custody

Blücher was held at the notorious Lefortovo Prison in Moscow, where he was tortured but maintained his innocence. There was no panel or show trial as there had been for Tukhachevsky. Some sources claim that he died from torture, while others say Stalin ordered him shot on November 9, 1938. His disappearance was a mystery for several weeks, and rumors surfaced—probably Kremlin-fomented—that he was fighting in China under an assumed name. A *New York Times* article dated December 16, 1938, mentioned his possible arrest and dismissal from army posts, but reported that he had merely been assigned to the War Office in Moscow. His wife was also arrested, according to Andrew Nagorski's 2007 book *The Greatest Battle: Stalin, Hitler, and the Desperate Struggle for Moscow That Changed the Course of World War II.* She later told a source that when she saw her husband in custody, he looked "as if he had been driven over by a tank," according to the book. "His tormenters continued to beat him, and blood flowed from one eye. 'Stalin, do you hear how they're beating me?' he'd shout."

The loss of Blücher, Tukhachevsky, and other skilled military leaders made the Soviet Union vulnerable, and Nazi Germany took advantage of this in June of 1941 when it invaded the Soviet Union from Poland. Blücher's name was rehabilitated in the late 1950s when Stalin's successor, Nikita Khrushchev, famously conceded that errors of judgment had been made during the Stalinist era.

Books

Murphy, John, Jr., "Stalin and Stalinism," in *Encyclopedia of Politics,* edited by Rodney Carlisle, *Volume 1: The Left,* Sage Reference, 2005.

Nagorski, Andrew, *The Greatest Battle: Stalin, Hitler, and the Desperate Struggle for Moscow That Changed the Course of World War II,* Simon and Schuster, 2007, p. 77.

Periodicals

New York Times, October 13, 1929; December 16, 1938, p. 20; February 23, 1964.

Time, September 2, 1929.□

Arlene Blum

The American mountaineer Arlene Blum (born 1945) has played a key role in breaking gender barriers in the world of elite level mountain climbing.

Best known for her leadership of the first group of women to reach the summit of the hazardous Nepalese peak Annapurna I, Blum was also part of the first all-female expedition that climbed Alaska's Denali. Blum wrote two books, one about the triumphant but tragic Annapurna expedition, and one a memoir exploring the roots of the instincts that led her toward mountain climbing, and recounting some of the episodes of gender discrimination she encountered on her way to the top of the world. There were numerous such episodes, since for most of its history mountain climbing had been an all-male activity.

Raised by Grandparents

The childhood that Blum explored in her memoir, *Breaking Trail,* was a restrictive one. She was born on March 1, 1945, in Davenport, Iowa. Blum's father, Ludwig Blum, was a German Jewish physician who escaped to the United States during World War II; her mother, Gertrude Isenberg Blum, was an American Jew who aspired to become a classical violinist. The two met in Chicago, but the marriage was already in the process of dissolving during Blum's mother's pregnancy. Gertrude Blum tried to provide an encouraging environment for her daughter but was often away from the house as she worked to fend for herself and provide for the family, and Arlene was raised mostly by her maternal grandparents, who were Orthodox Jews. Later Blum's mother suffered from mental illness and underwent a series of shock-therapy treatments.

The family moved to Chicago in 1951 and settled on the city's South Side. Blum was discouraged from becoming proficient on the piano, and despite her obvious intelligence was not allowed to enroll at the University of Chicago's prestigious Lab School. The atmosphere at home was not conducive to

who introduced her to mountain climbing. Her first attempt, on the slopes of Washington State's Mount Adams, was a failure; she failed to reach the top, took a long slide down on her backside, and was forced to carry a toilet seat around campus for weeks because sitting on a hard surface was too painful. But her conditioning and skills improved rapidly, and by 1965 she had climbed Mount Hood, at 11,237 feet the highest peak in Oregon. Thoroughly hooked, she arranged to study volcanic gas emissions from Mount Hood as part of her senior thesis research. She received her degree from Reed in 1966 and enrolled for graduate study at the Massachusetts Institute of Technology, turning Harvard University down partly because she was told that the venerable school's outing club was not open to women.

In 1967 Blum decided she was more comfortable on the West Coast, and switched to the doctoral program in bio-physical chemistry at the University of California at Berkeley. Before enrolling, she was part of a group that climbed 19,000-foot Nevado Pisco and 21,000-foot Chopiqualqui in Peru. Blum earned a Ph.D. from Berkeley, and her research contributed to the eventual banning of a flame retardant called tris that was used in children's pajamas but that Blum correctly suspected was carcinogenic. Blum balanced her studies in the lab with mountaineering throughout her graduate school career, however, and when she and her friends could not be on a peak in the Sierra or Cascade ranges, she honed her skills by rappelling up the sides of buildings on the Berkeley campus.

Up to this point, Blum's climbs had all been with groups that included friends, a romantic partner, and, on occasion, faculty members with whom she worked. By the late 1960s, however, she was ready for the more difficult mountains around the world, to be undertaken only with specialized gear and the cooperation of teams of top-flight mountaineers. As she tried to join these teams, Blum began to encounter discrimination. She applied to join a team that hoped to scale the then-unclimbed Koh-i-Marchech in Afghanistan, but, as she recalled in *Breaking Trail,* she received a letter saying that including a woman in the group could negatively affect "the camaraderie of the heights" and cause problems in "excre-tory situations high on the open ice." Setting her sights on Denali, then known as Mount McKinley, Blum encoun-tered similar prohibitions as well as the general notion that women were not physically strong enough for the rigors of high peaks. "Chicks? Climb Denali?" she was told at an American Alpine Club meeting she described in her memoir. "You must be joking. No way dames could ever make it up that bitch."

Blum's response was to organize an all-female Denali expedition of her own, putting together a team including women recommended by other climbers and women she found through placing advertisements. Blum persuaded Grace Hoeman, an Anchorage anesthesiologist and experienced Alaskan mountain climber, to serve as the expedition's leader, and she herself became deputy leader. Blum, however, had to take over a de facto leadership role when Hoeman developed severe altitude sickness as the group approached the summit. She also had to surmount a series of disagreements among team members. But on July 6, 1970, Blum's group became the first all-female team to scale Denali.

learning. Blum's grandmother "maintains the sanctity of her kosher kitchen with savage authority," Blum recalled in *Breaking Trail.* "If I break one of her rules, her eyes bore into me like bullets. 'Oy! You're a worthless child,' she barks. 'No good.' Slightly hard of hearing and addicted to television, she sits in her floral chair chain smoking and shouting at the full-volume TV set. Often I sit with her and watch *To Tell the Truth, I Love Lucy,* and *You Bet Your Life* until my head feels dull and my eyes ache."

Her grandparents argued frequently as well, and school became a refuge for the determined youngster. Blum was placed in an advanced program focusing on math and sci-ence, and from the start she was determined to compete with boys on an equal footing. Blum earned top grades, and a teacher encouraged her to look beyond the downtown Chi-cago branch of the University of Illinois, where most South Side kids went to college if they went at all. Blum, the teacher pointed out, could earn a scholarship that would allow her to attend any school she wanted to. Blum settled on an institu-tion that was far from home not only geographically but also in its atmosphere: Reed College in Portland, Oregon. "Reed was considered a radical place," Blum recalled to the school's alumni magazine. "It was all very mind-stretching and stimulating."

Climbed Mount Hood as Undergraduate

Blum majored in chemistry at Reed, and it was a freshman year lab partner, in whom she was romantically interested,

Planned Annapurna Attempt

Blum did not stay down to earth for long. She returned to Berkeley and did research for her Ph.D. dissertation, but in late 1971 she embarked on a 14-month around-the-world trip she called the Endless Winter. In eastern Africa, Iran, Afghanistan, India, and Nepal, she led teams that climbed 19 high peaks and passes, some of them almost untouched by human visitation. She visited the Great Barrier Reef and climbed mountains in New Zealand before returning home. Around this time Blum began to think about her greatest challenge yet: an expedition to the top of Annapurna I, the highest peak in a feared Nepalese mountain chain and the tenth-highest mountain in the world. It had never been climbed by an American team, male or female, and only eight men, and no women, had reached the summit.

Landing a teaching job at Wellesley College, Blum surprised the committee that hired her by immediately requesting a semester off so that she could climb Mount Everest as part of the American Bicentennial Everest Expedition in 1976. On many climbs of difficult peaks, only two climbers are chosen to attempt the summit, and Blum, suffering from a variety of medical problems, remained at a lower base camp, supporting two other members of the group who reached the top. But her ability to handle the most difficult situations in mountaineering was steadily growing. Back in the United States, Blum and her supporters sold T-shirts bearing the words "A Woman's Place Is On Top" in order to raise money for the upcoming attempt on Annapurna.

The story of the Annapurna expedition was recounted in Blum's book *Annapurna: A Woman's Place,* considered a classic of mountaineering literature. A team of women climbers left Berkeley in 1978 with Blum as leader. They ascended Annapurna, accompanied by a group of Sherpas, or members of a Nepalese ethnic group who live in the high mountains and are famous for their climbing abilities. The culmination of the trip encompassed both success and tragedy. The group planned to send members to the summit in groups, and the first group, including the female climbers Vera Komarkova and Irene Miller, along with Sherpas Chiwang Rinjing and Mingma Chering, reached the summit and became the first women ever to stand atop the mountain. The group's jubilation was cut short, however, when two members of the second ascent team fell to their deaths.

Blum continued to lead all-female climbing expeditions to the Himalayas and elsewhere, including a 2,000-mile Great Himalayan Traverse across a series of peaks from Bhutan through India. But after the birth of her daughter, Annalise, in 1987, she cut back on risky climbs, although she did carry her baby in a backpack on a trek across the Alps. (Annalise has been more interested in basketball than in mountain climbing.) "Once you have children you don't want to engage in life-threatening sports. It's a personal choice," she explained to Ramyata Limbu of the *Nepali Times.* Blum has led tours in the Himalayas, organized an annual Himalayan festival in Berkeley, and worked with the politically liberal organization MoveOn.org. Her main occupation has been conducting corporate workshops in leadership and decision-making. *Breaking Trail* was published in 2005. A group of Arlene Blum's personal papers is housed in the Stanford University Library.

Books

Blum, Arlene, *Annapurna: A Woman's Place,* Sierra Club Books, 1980.
Blum, Arlene, *Breaking Trail: A Climbing Life,* Scribners, 2005.
Great Women in Sports, Visible Ink, 1996.

Periodicals

Fortune, June 27, 2005.
Seattle Post-Intelligencer, October 28, 2005.

Online

"Interview with Arlene Blum," *Harcourt Books,* http://www.harcourt books.com/Breaking_Trail/interview.asp (October 29, 2009).
"Reaching the Summit," *Reed Magazine,* http://www.web.reed. edu/reed_magazine/feb2004/features/reaching_the_summit (October 29, 2009).
"Walking on Clouds," *Nepali Times,* http://www.nepalitimes.com. np/issue/2001/01/19/Travel/8627 (October 29, 2009).□

Augusto Boal

The Brazilian theater director and author Augusto Boal (1931–2009) created a unique set of democratically oriented innovations in the basic form of stage drama. He called these innovations the Theater of the Oppressed.

The Theater of the Oppressed took its name from a book, *Pedagogy of the Oppressed,* by Boal's friend, Brazilian writer and educator Paulo Freire. Freire believed that teaching should not be an authoritarian activity but rather a collaboration between a teacher and student who each learned from the other, and Boal's vision of theater likewise involved breaking down the traditional distinction between performer and audience. Audience members at a Boal performance might insert themselves into a play, step into a dramatic role as part of an ordinary activity, or even be unaware that they were an audience. Like Freire's ideas, Boal's Theater of the Oppressed drew inspiration from leftist political ideas, but Boal was adamant about avoiding theatrical propaganda. "Unlike the dogmatic political theatre of the 1960s, which told people what to do," Boal told Aleks Sierz of the London *Guardian,* "we now ask them what they want."

Studied Chemistry

Born in Rio de Janeiro, Brazil, on March 16, 1931, Augusto Boal (Bo-AHL) was the child of parents who had come to Brazil from Portugal. He was interested in theater from an early age, but at first planned to become an industrial chemist, studying chemistry in Brazil and then coming to Columbia University in New York for further training in 1952. While in New York he became acquainted with the city's rich progressive theater scene, and he took drama classes at Columbia on the side. He wrote a play, in English, called

The House Across the Street, and directed its first performance in New York in 1955. When Boal returned to Brazil, he was hired as director of the small Arena Theatre in São Paulo.

Boal's career seemed to be on the rise, but he remained dissatisfied. "I did theater like everybody else in that you call the spectator to come, you charge a price for the ticket and then you do plays, the best that you can," he recalled to Juan Gonzalez of the radio program *Democracy Now!* "But soon I understood that I was doing good plays, wonderful plays for people that were good writers for an audience that came just to look at it and say, 'Okay, it's nice.' And then they went away and nothing else happens." As Brazilian society became polarized between left and right in the 1960s, Boal began to think about ways in which theater could be used to aid Brazil's factory workers and its large class of landless farm workers. The Arena Theatre staged plays in union halls, schools, and churches, often operating on a financial shoestring.

During this period, Boal began to question traditional theatrical forms and to envision alternatives. He organized workshops for actors and playwrights, and he had audiences devise political topics for plays that the actors would improvise on the spot, a technique he called Newspaper Theater. Drama began to spill over into reality when a group of peasants threatened during one of Boal's performances to take up arms against a local landholder, and Boal began to run afoul of Brazil's military dictatorship. Later he expanded on the idea of audience participation, inviting audience members to shape a play as it developed. He called this Forum Theater, and the audience he called Spect-actors (Portuguese: Espect-atores). Boal knew he had struck a productive creative vein when a woman leapt onto the stage during an audience discussion and stepped into a role in the play.

Arrested and Tortured

In 1971 Boal was seized by Brazilian police while walking home from a performance of a play by the German writer Bertolt Brecht (a major inspiration for his own work). He was placed under arrest, held for three months, tortured, released, and deported to Argentina. There he was still working under an authoritarian government, and he had to resort to impromptu plays staged in public settings that might now go by the name of guerrilla theater; Boal called the technique Invisible Theater. In 1974 Boal codified his ideas in a book, *Teatro do Oprimido,* which was translated into English as *Theatre of the Oppressed* in 1979. The book combined some of Boal's essays from the 1960s with new material outlining the development of his theatrical ideas, all tied together by the idea of a spectator who was not simply part of a passive audience but actually an involved participant in a creative event. Where traditional theater, in Boal's view, served to reinforce ruling class control by making audiences passive, the theater of the oppressed made actors out of spectators.

Theatre of the Oppressed was eventually translated into more than 25 languages and remains the most influential of Boal's nine books, which include two novels, *The Miracle of Brazil* and *Americanos: Los Pasos de Murieta* (Americans: Murieta's Steps), and a practical manual, *Games for Actors and Non-Actors.* He continued to develop new techniques after his exile and to build on his core ideas. During a stint in Peru in 1973 he worked on a literacy campaign and developed the idea of Image Theater, with plays based on images rather than words.

From the early 1970s onward, Boal's ideas attracted the attention of theatrical innovators and progressive thinkers over much of the world, although at first he was somewhat less celebrated in English-speaking countries than elsewhere. In 1976 Boal moved to Lisbon, Portugal, and two years later he got a job teaching at the prestigious Sorbonne university in Paris, France. In addition to his teaching duties, Boal formed an annual Theater of the Oppressed festival and organized workshops, along with his wife, Cecilia, that were intended to jolt actors and directors out of their established habits of thinking about theater. Those established habits Boal called the Cop in the Head.

Elected to Rio City Council

A new phase in Boal's career began after Brazil undertook a gradual series of democratic reforms in the early and middle 1980s. Boal returned to Brazil in 1986 and threw himself into the revival of its oppositional theatrical scene. He formed a new Theater of the Oppressed Center and established a series of community theaters. Elected as a member of Rio de Janeiro's city council in 1993, Boal applied his theatrical ideas to the process of governing: in what he called Legislative Theater events, neighborhood-based audiences could discuss and even draft new laws and measures. Boal's Legislative Theater resulted in the enactment of 15 local and two state laws before he was defeated in his 1996 re-election bid. The experiment resulted in a new book, *Legislative Theater*, in 1998.

Boal's tendency toward theatrical experiment did not stop him from working within established organizations on occasion. In 1997 he was invited to direct a production of Shakespeare's *Hamlet* for the Royal Shakespeare Company in Stratford-on-Avon, England. "It means official recognition (for Shakespeare, I don't know how much more official you can get than the Royal Shakespeare Company) that the Theatre of the Oppressed is truly theatre," the director enthused in the *UNESCO Courier*. Yet Boal put his own characteristic twists on the production. In working with the actors he used a technique he called Rainbow of Desire, which involved a fusion of drama and therapy, and he structured the action so as to focus on minor characters in the production. While in England he also worked with Cardboard Citizens, a theater group operated by the homeless.

Partly because of the connection between Boal's ideas and those of the durably popular Freire, Boal continued to exert an influence long after radical theater and film went into decline. The British playwright John Arden, as quoted by Sierz, said that *Theatre of the Oppressed* "should be read by everyone in the world of theatre who has any pretensions at all to political commitment." In the new millennium, most of Freire's books remained in print in translations into English and other languages, and followers have issued guides for putting some of his ideas into action. One example is *Playing Boal: Theatre, Therapy, Activism*, edited by Jan Cohen-Cruz and Mady Schutzman. A full-length study of Boal's life and work, Frances Babbage's *Augusto Boal*, was published by Routledge in 2004.

In later years, Boal sometimes used theater as a direct means of peacemaking, arranging, for example, for Palestinians to perform plays by Israeli Jews and vice versa. Boal issued an autobiography, *Hamlet and the Baker's Son*, in 2001. In 1994 he was awarded the UNESCO Pablo Picasso Medal, and he received honorary doctorates from universities in several countries. He remained well known in the last decade of his life, often touring along a circuit of small theatrical companies and college theater departments with his son Julian in an effort to expand the worldwide corps of students trained in his methods. Shortly before his death, he was named UNESCO's 2009 Ambassador for Theater. Kyoung H. Park (of the *Korea Times*) quoted him as saying, "We are all actors: being a citizen is not living in society, it is changing it." Boal died in his native Rio de Janeiro on May 2, 2009.

Books

Babbage, Frances, *Augusto Boal*, Routledge, 2004.

Boal, Augusto, *Hamlet and the Baker's Son, My Life in Theatre and Politics*, Routledge, 2001.

Boal, Augusto, *The Theatre of the Oppressed*, 1974, English trans. Urizen, 1979 (repr. Routledge, 1982).

International Dictionary of Theatre, Volume 3: Actors, Directors, and Designers., St. James, 1996.

Periodicals

American Theatre, September 2009.
Guardian (London, England), May 6, 2009.
Korea Times, July 8, 2009.
New York Times, May 9, 2009.
UNESCO Courier, November 1997.

Online

"A Brief Biography of Augusto Boal," *Pedagogy & Theatre of the Oppressed*, http://www.ptoweb.org/boal.html (October 29, 2009).

"Famed Brazilian Artist Augusto Boal on the 'Theater of the Oppressed'" (interview), *Democracy Now!* (syndicated radio program), http://www.democracynow.org/2005/6/3/famed_brazilian_artist_augusto_boal_on (October 29, 2009).□

August Boeckh

The German classical scholar August Boeckh (1785–1867) took a wide-ranging approach to the study of ancient languages and culture, thereby helping to lay the groundwork for modern approaches to literary criticism and history.

Boeckh in his own time was known as a philologist, a scholar of languages, especially ancient ones. But he redefined the discipline of philology to a point where it was almost unrecognizable. Boeckh insisted that the texts that have come down to the modern world from ancient Greece and Rome had to be approached with every tool at the scholar's disposal—linguistic, historical, interpretive, critical, and so on. He did much to establish the discipline of hermeneutics, defined as the interpretation of a body of received texts. Boeckh had a long and influential career in the German university system, and as American education set itself up partly along German lines his influence was felt in the United States as well.

Raised by Single Mom

Boeckh (pronounced like "book," but with the last sound made guttural and the vowel produced with the lips more closely pursed) was born in the southwestern German city of Karlsruhe on November 24, 1785. His full name was Philipp August Boeckh, and his last name may also be written Böckh in German. The youngest of six children, he grew up in a family of scholars and civil servants. Boeckh's father, Mattäus, an official in the court of the local Margrave of Baden-Durlach, died when he was four, and his mother, Marie Salome, raised the family through dire financial circumstances. Even so, Boeckh was able to enroll at the *Gymnasium* or Latin-oriented high school, in Karlsruhe. He graduated in 1803 with a broad education and a certificate qualifying him to study theology, his first career plan.

In 1803 Boeckh entered the theology program at the University of Halle. He took a course in classical studies with one of the stars of the field at the time, Friedrich August Wolf, however, and, in the words of the 1911 *Encyclopedia Britannica,* "fell under the spell, passed from theology to philology, and became the greatest of all Wolf's scholars." He also studied with and was inspired by a scholar whose range of interests would mirror his own, the philosopher and theologian Friedrich Schleiermacher, under whose guidance he began to study the totalizing philosophy of Plato. He also studied what was known of ancient Greek music at the time, and wrote a dissertation about it. In 1807 Boeckh moved to Berlin but was unnerved by the unrest in the city that followed its invasion by Napoleon Bonaparte and returned home to southwestern Germany.

At the University of Heidelberg, Boeckh soon established himself as a privat-docent, or adjunct instructor supported by student fees. He was quickly given a special appointment as a professor and given a regular faculty position as a professor of classics in 1809. In 1811 he was hired away to the new University of Berlin under the title of Professor of Eloquence and Classical Literature, a position he would hold almost for the rest of his life. Boeckh was named to the Berlin Academy of Sciences in 1814 and became its secretary; in addition to his influential university lectures, he wrote and lectured in connection with that position.

Drew on Greek Music to Analyze Poetry

Boeckh made his academic reputation with translations of and commentaries on the writings of the Greek poet Pindar (c. 522–443 B.C.E.), which began to appear in 1811 with a volume of translations of Pindar's poetic odes. With the later volumes of his Pindar studies, he examined the question of poetic meters (or rhythms) in Pindar's Greek. Where treatments of the problem prior to Boeckh had relied merely on debate within the field of philology, Boeckh used a cross-disciplinary approach in which he drew on his knowledge of ancient music, pointing out that Greek drama and poetry were sung and could not be discussed in a vacuum.

The other writings from the early part of Boeckh's career were even more wide-ranging. His *Staatsaushaltung der Athener* (1817, published in English as *The Public Economy of Athens* in 1828) examined the political economy of the ancient Greek state—taxation, government spending, and public works. It was a fresh approach to the subject of ancient Greece, lying well beyond the usual purview of philology, and it opened the way for broader attempts to understand ancient Greek society as a whole. Yet Boeckh did not abandon the traditional tasks of the philologist. In 1825 he initiated a series of publications, called the *Corpus Inscriptionum Graecarum* and subsequently continued by others, that attempted to decode and interpret the inscriptions on ancient Greek buildings that had survived until that time.

Indeed, the essence of Boeckh's approach was that he believed each aspect of knowledge had something to offer other perspectives. Whereas philology and philosophy usually functioned as separate disciplines, Boeckh believed, as translator John Paul Pritchard put it in his introduction to Boeckh's *On Interpretation and Criticism,* that "neither functions satisfactorily without the other.... To formulate his concepts soundly, the philosopher needs an adequate fund of knowledge or data; too many philosophers, Boeckh charges, lack a basis in knowledge or tradition.... On the other hand, the philologist who attempts to work without some ordering concept in his view gathers a mere aggregate of facts, cannot digest his data into a system." Boeckh later in his career published studies of Plato and of the Pythagorean philosophers.

Very early in his career, Boeckh devised a general course outlining his vision of philology. He called it the *Encyklopädie und Methodologie der philologischen Wissenschaften* or *Encyclopedia and Methodology of the Philological Sciences,* using the word "encyclopedia" to mean a collection of knowledge rather than a multi-volume publication. Boeckh gave the course 26 times over the years of his teaching at the University of Berlin, and he became famous as a polymath, a person who has mastered many fields of knowledge. He attracted a total of 1,696 students to the course, averaging over 60 each time in an era when most university teaching was transmitted in small groups, and a large variety of German classical scholars of the following generation passed through the course.

Outlined Systematic Critical Method

The Encyclopedia, in addition to introducing the texts of the ancient world as they were then known, included a philosophical overview of the subject that proved to be of great importance for the development of literary criticism in general. Boeckh divided this overview into three parts: "The Idea of Philology," which described the uses of the field, "The Theory of Hermeneutics," which established a philosophical basis for the act of interpreting ancient texts, and finally the "Theory of Criticism," which laid out four ways of approaching an individual work: it could be approached with Grammatical, Historical, Individual, or Generic (related to its genre) Criticism. At a time when literary criticism was mostly undertaken by journalists, Boeckh laid out a systematic view of the subject that continues to resonate today.

Boeckh published many other books, covering subjects as varied as timekeeping and calendrical ideas among the ancients, an edition of Sophocles's play *Antigone,* Greek tragedy in general, and a study of Greek coinage. In the words of the 1911 *Britannica,* "Boeckh's activity was continually digressing into widely different fields." He wrote a vast number of smaller articles and commentaries, many of which were published in the *Transactions of the Berlin Academy.* These minor writings, as they were called, have been collected and fill seven volumes by themselves.

Boeckh gave his last course in 1866 in Berlin, where he died the following year on August 3. The *Encyclopedia* was compiled into book form by his students and issued in several different versions. In the U.S., Yale University professor Albert Stanburrough Cook introduced Boeckh's ideas after encountering them during his studies at the University of Jena. Many of his studies, translations, and editions remained the best available in their fields for decades or even a century or more after he wrote them, and the influence of his systematic and rigorous approach to scholarship was deeper still.

Books

Dictionary of German Biography, Saur, 2003.

Boeckh, August, *On Interpretation & Criticism,* trans. and ed. John Paul Pritchard, University of Oklahoma Press, 1968.

Encyclopedia Britannica, 11th ed., New York, 1910.

Mueller-Vollmer, Kurt, ed., *The Hermeneutics Reader: Texts of the German Tradition from the Enlightenment to the Present,* Continuum, 1985, repr. 2006.□

Arrigo Boito

With a very rare combination of musical and literary talent, Italian composer and poet Arrigo Boito (1842–1918) was involved creatively in several of the best known operas in the Italian repertory.

Although their relationship was not without strains initially, Boito cultivated a long friendship and creative partnership with the most famous Italian opera composer of all, Giuseppe Verdi. It was Boito who furnished the libretti (the texts) for the two great Shakespearean operas of Verdi's old age, *Otello* (1887) and *Falstaff* (1893). Boito himself produced only one work that became a classic— *Mefistofele,* which had its premiere in 1868. He labored for much of the rest of his life on a second opera but never completed it. Boito also wrote libretti for other composers and was a noted musical critic. Although the total size of his output either as writer or as composer was small, Boito made key contributions to the modernization of opera in Italy in the late nineteenth century.

Began Attending Conservatory at 11

Arrigo Boito was born on February 24, 1842, in Padua, Italy. His Italian artist father, Silvestro Boito, made a living from miniature paintings, and his mother was a Polish countess, Giuseppina Rodelinska. This unusual union dissolved when Boito was small, and he and his brother were raised in Venice by his mother. He took music lessons from two local teachers as a child, showed unusual talent, and was sent away to the Milan Conservatory when he was 11 years old because there was at the time no full-scale music school in the ancient city of canals. After a year of study Boito was given a scholarship that enabled him to complete his musical education in Milan. With a friend named Franco Faccio, he wrote a pair of cantatas, *Il quattro giugno* (The Fourth of June) and *Le sorella d'Italia* (The Sisters of Italy), as graduation exercises; both of them referred to the ongoing *risorgimento,* the nationalist movement that culminated in the establishment of Italy as a unified country.

The cantatas won the two young composers a prize of two thousand francs, which they used to travel to Germany and France to absorb the latest musical developments in those countries. In Germany they heard the operas of Richard Wagner, which had demolished the traditional Italian pattern of quasi-spoken recitatives and melodic arias. The Countess Clara Maffei, a noblewoman who played a key role in the *risorgimento,* gave them a letter of introduction to Verdi, who at the time was living and working in Paris. Boito and the celebrated composer got on well at the start, and Boito, who by that time had already written a good deal of poetry, was asked to write the text for a short Verdi choral piece called *Inno delle Nazione* (Hymn of the Nations).

That relationship changed, however, when Boito, after a detour to his ancestral Polish homeland, returned to Italy and became connected with a group of unconventional young artists and musicians known as the *scapigliatura* (literally, the unkempt ones). At a dinner following the premiere of an opera by Faccio, Boito gave a speech in which he said that the arts in Italy had the appearance of the walls of a whorehouse, a sentiment to which Verdi naturally enough took offense. Boito's poetry of this period, which included a long fable-poem called ''Re Orso'' (King Bear), often had a satirical tinge characteristic of the *scapigliatura* group. Another poem called ''Dualismo'' (Dualism) depicted a man on a tightrope between dreams of virtue and sin, and during this period Boito had been turning over in his mind the idea for a serious opera. It would be based on the duality of the virtuous and the satanic, as manifested in one of the most famous plays of the nineteenth century, Johann Wolfgang von Goethe's *Faust,* based on an old German story about a man who sells his soul to the devil in return for knowledge and perfect happiness.

Adapted Goethe Play

While *Faust* was known all over Europe, its complexities tended to get lost when the play was exported from Germany. French composer Charles Gounod's opera *Faust,* which had its Italian premiere at the La Scala opera house in Milan in 1862, reduced the story to its main romantic relationship between Faust and the play's innocent female lead character, Marguerite. As Boito's libretto for his new opera took shape, it included Goethe's entire story line, with all of its characters and philosophical ideas intact. The new opera was called *Mefistofele,* after the primary character Mephistopheles, the demonic figure and chaos sower in the opera. Boito's work on the opera was interrupted when he joined the army of Giuseppe Garibaldi, the principal leader of Italian unification, in 1865, but he returned to work on the libretto and music the following year.

When *Mefistofele* had its premiere at La Scala in 1868, it was the first opera in the theater's history, and one of very few in the entire history of opera, with both text and music written by the same person. Boito by this time was a controversial figure, with a coterie of supporters but a larger group of detractors. Controversy intensified as the libretto of Boito's opera was printed in advance of its first showing. The premiere of *Mefistofele* was one of opera's famous disasters. According to an account of the event written in 1906 by Enrico Fondi and published as part of a profile of Boito in the magazine *Outlook,* anti-Boito forces showed up at the premiere armed with large keys that they used to make amplified hissing noises showing their disapproval. Others in the audience just shouted, so loudly that the singer playing Faust was unable to hear the orchestra. "No work of art ever aroused such a warlike spirit," Fondi commented, adding that "the public deemed it unpatriotic to accept any reforming influence which an Italian, with such antecedents as Boito's, might draw from foreigners."

After the failure of *Mefistofele*—Boito closed down its run after just two chaotic performances—the composer retreated to lick his wounds, supporting himself by writing music criticism under the name Tobia Gorrio (an anagram of Arrigo Boito). He translated German operas and songs, including several of Wagner's operas, into Italian for the Ricordi publishing house, which began to ally itself with his supporters. After the Prologue section of *Mefistofele* was given a successful performance in the city of Trieste in 1871, Boito began to think about revising the work and presenting it once again. Musical fashions changed quickly, and, after a trial run of a shortened and altered version in Bologna in 1875, the opera was mounted again in Milan in 1881 without incident and became a part of the standard repertory, or regular rotation of operas performed by companies around the world. Apparently, no copies of the original version survived.

Even while he was first beginning to work on *Mefistofele,* Boito was pondering a follow-up on the subject of the decadent Roman emperor Nero, using for a title his Italian name, *Nerone.* Boito would work on the opera for almost his entire creative life, but never finish it. Partly this was because he was paralyzed by a lack of self-confidence after the premiere of *Mefistofele,* plunging himself anew into the study of music, classical literature, and foreign languages (he learned to speak both German and English fluently). He was also in demand as a librettist for operas by other composers, and the 1876 opera *La Gioconda,* by Amilcare Ponchielli, became another operatic standard in his list of credits. He also provided the texts for several other operas in the 1870s, and this prompted the publisher Ricordi and his friend Faccio to try to patch up the long history of bad blood between Boito and Verdi. In 1879 they suggested that Boito provide a libretto for *Otello,* an opera based on Shakespeare's play *Othello,* to be set by the older composer.

Wrote Verdi Libretti

Boito wrote the libretto, and Verdi, pleased with its high quality, agreed to a test role for Boito as librettist: Boito was to revise the libretto for Verdi's opera *Simon Boccanegra,* slated for an 1881 revival at La Scala. The revival was well received, and Verdi spent the next six years working on *Otello,* demanding numerous changes to the text from Boito. *Otello* has never been absent from the operatic repertory since its premiere in 1887, and it remains one of the few successful attempts to adapt the notoriously difficult language and structure of Shakespeare's plays for the operatic medium. Critics have pointed to Boito's ability to simplify complex plots and ideas and to think about them in musical terms as one of his greatest strengths. In 1892 Boito received an honorary doctorate from Cambridge University in England.

Verdi and Boito scored another success with *Falstaff,* which premiered in 1893 after delays that came this time from Boito's side: he took over the directorship of the Parma Conservatory temporarily so that his friend Faccio, incapacitated by syphilis, could continue to draw a salary from the institution. Boito's libretto this time drew on several linked Shakespeare plays: *The Merry Wives of Windsor* and *Henry IV,* parts one and two. Writing in the *New Grove Dictionary of Music,* William Ashbrook commented that Boito's "fondness for word-play, his knack for hitting on an epigrammatic phrase, and his mordant irony all found full scope" in *Falstaff.* Boito and Verdi planned a final Shakespeare opera, *Re Lear* (King Lear), but Verdi died in 1901, with Boito at his bedside.

By the time of the Verdi operas, Boito was a musical celebrity, and long profiles such as Fondi's, which discussed Boito's fondness for word puzzles, began to appear. In the late 1880s and 1890s Boito was romantically linked to the star Italian actress Eleanora Duse, increasing his renown. Yet that renown rested largely on a single work, *Mefistofele.* Boito worked on *Nerone* intermittently until about 1915, subjecting drafts to a lengthy process of revision. Verdi urged him to finish the opera, and he published the work's libretto in full in 1901. In 1904, however, he broke off his work in order to undertake a new study of the classical poetry on which the story was based. Finally he died in Milan on June 10, 1918, after a series of heart problems, leaving the work unfinished. It was completed by a group of musicians including the Italian conductor Arturo Toscanini and finally received its premiere at La Scala on May 1, 1924. Although not as commonly performed as *Mefistofele,* it too has found an ongoing presence in the operatic repertory. In Ashbrook's words, "*Nerone* possesses great originality, vividly contrasting pagan magic, imperial corruption, and Christian *caritas.* It is arguably Boito's finest achievement." Boito has been the subject of numerous Italian-language biographies but is less well researched by English-language writers.

Books

International Dictionary of Opera, St. James, 1993.

Kaufman, Thomas G., *Verdi and His Major Contemporaries,* Garland, 1990.

The New Grove Dictionary of Music and Musicians, 2nd ed., Oxford, 2001.

Periodicals

Opera News, December 24, 1994.

Outlook, 1906 (volume 82).

Washington Times, March 3, 1996.

Online

"Arrigo Boito," *Classical.net,* http://www.classical.net/music/comp. lst/boito.php (November 1, 2009). □

Robert Bolt

Well known in his native England as a playwright, Robert Bolt (1924–1995) turned screenwriter in the 1960s and penned scripts for several of the most acclaimed dramas of the period.

Those films were *Lawrence of Arabia* (1962), *Doctor Zhivago* (1965), and *A Man for All Seasons* (1966). All were popular on both sides of the Atlantic, and were chosen for multiple honors at major film awards ceremonies. These films had common elements that reflected Bolt's creative personality: they brought famous episodes in world history to life through devices of plot and construction that were innovative yet accessible to wide audiences. Bolt's stage plays, noted the *Times* of London, "formed a bridge between a slightly younger, more radical generation of writers including John Osborne, Harold Pinter and Arnold Wesker, who had started to make their mark in the mid-1950s and the [London] West End theatre of the 1960s," and in the cinematic realm he "became associated with intelligently crafted historical epics."

Forced to Work in Insurance Office

Robert Oxton Bolt was born on August 15, 1924, in Manchester, England. His father owned a small store that sold furniture and glass goods. Bolt tended toward mild troublemaking as a child; he liked to throw his father's glassware through open train windows, and he was caught shoplifting. Bolt was expelled from Manchester Grammar School for low academic performance, and his dismayed parents responded by forcing him to go to work in the most tedious place they could think of—an insurance office. This had the desired effect, and Bolt studied hard for university entrance exams. Before he could enroll at Manchester University, however, World War II intervened; he was drafted and served in Britain's army and Royal Air Force from 1943 until 1946.

After his discharge he entered the university and majored in English, receiving his degree in 1949. During and after the war he was a member of Britain's Communist Party, but he became disillusioned with Communism's anti-democratic tendencies and drifted away from the movement. In 1949 he married art student Celia Ann Roberts, known as Jo; the pair raised one son (Ben Bolt, who became a theater director) and two daughters. Bolt got a job teaching at a school in a small village near Exeter, England, in 1949. He had never shown much interest in writing, but when he was asked to direct a Nativity play in the little town, he discarded the script he was given and wrote one of his own. 'The three wise men came onstage and one said 'Hello' and another said 'Hello' and the third said 'Who's that?' And I felt the hair go up on the back of my neck," Bolt recalled in an interview quoted by John Ezard of the London *Guardian* in Bolt's obituary. "I thought, why does he say 'Who's that?' And I knew then that was what I wanted to do."

In 1950 Bolt moved on to a job at the more prestigious Millfield School in the village of Street. But he kept writing plays in his spare time, and he succeeded in getting some of them produced as radio plays on the national British Broadcasting Corporation (BBC) radio network. His first radio production, broadcast in 1953, was called *The Master.* Among the others was an early version of *A Man for All Seasons,* broadcast in 1954; 1955's *The Last of the Wine* depicted a family's reaction to the news that London was under threat of attack with a hydrogen bomb. Soon Bolt began submitting plays to agents in the West End theater district in London. The first four were turned down, but Bolt enjoyed his first hit with

Flowering Cherry in 1958. The play, which dealt with the dreams of a small-time insurance salesman, drew on both Arthur Miller's *Death of a Salesman* and Anton Chekhov's *The Cherry Orchard.* Aided by a performance by star actor Ralph Richardson in the leading role, the play ran for 435 performances and allowed Bolt to end his teaching career and live off his writing.

In 1960 Bolt ruled the West End with two plays mounted in theaters (the Globe and the Queen's) that were next door to each other. The Queen's entry, *The Tiger and the Horse,* featured actor Michael Redgrave as an emotionally impaired college professor. But the more significant play was *A Man for All Seasons,* newly expanded to full length. The play, noted Ezard, "was at once acknowledged as a modern classic when it opened with Paul Scofield as Sir Thomas More"—the complex English statesman, philosopher, and counselor to King Henry VIII who was executed after refusing to give his approval to the king's divorce from Catherine of Aragon.

The play's language, lightly flavored by Renaissance-era English but easy to grasp, was one of its main attractions. Bolt's play untangled the complex issues of Henry VIII's time, partly relying on an innovative stage device resembling the experiments of German dramatist Bertolt Brecht: a nonspecific figure called the Common Man recounted some of the background and served the function of the chorus in ancient Greek drama, commenting on the action. Thomas More, Bolt was quoted as saying by Ezard, "never regarded himself as martyr material. But he kept one small area of integrity within himself. And once the powers-that-be found out, they could not rest until they got at it. So he became a martyr against his desires, because he would not do what the authorities wanted." Bolt himself chose his growing career over martyrdom in 1961 after his arrest in a 1961 protest against nuclear weaponry: although many of his comrades, including the 89-year-old philosopher Bertrand Russell, served a one-month prison sentence after refusing to sign government papers promising not to disturb the peace, Bolt signed the agreement—he had just received an advance of 25,000 pounds for a new screenplay and was being pressured to get to work.

Asked to Revise Screenplay

The new screenplay was for *Lawrence of Arabia.* Bolt was brought on board after disagreements between director David Lean and the original screenwriter, the American Kevin Wilson, who had been a victim of the McCarthy-era blacklist in Hollywood. The film was based on the life and writings of British writer and military officer T.E. Lawrence, who aided Arab forces during their World War I-era revolt against Ottoman Turkish rule. While Wilson's script dealt with the complex political currents in the Middle East, Lean wanted a close character study of Lawrence, and this was something Bolt was ideally equipped to provide. The relative contributions of Bolt and Wilson to the screenplay have not been entirely clear, but the final dialogue in the film was largely Bolt's work. Bolt won a 1962 Academy Award nomination for Best Adapted Screenplay and a British Academy Award for Best Screenplay the same year.

Even as he reached the top rungs of the film industry, Bolt never gave up on playwriting. He returned to the

London stage in 1963 with *Gentle Jack,* starring the veteran British actress Dame Edith Evans. He teamed with Lean once again for his next film assignment, an adaptation of the Boris Pasternak novel *Doctor Zhivago.* Released in 1965, the film subordinated much of the rich historical detail of Pasternak's book to its romantic story line. Bolt's dialogue meshed perfectly with Lean's lush visuals, however, and the film became a major hit at the box office. Bolt's screenplay brought him his first Academy Award.

By this time, Bolt was hobnobbing with A-list stars in both England and the United States. In the autumn of 1965, he was invited to a party at the London townhouse of American actor Warren Beatty and French actress Leslie Caron, who were living together at the time. There he was introduced to Sarah Miles, an attractive starlet dressed in a miniskirt and high heels. "You look like a debauched Alice in Wonderland," Bolt said, according to author Adrian Turner, who wrote the tell-all biography *Robert Bolt: Scenes from Two Lives.* "Since I didn't dress myself, I can't be held responsible," Miles replied, to which Bolt rejoined, "It wasn't your clothes I was looking at." With sparks already flying, Bolt and Miles became inseparable and soon moved in together. They married in 1967, raised one son, divorced in 1976, and, after Bolt's five-year marriage to the noblewoman Lady Queensberry ended, married again in 1988. The marriage lasted until Bolt's death.

Won Multiple Awards

The 1966 film of *A Man for All Seasons,* directed by Fred Zinnemann, was another major hit and marked perhaps the high point in Bolt's career in terms of industry acclaim. The film was honored with six Academy Awards, including Best Picture and, for Bolt himself, Best Adapted Screenplay; it also received seven awards from the British Film Academy. Bolt shaved some of the more unusual edges off his stage play, eliminating the figure of the Common Man. *A Man for All Seasons* enjoyed yet another turn in the projection booth: it was filmed for American television in 1988 by actor Charlton Heston, who also appeared as Thomas More. This production restored the Common Man as a character. Critical evaluations of Bolt's work in general have been mixed, but Ezard noted in Bolt's obituary that *A Man for All Seasons* "outlasted most of [Bolt's] contemporaries' work and is still performed somewhere in the world every week."

Some of Bolt's more negative episodes of critical reception came after the release of his next two films, both written to showcase Miles in starring roles and both markedly less successful than Bolt's 1960s hits. Bolt and Lean joined forces once again for *Ryan's Daughter* (1970), another love story with a wartime background; this one was set in Ireland during the World War I-era uprisings that preceded Irish independence from Britain. The lengthy film tanked at the box office but has continued to attract interest. In 1972 Bolt wrote and directed another Miles vehicle, *Lady Caroline Lamb.* That year he was named Commander of the British Empire (CBE, a level of knighthood).

Bolt rejoined Lean in the late 1970s as the two worked on a new film version of the durable *Mutiny on the Bounty* story, but in 1979 he suffered a heart attack and stroke that left him mute and paralyzed on the right side. Gradually he regained the power of speech and was able to resume writing. He finished work on the *Bounty* script, which was filmed by the New Zealand director Roger Donaldson. Bolt's last finished screenplay was for *The Mission,* a film set in colonial South America. "Not a few reviewers," noted Mike Cummings of the *All Movie Guide,* criticized the film "for depicting Christianized natives in 18th-century South America as little more than talking mannequins à la the old Tarzan movies." But Bolt was given Best Original Screenplay nods by both the British Film Academy and the Hollywood Foreign Press Association in 1987. Bolt planned a final collaboration with Lean, an adaptation of the Joseph Conrad novel *Nostromo,* but it was interrupted by his death at his home in Petersfield, Hampshire, England, on February 21, 1995.

Books

International Dictionary of Theatre, Volume 2: Playwrights, St. James, 1993.

Turner, Adrian, *Robert Bolt: Scenes from Two Lives,* Hutchinson, 1998.

Periodicals

Daily Mail (London, England), January 26, 1998.

Guardian (London, England), February 23, 1995.

Sunday Times (London, England), February 1, 1998.

Times (London, England), February 23, 1995.

Online

"Bolt, Robert (1924–1995)," *Screenonline,* http://www.screenonline.org.uk/people/id/488286 (November 1, 2009).

"Robert Bolt," *All Movie Guide,* http://www.allmovie.com (November 1, 2009). □

Jim Bowie

James Bowie (1796–1836) was a colonel in the Texas Rangers and led the defense of the Alamo in 1836. Prior to that infamous battle he had earned a reputation as a notorious fighter and as the inventor of the famed Bowie knife, which still enjoys popularity today.

James Bowie was born to his frontier parents in the late 1700s. Due to poor record keeping during that era, scholars disagree about the exact date and place of his birth. The most common consensus is that he entered this world in Logan County, Kentucky, on April 10, 1796. His father, Rezin Bowie, was a soldier during the American Revolution, and his mother, Elve, had nursed Rezin back to health after the battle of Savannah. After the war the couple had ten children. Like most frontier families, the Bowies lived off the land. They moved frequently and are reported to have lived at varying times in Kentucky, Tennessee, and Louisiana. Rezin financed these moves by selling the land he had freely claimed to other families. It was a lucrative business.

Learned Three Languages

Elve insisted that all of her children be educated. In the juvenile series *Jim Bowie: Hero of the Alamo,* Ann Graham Gaines wrote, "None of the Bowie children ever went to school, yet all of them learned to read, write, and do arithmetic from lessons taught by Elve. Jim Bowie became fluent in Spanish, French, and English. His surviving letters are clear and well spelled. It is remarkable that Elve found time among the many jobs of each and every day to truly educate all of her children." These skills would serve Bowie well later in life.

Growing up, Bowie was close to his family, particularly his brother Rezin (sometimes spelled Reason) Pleasant. After the family arrived in Louisiana when Jim was six, the two boys spent much of their time exploring the land. They became known for their rough-and-tumble antics. Marianne Johnston noted one tale in the "Jim Bowie" edition of the children's *American Legends Series*: "The Bowie boys were . . . not scared of the alligators and snakes that lived in the bayou. . . . [They] liked to explore these swampy areas near the Bowie home in Louisiana. Legend says that Jim started riding alligators when he was a boy. He would rope shut the huge jaws of the dangerous alligators. Then he would jump on the alligators' backs and go for wild rides through the swamps!" Tall tales such as this were widely reported by writers capturing the spirit of frontier life.

Bowie set out on his own at around age 18. He began visiting New Orleans regularly, and soon became known as a gambler and fighter. Around this same time, he and his brother Rezin also entered the slave trade. According to this story recounted by Gaines, they would travel to Galveston Island in Texas to purchase slaves from famed pirate Jean Laffite. Even though slavery was legal in Louisiana, importing slaves was not. Anyone who reported such an act was later given one half of the price those slaves brought at auction. The brothers quickly learned how to work this law to their advantage. According to Gaines, "The Bowie brothers would turn in the slaves they bought from Jean Laffite to the customs agent. Later, they would buy the slaves back cheaply at public auction, while also receiving half that price from the government as their reward. They would then sell the slaves again for a large profit."

Popularized the Bowie Knife

Given the activities the Bowie brothers were engaged in, it is not surprising that they often found themselves in fights with the men that they crossed. One such fight around 1827, known as the Sandbar Duel, centered around a bank loan. Several men lost their lives and Bowie himself was shot multiple times before finally killing his attacker with a knife. Both the fight and the knife gained instant notoriety. According to Mark Stewart in the young people's book *The Alamo*, from the "American Battlefield Series," "This weapon was a long, curved hunting knife that was excellent for throwing and wide enough to gut whatever its user took a swipe at. In other words, it was a hunting knife that worked well on people." A guard protected the user's hand from the blade and helped gain leverage on the animal or person on the opposite end of the tool.

Like most of Bowie's life, it is difficult to separate fact from fiction in regard to the details of who invented the weapon. Unique in terms of the blade and the guard, the knife gained popularity on the frontier after the Sandbar Duel. While there is no dispute that Jim Bowie made the knife famous, it is possible that his brother Rezin actually designed the weapon. The *Encyclopedia of the American West* provided one explanation: "Although James Bowie is generally credited with the invention, it was Reason who made the first 'Bowie' knife. Reason, himself, wrote in 1838 that 'the first Bowie knife was made by myself. The length of the blade is 9½ inches, its width 1¼ inches, single edged and blade not curved.' Since the time that James successfully used the knife in a fight in Louisiana, the legendary weapon has been associated with him, not his brother."

Moved to Texas

It took Bowie several months to recover from the injuries he received during the Sandbar Duel. Not long after, he decided that he needed a fresh start, and decided to move to Texas, which was a part of Mexico at the time, to pursue the many land speculation opportunities available. According to the *Dictionary of American Biography*, "On October 5, 1830, he became a Mexican citizen and at once began to acquire extensive tracts of land, largely through the device of inducing Mexicans to apply for grants and then buying them, when obtained, at nominal prices." According to Donald S. Frazier

in *The United States and Mexico at War,* this scheme successfully garnered Bowie thousands of acres of Texas land.

Bowie was soon able to ingratiate himself with many of the leading families of San Antonio, due to his well-spoken and educated demeanor. In 1831 he married Ursula Veramendi, daughter of Vice-Governor Juan Martin de Veramendi. The couple had two children. Bowie soon became involved in Texas politics. He was unhappy with new laws being enacted by Mexican officials that threatened his land holdings. When it became obvious that Texas would seek independence from Mexico, he joined the Texas Rangers and was quickly promoted to the rank of colonel. In the summer of 1833, Bowie's wife and children contracted cholera during a summer outbreak. He was traveling for business and was not present when his family perished from the disease.

Mexican officials began restricting northern immigration to Texas in an effort to quell the revolutionary movement that was gaining steam in the region. In response to this and other actions, local politician Stephen Austin sent messages encouraging Texans to fight for their independence from Mexico. Mexican leader Santa Anna took immediate action by dispatching 1,200 troops to the region. When the small town of Gonzalez refused to relinquish a cannon to those troops and instead fired upon them, a war officially started.

Texas citizens answered the call for revolution for a variety of reasons. Stewart noted that Bowie's motives were land-based. He wrote, "Jim Bowie was the ultimate frontier opportunist—a man with a fearsome fighting reputation, a knack for working the system, and an excellent head for business. He was about to close a deal that would have given him control of more that a million acres in Texas when the trouble started in 1835. Historians have suggested that Bowie decided to stand and fight at the Alamo to protect his interests in Texas real estate."

Led Volunteers at the Alamo

Texans had to quickly establish a chain of command. Sam Houston, former governor of Tennessee, was chosen to lead the army. The Mexican strategy was to take away the resistance's weapons. After several skirmishes in the area, Houston sent Bowie to destroy the Alamo so Mexican troops could not use it to their advantage. The Alamo had an extensive history prior to the battle that made it famous. According to Michael Burgan, writing in the children's book *The Alamo,* "At first, the Alamo was a mission called San Antonio de Valero. Here, Spanish priests lived and taught Native Americans about the Roman Catholic religion. The mission closed in the 1790s and soon after was turned into a fort. It was named Alamo after the hometown of Mexican soldiers stationed there."

When Bowie arrived at the Alamo, he decided to defy Houston's orders to blow up the fort. Believing that it was a valuable military asset, he ordered the soldiers and volunteers to begin fortifying the defenses. Bowie shared command with Colonel William Barret Travis. Bowie led the volunteers while Travis was head of the soldiers. Not surprisingly, troubles arose from this shared responsibility. According to Edwin P. Hoyt, writing in *The Alamo: An Illustrated History,* "Bowie issued orders without consulting Travis. . . . Travis complained about

Bowie's drinking and high-handed manner, and threatened to send the regular troops out of town.''

The men reconciled their differences when Bowie fell ill with typhoid fever. He was confined to a sickbed the day after Santa Anna arrived in San Antonio on February 23, 1836, bringing with him approximately 1,800 troops. There were several small skirmishes in the days immediately following the Mexicans' arrival at the Alamo but the Texans did not lose a single soldier. The defenders of the Alamo sent desperate letters to Houston and other leaders, begging for supplies and more troops. The requests were not answered in time. Despite numbering fewer than 200 soldiers, the resistance held strong until March 6. On that day, the Mexicans laid siege to the fort. The attack took place at dawn. In the children's book *The Alamo: the Fight over Texas,* Gaines described the battle: ''Close to 2,000 soldiers advanced. The 190 men inside the Alamo tried to hold them back with cannon and rifle fire. Many Mexican soldiers fell, and for a moment their advance stopped. But their commanders reformed their lines and drove their men forward to the walls. At close range they started to shoot the Texans one by one. William Barret Travis was one of the first to die. He was shot while he stood on the north wall.''

Like the rest of his legendary life, Bowie's actual role in the final battle at the Alamo remains unverified. There is no question that he was suffering a high fever at the time. Some historians believe he was dead before Mexican soldiers ever entered the fort. Others have recounted the story that he fought valiantly from his sickbed using the very knife that carries his name.

Books

Burgan, Michael, *The Alamo,* Compass Point Books, 2001.

Dictionary of American Biography, edited by Allen Johnson, Charles Scribner's Sons, 1936.

Encyclopedia of the American West, edited by Charles Phillips and Alan Axelrod, Simon & Schuster, 1996.

Gaines, Ann, *The Alamo: The Fight Over Texas,* The Child's World, 2003.

Gaines, Ann Graham, *Jim Bowie: Hero of the Alamo,* Enslow Publishers, Inc., 2000.

Hoyt, Edwin P., *The Alamo: An Illustrated History,* Taylor Publishing Company, 1999.

Johnston, Marianne, *Jim Bowie, American Legends* series, Rosen Publishing Group, 2001.

Stewart, Mark, *The Alamo, American Battlefields* series, Enchanted Lion Books, 2004

The United States and Mexico at War, edited by Donald S. Frazier, MacMillan Reference USA, 1998. □

Anne Bracegirdle

Anne Bracegirdle (c. 1663–1748) was one of England's leading theater stars of her era. Along with Nell Gwyn and Elizabeth Barry, she belongs to the first generation of professional women actors in English-language drama and was a celebrated London beauty who was even involved in a deadly romantic triangle. On stage,

Bracegirdle specialized in comic roles and a number of leading dramatists wrote standard "innocent-heroine" roles for her.

B racegirdle's actual date of birth is unknown, and one source from her era claims that she first appeared on stage at the age of six in 1680. The contemporary scholar Elizabeth Howe, writing in *The First English Actresses: Women and Drama 1660–1700,* believed this to be an error, and that Bracegirdle was actually 16 years old when she made her debut. There is a record of a Northampton church showing a baptism under her name that took place on November 13, 1671, but Howe asserts she was probably born around 1663. Anthony Aston, a playwright and actor who died in 1731, refuted the claim that Bracegirdle was from Northamptonshire and instead asserted that she was from Staffordshire. Her father may have been a coach driver or operated a coach rental business and suffered some financial setbacks.

Whatever her origins, Bracegirdle became the ward of Thomas and Mary Betterton, two well-known London stage figures. Thomas Betterton was an actor who adapted plays and managed the Duke's Company after 1668. This was one of two theatrical production venues in London that operated under royal license and staged all of the leading plays of the Restoration period. This era, coinciding with the ''restoration'' of the monarchy that began with the reign of England's King Charles II in 1660, witnessed a tremendous flourishing of English drama after a period when all plays and stage performances had been banned under Puritan rule. Charles was the patron of the King's Company, while his brother the Duke of York was the official sponsor of the Duke's Company.

Demonstrated a Talent for Love Scenes

Bracegirdle's first stage role may have been at the Duke's Theater at Dorset Garden, a lavish structure on the Thames that was sometimes called Queen's Theatre and was demolished in 1709. She supposedly played Cordelio there in a 1680 production of a Thomas Otway play, *The Orphan*. Another possible part for her was as Clita in *A Commonwealth of Women*, written by Thomas D'Urfey and staged at the Theatre Royal of Drury Lane in 1685. By this point, the King's and Duke's companies had merged into one patent company, the United Company.

The first role on record for Bracegirdle was a lead in a new play by William Mountfort titled *The Injur'd Lovers, or The Ambitious Father*, which opened at the Drury Lane Theatre on February 6, 1688. She and Mountfort were rumored to have been romantically involved, and those rumors took a tragic turn in December of 1692, when Bracegirdle was appearing as the Countess of Essex in a play by John Banks, *The Unhappy Favourite, or The Earl of Essex*. Her co-star was Mountfort, and supposedly Bracegirdle had recently turned down a marriage proposal from Captain Richard Hill, an adventurer, soldier, and one of her legions of admirers. Hill was reportedly so incensed with the realistic love scenes Bracegirdle and Mountfort enacted on stage that he decided to take action. He enlisted the help of Lord Charles Mohun, a Whig politician known for his debauched lifestyle and penchant for duels.

Hill and Mohun hatched a plan to kidnap Bracegirdle on the night of December 9, 1692. Around ten p.m., as she and her companions were on their way home from a dinner party, Hill and Mohun tried to force Bracegirdle into their hired coach, but her party resisted, called for help, and Bracegirdle and her companions made it safely to her lodgings on Howard Street in The Strand area. Hill and Mohun decided to wait for Mountfort, who lived nearby. Two hours later, Mountfort passed Mohun on the street, words were exchanged concerning Bracegirdle, then Hill emerged from the shadows and struck Mountfort in the face before drawing his sword. One report claimed that Lord Mohun held the actor while Hill stabbed him to death. Hill fled to France. Mohun was tried at the House of Lords, and Bracegirdle testified, but the peer was acquitted of acting as accessory to a murder. Hill died in a bar fight a few years later, while Mohun died in a 1712 duel in Hyde Park along with James Hamilton, the 4th Duke of Hamilton.

Delighted Dryden, Then Congreve

Bracegirdle appeared in scores of United Company productions at the Theatre Royal at Drury Lane between 1688 and 1695. These included a so-called "breeches role" as Semernia in Aphra Behn's *The Widow Ranter* in 1689. Breeches roles featured female actors in male garb at some point in the plot in which the character disguises herself as a boy or young man, and these were popular with men in the audience, for the trouser costume permitted a rather daring highlighting of the female form at a time when there were tremendous social taboos against women wearing male clothing in public. Bracegirdle was said to have been a favorite of the playwright John Dryden, appearing in his 1691 work *King Arthur* as Emmeline, and gained immense fame in her first two Shakespeare roles—as Lady Anne in *Richard III* and Desdemona in *Othello*, both staged at Drury Lane in the early 1690s.

Dryden served as mentor to a young playwright named William Congreve, who would go on to write several roles specifically for Bracegirdle. She appeared as Araminta in his 1693 debut work, *The Old Bachelor*, at the Drury Lane Theatre, not long after the drama over Mountfort's murder had subsided. Congreve penned just five plays before entering a self-imposed retirement, but they were favorites with theatergoers and showcased Bracegirdle's talents as a comedic actor. The most acclaimed of all was *Love for Love* in 1695, which was staged at the new Lincoln's Inn Fields Theatre in London. According to Howe, Bracegirdle "inspired a special kind of witty heroine, the irresistible heiress who is pursued by admirers but who finds it difficult to be sure of the man who loves her."

Congreve's final play was *The Way of the World*, an enduring romantic comedy from 1700 that was still occasionally performed three centuries later. Scholars of English theater history consider it an exemplary piece of Restoration comedy and often judge it to be Congreve's best work. It featured Bracegirdle as the wealthy Millamant, who hopes to marry a young man named Mirabell, but their plans are thwarted by her villainous aunt, who wants the young woman's sizable dowry to remain in the family.

A colleague of Bracegirdle and Congreve was Colley Cibber, who wrote a 1740 autobiography in which he related anecdotes about his experiences as an actor and playwright at the height of the Restoration era. The work featured a paean to Bracegirdle as both lovely and talented, and a figure who "inspired the best Authors to write for her, and two of them, when they gave her a Lover, in a Play, seem'd palpably to plead their own Passions, and make their private Court to her, in fictitious Characters," he recalled in *An Apology for the Life of Colley Cibber: Comedian, and Late Patentee of the Theatre-Royal*.

Co-Founded New Company

After the United Company was badly mismanaged under a much-disliked director, Bracegirdle was one of several theater stars who essentially walked away from the company and petitioned the new king, William III, for a patent to form a new company on their own. This was known as Betterton's Company and its stage was erected over a former tennis court at Lincoln's Inn Fields, a large park in central London. Bracegirdle was listed as one of the company's co-managers, along with Betterton and Elizabeth Barry, the other leading female actor of the era. Barry was known for her tragic roles and appeared opposite Bracegirdle in several leading stage works of this era.

Barry was often vilified in the press, with speculation about her various off-stage romances with well-known figures of the day. Bracegirdle, by contrast, was slotted as the virtuous type, impervious to the pleadings of men who wished to marry her or, at the very least, set her up in her own household as a pampered mistress. Both women were stars, however, and delivered important prologues and epilogues at performances that often poked fun at their own celebrity. "Barry and Bracegirdle suggest that in order to succeed in her profession a woman had to be not only outstandingly talented and successful in a sphere which affected male profits," noted Howe, "but also persistent, hard-headed and unmarried."

There were rumors that Bracegirdle and Congreve had secretly wed, but their relationship had cooled by 1710. In the final decade of her career the stage star appeared in several revivals of Shakespeare's works, including *Measure for Measure* as Isabella, *King Lear* as Cordelia, and a 1701 version of *The Merchant of Venice* titled *The Jew of Venice* at Lincoln's Inn Fields. This last play was lost for a number of years, and the annals of English drama cited Bracegirdle as the first female actor to portray the beautiful heroine Portia, for in Shakespeare's time male actors played all roles.

Kept Admirers at Bay

Bracegirdle retired from the stage after a final performance on February 19, 1707, in *The Unhappy Favourite.* She was either 36 or 44 years old and lived for another 41 years in what was said to be quite comfortable financial circumstances, thanks to both her stage career and bequests from the wills of her late admirers. Among the well-born men who were said to have pursued her were Robert Leke, the 3rd Earl of Scarsdale; another was Lord Lovelace, whose "servant used to go every day to Mrs. Bracegirdle's house to ask how she did, and always brought back the same answer, that 'she was indifferent well, she humbly thanked his lordship,'" according to John Fyvie's book *Tragedy Queens of the Georgian Era.* "This, we are given to understand, was the utmost familiarity permitted to Lord Lovelace." The same volume also reported a tale mentioned by the English writer and political figure Horace Walpole, who noted that a Lord Burlington once had delivered an impressive gift of china to Bracegirdle's home. She took the accompanying letter, but instructed the servant that the sumptuous parcel was supposed to be delivered to Lord Burlington's wife, who, Fyvie wrote, "was so full of gratitude when her husband came home to dinner!"

All of the London newspapers reported the same obituary in mid-September of 1748—that Bracegirdle had died at her Howard Street home on September 12, and that she was laid to rest in the Cloisters of Westminster Abbey, one of the most hallowed of all burial grounds in England.

Books

"Anne Bracegirdle," in *International Dictionary of Theatre,* Volume 3: *Actors, Directors, and Designers,* St. James Press, 1996.

Cibber, Colley, *An Apology for the Life of Colley Cibber: Comedian, and Late Patentee of the Theatre-Royal,* Volume 1, R. and J. Dodsley, 1756, p. 127.

Fyvie, John, *Tragedy Queens of the Georgian Era,* E.P. Dutton, 1909, pp. 26–27.

Howe, Elizabeth, *The First English Actresses: Women and Drama 1660û1700,* Cambridge University Press, 1992, p. 32.

Howell, Thomas B. (compiler), *A Complete Collection of State Trials and Proceedings for High Treason and Other Crimes and Misdemeanors from the Earliest Period to the Year 1783,* Volume 12, Longman, Hurst, Rees, Orme, and Brown, 1816. □

Lydia Moss Bradley

Lydia Moss Bradley (1816–1908) was an American business person and philanthropist. She gave generously to the arts and sciences, and was the founder of Bradley University in Peoria, Illinois.

Lydia Moss Bradley was born on July 31, 1816, in Vevay, Indiana, to Zealy Moss, a farmer and Baptist preacher, and Jenny Glasscock Moss, a homemaker. Her parents valued education, and she spent many hours in a neighbor's kitchen learning to read from texts like the *Webster Speller,* the *English Reader,* and the Bible. Throughout her childhood she worked on the family farm alongside her siblings. The family denounced slavery despite its prevalence during that era. Prior to the birth of his children, Zealy Moss owned a plantation in Kentucky. During this time he discovered he could not support the institution of slavery. According to the article "Bradley Polytechnic Institute: The First Decade, 1897-1907," published on the *Internet Archive* web site, he was "too considerate of the welfare of the slaves for the profit of the plantation, and finally gave the place rent free to his negroes to work out their own living, while he crossed over into free territory to make his home and rear his family." He passed this attitude of working for oneself on to his children.

Became a Young Entrepreneur

When Bradley was a teenager, her father gave her a horse that she loved dearly. However, when the opportunity to trade her horse for a piece of land presented itself, she did not hesitate to enter into the transaction. The *Internet Archive* article noted, "Few young women would have thought of selling their riding horses to buy land at a time when a horse and saddle was the only means of communication and visiting in a sparsely settled country with few roads and fewer carriages." In exchange for her beloved colt, Bradley received 40 acres of forested land. With minimal help from her father she cleared the timber herself, and sold the wood to a local sawmill owner, Tobias Bradley. Shortly thereafter, Bradley became her husband.

Soon after the wedding, the Bradleys moved from Vevay, Indiana, to Peoria, Illinois. Bradley convinced her husband that Illinois was a better choice than Kentucky because it was a non-slave state. Like her father, she did not wish to make a living off the hard work of others. In order to purchase their new homestead, Bradley sold off the timberland she had acquired in the horse trade, as well as the family home she had inherited upon her father's death. An added benefit of living in Peoria was that it was also home to Lydia's brother, William Moss. Together, he and Tobias Bradley would enter into numerous business ventures, many of which were very successful.

Endured Multiple Tragedies

The Bradleys eventually had six children, although none lived to see adulthood. Most died due to accident or illness while toddlers. Laura, the youngest child, lived the longest, and was 14 years old when she died. The Bradleys were devastated by these losses and often discussed ways in which they could memorialize the lives of their offspring. They considered establishing an orphanage in Peoria, but soon rejected the idea. According to the article "Lydia Moss Bradley from Peoria," posted on the *Alliance Library System* web site, the couple felt that "such institutions were often ill-equipped to help young people acquire skills which they required to become independent." Soon, their thoughts turned to creating a place of learning.

Before any concrete plans could be developed in that regard, tragedy struck again. In 1867 Tobias Bradley died unexpectedly, leaving his entire estate, valued at approximately $500,000, to his wife. Part of that inheritance included controlling stock in the First National Bank of Peoria, which automatically gave the widow Bradley a place on the bank's board of directors. She went on to hold this position for over 30 years, and was the board's direct for 25 of those years. According to the "Lydia Moss Bradley" article, she was the only woman in the entire state to hold such a position and one of only a few across the country.

Two years after her husband's death, Bradley married again, to Edward Clark, a successful cotton dealer from Memphis, Tennessee. According to the *American National Biography*, "Bradley insisted that a prenuptial agreement be signed to protect her growing assets." This proved to be a fortuitous decision, because she divorced Clark after only four years and managed to be awarded all of her previous wealth in the proceedings.

As the sole recipient of a vast fortune, Bradley developed a strong business sense. She soon hired a business manager named W.W. Hammond, a local attorney well known for his business acumen. With his help, Bradley increased her fortune fourfold. She accomplished this by investing wisely in real estate and working tirelessly to improve the quality of her land holdings. She purchased 680 acres of swampland that she then drained in order to erect farm buildings and fences. When her crops did poorly, she had the soil analyzed and improved. She soon had a thriving farm, which prompted neighboring farmers to similarly improve their own lands, with the result that her own property value increased as well. In the end, the land she bought for $10 per acre sold for 14 times that much.

Known for Philanthropic Enterprises

Despite her success, Bradley did not intend that her money should only increase her personal coffers. She soon became well known in Peoria for her philanthropic tendencies and extensive charitable donations. The *Internet Archive* site described a few of her gifts, such as paying off a church mortgage, donating the site for a hospital, founding a home for elderly women, and founding a city park.

Throughout these undertakings, however, Bradley never stopped thinking about creating a school in memory of her husband and children. She planned to endow such an institution upon her own death. According to the *Internet Archive* article, Bradley's original will stated that "the first object of this institution [will be] to furnish its students with the means of living independent, industrious and useful lives by aid of the practical knowledge of the useful arts and sciences." Toward that end, Bradley began sending Hammond to meet with various heads of educational institutions, as well as with university professors and college presidents. William Rainey Harper of the University of Chicago advised Bradley to open her school as soon as possible, rather than merely to endow such an institution in her will, as was her plan. Once Bradley decided to heed Harper's advice, things quickly fell into place.

In 1892 Bradley purchased the Parsons Horological Institute, relocating the school from LaPorte, Indiana, to Peoria, where it was housed in the Peoria Watch Company building. In 1896 a charter for the Bradley Polytechnic Institute was obtained. Three years later Bradley Hall and Horology Hall were built. The school was set up to focus on providing practical courses. It was coeducational, and was open to students from 14 to 20 years of age. Bradley Polytechnic Institute went on to pioneer the study of domestic sciences as well as manual training and other vocational studies. The school was formally dedicated on October 8, 1897, and according to the *American National Biography,* the dedication simply stated that the undertaking was "for Tobias and the children." In 1920 Bradley Polytechnic Institute became a four-year college, offering baccalaureate degrees to students. In 1946 it became a university offering graduate courses in addition to a full range of undergraduate majors.

In seeming contrast to her wealth and status in the Peoria community, Bradley maintained the strong personal work ethic her father had instilled in her at an early age, and she continued running her own farm and performing other domestic duties. Much of her extraordinary success has been attributed to these humble actions. In an era that did not even afford women the right to vote, Bradley recognized the need to teach young people of both genders practical skills that would serve them throughout their lives. These were, after all, the skills she valued in her own life.

Despite the many tragic losses she faced in the untimely deaths of her children and husband, her friends noted that the school she created restored much of her happiness in the final years of her life. The *Internet Archive* article noted, "It was a common remark among those who knew her best, that the School had made her young again: life had taken on new meaning as the plan so long cherished and labored for took visible form before her eyes. Her face grew brighter and some of the lines graven by sorrows were softened and erased." Bradley fell ill in the early weeks of 1908. She succumbed to an unnamed illness on January 16 of that year. She left her entire estate to the school that she created.

Books

American National Biography, edited by John A. Garraty and Mark C. Carnes, Oxford University Press, 1999

Dictionary of American Biography, edited by Allen Johnson, Charles Scribner's Sons, 1964

Liberty's Women, edited by Robert McHenry, G. & C. Merriam Company, 1980

Women in World History: A Biographical Encyclopedia, edited by Anne Commire and Deborah Klezmer, Gale Group, 1999

Online

"Bradley Polytechnic Institute: The First Decade 1897-1907," *Internet Archive,* http://www.archive.org/details/bradleypoly techn00brad (November 23, 2009).

"Lydia Moss Bradley from Peoria," *Alliance Library System,* http://www.alliancelibrarysystem.com/IllinoisWomen/files/br/htm1/bradley.htm (November 23, 2009). □

Josef Breuer

The Austrian physician Josef Breuer (1842–1925), in addition to making several important discoveries in the field of physiology, conceived some of the key ideas and procedures of psychoanalysis, conducted the first long-term series of psychotherapy sessions with a single patient, and worked closely with and directly inspired Sigmund Freud during the early years of the development of the science of psychiatry.

Josef Breuer was born on January 15, 1842, in Vienna, Austria. He was born into a Jewish family that was only recently removed from the Jewish village culture of Eastern Europe; his father, Leopold Breuer, was a religious teacher but stressed the value of a Western education. Breuer's mother died when he was four; he was raised by his maternal grandmother and received his primary education at home, from his father. Breuer could read by the time he was four, and in 1850 he was sent to the Akademisches Gymnasium, a private school in Vienna that stressed classical studies and philosophy. Breuer excelled in school and particularly liked science courses. Early in life he decided to become a doctor.

Partly his decision was motivated by the fact that many professional careers were closed to Jews in Vienna in the middle of the nineteenth century, but medicine was one that remained generally open to those who could enroll at a school and pass its exams. Breuer began his studies at the University of Vienna in 1859, taking a year of general studies courses before beginning his medical specialization. He was fortunate to be studying under a variety of progressive anatomy and physiology professors, most notably his mentor, Johann Oppolzer, who were among the best in their fields. He received his medical degree in 1867 and became Oppolzer's assistant the following year. He also married Matilda Altmann on May 20, 1868; the couple had five children, and Breuer once wrote, as quoted by Albrecht Hirschmüller in *The Life and Work of Josef Breuer,* that "my home has always been a happy one, . . . my dear wife has given me five delightful and clever children," and that "none has been lost to me or caused me serious concern."

Even as an unpaid physician's assistant, Breuer was already involved in conducting groundbreaking research. His first publications were in the field of physiology, not psychology. Working with Ewald Hering, he demonstrated

that breathing was a reflex, involving the vagus nerve; the specific physiological mechanisms involved are still known as the Hering-Breuer Reflex, and the model Breuer proposed was among the first examples of the function of what is now known as the autonomic nervous system. Breuer's ideas were surprising at the time, and the exact locations of the receptors involved in the reflex function were not definitively established until the 1950s. In 1871, after Oppolzer's death, Breuer opened his own practice as a physician in Vienna.

Investigated Inner Ear Function

Breuer's lab work in the 1870s dealt mostly with the inner ear. Experimenting with animals (chiefly pigeons) and humans, he investigated the structure and function of the so-called labyrinth, a complex network of small bones and canals filled with a fluid known as endolymph. Breuer knew from the work of earlier scientists that injury to this area impaired the motor skills of animals; an immediate predecessor, Friedrich Goltz, suggested that pressure within a set of six semicircular canals (three in each ear) was crucial to human perception of position and movement. Breuer showed that the crucial factor was not pressure but the movement of the endolymph in the semicircular canals that contributed to the perception of position, and he pointed to the importance of another inner ear structure, the otolith. For many years, scientists did not even know of some of Breuer's experiments on the inner ear, much less accept the concepts, but his work, in the words of the *Dictionary of Scientific Biography,* "was correct, and today is recognized as the foundation of our knowledge of the sensory receptors for sensations of posture and movement."

In 1875 Breuer joined the internal medicine faculty of the University of Vienna, but he was never really happy in an academic environment and at one point turned down a colleague's offer to nominate him for the award of "professor extraordinarius." Breuer felt he was being shortchanged in the allocation of patients on whom he could perform research, although this was a common complaint among medical researchers at the time. Accordingly, Breuer continued to maintain his medical practice, and in 1885 he took the surprising step of resigning his professorship at the university.

The beginnings of Breuer's interest in psychological phenomena came about in 1880, almost by accident. While treating a seriously ill male patient, he observed the development of symptoms of psychological disturbance in the man's 21-year-old daughter, Bertha Pappenheim; in his accounts of subsequent events he referred to her by the pseudonym Anna O., and she has since been known by that name. Anna O. suffered from a variety of complaints, including intermittent paralysis, wild eye movements, confusion, inability to use or understand language, and an aversion to eating and drinking. Such problems among women were often lumped at the time under the catch-all name of hysteria.

Pioneered In-Depth Psychotherapy

Breuer noticed that Anna O., in the course of a single day, went through phases in which she behaved normally and some in which she was "clouded" or "absent," suffering from psychological symptoms. Sometimes using hypnosis, Breuer asked her to recall the circumstances under which a particular symptom had arisen. The patient responded enthusiastically, bringing up long chains of memories that, when they reached the first instance of a given symptom, resulted in that symptom's disappearance. Breuer undertook a series of these sessions with Anna O., regarded as the first example of in-depth, extended psychotherapy used to treat a single patient. He suggested that Anna's experiences had been trapped in her unconscious mind, and that the process of verbalizing them, which Breuer called catharsis, brought them to a conscious level and thus ameliorated the symptoms they caused. These ideas were central to what became the discipline of psychoanalysis.

Breuer's sessions with Anna O. were closely followed by a young Viennese physician and neurologist, Sigmund Freud. Breuer taught Freud his therapeutic method, and Freud began treating patients with it in 1888 or 1889. The two summarized their work in a joint article in 1893 and in a book, *Studien über Hysterie* (Studies on Hysteria), published in 1895. Breuer also served as Freud's personal physician, and Freud in later life attested to Breuer's influence on his ideas. Breuer was elected to the Viennese Academy of Science in 1894.

Although the events he set in motion permanently changed the treatment of mental illnesses, Breuer himself never treated another patient after Anna O. The reason was that he became uneasy with the strong attachment to him that she developed during therapy, and perhaps with the fact that a mutual attraction may have been present. Breuer eventually broke off the treatment sessions and left town with his wife, but Freud incorporated the patient's reactions to the therapist, which became known as transference, into his psychoanalytic procedures. The development was symptomatic of the growing frequency of disagreements between Breuer and Freud, who broke off contact with each other in 1896 and never spoke again, despite the close relationship between their respective families.

Disagreed with Freud About Childhood Memories

The reasons for this rupture were complex and have not been definitively elucidated. They may have had to do partly with the natural tension between an established older researcher and a talented younger investigator whose discoveries would eventually eclipse those of his teacher. Breuer and Freud specifically disagreed over the memories of childhood sexual abuse that often surfaced in therapy; Freud believed that they represented memories of actual events, while Breuer contended that they were inspired by childhood fantasies. The repercussions of their difference of opinion are still being felt more than a century later, but Freud later concluded that Breuer had been correct in many cases.

Breuer continued to write about memory, perception, and the phenomenon of hallucination, publishing a slender but influential body of about 20 papers over four decades. He was regarded later in life as one of Vienna's most distinguished scientists and physicians, with the prime minister of Hungary among his patients. Breuer had broad scientific and philosophical interests, and he wrote monographs on topics as diverse as the theoretical basis for Darwin's theory of evolution and the hearing apparatus of birds. He died in Vienna on Jun 20, 1925; his distance from traditional Jewish beliefs was illustrated by his request that he be cremated after his death. Most of Breuer's descendants left Austria during the period of Nazi rule, but one granddaughter died in the Holocaust.

Books

Breuer, Josef, and Sigmund Freud, *Studies on Hysteria,* Basic Books, 2000.

Cranefield, Paul, "Breuer, Josef," in *Dictionary of Scientific Biography,* edited by Charles Coulston Gillispie, Scribner's, 1970.

Hirschmüller, Albrecht, *The Life and Work of Josef Breuer,* New York University Press, 1978.

Gale Encyclopedia of Psychology, 2nd ed., Gale, 2001.

Periodicals

Times (London, England), June 7, 1994.

Online

"Josef Breuer," *Who Named It,* http://www.whonamedit.com/doctor.cfm/2649.html (November 16, 2009). □

Thomas Makdougall Brisbane

The Scottish administrator, military leader, and astronomer Thomas Makdougall Brisbane (1773–1860) had a colorful career that made an impact across the British Empire in the early nineteenth century.

Brisbane's name lives on mostly as a result of his four-year tenure as governor of New South Wales, the former British colony that is now the nation of Australia. The city of Brisbane, Australia's third-largest, is named for him, as are a host of less prominent places. Brisbane had a long military career as a younger man, rising through the ranks of the British army and fighting in both Britain's campaign against Napoleon Bonaparte on the Iberian peninsula and in the War of 1812, among other conflicts. He was also a noted astronomer, built a major observatory and, in the words of the Glasgow *Evening Times,* "is widely regarded as the founder of organized science in Australia."

Joined British Army

Thomas Brisbane was born on July 23, 1773, at the ancestral home of his old Scottish family, Brisbane House, located near the town of Largs in western Scotland's Ayrshire region. The middle name Makdougall was that of Brisbane's wife, Anna Maria, whom he married in 1819; he had her name legally added to his own. Brisbane's father had fought in the Battle of Culloden, in which Scottish forces backing the restoration of the Stuart line of British kings were defeated. The young Brisbane had an aristocratic upbringing and the best education Scotland offered; he was taught at home by tutors and moved on to the University of Edinburgh and an English boarding school in Kensington near London. His schooling completed, Brisbane was ready to enter the British Army's officer corps and was posted to the 38th regiment in Cork, Ireland, as an ensign.

Moving on to a posting in Galway, Brisbane made the acquaintance of the Duke of Wellington, who would go on to become one of Britain's greatest military heroes. The two, Brisbane recalled in his *Reminiscences of General Sir Thomas Makdougall Brisbane,* "used frequently to go out sporting together, and to kill our five-and-twenty couple of woodcocks between breakfast and dinner time. Brisbane spent most of the turbulent period on either side of the year 1800 in the field. In Flanders (now Belgium and the Netherlands) from 1793 to 1795, he led companies that engaged Austrian forces, at one point saving the town of Nieuport (now Nieuwpoort, Belgium) by leading a company that strategically opened a floodgate in the low-lying region and trapping the enemy fighters. In 1795 he returned to England and was sent to the West Indies, by then promoted to the rank of major.

Although as a rising officer he was increasingly protected from fighting on the front lines, Brisbane saw plenty of action in a series of campaigns across the Caribbean against forces consisting of French soldiers and Native Americans. In his *Reminiscences,* he recalled a group of Carib tribesmen who entered the British compound under a surrender flag. A British-affiliated slave informed Brisbane that the real intent of the Native group was to obtain fresh supplies, and Brisbane informed their leader, a chief named Taquin, that he was taking them prisoner. The Native group made a break for it, but Brisbane wrestled the chief to the ground and grabbed his knife, telling him that he would kill him if they did not break off the escape attempt. "I was obliged to carry my threat into execution," Brisbane wrote.

In 1800 Brisbane was promoted to lieutenant-colonel and, after a short rest in England, served for three years as commander of the British 69th regiment in Jamaica. The regiment was brought back to England in 1803. Brisbane remained its commander, but when the 69th was ordered to India, Brisbane pleaded ill health and gave up his command, accepting that his salary would be cut in half. He returned to Brisbane House, and for several years devoted himself to the study of astronomy, which had first caught his interest in 1795 when his ship, due to a navigational error, nearly crashed into a coastline. "Reflecting that I might often, even in the course of my life and services, be exposed to similar errors, I was determined to make myself acquainted with navigation and nautical astronomy," he wrote in *Reminiscences.* He ordered books, educated himself in the science of astronomy, and grew more and more interested as he saw the skies from different perspectives around the globe.

Built Observatory in Home

Back at home, Brisbane deepened his studies of astronomy and ordered the construction of an observatory, only the second in Scotland, at Brisbane House. More than a dilettante, he was elected in 1810 as a fellow of the Royal Society of London. But continuing military conflicts necessitated Brisbane's return to the ranks of active officers. Asking to serve under his friend Wellington, he was promoted to brigadier-general in 1812 and commanded a brigade that saw heavy fighting across Spain in the Peninsular War, a branch of the larger conflict between Britain and Napoleon Bonaparte's French empire. Brisbane participated in the Battle of Vitoria that marked a decisive setback for French forces. "So signal was this defeat," wrote Brisbane, that everything belonging to Spain's King Joseph (Napoleon's brother, Joseph Bonaparte) "fell into our hands, and that same evening I ate off his Majesty's plate and partook of his wine." Brisbane's troops shook down French stragglers, and Brisbane shared the plunder, parceling out five Spanish dollars to each of his men—small consolation, as some 1,800 of them, including 90 officers, had been killed.

Garlanded with various honors, including the thanks of the British Parliament and a designation as Knight Commander of the Bath (K.C.B.), Brisbane returned to the Western Hemisphere and led a British brigade during the unsuccessful (from the British point of view) Battle of Plattsburgh in the final stages of the War of 1812. Ready for civilian service, he applied unsuccessfully for the post of governor of New South Wales. Brisbane spent three years as a British commander in occupied France after Napoleon's final defeat and exile, and then took a command post in Ireland. In 1820, newly married and acting this time on a tip from Wellington, he applied again for the Australian post and was appointed. He was the young colony's sixth governor, succeeding Lachlan Macquarie and before him William Bligh, the Captain Bligh who survived the famous mutiny aboard HMS *Bounty.*

When Brisbane arrived in Sydney, Australia, in November of 1821, he found a society in transition. New South Wales had been established as a British prison colony, but over several decades it had also attracted a substantial population of free settlers. There was conflict between the ex-prisoners and new settlers, and the Australian colony shared problems typical to other lands in which the British Empire was expanding: land rushes, a lack of regulation, and the general problems of administering a far-flung population of speculators intent on quick financial gains.

Brisbane's four-year tenure as governor marked an important phase in the normalization of affairs in the colony. He introduced various administrative reforms, including one in 1823 calling for the requisitioning of supplies by tender (in writing). He regulated the system of land grants for new settlers and required them to employ one convict for every hundred acres to which they were granted rights, thus reducing the costs to the British government of maintaining those convicts. Brisbane established new vineyards and other plantations, and he attempted to establish a firm basis for the Australian dollar currency. Like other Britons of his time, Brisbane could not be called a friend of Australia's Aborigines, but he did favor compensation when aboriginal lands were seized, and he granted land to a British missionary society for an aboriginal reservation. Among the various European faiths, Brisbane was impartial, and he even refused an application for financial aid from members of his own Presbyterian church, believing that they had sufficient resources of their own.

Catalogued Stars of Southern Hemisphere

Brisbane did not neglect his pursuit of astronomy while in Australia, although he complained that his workload made it difficult for him to find the time. "In place of passing my time in the Observatory or shooting Parrots," he wrote, "I am seldom employed in either. . . . I cannot get thro' the various and arduous duties of my Government," he wrote, according to the *Australian Dictionary of Biography.* The observatory that he built at Parramatta near Sydney in 1822 was the first in Australia, and became the site of the first astronomical observations by telescope in the Southern Hemisphere since those of the French astronomer Nicolas Louis de Lacaille in 1751 and 1752. Despite the press of official duties, Brisbane and an assistant, Christian Rümker, catalogued 7,000 stars of the southern skies.

The British colonial government in Australia was beset by factional disagreements, and Brisbane often quarreled with the British colonial secretary, Frederick Goulburn. In 1825, both men were recalled to Britain. Brisbane and his wife had three children while they were in New South Wales, giving the second, Eleanor, the middle name of Australia, and the third, Thomas, that of Australius. A fourth child, Henry, was born at sea on the voyage home, off Rio de Janeiro, Brazil, in March of 1826, but died in his third month. The other children survived the trip, but Brisbane eventually outlived all four of his children.

Returning home to Largs, Brisbane busied himself with research and good works. He built a second observatory, in Makerstoun, became president of the Edinburgh Astronomical Institution, and picked up a treasured honorary degree that he had been given by Oxford University. In 1832 he was elected as president of the Royal Society in Edinburgh, succeeding the novelist and poet Sir Walter Scott. The British military attempted to lure him back with command posts in Canada and India, but he refused both. In later years he concerned himself with local affairs, supervising a drainage project and endowing a parish school and later the Largs Brisbane Academy. Its modern-day successor, the Largs Academy, was to be named the Brisbane Academy, but its headmaster scuttled the plan because he was concerned that mail for the school might be misdirected to Australia. In Australia itself, various places bear Brisbane's name. The Brisbane River was so named in 1823 during Brisbane's governorship, and the town of Brisbane, originally a prison colony, took its name from the river shortly after that. Perhaps the naming honor that would have pleased the soldier-astronomer the most was the establishment of the Sir Thomas Brisbane Planetarium in Brisbane in 1978. By the late 1850s Brisbane was calling himself "the oldest officer in the Army." Widely known and respected, he died at Brisbane House on January 27, 1860.

Books

Brisbane, Thomas Makdougall, *Reminiscences of General Sir Thomas Makdougall Brisbane, Bart.*, Thomas Constable, 1860.

Periodicals

Evening Times (Glasgow, Scotland), December 4, 1999.

Online

"Brisbane Academy," *Largs and Mill Port News,* http://www.largsandmillportnews.com/news/roundup/articles/2008/10/29/30082-brisbane-academy/ (November 2, 2009).

"Brisbane, Sir Thomas Makdougall (1773–1860)," *Australian Dictionary of Biography,* http://www.adb.online.anu.edu.au/biogs/A010141b.htm (November 2, 2009).

"Brisbane, Sir Thomas Makdougall (1773–1860)," *Dictionary of Australian Biography,* http://www.gutenberg.net.au/dictbiog/0-dict-biogBr-By.html#brisbane1 (November 2, 2009).

Sir Thomas Brisbane Planetarium, http://www.brisbane.qld.gov.au/planetarium (November 2, 2009). □

Herb Brooks

Herb Brooks (1937–2003) was a well-known and respected hockey coach in the United States and around the world. His most prominent victory was the "Miracle on Ice," the unlikely defeat of the Soviet Union by the United States in the 1980 Olympics in Lake Placid, New York.

Herbert Brooks Jr. was born On August 5, 1937, to Herb Brooks Sr., an insurance salesman, and Pauline Brooks. Born and raised in St. Paul, Minnesota, Brooks was inducted into a hockey lifestyle at an early age, and helped to lead Johnson High School to the 1955 state championship. He turned down a scholarship to play hockey for the University of Michigan and opted instead for a walk-on spot with the University of Minnesota hockey team. He played for three years with the University of Minnesota and graduated with a degree in psychology.

Played on National and Olympic Teams

In 1960 Brooks tried out for a spot on the U.S. Olympic team. He was a member of the team until just before the Olympics, when former Olympic player Bill Cleary agreed to join the team only if his brother Bob could play as well. Brooks was cut at the last minute and Bob's head was pasted on Brooks's body in the team photograph. The team went on to win the Olympic gold medal. In the book *The Boys of Winter,* author Wayne Coffey recounted the story that while Brooks and his father were watching the U.S. team win Olympic gold largely due to the efforts of the Cleary brothers, the younger Brooks quipped, "Well, I guess the coach cut the right guy." Brooks told this story often and indicated that it was a pivotal moment of motivation for him.

Brooks went on to play for several other national teams throughout the 1960s. He played on the U.S. National team in 1961, 1962, 1965, 1967, and 1970, acting as captain on the 1965, 1967, and 1970 teams. He also played in the 1964 and 1968 Olympic games, playing with his brother, David, on the 1964 team and captaining the 1968 team. Throughout this time he worked as an insurance salesman in order to keep his amateur status. He also played intermittantly for the semi-pro St. Paul Steers and Rochester Mustangs. It was after being brought to the emergency room after a Steers game that he met his future wife, who was a nurse there. They married in 1965 and had two children.

Began Coaching Career

In 1969 Brooks began his coaching career as an assistant coach for the University of Minnesota. From 1970-1971 he coached the University of Minnesota's freshman team, the Minnesota Junior Stars of the Minnesota/Ontario Junior League. He quit in 1971 because the University of Minnesota would not let him travel to the NCAA tournament with the varsity team. In spite of this dispute, on February 21, 1972, Brooks became the coach of the University of Minnesota Golden Gophers.

Brooks earned a reputation for his unique team style during his years with the Golden Gophers. He coached for the University of Minnesota's varsity team from 1972 to 1979. During those years, the team won three NCAA titles: 1974, 1976, and 1979. They also won the Western Collegiate

Hockey Association title in 1975. Here, his team began using a European-style hockey strategy mixed with traditional Canadian-American techniques. He left the Golden Gophers in 1979 to coach the U.S. National team, which finished seventh in the World Championships.

The Miracle on Ice

Brooks first applied for the job of coach of the 1980 Olympic hockey team in 1978. The Olympic Committee's first choice was Cleary, who had gone on to coach at Harvard University. But after Cleary turned down the position, the committee chose Brooks, who had impressed them with his plan for winning the Olympics. Instead of trying typical American strategies, he proposed attacking the Soviets using their own style of play.

At the time, Olympic players were required to be amateurs, and this suited Brooks's style of play. He repeatedly stated that he did not want an All-Star team. According to an Associated Press (AP) obituary posted on *ESPN Classic,* he said such teams were always "looking for players whose name on the front of the sweater is more important than the one on the back." He sought out players who were fast and flexible, players who would be able to adapt to a different style of play. He chose and trained 26 players for the 61 exhibition games that the team would play before going to the Olympics. Most of them were former collegiate players from the last three NCAA championship teams: Minnesota, Boston University, and Wisconsin. As these teams were former rivals, Brooks had his hands full. He chose Mike Eruzione from Boston University as the team's captain, and the team was narrowed down to just 20 before the Olympics.

Brooks was a demanding coach; in order to distract the players from their internal team rivalries, he encouraged them to direct their animosity towards him, rather than each other. He would single out players with a tirade, threatening to take away Eruzione's position as captain, or threatening to replace team members with new players. He also became famous for his "Brooksisms," motivational sayings which his players recorded. Some examples, according to the AP obituary, were, "You're playing worse and worse every day and right now you're playing like it's next month," and "You don't have enough talent to win on talent alone." His methods were effective in coalescing his players, and the team developed fast play, aggressive forechecking, and good puck possession.

Leading up to the Olympic games in Lake Placid, New York, Brooks's team played exhibition games both in Europe and the United States. The team didn't always measure up to his expectations. They played the Soviets only a week before the Olympics in an exhibition game, losing 10-3. When it counted, however, the team came through. In the early rounds of the Olympic games they recorded victories against Czechoslovakia, Norway, Romania, and West Germany, and tied Sweden.

On February 22, 1980, the U.S. Olympic hockey team faced their greatest challenge: the Soviet Union's powerful hockey team. According to *ESPN Classic,* Brooks told his players just before the game, "You're meant to be here. This moment is yours. You're meant to be here at this time." For

much of the game they were out-skated, and were down 3-2 in the third period. But Mark Johnson and Eruzione both scored in the third, leading the U.S. team to a dramatic 4-3 comeback win. As recorded on *ESPN Classic,* announcer Al Michaels recited one of sports' most memorable lines near the end of the game: "Do you believe in miracles? Yes!"

Two days later, the United States played Finland for the gold. The U.S. team was behind again, going into the third, 2-1, but forwards Phil Verchota, Rob McClanahan, and Johnson all scored in the third to bring the United States the gold medal, winning 4-2. That year, Herb Brooks was named "Sportsman of the Year" by *Sports Illustrated,* and many years later the same publication would name that victory over the Soviets as the greatest sports accomplishment of the twentieth century. The "Miracle on Ice," as it became known, was also immortalized in the movie *Miracle,* which focused on Brooks's coaching and starred Kurt Russell as Brooks.

Coached in NHL

Immediately after the Olympics, Brooks went to Switzerland to coach for a season for Daro in the Swiss Elite League, but he returned home shortly afterwards. From 1981-1985 he coached the New York Rangers of the National Hockey League (NHL), reaching the 100th victory mark more quickly than any other coach in Rangers' history. He was named the 1982 National Hockey League Coach of the Year in *Sporting News.* Still, while his first year went well, the subsequent years were more difficult. He was fired in January of 1985 with a record of 131 wins, 113 losses, and 41 ties.

He took a brief hiatus from hockey, but then returned to coaching. In this case, he went to coach at St. Cloud State College, which finished in third place in their NCAA Division III tournament championship. He returned to the NHL from 1987-1988, coaching the Minnesota North Stars. Having not turned the team around immediately, he was forced out. He then spent two years doing commentary for SportsChannel America and working as an industrial paper products salesman for Turnquist Paper Company.

In 1990 he was inducted into the U.S. Hockey Hall of Fame. In 1991 he coached the Utica Devils, members of the American Hockey League and a feeder team for the NHL's New Jersey Devils. In 1992-1993 he coached the Devils. The team lost in the first round of the playoffs, and Brooks left, citing a dispute with management. He went back to the Turnquist Paper Company for several years, while scouting for the Pittsburgh Penguins during the 1990s. While he put forth plans for coaching the 1992 and 1994 Olympic hockey teams, his ideas were rejected. He helped coach the 1998 French Olympic hockey team, although they did not make the playoff round.

Brooks coached the NHL's Pittsburgh Penguins from 1999-2000. His players, many of whom were European, thrived under his structured but creative coaching style. He mentored Ivan Hlinka, a Czech national coach, who then took over the team. This was his last time coaching NHL hockey, ending with a career record of 219 wins, 222 losses, and 66 ties. He later admitted that he found coaching in the NHL stifling and difficult.

In 1999 he was inducted into the International Ice Hockey Federation Hall of Fame. In 2002 he was again chosen to coach the Olympic hockey team. This time, though, his team was very different. They were NHL All-Stars instead of amateurs, and he needed to acclimate them to a different style of play and a wider rink. The team did well, winning the silver medal but losing to Canada 5-2 in the gold medal game. When asked why he had decided to coach the team again, Brooks replied, "Maybe I'm sort of like the players . . . there's still a lot of little boy in me," according to the AP obituary on *ESPN Classic.*

In 2002 he received the Lester Patrick Award for hockey service in the United States. He spent his last season as director of player development for the Pittsburgh Penguins, rejecting a multi-million dollar offer to coach the Rangers. He also worked part-time as a motivational speaker.

Died in Accident

Brooks died unexpectedly near Forest Lake, Minnesota, on August 11, 2003, in an automobile accident. He was driving home from the airport when his van veered off the road and flipped. Brooks was thrown from the car and died at the scene. His funeral was held in his hometown of St. Paul, Minnesota, where his casket passed under a canopy of hockey sticks.

His children went on to continue his work with American hockey, creating the Herb Brooks Foundation, which supports hockey development across the United States, particularly youth hockey. On April 25, 2004, his hockey jersey from Johnson High School was retired. On June 28, 2006, he was posthumously elected to the Hockey Hall of Fame.

Books

Coffey, Wayne, *The Boys of Winter: The Untold Story of a Coach, a Dream, and the 1980 U.S. Olympic Hockey Team,* Crown Publishers, 2005.

Jackson, Kenneth T., *Scribner Encyclopedia of American Lives Thematic Series: Sport Figures,* Charles Scribner's Sons, 2002.

Notable Sports Figures, Gale, 2004.

Scribner Encyclopedia of American Lives, edited by Arnold Markoe, Karen Markoe, and Kenneth T. Jackson, Vol. 7, Charles Scribner's Sons, 2007.

Periodicals

USA Today, August 12, 2003.

Online

"Coach known best for 1980 hockey gold," *ESPN Classic,* http://www.espn.go.com/classic/obit/s/2003/0811/1594173.html (January 2, 2010).

"Herb Brooks," *Biography Resource Center Online,* http://www.galenet.galegroup.com/servlet/BioRC (January 2, 2010). □

Hallie Quinn Brown

American educator, public speaker, and reformer Hallie Quinn Brown (c.1849–1949) dedicated her life to the improvement of educational and social

conditions for African Americans and for women. A well-respected lecturer who traveled the United States and Europe speaking about African American history and culture both as part of the Lyceum and on behalf of Ohio's Wilberforce University, Brown twice appeared before Great Britain's Queen Victoria. In addition to her long affiliation with Wilberforce, Brown served as an administrator at South Carolina's Allen University and Alabama's Tuskegee Institute in the late nineteenth century. As an activist, Brown advocated for women's suffrage, temperance, and civil rights, continuing to speak out in support of political and social causes well into her nineties. She was also the author of several books and pamphlets, including *Elocution and Physical Culture* (1910), *Tales My Father Told* (1925), and *Homespun Heroes and Other Women of Distinction* (1926).

B rown was born the fifth of the six children of two former slaves, Thomas Arthur Brown and Frances Jane Scroggins. Although her day of birth has been established as March 10, sources cite Quinn's birth year alternately as 1845, 1849, and 1850; her life's chronology suggests that a later year is more likely, but no records seem to directly support or refute any of these options. Originally from

Maryland, her father had purchased his own freedom at the age of 25 from his mother, a white Scottish plantation owner, and some years later also bought the freedom of his father, the plantation's African American overseer, as well as that of his two siblings. Brown's mother had been enslaved in Virginia but was freed by her owner before she turned 22, when she married Thomas Arthur Brown. The young couple settled in Pittsburgh, where Brown's father worked as a porter and conductor before becoming a riverboat agent. In the years before the Civil War, the Brown home served as a stop on the Underground Railroad, the secret network of private residences that provided food, shelter, and relative safety to fugitive slaves traveling to Canada to secure their freedom, and often offered hospitality to local African Methodist Episcopal (AME) clergy. On the University of Minnesota's *Voices from the Gaps* Web site, Brown's biographical entry argued that "her parents' commitment to the [Underground Railroad] would later influence the organizations Brown founded and participated in."

In 1864, the family moved to Canada, living for a time in Chatham, Ontario. There, Brown attended school—her first formal education—and helped her father support the family through farming. Troubles plagued the family, however; their Canadian home was seriously damaged in a fire in the years after the Civil War, and the Brown children experienced prejudice at their school. The family decided to return to the United States so that Brown and her younger brother could complete their education in a more welcoming atmosphere. In 1870, the Browns settled in Wilberforce, Ohio, and Brown enrolled at the town's Wilberforce College. Affiliated with the AME church, the school had been founded as a coeducational liberal arts college about fifteen years previously "to provide an intellectual Mecca and refuge from slavery's first rule: ignorance," according to the university's Web site. While at Wilberforce, Brown continued her study of rhetoric. She graduated second in her class with a bachelor's of science from the institution in 1873, and soon began working as a speaker with the traveling educational, performance, and entertainment troupe known as the Lyceum.

Educated Youth in the South and Midwest

Brown's primary focus during this era, however, was education. She taught throughout the South, including at Mississippi's Senora Plantation school and in Columbia, South Carolina's public school system. That city's Allen University appointed her Dean in 1875, a post she held until 1887. Brown continued other activities as well as her schedule permitted, attending the American Chautauqua Lecture School during the summer and graduating in 1886. At the Chautauqua School, she took a course with the Boston School of Oratory's Professor Robertson that greatly shaped her growing elocutionist, or public speaking, skills. During this period, Brown also seems to have continued her appearances with the Lyceum. She gave well-received speeches around the Midwest, and sang with the Wilberforce Concert Company, a group that performed around the country to raise money for the school. Upon her departure from Allen University in 1887, she returned to Dayton, Ohio, located about 20 miles from her alma mater. There, she taught in the city's public schools and founded a nighttime educational program for adult migrants to the area.

Brown's achievements in Dayton attracted the attention of respected Southern educator Booker T. Washington, and he offered her the post of lady principal—the equivalent of a modern Dean of Women—at his Tuskegee Institute in Tuskegee, Alabama, in 1892. She remained at Tuskegee for only a relatively short time before returning home to Ohio in 1893. That summer, Brown visited the Columbian Exposition—popularly known as the World's Fair—in Chicago as a speaker at the World's Congress of Representative Women. Seeking a spot on the fair's Board of Lady Managers in order to have the opportunity to exhibit the achievements of African American women, Brown was told that she did not qualify as she was unaffiliated with a formal women's organization. This rejection contributed to Brown's decision to found such an organization for African American woman, and she soon established the Colored Women's League.

Made Fundraising Tour of Europe

In 1894, Wilberforce offered its alumna a faculty position. Although Brown seems to have accepted the post promptly, she resumed her work with the Lyceum at about the same time and thus had little direct involvement with teaching. Instead, she traveled throughout Europe to raise money under the auspices of Frederick Douglass, lecturing on African American culture, promoting the cause of temperance, giving recitations of classic works of literature, and even singing. In 1895, she appeared at the World's Women's Christian Temperance Union conference in London. Two years later, she spoke before Great Britain's Queen Victoria, an honor she repeated in 1899. That same year, she participated in the International Conference of Women in London as a representative of the United States. Although her work primarily kept her in Britain, Brown also gave public lectures in France, Switzerland, and Germany during this period. By the time of her return to the United States in 1899, Brown had raised sufficient funds to support the construction of the Frederick Douglass Memorial Library.

Upon her return to the United States, Brown resumed her travels with the Lyceum and spent the next few years crisscrossing the country with that group. In 1900, she became the Secretary of Education for the African Methodist Episcopal Church, the first time a woman had held an administrative role of that caliber for the religious body. From 1906 onward, Brown served as a professor of elocution and traveling fundraiser for Wilberforce. In this latter role, she returned to Europe in 1910 to generate funds for the construction of a new women's dormitory. While in Great Britain, she acted as a representative of the Women's Parent Missionary Society of the AME at the 1910 World Missionary Conference in Edinburgh, Scotland. By 1912, Brown had persuaded a British woman, E. Julia Emery, to donate the necessary funds, and Keziah Emery Hall was built soon thereafter. During the latter half of the decade, Brown taught a freshman English course along with her fundraising duties, which often took her on speaking tours throughout the southern United States and occasionally back to Europe. In time, she also became a trustee of the university.

Campaigned for Political and Social Causes

Despite her advancing age, Brown remained active in public life throughout the 1920s and 1930s. A lifelong Republican Party supporter, in 1920 she worked on the successful Republican presidential bid of Ohio native Warren G. Harding and became the first woman to publicly speak from his home as part of his famed "front-porch" campaign. Four years later, she was a speaker at the party's national convention before campaigning to African American women on behalf of President Calvin Coolidge. With what A.L. Evans, A.E. Lamikanra, O.S.L. Jones, and V. Evans described as "a tremendous feeling for her people," Brown was a lifelong proponent of increased civil rights for African Americans. She made national news in 1925 when she and a group of other African American singers who had been scheduled to perform at the International Council of Women's conference in Washington, D.C., walked out in protest of their segregated seating arrangements. In 1932, she repeated her campaign efforts on behalf of incumbent President Herbert Hoover, although he logged a spectacular loss to Democratic challenger Franklin D. Roosevelt. She also served as vice-president of the Ohio Council of Republican Women.

Alongside her political efforts, Brown participated in the women's club movement that underpinned the rising feminist spirit of the late nineteenth and early twentieth centuries. In 1920, she became the seventh president of the National Association of Colored Women—the successor of the Colored Women's League that she had helped form some decades previously—and acted in that capacity until 1924. Under Brown's tenure, the women's association established a college scholarship fund for African American women that bore Brown's name, and undertook historical preservation efforts at Frederick Douglass's home in the Anacostia neighborhood of Washington, D.C. Thanks in part to the work of Brown and the National Association of Colored Women, the house is today a National Historic Site administered by the U.S. National Park Service. She retained an honorary presidency of the organization until her death.

Brown was also a prodigious author, producing volumes on topics ranging from public speaking to biography to women's rights. Her major published works include *Bits and Odds: A Choice Selection of Recitations* (1880), *First Lessons in Public Speaking* (1920), *The Beautiful: A True Story of Slavery* (1924), *Our Women: Past, Present and Future* (1925), *Tales My Father Told* (1925), *Homespun Heroines and Other Women of Distinction* (1925), *Pen Pictures of Pioneers of Wilberforce* (1937), and a dramatization of P.A. Nichols' *Trouble in Turkeytrot Church*. She also penned numerous pamphlets, with new publications appearing into the 1940s. Brown died at her home in Wilberforce, Ohio, on September 16, 1949, having reached (or very nearly so) her 100th birthday. She never married and had no children, but was survived by at least one niece, Frances Hughes, with whom she corresponded frequently during the last two and half decades of her life.

The multi-faceted Brown received recognition for her many accomplishments both during her life and after her death. In honor of her long affiliation with Wilberforce University, its nearby public offshoot Central State University designated its academic library the Hallie Q. Brown Memorial Library, and a community center in St. Paul, Minnesota, bears her name. Scholars continue to explore the legacy of her contributions to such diverse fields as education and rhetorical practices. Writing in *Black Pioneers in Communication Research*, Ronald L. Jackson II and Sonja M. Brown Givens proclaimed that Brown's "literary and oratorical works gave voice to thousands of disenfranchised people of her era... She is an inspiring example to us all as a champion for social justice and personal success."

Periodicals

Education, Summer 2004.
New York Times, May 6, 1925.

Online

"Brown, Hallie Quinn," American National Biography Online, http://www.anb.org/articles/ (January 8, 2010).
"Hallie Q. Brown Memorial Library," Central State University, http://www.centralstate.edu/academics/support/library/library/history.html (January 8, 2010).
"Hallie Quinn Brown," *Black Pioneers in Communications Research,* http://www.sagepub.com/upm-data/11830_Chapter3.pdf (January 8, 2010).
"Hallie Quinn Brown," Voices from the Gaps, University of Minnesota, http://voices.cla.umn.edu/artistpages/brownHallie.php (January 8, 2010).
"History," Wilberforce University, http://www.wilberforce.edu/welcome/history.html (January 8, 2010). □

John Moses Browning

The most prolific firearms inventor of all time, American gun genius John Browning (1855-1926) revolutionized the world of military and sporting arms, designing more than 80 firearms, from single-shot rifles to anti-aircraft cannons. Browning developed guns for the world's most renowned manufacturers, including Colt, Remington and Winchester. His most famous designs included the .45-caliber pistol and the Browning Automatic Rifle, or B.A.R., which consisted of a series of light and heavy machine guns used by U.S. forces from World War I through the Korean War.

Browning spent his childhood in Ogden, Utah, toddling around his father's gunsmith shop. Browning's father, Jonathan Browning, grew up in Tennessee, then landed in Nauvoo, Illinois, where he opened a gun-repair shop. At the time, Nauvoo was highly populated by Latter-day Saints, also known as Mormons. As tensions mounted between the Mormons and non-Mormons in the area, the Mormons decided to head west. Jonathan Browning made many of the guns the Mormon pioneers took in their mass exodus to the Salt Lake Valley, which began in 1846. Jonathan Browning followed in 1852 and opened a gunsmith shop in Ogden, a small frontier settlement in the

Utah Territory. Many Mormons practiced polygamy and Jonathan Browning was no exception. With his three wives, he fathered 22 children, including gun genius John Moses Browning, who was born January 23, 1855.

Raised in Father's Frontier Gun Shop

From an early age, Browning showed interest in his father's work and enjoyed sitting in the shop watching him work. When Browning was six, he made himself a makeshift workbench out of a box and spent hours tinkering with scraps of metal, pretending to work as a gunsmith. Browning's father soon put him to work and had the youngster scrubbing the rust off worn mechanisms and other rundown parts with a file and buffer. Browning attended school sporadically until the age of 15, preferring to stay in his father's shop. He was only interested in school so he could learn to write repair tags.

Some time between the ages of 10 and 13, Browning built his first gun using damaged, castoff parts from his father's shop. He took the crude gun for a test and returned home with a prairie bird for dinner. Browning was proud of his work, but his father admonished him, suggesting he should have taken more time and care with his design. His father's words stuck with him and for the rest of his life, Browning was meticulous and methodical with his designs. Browning spent the next decade working alongside his father and running the business in his absence. The shop did well in part because the railroad ran through Ogden bringing

passengers through town on their journeys out west—and no one wanted to head out west without a proper working gun. Around 1878, Jonathan Browning turned the shop over to his son and died a year later. Soon, Browning joined forces with his brothers to grow the business.

Sold First Firearms Patent

In 1879, Browning married Rachel Teresa Child. That same year, he applied for a patent for a single-shot rifle. It was the first of 128 patents he would receive. Browning's initial goal was to create guns that would help pioneers be more successful in hunting the big game that grazed out West. The Browning brothers built a primitive factory and began manufacturing Browning's single-shot rifle, which they sold in their hardware store alongside pistols and rifles from other manufacturers. The Browning guns became hugely popular in the region. The guns bore a stamp reading, Browning Bros. Odgen, Utah USA. In time, the gun landed in the arms of the Connecticut-based Winchester Repeating Arms Co. In 1883, Winchester's vice president traveled across the United States to Ogden to inquire about purchasing the gun's patent from Browning.

While Browning was semi-reluctant to sell his rights to the design, he also knew that deep down, he was more of an inventor than a manufacturer. He sold the rights, touching off what would become a 19-year relationship between Winchester and Browning. Less than a year later, Browning sold Winchester another design, this one for a repeating rifle that used large cartridges. The gun, known as the Winchester Model 1886 Lever Action Repeating Rifle, became one of the most popular rifles of all time and stayed in production until 1935. From 1884 to 1886, Winchester purchased 11 gun designs from Browning. Winchester did not manufacture every single one but purchased the patents to keep Browning's designs from its competitors.

Designed Machine Gun

Like his father, Browning was a member of the Church of Jesus Christ of Latter-day Saints and in 1887, the Mormon church sent him on a two-year mission to Georgia. During his mission, he did not have time to design any guns. After returning home, Browning's interest turned to designing a fully automatic gun. While watching members of the Odgen Rifle Club take target practice one day, Browning became mesmerized with watching the muzzles as members fired away. He noticed that a lot of energy was released from the muzzle with each blast and he began to ponder whether the energy could be "captured" and used to power the gun. The Gatling machine gun—the leading automatic weapon of the era—was powered by a hand crank. Browning believed that using the gasses to power the gun might be more efficient. He developed a way to capture the expanding gases from the exploding ammunition and use it to automatically eject the cartridge, reload, and fire the gun.

Once Browning had finished his gas-operated, water-cooled machine gun and tested the design, he contacted Colt, which manufactured military weapons. Browning and his brother traveled to Hartford, Connecticut, to demonstrate the weapon for Colt management. During the demo, the gun fired 200 rounds of ammunition in just a few seconds without a single misfire. While the gun performed extraordinarily, Colt officials were unsure whether it would be profitable to manufacture, so they sent the brothers on their way.

A few months later, Colt contacted Browning to tell him the U.S. Navy was interested in the gun; the Navy wanted a machine gun, however, only if it could fire continuously for three minutes. The gun, as designed, fired 600 rounds per minute, which meant it would need to handle 1,800 rounds to meet the three-minute specification. This posed several challenges, such as ensuring the barrel did not overheat and also sewing the 1,800 rounds into the canvas belts that fired the gun. Browning revamped the gun and tweaked the ammunition belt, then headed back to Colt to demonstrate the gun for the Navy. It fired all 1,800 rounds perfectly. One hundred years later gas-operated machine guns, like the one Browning invented, remained the standard.

Within a few years, the Colt Model 1895 Automatic Machine Gun was in production, outfitting troops in the Spanish-American War. Over the years, Browning designed several machine guns of different calibers. After the success of the machine gun, Browning developed semiautomatic pistols for Colt. Browning improved the pistol by engineering a "slide" mechanism, which gave the barrel covering the ability to slide back and forth, thus ejecting the spent cartridge after each shot and rotating a fresh round into the chamber. One hundred years later, most semiautomatic pistols still used Browning's slide design. Browning developed many pistols, but his most famous was the .45-caliber Colt, which came out in 1911. This gun became a standard issue for all branches of the U.S. service.

In 1900, Browning secured a patent for an auto-loading shotgun, the first of its kind. Winchester declined to buy the design so Browning sailed to Europe in 1902 to pitch the gun to officials at Fabrique Nationale (FN), a firearms manufacturer located in Liège, Belgium. FN officials liked the design and signed a contract to produce the gun, which Browning dubbed the Auto-5. In return, Browning received royalties on sales. Hunters loved the semiautomatic shotgun and by 1905, Remington was producing the Auto-5 for sale in the United States.

Developed Famed B.A.R. for Warfare

In 1917 the United States entered World War I, increasing the need for a more modern machine gun. Incidentally, the war occurred after a series of events that started with the 1914 assassination of Austrian Archduke Franz Ferdinand, who was killed by a Browning .32-caliber pistol. After engaging in the war, the U.S. military desired a machine gun that was more manageable than the guns of the day, which were so heavy they could not be carried around on the battlefield by soldiers advancing on the enemy. Browning once again came through, developing the Browning Automatic Rifle, or B.A.R., which he unveiled in 1917. Weighing just 17 pounds, the B.A.R. was highly portable and could be fired by a soldier from the hip or shoulder while walking. Like most Browning weapons, the gun was simple in design, comprising 70 pieces that fit together easily, allowing soldiers the ability to quickly disassemble the gun. Reassembly took less than a minute.

Government officials lauded the gun and soon adopted the B.A.R. for use in all U.S. military branches. Highly versatile, the B.A.R. was used by foot soldiers and mounted on planes, tanks and ships. Browning also developed another machine gun that could compete in the trenches—a .30-caliber, rapid-fire gun. In a show of patriotism, Browning sold the rights to his machine guns to the U.S. government for a fraction of what he could have made in the open market. When the guns were ready to be placed into service, Browning's son, Val Browning, traveled to Northern France to train U.S. soldiers in their use. The B.A.R. and the .30-caliber machine gun also played prominent roles in World War II. In describing his father, Val Browning told the *Deseret News* that his father was a humble man who never boasted about his inventions. "He was a most unpretentious man. You would never know he was a man of any renown to meet. There was never any kind of show."

Browning continued to develop firearms until the end of his life. In 1926 he traveled to the FN factory in Liège to oversee production of an over-and-under, double-barrel shotgun. At the time, most shotguns had side-by-side barrels. Browning liked the idea of stacking the barrels—this type of gun would need only one sighting plane. The gun, known as the Browning Superposed, was the last he ever designed. While at the factory in Liège, Browning became ill with chest pains and died on November 26, 1926. Browning's body was taken back to the United States by ship and received a military escort. Browning's son, Val, completed the gun's design and oversaw its initial production. The gun stayed in production until 1960, when the design was overhauled.

According to the *New American,* after Browning's death, Secretary of War Dwight Davis eulogized the humble gunmaker by saying, "It is not thought that any other individual has contributed so much to the national security of this country as Mr. Browning in the development of our machine guns and our automatic weapons to a state of military efficiency surpassing that of all nations."

Books

Browning, John and Curt Gentry, *John M. Browning, American Gunmaker,* Doubleday, 1964.

Schwing, Ned, *The Browning Superposed,* Krause Publications, 1996.

Winders, Gertrude Hecker, *Browning: World's Greatest Gunmaker,* John Day Co., 1961.

Periodicals

Deseret News (Salt Lake City, UT), April 4.

New American, August 17, 2009.

New York Times, November 27, 1926; November 28, 1926.

Salt Lake Tribune, August 3, 1992.

Wall Street Journal, March 20, 1918.□

Ned Buntline

One of the key originators of the mass market dime novel, the American writer Ned Buntline (Edward Carroll Zane Judson, c. 1821–1886) led an adventurous life that placed him among nineteenth-century America's most colorful characters.

B untline's novels of adventure featured outsized events and themes, but his own life was hardly less eventful. A partial listing of its significant moments might include his discovery of "Buffalo Bill" Cody; a role in organizing an anti-immigrant movement that later became the Know Nothing political movement, a leadership role in at least two riots, a 50-foot fall from a hotel window while trying to escape a lynch mob, and, not least important, authorship of some 130 books as well as an immense number of short stories, plays, essays, and nonfiction accounts of events, such as battles of the Mexican-American War, at which he was in all likelihood not present. Buntline exemplified as well as anyone else the development of a characteristically American popular culture.

Took Pen Name from Shipboard Rope

Buntline was born Edward Zane Carroll Judson on March 20, 1821 (or 1823), in Stamford, New York. As described in Jay Monaghan's Buntline biography, *The Great Rascal,* Buntline himself later penned a quatrain describing the scene: "Born when thunder loudly booming / Shook the roof above my head— / When red lightning lit the glooming / Which o'er land and sea was spread." Buntline's father, Levi Judson, was a writer, orator, patriotic historian, and an activist who defended the Freemasons fraternal organization against anti-Masonic political forces. Father and son argued, and one argument escalated to physical abuse. Buntline ran away, talked the captain of a fruit transport ship into taking him on as cabin boy, and later joined the U.S. Navy. He was promoted to the rank of midshipman by President Martin Van Buren after rescuing several other sailors in the aftermath of a collision with a ferry boat. By 1838 Buntline was turning his adventures into fiction, taking his pen name from the word for a rope supporting a sail. He participated in military action against the Seminole tribe in Florida, and issued 13 different challenges for duels as his ship sailed south. The expedition gave him more experiences on which he would draw in his writing. He went on to Cuba, where he met a woman named Seberina Marin, who became the first of his (at least) four wives.

Buntline's first story was published in the prestigious *Knickerbocker Magazine,* and he soon was sending exciting naval thrillers to other magazines like *Ballou's Pictorial.* He resigned his Navy commission in 1842. Soon, barely 20 years old, he decided that he was ready to assume the role of publisher. He made his way to Cincinnati, where he started the short-lived *Ned Buntline's Magazine,* and then moved to Paducah, Kentucky, editing a journal of political gossip he called *Ned Buntline's Own.* When that failed, he assumed the editorship of the *Western Literary Journal and Monthly Review,* and drove that into the ground as well. He moved south and claimed to have single-handedly arrested a pair of fugitive murderers in Eddyville, Kentucky. In 1846 in Nashville, Tennessee, he was alleged to have shot and killed the husband of a teenaged woman with whom he had been intimate. The husband's brother and some friends opened fire on him during his murder trial. Buntline escaped through a window, raced to the third floor of a nearby hotel, and tried to jump to an adjoining building but fell "forty seven feet three inches (measured), on hard, rocky ground, and not a bone cracked!," he boasted, according to Monaghan. But his injuries caused him gradually increasing problems throughout the rest of his life. A lynch mob caught him and hanged him, but sympathizers cut the rope. He was finally exonerated on grounds of self-defense.

None of this slowed down Buntline's literary productivity. In 1847 he returned to New York. He claimed to have fought in the Mexican-American War in 1848. Researchers have not been able to confirm that he actually did, but he certainly wrote about it and found a large audience for his war stories, as well as for the lurid vice tales of *The Mysteries and Miseries of New York: A Story of Real Life.* He published that book in installments with cliffhanger endings, printing the first one at his own expense and including a dictionary of criminal lingo as a glossary. A publisher quickly picked up the remaining installments. Soon two of Buntline's serialized stories had been turned into plays, and he was beginning to gain renown if not literary respect.

Charged with Astor Place Riot Role

He used his newfound fame to plunge into politics. Buntline was one of the organizers in the late 1840s of the Order of United Americans, a semi-secret anti-immigrant movement and later a political party known as the Know-Nothings because of the answer "I know nothing" that members agreed to give to questions about the group. Buntline has been credited as the originator of this idea. Buntline was a prime instigator of the Astor Place Opera House Riot of May 10, 1849. While supporters of American actor Edwin Forrest feuded with backers of the British tragedian William Macready, a mob with Buntline at the forefront ripped up cobblestones from the street and besieged a theater where Macready was playing the role of Shakespeare's *Macbeth.* The resulting clashes with police and National Guard forces left at least 23 people dead. Buntline served a year in prison for his part in the disorder, but upon his release was carried home by a group of supporters that included a band playing "Hail to the Chief."

In 1852 Buntline went to St. Louis and led a group of nativist rioters who confronted German-American immigrants as they attempted to vote in city elections. Buntline was arrested, but jumped bail and started a new newspaper in Illinois. As the Know-Nothing party declined in influence, Buntline temporarily moved back to his native Delaware County and became active in the new Republican Party. Buntline also supported the activities of temperance crusaders, although he personally did not follow an alcohol-free lifestyle.

A writer quoted by William B. Shillingberg in the *Kansas Historical Quarterly* characterized Buntline as "cheap, boisterous, an incorrigible liar, and a general bad egg," asserting that "his writing was all trash and he himself a rascal of the first order." Yet his role in the popular culture of the nineteenth century was significant. Buntline has often been named as the originator of the dime novel. John O. West, writing in the *Dictionary of Literary Biography,* characterized that as "probably an excessive claim" but agreed that Buntline "certainly was an early major dime novelist and one of the most prolific." Buntline claimed once to have written 60,000 words in six days, a play in four hours, and he recalled, according to Shillingberg, that "I once wrote a book of six hundred and ten pages in sixty-two hours. During that time I scarcely ate or slept. I never lay out plots in advance. I shouldn't know how to do it, for how can I know what my people may take it into their heads to do? . . . After I begin, I push ahead as fast as I can write, never blotting out anything I have once written and never making a correction or modification."

And, even if it would never achieve classic literary status, much of what Buntline wrote was exciting and effective. One of his favorite literary devices was to blur the line between fiction and reality, often creating a lead character named Ned Buntline. "This habit of Buntline was fixed—always he told the reader that his story was going to be true, and then told a whopper that nobody could believe," Monaghan noted. Buntline wrote poetry, political tracts, articles on fishing, and even a hymn. The settings of his fiction followed those of Buntline's own life, from the sea to the streets of New York. In 1862 he enlisted in the Union army. He was discharged two years later under murky circumstances, but claimed that he had been a scout in Indian country with the rank of colonel, asking thenceforth to be addressed by that title.

Promoted Buffalo Bill

After the war's end, Buntline quickly guessed that popular fiction was moving in the direction of the American West, and soon he headed west himself. In 1869 he met the then little-known bison hunter William Cody, dubbed him Buffalo Bill, and began a successful new series of dime novels featuring the colorful Western figure. Buntline brought Cody to Chicago and wrote a play, *Scouts of the Plains,* in which Buffalo Bill played the lead role. Critics ridiculed the work after its 1872 premiere. A *Chicago Times* reviewer quoted by Shillingberg wrote: "Such a combination of incongruous drama, execrable acting, renowned performers, mixed audience, intolerable stench, scalping, blood and thunder, is not likely to be vouchsafed to a city a second time, even Chicago." But the play moved on to New York in 1873 and earned handsome profits. Buntline and Cody argued over their share of the take, and the two parted ways. Most of the later mass market fiction featuring Buffalo Bill was written by Prentiss Ingraham, but it was Buntline who put him on the road to international stardom.

Buntline was also widely reported to have given a personalized set of revolvers called Buntline Specials, with 12- or 16-inch barrels, to Western lawman Wyatt Earp in Dodge City, Kansas, in 1876, although Shillingberg's article called the entire Earp story into question. Buntline, Shillingberg showed, was actually in New York in 1876, moving around in order to dodge court actions initiated by his ex-wife Lovanche Judson. In 1871 Buntline had married Anna (or Anne) Fuller; his last wife bore him two children, and he had one child by Annie Bennett, whom he married in the late 1840s. In his later years Buntline built a mansion and 120-acre estate in his native Stamford, calling it Eagle's Nest. The last decade of his life was calmer than its earlier chapters; he established a library with a bequest donated for that purpose by an uncle, and served as its director. After he became wealthy, Buntline was noted for his generosity to friends.

His rate of literary production slowed but never stopped, and he continued to churn out dime novels for the publishing firm of Beadle and Adams, the company that perfected the marketing of the form, and for other houses as well. One indicator of his popularity is that Mark Twain's Tom Sawyer imagines himself as "the Black Avenger of the Spanish Main"—a phrase apparently drawn from the title of Buntline's novel *The Black Avenger of the Spanish Main; or, the Fiend of Blood: A Thrilling Tale of the Buccaneer Times.* Buntline was finally slowed by the continuing effects of the injuries he suffered from the fall in Nashville. He died at his home on July 16, 1886.

Books

Jones, Daryl E., *The Dime Novel Western,* Popular Press, 1978.

Monaghan, Jay, *The Great Rascal: The Life and Adventures of Ned Buntline,* Little, Brown, 1952.

Nineteenth-Century American Western Writers, edited by Robert L. Gale, in *Dictionary of Literary Biography, Vol. 186,* Gale, 1997.

Online

"Wyatt Earp and the 'Buntline Special' Myth" (William B. Shillingberg), *Kansas State Historical Society* (*Kansas Historical Quarterly,* Summer 1976), http://www.kshs.org/publicat/khq/1976/76_2_shillingberg.htm (November 1, 2009). □

John Bernard Burke

British genealogist and publisher John Bernard Burke (1814–1892) possessed an encyclopedic knowledge of the titled families of the British Isles as the longtime editor of *Burke's Peerage,* the genealogical guide founded by his father in 1826. Burke also served as the Ulster King of Arms, a high-ranking royal appointment whose duties included overseeing the proper processional order when the British monarch visited Ireland.

B urke was born on January 5, 1814, in London, England, as the second son of John Burke. The family had centuries-old roots in Ireland: the Burke lineage included the earls of Clanricarde, a title that dated back to the 1330s conferred on the descendants of an illegitimate son of William de Burgh, who came to Ireland in 1175 with England's King Henry II. The family seat was in County Galway at Meelick Castle, but Burke's branch was situated at Elm Hall in County Tipperary. On his mother's side Burke was an O'Reilly, whose line stretched back to the princes of Breifne, two competing clans who established their own small kingdom in the center of Ireland in the 1200s that lasted until 1607.

Joined Family Firm

Burke's father left Ireland after marrying Mary O'Reilly and a failed attempt at a career in business. Deeply fascinated by history and genealogy, he became a writer and published his major opus, *A Genealogical and Heraldic Dictionary of the Peerage and Baronetage of the United Kingdom,* in 1826, when Burke was 12. In its shortened form it was called *Burke's Peerage,* and was designed as a competitor to *Debrett's Peerage,* a guide to the British aristocracy that began publication in 1769. Both titles were modeled after the imposing *Almanach de Gotha,* the compendium of European royal houses and ducal dynasties. Burke's father also created *Burke's Landed Gentry,* first published between 1833 and 1838. This was known as *The Commoners of Great Britain and Ireland* to distinguish its mere landowning listees from those who had been granted both domains and titles by reigning monarchs.

As a young man, Burke studied the classics at the College of Caen in Normandy, France, and began studying law at the bar of Middle Temple in London in 1835. He was "called to the bar," or formally admitted to the profession, in 1839, but never practiced. Instead he joined his father on another title being prepared, *The Royal Families of England, Scotland, and Wales, with their Descendants, Sovereigns and Subjects.* Its two volumes appeared in 1848 and 1851, but by then Burke's father had passed away and he took control of the family's growing publishing empire.

By the 1850s, Burke's years of experience in compiling the data on British aristocracy began to bring him a slew of honors, including a knighthood from Queen Victoria and several royal offices. In 1853 he was made Ulster King of Arms, which oversaw all Irish heraldic matters on behalf of the British monarch at a time when all of Ireland was under English control. Holders of the office were responsible for organizing official ceremonies in Ireland and maintaining the records and histories of the landed gentry, known as the Irish Peers. Burke also belonged to both of the elite chivalric orders created to reward Anglo-Irish nobles for their loyalty to the Crown. These were the Most Illustrious Order of Saint Patrick and the Order of the Bath. In 1867 he became Keeper of the State Papers in Ireland at Dublin Castle. A year later, he supervised what would be the most important state occasion of his career, when Queen Victoria's son, the Prince of Wales, was installed as a Knight of St. Patrick at the Cathedral of St. Patrick in Dublin. The heir-apparent would later become England's King Edward VII.

Weathered Criticism for Spurious Entries

Burke continued to oversee updated editions of *Burke's Peerage* and *Burke's Landed Gentry,* but the contents of both were sources of perennial controversy and occasional lawsuits. In 1865 the second title was targeted by the anonymous author of an essay called "Popular Genealogists, or the Art of Pedigree-making." Nearly a century later, *Times* of London journalist Anthony R. Wagner noted that the essay's author "went so far as to describe the majority of the pedigrees in the Landed Gentry as utterly worthless," and quoted a historian who called the *Peerage* a "gorgeous repertory of genealogical mythology." Burke's posthumous *Dictionary of National Biography* entry from 1909 cited his achievements in compiling the *Peerage* title but noted "it continued to be marred to some extent by the readiness with which doubtful pedigrees were accepted and unpleasing facts in family histories excluded."

In addition to his work on two flagship reference works, Burke also wrote, compiled, or annotated scores of other titles. There was *Royal Families of England, Scotland and Wales,* published between 1847 and 1851. Another was *The Roll of Battle Abbey,* which appeared in 1848. This was actually the title of an important historical document dating back to the Norman Conquest of Britain and of which only a handful of copies had survived. Burke also updated his father's *Dictionary of the Peerages of England, Scotland and Ireland, Extinct, Dormant and In Abeyance* in 1866 and 1883, and finished the *Encyclopaedia of Heraldry, or General Armoury of England, Scotland and Ireland* for publication in 1878.

Recognizing the public's appetite for genealogical history, Burke wrote more extensively about the rise and fall of Britain's richest and most powerful families. There was

The Romance of the Aristocracy, Or, Anecdotes and Records of Distinguished Families in 1855, and several editions of *Vicissitudes of Families,* which provided a wealth of anecdotal tales of the circumstances surrounding the granting of specific titles, and how some were lost. "Far oftener it is the spendthrift and the gambler who figure in these pages," noted a *Times* of London review of its third edition in 1884, "wrecking in a few years the inheritance which centuries have built up."

Descendants Assumed Control

Burke died on December 12, 1892, in Dublin at his home, Tullamore House. His wife, Barbara MacEvoy, preceded him in death five years earlier. They had eight children, including Henry Farnham Burke, who took over the stewardship of *Burke's Peerage* until his death in 1930. The new editions were issued in time for the holiday season and were, despite their exorbitant price, a popular New Year's gift. London's *Economist* declared that the title used to be "a standard reference book for just about every member of the 2,000-odd families whose kin inhabited its pages. It offered marriage guidance par excellence, it gave vital clues in pursuit of understanding how one family seemed to matter to another, and it was a comprehensive genealogical lexicon of the British upper class." In Sir Arthur Conan Doyle's Sherlock Holmes tales, the fictional detective often consulted *Burke's Peerage* or *Landed Gentry* titles as part of his sleuthing.

In the years following World War I, an important alteration was made to the *Burke's Landed Gentry* to include the terms "late of" and "formerly of" after many families were forced to sell their properties as a result of declining fortunes. *Debrett's* guides still maintained a strong presence, but the *Economist* article explained the differences between the two rivals. "Burke's was always more useful, for scholarly as much as for snobbish purposes...because [Debrett's] focuses on the current holder of a hereditary title and his (rarely her) close relations and immediate lineage, whereas Burke's offers a far wider genealogical canvas, exposing all the 'collateral' branches (that is, distant relations) of each family, thereby painting a much more detailed picture of consanguinity, achievement, endurance and (especially these days) decline."

The last edition of *Burke's Peerage* appeared in 1970. The holding company, Burke's Peerage Ltd., was sold in 1973 in the first of several transactions. It went into receivership and the company name was acquired by a firm that offered genealogical research into dormant titles that could be purchased for a hefty fee. The publishing rights to the Burke's books were eventually bought by a new company, Burke's Peerage & Gentry, which began issuing the flagship title once again in 1999. That 106th print edition of *Burke's Peerage and Baronetage* ran to more than 3,500 pages over two volumes, and cost $395. It also broke with longstanding tradition by listing children born outside of marriage. In 2009 the company announced that henceforth the print and online editions would list all children by order of birth, rather than the "sons first" standard.

Books

Dictionary of National Biography, Volume 22, edited by Sir Leslie Stephen et al., Oxford University Press, 1909, p. 338.

Periodicals

Economist, June 5, 1999.
New York Times, June 27, 1999.
Times (London, England), January 1, 1884; December 14, 1892; May 16, 1894; October 1, 1952; July 1, 2009. □

Susan Butcher

The American dog sled racer Susan Butcher (1954–2006) was one of the greats of her sport as well as one of its few female practitioners.

Although she was not the first woman to win Alaska's famed Iditarod race, her four wins, three of them consecutive, represent a record of accomplishment unmatched by any other dogsledder of either gender. Butcher's victories on the trail resulted from sheer determination, from courage, and often from an almost preternatural ability to communicate with animals. Butcher, more than other prominent figures in the world of dog sledding, became the face of the sport, and this was partly because she seemed almost to enter the world of the dogs she trained and raced, devoting herself to them full-time. "In a lot of respects," her husband David Monson told Viv Bernstein of the *New York Times,* "her greatest contribution to the sport itself was how she made year-round care and training really the standard rather than the exception." Asked once how she could keep track of the names of her pack of 150 Siberian huskies, she said (according to Mark Bechtel of *Sports Illustrated*), "It's easy when you know them. Like having 150 kids."

Walked 15 or More Dogs

Susan Howlet Butcher grew up a great distance from Alaska, both geographically and culturally. She was born on December 26, 1954, in Cambridge, Massachusetts, an intensely university-oriented suburb of Boston. Her father, Charles, was chief executive of a chemical company, her mother Agnes a social worker. Butcher crossed the space between Boston and the Alaskan wilderness in stages, the first of which was her parents' belief that Butcher and her sister should grow into self-sufficient women; they were given carpentry lessons and asked to help out as Charles Butcher restored a sailboat. From the start, Susan Butcher hated life in the city, saying so directly in a school essay she wrote at age eight. She also loved dogs and was good at managing them in groups. She walked the family's Labrador mix, Cabee, to a local park and picked up neighbors' dogs en route. Paying close attention to the sounds and attitudes of 15 or 20 dogs at once, she learned to gauge their needs and moods.

Butcher's parents divorced when she was 11, and she was further saddened by Cabee's death. An aunt gave her

a Siberian husky called Maganak, and she learned of the breed's association with sled dog racing and began to read about the sport. When she was 16, she moved out of her mother's house after being told she could not have a second dog. She joined her father in Colorado, a state with an active dog sledding scene, and she became fascinated by the Iditarod after reading about it in a magazine. Butcher took pre-vet classes at Colorado State University, but by the time she was 20 she had decided that the Iditarod was most important. She left Colorado for Fairbanks, Alaska, found a job in a salmon processing plant, and began to devote all her energy and money to the race. Often she lived in her car or in a tent to save money for a top-notch dog team.

Training her dogs while living in a cabin she built herself in the wilderness of Alaska's interior, Butcher worked seven days a week, 12 to 16 hours per day, running her team through courses of 50 to 70 miles. She fed herself and the dogs by killing caribou or moose, and one time she and her team survived a plunge through thin ice at a temperature of 25 below zero. After three winters, Butcher took a job as a dog trainer with Iditarod founder Joe Redington. She raised more money by donning a swimsuit on an Anchorage television broadcast, cutting a hole in some ice, jumping into the water, and asking for donations. In 1978 she entered her first Iditarod and placed 19th. The following year, she and Redington became the first dogsledders in history to lead a team up Denali (also known as Mount McKinley), the highest peak in North

America. That year, she also cracked the ranks of the top ten Iditarod finishers.

Saved by Dog That Sensed Danger

With a course running about 1,100 miles through snowbound Alaskan wilderness, the Iditarod is a rare test of endurance for human and dog alike. Butcher trained her dogs to pull 500-pound loads over distances of up to 70 miles, and they followed her orders unquestioningly—except for one day when a lead dog refused to make a left turn in response to Butcher's command. Butcher was puzzled, until the trail the dog had avoided collapsed into a river below. Butcher took fifth place in the 1980 and 1981 Iditarod races, finished second in 1982 after becoming lost in a snowstorm, dropped to ninth in 1983, and finished second once again in 1984.

Perhaps Butcher's most dramatic Iditarod was the 1985 race, although it was the only one between 1978 and 1994 that she did not finish. Midway through the course, Butcher's dogs were attacked by a hungry pregnant moose that became entangled in the team's harnesses. The moose killed two dogs, but Butcher protected the rest by fighting off the moose with an ax for 20 minutes until another racer arrived and shot it. Butcher withdrew from the race, which for the first time was won by a female dogsledder, Libby Riddles. As her injured dogs recuperated under a veterinarian's care, Butcher slept on the floor of the clinic. "They have to trust me and know that I care about them and that I won't ask them to do something they aren't capable of," Butcher was quoted as saying by Sonja Carberry in *Investor's Business Daily.*

One compensation for Butcher's Iditarod withdrawal in 1985 was her marriage to dogsledder (or musher) David Monson, whom she had met in 1980 when she ordered $6,000 worth of dog food from him but could not pay when billed. The two moved to remote Eureka, Alaska, where they opened Trail Breaker Kennels on the site of an abandoned mining camp. With Butcher often acting as a non-degreed veterinarian, the strength of her dog team grew. In 1986, Butcher won her first Iditarod and took home the $50,000 prize. She plowed that back into the kennel operation and won twice more, in 1987 and 1988, despite brutal conditions in the latter year that ranged from a dangerous melt to gale-force winds, and in the face of mounting criticism from multi-year champion Rick Swenson and other male mushers over the participation of female racers. Butcher finished second in 1989 and took home her fourth first-place trophy in 1990, setting a course record of 16 days, one hour, and 53 minutes. Only Swenson, with five wins, had more Iditarod victories than Butcher, and her dominance in the late 1980s with three consecutive and four total wins, remains unduplicated.

Worked to Improve Treatment of Dogs

In 1991 Butcher emerged as the leader of a group of racers and veterinarians who urged the sport of dog sledding to police itself in order to reduce the number of dog deaths on the course; the Iditarod had come under increasing scrutiny from animal rights organizations, and Humane Society of the United States investigator David Willis criticized the race on national television after one of Butcher's dogs died during the 1994 Iditarod. Partly because of reforms pushed by Butcher's group, however, the treatment of sled dogs improved during the 1990s and early 2000s, and dog deaths during the Iditarod became rare. Butcher continued to race until that year, never finishing lower than tenth after 1985. After the 1994 race she announced her intention to retire and start a family; she and Monson raised two daughters, Tekla (who shared her name with one of Butcher's favorite sled dogs) and Chisana.

In the 1990s Butcher was an Alaskan and national celebrity, often appearing on television to provide color commentary during the Iditarod. She and Monson continued to operate Trail Breaker Kennels, eventually opening parts of the operation to tourists who wanted to learn more about dog sledding. She also visited the White House, where she and her most successful lead sled dog, Granite, met with President George H.W. Bush.

In December of 2005, Butcher was diagnosed with acute leukemia. The cancer responded to chemotherapy and went into temporary remission. Butcher made the decision to pursue an experimental treatment involving a stem-cell transplant that offered her a chance at a complete cure. "There's no question she was a fighter, and she always chose to take risks for the hope she could be cured," her physician, Jan Abkowitz, told Bernstein. After the transplant, Butcher suffered from complications and soon the recurrence of the leukemia. She undertook a second round of chemotherapy, but her condition worsened, and she died at a hospital in Seattle, Washington on August 5, 2006. In 2008 the University of Alaska at Fairbanks announced the creation of the Susan Butcher Institute which is, according to the institute's web site, "dedicated to cultivating public service and leadership skills for Alaska's residents."

Books

Dolan, Ellen M., *Susan Butcher and the Iditarod Trail,* Walker, 1993.
Notable Sports Figures, Gale, 2004.
Wadsworth, Ginger, *Susan Butcher: Sled Dog Racer,* Lerner, 1994.

Periodicals

Anchorage Daily News, August 6, 2006.
Investor's Business Daily, October 20, 2006.
New York Times, August 7, 2006.
Sports Illustrated, August 14, 2006.

Online

"UAF Announces New Susan Butcher Institute," *University of Alaska–Fairbanks,* http://www.uaf.edu/news/a_news/200806 12135438.html (November 3, 2009).
"Wanted: Healthy, Happy Dogs," *Anchorage Daily News,* February 23, 1997, http://www.adn.com/adn/iditarod/25/ animal.html (November 3, 2009). □

C

Mary Steichen Calderone

Mary Steichen Calderone (1904–1998) has commonly been heralded—and criticized—for her efforts to create a science-based sex education curriculum for public schools in the United States. A physician and public health official, Calderone served as medical director for the Planned Parenthood Federation of America for more than a decade, but left the post in 1964 to co-found the Sex Information and Education Council of the United States, or SIECUS. For more than two decades she advocated for the inclusion of sex education in health and science, and was often vilified by conservative groups for her work. "We're still a strongly antisex society," Calderone told Nadine Brozan in the *New York Times*. "Fundamentally, we're scared, and still trying to repress others."

Calderone was the daughter of famed photographer Edward Steichen. She was born in Paris on July 1, 1904, and a year later, Steichen and his friend Alfred Stieglitz opened an art gallery at 291 Fifth Avenue in New York City, called Gallery 291. The Steichen family lived next door to the gallery for a time, but moved back to Paris permanently in 1906.

Calderone had a troubled relationship with her mother, Clara Smith Steichen, whose family's roots were near the Ozark Mountains. Clara followed the standard parenting cautions of the era about children's sexual self-exploration; at the time, respected medical professionals claimed this could cause later mental illness, and warned

parents to check it at an early age. Calderone later recalled that as a child her mother forced her to wear metal mitten devices when she went to bed, which she hated. The Steichen marriage, furthermore, was an unhappy one. At the outbreak of World War I, the family, which by then included Calderone's younger sister, Kate, returned to America for safety, but Clara then took Kate back to France, and Calderone opted to stay with her father. Her parents' marriage was effectively over by 1921, when Clara Steichen lost a $200,000 lawsuit she filed against another woman. In the case, Calderone's mother sued for alienation of affection, blaming a woman who had been a guest at the home for the end of the marriage, but a New York jury found the defendant not guilty.

Married and Became a Mother

Calderone was a gifted student at Brearley School, a private academy on New York's Upper East Side. She entered nearby Vassar College in 1921, majoring in chemistry at what was then also a single-sex school. After she graduated in 1925, however, Calderone gave up plans to enter medical school and instead enrolled in classes at the respected American Laboratory Theater in New York City for three years, and finally "gave it up when I found I wasn't good enough," she told Brozan.

Calderone was married for several years to an actor named W. Lon Martin, with whom she had two daughters, Nell and Linda. The marriage ended around 1933, and Calderone was devastated by the death of her eight-year-old daughter Nell from pneumonia two years later. Depressed, she underwent psychoanalysis and a battery of tests, which reaffirmed her natural aptitude for science. In 1935, at the age of 30, she entered the medical school at the University of Rochester in upstate New York.

Calderone earned her M.D. in 1939 and completed a pediatric internship at Bellevue Hospital in New York City. She also entered the graduate program of the Columbia University School of Public Health, where she met a physician who would become her second husband, Frank A. Calderone. At the time, he was a district health officer with the New York City Department of Health and Mental Hygiene, but would eventually became deputy commissioner of health for New York City and an executive officer with the World Health Organization (WHO).

Joined Planned Parenthood

Calderone's second marriage produced two more daughters, and for most of the 1940s she worked part-time as a school physician for the Great Neck public school system, not far from their home in the village of Old Brookville on Long Island. Both communities were part of a posh chain of North Shore suburbs that stretched eastward from New York City. It was during this period of her life that Calderone joined the Society of Friends, a religious denomination more commonly known as the Quaker faith. Quakers had a history of progressive activism, and had played an instrumental role in several social reform movements of the nineteenth century.

In 1953 Calderone took another part-time post, this one as medical director for the Planned Parenthood Federation of America (PPFA). Founded by family planning pioneer Margaret Sanger in 1921 as the American Birth Control League, PPFA offered both information and clinical services for women seeking to prevent pregnancy through the use of contraceptive devices, which still relied on what were known as barrier methods in this era. Most American women had a primary care physician and an obstetrician-gynecologist, but the profession was still dominated by men. Some medical professionals and religious authorities believed that to use any contraceptive methods at all was to interfere with the natural order of the world. There were also thorny legal issues surrounding birth control. In some states laws remained on the books that prohibited anyone from distributing such devices. In other jurisdictions it was illegal to provide contraceptive products to unmarried adults.

Calderone went to work at the PPFA to convince the medical profession to adopt less restrictive policies. One of her first initiatives was to survey all the major textbooks used in obstetric training in U.S. medical schools, and she found that the majority did not cover family planning. Securing cooperation from several authors who agreed to include current family planning information in subsequent editions, Calderone edited a work that became a standard text, *Manual of Family Planning and Contraceptive Practice,* that was revised several times in the 1960s and 1970s to include new breakthroughs.

Battled to Reduce Abortion Rates

One of the most significant breakthroughs was the introduction of the first combined oral contraceptive pill which, when taken as prescribed, prevented ovulation entirely. Its efficacy rate was phenomenally high, and its introduction in 1960 launched what is commonly referred to as the sexual revolution in America, when young men and women no longer feared the stigma of an unplanned pregnancy and either single parenthood or a rushed marriage. Calderone had worked with Searle and other pharmaceutical companies to set up clinical trials at PPFA clinics prior to "the Pill"'s approval by the U.S. Food and Drug Administration, and as medical director continued to support trials of new birth control methods, such as the intrauterine device (IUD) and contraceptive foam.

Without access to birth control, Calderone and other women's health advocates knew, pregnant women sometimes resorted to terminating pregnancies on their own. These included various toxic home remedies or paying a medical professional to perform an abortion under secretive and usually unsanitary conditions, because abortion was illegal in many states under most circumstances. As PPFA medical director, Calderone organized a 1955 conference of professionals from several fields, including noted sex behavior researcher Dr. Alfred Kinsey. The papers that resulted from the conference were published in 1958 as *Abortion in the United States.* This was the first serious text to assemble data on how many women died from illegal abortions and the estimated rates of permanent infertility due to infections and other complications. The publication of this work was considered a turning point in the movement to decriminalize abortion laws in the United States. All state laws barring first-trimester abortions were overturned by the 1973 U.S. Supreme Court decision *Roe v. Wade.*

Calderone and other family planning advocates knew that the key to reducing abortions was to make birth control methods more readily available. There was still major opposition, but Calderone and PPFA succeeded in persuading two major policy shifts from respected organizations. The first came in 1959, when the American Public Health Association declared that it endorsed responsible family planning as necessary to reduce soaring population rates in the developing world, which threatened the health of the entire planet. Five years later, the trustees of the American Medical Association reversed a policy that prohibited its members from providing birth control to patients.

Urged Schools to Implement Sex Education

That historic event occurred in December of 1964, but Calderone had already resigned from Planned Parenthood by then to take up the cause of sex education as her next crusade. Her decision was tied to a pair of factors: the volume of letters that Planned Parenthood received made her realize that Americans were vastly undereducated on the topic of human sexuality, and in 1961 she participated in The American Conference on Church and Family, convened by the National Council of Churches. "Attended by sociologists, religious leaders, educators and public health professionals, the conference highlighted the suffering of thousands of people because of ignorance about frigidity, impotence, homosexuality and contraception," noted Jane Brody of the *New York Times*. PPFA was still tightly focused on access to family planning methods, and Calderone knew she would have to leave the organization to continue her mission.

With a few participants from the American Conference on Church and Family, Calderone assembled a committee to urge the adoption of sex education standards in U.S. school curricula. The committee evolved into the Sex Information and Education Council of the United States, or SIECUS. Calderone served as its executive director from 1964 to 1975 and president from 1975 to 1982. She traveled around the country speaking to school boards, parent-teacher associations, and other groups, urging schools to implement the basic tenets of sex education as early as kindergarten. She pointed out that the increasing affluence of post-World War II America had brought major shifts for the generation of baby boomers who were turning 18 in 1964. Many parents were uncomfortable discussing sex with their children, she told a national convention of Parent-Teacher Association (PTA) delegates in May of that year, and it was best to provide correct, fact-based information on sexual health and reproduction, while stressing that intercourse had its rightful place inside the marital union. "We have given our children the keys and free access to cars, money with which to go to motels, empty houses and apartments," she said, according to a *New York Times* report, "and few rules about anything, including sex."

Not surprisingly, Calderone had numerous and well-organized foes, including the right-wing John Birch Society and various church-affiliated groups who "contended that her promotion of sex education in schools was encouraging a premature and unhealthy participation in sexual experience and usurping the role of parents in guiding their children's lives," wrote Brody. "Her reply was that if parents were doing their job properly there would be no need for school-based sex education."

Calderone left SIECUS in 1982 and took a post teaching at New York University. With co-authors she produced two classic texts, *The Family Book about Sexuality* and *Talking with Your Child About Sex*, both published in the early 1980s. She spent her final years in a Pennsylvania Quaker community, but suffered from Alzheimer's disease. She died on October 24, 1998, at a care facility in Kennett Square, Pennsylvania, at the age of 94.

Periodicals

Journal of Sex Research, May 1999.
New York Times, March 4, 1921; May 27, 1964; June 28, 1974; February 17, 1983; June 30, 1985; October 25, 1998.□

Hortense Calisher

The American author Hortense Calisher (1911–2009), noted Scott McLemee on the web site *Salon*, "has a reputation as a 'writer's writer.'" No fixed set of themes or settings linked her large production of novels, novellas, short stories, and nonfiction, but her craft as a writer was widely admired.

The diversity of Calisher's career makes a balanced summary difficult, and the difficulty is amplified by the variety of critical reactions her work has inspired. Some observers have preferred her intricately written short stories, while others favored her full-length novels with their often-unexpected themes and settings. In the memoir *Herself* and in some of her fiction, Calisher wrote in great detail about the upper-middle-class literary culture of New York in which she spent much of her life, but she could diverge into science fiction, mystery, and world affairs as well. McLemee opined that Calisher was "above all, a stylist—someone whose maneuvers are so inventive, supple and/or arcane that only readers similarly burdened with literary ambition are likely to appreciate the subtleties of her performance." Indeed, what ties Calisher's writing together is its tendency to make the observer as important as the observed, to insert an author's voice into the story. A *New York Times Book Review* essay quoted in the biographical essay appearing in *The Novellas of Hortense Calisher* asserted that she belonged to "a tradition descending from Henry James, in which the writer's own complex intelligence—his humming eloquence, his subtle knowingness—becomes essential to his equipment as a storyteller."

Drew on Southern Jewish Family Background

Hortense Calisher was born in New York on December 20, 1911. Calisher's family background was both Southern and Jewish, and, in a biographical sketch appearing on her web site she identified the combination as key to her development as a writer: "Jews have a pride of heritage, tradition and tragedy. So have Southerners, with different subject matter. Both are often anecdotalists, of humors peculiar to each—and run to large family gatherings.... The combination was odd all round, volcanic to meditative to fruitfully dull, bound to produce someone interested in character, society and time." Her father, Joseph Henry Calisher, came from Richmond, Virginia, where his father had been a leader of the local synagogue. "He could read Hebrew, no doubt with a drawl," Calisher wrote in *Herself*. A perfume manufacturer, he married the much younger Hedwig Lichtstern, a German Jewish immigrant, after meeting her at a horse race in upstate New York. The family moved from Richmond to New York in the years before Hortense was born.

Calisher had a writing instinct from the beginning; when she was seven she began keeping a record of her experiences in notebooks, which she saved and drew on in her writing as an adult. Growing up in an apartment house on Broadway, she wandered with other kids through Riverside Park and made keen observations of its geology. Calisher's parents valued literature and music, and she attended top schools despite a Depression-era family economic crisis that forced her father to hunt for a new job at age 70. She graduated from Hunter College High School and then, in 1932, Barnard College, majoring in English composition and philosophy. After finishing school she spent a year as a clerk at Macy's department store, also working stints as a model and social worker with the New York City Department of Public Welfare.

"Each of us had 175 families per month to visit—all of them, it seemed, on the top fifth floor," Calisher wrote in *Herself*. "I saw hall toilets for the first time—and all polyglot disease. One of my blocks had the highest TB rate in the U.S.A.: another was solidly prostitute. 'Family?' a girl said to me. 'There ain' no *families* here.'" Calisher's circumstances changed in 1935 when she married engineer Heaton Heffelfinger. The couple had two children, Bennet (whom she outlived) and Peter, and moved frequently because of Heffelfinger's work requirements. Eventually they settled in Nyack, New York, north of New York City in the Hudson River valley.

Enrolled in Writing Class

Although she wrote poetry from time to time, Calisher lacked the self-confidence to plunge into fiction. "I'd been fed on the best of literature, and I wanted to reach the summit," she was quoted as saying by Holcomb B. Noble of the *New York Times*. The press of marriage and family made it more difficult for her to find inspiration and concentration. "I got to be quite sick, since I wasn't doing what I was fitted for and craved," she continued. "Though I was a candidate for psychiatry, I always felt I had to fight it out alone, on the battlefield of myself. Finally I had something that was so important to me that I had to say it." Calisher enrolled in a writing class near her home in Nyack and wrote several semi-autobiographical short stories. She submitted them to *The New Yorker;* the first one published, "A Box of Ginger" (1948), impressed the magazine's editors

with details drawn on Calisher's childhood impressions of the rocks in Riverside Park.

Calisher's short stories were popular, and a group of them were collected in the book *In the Absence of Angels* in 1951. She won Guggenheim Fellowships in 1952 and 1955, using them to travel (to England) and write. In 1956 she became an adjunct professor of English at Barnard, the first in a long series of temporary and visiting professorships. She and Heffelfinger divorced in 1958, and that year she traveled around Southeast Asia under the auspices of the United States State Department. The following year she married writer Curtis Harnack. Finally, at the age of 50, Calisher published her first novel, *False Entry* in 1961.

The book attracted favorable critical notice with its compelling central figure, a man whose extraordinary memory enables him to insinuate himself into people's lives, leading into the book's variety of settings, from London to an Alabama town dominated by the Ku Klux Klan. The novel was a finalist in the annual National Book Award competition. For the rest of her long life, Calisher turned out novels and other books regularly, writing methodically for several hours a day. Rarely would a book give much of a clue as to what was coming in its successor, and *False Entry* was followed by *Textures of Life* (1963), an examination of the lives of young newlyweds.

Even further afield from Calisher's New York territory was *Journal from Ellipsia* (1965), a partly comic novel that was classed by publishers as science fiction; it dealt with a female human anthropologist who encounters and learns to deal with extraterrestrial life forms. At the same time, she was working on a novella, *The Railway Police*, that described a social worker who wore a wig; a television interviewer was so convinced it was autobiographical that he said on the air that Calisher must be wearing a wig herself. She offered to let him try to pull her hair off, but he refused. Calisher returned to home ground with the massive novel *The New Yorkers* (1969), which developed a family of Jewish characters first introduced in *False Entry*. Critics began to debate the relative merits of Calisher's novels and short stories, whereupon she surprised both camps with the unorthodox memoir *Herself* in 1972. The book's structure was complex and novelistic, using shifting time points and perspectives to gather the strands of the author's background.

Wrote Major Novels Past Age 70

Calisher's novels of the 1970s often took up contemporary themes. *Queenie* (1971) was a satirical New York coming-of-age story with sexual elements; the 60-year-old author reflected that "every 16-year-old is a pornographer." Other novels, such as *Eagle Eye* (1973) (the story of an upwardly mobile but troubled family) and *On Keeping Woman* (1977) dealt with crises of middle age. Entering her eighth decade, an age at which the productivity of many writers declines, Calisher became, if anything, even more prolific. *Mysteries of Motion* (1982) was called by novelist Joyce Carol Oates, writing in the *New York Times Book Review,* "as ambitious as anything we are likely to see published this season." The novel, set in the near future, was cast in the form of a space traveler's logbook; its complex structure reflected on ecological disaster on Earth and traced the relationships among a group of would-be colonists on a spaceship, the *Citizen Courier*.

Collections of Calisher's short stories continued to appear, and she also issued *Saratoga, Hot*, a collection of original stories, in 1985. The novel *The Bobby-Soxers* (1986) was a story of young women in an American small town, while *Age* (1987) featured a married couple in old age, each keeping a diary intended to be read after the other's death. Calisher served as president of the American Academy and Institute of Arts and Letters from 1987 to 1990, and in 1989 she received a Lifetime Achievement Award from the National Endowment for the Arts. She received honorary doctorates from Skidmore College, Grinnell College, and Hofstra University in the late 1980s. In 1986 she traveled to the People's Republic of China as a visiting lecturer under the U.S.–China Arts Exchange program.

Perhaps these honors were intended to put an elegant closing bookend to Calisher's long career, but they failed to slow her down. *Kissing Cousins* (1988) was an autobiographical nonfiction work exploring Calisher's Southern family background. Her 1992 novel *The Small Bang*, a sort of metaphysical mystery, was issued under the pen name Jack Fenno—and Calisher wrote an article about the pen name, "Portrait of a Pseudonym," for the journal *The American Scholar*. Issued just a year later, *In the Palace of the Movie King* traced the adventures of an Albanian filmmaker in America. *In the Slammer with Carol Smith* (1997) was the story of a 1960s radical who later became homeless on the streets of New York.

Calisher remained active well into her 90s. In 2001 she wrote an introduction to a new edition of a novel that had influenced her style, Henry James's *The Turn of the Screw*. Her last novel, 2002's *Sunday Jews*, was another Jewish family saga; it was followed by a third volume of autobiography, *Tattoo for a Slave*, in 2004. In 2006 she penned a recollection of her West Side New York childhood for the *New York Times*. She died in New York on January 13, 2009. Calisher's short stories were widely anthologized, but her novels remained for the most part more familiar to fiction aficionados than among the general public. "Ironically," wrote Kathleen Snodgrass in *Jewish Women: A Comprehensive Historical Encyclopedia*, "the protean nature of this writer may have contributed to her work not being better known."

Books

Calisher, Hortense, *Herself*, Arbor House, 1972.

Calisher, Hortense, *The Novellas of Hortense Calisher*, Modern Library, 1997.

Calisher, Hortense, *Kissing Cousins: A Memory*, Weidenfeld & Nicholson, 1988.

Contemporary Novelists, 7th ed., St. James, 2001.

Periodicals

Guardian (London, England), March 25, 2009.

New York Times, November 15, 2006, January 15, 2009.

Online

Biography, Hortense Calisher official web site, http://members. authorsguild.net/hcalisher (November 4, 2009).

"Hortense Calisher, 1911–2009," *Jewish Women: A Comprehensive Historical Encyclopedia*, http://jwa.org/encyclopedia/article/ calisher-hortense (November 4, 2009).

"JCO on Hortense Calisher," *Celestial Timepiece: A Joyce Carol Oates Home Page*, http://jco.usfca.edu/calisher.html (November 4, 2009).

"Review: *In the Slammer with Carol Smith*," *Salon*, http://www. salon.com/july97/sneaks/sneak970723.html (November 4, 2009).□

Cornell Capa

Hungarian-American photographer Cornell Capa (1918-2008) was a leading photojournalist renowned for his powerful photo essays. For a large part of his career, he worked with *Life* magazine, during the publication's greatest years. He was the younger brother of photojournalism pioneer Robert Capa. In 1974, he founded the International Center of Photography.

Cornell Capa enjoyed a long and distinguished career as a photojournalist. With the sensitivity he brought to his subject matter, he became a master of the discipline, yet he never considered himself an artist. Still, the photo essays he produced were more than a series of pictures; rather, they were characterized by compassion and empathy and communicated a moving narrative.

The famed photographer was born as Kornel Friedmann on April 10, 1918 into a Jewish family that lived in Budapest, Hungary. His parents, Dezso and Julia Berkovits Friedmann, were assimilated non-practicing Jews who owned a successful dressmaking shop. Dezso Friedmann served as head tailor.

Kornel was the youngest of the family's three sons. The oldest son, Laszlo, died of rheumatic fever in 1935. Middle son Robert also grew up to be a photographer. Kornel and Robert were very close, and Robert would be a strong influence on his younger brother's life.

Moved to France

From 1928 to 1936, Friedmann received his public education at the Imre Madacs Gymnasium in Budapest. While growing up, he wanted to become a doctor. After graduating from high school, he left Budapest for Paris, to join his brother Robert and to begin his medical education. Robert had left Hungary in 1931, to avoid political persecution. A leftist, his student activities attracted the unfavorable attention of his home country's anti-Semitic government officials. Before settling in Paris, Robert lived for a while in Germany, where he became a photojournalist. There, Robert became friends with two other photographers, Henri Cartier-Bresson and David Seymour. The three young men later became

famous photographers who helped pioneer the field of photojournalism.

Developed Interest In Photography

Joining his brother Robert in Paris in 1936 when he was eighteen years old, Kornel studied French at the Alliance Française. He supported himself by developing film for Robert, Cartier-Bresson and Seymour. He performed the work in an improvised darkroom that he set up in his hotel bathroom. In this way, Kornel became interested in photography, too, and he gave up his medical ambitions for a career in photojournalism.

By this time, Robert had changed his last name to Capa, a variation of the name of one of his favorite American film directors, Frank Capra. (Capra had received a "Best Director" Oscar in 1934 for *It Happened One Night* and he would later direct *It's a Wonderful Life*, the 1946 film that became a holiday classic.) Always close to his brother, Kornel took the last name, too. In 1937, and now known as Cornell Capa, he moved to New York City, where he lived with his mother and her four sisters.

Began Long Association with *Life*

Soon after, Robert joined his younger brother in New York. By now an established photographer, Robert began doing some work for Pix Inc., a new photography agency, where he helped Cornell secure a job as a printer and photographer.

A year later, Cornell again supported himself by developing film. However, now he worked in a professional darkroom and for a major publication, *Life* magazine. During this period, he published his first photo story, a spread about the New York World's Fair that appeared in *Picture Post* magazine.

In 1940, Capa married Edith Schwartz, who assumed a supportive role in her husband's career. She maintained his negatives and continually updated his archives, functions that she also performed for Robert Capa.

Served in World War II

Capa worked for *Life* until 1941, when he entered the military during World War II. That same year, he became a naturalized citizen. Until 1945, he served in the photo-intelligence unit in the United States Air Force, rising to the rank of sergeant.

In 1946, after returning from the military, Capa was hired by *Life* magazine as a staff photographer. A year later, brother Robert, Cartier-Bresson, and Seymour co-founded the Magnum Photos photography agency. Capa joined the firm in 1954, after his brother was killed while on assignment in Indochina, covering the French-Indochina war. The tragic death occurred on May 25, after Robert Capa stepped on a landmine. He was the first American war correspondent to die in the conflict that later evolved into the Vietnam War.

After Robert Capa's death, Seymour became Magnum Photo's president. But he, too, died while working as a war correspondent. On November 10, 1956, while covering the Suez War, he fell victim to Egyptian machine gun fire. Capa then became Magnum's president and held the position until 1960.

Meanwhile, he continued working for *Life* magazine, but as a contributing photographer. Capa was now highly renowned for his work. Writing in *The New York Times* in 2008, Philip Gefter said, "His work conformed to all the visual hallmarks of *Life* magazine photography: clear subject matter, strong composition, bold graphic impact and at times even a touch of wit."

Photographed John F. Kennedy

Unlike his brother Robert, Capa had no interest in covering war. Rather, he wanted to be a "photographer for peace." As such, Capa was much more interested in covering politics and chronicling social injustice. His coverage of the political campaigns of presidential candidates Adlai Stevenson and Nelson Rockefeller garnered substantial praise. It was his work related to John F. Kennedy, however, that provided him greater prestige. In 1960, *Life* magazine assigned him to cover Kennedy's ultimately successful presidential campaign, which allowed Capa to witness up close, and capture in a series of famous photos, the excitement surrounding the young, charismatic Kennedy.

Kennedy defeated Richard M. Nixon in the 1960 election. His moving inauguration address inspired Capa to develop a photo project to cover Kennedy's first one hundred days in office. He worked with nine other Magnum agency photographers. The project resulted in a book, *Let*

Us Begin: The First One Hundred Days of the Kennedy Administration. In the process, Capa became well acquainted with John and Jacqueline Kennedy. More than a decade later, Jacqueline Kennedy Onassis became one of the first trustees of the International Center of Photography, the archival organization that Capa founded.

Capa's Kennedy photographs pioneered political photojournalism. Wrote Stewart Kampel in *Encyclopaedia Judaica*: "[Capa and the Magnum photographers] developed a repertory of scenes: the candidate on the hustings, chin jutting over microphones; the sober chief conferring with his advisers; the burdened leader turning his shoulders to the camera for a moment of private contemplation."

Disavowed the "Artist" Label

Such images became staples of political coverage. Capa's work was considered revealing as well as artistic. Despite the outstanding quality of his pictures, however, Capa never considered himself an artist. He stated his case in the introduction of the 1992 book *Cornell Capa: Photographs.* "I am not an artist, and I never intended to be one," he wrote. "I hope I have made some good photographs, but what I really hope is that I have done some good photo stories with memorable images that make a point, and, perhaps, even make a difference."

Capa later came up with the phrase "concerned photographer" (the title of his 1968 book) that better defined his perceived purpose. A "concerned photographer," he described (as quoted by the *New York Times*), is one "who is passionately dedicated to doing work that will contribute to the understanding or the well-being of humanity" and who produced "images in which genuine human feeling predominates over commercial cynicism or disinterested formalism."

The phrase proved an apt self-definition. Capa's work, particularly the photo stories created in international settings, demonstrated the values he described. As a *Life* photographer, Capa often traveled to Latin America, where he documented the tragic, methodical destruction of native cultures. His photographic study of the Amahuaca Indians of the Amazon resulted in a well-received 1964 book *Farewell to Eden.* Other books that came out of his Latin American travels included *The Savage My Kinsman* (1961) and *The Andean Republics* (1966).

He also visited Argentina to cover the regime of President Juan Perón. Capa not only covered the administration's oppression of its people, but he also documented the revolution that drove Perón into exile. According to historian Richard Whelan, Capa often quoted photographer Lewis Hine, whose example guided Capa's approach. "There are two things I wanted to do," Hine said (according to the *New York Times*). "I wanted to show the things that needed to be corrected. And I wanted to show the things that needed to be appreciated." This quote perfectly encapsulated Capa's South American photo projects.

Covered Israeli Conflicts

Even though he was not keen on covering war, Capa's Jewish heritage compelled him to photograph major Middle East conflicts. In 1967, he traveled to Israel to document the Six Day War. In 1973, on assignment for *The New York Times*, Capa covered the Yom Kippur war in Israel. It was during this assignment that he decided he would not cover war again. Capa accompanied Terrence Smith, the award-winning journalist who was then serving as the newspaper's Israel bureau chief. At one point, Smith remembered, the two men were pinned down in a roadside ditch between the Syrian artillery and the advancing Israeli army, with shells exploding all around. After making it back safely to their hotel rooms, Capa transmitted his photographs and Smith filed his story. At about 1 a.m., Smith recalled, Capa told his colleague that he had come to a tough decision. "I can't do this anymore," the fifty-five-year-old Capa told Smith (as quoted on *The Huffington Post* web site). "I am the last surviving male in my family. I can't put them through any more of this."

Became a Versatile Practitioner

During his association with *Life,* Capa, a versatile lensman, covered a variety of assignments. Some of his best work involved smaller scale, more intimate portraits. For instance, he photographed movie legends Clark Gable and Marilyn Monroe on the set of *The Misfits.* The 1961 film would be the last for both Gable and Monroe, a circumstance that ultimately made Capa's arresting images even more poignant and historically significant.

For another project, Capa photographed mentally retarded children being educated in New England. The three-year undertaking, which began in 1954, culminated in the 1957 publication of the book *Retarded Children Can be Helped.*

His other books included *Adlai Stevenson's Public Years* (1966), *Israel, the Reality* (1969), *Jerusalem, City of Mankind* (1974), *Margin of Life* (1974), *Master Photographs* (1990), and *JFK for President* (2004).

Founded International Center of Photography

Along with his considerable photographic achievements, Capa founded the International Center of Photography (ICP) in New York City. Established in 1974 and located on Fifth Avenue, the ICP became one the world's most influential photography institutions. It provides a history of photojournalism and is comprised of archives that preserve the works of past and present practitioners, as well as galleries, a library and a school.

Essentially Capa's monument to "concerned photography," the ICP makes available to the public the finest examples of humanitarian pictorial work. It also provided Capa a way to memorialize his brother and to honor the photojournalism legacy he helped foster. Capa once commented that after his brother's death, he was haunted by the question of what happens to photographers' life work. By establishing the ICP, he found a way to keep their work alive.

The ICP has presented hundreds of exhibitions and showcased the work of thousands of photographers. Capa's own work has been highlighted in exhibitions that included "Cornell Capa-Photographer" (1994) and "Capa & Capa:

Brothers in Photography" (1990). Capa has also been exhibited at the Metropolitan Museum of Art and the Jewish Museum in New York City.

Died in New York City

Later in life, Capa suffered from Parkinson's disease. In 1994, he stepped down as the ICP's director, a position he held since the institution's founding. Despite his affliction, he remained active within the institute as its Founding Director Emeritus.

Capa died on May 23, 2008 at his home in Manhattan, New York. He was ninety years old. His wife Edith had passed away in 2001. Capa commented that she deserved so much of the credit for his accomplishments. The couple had no children.

During his career, Capa received numerous awards including the Honor Award from the American Society of Magazine Photographers (1975), The New York City Mayor's Award of Honor for arts and culture (1978), Leica Medal of Excellence (1986), the Peace and Culture Award from Japan's Sokka Gakkai International (1990), France's Order of the Arts and Letters (1991), the Distinguished Career in Photography Award from the Friends of Photography (1995) and a Lifetime Achievement Award in Photography from the Aperture Foundation (1999). Also, in 1995, he became an honorary member of the American Society of Museum Photographers.

Along with the ICP, Capa also founded the Robert Capa/David Seymour Photographic Foundation in Israel (1958) and the Bischof/Capa/Seymour Memorial Fund in New York City (1966).

Books

Capa, Cornell, *The Concerned Photographer*, Grossman Publishers, 1968.

"Capa, Cornell," *Encyclopaedia Judaica*, Macmillan Reference USA, 2007.

"Cornell Capa," *Contemporary Photographers, Third Edition*, St. James Press, 1996.

Periodicals

Art in America, September 2008.

The Guardian, May 26, 2008.

The New York Times, May 24, 2008.

Online

"Capa, Cornell," *Peter Fetterman Gallery*, http://www.peterfetterman.com/htmls/artists_detail.cfm?artistid=18 (December 7, 2009).

"Cornell Capa," *Jewish Virtual Library*, http://www.jewishvirtuallibrary.org/jsource/biography/Capa.html (December 6, 2009).

"Cornell Capa," *Magnum Photos*, http://www.magnumphotos.com/Archive/ (December 6, 2009).

"True Courage: Cornell Capa," *The Huffington Post*, http://www.huffingtonpost.com/terence-smith/true-courage-cornell-capa_b_103804.html (December 6, 2009). □

Richard D'Oyly Carte

The British theatrical producer Richard D'Oyly Carte was the executive who brought to the stage the classic comic operas of Gilbert & Sullivan, the preeminent creators of comic opera and operetta in English.

When Carte died in 1901, his obituary in the *Times* of London called him "the second of the famous triumvirate who may be said not only to have created English comic opera, but to have made for it a name that will live long in our national musical history." More than simply a producer or impresario, Carte conceived the idea of an English school of comic opera and recruited the librettist and the composer who were jointly best equipped to make it a reality. The Savoy Theatre and the D'Oyly Carte Opera Company that Carte created both outlived him, and, in modified form and under different ownership, both survive today. Musically talented himself, Carte was a visionary who laid the groundwork for a new art form that profoundly influenced musical theater for a century or more.

Born into Music Business

Richard D'Oyly Carte was born in London's Soho district on May 3, 1844. His family was not noble but was prosperous and distinguished. Despite his French name, Carte's family background was English. His grandfather had fought in the Battle of Waterloo against Napoleon. His father, Richard Carte, was a skilled flutist and composed several pieces for the flute; he later became a partner in the musical instrument manufacturing firm of Rudall, Carte and Co. The family had cosmopolitan interests and established a rule that French should be spoken in the household for two nights a week. The younger Carte attended London's progressive University College School and enrolled at the University of London. But, "the claims of his father's firm taking precedence of 'higher education'" (in the words of the *Times*), Carte dropped out of the university and joined the family business.

For a time, Carte (who sometimes signed letters as Richard D'Oyly Carte but was generally addressed by his last name alone) thought that he might like to become a composer himself. He wrote several short operettas and managed to get them produced, beginning with *Doctor Ambrosias—His Secret* at St. George's Hall in 1868. In 1871 his short opera *Marie* became the first production to grace the stage of London's new Opera Comique theater. But none of these was a notable success, and Carte also addressed a good deal of his energy to his business career. Gradually separating himself from his father's business, he became a manager or agent for several celebrated figures. He managed the career of the star soprano Adelina Patti for a time, organized the farewell tour of the single-named tenor Mario in 1870, and represented the business affairs of the French composer Charles Gounod in England. He,

along with his second wife, Helen Lenoir, booked tours for poet Matthew Arnold and playwright Oscar Wilde.

Around 1869, Carte hatched the idea of creating a distinctively English form of comic opera. At the time, according to an observer quoted by Tony Joseph in *The D'Oyly Carte Opera Company: An Unofficial History,* comic opera was "an unsavoury compound of ribald buffoonery and sentimental twaddle." Worse, from a business point of view, it was dominated by French composers and those from other foreign countries. It is not known exactly what gave Carte the idea of trying to stimulate homegrown competition, but he would certainly have been aware of the long run of French operetta hits by composer Jacques Offenbach, many of which had been produced in London theaters. When Carte, in late 1871 or early 1872, saw *Thespis,* the initial (and now mostly lost) collaboration between satirical poet William Schwenk Gilbert and composer Arthur Sullivan, the details of his plan began to fill in.

Reunited Gilbert and Sullivan

In 1874 Carte published an announcement stating (as quoted by Joseph) that he hoped to establish "a permanent abode for light opera" in London, where the genre would enjoy "all the completeness and attention to detail which is recognised in the representations given at even mediocre Continental theatres." He spoke to Gilbert and Sullivan separately about undertaking a new collaboration. They disregarded the suggestion at first, but early in 1875, when

Carte was looking for a curtain-raiser for a production of Offenbach's *La Périchole* he was mounting at the Royalty Theatre, Gilbert visited Carte's London office with *Trial by Jury,* a one-act spoof of British courts, that he had expanded from an earlier comic poem. Carte suggested Sullivan as a composer, and Sullivan agreed.

When *Trial by Jury* opened on March 25, 1875, it was an immediate success. The buzz among theatergoers was that it had upstaged the main Offenbach attraction, and indeed its run continued after the Offenbach operetta had closed. Carte took the show on tour, combining the short operetta with productions of *La Périchole,* one of a few other French operas, or a short opera of his own entitled *Happy Hampstead.* He began to bill his production organization as Mr. R. D'Oyly Carte's Opera Bouffe Company. The name came in advance of any actual organization, but Carte was working on rounding up investors for a more permanent entity. By 1877 he had formed The Comedy-Opera Company (Limited) and was ready to produce the first surviving full-length Gilbert and Sullivan collaboration, *The Sorcerer,* at the Opera Comique.

The Sorcerer enjoyed a strong 175-night run, but the work that made Gilbert and Sullivan household names was the next Carte production, *H.M.S. Pinafore.* The opera ran for more than 700 performances in London and became an international smash, stimulating such demand in the United States that in some cities it was booked into more than one theater simultaneously. With growing success, however, came disagreements between Carte and his partners; these culminated in an unsuccessful attempt by the Comedy-Opera Company Board of Directors to seize the *H.M.S. Pinafore* sets on July 31, 1879. The following night the production continued under the auspices of Mr. D'Oyly Carte's Opera Company, later shortened to simply the D'Oyly Carte Opera Company.

Opened Theater with All-Electric Lighting

in 1881 Carte constructed a new theater on the famed London boulevard the Strand, to be used at first exclusively for the production of Gilbert and Sullivan operas. The theater was called the Savoy, which gave rise to the collective term of "Savoy operas" for Gilbert and Sullivan's works. It was the first theater in London to be lit entirely by electric bulbs. Carte continued to operate the Savoy Theatre for the rest of his life, and in 1889 he added the nearby Savoy Hotel for the convenience of theatergoers. Gilbert and Sullivan kept the hits coming through the 1880s, with comic operas such as *The Pirates of Penzance, Patience,* and especially *The Mikado* becoming so popular that they added to the lexicon of the English language. The *Times* observed that "[i]n all of these works the hand of the brilliant manager, Mr. Carte, is visible, and his share of the honours was as well won and as richly deserved as those of his colleagues."

The three-way partnership of Carte, Gilbert, and Sullivan saw occasional strains along the way. Gilbert, as quoted by Gayden Wren in *A Most Ingenious Paradox: The Art of Gilbert and Sullivan,* wrote to Sullivan in 1885, "I confess I don't feel very keen about Carte. He owes every penny he possesses to us. . . . When *we* manage the theatre for him he succeeds splendidly. When he manages for himself, he fails. Moreover, when he succeeds, he shows a disposition to kick away the ladder by which he has risen." During the Savoy production of *The Gondoliers* in 1889 and 1890, tensions boiled over in an incident commonly known as the Carpet Quarrel. Gilbert accused Carte of improperly deducting expenses, including one charge for some carpeting at the theater, before reckoning profits for the show to be divided among the three. Sullivan backed Carte, and the Gilbert and Sullivan partnership dissolved. The team reunited twice in the 1890s but never experienced another major success.

Observers at the time pointed out that the actual sums involved were small, and to some degree the quarrel was the result of tension between two creative artists who wanted to take on new challenges. This was especially true of Sullivan, who after a decade of writing comic operas wanted to compose a serious work to rival the grand operas of Italy, Germany, and France. Carte, who hoped to repeat his success in creating an English school of comic opera with an ongoing group of serious works, backed the idea. Carte financed a second theater, the Royal English Opera House, with Sullivan's grand opera *Ivanhoe* as the premiere attraction. The opera's run was reasonably successful, but Carte had no follow-up ready from the thin ranks of British dramatic composers. After productions of several French operas and a year-long rental of the theater to actress Sarah Bernhardt, Carte gave up on the project and sold the building. The Royal English Opera House eventually was repurposed as the Palace Hall of Varieties.

Carte continued to produce comic operas at the Savoy, many of them with music by Sullivan, through the 1890s. He bought several other valuable London properties, including the grand hotels Claridge's and the Berkeley, and most of his holdings remained in the possession of the Carte family until the late 20th century. Carte had two sons, one of whom became his assistant and eventually passed the family operations on to a granddaughter, Bridget D'Oyly Carte. Carte died of heart disease in London on April 3, 1901. The D'Oyly Carte Opera Company, now headquartered in the city of Birmingham, continues to operate, and the Savoy Theatre, redesigned in the 1920s and completely rebuilt after a 1990 fire, remains an anchor of London's West End theater district.

Books

Joseph, Tony, *The D'Oyly Carte Opera Company, 1875–1982: An Unofficial History,* Bunthorne Books, 1994.

Sadie, Stanley, ed., *The New Grove Dictionary of Music and Musicians,* 2nd ed., Macmillan, 2001.

Slonimsky, Nicolas, editor emeritus, *Baker's Biographical Dictionary of Musicians,* centennial ed., Schirmer, 2001.

Wren, Gayden, *A Most Ingenious Paradox: The Art of Gilbert and Sullivan,* Oxford, 2001.

Periodicals

Daily Telegraph (London, England), April 5, 2004.

New York Times, July 22, 1993.

Times (London, England), April 4, 1990 (reprint of Carte obituary, April 4, 1901).

Online

"Richard D'Oyly Carte," *Boise State University,* http://math.boisestate.edu/gas/whowaswho/C/CarteRichardD%27Oyly.htm (November 11, 2009).☐

Rosalynn Carter

Rosalynn Carter (born 1927), the wife of United States president Jimmy Carter, was the First Lady of the United States from 1977 to 1981. She substantially expanded the role of that office, and she has been noted for leadership roles on issues relating to mental health and for a wide range of humanitarian activities.

Carter was born Eleanor Rosalynn Smith on August 18, 1927 in Plains, Georgia. She has always used the name Rosalynn; reports that she was named after Eleanor Roosevelt, who was not nationally prominent at the time of her birth, are inaccurate. Rosalynn's father, Wilburn Edgar Smith, served on the Plains town council and worked as a bus driver, auto mechanic, and clerk. When Rosalynn was 13, he died of leukemia at age 44. Her mother, Allethea, known as Allie, was left in charge of Rosalynn, three siblings, and an elderly father. She worked at a large variety of jobs to support the family, and Rosalynn, who had to pitch in as a teen by taking a job in a beauty parlor, gained a lifelong work ethic. Even with her varied responsibilities, Rosalynn graduated as valedictorian from Plains High School in 1944. She went on for a degree at Georgia Southwestern College (now Georgia Southwestern State University) in nearby Americus and received a degree there in 1946.

Soon after that, on July 7, 1946, she married James Earl "Jimmy" Carter. The wedding took place at Rosalynn's Plains Methodist Church, but she later adopted her husband's Baptist faith. As youngsters the two had been familiar with each other but did not know each other well; Jimmy Carter was three years older than Rosalynn, and at first she mostly had fantasies about him, stirred by photos of him in his U.S. Navy uniform. They began dating in the summer of 1945 after they were introduced by Jimmy Carter's sister Ruth, a friend of Rosalynn's; their first "date" was an afternoon the three of them spent cleaning up the grounds of the Carter family home. Jimmy Carter proposed marriage in December of 1945 but was turned down on the grounds that it was too early in their relationship. Rosalynn accepted his second proposal the following February.

Rosalynn, rooted in Plains, moved frequently with her husband during the first years of their marriage as Navy postings took him from place to place; they lived in Norfolk, Virginia, Philadelphia, Pennsylvania, New London, Connecticut, Pearl Harbor, Hawaii, San Diego, California, and Provincetown, Massachusetts. They quickly started a family, and sons Jack (born 1947), Chip (born 1950), and Jeff (born 1952) became mostly Rosalynn's responsibility.

"Jimmy was gone much of the time, and I had to take care of everything. It was very scary. But it taught me that I could do what I had to do," she explained to *People.*

Learned Peanut Farming Business

The family's move back to Plains in 1953—so that Jimmy Carter could take over his family's peanut farming business after his father's death—was not exactly to Rosalynn's liking, and things got even worse after drought conditions in their first year limited their earnings to $200 and forced the young family to move into public housing. But Rosalynn threw herself into the business, essentially serving as an unsalaried financial manager, and the Carters began to prosper. As Jimmy Carter's influence in the community grew, so did his political ambitions. He ran for and won a seat on the Sumter County school board in 1955, and in 1961 he was elected to the Georgia state senate. In 1966 he lost a complex three-way race for governor.

It was in that race that the pattern of Rosalynn's participation in her husband's campaign was set. She was a natural campaigner well suited to the task of introducing her rather bookish husband to wider audiences, and she would make cold calls on local journalists offering herself for interviews. The resultant exposure for Jimmy Carter in the 1966 campaign paid off as he was elected governor of Georgia in 1970. The Carters' political coming-of-age occurred during the height of the struggles over racial desegregation that were occurring across the South, and

their relatively liberal views sometimes caused them trouble in their small, conservative hometown. Campaigning in Georgia could be a rough-and-tumble experience as well. During the 1966 race, Carter handed a brochure to a man standing outside a shoe store and asked him to vote for her husband. "He was chewing tobacco, and it was drooling down his beard of several days' growth," Carter recalled in her autobiography, *First Lady from Plains.* "'I'm for Bo Callaway, lady,' he said. Then he spat on me."

During her husband's term as Georgia governor, Rosalynn Carter began to use her position to advance the cause of mental health reform. She had become interested in the issue as a youngster, when she was exposed to a developmentally disabled individual, and as she traveled the state campaigning she resolved to improve the way Georgia treated its mentally ill citizens. She served on the Governor's Commission to Improve Services to the Mentally and Emotionally Handicapped and volunteered at an Atlanta hospital. When Jimmy Carter launched his seemingly quixotic bid for the presidency in 1975, Rosalynn repeated her role as media advance woman. Her pledge to focus on mental health issues as First Lady played a role in the 1976 campaign, for it differed from the largely ceremonial status assumed by most presidents' wives up to that point, and her contributions overall were significant in helping her husband to his surprise victory in 1976. The populist flavor of the inauguration ceremonies the following January, in which the Carters walked together down Pennsylvania Avenue to the White House, was also partly Rosalynn's doing.

As First Lady, Carter continued her involvement with mental health issues and broadened her reach into other areas. Her influence on administration policies began even before President Carter's inauguration, when she reportedly convinced the President-elect to include mention of American families in his inaugural address. She often attended cabinet meetings, becoming the first presidential spouse to do so. Serving as Active Honorary Chair of the President's Commission on Mental Health, she helped to develop an advisory board and 30 task forces that worked toward a broad-based overhaul of federal support for the mentally ill. Her work culminated in the passage of the Mental Health Systems Act by the U.S. Congress in 1980. Aspects of that measure were rolled back by the subsequent administration of President Ronald Reagan, but she was also responsible for grants that generated further research into mental illness, and her open discussion of the subject was credited by Presidential historian Douglas Brinkley with helping to destigmatize mental illness.

Learned Spanish, Conducted Negotiations

Carter also formed a task force to evaluate federal programs for senior citizens and presided over the White House Conference on Aging. She was active in lobbying Congress in favor of measures designed to reduce workplace age discrimination, funding increases for senior services and clinics, and Social Security reform. Carter had an unusually active travel schedule as First Lady, acting as the president's personal representative on trips to countries across South America and the Caribbean, and often holding substantive discussions with leaders there in Spanish, a language she learned in an intensive course. Perhaps the most moving experience for Carter personally during her tenure as First Lady was a 1979 trip to Cambodia to learn more about the refugee crisis engendered by the mass slaughter carried out by that country's totalitarian government. Carter established a Cambodian Crisis Center that served as a clearinghouse for refugee aid, and she persuaded President Carter to increase U.S. immigration quotas for Cambodian refugees. Historian Carl Sferrazza Anthony told *People* that Carter's visits to refugee camps were a "horrific experience. There was tent after tent filled with sick and dying refugees." Her trip, he said, "wasn't sexy. It was the old-fashioned idea of touching people one by one."

After Jimmy Carter's loss to Ronald Reagan in the 1980 presidential election, the Carters found themselves in debt. They sold their peanut business and quickly got back on their feet by writing books that became strong sellers. Rosalynn Carter's *First Lady from Plains*, published by Houghton Mifflin in 1984, was written without the aid of a ghostwriter. She has published three other books: *Everything to Gain: Making the Most of the Rest of Your Life* (1987), *Helping Yourself Help Others: A Book for Caregivers* (1994), and *Helping Someone with Mental Illness: A Compassionate Guide for Family, Friends, and Caregivers* (1998). The last two were written with Susan K. Golant.

Perhaps the bulk of her energies were devoted to the operation of the Carter Center in Atlanta, which she and Jimmy Carter co-founded in 1982 and which by the 2000s had a staff of 150. An equal partner with the former president in the center's activities, she has served as chair of its mental health task force and has traveled around the world on missions ranging from campaigns to eradicate guinea worm disease to monitoring elections abroad. She has accompanied Jimmy Carter during peace negotiations in international hot spots including Bosnia, North Korea, and Ethiopia. Closer to home, she has served on the board of directors of the Rosalynn Carter Institute for Caregiving at Georgia Southwestern State University.

Rosalynn Carter and her husband remained in the news in the 2000s. In 2001 they cut their ties with the Southern Baptist Convention over its new prohibition against women serving as pastors and its statement that wives should be submissive to their husbands. The decision did not affect their membership in the Maranatha Baptist Church in Plains; Baptist churches (and individual believers) are autonomous and are not bound by the positions of the national convention. Rosalynn Carter was named to the National Women's Hall of Fame that year, becoming only the third First Lady so honored. Among her other awards are the Presidential Medal of Freedom and the Volunteer of the Decade Award from the National Mental Health Association. The two Carters were jointly given the 2009 American Peace Award, on which occasion Jimmy Carter said (according to the award committee's web site), "There's very seldom a decision that I make that I don't discuss with her, either to tell her after the fact what I've done, or very frequently, to tell her my options and seek her advice." The Carters continued to live in their hometown of Plains.

Books

Carter, Rosalynn, *First Lady from Plains*, Houghton Mifflin, 1984.

Periodicals

People, June 12, 2000.

U.S. Catholic, January 2001.

Online

"Eleanor Rosalynn Smith Carter," *National First Ladies' Library*, http://www.firstladies.org/biographies/firstladies.aspx?biography=40 (January 3, 2010).

"Jimmy and Rosalynn Carter," *The American Peace Award*, http://americanpeaceaward.org/recipient09.html (January 3, 2010).

"Rosalynn Carter," *New Georgia Encyclopedia*, http://www.georgiaencyclopedia.org (January 3, 2010).

"Rosalynn Carter—Biography of the Former First Lady of the United States," *The Carter Center*, http://www. cartercenter.org/news/experts/rosalynn_carter.html (January 3, 2010).□

Rosemary Casals

Growing up, American tennis champ Rosie Casals (born 1948) never trained with a professional coach, but instead learned the game through pickup matches on the public courts around her hometown of San Francisco. By the age of 16, Casals was ranked among the top five female singles players in the United States. She went on to win eleven professional singles titles and 112 doubles titles, making her mark with doubles partner and tennis whiz Billie Jean King. A fiery player-turned-activist, Casals spent her career fighting for equal pay and opportunities for female tennis players.

Rosie Casals was born September 16, 1948, in San Francisco to El Salvadorian immigrants. She was the great-niece of the famed Spanish cellist Pablo Casals. Once in the United States, Casals' immigrant parents struggled to earn a living and find their way. They gave custody of Casals and her older sister, Victoria, to their great aunt and great uncle, Maria and Manuel Casals, who raised them as their daughters. A talented soccer star who played for El Salvador's national team, Manuel Casals moved to the United States in his twenties and played soccer until a broken leg forced him to retire from the game. Manuel Casals enjoyed the thrill of competition too much to completely leave the sports world behind so he took up tennis to fill the void, figuring it would be easier on his leg. To help pay the bills, he ran a small vending machine business.

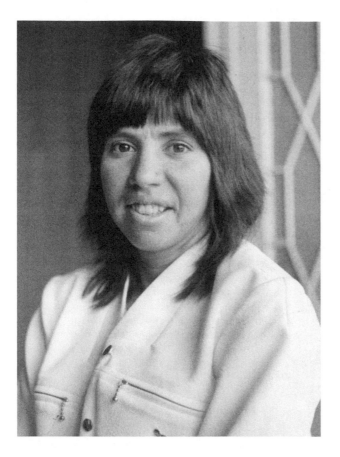

Took Up Tennis at Age Eight

As Manuel Casals developed his game of tennis, he began to take Casals and her sister with him to the tennis courts at San Francisco's Golden Gate Park. At first the girls were mere spectators but Casals insisted on playing and her great uncle finally gave in. Just eight, Casals took to the sport and enjoyed whacking the ball around with her great uncle for hours on end. She gave up piano and took to hitting tennis balls in her free time. As Casals improved, her great uncle lined up male opponents for matches. Casals played singles and doubles and mixed. It was during these friendly matches that Casals developed her scrappy style of play.

As Casals developed her skills, her great uncle continued to coach her. While Manuel Casals was no expert in the finer mechanics of the game, he was an athlete who understood sports psychology and encouraged Casals' court intelligence. "Good manners are important," he told *Sports Illustrated* in a 1966 profile on Casals. "And all the top-ranked players, they get to talking to themselves. I tell Rosie that's no good. When you start talking to yourself you can't concentrate. Your brain has got to be free."

Developed Scrappy, Scrambling Style

As a preteen, Casals began playing in junior tournaments, preferring to face opponents who were older. Early on, she stood out for her aggressive style and penchant for charging the net. Casals surprised opponents with her biting forehand and surprising quickness, which gave her the ability to cover the far corners of the court. She lacked the formal training of her opponents so she improvised a lot. Aside from her love of the game, Casals had little in common with her tennis-playing peers. Casals trained on public courts, coached by her great uncle, unlike many of her opponents who trained at country clubs with private coaches. When Casals was ten, she had to sleep in the family's late model Studebaker at one competition because the tournament's sponsors failed to provide rooms and her family could not afford a hotel. "It was a rude awakening," Casals told *People*. "The other kids had nice tennis clothes, nice rackets, nice white shoes and came in Cadillacs. I felt stigmatized because we were poor."

As a teenager, Casals was ranked number one in both the junior and women's divisions in Northern California. In 1964, at the age of 16, she cracked the top five ranking for U.S. female tennis players and stayed there for eleven years. Casals graduated from San Francisco's George Washington High School in June 1966 and intended to go to medical school but her tennis career took off and she never looked back. Casals surpassed expectations. At five-foot-two and weighing just 114 pounds, Casals was among the smallest female tennis players of her day. What she lacked in size, she made up for with spunk and gained fans for her entertaining, creative style of play. When opponents placed balls out of the reach of her racquet, Casals chased them down with her quick speed. She charged the net from every angle and blasted the ball with every scrambling shot. Casals pulled off tippy-toe volleys and behind-the-back shots. She was even known to loop the ball around the net post.

During the mid-1960s, Casals began to beat the more-seasoned players. She even knocked King out of tournaments. When Casals beat King at the Eastern grass-court championships in July 1966, *New York Times* reporter Allison Danzig paid tribute to Casals, noting that she beat King because she attacked "relentlessly with utter disdain for temporizing. Whacking her service, hitting her solid forehand with topspin, undercutting her backhand and bringing off dexterous low backhand volleys with sidespin, the little Californian challenges with every swing of her racquet."

Nonetheless, Casals and King became friends and joined forces, becoming one of the most formidable female doubles teams of all time. Through the mid-1960s and '70s, the tandem pair of Casals and King dominated the world of doubles. In 1966, they won the doubles title at the U.S. hard-court and indoor championships. In 1967, they won the women's doubles title at Wimbledon, as well as the U.S. Championships (now the U.S. Open) and the South African championships. They defended their Wimbledon title in 1968 and won again in 1970, '71 and '73. Casals also played mixed doubles. In 1970 and '72, Casals teamed with Romanian tennis star Ilie Năstase to win the mixed doubles title at Wimbledon.

Fought for Women's Equality On Court

As Casals' game improved, so did her dissatisfaction with women's place in the sport. During the late 1960s and early '70s, male tennis players received more prize money and more media attention than their female counterparts. Whenever there was a tournament, the women were often treated as sideshow entertainment. In some events, men out earned the women by a ratio of 10-to-1. In 1970, Casals was one of several female tennis players who rebelled against the unequal pay structure of the male-dominated United States Lawn Tennis Association—now known as the U.S. Tennis Association (USTA)—which governed the sport.

In 1970, Casals and eight other women boycotted the Pacific Southwest championships because it paid men $12,500 for first prize, while the female winner received $1,500. Casals believed women should be able to make a living playing tennis. She raged about the discrepancies to a *Time* magazine reporter in 1970. "We expend the same amount of energy as the men," she said, in arguing for equal pay. "We practice as much. We play just as hard. We contribute our share to the success of a tournament." Men's tennis star Arthur Ashe provided a counterpoint by noting that the men who play tennis "have families, and they don't want to give up money just for girls to play. Only three or four women draw fans anyhow, so why do we have to split our money with them?"

Tensions continued to mount and in 1970 Casals, King and seven other female players signed $1 contracts to participate in the first professional women-only tournament and tour organized by *World Tennis* magazine publisher Gladys Heldman. Heldman, a tennis buff, persuaded Phillip Morris CEO Joe Cullman to sponsor a series of professional women's tennis events—this became known as the Virginia Slims, the first women's professional tennis circuit. In 1970, Casals won the inaugural Virginia Slims tournament, which was held in Houston, earning $1,600. This was more than she was used to winning. In her entire first year of touring, Casals collected only $4,000. In 1970, Casals earned her career high ranking, coming in at number three.

The first full year of the Virginia Slims tour was 1971. That year, the tour hit seven cities. The women played their hearts out, touring the country and promoting their sport hoping for a brighter future with bigger sponsors and better, more equitable pay. Speaking to ESPN.com, Casals noted that the timing was right for female tennis players to make their move. "The women's movement was getting attention then. So why not us? We didn't just play. This was a fight for what we believed was right. You get militant; you have to fight a bit. We promoted, we put on clinics, we talked nonstop with media. It was like a circus." The women who participated in the Slims tour were temporarily suspended by the USTA, but they did not care. Slowly, things began to change. The Embassy Tournament in Wembley, England, raised the payout for the female champ from $2,000 to $10,000.

Another illustrious moment in Casals' career came in 1972 during Wimbledon. Held in England, Wimbledon is one of the most prestigious tennis tournaments in the world. When Casals came on court for her semi-final match against King, she was wearing a stylish tennis dress made by British fashion designer and tennis star Ted Tinling. The dress was mostly white, complying with Wimbledon's rules, but it also had some purple squiggles that read "VS" for Virginia Slims. The referee kicked her off the court and insisted she change. Later in life, Casals liked to joke that the dress made it to the Tennis Hall of Fame before she did.

Continued Winning Streak Into Late 30s

For Casals, 1973 was a good year. She beat King and U.S. tennis pro Nancy Richey on her way to winning the Family Circle Cup, a singles event that paid $30,000. It was the largest sum to date paid to a woman for winning a tennis event. Casals used her earnings to purchase a home in Sausalito, California. Casals and King combined for another Wimbledon doubles title that year, too. Off the court, Casals made a slam with her colorful television commentary during King's infamous 1973 matchup against male tennis champ Bobby Riggs, who challenged King to a match, boasting there was no way a woman could beat him. The match, which came to be known as the "Battle of the Sexes," took place in September 1973. During the match, Casals stood alongside ABC's Howard Cosell, adding commentary as King went on to win 6-4, 6-3, 6-3 before a prime time television audience. King's win helped increase recognition and respect for women's tennis.

In 1978, Casals underwent knee surgery, which slowed down her game, especially as a singles player. After having her knee worked on, Casals struggled in singles tennis, only making the finals one more time; however, she continued to play doubles effectively into the 1980s. In 1982, Casals teamed with Australian Wendy Turnbull to win the U.S. Open doubles title. In 1988, she hooked up with Czechoslovakian tennis phenom Martina Navratilova to win the Virginia Slims doubles title. Casals was 39, making her the second-oldest player to win a pro event. In 1990, Casals and King won the U.S. Open Seniors women's doubles championship. As a duo, their partnership was unmatched. No other tennis duo has won U.S. titles on grass, clay, indoor and hard surfaces.

Over the course of her career, Casals made it to at least the quarterfinals in every Grand Slam event, including the Australian Open, the French Open, the U.S. Open, and Wimbledon. Her 112 career doubles titles are second only to Navratilova. In 1996, she was inducted into the International Tennis Hall of Fame. Even after she quit playing, Casals worked as an ambassador for the sport promoting tennis and speaking with young girls, hoping to inspire the next generation of female athletes.

Periodicals

Daily News of Los Angeles, July 13, 1996.

Newsweek, January 2, 1967.

New York Times, July 28, 1966; September 9, 1970.

People, May 31, 1982.

Sports Illustrated, October 24, 1966.

Time, December 7, 1970.

Online

"Casals Far More Than King's Sidekick," ESPN.com, http://sports.espn.go.com/espn/womenshistory2009/news/story?page=Rosie casals (January 2, 2010).

"Rosie Casals," Sony Ericsson WTA Tour, http://www.sonyericssonwtatour.com/player/rosie-casals_2257889_1195 (January 2, 2010).

"Rosie (Rosemary) Casals," International Tennis Hall of Fame, http://www.tennisfame.com/ (January 2, 2010). □

Aimé Césaire

The Martinican writer and political leader Aimé Césaire (1913–2008) was among the most important cultural figures to emerge from the Caribbean region in the 20th century.

Césaire's activities extended into many different spheres, both literary and non-literary. He wrote poetry, drama, history, polemics, and political theory, taught school, and helped reshape the political status of the French colony where he was born and raised. He was among the black intellectuals from the French colonial world who advanced the idea of *négritude*, a common identity among Africans and African-descended peoples that manifested itself in cultural and political life. Césaire, in fact, coined the term "Négritude" in one of his most famous works, "Cahier d'un retour au pays natal" (translated as "Return to My Native Country"). What tied all his varied endeavors together was a lifelong resistance to colonialism and an attempt to use language to define his own identity and those of other French speakers of African descent.

Education Enhanced by Move to Capital

One of six children, Aimé Fernand David Césaire was born in the small town of Basse-Pointe, on the north side of the island of Martinique, then a French colony, on June 26, 1913. In "Cahier d'un retour au pays natal" Césaire wrote of 'the bed of planks' from which my race has risen," but the family qualified as middle-class; Césaire's father was a tax collector and sugar plantation manager, and his mother was a dressmaker. In the words of Robin D.G. Kelley, writing in the online magazine *Lip*, Césaire "lived close to the edge of rural poverty." He excelled in school, and his parents moved to the Martinican capital of Fort-de-France so that he could attend the elite Lycée Schoelcher.

By the time he graduated in 1931, Césaire was considered gifted enough to travel to France itself to continue his education. Studying at the Ecole Normale Supérieure, a top education school in Paris, he met other young intellectuals from around France's colonial empire. Among them was the future president of Senegal, Léopold Senghor. Césaire and his friends, while studying for the demanding exams of the French university system, founded a magazine called *L'étudiant noir* (The Black Student) and read whatever they could find about Africa, educating themselves to see its culture positively and questioning the views of European supremacy that they encountered in their schooling. It was in an essay in *L'étudiant noir* that Césaire first coined the word "Négritude."

After passing his exams in 1935, Césaire and a friend went on a short trip to the coast of Yugoslavia. Césaire spotted an island off the coast and began to think of Martinique. Told that the name of the island was Martinska, he took it as a sign and began writing a somewhat surrealistic poem about his homeland. The poem grew into "Cahier d'un retour au pays natal," which was published in 1939 in a small Paris journal called *Volontés*. At the time it was ignored. Césaire had married fellow student (and *L'étudiant noir* editor) Suzanne Roussy (or Roussi) in 1937, and two years later the pair returned to Martinique. The couple raised six children before the marriage broke up.

Impressed by Visit to Haiti

Césaire took a job teaching at his old high school, the Lycée Schoelcher. The revolutionary Afro-French psychiatrist Frantz Fanon, whose book *Black Skin, White Masks* would later draw inspiration from Césaire's anticolonialist writings, and the Martinican writer Edouard Glissant were among his students. The experience of living in Martinique during World War II, when the fascist Vichy government of France temporarily took control of the island, made a deep impression on Césaire, who joined the resistance-oriented French Communist Party. The war left Martinique's inhabitants surrounded by rings of hostile white forces after the United States Navy imposed a blockade on the island. Césaire's new magazine *Tropiques,* founded in 1941, had to adopt the guise of a folklore journal to evade government censorship. In 1944 Césaire slipped out of Martinique and visited Haiti, studying its history and its experience of throwing off French rule in the 19th century. Reportedly he had suffered from a speech impediment, a stammer, up to that time, but it disappeared during that trip.

In 1945, Césaire was elected mayor of Martinique's capital, Fort-de-France. He would hold that position, with only a short interruption, until 2001, and his accomplishments in the post–World War II era helped to shape the map of the Caribbean region as it still exists today. Although his own writings focused on a rejection of European cultural influences, Césaire as a politician pursued a more moderate course. He spearheaded legislation that ended Martinique's colonial status and made Martinique and three other French colonies—Guadeloupe, French Guiana, and Réunion island in the Indian Ocean—into full-fledged *départements* of the French government. After approving the change in a 1946 referendum, Martinicans became French citizens with full legal rights, and Césaire himself was elected one of the island's new deputies in France's national assembly. Among Martinicans themselves, Césaire is best remembered as a political leader.

At the same time, Césaire's literary career was taking off. The French surrealist writer André Breton, on a visit to Martinique in 1941, found a copy of the "Cahier d'un retour au pays natal" in a tailor's shop and began to champion Césaire as a writer who used surrealism in a new and unexpectedly political way. In the late 1940s and early 1950s Césaire wrote other long surrealist poems, treating such themes as slavery and oppression as well as describing natural environments in a way that owed little to poetic traditions. Some of his writings used the image of Martinique's Mount Pelée, a volcano near which Césaire grew up, as a symbol for his own personality and of the experience of African-descended peoples. Volumes of poetry such as *Soleil cou coupé* (literally, "The Sun's Throat Cut," 1948, translated as *Beheaded Sun*), or *Corps perdu* (1950, translated as *Disembodied*) gained Césaire a wide readership in France and beyond.

Became Disillusioned with Communism

In 1955 Césaire published his most famous nonfiction work, *Discours sur le colonialisme,* which included a comparison of the psychological effects of colonialism on its victims with that of Germany's Nazi regime on German citizens: both sets of victims hid gruesome truths from themselves. The book put Césaire somewhat at odds with orthodox Communists, who believed that the universal class struggle was more important than racial or cultural issues. Disillusioned by the Soviet Union's invasion of Hungary in 1956, Césaire left the French Communist Party, explaining his decision in a short book called *Lettre à Maurice Thorez* (Letter to Maurice Thorez). "It is true that, like so many of my contemporaries, I believed in what turned out to be a false Utopia," Césaire admitted to

Annick Thebia Melsan of the *UNESCO Courier.* "I am not at all ashamed about this. In the postwar context it expressed a heartfelt enthusiasm, a spiritual yearning." In 1958 he founded the leftist but non-Communist Martinican Progressive Party, which remains a major force in the island's politics.

Wrote Historical Dramas

Césaire did take to heart one claim of his former Communist associates, who had maintained that the difficult language of his surrealist works was unsuitable to mass art. In the 1960s he turned to the more accessible form of historical drama. His 1963 play *La tragédie du roi Christophe* (The Tragedy of King Christophe) dealt with a precursor to Haiti's 1963 revolution, while *Une saison au Congo* (A Season in the Congo, 1966) was concerned with the problems faced by Africa's newly independent countries and specifically with the assassination of Congolese leader Patrice Lumumba. Césaire's statements about Africa in the post-colonial era were often prophetic in identifying the devolution of political life in parts of the continent. The third of Césaire's trilogy of 1960s plays was *Une tempête* (A Tempest, 1968), an adaptation of Shakespeare's *The Tempest* in which the relationship between Prospero and Caliban on the play's tropical island is recast as a struggle between colonizer and colonized.

Césaire's works exerted a strong influence on black-power advocates in the 1960s and 1970s, but in his later years he found himself criticized by more radical younger figures. For example, younger Martinican writers believed that Césaire's use of the French language rather than the island's Martinican Creole variant marked him as a writer who assimilated himself to colonial influences. Césaire was unapologetic, telling Meslan that "the language I used was the language I had learned at school. That didn't bother me in the slightest; it didn't in any way come between me and my existential rebellion and the outpouring of my innermost being. I bent the French language to my purposes. Nature and history have placed us at the crossroads of two worlds, of two cultures if not more."

In his later years Césaire received various honors including designation as Commander of the Order of Merit by the West African nation Côte d'Ivoire. He lived to see the "Cahier d'un retour au pays natal" become part of the first-year French curriculum of Oxford University in England, and his home in Fort-de-France was often visited by French-speaking writers and intellectuals. By the time he died in Fort-de-France on April 17, 2008, at the age of 94, his work was the subject of numerous studies in both French and English.

Books

Arnold, A. James, *Modernism and Negritude: The Poetry and Poetics of Aimé Césaire,* Harvard, 1981.

Periodicals

Guardian (London, England), April 21, 2008.
Independent (London, England), April 19, 2008.
Times (London, England), April 18, 2009.
UNESCO Courier, May 1997.

Online

"Aimé Césaire (1913–2008)," *Books and Writers,* http://www.kirjasto.sci.fi/cesaire.htm (January 2, 2010).

"Aimé Césaire," *Contemporary Authors Online,* reproduced in *Biography Resource Center,* Farmington Hills, Mich.: Gale, 2010. http://galenet.galegroup.com/servlet/BioRC (January 2, 2010).

Kelley, Robin D.G., *Poetry & the Political Imagination: Aimé Césaire, Negritude, & the Applications of Surrealism, Lip,* http://www.lipmagazine.org/articles/featkelley_116.shtml (January 2, 2010).□

Leonard Chess

The Polish-born American recording company owner Leonard Chess (1917–1969), together with his brother Phil, founded Chess Records in Chicago in 1950. The label was of immense importance in the development of the urban blues and rock and roll music genres.

Chess was not a musician, and when he got into the music business he had little experience with music in general, much less that of the African American blues musicians, newly arrived in Chicago, whom he made into stars. He was a scrappy entrepreneur, looking for a break in a rough-and-tumble urban environment, just like thousands of other immigrant Jewish business entrepreneurs active in all kinds of businesses in American urban areas. Chess stood out for a variety of reasons, however. He worked hard, touring the United States ceaselessly to promote Chess releases as the company gained traction. He got along with the musicians he hired and often, through hands-on involvement in the recording process, drew from them their best performances. He was also in the right place at the right time—in a large city, in the central U.S., just as the great migration of Southern African Americans northward reached its peak and their music became the music of all America and much of the world.

Family Left Poland for Chicago

Leonard Chess was born Lejzor Czyz in Motele, Poland (also known as Motol or Motoul and now located in Belarus) in 1917; the exact date was not known, but his family observed his birthday on March 12. Motele, a village or *shtetl* typical of Jewish Eastern Europe, was also home to Chaim Weizmann, Israel's first president; it was almost completely destroyed by German troops in World War II. By that time, the Czyz family was long gone; shoemaker Yasef Czyz and his wife Cyrla settled on Chicago's South Side in 1922. Lejzor, the second of three surviving children, spoke Yiddish as his first language but was young enough that he adapted quickly to English; the family name was changed to Chess, and the children picked their own American names. Lejzor became Leonard, and his younger brother Fiszel became Phil Chess.

Leonard Chess spent much of his life living and working in the heart of Chicago's now solidly African American South Side. He worked in a shoe store as a teen and helped out at the family business, the Wabash Junk Shop on South State Street, later renamed Chess & Sons. He married Revetta Sloan in 1941, and the couple's son Marshall would become involved in many of the Chess label's operations. As a young man Leonard Chess acquired several failing small businesses in succession: Cut-Rate Liquor on South State, the 708 Liquor Store, and then, at 3905 South Cottage Grove Avenue, the Congress Buffet, which he renamed the Macomba Lounge. Chess took over ownership in 1946, just as the area was becoming a nightlife magnet for African Americans who had arrived to work in Chicago's booming factories.

At first Chess booked jazz saxophonists and crooner vocalists into the Macomba, and in 1947, encouraged by the success of the small record labels that were springing up around the country, he formed Aristocrat Records. The label's first artists were the same ones who performed at the Macomba; one was vocalist Andrew Tibbs (Melvyn Andrew Grayson), who had some success with a witty single, "Union Man Blues," a breakup song in which the vocalist asserted his right as a union member not to suffer bad treatment from his girlfriend. The label started slowly, but Chess's father had faith in the business and kept it afloat with repeated $10,000 cash infusions, and Phil Chess signed on to manage the company's business end. Finally Aristocrat struck gold in April of 1948 with a session devoted to its new blues vocalist and guitarist McKinley Morganfield, known as Muddy Waters.

Puzzled by Waters's Music

Chess did not immediately grasp the appeal of Waters's deep Southern blues sound, now transferred with explosive effect to the urban milieu of electric instruments. He had given scant attention to an earlier Waters recording session, in February, and then, as Waters launched into the heavily accented vocals of his classic "I Can't Be Satisfied," he was confused. "What's he saying? What's he saying?" Chess asked (according to biographer Nadine Cohodas). "Who's going to buy that?" But talent scout Evelyn Goldberg realized the music's appeal, and by 1949 Aristocrat releases were winning frequent mention in *Billboard* magazine's weekly roundups of singles in the rhythm-and-blues field.

Aristocrat prospered while other small labels failed not only because of its growing talent pool but because of Leonard Chess's efforts as a salesman. "A tireless promoter, he was constantly on the road, cementing his relationships with distributors, meeting disc jockeys, and learning more each time about the business itself," noted Cohodas. Chess often traveled to the South, especially the key blues city of Memphis, and he grew to know the juke joints and clubs where blues music flourished. On one trip to Memphis, distributor Buster Williams suggested that the Aristocrat label's name be changed to Chess, which was easy to remember and offered instant ideas for graphic designers. Leonard Chess agreed, and for the first release under the new name, saxophonist Gene Ammons's "My Foolish Heart," he used the record number 1425—the street address of the Chess family's first home in Chicago, at 1425 South Karlov Avenue.

Chess's Southern trips also helped him attract other bluesmen to Chess, and the label began to dominate the blues market in Chicago and beyond. The musicians who defined Chicago blues, including Howlin' Wolf and the blues harmonica powerhouse Little Walter, signed with Chess or its new subsidiary Checker (inaugurated in 1952), in the early 1950s. Chess also struck up a distribution deal with the new Memphis independent Sun Records and in 1951 issued Jackie Brenston's "Rocket 88," considered one of the first rock and roll records. Record keeping at the company was haphazard for its first several years, and Chess did not incorporate until 1952. Sometimes artists like Willie Mabon, who had an often-covered hit with "I Don't Know" in 1951, questioned Chess about royalty payments.

Participated in Influential Diddley Recording Session

Another rock and roll pioneer who came to prominence at Chess was Bo Diddley (Ellas McDaniel, born Ellis Otha Bates), who devised his stage name during rehearsals for his first recording session for Checker on March 2, 1955. According to Cohodas, Leonard Chess was closely involved in the making of the enormously influential single that came from that session, bearing the songs "Bo Diddley" backed with "I'm a Man." Chess provoked Diddley with rude, obscene orders, making the singer angry and contributing to the intensity that added much to the "I'm a Man" lyric. Chess, like other independent label owners of the period, was tight-fisted with his payments to artists, and he was not above engaging in so-called payola bribes to disc jockeys. But Diddley's complaints that other artists had succeeded by exploiting his characteristic "Bo Diddley beat" were echoed by Chess's own assertions later in life that white artists had traded in musical materials created by the African American artists Chess had nurtured.

Even more successful and influential among the stable of Chess artists was Chuck Berry, who was sent to Leonard Chess by Muddy Waters. Berry showed up at the Chess offices in May of 1955, asking to see Chess, and was asked to return with a demo tape. When he heard the tape, Leonard Chess heard potential in a country-flavored song, "Ida Red," which combined an old fiddle tune with several generations of country automobile chase songs. Wanting to avoid competition from the original "Ida Red" (probably the 1938 recording by Bob Wills & His Texas Playboys), Chess suggested the rhythmically similar title "Maybellene" after spotting a Maybelline cosmetics case on a windowsill. Intent on a certain sound, he insisted on 36 takes before wrapping up the session. Chess knew he had a hit on his hands and rushed to New York to hand-deliver a copy of the record to leading rock and roll disc jockey Allan Freed. For the rest of the 1950s Berry's recordings helped Chess prosper, and Leonard Chess and his family moved to a home in the luxurious north Chicago suburb of Glencoe, Illinois.

As rock music shifted away from the pure blues-based sounds of the late 1950s, the Chess label lost some of its dominance. But the Chess brothers continued to reap large profits as English rock bands discovered the sounds of classic American rhythm-and-blues, and covered many compositions copyrighted by Chess's publishing arm, Arc Music. The Rolling Stones recorded at Chess's new studios at 2120 South Michigan Avenue in 1964 (now home to Willie Dixon's Blues Heaven Foundation), and even recorded an instrumental song with that title as a tribute to the Chess label. The label continued to influence the blues genre, signing two powerful female vocalists, Etta James and Koko Taylor. Leonard and Phil Chess invested in the black-oriented radio station WVON, and in 1967 he took home a Man of the Year award from the Chicago Urban League in recognition of his efforts to employ African Americans.

The Chess brothers, wanting to focus on radio, sold Chess's music operations to the GRT label in 1969. Leonard Chess, who had suffered coronary problems, died of a massive heart attack a few months later on October 16, 1969. In 1987, the second year of the institution's existence, he was inducted into the Rock and Roll Hall of Fame in the Non-Performer category. Chess's life and personality, along with the label's musical history, were depicted in the 2009 film *Cadillac Records*, with Adrien Brody in the lead role of Leonard Chess.

Books

Cohodas, Nadine, *Spinning Blues into Gold: The Chess Brothers and the Legendary Chess Records,* St. Martin's, 2000.
Contemporary Musicians, volume 24, Gale, 1999.

Periodicals

Daily Telegraph (London, England), February 14, 2009.
Evening Chronicle (Newcastle, England), July 17, 2009.

Online

"Leonard Chess," *Rock and Roll Hall of Fame,* http://www.rockhall.com/inductee/leonard-chess (January 25, 2010). □

Swami Chinmayananda

The Indian spiritual leader known as Swami Chinmayananda (1916–1993) was one of the major modern interpreters and communicators of a strain of Hindu thought known as Vedanta, which is concerned with the self-realization of humans as they come to understand an ultimate reality.

Swami Chinmayananda was notable in several respects among the various Indian sages of the 20th century. He delivered his teachings in English, which enabled him to spread his philosophy in the West and particularly in the United States, where his ideas gained a foothold later in his life. He actively resisted Christian conversion activities in India and chided Indian immigrants in the U.S. for not paying enough attention to the religious traditions of their home country. And his presentation of ideas drawn from Hindu religion and philosophy was tailored equally to all groups in society; his publications ranged from annotations of ancient Hindu texts to books for children.

Attended English Schools

Swami Chinmayananda was born Balakrishnan Menon on May 8, 1916, in Ernakulam in the southern Indian region of Kerala. His parents, Kuttan and Parakutti Menon, were members of the local aristocracy. The family doted on young Balakrishnan, nicknamed Balan, and local religious figures claimed that he was destined for greatness. Menon's mother died when he was five, and his father remarried; his extended family, which valued both Indian traditions and British education, was also closely involved in his upbringing. He attended English schools and also became fluent in the southern Indian language of Malayalam and in Sanskrit, the language of the ancient Hindu scriptures.

As a child, Menon showed an inclination toward devotional practices. During family prayers, he would study a picture of the god Shiva. "Then I would shut my eyes to see whether I could see Him in my own mind, then open the eyes again and compare the picture. I would do that again and again, till I got it right to the smallest detail,

With practice I was able to picture Shankara with closed eyes, exactly as He was on the altar and later the picture would came readily as ordered" (as quoted in *Journey of the Master Swami Chinmayananda. The Man, The Path, The Teaching*). He gave little thought to a religious career, though, and enrolled at Maharaja's College in Ernakulam, at St. Thomas College in Trichur, and then, in 1940, Lucknow University, studying English literature and law. On one occasion he met Mahatma Gandhi during one of the independence leader's visits to Kerala.

Menon was a popular and active student who acted in plays, joined the debate club, and played on the tennis team. But the growth of serious Indian resistance to British rule in the early 1940s changed the direction of his life, He became involved in the struggle for Indian independence, giving speeches, distributing literature, and organizing labor unions. Sought by British troops, he spent a stretch in hiding and was finally arrested. Spending several months in prison in miserable conditions, he often saw his cellmates pass away, and it was during this period, according to Swamini Shivapriyanandaji, that he began to think more deeply about the meaning of human existence.

Saved by Passerby

Menon almost died himself—he contracted typhus in prison, and the prison's British commanding officer, fearful of inflating the institution's already high death toll, ordered him released. He was dumped beside a road and left for dead, but he was taken in by an Indian Christian woman who cared for him, she said, because his nose reminded her of that of her son, who was away on military service. Menon returned to the university, graduated, and took a reporting job with the *National Herald* newspaper in Delhi. Again he acquitted himself well and seemed headed for a prosperous career, but he was dissatisfied and felt that the lifestyles of the upper-class Indians among whom he was spending time were hollow and selfish. He began to think again of the devotional practices he had enjoyed as a child.

Menon renewed his spiritual quest, studying both Indian and Western philosophy. His studies led him to the holy city of Rishikesh, partly with the intention of writing a journalistic exposé on the city's leading guru, Swami Sivananda, the founder of both Sivananda Yoga and the Divine Life Society. He had first heard of the guru when he ran across an article about him in a magazine. Arriving in a skeptical frame of mind, Menon was fascinated by the swami, who in turn urged the young journalist to devote his life to spiritual pursuits. The transition was not instantaneous; he returned to Delhi and continued his journalistic work. But on February 25, 1949, Balakrishnan Menon became Swami Chinmayananda Saraswati; Chinmayananda meant "filled with the bliss of pure consciousness" ("Swami" is a title, meaning "owner of oneself" in Sanskrit). He would be known affectionately among his followers as Gurudev or Swamiji.

For several years he lived in the Himalaya mountains, studying the ancient scriptures of Hinduism—the Upanishads (which are the final sections of Vedas and which form the core of Vedanta teachings on consciousness), the Bhagavad Gita, and other writings. By 1951 he felt ready to begin his career as a religious leader, delivering talks he called *jnana yajna,* or Homage to Knowledge. But his teacher, Swami Tapovanam, told him that he was not ready, and that he should spend six months living as a homeless person in different parts of India, sleeping in temples or simply under trees. After he completed this tour, he was given permission to begin his *jnana yajna* on condition that at least four people showed up to hear his first talk. It so happened that exactly four came to the first one, held in Pune in November of 1951.

Swami Chinmayananda met resistance at first. Traditional Hindu teachers thought little of his folksy approach, punctuated with humor and short fables that anyone could understand. Nor did he make much headway among the Western-educated Indians with whom he had not so long ago identified; Indian elites in the early 1950s were looking toward modern statehood and the growth of industry, not toward rigorous religious teachings. Yet crowds at Swami Chinmayananda's lectures grew, and he declined to adopt a more opulent lifestyle as they did so. On being asked by a child where he lived, he answered (according to Swamini Shivapriyanandaji), "At the airports and the train stations." He moved around frequently, and until the end of his life, he seldom stayed in one place for more than a week.

Founded Educational Institutions

At his lectures, Swami Chinmayananda asked that listeners bring copies of the *Bhagavad Gita* and the Upanishads and be ready to join him in chanting their texts. He spoke in English, often in short parables designed to illustrate points of Vedantic philosophy, punctuated with humorous remarks in the local language. Swami Chinmayananda wrote some 82 books about various aspects of Hinduism. Like other Indian sages, he sponsored the construction of charitable institutions such as orphanages and hospitals as his organization grew. That organization became formalized under the name Chinmaya Mission in 1953. Swami Chinmayananda also founded two educational institutions in India for the propagation of his ideas, Sandeepany Sadhanalaya in Mumbai and Sandeepany Himalayas in Sidhbari, in the Himalaya mountains.

Swami Chinmayananda came to the U.S. for the first time in 1965, after which Chinmaya Mission opened branches in various American states. A U.S. counterpart to Sandeepany Sadhanalaya, Sandeepany West, opened in northern California. The movement's international growth was hampered by the departure of Swami Chinmayananda's protégé, Swami Dayananda, in 1982, but Swami Chinmayananda lectured at various U.S. universities and even appeared at the United Nations in 1992. He was more aggressive as a defender of Hinduism than other sages; when Pope John XXIII visited India in 1962, Indian Catholics announced a plan to gain 108 converts to Catholicism in every city he visited. Swami Chinmayananda responded with a campaign to attract 1,008 Christian-to-Hindu converts in each city. In America he urged Indian immigrants to reconnect with their spiritual heritage.

After suffering a heart attack in 1980 and undergoing quadruple bypass surgery, Swami Chinmayananda continued to travel and preach. He died from a second heart attack in San Diego, California, on August 3, 1993. His body was flown back to India, where it was transported with a military escort to his funeral, attended by a range of dignitaries. "Following traditional Hindu custom," noted *Hinduism Today,* "Swami was entombed in a specially prepared sepulcher at the Sidhbari ashram. Great yogis are interred not in a casket but seated in the lotus posture. Salt, camphor and sandalwood powder fill the cavity. The samadhi shrine is behind his simple living quarters and faces the majestic Himalayas."

Books

Krishnakumar, Radhika, *Ageless Guru: The Inspirational Life of Swami Chinmayananda,* Eeshwar, 1998.

Patchen, Nancy, *Journey of the Master Swami Chinmayananda. The Man, The Path, The Teaching,* Chinmaya Publications, USA and Central Chinmaya Mission Trust, India, 1994.

Religious Leaders of America, 2nd ed., Gale, 1999.

Online

"Chinmayananda: 1916–1993," *Hinduism Today,* http://www.hinduismtoday.com/modules/smartsection/item.php?itemid=1176 (January 24, 2010).

"Short Biography of Swami Chinmayananda," *Chinmaya Chicago,* http://www.chinmaya-chicago.org/chinmaya.htm (January 24, 2010).

"Journey Through Timeless India," http://www.timelessindia.us/chapter3.htm (January 24, 2010).

"Swami Chinmayananda," *Central Chinmaya Mission Trust,* http://www.chinmayamission.com/swami-chinmayananda.php (January 24, 2010). □

Conchita Cintrón

Chilean-born American-Peruvian bullfighter Conchita Cintrón (1922–2009) is regarded as the greatest among the few female bullfighters who have ever entered the ring as professionals.

Known as *La Diosa Rubia* or the Blonde Goddess, Cintrón possessed in abundance the star quality, the grace known as *duende,* that marked famous bullfighters through the ages. "The arena," Cintrón wrote in her autobiography, *Memoirs of a Bullfighter,* "is a microcosm of the world. Within its small circle one finds life, death, ambition, despair, success, failure, desperation, valor, cowardliness, generosity, and meannness—all condensed into the actions of a single afternoon or even a single moment." Cintrón killed an estimated 750 bulls over a career that lasted from 1936 until 1949, and her fame spread across Latin America and the Iberian peninsula. Indeed, even the end of her career remains a famous episode in bullfighting history.

Born to American Parents

Concepción Cintrón Verrill was born in the northern Chilean city of Antofagasta on August 9, 1922. Her family soon moved to Lima, Peru, where Cintrón grew up. But her background was neither Chilean nor Peruvian: her father, Francisco Cintrón Ramos, was from Puerto Rico and was only the second Puerto Rican admitted to the United States Military Academy in West Point, New York. Stationed in Panama after graduating, he met Loyola Verrill, daughter of the American adventurer and later science fiction writer Alpheus Hyatt Verrill. Cintrón's father went into business after leaving the military, and her childhood, she wrote in her autobiography, "was similar to that of many American children. I knew nothing of bulls and never heard of bullfighting except in passing." She attended school in England for a time, which did nothing to further her knowledge.

An only child until she was ten, Cintrón acquired a younger brother in her 11th year. Around the same time she spotted a sign advertising lessons in "equitation"—horseback riding—and asked what it was. Her parents agreed to sign her up when she turned 11, and she began to pay closer attention to the school. "One morning I saw Ruy da Cámara . . . ," she wrote. "He came mounted on a beautiful sorrel mare that did the most fantastic steps . . . A horse that danced! The rider was elegant and distinguished. He wore a monocle, something I had seen only at the movies. I was stunned." Cintrón quickly showed talent as a rider, but the first time she attended a bullfight she was distressed by the blood and gore.

Yet da Cámara, himself once a famed *rejoneador,* encouraged her, and when she saw her fellow riders enter the bullring she felt a strong desire to try it herself. Cintrón practiced her moves on a chair, and she steeled herself to kill by stabbing oxen in a slaughterhouse. Failing at first to kill them cleanly because her eyes were closed, she resolved to take six swings with a knife at six oxen, vowing to give up bullfighting if she did not kill each one with a single stroke. She succeeded, and returned home singing. Cintrón entered the bullring for the first time at age 13, on a trip to Portugal, and killed her first bull at 15. From then on, she was untroubled. "I have never had any qualms about it," she was quoted as saying by Bruce Weber of the *New York Times.* "A qualm or a cringe before 1,200 pounds of enraged bull would be sure death." Da Cámara remained Cintrón's mentor throughout her bullfighting career.

Fought on Horseback and on Foot

In 1937 and again in 1938, Cintrón appeared at Lima's main bullfighting arena. On the second occasion she wore the traditional garb of the bullfighting *novillero* or initiate: breeches, a short silk jacket, and a wide-brimmed hat. Bullfighting columnists took note of her skills, and her career as a professional *rejoneadora,* the only one on the circuit that led from Peru to Colombia, Venezuela, Mexico, Portugal, southern France, and finally Spain. A *rejoneador* was a bullfighter who rode on horseback, but Cintrón, was exceptionally skilled in the ring both as a rider and on foot. She was not the first female bullfighter, but she was the only one active during much of her career. She faced the bull directly in many of these countries, but in Spain it was illegal for a woman to enter the bullring except on horseback.

Cintrón became an American citizen when her family registered her existence at the American embassy in Lima when she was a baby. "In Peru all North Americans are called *gringos,* and I, too, was a gringa," Cintrón recalled in her autobiography. "But as time went on, I became increasingly Latinized, a process which ended, eventually, in my petitioning for Peruvian citizenship." In one way, however, Cintrón would always be exotic: a female bullfighter was unusual enough, and one with long blond hair was unheard of. Cintrón, instantly recognizable, caused great excitement among spectators even on those rare occasions when she delivered a subpar performance. She was gored by a bull only twice, once in each thigh, and each time she killed the bull before receiving treatment. On the second occasion, in 1949 in Guadalajara, Mexico, Cintrón was dragged from the ring but threw off her protectors and climbed back into the ring to dispatch the bull by driving a sword between its shoulder blades.

As her fame grew, Spanish audiences began to express an interest in seeing Cintrón fight on the ground rather than on horseback. She gained backers such as bullfighting authority Josée María de Cossio, who wrote (according to Mark Mulligan of the *Financial Times*), "For the systematic detractors of female bullfighting, the appearance . . . of this beautiful, svelte, magnificent *rejoneadora* and standing *torera* was a hard blow. The stupid legend of the butch woman bullfighter has been roundly defeated by the extraordinary femininity of Conchita Cintrón." Promoters got around the ban against women by mounting bullfights at private parties or in the Spanish enclaves of Ceuta and Melilla in North Africa, but authorities on the Spanish mainland refused to relent.

Defied Spanish Law

Probably in October of 1949—various dates have been given for this event, but Cintrón's autobiography appears to place it in 1949—Cintrón entered a bullring in Jaén, in southern Spain's Andalusia region. The crowd urged that she be allowed to fight on foot, and despite the refusal of the Spanish president in the crowd, she took off her spurs and dismounted. "The people's enthusiasm was only the echo of my own heart," Cintrón wrote in her memoir. She faced the bull. "Eh! Lovely toro," she wrote.

"Finally I was answering him. There he had me face to face. His eyes were coal black, and the curls on his neck were of fine copper. He charged, his black muzzle lowered, his white horns coming closer and closer. And then feeling the brave bull whirl around me, I shuddered like the very sand beneath us, burned like the sand on this golden afternoon, glowed like the sand with the red of flowers and blood. I was dreaming. It was sublime." Many accounts have stated that instead of stabbing the bull at the vulnerable spot between its shoulder blades, Cintrón touched the spot with her hand. In her memoir, however, she wrote merely that she dropped her sword.

Cintrón was placed under arrest but was almost immediately released; the regional governor, responding to the demands of the crowd, pardoned her. She left the arena weeping, carrying the ears and tail of the bull, which had been killed by a young *novillero.* The fight marked Cintrón's last professional appearance in the ring. A year later, she married da Cámara's nephew Francisco de Castelo Branco, a Portuguese businessman and big-game hunter whom she had first met when she was 12. The couple settled in Lisbon, Portugal, and raised a son. She also worked as an aide at Peru's embassy in Lisbon and bred Portuguese water dogs. Cintrón's autobiography, which ends with the Jaén episode, first appeared in Spain in 1962 and was translated into English and published with an introduction by film director Orson Welles in 1968. "Nobody was ever more perfectly feminine, and she triumphed absolutely in the most flamboyantly masculine of all professions," Welles wrote of her. There also exists a biography of Cintrón by her mother *Goddess of the Bullring,* published under the name Lola Verrill Cintrón. Cintrón made a ceremonial entrance into a bullring in France in 1991, riding beside the *rejoneadora* María Sara, who had been inspired by her own exploits. She died in Lisbon on February 17, 2009, at the age of 86.

Books

Cintrón, Conchita, *Memoirs of a Bullfighter,* Holt, Rinehart & Winston, 1968.
Cintrón, Lola Verrill, *Goddess of the Bullring,* 1960.

Periodicals

Financial Times, February 28, 2009.
Independent (London, England), March 7, 2009.
New York Times, February 20, 2009; February 21, 2009.
Times (London, England), March 2, 2009.

Online

"Conchita Cintrón," *Women of Action Network,* http://www.woa. tv/articles/at_cintronc.html (January 3, 2010). □

Mamie Phipps Clark

American psychologist Mamie Phipps Clark (1917–1983) is best known for her groundbreaking research on the racial identity and self-esteem of African-American children. Her work helped overturn institutionalized segregation policies in United States public schools. With her husband Kenneth B. Clark, she co-founded the Northside Center for Child Development in Harlem, which provided previously unavailable psychological services to that community's families.

Mamie Phipps Clark was a pioneer in the field of psychology in terms of race and gender. She was the second African-American to receive a doctor of psychology degree from Columbia University (her husband, Kenneth B. Clark, was the first). As such, she was also the first African-American women to earn a doctorate from the university.

The doctorate represents a significant personal accomplishment, but Clark's career achievements would have much more far-reaching impact: She collaborated with her husband to provide much needed psychological testing for minority and low-income children, and the couple's collaborative research would play a significant part in the Supreme Court case (Brown v. Board of Education of Topeka, Kansas) that ended years of segregation in American public schools.

Encouraged by her Mother

Mamie Phipps Clark was born Mamie Katherine Phipps on October 18, 1917, in a segregated community in Hot Springs, Arkansas. She was the older of two children of Harold Hilton Phipps, a British West Indies native and physician, and Katie (Florence) Phipps. She grew up in a strongly supportive home environment. Katie Phipps assisted her husband in his medical practice and she encouraged her children to succeed. As a result of this positive maternal influence, Mamie's brother became a successful dentist, and Mamie became an accomplished psychologist who positively influenced the nation's race relations.

Clark attended the segregated Langston High School and proved an intelligent, resourceful student. When she graduated in 1934, however, her prospects for higher education appeared slim: She was a child of the Great Depression and, more significantly, she was black. Existing discriminative admittance policies restricted African Americans from enrolling in southern universities, but Clark overcame the odds by her innate talent. She received scholarships to Fisk University in Nashville, Tennessee and Howard University in Washington D.C. She chose Howard and majored in mathematics and physics.

Became Interested in Mental Health

At Howard University, she shifted her academic direction after meeting future husband Kenneth B. Clark, who was a psychology post-graduate student and teaching assistant. She was a student in Clark's abnormal psychology course and became fascinated by the subject. Recognizing her intelligence and curiosity, Clark persuaded her to switch majors to psychology. At the time, Francis Cecil Sumner, the first African-American to ever receive a Ph.D. in psychology, headed Howard University's psychology department.

Mamie Clark supplemented her studies by becoming a departmental part-time worker who also participated in research. In the process, she developed a deep, abiding interest in the mental health of black children. Subsequently, during her undergraduate years, she administered psychological testing to about 200 pre-school children in the area, an activity that provided her insight into their self image and the impact that racism had on their mental development.

Began Collaboration with Husband

In 1938, she graduated magna cum laude with a B.S. degree in psychology. That same year, she married Kenneth Clark. Supported by a three-year grant from the Julius Rosenwald Fellowship program, the Clarks began collaborating on research about racial identification in black children. In 1939, they published "The Development of Consciousness of Self and the Emergency of Racial Identification in Negro Pre-school Children." The article, which was based on Mamie Clark's undergraduate research, was published in the *Journal of Social Psychology*. In the same year and in the same journal, the Clarks published "Segregation as a Factor in the Racial Identification of Negro Pre-School Children." In 1940, the journal also published their article called "Skin Color as a Factor in Racial Identification of Negro Pre-school Children."

In 1939, Kenneth Clark entered the Ph.D. program in psychology at Columbia University in New York City and earned his degree in 1940. Mamie Clark remained at Howard University to finish her master's work. She received her M.A. in psychology in 1939 with a thesis entitled "The Development of Consciousness of Self in Negro Pre-School Children."

A year later, with the Rosenwald Fellowship financial support, Clark followed her husband to Columbia University, where she became the only black student and one of two women in the psychology department's doctoral program. Ironically, she was sponsored by Dr. Henry Garret, who supported segregation in public schools. When she received her Ph.D. in 1943, she became the second black individual to earn a psychology doctorate from Columbia. During her studies, she administered psychological tests to about 300 youths in the city schools. Her dissertation, which involved the development of mental abilities in children, was titled "Changes in Primary Mental Abilities with Age." Her thesis was published in the *Archives of Psychology* in 1944.

After earning her Ph.D., Clark found employment as a research associate at the New York Examination Center of the United States Armed Forces Institute at Teachers College, Columbia University. She also worked as a research psychologist for the American Public Health Association.

Co-founded Northside Center

In 1945, she became chief psychologist at the Riverdale Home for Children in New York. While at this private protection agency for homeless African-American girls, Clark administered about 345 individual psychological tests to children. These tests measured their intelligence, aptitude, and personality.

While at Riverdale, Clark recognized an urgent need for psychological services to Harlem's black and minority children and their families. With her husband, she co-founded the Northside Center for Child Development, in March 1946. Initially, the Center was located in the basement of a Harlem housing project and was run by volunteers who donated their time and money. It provided psychological, psychiatric, and casework services. Families were only charged according to how much they could afford, and many received services for free. Mamie Clark would serve as executive director until she retired in 1980.

Later, the Center became involved in psychological testing of minority and underprivileged children in the New York City public school system. The Clarks discovered that many of these children were being transferred into classes for the mentally retarded. This often occurred illegally and without parental consent. Subsequent testing performed by the Clarks revealed many of the children were too intelligent for such placement. Mamie Clark fought the school system and helped children return to their normal classes. Afterward, the Center supplemented its services with a remedial education program.

The Center became a success and the Clarks eventually had more clients than they could handle. Because it was essentially nonprofit in nature, the Center attracted funding from philanthropic individuals and organizations. By 1968, the Center moved to the New Lincoln across from Central Park and serviced 600 patients a year. With an annual budget of $450,000, the Center was able to hire a full-time staff that included psychiatrists, psychologists, social workers, remedial reading, and arithmetic specialists, a consulting pediatrician and clerical workers. Efforts were enormously successful: Mamie Clark once estimated that about seventy-five percent of the children it served showed improvement at school as well as at home.

Developed "Doll" Experiment

Meanwhile, the Clarks continued their research activities. In 1950, they published "Emotional Factors in Racial Identification and Preference in Negro Children" in the *Journal of Negro Education*. They also published a chapter in *Readings in Social Psychology*, ("The Emergence of Racial Identification and Preference in Negro Children"), that described their "doll test" experiment designed to analyze children's self image and racial self-identification. The study, which included black children between the ages of three and seven, would have enormous social impact.

The experiment arose from Mamie Clark's 1939 master's thesis, "The Development of Consciousness of Self in Negro Pre-School Children." In the thesis, Clark described a previous experiment involving one black and one white doll shown to black children. The children almost always preferred the white doll. For their own experiment, the Clarks purchased four diaper-clad dolls, two white and two black, from a local toy store. They showed these dolls to the children and asked them questions designed to reveal racial perceptions and preferences. Nearly all of the children indicated that they were aware of the racial differences among the dolls. But when the children were asked which doll they preferred, most picked a white doll. Also, as part of the experiment, the Clarks asked the children to draw pictures of themselves. The Clarks observed that the task often produced anxiety in the subjects. Further, and more disturbingly, in their drawings, many of the children portrayed themselves as white-skinned. Based on their results, the Clarks concluded that prejudice, discrimination and segregation had a negative impact on children's development.

Specifically, many black children felt inferior and even developed a capacity for self-hatred.

Research Supported Desegregation

The Clarks' research not only demonstrated the psychological damage of prejudice and segregation, but it also served as supportive evidence in court cases involved in overturning segregation in public schools throughout the United States. In particular, the National Association for the Advancement of Colored People, or NAACP, used the Clarks' research and publications in court cases that culminated in the 1954 landmark United States Supreme Court decision. In the Brown v. Board of Education case, the Supreme Court overruled the previous "separate but equal" ruling that came out of the Plessy v. Ferguson case in 1896.

Essentially, in its unanimous decision, the Supreme Court indicated that segregation implied inequality. Thus, the Court overturned school-based segregation. It declared that "segregated schools are not equal and cannot be made equal, and hence they are deprived of the equal protection of the laws." In writing the decision, Justice Earl Warren referenced the Clark's research. Indeed, the court case was one of the first that included evidence from psychological research.

Mamie Clark's research on racial identity and self-image became part of a summary prepared by a group of social scientists that included Gordon Allport, Otto Klineberg, and her husband. The summary was submitted to the court lawyers working with the NAACP. Among these lawyers were Thurgood Marshall and Robert Carter. The court's eventual decision included a summarization of the impact of the Clark's research: "To separate [children] from others of similar age and qualifications solely because of their race generates a feeling of inferiority as to their status in the community that may affect their hearts and minds in a way unlikely ever to be undone," (as quoted by the Library of Congress web site).

Later Career

With the impact that her research had on desegregation and civil rights, Clark was now considered more than just an advocate for minority and underprivileged children. She became an influential figure in areas of academia, culture, and social policy.

She served on the board of directors of Teachers College at Columbia University, Mount Sinai Medical Center, and Haverford College. Also, from 1958 to 1960, she was a visiting professor of experimental methods and research design at Yeshiva University in New York City.

Outside of academic settings, Clark became the first woman trustee of Union Dime Savings Bank in New York City. She also served on the boards of the American Broadcasting Company, New York Public Library, Museum of Modern Art, Institute of Museum Services, the Museums Collaborative, The New York Mission Society, and the Phelps Stokes Fund.

In addition, she was a member of advisory groups for the National Head Start Planning Committee of the Office of Economic Opportunity and for Harlem Youth Opportunities Unlimited; a fellow of the American Association of Orthopsychiatry; served as a commissioner for the Palisades Interstate Park Commission; and was a member of Phi Beta Kappa and the American Psychological Association.

Continuing as the executive director of the Northside Center, she helped initiate the construction in the 1960s of Schomburg Plaza in Harlem, which included housing for 600 low- and middle-income families. Clark retired as director in 1980, but she remained active. Until her death in 1983, she served as treasurer of Clark, Phipps, Clark and Harris, Inc., her husband's human-relations consulting firm.

Died of Cancer

Clark died of cancer on August 11, 1983 at her home in Hasting-on-Hudson in New York City. She was sixty-five years old. She was survived by her two children, Kate Harris and Hilton Clark, three grandchildren, and her husband. Kenneth Clark died on May 1, 2005.

During her career, Mamie Clark received high honors for her accomplishments. In 1957, she received the Alumni Achievement Award from Howard University. In 1972, she received an honorary Doctor of Humane Letters degree from Williams College in Williamstown, Massachusetts.

Her career epitomized profound gender and race-related changes taking place in America. Moreover, her work hastened those changes. A chapter on Clark that appeared in *Women in Psychology: A Bio-Bibliographic Sourcebook* (1990) stated that her "research into the importance of self in black children, completed fifteen years before the Brown decision, paved the way for an increase in psychological research into the areas of self-esteem and self-concept."

Mamie and Kenneth Clark's contribution to that decision helped initiate the steps toward desegregation of American schools and proved a milestone for the emerging Civil Rights movement.

Books

"Mamie Phipps Clark," *Notable Black American Women* Book 3, Gale Group, 2002.

"Mamie Phipps Clark," *The Scribner Encyclopedia of American Lives, Volume 1: 1981-1985*, Charles Scribner's Sons, 1998.

Periodicals

The New York Times, August 12, 1983; May 2, 2005.

Online

"Mamie Katherine Phipps Clark (1917–1983)," *The Encyclopedia of Arkansas History and Culture*, http://www.encyclopediao farkansas.net/encyclopedia/entry-detail.aspx?entryID=2938 (December 14, 2009).

"Mamie Phipps Clark 1917–1983," *WebsterUniversity.edu,*, http://www.webster.edu/~woolflm/mamieclark.html (December 14, 2009).

"'With an Even Hand'-Brown v. Board at Fifty," *Library of Congress*, http://www.loc.gov/exhibits/brown/brown-brown.html (December 14, 2009).□

Carlo Collodi

Italian author Carlo Lorenzini (1826–1890), often known by his pseudonym Carlo Collodi, is best known as the creator of the beloved children's story *The Adventures of Pinocchio*. A longtime freelance journalist, Lorenzini had established a political newspaper *Il lampione* (The Streetlamp), served with the regional Senate of his native Tuscany, and written several plays before turning to children's literature in the 1870s. During this latter stage of his career, Lorenzini published a number of fictional and educational children's works under the name of Carlo Collodi, including the *Giannettino* series (1877–1890) and *The Adventures of Pinocchio* (1882), now widely regarded as the most successful and best known Italian children's story of all time. Translated into English in 1892, the work and its political and cultural subtexts continue to inspire debate among scholars even today.

Interpretations of Lorenzini's politics, personality, and purposes vary widely. Writing in *Pinocchio Goes Postmodern: Perils of a Puppet in the United States*, Richard Wunderlich and Thomas J. Morrissey argued, "Since most readers—and scholars, too, for that matter—learn of or actively study Collodi's life only *after* reading *Pinocchio*... and since biographical information in English is not abundant, it seems fair to assume that for most an interpretation of the life is at least as likely to be dependent on an interpretation of the novel as the other way around." Certain facts about Lorenzini's life apart from *Pinocchio* have been firmly established, however. He was born the eldest of ten children on November 24, 1826, in Florence, then the capital of the Grand Duchy of Tuscany and today the center of Italy's Tuscany region. Both of Lorenzini's parents worked as servants in the household of Marquis Carlo Ginori, whose family owned the respected Doccia porcelain factory; Lorenzini's father was the marquis's cook, and his mother a seamstress who originally hailed from the nearby village of Collodi, from which the writer would later adopt his pseudonym. Despite his humble origins, the young Lorenzini impressed the marquis with his intelligence, and the nobleman funded his education at a local Catholic seminary.

Lorenzini, however, did not wish to join the priesthood, and after completing his education at about the age of eighteen began working at Florence's Piatti bookstore. There, Ann Lawson Lucas argued in *The Oxford Encyclopedia of Children's Literature*, "Lorenzini became deeply committed to the creation of a unified Italy, was a moderate follower of [Italian activist and thinker] Giuseppe Mazzini, and advocated political and social reform." Driven by this nationalistic commitment, the young man fought in the unsuccessful 1848 revolution against Austrian control. The following year, he co-founded a satirical political newspaper called *Il*

lampione with a brother and some friends. Italian authorities soon closed the paper down, but Lorenzini had won a secretariat to the Tuscan Senate that provided him with a sufficient salary to continue his journalistic activities. Subsequent civil service positions along with writing continued throughout the 1850s, with Lorenzini again establishing a newspaper, *Lo scaramuccia* (Scaramouche), in 1853; this time, however, he wrote about dramatic news rather than political figures. His appetite for theater whetted, the journalist turned to playwriting and published a collection of plays in 1856. The following year, he issued a novel, *I misteri di Firenze* (The Mysteries of Florence). As revolution again swept the Italian peninsula, Lorenzini rejoined the army, fighting for independence in 1859 and 1860. With the fall of the Tuscan monarchy and the unification of Italy, he was able to bring *Il lampione* back into production during the 1860s. He continued to write and publish extensively over the next several years, working on projects ranging from newspaper articles to an edition of a standardized Italian dictionary, a necessity for a country coming together after centuries of regional differences in culture and dialect.

Wrote *The Adventures of Pinocchio*

Lorenzini's first jaunt into the world of children's literature came in 1875. Despite the writer's lack of experience writing for juveniles, the Florentine publishing company of the Brothers Paggi offered him the job of translating a number of popular fairy tales by such writers as Charles

Perrault, Madame Leprince de Beaumont, and Madame d'Aulnoy from the original French into Italian. "It is true that Lorenzini was a chameleon writer; variety and quicksilver were the hallmarks of his writing life. And yet, why ask him to translate from French? Why ask him to tackle fairy tales? Why ask him, a novice in the medium, to write for children?" wondered Ann Lawson Lucas in her introduction to the Oxford World's Classics edition of *The Adventures of Pinocchio*. Whatever the publishers' impetus, Lorenzini accepted the challenge, and the completed work "established a new, important partnership between himself the Fratelli Paggi, and opened a new chapter in the history of children's literature," Lucas concluded. Published as *I racconti delle fate* (Fairy Tales), this translated volume marked not only Lorenzini's emergence as a children's author, but also the book-length debut of the Carlo Collodi pen name.

The success of Lorenzini's translations led to additional work in the genre, beginning with 1877's *Giannettino* (Little Johnny). A revamp of the then fifty-year-old children's story *Giannetto* by Alessandro Luigi Parravinci, *Giannettino* was a massive popular success—so great, in fact, that Lorenzini was made a Cavaliere della Corona d'Italia (Knight of the Crown of Italy) the year after its publication in honor of his work. Combining entertainment with instruction in a new, more modern way, the book became the first in a lengthy educational series of *Giannettino* volumes that offered lessons in topics including Italian grammar, geography, and mathematics. New *Giannettino* stories appeared regularly until the author's death in 1890 put a close to the series.

Despite the wild success of the *Giannettino* series, however, Lorenzini's greatest literary legacy is unquestionably his fable *The Adventures of Pinocchio*. The story of a puppet who comes to life after being crafted by the puppeteer Geppetto, *The Adventures of Pinocchio* in its original form was fronted by a remarkably unsympathetic protagonist. Pinocchio ran away from home almost immediately after coming into being, and promptly murdered the Talking Cricket immortalized by Disney as the sprightly Jiminy Cricket. He burns off his feet, squanders what possessions Geppetto has given him, is nearly murdered, commits any number of what Pamela Loy characterized in *Italian Literature and Its Times* as "naughty and recalcitrant" acts before undergoing a change of heart and, eventually, becoming a live human boy at the end of the tale. Originally published in installments in the Italian *Il gionale per i bamini* (The Newspaper for Children) between July and October of 1881, the story had initially concluded on the distinctly down note of the puppet hung from a tree. Public response was so great, however, that Lorenzini took the story back up in February of 1882, leading the moralizing story to its ultimately happier conclusion. *The Adventures of Pinocchio* made its book debut in February of 1883, shortly after the serialized version ran its course.

Pinocchio's Legacy Endured

Interpretations of the book have been various and diverse, although many familiar with its story remain unaware of its perceived deeper meanings. In his introduction to the

University of California edition of Collodi's tale, Nicolas J. Perella lamented that "outside Italy Collodi's tale is still taken almost exclusively as a story for children, who... are hardly capable of fully understanding the tale's underlying linguistic sophistication and narrative strategy, its various levels of irony and sociocultural innuendo, or its satirical thrusts against adult society. Nor do the numerous translations... indicate much awareness of these nonchildish features; such versions are so monolithically reductive that most non-Italian adults are unlikely to suspect the book's subtleties and multi-faceted content." Beginning in the 1980s, however, improved translations have opened these subtleties to a wider audience, and serious literary explorations of the volume have increased in the English-speaking world. Scholars have compared the story to that of *La Divina Commedia* (The Divine Comedy) by fellow Italian Dante Aligheri, and argued for the puppet's seeming spiritual links to more modern figures produced by the writer Franz Kafka. "Pinocchio is deeply enmeshed in a national and theoretical apparatus," wrote Suzanne Stewart-Steinberg in *The Pinocchio Effect: On Making Italians (1860–1920)*, "that has turned him into a 'representative' of [Italy] and made him able to bring into focus those mechanisms that pertain to the making of the modern, postliberal Italian subject."

Lorenzini continued writing children's books until his apparently sudden death on October 26, 1890, at the age of 63, in Florence. He never married, and history records no children—just as history has brought down little of the biographical detail that could further enrich modern understanding of the man and his work. "So, this conservatively educated bachelor, rebel, political satirist, novelist, playwright, arts critic, and civil servant, who may or may not have had a gambling problem, suffered from depression, and/or fathered a daughter out of wedlock, is known to us because of a children's book that he could not tell was not finished until children told him so, and which he could have hardly imagined would become a national treasure and a global success," summarized Wunderlich and Morrissey. In fact, Lorenzini's *Pinocchio* did not receive an English-language publication until after the author's death, and one of its first American editions completely failed to acknowledge him as the author altogether. Supported by a classic story and a famous Walt Disney animated film version that is widely considered to have greatly watered down Lorenzini's original tale, *Pinocchio* has become an immortal children's classic.

Indeed, in his native Italy, Lorenzini and Pinocchio have long been figures of much reverence. *The Adventures of Pinocchio* had already enjoyed several reprints during the brief span between its initial release and Lorenzini's death, and new editions have appeared like clockwork in the decades since. During the mid-twentieth century, Professor Rolando Anzilotti, mayor of the town of Pescia—a small community located scant miles from Collodi—established a Committee for the Monument to Pinocchio. This group sponsored a competition to design an honorary sculpture to which nearly 85 artists submitted entries. The two winning monuments became the heart of the town of Collodi's *Parco di Pinocchio* (Pinocchio Park), a sprawling

literary theme park established in 1956 that offers cultural activities and entertainment inspired by the titular puppet. In the early 1960s, the original Committee for the Monument to Pinocchio evolved into the Fondazione Nationale Carlo Collodi (Carlo Collodi National Foundation) with the stated aims of promoting Collodi, Pinocchio, and other children's literature to young readers both in Italy and around the world. Yet outside of Italy, Lorenzini remains something of an unknown, vastly overshadowed by his wildly popular creation; indeed, for many years Collodi was erroneously known as Charles, rather than Carlo, Collodi in the United States. Just as the practical popular anonymity of the author cannot be ignored, however, the lasting cultural presence of his most famous creation cannot be denied.

Books

Collodi, Carlo, *The Adventures of Pinocchio,* Oxford University Press, 1996.

Collodi, Carlo, *The Adventures of Pinocchio,* University of California Press, 1986.

Loy, Pamela. *World Literature and Its Times: Profiles of Notable Literary Works and the Historic Events that Influenced Them,* Volume 7: Italian Literature and Its Times, Gale, 2005.

Stewart-Steinberg, Suzanne, *The Pinocchio Effect: On Making Italians (1860—1920),* University of Chicago Press, 2007.

Wunderlich, Richard and Thomas J. Morrissey, *Pinocchio Goes Postmodern: Perils of a Puppet in the United States,* Routledge, 2002.

Zipes, Jack, ed. *The Oxford Encyclopedia of Children's Literature,* Oxford University Press, 2006.

Online

Carlo Collodi National Foundation, http://www.pinocchio.it/eng/fondazionecollodi/ (January 9, 2010).□

Realdo Colombo

Italian anatomist Realdo Colombo (c. 1516–1559) was a pioneer in the science of cadaver dissection and vivisection in sixteenth-century Italy. With the artist Michelangelo, he planned to publish a comprehensive illustrated tome on human anatomy, but the work never came to fruition. Colombo's only surviving work is *De Re Anatomica,* a text in which he correctly identified some functions of the pulmonary arteries. His research findings influenced British physician William Harvey, who made important discoveries about the human circulatory system a generation later.

E xact birth and death dates for Colombo have been lost to time. He was likely born around 1516 in Cremona, the capital city of Lombardy in northern Italy. It is known that his father was an apothecary, or druggist, and that a relative of theirs, Paolo Colombo, served as professor of anatomy at the University of Padua. This school, founded in 1222, was one of the oldest universities in Europe and renowned as a center of medical training by Colombo's lifetime.

Around 1529, Colombo began a liberal arts course of study in Milan, and is believed to have entered his father's profession for a time. In 1533, father and son moved to Venice when the senior Colombo took a post with Giovanni Antonio Lonigo in the Adriatic seaport city. Venice was actually an independent republic at the time, and Padua was part of its realm of authority. Lonigo was a surgeon who was the official dissector for Paolo Colombo, and Colombo began studying under Lonigo.

Harbored No Squeamishness

At the time, there were taboos against the deliberate cutting of the human body, either dead or alive, and thus surgery and medicine were essentially two separate professions. Anatomists like Paolo Colombo delivered lectures to medical students by presiding over the dissection of a cadaver conducted by surgeons like Lonigo. Using cadavers of executed criminals, these professors of surgery and medicine pointed out the various organs and their functions in a lecture setting. Anatomists, working on their own, also dissected cadavers for research purposes. "The dissector worked with knives and scalpels for a variety of tasks," wrote William E. Burns in *The Scientific Revolution: An Encyclopedia*, "with a saw for cutting bones, and sometimes, as when digging veins out of fat, with his fingers. Bellows and pipes inflated the lungs. A wicker basket next to the dissecting table received the body parts when the dissector was finished with them."

After thorough training under Lonigo, Colombo entered the University of Padua to study medicine. His previous studies in liberal arts also permitted him access to a teaching post at the school, as an instructor in philosophy. At Padua's medical college, his teacher was John Caius, a British physician who would later be honored with a namesake college at Oxford University. Padua's renowned medical school was also home to the most famous anatomist in all of Europe, Andreas van Wesel, who was called by the Latinized form of his name, Vesalius. A native of Brussels, Vesalius came from a long line of highly regarded physicians and had come to Padua after studies at the University of Paris.

In France Vesalius had become familiar with a text from classical Rome that was more than 13 centuries old by then. This was *Methodus medendi*, also known as *The Description and Treatment of the Principal Diseases Incident to the Human Frame*. It was written by a second-century Roman physician named Galen, who had treated the gory wounds of gladiators inflicted in ancient Rome's favorite public sport. Galen's book survived Europe's Dark Ages, and for medieval anatomists and physicians was the only reference text available. When Vesalius finished his studies at Padua, he was offered the chair of surgery and anatomy at the university. He conducted dissections on his own for classes, and began making detailed notes and illustrations.

Succeeded Vesalius at Padua

While Vesalius was considered the foremost expert on human anatomy of the era, Colombo also emerged as a formidable scholar, in part because of his own extensive background in dissection under Lonigo. In 1541 he was named assistant to Vesalius at the University of Padua, and a year later took over the Belgian's teaching duties when Vesalius took a leave of absence in order to complete his book on human anatomy.

In the 1543 first edition of *De humani corporis fabrica* (On the Fabric of the Human Body), Vesalius referred to his assistant as "my friend Colombo, skilled professor at Padua, most studious of anatomy," according to Garabed Eknoyan and Natale G. De Santo in the *History of Nephrology*. In the interim period, however, the two anatomists had a falling out that likely arose from Colombo's challenges to Vesalius's claims. "It is not unexpected that during the course of dissection, Colombo, in his pursuit of anatomical accuracy, would have pointed to the errors of several others, including those of Vesalius," wrote Eknoyan and De Santo. "This was the very essence of the method Vesalius had promulgated, and something he had done himself to his own predecessors and contemporaries."

Vesalius's *Fabrica* was hailed as a major achievement and quickly became the standard textbook for medical students. The Belgian returned only temporarily to Padua, and went on to take a post as physician to the Holy Roman Emperor, Charles V. Following this, Colombo succeeded Vesalius as permanent chair of surgery and anatomy at Padua. In subsequent editions of *Fabrica* Vesalius excised all references to Colombo.

Spent Final Years in Rome

In 1545 Colombo was invited to the University of Pisa by Cosimo I de' Medici, the Duke of Florence. Cosimo had reorganized the university and wanted to make the revitalized school a rival to that of Padua, which was supervised by the Signoria, or Senate of Venice. Colombo spent three years in Pisa before moving to Rome in 1548, when he was invited to become chair of anatomy at *La Sapienza— Università di Roma*, which was the official Papal University at the time. He held this position until his death eleven years later, in 1559.

There are scarcely any other details about Colombo's life that survive the ages, save for the fact that he was known for his masterful dissection of cadavers, which in Rome attracted large audiences at Sapienza University. By this point, there were fewer official restrictions on dissection for scientific purposes, and scores of high ranking church officials were said to have been among the audience members for these gruesome demonstrations. The most famous artist of the Italian Renaissance, Michelangelo, came to know Colombo, and they made plans to collaborate on an illustrated text on anatomy to compete with Vesalius's work. The artist was in his early seventies by the time Colombo came to Rome, however, and his health was failing. Colombo treated Michelangelo for kidney stones, and the artist's biographer, Ascanio Condivi, mentioned Colombo in the 1553 *Vita di Michelangelo*

Buonarroti (The Life of Michelangelo Buonarroti); Condivi noted that Colombo sent Michelangelo a dead Moor—probably referring to a Muslim slave or prisoner of war originally from North Africa—so that Michelangelo could carry out his own inquiries.

Colombo began working on *De Re Anatomica* as early as 1542. He had finished it by 1558, and it was published in Venice a year later, either shortly before his death or posthumously. Totaling nearly 500 pages in Latin, the work has no illustrations and is dedicated to Pope Paul IV, born Giovanni Pietro Carafa, a friend of Colombo's who was elected head of the Roman Catholic Church in 1555. The book was translated into English in 1578 and contains Colombo's extraordinary discoveries about the pulmonary arteries, which carry blood from the heart to the lungs.

Made Breakthrough Pulmonary Discovery

For anatomists of Colombo's era, there was a great deal of guesswork involved in deciphering the ways in which the major organs were connected to one another. This was especially true of the heart, because it was virtually impossible to observe the live muscle in action, pumping blood to the lungs, where it mixes with inhaled oxygen. The oxygenated blood is then carried to other organs via several main arteries. Veins, by contrast, bring blood back to the heart. None of this was known in Colombo's era.

Galen, however, had written about the differences he saw in arterial blood and venous blood. Venous blood was much darker, and Galen asserted that it originated in the liver. When it arrived at the chambers of the heart, Galen theorized, it reached the pulmonary arteries—which take blood to the lungs to become oxygenated—via a series of tiny pores in the cardiac septum. There, Galen assumed, it became arterial blood, which was lighter in color because of the oxygen cells it contained.

Galen's premise was incorrect. Colombo discovered that it was the pulmonary arteries that carried blood from the heart to the lungs. As Lawrence I. Conrad explained in *The Western Medical Tradition: 800 B.C.–1800 A.D.,* Colombo "cut the pulmonary vein of a living dog as far away as possible from the heart and found that it always contained blood and not air (in the cadaver it was also always full of blood)." Conrad added, "Colombo observed that the blood in the pulmonary vein was like arterial blood, and concluded that it was in the lungs rather than in the heart that venous blood and air were mixed and altered into 'shining, thin, and beautiful' blood."

Colombo's dissections had also yielded another important breakthrough that would not earn full scientific recognition until nearly 70 years after his death. He postulated that blood traveled from the right side of the heart to the left side, and did so by the pulmonary arteries. Those pathways took blood into the lungs where it underwent two functions: the lungs added oxygen and removed carbon dioxide, which mammalian systems exhale as part of the respiratory process.

Influenced William Harvey, Argentine Novelist

The actual movement of the heart was another mystery that Colombo wrote of, but a full understanding of the circulatory system would not come about until British physician William Harvey published *Exercitatio Anatomica de Motu Cordis et Sanguinis in Animalibus* (An Anatomical Exercise on the Motion of the Heart and Blood in Living Beings) in 1628. Harvey cited Colombo's discoveries in several places in this work, which became one of the most significant breakthrough texts in human anatomy since Vesalius's opus.

Colombo's own 1559 work, *De Re Anatomica,* received little attention upon publication, and indeed was even challenged by some of his peers on the Italian peninsula. There is an intriguing footnote to his discoveries, and one considered all the rarer for the fact that it was nearly impossible to find female cadavers on which to perform dissections. In *De Re Anatomica* Colombo identified "the seat of woman's delight," according to Thomas Laqueur's *Making Sex: Body and Gender from the Greeks to Freud.* "If it is permissible to give names to things discovered by me, it should be called the love or sweetness of Venus." It later came to be called the clitoris.

How Colombo came by his knowledge was the inspiration for *El Anatomista,* a 1997 novel by Argentinean author Federico Andahazi. Andahazi's fictional tale of Colombo's "research" with a Venetian prostitute was published in English translation in 1998 as *The Anatomist.* The book was a bestseller in Argentina and even won the prestigious Fortabat Prize for best debut novel of the year, but the prize's benefactor, cement heiress Amalia Lacroze de Fortabat, cancelled the awards ceremony, deeming the novel's subject matter too provocative, though she did give Andahazi the $15,000 prize money.

Books

Burns, William E., *The Scientific Revolution: An Encyclopedia,* ABC-CLIO, 2001, p. 87.

Bylebyl, Jerome J., "Colombo, Realdo," *Complete Dictionary of Scientific Biography,* Volume 3, Charles Scribner's Sons, 2008, pp. 354–357.

Conrad, Lawrence I., *The Western Medical Tradition: 800 B.C.–1800 A.D.,* Volume 1, Cambridge University Press, 1995, pp. 328–329.

Eknoyan, Garabed, and Natale G. De Santo, "Realdo Colombo (1516–1559): A Reappraisal," in *History of Nephrology,* Volume 2, *Reports from the First Congress of the International Association for the History of Nephrology,* edited by Garabed Eknoyan et al., Karger Publishers, 1997, pp. 261–267.

Laqueur, Thomas, *Making Sex: Body and Gender from the Greeks to Freud,* Harvard University Press, 1990, p. 64.

Walsh, James Joseph, "Mateo Realdo Colombo," *Catholic Encyclopedia,* Volume 4, Robert Appleton Company, 1908.

Periodicals

New York Times, May 17, 1997; September 13, 1998. □

Mary Colum

Irish literary critic and writer Mary Gunning Maguire (1884–1957) was a part of the vibrant Irish literary scene of the early twentieth century. Better known by her married name, Mary Colum, Maguire left her native country for the United States in 1914 after marrying fellow Irish writer Padraic Colum. She wrote articles for several major American publications and served as literary critic for both *Forum* and the *New York Times Book Review,* as well as teaching comparative literature for several years at New York City's Columbia University. Additionally, Maguire published two books during her lifetime, a 1937 discussion of literary movements entitled *From These Roots: The Ideas that Have Made Modern Literature* and her 1947 autobiography *Life and the Dream;* the year after her death, her husband published their jointly written memoir, *Our Friend James Joyce.* Respected for her critical efforts during her lifetime, Maguire is largely remembered today for her connections to other, better-known Irish literary figures.

Born Mary Catherine Gunning Maguire on June 13, 1884, in Collooney, County Sligo, Ireland, the future literary figure grew up in the households of her grandmother and an aunt and uncle after the death of her parents when she was quite young. She developed a love of reading and writing at a young age, taking on the task of helping illiterate relatives correspond with family members who had immigrated to the United States and treasuring her at times limited opportunities to delve into books. The further deaths of both grandmother and aunt led to Maguire's enrollment in a convent school in Monaghan. "The first night...there rushed over me, not exactly a homesickness, for I was glad to be at the school, but the sense of loneliness that comes over one in unaccounted surroundings," she later recalled in her autobiography *Life and the Dream.* Although she at times felt stifled by the rigidity of the school's world, she enjoyed the educational experience, particularly the study of Latin and other languages. Maguire visited relatives on her school holidays until she turned eighteen, when she enrolled at Dublin's National University to study modern languages. She supplemented her formal education by attending plays at the city's Abbey Theater, then under the direction of Irish literary figures John Synge, Lady Augusta Gregory, and William Butler Yeats, the latter of whom she came to know personally.

After completing her university degree, Maguire—known as Mollie to her friends—took a position teaching English at St. Ita's, a respected Dublin girls' school run by educator Padraic Pearse. In March of 1911, Maguire produced her first notable piece of critical writing: an essay on the *Collected Works of John Synge,* published in the

newly-established *Irish Review,* a journal founded by Maguire and three friends and colleagues. The piece established her as a new Dublin literary voice; in *Modern Irish Writers: A Bio-Critical Sourcebook,* Taura S. Napier observed that it "attracted the attention of academics and general readers alike for its unconventionality, comparing great artists with makers of melodrama and serial shockers in that both find their audience not in rarefied cliques but among the multitudes, 'strong men and thieves and deacons.'" Maguire quickly assumed the critic's chair at the *Irish Review,* writing numerous reviews in addition to a handful of features for the publication.

Moved to the United States

Although apparently somewhat ambivalent about the prospect of marriage, Maguire wed fellow writer and *Irish Review* co-founder Padraic Colum in 1912 after a singularly unromantic proposal; finding Maguire distraught at home after dramatically rejecting the proposal of another, rather determined suitor, Colum said reasonably, "I think that to save yourself trouble, you should marry me. Then these fellows will all leave you alone and you won't have to go through any more of these scenes," according to Maguire's autobiography. Soon after their marriage, the couple received an invitation to visit one of Padraic Colum's relatives in Pittsburgh, Pennsylvania, but as they had already leased a house in Dublin the newlyweds declined. As the first stirrings of World War I began to rattle Europe, however, they decided to travel to the United States after all. Setting out on steamship from Liverpool, Maguire became intrigued both by the native American citizens— she met a young Alain Leroy Locke, an African American writer who had a profound influence on the Harlem Renaissance during the following decade—and by the European emigrés who had adopted the country as their own. "That people would call themselves American so determinedly after being only a few years in the United States...was impressive,...These Americanized Europeans gave me the first direct notion of the United States democracy," she recalled in her autobiography. After landing, Maguire and her husband passed through Ellis Island, which inspired mingled anxiety and awe at the immigration station's efficiency in the arriving critic, and spent a brief time in New York City before continuing on to the Pittsburgh relatives' home.

Upon leaving Pittsburgh, the couple planned to make a lengthier visit to New York City and then return to Dublin. That return did not come to pass, however, and they settled into a small apartment in the city that would largely be their home for the rest of their lives. As Padraic Colum was a respected young writer of the Irish Literary Renaissance, Maguire had the opportunity to meet many new people and develop a new circle of artistic friends, most of whom originally hailed from Europe. Slowly realizing that a return to Dublin was unlikely, she set to work building a new life for herself in the United States. During the early 1920s, she made a visit to Ireland, finding it at once pleasantly familiar and greatly changed in the wake of the Irish Revolution. Brief sojourns in London and Paris preceded their return to New York City. Through the rest of the

1920s, Maguire traveled often, visiting the Hawaiian Islands, Ireland, France, and Italy, and entertained literary figures such as playwright Eugene O'Neill and poet Elinor Wylie at home in New York. She lived for a time in Connecticut, but craved the excitement of the city. After the couple moved back to New York in the late 1920s, Maguire took up her efforts at literary criticism in earnest, a career suggested to her some years previously by no less a figure than Yeats.

By March of 1930, Maguire and her husband had moved to Paris, and there Maguire learned that she received a fellowship in literary criticism from the Guggenheim Fellowship. Having missed seeing Paris resident James Joyce, who had been a friend of Padraic Colum's since their early days in Dublin, on their previous trips to the city, Maguire was pleased to at last meet the respected author. "Joyce," she wrote in her autobiography, " was a very lonely man who paid dearly for his fame, though, maybe, if he had not had the fame, things might have been even more desolate for him: he did actually enjoy the attention[.] . . . No doubt he had what might be called a persecution complex, but really this was not surprising, for he was actually persecuted." Together with her husband, Maguire worked to shield Joyce from some of the most hurtful things written about him, and the pair formed a close friendship with Joyce and his wife and even served as godparents for his grandson Stephen. After a stay on the Riviera, Maguire returned to New York City in 1933.

Wrote Literary Criticism for Major Publications

From the late 1930s until the 1950s, Maguire was a regular contributor and reviewer for the *New York Times Book Review;* she wrote the poetry criticism column for that publication during the 1940s. According to her obituary in the *New York Times,* "She was forthright in criticism and apparently enjoyed drawing printed replies, to which she would respond in the spirit of one to whom poems, plays, and books, the persons who write them and the controversy about them are the essence of life." Maguire was also the literary critic for *Forum* from 1934 until 1940. She channeled her knowledge of literary history and criticism into a 1938 book-length discussion of the topic, *From These Roots: The Ideas that Have Made Modern Literature.* Stating in the work's introduction that it was "an attempt to describe and interpret the movements behind the various [literary genres], to give the history of the development of literary tendencies and forces since modern literature began in the middle of the eighteenth century," Maguire explored the creative relationship between prose and poetry across a broad swath of space and time. Although scholars received the book with somewhat mixed response, it became a popular success in the United States and went through at least three print runs in short order. That same year, Maguire received a second Guggenheim fellowship in literary criticism.

Maguire's second book-length volume, *Life and the Dream,* appeared in 1947. Recounting her personal and professional life up to the World War II era, the autobiography, according to Napier in *Seeking a Country: Literary Autobiographies of Twentieth-Century Irishwomen,* "is a

key text in the development of Irish autobiography as a distinct component of modern literature. . . . It embodies the alternative narrative strategies of Modernist literature, yet lucidly situates its author within the social realities of the early and middle twentieth century." Because of Maguire's long acquaintanceship with notable Irish literary figures such as Yeats and Joyce, the work has also attracted popular and scholarly attention due to its anecdotes and observations on these more famous individuals. In fact, a contemporary review in *Time* magazine dedicated half of its column space to describing Maguire's descriptions of others, rather than focusing on the tale of the autobiographer's own life.

From 1952 to 1956, Maguire served as a guest professor in comparative literature at Columbia University, and in 1953 she gained membership in the National Institute of Arts and Letters. She suffered from increasingly poor health complicated by the effects of anemia in her declining years, but continued to pursue her literary efforts. In fact, Maguire was working on *Our Friend James Joyce* with her husband at the time of her death on October 22, 1957, at the couple's home in New York City, New York. Her husband published the book the following year, and outlived his wife by nearly fifteen years. In the decades since her death, Maguire's public recognition and literary reputation have dwindled into near-obscurity. As Andrew Goodspeed argued in *Ireland and the Americas,* however, she "may have been the better literary mind—she simply lacked Padraic's literary gift." Yet Maguire's legacy lies largely in her efforts to bring Irish literature to an American audience through her criticism; Goodspeed continued, "Because of her interest and ability to explicate difficult literature, she helped writers, even those of Joyce's stature find a greater reading public in the United States." Her anecdotes on the personalities and times of some of Ireland's most respected writers have also added to a fuller understanding of their lives and contributions, and assured her literary value if not necessarily her enduring fame.

Books

Byrne, James P., Philip Coleman, and Jason Kings, eds., *Culture, Politics, and History,* ABC-CLIO, 2008.

Colum, Mary, *From These Roots: The Ideas That Have Made Modern Literature,* Columbia University Press, 1937.

Colum, Mary, *Life and the Dream,* Doubleday, 1947.

Gonzalez, Alexander G., *Modern Irish Writers: A Bio-Critical Sourcebook,* Greenwood, 1997.

Napier, Taura S., *Seeking a Country: Literary Autobiographies of Twentieth-Century Irishwomen,* University Press of America, 2001.

Welch, Robert, ed. *The Concise Oxford Companion to Irish Literature,* Oxford University Press, 2000.

Periodicals

American Literature, November 1938.

Modern Language Review, July 1946.

New York Times, October 23, 1957.

Time, March 31, 1947. □

James J. Corbett

American boxer and actor James J. Corbett revolutionized the sport of boxing, in both technique and image. A sophisticated and educated man, he went on to a career as a minor matinee idol on stage and in film—something that would have been inconceivable for the generation of boxers before him.

Corbett's bout against John L. Sullivan in 1892 was one of boxing's great turning points. "The style of boxing which Corbett flashed in New Orleans on the night he fought John L. was a radical departure from anything ever seen before in the ring," recalled the author of a 1919 *Tacoma News Tribune* article quoted on the Web site of the *Boxrec Boxing Encyclopedia.* "He had speed, was panther-like in his movements and was scientific to a bewildering extreme. He...demonstrated that a light hitting fighter who had perfected his speed and built up a great defense had just as much of a chance to win a decision by knockout as had the heavy hitter." Yet equally important was Corbett's debonair image. He dressed in expensive suits and ties, and even before the end of his boxing career he began a new one as a touring actor. "Gentleman Jim" Corbett took boxing from an ill-regulated carnival on the margins of society into a respectable sport and brought it numerous new fans, many of them women.

Father Operated Livery Stable

James John Corbett was born to Irish immigrant parents in San Francisco on September 1, 1866. His father, Patrick Corbett, ran a carriage-horse stable in a rough part of the city where working men spilled out of the doors of the many saloons on the street where Corbett grew up. He was one of ten children to reach adulthood in his family. Serious Catholics, Corbett's parents hoped that he might pursue a career as a priest, but Corbett showed little talent for study or books. His instincts as a fighter, on the other hand, were good from the start; he nearly won a fight with a feared bully at his local parochial school, losing only when the larger boy succeeded in sitting on him.

Both boys were expelled from the school, and Corbett was soon thrown out of another school for similar reasons. That put an end to his education, and when he was 14 his father got him a job as a clerk. Corbett moved on to another job at San Francisco's Nevada Bank, starting as a messenger boy and advancing over several years to the position of teller. Corbett took on his co-workers in informal boxing matches, and then, with disposable income available, joined the Olympic Athletic Club. Trainers there noted his unspectacular physique and tried to steer him toward baseball instead, but after suffering a hand injury Corbett returned to boxing. Corbett worked hard to develop his left-hand punches, and later claimed to have developed the left hook.

Corbett soon won the club's middleweight championship, and then, when he was 18, its heavyweight crown. He eloped with his sweetheart, Olivia Lake, that following year, and as the newlyweds traveled around the West, Corbett took to the ring to raise money, sometimes fighting under a pseudonym in order to conceal their whereabouts from the couple's parents. In Salt Lake City, Utah, he earned a $460 prize by beating the state champion, Frank Smith. Back in San Francisco, Corbett split his time between an insurance job and coaching boxers at the Olympic Club. By that time, word of his talents had spread, and promoters saw money to be made from matches in which he was involved.

Corbett's professional debut was set for May 30, 1889, when he took on Joe Choynski. Choynski was Jewish, and ethnic passions ran high in advance of the fight as promoters played up the clash. The fight was banned by the city government as a result, after which the organizers tried to stage it in a barn in rural Marin County. Police shut it down, but a week later, on a barge in San Francisco Bay, Corbett outlasted Choynski in a 28-round fight. Boxing matches in those days were not limited to 12 or 15 rounds but continued until one fighter had been knocked out or was unable to continue.

Appeared Opposite Maurice Barrymore

In fact, Corbett's next major opponent, New Yorker Jake Kilrain, had recently fought for 106 rounds against a British boxer, emerging with a draw. When Corbett defeated Kilrain in a bout in New Orleans in early 1890, it propelled him to a national level. He fought and beat Dominick

McCaffrey in Brooklyn, New York, in April of 1890, and that victory launched him to the ranks of viable challengers to the reigning heavyweight champion, John L. Sullivan. Corbett enjoyed the limelight and capitalized on his growing fame by seeking out roles as a stage actor. It was probably a first for a boxer, but the debonair Corbett took naturally to the stage and was cast in the classic play *Camille* opposite star actor Maurice Barrymore (father of Lionel Barrymore, great-grandfather of Drew Barrymore) in an 1890 production.

Another top contender was Peter Jackson, a Virgin Islands native of African descent who fought out of Australia. Sullivan had refused to fight Jackson purely to preserve racial segregation in the ring, but Corbett agreed to a bout with Jackson. The two met in San Francisco on May 21, 1891, and after 61 grueling rounds the fight was declared a draw as both boxers became too exhausted to continue. That definitely established Corbett as Sullivan's top challenger. Corbett hired a manager, William Brady, who was as interested in his growing acting career as in his boxing skills. As he waited for the details of a fight with Sullivan to be worked out, Corbett commissioned a play written specifically for him, *Gentleman Jack.*

The heavily hyped Corbett-Sullivan bout took place in New Orleans on September 7, 1892. It was the first world heavyweight championship held under the Marquess of Queensberry Rules, which had introduced such modern features of the sport as boxing gloves, three-minute rounds, and the count of ten given a boxer who has been knocked down. The *Tacoma News Tribune* article noted that whereas most boxers of the time "were fellows who made a specialty of looking as rough and as tough as they could," Corbett "wore a suit of 'ice cream' clothes, a natty straw hat, a silk shirt, a necktie that must have set him back $3 at the very least, a pair of fashionable tan shoes and silk socks to match—and he carried a cane. That was the climax—the cane."

Some in the crowd ridiculed Corbett, whom Sullivan outweighed by some 30 pounds. But the challenger ducked Sullivan's hard punches, landed a nose-breaker of his own in the third round, and wore Sullivan down over the rest of the fight, scoring a knockout in the 21st round. The fight was recognized from the start as a major accomplishment for what was called scientific boxing—the application of technique as a counterweight to brute force. Corbett, by now a national celebrity, began to tour with a production of *Gentleman Jack* that traveled around the United States and eventually to Europe. A staged fight featuring Corbett was filmed in 1894; the resulting film was among the first films to rely on a celebrity star.

Fight Filmed by Edison

Corbett fought an overmatched Peter Courtney on September 8, 1894; the fight was filmed by Thomas Edison. Corbett successfully defended his title in a bout against Britain's Charley Mitchell with a third-round knockout in Jacksonville, Florida, on January 25, 1894. With a growing taste for the high life, Corbett in the mid-1890s moved to New York, divorced his first wife, and married a woman from Nebraska named Vera Stanwood (born Jessie Taylor).

The marriage was troubled and by some accounts violent, and Corbett embarked on a series of affairs, including one in his later years with actress Mae West. The marriage endured, however, for the rest of Corbett's life. Corbett announced his retirement but soon agreed to fight British-born New Zealander Bob "Ruby Robert" Fitzsimmons. The fight was delayed for several years as anti-boxing Southern governors put legal roadblocks in its way.

Perhaps rusty from infrequent fights and sporadic training, Corbett lost his heavyweight title to Fitzsimmons in a 14th-round knockout in Carson City, Nevada, on St. Patrick's Day, 1897. A film of the fight by Edison associate Enoch Rector, using more than two miles of film, became the first feature-length presentation in cinema history. Reviewers noted the preponderance of women among the film's audiences after it opened at New York's Academy of Music. The film was a hit, and with a lack of available facilities for reproducing it, a second version, with railroad workers standing in for Corbett and Fitzsimmons, was rushed into production. Corbett's loss was followed by personal tragedy; Corbett's father, Patrick, bet and lost his entire net worth on the bout; the following year, probably suffering from dementia, he killed his wife and then himself. To raise money, Corbett appeared in a series of exhibition bouts against his brother Tom. After Fitzsimmons lost his title to the preeminent fighter of the next generation, James Jeffries, Corbett had another shot at the title.

The Corbett-Jeffries bout on New York's Coney Island on May 11, 1900, was another classic heavyweight contest, with the advantage seesawing several times. Jeffries, who was nine years younger than Corbett, finally landed a knockout punch in the 23rd round. Jeffries won a 1903 rematch against the 37-year-old Corbett in the tenth round. Corbett later served as Jeffries's trainer, commented on boxing for journalists, and generally remained on the edges of the boxing world. He continued to act in vaudeville and, beginning with 1920's *The Prince of Avenue A,* acted in films. He remains best known among film audiences not for any of his own efforts but for the 1942 film *Gentleman Jim,* based on his 1925 autobiography, and *The Roar of the Crowd,* in which Corbett's role was portrayed by actor Errol Flynn. Corbett died of liver cancer or heart disease at his home in Queens, New York, on February 18, 1933. He was inducted into the International Boxing Hall of Fame in 1990.

Books

Corbett, James J., *The Roar of the Crowd: The True Tale of the Rise and Fall of a Champion,* Putnam, 1925.

Fields, Armond, *A Biography of the Heavyweight Boxing Champion and Popular Theater Headliner,* McFarland, 2001.

Myler, Patrick, *Gentleman Jim Corbett: The Truth Behind a Boxing Legend,* Robson, 1989.

Niemi, Robert, *History in the Media: Film and Television,* ABC-CLIO, 2006.

Notable Sports Figures, 4 vols., Gale, 2004.

Periodicals

Independent on Sunday (London, England), January 17, 1999.

Online

"Biography: James J. Corbett," *Internet Movie Database,* http://www.imdb.com (November 5, 2009).

"James J. Corbett," *All Movie Guide,* http://www.allmovie.com (November 5, 2009).

"James J. Corbett," *Boxrec Boxing Encyclopedia,* http://www.boxrec.com/media/index.php/James_J._Corbett (November 5, 2009).

"James J. Corbett," *International Boxing Hall of Fame,* http://www.ibhof.com/pages/about/inductees/oldtimer/corbettjamesj.html (November 5, 2009).□

Gaspard Gustave de Coriolis

Best known for his discovery of the Coriolis effect, the French engineer and mathematician Gaspard Gustave de Coriolis (1792–1843) also established the terminology of two of the fundamental concepts of engineering mathematics, work and kinetic energy.

The Coriolis effect is a principle that relates to the motion of objects as observed from a rotating frame of reference. The path of an object moving across something that is rotating seems to curve, and this is because when something is rotating, the outer parts (of a disc) or the parts with the largest circumference (of a sphere, such as the Earth) are moving faster than the parts closer to the inner or smaller parts. The Coriolis effect was an explanation of this seeming paradox, and it showed that the classical laws of mechanics were valid even in a rotating frame of reference. Coriolis's discovery helped to explain the large-scale motion of ocean currents and tropical cyclones—but generally not, contrary to popular belief, the rotational motion of water in a draining bathtub.

Father Fled French Revolution

Gaspard Gustave de Coriolis, who usually signed his name simply as G. Coriolis, was born in Paris, amidst the turmoil of the French Revolution, on May 21, 1792. His father, Jean-Baptiste-Elzéar Coriolis, was a career soldier who had fought with French forces supporting the American side in the Revolutionary War. With the capture and subsequent execution by guillotine of King Louis XVI, the situation of the elder Coriolis, an aristocrat, became very precarious. The family fled Paris, with the infant Gaspard in hand, and settled in the provincial city of Nancy, where Coriolis's father went into business.

Coriolis was educated in Nancy and applied successfully to the recently established École Polytechnique in Paris in 1808. Under Napoleon Bonaparte, the school had become a path to a position in France's civil service, and Coriolis's score was the second highest of all the applicants that year. He was on his way to a prosperous career as a civil engineer but was troubled by poor health. After graduating, Coriolis joined the engineering corps

associated with another Parisian engineering institution, the École des Ponts et Chaussées (School of Bridges and Roads). He spent several years in the Vosges mountains with engineering teams assigned to public works projects.

Health problems combined with financial pressure resulting from his father's death caused Coriolis to take a position as a tutor at his alma mater, the École Polytechnique, in 1816. He was recommended for the position by the mathematician Augustin-Louis Cauchy, who like Coriolis was a Catholic of royalist sympathies. It was this decision that turned Coriolis's career from engineering toward mathematical and physical research. He spent the rest of his life as an educator with research interests on the side. Inspired partly by the research into military artillery carried out by Napoleon's minister of war Lazare Carnot, he began the work that culminated in 1829 with the publication of his *Du Calcul de l'effet des machines* (On the Calculation of Mechanical Action).

That book first propounded a concept known since then to generations of high school physics students, that of work in the sense in which the word is used in physics. Work (in French, *travail*) is the amount of energy produced by the application of a force. Coriolis synthesized the idea from various similar concepts that were in the air at the time, but engineer Jean-Victor Poncelet, with whom Coriolis shared ideas, credited the term "work" to Coriolis explicitly. The term kinetic energy (in French, *force vive*), which Coriolis used to denote the energy contained in an object's motion, was introduced in the same work; it summed up earlier and more complex ways of expressing the same concept. Coriolis also tried to introduce a unit of measurement, the dynamode, as a standard quantity of work in the metric system, equivalent to 1,000 kilogram-meters, but the measurement did not come into general use.

With the publication of his book, Coriolis was offered the position of professor of mechanics at the brand-new École Centrale des Artes et Manufactures (Central School of Arts and Manufacturing, now the École Central Paris), and accepted. The following year, when his mentor Cauchy was forced out of Paris by revolutionary activity, Coriolis was offered his position at the École Polytechnique. Increasingly interested in doing research, he turned the position down.

Installed Water Coolers in Classrooms

Coriolis did begin teaching at the École des Ponts et Chaussées in 1832 and assumed a permanent professorship there in 1836. In the same year he was elected as a member of the French Academy of Sciences, a select group of academics, in its mechanics division. He also taught classes at the École Polytechnique and in 1838 became that institution's Director of Studies. This position, involving supervision of the school's general operations as well as research activities, suited him well. He tried to improve the working conditions for faculty and researchers. Among other measures, he had water coolers installed in each classroom; nearly a century and a half later they were still known as Corios among their users.

The research that led to the formulation of the Coriolis effect was a mix of applied engineering and pure physics. Coriolis worked with water wheels and other pieces of rotating hydraulic machinery, trying to devise principles with practical applications in engineering problems of the time. But he also believed that theory and technology each benefited when they were closely related. As Pierre Costabel put it in the *Dictionary of Scientific Biography,* "While many scientists seemed to favor a radical separation of theory from technology, Coriolis voiced the belief that rational mechanics should be developed as a discipline for the enunciation of general principles applicable to the operation of motors and analysis of the functioning of machinery."

In the early 1830s Coriolis undertook a series of investigations of how work and energy functioned under various conditions, such as where friction or rotation was present. He developed general equations that expanded the ideas of classical mechanics in ways that were generally recognized as concise and useful. The Coriolis effect was first set forth in an 1835 paper entitled "Sur les équations du mouvement relatif des systèmes de corps" (On the Equations of Relative Movement of Systems of Bodies). A charming byproduct of his work was another treatise, *Théorie mathématique des effets du jeu de billard* (A Mathematical Theory of the Effects in the Game of Billiards), written the same year but not published until 1844.

Theory Operated at Macro and Micro Levels

What became known as the Coriolis effect was a distillation of Coriolis's observations of the behavior of bodies in a rotating frame of reference, which might be as small as a water wheel or as large as the Earth. Essentially, Coriolis stated that in that situation, a set of new equations had to be added to the laws of classical mechanics in order to explain the curved paths a moving body, such as an object moving through the Earth's atmosphere, will follow. His discovery helped to explain a wide range of physical phenomena, including curves and directional rotation in ocean currents, winds, and cyclonic storms such as hurricanes, which behave differently depending on whether they occur in the Northern or Southern Hemisphere.

In theory, the Coriolis effect operates even in a very small-scale system such as a bathtub drain, and experiments have shown that, with all other factors strictly controlled and the water in the tub left to settle long enough that it contained very little residual motion, water will indeed drain out in a clockwise spiral in the Southern hemisphere and counterclockwise in the Northern hemisphere. In practice, however, the Coriolis effect is much less significant than other factors, such as the shape of the drain and existing currents in the water, in determining which way the water drains out. The idea that the Coriolis effect determines the direction of water rotation in a draining bathtub, however, has often been repeated.

Coriolis's health worsened in the spring of 1843, and he died on September 19 of that year in Paris. He was buried at the Montparnasse Cemetery. Working until the end, he was in the midst of preparing the proofs of his last book, *Traité de la mécanique des corps solides et du calcul de l'effet des machines* (Treatise on the Mechanics of Solid Bodies and on the Calculation of the Effect of Machines) when he died; it was published the following year. His life was well chronicled in France later in the 19th century, and in 1963 a French oceanographic ship was named in his honor.

Books

Complete Dictionary of Scientific Biography Scribner's, 2008.

Online

"Do Bathtubs Drain Counterclockwise in the Northern Hemisphere?," *The Straight Dope,* http://www.straightdope.com/columns/read/149/do-bathtubs-drain-counterclockwise-in-the-northern-hemisphere (February 2, 2010).

"Gaspard Gustave de Coriolis," *The MacTutuor History of Mathematics Archive* (School of Mathematics and Statistics, University of St. Andrews, Scotland), http://www-history.mcs.st-andrews.ac.uk (February 2, 2010).

"Gaspard-Gustave de Coriolis." *World of Physics,* reproduced in *Biography Resource Center,* http://galenet.galegroup.com/servlet/BioRC (February 2, 2010).

Van Domelen, Dave, "The Coriolis Effect: A (Fairly) Simple Explanation," *Department of Polar Satellite Meteorology and Climatology, University of Wisconsin,* http://stratus.ssec.wisc.edu/courses/gg101/coriolis/coriolis.html (February 2, 2010). □

Martín Cortés de Albacar

Spanish cosmographer Martín Cortés de Albacar (1510–1582) authored *Arte de navegar*, a landmark guide for seafarers of the sixteenth century. Its 1561 English translation, *The Arte of Navigation*, was relied upon by Sir Francis Drake, Martin Frobisher, and other important explorers of the era. In his book *The Art of Navigation in England in Elizabethan and Early Stuart Times*, scholar David Watkin Waters called the English edition of Cortés's opus "one of the most decisive books ever printed in the English language. It held the key to the mastery of the sea."

Cortés was born in 1510 in Bujaraloz, a town in the province of Zaragoza in northeastern Spain. At the time of his birth, Zaragoza was part of the kingdom of Aragon, whose influential ruler was King Ferdinand II. Ferdinand's 1469 marriage to Queen Isabella I of Castile brought their two separately ruled territories to power and formed the basis of the Spanish Empire, but the sovereigns also provided financial support to a little-known Italian mariner, Christopher Columbus, who claimed he could reach India by sailing westward instead of south and east around the African continent. Columbus's 1492 discovery of the Caribbean islands and the Americas launched Spain's Age of Exploration. Ferdinand and Isabella sent out exploratory missions to this "New World," and a generation of Spanish *conquistadores* subjugated indigenous populations on the islands of Hispaniola, Cuba, and Puerto Rico while uncovering vast mines of gold and silver in Mexico and South America.

Ferdinand and Isabella's grandson was Charles I of Spain, who became Charles V, the Holy Roman Emperor, in 1519. He wielded immense power over large parts of Europe and also supported Spain's increasingly profitable colonization strategy. By law all Spanish ships bound for the Americas sailed from Cádiz, a city on the southwestern tip of Spain in what was then the Kingdom of Andalusia. Cádiz had been a great port of the pre-modern age, used by the Phoenicians for their Mediterranean trade as far back as the tenth century B.C. It underwent a renaissance as the center of Spain's growing maritime ambitions after the 1495 decree that its port held primacy, and a few years later a navigators' guild was established in the city, which offered course instruction for ships' pilots. This was *El Colegio de Pilotos Vizcaínos*, or College of Vizcayan Pilots. "Vizcaíno" referred to Vizcaya, the part of northern Spain from which Basque fishing boats had been departing to troll for cod in the waters off Newfoundland in present-day Canada.

Taught in Cádiz

It was in Cádiz that Cortés started his career as an instructor in cosmography, the study and mapping of the known world. He was later associated with *La Casa de la Contratación*, or House of Trade. This was founded in Seville by Isabella in 1503 and played a vital role in all Spanish missions abroad. The Casa levied taxes on incoming goods and issued licenses to pilots, who were hired by ship captains to ensure that their vessels reached the targeted destination.

Knowledge of the Western Hemisphere was a closely guarded imperial secret during Cortés's time. After 1508 there was a master map, called the *Padrón Real*, which was updated regularly by returning navigators under oath at the Casa headquarters in Seville. They reported on ports discovered, islands, elevations, as well as latitudes and longitudes. Casa-licensed navigators would be given new charts based on all current information from the keepers of the Padrón Real. The competing Iberian peninsula kingdom of Portugal kept a similar master map for use by its maritime explorers and trade ships.

Lines of latitudes and longitude divide the earth's surface into grids. One of the precursors to Cortés's landmark work on navigation came from Portuguese cosmographer Francisco Faleiro, whose 1535 tome *Tratado del la Esphera y del arte del marear: Con el regimiento de las alturas, con algunas reglas nuevamente escritas muy necesarias* helped establish a scientific method for determining latitude and longitude. This was essential for ship's pilots, where errors in estimating course could result in weeks lost at sea, shipwrecks, or other disastrous consequences of not reaching the intended destination. Another forerunner was a guide also called *Arte de navegar*, written by Spaniard Pedro de Medina in 1545. Medina's work, published in Valladolid in 1545, was essentially a test preparation for the Casa examination for pilots' licenses.

Dedicated to the King

Cortés completed his own *Arte de navegar* and published it in 1551. Its full title was *Breve compendio de la Sphera y del arte de navegar: Con nuevos instrumentos y reglas, exemplificado con muy subtiles demonstraciones,* or "Short Compendium of the Sphere and of the Art of Navigation: With New Instruments and Rules, Exemplified with Very Simple Demonstrations." It was published in Seville by Casa de Antón Álvarez and dedicated to Charles V. As María M. Portuondo wrote in *Secret Science: Spanish Cosmography and the New World*, Cortés "explained in the dedication and prologue that he wrote the book out of frustration with the ignorance of pilots and their reluctance to learn the principles of astronomical navigation that could turn their dangerous craft into a more certain science...Cortés's book began with a theoretical section where he discussed the sphere and the composition of the earth according to Aristotle. This is followed by a discussion of the movements of the sun and moon and their effect on earth."

Cortés's *Arte de navegar* provided instructions for pilots to build their own navigational instruments to determine a ship's position on the open seas according to the known markers in the sky. One of these was a sundial, a device used since ancient times to determine high noon. Because a sundial must be in alignment with the axis of the earth's rotation, Cortés's design for a sundial featured pivotal supports known as gimbals. He also described an instrument called the "nocturnal," also known as a noctur-labe. The nocturnal, to be used at night, was a circular device with the months of the year. By fixing the position of the North Star, or Polaris, in the night sky, mariners could determine the time and anticipate tides, which ebb and flow with the moon and are another crucial element in maritime navigation. Cortés also revealed details on how to construct and use a sea astrolabe, used for determining the altitude of the sun. By using these instruments and following Cortés's principles, navigators could more accurately plot their course with the help of the charts provided by the Casa.

The *Arte de navegar* was discovered by English navigator Steven Borough, the chief pilot of the Muscovy Company and the first known person to reach Russia from England by sea. Borough was invited to visit Seville and the Casa pilots' school in 1558, and brought back a copy of Cortés's work. Richard Eden, an Oxford-educated cloth merchant, alchemist, and translator, was hired by Borough to create the English-language version. Published in 1561 as *The Arte of Navigation,* it was the first work of its kind in English and went through several editions over the next half-century. It became an indispensable aid to several important English explorers who followed Borough. One of them was Martin Frobisher, who sought a route to Asia through the fabled Northwest Passage. Another was Sir Francis Drake, the privateer who carried out attacks against vessels of Spain's gold- and silver-laden "treasure fleet" and circumnavigated the globe in a 1577–80 journey.

Aided Founding of the British Empire

Drake was a key figure in England's own Age of Exploration under Queen Elizabeth I, as was a lesser-known figure, John Davis, who also sought a northwest route to China, Japan, and India in the 1580s but inadvertently mapped out much of the land masses and seas surrounding and below the North Pole instead. In the introduction to an 1880 edition of *The Voyages and Works of John Davis, the Navigator,* Albert Hastings Markham noted that Davis used both Cortés's and Medina's volumes, which "contained an account of the Ptolemaic hypothesis; a calendar and rules to find the prime and epact, the moon's age, and time of tides; use of the compass; tables of the sun's declination for five years; and descriptions of the sea chart, astrolabe, and cross staff."

For English explorers, Cortés's *Arte de navegar* was eventually superseded by William Bourne's *A Regiment for the Sea,* which was actually a revised edition of Cortés's work. Bourne was an English mathematician and corrected what he felt were *Arte de navegar*'s errors. It, too, went though several editions and was translated into several other European languages. For Spanish mariners, *Arte de navegar* fell into disuse after the 1588 publication of Rodrigo Zamorano's *Compendio del Arte de Navegar.*

Cortés's important work was the only one of his career. He died in 1582 at the age of 72. Nevertheless, "Cortés de Albacar belongs to that first generation of cosmographers and pilots who sought to establish an instrumental method of transatlantic navigation and to make that method available to other pilots," wrote a

scholar, Antonio Barrera-Osorio, on the Folger Institute Web site. Barrera-Osorio called Cortés's guide "the foundational text for England's long tradition of sea-dominance and colonization."

Books

Barrera-Osorio, Antonio, *Experiencing Nature: The Spanish American Empire and the Early Scientific Revolution,* University of Texas Press, 2006, p. 131.

Markham, Albert Hastings, *The Voyages and Works of John Davis, the Navigator,* printed for the Hakluyt Society, 1880, p. li-lii.

Portuondo, María M., *Secret Science: Spanish Cosmography and the New World,* University of Chicago Press, 2009, p. 53.

Waters, David Watkin, *The Art of Navigation in England in Elizabethan and Early Stuart Times,* Yale University Press, 1958, p. 104.

Online

Barrera, Antonio, "Navigational Manual of Cortés," Folger Institute, http://www.folger.edu/html/folger_institute/experience/disciplining_barrera.htm (November 17, 2009). □

R. Crumb

The American cartoonist Robert Crumb (born 1943), who used the name R. Crumb in his artwork, revolutionized the world of comics and gave voice to the anarchic spirit of the 1960s counterculture in images and outrageous concepts that became icons of the era.

Crumb has often struck even his fans as an infuriating figure who was critical of nearly everything and everyone, not least himself. His comics have given voice to unpleasant attitudes, sometimes racist or sexist, that he has contended are embedded in not only his own psyche but also the structure of American society. Many of Crumb's cartoons were meant to shock, and shock they did. Yet Crumb has, somewhat to his own chagrin, become successful, rising from the world of underground comics in the counterculture of San Francisco in the 1960s to art museum exhibitions and serious critical writing four decades later. Even Crumb himself, who despite the total irreverence of his comics thought hard about his status as a force for change, would probably agree that the tradition of using comics for purposes of satire and social criticism was enriched by his work.

Drew Comics with Older Brother

Robert Crumb was born on August 30, 1943 in Philadelphia, Pennsylvania. He had two brothers, both of whom became even less well adjusted as adults than he was, and two sisters. Crumb's father, Charles Crumb Sr., was a career member of the U.S. Marine Corps; he was strict and, according to the documentary biography *Crumb* (whose account has been challenged by Crumb's sister Carol

Gilliam of the *Monty Python* series of films. Crumb himself worked for *Help!* for several years in the mid-1960s, moving to New York and at one point taking a job with the Topps trading-card company on the side. During this period he created one of his enduring comic characters, the heavily bearded, and genial but essentially disreputable guru Mr. Natural. He also began experimenting with the drug LSD. In 1967 Crumb moved to San Francisco, just as the counterculture of the Haight-Ashbury neighborhood was reaching its peak.

Sold Comics on Street

In the open atmosphere of San Francisco, Crumb continued using drugs, although he later gave them up. His drawing became less true-to-life and more fantastic, resulting in the creation of new and distinctive visual imagery. Soon after arriving in San Francisco Crumb launched a new comic book, *Zap*, which he and his wife sold on street corners at first. It virtually launched an underground comics scene in San Francisco and the rest of the West Coast. A copy made its way to future Seattle cartoonist Lynda Barry, who recalled her reaction to *Entertainment Weekly:* "You know how people know where they were when Kennedy was shot? I know exactly where I was when I saw my first R. Crumb comic book. It was in the eighth grade and I was in row three, seat three, and it was Zap number zero, and it completely blew my mind."

The *Zap* series was enormously successful and, for a time, made Crumb a counterculture star. He and Dana had a son, Jesse (who later became a commercial illustrator), but their marriage broke up as the previously shy Crumb began to receive large amounts of attention from young women. An image originally published in *Zap #1*, showing four men with oversized legs and feet striding beneath the words "Keep on Truckin'" became one of Crumb's most famous images. The phrase was derived from various old blues and country lyrics that Crumb heard on the 78 rpm records he collected avidly for most of his life; he formed a band, the Cheap Suit Serenaders, to perform the music he loved, playing the banjo himself.

The 1970s were difficult times for Crumb, financially and artistically. His style spawned a host of imitators who became competitors, and the "Keep on Truckin'" image, which he had never properly copyrighted, became the subject of a royalty lawsuit he eventually lost. Fritz the Cat became the subject of a notorious X-rated film by animator Ralph Bakshi in 1971, but Crumb disliked the film and had little input on the script. Crumb fell in debt to tax authorities to the tune of $40,000. During this period Crumb mused on his place in society, in a mixture of hand-lettered text and drawings, in an unpublished sketchbook called "What are the responsibilities of a Cartoonist in the REVOLUTION?" In 1978 he married fellow cartoonist Aline Kominsky, who tried to set his affairs in order and eventually succeeded to an extent, but at one low point the couple lived in a shack in rural California with no running water. In 1981 they had a daughter, Sophie.

Crumb's cartoons in the 1960s sometimes featured stereotypical, crude images of African Americans and women, and he took considerable criticism for this aspect

DeGennaro), sadistic and physically abusive. Crumb's mother, Bea, suffered from mental illness and may have abused diet pills. Crumb and his brothers retreated from their dysfunctional family atmosphere into the world of comics, and from the start Crumb liked edgy comics such as Walt Kelly's "Pogo" and later, in the mid-1950s, the new satirical comic book *Mad*. Crumb and his older brother Charles, who was also an emotionally domineering figure, drew comic books together, introducing a sensualist cat named Fritz while they were still very young.

After graduating from high school, Crumb landed a job in 1962 as an illustrator with the American Greetings card publisher in Cleveland, Ohio. He did well there—his supervisor, "Ziggy" comic creator Tom Wilson, recognized his talent and gave him opportunities to develop humorous cards but also urged him to shave the grotesque edges off his drawings. After working for American Greetings for several years, Crumb married Dana Morgan in 1964. Almost penniless, the couple traveled around Europe as Crumb occasionally mailed drawings back to American Greetings and Dana stole food to keep them going. He mailed a Fritz the Cat cartoon to his idol, *Mad* creator Harvey Kurtzman, who, according to Steve Burgess of *Salon,* sent it back with the comment, "We really liked the cat cartoon, but we're not sure how we can print it and stay out of jail."

The publication to which Crumb sent the cartoon was *Help!,* a short-lived but influential magazine that also spawned the career of comedian and animator Terry of his work. One of his recurring characters, Angelfood McSpade, was an African woman brought to the U.S. by whites and forced to work at low-level jobs. Crumb, however, appeared in his own cartoons and mercilessly lampooned his own attitudes as well as those he saw in the society around him. In a discussion with Stella McCartney in *Interview,* Crumb responded to the criticism this way: "I can't blame women for having that reaction to my work. I certainly see why they would, or why black people might think my work is racist. I can see why they might think those things, even though I feel that I have to reveal all of the various complicated contradictions and emotions and feelings that are in me. I just have this compulsion to lay it all out there."

Illustrated Abbey Book

The outrageous aspect has never disappeared from Crumb's work, but in the later part of his career he took on a greater variety of projects. In 1985 he illustrated a new edition of Edward Abbey's ecological-activist novel *The Monkey Wrench Gang.* Crumb created new characters such as the urban professional social climber Mode O'Day and formed a new magazine, *Weirdo.* Despite the continuing satirical edge to his work, and despite his own aversion to publicity and any form of commercial success (he often turned down commissions from large-circulation magazines such as *Playboy),* there were signs by the mid-1980s that Crumb was making the transition from underground figure to cultural icon. The first of a number of art gallery and museum exhibitions devoted to Crumb's drawings took place in San Francisco in 1983; all of the Crumb drawings for sale at the gallery show sold out on the first night of its run. Exhibitions followed at New York's Alexander Gallery and even abroad, at the Museum Ludwig in Cologne, Germany.

One of the major projects with which Crumb was involved in the 1990s was the documentary *Crumb,* made by his friend Terry Zwigoff. Filming on the project took six years and covered a wide range of topics, from Crumb's own childhood to the development of the lives of his brothers (younger brother Maxon lived in a cheap hotel in San Francisco and was shown meditating while lying on a bed of nails), to critical evaluations of Crumb's work. Among Crumb's champions in the film was *Time* magazine critic Robert Hughes, who compared Crumb's drawings to the complex and satirical visions of society in the classic works of Dutch artist Pieter Brueghel and Spain's Francisco Goya; his detractors included magazine editor Deirdre English, who (according to Burgess) characterized his 1969 incest-themed comic *Joe Blow* (which faced obscenity charges when it was first published) as "an arrested juvenile vision." Crumb's older brother, Charles Jr., committed suicide after filming was completed.

During filming, Crumb and his wife moved to the village of Sauve in southern France and have continued to live there, granting only occasional requests for interviews. In 2005 Crumb and collaborator Peter Poplaski issued *The R. Crumb Handbook,* an account of the artist's life mixed with a selection of reprinted comics. By that time much of Crumb's earlier work had been reissued, in handsome hardbound volumes, in an ongoing multivolume series called *The Complete Crumb.* An entirely unexpected Crumb project appeared in 2009: an illustrated edition of the biblical Book of Genesis. Crumb, although he had stated that he was an atheist, approached the story without mockery, in a spirit of pure realism. "This version of Genesis works so well because it is not reverential," wrote Malcolm Jones in *Newsweek.* "The artist always honors the story, never dodging or minimizing the occasions when God or one of his emissaries enters the action, but by keeping everything as grittily real as possible, Crumb achieves a miracle all his own: he makes one of the world's oldest stories new again."

Books

Crumb, Robert, *The R. Crumb Handbook,* MQ Publications, 2005.
Newsmakers 1995, issue 4, Gale, 1995.

Periodicals

Artforum International, March 2005.
Entertainment Weekly, April 28, 1995; June 2, 1995.
Interview, April 2005.
New Statesman, March 21, 1005.
Newsweek, November 2, 2009.

Online

"R. Crumb," *Salon* (May 2, 2000), http://archive.salon.com/people/bc/2000/05/02/crumb/index.html (January 30, 2010).
"Robert Crumb," *Comic-Art.com,* http://www.comic-art.com/biographies/crumb001.htm (January 30, 2010).□

D

Paulina Wright Davis

The American social reformer Paulina Kellogg Wright Davis played a key role in the first wave of feminism in the United States. She was an organizer of the first annual National Women's Rights Convention, held in 1850, and she served as president of the convention for its first two years of existence, giving the keynote address at both gatherings.

In those roles, Davis helped set the tone and devise the intellectual framework for early American feminism. Unlike Elizabeth Cady Stanton and some of her other compatriots in the movement, she preferred action to written polemic; she left one written history of the early women's rights movement among a slender body of writings. Davis's thinking, however, was daring and wide-ranging. She accomplished practical goals, such as reform in the area of the property rights of married women, but her famous speeches were broad inquiries into the nature of women's capabilities, combined with stirring calls to action. The roots of her activism grew from the fertile soil of nineteenth-century American reformism, and her importance in the development of the women's rights movement remains underappreciated.

Orphaned at Age Seven

Paulina Kellogg was born in Bloomfield, in central New York state, on August 7, 1813. She came from what qualified at the time as an old American family; her maternal grandfather had fought in the Revolutionary War and served on the staff of the French general Lafayette. Her father, Ebenezer Kellogg, served in the U.S. Army himself,

and the family, well provided for, settled in an undeveloped area on the frontier near Niagara Falls. When Paulina was seven, however, she was orphaned. She was raised in Le Roy, New York, near Rochester, by an aunt who was a devout Presbyterian.

As Paulina grew up, the fiery Protestant revivalism of the Second Great Awakening helped to shape her attitudes. Western New York at the time was known as the Burned-Over District because, it was said, the population of the area was already so thoroughly converted to Christianity that there were few souls left to draw to the holy fire. Paulina joined the Presbyterian Church at 13 and became involved with its numerous women's organizations. She hoped to embark on a career as a missionary but was disappointed to learn that the church forbade single women in that capacity. A Utica merchant, Francis Davis, pointed out that his city was full of souls, including his own, that were in need of spiritual guidance, and the two married in 1833.

Although Francis Davis forbade his 19-year-old wife to give speeches in public, he shared her forward-thinking spirit. Both spouses were active in the abolitionist movement and served on the executive committee of the Central New York Anti-Slavery Society, a stance that put them in the sights of pro-slavery agitators. After one of the society's conventions, rioters surrounded the Wrights' house (or that of a friend where Paulina was hosting convention delegates—sources differ), stacked hay bales around the foundation, and approached the house with lit torches. According to the nineteenth-century reference book *Daughters of American Women of the Century* by Phebe Hanaford, quoted on the *Sunshine for Women* web site, the women in the house went ahead with their usual prayers, whereupon "the leaders [of the riot], peeping through the blinds, saw a number of women on their knees, in prayer: the sight seemed to soften their wrath, and change their

133

purposes; for they quietly withdrew, leaving the women in undisturbed possession of the house."

Both Francis and Paulina Wright, disturbed by their church's pro-slavery attitude, resigned their memberships, and from the late 1830s onward Paulina began to devote her energies increasingly to social causes. It was during this period that she met American feminist pioneer Elizabeth Cady Stanton. Her first foray into women's rights activism was a petition drive in support of a Married Women's Property Act that had been introduced in the New York State Legislature. The measure was aimed at insuring married women's control over their own property. After a decade of work, the efforts of Wright and her collaborator, Russian-born American feminist Ernestine Rose, were crowned with success when the Married Women's Property Act was implemented in 1848.

Imported Anatomically Correct Mannequin

Francis Wright died in 1845. Modern accounts of Paulina's life have stated that his will left her a wealthy woman, but according to *Daughters of American Women of the Century*, Francis Wright had suffered business setbacks in his later years, and Paulina "was thrown on her own resources for support." From France she imported an anatomically correct female dummy, said to be the first one in the United States, and moved to New York to study medicine in 1846. She also began to give lectures on female physiology, a controversial move in its time but one that inspired many young women to take up the study of medicine themselves. Anti-slavery leader Abby Kelley asked Wright to attend the

birth of her first child. In the 1840s Wright's ideas about women's rights became more wide-ranging and more oriented toward a fundamental questioning of societal assumptions. Mary P. Ryan, in *The Cradle of the Middle Class: The Family in Oneida County, New York, 1790–1865,* asserted that Wright's experiences had "bred a radical feminism."

Around 1848 Wright met Rhode Island state senator and abolitionist Thomas Davis, an associate of the leading New England anti-slavery activist William Lloyd Garrison. The couple married, and adopted two daughters. Thomas Davis favored women's equality and backed his new wife's efforts in that direction, and Paulina began to devote herself full-time to direct action. She broke off her anatomy lectures and began to work with Stanton and other feminists to organize the first National Women's Rights Convention, to be held in 1850 in Worcester, Massachusetts. The convention was originally an offshoot of the large annual Anti-Slavery Society meeting in Boston.

Davis was a key player in organizing the first convention, sending letters and taking out newspaper advertisements to help draw the country's far-flung feminist activists, many of whom lived in the feminist heartland of far western New York State, to Massachusetts in an era of primitive train travel and horse-and-carriage transportation. The first convention drew participants from nine states, and Davis was chosen to serve as president for a second year. Her two keynote addresses were founding documents of American feminism. Rather than focusing on narrow goals, they inquired into the basic nature of the relationship between men and women, and into the inequalities built into the structure of society as it was then constituted.

"When the argument for restraint [of women] is rested upon Woman's alleged incapacities, we might triumphantly answer, that where an actual and obvious incapability is seen and known among men, their eligibility is not therefore taken away," Davis pointed out in her 1851 address, found on the Vassar College Libraries web site. Later she outlined the extremely limited educational opportunities available to women. "We say that Women are not proved incapable, but that they are kept in ignorance; first, by the denial of systematic education, ample and adequate; and next, by the withdrawal and withholding of all those useful and honorable posts, places and functions, from them as a sex, which are the proper incentives to the successful pursuit of learning," she said.

Founded Magazine

In 1852 Davis gave up the convention presidency, and the following year she founded a magazine, *The Una,* named for a character in the Edmund Spenser poem "The Faerie Queene," and her plan was to make the magazine into a forum for cutting-edge feminist ideas. After Davis and her husband moved to Washington, D.C., in 1854, following the latter's election to the U.S. House of Representatives, the magazine's editorial responsibilities were split between Davis and an another early feminist, Caroline Healey Dall, who envisioned it instead as a literary magazine. Without Davis's visionary energy at the helm, *The Una* ran aground.

Davis, however, continued to take an active role in women's rights issues. She supported and wrote in favor of the campaign for woman suffrage led by Stanton and Susan B. Anthony as that campaign split from the anti-slavery movement in the mid-1850s, and after the Civil War she was a co-founder of the New England Woman Suffrage Association. Davis and her husband had returned to Providence after the end of his term in Congress in 1855, and she lived there for the rest of her life. In what was then a small city of fewer than 50,000 inhabitants, Davis created a forward-thinking salon of her own, inviting guests such as the poet Walt Whitman to her comfortable house just outside the city.

In her later years, Davis often made trips to Europe that combined her social reform activities with her interest in fine art. She met with various European thinkers and copied paintings in the Louvre and the Luxembourg Palace, bringing her paintings back to the United States. and hanging them in her own home. She had less success finding art classes, however, finding most of them closed to women students. In 1870 she helped organize a 20-year reunion of participants in the Woman Suffrage movement in New York, and the following year she published the reunion's proceedings as *The History of the National Woman's Rights Movement.* On a return voyage from Europe in 1876, a longstanding problem with gout worsened, and she found great difficulty in walking. Hanaford met with her near the end of her life, and recorded these words from Wright: "How petty the ridicule and persecution we have passed through, that seemed so grievous at the time, now appear, compared with the magnitude of the revolution we have inaugurated!" Davis died in Providence on August 24, 1876.

Books

Ryan, Mary P., *The Cradle of the Middle Class: The Family in Oneida County, New York, 1790–1865,* Cambridge, 1981.

Online

"Guide to the Paulina Wright Davis Papers," *Vassar College Libraries,* http://www.specialcollections.vassar.edu/finding aids/davis_paulina_wright.html (November 9, 2009).

"Paulina Kellogg Wright Davis," *National Women's Hall of Fame,* http://www.greatwomen.org/ (November 9, 2009).

"Paulina Kellogg Wright Davis (1813–1876)," *Sunshine for Women,* http://www.pinn.net/~sunshine/whm2002/p_davis.html (November 9, 2009).☐

Doris Day

American singer and actress Doris Day (born 1924) enjoyed a long career that extended through the Big Band era, the Golden Age of Hollywood musicals, sophisticated 1960s comedies, and into the 1970s. Often the target of critical ridicule, Day became regarded as a versatile performer whose talents were not fully appreciated until after her retirement.

D uring a performing career that lasted almost a half-century, Doris Day developed a reputation as a too-wholesome heroine of saccharine films. Also, because of her seemingly cheerful disposition, people

believed her screen persona carried over into her private life. The existing record, however, belies both assumptions and intrudes upon Hollywood fantasy.

While Day was perceived as a chaste, girl-next-door, a close analysis reveals that the typical Doris Day character—particularly in the films produced in the late 1950s and early- to mid-1960s—was a strong minded, resilient, independent woman who achieved success in a male-dominated world while spurning the advances of arrogant, smooth-talking, would-be seducers. As such, she could serve as a role model for modern, young women. Indeed, the Day persona predated Mary Tyler Moore's "Mary Richards" character from the ground-breaking 1970s television series.

In addition, many of the films that depicted her fending off advances from male co-stars (Rock Hudson, Cary Grant, and James Garner, among others), were far from innocent. Scripts were replete with blatant (but tasteful) sexual innuendo and frequently demonstrated mature, sophisticated attitudes about adult relationships.

As far as her personal life, Day led anything but a chastity-rewarded existence. She endured a great deal of emotional, physical, and financial turmoil. To her credit, she continually conveyed cheerfulness and positivism.

Day was born on April 3, 1924 as Doris von Kappelhoff. A small-town girl, she grew up in Evanston, Ohio, the only daughter of William von Kappelhoff, a music teacher, and Alma Sophia Welz, a housewife. The family also included two sons. The pattern of her troubled life was established early: In 1931, her parents divorced, and Day was raised by her mother.

The future star's education was unconventional. She attended local parochial schools but never attained a high school degree. She became interested in dancing at an early age and took ballet and tap lessons at the Hessler Dancing School. By 1936, she partnered with a fellow aspirant, Jerry Doherty. The young pair won a local amateur dance contest and traveled to Hollywood, where they worked in the Fanchon and Marco stage show.

Dancing Aspirations Shattered

Day's dancing ambitions were thwarted when she suffered serious leg injuries. On October 13, 1937, in Hamilton, Ohio, she was a passenger in a car that was struck by a train. Injuries included compound fractures and a shattered right leg. These were aggravated when Day suffered a fall during her fourteen-month recuperation.

Undaunted, Day sought other outlets for her performing ambitions, directing her efforts and innate talent toward a singing career. Influenced by the Ella Fitzgerald performances that she heard on the radio, and bolstered by requisite vocal training, Day began performing on local radio programs. While she received no pay, Day gained exposure and garnered attention. As a result, by the time she was sixteen years old, she began singing professionally for regional bandleader Barney Rapp.

As her career progressed, she didn't fare well in personal relationships. She suffered two bad marriages. In 1941, she wed trombonist Al Jorden. The couple had one son (Day's only child, Terry) but the union ended in divorce in 1943. Reportedly, Jorden was a jealous and abusive husband. Day later wed saxophonist George Weidler, but the union only lasted eight months.

Meanwhile, Day changed her name. Now officially and professionally known as Doris Day, she sang with two well-known, popular 1940s bands: Bob Crosby and the Bobcats and Les Brown and his Band of Renown. Her fame increased. She appeared on the "Your Hit Parade" radio program, which led to recording opportunities. Two of her records, "My Dreams are Getting Better All the Time" and "Sentimental Journey," became number-one hits. The latter was a major milestone in her early career. It remains one of her best-know recordings and it eventually became Les Brown's theme song. Day remained with Brown until 1946. The following year, she signed a contract with Columbia Records, entering into an association that would last two decades.

Audition Led to Film Career

Day was now living in California, close to the Hollywood film industry. Her movie career began in 1948, under serendipitous circumstances. The Warner Brothers film company was producing a movie called *Romance on the High Seas* and needed an emergency replacement for star Betty Hutton, who became pregnant during filming. Someone suggested Day and she made the most of the opportunity. After belting out a vibrant rendition of "Embraceable You," she won the audition.

In this film debut, Day played "Georgia Garret," a torch singer who performed in a seedy nightclub, a role that was far removed from Day's later reputation. She made a strong impression and became an "overnight" star. Warner Brothers signed her to a contract. This impressive debut was followed by two more films, *My Dream is Yours* and *It's a Great Feeling*, both produced in 1949.

In the next four years, Day made at least two films each year. During this first phase of her film career, she performed in many musicals, which allowed her to display both her acting and singing talents. She worked with Warner Brothers' best directors, including Michael Curtiz and Roy Del Ruth. In 1950, she appeared in *Young Man With a Horn, Tea for Two, The West Point Story*, and *Storm Warning*. These were followed by *The Lullaby of Broadway, On Moonlight Bay, I'll See You In My Dreams*, and *Starlift*, all in 1951; *The Winning Team* and *April in Paris* in 1952; and *By the Light of the Silvery Moon* and *Calamity Jane* in 1953. Best-selling Day recordings spun off from these films (e.g., "Secret Love" from *Calamity Jane*) further established Day as a top-ranked vocal performer.

Married Marty Melcher

Day's leading men included established and rising stars such as Gordon MacRae, Kirk Douglas, and future United States president Ronald Reagan, her co-star in *The Winning Team*, a biography of baseball pitcher Grover Cleveland Alexander. During the filming, Day dated Reagan, but she also became romantically involved with her new agent, Marty Melcher. On April 3, 1951, Day and Melcher married. After Warner Brothers released Day from her contract in 1955, she and Melcher formed Arwin Productions, which co-produced Day's subsequent films with major studios. The third time appeared the charm for this latest marriage, which lasted until Melcher's death in 1968. But trouble resided beneath the surface. Day's friends later suspected that Melcher only married Day to gain control of her money (subsequent events seemed to confirm this suspicion), and Melcher's relationship with Day's son, Terry, became troubled over the years.

During this period, Day's best-known and most highly regarded films were *Love Me or Leave Me* (1955) and *The Man Who Knew Too Much* (1956). The former co-starred her with James Cagney, who played a gangster, the kind of role that made him an American film icon. Day played Ruth Etting, a nightclub singer who gained fame in the 1920s. Today, the film is of interest to modern audiences because of Cagney's presence. Day gave one of her finest screen performances, however, in a film that allowed her to place her vocal talents on full display. *The Man Who Knew Too Much* was directed by Alfred Hitchcock, and it is regarded as one of his greatest suspense films. It included the song "Que Sera, Sera," which became a Doris Day trademark. While the cloying number is considered the film's single flaw, Day's recording sold more than a million copies and earned her a Gold Record.

Toward the end of this productive decade, Day also starred in *The Pajama Game* (1957), a successful filming of the Broadway hit, and *Teacher's Pet*, which paired her with screen legend Clark Gable. She was now considered a top box-office draw and became a highly recognizable international celebrity.

New Persona for a New Era

As with all enduring performers, Day realized the need for self-reinvention. She helped engineer her own in 1959, when she signed to star in *Pillow Talk*. At this point, public tastes were changing, and the kind of musicals she once appeared in fell out of fashion. Moreover, Day was now in her mid-thirties and far too old to continue playing the kind of roles that made her famous. By agreeing to do *Pillow Talk*, she successfully transitioned herself from a twenty-something ingénue to a thirty-something professional career woman. Furthermore, she switched genres from cornpone musicals to sophisticated comedy. As a result, Day would become more popular than ever. *Pillow Talk* provided a template for many of Day's subsequent films, which were replete with sexual innuendo and wherein Day played a sophisticated professional woman who fended off the advances of predatory males. Also, it was her first on-screen pairing with Rock Hudson, who would become a frequent co-star. Her role as "Jan Morrow" earned her an Oscar nomination.

Subsequent similarly themed romantic comedies included *Lover Come Back* (1962), *That Touch of Mink* (1962), *The Thrill of it All* (1963), *Move Over, Darling* (1963) and *Send Me No Flowers*, a 1964 film preceded by a marketing campaign that included the tag line, "Send me no flowers—just send me!" Day also appeared in *Do Not Disturb*, a 1965 film whose movie trailer advised moviegoers "Do not disturb Doris Day! Do not disturb Rod Taylor!" The suggestion was clear, if not explicit.

But Day's film activities weren't restricted to this kind of fare. During this new period, she also starred in the suspense film *Midnight Lace* (1960), wherein she was menaced by Rex Harrison; *Billy Rose's Jumbo*, a 1962 musical comedy that involved a circus and its beloved elephant; a western *The Ballad of Josie* (1967), as well as family comedies such as *Please Don't Eat the Daisies* (1960) and *With Six You Get Egg Roll* (1968). No matter the genre, however, the Doris Day name on a theater marquee assured box-office success, as it had become a familiar and popular commodity.

More Personal Problems Surfaced

Despite the ongoing success, Day's personal life would continue to be plagued by turmoil. By all appearances, her relationship with Marty Melcher seemed to be a Hollywood anomaly—that is, a happy marriage. But subterfuge was transpiring behind the façade. Throughout most of Day's career, Melcher acted as her agent and investment advisor. Working with Hollywood lawyer, Jerome B. Rosenthal, Melcher invested Day's money in hotels, oil and cattle. When Melcher died in 1968, however, Day's son Terry Melcher (Marty had adopted his wife's only son) reviewed her investments. To their shared dismay, Terry Melcher, who had become one of the most successful record producers in the Los Angeles music scene, discovered that Day's investments were essentially worthless. Moreover, Day now owed hundreds of thousands of dollars in back taxes, which essentially bankrupted her. Day also discovered that Marty Melcher had committed her, without her knowledge, to a television series. (This wasn't the first time something like this happened. Day revealed in her autobiography that she didn't want to do the 1965 film *Do Not Disturb*. But Marty Melcher, with his power of attorney, signed Day up for the picture without informing her. Day had no choice but to complete the assignment.)

Following the revelations of her late husband's business transactions, Day suffered nervous exhaustion and then a complete physical and emotional breakdown. But she recovered in time to fulfill her television commitment. "The Doris Day Show" ran from 1968 to 1973. Meanwhile, in 1969, Day sued Rosenthal. The five-year court battle finally ended in Day's favor: the judge awarded her $22 million in damages. By this time, Day's television show had been cancelled, and she assumed a much lower profile, appearing only in commercials and an occasional television special. By 1975, she announced her retirement, which allowed her to devote time and energy to a new passion: animal rights. A year later, she married again, but this union with Barry Comden ended in divorce four years later.

Subsequently, Day secluded herself on her Carmel, California ranch where she continued to advocate for animal rights. She established several organizations, including the Doris Day Pet Foundation and the Doris Day Animal League, both of which lobby for the welfare of animals.

Recognized for Accomplishments

Meanwhile, her career underwent positive critical reevaluation. Day became a star once again *in absentia*. In 1989 the Hollywood Foreign Press Association awarded Day a Golden Globe Lifetime Achievement Award. In addition, she received a Lifetime Achievement Comedy Award in 1991 from the American Comedy Awards.

Day was also the subject of two highly regarded biographies, *Doris Day: Her Own Story* (1976) by A. E. Hotchner and *Doris Day* (1991) by Eric Braun.

In 2004, Day, who is honored on Hollywood's Star Walk of Fame, received the Presidential Medal of Freedom. In 2008, she received a Grammy Award for Lifetime Achievement in Music. The recent awards underscored the reassessment of her work. Day became regarded as a versatile singer and actress whose talents were often under-appreciated. Also, books such as *The Films of Doris Day* (Christopher Young, 1977) and *Move over Misconceptions: Doris Day Reappraised* (Jane Clarke, 1980) provided positive career overviews.

Books

"Doris Day," *Contemporary Musicians*, Gale Group, 1999.

"Doris Day," *International Dictionary of Films and Filmmakers, Volume 3: Actors and Actresses*, St. James Press, 2000.

"Doris Day," *St. James Encyclopedia of Popular Culture*, St. James Press, 2000.

"Doris Day," *The Scribner Encyclopedia of American Lives Thematic Series: The 1960s*, Charles Scribner's Sons, 2003.

Online

"Doris Day," *Dorisdaytribute.com*, http://www.dorisdaytribute.com/biography.htm (October 20, 2009).

"Doris Day Biography," *Biography.com*, http://www.biography.com/articles/Doris-Day-9268553 (October 20, 2009).

"Doris Day," *TCM.com*, http://www.tcm.com/tcmdb/participant.jsp?participantId=45686 (October 20, 2009) □

Marian de Forest

American dramatist and journalist Marian de Forest (1864–1935) rose to great prominence in her own lifetime as part of the women's movement of the late nineteenth and early twentieth centuries. One of the United States' first female journalists, de Forest wrote for three different newspapers in her native Buffalo. In 1911, she expanded her written efforts to the stage with a well-respected dramatization of Louisa May Alcott's classic novel *Little Women*, the first of a number of plays that were produced both locally and nationwide. An avid supporter of cultural growth for western New York State, de Forest campaigned for the establishment of the Buffalo Philharmonic Orchestra. Although most famous for her dramatic work during her lifetime, her most lasting achievement is arguably the establishment of Zonta, a global professional women's organization that grew its membership from just a handful in 1919 to over 33,000 by 2010. In 2001, the National Women's Hall of Fame in Seneca Falls, New York, inducted de Forest for her far-reaching contributions to women's history.

Born on February 27, 1864, in Buffalo, New York, Marian de Forest was the daughter of furniture manufacturer and businessman Cyrus M. de Forest and his wife Sarah Germain Sutherland de Forest. While still a child, de Forest injured her eyes; this decline in vision required her to spend three years out of bright light, so she was privately tutored at home in a dim room. By memorizing all of her school lessons, the young de Forest developed an excellent memory that served her well throughout her later career. After her eyes had sufficiently recovered, she enrolled in the Buffalo Seminary. When she completed her studies at the institution in 1884, she became the youngest person up to that time to have graduated from the school.

Was Among Buffalo's First Female Journalists

Undeterred by the era's views of women in the workplace, de Forest decided to pursue a career in journalism. Between the mid-1880s and 1901, she reported first for the *Buffalo Evening News* and later for the *Buffalo Commercial*. When Buffalo hosted the Pan-American Exposition in 1901, de Forest served as executive secretary of the Board of Women Managers. Unusual for the time, the board decided not to separate women's achievements into their own separate exhibition; in a historical brochure transcribed on the Web site Doing the Pan, the board explained, "Wherever her skill or genius has given [woman] a title to excellence there her work will be shown and judged on its merits. The progress of science and the conquest of nature by means of invention, the increased perfection of machinery which eliminates the factor of human physical strength, and, above all, the successful prosecution by

woman of studies in superior education, makes the achievement of her ideal only a matter of time."

The following year, de Forest joined the staff of the *Buffalo Express,* where she soon rose to become drama critic and editor of the Women's Department. Her column "As I Go to the Play" ran in the newspaper until her departure from journalism in 1924, and afforded de Forest the opportunity to befriend some of the best known theatrical figures of her day. She met and befriended such famous performers as French actress Sarah Bernhardt and Italian opera singer Enrico Caruso, as well as the American actress Minnie Maddern Fiske. At the urging of Fiske, de Forest embarked on what would be one of the two most defining endeavors of her career: playwriting.

Brought *Little Women* to the Stage

In 1911, de Forest undertook the challenge of dramatizing Louisa May Alcott's *Little Women.* The novel explores the personalities, family relationships, and social and cultural world of sisters Meg, Jo, Beth, and Amy March and has been a popular hit from the time of its first publication in 1868. *Little Women* presented the nascent playwright with the somewhat daunting task of reinterpreting a much-beloved story in a new medium; added to this was the Alcott family's initial resistance in allowing the novel to be dramatized as many of the characters were inspired by the novelist's sisters and other relatives. De Forest—who had enjoyed the book since childhood—persevered, however, and her adaptation made its stage debut at Buffalo's Teck Theater in January of 1912. A warm reception in Buffalo preceded an equally successful Broadway production at the Playhouse in New York City, which opened in October of the same year. "It's a chastening experience, dramatizing a novel," de Forest later wrote in the *New York Times,* continuing, "also a valuable experience, provided one has a sense of humor; and it demonstrates afresh that books don't talk, that characters cannot be transferred unchanged from the printed page to the theater." She later traveled to London and Paris for productions of *Little Women,* which has also enjoyed occasional revivals in its now-lengthy history.

De Forest's next significant theatrical success came in 1916, when she dramatized Helen R. Martin's 1914 novel *Barnabetta.* Set in Pennsylvania Dutch country, the novel had told the story of title character Barnabetta Dreary's downtrodden existence until the girl's father remarries to the lively Juliet Miller. Miller develops a motherly affection for Barnabetta, and pays to send her away to boarding school where her existence takes a distinct turn for the better. Although de Forest's initial interpretation of the story had held true to the events of the novel, she later determined that some creative editorial work was called for. "I took [the manuscript] out again," she wrote in the *New York Times* article, "and, equipped with my trusty blue pencil, cut every line I thought was 'booky,' killed off a few characters with cheerful disregard for human life, boiled down the college experiences of Barnabetta, and introduced some of Barnabetta's people from her hometown, trusting to Juliet...to supply the something I knew was lacking in the college scene."

After a few more revisions, the completed drama—retitled *Erstwhile Susan,* a nod to Miller's nickname—entered production. Starring Fiske in the role of Juliet Miller, *Erstwhile Susan* opened at New York City's Gaiety Theatre in January of 1916. Although the *New York Times'* drama critic characterized the play as "a comedy with a slender, unpretentious, and quite insignificant story, scant dramatic value, a half-dozen unusual and rather interesting types, and then one all-absorbing character...Juliet," the review later went on to admit "there is some pleasant, flavorous comedy in the glimpses of...life among the Pennsylvania Dutch." Public reception of the work was strongly positive, however, and the play enjoyed a successful run of several weeks with a one-off revival at the end of the year. A 1919 film version starring Constance Binney and Anders Randolph followed. De Forest wrote a number of other plays, including *The Lovers of Yesteryear* and *Mr. Man,* although these efforts failed to attract the level of public notice of her first two efforts. In fact, de Forest considered publicity efforts for *Mr. Man* so disappointing that she had an airplane drop leaflets promoting it over the city of Buffalo. "She knew how to make a splash," Vivian Cody commented to Paula Voell of the *Buffalo News* about the incident in 2001.

Founded Women's Club Zonta

Back in Buffalo from her European jaunt, the journalist and playwright hosted a meeting in November of 1919 at the city's Hotel Statler that proved to be the commencement of a far-flung organization that long outlived de Forest herself: Zonta. The organization's Web site explained that "de Forest conceived the idea of an organization that would bring together women in executive positions. She envisioned a strong network that would help women reach their rightful place in the professions. She understood how important it was to break through the 'glass ceiling' long before the term was ever used." Taking its name from a Lakota Sioux word meaning "honest and trustworthy," the burgeoning group appointed de Forest as its first president. Women's clubs were popular social and cultural institution for progressive women of the era, and Zonta soon found a ready audience outside of Buffalo. The Confederation of Zonta Clubs initially took shape in nine cities, including Binghamton, New York; Buffalo; Detroit; Elmira, New York; Erie, Pennsylvania; Ithaca, New York; Rochester, New York; Syracuse, New York; and Utica, New York. By 1927, Zonta had become an international organization with the establishment of a club in Toronto, Ontario, Canada, and by the time of de Forest's death in 1935 Zonta claimed nearly 125 chapters in North America and Europe.

Along with her work with Zonta, de Forest worked tirelessly to promote greater cultural offerings around Buffalo. In 1924, she resigned from her longtime position at the *Buffalo Express* to found the Buffalo Musical Foundation. Committed to bringing symphony orchestra music to western New York, the foundation developed a program with the city's public schools to sponsor a series of visits by such major orchestras as the Boston Symphony Orchestra, the Detroit Symphony Orchestra, and the Cleveland Orchestra. After the onset of the Great Depression in the early 1930s, de Forest helped stage a Pop Concert to feature the talents of musicians who had lost their jobs. The Buffalo Musical Foundation at last achieved one of its greatest goals, the city hosting its own symphony. The Buffalo Philharmonic Orchestra played its first notes in 1935. De Forest also served on the board of directors of several prominent local organizations, including the Buffalo Public Library, the Humane Society, and the Society for the Prevention of Cruelty to Animals. Her lifelong devotion to animals was so great that after the death of her beloved pet cat, Sammy, in 1924, she had it interred at one of the state's earliest pet cemeteries.

During her declining years, de Forest remained active despite a lengthy battle with cancer. Her last major writing work came in 1933, when she collaborated with fellow playwright Zona Gale on a series of radio dramas that were broadcast by NBC as "Neighbors." De Forest died as a result of her illness at the age of 70 on February 17, 1935, at Buffalo's General Hospital. Although her international renown was great at the time of her death, de Forest slowly dropped out of the public consciousness even in her native Buffalo. Writing in 2001, Voell observed that "it seems the city really did lose her. No streets named for her, no schools, no municipal buildings. No public recognition of a woman [at the time of her death] called Buffalo's 'most renowned' and 'its first woman citizen.'" Indeed, although de Forest remains a remarkably obscure figure in light of her widespread fame only decades previously, she has gained increased recognition—at least in her hometown—in the new millennium. In 1998, members of the Zonta Club of Buffalo won induction for their founder to the Western New York Women's Hall of Fame. Three years later, the National Women's Hall of Fame in Seneca Falls, New York, inducted her into its ranks for her achievements in the arts and humanities. Later that decade, de Forest had a statue dedicated to her, and in June of 2009, the city of Buffalo granted de Forest a spot on its cultural walk of fame. Her indisputably significant cultural legacy, however, which includes not only her own creative works and the foundation of Zonta but also her efforts to propel women to a more equitable social role, does not seem to have guaranteed de Forest the kind of enduring fame that such contributions might seem to demand.

Periodicals

Buffalo News, March 17, 2001; September 14, 2002; June 25, 2009.

New York Times, December 22, 1911; January 19, 1916; January 23, 1916; March 5, 1916; December 4, 1916; February 18, 1935.

Online

"Marian de Forest," National Women's Hall of Fame, http://www.greatwomen.org/women.php?action=viewone&id=185 (January 8, 2010).

"Marian de Forest," Zonta International, http://www.zonta.org/site/DocServer/MariandeForestBiography.pdf?docID=701 (January 8, 2010).

"No 'Women's Department'," Doing the Pan, http://panam1901.org/womens/brochure_excerpt.htm (January 8, 2010). □

Thomas West De La Warr

English colonial official Thomas West, the Baron De La Warr (1577–1618), served as governor and captain general of the colony of Virginia. He is remembered for his refusal to let the early colonists abandon the Jamestown settlement after starvation, disease, and war with Native Americans decimated their ranks. Though his actual tenure at the colony was brief, he implemented tougher disciplinary rules and ordered new fortifications built. "If not for his appearance, Virginia might have gone the way of so many lost colonies," wrote Adam Goodheart in the *New York Times*. "What is now the Southeastern United States could well have ended up in the French or Dutch empires."

De La Warr came from a family that claimed to have come to the British Isles during William the Conqueror's Norman Conquest of England in 1066. The first ancestor to be ennobled was Roger La Warr, who served King Edward I. The third Baron De La Warr, also named Roger, took part in two notable victories in England's Hundred Years' War with France, the Battle of Crécy and the Battle of Poitiers. The title went through various permutations over the next three centuries, including passing over to the children of a sister of one late baron who had married into another titled family, the Wests. At one point, the title and its accompanying privileges were revoked when one heir was accused of trying to poison his uncle. That was De La Warr's grandfather, William West. The title was restored to the family in 1563, 14 years before De La Warr's birth in 1577.

Born in Hampshire

The future Virginia governor is thought to have been born at the family's manor home at Wherwell Abbey in Hampshire, a property granted to the family by Thomas Cromwell, who supervised King Henry VIII's famous Dissolution of the Monasteries in the 1530s. The original Wherwell Abbey was a convent of Benedictine nuns that dated back to 986 and had been founded by the wife of one of England's Saxon kings.

De La Warr's mother was Anne Knollys West, whose father was a courtier during the reign of Henry and his daughter, Queen Elizabeth I. In the early 1590s, De La Warr entered Queen's College of Oxford University, but left before earning a degree. He traveled in Italy before returning to marry Cecilia Shirley in a ceremony that took place at St. Dunstan's in the West Church in London in November of 1596. Shirley's soldier-father was a Member of Parliament and knighted by Elizabeth, but later resorted to piracy to repay debts owed to the crown by the family.

De La Warr's career followed some of the same turns as his father-in-law's, with the exception of the piracy. He was elected to Parliament and served in England's army stationed in the Low Countries. In 1599 he followed his cousin, Robert Devereux, to Ireland when Devereux became Lord Lieutenant of Ireland. Devereux, also known as the second Earl of Essex, was a top advisor to Elizabeth, and foolishly convinced the regent to send him to Ireland with a massive military force. At the time, the neighboring British isle was technically held by the crown, but English authority there was weak. Both Henry and Elizabeth tried to reassert power in what was called the Tudor Reconquest, which prompted a full-scale rebellion in 1594 by Irish chieftains under Hugh O'Neill.

Battled the Irish

De La Warr was one of the military commanders among the 16,000 troops that Devereux brought to Ireland to subdue O'Neill's forces. Devereux knighted him in Dublin on July 12, 1599. These knighthoods were controversial, however, as was Devereux's failed military campaign in which he was forced to agree to a truce with O'Neill. Devereux returned to England, was arrested, and many of his privileges were revoked. De La Warr remained loyal to him, however, and was implicated in the Earl of Essex's rebellion against Elizabeth in February of 1601. Devereux was ultimately beheaded as a traitor. De La Warr was held in the Wood Street Counter, a jail in the City of London district, but was eventually pardoned.

De La Warr's father died on March 24, 1602, and with that he inherited the title and all family assets. He also took a seat at the Privy Council, a group of core advisors to Elizabeth. She died in 1603, but a succession crisis was prevented by her deathbed proclamation that the son of Mary I of Scotland should succeed her on the throne. De La Warr retained his seat on the Privy Council under the new monarch, James I.

James was eager to establish settlements in the New World, as Spain had done. In fact, the Spanish had reaped massive financial rewards through discoveries of gold and silver in South and Central America. Sir Walter Raleigh, a favorite of Queen Elizabeth, was granted a charter to establish a colony on a piece of Virginia land in the 1580s, but the settlers vanished and were thought to have either died or been absorbed into the Native American population. In 1606 James granted charters to a pair of joint-stock companies, the Virginia Company of London and the Virginia Company of Plymouth. The Plymouth venture was assigned the lands between latitude 45 degrees and 38 degrees North, while the London Company was granted permission to settle on the coastline between latitudes of 34 degrees and 41 degrees North. The rights held by the Plymouth shareholders eventually passed over to members of the Puritan sect, who sent their first expedition to settle what is present-day Massachusetts in 1620.

Invested in Virginia Company

The first Virginia Company settlers arrived in 1607 in a place they named Jamestown in honor of the king. This was an uninhabited spit of land formed by a lesser southern inlet of the Chesapeake Bay, and some distance from the ill-fated Roanoke Island settlement. The first colonists thought the place had excellent geographic advantages—but it was uninhabited for a reason. The brackish water was unfit to drink and became a breeding ground for mosquitoes and other pests in the long, humid summer.

The first colonists were affluent gentlemen farmers who were, historians caution, somewhat averse to actual hard labor. Furthermore, they found the climate unbearable. There were scores of other problems, including relations with nearby Powhattan Nation residents and outbreaks of illnesses like dysentery, an intestinal infection caused by drinking impure water. In 1609 De La Warr was named to the superior council of the Virginia Company and charter-holder in a second joint-stock venture reconstituted from the original one. This time, a governor would be appointed to head the colony, and Captain John Ratcliffe was named to the post.

The new London Company sent out a second expedition of supplies and new settlers in June of 1609. On July 25, 1609, the main vessel, the *Sea Venture*, was separated from two smaller ones by a hurricane off the coast of Bermuda, an uninhabited atoll about 650 miles from the coast of present-day North Carolina. The party was forced to winter over on the island to rebuild the vessel. This second Jamestown expedition finally reached the Virginia settlement in May of 1610 after what had been the most terrible winter, forever commemorated as the Starving Time. Scores of the Jamestown colonists had died from sickness or malnutrition, while others had been killed by Powhattan while stealing food. Some had escaped and gone to live elsewhere, possibly in Native American communities. The two commanders in charge of the *Sea Venture* decided that they would look for the others and then return to England with all surviving settlers.

Ordered Colonists to Remain

De La Warr, meanwhile, was appointed "Lord Governour and Captaine Generall of Virginia" for life on February 28, 1610,

and he left England on April 1 of that year with his own ship. He brought another two vessels loaded with supplies and 150 additional colonists. They arrived at Cape Henry on June 5, and reached Jamestown on June 10. They came across the *Sea Venture* group and were told of the plan to head back to England. As governor, De La Warr possessed absolute authority, and ordered everyone to stay. He sent one of his top aides to Bermuda for more provisions, and another to England for further help.

The military-style disciplinary tactics De La Warr implemented were the same deployed on campaigns in Ireland to maintain control—in order to receive food rations, the men had to work. While some colonists were assigned the task of building stronger fortifications, others were sent out on raiding parties to steal food and burn the Powhattans' crops.

Fears that Jamestown had been a poor choice for a settlement rose again, however, for almost as soon as he arrived De La Warr himself became ill. Finally, when the winter passed and he had effected an uneasy truce with the Powhattan, he departed for a place he called "Mevis" in late March of 1611. This was possibly the island of Nevis in the West Indies, but his ship was blown off course to what he called the "Western Iles" (islands), possibly the Bahamas. He recovered and arrived in England in June of 1611.

Virginia Killed Him

De La Warr wrote a well-preserved report that was entered into the record at Stationers' Hall, London, on July 6, 1611 as *The Relation of the Right Honourable the Lord De-la-Warre, Lord Governour and Captaine Generall of the Colonie, Planted in Virginea*. He delivered the document to the unhappy shareholders of the London Company, who were dismayed by the meager return on their investment to date and were themselves clamoring for an end to the project; some were threatening to halt their regular subscription payments to fund the colony. In his report, De La Warr recounted his illnesses, including a terrible bout with dysentery. It was, he nevertheless asserted, a fine spot for settlement. "The countrey is wonderfull fertile and very rich," he wrote, "and makes good whatsoever heretofore hath beene reported of it, the Cattell already there, are much encreased, and thrive exceedingly with the pasture of that Countrey."

De La Warr himself was the largest investor in the Virginia colony by that point, as were his three brothers, all of whom had gone with him. He had left Sir Samuel Argall in charge, but Argall was an ineffective manager and so De La Warr made plans, once more, to return to Virginia. His ships left in March of 1618, stopping in the Azores, the Portuguese-held islands in the middle of the Atlantic Ocean. There are conflicting reports whether De La Warr died there, died at sea, or died after the main vessel, the *Neptune*, reached Virginia. His date of death is usually cited as June 7, 1618.

One of the colonists who had been delayed by the Bermuda hurricane of 1609 was John Rolfe, who famously married Pocahontas, the daughter of a Powhattan chief. Rolfe was also responsible for introducing the first tobacco crops to Virginia, which helped the colony thrive. De La Warr's survivors, including his wife and five daughters, received a sum of 500 pounds per year from the customs duties on Virginia tobacco and other exports. After De La Warr's death, the

English named a bay to the north, called Poutaxat by the Lenape Indians, in his honor. From this the Delaware River and state of Delaware take their names.

Books

Calder, Isabel M., "Thomas West De La Warr," in *Dictionary of American Biography Base Set,* American Council of Learned Societies, 1928-1936.

De La Warr, Thomas West, "The Relation of the Right Honourable the Lord De-la-Warre, Lord Governour and Captaine Generall of the Colonie, planted in Virginea," in *Narratives of Early Virginia, 1606-1625,* Volume 5 of *Original Narratives of Early American History,* edited by Lyon Gardiner Tyler, C. Scribner's Sons, 1907, pp. 205–214.

Horn, James, *A Land as God Made It: Jamestown and the Birth of America,* Basic Books, 2006.

Periodicals

New York Times, July 2, 2006. □

Oscar Stanton De Priest

The American politician Oscar De Priest (1871–1951) was the first African American elected to the United States Congress in the post-Reconstruction era, and the first elected from a northern state.

After a long rise through Chicago's cutthroat political structure, De Priest served three terms in the House of Representatives in the late 1920s and early 1930s. His influence is measured less by his legislative contributions or even by his pioneer status than by his outspokenness in attempting to further African-American political influence—at a time when few African-American politicians could be described as outspoken. De Priest was a Republican, and he shared many of the conservative views of the party of which he was a member. When it came to racial issues, however, De Priest was surrounded by controversy almost as soon as he arrived in Washington. He relished his new role, which gave him the opportunity to confront the entrenched influence of Southern segregationists.

Witnessed Political Violence

The son of former slaves, Oscar Stanton De Priest was born in a cabin in Florence, Alabama, on March 9, 1871. His father, Neander De Priest, was a teamster and part-time farmer, and his mother, Martha, did laundry to help the family get by. Growing up at a time when white Southerners were trying to reassert control over newly freed African Americans during the Reconstruction era, De Priest witnessed several instances of terrorism and political violence while he was still a small child. His father protected the African-American Republican congressman James Rapier from a kidnapping attempt. A white Republican politician was shot near the De Priest family home, and a neighbor was shot a dozen times and then hanged in front of his house. In 1878 the De Priest family joined other African-American "Exodusters" (as they were known) in a migration west to Kansas.

De Priest was safer in his new home of Salina, Kansas. He and his siblings were the only African Americans enrolled at the local elementary school. Although they were on the receiving end of racial taunts, De Priest was able to defend himself against them in a way that had been impossible in the Deep South. He took bookkeeping courses at the Salina Normal School, and in 1888 he and two white classmates ran away from home and got as far as Dayton, Ohio. The following year he made his way to Chicago, becoming one of the first wave of African-American arrivals in that growing city of stockyards and trade.

Sometimes passing for white in order to land jobs (and sometimes losing them when his identity was revealed), De Priest found work as a house painter and carpenter's apprentice. He realized that there was money to be made in providing housing for the growing tide of African-American migrants fleeing oppression in the South, and in the 1890s he started a painting and decorating business that evolved into a real estate agency. In 1898 he married Jessie Williams, and the pair had one son, Oscar Jr., born in 1906. By that time De Priest had begun to get involved in local politics. He attended a local Republican precinct meeting and agreed to cast a deciding vote in a deadlocked contest for precinct captain on condition that the winner would in turn name De Priest precinct secretary.

As Chicago's African-American population grew, De Priest took the lead in organizing newcomers to the South

Side's Second and Third Wards. This made him a player in the city's machine-dominated politics, in which street-level work was rewarded by patronage and low-level political office. In 1904 De Priest was slated for and elected to a seat on the Cook County Board of Commissioners. He was re-elected in 1906 but ran afoul of Republican U.S. Representative Martin B. Madden in 1908 and was not renominated. For several years De Priest concentrated on building his real estate business, which brought him considerable wealth. He acquired properties whose prices were depressed due to white flight from integrating neighborhoods, and rented them out to new arrivals at high prices. In 1915, after cultivating relationships with Madden and Chicago's Republican mayor, William "Big Bill" Thompson, De Priest was elected to the Chicago City Council, becoming its first African-American alderman.

Charged with Accepting Bribes, Exonerated

Over his two terms on council, De Priest faced charges that he had accepted payoffs from club and theater owners involved in gambling, prostitution, and police bribery. Convinced to step down from office in 1918 rather than run for a third term, he went to trial and was defended by the prominent trial lawyer Clarence Darrow. De Priest was acquitted, and though he was plagued by corruption charges at various points in his career, he was never convicted of any wrongdoing.

After his acquittal De Priest ran again for council as an independent, but lost. During Chicago's largely white-instigated race riots in 1919, black Chicagoans reported that he worked to free black stockyard workers trapped by white mobs and armed himself in order to carry food supplies through white neighborhoods. He continued to work behind the scenes politically, serving as an alternate delegate to the Republican National Convention in 1920 and becoming the Third Ward Republican Committeeman in 1924. In 1928 he announced his support for Madden's re-election bid although William Dawson, an African-American Democrat, was also running for the seat.

When Madden died soon after the 1928 primary elections, De Priest saw his chance. Thompson agreed to back him as Madden's replacement on the Republican ticket, and De Priest faced a white Democrat, Harry Baker, and an African-American independent, William Harrison, in the November election. The lakefront First Congressional District was split between the predominantly white downtown area and the South Side's historically African-American neighborhoods. De Priest emerged the winner with 48 percent of the vote; in his re-election campaigns in 1930 and 1932 he won outright majorities.

Almost from the day he arrived in Washington, De Priest faced resentment from segregationist Southern Democrats, and he responded aggressively. Some conspired to prevent him from being seated at all, based on charges that De Priest had protected South Side gambling rings, although De Priest had been cleared of all charges before the election. De Priest's secretary, who was black, was refused seating in the House restaurant at the behest of North Carolina Representative Lindsay Warren, and De Priest responded with a petition urging investigation of Warren's right to do so. A group of Howard University students showed up at the restaurant to support De Priest and demanded seating.

A speech De Priest gave on the House floor in support of his petition quoted a letter he had received from another Southern congressman that said (according to *Time*), "I neither eat nor sleep with the Negroes, and no law can make me do so." "Nobody asked the gentleman to sleep with him," De Priest retorted. "That was not in my mind at all. I do not know why he thought of it. I am very careful about whom I sleep with." A Tennessee newspaper warned readers that De Priest was coming to town to talk about social equality. "Nothing was further from my mind," De Priest declared in the same speech, "but after they had made that charge and in order to make the papers of Chattanooga say something that was true for once in their lives, I did say something about it. This is what I said: 'When the Negroes came to this country originally they were all black; they are not now, because somebody has had a good deal of social equality.'" Despite De Priest's energetic rhetoric and the students' early use of the sit-in technique, the protest was ultimately unsuccessful.

Controversy Followed Wife's Invitation

The biggest controversy flared in the summer of 1929 when First Lady Lou Hoover, following longstanding custom, invited the wives of House members to the White House for tea. Although African Americans, back as far as abolitionist Frederick Douglass, had been invited to the White House before, the issue became controversial. On July 1, *Time* noted dryly that De Priest "continued last week to be the most conspicuous Negro in the U.S." Finally Mrs. De Priest was invited, along with a small group of carefully selected congressional wives, and appeared at the White House in a blue chiffon dress. The White House police force was advised in advance not to turn away its black female visitor. "It can be stated that Mrs. De Priest conducted herself with perfect propriety," recalled a White House usher quoted by Henry Chase in *American Visions*. "She really seemed the most composed one in the group."

Southerners, according to press accounts quoted by Chase, were "outraged," "affronted," "insulted," and "humiliated." South Carolina senator Coleman Blease inserted racist verse about the incident in the Congressional Record; it was later expunged. The *Jackson Daily News* in Mississippi warned President and Mrs. Herbert Hoover not to visit the South and, according to *Time*, editorialized that "the De Priest incident has placed President and Mrs. Hoover beyond the pale of social recognition by Southern people." Unintimidated, De Priest used his congressional prerogative to nominate Benjamin O. Davis for enrollment at the U.S. Military Academy in West Point, New York; according to *Time*, he warned that if Davis was not allowed to graduate he would send "bigger and blacker" recruits on subsequent occasions.

De Priest commanded sizable crowds at African-American events and used his position as a bully pulpit. "If your district leader is a white man, pitch him out," he told a crowd in New York's Harlem neighborhood, according to *Time*. "You have a jimmy in your votes to better conditions. Use it. Don't complain about race discrimination; change it through practical politics. When a Negro doesn't want to elect a Negro, there is either jealousy or dirty money behind him." Where race was not involved, though, De Priest was a loyal Republican. He warned against Communist influence in urban areas, and for several years opposed the New Deal social welfare and economic recovery policies of President Franklin Roosevelt, although he did sponsor a 1933 measure that outlawed racial discrimination on work crews created by Roosevelt's Civilian Conservation Corps.

Some of De Priest's views changed as the effects of the Great Depression deepened in his South Side Chicago district, but by then it was too late for him to resist the realignment from Republican to Democrat that occurred in African-American communities in the 1930s. De Priest faced criticism from civil rights activists for opposing Roosevelt's reforms, although he was applauded for giving speeches in the South in the face of death threats. In the 1934 election De Priest was challenged by Arthur Mitchell, a Republican turned Democrat, and was defeated, losing to Mitchell again in 1936. Between 1943 and 1947 De Priest served two more terms on the Chicago City Council. He continued to operate his real estate business until his death in Chicago on May 12, 1951, after being hit by a bus.

Books

Notable Black American Men, edited by Jessie Carney Smith, Gale, 1998.

Periodicals

American Visions, February–March 1995.

New York Post, January 20, 2009.

Time, July 1, 1929, July 15, 1929, September 2, 1929, April 2, 1934, November 19, 1934.

Online

"De Priest, Oscar Stanton (1871–1951)," *Biographical Dictionary of the United States Congress,* http://www.bioguide.congress.gov/scripts/biodisplay.pl?index=D000263 (November 12, 2009).

"Oscar Stanton De Priest," *Black Americans in Congress, 1870–2007: U.S. House of Representatives,* http://www.baic.house.gov/member-profiles/profile.html?intID=28 (November 12, 2009).

"The Oscar Stanton De Priest House," *National Park Service,* http://www.nps.gov/history/nr/travel/civilrights/il1.htm (November 12, 2009). □

Donna de Varona

American swimmer Donna de Varona (born 1947) competed for just seven years, yet during that time she broke 18 world records, captured 37 national titles and earned two Olympic gold medals. After retiring from swimming at 17, de Varona worked for ABC, becoming the first female sports broadcaster on a major network. Passionate about promoting amateur sports and opportunities for women in sports, de Varona advocated for 1972's landmark Title IX legislation (which allowed equal opportunity for female athletes), as well as 1978's Amateur Sports Act.

The second of four children, Donna Elizabeth de Varona was born April 26, 1947, in San Diego to David and Martha de Varona. She was of Spanish, Welsh and German descent. By the time de Varona entered grade school, the family lived in Lafayette, California, near the San Francisco Bay. Each of the de Varona children participated in sports, inspired by their athlete-father. An All-American left tackle, David de Varona represented the University of California-Berkeley at the 1937 Rose Bowl. He also crewed for the college's championship rowing team. While David de Varona's sports career ended after college—he worked as an insurance salesman—he enjoyed coaching his children and their sports-minded friends. De Varona's little sister, Joanna, was a gymnast. Her older brother played football at the University of Oregon and her little brother became an avid golfer.

As a young girl, de Varona fell in love with baseball and followed her older brother, David Jr., to his Little League games. She spent her allowance on bubble gum so the players would let her into the dugout. De Varona thought they might let her play but this was long before the passage of Title IX afforded U.S. girls an equal opportunity on the nation's playing fields and courts. To appease her desires, de Varona was given a uniform and made a bat girl. "I wore a cap with my ponytail sticking out the back, and I really got into the spirit of the games," de Varona recalled in the book *After Olympic Glory* by Larry Bortstein. "But I always wondered why I couldn't play. I assumed at first that I would somehow get to play just because I was around all the time, but nothing like that ever happened."

Discovered Swimming

De Varona took diving lessons but was not overly enthusiastic about the sport. In 1957, her older brother injured his knee and had surgery. To help rehabilitate his leg, he attended a recreational camp and de Varona followed along. While there, she discovered a passion for the water and knew she wanted to compete against other swimmers the way her brother competed on the baseball diamond. De Varona's father took her to visit several swim coaches and one of the first ones they spoke with refused to take her, despite her obvious talent. Just 10, de Varona had yet to master each stroke and the coach thought she was too old to start.

Undaunted, de Varona began training under her father's direction. She started competing in novice meets and fared well. Soon, other coaches took notice and she was asked to join the Berkeley YMCA swim program. De Varona was thrilled. While she knew the YMCA swim program would probably not be as rigorous as a private-club program, she was happy to find a place to train. Getting to the Berkeley Y took dedication—de Varona had to take two buses and walk about a mile to meet her ride. By the age of 11, she was completing daily workouts at the Y to improve her stroke proficiency. The place was not ideal, however—the pool at the Berkeley Y was only 20 yards long, whereas competition pools were 50 meters, or about 51.5 yards.

One of de Varona's coaches at the Berkeley Y included Weikko "Finn" Ruuska, an established coach who pushed his swimmers with grueling workouts. The team included Ruuska's daughter, Sylvia, who was the star athlete. De Varona learned many skills from Ruuska, such as how to breathe on both sides and how to work hard. However, the more de Varona's times and techniques improved, the less Ruuska helped her. He concentrated his coaching efforts on his daughter, who did become an Olympic medalist. Ruuska even went so far as to accuse de Varona of taking pep pills to enhance her performance. Tensions mounted, yet de Varona stayed at the Berkeley Y and began training under a different coach, Tatto Yamashita. By now, she was a serious competitor, swimming both before and after school.

Qualified for Olympics at 13

In July 1960, de Varona traveled to Indianapolis to swim in the Amateur Athletic Union (AAU) outdoor nationals. Just 13, the 5-foot-2 de Varona, weighing about 100 pounds, was ranked among the top swimmers in the 400-meter individual medley. In the medley, swimmers compete with four different strokes, swimming each for 100 meters. They have to race each stroke in order—butterfly, backstroke, breaststroke and freestyle. At the nationals, de Varona broke the 400-meter individual medley world record with a time of 5 minutes, 36.5 seconds. The old record, which de Varona bested by nearly four seconds, was held by her rival, Sylvia Ruuska. Unfortunately for de Varona, the 400-meter individual medley was not yet an Olympic event—for women. In 1960, male swimmers could compete in the event, but not women. De Varona did, however, make the 1960 U.S. Olympic swim team, qualifying as an alternate for the 400-meter freestyle relay.

De Varona turned 13 four months before the 1960 Summer Olympics, held in Rome, and was the youngest member of the U.S. Olympic team. Her parents could not afford to make the trip, so she went alone with the team and befriended many of the older athletes during her time at the Olympic Village. Her Olympic teammates included boxer Muhammad Ali and sprinter Wilma Rudolph, who each won gold. In Rome, de Varona worked out with the team and swam in the races to qualify the relay team for the finals. As an alternate, de Varona did not get to swim in the finals when the team came in first. In later years, this would have qualified de Varona for a medal. Olympic rules changed and by the 21st century, swimmers who helped qualify their teams for the finals also received medals even if they did not swim in the finals. While de Varona enjoyed the experience, she also found it frustrating to hold a world record in an event and not get to officially swim at the Olympics.

De Varona returned home and continued to improve her times. At the AAU nationals in August 1961, de Varona broke her world record, swimming the medley in 5 minutes, 34.5 seconds. At 14, de Varona set a world record in the women's 200-meter individual medley in Tenri, Japan. By the time de Varona was in high school, the family had moved to Santa Clara so she could join the Santa Clara Swim Club and train under George Haines, who later coached Olympic phenom Mark Spitz. During the early 1960s, de Varona continued her hot streak. A competent backstroke swimmer, de Varona broke the 100-meter backstroke world record in 1963 with a time of 1 minute and 8.9 seconds. De Varona's enthusiasm for swimming increased after it was announced that the women's 400-meter individual medley would be added to the 1964 Summer Olympics.

Won Double-Gold in 1964

During the 1964 Olympic trials, de Varona set a new world record in the 400-meter individual medley, winning with a time of 5 minutes, 14.9 seconds. She became a media darling. Swift in the water and spunky on land, the press could not get enough of her. In the months leading up to the Olympics, de Varona appeared on the covers of *Life, Time, Sports Illustrated,* and the *Saturday Evening Post.*

De Varona traveled to Tokyo in October 1964 to compete in the games. The United States swept the 400-meter individual medley, with de Varona taking first with a time of 5 minutes, 18.7 seconds. She also competed in the 100-meter butterfly, but placed fifth. De Varona brought home a second gold, however, as a member of the 400-meter freestyle relay team, which won first place with a world-record time of 4 minutes, 3.8 seconds.

In an article profiling female athletes in *Joe Weider's Shape,* de Varona said she returned home from the Olympics disillusioned when she realized her male teammates were going to continue swimming, having earned scholarships to Yale and Stanford, "while the message to me was, 'You're a girl, so now you have to stop.' I said, 'Is my gold medal less valuable?' Because of my gender, the rewards weren't there." With no scholarships available, she decided to quit swimming and became determined to increase the opportunities available to female athletes in the future. De Varona entered the University of California-Los Angeles in 1965 to study political science and pledged Kappa Kappa Gamma.

Became Broadcaster, Activist

De Varona called ABC and asked for a job. Over the years, de Varona had befriended Jim McKay, host of ABC's *Wide World of Sports.* McKay had interviewed de Varona several times. During the 1964 nationals, de Varona allowed McKay's crew to place a camera under her in the lane to capture live footage. This was long before underwater cameras were placed in tracks below the athletes. The task involved submerging a scuba diver under de Varona. In a 2005 interview with *Swimming World,* de Varona recalled the spectacle. "After the race, the frogman asked me how it went, and I told him, 'In the future, just don't breathe when I swim over you—the bubbles are distracting.'"

In 1965, de Varona began her broadcast career with ABC's *Wide World of Sports,* offering commentary at the AAU's indoor swimming men's championships. De Varona was the first female sportscaster hired by a major network television. She went on to cover 17 Olympic Games and also did work for Sporting News radio. In 1991, she won an Emmy Award for producing a story about a one-armed Special Olympics swimmer. Breaking into the male-dominated world of sports reporting was no easy task, though, as de Varona recalled in the *San Francisco Chronicle.* "I had two things I had to fight: one was how young I was and the other was a stereotype, 'Do we put women on a football or baseball interview?' It took me years to convince people that was OK."

During the early 1970s, de Varona advocated for the passage of Title IX, which opened equal opportunities for females in sports. After the law passed, she pushed for its implementation, as many schools were slow to institute changes. In 1974, de Varona helped tennis great Billie Jean King found the Women's Sports Foundation, which advocates for female athletes at all levels and helps them find scholarships. De Varona also worked for the United Nations' Right to Play program, which provides children around the globe with opportunities for physical and social development through sports. She also spent time in Washington, D.C., stumping for congressional reform in the area of amateur sports and pushing funding for physical education programs in public schools. She continued her involvement with the Olympics by serving on the International Olympic Committee's Women in Sport commission in the early 2000s. During the late 1980s, de Varona married investment banker John Pinto. The couple had two children, John and Joanna, who grew up playing sports like their mother.

Books

Bortstein, Larry, *After Olympic Glory,* Frederick Warne & Co., 1978.

Thomas, Bob, *Donna de Varona: Gold Medal Swimmer,* Doubleday & Co., 1968.

Periodicals

Advocate (Stamford-Norwalk, CT), December 3, 2005.
Joe Weider's Shape, April 1999.
New York Times, July 16, 1960.
San Francisco Chronicle, February 12, 1987; May 6, 2001.
Swimming World, December 2005.

Online

"One on One-Donna de Varona-12 Dec 09-Part 1," CastTV, http://www.casttv.com/video/. □

Dolores Del Rio

Actress Dolores Del Rio (1905–1983) was one of the first film performers from Mexico to gain an international reputation, and she rivaled Greta Garbo in providing images of exotic foreign beauty in the Hollywood film industry of the 1930s.

Del Rio was a pioneer both in the United States and in her home country. Often typecast in ethnic roles, she resisted such stereotyping to a degree and managed the financial aspects of her career astutely. She made appearances in several key films that marked the beginning of a serious film industry in Mexico, and her stage career eventually brought her the unofficial status of First Lady of Mexican Theater. Even if her career was hampered by American attitudes toward Latin culture at several points, she has continued to be recognized as a major star of the silent era and to exert a fascination related to her cultural background.

Family Fled Pancho Villa

Del Rio was born in the northern Mexican city of Durango on August 3, 1905. Her family was well off, and her birth name reflected the aristocratic Spanish and Latin American practice of combining the father's and mother's family names; it has been reported as Lolita Dolores Martínez Asúnsolo López Negrete and as Lolita Dolores Asúnsolo y López Negrete. Del Rio's father, Jesús Asúnsolo, was the director of the Bank of Durango. When conflict broke out in northern Mexico during Del Rio's childhood, her father had to flee the armies of revolutionary general Pancho Villa and seek refuge in the U.S. Dolores and her mother, Antonia, were sent to Mexico City, where Dolores attended a French-language convent school and studied dance.

In 1921 she married lawyer Jaime Del Río. The couple spent their honeymoon in Europe, and Dolores made her stage debut in entertainment revues mounted for members of the Spanish military. Back in Mexico, she met U.S. silent film director Edwin Carewe through a mutual friend, artist Adolfo Best Maugard, and Carewe invited her to come to Hollywood. She arrived in August of 1925 and was cast in a small part in Carewe's film *Joanna.* Publicity for the film billed Del Rio as a Spanish actress, but she demanded that the billing be changed to accurately reflect her Mexican origins. After she landed a few more substantial parts, Del Rio was picked as one of the "Baby Stars" of the year by the Western Association of Motion Picture Advertisers in 1926.

She made the most of her turn in the spotlight that year with the controversial *What Price Glory?,* directed by Raoul Walsh. Del Rio played Charmaine, a French girl desired by both of the film's brawling U.S. Marine male leads. The film

became a box-office hit and propelled Del Rio to a leading position during the last few years of the silent era, although her ethnicity remained fluid on film. In 1927 she appeared as a Russian peasant in *Resurrection,* an adaptation of a novel by Leo Tolstoy. Between 1925 and 1929 Del Rio appeared in 15 silent films. Her starring performance in 1928's *Ramona* was praised by the *New York Times,* which noted: "Not once does she overact, and yet she is perceived weeping and almost hysterical. She is most careful in all the moods of the character. Her beauty is another point in her favor."

Learned English Because of "Talkies"

In silent films Del Rio's poor command of English did not present a problem, but that would soon change. "When sound arrived in 1929 I was faced with the awful fact that I had to learn English," she recalled to Stan Maays of the *Palm Beach Post.* "So at first I turned to people I'd worked with. You know, Victor MacLaglen played a trick on me. He taught me some terrible things to say. But I eventually hired a coach and worked hard." She retained a Latin accent, however, and this continued to circumscribe somewhat the roles that were available to her during the 1930s.

After singing several French-language songs in the otherwise silent 1929 film *Evangeline,* Del Rio released her first "talkie," the melodramatic *The Bad One,* in 1930. She signed a contract with the United Artists studio that promised her the impressive salary of $9,000 a week but was unable to honor it due to an illness that sidelined her for some months in 1930 and 1931. Del Rio married her second husband, MGM studio

art director Cedric Gibbons (the designer of the Academy Award Oscar statuette), in 1930, and the couple moved into a palatial home in Santa Monica, California. In 1932 Del Rio signed with the RKO studio and appeared in *Bird of Paradise,* playing a Polynesian girl who throws herself into a volcano at the climax of the film. Producer David O. Selznick had ordered that a story be written around that scene and had specified Del Rio as the lead. Del Rio also appeared in *The Girl of the Rio* that year.

The Girl of the Rio was successful, but its views of Mexico were negative enough that the Mexican government lodged a formal protest against it, and it was banned in several Latin American countries. In 1933 Del Rio co-starred with Fred Astaire and Ginger Rodgers in *Flying Down to Rio,* a film notable for its dual introductions of Astaire and Rodgers as a dance team and of the two-piece bathing suit in Hollywood film, worn by Del Rio. A feature on Del Rio in *Photoplay* magazine in 1934 emphasized her physical attributes; after consulting with "medical men, artists, and designers" (as quoted by Kristin Tillotson of the Minneapolis *Star Tribune*), the magazine issued the pronouncement that Del Rio had an ideal feminine figure.

Del Rio represented an evolution in the favored look of Hollywood's lead actresses, from the heavily made-up round faces of the silent era to the sculpted, high-cheekboned face of the 1940s and beyond. She was often compared to another foreign actress, Sweden's Greta Garbo, and the German actress Marlene Dietrich pronounced her even more beautiful than Garbo. Over the rest of the 1930s and early 1940s, Del Rio's on-screen ethnicity varied from French (*International Settlement*) to Arabic (*Ali Baba Goes to Town*) to unspecified South American (*I Live for Love*) in a series of mostly forgettable films, but her own Mexican heritage was rarely on view.

Denied Flower Petal Consumption Rumors

Although Del Rio was rarely under consideration at season-ending awards presentations, she got plenty of press. Del Rio's youthful good looks—which caused Hal Erickson of the *All Movie Guide* to write that even in 1960 she looked "far too young to play Elvis Presley's mother" in *Flaming Star*—spawned bizarre rumors that she slept for 16 hours a day and subsisted mostly on gardenia (or orchid) petals in an attempt to maintain her favorable complexion. Del Rio categorically denied the rumors to Maays, saying, "That's all part of some silly legend. And to say that I sleep 16 hours a day, why, that's ridiculous. How could I possibly sleep that long when I have so much to do?" After Del Rio's marriage to Gibbons ended in divorce, she became one of Hollywood's most sought-after single actresses. She dated director Orson Welles during the creative period that included his classic *Citizen Kane,* and one of the best films of the first part of her career was the Welles-produced spy thriller *Journey Into Fear* (1942). Soon after that, disillusioned by the direction of her career and by negative publicity surrounding Welles's new relationship with actress Rita Hayworth, Del Rio decided to return home to Mexico.

Del Rio's work in Mexico brought her the critical acclaim she had mostly missed in the U.S. She released two important Mexican dramas in 1943: *Flor silvestre* (Wildflower) and *María Candelaria,* both directed by Emilio Fernández. The latter film, about a young woman in a small town who is stoned to death after a false accusation that she has posed nude for a painting, won the Golden Palm award at the Cannes Film Festival in 1946 when European film festivals resumed after World War II. Del Rio appeared frequently in Mexican films in the 1940s and 1950s, winning several best-actress awards, and in 1948 she had a starring role in *The Fugitive,* a film by American director John Ford that was made mostly in Mexico. Del Rio's career in the 1950s may have been slowed by restrictions in place in Hollywood during the period of artistic pressure from the anti-Communist investigations of Senator Joseph McCarthy; she had aided refugees from the Spanish Civil War who had fought against the armies of future authoritarian leader Francisco Franco.

In Mexico, Del Rio was widely recognized for her work as a stage actress and was even (according to *Turner Classic Movies*) dubbed "the first lady of Mexican theater." In 1956 she appeared in summer stock shows in the New England area. Her Mexican theatrical career began at the suggestion of American producer Lewis Riley, who suggested that she appear in a 1958 Mexican production of the Oscar Wilde play *Lady Windemere's Fan.* Riley and Del Rio married in 1960 and took up residence near Mexico City. In the 1960s she appeared in several films and television programs, rejoining John Ford for the western *Cheyenne Autumn* in 1964. In the 1970s Del Rio established the Estancia Infantil, a government-supported child care center for the children of performers, not only serving on the board but maintaining hands-on involvement with the center's programs. Plagued by hepatitis, she died at her home in Newport Beach, California, on April 11, 1983.

Books

Hadley-Garcia, George, *Hispanic Hollywood: The Latins in Motion Pictures,* Citadel, 1990.

Notable Hispanic American Women, Book 1, Gale, 1993.

Periodicals

New York Times, April 13, 1983.

Palm Beach Post, January 10, 1970.

Star-Tribune (Minneapolis, MN), January 13, 2002.

Online

"Dolores Del Rio," *All Movie Guide,* http://www.allmovie.com/artist/18330 (January 18, 2010).

"Dolores Del Rio," *Turner Classic Movies,* http://www.tcmdb.com/participant.jsp?participantId=47807 (January 18, 2010). □

Willie Dixon

The African-American songwriter, vocalist, bassist, and producer Willie Dixon (1915–1992) was a central figure in the evolution of the blues from a rural folk form into an internationally significant genre of popular music that shaped rock and roll at a fundamental level. His career encompassed much of the history of the blues in the 20th century.

As a staff session musician and producer at the Chicago label Chess Records in the 1950s and 1960s, Dixon was, in the words of Peter Watrous of the *New York Times,* "the architect of the Chicago blues sound," who "knew exactly what he wanted and how to get it." As a songwriter who composed more than 500 blues pieces, many of them classics of the genre, he was, as Jas Obrecht of *Guitar Player* put it, "the poet laureate of modern blues." After his long career at Chess and other Chicago labels, Dixon became prominent as a blues recording artist himself, frequently performing in the blues revival concerts that established blues as an art form in Europe and enriched the repertory of classic British rock bands. Toward the end of his career he emerged as a spokesman for the rights of blues artists who, like himself, had never been adequately compensated for their creative contributions.

Sent to Prison Farm as Preteen

Willie Dixon was born in Vicksburg, Mississippi on July 1, 1915. He had vivid memories of racial segregation in the southern United States, and he grew up in dire poverty. "I lived around there under starving conditions, until I had to get the hell out, so somebody else could eat," he told Worth Long of the *African American Review*. Getting out involved running away at the age of 11 to a farm, where his life was even more difficult than it had been in Vicksburg. The area, however, was musically rich; in Vicksburg he heard gospel music, the early blues pianist Little Brother Montgomery and other pianists playing a pattern he called "Dudlow" after a nearby town but that soon became known as boogie-woogie, and country music on his brother's small radio. After he was arrested for vagrancy at age 12 and sent to a prison farm, the Harvey Allen County Farm, he heard Mississippi Delta–style blues from other prisoners and began to understand the grim circumstances from which they sprang.

Dixon began composing original music while still in Vicksburg. A major influence, he told Long, was his mother, who "used to write all types of poems and things. . . . She made a lot of little poem books when I was a kid. They consisted of nothing but spiritual ideas and things out of the Bible. Some of them I remember. Then I had a whole book of poems that I wrote as a kid." Physically abused at the prison farm, Dixon was temporarily deafened by a blow to the head that he received there. He escaped, made his way to Memphis, and rode a freight train to Chicago, settling there for good in 1936.

Weighing in at 250 pounds, Dixon tried out his skills as a boxer and won an Illinois Golden Gloves title in the novice heavyweight category in 1937. He was suspended from professional boxing after a pay dispute, however, and turned back to music. Having already gained a strong grasp on harmony singing in Mississippi, he began singing gospel music with the Union Jubilee Singers. He also received a homemade bass from another musician, Leonard "Baby Doo" Caston. It was built from an oil can with a single string, and Dixon believed that it followed African models.

Refused Draft Order

Dixon also joined a band called the Five Breezes, which recorded for the Bluebird label in 1939, and another called the Four Jumps of Jive. Dixon's growing success was interrupted when he was drafted into the U.S. Army during World War II and refused to report for duty, claiming conscientious objector status on grounds of the historical mistreatment of African Americans in the U.S. He served another year in prison.

After his release, Dixon resumed where he had left off. In 1945 he joined, on bass, a group called the Big Three Trio, which had a minor hit called "Wee, Wee Baby, You Sure Look Good to Me" and generated steady nightclub work. That brought Dixon into contact with the Polish-born brothers Leonard and Phil Chess, whose Aristocrat label was renamed Chess in 1950. They hired Dixon as a bassist for session work in the late 1940s and soon realized that he had both songwriting skills and a grasp of the entire music-making process, from leading a band to arranging and what was becoming known as producing. Dixon became a full-time employee at Chess, receiving a modest salary of $100 a week for a large variety of musical contributions to a new style of blues that was growing rapidly as Southern African Americans migrated northward in search of opportunity.

Dixon hit his peak as a songwriter in the early-to-middle 1950s when he began to work with Chess's hottest blues guitarist, McKinley Morganfield, known as Muddy Waters. In 1954 he penned Waters's top-five rhythm-and-blues hit "Hoochie Coochie Man," following it up with similarly economical and memorable lyrics in "I'm Ready" and "I Just Wanna Make Love to You." "My Babe," recorded by harmonica player Little Walter the following year, topped rhythm-and-blues charts and became an instantly recognizable blues classic with

its close integration of Dixon's lyric and the song's basic harmonica line. During the 1954–1956 period, Dixon's songwriting output dominated the Chess release catalogue.

Dixon wrangled with the Chess brothers over his scanty royalty payments and left the label temporarily for its crosstown rival, Cobra, in 1957. He continued to play the bass for Chess sessions, however, backing the pioneering rock and roll vocalist and songwriter Chuck Berry on many of his Chess recordings in 1956 and 1957. Dixon's work as a producer for Cobra in the late 1950s was especially significant as he defined a distinctive West Side Chicago blues style in his work with such artists as Buddy Guy, Otis Rush, and Magic Sam, placing a consistent emphasis on lead guitar. As a songwriter he was responsible for Rush's hit "I Can't Quit You Baby."

Toured Europe

As the blues began to lose popularity to soul and pop styles in African-American communities, it gained new audiences among young white music fans. Dixon appeared with pianist Memphis Slim at the Newport Folk Festival in Rhode Island in 1959 and made several tours of Europe under the auspices of the American Folk Blues Festival between 1962 and 1971. Dixon had some of his greatest European successes in Britain, where he found that young rock musicians were already very familiar with his work at Chess, not only covering Dixon's Chicago blues (the Rolling Stones, for example, recorded the Dixon-composed Howlin' Wolf song "Little Red Rooster" in 1964) but even seeking out new material. Dixon continued to write music for Chess artists as well, penning the blues standard "You Can't Judge a Book by Looking at the Cover," recorded by Bo Diddley in 1962, and launching the career of Koko Taylor in 1966 with "Wang Dang Doodle."

Among younger blues fans Dixon may be better known as a solo artist than for any of his previous activities, but his solo career did not begin in earnest until quite late in his life. Although he recorded one album, *Willie's Blues,* for the jazz-oriented Prestige label in 1959, he did not release solo albums consistently until 1969, when he released *I Am the Blues* on the major Columbia label and followed it up with a series of albums on small labels like Ovation and his own Yambo imprint. He frequently toured with a group called the Chicago Blues All-Stars that he formed in 1969, and he toured for up to six months a year in the 1970s, until problems resulting from diabetes slowed his schedule. In the early 1980s he left Chicago for southern California, where he continued to record and contributed blues elements to movie soundtracks. Dixon received Grammy award nominations in 1973 (for the album *Catalyst*), 1977 (for *What's Happened to My Blues?*), *15 July, 1983 Live,* and *Hidden Charms,* which won the Best Traditional Blues Album Grammy in 1988. The three-CD *Chess Box* set that appeared the following year attested generously to Dixon's musical influence. In 1990 Dixon published an autobiography, *I Am the Blues.*

By that time, Dixon had recovered some of the royalties from his earlier music in a series of court actions against Chess, which had been acquired by other labels, in the 1970s. Early in his career he had often sold songs outright for as low as $30 apiece, but now he became an advocate for younger musicians. He formed the Blues Heaven Foundation as a general support mechanism for blues musicians and to ensure, he told Long, that the blues "will be properly advertised, publicized, emphasized, talked about, and understood." The foundation moved into the former Chess offices at 2120 South Michigan Avenue in Chicago and continued to operate after Dixon's death in Burbank, California, from complications of diabetes, on January 29, 1992.

Books

Contemporary Black Biography, Volume 4, Gale, 1992.
Dixon, Willie, with Don Snowden, *I Am the Blues: The Willie Dixon Story,* Da Capo, 1990.

Periodicals

African American Review, Summer 1995.
Guardian (London, England), January 31, 1992.
Guitar Player, October 1993.
New York Times, February 9, 1992.
Rolling Stone, March 23, 1989.

Online

"Willie Dixon," *All Music Guide,* http:;//www.allmusic.com (February 7, 2010).
"Willie Dixon," *Rock and Roll Hall of Fame,* http://www.rockhall. com/inductee/willie-dixon (February 7, 2010). □

Larry Doby

Often overlooked in the annals of baseball history, Larry Doby (1923-2003) became the first African-American to play in Major League Baseball's American League when he took the field for the Cleveland Indians in July 1947, just eleven weeks after Jackie Robinson integrated the National League. Despite the pressure of playing alongside teammates and opponents who wanted him off the field, Doby drove in 970 runs and hit 253 homers in a career spanning 13 seasons, twice leading the American League in homers and once in runs batted in (RBI). A Hall of Fame outfielder, Doby made the All-Star team seven times.

The grandson of a slave, Lawrence Eugene Doby was born December 13, 1923, in Camden, South Carolina. Doby's father, a semipro baseball player, died when he was eight. By the time Doby was 14, the family had relocated to Paterson, New Jersey. A talented athlete, Doby attended Eastside High School, participating in baseball, basketball, football, and track. Though the high school had been integrated, Doby was the only black athlete on the football and baseball teams. He met his future wife, Helyn Curvey, while in high school. They lived in the same neighborhood and walked to school together.

Started Career in Negro League

After graduating in 1942, Doby spent the summer playing for the Negro League's Newark Eagles, competing under the name "Larry Walker" so as to maintain his amateur status. During his rookie season with the Eagles, Doby hit .391. The next fall, he enrolled at Long Island University in Brooklyn, New York, and earned a spot on the basketball team. Originally, Doby studied to become a teacher, or maybe a coach.

Doby never finished his first year of college. With World War II in full swing, Doby received a draft notice and reported to the Great Lakes Naval Training Station in Chicago. He was sent to a small and scarcely inhabited South Pacific island called Ulitihi. The United States used Ulitihi to support naval operations in the Pacific. The servicemen on Ulitihi had a radio and Doby learned quickly about the Dodgers organization and how it signed Robinson in late 1945 to play in its farm system. Doby began to wonder if black athletes might actually be allowed to play in the major leagues some day soon.

In January 1946, the Navy discharged Doby and he returned to the Newark Eagles in the spring. The Eagles, propelled by Doby's .348 batting average, made it to the Negro World Series that year, where they faced the Kansas City Monarchs. During the series, Doby batted .272, helping drive his team to victory. Another important milestone that season included Doby's marriage to his high school sweetheart, Helyn, on August 10, 1946. They married in the morning so Doby could make his evening game.

Integrated American League

By the time the 1947 season rolled around, Cleveland Indians owner Bill Veeck was anxious to sign an African-American player. Veeck's scouts focused on second-baseman Doby. The Cleveland Browns football team had recently become integrated and Veeck figured local fans would be equally accepting in baseball. Veeck's biggest motivation, however, was to field a winning team and he wanted to be the first to grab the Negro League's best talent. Unlike Dodgers president and general manager Branch Rickey, Veeck was low-key in his approach to integration. "I'm not going to sign a Negro player and send him to a farm club," Veeck said at the time, according to Andrew O'Toole's book *The Best Man Plays.* "I'm going to get one I think can play with Cleveland. One afternoon when the team trots on the field, a Negro player will be out there with them."

On July 3, 1947, Veeck purchased Doby's contract from the Newark Eagles. The following day, Doby played his last game as an Eagle, hitting a homer in his last at bat and leaving with a mid-season average of .415. Plucked from the fields of the Negro League, Doby was taken by train to Chicago and given less than 24 hours to prepare for his MLB debut. On July 5, the Cleveland Indians faced the Chicago White Sox at Comiskey Park. Before the game, Veeck introduced Doby to his new, all-white teammates, several of whom refused to shake his hand. As the Indians began warm-ups, Doby stood alone for several uncomfortable minutes until Joe Gordon, the second baseman, waved his glove at Doby. Eleven weeks earlier, Robinson had integrated the National League when he donned a Brooklyn Dodgers uniform and now Doby, wearing a No. 14 Cleveland Indians jersey, was attempting to integrate the American League.

In the seventh inning, shortstop/manager Lou Boudreau sent Doby in to pinch hit. He struck out. After the game, Doby headed to a separate hotel from his teammates because segregation laws at the time prohibited him from staying at the same establishment. For Doby, the transition was rough. "I had no roommates on trips," Doby recalled in later years, according to O'Toole's book. "On trains no one invited me to play cards or talk over games. The worst thing was not having anyone to communicate with, talk over the game with after it's over and start me thinking about the next game . . . it was very lonely."

Faced Discrimination, Name-Calling

Being one of two African-Americans in the major leagues proved tough. Players spit tobacco juice on Doby as he slid into second base. They called him names, such as coon and jigaboo. Pitchers threw the ball at his head. In many cities, Doby struggled to even reach the stadium because cabdrivers refused black passengers. Robinson endured similar situations and often made headlines for being a pioneer in the struggle, whereas Doby's plight was often overlooked. According to the *Washington Times,* Doby summed up his struggle this way: "You didn't hear much about what I was going through because the media didn't want to repeat the same story. I couldn't react to [prejudicial] situations from a physical standpoint. My reaction was to hit the ball as far as I could."

Though Doby tried to ignore the slights, it was hard to take. Later in the season, in a game against the St. Louis Browns, Doby lost his poise after a fan pelted him with non-stop racial slurs. Armed with a bat, Doby began climbing into the grandstand but was intercepted. In another game, a quick-witted umpire positioned himself between Doby and an offending opponent after the player spit on Doby. Mostly, Doby kept his cool, realizing that if he fought back and created problems, he would be banished from the league and disrupt the chances of other Negro League players. When a bad call was made, Doby did not directly confront the umpire but instead quietly pointed to the back of his hand, indicating that he knew the color of his skin influenced the call. Because Doby's integration got off to a rough start, he hardly played the rest of the 1947 season. He made only 29 appearances, mostly as a pinch hitter, and collected just five hits.

Doby's performance was underwhelming, but Boudreau recognized a solid athlete under the strain and stress and wanted to give Doby a better chance. Because the team already had a solid second baseman in Gordon, Doby was told to learn to play the outfield over the off-season. Doby reported to spring training in Tucson, Arizona, in 1948, ready to take up his new position. Former Cleveland outfielder Tris Speaker, who was working as a scout and coach for the team, tutored Doby by hitting him endless fly balls. Doby's performance during spring training earned him a small degree of acceptance among his teammates. He batted .358 and smacked a 500-foot homer during the preseason.

Segregation laws continued to be a problem. In Tucson, Doby had to bunk with a local African-American family because the hotels refused to take him. At some parks Doby was forbidden from entering by the front gates and had to be escorted through the rear. Through all the challenges, Veeck proved to be Doby's biggest ally. In a 1998 interview with the *New York Times,* Doby praised Veeck, saying Veeck "knew I needed someone to talk to outside my wife and family. He loved jazz so he would call up and say, 'I'll see you tomorrow,' and we'd sit down and listen to Dizzy Gillespie, George Shearing, Count Basie, Errol Garner. That relaxed me and gave me a good feeling."

Led Team to World Series Win

Boudreau placed Doby in the starting lineup for the 1948 opener and the new outfielder flourished, batting .301 that year. In mid-season, ace Negro League pitcher Satchel Paige joined the team, adding another black face to the lineup. During the final three-week run of the season, Doby helped his team chase down the pennant for the first time in 28 years by batting .396 with ten RBI and three homers. After becoming the American League champs, the Indians faced the Boston Braves in the World Series. When the teams entered Game 4, the Indians held the advantage—2-to-1—in the best-of-seven series. The game was close but Doby smashed a homer to give his team a 2-1 victory. Cleveland's winning pitcher, Steve Gromek, took hold of Doby for a post-game hug as photographers snapped away, capturing their grinning faces.

According to Steve Jacobson, author of *Carrying Jackie's Torch,* Doby cherished the photo, which hit papers across the United States. "That's what America is all about, or what it's supposed to be all about. We could have rehearsed all day and never got that joy on our faces. It was genuine. I hit a home run to win the game for him." When Gromek returned home to Michigan, he took a lot of heat for the photo, one of the first to show affection between a white and black player during the tense years of integration. The Indians went on to win the series with the help of Doby's bat. Over the series, Doby batted .318 with seven hits. Doby returned home to a parade and banner reading "Welcome Home Larry Doby Paterson Is Proud Of You," yet when Doby tried to use his baseball earnings to purchase a new home, residents circulated a petition to bar him from buying in a white neighborhood.

Over the next several years, Doby proved to be a solid and productive player. In 1949, Doby appeared in his first of seven consecutive All-Star games. In 1952 and '54, he led the American League in homers, whacking 32 each season. In 1954, he helped deliver the Indians to the World Series again as the team set an American League record for most regular-season wins with 111. Doby led the league in RBI that year with 126. Heavily favored, the Indians lost to the New York Giants. Following the 1955 season, Veeck traded Doby to the Chicago White Sox.

After enduring a decade of taunts, Doby finally lost his temper and became the first African-American player to start a fight on the field. It happened in June 1957, when Yankees pitcher Art Ditmar knocked Doby off the plate with a high inside pitch. Doby jumped up from the dirt, charged the mound and let go a left hook, emptying both benches for a 20-minute brawl. After the season ended, Doby was traded around several times and retired in 1959. Doby continued his involvement with baseball, integrating Japan's professional league in 1962 and coaching in the minor leagues. In 1978, Veeck bought the White Sox and made Doby the manager for half a season, making Doby the second African-American to become a manager in the major leagues.

Over the course of his career, Doby was often overshadowed by Robinson because Robinson was the first to break baseball's color line. Doby's career batting average of .283 is lower than Robinson's average of .311. While Doby drove in 970 runs over his career and hit 253 homers, his statistics are not phenomenal. What was phenomenal, however, was the fact that he rose to the challenge and played without the support system Robinson enjoyed. Nonetheless, Doby compiled many firsts—he was the first black athlete on a World Series winning team. He went 166 games in center field without an error and was the first black player to lead either league in homers. In 1998, Doby was duly awarded for his accomplishments when he was inducted into the Baseball Hall of Fame five years before his death.

Books

Jacobson, Steve, *Carrying Jackie's Torch: The Players Who Integrated Baseball-and America*, Lawrence Hill Books, 2007.

O'Toole, Andrew, *The Best Man Plays: Major League Baseball and the Black Athlete, 1901-2002*, McFarland & Co., 2003.

Periodicals

Daily News (New York), February 27, 1998.

New York Times, February 23, 1997; March 4, 1998; July 26, 2001; June 19, 2003.

Toronto Star, July 6, 1997.

Washington Times, June 21, 2003.

Online

"Larry Doby," Baseball-Reference.com, http://www.baseball-reference.com/players/d/dobyla01.shtml (December 29, 2009). □

Allen Dulles

American governmental official and espionage officer Allen Welsh Dulles (1893–1969) presided over the growth of the United States Central Intelligence Agency (CIA) and was the architect of several of the most controversial covert operations of the 1950s and 1960s—operations that, successful or not, aimed to destabilize foreign governments.

T he projects Dulles oversaw, involving Latin America and the Middle East, had repercussions that stretched far into the decades after his own death. They were fundamental to American foreign policy, for Dulles was, to use colloquial language, the quintessential mover and shaker: he was a member of a powerful family that, in the words of biographer Leonard Mosley, "consolidated its control over the external policies of the United States" with his ascension. Dulles's career began amid the reorganization of the world order that followed World War I and came to full flower during World War II as he directed intelligence operations against Nazi Germany. Although he later helped to design large geopolitical strategies, he perhaps remained at heart a case officer—an intelligence officer who manages the efforts of agents in the field.

Born with Foot Defect

Born April 7, 1893, Allen Welsh Dulles was a native of Watertown, New York. His father, Allen Macy Dulles, was the minister at the local Presbyterian church; his mother, Edith Foster Dulles, was the daughter of John W. Foster, who served as U.S. Secretary of State in the administration of President Benjamin Harrison. The third of five children, Dulles was born with a club foot. It was for the most part repaired by a surgeon while he was still a baby, but he limped and later was troubled by gout in the same foot (the left). When Dulles was eight, he wrote a little book of his own about the recently concluded Boer War in South Africa. He and his older brother, future U.S. Secretary of State John Foster Dulles, both excelled in school and attended Princeton University, where Allen Dulles won a prize for a paper in the field of philosophy, his major.

After graduating with honors from Princeton in 1914, Dulles spent a year teaching at a Christian college in Allahabad, India, becoming fluent in Hindi and later traveling through Singapore and China. He returned to Princeton as a graduate student, earned a degree in international law, and joined the U.S. diplomatic corps in 1916. His first posting, before the U.S. entered World War I on the side of the Allies against the Central Powers (of which Austria-Hungary was a member), was to Vienna, Austria. He soaked up enough knowledge of the quickly decaying Austro-Hungarian Empire that when he was transferred to Bern, Switzerland later in the war, he had the reputation of an expert on Austria. Dulles began compiling what were, in effect, intelligence reports on Eastern Europe, monitoring newspaper opinion, consulting expert informants and emigrés, and writing up what he learned in reports to his superiors in Washington. As a result, Dulles was named to the U.S. diplomatic team that negotiated a peace treaty after World War I ended with an armistice on November 11, 1918.

In October of 1920 he married Clover Todd. The marriage lasted until Dulles's death but was strained by a series of extramarital relationships on the part of Dulles, who even prior to the marriage had turned down the chance to meet Vladimir Lenin, soon to emerge as the leader of the Russian Revolution, because he had a date with a girl. (He later told the story to intelligence recruits as an illustration of the importance of keeping work separate from their personal lives.) "There were at least a hundred women in love with Allen at one time or another," Dulles's sister Eleanor was quoted as saying by

Melrose, "and some of them didn't even get to close quarters with him." Allen and Clover Dulles raised three children: Clover, Joan, and Allen.

Dulles served in diplomatic posts in Berlin, Constantinople (now Istanbul), and Washington, D.C. in the early 1920s, but the financial pressures of a growing family induced him to leave the diplomatic corps and enroll in law school at George Washington University. In 1926 he joined the staff of the law firm of Sullivan & Cromwell, where his older brother already worked. His cosmopolitan ways and enthusiastic willingness to undertake international travel made him invaluable to Sullivan & Cromwell, which vigorously pursued international business and by 1930 had grown into one of the largest law firms in the world.

Warned Against German Threat

Despite his success in private enterprise, though, Dulles remained a passionate and keen observer of international events. He was especially alarmed by events in Germany, where as early as 1934 he warned against the aggressive streak in the ideology of Adolf Hitler's government. As the situation in Europe worsened in the early months of World War II, Dulles backed U.S. intervention in the war, running counter to the isolationist tendencies of other members of his Republican party. A New York lawyer and friend, William J. Donovan, identified Dulles as an individual whose talents could be tapped as the U.S. built up its lagging intelligence capabilities. When Donovan was named Coordinator of Information (COI) by President Franklin Roosevelt in the aftermath of the Pearl Harbor attack, he hired Dulles to run the agency's New York Office and to research the backgrounds of the German leadership.

In 1942 the office of the COI evolved into the Office of Strategic Services (OSS), the immediate World War II–era ancestor of the CIA and the key American intelligence agency during the war. Dulles returned to Bern, where he had spent part of World War I, to take charge of the OSS office there. "Bern," noted Dulles biographer Peter Grose, "established Allen's standing as a spymaster." Working with contacts among a tightly knit group of anti-Nazi German officials, he recruited and turned German foreign service official Fritz Kolbe, whom he code-named George Wood after an old family friend. Kolbe made microfilm copies of over 1,600 secret German documents and transmitted them to Dulles, who was at times overwhelmed by the flow of information. At the end of the war Dulles helped negotiate the surrender of German troops in Italy.

The aftermath of the war nourished the roots of Dulles's activities as a fervent anti-Communist. Stationed in Berlin, Dulles observed the growth of Russian influence in the zone it occupied. In a *Foreign Affairs* transcript of a Dulles appearance before the Council on Foreign Relations in December of 1945, he said, "Until the Russians get out—and there is no indication that they intend to—there can be no central administration [in Germany]." As Dulles guessed, Germany was soon partitioned into Eastern and Western entities.

In 1947 Dulles participated in the drafting of legislation for the new Central Intelligence Agency, and when Walter Bedell Smith became the CIA's second director in 1950, Dulles became his director of covert operations. From 1951 to 1953 he served as deputy CIA director and oversaw the basic development of the agency's Cold War intelligence-gathering operations. In 1953, newly elected President Dwight D. Eisenhower appointed Dulles to succeed Smith as Director of Central Intelligence—the chief executive office of the CIA. In his first months in office he resisted the anti-Communist crusades of Senator Joseph McCarthy, which as a result left the CIA largely untouched.

Spearheaded Regime Change Operations

Dulles, however, had become an anti-Communist crusader himself. Like many in government at the time, he saw the conflict between capitalism and Communism as a global struggle, with the U.S. and the Soviet Union as central combatants jockeying for influence everywhere. In 1953 Dulles was instrumental in the decision to provide aid—how much is still disputed—to opponents of left-leaning Iranian leader Mohammed Mossadegh, resulting in the installation of Shah Reza Pahlavi as a pro-Western but unpopular Iranian ruler. The Shah was overthrown in 1979, and the Islamic Republic of Iran established.

An emboldened Dulles repeated his success the following year, again at a cost of antagonizing many inhabitants of countries in the region. In response to a request from President Eisenhower, he spearheaded a plan to destabilize the democratically elected government of Guatemalan president Jacob Arbenz by harassing Guatemalan forces with small attacks and clandestine radio broadcasts designed to sow panic among government loyalists. The plan worked as Arbenz was forced to resign and was replaced by a government friendlier to U.S. interests. By the mid-1950s, Dulles could look back on major successes that had brought the CIA to a peak of influence. Dulles's star only rose further as the agency deployed the high-altitude U-2 spy plane, the first generation of devices that provided photographic images of what was occurring in the Soviet Union itself. Another covert operation within the Soviet Union brought to light struggles within the Communist government there; Dulles obtained a secret speech in which Soviet Communist Party First Secretary (and later Premier) Nikita Khrushchev denounced the practices of the late dictator Josef Stalin.

In the late 1950s and early 1960s, however, Dulles suffered a series of reversals. An early harbinger was a failed attempt to displace Indonesian president Sukarno (who used only one name). Then, in the spring of 1960, the Soviet Union succeeded in shooting down a U-2 plane piloted by Francis Gary Powers. A CIA-provided cover story that the plane was a weather research aircraft was soon shown to be false as the Soviets produced the intact wreckage of the plane along with Powers himself, who had parachuted to safety. Dulles suffered his first major propaganda setback.

The plan that ended Dulles's illustrious career was the Bay of Pigs invasion of Cuba on April 17, 1961. Dulles and his team planned to repeat the sequence of events that had worked in Guatemala, with a small invasion force of Cuban exiles and American personnel, backed by a massive propaganda effort. The invasion collapsed after three days of fighting in which resistance from Cuban troops proved unexpectedly strong, handing a major propaganda victory to the

Soviet Union and a public-relations headache to the recently inaugurated U.S. President John F. Kennedy. Dulles maintained, for the most part privately, that the plan had failed partly because the Kennedy administration failed to devote sufficient resources to it and had acted hesitantly in several respects. Nevertheless, Dulles was forced to resign in 1962. He served on the Warren Commission that investigated Kennedy's assassination in 1963 and 1964. In the late 1960s he is thought to have suffered one or more strokes, and he died in Washington on January 29, 1969. Dulles was the author of several books, including *Germany's Underground, The Craft of Intelligence,* and *The Secret Surrender.*

Books

Ambrose, Stephen E., *Ike's Spies: Eisenhower and the Espionage Establishment,* Doubleday, 1981.
Brands, William H., Jr., *Cold Warriors: Eisenhower's Generation and American Foreign Policy,* Columbia, 1988.
Frankel, Benjamin, ed., *The Cold War: 1945–1991,* Gale, 1992.
Grose, Peter, *Gentleman Spy: The Life of Allen Dulles,* Houghton Mifflin, 1994.
Mosley, Leonard, *Dulles: A Biography of Eleanor, Allen, and Foster Dulles,* Dial, 1978.

Periodicals

Foreign Affairs, November–December 2003.

Online

"Allen Welsh Dulles, *CNN,* http://web.archive.org/web/200801071 01249/http://www.cnn.com/SPECIALS/cold.war/kbank/profiles/ allen.dulles (December 20, 2009). □

Eleonora Duse

Italy's Eleonora Duse (1858–1923) was among the first true modern actresses, developing a personal philosophy of the art of acting and seeking to apply her own interpretations to theatrical roles instead of portraying emotions in ways prescribed by tradition.

H ers was a novel approach at the time, and audiences flocked to see her. To Duse, playing a character meant surrendering herself completely to the role. She became a star on both sides of the Atlantic Ocean, and her romantic life, which involved several prominent male creative figures of her time, provided plenty of raw material for her art. To audiences of the late 19th and early 20th centuries, Eleonora Duse was simply "La Duse"—an instantly recognizable and well-known figure even for those not lucky enough to see her in person on big-city stages.

Born into Theatrical Family

Eleonora Giulia Amalia Duse (doo-ZAY) was quite literally born into acting, to a ragged, impoverished troupe of traveling players passing through the town of Vigevano, Italy, on October 3, 1858. Reportedly she was born on a train. The

Compagnia Duse, run by Eleonora's father Vincenzo, was truly a family affair, and all members had a part to play. It was only natural, then, that when the company performed *Les Misérables* in 1862, there was nobody better suited to play young Cosette than little Eleonora, so at just four years of age, Eleonora Duse played her first stage role. Too young to understand what it all meant, she was frightened. After enduring real kicks from the horrible Madame Thenardier, Eleonora began to cry for her mother, who was offstage trying to reassure her.

After ten years of dutifully portraying role after role, Duse achieved a breakthrough as an actress in 1873 with Compagnia Duse's performance of Shakespeare's *Romeo and Juliet.* Eleonora was 14, Juliet's age when she met her Romeo, and for the first time she felt herself truly empathizing with a character. There was also the coincidence of playing the part in Verona, Juliet's own city. Duse (according to biographer Frances Winwar) said of the experience, "Then on a Sunday in May in the ancient amphitheater under the open sky, before a multitude of simple burghers who had lived in that legend of love and death, I was Juliet. . . . No triumph ever gave me the intoxication and the fullness of that great hour. Truly, when I heard Romeo say, 'Oh, she doth teach the torches to burn bright,' I was on fire, I became a flame." She would later refer to this moment as a state of grace and to her connection with the character of Juliet as a sense of abandonment. She found herself guided by what she called (as quoted by biographer Helen Sheehy) an "echo of the pain of the world," and would from then on strive for a "transformation of life" in the roles she played.

In 1878 Duse joined the company Cotti Belli-Blanes for a season in Naples. There she was finally given the opportunity to play main roles, though this was at first only because of lead actress Giulia Gritti's illness during the season. Cotti Belli-Blanes was an acting company of great notoriety, and the opportunity got Duse noticed. While substituting for Gritti in the role of Maia in the play *I Fourchambault,* Duse made such an impression on actor Giovanni Emanuel that he formed an acting company at the Teatro dei Fiorentini and hired Duse as one of his leading ladies. "They saw her as a Desdemona of incomparable meekness and innocence. They saw her as the mad Ophelia shredding the wildflowers in her hands," noted biographer Frances Winwar, writing in reference to Duse's various Shakespearean roles during this formative period. She had another milestone performance as Thérèse in Emile Zola's *Thérèse Raquin,* which won her a spot in Cesare Rossi's acting company.

Had Child by Publisher

It was during this time that Duse had her first off-stage experience with love. A brief and passionate relationship with newspaper magnate Mattino (or Martino) Cafiero ended in pregnancy and heartbreak for Duse. Cafiero, more interested in the thrill of the hunt, hardly batted an eyelash when Duse's company obligations took her to Turin. She left the company only briefly to give birth to her son, who died shortly thereafter. The experience tormented Duse throughout her life. Not long after her return, Rossi made Duse the company's leading lady, giving all the main parts to her. He acknowledged Duse's genius and afforded her the freedom to interpret her characters as she saw fit. He also became enamored with her, and to escape his advances, she married Teobaldo Checchi, a fellow member of the company, in 1881. It was yet another lopsided love affair, for Duse did not share Checchi's feelings, though she admired him greatly and valued his friendship and devotion. Nonetheless, the union produced a daughter, Enrichetta, born in 1882.

During this stint in Rossi's company came another turning point in Duse's life. The French diva Sarah Bernhardt, a living legend of the stage, came to Rossi's Teatro Carignano to give a handful of performances. It was Duse's first encounter with international-level professional acting, and it inspired her greatly. Later she recalled the event (as quoted by Emil Alphons Rheinhardt in his biography of Duse), saying, "To me it was as if with her approach all the old, ghostly shadows of tradition and of an enslaved art faded away to nothing. It was like an emancipation."

No sooner had the famous Bernhardt left Turin than Duse was begging Rossi to put on Alexandre Dumas' play *The Princess of Baghdad* (1883); Duse would portray Lionette, a role Bernhardt herself had played. Rossi's previous experience with the play had been in Paris, where it was practically booed off the stage, and he was reluctant to give it another try. After Duse declared that she would either play in *The Princess of Baghdad* or leave the company, Rossi let her have her way. It would be one of Teatro Carignano's most memorable and successful shows, starting a string of performances that helped revitalize the struggling theater and brought Duse's genius further into the limelight. When the company's obligations in Turin ended, they moved on to Rome, and Duse persuaded Rossi once again to put on another virtually unknown play by Dumas, *La Femme de Claude*. After the poorly attended first night, Rossi was on the verge of canceling the show for the next evening, but Duse and other members of the cast changed his mind.

The second performance of *La Femme de Claude* was played to a packed house, theatergoers having heard of the extraordinary performance by the then-unknown Duse the night before. Rome was a notoriously difficult audience, and with this triumph Duse was catapulted into fame. In 1884 Dumas wrote a play especially for her, *Denise*, which she agreed to do despite the fact that the play affected her in a personal way. Both Duse and the character of Denise had lost sons in infancy at a young age. Duse took this painful life experience with her to rehearsals, giving herself over to the part of Denise so fully and passionately that her health was affected. On the eve of the play's opening, Duse suffered a hemorrhage in her lungs, and doctors were not optimistic about her chances. Count Giuseppe Primoli, a friend of both Duse and Dumas, wrote (according to Winwar) to the playwright during the ordeal: "But she did not want to die, not before playing Denise!" She ended up recovering and taking the stage in the part, to great acclaim.

Toured South America

In 1885 Duse went with Rossi's company on a tour of South America. It was the first time she had left Italy, and the experience marked another stage in her personal development. The cracks in Duse's marriage began to show during the voyage, and before the engagement in South America was over, she and Checchi had agreed to separate; he left the company, and they returned to Italy without him. Upon her return, she broke with Rossi and formed the Drammatica Compagnia della Città di Roma, her own company. With this move she was afforded more freedom and control over what she played, and she took the opportunity to introduce Italy to some forgotten plays, as well as to the writings of Norwegian playwright Henrik Ibsen and his controversial proto-feminist drama *A Doll's House*. For the rest of her career, Duse would be known for her Ibsen interpretations.

Duse gave her first performance in the United States in 1893, in Dumas' *La Dame aux Camélias*. The public was at first less than fully interested, unaccustomed to Duse's anti-publicity philosophy and refusal to do interviews. Additionally, Duse was quite unlike the stars of the American stage in that day; she wore no makeup, preferring to let the parts speak for themselves, and played only in Italian. Despite all this, she won American audiences over with her talent much as she wooed Rome at the dawn of her success. In England, too, her fame grew; after seeing both actresses play in *La Dame aux Camélias* within a few days of each other, British playwright George Bernard Shaw famously declared Duse's performance superior to Sarah Bernhardt's. The rivalry between the two actresses became the subject of a play, *The Ladies of the Camellias,* by Lillian Groag.

After a romantic involvement of several years' duration with operatic composer and librettist Arrigo Boito, Duse met the writer Gabriele d'Annunzio shortly before her second American tour, and the two began a love affair. It would ultimately find immortality in d'Annunzio's book *Il Fuoco* (The Fire), a somewhat scandalous semi-fictionalized account of their relationship that d'Annunzio published against Duse's wishes. The pairing would produce great plays, among them *La Città Morta* (The Dead City). Despite Duse begging to play the main part in *La Città Morta*, d'Annunzio gave it to Bernhardt, whom he secretly regarded a superior actress. The move wounded Duse, who reportedly had to be stopped from burning down d'Annunzio's house, but she graciously accepted a part in d'Annunzio's *Sogno d'un Mattino di Primavera*, (Dream of a Spring Morning), which he gave her as a sort of consolation. Their affair ended in 1904 after d'Annunzio promised her a part in his new play, *La Figlia di Iorio* (Iorio's Daughter) but gave the part to another actress instead of waiting for her when she fell ill with a case of tuberculosis she kept hidden from the public.

Directed Film

In 1909 Duse retired from acting—almost on a whim, it seemed to friends. After a performance of Ibsen's *The Lady from the Sea* in Berlin, at the age of 51, she left the stage. Over the next several years, she may have engaged in a lesbian relationship with the Italian feminist Lina Poletti. When World War I broke out, she traveled to hospitals all over Italy, offering support to wounded soldiers, helping however she could, and running errands for them. In 1916 she appeared in and directed a film, *Cenere*. When she returned to her home in Asolo after the war was over, she found her savings completely obliterated by currency fluctuations. So, in 1921, after 12 years in retirement, she returned to the stage at age 63 much in the way she had first come to it at age four, out of obligation and necessity. Her first performance upon her return was once again *The Lady from the Sea*, this time in Rome. Her tuberculosis had progressed to the point where she had to carry an oxygen tank as she traveled.

Duse returned to the U.S. in October of 1923, giving her opening performance at the Metropolitan Opera House. The *New York Times* reported (as quoted by actress Eva Le Gallienne in her biography of Duse) that "[e]very seat and all the standing-room at the Metropolitan Opera House was filled last night by the crowd that went to see Eleonora Duse in her first appearance on the American stage for 20 years. People stood three and four deep in the space at the rear of the orchestra seats. . . . More than one-hundred-and-fifty extra seats in the musician's pit helped take care of the crowd." Her arrival was so well anticipated that *Time* magazine spoke of it four months in advance in its June 30, 1923 issue; Duse herself graced the cover of that issue, becoming the first Italian and woman to have the honor.

In April of 1924, after playing most of her 20 obligations on the U.S. tour, Duse was forced to play in Pittsburgh, which she called "the most hideous town in the world" because of its harsh Eastern weather. Duse stayed at the Schenley Hotel (now the Union Building of the University of Pittsburgh) and insisted on walking to and from the Syrian Mosque auditorium, even in the cold and rain of the Northeastern early spring. After playing one show at the Mosque on April 5, she came down with pneumonia, and after battling for her life for two weeks, she died in Pittsburgh on April 21, 1923, at the age of 64. Her final words, according to Le Gallienne, were, "Pack the trunks. We must move on!'' Her body was buried in a small cemetery near her home in Asolo, Italy.

Books

Le Gallienne, Eva, *The Mystic in the Theatre: Eleonora Duse,* Farrar, Straus & Giroux, 1966.

Rheinhardt, Emil Alphons, *The Life of Eleonora Duse,* Blom, 1969.

Sheehy, Helen, *Eleonora Duse: A Biography,* Knopf, 2003.

Winwar, Frances, *Winged Victory: A Biography of Gabriele d'Annunzio and Eleonora Duse,* Harper, 1956.

Periodicals

Rocky Mountain News, March 23, 2006.

Time, July 30, 1923.

Online

''Duse, Eleonora,'' *GLBTQ: An Encyclopedia of Gay, Lesbian, Bisexual, Transgender, & Queer Culture,* http://www.glbtq.com/arts/duse_e.html (January 10, 2010)

''Duse, Eleonora Giulia Amalia,'' *Pennsylvania Center for the Book,* http://pabook.libraries.psu.edu/palitmap/bios/Duse__Eleonora.html (January 10, 2010).☐

E

José Maria Eça de Queirós

The Portuguese writer José Maria Eça de Queirós (1845–1900) is regarded as the foremost practitioner of the realist novel in his country, and as one of the greatest writers Portugal has ever produced.

Eça de Queirós wrote in Portuguese, a language that at the time was seldom spoken internationally, and this hindered the general appreciation of his work. In an interview quoted on the *Vidas Lusofonas* web site, Eça de Queirós, with tongue in cheek, conceded that "struggles in the field of literature are fruitless when you write in the Portuguese language," and that he should have opened up a gourmet food shop where he could have said, "with an air of delicate superiority, 'Hi there, Mr. Journalist! We have a wonderful cheese that will make your mouth water.'" The comment was typical for Eça de Queirós, whose writing took a sharply satirical attitude toward middle-class Portuguese life. His books eventually appeared in English during and after his lifetime, and he has gradually amassed an international readership.

Supported After Out-of-Wedlock Birth

José Maria Eça de Queirós (also spelled Queiroz) was born in the small town of Póvoa de Varzim, Portugal, on November 25, 1845. He was the illegitimate son of a Brazilian judge. His teenage mother had come to Póvoa de Varzim to keep her pregnancy secret. Eça de Queirós was raised by his father's parents. His father made financial contributions to his education and helped him establish himself as a young man, but did not acknowledge paternity until Eça de Queirós married in middle age. Eça de Queirós attended a top boarding school in the city of Porto and went on to law school at the University of Coimbra.

Eça de Queirós had watched during his teenage years as his father presided over two cases, one involving counterfeiting and the other adultery, that showed both the corruption of Portugal's judicial system and the dubious morality of its social upper crust. At the university, he spent less time studying than conversing with aspiring writers and malcontents. He received his law degree in 1866 and spent several years mostly going out with his friends, who tended to be young intellectuals. Eça de Queirós edited a newspaper opposed to Portugal's government, worked intermittently as a lawyer, and wrote several long poems, including one that may have been based on a prank in which a friend contrived to make him and his friends believe they had heard a ghost running through a cathedral at night. In 1869 one of Eça de Queirós's friends, the nobleman Luís de Castro Pamplona, treated Eça de Queirós to a trip to Cairo, Egypt, to witness the opening of the Suez Canal.

In 1870 Eça de Queirós became an administrator in the Portuguese city of Leiria, but he continued to devote his energy to writing. He and Ramalho Ortigão wrote a novel, *O mistério da estrada de Sintra* (The Mystery on the Road to Sintra), that was told in the form of a series of letters, with the last one explaining that the entire set was fictional. The book is considered Portugal's first example of the police novel. Later in 1870 Eça de Queirós took a civil service exam for an open diplomatic post and achieved the top score, but the post went to the second-place finisher instead. Eça de Queirós, disillusioned, returned to Leiria and began an affair with a local noblewoman. His position in that small city became more difficult when the two were discovered in a bedroom during a party they were both attending.

Posted to Cuba

Eça de Queirós and Ortigão began publishing the satirical magazine *As Farpas* in 1871. In Portuguese terms Eça de Queirós was a progressive, but he did not have a radical temperament and avoided international socialist organizations. He finally entered Portugal's diplomatic corps in 1872, gaining a posting to the French Antilles. Diplomatic work seems to have appealed to Eça de Queirós—he enjoyed observing the new societies he encountered and describing them in letters, and he had plenty of time for his own writing. In 1872 he began a two-year stint in Havana, Cuba, during which he also visited the United States (he admired Chicago but was ambivalent toward the hubbub of New York) and Canada. During this time he wrote *Singularidades de uma rapariga loira* (translated as *Singularities of a Blonde Girl*), a tale of a young woman whose kleptomania leads to the cancellation of her impending marriage.

In 1874 Eça de Queirós was transferred to a Portuguese consulate in Newcastle, England, and he spent much of the next two decades working there and in the city of Bristol. His witty correspondence from this period was issued as *Letters from England* in 1905 and again in a new translation as *Eça's English Letters* in 2000. All through his travels, he had been at work on a novel that drew on his experiences in Leiria, and in 1876 *O Crime de Padre Amaro* (The Crimes of Father Amaro) was published.

The book follows the career of the title character, who has reluctantly agreed to enter the priesthood. He has sexual relations with a young woman who becomes pregnant and later commits suicide. *The Crimes of Father Amaro* may have been inspired by French novelist Emile Zola's *The Transgression of Abbé Mouret,* published the previous year, and in general Eça de Queirós's grimly satirical treatment of the hypocrisy present through several layers of Portuguese society owed much to the realistic school of French writing in the later 19th century, and Eça de Queirós was sometimes referred to as the Portuguese Zola. In 2002 *The Crimes of Father Amaro* was filmed in Mexico, with its setting transferred to that country in contemporary times, complete with church corruption resulting from large cash contributions by narcotics traffickers. The film became the highest-grossing Mexican-made release in Mexican cinema history.

Eça de Queirós issued other books in quick succession. *O Primo Basilio* (1878, translated as *Cousin Bazilio* in 1953 and also the basis for films and television programs) resembled not Zola but Gustave Flaubert in its tale of adultery in a middle-class Lisbon family. Adultery was a theme common to several of Eça de Queirós's novels and shorter novellas, including the comic *Alves & Cia.,* (Alves and Company, translated as *The Yellow Sofa*), which was not published until 1925. His 1880 story collection *O Mandarim* (The Mandarin) departed from the author's usual realistic style and explored fantasy elements.

Formed "Life's Losers" Discussion Group

In 1886 Eça de Queirós married Emília de Castro Pamplona Resende in Porto, Portugal. They had a daughter, Maria, and a son, José Maria. In 1887 he published the novel *A relíquia* (translated in 1930 as *The Relic*), a satirical farce involving a young hipster who pretends to be religious so that he can inherit money, counterfeit relics from the Middle East, and a pair of switched packages, one containing a copy of Christ's crown of thorns and the other a woman's nightgown. The book has been praised by one of the foremost American literary critics, Harold Bloom. At the end of 1887 Eça de Queirós joined a new intellectual discussion group in Lisbon, this one called *Vencidos na Vida,* (Life's Losers).

In 1888, after working on it for several years, Eça de Queirós published his most ambitious novel, *Os Maias,* meaning The Maias, or The Maia Family. The book traced the gradual disintegration of an old Portuguese family through a series of romantic events that exposed many layers of the development of Portuguese society in the 19th century. The book has been translated into English several times, most recently as *The Maias: Episodes from Romantic Life* in 2007.

Eça de Queirós's career as a diplomat also hit a high point in 1888 as he was appointed Portugal's consul in Paris, France. He lived in Paris for the rest of his life, and while conflicts involving Portugal's colonial holdings in Africa took up some of his energy, he still found time to write short fiction, translate literature into Portuguese, and found a new magazine, the *Revista Moderna,* in 1897. Eça de Queirós suffered for some years with an undetermined illness that may have been tuberculosis; a visitor who saw him late in his life described him as coughing heavily and out of breath. Eça de Queirós died in Paris on August 16,

1900, but his literary reputation continued to increase with posthumous publications and new translations of his works in the years and decades after his death.

Books

Portuguese Writers, ed. Monica Rector and Fred M. Clark, *Dictionary of Literary Biography,* Vol. 287, Gale, 2004.

Periodicals

Guardian (London, England), July 11, 2009.
New York Sun, August 15, 2007.
New York Times, November 15, 2002.

Online

"Consul Yourself," *The Guardian* (London, England), http://www.guardian.co.uk/books/2000/dec/23/biography1 (February 8, 2010).
"Eça de Queiroz," *Vidas Lusofonas* (Portuguese Lives), http://www.vidaslusofonas.pt/eca_de_queiros2.htm (February 8, 2010).
"José Maria Eça de Queirós," *Books and Writers,* http://www.kirjasto.sci.fi/ecade.htm (February 8, 2010). □

Jake Ehrlich

American lawyer and author Jake W. Ehrlich (1900–1971) was a famed criminal and civil defense attorney in San Francisco, California that earned him the nickname "The Master." Known as a sharp dresser and sharper legal performer, Ehrlich developed a nationwide reputation during his 40-year career. His flamboyant courtroom style, high-profile cases, and famous client list became the inspiration for Perry Mason—a fictional character who appeared in popular crime novels by Erle Stanley Gardner and was later portrayed on the small screen by Raymond Burr—and television lawyer Sam Benedict. None of his over 100 clients charged with murder received the death penalty, and one was found not guilty in a mere four minutes. Along with his legal work, Ehrlich wrote more than ten works on the law as well as an autobiography, *A Life in My Hands.* Nearly three decades after his death, Ehrlich remained a pop culture presence, with actor Jon Hamm portraying the famed attorney in the 2010 film *Howl.*

Jacob Wilburn Ehrlich was born on October 15, 1900, on a plantation in Montgomery County, Maryland, located between Washington, D.C., and Baltimore. The eldest of the seven children of Harry and Sarah Ehrlich, the young Ehrlich became fascinated by the law through occasional trips to watch court sessions in nearby Rockville with his grandfather. After a brief stint in the army, during which he served along the Mexican border, Ehrlich enrolled at Washington, D.C.'s Georgetown University to pursue his dream of becoming an attorney. World War I interrupted his studies, however, and the young man returned to the army, this time to serve as a lieutenant in France. After the war ended in late 1918, Ehrlich spent only a short time back in Maryland before working his way across the country to San Francisco. There, he supported himself with jobs at a railroad office and as a professional boxer while continuing his legal studies, ultimately earning a law degree from the San Francisco Law School. He also met and married a hospital dietician, Marjorie Mercer; the couple soon had a son, Jacob Jr. and a daughter, Dora Jane.

In 1922, Ehrlich joined the California Bar Association and his career began in earnest. That career took a different form than the young hopeful had anticipated, however; in *Never Plead Guilty: The Story of Jake Ehrlich,* John Wesley Noble and Bernard Averbuch quoted him as recalling, "I discovered that I was not going to be engaged by Standard Oil, Bank of America or the California Packing Corporation. I had to take whatever cases came to me. Some of my clients were not the wholesome type. They came to the bar of justice seedy and tarnished, in body and spirit." Taking on primarily divorce cases and forced at first to work a night job at a tire factory, the novice attorney focused on building his reputation and developing his personal and professional style. His sartorial choices contributed to his renown nearly as much as did his courtroom skills, with the fastidious Ehrlich refusing to keep a pencil in his pocket so as not disarrange his suit jacket and forsaking briefcases in favor of accordion files. An unsuccessful run for State Attorney General—Ehrlich's only venture into politics—preceded his first major trial success in the 1931 rape trial of theater owner Alexander Pantages. Although Pantages had already been convicted of the crime once, he won a retrial and brought Ehrlich on board. The young lawyer mounted a dramatic defense that led to both the jury finding Pantages not guilty and to a sharp rise in Ehrlich's public profile.

Defended Famous Cases

For over three decades, Ehrlich defended high-profile clients including film stars, and famous singers, and murder suspects. He counted Errol Flynn, Billie Holiday, and Howard Hughes among his clients, and promulgated his reputation through both legal victories and such public outbursts as reputedly pulling a gun on a waiter at a popular San Francisco restaurant to demand faster service. He split his time between criminal and civil cases, taking on numerous divorce suits in a time when ending a marriage was not a simple task, and acted as counsel for the San Francisco Policeman's Association. In this role, Ehrlich defended numerous city officers in suits ranging from corruption to murder. Propelled by the motto "never plead guilty," Ehrlich saved clients from the death penalty even when their conviction seemed unquestionable.

One famous example of this sort of victory came in 1941. A young woman named Jean Collins called Ehrlich and informed him that she had just shot her boyfriend, Tony Barcelona, because he had been threatening to throw her out of the couple's thirteenth-floor hotel room. At the trial in February of that year, the prosecution read aloud Collins' dramatic confession to the crime, which described Barcelona's abuse and culminated in her shooting him three times. To present a case of justifiable homicide in self-defense, Ehrlich had a life-size dummy of the much-larger Barcelona constructed and engineered a situation for the petite Collins to stand next to it, visually stunning the jury with their relative difference in sizes. Further arguments focused on Barcelona's police record and history of violence. The combination of drama and persuasion prevailed, and after deliberations of just thirteen minutes the jury returned a verdict of not guilty.

Ehrlich's legal showmanship was so great that it could overcome even the wishes of his own clients. In the early 1950s, he defended housewife Gertrude Morris, a woman charged with murdering her husband Milton Morris in a fit of what was apparently mingled rage and sorrow over a suspected extramarital affair. The horrified wife later deeply regretted her action, and by the time Ehrlich entered the picture soon after, the accused murderess had come to a perhaps unexpected decision. Noble and Averbuch quoted her as telling her attorney that "Everything will be all right because I will be executed." Morris had seemingly given up all desire to live and tried to commit suicide while in jail awaiting trial; she later refused to speak with Ehrlich regarding her defense, much to his amazement. Morris's behavior led Ehrlich to attempt to have her declared incompetent to stand trial in November of 1951, but the jury declined his request. When her murder trial proceeded in January of the following year, the courtroom was packed with reporters and curiosity seekers alike. While acknowledging that Morris had killed her husband, Ehrlich presented that she had done so because she loved him rather than because she had hated him, and that she had failed to grasp the consequences of her actions at the time of the crime. Morris, however, repeatedly asked for the strongest possible verdict and by all accounts yearned for the death penalty. Ehrlich overcame, however, with an impassioned closing argument that brought members of the jury to tears. Morris was found guilty of manslaughter and sentenced to one to ten years in prison.

Later in the decade, Ehrlich led the defense of the obscenity trial of Beat poet Allen Ginsburg's "Howl." Filled with references to sexual activities and illicit drug use, the poem had been sold in a collection entitled *Howl and Other Poems* at the City Lights bookstore in San Francisco for several months before police arrested store owner Lawrence Ferlinghetti and sales clerk Shigeyoshi Murao for pandering obscene materials. Although the charges against Murao were dropped, Ferlinghetti's resulting 1957 trial became a significant milestone in the history of American censorship in a time of changing legal and social boundaries based on the freedom of speech and press protections granted in the United States Constitution's First Amendment. In a similar case that year, Supreme Court Justice William Brennan wrote, "All ideas having even the slightest redeeming social importance—unorthodox ideas, controversial ideas, even ideas hateful to the prevailing climate of opinion—have the full protection of the [First Amendment] guaranties . . . But implicit in the history of the First Amendment is the rejection of obscenity as utterly without redeeming social importance," according to a contemporary *Time* magazine report. Establishing a definition of obscenity proved more difficult, however, and ultimately hinged on whether the work appealed overwhelmingly to prurient, or purely sexual, interests. Joined by the American Civil Liberties Union, Ehrlich argued that Ginsberg's work deserved First Amendment protection due to its inherent literary and social merit—and the court agreed, finding Ferlinghetti not guilty and declaring that *Howl and Other Poems* was not an obscene work.

Career Became Basis for Television Shows

Such notable trials combined with an almost vaudevillian approach to the courtroom made Ehrlich a national figure. The same year that the lawyer made headlines over "Howl," he also came into living rooms across the United States, albeit in fictional form as the inspiration behind television program *Perry Mason*. Mason had made his first appearance in Erle Stanley Gardner's 1933 novel *The Case of the Velvet Claws* as a sharp Los Angeles defense attorney who, over the course of his printed, radio, and televised career, routinely cleared innocent clients from blame while simultaneously forcing the guilty parties to incriminate themselves. Mason exhibited the same kinds of courtroom performances that Ehrlich employed, and television actor Raymond Burr spent two weeks observing the San Francisco attorney in action as he developed his characterization of the title character. *Perry Mason* went on to become one of the most successful legal programs in television history, inspiring numerous later crime and legal dramas. Among these was *Sam Benedict,* a San Francisco-based legal drama that not only drew on the career of Ehrlich for its premise but also employed him as a scriptwriter and editor.

A prolific writer on legal matters, Ehrlich also published numerous books during the latter years of his career. His legal works include *Ehrlich's Blackstone* (1959), an updated edition of eighteenth century legal scholar William Blackstone's classic text *Commentaries of the Laws of England; Ehrlich's Criminal Law (1960); Howl of the Censors* (1961), discussing the Ginsburg case and later adapted as the 2010 film *Howl; The Holy Bible and the Law* (1962), *A Reasonable Doubt* (1964); *The Lost Art of Cross-Examination* (1970); and three with Brad Williams: *A Conflict of Interest* (1971), *A Matter of Confidence* (1973), and *Mord in Chinatown* (1973). Noble and Averbuch's 1955 biography of Ehrlich *Never Plead Guilty* had sales figures tallying over two million in paperback alone—a testament to Ehrlich's widespread popular appeal—and Ehrlich published his autobiography, *A Life in My Hands,* in 1965. He also worked with charitable causes during his career, serving as the president of children's relief organization Saints & Sinners for several years.

Ehrlich passed away at the age of 71 on December 24, 1971, as the result of a heart attack. His death attracted nationwide notice, with the *San Francisco Examiner* mourning the loss of a "tough, outspoken little attorney with the snowy crest of linen issuing from his breast pocket, the baroque gold jewelry and the snub-nosed police special in a holster under his arm, [who] was San Francisco in very special ways." A flamboyant public figure whose fame has endured perhaps in the memory of his fictional alter ego Perry Mason more than in his own name, Ehrlich was certainly one of the preeminent legal figures of his day as well as a celebrity in his own right for both his courtroom skills and showmanship.

Books

Morgan, Bill, and Nancy Joyce Peters, eds., *Howl on Trial: The Battle for Free Expression,* City Lights Books, 2006.

Noble, John Wesley, and Averbuch, Bernard, *Never Plead Guilty: The Story of Jake Ehrlich,* Farrar, Straus, and Cudahy, 1955.

Periodicals

New York Times, December 25, 1971.
San Francisco Chronicle, October 20, 1998.
San Francisco Examiner, December 24, 1971.
Time, July 8, 1957.

Online

"'Howl' obscenity prosecution still echoes 50 years later," First Amendment Center, http://www.firstamendmentcenter.org/news.aspx?id=19132 (January 11, 2010).

Never Plead Guilty, http://www.neverpleadguilty.com/index.html (January 11, 2010).

"Perry Mason," The Museum of Broadcast Communications, http://www.museum.tv/eotvsection.php?entrycode=perrymason (January 11, 2010).□

Ahmet Ertegun

The Turkish-American recording producer and music executive Ahmet Ertegun (1923–2006) founded the Atlantic label and helped to develop the careers of some of the most famous musicians in the fields of rhythm and blues and rock and roll.

Pierre Perrone of the London *Independent* asserted flatly that "Ahmet Ertegun was the most important figure in the record industry of the 20th century," and few observers would disagree substantially with that statement. In 1987 Ertegun became the first non-musician inducted into the Rock and Roll Hall of Fame, and Atlantic, the label he co-founded in 1947, remained a significant force in the music industry decades later. The musicians who owed their fame partly to Ertegun include Ray Charles, Aretha Franklin, and the band Led Zeppelin. Ertegun was modest about his own abilities as a talent spotter; music executive David Geffen recalled to Jon Pareles of the *New York Times* that "[i]f you're lucky, you bump into a genius, and a genius will make you rich in the music business." But Ertegun's ability to recognize genius when he saw it rested on a unique background involving a long acquaintance with American, and specifically African-American, musical traditions.

Heard Jazz in Paris and London

Ahmet Ertegun (originally Ertegün) was born in Istanbul, Turkey on July 31, 1923. His father, Mehmet Munir, was a Turkish diplomat and a close confidant of Kemal Ataturk, the founder of the modern nation of Turkey. The family took the last name Ertegun, meaning "the next day," when Ahmet was young because of a Turkish government decree mandating surnames. Ahmet was educated at home in Switzerland, France, and England as his father took up ambassadorial posts in those countries. In 1934 Mehmet Munir was named Turkey's ambassador to the United States. By that time Ahmet and his brother Nesuhi had already discovered and become fascinated by American jazz as played by expatriate musicians in Paris and London—the first black people they had ever seen.

Soon the Ertegun brothers were frequenting black-oriented music stores in Washington and amassing what became a collection of 25,000 78 rpm records. The Turkish embassy hosted concerts by jazz musicians, disregarding Washington's persistent racial segregation customs. Ertegun attended St. John's College in Maryland and then Georgetown University, majoring in philosophy, but his financial independence came to an end with his father's death in 1944. "I was totally unemployable," he

was quoted as saying by Perrone. "So naturally I decided to go into the music business."

Ertegun and a friend who had worked briefly as a talent scout, Herb Abramson, formed a pair of small labels, Jubilee and Quality, with financing from Washington record store owner "Waxie Maxie" Silverman. Neither venture lasted. Ertegun then borrowed $10,000 from his dentist, and he and Abramson launched Atlantic Records, whose name was originally inspired by that of the Pacific Jazz label both young entrepreneurs admired. They rented a space, which for some years served as both office and studio, in the decrepit Jefferson Hotel on Manhattan's West 56th Street. Atlantic was part of a large group of new labels that sprouted up all over the U.S. in the years after World War II, and Ertegun's first releases went nowhere.

Incorporated Southern Component into Sound

Atlantic's first breakthroughs came after the two partners took a tour of Southern cities, visiting clubs to measure their own releases against what they heard young African Americans listening and dancing to. They added Southern African-American artists to Atlantic's roster and pushed their New York bands to record in a more rhythmically vigorous style, creating a big-beat rhythm-and-blues idiom that became one of the streams feeding into early rock and roll. Their efforts were rewarded in 1949 with Atlantic's first major hit, Tennessee guitarist Stick McGhee's "Drinkin' Wine Spo-Dee-O-Dee." Soon after that, Ertegun heard a recording by an unknown vocalist and piano player who

then visited Atlantic's offices. "Ray Charles, you are the greatest singer. You're the greatest piano player. Man," Ertegun said (as he recalled to A.L. Bardach of the online magazine *Slate*), "you are home now!" Charles remained with Atlantic as he recorded "What'd I Say?" and other pioneering fusions of rhythm and blues with gospel techniques.

Ertegun continued to prowl nightclubs in New York and elsewhere, discovering new artists like vocalist Ruth Brown or the group the Drifters, and often producing their records. If there was not enough new material on hand for a session, Ertegun was happy to furnish a composition of his own, rendering his name as "A. Nugetre" (Ertegun spelled backward) on the label because he still harbored occasional thoughts of returning to Turkey and taking a sensitive government job there. Ray Charles's hit "Mess Around" was among Ertegun's songwriting credits. Nesuhi Ertegun joined his brother in the business in the late 1950s, adding a jazz component to Atlantic's catalogue and becoming responsible for jazz recordings by Charles and the tenor saxophonist John Coltrane, among others. Among Ertegun's protégés at Atlantic in the late 1950s was the pioneering 1960s producer Phil Spector.

Among Ertegun's few regrets in the music business was his decision to bow out of a bidding war for the services of the young Elvis Presley, but he made up for it by signing the hugely successful Italian-American vocalist Bobby Darin. As Atlantic grew, Ertegun showed the same expertise in choosing employees, such as producers and talent spotters, as he had in signing artists himself in the label's early days. Among the historically significant figures he brought on board at Atlantic was producer Jerry Wexler, who made the label into a major force in soul music in the 1960s. After Ertegun signed the Detroit vocal powerhouse Aretha Franklin, Wexler supervised sessions in which she was recorded with Southern musicians in Memphis, Tennessee and Muscle Shoals, Alabama.

Up to that point, most of Atlantic's artists had been African Americans or white artists working in predominantly African-American idioms. In the mid-1960s, however, Ertegun steered Atlantic into rock, signing groups such as Iron Butterfly and Buffalo Springfield, and forming the new Atco imprint. "I should have gotten the Beatles," he told Bardach. "But one of my lawyers kind of messed up." The signing of the hard-rock band Led Zeppelin and a 1971 agreement to distribute the Rolling Stones Records imprint, reportedly reached because Stones frontman Mick Jagger felt comfortable with Ertegun, who dozed off during negotiations, helped compensate for that loss.

Suggested Feature of Collins Hit

In 1968 Ertegun had sold Atlantic to the Warner–Seven Arts label; Atlantic later became one leg of the major WEA (Warner-Elektra-Atlantic) group and continues to exist today as part of the Warner Communications colossus. Retaining the title of founding chairman, Ertegun maintained close involvement with Atlantic's day-to-day operations, and during the 1970s and 1980s he signed such major acts as the bands Foreigner and ABBA to Atlantic. The prominent drum solo on Atlantic artist Phil Collins's evergreen 1981 hit

"In the Air Tonight" was the result of a suggestion from Ertegun. Atlantic or its Atco and Cotillion subsidiaries issued multimillion-selling LP albums by rock guitarist Eric Clapton, rock-classical fusion group Emerson, Lake & Palmer, Australian pop group the Bee Gees, and many others.

While successful, these groups for the most part were not on the forward edge of musical development like those Ertegun had discovered in the 1940s and 1950s. Ertegun took some criticism for this development: Wexler, complaining (according to the London *Daily Telegraph*) that Ertegun had become "less judgmental and more commercial," left Atlantic in 1975. But Ertegun, whose fondness for going to nightclubs to soak up the latest trends persisted into the hip-hop era, became a wealthy man, entertaining a steady crowd of jet-setting stars in homes he owned in Manhattan, the posh Hamptons area of Long Island, Paris, and Turkey (on the Aegean seacoast in Bodrum). An elegant figure in his tailored suits, Ertegun was also known as a practical joker. After his first marriage, to Jan Holm, dissolved, he wooed his second wife, designer Mica Banu Grecianu, by hiring an orchestra to hide in her hotel room and surprise her with a rendition of "Puttin' on the Ritz."

More serious criticism came from Ruth Brown, who wrote (as quoted by Adam Sweeting and Richard Williams of the London *Guardian*) that "[f]or every Picasso he had on his wall, I had a damp patch on mine." She was referring to Ertegun's large collection of modern art and her own poverty in later life, the result of the sort of contract, often viewed as exploitative, that deprived Brown and many other African-American artists of her generation of most of the profits their recordings reaped. After an initial unsatisfactory exchange in which Ertegun wrote a $1,000 check while reminding Brown that she still owed the company $30,000, the episode resulted in the formation of the Rhythm and Blues Foundation, set up with the help of a $1.5 million donation from Ertegun. The aim of the foundation was to provide financial and medical help for rhythm-and-blues artists of advancing age.

Another organization with which Ertegun was closely involved in its early years was the Rock and Roll Hall of Fame in Cleveland, which inducted Ertegun himself in 1989 as its first non-musician member. Ertegun received various other awards in his later years, including designation as a Living Legend by the U.S. Library of Congress in 2000. But he preferred hands-on projects such as supervision of Atlantic and Ray Charles box sets, as well as soundtrack albums for the Charles film biography *Ray* (2004), in which Ertegun was portrayed by Curtis Armstrong, and an Atlantic picture history, *What'd I Say: The Atlantic Story.* In 1990, Ertegun was the subject of an industry-oriented biography, *Music Man: Ahmet Ertegun, Atlantic Records, and the Triumph of Rock 'n' Roll.* An autobiography project remained unrealized at Ertegun's death, after a fall and head injury at a Rolling Stones concert, in New York on December 14, 2006. Led Zeppelin reunited for a concert in his honor the following year. "The popular notion is that without Elvis Presley, Chuck Berry and Little Richard, there wouldn't have been rock 'n' roll," wrote rock historian Robert Hilburn in the *Houston Chronicle.* "But it may be closer to the truth to say there wouldn't have been rock 'n' roll without Ahmet Ertegun."

Books

Contemporary Musicians, volume 10, Gale, 1993.
Ertegun, Ahmet, and others, *What'd I Say: The Atlantic Story,* ed. C. Perry Richardson, Welcome Rain, 2001.
Wade, Dorothy, and Justine Picardie, *Music Man: Ahmet Ertegun, Atlantic Records, and the Triumph of Rock 'n' Roll,* Norton, 1990.

Periodicals

Daily Telegraph (London, England), December 18, 2006.
Guardian (London, England), December 16, 2006.
Houston Chronicle, December 16, 2006.
Independent (London, England), December 16, 2006.
New York, July 16, 1973.
New York Times, December 16, 2006.
USA Today, December 11, 2007.

Online

"Ahmet Ertegun," *Rock and Roll Hall of Fame,* http://www.rockhall.com/inductee/ahmet-ertegun (January 2, 2010).
"Interrogating Ahmet Ertegun: The Atlantic Records Founder on Ray Charles, Islamic Fundamentalism, and His Own Hipness," *Slate,* http://www.slate.com/id/2114074 (January 2, 2010). □

Bartolomeo Eustachi

Italian anatomist Bartolomeo Eustachi (died 1574) made important discoveries as a medical professor at Rome's Sapienza University. Also known by the Latinized form of his name, Eustachius, the physician and researcher is credited with discovering the canal that connects the middle ear to the throat. They were named the "Eustachian tubes" in his honor, but are also referred to as the pharyngotympanic tubes.

There are several conflicting dates for Eustachi's birth, ranging from 1500 to 1520. It is known that he came from San Severino, a town in the Marche region in coastal central Italy, and that his father was Mariano, a physician. Historians believe he studied medicine in Rome and Padua. The latter city was home to Italy's second oldest university and was acclaimed as a center of excellence in scientific research, especially medicine.

The details concerning the earliest years of Eustachi's professional career are unclear, but it is known that he served as personal physician to the Duke of Urbino and then to the Duke's brother, a cardinal. When that cardinal, Giulio della Rovere, was called to Rome to become head of San Pietro in Vincoli in Rome in 1548, the physician Eustachi went with him. The appointment of della Rovere as cardinal-priest of San Pietro in Vincoli signified the close ties between the family and the Vatican authorities. San Pietro was also called the Basilica Eudoxiana and dated back to the 430s, when a site of worship was erected to house what were believed to be the remnants of chains once used to confine St. Peter, one of Christ's twelve apostles.

Dissected Cadavers

In Rome, Eustachi was hired to teach at *La Sapienza—Università di Roma*, the Sapienza part of which means "wisdom." He lectured in anatomy and was apparently granted permission to conduct scientific research on corpses from two different hospitals in Rome. One of these medical facilities was attached to Santo Spirito in Sassia, a church originally founded for Saxon pilgrims to Rome around 700. By Eustachi's lifetime it was attached to an adjacent hospital that cared for foundlings, or abandoned children, on the street Borgo Santo Spirito near the Vatican. The other hospital that provided Eustachi with cadavers was affiliated with the church Santa Maria della Consolazione at the foot of Rome's Palatine Hill. In ancient Roman times, criminals facing a sentence of death were thrown off the cliff above this site, and later a statue of the Virgin Mary was placed at the site, around which grew the church and then, in 1506, the hospital that served the poor Trastavere neighborhood.

Conducting autopsies was a relatively new phenomenon in Western Europe at the time. Italy and other lands were still ardently religious societies, with laws based on Christian tenets that governed all aspects of life and, in this particular instance, the handling and burial of the dead. Regarding the disturbance of corpses, the Church's guidelines were essentially a continuation of ancient Roman laws prohibiting the dissection of cadavers for any reason, including scientific investigation. In the fourteenth century, however, some of the duchies and other states of northern Italy granted exceptions to the ban on cadaver autopsies in the cases of executed criminals, which could be examined for instructional purposes only. So strong was the prohibition that a barber-surgeon was employed for the task at medical colleges; physician/professors would preside over the event and point out the anatomical parts and their functions.

The practice, which could only be carried out in winter months due to lack of effective methods of refrigeration, seems to have spread to Rome by the time of Eustachi's stint at La Sapienza. Eustachi's autopsies for students were apparently open to curious onlookers, too, according to Andrea Carlino in *Books of the Body: Anatomical Ritual and Renaissance Learning*. From these autopsies Eustachi began to compile a treatise on anatomy that he hoped would surpass that of the Belgian anatomist Andreas van Wesel, called Vesalius. In 1543 Vesalius published his famous *De humani corporis fabrica* (On the Fabric of the Human Body), and it was the standard textbook for medical students.

Challenged Vesalius

Vesalius had been a member of the faculty at Padua's college of medicine, and his book was the first to be used since the error-ridden *Methodus medendi,* written by the Roman physician Galen in around 180 C.E. Also known as *The Description and Treatment of the Principal Diseases Incident to the Human Frame,* Galen's work was drawn from his studies of gladiators' wounds and dissections of monkeys and other animals, and it was the only anatomical textbook available to medical students in the late Middle Ages.

The historic *Fabrica* work from Vesalius refuted many of Galen's claims, but Eustachi wanted to author a more complete version of Vesalius's findings. He seems to have carried on a professional rivalry with Vesalius, and his first two books contained refutations of some of Vesalius's claims against Galen. These titles were *Ossium examen* (A Consideration of Bones) and *Demotu capitis* (roughly translated as "On the Motion of the Head"). These appeared in the early 1560s.

By this point in his career Eustachi had already finished a tremendous amount of research on human anatomy. With his assistant Pier Matteo Pini he made nearly four dozen drawings of the human body and its systems, and then hired an engraver named Giulio de Musi to etch images on copper plates for the printing process. In total, Eustachi, Pini, and de Musi created 47 plates that Eustachi hoped so see published in full. The plates were finished by 1552, but the complete work was never published in his lifetime. Historians surmise that Eustachi, who likely earned only modest salaries from della Rovere and La Sapienza, was unable to financially underwrite the expensive printing process himself.

Correctly Identified Parts of Kidney

Instead the findings were published in smaller volumes in the first half of the 1560s. The first of these was *De renibus libellus* (roughly translated as "Little Book on the Structure of the Kidneys"). It featured seven of his detailed plates and explained the function of the kidney in excreting waste from the body. In the 1997 collection of papers published as *History of Nephrology,* Mabel L. Purkerson noted that "Eustachi's contributions concerning the kidney are several: he was the first to describe the adrenal glands, he noted correctly that the right kidney is lower than the left, he clearly and accurately illustrated the intrarenal vasculature," among other breakthroughs. His work was also notable for the grid overlay, with corresponding numbers in the text using letters and numbers as "coordinates because Eustachio felt quite strongly about letters being placed on his artwork," Purkerson wrote.

Another work was *De dentibus libellus,* a treatise on teeth. The Eustachian tube is named in honor of Eustachi's findings in *De auditus organis* (On the Auditory Organ). He described a canal of three to four centimeters in length that led from the middle ear to the throat. This was actually first discovered by a fifth-century BCE medical theorist, Alcmaeon of Croton, whom the philosopher Aristotle reported as claiming that goats could breathe through their ears as well as their noses. This information was lost over time, however; in Eustachi's day, physicians believed the ear was a closed orifice—that is, if a substance entered it, it would not be able to reach the inside of the body.

Discovery Linked to *Hamlet*

Instead, as Eustachi showed in his plates, the middle ear is connected to the pharynx, a cavity that has both respiratory and digestive functions. "Knowledge of this passage will be very useful to physicians for the correct use of medicaments, because now they will know that even thick material can be expelled or purged from the ears by a very ample pathway, either by nature or by the aid of those medicaments which are called *masticatoria*," Eustachi wrote, according to Tanya Pollard's *Drugs and Theater in Early Modern England*. The discovery that the ear was a permeable orifice seems to have found its way into the 1599 play *Hamlet* by William Shakespeare, in which the late king, Hamlet learns, has been killed by an assassin who poured poison into his ear.

Eustachi's books were collected into one volume, *Opuscula anatomica*, which was published in 1564. These included all of the previous titles as well as an expansion of his work on teeth; he asserted that the fourth-century B.C.E. Greek physician Hippocrates was correct in his belief that teeth begin to grow in the fetus in the womb, and he also declared that teeth are not containers of bone marrow, as some thought at the time.

In his later years Eustachi gave up his teaching post in Rome because of gout, but still served as della Rovere's physician. He was also known to have treated Philip Neri and Charles Borromeo, two esteemed clerics who would later be canonized as saints by the Church. In August of 1574, della Rovere fell ill while in Marche, and Eustachi was summoned to his side. Eustachi, however, fell ill in Umbria, and died on the 27th of that month.

"Rescued from Obscurity"

In 1564's *Opuscula anatomica*, Eustachi wrote of having completed 47 copper engravings with de Musi—but only eight of these were featured. For more than a century the remaining illustrations were thought to have been lost, but Eustachi had bequeathed them to his assistant Pini, and the 39 missing plates were discovered in the 1700s by a descendant of Pini's. They were bought by Pope Clement XI, who gave them to his personal physician, Giovanni Maria Lancisi. Lancisi added some notations and the complete set was published in 1714 as *Tabulae anatomicae Bartholomaie Eustachi quas a tenebris tandem vindicatas* (Anatomical Illustrations of Bartholomeo Eustachi Rescued from Obscurity).

Subsequent editions of Eustachi's opus were tremendously popular among medical professionals across Europe for the next few decades, and his grid system of notation was widely adopted by medical book publishers. "Although devoid of Eustachi's planned text, the plates alone assure him a distinguished position in the history of anatomy," noted C. D. O'Malley in the 2008 reference work *Complete Dictionary of Scientific Biography*. O'Malley also asserted that "had the Eustachian anatomical illustrations not been lost to the medical world for over a century, it seems likely that anatomical studies would have reached maturity in the seventeenth rather than the eighteenth century."

Books

Carlino, Andrea, *Books of the Body: Anatomical Ritual and Renaissance Learning,* University of Chicago Press, 1999.

Fisher, George Jackson, "A Series of Sketches of the Lives, Times and Works of the Old Masters of Anatomy and Surgery," in *Annals of the Anatomical and Surgical Society,* Volume 2, edited by Charles Jewett, Brooklyn, NY, 1880, pp. 113–117.

O'Malley, C.D., "Eustachi, Bartolomeo, in *Complete Dictionary of Scientific Biography,* edited by Charles Gillispie, Volume 4, Cengage, 2008, pp. 486–488.

Pollard, Tanya, *Drugs and Theater in Early Modern England,* Oxford University Press, 2005, p. 128.

Purkerson, Mabel L., and L. Wechsler, "Depictions of the Kidney through the Ages," in *History of Nephrology,* Volume 2, *Reports from the First Congress of the International Association for the History of Nephrology,* edited by Garabed Eknoyan et al., Karger Publishers, 1997, pp. 142.□

F

Girolamo Fabrici

Italian anatomist and surgeon Girolamo Fabrici (1537-1619) conducted pioneering research in fetal development. He also advanced knowledge about human physiology, particularly related to the circulatory system and the structure and function of venous valves.

Because of his influential work, Girolamo (also Geronimo) Fabrici (also Fabrizio or Fabricius) became known as the founder of embryology. During a twenty-year period which extended from 1600 until his death in 1619, Fabrici conducted groundbreaking studies related to the fetal development of different animals. In 1612, he described for the first time how chicken embryo development proceeds from its earliest days. His work in this area led to better understanding of how the human embryo develops from fertilization to the fetal stage.

Fabrici also helped advanced the field of anatomy and physiology. In particular, he provided new information about organ structure (the eye and the larynx), the respiratory system, muscle mechanics, and the structure and function of the semi-lunar valves in the veins. Further, in the anatomical theater of the University of Padua, Fabrici advanced the comparative approach to anatomy and embryology.

Attended University of Padua

Fabrici was born on May 20, 1537, near Orvieto in Italy. He was also known as Hieronymus Fabricius ab Aquapendente, with his surname indicating the town in which he was born. He was the oldest son of Fabrico Fabrici, the patriarch of a noble, but not wealthy, family. He attended the University of Padua. Founded in 1222, and located in Padua, Italy, the institution is one of the oldest universities in the world. It was there that Fabrici first studied humanities (logic, philosophy, Greek, and Latin). Reportedly, his nine-year education (1550-1559) was financed by the patronage of the aristocratic Loredan family.

While at Padua, Fabrici's interests shifted from humanities to medicine; he received the finest education. His instructor in anatomy and surgery was Gabriel Fallopius (1523-1562), considered one of the sixteenth century's most illustrious anatomists. Fallopius' research added to the early knowledge about the ear. He also studied the human sex organs (the fallopian tube in women is named after him).

Became Medical Professor

In 1559, Fabrici concluded his nine-year university education, graduating with degrees in medicine and philosophy. Subsequently, he supported himself by giving private lessons in anatomy.

He returned to the University of Padua in 1565, three years after Fallopius died, taking over for his mentor as a professor of anatomy and surgery. In this way, he became part of a rich heritage: Fallopius' own predecessors included renowned anatomist such as Realdo Colombo (died 1559), Bartolomeo Eustachi (died 1574) and Andreas Vesalius (1514-1564). In 1600, Fabrici was awarded tenure and remained at Padua for the rest of his career. He retired from teaching in 1613, after spending nearly fifty years at the university.

Carried out Groundbreaking Studies

At Padua, Fabrici conducted the research that would advance the fields of anatomy and embryology. In 1579, he demonstrated the valves in the veins residing in the limbs. In 1603, he published *De venarum ostiolis* ("On the Valves of the Veins"), in which he specifically described the structure

and function of venous semi-lunar valves. While these valves had been previously observed, Fabrici's paper pushed knowledge a step further by providing description much more detailed than previously offered. Even though his explanation of valve function—the valves, he stated, served to slow down blood flow, which enabled body tissues to absorb nutrients— later proved to be incorrect, he still accurately identified how blood moves throughout the body.

Beyond the notoriety his research fostered, Fabrici gained considerable renown as an educator. One of his students was the famed English physician William Harvey (1578-1657), who studied under Fabrici from 1597 to 1602. Harvey would become the first to accurately and explicitly describe the human body's circulatory system and the role that the heart plays in this physiological function. Fabrici's earlier research helped Harvey develop this description.

Performed Surgery and Wrote Papers

Along with his research activities into anatomy, physiology and embryology, Fabrici also performed surgery. Important individuals and families in Italy sought him out for consultation, including the Duke of Mantua (in 1581) and the Duke of Urbino (in 1591). In 1604, the Grand Duke asked Fabrici to treat his son. In the first decade of the seventeenth century, Fabrici traveled to Venice to administer treatment to the wounded Paolo Sarpi (1552-1623). Fabrici successfully treated the Venetian patriot and religious reformist and, as a result, he became a knight of Saint Mark by the Republic of Venice. He was also highly regarded in

medical circles: From 1570 to 1584, he served on the commission that administered examinations and granted licenses to surgeons.

Fabrici made himself rich by his combined academic and surgical activities, but his most substantial accomplishments came through his research. In the area of embryology, Fabrici wrote two hugely significant papers. In 1600, he penned *De formato foetu* ("On the Formation of the Fetus"), the first study to compare late fetal stages of different animals and the first to describe the placenta in detail. The second paper, *De formatione ovi et pulli* ("On the Development of the Egg and the Chick"), was written in 1612.

Both works were remarkable in their detail. While Fabrici conducted his research without the use of magnifying lenses, he accompanied his writings with astonishingly intricate illustrations. In *De formatione ovi et pulli*, five plates represented the first illustrations of a chick egg in development, starting from the earliest days of incubation.

In his embryological research, Fabrici combined the philosophical with the physiological, as he sought to describe the purpose of the fetal organs. In *De formato foetu*, Fabrici described how he believed nature appears to provide for the needs of the fetus during gestation. He also discussed the elements such as the umbilical vessels, fetal membranes, placenta and the uterus.

Became Influential Anatomist

Meanwhile, Fabrici became the most influential anatomist of the late sixteenth and early seventeenth centuries, as he elevated the status of anatomy at European universities. At the University of Padua, he helped establish the first permanent anatomical theater. His anatomy lectures included dissections, wherein he demonstrated the anatomy of a fetal horse, a fetal sheep and a pregnant ewe. One lecture involved the dissection of a woman who died while in labor.

Fabrici also helped elevate the tone of public anatomies in terms of civility and dignity. In an article published in the summer 2007 issue of *Renaissance Quarterly* ("Civility, comportment and the anatomy theater: Girolamo Fabrici and his medical students in Renaissance Padua"), author Cynthia Klestinec described how, in the Renaissance era, public anatomy studies coincided with public carnival events and, as a result, became a boisterous celebration of the human body. At Padua University, however, Fabrici changed the tenor of the occasion. Fabrici always initiated the dissection process with a philosophically disposed introduction to his research. For medical students, the overall tone of the occasion fostered silence, observation, and respect.

As Klestinec related: "The anatomy theater became a place for Fabrici to develop and to publicize his innovative research on the philosophical causes (rather than physical structures) of anatomy. For his students as well, the demonstration was defined not by manual activity but rather by philosophical weight—that is, not by a physicality that might bleed into the Carnival season but rather by conceptual rigor. This distinction, however, led students to reconsider the anatomy demonstration as an integral part of their wider university education. They associated it with natural philosophy."

Subsequently, Venice officials recognized Fabrici with many honors and built for him an anatomical theater.

Died Near Padua

Fabrici continued at Padua until 1613, when his poor health compelled him to retire. He died six years later, on May 21, 1619. He passed away at his villa, La Montagnola, located in Bugazzi, near Padua.

Besides *De venarum ostiolis, De formato foetu* and *De formatione ovi et pulli*, his major works include *De visione, voce et auditu* (1600) and *De motu locali animalium secundum totum* (1618). His written works related to surgery were collected in *Pentateuchos cheirurgicum*, published in Frankfurt, Germany in 1592, and in *Operationes chirurgicae*, published in Venice, Italy in 1619, the year of his death.

In addition, his collected works were published as *Opera omnia Anatomica et Physiologica*, in Leipzig, Germany in 1687. During his career, Fabrici was a member of the medical colleges at the universities of Padua and Venice.

Books

"Girolamo Fabrici," *Merriam-Webster's Biographical Dictionary,* Merriam-Webster Incorporated, 1995.
"Girolamo Fabrici," *World of Anatomy and Physiology,* Thomson Gale, 2006.
"Girolamo Fabrici," *World of Biology,* Thomson Gale, 2006.
"Girolamo Fabrici," *World of Genetics,* Thomson Gale, 2006.

Periodicals

Renaissance Quarterly,, Summer 2007.

Online

"Fabrici [Fabricius, Fabrizi], Girolamo," *The Galileo Project,,* http://galileo.rice.edu/Catalog/NewFiles/fabrici.html (December 15, 2009).
"Fabricius, Hieronymus (1537Û1619)," *Hutchinson Encyclopedia,,* http://encyclopedia.farlex.com/Fabricius,+Hieronymus (December 15, 2009).
"Girolamo Fabrici," *NNDB.com,* http://www.nndb.com/people/017/000100714/ (December 15, 2009).
"William Harvey," *San Jose State University.edu,* http://www.sjsu.edu/depts/Museum/harvey.html (December 15, 2009). □

W. Mark Felt

American former associate FBI director W. Mark Felt (1913–2008) made headlines during the 1970s as "Deep Throat," the anonymous source who, by passing information to *Washington Post* reporter Bob Woodward, brought about the Watergate scandal that led to the resignation of then-United States President Richard M. Nixon. After guarding his identity closely for over three decades, Felt revealed himself as the legendary source in 2005, ending years of speculation but not closing the book on the famed scandal, which

continues to fascinate the public long after its conclusion. Three years after unmasking himself, Felt died in Santa Rosa, California, at the age of 95.

William Mark Felt was born on August 17, 1913, in Twin Falls, Idaho, where he grew up in relatively comfortable circumstances until his father's building contracting job ran into difficulties with the onset of the Great Depression in 1929. Although Felt was not an outstanding student, he—as he declared in his autobiography, *A G-Man's Life: The FBI, Being "Deep Throat," and the Struggle for Honor in Washington*—"always felt attracted to adventure and advancement and saw [himself] as a leader." He attended the University of Idaho, where he served as president of the Beta Theta Pi fraternity and worked part-time to pay for college. After graduating in 1935, Felt decided to move to Washington, D.C., in the hopes of landing a government job that would enable him to attend law school. As luck had it, Idaho Senator James P. Pope offered the aspiring attorney a job as a correspondence clerk in his Washington office, and Felt accepted eagerly.

Rose Through Ranks of the FBI

In the nation's capital, Felt began taking law classes at George Washington University Law School in the evening while working first for Pope and later for his successor, D. Worth Clark.

He also found time to court and marry fellow Idahoan Audrey Robinson in 1938. Two years after his marriage, Felt completed his law degree. After successfully standing his bar examination, he took a position with the Federal Trade Commission; however, Felt found the work unsatisfying—his first and only assignment involved researching a brand of toilet tissue—and decided to apply for a role with U.S. Federal Bureau of Investigation (FBI) in November of 1941. After several weeks of interviews, exams, and background checks, Felt was offered a position as a special agent. He reported for his first day of work with the organization that would become his lifelong employer in January of 1942.

Felt's years at the Bureau were hectic ones. Organization chief J. Edgar Hoover required new agents to transfer frequently, and within the first three years of Felt's career he was on staff at the FBI offices in Houston, San Antonio, Washington—where he worked extensively on Nazi counterspy efforts—and Seattle. This final location provided a few years of welcome stability for the by-then growing Felt family, supplemented in 1943 by daughter Joan and four years later by son Mark Jr. The city did not offer the kind of career-making exposure that Felt sought, however, so he lobbied for a position higher on the ladder. A brief return to the nation's capital was followed by stints in New Orleans, Los Angeles, and Salt Lake City, where Felt became at last a special agent in charge. After a short tenure in Kansas City, the agent again returned to Washington in 1962, where he became the second in command of the FBI's Training Division. After two years, Felt was promoted to a much more powerful position: chief inspector of the agency's Inspection Division, a job Felt termed "a virtual extension of the director" in his memoirs. Felt retained this role until 1971, when he advanced to become the FBI's associate director, the agency's second-highest ranking slot.

Provided Information During Watergate Scandal

The events that kicked off the Watergate scandal were simple ones: in June of 1972, five men linked to the Republican Party's Committee to Re-elect the President broke into Democratic campaign offices located in Washington, D.C.'s Watergate building. Led by Felt, the FBI quickly began investigating the burglary for any connections to the Nixon White House. The administration came out apparently cleared of all charges, and Nixon won re-election in late 1972. *Washington Post* reporters Bob Woodward and Carl Bernstein remained interested in the affair, however, and Woodward made contact with someone he initially identified only as "my friend." This friend—soon dubbed "Deep Throat" by *Post* managing editor Howard Simons—initially simply confirmed information that the reporters had obtained through other sources. In time, however, Deep Throat began to steer the pair down the path to unraveling the Nixon White House's conspiracy to cover up their involvement with the Watergate burglary. This revelation quickly led to Nixon's famed resignation in 1974.

As the scandal unfolded, Deep Throat became a figure of great mystery and speculation. Characterized in Bernstein and Woodward's book on the affair, *All the President's Men,* as a shadowy, cigarette-smoking source who met with Woodward under terms of the greatest secrecy late at night in a parking garage, Deep Throat carefully guarded his true identity. In fact, before Felt formally revealed himself as the source in 2005, only four people were publicly known to have been aware of Deep Throat's real name—a number which did not include reporter Bernstein, despite his intimate involvement with the scandal. In describing a 1973 meeting between himself and Felt in a bar in *All the President's Men,* however, Woodward "wondered if his friend was intentionally flirting with the danger of being discovered. Did Deep Throat want to get caught so he would be free to speak publicly? . . . Woodward started to ask, then faltered. It was enough to know that Deep Throat would never deal with him falsely. Someday it would all be explained." The mystique surrounding the source was only heightened by Woodward and Bernstein's popular book and the following movie version, which featured Hal Holbrook as the anonymous tipster. Felt retired from the FBI in June of 1973 in the midst of the affair, but almost immediately the press began to speculate that he had been Deep Throat.

Even decades after the events and Felt's acknowledgement of his role, the complete story of his involvement remains somewhat hazy. Writing in Felt's autobiography, John O'Connor identified three key pieces of information still lacking: "why he initiated his high-stakes garage meetings with Woodward, how he planned and managed those meetings, and how he escaped detection at the FBI." Indeed, Felt seems to have deftly balanced his public role as the head FBI investigator into the break-in, maintaining apparent loyalty to FBI interim director L. Patrick Gray III—who was himself passing information from the FBI to the White House—and his private persona as press informant. Yet speculation of Felt's motivations continues to this day. Some have argued that he simply felt compelled to speak out against what he saw as rampant corruption in the Nixon administration, while others have postulated that the actions were in response to the White House's efforts to subsume the independence and power of the FBI in the wake of Hoover's death.

In the later part of the 1970s, the Civil Rights Division of the Justice Department began investigations into actions taken by the FBI against the radical group the Weather Underground Organization (WUO) earlier in the decade. After splintering from the activist Students for a Democratic Society in the late 1960s, the WUO engaged in a series of bombings that have been classified as domestic terrorism. During the period of the bombings, the FBI had searched the homes and placed wiretaps on the telephone lines of those known to be affiliated with members of the WUO. By the time of the Carter Administration in the late 1970s, however, the legality of these actions began to come into question, and the Civil Rights Division called FBI agents in for investigation. Attempting to protect these low-level employees, Felt, Gray, and fellow FBI official Edward S. Miller took responsibility for the actions, claiming that they were fully justified. The three went to trial for civil rights violations in 1978, and were found guilty. Felt was devastated; his good record of years of service was shattered. He appealed the verdict and was later pardoned by President Ronald Reagan, yet the lingering effects of the trial proved difficult for Felt. Despite his pardon, he retained the psychological scars from the affair. The pressure of the situation ultimately overwhelmed his wife, who committed suicide in 1984. Although Felt kept the nature of his wife's death a secret, he began to forge closer ties with his remaining family members. Regular visits to his daughter and her sons in California became the norm, and in the early 1990s the former informant left Washington for good in favor of Santa Rosa, California. There, he helped raise his grandsons even after a stroke partially debilitated him in 1996.

Revealed Himself as Deep Throat

While many had speculated that Felt had played the key informant role in the Watergate scandal, he offered no confirmation of this rumor even to his family until the new millennium. After former paramour and continued close friend of the retired agent, Yvette LaGarde, inadvertently revealed Felt's secret to his daughter, Joan Felt began persuading her father to reveal his secret. Felt had long intended to keep his involvement clandestine until after his death, and grappled with his own concerns over how the role of Deep Throat had been perceived within the FBI. Eventually, however, Felt agreed to unveil himself, answering one of modern history's most hotly debated questions. "I'm the guy they used to call Deep Throat," he told family friend John O'Connor in *Vanity Fair*. The press responded quickly and enthusiastically to this revelation, profiling the aging Felt and revisiting the events of 1972. The historic nature of Felt's public acknowledgement of his role was noted; in the *New York Times*, Sally Quinn, the wife of former *Washington Post* executive editor Benjamin C. Bradlee, commented that, "there's been a certain mystique about the story that will not be there anymore. Everybody loves a secret that can be kept. Deep Throat has become this living legend, like Camelot. And now it isn't anymore."

On December 18, 2008, Felt passed away in Santa Rosa, California, at the age of 95. His death attracted national attention, again raising questions of Felt's motivations and the legacy of the Watergate scandal. Speaking in the *Washington Post*, Watergate authority Ronald Kessler argued, "Some think he abused his position by cooperating with Woodward. Others think he was a patriot because he helped bring down Nixon who was engaged in criminal activity and might have abolished elections. I agree with those who think he was a patriot. People ascribe a number of motives to him, both bad and good. Some say he helped Woodward because he wanted to be named FBI director by a new president. I suppose that was part of it but I believe he was personally outraged by Nixon's actions and some of the instructions that Nixon was giving the FBI." Regardless of Felt's true goals in putting Woodward on the path to Watergate—and of the circumstances surrounding the FBI's actions toward the Weather Underground—the legacy of Felt's actions is unquestionable and his status as the most famous anonymous source in American history undeniable.

Books

Bernstein, Carl, and Bob Woodward, *All the President's Men,* Simon & Schuster, 1974.

Felt, Mark, and John O'Connor, *A G-Man's Life: The FBI, Being "Deep Throat," and the Struggle for Honor in Washington,* PublicAffairs, 2006.

Woodward, Bob, *The Secret Man: The Story of Watergate's Deep Throat,* Simon & Schuster, 2005.

Periodicals

New York Times, June 1, 2005; December 19, 2008.
Vanity Fair, July 2005.

Online

"Deep Throat Dies; Most Famous Anonymous Source in U.S. History," WashingtonPost.com (December 24, 2009). □

Horton Foote

American playwright and screenwriter Horton Foote (1916–2009) was among the most widely acclaimed and frequently produced playwrights, drawing on life in the southern United States in the 20th century.

To casual moviegoers, Foote may have been best known for his adapted screenplay for the hit film *To Kill a Mockingbird* (1962) and for his own original screenplay, *Tender Mercies* (1983). But his stage plays likewise form an important part of his legacy. They are rooted in the east Texas town of Wharton (renamed Harrison in many of his plays) where Foote grew up and lived for large parts of his life. Foote's quiet, realistic dramas, with characters who absorb life's blows and try to find inner strength, have fallen in and out of theatrical fashion, but Foote lived long enough to witness and participate in a major revival of his writing that seemed likely to establish it in the theatrical canon. Actor Robert Duvall, who appeared in both *To Kill a Mockingbird* and *Tender Mercies,* told Wilborn Hampton of the *New York Times* that "Horton was the great American voice. His work was native to his own region, but it was also universal."

Grew Up in Storytelling Family

Albert Horton Foote Jr. was born in Wharton, Texas on March 14, 1916. He was called Little Horton; his father ("Big Horton") owned a clothing store. Everyone knew everyone else in the small town, and branches of Foote's family extended into nearby communities. Theater was almost unheard-of, except for a troupe of traveling players that came through Wharton once a year, but storytelling, often pertaining to family affairs of all kinds, was a valued art, and Foote, a quiet but curious child, picked up a fund of tales that would last him a long lifetime; he later said that more than half his plays originated with stories he heard from his father. When he was 12, Foote announced that he wanted to become an actor.

Although initially taken aback, Foote's family backed his ambitions, selling off their small landholdings in order to pay his acting-school tuition at California's Pasadena Playhouse. Foote moved after graduating to New York City, and the young man from small-town Texas flourished in the theatrical capital of the U.S. Working at various jobs, including elevator operator and bookstore clerk, he landed occasional acting roles and made friends with another small-town Southern theatrical figure, Tennessee Williams. At the bookstore he

met a customer, Lillian Vallish; the two married in 1945 and raised four children.

Foote plunged eagerly into New York's performing arts scene, making contacts not only in the theater world but also with avant-garde dancers such as Martha Graham and Agnes de Mille. It was de Mille who, after observing a Foote improvisation in an acting class, suggested that he try his hand at playwriting. When he asked her what he could write about, she gave him the time-honored advice that writers should write about what they know.

Taking the advice to heart, Foote returned home and wrote a one-act play called *Wharton Dance,* following it up with a full-length play called *Texas Town* after *Wharton Dance* was presented as part of a group of short plays. *Texas Town* was staged in a production by the American Actors Company in 1941, with Foote himself playing the lead, and, somewhat to Foote's surprise, *New York Times* theater critic Brooks Atkinson showed up at the performance and praised the play as (according to Hampton) an "engrossing portrait of small-town life," "simply written," leaving "a real and languid impression of a town changing in its relation to the world" and "an able evocation of a part of life in America."

Wrote Radio and Television Plays

After a stint as manager of the theater program at the King-Smith Studio School in Washington, D.C., where he desegregated the school's theater (becoming the first Washington theater operator to do so), Foote returned to New York in the early 1950s and

devoted himself fully to playwriting. His early works had little impact at the time, but he found himself in demand as a writer of short dramas for radio and, increasingly as the 1950s progressed, television. "The Trip to Bountiful," the story of a Houston widow who eludes her children in order to make a trip to her childhood home, was originally written as a one-hour television play in 1953, with actress Lillian Gish in the lead role. Expanded to a full-length Broadway play two years later it had only moderate success, but a 1985 film of the play won a Best Actress Academy Award for star Geraldine Page. In the 1950s and early 1960s Foote's dramas were somewhat overshadowed by the more flamboyant and intense works of Tennessee Williams and Arthur Miller, but they possessed a timeless quality that served them well over the long term.

Dividing his time between New York and Hollywood as the focus of television production shifted westward, Foote began to flesh out his dramatic vision of his hometown in a series of teleplays, collected as *Harrison, Texas: Eight Television Plays* in 1959. Two years later, Foote's wife knocked on the door of his study, holding a copy of Harper Lee's recently published gothic novel of small-town racial injustice, *To Kill a Mockingbird,* and told him he should read it. Foote's 1962 screenplay based on the book helped make a star of Duvall, in the role of Boo Radley, and earned Foote himself an Academy Award. The screenplay won the admiration of Lee, who called it (according to John Lahr of the *New Yorker*) "a work of such quiet and unobtrusive excellence that many people have commented the film's dialogue was lifted chapter and verse from the novel. This is simply not so." Foote and Lee became lifelong friends, and Lee (according to Wilborn) once quipped that Foote "looked like God, only clean-shaven."

Foote had another successful screenplay with the Steve McQueen vehicle *Baby, the Rain Must Fall* in 1965 but grew disillusioned when he lost creative control over subsequent scripts for *Hurry Sundown* and an adaptation of his own early play *The Chase.* Foote moved back east, to a farm in New Hampshire, and then, after the deaths of his parents, to the family homestead in Wharton. He began to devote himself fully to stage drama once again, encouraged by consistently positive notices from *New York Times* critic Frank Rich. In the 1970s Foote issued an entire cycle of nine plays entitled *The Orphans' Home Cycle,* tracing the lives of a pair of characters based on Foote's own parents. All nine plays were written over a span of two years. One of the cycle's central plays, *1918,* showed Foote at perhaps his very best, setting family dramas against an overwhelming outside force—in this case the deadly influenza epidemic of 1918.

Penned Country Music Screenplay

Foote did not abandon screenwriting completely, however. In 1983, inspired partly by his nephew's experiences in a rock band, he began work on a screenplay featuring an alcoholic country singer, Mac Sledge, who is on a downward trajectory in both the music business and life in general. The resulting film, made for a mere $4.5 million in Waxahachie, Texas by Australian director Bruce Beresford, reunited Foote with Duvall, both of whom won Academy Awards for their work. The sparse dialogue strokes in which Foote traces the growing and redemptive romance between Sledge and the young widow Rosa Lee have made the film one of Foote's most enduringly popular works. Foote's screenplay for *The Trip to Bountiful* two years later won him another Academy Award nomination.

Crediting his productivity partly to the Christian Science faith he adopted in 1953 (but studiously kept out of his work), Foote continued writing prolifically into his tenth decade and often engaged himself with contemporary themes. *The Young Man from Atlanta* (1995), which told the story of a couple trying to deal with their son's suicide and probable homosexuality, won a Pulitzer Prize. His play *Dividing the Estate,* produced on Broadway in 1997, dealt with the effects of the collapse of Texas's oil-based economy in the 1980s. One of his last plays, *The Carpetbagger's Children,* toured the U.S. before being mounted at New York's Lincoln Center in 2002. In his later years, Foote also was active as a director of his own plays.

In early 2009, Foote took up temporary residence in Hartford, Connecticut, in order to work on an adaptation of *The Orphans' Home Cycle* into a three-play production for the Hartford Stage Company. He died suddenly on March 4, 2009, at the age of 92, having written about 60 plays of various lengths, plus television scripts and screenplays. Lahr summed up his legacy this way: "He examined the ripple, not the wave. His was a quiet voice in noisy times."

Books

Contemporary Southern Writers, St. James, 2009.
Hampton, Wilborn, *Horton Foote: America's Storyteller,* Free Press, 2009.

Periodicals

American Theatre, July-August 2009.
Atlanta Journal-Constitution, December 13, 2009.
Houston Chronicle, March 5, 2009.
Independent (London, England), March 7, 2009.
New York Times, March 5, 2009.
New Yorker, October 26, 2009.
Variety, March 9, 2009.

Online

"Horton Foote Biography," *Horton Foote Society,* http://horton footesociety.org (January 12, 2010). □

Cornelia Funke

The German author Cornelia Funke (born 1958) rocketed to international fame in the first years of the 21st century after one of her books, *The Thief Lord,* was translated into English.

Funke's books have had one trait that historically has defined any children's literature that has lasted: they are interesting for adults as well as children. She typically began writing only after doing several months of research into a book's setting, and her plots are complex and sophisticated. Yet her characters also compel strong

identification from children. "It all starts with character," Funke told Anne Johnstone of the Glasgow (Scotland) *Herald.* "When you give the readers characters they love, they can go anywhere and do anything, and the reader will follow them. But if you don't love them the story can't hold you. Funke has been compared to British children's book writer J.K. Rowling and even to the classic fantasy writer J.R.R. Tolkien, and filmmakers have begun to explore adaptations of her work.

Frequently Met Father at Library

Cornelia Funke (pronounced Cor-NAY-lia FOONK-uh in German, but Funke has stated that she enjoys the "funky" pronunciation used by children in the United States) was born in the small city of Dorsten in northwestern Germany on December 10, 1958. Her grandfather was a well-known maker of etchings. Cornelia's father Karl-Heinz, a lawyer, "was humorous and gentle," she told Johnstone, "and books were important. They suggested there was something exciting beyond the horizon of this small gray place. We had this nice ritual of taking different bridges across the river, meeting at the library, and coming home together with piles of books." As a child Funke had various career plans, including astronaut, pilot, and wife of the chief of a Native American tribe. She enjoyed famous children's books such as the Narnia chronicles of C.S. Lewis, Astrid Lindgren's *The Brothers Lionheart,* and Mark Twain's *Tom Sawyer,* but she never showed any special inclination toward writing.

Funke studied education in college and spent several years as a social worker, spending her days among children on a playground. She married Rolf Funke, a printer, in 1981, and the couple settled near Hamburg and had two children, Anna and Ben (her maiden name was also Funke). Then she decided she wanted a more artistic career and enrolled in a book illustration program at the Hamburg State College of Design. "Most adults will want to make you believe that with [the age of] 18 at the latest you should have figured out what kind of profession is the right one for you," Funke wrote in her official web site biography. "Don't believe a word of that!" Indeed, Funke did not begin writing seriously until she was in her mid-30s.

She had no trouble finding work as an illustrator of children's books, but from her contact with children as a social worker she thought she knew the kinds of books she liked, and she was dissatisfied with the quality of the books she was given and thought she could do better. Once she started to write, books came quickly despite a rigorous self-editing process that often saw her discarding paragraphs or even fully written chapters. By 2004 Funke had written 40 books, most of which, surprisingly in view of her later success, have remained untranslated into English. In Germany she became well known for book series entitled *Die Gespensterjäger* ("Ghost Hunters," a few of which have been translated) and *Die wilden Hühner* ("Wild Chicks"). Funke has illustrated many of her books herself.

Funke's breakthrough novel was *Herr der Diebe,* written in 2000 and translated in 2002 as *The Thief Lord.* The book was about two orphaned children who run away to Venice, Italy and meet a variety of colorful characters in an abandoned movie theater, including the one named in the title. Funke chose Venice partly because, as she explained to Jean Westmoore of the *Buffalo News,* "I wanted children to know that there is a magical place like this—and that they can really go there, touch it, smell it, explore it. Many magical places in books are out of reach, Venice is not—and many children went there with their parents to find all the places I described in the book."

English Publisher Alerted by 11-Year-Old Reader

The Thief Lord was translated because a bilingual 11-year-old German girl living in England wrote to publisher Barry Cunningham—the discoverer of J.K. Rowling—saying that Funke was her favorite writer and asking why it wasn't possible to read her books in English. Cunningham, intrigued, soon agreed to issue *The Thief Lord* at his new publishing operation, Chicken House. In the U.S., where *The Thief Lord* spent four months on the *New York Times* best-seller list, Funke's books were published by Scholastic, Inc.

Funke's next book, *Inkheart* (published in German as *Tintenherz* and immediately issued in English) showed the author at her most ambitious. The book and its two sequels, *Inkspell* (*Tintenblut,* literally "Ink Blood," 2005) and *Inkdeath* (*Tintentod,* 2007), depended on a conception that served to instill in young readers an idea of the power of literature: the books featured a character named Mo whom Funke called a Silvertongue, with the ability to make a character in a book come alive—as long as a real-life person was transported into the book in return. This device gave rise to a complex structure

of parallel plots taking place in real life, in books within books, and in the interaction between the two.

Funke also wrote simpler books for younger children, including *Dragon Rider* (*Drachenreiter,* depicting a dragon named Firedrake on an extended quest), *The Princess Knight* (*Der geheimnisvolle Ritter Namenlos,* literally "The Mysterious Rider Without a Name"), and *Pirate Girl* (*Käpten Knitterbart und seine Bande,* literally "Captain Wrinklebeard and His Band"). Funke spoke English fluently, and due to the success of her books the family was able to move from Germany to Beverly Hills, California, purchasing a home with a detached writing cabin once owned by actress Faye Dunaway. She continued to write in German, however, finding that the effort of writing in English interfered with the free flow of her imagination.

Suffered Husband's Death

Just as Funke was reaching new heights of popularity her life was struck by tragedy. A little more than a year after the family moved to California, Rolf Funke was diagnosed with incurable colon cancer. Given two weeks to live, he lived for four, during which he asked Funke to bring a computer to his hospital room and work so that he could feel that daily life was going on around him. After his death, Funke felt a deepened tie to her new home. "In Germany, my friends would have left me alone but the pragmatism of Americans when faced with grief is amazing," she told Johnstone. "I was bombarded with help. 'Shall we pick up the kids?'" Her husband's death, she continued, taught her "never to succumb to fear and postpone something you really want to do. It's given me a 'Carpe diem' attitude to life."

Readers might have assumed that the dark tone of *Inkdeath* resulted from this experience, but actually the book had been completed before Rolf's diagnosis. To adults who might have wondered whether the occasionally gruesome scenes in her books might make them inappropriate for children, Funke responded to Mike Wade of the London *Times* that "[i]n children's literature a writer can be incredibly free with fear, or even cruelty, because a child, hopefully, has no experience. The emotional impact is lost." Of a scene in *Inkdeath,* where the storyteller and bookshop owner Mo fears he is losing his mind because he is under a spell, she said, "Adults said they couldn't bear to read that. Children didn't have a problem; they play with the imaginative material much more than we do as adults. They can deal easily with cruelty. I was very humbled when a group of eight and nine-year-olds told me they had no problem with that." She has encouraged readers to read her books aloud but also has expressed her love for the physical feel of books, and she has accumulated a collection of first editions.

The first of what promised to be many film versions of Funke's writings, a film of *Inkheart,* appeared in 2009, with actor Brendan Fraser, whom Funke had imagined in the part while writing the book, in the lead role of Mo. Funke herself served as a producer for the film. The year 2010 was slated to bring a new Funke novel, *Reckless,* based on the fairy tales of the Brothers Grimm. Funke's plans were to have the book inaugurate a new series of novels drawn on myths and legends from around Europe. She collaborated on *Reckless* with British filmmaker Lionel Wigram, and despite the mixed critical reception given the film of *Inkheart* in the U.S., her work seemed a likely contender to fill the void left by the completion of Rowling's *Harry Potter* series in the coming years.

Books

Authors and Artists for Young Adults, Vol. 68, Gale, 2006.

Periodicals

Buffalo News, April 7, 2004.
Herald (Glasgow, Scotland), November 1, 2008.
Observer, July 11, 2004.
Seattle Post-Intelligencer, January 23, 2009.
Times (London, England), August 12, 2009.
Virginian Pilot (Norfolk, VA), January 24, 2009.

Online

''Cornelia Funke: Biography,'' *Cornelia Funke Official Web site,* http://www.corneliafunke.de/en (February 2, 2010).
''Meet Cornelia,'' *Scholastic,* http://www.scholastic.com/corne liafunke/bio.htm (February 2, 2010).
''The 2005 Time 100: Cornelia Funke,'' *Time,* http://www.time.com/ time/subscriber/2005/time100/artists/100funke.html (February 2, 2010).□

G

Alexander Garden

Scottish-born Alexander Garden (1730–1791) had a successful medical practice in Charleston, South Carolina, before the American Revolutionary War, but is best remembered for his work as a botanist and naturalist. Garden collected and categorized hundreds of plant and animal species native to the North American continent, sending some to the founder of modern taxonomy, Sweden's Carl Linnaeus, with whom he corresponded for many years. The fragrant gardenia flower was named in Garden's honor for his service to science.

Garden was born in January of 1730 in Birse Parish, Aberdeenshire, in east-central Scotland. His father was a Church of Scotland minister also named Alexander Garden. In his teens, he entered Marischal College at the University of Aberdeen to study medicine, and traveled to London to sit for the Royal Navy examination to become a ship surgeon's assistant. He served for four years, and then entered the medical school of the University of Edinburgh. He had difficulty paying the university fees at Edinburgh, and would eventually receive his medical degree from Marischal College in 1753.

Interested in Healing Herbs and Flowers

Garden's stint at Edinburgh, however, was notable for the time spent studying under Charles Alston, who taught courses in what was called *Materia medica* in Latin, the language widely used in science at the time. Materia medica referred to the treatment of illnesses through plant or other remedies, and the field would eventually come to be called "pharmacology." It was here that Garden's interest in botany was sparked by the study of plants that possessed curative properties. Edinburgh was a leading center for this field when Garden was there: at the time, Alston held the post of Keeper of the Garden at Holyrood Palace in the city. Founded in 1670, the Holyrood garden cultivated a wide variety of plants for scientific purposes under royal authority. It was the first such botanical garden in Scotland and only the second in the British Isles.

There are several known figures from this period named "Alexander Garden," including a minister of St. Philip's Church in Charleston, South Carolina. Some sources cite this as Garden's father, but it may have been merely a relative who allegedly wrote to encourage him to come to the royal colony and establish a medical practice in the thriving port city. He arrived in April of 1752, and on Christmas Eve three years later married Elizabeth Peronneau, daughter of a prominent French Huguenot family in Charleston. Still fascinated by botanical science, he kept in touch with Alston and other professors in Scotland, who likely put him in contact with others in the Crown colonies who shared his interest.

Garden was unused to the tropical climate of the Carolinas. In the summer of 1754, he traveled to New York State to meet with a prominent botanist with whom he was corresponding. Cadwallader Colden was a fellow Scot and physician who also held several important political posts over the course of a long career, including Surveyor General of the Colonies and Lieutenant Governor of New York. Colden had a vast estate near Newburgh, New York, called Coldengham, and was a plant collector in North America for the Swedish botanist Carl Linnaeus. It was here that Garden was thought to have first encountered Linnaeus's groundbreaking 1753 work, *Species Plantarum*. The double-volume reference work contained descriptions of all known plants in the world as cataloged by Linnaeus, and introduced his binary, or two-part, nomenclature system for plants. This system enabled Alston, Colden, Garden, and other botanical experts to classify newly discovered plants, and was a major breakthrough in natural sciences. A plant that differed from others was named as a species, which belonged to an already-named genus. Linnaeus also created artificial classes and orders to further organize the earth's plant life. He would later use it to classify the planet's animal species.

Began Correspondence with Linnaeus

During this same period Garden also visited Philadelphia botanist John Bartram. Like Colden, Bartram collected plant specimens for Linnaeus and traveled widely through the Great Lakes region and the South searching for new types of wildflowers and trees. Garden took up the line of work himself in the Carolinas, and was made the first colonial correspondent of the Royal Society of Arts. One of his first significant forays was in 1755, when he took part in an expedition into Cherokee country organized by South Carolina's governor. The party likely ventured as far as west as Caesar's Head in present-day Greenville County, South Carolina, where the Blue Ridge Mountains reach into South Carolina.

For the better part of a quarter-century Garden sent back hundreds of plants and animals he discovered in the Carolinas. Many of the parcels were addressed to a London zoologist named John Ellis, who had a thriving business as a linen merchant that linked him to the British colonies in North America and the Caribbean. It was Ellis who suggested that Garden write Linnaeus, and after 1758 there was a prolific correspondence between the three. The Swedish scientist requested more research into insects and aquatic creatures of the central coastal regions of North America, and after 1760 Garden began sending specimens to Linnaeus in Uppsala, Sweden.

In the twelfth edition of Linnaeus's master work, *Systema naturae* (System of Nature) published between 1766 and 1768, Garden was mentioned several times as the source for many new citations. He was credited with the discovery of the mud eel common throughout the southern United States, which Linnaeus named *Siren lacertina*. *Amphiuma means* was another important find. This was a two-toed salamander also known as the Congo snake or Conger eel. Also common to the southeastern United States, the species was known to grow up to three feet in length, and could bite when provoked.

Wrote About Electric Eels

Garden played a significant role in introducing European scientists to the electric eel, which gave off a powerful electric shock as a self-defense mechanism. Linnaeus called it *Electrophorus electricus,* but it is more commonly known as the knifefish. The fish, native to South America, had been brought to Charleston, and caused a sensation both there and in Europe. Many of the principles of electricity were known by scientists of the day, but no human had yet managed to successfully harness and reproduce this source of energy. There were electric rays known as torpedo fish in the Mediterranean, but they were bottom-dwelling creatures and the Western Hemisphere eels produced a much more powerful charge.

Garden saw his first electric eel at a 1774 demonstration in Charleston, and wrote a paper on it that Ellis read at a 1775 London meeting of the Royal Society. Garden wrote in "An Account of the Gymnotus electricus, or Electrical Eel," according to James Delbourgo's *A Most Amazing Scene of Wonders: Electricity and Enlightenment in Early America,* "This fish hath the amazing power of giving so sudden and so violent a shock to any person who touches it, that there is, I think, an absolute impossibility of ever examining accurately a living specimen."

George Baker was the ship captain who brought the electric eel to Charleston. Baker traveled regularly between England and Guiana, at the northeastern tip of South America, and wanted to bring live specimens back to England. Garden advised him to bring an extra cask of rum should any of the five live eels die en route to England. Baker arrived in Falmouth in November of 1774, and there was just one still alive, which Baker demonstrated to astonished onlookers. It died before the vessel reached London. The eels in rum were dissected by a famous surgeon, John Hunter, who would later serve as physician to King George III. Finally, in 1800 the famed German scientist and explorer Alexander von Humboldt traveled to what is now Venezuela and rode with his men and horses into a shallow lake full of the eels. The eels went into a frenzy of shocking, and two of the horses died. But Humboldt correctly surmised that at least a few of the eels had exhausted their powers, at least temporarily, and could be seized for experiments.

After the death of Linnaeus, Garden corresponded with other notable taxonomists abroad. He provided information for the Welsh naturalist Thomas Pennant's 1785 work *Arctic Zoology,* and sent dried fish specimens to Laurens Gronovius of Holland, who made important advances in the classification of the world's fishes. On Linnaeus's recommendation, Garden had been elected a member of Royal Society of Uppsala in 1763, and became a fellow of the Royal Society in London a decade later. More than 200 years later, 16 of the specimens Garden sent to Gronovius are displayed in the British Museum of Natural History in London. Burlington House in London houses the vast collection of the Linnaean Society of London; of its 158 dried fish specimens, 85 were sent by Garden from South Carolina.

Fled the Carolinas

Notwithstanding his contributions to science, Garden was by profession a doctor in Charleston. He worked valiantly to inoculate around 2,500 residents during a particularly deadly outbreak of smallpox in the city in 1760. He also wrote about the medicinal uses of pinkroot (Spigelia marilandica), which the Cherokee knew as a treatment for roundworm. As a physician, Garden was indirectly involved in one of Charleston's most lucrative areas of commerce, the slave trade. He inspected incoming ships from Africa, where he reported that the casualty rates could be as high as one third to one half of the original captives. The dead were simply thrown overboard. "I have never yet been on board one that did not smell most offensive . . . what for filth, putrid air, putrid dysenteries," he once wrote, according to a 2008 article by Jessica Johnson in the Charleston *Post and Courier.* "It is a wonder any escape with life."

Garden barely escaped the colonies with his own life. During the American Revolution, he remained a staunch Loyalist. His son and namesake served on the other side, a familial breach that never healed. In December of 1782, Charleston was evacuated after a long and troubled period, including a six-week siege. As a known supporter of the Loyalist cause, Garden was subject to the terms of an earlier Act of Confiscation and his property was seized. He sailed for England and suffered terrible seasickness on the voyage. His health was permanently compromised, and he sought treatment for tuberculosis at clinics in Scotland, France, and Switzerland. In the remaining years of his life he lived in a house on Cecil Street in the Westminster district of London with his wife and two daughters, and served as vice president of the Royal Society. He died on April 15, 1791.

Garden's son Alexander fought in George Washington's Continental Army and became a major. He managed to save his family's 1,600-acre parcel of land, called Otranto Plantation, near Goose Creek, South Carolina, after it was confiscated. The younger Garden wrote two volumes of *Anecdotes of the Revolutionary War in America* before his death in 1829.

It was the London merchant and zoologist John Ellis who persuaded Linnaeus to name a plant in Garden's honor. The Cape jasmine, a shrub native to Asia but brought to the West from South Africa's Cape Colony and known for its fragrant blossoms, was chosen. This is *Gardenia jasminoides,* or the gardenia.

Books

Delbourgo, James, *A Most Amazing Scene of Wonders: Electricity and Enlightenment in Early America,* Harvard University Press, 2006, p. 166.

Peattie, Donald Culross, "Alexander Garden," in *Dictionary of American Biography,* American Council of Learned Societies, 1928-1936.

Sanders, Albert E., *Natural History Investigations in South Carolina: From Colonial Times to the Present,* University of South Carolina Press, 1999.

Periodicals

Journal of the History of Medicine and Allied Sciences, 1971.

Post and Courier (Charleston, SC), January 24, 2008. □

Gerald Gardner

British witch, writer, and occultist Gerald Gardner (1884–1964) established and popularized the modern Wiccan religion through his writings, particularly the seminal 1954 work *Witchcraft Today* and its 1959 successor, *The Meaning of Witchcraft,* and in doing so helped kick start the neo-pagan movement of the twentieth century. Having spent much of his life abroad working as a tea planter, rubber plantation manager, and customs officer, Gardner was middle-aged by the time he returned to England and began to pursue his interest in traditional witchcraft. In 1939, he joined a coven dedicated to practicing what he believed were centuries-old religious rites, and over the next several years fully developed the series of rituals and beliefs that formed the benevolent pagan religion Wicca. In time, the number of adherents to this movement has grown considerably, with 134,000 Americans identifying themselves as practicing Wiccans in 2001 over a mere 8,000 a decade previously.**

orn on June 13, 1884, in Great Crosby, Lancashire, England, Gardner was the third of the four sons of William Robert Gardner and his wife Louise Barguelew Ennis Gardner. The elder Gardner was a successful timber merchant in the nearby city of Liverpool and served as a justice of the peace, providing the family with a comfortable standard of living. Neither he nor his wife had much involvement in the raising of their family, however. Instead, they hired Irish nursemaid Josephine McCombie, who assumed the primary care of the young Gardner. As a child, he suffered from asthma which limited his ability to engage in play and other physical activities. He did not attend school, but developed an interest in history while traveling throughout Europe with McCombie. When Gardner was sixteen, his nurse married a tea planter who lived in Ceylon—now known as Sri Lanka—and the teenager accompanied her to the tropical island.

In Ceylon, Gardner took a position of a planter on a tea plantation. Over the next seven years, he worked on two tea plantations and as a manager of a rubber plantation on the island. In 1908, he moved to the Southeast Asian island of Borneo, where he continued his work on local rubber plantations as a manager and planter. Fifteen years later, he shifted from planter to inspector for the British government. Later, he advanced to become the principal British customs officer in the Malaysian state of Johor; Gardner also served as an inspector of opium dens. Although the emigrant made at least four lengthy visits back to England—he married British nurse Dorothea (Donna) Frances Rosedale during one such trip in 1927—Gardner became deeply interested in Malaysian culture and history during his lengthy stint in the region. He researched ancient Malaysian civilization, with a particular attention to archeological artifacts and weaponry. Although—or perhaps because—Gardner had not been raised in any religious tradition, he was also drawn to the study of Eastern mysticism, ranging from Buddhism to regional tribalism. In time, he published articles in the journal of the *Royal Asiatic Society* and so developed a reputation as an expert on ancient Malaysian artifacts.

Joined Coven of Witches

After Gardner retired from the civil service in 1936, he and his wife returned to England, where they first settled in the London area. He lived by all accounts a quiet if somewhat unconventional life there, joining a nudist club based in the North London suburb of Finchley, taking part in the city's Folklore Society, and spending the better part of the winters of 1936 and 1937 in the more hospitable climate of the island of Cyprus. According to the *World Religions Reference*

Library, on one of these voyages, Gardner "discovered what he described as places that he dreamed about earlier. He became convinced that he had lived on Cyprus in another lifetime." This conviction led to the writing of Gardner's first historical novel, 1939's *A Goddess Arrives,* and contributed to his growing interest in the ancient practice of goddess worship. During this period, Gardner also continued to publish works based on his research in Malaysia; his debut book-length study, *Kris and Other Malay Weapons,* appeared in 1936. According to Ronald Hutton in *The Triumph of the Moon: A History of Modern Pagan Witchcraft,* these "monographs... testify to the range and energy of [Gardner's] mind and his particular preoccupation with swords and daggers (especially the latter) and their magical associations." As the first stirrings of World War II began to raise concerns in Europe in 1938, the Gardners—perhaps at the behest of associates from the Finchley nudist group—left the capital for the small town of High-cliffe, Dorset, along the country's southern coast in what is called the New Forest.

Soon after moving to the countryside, Gardner became a part of a local witches' coven, the Fellowship of Crotona. Led by a woman he called "Old Dorothy" and whom historians believe to have to been what the *World Religions Reference Library* described as the "very prim and seemingly conservative lady" Dorothy Clutterbuck, the coven claimed that it practiced a set of religious beliefs dating from at least the medieval period. Although Gardner seems to have accepted this statement, Hutton noted in *The Triumph of the Moon* that "No academic historian has ever taken seriously Gardner's claim to have discovered a genuine survival of ancient religion, and it was dismissed... by the journal of the Folk-Lore Society. Members of the latter generally found the religion described as by so totally unlike the traditional English witchcraft beliefs which they had recorded themselves and found recorded by earlier collectors, that they rejected his assertions out of hand." Regardless of the practices' actual age, they intrigued Gardner and he sought permission from the group to publish a book detailing their rites. The following decade, he met influential occultist Aleister Crowley, who provided him with additional information about witchcraft from his own personal experience. This association also resulted in Gardner's entry into the Ordo Templi Orientis, a sect that Crowley had formed which practiced a series of rites loosely inspired by Eastern Tantric practices.

Established Wiccan Religion

Based on his membership in the Fellowship of Crotona and his lessons with Crowley, Gardner wrote a book on witchcraft published as *High Magic's Aid* in 1949. Because of England's anti-witchcraft laws, Gardner used the pseudonym Scire and presented his piece as a fictional novel rather than a non-fictional guide. *High Magic's Aid* contains several rites central to the practice of Wicca, however; writing in the *Oxford Dictionary of National Biography,* Hutton argued that although Gardner's "beliefs were fully elaborated by 1948... but the extent to which he personally devised the religion is unclear." Gardner is generally credited, however, with the creation of the religion due to his writings and to the extensive promotion of Wicca that he began in 1950, when he started describing its practices to potential adherents in the capital. With the end of

Britain's anti-witchcraft laws in 1951, Gardner commenced a series of interviews and appearances in mass media outlets to spread information about the new faith. That same year, he traveled to Castletown on the Isle of Man off England's north-western coast and began working with the newly-opened Museum of Magic and Witchcraft. After a stint as a lecturer at Ghana's University College, he settled in Castletown and bought the museum, which he operated for many years.

At about this time, Gardner initiated Doreen Valiente into his coven. She rose to become its high priestess and helped shape the form of the Wiccan practices that Gardner published in the *Book of Shadows.* With a focus on nature, feminine supremacy, and witchcraft, Wicca as laid out by Gardner followed a distinctly hierarchical structure with initiates advancing through three successive levels as they gained knowledge of the religion's rites. Despite witchcraft's status as a mystery religion—one in which only practitioners have full knowledge of its workings—Gardner wrote a book for a general audience about Wicca in 1954, the influential *Witchcraft Today.* Its publication generated public interest in witchcraft and contributed to the spread of Wicca throughout the country. Gardner himself also became a well-known public figure, much to the consternation of some witches who preferred to keep their practices and beliefs within their own covens. A second book describing Wiccan beliefs, *The Meaning of Witchcraft,* appeared in 1959.

Wicca Grew After Death

Although Gardner remained an active practitioner and a voluble public advocate of witchcraft in his later years, he did not produce any further significant writings after *The Meaning of Witchcraft;* his 1960 autobiography, *Gerald Gardner: Witch,* was completed by ghostwriter Idries Shah writing under the pseudonym Jack L. Bracelin. On February 12, 1964, Gardner suddenly collapsed and died as the result of a cerebral hemorrhage while eating breakfast aboard the cruise ship *Scottish Prince,* which was sailing along the North African coast of the Mediterranean Sea. At the time of his death, he was 80 years old. Gardner was interred the following day in the port city of Tunis, Tunisia. His legacy as the founder of Wicca has had a wide geographic and cultural impact, and Gardner has achieved the singular distinction of promulgating the only complete set of religious beliefs, rather than a branch or denomination that built upon those of an existing religion, to originate in England.

Although Hutton pointed out in the *Oxford Dictionary of National Biography* that Gardner's "status as a scholar remains controversial," he also acknowledged that "Gardner was clearly a man of considerable charm and kindness, an excellent raconteur with a love of jokes and a zest for life." Even contemporary Wiccans admit that not all of Gardner's claims about the foundation their faith may have been true. "Gardner may have been an utter fraud; he may have actually received a 'Traditional' initiation; or, as a number of people have suggested, he may have created the Wicca as a result of a genuine religious experience, drawing upon his extensive literary and magical knowledge to create, or help create, the rites and philosophy. What I think we can be fairly certain about is that he was sincere in his belief. If there had been no more to the whole thing than an old man's fantasy, then . . . Wicca would not have grown to be the force that it is today," commented Julia Phillips in *History of Wicca in England: 1939 to the Present Day.*

Unquestionably, in the decades since Gardner's death, ever increasing numbers have joined the religion that he popularized; a 1963 Gardnerian initiate named Raymond Buckley brought Wicca to the United States, where it found a ready, if small, audience. By 2004, however, estimates placed the highest levels of Wiccans in the United States and Australia, with estimates placing American adherents from about 135,000 to three times that amount. Smaller populations also practice the faith in such far-flung locales as Japan, South Africa, Canada, and New Zealand. If historical figures are any indication, Wicca and other neo-pagan movements will likely continue to steadily attract new adherents for some time to come, perpetuating Gardner's teachings to new generations of witches.

Books

Hutton, Ronald, *Oxford Dictionary of National Biography,* Oxford University Press, 2004.

Hutton, Ronald, *The Triumph of the Moon: A History of Modern Pagan Witchcraft,* Oxford University Press, 1999.

Jones, Lindsay, ed. , *Encyclopedia of Religion,* Macmillan Reference USA, 2005.

O'Neal, Michael, and J. Jones, eds., *World Religions Reference Library,* UXL, 2007.

Witchcraft, Greenhaven Press, 2002.

Periodicals

New York Times, October 3, 1999.

Online

"American Religious Identification Survey 2001," City University of New York, http://www.gc.cuny.edu/faculty/research_briefs/aris.pdf (January 10, 2010).

"History of Wicca in England: 1939 to the Present Day," The History of Wicca, http://www.geraldgardner.com/History_of_Wicca_Revised.pdf (January 10, 2010). □

Pat Garrett

American lawman Pat Garrett (1850–1908) is best known for killing Billy the Kid, a legendary New Mexico outlaw. After heading west at age 18, Garrett lived an adventurous life on the frontier: he hunted buffalo, tended bar, raised cattle, bought mining and ranch land, worked as a customs collector and a sheriff, and shot at least four men to death.

Patrick Floyd Jarvis Garrett was born in Chambers County, Alabama, on June 5, 1850, to farmer John Lumpkin Garrett and Elizabeth Ann Jarvis. He grew up on a Louisiana cotton plantation his father purchased in 1853. After the Civil War, Union soldiers confiscated

cotton from the Garrett plantation, plunging the family deep into debt. Garrett's parents died within a year of each other in the late 1860s, leaving their children the insolvent plantation. In January of 1869, after a financial dispute with his brother-in-law, Garrett left Louisiana to seek his fortune in Texas.

A Western Frontiersman

After several years as a farmer near Dallas, Texas, Garrett joined a party of buffalo hunters in 1875. It was among the last years that giant hordes of buffalo still roamed the American West. Garrett spent about two years as a hunter, proving himself a skilled marksman who could kill dozens of buffalo a day. While on the buffalo hunt, however, he got into a fatal fight with Joe Briscoe, a member of his hunting party, in November of 1876. Briscoe took offense to a derogatory comment Garrett made about him being Irish and started a fistfight. When Garrett knocked him down, Briscoe came after him with an ax, and Garrett shot him to death in self-defense. Garrett turned himself in at Fort Griffin, Texas, but authorities there declined to prosecute.

By the end of 1877, the over-hunted buffalo were fast disappearing. Garrett and his remaining partners abandoned the hunt and moved to Fort Sumner, New Mexico. Garrett began working as a hog rancher there. He married his wife, Apolinaria Gutierrez, daughter of a freight company owner, on January 14, 1880. The wedding came soon after a hog trampled Garrett; Apolinaria had taken care of him as he recovered. (Garrett may have also been briefly married to another woman around 1877, but details are unclear.) While his former hunting partners moved on, Garrett chose to stay in Fort Sumner and began working as a bartender in a local saloon.

Shot Billy the Kid

During Garrett's first years in Fort Sumner, local ranchers were caught up in the Lincoln County War, a bloody, lawless battle for power. The war pitted John Chisum, a wealthy ranch owner who controlled much of the area's property and cattle, against several smaller ranchers. Working as a bartender, Garrett stayed out of the war, though he would later kill some of the outlaws who had taken part in it, including a young gunslinger named Henry McCarty who usually went by the aliases William Bonney or, more often, Billy the Kid.

Garrett's involvement in the conflicts in Lincoln County began in April of 1879, when Chisum wrote to New Mexico Governor Lew Wallace, recommending that he deploy a squad of ten armed men near Lincoln, New Mexico to deter robbers. Chisum suggested that Garrett lead the squad. Garrett had probably impressed Chisum by leading a posse that pursued several Comanche Indians who had stolen horses from a ranch near Roswell, New Mexico. Garrett's posse had tracked down the Comanches, likely killed them, and returned many of the stolen horses.

With backing from Chisum and several other powerful cattle ranchers, Garrett ran for Lincoln County sheriff against the incumbent, George Kimball. He defeated him, 320 to 179, in November of 1880. Kimball deputized Garrett soon after, so that he could begin enforcing the law immediately, before his term as sheriff officially began in January. By then, Billy the Kid had launched a crime spree, robbing travelers on the remote roads and trails of southeast New Mexico. Wallace, the governor, advertised a $500 reward for anyone who captured the Kid and delivered him to a sheriff. Garrett made capturing the Kid his top priority and rounded up several men to help pursue him.

On December 20, 1880, Garrett's posse surrounded Billy the Kid and his gang in a one-room house near Fort Sumner and shot one of the gang members. The Kid surrendered, and Garrett took the gang to the state prison in Santa Fe. After a trial, a judge sentenced Billy the Kid to death on April 15, 1881, and turned him over to Garrett, who was to have him hanged in Lincoln on May 13. Garrett and his deputies imprisoned Billy the Kid in a room on an upstairs floor of the Lincoln County Courthouse. On April 28, however, the Kid killed the two men guarding him and escaped. Garrett set out to track him down again.

Three months later, Garrett was tipped off that Billy the Kid might visit the ranch of their mutual friend Pete Maxwell in Fort Sumner. Garrett visited Maxwell with two of his men on July 13. The tip was correct: the Kid was elsewhere on Maxwell's property, attending a dance. Decades later, while revisiting the site where Maxwell's house had stood, Garrett retold the story of what happened next to writer Emerson Hough.

"I was sitting in the dark and talking to Pete, who was in bed," Garrett told Hough (as quoted in Jack DeMattos' book *Garrett and Roosevelt*). "The Kid passed John Poe and Tip McKinney, my deputies, right over there [in] what then was the gallery, and came through the door right here. He could not tell who I was. 'Pete,' he whispered, 'who is it?' He had a pistol, a double-action .41 in his hand." Garrett drew his gun before the Kid drew his. "I was just a shade too quick for him," Garrett told Hough. "His pistol went off as he fell, but I don't suppose he ever knew who killed him or how he was killed."

Killing Billy the Kid "haunted Garrett to the day of his death," wrote Richard O'Connor in his biography, *Pat Garrett*. "No matter what pursuit he took up, no matter how peaceful—actually he served as a lawman only a half-dozen years of a fairly long life—he could not eradicate the popular impression of himself as a man who lived by the gun." Worse, O'Connor added, Billy the Kid's many fans considered Garrett "a legally employed and authorized assassin." Garrett defended his pursuit of the outlaw in an 1882 book *The Authentic Life of Billy the Kid*. The book was not successful, and historians have attacked it as poorly written and inaccurate (though the fiercest criticism was directed at the chapters penned by co-writer Ashton Upson, not the chapters they believe Garrett wrote or dictated).

Garrett and Theodore Roosevelt

Between 1881 and 1890, Garrett served a year as a Texas Ranger, ran unsuccessfully for the New Mexico territorial council and sheriff of Chaves County, discovered a source of artesian water in the Pecos Valley area, and helped irrigate a stretch of land using water from the Hondo River. He moved his family to Uvalde, Texas, in 1891 and bought a ranch there. In 1896, New Mexico Governor William Thornton appointed Garrett sheriff of Dona Ana County, entrusting him to hunt down the kidnappers and presumed killers of prominent businessman Albert Fountain and his son, Henry. Garrett spent years building a case against Oliver Lee, a rancher and ally of Fountain's political rival, and a gunman named Jim Gililland. Garrett eventually filed murder charges against the two men, but they were acquitted at trial.

When Theodore Roosevelt became President of the United States, Garrett decided to apply for a federal customs appointment, calculating correctly that his candidacy would appeal to Roosevelt, a fan of tough Western lawmen. In December of 1901, Roosevelt nominated Garrett collector of customs for El Paso, Texas. The appointment was controversial, and once in office, Garrett gave his opponents plenty of new reasons to oppose him. Garrett got into a public fight with a former employee whom he thought had slandered him. Invited to a reunion of the president's Rough Riders, the cavalry unit Roosevelt had led in the Spanish-American War, Garrett brought his friend Tom Powers, owner of a saloon and gambling house. He introduced Powers to the president and got Roosevelt to pose for a photograph with the two of them. Roosevelt, who had not known Powers was a gambler, was embarrassed when the photo became public.

In 1905, on the recommendation of Treasury Secretary Leslie Shaw, Roosevelt declined to appoint Garrett to another term as customs collector. Roosevelt wrote letters to several Garrett supporters explaining his decision. "The Secretary of the Treasury reported very strongly against Garrett's reappointment on the ground that he was an inefficient collector;

that he was away a large part of the time from his office; that he was in debt and that his habits were bad," Roosevelt wrote in one letter, reprinted in Jack DeMattos' book *Garrett and Roosevelt.* The president admitted that he found it "annoying" that Garrett had gotten him to pose for a photo with a gambler, but added that he had no problem with Garrett's violent past: "I am not in the least sensitive to the past career of one of these Vikings of the border. I do not mind at all Garrett having killed four men. I think he was justified in killing them."

A Mysterious Murder

When Garrett's term as collector expired in January of 1906, he returned to his ranches in New Mexico. Garrett's debts grew worse; that September, creditors auctioned off his personal property. Desperate to improve his finances, Garrett became entangled in a business deal that led to his death.

In 1907, Garrett's son, Dudley, leased Garrett's Bear Canyon Ranch to Jesse Wayne Brazel, a 31-year-old cowboy. Brazel moved more than a thousand goats onto the ranch, which offended Garrett, a cattle rancher and horseman. Garrett tried to cancel Brazel's lease, with no luck. The conflict grew tense. Two men of questionable reputations, Carl Adamson and his cousin, James P. Miller, expressed interest in leasing or buying Garrett's land.

On February 29, 1908, while traveling to Las Cruces, New Mexico, Garrett was shot to death on the roadside. Brazel was arrested and charged with murder but was acquitted at trial. Many historians believe Brazel was the culprit, while others say Miller, a notorious killer, was involved in the murder.

Today, Pat Garrett and his enemy, Billy the Kid, are among the most legendary names connected to the old West. Their story was fictionalized in a 1973 movie, *Pat Garrett and Billy the Kid,* starring the singer Bob Dylan. The Museum of the American West in Los Angeles displays two of Garrett's guns, a Hopkins and Allen revolver and a Merwin and Hulbert .38 caliber revolver.

Books

DeMattos, Jack, *Garrett and Roosevelt,* Creative Publishing Company, 1988.

Epstein, Dwayne, *Lawmen of the Old West,* Thomson Gale, 2005, p. 49-59.

Metz, Leon C., *Pat Garrett: The Story of a Western Lawman,* University of Oklahoma Press, 1974.

O'Connor, Richard, *Pat Garrett: A Biography of the Famous Marshal and the Killer of Billy the Kid,* Doubleday and Company, 1960.

Online

"Garrett, Pat." World Book Advanced. http://www.worldbook online.com (January 1, 2010).

Other

Additional information was gathered during a visit to the Autry Center's Museum of the American West in Los Angeles on September 18, 2009. □

Zinaida Gippius

The Russian poet and fiction writer Zinaida Gippius (1869–1945) exerted a strong influence on the development of contemporary Russian literary culture. She was a novel thinker in the realms of both human sexuality and religion.

Gippius left Russia after the revolutionary events of 1917, and in the years after her death she was gradually forgotten, expunged from literary histories in the Soviet Union because of her strong anti-Communist attitudes, yet far too radical in other ways for the culture of conservative Russian emigrés. Few studies or editions of Gippius's works appeared in English, and those that did tended to downplay her ideas about sexuality, both her own and in human society in general. An ongoing re-evaluation of Gippius's work, however, has made clear its strong connections with the strain of mystical religion in modern Russian writing and its originality in considering the nature of gender. In the words of her biographer Temira Pachmuss, Gippius's poetry "reveals—more than the works of any other Russian modernist writer—that special love for beauty, that antinomy between the poet's religious impulses and simultaneous blasphemy, and that bond between religion, poetry, and mystical sensuality which characterized Russian belles-lettres" in the years on either side of 1900.

Zinaida Nikolaevna Gippius, the oldest of four daughters, was born on November 8, 1869, in Belev, Russia. Her father, Nikolai Romanovich Gippius, was an influential court official, and Gippius had a top-notch education at home from private tutors and at girls' schools in Kiev and Moscow. Her name can also be written as Hippius in Western lettering, a spelling she preferred in later life. When she was 19, Gippius married the poet and literary critic Dmitri Merezhkovsky, and the couple settled in St. Petersburg.

Influenced Modern Russian Poetry

Gippius started writing poetry when she was young, and by the late 1880s she was publishing poetry in the romantic and emotional modes of the day. Soon she became acquainted with the cream of the Russian literary scene in St. Petersburg, meeting Tolstoy and Maxim Gorky. She was also heavily influenced by the novels of Fyodor Dostoevsky, whose brand of Russian Orthodox religion influenced her own conception of Christianity as a mystical, transfiguring force. By the early 1890s, Gippius was writing poems with a distinct, even radical style of her own. In the words of Simon Karlinsky, in a biographical sketch written as an introduction to Vladimir Zlobin's *Zinaida Gippius: A Difficult Soul,* Gippius's poems of 1893 and 1894, "initially rejected by some of the best literary journals of the time, marked the beginning of modern Russian poetry." Gippius experimented with rhyme and meter, and her innovations were studied by a younger generation of Russian poets who later became more famous, including Alexander Blok and Anna Akhmatova.

Gippius's innovations were not only formal in nature, however. She is considered the founder of the Russian Symbolist movement, a loosely connected set of trends, drawing on influences from Western Europe that generally exalted the creative, the spiritual, inner experience, and the irrational. Gippius and Merezhkovsky often hosted like-minded writers and artists at their St. Petersburg apartment, which gradually evolved into one of the city's leading salons or intellectual gathering places. Gippius began to write short stories, an occasional play, and unusual pieces of literary criticism that she cast in the form of conversations. Many of Gippius's writings were religious in nature. She and Merezhkovsky traveled extensively in western Europe and absorbed the latest developments in French poetry as well as in visionary European thought.

Around 1900, the religious strain in Gippius's writing began to develop in unusual directions. Joined by other writers whose works had been published in the journal *Mir iskusstva* (The World of Art), Gippius, Merezhkovsky, and the critic Dmitri Filosofov (a cousin of the ballet impresario Serge Diaghilev) began to explore the idea of what they called a new religious consciousness. They envisioned a Third Testament leading to the kingdom of God on Earth, in which the existing divisions of human society, including that between male and female, would be transcended. The trio began to devise their own liturgy, and held services at the Gippius-Merezhkovsky home. Between 1901 and 1903 they began to invite others to these gatherings, which they called Religious-Philosophical Meetings; attendees included not only literary figures but open-minded Orthodox priests and monks. After 25 gatherings, the Religious-Philosophical Meetings were disbanded in 1903 upon the orders of the Tsar's Ober-Procurator or religious supervisor, Konstantin Pobedonostsev.

Explored Merging of Male and Female Characteristics

Gippius incorporated many of her new ideas into such new works as the *Third Book of Stories* (1902) and a set of diaries called *About the Cause.* Her religious metaphysics had a strong sexual component; central to her view of the divine was what she called the Mystery of the Two. Sexual intercourse was, in Gippius's view, a portal to religious experience, but sexual desire in itself was an obstacle to the sublimation of sexual impulses in Christ. Gippius believed that a perfected human would be androgynous, uniting male and female characteristics, and she believed that God and Christ united the male and female natures found among human beings.

For Gippius's contemporaries as well as for modern readers, ideas of this kind stoked speculation about the extent to which Gippius's views were embedded in the circumstances of her own life. A 1905 portrait of Gippius in a page uniform by Leon Bakst shows a rather androgynous figure, and guesses about the nature of Gippius's sexuality have been repeated and examined by various writers. One rumor that appeared during Gippius's own lifetime was that her marriage to Merezhkovsky remained unconsummated. Karlinsky's essay presents an interpretation of Gippius's life and art involving the supposition that Gippius was a hermaphrodite who pursed

a relationship with the homosexual Filosofov because she thought of him as a potential sexual partner. Gippius's main biographer, Temira Pachmuss, has cast doubt on such claims, pointing out that a friend of the Gippius-Merezhkovsky couple in later life specifically rejected the claim that their marriage was celibate. Karlinsky in turn suggested that Pachmuss edited Gippius's diaries to remove passages that she considered scandalous.

Whatever the truth of the matter might have been, Gippius indisputably revealed unusual attitudes toward gender in her writings. The Russian language distinguishes much more clearly than English between masculine and feminine modes of speaking, and Gippius often used masculine pronouns and narrated stories from a masculine point of view. Sometimes she alternated between masculine and feminine pronouns. Gippius also published various kinds of writings under male pen names, but this was not unusual for a female writer of her time. Many details of Gippius's attitudes toward love and sex show through in her *Contes d'amour* (Stories of Love), diaries published after her death.

Some of them have appeared in English under the title *Between Paris and St. Petersburg.* Gippius spent the summer of 1899 visiting the gay German photographer Wilhelm von Gloeden in Italy, and in one diary from that year quoted by Karlinsky, she wrote: "It is equally good and natural for any person to love any other person. Love between men *may be* bounteously beautiful and God-given, like any other love." Of one gay man she wrote (in the same entry): "What appeals to me in all this is the illusion of a possibility, a kind of hint at bisexuality, so that he seems to be both a woman and a man. This is terribly close to what I need." In other places Gippius wrote negatively about homosexuality, which she encountered in the circle of the German-Italian photographer Wilhelm von Gloeden.

Supported Revolutionary Movements

Gippius was a supporter of the various revolutionary movements that flourished in Russia during the early years of the twentieth century, and she viewed the failed anti-Tsarist Revolution of 1905 as the first step in a religious awakening that would reconstitute the Russian state and society on an entirely new basis. She was an associate of the political assassin Boris Savinkov and even ghostwrote his novel *The Pale Horse.* Gippius and her husband remained influential and widely read literary figures in St. Petersburg, and her two best-known novels *Chortova kukla* (The Devil's Doll, 1911) and *Roman-Tsarevich* (1913), both explored the theme of a progressive religious revolution. Gippius also wrote a book of stories, *Lunnye murav'i* (The Moon Ants, 1912) and several plays that emphasized spiritual themes.

World War I posed a philosophical problem for Gippius, who initially opposed the fighting on religious grounds. The revolutionary events of 1917 did even more to throw her world into disarray. After greeting the establishment of the liberal Provisional Government with high hopes, Gippius was horrified by the rise of the atheistic and totalitarian Communists, whose actual takeover she watched from her apartment balcony. Gippius, Merezhkovsky, Filosofov, and Gippius's secretary, Vladimir Zlobin (from whom many of the details of her personal life have come down) left St. Petersburg on Christmas

Eve of 1919, made their way to Minsk (now in Belarus), and sneaked across the Polish border. For a time Gippius was involved in trying to organize Russian forces for an attempt to overthrow the Bolshevik government, but in 1920 she left for Paris.

Gippius continued to write poetry in Paris, often traveling in circles of Russian emigrants. She explored the themes she had taken up before World War I; her 1927 short story collection *Memuary Martynova* (The Memoirs of Martynov) concerned bisexual love. But she was generally less prolific during this period, "as if," noted Pachmuss in a *Dictionary of Literary Biography* essay, "fatigue, disenchantment, and her unsuccessful attempt to defeat Bolshevism had overwhelmed her." A final factor depressing Gippius's posthumous reputation was her flirtation with German fascism; she disdained Adolf Hitler's autocratic personality but hoped that the Germans would overthrow the Soviet Communist Regime. In her last years, Gippius wrote the philosophical poem *Poslednii krug* (The Last Circle), modeled on Dante's *Divine Comedy*. She died in Paris on September 9, 1945.

Books

Kalb, Judith E., ed., *Russian Writers of the Silver Age: 1890–1925,* (*Dictionary of Literary Biography,* vol. 195), Gale, 2004.

Pachmuss, Temira, *Zinaida Gippius: An Intellectual Portrait,* Southern Illinois University Press, 1971.

Poggioli, Renato, *The Poets of Russia,* Harvard University Press, 1960.

Zlobin, Vladimir, *A Difficult Soul: Zinaida Gippius,* introduction by Simon Karlisky, University of California Press, 1980.

Online

"Zinaida (Nikolaevna) Gippius." *Contemporary Authors Online,* Gale, 2009.

"Zinaida Gippius and *Vyliublennost:* An Early Modernist's Sexual Revolution," *International Institute of Social History* (Amsterdam), http://www.iisg.nl/womhist/hetherington.doc (November 15, 2009).□

Steffi Graf

The German professional tennis player Steffi Graf (born 1969) dominated the sport of women's tennis from the late 1980s through the mid-1990s.

Graf won a total of 107 singles titles over her 15-year career as a professional. Of those, 22 were in Grand Slam events: major championships in Australia, France, Britain, and the United States that form the high points of the annual tennis tournament circuit. When Graf came on the scene in the 1980s, she was competing with a large group of teenage tennis prodigies. Most of them flamed out, but Graf went on to notch several years of crushing triumphs—and a comeback for a renewed run at the top when it seemed that her reign had been broken. While other players specialized in clay, or grass, or hard-surface courts, Graf was a threat on all these surfaces. Steffi

Graf was, in the words of *BBC News,* "arguably the greatest female player ever."

Became Junior Champion

Stefanie Maria Graf was born in Mannheim, in what was then West Germany, on June 14, 1969. Her father, Peter, and her mother, Heidi, both played tennis, and Peter Graf was a nationally ranked player in West Germany. When she was three, Steffi demanded that she be allowed to play with an old tennis racket, and soon she was hitting the ball hard enough that she had broken all the lamps in the house. The family moved to the Mannheim suburb of Brühl, and soon set up a makeshift tennis court in the basement of their house with a pair of chairs and some string. Once Peter Graf realized that Steffi was serious about tennis, his encouragement of her talents became more than casual.

He began to enter her in tournaments, and she won her first one at age six. In 1982 he pulled her out of school so she could concentrate on tennis—and she became West German junior champion. That year she entered the French Open in Paris, where she was taken for a ball girl. In 1984, while lawn tennis was still a demonstration sport at the Summer Olympics, she traveled to the games in Los Angeles and returned home with a gold medal. The following year, the teenaged Graf joined the international Women's Tennis Association tour. She reached the semifinals of the U.S. Open in New York City, losing to reigning 1980s champion Martina Navratilova.

The year 1986 marked Graf's breakthrough. At one point she won 24 consecutive matches. She won her first tournament on the official tour, the Family Circle Cup in Charleston, South Carolina, and soon she was winning major events like the U.S. Clay Court Championship and the German Open. She beat Navratilova and another durable champion, Chris Evert, in quick succession, vanquishing both in less than one hour each. That made Graf a millionaire, but she was far from satisfied. While other teenage players enjoyed the limelight, Graf redoubled her efforts with a fresh regimen of weightlifting, running, and jumping rope. The efforts paid off: in 1987 she beat Navratilova in the French Open to win her first Grand Slam event, and in August of that year she attained the world number one ranking among women tennis players. She would hold that ranking for the next 186 weeks.

Won Grand Slam

In 1988 Graf exceeded even these considerable accomplishments, winning the Grand Slam—victories in all four Grand Slam tournaments. She beat Evert in the Australian Open; crushed Natalia Zvereva of the Soviet Union by a score of 6-0, 6-0 in the French Open final, becoming the first woman to score a complete shutout in a Grand Slam event; ended Navratilova's run of eight consecutive championships at the Wimbledon tournament in London, England; and completed the Slam with a victory over Gabriela Sabatini at the U.S. Open. The Grand Slam, a quartet of tournaments played on different surfaces in sharply differing environments, was notoriously difficult to win in its entirety; Graf was only the third woman (after Maureen Connolly and Margaret Court) to do so, and she won convincingly. She followed up this feat with a second gold medal at the 1988 Summer Olympics in Seoul, South Korea, becoming the first and thus far only player in history to win a so-called Golden Grand Slam. In Seoul she took track practice with members of the West German men's Olympic team, and her speed on the court inspired more than one observer to suggest that if she had not taken up tennis, she would have excelled as a sprinter.

Not yet 20 years old, Graf faced only half-facetious questions about whether she was considering retirement, since she apparently had little more to accomplish. In 1989, however, she had arguably an even better year than in 1988. She was robbed of an unheard-of second consecutive Grand Slam when she lost a close French Open final to Aranxta Sanchez-Vicario, but she won 14 other tournaments and finished with an 86-2 record for the year. For a time she thought that she might go undefeated. Indeed, most of Graf's thoughts revolved around the game. She was discouraged by her father from dating, and she had few friends among other players. "I think only of tennis, tennis, tennis," she was quoted as saying by Bob Carter of *ESPN*.

In the early 1990s Graf continued to rack up tournament victories. She was rivaled during this period only by the Yugoslavia-born Monica Seles, who finally dethroned Graf as the world's number-one player in March of 1991. The top spot alternated between the two players for several months, and their exciting rivalry brought new fans to the game. Then, on April 30, 1993, a crazed Graf fan, Gunther Parche, stabbed Seles in the back as she walked around the net to switch ends of the court during a match. He stated that he hoped to eliminate Seles as a rival to Graf, and in this he succeeded; Seles was forced off the court for 27 months and never regained her former dominance.

The once-sheltered Graf had to deal with other problems in the 1990s, and most of them came from the man who had sheltered her: her father. In 1990 he was named in a paternity suit by a model who had posed for *Playboy* magazine. He was exonerated by testing, but Graf found her name splashed across Germany's tabloid newspapers. And Peter Graf was not so lucky in 1995; after being charged with income tax evasion, he was sentenced to 45 months in prison. He was released after 27 months when Steffi Graf paid a $775,000 fine on his behalf.

Inducted Into Hall of Fame

None of this slowed Graf down very much on the tennis court. She won at least one Grand Slam title every year from 1990 to 1993, when she won three. Graf retained her number one ranking through the mid-1990s, gradually reducing her schedule in order to counter the physical toll that top-flight tennis takes on an athlete's body. Between 1993 and 1995 her overall record was 181-14, and a run of victories at Wimbledon was interrupted only by a first-round loss to Lori McNeil in 1994. Graf's all-around game was a key contributor to her ongoing success; she had a strong net game and a dangerous spinning backhand, but the centerpieces of her attack were her powerful forehand and her blistering speed on the court.

It took a series of physical problems to end Graf's dominance of the game. In 1997 the star injured her knee at a tournament in Japan and was forced to undergo surgery twice. Still ranked number one at the beginning of the year, she fell out of the top ten and finally to number 28 by the end of the year, displaced at the top of the rankings by the volatile Swiss teenager Martina Hingis. Graf slowly recovered, fighting back pain and playing tournaments mostly on slow clay courts. She won her last Grand Slam tournament against Hingis at the French Open in the late spring of 1999 and retired from professional tennis on August 13 of that year, at the age of 30.

Graf's long-deferred love life made some headlines after her retirement. Through much of the 1990s she had dated race car driver Michael Bartels, but her new relationship with Iranian-American tennis champion Andre Agassi came to light in 1999. On their first date, Agassi reportedly asked whether she wanted children. Four days after their marriage in October of 2001, the couple became parents of a son, Jaden, and in 2003 they had a daughter, Jaz. The following year, Graf was inducted into the International Tennis Hall of Fame. After leaving tennis, Graf marketed a line of handbags bearing her name and worked for the World Wildlife Federation. In 2005 she made a brief return to the court at a Houston Wranglers World Team Tennis match, losing one singles and one doubles match. She and her family have made their home in Las Vegas, Nevada.

Books

Hilders, Laura, *Steffi Graf,* Time, 1990.
Notable Sports Figures, Gale, 2004.

Periodicals

Asian News International, November 9, 2009.
Evening Standard (London, England), April 22, 2003; July 13, 2005.
Guardian (London, England), August 14, 1999.
Independent (London, England), August 14, 1999.
New York Times, July 4, 1988.

Online

"Graf: Queen of the Lawn," *ESPN,* http://www.espn.go.com/classic/biography/s/Graf_Steffi.html (November 29, 2009).
"Life in Las Vegas," *Stefanie Graf Official Web site,* http://www.steffi-graf.net/en/?p=688 (November 29, 2009).
"Steffi Graf," *International Tennis Hall of Fame,* http://www.tennisfame.com/famer.aspx?pgID=867&hof_id=125 (November 29, 2009).
"Wimbledon Legends: Steffi Graf," *BBC News,* http://www.news.bbc.co.uk/sport2/hi/tennis/wimbledon_history/3742103.stm (November 29, 2009). □

Hetty Green

American financier Henrietta "Hetty" Howland Green (1834–1916) was the world's richest woman when she died in 1916. A whaling fortune heiress, Green made savvy long-term investments but lived so frugally that her name became a byword for parsimony during her lifetime. Even decades after her death, a picture of her appeared in *The Guinness Book of World Records* under the entry for "World's Greatest Miser."

Green came from an old Massachusetts Quaker family whose fortunes were made in the whaling industry. She was born Henrietta Howland Robinson on November 21, 1834, in New Bedford. Her formidable father had married into the prosperous Howland family—whose roots in New England stretched back to the Mayflower era—after attaining some business success in textile manufacturing in Rhode Island. Her mother, Abby, gave birth to a much-anticipated son in May of 1836, but the baby did not survive infancy, and Abby was devastated. She remained a distant figure during Green's childhood, much of which was spent at the home of her grandparents, where she had been sent to stay during her mother's pregnancy. The headstrong, active girl was raised by her father and her Howland relatives, including her mother's invalid sister, Sylvia.

Schooled by Her Father

The time Green spent with her father largely revolved around his workday and financial dealings. She accompanied him to the great whaling wharves in New Bedford, the center of the U.S. whaling industry at the time, and to the offices of the Howland Company. "As soon as I learned to read it became my daily duty to read aloud to them the financial news of the world," she once told a reporter, according to Charles

Slack's *Hetty: The Genius and Madness of America's First Female Tycoon.* "In this way I came to know what stocks and bonds were, how the markets fluctuated, and the meaning of 'bulls' and 'bears.'"

Green's more formal education came from a pair of Quaker schools she attended. At the age of 15, she was sent to a posh "finishing" school in Boston, and was later sent off to stay with relatives in New York City, likely with the hope that she would find a suitable husband; but Green was wary of fortune-hunters. She returned to New Bedford, though she occasionally made extended visits to New York. In 1860, she was a guest at a ball to honor the young heir to the British throne, England's Prince Edward VII, and danced twice with him. But Green was far more preoccupied with her family's fortune during this period of her life, especially that of her invalid aunt, the bulk of which she hoped to inherit. Back in New Bedford, Green kept a careful watch on her Aunt Sylvia's household and objected to the retinue of staffers who cared for and befriended the virtual shut-in. There were several dramatic incidents over Sylvia's various wills, one of which Green wrote out herself and another that installed a new physician, whom Green loathed, as trustee of the inheritance.

Vilified in Sensational Trial

Green's father died first, however, and left her $5.7 million. Just under a million dollars of that was in cash, with the rest locked in a trust administered by two of Edward Robinson's trusted business associates. Her aunt's death followed just two weeks later, in July of 1865. Green then entered into a protracted legal battle to contest her aunt's will, based on a piece of paper she claimed to have retrieved from Sylvia's vault of important documents on the day of the funeral. This "second page" contained Sylvia's assertion that any subsequent will made after the 1862 one—which left the bulk of her fortune to her niece, free and clear—was hereby invalidated. The case dragged on for months, and was amply chronicled in the Boston and New York newspapers of the day. There were sensational claims made by both sides. Attorneys for her aunt's estate claimed the document was a forgery, while Green maintained that Sylvia's doctor had dosed her with laudanum—a highly addictive mixture of morphine and opium—while a cabal of servants conspired to profit from their longtime employer's death. In court, the maids and nurses testified that Green had terrorized her aunt over the matter of the 1862 will and constantly berated her over household expenses.

By this point in her life Green had settled in New York City and was engaged to be married. Her fiancé was Edward Henry Green, who came from a prosperous family in Bellows Falls, Vermont, but had made his own fortune in trade with Asia, where he had also lived for a number of years. He was 14 years her senior, and they were likely introduced by Green's father. The couple wed on July 11, 1867, while awaiting a verdict in the lengthy legal battle over her aunt's will, and immediately moved to London in the wake of rumors that Green might face criminal charges if found guilty of forgery.

Unlike his new bride, Edward appreciated certain extravagances, such as gourmet food, rare wines, and custom-made clothing, and the couple lived in a luxury hotel overlooking Regent's Park. She gave birth to both of her children there. Edward "Ned" Howland Robinson Green was born in August of 1868, followed by a daughter they named Hetty Sylvia Ann Howland Green in January of 1871.

Invested for the Long Term

Green eventually reached a settlement with the trustees of her aunt's estate, but remained in England until 1874. In London, her husband served on the board of several banks, while she occupied herself investing the money she had inherited from her father. "Greenbacks" were her first major purchase. These were U.S. government bonds issued just after the end of the Civil War, and their price had plummeted along with investor confidence. Green bought them cheap, held onto them, and earned hundreds of thousands of dollars as the nation recovered and began rebuilding its infrastructure. Railroad bonds were another sure bet for Green, and she also began to deal with banks in both London and New York. They traded her loans in return for cash, and sometimes the borrowers defaulted. The property used as collateral became hers. Eventually she owned vast tracts in the West and entire city blocks in Chicago.

The Greens returned to the United States to live with Edward's aged mother in Bellows Falls. Once again, the household staff reported terrible battles with Green over grocery purchases and any expense she deemed unnecessary. Her children wore the same shabby clothes she preferred, and grew accustomed to being mistaken for beggar children

while out in public. Out of this period came one of the most dramatic tales about Green's miserliness. Her son, named after his father but called Ned, was involved in a sledding accident. It may have involved a dislocated kneecap, and he could still walk on the leg, but it worsened over the years. Stories about Green's penny-pinching were already legion in Bellows Falls, and she already harbored a deep mistrust of doctors, who she felt overcharged the wealthy. She tried various remedies on her son, who began to walk with a pronounced limp as his leg withered. Finally, she took him to see several specialists, but presented herself and her son as charity cases. At New York City's famed Bellevue Hospital, a doctor recognized her and exposed her as one of America's richest citizens. Finally, Ned's leg had to be amputated below the knee in 1888, about a decade after the original accident. He wore a cork leg for the rest of his life.

Dubbed "The Witch of Wall Street"

Green's parsimony took its toll on her marriage, too. In January of 1885 the Wall Street bank John J. Cisco and Son collapsed. She attempted to remove the $200,000 in negotiable securities she kept there, but then learned that the Cisco partners had made large loans to her husband totaling more than $700,000. Once again, she entered into a drawn out, well publicized battle with the trustee appointed to oversee Cisco's ruinous situation. She eventually extracted her assets by settling her husband's debt and then ejected him from their home. They never divorced, and several years later she later nursed him when he was near death from heart disease and chronic nephritis.

The Cisco fiasco only heightened the public's fascination with Green. Other Wall Street financiers respected her as a savvy investor, and she was among several leading names who made loans to the City of New York during a financial crisis known as the Panic of 1907, but she was derided in the tabloids as "the Witch of Wall Street." The stories mocked her shabby attire and recounted her relentless haggling with merchants, waiters, and almost any other unfortunate person involved in a financial transaction of any sort with her. Reporters followed her everywhere, and she frequently changed residences in order to avoid having to pay local taxes. She lived under aliases at apartment houses in Manhattan, Brooklyn, and Hoboken, New Jersey, took streetcars everywhere because she considered a carriage and driver a waste of money, and was one of the rare women who had a police permit to carry a pistol in New York City. She claimed she needed this because of her numerous enemies. "I often carry many valuables and vicious people know it," she told a New York Police Department sergeant, according to a *New York Times* report.

In the same article, Green claimed that her father had been the victim of foul play when he died in 1865. She repeated this claim to others, and also suggested that her aunt had been poisoned. Closer to home, she kept a strict watch over her grown children's suitors, fearful that they would fall prey to fortune hunters. Her daughter, Sylvia, was married in 1909 at the age of 38 to Matthew Astor Wilks, a great-grandson of John Jacob Astor. Ned, who spent long stretches of his adult life out West as his mother's business agent, eventually rose to become chair of the Texas Republican

Party. Outside of New York, he lived with Mabel Harlow, a reported Chicago prostitute who had followed him out to Texas as his "housekeeper." They wed a year after his mother's death.

Left $100 Million Fortune

Green died at the age of 81 in New York City on July 3, 1916, after suffering a series of strokes. In her later years she had stopped taking the 7 a.m. ferry from Hoboken to Manhattan, where she had a desk at Chemical Bank, and had divested many of her holdings. Not surprisingly, her estate was tied up in legal matters for several years; both New York and New Jersey battled in court to have her declared a resident in order to claim inheritance taxes, which were estimated at $5 million. Aside from a total of $25,000 in bequests to others, she left everything to her two children, and was buried next to her husband in Bellows Falls. Her holdings included real estate in New York and Chicago, mining securities, tracts of farmland, and oil-rich lands parcels.

Green also owned a building at 74 Broad Street in Lower Manhattan, which she let empty out of its tenants over the years, using its sixth floor as storage for some things that were apparently of sentimental value to her. Among these items were a sleigh in which she used to ride with her father in New Bedford and the dress she wore at the ball when she danced with the future King Edward VII. "Probably her life was happy," an editorial in the *New York Times* wrote of Green two days after her death. "At any rate, she had enough of courage to live as she chose and to be as thrifty as she pleased, and she observed such of the world's conventions as seemed to her right and useful, coldly and calmly ignoring all the others."

Books

Slack, Charles, *Hetty: The Genius and Madness of America's First Female Tycoon,* Ecco, 2004.

Periodicals

Forbes Global, November 1, 2004.
New York Times, May 9, 1902; July 5, 1916.□

Marjorie Grene

American philosopher Marjorie Grene (1910–2009) was a pioneer in her discipline several times over.

Grene was a woman in a field almost totally dominated by men, and she generally rejected the notion of consciousness that was central to many systems of both classic and contemporary philosophy. She is regarded as a founder of the philosophy of biology, and she helped to introduce existentialism to the English-speaking world even as she herself rejected it. Grene's long career began with her study of contemporary European philosophy in Germany and Denmark in the 1930s. She studied under some of the most famous philosophers of the twentieth century, developing a powerful grasp of philosophical thinking but following directly in the footsteps of none of them. Grene often said that all knowledge was orientation. She emphasized the relationships between organisms, including humans, and their environments, and she examined how those relationships combined to create what is known as perception.

Studied in Germany

Grene was born Marjorie Glicksman in Milwaukee, Wisconsin on December 13, 1910. Her father, Harry Glicksman, was an English professor. Grene attended Wellesley College in Massachusetts, majoring in zoology and graduating in 1931. All through her intellectual and professional career, an interest in animals and natural history would inform her philosophical ideas. She also had a strong interest in philosophy but from the beginning rejected one of its central ideas: that humans possess something called consciousness, an inner facility of awareness. After graduating from Wellesley, Grene moved on to the University of Freiburg in Germany as an exchange student. After one seminar there, she recalled in an autobiographical essay published in *The Philosophy of Marjorie Grene,* she emerged into the hallway saying "Was wär ich ohne meine Umwelt?" (What would I be without my surroundings?)

In Germany (at Freiburg and the following year at the University of Heidelberg), Grene attended the lectures of Martin Heidegger and Karl Jaspers, two giants of contemporary German philosophy who both offered dense overall theories of the nature of human existence and knowledge. The rise of fascism in Germany necessitated Grene's return to the United States, where she earned an M.A. (1934) and then a Ph.D. (1935) from Radcliffe College. Radcliffe was, Grene recalled in her autobiographical essay, "the nearest a woman could get to Harvard in those days," and she took classes from Harvard faculty members including Alfred North Whitehead. After a stint in Copenhagen studying the writings of Danish philosopher Soren Kierkegaard (whose works she read in the original Danish), and a brief period teaching at Monticello College in Illinois, Grene landed a job as an instructor at the University of Chicago in 1937.

At Chicago, Grene came into contact with the originally Austrian doctrines of logical positivism, in the person of professor Rudolf Carnap, and the durable American viewpoint of pragmatism. Each of these left a mark on her own thinking, although she did not follow either group of thinkers in a systematic way. She married classical scholar David Grene in 1938, and the couple had two children, Ruth and Nicholas, before divorcing in 1961. Grene published a philosophy anthology, *From Descartes to Kant,* in 1940; it was credited to Grene and T.V. Smith, but, Grene wrote, "it was entirely my work." Nevertheless, she lost her job at Chicago in 1944, and the family moved to an Illinois farm. Beginning in 1952 they lived on a farm in Ireland, and until the late 1950s she had no connection to an academic institution, even though she continued to write philosophical essays in the morning before beginning her farm chores. "As has long been the case with most women, and still holds today for very many, my personal history has had a very important influence on my professional work, keeping me from it in large measure for many years and encouraging me . . . to work in areas I would not myself have chosen." It was during this period that Grene systematically investigated and wrote about existentialism, becoming one of the first philosophers writing in English to do so. Among the demands of running a farm she wrote two books, *Dreadful Freedom: A Critique of Existentialism* (1948) and *Heidegger* (1957).

Two developments in Grene's middle age helped to shape her ideas into coherent forms that provided the basis for more than a dozen books and numerous articles. The first was her acquaintance with Michael Polanyi, a chemist who in the 1950s turned his attention to philosophy. Grene served as Polanyi's editor, advisor in the history of philosophy, general sounding board, and, often, philosophical partner. Polanyi wrote (as quoted by Douglas Martin of the *New York Times*) in his book *Personal Knowledge* that "[t]here is hardly a page that has not benefited from her [Grene's] criticism. She has a share in anything I may have achieved here." Grene's interest in the philosophy of science, and in the relationship between philosophy and science, began and blossomed during this period.

Wrote Book on Aristotle

A second important influence on Grene's thinking came about as a result of her return to teaching. After short periods teaching and doing research at the universities of Manchester and Leeds in England, she was hired as a lecturer in philosophy at the Queen's University of Belfast in Northern Ireland in 1960, remaining there until 1965. Grene's teaching responsibilities there focused on ancient Greek philosophy, and for the first time she made a systematic study of the writings of Aristotle. One result was her book *Portrait of Aristotle,* a standard text published in 1963 and reissued in 1998. Beyond that, Grene found in Aristotle a philosopher whose more abstract ideas were related to his study of biology, of living organisms, and who did not try to reduce the variable nature of the world to a set of physical or philosophical principles. In a 1972 article entitled "Aristotle and Modern Biology" (quoted in her autobiographical essay), Grene wrote that "Aristotle can remind us of the many-leveled structure both of inquiries into complex systems and of the systems themselves, and thus of the inadequacy of a one-leveled atomism for the understanding of such systems."

Moreover, Grene began to develop her ideas about the connections between philosophy and biology into an ongoing body of thought. "She was arguably the founding figure in the new field of the philosophy of biology," philosopher Michael Wedin was quoted as saying in the *New York Times.* In books such as *Approaches to a Philosophical Biology* (1968), *The Understanding of Nature: Essays in the Philosophy of Biology* (1974), and, at age 94 in 2004 (with David Depew as co-author), *The Philosophy of Biology: An Episodic History,* Grene inquired into the nature of biological knowledge. She focused especially on evolution, evaluating the fundamental role of unpredictability in the process, asking such questions as what the evolution of an organism meant in regard to its basic nature. Grene was a founding member of the International Society for the History, Philosophy and Social Studies of Biology.

Grene credited her late-life intellectual productivity partly to her return to the U.S. in 1965, in order to take a position as professor of philosophy at the University of California at Davis. "Returning to our system, where instructors are relatively at liberty to develop their own courses and where students actually like to ask questions . . . was positively exhilarating," she wrote in her autobiographical essay. Grene remained at Davis until she reached the school's mandatory retirement age in 1978, moving on to a long series of visiting professorships through the 1980s. In 1985 and 1986 she served a year as a research fellow at the American Museum of Natural History in New York. In 1988 Grene settled into a position as honorary university distinguished professor and adjunct professor of philosophy and science studies at Virginia Polytechnic Institute and State University, generally known as Virginia Tech, in Blacksburg, Virginia.

Penned Critique of Descartes

In the later part of her career Grene tried to codify her objections to the idea of consciousness, most succinctly stated by French philosopher René Descartes in his famous dictum "Cogito ergo sum" (I think, therefore I am). Grene developed her critique of Descartes in her books *Descartes* (1985), *Descartes Among the Scholastics* (1991), and, as editor with Roger Ariew, *Descartes and His Contemporaries: Meditations, Objections, and Replies.* Philosopher Richard Burian told the *Times* of London that by rejecting Descartes' idea of consciousness, Grene was "bucking the mainstream of philosophic thought for her entire career." Later in life she drew on the ideas of French philosopher of perception Maurice Merleau-Ponty and American philosopher-psychologist James Jerome (J.J.) Gibson.

Grene's independence of mind was all the more impressive in that she was a woman in the almost entirely male field of philosophy. Grene could more than hold her own in intellectual debate, however. With the publication of *The Philosophy of Marjorie Grene* in 2002 Grene received the honor of becoming the first woman included in the Library of Living Philosophers series (earlier writers so honored included Bertrand Russell and Albert Einstein). In the introduction to that volume, Randall E. Auxier and Lewis Edwin Hahn wrote: "Many more philosophers than would confess it have approached with considerable trepidation a public disputation with Professor Grene, and not a few have quietly declined the opportunity to argue with her altogether."

Grene's students benefited from her argumentative ways, and many of them contributed essays to *The Philosophy of Marjorie Grene* in which they probed her ideas. Each was accompanied by a rebuttal from the nonagenarian Grene herself. Greene's vinegary personality was balanced by a kind and gregarious side; at Virginia Tech, she could often be found walking the halls and offering candy or cookies to anyone she met. Grene remained active into her mid-90s. She died in Blacksburg at the age of 98 on March 16, 2009.

Books

Auxier, Randall E., and Lewis Edwin Hahn, *The Philosophy of Marjorie Grene,* Open Court, 2002.

Periodicals

New York Times, March 29, 2009.
Roanoke Times, February 25, 2003.
Times (London, England), April 22, 2009.
Virginian Pilot, March 23, 2009.

Online

"Marjorie Grene" (interview), *Believer* (March 2005), http://www.
 believermag.com/issues/200503/?read=interview_grene
 (December 20, 2009).
"Marjorie Grene: 1910–2009," *Contemporary Authors Online,*
 Gale, 2010. Reproduced in Biography Resource Center.
 Farmington Hills, Mich.: Gale, 2010. http://galenet.
 galegroup.com/servlet/BioRC (December 20, 2009). □

Carlotta Grisi

Italian dancer Carlotta Grisi (1819–1899) captured the hearts of Europe as one the most acclaimed dancers of her time. Grisi is best known for her creation of the title role in the ballet *Giselle.*

Carlotta Grisi was born on June 28, 1819, in Visinada, Italy, into a family known for their operatic singing talent. Carlotta, though, showed an early love of dancing. She started taking classes in Milan at the age of seven. Three years later she was singled out from the children's ballet corps to perform individually, and became their premier dancer. Because of her early success, Grisi went without a ballet-master. In 1833 her parents allowed her to tour Italy where, in Naples, she met Jules Perrot, an established dancer, who became her teacher and lover.

Ignored in Paris Debut

In addition to being able to teach Grisi many of the techniques that she had missed due to her young age, Perrot became her personal choreographer, creating dances specifically to accentuate her strengths and de-emphasize her weaknesses. After traveling throughout Europe, Perrot arranged Grisi's debut in Paris. On February 28, 1840, she danced in *Le Zingaro* at the Théâtre de la Renaissance. Billed as Madame Perrot, Grisi danced and sang while Perrot danced as her partner. Perrot's performance was highly acclaimed, while that of Grisi was largely rebuked or ignored.

Because Grisi had little success in her Paris debut, Perrot had to find another way to obtain a contract for her at the Paris Opéra. The Baron de Vidil, an influential patron, intervened on Grisi's behalf with Louis Perrot (no relation to Jules), who was the director of the Beaux-Arts at the Opéra. With his intercession, Grisi signed a contract with Léon Pillet for a salary of 5000 francs per year, with no added fee per performance, a mere pittance compared to her later contracts. In her debut at the Paris Opéra, Grisi was partnered with Lucien Petipa in *La Favorita* on February 12, 1841. Their pas de deux, or partnered dance, was well received by the public, but had mixed reviews from critics. The same was true of her next two pas de deux, occurring a month later, in *La Juive* and *Don Juan.*

Met Théophile Gautier

One of the foremost writers of his times, the critic Théophile Gautier was no stranger to Grisi; he had fathered her sister Ernesta's two children, Judith and Estelle. He first reviewed Grisi in 1840 in *Le Zingaro* at the Théâtre de la Renaissance. It wasn't until the beginning of 1841, though, that Carlotta Grisi met Gautier, and he became enamored with her. There is no clear evidence that they had an affair, but there was much speculation. It seems clear from his poetry, however, that his love was probably unrequited. The only indication of a possible reciprocity was needlework that she sent to him, which was often hidden by his daughter Judith.

Starred in *Giselle*

If Grisi did not know the importance of the success of *Giselle* during its production, Perrot did. Perrot fought to be the choreographer of the work. He was aware that Grisi's first contract with the Opéra would expire just a month and a half after *Giselle,* and he was determined to acquire a better deal for her in the future.

Many different hands went into the creation of *Giselle.* Vernoy de Saint-George wrote the script. Adolphe Adam composed the music. Ciceri designed the sets. Coralli was the choreographer. Petipa was once again Grisi's partner.

Perrot, in spite of his hand in the choreography, was not billed in the show.

Giselle debuted on June 28, 1841, to spectacular reviews. The public came to know Grisi simply as "La Carlotta." In the book *Carlotta Grisi,* author Serge Lifar quoted Gautier writing of her performance: "More than one eye which had expected to see merely points and *rond de jambe,* was surprised to find itself dimmed with tears, a thing that does not happen often at the ballet. This rôle will henceforward be impossible for any other dancer, and the name of Carlotta has become inseparable from that of Giselle."

Grisi was rewarded for her hard work when her contract was renegotiated shortly thereafter. Her terms increased to a two-year contract, the title of première danseuse (primary dancer), a salary of 12,000 francs for the first year, 15,000 francs for the second year, 43 francs per performance the first year, 72 francs per performance for the second, and seven guaranteed performance fees each month. The public and the critics hailed her as one of the best dancers in the world, among the ranks of Fanny Elssler and Marie Taglioni.

Grisi also made a personal decision shortly after the first production of *Giselle*: she separated from Perrot and went to live with her mother and sister in Paris. Professionally, she received a new rank within her own company as well. The Opéra's former première danseuse, Pauline Leroux, became bitter when she lost practice time for her new work *La Jolie Fille de Grand* to Grisi and *Giselle.* She soon lost more than that when Grisi was given her part in *La Jolie Fille de Grand.* Grisi originally refused to accept the part, in support of Leroux, but gave in after several months. Critics continued to praise her in this role as well.

Enjoyed Continued Success

Carlotta soon brought *Giselle* to London, opening in Her Majesty's Theatre on March 12, 1842. She quickly returned home and opened as Beatrix in *La Jolie Fille de Grand* in June of that year. The production costs for *La Jolie Fille de Grand* became exorbitant. It contained nine scenes and cost more than 50,000 francs (compared to that, *Giselle* cost only 20,000 francs to produce).

In her next production she danced one of her most famous parts. Opening on February 22, 1843, Grisi performed in *La Peri,* in two acclaimed numbers. In the *Pas du Songe* she leapt from a cloud, falling into the arms of her partner, risking serious injury in the process. In the *Pas de l'Abeille* she was an innocent girl pursued by a bee from a flower.

She once again went to London, where *La Peri* opened at the Theatre Royal on September 20, 1843. When she returned to Paris, she did not attempt any new roles. Pillet was not mounting new productions as the old ones were still bringing in a full house.

Starred in *La Emèralda*

She created the titular role in *La Emèralda* at Her Majesty's Theatre in London, which opened March 9, 1844. This ballet, inspired by Victor Hugo's work *Notre Dame de Paris* (The Hunchback of Notre Dame), has never been performed in France, though many dancers have revived the role. In 1845 the director of Her Majesty's Theatre,

Benjamin Lumley, tried to restage the ballet as a divertissement with the four greatest dancers of the age: Taglioni, Elssler, Grisi, and Fanny Cerrito. It seemed an unreasonable idea because of the production cost as well as personality clashes among the four ballerinas. After Lucile Grahn replaced Elssler, however, the ballet became a reality and opened on July 12, 1845. Grisi had made financial and personal sacrifices in order to participate, as she was contractually obligated to be in Paris and could only arrive to rehearse a few days before opening night.

Commissioned New Works

Grisi reopened in *Giselle* on July 25, 1845, and then commissioned a new ballet by Adolphe Adam, *Le Diable à Quatre.* The ballet was written expressly to highlight Grisi's talents. It opened on August 11, 1845. Her next work, *Paquita,* opened on April 1, 1846, in Paris and then debuted in London on June 3, 1846.

Grisi once again joined with Cerrito and also with Carolina Rosati for the work *The Elements,* which debuted in London on June 26, 1847, at Her Majesty's Theatre. She returned to Paris to create *Griséldis* or *Les Cinq Sens,* which debuted on February 16, 1848. This endeavor, though, was complicated by the Revolution of 1848 in France. Grisi returned to London to dance with Cerrito, Rosati, and Taglioni's niece, Marie Taglioni. Their work, *Les Quatres Saisons,* debuted on June 13, 1848, at Her Majesty's Theatre.

Left Paris

Grisi's contract with the Opéra ended on January 31, 1849. She chose not to renew, as she saw the future of the ballet elsewhere. Grisi continued to dance, while not under contract, at the Opéra until the end of 1849. She played the titular role of *Electra* or *La Pléïade Perdue,* opening on April 19, 1849. She debuted for the last time in Paris on October 8, 1849, in *La Filleule des Fées.* She danced for the last time in London in *Les Métamorphoses,* debuting on March 12, 1850.

Grisi wanted to visit Russia, and Perrot, her former ballet-master and lover, helped to arrange her visit. This was a strategically bad move for him, as the Imperial Theatres already had a star, Andreyanova, who might feel threatened by Grisi. Still, Grisi appeared in Russia throughout 1850 and 1851. She appeared in *Giselle* on October 8, 1850. Her reception, though, was lukewarm, as Elssler had already performed the role in Russia to great acclaim.

She gave several more performances in Eastern Europe, notably in St. Petersburg and Warsaw. On January 30, 1851, she appeared in *Ondine* or *La Naïade,* which was first produced in London for Cerrito. In this number, also known as *The Naiad and the Fisherman,* her reviews were better. This, though, may be due to the fact that Perrot became ballet-master in 1831. On November 11, 1852, Grisi appeared in *La Guerre des Femmes* or *Les Amazones du IXe Siècle.* On February 12, 1853, she appeared in *Gaselda* or *Les Tziganes.* This was her last time on stage. Grisi was forced to give up dancing during negotiations to return to the Opéra in 1854, after falling down some stairs and injuring her leg.

Retired to Domesticity

Prince Radziwill had given a home to Grisi at Saint-Jean, near Geneva. At the age of 34, Grisi bore him a child and named her Ernestine Grisi. They lived happily at Saint-Jean in relative anonymity. Gautier was a frequent visitor, but there was still no indication of an additional closeness in their relationship. In 1875 Ernestine married the painter Emile-Auguste Pinchart and later bore Grisi several grandchildren.

Grisi died peacefully on May 20, 1899, at the age of 79. She was buried near Geneva.

Books

International Dictionary of Ballet, St. James Press, 1993.

Lifar, Serge, *Carlotta Grisi,* John Lehmann Ltd., 1947.

Migel, Parmenia, *The Ballerinas: From the Court of Louis XIV to Pavlova,* Macmillan Company, 1972.

Wilson, G.B.L., *A Dictionary of Ballet,* Third Edition, Theatre Arts Books, 1974.

Periodicals

New York Times, September 16, 1877; May 23, 1899.□

Victor Gruen

Victor Gruen (1903–1980) was an Austrian-born architect who created twentieth-century America's most enduring symbol of affluent consumer culture, the shopping mall. In the decades that followed his widely copied design, Gruen decried suburban sprawl and careless regional planning in the United States. He gave voice to his disappointment in a 1975 science fiction novel, *Is Progress a Crime?,* in which a fictional architect at the tail end of his career described his adopted homeland as a nation "where everybody is persuaded to buy what he doesn't need with money he doesn't own in order to impress people he actually can't stand."

Gruen was born Viktor David Grünbaum on July 18, 1903, in Vienna, Austria. When he was 15 years old, World War I ended, and with it the mighty Austro-Hungarian Empire. Austria became a republic, and the great artistic movements that had been coalescing over the past few decades in the city of Vienna began to flourish in a new, Modernist style of art and architecture that would greatly influence the direction of his own career.

Trained in Modernist Style

Gruen came from an affluent Jewish family, but his father's death forced the teen to leave school in order to support the family. A gifted artist, he found a job as a draftsperson at a construction firm owned by a friend of the family. The firm was building some of the new high-rise apartment buildings for Vienna's postwar landscape in the 1920s, and after taking courses at the Technological Institute and Vienna Academy of Fine Arts, Gruen found a job as an architect with the firm of Peter Behrens, a German who taught at the Vienna Academy in the 1920s. Behrens was dedicated to the idea that architecture and the arts should further the goals of a modern, egalitarian society.

Gruen shared similar ideals. As a young man he joined Austria's left wing Socialist Party, and in the late 1920s and early 1930s appeared with cabaret theater groups that performed satirical political skits. That period of artistic freedom ended in 1934 when a right wing political party called *Vaterländische Front,* or Fatherland's Front, came to power and began implementing strict censorship laws. From 1934 to 1936 Gruen operated his own residential architecture firm in Vienna out of the apartment he shared with his wife, Lizzie Kardos.

The Fatherland's Front was one of two major right wing elements in Austria, and in 1938 it was usurped by the Austrian Nazi Party. That same year, Austria was absorbed in its entirety into neighboring Nazi Germany. This was known as the Anschluss, or annexation, and immediately imperiled all Jewish citizens in Austria, who now anticipated the same anti-Semitic laws and deportations to labor camps that Germany's Jews faced.

Fled Nazi Regime

Gruen and his wife decided to leave. A friend from his theater days managed to obtain a Nazi uniform and wore it to drive the couple to the airport, where they boarded the first plane to Switzerland. From there, they escaped to London and eventually found passage on an ocean liner bound for New York City. When Gruen walked off the S.S. *Statendam* in the spring of 1939, he had just eight dollars to his name, and spoke very little English. He shortened his surname to "Gruen," changed the spelling of his first name to a more Americanized version, and found a job as a draftsperson for an architectural firm that was working on a highly anticipated General Motors exhibit called "Futurama" for the 1939 New York World's Fair. The enormous "world of tomorrow" theme park ride promised Americans their own personal vehicles on automated highways in just 20 years' time.

Gruen's chance encounter on the street with another Viennese refugee of 1938, Ludwig Lederer, brought him his first major commission in the United States. Lederer was an established retailer in Europe with his Lederer de Paris chain, and he hired Gruen to design the first store in New York. The elegant Fifth Avenue space won Gruen several new commissions, including a new outpost of the London nightclub Ciro's, also on Fifth Avenue. For a period of time in the 1940s he lived in Southern California after winning a job to design stores for Grayson's, a clothing retailer.

The metropolitan Los Angeles area saw enormous growth during this period, as World War II raged on both the Pacific and European fronts and the U.S. aircraft industry in California converted to wartime production. Factory workers moved west there for jobs, liked the sunny climate, and stayed. This was one of the first places where the elements of single family residential housing developments and the modern highway intersected, and Gruen's work for Grayson's prompted him to consider how Americans spent their leisure time in such places. He began sketching out ideas for shopping centers which approximated a convenient "downtown-like" experience, but which included parking spaces for an enormous number of cars.

America's Leading Retail Architect

Gruen founded his own firm, Victor Gruen Associates, in 1951. Two years later, the *New York Times Magazine* ran a feature story about these new regional shopping centers that were designed with innovative truck tunnels underneath to deliver goods to their dozens of stores. Gruen told the story's writer, C. B. Palmer, that these new retail sites "are re-creating something lost—something we had in the Greek Agora, the medieval markets, the rural New England town of past centuries. ... In the old days the cathedral towns were market centers. Farmers brought their produce in one day a week. Market stalls were set up and as trade increased permanent stores were built, and so were homes. The atmosphere counted for a great deal—the atmosphere of meeting people, exchanging news and ideas, watching the steadily changing picture."

The same article noted there were several of the new concept shopping centers in the planning stages, but it was the home of the U.S. automotive manufacturing industry, Detroit, that saw the sharpest rise in personal vehicle ownership and changes in consumer patterns in the post-World War II era. A local real estate mogul named A. Alfred Taubman hired Gruen to build a shopping center on a piece of land a little north of Detroit in the now rapidly proliferating suburbs. Taubman had already secured the metro Detroit area's largest and most prestigious department store, J. L. Hudson & Company, to serve as the anchor store at Northland Center, which received national attention when it opened in March of 1954. Set on 163 acres, Northland boasted 80 stores and 8,800 parking spaces. It was the first suburban open-air shopping center in the world, and was quickly replicated by Gruen, Taubman, and Hudson's across the Detroit suburbs.

Years later, the Hudson family would merge their chain with a Minneapolis retailer called Dayton's. It was the three Dayton brothers who hired Gruen to build another first in retailing, the world's first fully enclosed, climate-controlled shopping center. Southdale opened in the suburb of Edina, Minnesota, in October of 1956 as the world's first two-story mall. The Dayton family had wanted to replicate the success of Northland, but Gruen convinced them to put a roof over the project, presenting evidence that Minnesota temperatures offered less than 30 days a year of pedestrian-friendly weather. "Underneath a center skylight was a garden courtyard, which at the time was one of the largest indoor public spaces in America, complete with a goldfish pond, an aviary, hanging plants, and artificial trees," wrote Paul Lukas in *Fortune* about Gruen's Edina landmark. "By creating a completely enclosed environment with no exterior windows, mall developers were able to use an array of cues to keep shoppers moving," Lukas continued, citing see-through Plexiglas handrails on the second floor and "lighting to simulate an eternal sense of midafternoon so that people didn't get a sense of how long they'd been shopping."

Disappointed by Commercial Landscapes

Gruen was the most famous retail architect in the United States following these triumphs in Michigan and Minnesota. He became an ardent advocate of more humane urban planning, warning that highways and suburban sprawl were creating a nightmarish vision far removed from the pleasant, efficient communal experience forecasted by the Futurama exhibit. Asked on the eve of the 1960s to imagine what American life would be like in 1975, he predicted a gloomy prognosis if commercial interests remained unchecked by regional development authorities. "Otherwise," he wrote in *Life,* "we will spend our precious hard-earned leisure time within our own four walls, cut off from society by the foes we have created: murderous traffic, smog, disorder, blight and ugliness."

With offices in five cities by then, Gruen's firm designed many of the first enclosed shopping centers across the United States and later focused on urban planning and large-scale residential architecture. Gruen was disappointed, however, that developers brushed off his more ambitious plans. "Gruen, true to his socialist ideals, usually included land in his mall designs to be set aside for community and civic functions," wrote Lukas. "But those provisions rarely made it into the final projects, primarily because building a mall usually raised surrounding land values, so developers—who tended not to share Gruen's high-minded politics—found it more profitable to sell off the civic-targeted land to speculators, who inevitably put commercial enterprises on it.''

Gruen's malls quickly changed the way Americans shopped. They were particularly favored by a new generation of stay-at-home mothers, with newspaper reports about some of his first malls noting that they seemed to be a gathering place where women could socialize during the daytime hours and even wear ''slacks'' in public. The stores were closed on Sundays, but Americans made them part of their day-off ritual anyway and came to browse the window displays.

Died in 1980

Gruen's best-known residential projects included the Wilshire Terrace in Beverly Hills, a prime piece of Southern California real estate erected in 1958 at the intersection of Wilshire and Beverly Glen boulevards that featured staggered terraces to maximize privacy. In Boston, he designed Charles River Park, a luxury housing development that was an early attempt to create an urban gated community. He retired in 1967, and returned to his native Austria, where he died on February 14, 1980. Married four times, Gruen was survived by former spouse Elsie Krummeck Crawford, his fourth wife Kemija Gruen, and his son Michael.

In a somewhat ironic twist, the malls that Gruen created fell out of favor in the decades following his death, and American retail developers began favoring an open-air design that more faithfully mimicked the village commercial districts of yore. In March of 2004, journalist Malcolm Gladwell wrote an article in the *New Yorker* commemorating the 50th anniversary of the mall. ''Postwar America was an intellectually insecure place, and there was something intoxicating about Gruen's sophistication and confidence,'' wrote Gladwell about Gruen's dream of a more connected world anchored by a communal retail experience. ''He was a European intellectual, an émigré, and, in the popular mind, the European émigré represented vision, the gift of seeing something grand in the banality of postwar American life.''

Books

Hardwick, M. Jeffrey, and Victor Gruen, *Mall Maker: Victor Gruen, Architect of an American Dream,* University of Pennsylvania Press, 2004, p. 218.

Periodicals

Fortune, October 18, 2004.
Life, December 28, 1959.
New Yorker, March 17, 1956; March 15, 2004.
New York Times, February 16, 1980; August 30, 1992.
New York Times Magazine, November 29, 1953.
Star Tribune (Minneapolis, MN), October 7, 2006.□

Gary Gygax

The American game designer Gary Gygax (1938–2008), best known for his creation Dungeons & Dragons, was the primary originator of an entirely new kind of entertainment: the role-playing game, in which participants are represented by a single character or figure rather than marshaling and controlling a group of pieces.

Ernest Gary Gygax was born in Chicago on July 27, 1938. His father, a Swiss immigrant, was a professional violinist who liked to read fantasy fiction and mythology, while his mother enjoyed games and introduced him to card games and chess at an early age. The family moved to Lake Geneva, Wisconsin, when Gygax was eight, and he lived there for most of the rest of his life. As a child he discovered and explored a set of tunnels running underneath a disused insane asylum. Gygax began reading science fiction in his teens and soaked up the works of the top authors in the genre, including Fritz Leiber, Michael Moorcock, and Robert E. Howard and others. Sometimes he imagined game scenarios based on the stories he had read. He later said that he disliked the fantasy novels of J.R.R. Tolkien, but these are nevertheless thought to have influenced the Dungeons & Dragons cast of characters. Gygax also enjoyed pulp sword-and-sorcery stories like those featuring the hero Conan the Barbarian. His imagination did not result in good grades in high school, and he dropped out as a junior. For a time he drifted from job to job, taking some anthropology classes at a local junior college.

Gygax married in 1958, and by the early 1960s, with two children to support (he eventually had six), he settled into a full-time job as an insurance underwriter with the Fireman's Fund firm. Insurance analysis might seem to have little to do with the rich fantasy environments of Dungeons & Dragons, but screenwriter and Gygax collaborator Flint Dille told Leigh Buchanan of *Inc.* magazine that the two phases of Gygax's career were actually closely related: ''If you squint at a D&D character record sheet, you'll see it's an actuarial table. Insurers take facts about a person's life and build stats on it to figure out when they're going to die and of what. Gary said, 'Let's do that for a dragon. We'll roll a die for the odds.'''

The intermediate step that allowed Gygax to put together fantasy and probability studies was his involvement in wargaming, which he took up as a hobby in early adulthood. Gygax and his friends started out with tabletop reenactments of the Battle of Gettysburg and other famous military events. Generally they used a preexisting game as a framework, but Gygax felt free to make up his own rules. Soon he and his friends had devised a World War II tank game of their own and had rejected ordinary dice as a way of introducing the element of chance. Looking for a way of generating a large number of equally likely outcomes, they drew from a set of 20 numbered poker chips in a hat. Gygax improved on this method when he spotted a set of Platonic solids—bodies with four, six, eight, 12, or 20 equal sides—in a school equipment catalogue. The 20-sided icosahedron became central to Dungeons & Dragons.

Home Gathering Grew Into Festival

In 1967 Gygax invited about 20 friends to the basement of his home for a mass wargaming meeting, and the following year he rented Lake Geneva's Horticultural Hall and charged a one-dollar admission fee for the meeting's second year. Several dozen war game enthusiasts from various states and Canadian provinces came to the event Gygax named the Lake Geneva Convention, or GenCon for short; by the 2000s, GenCon was among the biggest gaming conventions on the North American continent. The early meetings helped Gygax widen his circle of gamer acquaintances, and one of them brought him a medieval-themed game called Siege of Bodenburg, governed by a then-unusually elaborate rule book that was four pages long. Gygax modified the game in two ways, to the delight of his friends. "Well, they loved it. They went absolutely crazy for it," he was quoted as saying in the London *Times*. Gygax introduced a dragon, a troll, and other figures, drawing on the vaguely Celtic Conan the Barbarian books and other medieval fantasies he had long enjoyed. Second, he expanded the rule book to 16 pages. By 1971, the game had evolved into a distinct creation Gygax called *Chainmail*; it is still played today.

Convinced that game design was his future, Gygax quit his insurance job and for a time operated a small shoe repair business to make a living. With an associate, Dave Arneson, a University of Minnesota student who attended the 1969 GenCon event, he began to refine *Chainmail*. The most important new development was that instead of having players competing to win a battle by advancing miniatures on a board, each player would choose just a single figure, a hero with distinct strengths and weaknesses, who would encounter a series of hazards and challenges. Accounts differ as to whether it was Arneson or Gygax who first devised the idea of having each player inhabit a single role; an extensive account of Gygax's career published in *Wired* in 2008 attributed the innovation to Gygax, stating that Arneson saw the idea's potential for "free-form, improvisatory play" as similar to games he had developed with a group of players in the Minneapolis–St. Paul area. According to David Kushner of *Wired*, it was Arneson who devised the idea of a referee or game master who would structure each individual game episode and set challenges for the players; this figure evolved into the Dungeon Master of Dungeons & Dragons.

Gygax and Arneson began to work out the details of their new game idea, exchanging mail and long distance phone calls between Wisconsin and Minnesota. Gygax added new medieval monsters to the game's cast of characters, and he codified Arneson's unstructured ideas. "He could type, and I couldn't," Arneson told Kushner. Gygax began to believe he was in possession of a successful new concept, and after trying out the new game on two of his children and one of their friends, he was more convinced than ever. A third Gygax child, four-year-old Elise, named the game Dungeons & Dragons. Gygax took the game to an established manufacturer, Avalon Hill, whose representatives were baffled by a game with no board and generally no clear winner. A game might go on for hours, days, or longer with no resolution, as players explored the implications of various campaigns. "People said, 'What kind of game is this? You don't play against anybody. Nobody wins. It doesn't end. This is craziness,'" Gygax was quoted as saying in the London *Times*.

Gygax and his associate Donald Kaye responded to Avalon Hill's skepticism by forming a company of their own, Tactical Studies Rules, or TSR, in 1973. Dungeons & Dragons, introduced early the following year, was minimal in its equipment, including rule books explaining in precise terms the powers and flaws of each character and perhaps, depending on the version, some maps, figurines, and dice. Dungeons & Dragons was not a traditional board game but, in the words of the London *Independent*, "a system for imagining characters and situations—cityscapes, conflicts, confrontations, alliances—within a tightly rule-based structure and driven by the throw of dice." Although the rules were complex, the point of the game, for Gygax and many participants, was to collaborate imaginatively in a social environment. Startup costs for TSR were $2,400, and the company was headquartered in Gygax's basement. The rule book, originally titled *Dungeons & Dragons: Rules for Fantastic Medieval Wargame Campaigns Playable with Paper and Pencil and Miniature Figures,* cost ten dollars, and 20-sided dice were $3.50 apiece. After ten months the initial run of 1,000 books had sold out, and a second printing, twice as large, was soon exhausted as well. Gygax added new creatures, new manuals to go with them, and, by 1977, an *Advanced Dungeons & Dragons Monster Manual,* as he struggled to keep up with burgeoning interest in the game among students and hobby enthusiasts.

Faced Controversy

Attacks by Christian fundamentalist tract publisher Jack Chick and others may have helped further the game's popularity in the late 1970s and early 1980s. The 1981 Rona Jaffe novel *Mazes and Monsters,* which depicted a fantasy game clearly based on Dungeons & Dragons, suggested that players might lose the ability to distinguish between fantasy and reality and even be inspired to commit violence or suicide. The book was made into a television film starring a then-unknown Tom Hanks. Gygax received death threats and was forced to hire private security guards. He made an appearance on the CBS television program *60 Minutes* to defend *Dungeons & Dragons,* generating still more publicity. As of 2008, TSR's initial $2,400 investment had resulted in estimated sales of $1 billion, with some 25 million people worldwide having been at some point involved with the game. A Dungeons & Dragons subculture burgeoned, and players began to customize the game for themselves in various ways.

In the early 1980s Gygax temporarily left Wisconsin for California in order to oversee a television cartoon version of Dungeons & Dragons. Donald Kaye had died in 1975, and the move sidelined Gygax from TSR's operations at a critical time. He felt that he was being forced out of a decision-making role at the company he had created, and in 1985 he left TSR altogether. Gygax designed a new role-playing game, *Dangerous Journeys,* and wrote a trio of fantasy novels based on it; he also wrote books loosely based on Dungeons & Dragons–like settings, including five books featuring an orphan character named Gord the Rogue and (with Dille) a "Sagard the Barbarian" series.

Dungeons & Dragons itself was acquired in the late 1990s by the publisher Wizards of the Coast, which in turn was absorbed by the long-established game maker Hasbro. Gygax held the title of consultant for a time. In 1999 he created a final role-playing game, Lejendary Adventure, for the Arkansas publisher Troll Lord; the game was notable for its streamlined, intuitive set of rules. Gygax suffered two strokes and a heart attack during his final years but remained active and involved in creating new products based on the games he had invented almost until his death in Lake Geneva on March 4, 2008. He was survived by his second wife, Gail Gygax.

By that time, the popularity of Dungeons & Dragons had been dented somewhat by computer gaming, but Gygax's ongoing influence was easy to detect in the character-centered narratives of computer adventure games. Even the MMORPGs or Massively Multiplayer Online Role-Playing Games made popular by social networking applications bore traces of Gygax's innovations; the MMORPG "World of Warcraft" was a close D&D relative. Gygax himself disliked online games and rarely played them. "Computer games can be so isolating," he was quoted as saying in the *Times.* They're not anything like sitting in a group and laughing, telling stories. You can't share a bag of Cheetos online." Nevertheless, the gaming site Gamespy.com named Gygax the 17th most influential person in computer game history.

Books

Authors and Artists for Young Adults, vol. 65, Thomson Gale, 2005.

Periodicals

Economist, March 15, 2008.

Guardian (London, England), March 7, 2008.

Inc., June 2008.

Independent (London, England), March 8, 2008.

New York Times, March 15, 2008.

San Francisco Chronicle, March 6, 2008.

Times (London, England), March 6, 2008.

Online

"Dungeon Master: The Life and Legacy of Gary Gygax," *Wired,* March 10, 2008, http://www.wired.com/gaming/virtualworlds/news/2008/03/ff_gygax%3FcurrentPage%3D4 (November 12, 2009). □

H

Mia Hamm

Mia Hamm (born 1972) has been one of the most accomplished and ground-breaking female soccer stars in the United States. With four NCAA championships, two World Cup Championships, and two Olympic Gold Medals, she is also one of the most decorated. She was a consistent high scorer, holding the title of All-Time Leading Scorer in international soccer with 158 goals. She retired from soccer in 2004.

ariel Margaret Hamm was born on March 17, 1972, in Selma, Alabama, to parents Bill and Stephanie. She was the fourth of six siblings, with three sisters and two brothers. Her mother was a former ballerina who tried to steer her young daughter towards dance, but found her reluctant, even at the age of six. In spite of that, she nicknamed her daughter "Mia," after the ballerina Mia Slavenska. Her father was a colonel and fighter pilot in the Air Force. Because of his military career he moved his family often: Texas, California, Virginia, and even Florence, Italy. He also shared his passion for soccer with his young daughter. While living in Italy, he bought season tickets to the local Italian soccer team and often brought his daughter along with him.

By her own admission, Mia grew up on the soccer field. When she was five years old, her parents adopted her brother Garrett, who was eight years old at the time, and very athletic. He had a large impact on her development as an athlete. She told Jere Longman of the *New York Times,* "When he'd go play pickup football or baseball, I was always right behind him. He always picked me for his teams."

Mia Hamm joined her first soccer team at the age of five. She was in a co-ed pee wee league in Wichita Falls, Texas. This was not the only sport that she played. She was a shortstop and a pitcher on a boys' baseball team; she played point guard on the basketball team and played softball and tennis; she even played wide receiver and cornerback on the boys' football team at Notre Dame Middle School. Eventually she became the only girl to play in a boys' soccer league. She was incredibly dedicated to the sport. She awoke early in the summers to practice, and it showed on the field. The boys were not enthusiastic when a girl scored against them, and she became a target for their rough aggression, but quickly learned how to avoid on-field collisions.

Early Career

At the beginning of her high school career she played for coach Lou Pearce at Notre Dame High School in Wichita Falls, Texas. She moved to Burke, Virginia, and played at Lake Braddock Secondary School. In her sophomore year of high school she was named a scholastic All-American.

While she was in high school, she began to play on an "Olympic development team," even before women's soccer was declared an Olympic sport. Her coach on that team was John Cossaboon. Cossaboon was impressed by the young woman and called his friend, Anson Dorrance, the coach of the women's national team. In 1987, at the age of 15 years, Hamm became the youngest soccer player to play on a national team, male or female. She made her first appearance on August 3, 1987, in a U.S. Soccer Federation tournament. Of that day, Mia Hamm told *Sports Illustrated,* "I was a nightmare. I had no idea how to play, and when I first did fitness with the national team, I thought I'd die." In 1991, at age 19, she took a year's sabbatical to

play as the youngest player on the U.S. National Team that won the FIFA Women's World Cup.

After graduating from high school, Hamm enrolled at the University of North Carolina, where the coach was Anson Dorrance. With that team, the North Carolina Tar Heels, she won four NCAA championships in 1989, 1990, 1992, and 1993 (taking 1991 off to play with the U.S. National Team). She was named to the NCAA All-Tournament Team in 1989 and 1990, and led the country in scoring at the college level in 1990, 1992, and 1993. She was the Atlantic Coast Conference (ACC) Player of the Year in 1990, 1992, and 1993. In her years with the University of North Carolina, she was a three-time collegiate All-American. She was also the winner of the prestigious Hermann Award for the best female college soccer player and the Missouri Athletic Club Award in 1992 and 1993. She left her collegiate soccer career as the highest scorer, with 103 goals, 72 assists, and 278 points, in 1993. In 1994, shortly after her graduation, the University of North Carolina retired her number, 14.

In 1994 she earned a degree in political science from the University of North Carolina. In another milestone in her personal life that year, she married Christian Corey, an officer in the Marines.

Rose to Fame

Hamm continued to be acclaimed after her collegiate career. She was named U.S. Soccer's Female Athlete of the Year from 1994 through 1998. She was the first person to receive the honor more than twice, and only the second person to receive it two years in a row. In 1995 she led the U.S. team to an overall record of 19-2-2, netting 19 goals and 18 assists. She helped lead them to a Bronze medal in the Women's World Cup.

In 1996, the first year that women's soccer was an Olympic sport, she reached international fame when she led the U.S. Women's soccer team to an Olympic gold medal, playing in front of more than 78,000 fans and a national television audience. The team beat China 2-1. This was the first time that women's soccer had taken a central role on an international stage.

Hamm continued to dominate on a national and international level. In 1997 she won the U.S. Women's Cup MVP for the second time (the first time was in 1995). She was also the Women's Sports Foundation Team Athlete of the Year. She was a nominee and finalist for the U.S. Olympic Committee's Sportswoman of the Year in both 1996 and 1997. She was the Amateur Athletic Foundation's World Trophy recipient in 1998. She was a member of the gold medal-winning team at the Goodwill Games, and in 1998 became the first U.S. player to score 100 goals. She was named Female Athlete of the Year by cable television sports network ESPN.

Enjoyed Success On and Off the Field

Hamm had a banner year in 1999. Professionally, she raised the profile of American women's soccer with the U.S. Women's Soccer Team at the FIFA World Cup. Playing against China in front of a sold-out Rose Bowl and a television audience of 40 million, she and her teammates won the World Cup. It's a game that has gone down in history: In 120 minutes of scoreless play, with two overtimes, Brandi Chastain scored a goal with a single penalty kick, winning the game. The team became role models for girls across the country, not only for their prowess on the field but also for their personal and professional successes. All of the women on the team either had college degrees or were full-time students. Many were married and had children. Hamm and her teammates were named the Associated Press's Female Athletes of the Year.

Beyond that victory, Hamm met several other professional goals. She was a part of the team that won the U.S. Women's Cup tournament in Louisville, Kentucky. She also became the all-time leading scorer in international soccer. She surpassed Elisabetta Vignotto, a retired Italian soccer star, when she scored her 108th goal on May 22, 1999. She would, in fact, become the world's leading goal scorer in international competition, male or female.

In 1999 Hamm repeated her performance as ESPN's Espy winner of the Female Athlete of the Year award, as well as Soccer Player of the Year. In addition, Hamm had several personal successes. The first was the publication of her autobiography, *Go for the Goal: A Champion's Guide to Winning in Soccer and Life,* co-authored by Aaron Heifetz; the book was part autobiography, part self-help, and part soccer instruction. That year, Nike named a building after Hamm.

Created the Mia Hamm Foundation

The year 1999 also marked a personal milestone for Hamm when she created the Mia Hamm Foundation. Mia's success as a soccer star and the influence of her brother Garrett were the inspiration for the foundation. In 1975 Garrett contracted a rare blood disease called aplastic anemia. He died of the disease in 1997. When Mia started the foundation it had a two-fold goal: to raise funds to research bone marrow diseases and to assist young female athletes.

By 1999 Mia Hamm had become a hot commodity. She did commercials for Pert Shampoo, AT&T, Power Bars, Nike, Sportmart, and Pepsi. Probably her most memorable commercial was with Michael Jordon, a basketball superstar, for the sports drink Gatorade. In it, she consistently beat Jordan at sports such as soccer, basketball, fencing, and judo while the song "Anything You Can Do, I Can Do Better" played in the background. She helped create a special edition Barbie doll that was a soccer player.

In 1996, after the Olympics, she appeared on the television show *Late Night with David Letterman*. In 1997 she was named one of the 50 most beautiful people in *People* magazine. In 1998 a *Sports Business Daily* survey found her to be the most marketable female endorser in America.

Helped Found Women's United Soccer Association

Hamm's success did not stop after 1999. She was a part of the U.S. Women's Soccer Team that won the Silver Medal at the 2000 Olympics. In 2001 she became a founding member of WUSA, or Women's United Soccer Association, and a member of the Washington Freedom franchise. She won another gold medal with her performance as a part of the U.S. Women's Soccer Team in the 2004 Olympics. She participated in a ten-game "Fan Celebration Tour," retiring shortly thereafter. At her final game, she assisted on two goals in an exhibition win against Mexico in Carson, California. By that time she had scored more goals than any other player in women's soccer history, at 158 goals.

Some final professional goals that she reached included being named again as Best Soccer Player at the Espy Awards in 2005. She was inducted into the Texas Sports Hall of Fame on March 11, 2008. She also wrote a children's book, *Winners Never Quit.*

Exemplified Title IX Ideal

Hamm's name has been used on many occasions as an example of the success of Title IX. Signed into law by Richard Nixon in 1972, the year that Hamm was born, Title IX gave full equality to women in intercollegiate athletics. Because of this, female athletes like Hamm were better able to become role models to young women. Her national team coach, Tony DiCicco, told Longman, "She's not only a soccer icon, but she's an icon for women's athletics. That's a huge responsibility." Many have seen her that way, and in her work as a teacher at clinics and as a speaker, she has helped to support women's athletics across the country.

In 2003 she married her second husband, then-Boston Red Sox shortshop Nomar Garciaparra, after divorcing Corey in 2001. They have a set of twins.

Books

American Decades 1990-1999, edited by Tandy McConnell, Gale Group, 2001.

Contemporary Heroes and Heroines, Book IV, Gale Group, 2000.

Great Women in Sports, Visible Ink Press, 1996.

Hamm, Mia, with Aaron Heifetz, *Go for the Goal: A Champion's Guide to Winning in Soccer and Life,* HarperCollins, 1999.

Hamm, Mia, *Winners Never Quit,* Illustrated by Carol Thompson, HarperCollins, 2004.

Notable Sports Figures, Gale, 2004.

Scribner Encyclopedia of American Lives Thematic Series: Sports Figures, edited by Kenneth T. Jackson, Charles Scribner's Sons, 2003.

Sports Stars, U*X*L, 1996.

Periodicals

New York Times, June 11, 1999.

Sports Illustrated, December 14, 1992.

Online

"About Mia," *Mia Foundation,* http://www.miafoundaiton.org/aboutmia.asp (September 12, 2009). □

Caroline Harrison

American First Lady Caroline Lavinia Scott Harrison (1832–1892) is best remembered today for her efforts to renovate, preserve, and modernize the White House during the administration of her husband, United States President Benjamin Harrison. Although the First Lady failed to gain needed funding for her planned physical expansion of the structure, she oversaw such efforts as installing electric lighting and modern plumbing. An educated woman and skilled political hostess, Harrison was also active in social and charitable work and became the inaugural President-General of the National Society of the Daughters of the American Revolution in 1890. Tuberculosis cut short her varied activities in 1892, leaving her daughter to serve as official White House hostess for the waning months of the Harrison Administration.

Born Caroline Lavinia Scott on October 1, 1832, in the small town of Oxford, Ohio, Harrison was the second daughter of professor and Presbyterian minister John Witherspoon Scott and his wife, Mary Potts (Neal) Scott. Growing up, Harrison—nicknamed "Carrie"—received an excellent education, showing an

early interest in literature, music, and painting. The Scott family, which included daughters Mary and Elizabeth and sons John and Henry in addition to the future First Lady, enjoyed a comfortable if relatively modest standard of living thanks to the family patriarch's teaching positions, first at Oxford's Miami University and later at nearby Cincinnati, Ohio's Farmers' College. Through this latter position, the Scott family came to know a student at the college named Benjamin Harrison. Soon, he developed a great affection for the family's vivacious daughter, even transferring to Miami University after the Scotts returned to Oxford, where John Witherspoon Scott founded the Oxford Female Institute. In 1852, the young couple became engaged; Benjamin Harrison then went back to Cincinnati to study law, while his fiancée continued her academic studies in Oxford and began teaching piano at her father's school. On October 20, 1853, the two were wed by John Witherspoon Scott.

Rose to Prominence in Midwest

After their marriage, the newlyweds lived briefly at the Harrison family home in North Bend, Ohio—a small town west of Cincinnati on the Ohio River—before settling in Indianapolis, Indiana, where Benjamin Harrison planned to practice law. The young bride spent much of her time at her family's home in Oxford, however, first to give birth to her son Russell on August 12, 1854, and then to recuperate from a series of illnesses. The Harrison family faced considerable financial hardship until 1855, when Benjamin Harrison

formed a partnership with more experienced attorney and politician William Wallace. As her husband's practice flourished, Harrison was able to focus her energies on domestic matters and to participating in the congregation of the city's First Presbyterian Church. She taught Sunday school and took part in the church choir, continuing her involvement with social causes even after the birth of the second Harrison child, daughter Mary, on April 3, 1858.

Meanwhile, Republican Benjamin Harrison began his political career with election as city attorney in 1857. Three years later, he won the office of reporter of the state supreme court—a position that did not prevent him from taking part in the Civil War as a colonel in the Union Army beginning in 1862. Left to manage the household and care for two children alone, Harrison nevertheless found time to work with charitable organizations supporting the war effort and even to occasionally visit her husband in the field. After the close of the conflict in 1865, Benjamin Harrison returned to take up his law practice in Indianapolis, and the family settled into a comfortable upper-middle-class existence with Harrison taking an active role in the management of her household and children. By 1875, the family had reached sufficient financial comfort to construct a nine-bedroom residence in Indianapolis, at which the matron hosted numerous social and political parties, culminating in a visit by President Rutherford B. Hayes and First Lady Lucy Ware Webb Hayes in 1879.

A failed 1876 bid for the Indiana governorship did not stifle Benjamin Harrison's political ambitions, and in 1880, he won election to the U.S. Senate. The Indiana-based family soon took up part-time residence in Washington, D.C. There, Harrison continued her life much as she had done in Indianapolis, holding what social events the family's smaller city apartments allowed and joining the board of lady managers for the capital's Garfield Hospital. Illness often encroached on Harrison's daily life, however, and she welcomed the chance to leave the city during the lengthy Congressional recesses common in the era.

Although Benjamin Harrison lost his bid for re-election to the Senate in 1886, he remained a prominent Republican political figure and was named the party's nominee for the 1888 presidential election. Conducting a "front-porch" campaign, the candidate spent much of the campaign season at home in Indianapolis, where he and his wife met with supporters and political figures on a daily basis. Harrison's experience as a political hostess proved vital as the weeks wore on, and she accepted the inevitable damage to her home and belongings and increased press attention on her family with equanimity. The Harrisons' welcoming campaign efforts came to fruition when Benjamin Harrison was elected to the presidency through the auspices of the Electoral College despite losing the popular vote.

Updated the White House

Following Harrison's inauguration in March of 1889, the new President and his First Lady—who wore, with much fanfare, an inaugural dress designed and produced exclusively in the United States as a reflection of her husband's support for domestic manufacturing—settled into a White House that was greatly scarred by the passage of time. Constructed at the beginning of the nineteenth century, the imposing edifice had seen little renovation during its lifetime. Harrison, who brought her daughter's family and other relatives to live in the White House, found the quarters cramped and outmoded in comparison to her stately Indianapolis home. With eleven people sharing just five bedrooms and one bathroom, perhaps unsurprisingly Harrison turned her influence to promoting a marked expansion of the presidential residence. Citing the recent additions to the Capitol building, the First Lady began lobbying for Congress to fund the construction of two new wings to the White House. Architect Fred David Owen presented plans for a new west wing containing administrative offices and an east wing holding an art gallery linked by an interior botanical garden in what would have been a significant reimagining of the original structure's architectural design at a cost of the hefty sum of nearly one million dollars.

Congress refused to approve these plans, however, but did allocate a considerable sum to renovation and upkeep for the White House. Harrison set to work on the structure, overseeing everything from a thorough cleaning—history recounts her horror at the rats in the White House basement—to the installation of electric lighting, new private bathrooms, and freshly redecorated public rooms. She evaluated stored furniture and selected pieces for preservation, and presided over the installation of the first White House Christmas tree in 1889. Additionally, the First Lady, who had won prizes for her artwork at expositions in Indiana, took a particular interest in the White House formal dinnerware. Importing her previous watercolor instructor Paul Putzki from Indiana, Harrison designed a new presidential china pattern. In the process of doing so, she unearthed pieces from earlier White House residents that she had repaired and cleaned. These settings became the heart of the White House China Collection, a popular part of the White House Museum to this day. Although some contemporaries dismissed her efforts as overly domestic and Harrison herself as provincial, the First Lady soldiered on and ultimately became a well-respected national figure.

Alongside her work at the White House, Harrison continued her charitable and social efforts in the capital, mounting French classes and lending her influence to a fundraising drive for Johns Hopkins School, contingent on that institution's acceptance of women—a sign of the growing feminist movement in the country. Equally, a national resurgence of interest in American history contributed to the foundation of the Daughters of the American Revolution (DAR), a women's organization dedicated to promoting patriotic preservation and education. Harrison agreed to become the organization's first President-General, and took an active role in the management of the nascent group. According to historian Carl Sferrazza Anthony in *First Ladies: The Saga of the Presidents' Wives and Their Power, 1789–1961*, "by inviting the group to meet in the [White House] Blue Room, guiding the election of officers to women with political connections, listening to their objectives, and supporting 'every move that had political implications,' the First Lady helped the DAR immediately

establish credibility." Long after Harrison's death, the DAR continued to honor her memory, using her favorite orchid as an organizational symbol.

Death Led to Scandal

Long plagued by sporadic illness, Harrison's final decline in health began in the spring of 1892 when she was diagnosed with the respiratory disease tuberculosis. The First Lady ventured to the Adirondack Mountains in upstate New York in the hopes of easing the disease, but she steadily worsened. In September of 1892, she returned to the White House, where she died from her illness on October 25. Soon after a funeral service in the nation's capital, Harrison was interred at Crown Hill Cemetery in Indianapolis, Indiana. The following month, a reportedly devastated Benjamin Harrison lost the presidential election when Democrat Grover Cleveland won a second nonconsecutive term. Upon Harrison's death, the *New York Times* eulogized her memory, proclaiming that "her personality was exceedingly sweet and winning, her domestic life serene, happy, and useful, and the circumstances of her last illness were exceedingly sad. Without the least apparent effort to be widely known she made a strong impression on the public mind…and the news of her death will be received with great sorrow throughout the land."

These proclamations may have come too soon, however, for domestic scandal haunted Benjamin Harrison shortly after his wife's death. The erstwhile president remarried in 1896 to one of his former wife's nieces, Mary Scott Lord Dimmick, who had worked for the First Lady as secretary when she had resided in the White House. Rumors regarding a possible relationship between the then-President and Dimmick while the First Lady had still lived began to fly, and Harrison's two elder children refused to accept the second marriage. Conflicting stories of the domestic happiness of the Harrisons during the latter years of their marriage circulated widely, suggesting alternately that Benjamin Harrison had loved his wife dearly and was simply seeking companionship in his advancing age and that he had an inappropriate relationship with his second wife before his first had passed away. Writing in *American First Ladies: Their Lives and Their Legacy*, Charles W. Calhoun noted that "if…the stories of domestic turmoil in the Harrison White House are true, they bespeak a deep suffering on Caroline Harrison's part that simply throws into higher relief her achievements as First Lady." Indeed, it is largely for these accomplishments that Harrison remains known today. Her legacy can be readily seen in the physical aspect of the modern White House, an edifice that evolved greatly under the former First Lady's watch.

Books

Anthony, Carl Sferrazza, *First Ladies: The Saga of the Presidents' Wives and Their Power, 1789–1961*, William Morrow, 1990.

Gould, Lewis L., ed., *American First Ladies: Their Lives and Their Legacy*, 2nd ed., Routledge, 2001.

Watson, Robert P., ed., *American First Ladies*, Salem Press, 2002.

Periodicals

New York Times, October 25, 1892.

Online

"Carolina Lavinia Scott Harrison," The White House, http://
www.whitehouse.gov/about/first-ladies/carolineharrison
(January 2, 2010). □

Ernie Harwell

The American broadcaster Ernie Harwell (1918–2010), over a career in baseball lasting more than 75 years, became an icon of the Detroit Tigers franchise and a legendary figure in the world of sports radio.

arwell grew up reading baseball publications from near the dawn of the modern game, and his career stretched into the era of digital broadcasting and the Internet. He had a style that was distinctive in its precision and economy, and, like other famous broadcasters, he repeated favorite expressions that became his trademarks. Beyond these characteristics, which he shared with other famous broadcasters, Ernie Harwell was loved for his personality, defined by an unassuming warmth and humor that made friends of all who encountered him. "Ernie Harwell is arguably the best who ever announced, right there with anyone who ever did baseball games," former Baltimore Orioles player Brooks Robinson told National Public Radio. "And he's a warm, wonderful gentleman. He never has changed. And his voice has never changed."

Overcame Speech Impediment

The youngest of three brothers, William Earnest Harwell was born in Washington, Georgia on January 25, 1918. His father operated a furniture store and a funeral home—a combination that made sense in the small Georgia town because, as Harwell pointed out to Mel Antonen of *USA Today,* "furniture people make coffins." Harwell liked baseball from the start and immersed himself in season guides dating back as far as 1905—"I read that stuff like it was fiction," he told King Kaufman of *Salon.* As a child he suffered from a speech impediment that made him confuse the letters F and S, but his family, although not well-off, sent him to a speech teacher whose treatment involved repeated readings of the Sam Walter Foss poem "The House by the Side of the Road." The phrase found its way into Harwell's usual on-air description of a batter called out on strikes: "He stood there like the house by the side of the road."

When Harwell was 16, he wrote to the magazine *Sporting News* offering his services as Atlanta correspondent and signing his name W. Earnest Harwell to make himself appear older. He got the job. In his senior year he won a national high school literary competition called

Quill and Scroll, taking home a Royal typewriter as a prize. He was the first Southerner to win the contest. Harwell attended prestigious Emory University in Atlanta, holding down a job on the side as a copy editor at the *Atlanta Constitution.* "That's the best training I ever got as a writer, looking at other people's stories, seeing what worked and what didn't," he told Kaufman.

After graduating from Emory, Harwell auditioned for and was given his first job in broadcasting, covering games of the minor-league Atlanta Crackers for Atlanta radio station WSB. Sometimes, instead of live broadcasts, this involved recounting a game based on results found in wire service reports, and Harwell became expert at creating the feeling that the listener was present at the game by including just the right amount of detail. In 1941 Harwell married Lulu Tankersley, beginning an affectionate partnership that would last for the rest of his life. They raised four children. Harwell joined the Marine Corps during World War II and served as a correspondent for the armed services magazine *Leatherneck.* He covered the Japanese surrender at Wake Island. After returning to the U.S. Harwell resumed his broadcasting career in Atlanta.

Harwell made the jump to the major leagues in 1948, when he was recruited by Brooklyn Dodgers president Branch Rickey as a possible replacement for the ailing voice of the Dodgers, Red Barber. The Atlanta team's owner refused to sign the contract unless a minor-league player from the Dodgers' Montreal farm team, catcher Cliff

Dapper, was added to the deal in return, and Harwell became the only broadcaster ever directly involved in a major-league trade. Harwell worked under Barber in Brooklyn during second baseman Jackie Robinson's second season there, and Lulu Harwell and Robinson's wife, Rachel, became friends. In 1950 Harwell moved to the New York Giants, where, in October of 1951, he covered the so-called Shot Heart Round the World, Bobby Thompson's pennant-winning home run on the first nationally televised sports playoff series. In 1954 he moved to the Baltimore Orioles.

Hired by Tigers

In 1960 Harwell was hired by the Detroit Tigers after being recommended for the job by former third baseman George Kell, who had moved from the Baltimore broadcast booth to Detroit a few years earlier. With only a few interruptions, Harwell would be a reliable fixture of Detroit radio in the spring and summer until 2002, broadcasting from "the great voice of the Great Lakes," clear-channel radio station WJR. While employed by the Tigers, Harwell missed only two games, one for his brother's funeral in 1968, and the other when he was inducted into the National Sportscasters and Sportswriters Association Hall of Fame in 1989.

When it came to colorful turns of phrase, Harwell could match any of his contemporaries from the golden age of sports radio. Kaufman summarized some of the "Ernieisms" that became familiar to Detroit sports fans: a team with men on base had "more runners than a sled factory," while an umpire might be "the ol' maître d' from Tennessee." A batter called out on strikes, Harwell said, was "called out for excessive window shopping," and a team that executed a double play got "two for the price of one." Most familiar of all was the forceful "Looong gone!" with which Harwell greeted a Tiger home run.

As Harwell outlasted most of his contemporaries (except for Dodgers broadcaster Vin Scully, a protegé whose skills he insisted were greater than his own), his microphone artistry began to seem rarer and more valuable. "Ernie Harwell still sounds like old radio," noted Kaufman. "He projects his voice, rather than caressing the microphone with it, the way younger announcers do. His style is conversational, sure, but he's not just talking. He's broadcasting." The kind of bond Harwell had with Detroit fans, too, became rarer, not only because baseball could be viewed on television or the Internet, but also simply because distinctive voices were rarer, and broadcasters who took the time to sign autographs and cultivate one-to-one relationships were no longer the norm.

Fired, Then Rehired

For these reasons, Tiger fans were shocked when, in 1990, Harwell was asked to retire after the 1991 season. The move, a public-relations disaster for the club, was variously blamed on team president and former University of Michigan head football coach Bo Schembechler and owner Thomas Monaghan, but no Tiger executive ever fully owned up to it. Harwell did not accede to the club's demands that he portray the firing as a retirement, and he remained in the game in 1992 with stints on the CBS radio network and as a California Angels broadcaster. Harwell was rehired in 1992 by the Tigers' new owner, Mike Ilitch, owner of the Little Caesars pizza chain. Between 1994 and 1998 Harwell appeared in Tigers television broadcasts, but he returned to the radio in 1999.

Harwell, who became a born-again Christian at a Billy Graham Crusade in 1961 but rarely proselytized or discussed faith in anything other than general terms in public, wrote eight books, beginning with 1985's *Tuned to Baseball*. Titles such as *Ernie Harwell's Diamond Gems* (1993) and *Stories from My Life in Baseball* (2001) drew on his encyclopedic knowledge of the game; listeners during his later years were amazed at his ability to recall even obscure statistics from decades before. Harwell's most recent title as of 2010 was *Breaking 90*, issued just in advance of his 90th birthday. He was inducted into the Baseball Hall of Fame in 1981 and the Radio Hall of Fame in 2002, among many other awards.

In 2002 Harwell retired of his own accord, quipping (according to Kaufman) that he did not want to hear anyone say "I heard your last show, and it should have been." At the end of his last broadcast (quoted by Antonen) he thanked listeners for "taking me to the cottage up north, to the beach, the picnic, your workplace and your backyard. Thank you for sneaking your transistor under the pillow as you grew up loving the Tigers. God has a new adventure for me." The Tigers organization commemorated his tenure with a statue of Harwell holding a microphone near the entrance of its newly built stadium, Comerica Park. Harwell continued to write a regular baseball column for the *Detroit Free Press* even after his diagnosis with inoperable bile duct cancer in the autumn of 2009. Harwell told Scott Michaux of Georgia's *Augusta Chronicle* that news of his illness was "plastered all over the papers here. It's been a whole lot of attention I don't really deserve." Harwell died of his illness on May 4, 2010, having continued writing his newspaper column until the end.

Books

Harwell, Ernie, *My 60 Years in Baseball,* Triumph, 2002.

Notable Sports Figures, Gale, 2004.

Periodicals

Augusta Chronicle (Augusta, GA), September 6, 2009.

USA Today, September 23, 2009.

Online

Kaufman, King, "Baseball Greetings, Ernie Harwell," *Salon,* August 27, 2002, http://www.salon.com/people/feature/2002/08/27/harwell (February 20, 2010).

"Ernie Harwell," *Museum of Broadcast Communications,* http://www.museum.tv/rhofsection.php?page=214 (February 20, 2010).

"Ernie Harwell to Receive Lifetime Achievement Award in May," *Detroit Free Press,* February 11, 2010, http://www.freep.com/article/20100211/BLOG18/100211046/Ernie-Harwell-to-receive-lifetime-achievement-award-in-May (February 20, 2010).

Harwell, Ernie, "This Column the Result of Mr. Ego's Victory over Mr. Lazybones," *Detroit Free Press,* January 24, 2010, http://freep.com/article/20100124/SPORTS02/1240431/1322/This-column-the-result-of-Mr.-Egos-victory-over-Mr.-Lazybones (February 20, 2010). □

Gladys Heldman

Fed up with the unequal pay structure that rewarded male tennis champions with more money than their female counterparts, Jewish American tennis activist Gladys Heldman (1922-2003) organized the first all-women's tennis circuit in 1970, which became known as the Virginia Slims. Heldman also gained notoriety as the founder and publisher of *World Tennis* magazine, which became the literary voice of the game. Over the course of her lifetime, Heldman used her influence to become one of the world's leading ambassadors for the sport.

Gladys Medalie Heldman was born May 13, 1922, in New York City. Heldman's mother, Carrie Medalie, was a Latin and Greek scholar. Her attorney father, George Medalie, served as a judge on the New York Court of Appeals, the highest court in the state of New York. Heldman attended Stanford University in California and graduated in 1942, earning Phi Beta Kappa honors for her academic achievement. The day after she graduated, she married Julius Heldman, a 1936 U.S. junior (18 and under) tennis champion with a doctorate in chemistry.

Raised as Scholar, Not Athlete

While Julius Heldman enjoyed tennis, he did not desire a professional career in the sport. After finishing his graduate degree at Stanford, he took a job teaching chemistry at the University of California at Berkeley. Heldman enrolled at Berkeley, too, and earned a master's degree in medieval history. She was going to work on her doctorate but found a job as an instructor at the Williams Institute in Berkeley and never went back to school. The Heldmans left Berkeley when Julius Heldman was selected to work on the Manhattan Project—a secret World War II military assignment aimed at producing the first atomic bomb. Julius Heldman was sent to a research lab in Oak Ridge, Tennessee, where uranium ore was processed. After the war ended, the Heldmans left Tennessee and returned to Berkeley.

Discovered Tennis After Marriage

Gladys Heldman did not grow up playing sports and never held a tennis racquet until she married Julius Heldman. After moving back to Berkeley, Heldman started playing tennis in earnest. Speaking to *Sports Illustrated,* Heldman recalled that time. "Those were the days when I just couldn't wait to go to bed so it would be time to get up again and play tennis. I played eight or nine sets a day." Sometimes, Heldman even competed in two separate tournaments on the same day, each located in a different city. She drove all around the San Francisco Bay area competing in tournaments, playing everything from singles and doubles to mixed. As an amateur, Heldman collected some 80 tennis trophies.

Meanwhile, Julius Heldman left teaching to work at Shell Oil Co. and in 1949 was sent to Houston. By this time the Heldmans had two daughters, Julie and Carrie. The Heldmans settled just outside of Houston in Genoa. They bought a small farm, where they boarded horses, raised turkeys and kept a pig. Heldman continued to work on her game and her daughters began playing, too. In 1951 and '52, Heldman was ranked the No. 1 female amateur in Texas. Heldman made her first—and only—appearance at Wimbledon in 1954, but was eliminated quickly. She made four appearances at the U.S. National Championships, now the U.S. Open. She was also busy with men's amateur tennis, organizing the teams her husband competed with. Despite the rigors of a career as a petroleum chemist, Julius Heldman kept up his game and won a U.S. Senior indoor championship in the 1960s.

As Heldman's involvement and enthusiasm for tennis flourished, she came up with the idea to produce a publication to inform area tennis fans about what was going on. She dubbed her publication the *Houston Tennis News.* The first several editions were merely a single mimeographed sheet. Eventually, the publication grew into four pages of printed materials. By 1951 she had renamed her tennis rag the *Round-Up,* which matured into 16 pages of colorful commentary written by tennis players. The *Round-Up* featured regular commentary from U.S. men's doubles partners Gardnar Mulloy and Billy Talbert. The duo won the U.S. National Championships doubles titles in 1942, '45, '46 and '48. Heldman produced the publication on her own. She served as writer, editor, publisher and mailer of copies. At first, Heldman offered the publication free of charge but later started selling it. In 1953 she killed the *Round-Up* when Mulloy suggested they do a glossy magazine instead.

Founded *World Tennis* Magazine

The first issue of *World Tennis* magazine came out in the spring of 1953. Mulloy took care of the ads while Heldman did the writing. Initially, they lost thousands of dollars because they had trouble attracting big advertisers to offset their costs, and there were only about 200 subscribers. After three years Mulloy wanted to quit but Heldman refused to back down. *World Tennis* started in Houston but moved to New York City when Julius Heldman was transferred again by Shell.

In New York, Heldman began publishing from her mother's apartment, then moved to a tiny upstairs office above a small, smelly shop that sold ice and kerosene. In those early days, Heldman worked relentlessly to keep the magazine afloat, serving as editor-in-chief, publisher and writer. Her days started at 6 a.m. and she often worked late into the night and on weekends. She also served as the art director, the layout consultant and the circulation manager. When Heldman started the publication, tennis received little, if any, coverage from the news media. *World Tennis* was the first magazine dedicated entirely to the sport. The magazine's friendly tone provided readers with an in-depth look at the game and also contained a comprehensive results section reporting on recent events.

As the publisher, Heldman quickly became an ambassador for the game. She was known to let players bunk at her New York home if they had trouble affording accommodations. In 1959, Heldman organized the U.S. National Indoor Championships after the United States Lawn Tennis Association (USLTA) canceled the event because it had become such a money-loser. Under Heldman's direction, the competition turned a profit. In 1962 Heldman brought more than 80 female players from overseas to participate in the U.S. Open. To fund the ordeal, Heldman lined up sponsors and found accommodations.

By the mid-1960s, the magazine had lured readers from around the globe. Heldman received letters from tennis buffs in Indonesia, Hungary, Czechoslovakia and the Soviet Union begging for subscriptions. These readers offered to send gifts if Heldman would send them the magazine. Laws at the time forbade money from leaving those countries. Heldman, of course, accepted this arrangement. Tennis champ Martina Navratilova read the magazine while growing up in communist Czechoslovakia. She credited *World Tennis* with keeping her inspired and informed about the sport. Eventually, Heldman's hard work began to pay off. By 1964, *World Tennis* boasted some 43,000 readers. When Heldman sold the magazine to CBS Publications in 1972, circulation stood at 125,000. The magazine later folded in 1991.

Led Drive to Level Playing Court

The more Heldman became entrenched in the tennis world, the more she was bothered by the inequity women faced. At pro-sanctioned tennis tournaments, it was common practice for the male champion to win a much larger purse than the female champ. In 1970, the Pacific Southwest championships in Los Angeles offered a $12,500 prize for the male winner and a $1,500 prize for the female winner.

In an act of defiance, Heldman encouraged a group of nine disgruntled female players to boycott the Pacific Southwest tour stop and instead play in a renegade, women-only tournament in Houston, which Heldman organized. She put up her own money for the event and also persuaded Phillip Morris CEO Joe Cullman to join as a sponsor. Phillip Morris was the tobacco company that produced Virginia Slims, a cigarette aimed at women. Heldman convinced Cullman it would be a great advertising move. The inaugural Virginia Slims tournament took place in late 1970 in Texas. The women who played in the tournament became known as the "Houston Nine" and included Billie Jean King, Rosie Casals, Nancy Richey, and Heldman's own daughter, Julie Heldman. Of the Heldman girls, Julie Heldman was the standout tennis star. She reached a world ranking of No. 5 in 1969; that year she won the Italian Open.

Following the successful tournament, which was won by Casals, Phillip Morris sponsored a series of professional women's tennis events in 1971. Known as the Virginia Slims, it was the first female-only tennis circuit. The players who participated were suspended by the USLTA, but they did not really care. Over the course of 1971, the women on the Virginia Slims circuit staged tournaments in seven cities. At each stop, they played their hearts out, hoping to bring greater recognition to the sport and to its female athletes.

While Heldman is often honored for starting up the women's pro circuit, she credited the players for turning the Virginia Slims tour into a winner. Speaking about the success of the tour to the *New York Times* in 1995, Heldman put it this way: "The reason it worked was because the women gave so much of themselves. ... Billie Jean was incredible, always available for a clinic, a pro-am, an interview. She had the most to give, and she gave it. But everyone gave. The women who lost in early rounds would fly to the next city to beat the publicity drums for the upcoming tournament." While the players used the tennis court to stump for change, Heldman used the pages of her magazine as a forum to discuss the inequalities.

After a three-year power struggle, the USLTA and the Virginia Slims players reached a reconciliation. The breakaway players had done their job creating publicity the USLTA could not ignore. The result: prize monies were evened out between the sexes. By promoting themselves on the circuit, the female tennis stars became as well-known as their male counterparts. There was no denying that the female players could deliver the fans. By 1980, there was more than $7 million of prize money available to female players through 47 events worldwide. The Virginia Slims circuit eventually evolved into the WTA (Women's Tennis Association) Tour, later featuring such U.S. stars as Serena and Venus Williams and Jennifer Capriati, as well as Russia's Nadia Petrova.

Remembered as "Mother" of Tennis

In the early 1980s, the Heldmans retired and moved to Santa Fe, New Mexico. Gladys Heldman continued to work on her game up until the end of her life. The Heldmans' estate included an indoor tennis court in an adobe outbuilding. "She loved the sport more than anybody I have ever seen," Heldman's coach, Claudia Monteiro, told the *Santa Fe New Mexican* shortly after Heldman's death. Monteiro noted that Heldman's tennis "improved enormously" during her 70s. Despite all that she accomplished, Heldman always lamented that she never had a decent overhead.

Heldman died June 22, 2003, at her Santa Fe home from a self-inflicted gunshot wound. She had been in ill health for some time. After her death, many players paid tribute to Heldman, who was sometimes called the "mother" of the modern game of tennis. According to the *Boston Globe*, King released this statement in remembrance of Heldman the week she died: "Without Gladys, there wouldn't be women's professional tennis as we know it. She was a passionate advocate, and driving force behind the start of the Virginia Slims Tour, and helped change the face of women's sports."

Periodicals

Boston Globe, June 27, 2003.

Gazette (Montreal, Quebec), June 27, 2003.

Globe and Mail (Canada), August 20, 1991.

New York Times, August 31, 1958; March 26, 1961; November 17, 1995; June 25, 2003.

Santa Fe New Mexican, June 24, 2003.

Sports Illustrated, June 22, 1964.

Online

"Gladys Medalie Heldman," International Tennis Hall of Fame, http://www.tennisfame.com/famer.aspx?pgID=867&hof_id=143 (December 24, 2009).

"The Mother of Tennis," *Stanford Magazine,* http://www.stanfordalumni.org/news/magazine/2003/novdec/classnotes/heldman.html (December 24, 2009). □

Albert Hofmann

Swiss chemist Albert Hofmann (1906–2008) earned a place in counterculture history as the creator of LSD, a powerful hallucinogenic that became a popular recreational drug in the 1960s and 1970s. Hofmann was a respected pharmaceutical scientist who was perplexed by the odd sensations he experienced when he accidentally came into contact with the substance in his lab one day in 1943. "LSD wanted to tell me something," he said, on the occasion of a symposium honoring him on his hundredth birthday in 2006, according to Wired.com. "It gave me an inner joy, an open mindedness, a gratefulness, open eyes and an internal sensitivity for the miracles of creation."

Hofmann was born on January 11, 1906, in Baden, Switzerland, where his father was a toolmaker. Baden was located in a picturesque mountain area and Hofmann loved exploring the forests near his home as a child; he recalled that even as a youngster he had revelatory experiences while marveling at the natural world's seemingly perfectly managed ecosystem. These experiences fueled his interest in science, and with financial support provided by a friend of the family he entered the University of Zurich at the age of 20. Four years later, he completed his doctoral thesis in chemistry after conducting studies on vineyard snails and a carbohydrate they produce called chitin.

Experimented with Ergot

Hofmann was already working at Sandoz Laboratories by the time he appended the title "Dr." to his name when he earned his Ph.D. in 1930. Sandoz was one of several pharmaceutical companies based in Basel, Switzerland, that had become major international players in the previous century. The first profitable product sold by Sandoz was phenazone, a fever reducer that was widely used before the invention of aspirin, and in the 1920s the company began introducing drug compounds derived from ergot, a grain fungus. Gynergen, a headache remedy, was one of these products.

It was to this project that Hofmann was assigned as a research chemist. Gynergen, which worked by constricting blood vessels, was effective, but scientists also knew that the body seemed to be able to store ergot to a level of toxicity, and numbness, gangrene, and blindness could result. In medieval Europe, grain supplies sometimes became infected with ergot, and entire communities experienced perplexing and often fatal symptoms. The limbs tingled, then became gangrenous; in the final stages sufferers experienced convulsions and hallucinations. Pregnant animals who became infected from ingesting tainted grain often miscarried. The first known reports of such outbreaks came from a northern German town called Xanten in the

830s. Around 945, there was a similar episode near Paris of what became known as "St. Anthony's Fire."

Interest in ergot and its effects was carried into the modern era by midwives, who sometimes used minute doses to speed childbirth. Chemists in the United States had already isolated the active ingredient as lysergic acid, and in the 1930s Hofmann worked on experiments to fuse lysergic acid with other compounds. Lysergic acid itself was highly unstable; in other words, its effects could be variable, which made it a poor choice for a pharmaceutical building block. In November of 1938, Hofmann finally created a more stable synthetic version, giving it the German name "lyserg-saure-diathylamid-25," or LSD. *Säure* is the German term for "acid," and is etymologically linked to the English term "sour." The "25" designation came from the fact that it was the 25th compound that Hofmann had made for this particular Sandoz project.

Ingested LSD Accidentally

Hofmann never did anything with that original LSD-25, and the ergot project was wrapped up. In 1943, however, he reconsidered it when searching for botanically based products that had stimulant effects on mammalian respiratory and circulatory systems. It was a Friday afternoon, April 16, 1943, and Hofmann began to feel lightheaded while working in the lab, and then an interior window opened up that he "recognized . . . as the same experience I had had as a child," he told *New York Times* journalist Craig S. Smith, citing the epiphany-like experience in the forest. "I didn't know what caused it, but I knew that it was important."

Hofmann originally thought that it was the fumes from LSD that had caused the sensation, but he realized that he had handled the substance with his fingers, then inadvertently rubbed his eye before the sensations began. He left the lab and rode home on his bicycle, because it was wartime and vehicles and gasoline were scarce. "At home I lay down and sank into a not unpleasant intoxicated-like condition, characterized by an extremely stimulated imagination," he wrote in a report to his Sandoz employers, according to an article in the *New York Times Magazine*. Back at work on Monday, he deliberately took a dose of 0.25 milligrams, and had to ask his assistant to help him get home. Hofmann had actually taken about ten times more than he should have, and felt some extremely unpleasant effects. "Everything in my field of vision wavered and was distorted as if seen in a curved mirror," he wrote in his autobiography, according to the London *Guardian*. "I also had the sensation of being unable to move from the spot. Nevertheless, my assistant later told me that we had travelled very rapidly."

Hofmann was a husband and father, but fortunately his wife and children were away at the time. At home, he was disturbed by the way the furniture seemed to move, and when a neighbor brought over some milk he saw her as a malevolent witch wearing a colored mask. "A demon had invaded me, had taken possession of my body, mind and soul," he recalled, according to the *New York Times Magazine*. A doctor was summoned, who found no physical symptoms of anything wrong except that Hofmann's pupils were dramatically dilated. The confirmation that he was not about to die reassured him, and he began to relax, letting the hallucinations float past. He fell asleep and the next morning felt reborn and his senses seemed renewed, for his breakfast tasted especially delicious and the colors around him looked more vivid than usual.

Hailed as Major Breakthrough

Hofmann delivered a full report to his supervisors at Sandoz, and three employees tried it themselves. A decision was made to share the results with a University of Zurich psychiatric researcher, who identified LSD as a nontoxic psychotropic compound, and Sandoz began offering it to qualified researchers and medical professionals for experimental trials under the brand name Delysid after 1947. Psychiatric and psychotherapy professionals soon hailed it as an exciting new breakthrough to unlocking the secrets to schizophrenia, whose sufferers sometimes experienced hallucinations.

U.S. military officials, working with the Central Intelligence Agency, conducted scores of experiments using LSD under a covert project known as MKULTRA, which administered LSD and other powerful drugs during the interrogation of enemy combatants and captured foreign intelligence agents; they also experimented on unwitting U.S. military personnel and even civilian subjects in psychiatric hospitals. All of the Project MKULTRA files were ordered destroyed during the Watergate era in 1973.

By then, the counterculture movement was in full bloom. Hofmann's discovery had unusual parallels with the origins of the youth subculture that emerged during the 1960s, as a generation of teens and young adults began questioning the rigid belief systems of their parents and other adult authority figures. The movement also dovetailed with the civil rights movement, the women's liberation movement, and opposition to an ongoing war in Vietnam where, due to the military draft, U.S. males over the age of 18 could be called up for service.

Participated in Experiments

Though Project MKULTRA was top secret, word of LSD's stunning psycho-pharmaceutical effects leaked out. Hofmann himself participated in several "acid trips," as the six- to 12-hour experience became known. He corresponded with Ernst Jünger, one of Germany's most acclaimed living novelists, and Jünger traveled to Switzerland to take LSD at Hofmann's home, where they listened to Mozart. Others contacted him, including some who had conducted research into the naturally occurring drug peyote, which was a longtime part of spiritual rituals practiced by Native Americans and their ancestors in the southwestern United States and Central America where the peyote cactus flourished.

Academic professionals were intrigued by the promise of LSD, peyote, and other dramatically powerful drugs that users claimed could result in a breakthrough "ego death" when ingested under proper conditions. One of these scholars was Dr. Timothy Leary, a professor of psychiatry at Harvard University, who began promoting it in his classes and writings. In the spring of 1961 a book titled *Exploring Inner Space: Personal Experiences Under LSD-25,* written by a pseudonymous author, sparked further interest, and by the summer of 1962 there were newspaper reports of an illicit trade in LSD in Southern California. Sandoz's patent on LSD had expired by then, and a *New York Times* article described the drug as relatively easy to make inside a standard laboratory by a professional with an organic chemistry background.

Leary, Jünger, the British writer Aldous Huxley, and scores of others wrote extensively about the life-changing effects of taking LSD. But when the drug became part of the counterculture scene, manufactured in impure settings and taken without supervision or in incautious amounts, it was demonized as dangerous and liable to cause brain damage or even permanent psychosis. Indeed, based on his own negative experience on that Monday in 1943, Hofmann was vociferously opposed to the casual use of LSD, and even met with Leary to urge him to rescind his enthusiastic pronouncements—but to no avail. By the end of the 1960s, LSD was formally outlawed by most countries, including the United States, and all scientific trials were halted.

Criticized Casual Use

Hofmann was a hero to the counterculture movement, but wrote of his disappointment with the misuse of LSD in his 1983 autobiography *LSD, My Problem Child: Reflections on Sacred Drugs, Mysticism and Science.* Since its discovery, he had carried out further research into entheogenic shamanism, or rituals involving the use of psychedelic compounds to induce an ecstatic or hallucinatory state. Scores of ancient and non-Western civilizations practiced this, he explained, but in the West the ritual fell out of favor officially in 392 C.E., after the Roman emperor Theodosius I banned an ancient Greek ritual called the Eleusinian Mysteries that had been practiced by pagan priests since 1500 B.C.E., or nearly two thousand years. The rites took place at a sacred site to honor the Greek goddess of grain, Demeter. Participants drank a beverage known as *kykeon,* made from barley, which may have contained the ergot virus or some other hallucination-inducing element. Early Christian church leaders condemned the highly secretive ritual, which was said to reveal to participants the promise of life after death. Hofmann contributed to a 1978 book, *The Road to Eleusis: Unveiling the Secret of the Mysteries,* an exploration of the Greek rite and other entheogenic practices.

Hofmann and his wife traveled to Central America to conduct research on peyote and psilocybin, a plant used by the Mazateca, an indigenous group in Oaxaca. In 1971 he retired from his long career at Sandoz as director of the natural products department. He lived near Switzerland's Jura Mountain range and celebrated his 100th birthday in 2006. He used the occasion to give interviews calling for the renewal of legitimate scientific trials on LSD and other hallucinogens. "It should be a controlled substance with the same status as morphine," he told Smith, and said he might consider using it himself at the end-of-life stage.

Hofmann died on April 29, 2008, of a heart attack at the age of 102. His wife, Anita, predeceased him, as did two of his children. The mysteries of humankind's relation to the universe had already apparently been revealed to him, for when Smith asked him if had any advanced theories about death, "he appeared mildly startled and said no. 'I go back to where I came from, to where I was before I was born, that's all.'"

Periodicals

Economist, May 10, 2008.

Guardian (London, England), May 1, 2008.

New York Times, July 14, 1962; January 3, 1965; August 11, 1975; January 7, 2006.

New York Times Magazine, December 28, 2008.

Times (London, England), April 15, 1993.

Online

"LSD: The Geek's Wonder Drug?," Wired.com, January 16, 2006, http://www.wired.com/print/science/discoveries/news/2006/01/70015 (January 6, 2010). □

James Wong Howe

The Chinese-born cinematographer James Wong Howe (1899–1976) was one of the first figures in the field of cinematography to be recognized for his distinctive stylistic contributions.

Growing up in the American West, Howe experienced the height of anti-Asian prejudice in the region. But he prospered through hard work and total dedication to his craft in a career saga that embodied classic American narratives of success. Howe's work in movies spanned much of the history of the art form, from silent film to the age of the blockbuster. He did not have a single style, but, in the words of Scott Eyman (writing in *Five American Cinematographers*), his strong point "was always his adaptability. His ego never felt the need to bolster itself by artificially forcing a uniform style onto every film he photographed. He preferred...a style individually crafted to draw out the specific story and characterizations." The result was a body of classic American films remembered as much for visual appearance as for spoken dialogue.

Father Joined Railroad Worker Migration

James Wong Howe was born Wong Tung Jim in Yong'an village, near Taishan, China, on August 28, 1899. Wong, in the Chinese naming system, was his family name, and his father was named Wong How. The Chinese actress Anna May Wong was Howe's cousin. The elder Wong left China for the United States the year Howe was born, following a large migration of Chinese who built much of the railroad system in the western U.S. He later opened a general store in Pasco, Washington, and when Howe was five, he was sent to join his father there. Howe told Eyman that he had

latest camera equipment. By 1919 he had graduated to "slate boy," holding the chalkboard that identified each scene during shooting, and he caught the attention of director and film impresario Cecil B. DeMille when he induced a reluctant canary to "sing" by pushing chewing gum into the bird's beak. The canary began to move its beak rapidly to throw off the gum, and the pleased DeMille got his illusion of birdsong and increased Howe's salary by half. Over the next several years Howe gained other practical experience in camera work.

Howe's breakthrough came when he photographed ingénue actress Mary Miles Minter (Juliet Reilly) in 1922. Minter was pleased with the photos because, unlike most black-and-white shots of the time, they showed her blue eyes clearly, and she demanded that Howe be made her cameraman. Howe, who had no idea how he had produced the effect, frantically experimented with different fabrics and backdrops, striking pay dirt with a framed piece of black velvet he mounted on his movie camera; it turned out that it had been black cloth reflected in Minter's eyes that had darkened them. Here Howe's Asian ethnicity worked to his advantage; the Hollywood rumor mill churned out news that Minter had located an exotic foreign cameraman who had worked wonders with her face, and other actresses began to request his services. By 1923 Howe had been promoted from operating cameraman to director of photography at Lasky Studios' successor, Paramount.

Hoped to Film in China

Howe's real breakthrough came in 1926 with *Mantrap,* a vehicle for silent-film sex symbol Clara Bow. His cinematography, using natural light to surround the actress with a soft glow, was key in developing Bow's image in the film. In the late 1920s Howe worked on his proposed directorial debut, a film set in China. The project gave him the opportunity to visit his home country, but it eventually foundered; although most of the footage was lost, some of it found its way into the 1932 film *Shanghai Express.* Unlike Bow, Howe made the transition into sound film in the early 1930s after a few initial roadblocks.

After a period as a freelance cinematographer, Howe moved to the MGM studio in 1933. According to Rainsberger, his preference for plain, low-contrast interior shots during this period earned him the nickname "Low-Key Howe." Again, there was method in Howe's decisions; he was staying out of the way of the stars of such fast-moving, dialogue-oriented films as *The Thin Man* (1934). Howe was first billed on film as James Wong Howe during this period. By the mid-1930s Howe's talent had been recognized financially if not with general celebrity; he purchased a Duesenberg automobile for $37,000 but found that passers-by assumed he was a house servant being allowed to drive a wealthy family's car.

In 1938 Howe moved to the Warner Brothers studio and garnered the first of his ten Academy Award nominations, for *Algiers.* He had another long run of success at that studio, working on 26 films between 1938 and 1947 and helping to build the career of another major female star, *Algiers* star Hedy Lamarr. During World War II, Howe

no recollection of his life in China except that the family lived in a village.

Howe's family were the only Chinese people in the immediate area, and as a child Howe suffered various forms of schoolyard harassment and worse; one teacher refused to admit him to class on account of his race. That teacher's replacement, according to Howe biographer Todd Rainsberger (writing in *James Wong Howe, Cinematographer*), coined the name James Wong Howe by changing Howe's name Jim to James and adding it to a respelled version of Howe's father's name. Howe's interest in film began early but inauspiciously; he bought a Brownie camera at a local store in 1911 but, on his first try, tried to develop the film wrapper instead of the film itself. Persisting through other mistakes, he learned basic photographic skills. Howe's father, who disliked cameras and avoided being photographed, hoped that Howe would become a doctor or take over his store in Pasco. But Howe was restless. Hoping to assimilate into American life, he dreamed of careers as an airline pilot or as a boxer. Active as a boxer in Oregon for several months, he is listed in boxing record books and on web sites.

In 1916 Howe, who used the first name Jimmie at this point (and for much of the rest of his life among friends), made his way to California. After brief stints as a busboy and commercial photographer's assistant, he applied at the Lasky Corporation film studio. Given a ten-dollar-a-week job as a janitor by camera department head Alvin Wykoff, he used the opportunity to familiarize himself with the began wearing a button that read "I am Chinese" after ugly incidents of prejudice directed against Asians in general, despite the fact that China and the U.S. were allied against China's Japanese invaders. Actor James Cagney wore a similar button for a time in solidarity with Howe.

Marriage Plans Delayed by Discriminatory Laws

In the late 1930s, Howe began a long-term relationship with white writer Sanora Babb. The two hoped to marry but could not do so until 1949, when California's laws prohibiting interracial marriage were repealed. Howe's application for American citizenship, long ruled out by California immigration laws, had to wait even longer, but he became an American citizen in 1958. After the end of the war Howe's career slowed somewhat as color film and other new technologies took hold. In the late 1940s he began working again on a freelance basis and enjoyed the chance to explore innovative ideas. The 1947 boxing film *Body and Soul* was unusually realistic, for Howe, a boxer himself, climbed into the ring with a handheld camera to get close-ups of star John Garfield. For *The Brave Bulls* (1951), he attached cameras to actors' waists. Despite his flexibility behind the camera, however, the cinematographer who had done so much to make directors look good had little success in his two outings as a director, *Go, Man, Go!* (1954) and *The Invisible Avenger* (1958).

Because of his associations with Hollywood liberals such as Garfield, Howe was regarded with suspicion by investigators from the House Un-American Activities Committee during the mid-1950s but was never blacklisted. The intense dramas popular in that decade fit Howe's talents perfectly, and he earned his first Academy Award for his work on *The Rose Tattoo* (1955), which depended on complex lighting of the interior space in which much of the film unfolds. Howe earned another Oscar nomination for the color film *The Old Man and the Sea* (1958), based on a story by Ernest Hemingway, and he took home a second statuette for *Hud* (1963), a film set in the bleak landscape of West Texas and based on a Larry McMurtry novel. Howe recalled that he emphasized the harsh bleakness of the scenery. "I'd look through the camera and there would be clouds there," he told Eyman. "I'd say, 'It's too pretty, Marty [director Martin Ritt].' He'd say, 'Yeah.' I'd put in a filter and take the clouds out and say 'Looks better now.' He'd say, 'Yeah, not so decorative.'"

Howe reunited with Ritt for the labor saga *The Molly Maguires* in 1968, but after that film he began to suffer a variety of health problems. Offered the position of cinematographer on the film *The Godfather,* he was forced to turn it down. He was brought out of retirement for 1975's *Funny Lady* by producer Ray Stark, who hoped that Howe could re-create his female star power magic for that film's female lead, Barbra Streisand. Shooting on the film was suspended when Howe was hospitalized, and he returned to finish his work on it. *Funny Lady* brought him his final Academy Award nomination. Howe died from cancer in Los Angeles on July 12, 1976, with about 130 films to his credit. By that time his work was beginning to come under examination from cinema historians, and retrospectives of his work— rare for any cinematographer—were mounted at the Seattle

International Film Festival in 2002, and in a weeklong tribute in San Francisco, California in 2004.

Books

Eyman, Scott, *Five American Cinematographers,* Scarecrow, 1987.

Notable Asian Americans, Gale, 1995.

Rainsberger, Todd, *James Wong Howe: Cinematographer,* A.S. Barnes, 1981.

Periodicals

San Francisco Chronicle, October 20, 2004.

Online

"James Wong Howe, ASC," *International Cinematographers Guild,* http://www.cameraguild.com/index.html?news/guild/guild_selects.htm~top.main_hp (January 10, 2010).

"James Wong Howe," *Internet Encyclopedia of Cinematographers,* http://www.cinematographers.nl/GreatDoPh/howe.htm (January 10, 2010).

"James Wong Howe," *Internet Movie Database,* http://www.imdb.com/name/nm0002146/bio (January 10, 2010). □

William Ambrose Hulbert

American sports executive William Ambrose Hulbert (1832–1882) founded baseball's National League. He also served as the league's president from 1877 until his untimely death in 1882. He was posthumously inducted into Major League Baseball's Hall of Fame in 1995.

I t is one of sports history's great ironies. Pioneering baseball executive William Ambrose Hulbert was born a mere thirteen miles from Cooperstown, New York, the site of Major League Baseball's national Hall of Fame. Few men did more for the sport of baseball, yet his path to enshrinement was far from straightforward. His well-deserved induction did not come until more than a century after his death— a delay proved puzzling. After all, Hulbert was the driving force behind the creation of the National League, the first of the sport's only two existing major leagues.

Baseball historians agree that Hulbert should have received a plaque in 1937, the year that the Hall of Fame began inducting non-players (e.g., notable managers, executives, etc.) for contributions to the sport. After all, during the sport's eighteenth-century infancy, Hulbert replaced an unsteady organization (the National Association) with the far more stable "senior circuit," helped rid the burgeoning sport of its corrupting influences (gambling, alcohol, rowdiness), and initiated organizational changes that promoted baseball's growth and increased its popularity.

"In all the history of Base Ball no man has yet appeared who possessed in combination more of the essential attributes of a great leader than did William A. Hulbert," commented Al Spalding (as quoted by the National Baseball Hall of Fame web site), a player, manager, and sports executive during Major League Baseball's early years, and co-founder of the A.G. Spalding sporting goods company, which has endured since 1876. "He stood like a stone wall, protecting the game of Base Ball in its integrity and turning back the assaults of every foe who sought to introduce elements of dishonesty, discord or degeneration."

A businessman first, Hulbert, who made his money in the coal industry, imbued the sport with his corporate sensibilities, which helped make baseball a profitable enterprise. Described on his Hall of Fame plaque as a silver-tongued, vigorous and influential director, Hulbert aligned baseball with other industries (transportation, hotels, landscaping firms and sporting goods suppliers).

Moved from Business to Baseball

William Ambrose Hulbert was born on October 23, 1832 in Burlington Flats, a New York state hamlet close to Cooperstown. When he was two years old, his family moved to Chicago, Illinois. In 1847, he enrolled in Beloit College in Wisconsin, where he studied business. When he returned to Chicago, he married the daughter of a thriving grocer and then started a successful coal dealership. He also became a fan of baseball, at that time a new sport.

In 1871, Hulbert supported Chicago's professional baseball club, the White Stockings, a charter member of the National Association (the team later evolved into the Chicago Cubs). But the association encountered a significant detour. On October 8 of that year, the famous Chicago fire, which lasted two days, destroyed about four square miles of the city. The apocalyptic conflagration consumed the White Stockings' Lake Park playing field. As a result, the team withdrew from the then-existing National Association baseball league.

The team managed to resuscitate itself, however, and within three years of the historic fire, returned to competition. Hulbert, still one of its biggest boosters, became club officer and part owner. By 1875, he became the White Stockings' president.

Became a Savvy Contract Negotiator

In his new role, Hulbert sought to make the White Stockings a competitive organization. This propelled him into the prevalent and tricky contract negotiations. One of his first orders of business involved retaining the services of shortstop Davy Force. Like other talented players of the era, Force did not remain in one place too long. Realizing that Force was a reputed team-jumper, Hulbert negotiated an attractive contract in September 1874 that would secure the shortstop's services for the 1875 season. Hulbert drew up the contract in the final months of the existing baseball season, however. The timing ran counter to National Association rules that forbade in-season negotiations, so league officials voided the agreement. Undaunted, Hulbert tried again in November, but a clerical error invalidated the revised contract. The roadblocks enabled the Philadelphia Athletics to intercede and eventually acquire Force. Angry and frustrated, Hulbert protested, but the National Association's Council, which was headed by a Philadelphia official, approved Force's most recent contract offer. Hulbert had run out of luck.

Now convinced that an Eastern ball club bloc plotted against Western-based franchises, Hulbert, who already had demonstrated a ruthless business approach as a coal baron, was ready to get down and dirty. He responded by engaging in the common practice of "pirating" players. Specifically, he entered into secret negotiations with star players from Eastern teams, tempting them to jump ship and board his club. In this way, he obtained the services of the Philadelphia Athletics' first baseman Adrian "Cap" Anson, a future Hall of Famer. Hulbert also signed star players from the Boston franchise, including Ross Barnes, Cal McVey, Deacon White and, most significantly, Al Spalding. Again, these signings bucked the National Association's established strictures, but Hulbert developed a plan to circumvent the anticipated disciplinary action: He would form his own baseball league.

Founded the National League

In late 1875 and early 1876, Hulbert began laying the groundwork for his envisioned league. Collaborating with

Spalding (the player he recruited from Boston) he developed the league's constitution, which still exists. Potential allies made it easy for him to proceed. At least seven other sympathetic team owners sought to wrest control of the sport from the National Alliance. On February 2, 1876, Hulbert gathered the owners for a meeting at the Grand Central Hotel in New York City, where he outlined his plan. Avidly listening to his pitch were team owners from Boston, Massachusetts; Cincinnati, Ohio; St. Louis, Missouri; Hartford, Connecticut; Philadelphia, Pennsylvania; Louisville, Kentucky; and New York City.

According to the Hulbert plan, the new National League would establish charter teams in cities with at least 75,000 potential paying customers. Further, new league rules would prohibit more than one team in each city. Also, as Hulbert originally outlined in 1876, the National League would operate by the highest business principles. Team owners bought into the plan.

Moving forward, Hulbert established a central office. Connecticut politician Morgan Bulkeley, who owned the Hartford baseball franchise, was appointed president. Burkeley proved to be little more than a figurehead, however. While his assigned duties included maintenance of team records, instigation of rule changes, management of umpiring staff, and general arbitration, he actually accomplished virtually nothing. In fact, Hulbert masterminded league development behind the scenes. Ultimately, Bulkeley's insubstantial one-year tenure ended when he failed to show up for the 1877 National League meeting. Team owners insisted that Hulbert take over as president.

Strived to Clean up the Game

Offered the reins, Hulbert became an iron-fisted ruler. But more than just an implacable tyrant, Hulbert sought to advance the game of baseball at the professional level. Changes that he initiated influenced Major League Baseball's subsequent development. True, the league's creation was driven by expedience, but Hulbert was guided by higher goals. He sought to provide an alternative to the struggling National Association, which had been weakened by ineffectual leadership and corrupted by gambling, drunkenness, and a general rowdiness. These elements, Hulbert believed, threatened the sport's survival. As such, he established a partial ban on alcoholic beverages served at ballparks and strived to eliminate the gambling faction. In addition, to uphold the integrity of games played, he established completely impartial umpiring. No longer would team captains be allowed to selected members of umpiring crews.

Hulbert also introduced the concept of regular game scheduling, a duty he removed from clubs and assigned to league officials. In one of his first official actions, he threw out two teams (the New York Mutuals and the Philadelphia Athletics) for failing to complete league-designated schedules.

Later, he kicked the Cincinnati Red Stockings out of the league because the team refused to follow his edict that banned ballpark beer sales on Sunday. But this move resulted in a major-scale mutiny and the 1882 creation of the American Association (AA), a league that was more liberal as far as alcohol sale. The AA, which became known as the "beer and whiskey league," proved a viable competitor for the next ten years.

Meanwhile, observers viewed the National League's missionary zeal and pious proclamations with suspicion. Newspapers such as the *New York Clipper* considered the league's creation as a play to gain power. In a February 12, 1876 sports editorial, the *Clipper* described the National League as a baseball *coup d'etat* and pointed out the apparent hypocrisy of its rulings related to business transactions and one-city, single-team rule: "... we do decidedly object to the secret and sudden coup d'etat of the Western club-managers, and the glaring inconsistency of their action in throwing out one club, open to the charge of crooked work last season, while retaining another club equally amenable to censure for the doubtful character of the play of its team."

The Clipper continued its relentless attack: "Then, too, they leave out the New Haven Club—an organization which, in the high character of its officials, the strength of its team, and its reputation for carrying out its obligations, stands as high as the clubs in the League—under the rule of limiting League clubs to cities having not less than 75,000 inhabitants, while they allow the Hartford Club in their League, though that city has not so many inhabitants by 13,000 as New Haven."

Banned Corrupt Players

Despite such indictments, the eight-team National League became a success, and the National Association later folded. Hulbert faced another major crisis only a year after forming the new league, however, and it involved gambling. Late in the 1877 season, the Louisville club, against all odds, lost a three-and-a-half-game lead in the standings. This led to suspicions of game fixing and a call for investigation. As he looked into the matter, Hulbert learned that four prominent Louisville players (Bill Craver, Jim Devlin, George Hall and Al Nichols) were in on the fix. It was baseball's first major gambling scandal, even before the infamous "Black Sox" scandal of 1919 (when players from the Chicago White Sox conspired with gamblers to throw that year's World Series).

Hulbert banned the four players from baseball for life. Devlin, who was a star pitcher, pleaded for mercy, reportedly falling to his knees before the league president. Hulbert was moved by the gesture and by Devlin's personal situation, but he remained adamant. According to Spalding (as quoted by Steve Wulf in a 1990 *Sports Illustrated* article), he handed Devlin a fifty-dollar bill and said, "That's what I think of you personally, Devlin. But, damn you, you are dishonest and sold out a game. I can't trust you. Now go on your way, and never let me see your face again, for your act against the integrity of baseball will never be condoned as long as I live."

As a result of the four-player ban, the Louisville team removed itself from the league, soon followed by the St. Louis and Hartford clubs. To fill the gaps left by the deserting clubs, Hulbert installed franchises in Indianapolis, Indiana, Milwaukee, Wisconsin and Providence, Rhode Island. These weren't the strongest baseball towns, but the team placements served its purpose. The National League had weathered its first storm.

Died of Heart Failure

The National League not only survived, it thrived, although Hulbert would not be around to witness its ongoing success. In 1882, when he was only forty-nine years old, he died of heart failure. He passed away in Chicago on April 10, just as a new baseball season was starting.

Hulbert was inducted into the Major League Baseball's Hall of Fame in 1995, but the sport's historians feel that the honor was too long in coming. The Hall was established in 1936. Initial inductees included players Ty Cobb, Babe Ruth, Honus Wagner, Christy Mathewson, and Walter Johnson. The following year, the Hall formed a committee to select non-player inductees that provided outstanding service to the game. The first honorees included managers Connie Mack, John McGraw, and George Wright, who established baseball's first professional team. The Hall also inducted Ban Johnson, as he was the American League's first president, and Morgan Bulkeley, because he served as the National League's first president. An injustice became evident: The ineffectual Bulkeley superceded Hulbert, who not only founded the National League but performed the tasks that Bulkeley should have performed.

The Hall of Fame's Veteran Committee finally redressed the injustice in 1995. The inscription on Hulbert's Hall of Fame plaque summarizes his contributions (as recorded on the National Baseball Hall of Fame web site): "Wavy-haired, silver tongued executive and energetic, influential leader. While part-owner of Chicago National Association Team, was instrumental in founding National League in 1876. Elected N.L. President later that year and is credited with establishing respectability, integrity and sound foundation for new league with his relentless opposition to betting, rowdiness, and other prevalent abuses which were threatening the sport."

Periodicals

New York Clipper, February 12, 1876.
Sports Illustrated, February 26, 1990.

Online

"National League," *Ringsurf.com,* http://www.ringsurf.com/online/1749-national_league.html (December 23, 2009).
"William Hulbert," *American Studies at University of Virginia,* http://xroads.virginia.edu/~HYPER/INCORP/baseball/hulbert.html(December 23, 2009).
"William Hulbert," *Baseball Library.com,* http://www.baseballlibrary.com/ballplayers/player.php?name=William_Hulbert_1832 (December 23, 2009).
"William Hulbert," *Sports Encyclopedia,* http://www. sportsecyclopedia.com/mlb/nl/hulbert.html (December 23, 2009).
"William Hulbert's Hall of Fame Plaque," *National Baseball Hall of Fame,* http://209.23.71.87/hofers_and_honorees/plaques/hulbert_william.htm(December 23, 2009).□

J

John Hughlings Jackson

The British neurologist and researcher John Hughlings Jackson (1835–1911) shaped how scientists understood the localization of specific functions within the brain.

Jackson was an unusual kind of scientist: he never conducted experiments, and he rarely used a microscope. Nevertheless, he advanced the study of human physiology in many ways, and a variety of medical conditions still bear his name. Jackson made his discoveries through a combination of keen observation and a commitment to the broad application of reasoning from known facts. His observations grew partly out of his own life circumstances: he closely scrutinized the symptoms of his wife, an epileptic, and he was brilliant when it came to deducing normal brain function from his observations of abnormalities. In the words of Edwin Clarke, writing on Jackson in the *Dictionary of Scientific Biography,* Jackson has been "acclaimed as the greatest British scientific clinician of the nineteenth century."

Learned Medicine Through Apprenticeship

Named for his father, farmer John Jackson, and his mother, Sarah Hughlings Jackson, John Hughlings Jackson was born in Providence, in Britain's Yorkshire region (it is now part of North Yorkshire), on April 4, 1835. He was one of five children, all of whom were ambitious; his three brothers all settled in New Zealand. Little is known of Jackson's early life. He attended small English country schools, and from all evidence had only a modest education. At the age of 15 he apprenticed himself to a doctor at the York Hospital Medical School, and in 1855 he moved to London to finish his schooling at the St. Bartholemew's Hospital Medical School. That gave him the basic medical certification current in Britain at the time: he was made a Member of the Royal College of Surgeons and Licentiate of the Society of Apothecaries. Returning to Yorkshire, he took a job as house surgeon to the dispensary, essentially a pharmacy that provided treatment, at York Hospital. He worked there with the brain researcher Thomas Laycock and began to read more widely, absorbing the ideas of proto-evolutionist Herbert Spencer among others.

Jackson remained hungry for broader knowledge, and in 1859 he returned to London and made plans to study philosophy. But another physician from Yorkshire, Jonathan Hutchinson, recognized Jackson's talent and encouraged him to remain in the field and seek out a better position. He joined the staff of London's Metropolitan Free Hospital in 1859 and, by correspondence, earned an M.D. degree from the University of St. Andrews in Scotland the following year. In 1861 he was made a member of the Royal College of Physicians of London, a top professional group.

Joining the staff of London Hospital in 1863 as assistant physician, Jackson was on staff there and at other London hospitals for most of the rest of his life. Most consequential for his research was a longtime appointment at the National Hospital for the Paralysed and Epileptic. He also worked at the Moorfields Eye Hospital, which gave him access to new ophthalmologic equipment that also played an important part in his early research. He wrote some of his early papers about the relationship between vision and the brain, and the diseases that could result if something went wrong in this relationship. As his fame grew, he was elected a Fellow of the Royal College and gave a number of lectures at the group's meetings.

Married Epileptic Cousin

Jackson's interest in epilepsy grew partly from his immediate surroundings. He himself was a chronic vertigo sufferer. In 1865 he married a cousin, Elizabeth Dade Jackson. She suffered from what later became known as Jackson's or Jacksonian epilepsy: a form of the disease involving seizures on one side of the body only. The couple had no children, and Elizabeth Jackson died in 1876 after stroke-related complications.

Epilepsy had been observed by doctors for many centuries, and researchers had even begun to establish its status as a brain-related disease and to speculate that it might originate in the medulla oblongata, the lower part of the brainstem. But Jackson was frustrated by what he called the great vagueness of the word epilepsy. He began to systematically observe and catalogue the symptoms of hundreds of epilepsy patients he encountered, finding that those symptoms included such phenomena as hallucinations, jerks and twitches, dreamlike states, and involuntary chewing as well as the familiar but frightening grand mal seizure. Jackson concluded that epilepsy was not a single disease but a complex of related disorders occurring in the brain.

Jackson's next step was to correlate his observations with what was known about the structure of the brain. Widely familiar with existing literature in the field in both English and French, Jackson had a synthesizing mind that led him intuitively in productive directions. Drawing especially on the work of French anatomist Paul Broca, Jackson used his data to identify specific parts of the brain involved with

epileptic seizures and other disorders. His hypotheses confirmed much of Broca's work and established a basis for much of the map of the brain as it is known today. By observing abnormal conditions, Jackson correctly located the sites of motor activity, physical sensation, and language ability in the brain. For example, he noticed that aphasia, or loss of language production ability and comprehension, occurred in right-handed patients when they had suffered an injury in the left cerebral hemisphere, and vice versa. From these observations, Jackson made accurate hypotheses about the location of the language centers in the brain and correctly guessed that they vary according to an individual's dominant hand.

Founded Long-Lasting Journal

It was with epileptics that Jackson made his most valuable observations. He was the first to identify epileptic seizures as the results of electrical discharges in the brain, and he noticed that seizures often started in a specific part of the body and then became more general. Jackson's general description of the brain as being divided into a fixed structure, with individual sections controlling different parts of the body, came from his work on epilepsy. His writings formed a link between the work of German researchers Gustav Theodor Fritsch and Julius Eduard Hitzig, who had used experiments with dogs to show that electrical stimulation of the brain cortex produced limb movements on the opposite side of the dog's body, and the work of David Ferrier, the first major synthesizer of ideas on brain structure, whose book *The Functions of the Brain* (1876) was dedicated to Jackson. Two years later Jackson joined Ferrier and two other scientists to founded the influential journal *Brain,* which is still in existence.

The implications of Jackson's work for clinical practice were numerous. No fewer than seven conditions, symptoms, or principles bear his name: Jackson's cerebellar syndrome, Jackson's epilepsy, Jackson-Mackenzie syndrome (a type of localized paralysis), Jacksonian march, Jackson's rule, Jackson's law, and Jackson's sign. Jackson was a modest figure who showed no inclination to become a scientific star and was quick to give credit to other researchers. Overall, his conception of epilepsy is not far from the modern understanding of the condition. Jackson was better known among those who heard his lectures and read his 300-odd papers than he was among the British public in general. Many who did know him were fond of calling him "The Sage."

Jackson also wrote more generally about the relationship between the brain and the body, drawing on Spencer's theories in order to argue that the nervous system evolved from simple to complex, and that the various stages were all present in the human organism. These ideas helped lay the groundwork for Sigmund Freud's theory of psychoanalysis, which posited the existence of simple, largely unconscious drives relating to physical matters, as well as more complex mental functions that could partly restrain the simpler drives. Freud was directly influenced by Jackson's writings, which came close to suggesting the key Freudian idea of the unconscious. Like Freud, Jackson had little interest in religion and refused to accept the idea of life after death. On a lighter note, Jackson also wrote an article about humor in 1887; he similarly attempted to classify it according to a hierarchical scheme in which puns formed the bottom layer.

In his later years, Jackson was rewarded with modest professional honors. Britain's Neurological Society inaugurated an annual Hughlings Jackson lecture, and Jackson delivered the first one in 1889. He received honorary doctorates from the universities of Leeds, Glasgow, and Edinburgh. Jackson died in London on October 7, 1911; a plaque marks his longtime residence on London's Manchester Square. The popular neurological writer Oliver Sacks, whose writings have similarly been based on close observations of individual patients rather than on scientific observations, has cited Jackson as a forerunner in *The Man Who Mistook His Wife for a Hat* and other writings.

Books

Biographical Dictionary of Psychology, edited by Noel Sheehy, et al., Routledge, 1997.

Critchley, MacDonald, and Eileen A. Critchley, *John Hughlings Jackson, Father of English Neurology,* Oxford, 1998.

Dictionary of Scientific Biography, Vol. 6, edited by Charles Coulston Gillispie, Charles Scribner's Sons, 1981.

Online

"John Hughlings Jackson," *Who Named It?,* http://www.whonamedit.com/doctor.cfm/2766.html (January 10, 2010). □

Nell Jackson

American track and field athlete and coach Nell Jackson (1929–1988) set records in sprinting events, participated in Olympic games, coached Olympic teams and enjoyed a long and successful academic career. An influential and inspirational sports figure, she helped increase career opportunities for women and minorities in sports. In 1989, she was posthumously inducted into the National Track and Field Hall of Fame.

Most likely, Nell Cecelia Jackson never envisioned herself as a pioneer, but she became just that through the significant achievements that she accomplished between 1948 and 1988—a forty-year period that saw her advance from a record-setting athlete to an influential coach, scholar and administrator. Her career witnessed both personal and historic milestones that transformed sports in terms of gender and race. Beyond her record-setting accomplishments, she became the first African American assistant athletic director at a major educational institution and the first African American head coach of a U.S. Olympic team. But she did not set out to change the world. She simply wanted to excel—and this she did well, both on the playing field and the professional arena.

The future women's track and field star was born on July 1, 1929 in Athens, Georgia, to Burnette L. and Wilhelmina G. Jackson. She was one of the family's three children (her brothers were Burnette L. Jackson, Jr. and Thomas O. Jackson). When Jackson was a child, she moved with her family to Tuskegee, Alabama. Home of Tuskegee University, the community was strongly focused on academic and athletic success, and this supplied Jackson with a powerful will to succeed in both areas.

A gifted athlete, the young Jackson demonstrated natural abilities in diverse activities that included swimming, tennis, and basketball. She was also an exceptional runner, though, and ultimately focused on track and field, specializing in sprint events. Success came early and often for the five-foot seven-inch, 126-pound Jackson. In 1944, when she was only fifteen years old, she qualified for national competition. A year later, she place second in the 200-meter race in both indoor and outdoor events sponsored by the Amateur Athletic Union (AAU), the national organization that promotes nonprofessional athletes in non-profit competition. On both occasions, Jackson finished behind Stella Walsh, an Olympic gold medalist.

Reached Olympian Heights

In 1946, when she was still a high school student, Jackson was selected to the United States All-American team for the 200-meters event. The following year, she graduated from Tuskegee High School and enrolled at Tuskegee University, where she majored in physical education. The university boasted one of the country's best women's track and field programs, and Jackson became a leading sprinter. Mentored by USA Track and Field Hall of Fame coach Cleve Abbott, Jackson participated in the 200-meter and the 400-meter relay events. In 1948, and only a college freshman, Jackson qualified for the United States Olympic team. She disappointed herself in that year's Summer Olympic Games held in London, England, however, as she failed to place in either of her chosen events.

Undaunted, Jackson responded by setting a new American record the following year: she recorded a 24.2-second finish in the 200-meter event. It would take six years for another sprinter to break the record. In addition, she won the national AAU 200-meter championships for three successive years (1949–1951). The 1950 competition included an interesting footnote: Jackson beat out Walsh. That same year, Jackson, because of her splendid speed, assumed the pivotal anchor position on Tuskegee University's 400-meter relay team.

In 1951, she once again participated in Olympic competition. Also, she participated in the first Pan-American games, which were held in Buenos Aires, Argentina. She brought home a silver medal in the 200-meter race and a gold medal in the 400-meter relay race.

Earned Academic Degrees

At the same time that Jackson compiled these impressive athletic accomplishments, she also garnered important academic credentials. In 1951, she earned her bachelor's of science degree in physical education from Tuskegee University. She then enrolled in Springfield College in Massachusetts for graduate work. She eventually received her master's degree in physical education in 1953. Two years later, she participated in a summer study program at the University of Oslo, in Norway. In 1962, she received a doctorate in philosophy in physical education from the University of Iowa, located in Iowa City.

Academic success extended her sports career beyond the playing field, and she achieved substantial personal and historic milestones. In 1953, she became a physical education instructor at Tuskegee University and, a year later, realized a dream when she became the institution's head track and field coach, a position she held until 1962. The Olympic committee duly noted her outstanding work as a head coach and, in 1956, the organization asked her to coach the women's track and field team. In accepting the assignment, Jackson became the first African American head coach, male or female, of a U.S. Olympic team. She also remained physically active in swimming competition. The same year that she became an Olympic coach, the Associated Press named her the Female Athlete of the Year for diving. (Beside track and field, Jackson also coached swimming and, in 1958, she became the first men's swimming coach at Tuskegee University, heading a program that she started.)

Subsequently, Jackson's academic and coaching accomplishments intertwined in an ever upwardly mobile career path. After completing her doctorate work at the University of Iowa in 1962, Jackson became an assistant professor of physical education at Illinois State University in Normal, Illinois. She held the position for two years, from 1963 to 1965. She then transferred to the University of Illinois in Urbana-Champaign, where she served as an associate professor for eight years. At Illinois, she coached the track team to a national championship in the 1970 outdoor season.

During the same period, she became the assistant manager and then manager of the United States women's track and field team. She held the position for twenty-three years. Further, in 1972, she coached the United States track and field team that participated in Martinique and, once again, she coached the United States women's Olympic track and field team.

In 1973, she moved to Michigan State University in East Lansing, where she became the women's track coach and professor of physical education. She also became the first African American assistant athletic director at a higher education institution.

Entered Track Hall of Fame

Jackson retired from full-time coaching in 1981, but she remained very active. In her last position, Jackson was director of physical education and intercollegiate athletics and professor in the department of physical education at the State University of New York at Binghamton. She assumed the position in 1982 and held it until her untimely death in 1988. She died in Vestal, New York on April 1. She was only fifty-nine years old. A year later, Jackson was inducted into the National Track and Field Hall of Fame.

Even though her career was cut short, she achieved a great deal and earned well-deserved recognition. She was not only an accomplished athlete and coach but she also gained a reputation as a researcher. She developed numerous workshops and clinics and contributed to medical publications. In all, she published more than twenty articles, papers and chapters in professional journals. She also contributed to textbooks, and she wrote *Track and Field for Girls and Women*, a book that became a standard text and helped advance women's athletics.

She also applied her scholarship to film: Jackson produced *Grace in Motion* and helped develop instructional film loops that were widely utilized by the National Collegiate Athletic Association (NCAA).

Mentored Successful Athletes

As a coach, Jackson had the opportunity to work with many talented athletes who went on to achieve significant success in their own right. The talented student-athletes she mentored included Mildred McDaniels, a 1956 Olympic gold medal winner in the high jump; Neomia Rodgers, a high-jumping member of the 1960 Olympic team; Maeoper West, a competitor in the 1973 World University Games; and Sue Latter, the 1977 winner of The Athletic Congress (TAC) 800-meter event. While at Tuskegee University, Jackson coached Barbara Jacket, a fellow member of the United States Track and Field and Cross Country Coaches Association Hall of Fame (USTFCCCA) and a 1992 United States Olympic coach. Also, one of Jackson's students at Michigan

State was Karen Dennis, who later became the women's track and field coach at Ohio State University.

Jackson also mentored renowned educators and administrators such as Dorothy L. Richey, of Slippery Rock University, and Annie Croom of West Georgia College.

Affiliated with Numerous Athletic Organizations

In addition to her athletic achievements, Jackson carved out many important affiliations throughout her career. She was a member of the American Alliance of Health, Physical Education, Recreation and Dance, the American College of Sports Medicine, and the Athletic Congress.

During the 1960s, she coordinated the track and field sections for the first and fifth National Institute on Girls Sports (in 1963 and 1968, respectively). From 1964 to 1969, she was a member of the women's board of the United States Olympic Development Committee. In 1965, she organized the Illini Track Club for Girls. Also during the decade, Jackson was the Division of Girls and Women in Sports liaison chairperson (1966 through 1968) and the track and field Principles and Techniques of Officiating chairperson (1964 through 1966).

As her career progressed, she was a member of the AAU Women's Track and Field Committee (1968–1971) and served on the board of directors of the United States Olympic Committee (1969–1972). During the 1970s she was a member of the Urbana, Illinois YWCA corporation board and the Lansing, Michigan YWCA board of directors. From 1978 to 1981, she was field sports committee chairperson for the Association for Intercollegiate Athletics for Women (AIAW) and, from 1979 to 1982, she was vice president of TAC. In 1982, Jackson became AIAW's Ethics and Eligibility chairperson.

In 1980, Jackson was selected as one of five United States educators to attend the International Olympic Academy in Greece. From 1985 to 1988, she was a member of the International Relations Committee of the United States Olympic Committee. From 1982 through 1988, she was a member of the Binghamton, New York, Urban League board of directors. At the time of her death, she was secretary of The Athletics Congress (TAC).

Hall of Fame Honors

Besides being elected to the National Track and Field Hall of Fame and the USTFCCCA Hall of Fame, Jackson also was inducted into the Southern Intercollegiate Athletic Conference Hall of Fame, the USATF Hall of Fame, the Tuskegee University Hall of Fame, the Black Athletes Hall of Fame, and the International Women's Sports Hall of Fame.

Jackson received many other honors and awards. The most notable include Tuskegee University's Alumni Merit Award (1973); National Alumni Merit Award (Tuskegee University, 1977); National Association for Girls and Women in Sports (NAGWS) Presidential Citation (1977); and the University of Iowa's Department of Physical Education Alumni Merit Award (1984). In 1989, she was posthumously honored with the Robert Giegengack Award.

Following Jackson's death, several awards were created to honor her memory, accomplishments and positive impact on women and minorities in sports. In 1992, the NAGWS established the Nell C. Jackson Award to recognize the contributions of minority women who have demonstrated outstanding potential in scholarship, coaching, administration, and leadership through distinguished service to girls and women's sports. The award is presented at three levels: professional, college/university, and high school. Other awards to honor Jackson were established by the National Association of Collegiate Women Athletic Administrators, Michigan State's Varsity Alumni ''S'' Club and Binghamton University.

Books

''Nell Jackson,'' *Great Women in Sports,* Visible Ink Press, 1996.

''Nell Jackson,'' *Notable Black American Women,* Book 1, Gale Research, 1992.

Online

''Dr. Nell Jackson,'' *U.S. Track and Field and Cross Country Coaches Association,* http://www.ustfccca.org/ustfccca-hall-of-fame/ustfccca-hall-of-fame-special-inductees/nell-jackson-ustfccca-special-inductee (December 29, 2009).

''Nell Jackson,'' *USATF.org,* http://www.usatf.org/halloffame/TF/showBio.asp?HOFIDs=80 (December 29, 2009)

''Nell Jackson Athlete-Coach,'' *USATF.org,* http://www. usatf.org/athletes/hof/jackson.asp (December 29, 2009).

''Nell C. Jackson Award,'' *American Alliance for Health, Physical Education, Recreation and Dance,,* http://www.aahperd.org/nagws/programs/awards/Nell-Jackson-Award.cfm (December 29, 2009).□

James Jamerson

The American string bassist James Jamerson (1936–1983) contributed fundamentally to the sound of the hit recordings released by Detroit, Michigan's Motown label in the 1960s.

Trained in jazz, Jamerson expanded the range of the bass far beyond its usual role in the popular music of the day. His adventurous and rhythmically complex bass playing gave a fresh profile to Motown recordings from Martha Reeves & the Vandellas' ''Dancing in the Street'' to Marvin Gaye's ''Ain't That Peculiar,'' as well as to recordings on other labels. Like other Motown session musicians, Jamerson labored in obscurity during his lifetime, and when he died in 1983 few outside his own musical and social circles took notice. The biography and film documentary *Standing in the Shadows of Motown,* appearing respectively in 1991 and 2002, did a great deal to document Jamerson's musical contributions.

Constructed Homemade Bass

James Lee Jamerson Jr. was a native of Edisto Island, South Carolina, born on January 29, 1936. His father, James Sr., was a shipyard worker in nearby Charleston; his mother, Elizabeth, worked as a maid. After spending his early childhood on the island, Jamerson lived with relatives in the city of Charleston. He maintained a lifelong affection for the food and culture of the South Carolina low country, and later in life he would sometimes entertain his friends by cooking exotic dishes from the area such as raccoon and opossum. Jamerson soaked up the gospel music, blues, and jazz he heard in local homes and churches, and at one point he constructed a homemade bass by attaching a large rubber band to a stick—because, his son James Jr. said in the *Standing in the Shadows of Motown* film, he wanted to make the ants dance. As a child he was confined to a wheelchair for a year following a bicycle crash, leaving him with a limp.

In 1953 Elizabeth Jamerson moved to then-booming Detroit, and she did well enough that she could send for her son to join her the following year. Attending Northwestern High School, he picked up a bass that was resting on the floor of a music room and was encouraged to continue. He bought a bass and joined the high school's jazz band. Jamerson made enough progress that he was offered a music scholarship to Wayne State University, but by that time he was already earning money playing at dances and weddings. His skills were growing rapidly as he sat in on jam sessions with Detroit's large crop of progressive jazz

musicians, including guitarist Kenny Burrell and wind player Yusef Lateef. So he turned the scholarship down. Before graduating from high school, Jamerson married Annie Wells. The couple raised four children, James Jr. (later a Los Angeles session musician), Joey, Dorene (known as Penny), and Derek.

Often riding around the city with a bass protruding from his car window, Jamerson became well known in Detroit's musical community. He joined a blues band called Washboard Willie and the Super Suds of Rhythm, performing in tough clubs like the Bucket of Blood where he sometimes had to rely on his martial-arts skills to make it out unscathed. Somewhat more sedate was the cluster of jazz clubs around Detroit's New Center area, an important musical breeding ground where Jamerson played and met with many of the instrumentalists who would soon become part of the roster of Motown at its nearby headquarters. By about 1960 he was finding session work as a bassist on recordings issued by the small Detroit labels Fortune and Anna, the latter co-owned by Gwen Gordy, the sister of young African-American entrepreneur Berry Gordy.

Joined House Band at Tamla

In 1959 Berry Gordy asked Jamerson to become part of the house band of musicians associated with his own growing label, Tamla. As Anna was folded into Berry Gordy's new label Motown in the early 1960s, the group of backing musicians known as the Funk Brothers took shape, with Jamerson at the center of its sound. His style took a step forward when he incorporated an electric bass, a Fender Precision model he acquired in 1961. By the time Motown broke through to international popularity in 1964, vying for control of the top of the charts with the Beatles and other British Invasion bands, Jamerson's bass line had become crucial to the way Motown hits like the Temptations' "My Girl" developed in the studio.

Jamerson mostly gave up playing live gigs and became a full-time employee at Motown that year. In Gordy's assembly-line-like system for the production of hit recordings, the session musicians were mostly anonymous, and in the 1960s few fans or even music writers knew who Jamerson was. He gained a measure of recognition, however, from the range of musicians who tried to imitate his style, including Beatles vocalist and sometime bassist Paul McCartney, who told *Bass Guitar* (as quoted on the website of the Rock and Roll Hall of Fame) that "James Jamerson became my hero, because he was so good and melodic." There was no doubt within Motown headquarters of Jamerson's value; even under Gordy's strict scheduling regime a session might be delayed so that Jamerson could play—and this despite a mercurial personality that led Elvis Mitchell of the *New York Times* to call the musician "a genius as wily and autocratic as Fidel Castro and far more unpredictable." In 1968 Jamerson demanded and received a salary increase to $1,000 a week.

The list of Motown hits on which Jamerson performed would read like a nearly complete discography of the label's releases in the mid-1960s. In general, the interplay between Jamerson, the Funk Brothers percussion players, and the hook-oriented music and lyrics of Motown's stable of songwriters was critical to the label's success. The Rock and Roll Hall of Fame lists the following as "essential" Jamerson recordings: Stevie Wonder's "I Was Made to Love Her," Martha and the Vandellas "Dancing in the Street," "Reach Out (I'll Be There)" and "I Can't Help Myself" by the Four Tops, "You Can't Hurry Love" and "You Keep Me Hangin' On" by the Supremes, "Ain't That Peculiar" and "What's Going On?" by Marvin Gaye (the latter named by Jamerson as his own favorite performance), "My Girl," and "Going to a Go-Go" by the Miracles.

Overdubbed Acoustic Bass with Electric Instrument

Jamerson's innovations in terms of the vocabulary of the bass were numerous, and more and more of them emerge in repeated hearings of Motown recordings. He pushed and pulled the beat, adding variations to the basic bass line as a jazz player might do. Sometimes he created an unusual sound by playing an acoustic bass line and overdubbing it with an electric bass. He used only his index finger to play the instrument. Bassist Clark Dorman told the Charleston *Post & Courier* that "[l]istening to any one of his tunes is like going to a bass clinic."

Jamerson adapted to the more heavily arranged style of later Motown releases and remained with the label through its move from Detroit to Los Angeles in 1973. Shortly after that he left the label. His work in mid-1970s Los Angeles was still significant; he recorded music ranging from the folk styles of vocalists Maria Muldaur and Joan Baez to dance pop and early disco records like the Hues Corporation's "Rock the Boat" (1974) and the Sylvers' "Boogie Fever" (1975), rock (Robert Palmer's "Which One of Us Is the Fool" (1976), and pop (Marilyn McCoo and Billy Davis Jr.'s "You Don't Have to Be a Star (To Be in My Show)" (1976). In the late 1970s, however, Jamerson was increasingly troubled by the effects of chronic alcohol abuse and was frequently hospitalized; raised in a Christian environment, he never drank as a teen but had been introduced to liquor during his early years performing in Detroit.

Jamerson died in Los Angeles on August 2, 1983; the immediate cause was pneumonia, complicated by heart failure and cirrhosis of the liver. The 25th anniversary *Motown 25* special broadcast on television shortly afterward gave scant notice to his contributions, but the *Motown 40: The Music is Forever* program broadcast in 1997 was more generous, and the general trend toward recognition of how much instrumentalists in general, and Jamerson in particular, had contributed to the Motown sound continued with Jamerson's induction into the Rock and Roll Hall of Fame in 2000 and the release of the *Standing in the Shadows of Motown* film in 2002. He was the first sideman inducted into the Rock and Roll Hall of Fame.

Books

Contemporary Black Biography, Vol. 59, Gale, 2007.

Slutsky, Allan, *Standing in the Shadows of Motown: The Life and Music of Legendary Bassist James Jamerson,* Hal Leonard, 1991.

Periodicals

New York Times, November 15, 2002.

Post & Courier (Charleston, SC), September 21, 2003; July 28, 2005; April 30, 2009.

Online

"James Jamerson," *All Music Guide,* http://www.allmusic.com (February 3, 2010).

"James Jamerson," *Rock and Roll Hall of Fame,* http://www.rockhall.com/inductee/james-jamerson (February 3, 2010). □

Emil Jannings

German actor Emil Jannings (1884–1950) was one of cinema's first international stars. Jannings appeared in scores of films from some of the leading directors in both Germany and Hollywood, and won the first Academy Award for Best Actor in 1929. The portly thespian excelled in tragic roles, and may be best remembered for his role as the hapless, lovestruck teacher seduced by Marlene Dietrich in the 1930 classic *The Blue Angel.*

Jannings was born Theodor Friedrich Emil Janenz on July 23, 1884, in Rorschach, Switzerland. Some sources falsely claim he was born in Brooklyn, New York, but it was his father who was an American; Jannings's mother was German and the family moved from Switzerland to Germany around 1895. As a teen, Jannings disliked school and developed a habit of truancy. He ran away from home and talked his way into a job with a kitchen crew on board a North Sea cargo ship, but was discovered and returned to his parents. Disdaining his parents' plan for him to enter college and become an engineer, Jannings ran away a second time, this time signing on with a traveling theater group as a bill poster and prop master. Authorities found him again, but this time his father decided to let him stay, thinking that such a low-level job would soon prove dispiriting to the teen.

Rose to Fame on German Stage

Instead, Jannings stuck with it and discovered a passion for acting. He spent a few years traveling around various Central European cities with other theater companies. In his early twenties, he settled in Berlin to train under Max Reinhardt at the famed Deutsches Theater. Reinhardt was a tremendously influential figure in early-twentieth century modern drama, and inadvertently trained some of the most highly regarded film actors in the early history of cinema. In the era before the first full-length feature films, however, Jannings was known as a specialist in the great Shakespearean leading roles.

Portrayed Classic Mephistopheles

F.W. Murnau was another prominent filmmaker in the UFA stable who cast Jannings in several career-making roles. Murnau had incited an international sensation with his 1922 vampire thriller, *Nosferatu,* and gave Jannings the title role in a new UFA project, *Der letzte Mann.* One of the most acclaimed films of the silent era, the 1924 release featured Jannings as the doorman of a luxury Berlin hotel whose manager decides he is too elderly to handle the trunks and other baggage the job requires. He is forced to give up his grand uniform and the front-of-the-house job for a position as a lowly restroom attendant. UFA also released it worldwide, and its English-language premier as *The Last Man* earned critical accolades. Writing in the *New York Times* in January of 1925, Mordaunt Hall praised Murnau's "highly artistic film masterpiece" that related a story with the fewest possible title cards and highlighted its lead actor's performance. "Jannings tells the story with amazing strength by his actions and his expressions," Hall declared.

Jannings also appeared in two more major productions at UFA under Murnau's direction. These were *Herr Tartüff,* an adaptation of the classic Molière play of seventeenth-century France, and *Faust,* an extravagantly budgeted film retelling of the classic German folkloric saga set down by Johann Wolfgang von Goethe. Jannings was cast as Mephistopheles, the devil, who wagers with an angel that it is indeed possible to corrupt an honest person's soul. The *New York Times* called it a movie that "inspires with its wealth of imagination, its shadows and soft lights, its astounding camera feats and its admirable portrayals." Murnau also included a novel sequence in which Jannings's satanic character flies over the village while seeds of a deadly plague rain down from his wings.

The great *Faust,* also considered one of the silent era's masterpieces, would be Jannings's final film with Murnau, though both came to the United States to work shortly before the film's U.S. premiere in December of 1926. Jannings had appeared in a widely acclaimed 1925 film, *Variété,* from director E.A. Dupont, and its tale of love and anguish among circus performers also brought rave reviews and interest from Hollywood studios. Murnau would go on to make *Sunrise,* a 1927 film from the Fox Film Corporation that won one of the first Academy Awards, while Jannings was signed to a three-year contract with Famous Players-Lasky, the forerunner of Paramount Pictures. Not long after his arrival, a reporter for the *New York Times* interviewed Jannings, apparently with the help of a translator, because the article noted that the only phrase the actor knew in English was "I am happy to be here."

Won First Oscar

Jannings made his first Hollywood film in 1927 under Josef von Sternberg, the Austrian-born director who had spent much of his life in America. *The Last Command* featured Jannings as a high-ranking noble in tsarist Russia, Grand Duke Sergius Alexander, and portrayed his love for a left-wing sympathizer whose Bolshevik boyfriend the duke has been sent to prison. After the Bolsheviks triumph in the 1917 Revolution, Sergius is forced into exile and works as

Jannings made his film debut in 1914's *Im Schützen-graben* (In the Trenches), a silent film made to bolster support for imperial Germany's entry that year into World War I. He went on to appear in several more films from the proliferating German movie studios of this era, including an early horror film from 1916, *Nächte des Grauens* (A Night of Horror). He made his first film for director Ernst Lubitsch, *Die Augen der Mumie Ma* (The Eyes of the Mummy Ma), in 1918. The movie also starred a popular Polish actor, Pola Negri, and was made at the new UFA Studios in Berlin. This was a newly created consortium of German film studios whose acronym stood for Universum Film Aktiengesellschaft. Lubitsch, Negri, and scores of other UFA talents would go on to successful careers in Hollywood along with Jannings.

UFA emerged as a top European producer of generously budgeted feature films that showcased state-of-the-art cinematography and special effects in the era before the advent of sound. It gave free rein to its leading filmmakers, like Lubitsch, who cast Jannings in several starring roles. One of the first of these was *Madame DuBarry,* released in the United States as *Passion* in late 1919 after a wartime embargo on German exports came to an end. Jannings played France's Louis XV, with Negri as the titular courtesan. In another historical epic from Lubitsch, 1920's *Anna Boleyn,* the actor starred as England's Henry VIII with another leading female actor of the era, Henny Porten, as the doomed queen.

an extra in Hollywood films. The role cemented Jannings's position as one of the world's best dramatic actors, especially in the tragedian roles, and he won the first Academy Award for Best Actor from the newly created Academy of Motion Picture Arts and Sciences for that role, as well as for a second one, *The Way of All Flesh.* The latter was an intensely melodramatic tale of a bank clerk led astray. Jannings's character, Schilling, is depicted as a doting father of six and a trusted employee whose downfall begins on a business trip in which a con artist seduces him, plies him with champagne, then steals the securities he is carrying. The films were released in 1927 and 1928, respectively, and both were eligible for consideration under the Academy's newly created guidelines.

Jannings's dual Oscar win marked the only time the Best Actor/Actress award would be given for multiple performances. At the time, the industry event was a small-scale affair, just a banquet held on May 16, 1929, at the Hollywood Roosevelt Hotel. The year's winners were announced in a press release beforehand, and Jannings decided to skip the event because he was already preparing to leave America. A Warner Brothers movie of 1927, *The Jazz Singer,* ushered in the era of sound pictures, and suddenly foreign stars like Jannings with their heavily accented English were deemed unwise casting choices.

Immortalized as Tragic Cuckold

Newspaper reports stated that Jannings would return to Hollywood to make his first talking picture, but that did not happen. Instead he reunited with Sternberg at the UFA Berlin studio to make *Der blaue Engel,* an adaptation of the 1904 novel *Professor Unrat* by Heinrich Mann. Jannings played the stern, moralistic Professor Immanuel Unrath, a teacher at a high school for boys. He learns his unruly students are beguiled by a new act at the town's Blue Angel nightclub featuring a *femme-fatale* cabaret singer named Lola Lola, played by Marlene Dietrich, and he visits the club to chastise her. He leaves behind the formal top hat he customarily wears, and finds some of her lingerie in his coat the next day. He returns the next night, and his downfall begins. In quick succession, he is seduced by Lola, loses his job, marries her, and becomes part of the touring cabaret act.

Der blaue Engel made Dietrich a star, and was also noteworthy as one of the first films to be shot simultaneously in two languages, for two separate versions. *The Blue Angel*'s English-language version premiered in New York in December of 1930, with Hall finding that "as an actor who speaks his lines, Mr. Jannings is perhaps even better than he was in his mute productions." Writing in the London *Observer* a decade later, the critic Philip French called it "the first truly great sound movie to be produced in Europe." One of its later scenes features Unrath dressed as a clown while crowing like a rooster as the magician breaks eggs on his head before his old hometown audience at the Blue Angel, and this scene, asserted French, "remains unsurpassed for its depiction of humiliation."

Jannings remained in Germany, and also had a lakeside home in Austria. He continued to appear in UFA films, though the dubbed versions were poorly received

elsewhere. He also won major stage roles in new plays staged at the Deutsches Theater, which was still under Reinhardt's direction.

Reportedly Hitler's Favorite Actor

In January of 1933, Germany's right-wing extremist party, the National Socialists (Nazis), came to power with Adolf Hitler as chancellor. Harassment of opponents of the regime followed soon afterward, and then harsh anti-Semitic laws, the start of a world war, and the formulation of a policy to eliminate the entire Jewish population of Europe. Many talented artists, writers, directors, and actors fled Nazi Germany along with other members of the intelligentsia. Jannings was among those who stayed. UFA came under control of Joseph Goebbels, Hitler's minister for propaganda, and films became stridently pro-German. Among these were 1941's *Ohm Krüger* (Uncle Krüger), an historical epic about South Africa's Boer War. It was a vehemently anti-British piece of work, and for his title role as the Boer leader, Jannings was awarded the Ring of Honor of the German Cinema by Goebbels. He also earned other Nazi state honors, including Reichskultursenator and *Staatsschauspieler,* or Actor-Artist of the State.

At the end of World War II in 1945, those who had publicly supported the Nazi regime underwent a review process called de-Nazification. One of the UFA's most respected producers during its 1920s heyday was Erich Pommer, who had spent the war years in the United States after producing *Der letzte Mann, Der blaue Engel,* and other classics. Pommer returned to Germany after the war and to a key position at UFA, which had come under control of the U.S. occupation authorities. Pommer denied Jannings the necessary license to work again in German films. After an attempt to emigrate to Argentina, Jannings settled at his home near Salzburg in 1947. He died on January 2, 1950, at Stroblhof, his home on Lake Wolfgang. The cause was liver cancer and pneumonia. His third wife, Gussy Holl, was a well-known cabaret singer and actor of the 1920s who had previously been married to Conrad Veidt, another leading German actor of the silent era.

Books

Fox, Jo, *Film Propaganda in Britain and Nazi Germany: World War II Cinema,* Berg Publishers, 2007.

O'Leary, Liam, "Jannings, Emil," in *International Dictionary of Films and Filmmakers,* edited by Sara Pendergast and Tom Pendergast, fourth edition, Volume 3: *Actors and Actresses,* St. James Press, 2001, pp. 617–619.

Weimar Cinema: An Essential Guide to Classic Films of the Era, edited by Noah Isenberg, Columbia University Press, 2008.

Periodicals

New York Times, January 28, 1925; June 28, 1926; October 24, 1926; December 7, 1926; July 3, 1927; December 6, 1930; January 3, 1950.

Observer (London, England), October 19, 1997. □

Michaëlle Jean

Haitian-born Canadian government official Michaëlle Jean became the 27th governor general of Canada in September of 2005. She is the first Canadian of African descent to hold the position.

The governor general is the official representative of the British Crown, or monarchy, in Canada, and as such is the country's acting head of state. Until recently, given the largely symbolic nature of the association between Canada and the British monarchy, the post of governor general has been mostly ceremonial. Michaëlle Jean, however, has become a Canadian celebrity who has used her position to establish rapport with Canadians of various ethnicities as well as participating in the required goodwill appearances abroad. And she played a key role in a Canadian governmental crisis in 2008—a situation in which she was called upon to invoke one of the few actual powers reserved for her office.

Father Tortured by Haitian Police

Michaëlle Jean was born on September 6, 1957, in the Haitian capital of Port-au-Prince. She has one sibling, a sister. Her grandmother, Dianira Oriol, was an *audiencière,* or Haitian village storyteller. Jean's father, Roger, was a philosophy teacher and school principal who had a tense relationship with Haitian dictator François "Papa Doc" Duvalier, and he and Michaëlle's mother, Luce, had her tutored at home rather than letting her attend a school where she would be subjected to government indoctrination. Roger Jean was arrested by the government in 1965 and imprisoned and tortured, and Luce also encountered trouble from the police. Her parents' sufferings, and those of Haitian dissidents in general, were not hidden from Michaëlle. "You would go to a police station and you would find blood everywhere on the walls. I know that because my father was arrested and tortured," she told Alexander Panetta of the *Guelph Mercury.*

in 1967 Roger Jean left Haiti for Canada, and he was able to bring his wife and daughters to live with him the following year. He took a job teaching at a college in Thetford Mines, Quebec. There, Michaëlle experienced schoolyard insults of a racist nature. To make matters worse, perhaps because of the stress he had endured during his own imprisonment, Roger Jean became more and more violent at home. Finally, mother and daughters left for the city of Montreal, where Luce Jean worked in a factory and took all-night shifts at the Louis H. Lafontaine psychiatric hospital. "She was a rigorous woman who expected a lot from her daughters, reading, learning languages," an uncle, writer René Depestre, told Tu Thanh Ha and Ingrid Pertiz of the Toronto *Globe & Mail.* Michaëlle flourished at the Ecole Marguerite-de Lajemmerais, a public school for musically talented girls.

Jean earned a bachelor's degree in Italian and Hispanic languages at the University of Montreal around 1984; she speaks French, English, Italian, Spanish, and Haitian Creole fluently, and Portuguese competently. She went on for a master's degree in comparative literature at the same institution. Serving as a graduate student instructor, she entered a classroom to begin teaching a course in Italian literature. "The students took one look at me, and then there was a deafening rustle as they pulled out their schedules to see if they were in the wrong classroom," Jean recalled to Ray Conlogue of the *Globe & Mail.* Sometimes she worked for a domestic violence shelter in Montreal.

She had journalism in mind as a possible career goal through much of her education, and in February of 1986 she got her chance to break into the profession in a dramatic fashion. A graduate student friend, Ghila Benesty-Sroka, asked Jean to come with her on a trip to Haiti to do research for an article she was writing for a new magazine she had founded, aimed at immigrant women. When the two arrived in Port-au-Prince, the Duvalier dictatorship had just collapsed, and the streets were chaotic. With Benesty-Sroka speaking French and Jean using her native Creole, the pair shot valuable on-the-spot footage of the fast-moving changes in Haiti. The trip, Depestre told Ha and Peritz, brought Jean into renewed contact with her roots. "Even when you adopt another nationality, you remain attached to your childhood, to the land of Haiti, to the Creole tongue," he said.

Hired as CBC Reporter

Back in Montreal the two edited the material into a successful documentary that brought Jean to the attention of the French language service of the Canadian Broadcasting

Corporation (CBC). She was hired as a reporter in 1988, becoming the first French-speaking CBC news reporter of African descent, and the following year she married French filmmaker Jean-Daniel Lafond. The couple settled in Montreal's historically black Little Burgundy neighborhood and adopted a daughter, Marie-Eden, from Haiti. As the wife of a French citizen, Jean added French to her list of official nationalities.

Jean worked her way up at the CBC from reporter to anchor to talk show host. She appeared on the news programs *Montréal ce soir* (Montreal Tonight), *Le Point, Le Monde ce soir* (The World Tonight), *Virages* (Changes in Direction), and *Horizons francophones*. Jean, sometimes working with Lafond, maintained her connection with Haiti by making a documentary of her own, *Haiti in All Our Dreams* (1996). Around the year 2000 she made the leap to the CBC's English-language broadcasting service. "I'm worried about working in English," she confessed to Conlogue. "Even if they say I have a 'delightful' French accent." Indeed, Jean's speech was peppered with French words. "I'd like to get away from this ronflant [sleep-inducing] kind of public conversation. Otherwise we'll never get out of it and politicians will keep leading us by the nose," she told Conlogue.

Jean soon became a familiar face and voice to English-speaking Canadians as well, hosting a pair of documentary film programs and launching her own radio show, *Michaëlle,* on the Radio Canada network. She insisted, however, that she be allowed to continue living and working in Quebec, where she felt her status as a black celebrity had more impact. In 2000 she received the Raymond-Charette award, honoring a broadcast journalist for effective use of the French language. By 2005 Jean was riding high with a constantly growing career. She had even reestablished contact with her father, who sent her a letter after nearly 30 years with no communication.

In August of that year, Canadian prime minister Paul Martin named Jean as the new governor general. Jean was uncertain about the idea. "My first reaction was to propose names," she told Aaron Wherry of the Canadian magazine *Maclean's.* "I came up with 30 right away and they said, 'No, we took care of that. We had a committee, you know, but the idea was to ask you.' So I took about four weeks and I knew that to have a person like me becoming governor general would actually provoke a lot of hope in so many people. I knew that. I knew it. And just for that reason it was worth considering."

Denied Separatist Ties

The selection of a media personality was not controversial; Jean's predecessor, Adrienne Clarkson, had also come from the world of the media, and the job, which involved frequent public appearances but little or no actual policy-making, seemed to call for a confident public figure with a wide knowledge of world affairs. Jean's French citizenship was a more important issue. Most controversial of all was the claim, published in a Quebec magazine, that Jean and her husband supported the longstanding movement to make Quebec independent from the rest of Canada. Jean gave up her French citizenship and, after at first refusing to comment, issued a statement saying she had never been a Quebec separatist. On September 27, 2005, she was

sworn in as Canada's 27th governor general, officially becoming Her Excellency the Right Honourable Michaëlle Jean, Chancellor and Principal Companion of the Order of Canada, Chancellor and Commander of the Order of Military Merit, Chancellor and Commander of the Order of Merit of the Police Forces, Governor General and Commander-in-Chief in and over Canada. With the English monarch as Canada's official head of state, Jean was the country's vice-regal.

Jean made full use of the national prominence her position afforded her. Wherry, while noting that the common comparison of Jean to American television host Oprah Winfrey was "easy," also claimed that it was "not entirely without merit....Oprah's primary gift is an ability to appeal intimately on an emotional level. To feel publicly and deeply. And there is some of this in Jean." The governor general, indeed, credited herself with a degree of empathy that she ascribed to cultural factors, telling Wherry that "I come from a culture where we can be physically very close to people. I think people sense that. At every ceremony, every occasion, people say, 'You make me feel comfortable.'"

The charismatic Jean was a familiar face on news broadcasts, making appearances abroad and in Canada. She generally attended repatriation ceremonies for Canadian soldiers killed in the war in Afghanistan. There were a few controversies, such as a European trip in which she twice referred to herself as Canada's head of state (she was the vice-regal representative of the actual head of state, Queen Elizabeth II), but mostly she navigated the pitfalls of a position that, historian David Mitchell told Wherry, "I think it's safe to say, is harder than it looks," and she became a popular figure with strong appeal among young Canadians of African descent.

For the most part, Jean's duties were ceremonial; the office of the governor general has almost no policymaking role in Canada's governance. In 2008, however, Jean played a major role in an unusual event in the country's political life. The Conservative Party of Canadian Prime Minister Stephen Harper had increased its share of seats in the Canadian Parliament in federal elections held on October 14 of that year, but a coalition between two opposition parties, the Liberals and the New Democratic Party (NDP), with support from the Green Party and the separatist Bloc Québécois, threatened to join forces and bring down the new government with a vote of no confidence over an upcoming fiscal measure. The response of the governing Conservatives was to ask Jean to suspend, or "prorogue," Parliament—a procedure with roots deep in the history of the British Empire. After cutting short a European visit and sitting down for a two-and-a-half-hour meeting with Harper, Jean agreed to the Conservatives' request and prorogued Parliament, providing a cooling-off period for all the parties involved. When Parliament met again in January of 2009, the Liberal-NDP coalition dissolved.

The controversy was perhaps symptomatic of increasing political polarization in Canada, but it did not significantly impede Jean's activities. In 2009 she made an emotional visit to Haiti in connection with the Harper government's announcement of a new $555 million aid package for that impoverished country. She applauded Haiti's ongoing attempt to professionalize its police forces. There was no fixed end to Jean's term as governor general, and she seemed likely to assume an increasingly prominent place in Canadian life, inside or outside of government. Her many awards and honors have included one for Woman of the Year from *Elle Québec* magazine.

Two days after the magnitude 7.0 earthquake that struck Haiti on January 12, 2010, Jean appeared on Canadian television and appealed to the world community to come to the aid of her home country. She had to pause several times during her speech to collect herself, and toward the end she broke down completely. In Haitian Creole, she said (according to Daniel Leblanc in the *Globe & Mail*), "Women and men of Haiti, we must not lose hope. We are known for our strength and resilience, and need to stand courageously before this challenge that is affecting us again." Jean made an official but emotional visit to Haiti in March of 2010, meeting with Canadian troops who were spearheading relief efforts and also with friends, relatives, and ordinary Haitians on an unscripted walk through the streets of the devastated town of Jacmel, where she had spent part of her childhood. As she boarded a helicopter to leave Jacmel, reported Jessica Leeder of the *Globe & Mail*, Jean "buried her head in her hands and began to sob."

Books

Contemporary Black Biography, vol. 70, Gale, 2009.

Periodicals

Globe & Mail (Toronto, Ontario, Canada), October 26, 2000; August 5, 2005; January 14, 2010; March 10, 2010.
Guelph Mercury (Guelph, Ontario, Canada), January 17, 2009.
Maclean's, January 14, 2008; October 26, 2009.
Time Canada, August 15, 2005.
Toronto Star, January 19, 2010.

Online

"GG agrees to suspend Parliament until January," *Canadian Broadcasting Corporation,* http://www.cbc.ca/canada/story/2008/12/04/harper-jean.html (November 20, 2009).
"Governor General Michaëlle Jean," *The Governor General of Canada,* http://www.gg.ca/document.aspx?id=41 (November 20, 2009).
"Jean, Michaëlle," *The Canadian Encyclopedia,* http://www.thecanadianencyclopedia.com/ (November 20, 2009).
"Michaëlle Jean," *CBC News Indepth,* http://www.cbc.ca/news/background/governorgeneral/michaelle_jean.html (November 20, 2009).□

Fergie Jenkins

In a Major League Baseball career spanning 19 seasons, Canadian hurler Ferguson Jenkins (born 1942) won 284 ballgames, posted seven 20-win seasons

and pitched 267 complete games with 49 shutouts. A mainstay of the Chicago Cubs during the late 1960s and early '70s, Jenkins won the Cy Young Award in 1971. He was elected to the Baseball Hall of Fame in 1991, becoming the first Canadian enshrined in Cooperstown, NY.

Ferguson Arthur Jenkins was born December 13, 1942, in Chatham, Ontario, Canada. His mother, Delores Jenkins, was descended from a slave who traveled north to freedom on the Underground Railroad. She went blind as a result of complications related to his birth. Jenkins' mother never saw him play baseball, though she played a significant role in his success. "I remember she always walked with a white cane and always made sure that my baseball uniform was sparkling clean and my baseball shoes were polished," Jenkins told the *New York Times.* "I'm not sure how she knew, but she never let me out of the house to play ball unless I was all in order."

Excelled in Several Sports

Jenkins developed a fondness for baseball from his father, Ferguson Holmes Jenkins, who played center field for the Windsor Black Barons, a semi-pro team based in Ontario. He also played in the Negro League. The elder Jenkins gave up baseball, however, and settled into life as a chauffeur and cook on Great Lakes shipping-line vessels because Major League Baseball was not open to black players at the time.

An all-around athlete, Jenkins excelled at several sports. He started playing hockey when he was about six or seven and by high school was good enough to play defense on the local Junior B hockey team. In Canada, Junior B is the highest amateur league athletes play in before turning pro. Jenkins started playing baseball around the age of nine but only during the summers because his high school did not have a baseball team. Chatham Vocational School did have a basketball team, of which Jenkins was the star center during 1961 and '62. Despite his talent on the court, Jenkins did not receive any college scholarship offers. He did catch the attention of the Harlem Globetrotters, however, and toured with them in the late 1960s during two of his off-seasons from baseball.

Found Home in Baseball

Jenkins, a rightie, did not start pitching until he was a teenager, but as a child he unwittingly honed his throwing-arm accuracy by tossing rocks down the ice chutes at the local coal yard and through the open doors of speeding boxcars as trains moved through town. Little did he know those activities would pay off later in life as he tossed balls toward home plate with uncanny accuracy. Career-wise, baseball was Jenkins' third choice, but when he graduated from high school it proved the brightest prospect.

Jenkins' English teacher and gym assistant alerted a baseball scout about his student's talent. He signed with the Phillies in 1962 and headed for the minor leagues. Jenkins played in the minors during the years when segregation ran rampant in the United States. Growing up, Jenkins experienced some taunting in his native Canada, but it was nothing like the racial prejudice he encountered in the Southern United States during his time in the minor leagues. In Florida, he and his black teammates could not find any hotels that would admit them, so they were forced to sleep in a funeral parlor, along with the dead bodies. Jenkins pushed through, though, realizing the prize of playing in the majors would be worth the struggle. He showed remarkable control from the mound and quickly moved up through the minors, making his major league debut for the Phillies in 1965, toward the end of the season.

Dominated at Wrigley Field

In 1966, the Phillies traded Jenkins to the Chicago Cubs, where he continued in his role as a relief pitcher. From the start, Jenkins proved productive. During Jenkins' first outing in a Cubs uniform, he entered in the middle of a game, hit a home run and earned a win. Jenkins pitched in 60 games his first year as a Cub, earning five saves and six wins. As the 1967 season got under way, Cubs manager Leo Durocher decided to turn the six-foot-five, 210-pound Jenkins into a starter. Jenkins rose to the occasion and quickly became a staple in the Cubs' pitching rotation. He made his first of three All-Star appearances that year, too. The first batter Jenkins faced in his first All-Star game was New York Yankee MVP Mickey Mantle. Jenkins struck him out, fanning six in three innings.

As a pitcher, Jenkins did not overpower batters—the fastball was not his weapon. What he possessed was incredible durability and a supernatural ability to take command of the ball. "I had decent control because I worked at it," Jenkins told *Baseball Digest*. "I had a good sinker, a good slider. I tried to get hitters to hit the top half of the ball." In 1967, Jenkins posted his first 20-win season and led the league with 20 complete games. He won 20 games again in 1968 but also posted 15 losses, mostly due to the Cubs' lack of production from the batter's box.

While Jenkins dominated at Wrigley Field, his teammates did not. During the 1968 season, Jenkins set an MLB record for most 1-0 losses in a season, with five. In fact, over the course of his career Jenkins lost 13 outings by a 1-0 margin, despite going the distance in all those games. Another disappointment for Jenkins was that he never got to enjoy the national spotlight during a championship series because he never pitched for a pennant-winning team. In 1969, the Cubs took a double-digit lead over the New York Mets in the National League East division, but blew it in the run-up to the playoffs.

Won Cy Young Award

Jenkins led the National League in 1971 in wins (24), innings pitched (325), games started (39), and complete games (30). In addition, he averaged only one walk every nine innings and went on to win the Cy Young Award. In six straight seasons with the Cubs, Jenkins won at least 20 games. He struggled, however, in 1973, posting a 14-16 record and was traded to the Texas Rangers, where he played under the infamous Billy Martin. In 1974, Jenkins won 25 games and collected the American League's Comeback Player of the Year Award. In 1975, the Rangers dealt Jenkins to the Boston Red Sox, who traded him back in 1977. Jenkins returned to Chicago in 1982 and retired in 1983 a few months before his 41st birthday.

After retiring, Jenkins withdrew to his ranch in Ontario, Canada. He divorced his wife, Kathy Williams, in 1987. The couple had three daughters. Jenkins continued his involvement with baseball, serving as Team Canada's pitching coach for the 1987 Pan Am games. He married Maryanne Miller in 1988, then moved to a 160-acre ranch near Guthrie, Oklahoma, complete with horses, cattle and several acres of wheat. Jenkins worked part-time as a pitching coach for an Oklahoma City AAA team. He spent the rest of his time working his ranch.

A calm and collected sportsman, Jenkins was ejected just once from a game. His most awkward moment came in 1980 when he was arrested in Toronto after small amounts of marijuana and cocaine were found in his luggage. Jenkins claimed he was innocent. The baseball commissioner suspended Jenkins but he was reinstated after his attorney persuaded the commissioner that he could not rule on Jenkins' fate until the matter was decided in court. An Ontario provincial judge found Jenkins guilty during a December 1980 trial, yet the judge gave him an absolute discharge, meaning there was no fine, no sentence, and no criminal record. According to a report of the proceedings in the *Washington Post,* the judge told Jenkins, "You seem to be a person who has conducted himself in exemplary fashion in the community and in the country, building up an account. This is the time to draw on that account."

Inducted Into Hall of Fame

In 1991, Jenkins became the first Canadian elected to the Baseball Hall of Fame. He received votes on 333 of 443 ballots cast by the Baseball Writers' Association of America, barely giving him the 75 percent needed. His arrest for cocaine and marijuana and the peculiarity surrounding how Jenkins handled the matter tarnished his image, despite his numbers from the mound. He did not make it into the Hall until his third try. "I thought he was a great pitcher, with great control," former MLB outfielder Cito Gaston told the *Toronto Star* shortly after Jenkins made the Hall of Fame. As a player, Gaston batted against Jenkins several times. "He wasn't really overpowering, but he had a great slider and he kept it low and away. He could paint the black [the border around the plate] with that slider. And he had one heck of a changeup."

According to the *Toronto Star,* Jenkins invoked his father during his Hall of Fame induction ceremony. "My father played baseball from 1925 to the 1940s in the Ontario Baseball League and also the Negro League. The opportunity for him to play professional ball was limited because of the history of that era. Fortunately, he outlived history and witnessed change." Jenkins went on to thank his father for teaching him the game. "Today, I am not only being inducted alone. I am being inducted...with my father, Fergie Jenkins Sr."

Endured Heavy Losses Off Mound

While Jenkins' baseball career was filled with triumph and wins, his personal life included many hardships and losses. In December 1990 his wife, Maryanne, broke her neck in an auto accident and contracted pneumonia. She died the same week Jenkins was elected to the Hall of Fame. Her death left Jenkins with two children to raise—Samantha, their toddler, and 10-year-old Raymond, who was Jenkins' stepson. By 1992, Jenkins was engaged to Cindy Takieddine.

In December 1992, Jenkins faced tragedy again when Takieddine picked Samantha up from day care and drove her out to a rural road, where she attached a vacuum cleaner hose to her vehicle's exhaust pipe. Takieddine then threaded the hose back in through the window, sealed it with tape, turned on the vehicle and held Samantha in her arms. They died of carbon monoxide poisoning. Takieddine's suicide note left little explanation. She was upset Jenkins was considering a job with the Reds that would force him to travel for long periods and she did not want to spend months alone on the ranch. Jenkins ended up working as a pitching coach for the Reds' organization in 1993 and '94, then for the Cubs in 1995 and '96. By the early 2000s, Jenkins had married former Las Vegas showgirl Lydia Farrington. They later moved to a ranch in Arizona. In 2003, Jenkins served as commissioner of the independent Canadian Baseball League, a minor league division.

For most of his career, Jenkins flew under the radar because his teams never played in the national spotlight. He was, however, a formidable pitcher in his own right, posting seven seasons with 20 or more wins. Jenkins' strike-out-to-walk ratio remains among the finest of all time. Only a handful of pitchers—including Jenkins—have posted more than 3,000 strikeouts with fewer than 1,000 walks. His stats include 3,192 career strikeouts with 997 walks. As of 2010, Jenkins remained the only Canadian in baseball's Hall of Fame.

Periodicals

Baseball Digest, September 2008.
Gazette (Montreal), June 6, 2009.
Globe and Mail (Canada), March 31, 1993.
New York Times, January 3, 1993.
Sports Illustrated, June 9, 2003.
Toronto Star, January 10, 1991; July 22, 1991.
Washington Post, December 19, 1980.

Online

"Glory Amid Grief," *Sports Illustrated,* http://sportsillustrated. cnn.com/vault/article/magazine/MAG1139688/index.htm (30 December 2009). □

Ban Johnson

American Major League Baseball executive Byron Bancroft "Ban" Johnson (1864–1931) founded professional baseball's American League. In the early part of the twentieth century, he was one of the most influential and powerful forces in the sport's growth. He was elected to the Baseball Hall of Fame in 1937.

Before and during his reign as the president of the American League, Byron Bancroft "Ban" Johnson became one of professional baseball's most influential executives. But he developed a reputation as a power-hungry, arrogant dictator, which earned him his "Czar of Baseball" nickname. Still, few of his contemporaries could dispute his skills as a highly effective administrator.

Effectiveness would combine with failings to produce a fall of Shakespearean intensity. During his career rise, Johnson made some important friends. Conversely, during his declining years, he made some important enemies, which precipitated his eventual abdication. In the end, however, his influence proved enormous. Professional baseball, as it currently exists, is in great part attributable to Johnson's efforts: He established the second of two major leagues and helped transform a rough-and-tumble sport into the "National Pastime."

Johnson was born on January 6, 1864 in Norwalk, Ohio. His parents were Alexander Byron Johnson, a school administrator, and Eunice C. (Fox) Johnson. He was one of three sons.

Johnson's deeply religious parents attended Oberlin College in Oberlin, Ohio, an academic institution founded by Presbyterian ministers. In Avondale, Ohio in 1867, Alexander Johnson helped establish the Avondale Presbyterian Church, where he taught Sunday School. Johnson's parents hoped their son would enter the ministry, and they enrolled him in their alma mater. But Johnson didn't follow their envisioned path: He later transferred to Marietta College in southeast Ohio, and decided that he wanted to become a lawyer. He enrolled at the University of Cincinnati Law School, but he dropped out before he earned a degree.

The future baseball executive actively participated in the sport as a boy, and he later became a catcher on semi-pro and college baseball teams. He developed a reputation as a tough competitor. Playing baseball's most physically demanding position, he worked behind the plate without wearing a mask or body protection. Johnson was physically well suited for the position. He was five-feet eleven-inches tall and weighed one hundred and eighty pounds. He was good enough to receive a contract offer from a major league team. His father wouldn't let his son sign, however, and Johnson never played professional baseball.

Became a Journalist

After Johnson dropped out of the University of Cincinnati in 1886, he entered the newspaper field. In his first job, the twenty-one-year-old Johnson earned twenty-five dollars a week covering news and sports for the *Cincinnati Commercial-Gazette*. In 1887, he was promoted to sports editor.

His position provided him access to the region's leading sports figures, including baseball players and team owners from existing professional clubs. An opinionated individual who assumed strong stances in print, Johnson both alienated and attracted members of the Cincinnati sports establishment. One of his friends was Charles A. Comiskey (1859-1931), who eventually gained national fame as the owner of the Chicago White Sox baseball franchise. At the time, Comiskey was the player-manager with the Cincinnati Reds, a National League baseball team. The two men became card-playing and drinking buddies and spent many hours discussing the state of professional baseball. Johnson and Comiskey agreed that general rowdiness and profanity was getting out of hand, and they shared ideas on how to clean up the sport. Johnson would later transform some of the ideas into reality when he became a baseball executive.

Resuscitated the Western League

In November 1893, Comiskey and Cincinnati Reds team owner John T. Brush recommended Johnson for the position of president of baseball's Western League. The troubled organization had been founded only a year earlier and already faced financial collapse. At the time, it was a minor league organization with teams in Detroit and Grand Rapids in Michigan; Indianapolis, Indiana; Kansas City, Kansas; Minneapolis, Minnesota; Milwaukee, Wisconsin; Sioux City, Iowa; and Toledo, Ohio.

Johnson accepted the position, but continued working as a sports editor. In 1894, however, he left the journalism field to focus entirely on baseball. With his passion for the sport, he quickly turned a moribund organization into a profitable enterprise. This was largely due to his forceful personality that, combined with his large physical size, created a formidable presence. He was described as ambitious and even egotistical. While he coveted power, he was also noted for his intelligence and strong organizational skills, as well as his fervid desire to improve baseball's reputation. Once installed as president, he immediately began implementing changes: He bolstered the authority of umpires, discouraged liquor sales at baseball parks and curtailed the on-field and off-field rowdiness. As a result, baseball stadiums became a more family-friendly environment, and attendance dramatically increased. Comiskey followed his friend into the Western League when he purchased the Sioux City ball club in 1894. By 1897, some Western League teams were earning more money than teams in the National League which, at the time, was the sport's single major league operation.

Expanded and Renamed the League

In 1899, the twelve-team National League cut back to eight teams, dropping the Cleveland, Ohio; Washington D.C.; Louisville, Kentucky; and Baltimore, Maryland franchises. Johnson, who wanted the Western League to compete on an equal basis with the National League, saw this development as an opportunity for expansion. He added teams and shifted franchises around, moving one team from Columbus, Ohio to Cleveland to fill the vacancy left by the National League team reduction.

Johnson faced opposition from National League team owners, but his Western League garnered increasing popularity. In 1900, at a Western League business meeting, Johnson renamed the organization the American League. Team owners awarded him a multi-year contract.

In 1901, Johnson proclaimed that the renamed organization was a major league enterprise. Befitting Johnson's personality, it was a bold and even presumptuous declaration. Nevertheless, it seemed justified. He had attracted the services of National League players by eliminating the annual salary cap that existed in the rival organization. As a result, the National League lost some of its star players. Also, Johnson established teams in Boston, Massachusetts; Philadelphia, Pennsylvania; Washington D.C.; and Baltimore. Some American League teams competed directly with National League franchises, and the new major league was outscoring the opposition at the gate. As early as 1902, overall American League attendance topped the National League's.

Increased Power

The American League success compelled the National League to recognize the upstart as a viable organization and a powerful, emerging force in the sport. As a result, the competing organizations developed terms of agreement that would allow them to peacefully co-exist. For one thing, they agreed to respect one another's player contracts. More significantly, the leagues created a National Commission that would settle disputes. This three-man governing body included Johnson, National League President Harry Pulliam and Garry Herrmann, owner of the National League's Cincinnati Reds teams, who was appointed to the commission by other team owners. Johnson and Herrmann were old friends and Herrmann often sided with Johnson on important decisions. This relationship unofficially provided Johnson with the greatest share of power within the Commission. Indeed, during the next fifteen years, Johnson became the sport's most powerful man, a position that earned him the nickname "the Czar of Baseball." He demonstrated his full measure of control in 1914, when the new Federal League tried to become a major league organization. Johnson used his influence to keep it out of the two-league fraternity.

Meanwhile, the American League continued prospering under Johnson's leadership. Capitalizing on this development, the two major leagues came up with the idea of a "World Series," which would pit the American and National league champions in a post-season battle. The first series was held in 1903, and the concept proved a huge success that furthered baseball's increasing popularity.

Made Enemies Among Team Owners

Johnson did not fare as well in ensuing years. He had always been considered arrogant, but as the leading figure on the National Commission, he developed a reputation as an autocratic ruler. He also began making enemies through controversial rulings. For instance, in 1915, he invalidated a contract that George Sisler, a future baseball Hall of Famer, had signed with the Pittsburgh Pirates, a National League team. Johnson assigned Sisler to the St. Louis Browns. With this ruling, Johnson not only made an enemy of Pittsburgh owner Barney Dreyfuss, but he also lost the support of other owners.

Additionally, during this period Johnson's relationship with his old friend, Charles Comiskey, transformed from friendship to feud. It began when Johnson suspended one of Comiskey's star players, White Sox outfield Danny Greene, for three games. The enmity escalated at the start of the 1919 baseball season, when Johnson ruled that Jack Quinn, a rising pitcher in the Pacific Coast minor league system, be sent to the New York Yankees. Quinn had pitched for Comiskey and the White Sox in 1918, and Comiskey had hoped that Quinn would bolster his pitching staff in the upcoming season. Instead, the Pacific Coast League team owner sold Quinn to the Yankees. Johnson approved the sale, which dashed Comiskey's hopes. Comiskey was furious that his old friend didn't side with him in the protracted contract dispute.

"Black Sox" Scandal Taints Baseball and Johnson

By initiating a feud with Comiskey, Johnson lost a valuable team-owner ally. But things truly began to unravel for him in 1919, which was a pivotal year in baseball history as well, as it witnessed a major scandal that set in motion the subsequent destruction of the National Commission. It all revolved around the 1919 World Series. Two related developments contributed to the National and American team owners' disenchantment with the governing body: The perceived mishandling of the 1919 World Series so-called "Black Sox" scandal and a subsequent and controversial ruling that involved purse money earmarked for the New York Yankees.

Specifically, the "Black Sox" scandal involved the 1919 World Series between Comiskey's Chicago White Sox and the Cincinnati Reds. Eight members of the White Sox team were charged with conspiring with gamblers to fix the outcome of the series. The players (pitchers Eddie Cicotte and Claude Williams, outfielders Joe Jackson and Happy Felsch, first baseman Chick Gandil, shortstop Swede Risberg, third baseman Buck Weaver, and reserve infielder Fred McMullin) were accused of throwing games to ensure a Red's series victory. Reportedly, their motivation was to get back at Comiskey, who they felt was tightfisted with his money. The following year, the players were banned for life from baseball, even though actual participation of several players (particularly Jackson and Weaver) has always been disputed.

The fix was suspected after Game 1 of the best-of-nine-game series. White Sox manager Kid Gleason discussed rumors with Comiskey, who went to Johnson and National League President John Heydler (who had succeeded Pulliam as a Commission member). Johnson reportedly dismissed Comiskey's suspicions with an insulting remark. After Game 2, White Sox Secretary Harry Grabiner called Heydler to discuss the possible fix. Heydler promised that he would talk it over with Johnson and get back to Grabiner, but he never followed through.

Meanwhile, Grabiner was keeping a diary, which later became an open book. The contents revealed that Johnson and fellow Commission member Herrmann both averred that nothing amiss transpired, despite overwhelming contradictory evidence.

Johnson eventually conceded that the 1919 World Series was indeed tainted by gamblers' involvement, and he launched his own investigation. By June 1920, he gathered enough evidence to develop a case against the White Sox players. But he delayed moving forward, waiting for his friend Charles A. McDonald to be appointed chief justice of the Cook County criminal court in Chicago. Grabiner revealed in his diary that the delay was part of Johnson's plot to have Comiskey removed from the sport. Johnson, Grabiner related, hoped to buy Comiskey's White Sox team and give it to one of his allies.

The problems did not stop there, however. After the World Series, Johnson and Commission Chairman Herrmann withheld third-place purse money from the New York Yankees. Earlier in the 1919 baseball season, the Yankees had acquired pitcher Carl Mays from the Boston Red Sox, which angered Johnson. Withholding of the third-place purse money was perceived as Johnson's revenge.

At this point, team owners decided to unite against the National Commission. On November 12, 1920, they passed a resolution that would replace the Commission with a single authority figure. As a result, Kenesaw Mountain Landis became the sport's first Commissioner of Baseball. Determined to clean up baseball's sullied reputation, Landis ruled with an iron first.

Retired as Influence Waned

In ensuing years, Johnson often quarreled with Landis, but the American League president received little if any support from team owners. With his power now drastically diminished, and in increasingly poor health (he suffered from diabetes), Johnson resigned as American League president in July 1927. He still had eight years left on his contract, but he refused to accept the $40,000 annual salary.

His health worsened during retirement, and he passed away on March 28, 1931, in St. Louis, Missouri. He was sixty-seven years old. Johnson was survived by his wife, Sarah Jane Laymon, who he married in 1894. The couple had no children.

In 1937, he was posthumously inducted into Baseball's Hall of Fame. His plaque reads, "Byron Bancroft Johnson, organizer of the American League and its President from its organization in 1900 until his resignation because of ill health in 1927. A great executive."

That is how many people chose to remember him. "He was the most brilliant baseball man the game has ever known," recalled another Hall of Fame baseball executive, William Harridge (as quoted by the Baseball Hall of Fame website), who served as American League president from 1931 to 1958. "He was more responsible for making baseball the national game than anyone in the history of the sport."

Books

"Bryon Bancroft Johnson," *Dictionary of American Biography Base Set*, American Council of Learned Societies, 1928-1936.

Online

"1919 Ban Johnson," *National Baseball Hall of Fame and Museum,,* http://www.baseballhalloffame.org/hofers/detail. jsp?playerId=473431 (October 24, 2009).

"1919 Black Sox," *1919blacksox.com*, www.1919blacksox. com/story.htm (October 24, 2009).

"Ban Johnson," *Baseball-reference.com*, http://www.baseball-reference. com/bullpen/Ban_Johnson (Oct 24, 2009).

"Ban Johnson," *National Baseball Hall of Fame and Museum,,* http://www.baseballhalloffame.org/hofers/ (October 24, 2009).

"Ban Johnson (1901-1927), *Sports encyclopedia.com*, http://www. sportsecyclopedia.com/mlb/al/bjohnson.html (October 24, 2009).

"Harry Frazee and the Ban Johnson Book," *Baseball Daily Digest*, http://seamheads.com/blog/harry-frazee-ban-johnson-and-the-feud-that-nearly-destroyed-the-american-league/ (October 24, 2009).□

Georgia Douglas Johnson

American poet and playwright Georgia Douglas Johnson (c.1880–1966) was the foremost African American female poet of her time and among the group of artists who made up the famed 1920s Harlem Renaissance. After a handful of early poems appeared in *Voice of the Negro* and *Crisis*, Johnson published her first volume of poetry, *The Heart of a Woman and Other Poems* in 1918. Further poetry collections followed, along with well-regarded dramas, a regular newspaper column entitled "Homely Philosophy," and a number of short stories published under often now-lost pseudonyms. Although some contemporaries criticized Johnson's poetry for failing to sufficiently explore racial issues, her plays delved deeply in such controversial topics as lynching and miscegenation (marriage or cohabitation between a man and woman of different races). Johnson spent much of her life in Washington, D.C., where she presided over gatherings of fellow writers and intellectuals, including poets Langston Hughes and Countee Cullen, at weekly literary salons at her home.

Although Johnson's birth year has been alternately identified as 1880, 1886, and 1887—the middle year has traditionally been ascribed to her, but the earliest is the most likely—unquestionably she was born Georgia Blanche Douglass Camp on September 10 in Atlanta, Georgia. Her father, George Camp, was of mixed white and African American heritage, while her mother, Laura Jackson, came from a mingled Native American and African American background; this diverse ethnic ancestry informed Johnson's outlook and writing throughout her life. Her father and mother separated while Johnson was still a small child, and she seems to have had little if any contact with him after this split. Growing up largely in Rome, Georgia, where her mother had taken Johnson and her sister, the future writer presumably attended public schools and studied music. By 1893 Johnson was back in Atlanta, where she attended the Normal School at Atlanta University. After graduating in 1896, she traveled north to Ohio to study violin, piano, and voice among other skills first at the Oberlin Conservatory in Oberlin and later at the nearby Cleveland College of Music. During this period, Johnson was particularly interested in composition; in *Color, Sex, & Poetry: Three Women Writers of the Harlem Renaissance*, Gloria T. Hull contended that "this love of music sings through the lines of her verse, for, as [Johnson] put it, 'Into my poems I poured the longing for music.'"

Published First Poems

Her dreams of composition failed to materialize, however, and Johnson returned to Atlanta to take up a career as a teacher and assistant principal in that city's public school system. On September 28, 1903, she married Henry Lincoln "Link" Johnson, a lawyer and Republican Party delegate-at-large for the state of Georgia who was some ten years her senior. Upon her marriage, Johnson gave up her educational position, dedicating herself to her family which grew to include sons Henry Lincoln Jr. in 1906 and Peter Douglas in 1907. In 1910, the Johnson family moved to Washington, D.C., where Link Johnson founded a law practice and later served as the city's Recorder of Deeds. The shift to the capital was a portentous one for Johnson, who began to discover her poetic talents after sharing some of her early poems with Kelly Miller, then Dean of the city's Howard University. Flush with confidence, Johnson saw her poems "Gossamer," "Fame," and "My Little One" make their publication debut in W.E.B. Du Bois's *Crisis* in 1916.

Two years later, Cornhill Company published Johnson's debut full-length volume, *The Heart of a Woman and Other Poems.* Contemporary critics largely embraced the work, announcing that it heralded the arrival of a powerful, if not completely formed, new literary voice. Writing in the volume's introduction, poet William Stanley Braithwaite declared the poems "intensely feminine...It is a kind of privilege to know so much about the secrets of woman's nature, a privilege all the more to be cherished when given, as in these poems, with such exquisite utterance, with such a lyric sensibility." Some challenged Johnson's work as not offering sufficient commentary on the specific issues then facing the nation's African Americans, however; in a time when black writers were calling for change in many of their pieces, Johnson focused on the race-blind nature of womanhood. In the *Journal of Negro History*, J.R. Fauset dismissed Johnson's critics, declaring that "Johnson, although a woman of color, is dealing with life as it is regardless of the part that she may play in the great drama...there is no reason why she should not in the near future take rank among the best writers of the world." Despite Johnson's early literary success, her husband—who subscribed to the traditional view that women should forswear employment in favor of dedicating themselves exclusively to the care of their families—seems to have offered little if any support to her endeavors.

Headed Washington, D.C. Literary Salon

Regardless of this absence of marital encouragement, Johnson soldiered on with her poetry. In response to those who had criticized her perceived lack of racial sensibility, she next focused on a series of poems informed by the African American experience. In 1922, these were published as *Bronze: A Book of Verse,* and featured a somewhat half-hearted introduction by W.E.B. Du Bois. Hull argued that "much of *Bronze*—which is her weakest book—reads like obligatory race poetry," but contemporaries applauded the volume, with Alain Leroy Locke proclaiming in *Crisis* that "Johnson has at last come to her own...it is the homecoming of the mind and heart to intimately racial thought and experience which is to be especially noted and commended." At about this time, Johnson also began hosting regular gatherings at her home. Attended by African American literary and political luminaries including Du Bois, Langston Hughes, Zora Neale Hurston, and Alice Dunbar-Nelson, the "Saturday Nighters" became an opportunity for a veritable Who's Who of African American thinkers to gather to discuss the issues of the day. This salon continued for a decade, making Johnson's Washington, D.C. home a nexus of the city's intellectual culture.

After Link Johnson died in September of 1925, the burgeoning poet's life changed considerably. While the loss of her husband and the growth of her two sons—by then in their middle to late teens—allowed her greater freedom to pursue her own course, it also brought increased financial pressures. Johnson again took up regular employment with the Department of Labor as the Commissioner of Conciliation, a position responsible for inspecting the living conditions of workers. Beginning in 1926, she penned a newspaper column called "Homely Philosophy" that appeared in 20 newspapers across the country, including the Boston *Guardian* and the Chicago *Defender*. Nevertheless, Johnson found time for her craft, writing poems, plays, and short stories, and traveling on the lecture circuit. Chief among her literary output of the latter half of the 1920s was Johnson's third volume of poetry, 1928's *An Autumn Love Cycle.* Notable particularly for its inclusion of what has become the writer's best-known poem, "I Want to Die While You Love Me," the book returned to many of the same themes of femininity that had pervaded *The Heart of a Woman.*

During the later 1920s and into the 1930s, Johnson also wrote several racially-charged plays. *Blue Blood,* a play that hinges on the rapes of the mothers of a couple planning to be married until they discover that they share a father as a result of those events, somehow turned that historically quite viable but distinctly unsettling premise into a well-received comedy. Staged by the Krigwa Players in New York City in 1926, *Blue Blood* won an honorable mention in the *Opportunity* play contest. Follow-up *Plumes,* an exploration of the conflict between modernity and folkways in the early twentieth century South, garnered first prize in that event the next year. Plays including *Safe* and one-acts "A Bill to be Passed" and "Blue-Eyed Black Boy" dealt with the highly topical subject of lynching, a practice that claimed the lives of hundreds of African Americans during the first quarter of the century. Although Johnson identified nearly 30 dramatic works in a literary catalogue that she produced in the early 1960s, only four made their way to the stage and very few have survived to the present day.

Career Waned in Later Years

From 1930 until nearly the time of her death over 35 years later, Johnson also operated a pen pal club, the "One World" Washington Social Letter Club, under the pseudonym Mary Strong. For a small fee, Johnson reviewed an applicant's informative questionnaire and provided that person's address to a number of like-minded individuals around the world. Whether her motivation was financial or beneficent, the long-lasting existence of the club speaks to the support of its members. She also dedicated the latter decades of her life to writing short stories and poems, many of which likely appeared under pseudonyms and are now thus lost or forgotten. She optimistically entered her name in consideration for awards from various foundations, but was never successful. During the 1940s, she returned to her early love of music, scoring and providing lyrics for several songs. Although Johnson strove to have wide-ranging manuscripts published, however—including further volumes of poetry and a book on her famed "Saturday Nighters"—the literary world had shifted and her style was no longer fashionable or reflective of the contemporary African American sensibility.

Self-published in 1962, her final work *Share My World* anthologized some of her better-known earlier pieces, such as "I Want to Die While You Love Me," but largely offered brief poems of the themes of universality and reminiscence. Hull described *Share My World* as "a twilight volume, casting a retrospective glow on the life and work it encompasses." An introductory essay to poet Robert E. Fennell's *Second Movement* rounded out Johnson's lengthy career. In 1965, Atlanta University acknowledged her literary contributions with an honorary doctorate. She died on May 14 of the following year at Freedman's Hospital in Washington, D.C., soon after suffering a stroke, and was later interred at Lincoln Cemetery in her native Atlanta. Scholars believe that after her death, a great deal of unpublished writings, including a novel, poems, essays, short stories, and even a biography of her husband, were lost. Friend Owen Dodson recalled seeing a cleaning crew throw away many of the writer's manuscripts even as he drove past her longtime home on the way back from her funeral.

Johnson's published poetry and other literary works live on, however, and her contributions continue to be honored decades after her death; in 2010, the Georgia Writers Hall of Fame at the University of Georgia inducted the poet in recognition of her work. Her legacy encapsulates not only her own written output, but also that of the literary community that she fostered at her Washington home. Writing in the *Washington Post,* Sarah Booth Conroy quoted George Mason University associate professor of history Jeffrey Stewart as arguing that Johnson's weekly gatherings allowed some of the greatest African American literary figures of the day to "[rail] against 'drawing-room literature of manners and class snobbery.'" Conroy went on to note, however, that "ironically, Mrs. Johnson used her drawing room, affluence and good manners as a way to change the world, while still treating people pleasantly." By encouraging the open discussion of race and class, Johnson contributed to the development of a new African American consciousness in the twentieth century, an achievement that arguably stands alongside her poetry as among her greatest successes.

Books

Contemporary Black Biography, Gale, 2004.
Hull, Gloria T. *Color, Sex, & Poetry: Three Women Writers of the Harlem Renaissance,* Indiana University, 1987.
Johnson, Georgia Douglas. *The Heart of a Woman and Other Poems,* Cornhill Company, 1918.

Periodicals

Crisis, February 1923.
Journal of Negro History, October 1919.
Washington Post, May 17, 1966; March 4, 1990.

Online

Georgia Writers Hall of Fame Official Website, http://www.libs.uga.edu/gawriters/index.html (January 6, 2010).

"Georgia Douglas Johnson," *Beltway,* http://washingtonart.com/beltway/gdjohnson.html (January 6, 2010).
"Georgia Douglas Johnson (ca. 1877–1966), *New Georgia Encyclopedia,* http://www.georgiaencyclopedia.org/nge/ArticlePrintable.jsp?id=h-989 (January 6, 2010).
"Georgia Douglas Johnson," Modern American Poetry, University of Illinois, http://www.english.illinois.edu/MAPS/poets/g_l/douglas-johnson/johnson.htm (January 6, 2010).
"Johnson, Georgia Douglas," American National Biography Online, http://www.anb.org/articles/home.html (January 6, 2010).□

Johnnie Johnson

American pianist Johnnie Johnson (1924–2005) has been hailed as the 'father of rock & roll piano' for his role as the longtime keyboardist and musical collaborator of the legendary musician Chuck Berry. The inspiration for the title character of rock classic "Johnny B. Goode," Johnson taught himself to play piano as a child and first played on the radio at just eight years old. In 1953, chance brought the keyboardist and Berry together for what was supposed to be merely a one-off performance but turned into a partnership spanning three decades. Although Berry long overshadowed his band mate, Johnson began to win recognition as a solo artist in the 1980s and released several albums under his own name, including *Blue Hand Johnnie* (1987), *Johnnie B. Bad* (1991), *Johnnie B. Back* (1995), and *Johnnie Be Eighty, and Still Bad!* (2005). He won induction into the Rock & Roll Hall of Fame in 2001.

Born Johnnie Clyde Johnson on July 8, 1924, in Fairmont, West Virginia, the future rock & roll innovator first encountered the piano at the age of four or five. "I imagine it was just for decoration in the house, because no one in the family was musical, not a one," he recalled to Ben Sandmel of the Rockabilly Hall of Fame website. "But I sat down and started playing right off the bat, something simple like 'Chopsticks.' My mother cried, and said it was a gift from God." In time, Johnson's simple explorations on the instrument advanced from tinkling to playing, and the young musician soon developed the ability to reproduce songs that he heard on the radio or his parents' record player himself—a skill that Johnson, who never received formal training or learned to read music comfortably, relied on throughout his life. Because of his parents' diverse musical interest, the budding keyboardist developed genre-spanning tastes and skills from the beginning. As Johnson told Sandmel, "I consider myself a piano player, period. I play rock, I play jazz, I play blues." When he reached high school, Johnson formed a band with some friends called the Blue

band's business matters, as well. Now-legendary Chicago label Chess Records signed the trio on the strength of a demo Berry had given to label head Leonard Chess and a recommendation by blues musician Muddy Waters, and the group soon cut their first single, "Maybellene." Released in July of 1955, the song revolutionized music. "Rock & roll guitar starts here," proclaimed *Rolling Stone* in 2004; yet critics also acknowledge the vital contributions of Johnson's rhythmic piano beats to underscore Berry's blazing guitar. Contemporary listeners sent the track to number five on the charts, making it an undisputed hit.

Johnson continued to provide the keyboard beats for many of the group's songs over the next several years, with some arguing that Berry's guitar riffs pull directly from the pianist's combination of boogie-woogie, blues, and honky tonk. Many of the guitarist's signature compositions are written in key signatures uncommonly used on the guitar, but popular on the piano, indicating that Berry simply transposed Johnson's melodies from one instrument to another. Now-classic rock songs such as "Roll Over Beethoven," "Sweet Little Sixteen," and "Rock and Roll Music" strongly feature Johnson's distinctive piano sound alongside Berry's guitar work.

With the success of these singles, Johnson was able to quit his job at the steel mill and play music full-time. The combo performed around the United States despite being banned from clubs and hotels in certain parts of the country due to local segregation laws; years later, Johnson recalled playing in bars and staying with local African American families. Despite this outward success, the keyboardist became increasingly erratic as he sank deeper in alcohol dependency, and Berry complained of his frequent lateness to practice and performances. Legend recounts that about this time Berry wrote the lyrics to the seminal rock & roll song "Johnny B. Goode" alternately as a tribute to the virtuosity of his pianist and as a plea to Johnson to arrive to gigs on time and cease leaning heavily on alcohol, although Berry himself has never fully confirmed either of these suppositions. After Berry attacked Johnson's alcoholism in his own 1989 autobiography, the keyboardist told the *Los Angeles Times* that "it didn't hurt, because it was true...I was a heavy drinker, and it did interfere with my playing," according to the artist's entry in *Contemporary Musicians.*

Career Declined and Revived

During the early 1960s, Berry was convicted of transporting a minor across state lines after a fourteen-year-old Arizona girl that he had hired to work at his racially-mixed St. Louis venue, *Club Bandstand,* was arrested on prostitution charges. The front man spent two years in federal prisons, while Johnson returned to play with guitarist Albert King. The pair reunited after Berry's release but their musical songwriting collaboration began to dwindle. Although they performed together for several more years, no new songs of the caliber of "Maybellene" or "Roll Over Beethoven" emerged from their sessions. In the late 1960s, Johnson passed on an opportunity to record his own solo album for Chess Records, later telling Ken Burke of the Rockabilly Hall of Fame (as quoted the website) that "I don't regret

Rhythm Swingsters, although he acknowledged that their efforts were strictly amateur.

In 1941, Johnson left West Virginia to seek work in the booming manufacturing center of Detroit. He spent the next two years working at a Ford-owned defense plant by day and performing around the city by night. With the rise of American involvement in World War II, Johnson enlisted in the U.S. Marine Corps in 1943 and soon landed a spot in a Special Service Band, the Barracudas. "We played USO shows, that type of thing. This is where I really got the feeling that I wanted to be a professional musician, so I stuck with it after I got out of the service," he told Sandmel. Back in the United States after the close of the war in 1945, Johnson passed through Detroit and Chicago, where he played occasionally with guitarist Albert King, before landing in St. Louis in 1952 and taking a job at a steel mill.

Began Collaboration with Chuck Berry

This move proved to be a turning point in the pianist's career. He formed a three-piece combo called Sir John's Trio, which played the popular standards of the era. Booked to perform a 1953 New Year's Eve gig with his band at St. Louis's Cosmopolitan Club, Johnson found himself unexpectedly down a musician after his regular saxophonist fell ill. He hired local singer and guitarist Chuck Berry—despite his relative inexperience—to fill in with the combo for the evening's performance, and music history was born. Berry and Johnson soon began playing together at the club, with the charismatic front man taking the lead in the nascent [the decision] because at that time I don't think I could've handled it. It would've been a mistake for them to waste some money on trying to do something with me, because I just wasn't ready, that's all." A few years later, Johnson and Berry parted ways for good, and the pianist again took up playing with King, albeit on a smaller scale.

By the mid-1980s Johnson's musical career had practically vanished. For a time, he was making a living in St. Louis as a bus driver for senior citizens, but his contributions to Berry's oeuvre had been largely forgotten and Johnson himself wound up living at a local flophouse. Rolling Stones' guitarist Keith Richards had become intrigued by the pianist's style, however. Richards got in touch with Johnson and asked him to take part in the filming of a Berry tribute film, *Hail! Hail! Rock 'n' Roll!* Speaking to *Rolling Stone*'s David Fricke, Richards later recalled, "it was very fortuitous that I got to do the *Hail! Hail! Rock 'n' Roll* movie with him. I knew Johnnie and Chuck hadn't been together for years and years, and I didn't honestly know if Johnnie was still playing.... And it was such a beautiful thing, the way he slipped in and, through that movie, had a whole new career." After the documentary wrapped, Johnson joined Richards as part of the backing band for the latter's 1988 solo album *Talk Is Cheap*, cementing his return to rock 'n' roll. Work with other contemporary music greats, including Eric Clapton, Bo Diddley, and Aerosmith, soon followed.

In 1988, Johnson released his own debut solo effort, *Blue Hand Johnnie*, on St. Louis label Pulsar. Four years later came *Johnnie B. Bad*, a major label outing that also featured Richards, Clapton, and the rock band NRBQ, and introduced music fans on a large scale to his independent work for the first time in his lengthy career. "Johnson is the consummate sideman, a medium for musical expression rather than a charismatic group leader, so his solo project had to be carefully assembled around him by respected peers ... [he] shows off his considerable skills as a blues piano player and surprising ability as a singer, while his special friends clearly have a hell of a good time providing the context," lauded John Swenson of *Rolling Stone*. Johnson's next album, 1994's *That'll Work*, paired him with country-rock act the Kentucky Headhunters, but he returned to true solo work with 1995's *Johnnie B. Back*. He continued to perform throughout the decade, overcoming his fear of flying to tour the world and finally kicking his dependence on alcohol with the help of his third wife, Frances.

Won Recognition in Final Years

In 2000, Johnson sued his former collaborator Berry for back royalty payments, claiming that the singer had taken advantage of his alcoholism and resulting lack of business savvy. Arguing that he had written the music for over 50 popular songs including "Roll Over Beethoven" and "No Particular Place to Go," the pianist claimed that he had lost out on millions of dollars in revenue because Berry had copyrighted the songs in his name alone. "I'm so surprised that a lawsuit could come down 45 years later," commented Berry associate Dick Alen to *Billboard*. "When I spoke to Chuck, he said, 'I'm just disappointed that Johnnie would do something like this.'" In fact, the case was eventually dismissed in federal court, however, because the statute of limitations

on copyright disputes had long since expired and the judge deemed the lapse in time too great to pursue the suit. Nevertheless, Johnson's contributions received increased public recognition—if not financial recompense—in the new millennium. In 2001, the Rock & Roll Hall of Fame inducted the pianist, declaring him "one of the unsung heroes of rock and roll" on its web site. The following year, Fairmont State College in Johnson's native Fairmont, West Virginia, granted him an honorary doctorate in music, and in 2004 New York City's New School University granted him a Beacons in Jazz Award.

Despite advancing age and faltering health, the pianist resisted retirement, recording and performing steadily until the end of his life. Johnson's final solo recording *Johnnie Be Eighty, and Still Bad!* was released shortly before the musician passed away at his home in St. Louis on April 13, 2005, a mere ten days after his final performance in his adopted hometown. The press and Johnson's fellow musicians alike paid tribute to the man that Ernie Rideout of *Keyboard* characterized as "one of the greats of rock 'n' roll piano." He was interred at Jefferson Barracks National Cemetery in St. Louis, an honor earned through his World War II-era military service.

Books

Contemporary Black Biography, Volume 56, Gale, 2006.
Contemporary Musicians, Volume 56, Gale, 2006.

Periodicals

Billboard, December 16, 2000; May 1, 2004.
Guitar Player, April 2001.
Hollywood Reporter, October 25, 2002.
Keyboard, June 1, 2005; October 1, 2005.
New York Times, April 14, 2005.
Rolling Stone, August 22, 1991; December 9, 2004; April 15, 2005.

Online

"The Doctor Is In," Rockabilly Hall of Fame, http://www.rockabillyhall.com/DrIJJohnson.html (January 6, 2010).
"Johnnie Johnson," Allmusic Guide, http://www.allmusic.com/ (January 6, 2010).
"Johnnie Johnson," Rock & Roll Hall of Fame, http://www.rockhall.com/inductee/johnnie-johnson (January 6, 2010).
"Johnnie Johnson," Rockabilly Hall of Fame, http://www.rockabillyhall.com/JohnnieJohnson1.html (January 6, 2010).
"Johnnie Johnson: Father of Rock 'N Roll," The Johnnie Johnson Blues and Jazz Society, http://www.johnniejohnsonbluesandjazz.com/johnnie.html (January 6, 2010).□

William Joyce

British fascist William Joyce (1906–1946) earned the scorn of a nation during World War II for his radio propaganda broadcasts from Nazi Germany. Dubbed "Lord Haw Haw" by the British newspapers, Joyce

trial. In it, he declared that he had been born in America but described his "loyalty to the Crown" and repudiated any ties to the United States, according to the *Times* of London.

Joyce was a gifted student and went on to Birkbeck College of the University of London to study for a degree in English language and literature. He met his first wife, Hazel Barr, at Birkbeck, and also became involved in a new right-wing political movement initially centered on an opposition to Communism. The new "British Fascisti" borrowed their name from the Italian Fascist movement led by Benito Mussolini, and some adherents were also members of the more mainstream Conservative (Tory) Party. At a campaign meeting before the 1924 British parliamentary elections, Joyce was serving as a security guard for the speakers on the dais at Bath Hall in Lambeth when a brawl erupted; he was slashed in the face and would carry a lifelong scar across his right cheek, from the ear to the mouth, which he blamed on "Jewish Communists."

After graduating from Birkbeck College in 1927, Joyce began working toward a master's degree, but claimed that a Jewish tutor had thwarted his academic ambition. His anti-Semitic views prompted the Foreign Office to reject his 1928 application to join its diplomatic corps, and he was also spurned by the Tories for these views. In the early 1930s he drifted into the British Union of Fascists (BUF), an organization formed by Sir Oswald Mosley, an aristocrat and former Member of Parliament.

delivered scathing assessments of England's military prowess and urged the nation to surrender. He was hanged for treason at London's Wandsworth Prison on January 3, 1946.

Joyce was actually born in Brooklyn at 1377 Herkimer Street to immigrant parents on April 24, 1906, qualifying him automatically for American citizenship. His father was from Galway, Ireland, and his mother was of English extraction, and they returned to Galway in 1909. There Joyce attended Roman Catholic schools, where he emerged in his teens as a fierce supporter of the Union side, which was unusual for a Roman Catholic in the bitterly divided Ireland. He would later claim that he had been the target of an Irish Republican Army death squad for hanging around the barracks of the so-called Black and Tans, the demobilized British Army troops who were stationed in Ireland after the end of World War I to suppress the Irish rebellion.

Moved to London

Joyce, his father, and at least one of his brothers eventually settled in England. He finished his education at King's College School in Wimbledon, and then entered Battersea Polytechnic University in 1922. That same year, he applied for a slot in the Officer Training Corps of the British Army, and submitted a letter that later turned up at his treason

Became Prominent Fascist Propagandist

Mosley, recognizing Joyce's gift for oratory, made him the BUF's director of propaganda. Around this same time Joyce applied for a British passport, stating on the application that his birthplace was Galway, Ireland. The documents were not vetted, and his application was approved. Over the next few years he was involved in several outbreaks of violence at political rallies that eventually prompted the British Parliament to approve a new Public Order Act that barred the wearing of political uniforms in public.

Joyce was one of three BUF candidates who ran for a seat in the 1937 municipal election in London, but all of them lost. After that, Mosley dismissed nearly all of the BUF's paid staffers, including Joyce, who then formed the National Socialist League. Its platform centered on support for an alliance between Britain, Italy, and Nazi Germany. By this point, German Chancellor Adolf Hitler and his National Socialist Party had begun enacting draconian laws against German Jews. The anti-Semitic policies were also carried out in neighboring lands that an increasingly aggressive Germany began annexing. Another world war loomed, and British intelligence services kept a close watch on Joyce, Mosley, and other Nazi sympathizers.

By this point Joyce's first marriage had ended in divorce and he wed another BUF member, Margaret White. Receiving word that an Emergency Powers Act was about to go into effect and that would mean his likely detention as a German sympathizer, the Joyces fled to Germany in the last week of August 1939. On September 1,

Nazi troops invaded Poland, an act that provoked World War II. Stranded, he found work as a translator but within a few weeks had landed a job in Berlin with Germany's state-controlled radio network, Grossdeutscher Rundfunk (Greater Germany Radio) as part of its special international broadcasting service. He worked from the Rundfunkhaus (Radio House) in Berlin's Charlottenburg district, and was provided with an apartment in the posh neighborhood, an official work permit, and a comfortable salary.

Germany Calling

The derogatory name "Lord Haw-Haw of Zeesen" was given to the pro-German propagandists who preceded Joyce by a writer for London's *Daily Mail*. Joyce's infamous *Germany Calling* program began on September 18, 1939, and was beamed at the British Isles from the North Sea ports of Bremen and Hamburg. The nighttime broadcasts were aimed at demoralizing the British populace. In the early weeks of the war, for example, Joyce claimed that Dover and Folkestone had been destroyed by German forces but that the British government was hiding this information. He presented himself as an ardent British patriot, despite his presence in Germany, and he exhorted Britain to surrender.

Joyce's *Germany Calling* broadcasts quickly gained a sort of cult following in Britain. Comedians and ordinary folk imitated his voice for laughs by pinching their noses to yield Lord Haw Haw's curious drawl, which was initially assumed to be that of another German who spoke flawless English. Privately, British officials were apprehensive, for in the first year of the war some of the broadcasts revealed a shocking level of information. The fears of a leak at the U.S. Embassy in London proved true, and in the spring of 1940 an American embassy employee was arrested for providing top secret documents to a young Russian woman he hoped to date who, in turn, passed them on to German intelligence sources.

In a world before television and the Internet, the telephone, telegrams, and regular mail were the main forms of communication besides radio broadcasts. Phone calls and mail were of course embargoed under special wartime laws. As James B. Reston wrote in a *New York Times Magazine* article in February of 1940, the mysterious Lord Haw Haw "is the last voice across the blackout from Germany, the final human contact between the Nazis and the English...and in some ways the most dangerous new personality of the war."

Honored with Nazi Medal

Reston noted that Lord Haw Haw's tirades exploited both a sense of pride in the mighty British Empire and longstanding class prejudices in Britain. "He tells them that rationing should have been introduced in Britain on the very day that war broke out and points out that the delay enabled the rich to stock up on food that the poor couldn't afford to buy," Reston wrote. Joyce also volleyed continual taunts about certain Royal Navy warships, asserting they had been sunk by German U-boats. During these years he also wrote scripts for another Grossdeutscher Rundfunk effort that was even more nefarious in its mission: these were pro-Germany broadcasts that purported to be coming from underground stations operating somewhere in England.

Germany Calling proved such a sensation that even Americans on the East Coast were intrigued and at times could catch the signal out of Radio Bremen transmitters. It was Joyce's ex-wife who identified his voice in March of 1940 upon hearing one of the broadcasts, and after 1941 he used his real name and the comical moniker by which nearly all Britons knew him. He and his second wife lived comfortably in Berlin during the early part of the war, but they were both heavy drinkers, and the marriage foundered when she had an affair. They divorced, but reunited outside the courthouse that same day and were remarried.

During his six years in Germany, Joyce applied for and was granted German citizenship, and penned an autobiography titled *Twilight Over England*. In 1944 he was honored with the *Kriegsverdienstkreuz,* or War Merit Cross for his work. The document authorizing his medal was signed by Adolf Hitler, whom Joyce never met. As joint efforts by British, American, and Russian troops turned back the Nazi threat, Berlin came under heavy bombardment. In the last weeks of the war, Hitler committed suicide on April 30, 1945, which was also the date of Lord Haw Haw's final broadcast. Listeners would later report that he sounded as if he had been drinking heavily. Britain, he warned, would be bankrupt from the war, and he signed off with his typical "Heil Hitler!"

Captured in Flensburg

After that, the airwaves of Greater Germany Radio went silent for several days. The next voice to follow Joyce's was a rebroadcast of a speech by the commander of the Allied forces in Europe, U.S. Army General Dwight D. Eisenhower. British military personnel quickly took over the radio stations in the north German cities and officially condemned the traitorous Lord Haw Haw. His whereabouts were unknown. Later, Joyce revealed that he and his wife had been escorted from Berlin and he broadcast his final messages from the Radio Hamburg studios. German officials also provided them with false identity documents. He and his wife planned to sail for Sweden and made it as far as Flensburg, near Germany's border with Denmark.

On the evening of May 28, a disheveled-looking Joyce was walking in a wooded area that had a view of the Flensburg harbor when he came upon two British intelligence officers searching for firewood. He pointed out a couple of logs for them, speaking in French, and they thanked him in German. He then spoke in English, and at that point they recognized the voice of Lord Haw Haw. They asked him if he was William Joyce, and in response he claimed to be "Fritz Hansen" and reached into his pocket to pull out his fake passport. At that, the British officers fired several shots into his backside, and he was taken into custody.

The London trial of Lord Haw Haw was a sensation. He was tried under the terms of a new Treason Act of 1945, but his attorneys argued that because he had been born in the United States, he was never technically a British citizen and thus not subject to British treason laws. The Crown prosecutors countered that his British passport had, in the first weeks of the war, still entitled him to British diplomatic protection in Germany, and that he had begun his broadcasts before attaining German citizenship in September of 1940. The jury agreed with the prosecutors, and his death sentence was handed down on September 19, 1945. A Court of Appeal upheld the conviction on November 1, and it was appealed then to the House of Lords, which also upheld the sentence. He was hanged on January 3, 1946, at Wandsworth Prison. He remained unrepentant until the end. "I am proud to die for my ideals," the *New York Times* quoted him as saying in a statement released by his brother, "and I am sorry for the sons of Britain who have died without knowing why."

Books

Lerner, Adrienne Wilmoth, "Lord Haw-Haw," in *Encyclopedia of Espionage, Intelligence and Security,* edited by K. Lee Lerner and Brenda Wilmoth Lerner, Volume 2, Gale, 2004, pp. 238-239.

Periodicals

Daily Mail (London, England), December 12, 2003.

New Statesman, June 2, 2003.

New York Times, January 14, 1940; January 4, 1946.

New York Times Magazine, February 25, 1940.

Telegraph (London, England), October 13, 2000.

Times (London, England), September 18, 1945. □

K

Keokuk

Sauk chief Keokuk (c.1780–1848) led his people through the most wrenching and divisive decision they ever faced: to abandon their tribal lands in Illinois to white settlers and relocate to villages west of the Mississippi River. While rival leader Black Hawk rallied the Sauk who insisted on staying in Illinois and fought the Black Hawk War of 1832, Keokuk maintained cooperative relations with the United States government and led the Sauk who chose to relocate, not fight. Keokuk and Black Hawk remain intertwined in histories of the American frontier, symbolizing the choices Native Americans faced when white settlers coveted their land.

Keokuk was born around 1780 in the Sauk tribe's settlement near the Rock River, in what is now northwest Illinois. Though Keokuk was born into the martial, or military, branch of the Sauk, which normally meant he could not become a civil chief, he showed an early talent for public speaking. Civil leaders grew to respect his public talks at tribal councils about matters such as treaties. Between 1804 and the War of 1812, the Sauk and their allies, the Foxes, began looking to Keokuk to participate in their frequent negotiations with whites over annual payments to the tribes, whites' insistence that they leave certain lands, and wars between the Sauk and other tribes.

During the War of 1812, Keokuk's bravery made him a leader at a young age. Most Sauk were allied with the British against the Americans. When they heard that American soldiers were on the march in the region, the Sauk feared the troops would attack their village, Saukenuk. Few Sauk warriors were in the village at the time, and the chiefs considered surrender. Keokuk addressed the war council, however, and offered to lead the resistance to an American attack. The chiefs let Keokuk take charge of a war party and made him a chief — a great departure from custom, which normally held that a warrior could not become a chief, or even address a council of chiefs, until he proved himself in battle. The Americans never attacked Saukenuk, but the decision set in motion Keokuk's future as a Sauk leader.

Respected as Negotiator

After the war, white settlers began streaming into traditional Sauk lands, pursuing fur trading and lead mining, especially after Illinois was established as a state in 1818. The Sauk were divided over how to respond. Some, including Black Hawk, became known as the British Band because they felt a continued alliance with the British, in Canada, would save them from American domination. Other Sauk, including Keokuk, felt they had no alternative but to negotiate and cooperate with the Americans. White settlers had begun to outnumber natives in Illinois, and their numbers increased every year, making violent resistance futile.

In 1821, Keokuk and several other Sauk leaders agreed to turn over to the Americans two Sauk accused of murdering two whites the year before. Keokuk eventually traveled to St. Louis in the party that turned over the accused men to William Clark, the territorial governor of Missouri. The gesture led to a period of peaceful negotiations between the Americans and the Sauk.

American officials cultivated Keokuk as a contact. "If things are well managed[,] in two or three years more [Keokuk's] word among the Sauks and [F]oxes will be their law," Thomas Forsyth, an Indian agent to the Sauk and Foxes, wrote to Clark in 1821 (as quoted by Kerry Trask in his book *Black Hawk*). During the 1820s, the United States government gave Keokuk more gifts of flour, meat, salt, and whiskey than they gave to any other Sauk leader. The gifts made Keokuk more influential among the Sauk, since giving presents was an important measure of power in the tribe.

Keokuk affixed his mark to several treaties with American officials between 1814 and 1832, always signing under the heading of Sauk warriors or braves, not the chiefs. He joined negotiations because of his gifts as a speaker, but he was expected to defer to the civil chiefs' decisions. While maintaining relations with the Americans, Keokuk led Sauk war parties in battles against the Sioux and supported other war parties' fights against the Sioux and the Menominees, even though the Americans pushed the tribes to stop warring. In 1822, for instance, when Forsyth tried to stop a Sauk attack against the Sioux, Keokuk told him he did not understand the tribes' notions of honor and vengeance. "The Sioux Chiefs will never come forward [to negotiate], and as the war has commenced we must not let our guard down," Keokuk told Forsyth (as quoted by Thomas J. Lappas in the book *The Boundaries Between Us*). This stance helped Keokuk maintain his status as a leader among the Sauk, even as he became a mediator with Americans.

In 1824, Keokuk was one of several Sauk leaders who traveled to Washington, D.C., Baltimore, Philadelphia, and New York City to talk with American officials about the government's desire to end wars among tribes. Keokuk had never seen cities so large, and the trip helped convince him of the Americans' vast power. By the late 1820s, gradually adjusting to American influence, Keokuk tried to stop Sauk war parties from fighting the Sioux and Osages. In 1827, he warned Forsyth that Black Hawk was putting together a war party to fight the Sioux. Under pressure from Keokuk and Sauk civil chiefs, Black Hawk decided not to go to war, but the disagreement between him and Keokuk worsened. Black Hawk felt Keokuk had sided with the Americans to prevent an honorable war against the tribe's enemies.

By then, American officials were pressuring the Sauk to leave their lands in Illinois and move west of the Mississippi River. The Americans cited an 1804 treaty that had given the United States the right to the Sauk lands. It is unclear, however, whether the Sauk leaders of 1804 had understood what they had agreed to. A generation later, the Sauk were divided about what to do.

Keokuk did not like the 1804 treaty. In 1829, he rejected an American attempt to buy more Sauk land west of the Mississippi River by arguing that "The Americans cheated my Grand Father" in 1804, "and we are not going to be taken in....that way again" (as quoted by Patrick Jung in *The Black Hawk War of 1832*). Keokuk chose to abide by the 1804 agreement, however, likely calculating that the Sauk could not successfully resist the Americans. Around 1829, many Sauk, including Keokuk's relatives, moved west to a new village in present-day Iowa, near the Des Moines and Iowa rivers.

In August of 1829, Keokuk and several other Sauk, Potawatomi, and Chippewa leaders signed a treaty that cemented the Americans' 1804 claim to the Sauk and Fox lands. Keokuk remained a savvy negotiator, insisting on greater payments for the tribal lands while retaining wide respect among American officials. One, Lt. George A. McCall, called Keokuk "a perfect Apollo figure" (according to Lappas in *The Boundaries Between Us*) and "one of the most graceful and eloquent speakers I have seen among the Indians of any tribe."

Keokuk Versus Black Hawk

Meanwhile, the British Band, a minority among the Sauk by most accounts, insisted they would not give up Saukenuk, the tribal village in Illinois. White settlers began moving into Saukenuk in the winter of 1829 while the Sauk were out west hunting. Each summer, tensions increased between the Sauk and the settlers, as the natives returned from their hunt to find whites on more of the tribal land. Keokuk returned to Illinois in 1830 and 1831 to try to persuade the British Band to move west.

Black Hawk refused to go. He grew increasingly embittered toward his rival, complaining that Keokuk "accomplished nothing towards making arrangements for us to remain, or to exchange other lands for our village" (according to Lappas in *The Boundaries Between Us*). "There was no more friendship existing between us. I looked upon him as a coward, and no brave, to abandon his village to be occupied by strangers."

When Black Hawk and the British Band returned to Illinois in April of 1832, the famous Black Hawk War broke out. Though the war bears his name, Black Hawk later said American troops had started the fighting by attacking warriors he had sent out under a white flag of truce. After several battles in Wisconsin and Illinois, the war ended in August of 1832, when Illinois militiamen massacred Black Hawk's band, including women and children as well as warriors. Black Hawk surrendered soon afterward.

Keokuk and several other tribal leaders met with American general Winfield Scott that September. Scott demanded that the tribes give up their land on the west bank of the Mississippi River in exchange for annual payments. Keokuk agreed. The treaty made Keokuk the Sauk's main chief by directing all annuity payments to him, a controversial decision among the Sauk.

After the Black Hawk War

In the fall of 1837, Keokuk, Black Hawk, and several other Sauk leaders traveled to Washington, D.C. for a meeting to attempt to resolve their long-simmering conflict with the Sioux. The meeting, held at a church and hosted by the U.S. Secretary of War, did not go well. A Sioux speaker insulted the Sauk as warlike and untrustworthy, and Keokuk responded with clever retorts. "They tell you that our ears must be bored with sticks, but...you could not penetrate their thick skulls in that way—it would require hot iron," Keokuk shot back, according to Benjamin Drake's 1838 book *The Great Indian Chief of the West, or, Life and Adventures of Black Hawk*. "They say they would as soon make peace with a child, as with us — they know better, for when they made war upon us they found us men.''

On their way home, the Sauk leaders visited Cincinnati, where Drake, the author, met Keokuk. ''In person, Keokuk, is stout, graceful and commanding, with fine features and an intelligent countenance,'' Drake wrote in *The Great Indian Chief of the West.* ''His broad expanded chest and muscular limbs, denote activity and physical power.'' Drake collected other biographical details from acquaintances of Keokuk. ''He is known to excel in dancing, horsemanship, and all athletic exercises,'' Drake added. ''He has acquired considerable property, and lives in princely style.''

In 1841, United States officials visited the Sauk and Fox and pressured them to relocate farther west. Keokuk protested. ''We were once powerful; we conquered many other nations, and our fathers conquered this land,'' he said (as quoted by John P. Bowes in *Black Hawk and the War of 1832*). ''We now own it by possession, and have the same right to it that the white men have to the lands they occupy.'' A year later, however, with more white settlers pouring into Iowa, Keokuk and other tribal leaders felt they had no choice. They sold their land in Iowa and agreed to relocate to Kansas within three years. Keokuk and his tribe moved to a reservation in Kansas in October of 1845. Keokuk died there in 1848. His son, Moses Keokuk, became chief of the Sauk.

Historians still debate Keokuk's character and leadership. Their opinions of him often depend on their evaluation of Black Hawk, now a folk hero and symbol of Native American resistance to white incursion and tribal expulsion. ''We were a divided people, forming two parties,'' Black Hawk said in his autobiography (as quoted by Lappas in *The Boundaries Between Us*), ''Ke-o-kuk being at the lead of one, willing to barter our rights merely for the good opinion of the whites; and cowardly enough to desert our village to them.'' Historians sympathetic to Black Hawk's view tend to focus on Keokuk's streak of vanity and say American officials successfully maneuvered to buy his friendship and increase his standing among the Sauk. Other historians note that Keokuk often asserted himself in negotiations with the Americans and say Keokuk's pragmatic view reflected the feelings of most Sauk and Foxes at the time. ''The dissidents [such as Black Hawk],'' Lappas wrote, ''idealized the path of resistance without giving much credit to the prudence and shrewdness of Keokuk's dealings with whites.''

Books

Barr, Daniel P., ed., *The Boundaries Between Us: Natives and Newcomers along the Frontiers of the Old Northwest Territory, 1750-1850,* Kent State University Press, 2006, p. 219-234.

Bowes, John P., *Black Hawk and the War of 1832: Removal in the North,* Chelsea House Publishers, 2007.

Drake, Benjamin, *The Great Indian Chief of the West, or, Life and Adventures of Black Hawk,* Queen City Publishing House, 1857, p. 118-142.

Jung, Patrick J., *The Black Hawk War of 1832,* University of Oklahoma Press, 2007.

Nichols, Roger L., *Black Hawk and the Warrior's Path,* Harlan Davidson, Inc., 1992.

Trask, Kerry A., *Black Hawk: The Battle for the Heart of America,* Henry Holt and Company, 2006.□

Jack Kirby

The American comics artist Jack Kirby (1917–1994) created or helped create some of the most familiar figures in the field of adventure comics. Several of his creations have inspired popular feature films.

Kirby was equally well known for his drawing style. His ''bold and sculptured hero drawings have been emulated for decades,'' noted Elvis Mitchell of the *New York Times,* and while he did not create the comic-book superhero he made important original contributions to the appearance of the superhero genre at several stages of his career. The high point of Kirby's creative activity came perhaps with his sometimes stormy but highly productive collaboration with Stan Lee at Marvel Comics in the 1960s, when he essentially gave comic books the look on which a generation of American youngsters grew up. Comic book characters that Kirby created or co-created include Captain America, the Incredible Hulk, the X-Men, and the Fantastic Four.

Grew Up Streetwise

Jack Kirby was born Jacob Kurtzman in New York on August 28, 1917, and grew up on Manhattan Island's Lower East Side. His father worked in a clothing factory and was an adherent of Conservative Judaism. Kirby grew up attending both public school and a Hebrew school, but he also learned lessons on New York's streets; the *Comic Book Database* web site has even suggested that his artistic style owed something to ''a rough-and-tumble childhood with much fighting among the kind of kid gangs he would render more heroically in his future comics.'' He loved newspaper cartoons as a child, learned to imitate them, and soon was selling caricatures to his neighbors for a few pennies apiece.

As a teen Kirby was admitted to the Pratt Institute, a prestigious art school in Brooklyn. But he dropped out almost immediately and began an effort to hone his skills on his own, subscribing to a cartooning correspondence course he found in a comic book and making careful studies of elaborate Sunday newspaper adventure comics, especially *Flash Gordon.* He worked for a short time for the Lincoln newspaper chain, working on comic strips and single-panel advice drawings like *Your Health Comes First.* In his late teens Kirby landed a job at the Max Fleischer film studio as an ''in-betweener''—an animator who filled in the action between main frames. He often worked on *Popeye* cartoons.

The assembly-line quality of animation work did not appeal to Kirby, however. He called the Fleischer studio (according to *Comic Book Database*) "a factory in a sense, like my father's factory. They were manufacturing pictures." Looking around for new opportunities, he noticed the increasing popularity of original comic books, stimulated by the introduction of Superman in 1934. He soon landed a job with a company called Eisner & Iger that produced comic books for a variety of publishers. During this period he tended to work under different pseudonyms for each separate comic; he drew a crime fighter comic called *Wilton of the West* as Fred Sande and a Popeye knockoff, *Socko the Seadog,* simply as Teddy. Among his pseudonyms were several that began with the first name Jack, and he drew a Western comic under the name Lance Kirby. Out of these names came the pseudonym Jack Kirby, which he adopted legally in 1942. That year he married Rosalind Goldstein; the couple raised three children, Susan, Neal, and Barbara.

Drew Captain American Comics

In the early 1940s Kirby moved among various small companies, including Novelty Comics and Fox Publishing. When he met Joe Simon, an editor at Fox, the two clicked creatively and formed a partnership that lasted until 1954. Their most famous creation was Captain America, who first appeared with his super powered shield and American flag costume in 1941—just in time to become a national icon during the World War II years. The publisher was Timely Comics, the corporate predecessor to Marvel. Kirby and Simon followed up Captain America with other war-oriented comics, the Boy Commandos and the Newsboy Legion. As of 2010, new Captain America comic books were still appearing.

The appeal of the duo's creations did not depend just on the timeliness of their storylines, however. From the start, Kirby's drawings had an imaginative, unprecedented kinetic quality that grabbed the attention of young readers. The unique physical distortions that have become part of the basic visual grammar of comics often originated with Kirby. Playwright Jules Feiffer (quoted by Mitchell) described Kirby's style in a book he wrote about early comic book heroes: "Muscles stretched magically, foreshortened shockingly. Legs were never less than four feet apart when a punch was thrown. Every panel was a population explosion—casts of thousands: all fighting, leaping, falling, crawling." One *Captain America* comic contained the first full-page panel in comic-book history.

Kirby was drafted into the U.S. Army in 1943 and landed in Normandy, France several weeks after D-Day. He served in the Third Army, 11th Infantry unit and saw action in the Battle of Metz in November of 1944. Suffering from trench foot, he was hospitalized in France and Britain before returning home in 1945. In the postwar environment, Kirby found superhero comics losing popularity. He and Simon responded with new titles in other genres. Their *Young Romance* series, which made its debut in 1947, is thought to have been the first romance comic. Kirby combined the romance and Western genres in *Real West Romances* and drew crime, horror, and humorous comic books for a variety of publishers.

Kirby was most in his element with fantastic settings, however. As Timely evolved into Atlas Comics, Kirby returned to the publisher's stable and gained new fans with his elaborate drawings of unearthly monsters in such series as *Strange Tales*. Atlas became Marvel Comics in 1961, and Kirby formed a historic new partnership with Marvel editor and chief writer Stan Lee. The new company launched with a comic featuring a unique new superhero team, the Fantastic Four, and over the rest of the 1960s decade it was Marvel and the creations of the team of Kirby and Lee that dominated the comics field. In addition to the Fantastic Four, the Incredible Hulk, and the X-Men, the duo introduced Iron Man, the Watcher, Magneto, the Silver Surfer, Galactus, and many other characters. The last two of these first appeared in Fantastic Four books.

Worked from Synopses by Lee

The nature of the creative relationship between Kirby and Lee was a matter of debate, both within the Marvel firm and beyond. Generally, Lee wrote out a synopsis of a comic's storyline, leaving Kirby to fill in the details with his artwork—a process that gave Kirby a great deal of latitude. Kirby is thought to have created the Silver Surfer, the Sentinel of the Spaceways (a noble figure with a surfboard-like craft that could exceed the speed of light), entirely on his own, introducing the character into a Lee story that did not include any mention of him. Other Marvel artists, on Lee's orders, imitated Kirby's detailed, elegant style. In 1966, however, the *New York Herald Tribune* newspaper ran a feature on Marvel that minimized Kirby's contributions.

Lee apologized to Kirby for his part in the story, but the episode marked the beginning of a period of tensions in the partnership, which fell apart altogether by the mid-1970s. Still, Kirby continued to create prolifically for Marvel. His working conditions were good, for one thing. Whereas early in his career he had sometimes been pressured to create up to six pages a day, including drawing, inking, and text, he now had the time to create the kind of detailed artwork at which he excelled. Kirby left Marvel for DC Comics in 1970 but returned in 1975. Around that time he was able to purchase a home in California, mailing his artwork back to the Marvel offices in New York.

Although his work never regained the overwhelming popularity it had attained in the 1960s, Kirby remained active and successful until his retirement in 1987 at age 70. He worked for DC on a series called Fourth World that by the release of 1985's *Hunger Dogs* had expanded to full graphic novel scope. Some of Kirby's energy in the 1980s was devoted to legal battles with Marvel over the return on his original artwork from his classic strips of the 1960s; about 20 percent of them were eventually restored to his possession. In his later years Kirby frequently attended the Comic-Con convention in San Diego, California, where he was treated as an elder statesman of the art. He died of heart failure in Thousand Oaks, California, on February 6, 1994. Almost ten years later, novelist Michael Chabon told Mitchell that "[I]t just says something awful and it says something about comics that someone like Jack Kirby is so little known, and the characters he created are everywhere still." The *Jack Kirby Quarterly* provides scholarly documentation of the work of the artist many comics fans simply called The King.

Books

Evanier, Mark, *Kirby: King of Comics,* Abrams, 2008.

Periodicals

Independent (London, England), February 11, 1994.

New York Times, February 8, 1994; August 27, 2003.

Online

"Jack Kirby," *Comic Book DB,* http://comicbookdb.com/creator. php?ID=100 (January 17, 2010).

"Jack Kirby (Jacob Kurtzman)," *Comiclopedia,* http://lambiek. net/artists/k/kirby.htm (January 17, 2010).

"Jack Kirby Biography," "Jack Kirby Timeline," *Jack Kirby Museum & Research Center,* http://kirbymuseum.org/ biography (January 17, 2010).□

Charles R. Knight

American artist Charles R. Knight (1874–1953) was the first artist to visually conceptualize on a wide scale the appearance and environment of prehistoric creatures. His depictions of the natural world—particularly his illustrations of dinosaurs— have informed popular and scientific ideas about the appearance of these creatures for over a century. After beginning his career as an illustrator, Knight became the preferred artist of New York City's American Museum of Natural History, producing numerous paintings, illustrations, and murals of dinosaurs and other ancient animals. His pieces also grace the halls of the Carnegie Museum, the Field Museum of Natural History, and the Natural History Museum of Los Angeles. Respected to the present day for their naturalistic style, Knight's works have increasingly been the focus of major exhibitions and publications.

Born on October 21, 1874, in Brooklyn, New York, the artist was the only child of Englishman George Wakefield Knight and his Maine-born and bred wife, Lucy. From a young age, Knight showed a marked interest in the natural world, and his family encouraged his budding zoological interest, providing him with illustrated books on nature and introducing him to New York City's American Museum of Natural History at the age of five. This fascination with the natural world was mirrored by Knight's growing fondness for drawing, despite a childhood eye injury that permanently impaired the vision in his right eye, leaving him legally blind and helping form his high-strung personality. Describing the accident in *Dinosaurs, Mammoths, and Cavemen: The Art of Charles R. Knight,* Sylvia Massey Czerkas and Donald F. Glut quoted the artist as recalling, "I have no doubt that the accident contributed a great deal to my later nervous condition as my vision was always under a strain which reacted upon my entire nervous system." Despite his limited vision, Knight continued to draw and paint throughout his life, a task which often necessitated that the artist view his work at a very close distance.

Began Career as Natural Illustrator

Short months after this incident, Knight's mother died from complications of pneumonia; in 1882, his father remarried an amateur artist, Sarah Davis. Although Knight and his stepmother had an at times contentious relationship, she contributed to his artistic development both by instructing him herself and, later, by enrolling him in the city's Froebel Academy. There, the young Knight studied artistic techniques before progressing to first the Polytechnic Institute then to the new Metropolitan Art School at the Metropolitan Museum of Art. He supplemented this formal education by taking classes at the Art Students League, where he practiced more contemporary techniques in addition to the classical forms taught at the Metropolitan. Although still a teenager, Knight made the leap from student to professional in 1890 when he was hired on at the firm of J. & R. Lamb. This company produced stained glass windows for churches, and before long Knight was drawing animals and flowers for Lamb's designs. Knight's career with the company was cut short after two years, however, when his father died following a sudden stroke. His passing affected the young artist greatly, and Knight stopped working, instead living with his stepmother and grandparents.

By 1893, these living arrangements had soured, and Knight left his family home to return to Manhattan. He found a freelance position illustrating animals for *McClure's* magazine, and soon after began supplementing that work with pieces for the American Book Company. These efforts contributed to Knight's growing reputation as an animal artist, and he relished the opportunity to observe animals up close at the city's Central Park Zoo and American Museum of Natural History. Through his regular visits to the latter institution, the artist became acquainted with members of the museum's scientific staff; this led to an offer from Dr. Jacob Wortman to produce a drawing of a prehistoric pig-like creature called an *elotherium* based on Wortman's fossil reconstruction. Knight accepted, and with the completion of the drawing in 1894 began a long association between artist and institution. "Everything seemed to come my way in those days," he later recalled in his autobiography, "or at least a fair amount of work and a moderate income." Indeed, soon after, the artist's continuing association with *McClure's* garnered him a trip to Europe sponsored by the publication's owner.

Upon his return in 1896, Knight developed a friendship with American Museum of Natural History paleontologist Henry Fairfield Osborn. The head of the museum's Vertebrate Paleontology Department, Osborn recognized Knight's talents and charged the young artist with producing illustrations of living dinosaurs based on their fossilized remains. To accomplish this task, Knight learned to sculpt and produced small models of the creatures to use as guidance for his paintings. He also spent a short period under the tutelage of respected Philadelphia paleontologist, Edward Rinker Cope, in 1897. This study gave the artist a new understanding of scientific thought on the nature of prehistoric creatures. His thirst for knowledge and dedication to detail helped propel Knight to new artistic heights, and his illustrations became among the museum's most popular features. The following year, Osborn persuaded financier J.P. Morgan to fund Knight's creation of a series of paintings and sculptures depicting ancient creatures; Morgan then purchased the originals and gave them to the museum, while copies were distributed for educational use. A personal success mirrored the artist's rising professional standing, when Knight married Annie Humphrey Hardcastle, a native of the southern United States who worked at a publishing house in New York City, in 1900. The couple later had a daughter, Lucy.

Gained National Prominence

The dawn of the twentieth century found Knight beginning to earn recognition outside of the New York metro area for his art. A 1901 trip to Washington, D.C. landed the artist's work in a scientific book, *Animals Before Man in North America,* on display at the Smithsonian Institution, and on the ten dollar bills issued to commemorate that year's Pan-American Exposition. Back in New York City, he took a jaunt into sculpture, creating two large elephant heads, a tapir, and a rhinoceros for the Bronx Zoo. His primary employer remained the American Museum of Natural History, however, and Knight painted numerous works for the museum over the ensuing decades. During the 1910s, Morgan again funded Knight's work at the museum, supporting the construction of a studio in Bronxville where the artist created several murals for the institution's Hall of the Age of Man. This significant undertaking was not completed until 1923. Two years later, Knight again turned his hand to mural-making, this time creating a depiction of the fossils from the La Brea Tar Pits for the Natural History Museum of Los Angeles.

In 1926, Knight undertook a significant project decorating a new fossil gallery, Graham Hall, at Chicago's Field Museum. Painting the murals of the development of prehistoric animal life consumed four years of the artist's time, and afforded Knight and his family the opportunity to visit prehistoric sites in Europe alongside museum curator Henry Field in 1927. The cave paintings made by ancient people in France and Spain enthralled the artist who had dedicated his life to creating representations of many of these same ancient creatures. Of the original 28 murals that Knight painted between 1926 and 1930, 23 remain on display at the Field Museum. Endeavors such as these only served to bolster the artist's reputation, and by the 1930s, Knight's profile had grown so significantly that a longtime admirer of his work, Dr. George Kunz, initiated plans to build a museum dedicated to his art. Conceived as The Kunz Museum of Charles R. Knight's Work, the institution failed to materialize before Kunz's death ended the possibility.

After Osborn—still Knight's strongest proponent at the American Museum of Natural History—died in 1935, the artist found that his long-standing relationship with the institution began to wane. Turning to new endeavors, Knight dedicated part of his later career to writing text and creating artworks for his own illustrated nature books. The first of these, *Before the Dawn of History,* appeared in 1935 and featured numerous reproduction of Knight's famed museum pieces. "Those who are familiar with the murals and other work of Charles R. Knight...will hardly need to be told of the character, the beauty, and the interest of the illustrations in the volume," proclaimed a 1935 *New York Times* review. He went on to write and illustrate three additional books over the next fifteen years: *Life Through the Ages* (1946), *Animal Drawing: Anatomy and Action for Artists* (1947), and *Prehistoric Man: The Great Adventure* (1949). Of these, *Animal Drawing* offered practical instruction in the nuances of drawing animals and encouraged artists to consider both psychological and physical features in their works. Knight also shared his knowledge of prehistoric life through a series of radio broadcasts, educational lectures, and magazine articles for *National Geographic.*

Significantly Influenced Later Artists

Knight embarked on his final series of new paintings between 1944 and 1946. A group of 24 small works depicting various plant and animal life forms during a succession of ancient geological eras, the series quickly found a home at the Natural History Museum of Los Angeles County despite having been produced without a commission. After the completion of these works, Knight essentially retired, wishing to spend more time with his family. A commission from the Everhart Museum of Scranton, Pennsylvania for a large mural depicting the Carboniferous Period—an epoch stretching from roughly 350 million to 290 million years ago—drew the artist back to work in 1951. This mural, entitled *Pennsylvania Coal Age Landscape,* offered a glimpse of a probably prehistoric swampy Pennsylvanian scene that sprawled over four by fifteen feet. This piece became Knight's last, and he passed away at the age of 78 on April 15, 1953, at Polyclinic Hospital in Manhattan. Czerjas and Glut recorded his final instruction to his daughter, Lucy, as, "Don't let anything happen to my drawings."

Indeed, this concern has proved misplaced; more than half a century after Knight's death, his artworks remain on display at such prestigious institutions as the American Museum of Natural History, the Smithsonian Institution, and the Field Museum of Natural History. As one of the first artists to depict prehistoric times in an observational, realistic way, Knight set the bar for later interpretations of both ancient creatures such as dinosaurs and of contemporary animal life. His influence can also be readily seen in popular film depictions of long gone life forms inspired by such movie classics as *The Lost World* and *King Kong.* Museums across the United States showed Knight's work in the early 2000s, with the Mesa Southwest Museum in Mesa, Arizona; the George C. Pace Museum in Los Angeles, California; the Academy of Natural Sciences in Philadelphia, Pennsylvania; and the Museum of the Earth in Ithaca, New York, all hosting special exhibitions. A planned coffee table book and documentary film were underway by the end of the decade, a testament to Knight's enduring appeal. Writing in the foreword to the 2005 edition of Knight's autobiography, science fiction author Ray Bradbury commented, "when you do excellent things, you live forever. So the work that Charles R. Knight did—it's there forever, and it's going to stay forever."

Books

Czerkas, Sylvia Massey and Donald F. Glut, *Dinosaurs, Mammoths, and Cavemen: The Art of Charles R. Knight,* E. P. Dutton, 1982.

Knight, Charles R., *Autobiography of an Artist,* 2005.

Peoria Art Museum, *Charles Robert Knight 1874–1953,* 1969.

Periodicals

New York Times, January 20, 1935; April 17, 1953.

Online

"A Look Inside," The Everhart Museum of Natural History, Science, & Art, http://www.everhart-museum.org/Education/Kids/Dinosaurs/Dino.Inside.htm (January 4, 2010).

"Exhibition Highlights: Illustrators," Field Museum, http://www.fieldmuseum.org/EVOLVINGPLANET/exhibition_4.asp (January 4, 2010).

The World of Charles R. Knight, http://www.charlesrknight.com (January 3, 2010). □

Leonhard Koeppe

The German ophthalmologist Leonhard Koeppe (1884–1969) popularized the slit lamp that remains a common feature of eye examinations today.

The slit lamp was invented by Swedish ophthalmologist Allvar Gullstrand, but it was Koeppe who first reached a full appreciation of the uses to which it could be put. He suggested several key improvements to the device, subsequently incorporated into the machines manufactured by the world-leader German optics firms of the 1920s. Koeppe was more generally an expert in the internal structure of the eye and in its microscopic examination. He was the author of the textbook *Die Mikroskopie des lebenden Auges* (The Microscopy of the Living Eye).

Switched from General Medicine to Ophthalmology

Leonhard Koeppe was born in Torgau, in the Saxony region of eastern Germany, on November 20, 1884. He was of Protestant background, and his father was a district physician. Koeppe himself began his career with the general study of medicine at the universities of Freiburg and Halle, and at the latter institution he obtained a doctoral degree in medicine in 1911 (the equivalent of an M.D. degree in the German system, where the recipient is called a *Doktor der Medezin* or Doctor of Medicine). He worked for two years as a practicing physician in the town of Dommitzsch on the Elbe River, and then, motivated by a desire to specialize in ophthalmology, returned to Halle for further study.

In May of 1914 Koeppe took a job as an assistant at the University of Halle Eye Clinic, working under ophthalmologist Franz Schieck. After Schieck took over the clinic when its director, Eugen von Hippel, departed for a teaching job, Koeppe was able to work closely with him and to carry out several years of intensive research. The results of this work were seen in *The Histology of the Living Human Corpus Vitreum and Its Genetically and Age-Related Changes,* a close study of part of the eye's microscopic-level anatomy. That thesis served as Koeppe's

Habilitationsschrift—in the German university system, a piece of writing that qualifies its author, if approved, to become a professor.

Koeppe had interests beyond medicine, and he used the period of several years before a professorship opened up to undertake further studies in higher mathematics and physics. These studies served him well when he turned to a self-directed broad survey of the eye's microscopic structure. Between 1916 and 1919 he was the author of the most important papers published in the field of German ophthalmology. He summarized his findings in *The Microscopy of the Living Eye* (1920, with a second volume issued in 1922). That year, Koeppe was named a professor at the University of Halle, a position he held until the end of World War II.

Perfected Slit Lamp

Koeppe's studies exposed him to a new device that had recently begun to be manufactured by the prestigious German optics firm of Carl Zeiss: the slit lamp, for which Gullstrand had won the Nobel Prize in 1911 but which had not yet come into common use. In the words of a modern guide to the use of the slit lamp published by Zeiss, "It seems that Koeppe was the first to really recognize the value of the invention of Gullstrand." The bright bar of light applied to the eye of most people undergoing an optical exam was partly Koeppe's creation, for it was he who devised a way of incorporating a small microscope into the device for use by the examiner.

In the early 1920s Koeppe began giving introductory lectures on optical microscopy, and these yielded further discoveries on his own part and among his students. Koeppe's research was mostly concentrated on the anterior chamber of the eye, including the so-called chamber angle, and the diseases associated with that part of the eye, most importantly glaucoma. He devised a lens, still known as a Koeppe lens, for the examination of this part of the eye. It is still in use today among other lens types; in the words of *Glaucoma Today*, "The Koeppe lens is an excellent teaching tool but is complicated to set up. It provides a panoramic view of the angle and allows great maneuverability to see into a narrow angle and identify the scleral spur or angle recess." One disorder of the iris, called Koeppe's nodules, also bears his name.

In 1922 Koeppe won the Gräfe Prize, named after the founder of modern German ophthalmology, Albrecht von Gräfe. He was a member of the Leopoldina society of German natural science investigators. Koeppe's other books include *Die Bedeutung der Gitterstruktur in den lebenden Augenmedien für die Theorie der subjektiven Farbenerscheinungen* (The Significance of the Lattice Structure in the Living Eye Medium for the Theory of Subjective Color Appearances, 1922), and *Methoden zur Untersuchung der Sinnesorgane (Lichtsinn und Auge)* (Methods of Investigation of Sense Organs (Light Sense and the Eye), 1937).

Koeppe was internationally famous in the field of ophthalmology, and he was active for some years as a teacher and researcher outside of Germany. His international career began with an honorary visiting professorship at the University of Madrid in Spain in 1921. He also taught at universities in Czechoslovakia, Yugoslavia, Italy, the Netherlands, Canada, and the United States. Koeppe twice seemed ready to take up a new career in the U.S. but returned to Germany both times. Between 1923 and 1925 he worked in Rochester, New York as a research scientist at the leading American optics firm, Bausch & Lomb (which issued a new slit lamp based on his work), and during the 1930–1931 academic year he served as research professor of ophthalmic microscopy at Iowa State University. Apparently disillusioned by life in the U.S., he returned to Halle and devoted himself anew to ophthalmological research.

Worked on German Military Optics

As the German fascist state under Adolf Hitler assumed totalitarian powers in the spring of 1933, Koeppe joined the National Socialist Party on May 1 of that year. Probably as a result, he was able to maintain his professorship in Halle through the World War II years. In the late 1930s he worked for the army-associated Heeresnachrichtenschule in Halle, doing research on optical problems associated with air and undersea warfare. After the war, however, he was removed from his post, although beginning in 1957 he was reappointed for a short period. In 1927 he had begun a small ophthalmology practice, and he turned to this work anew.

Koeppe remained interested in scientific research, however, and he was fascinated by the phenomena of apparitions and inner visions, and he presented his ideas in small gatherings after his deteriorating hearing made it impossible for him to attend larger academic conferences. Koeppe remained interested in the latest scientific developments and conscientious in the treatment of his patients even as he himself was suffering from a long illness and was under the care of his wife. He died in Halle on March 18, 1969. A biography, *Leonhard Koeppe—eine biographische Betrachtung* (Leonhard Koeppe—A Biographical Treatment) was written by Kerstina Anton and submitted as a dissertation at the University of Halle in 1984.

Books

Deutsche Biographische Enzyklopädie (German Biographical Encyclopedia), Saur, 1997.

Periodicals

Klinische Monatsblätter für Augenheilkunde (Clinical Monthly Pages for Eye Treatment), 1969.

Online

"Gonioscopy: A Review," *Glaucoma Today*, September 2008, http://bmctoday.net/glaucomatoday/2008/09/article.asp?f=GT0908_06.php (February 15, 2010).

"Leonhard Koeppe," *Online Catalogue of Professors from the University of Halle*, http://www.catalogus-professorum-halensis.de February 15, 2010). □

Ray Kurzweil

Ray Kurzweil (born 1948) is best known for his inventions and software advancements such as the Kurzweil Reading Machine and Optical Character Recognition. He has also become well known for his work in Artificial Intelligence (AI) and pattern recognition.

Ray Kurzweil was born on February 12, 1948, in Queens, New York. He was the son of Fredric and Hannah Kurzweil; the former was a concert pianist and conductor, and the latter was an artist. Kurzweil found his calling to be an inventor at an early age, as early as five years old, and he claimed never to have wavered. He enjoyed tinkering with musical instruments and second-hand electronics when he wasn't playing with the erector sets and other construction toys that his parents bought for him.

Kurzweil constructed his first computer at the age of 12, using logic circuits from telephone relays, and entered it into his school science fair. Soon after that, he wrote a statistical computer program, which was later distributed by IBM. At 15 he created a machine that recognized music patterns and created original musical works. This success brought him onto the 1960s television show *I've Got a Secret.* He was also invited to the White House to meet President Lyndon B. Johnson as one of 40 finalists in the Westinghouse Talent Search. He even won first prize in the International Science Fair in 1964.

He enrolled at the Massachusetts Institute of Technology (MIT) in 1967, where he majored in computer science and literature. Other students often referred to him as "The Phantom" because he often left his college activities behind to engage in his own pursuits. It was at MIT that he met the AI lab founder and director, Marvin Minsky, who became a mentor to Kurzweil. As a sophomore, Kurzweil, with several other students, developed SELECT, a software program designed to help high school students choose a college. Publisher Harcourt, Brace & World bought the software program for $100,000 plus royalties. Kurzweil graduated from MIT in 1970.

Founded Company

Kurzweil went into the field of pattern recognition, a subdomain of AI. Many of his technological firsts and future discoveries came from his work in this field. In 1974 he founded his first company, Kurzweil Computer Products (KCP). During this time he attempted to create a product that could recognize printed characters. The company started out with many difficulties, and Kurzweil had to pawn his possessions in order to keep the company afloat. Soon after, though, the company designed Omnifont, an Optical Character Recognition (OCR) software that could read the letters in virtually any font, as opposed to most OCR programs that could only read characters in a specific font. KCP combined this technology with the flatbed scanner, which Kurzweil developed in 1975. This meant that a user could scan a document and be able to render the image into text.

Kurzweil expanded this technology to include a new aspect: text-to-speech software. This software could interpret the rules of language and combine them with OCR technology that could read scanned documents to a user. He developed this after a passing encounter with a blind passenger he met during an airline flight. Of the encounter, Kurzweil told *Electronic Design,* "He described to me how there wasn't too much he couldn't do, but he acknowledged one handicap: an inability to read ordinary printed materials such as his memos. So at that point, I decided to apply the OCR to a reading machine." In an article in *Business Week,* Stevie Wonder, the well-known blind musician, said of the software that "it gave blind people the one life goal that everyone treasures, and that is independence."

OCR software combined with the text-to-speech software became known as the Kurzweil Reading Machine (KRM), and was released in 1976. In 1978 he received the Association of Computer Machinery (ACM) Grace Murray Hooper Award.

In the early 1980s, Kurzweil sold KCP to Xerox Imaging Systems for about six million dollars. Soon after this, he founded Kurzweil Applied Intelligence, Inc., which grew to become the largest speech recognition company in the world, with Kurzweil as its chair and co-chief executive officer. In 1983 he created the K250 synthesizer, the first advanced computer music keyboard. This creation came after a 1982 visit to Stevie Wonder's studio, where Wonder asked Kurzweil to create an instrument that would allow someone to play several different instruments simultaneously. The K250 synthesizer could not only accurately mimic the sound of different instruments, it also created realistic decay, sustain, and release of different instruments. He sold this invention to Young Chang Akki Co, Ltd.

Kurzweil continued to receive awards for his innovations. In 1986 he was named the honorary chair for innovation for the White House Conference on Small Business by then-President Ronald Reagan. In 1987 he marketed the first commercial large vocabulary speech recognition technology, including the Kurzweil VoiceWriter that recognized about 10,000 words. In 1988 he was named Inventor of the Year by MIT, the Boston Museum of Science, and the Boston Patent Law Association. In 1990 he was voted Engineer of the Year by more than one million readers of *Design News* magazine, receiving their Technology Achievement Award.

Wrote *The Age of Intelligence Machines*

After many successful inventions, Kurzweil wrote his first book, *The Age of Intelligent Machines,* a history of AI, along with his ideas about trends in technology that could be modeled through pattern recognition in order to predict the future. He released the book in 1990 and it was considered a positive approach to the subject. He wrote in his book that "being a high-tech entrepreneur is like being a surfer.... You have to ride the wave at exactly the right time. You have to have some idea of where things are going. If your project's going to take three years, you want it to be relevant when it comes out. If it's ahead of its time, it won't be affordable. If it's behind its time, you'll be the eighteenth person out in the field."

Kurzweil used history and politics in making his predictions. He made several very accurate predictions in the book, lending it credibility. For example, he predicted the creation of a world-wide computer network, which we now know as the Internet. He foresaw intelligent weapons, which were used beginning in the Gulf War. He even predicted the defeat of a human chess champion by a computer program, though his prediction was one year off. He anticipated that the defeat would occur in 1998, but Deep Blue, the chess playing computer program, won in 1997.

Kurzweil continued to be acclaimed for his designs. In 1991 he received the Louis Braille Award and in 1992 he received the Massachusetts Quincentennial Award for Innovations and Discovery.

Discussed Diabetes Diagnosis

Released in 1992, Kurzweil's next book, *The 10% Solution for a Healthy Life,* discussed his battle with Type II diabetes. He was diagnosed at age 35 and was prescribed conventional treatments, such as insulin treatment. After gaining weight, he switched doctors and began to do his own research. In his book, Kurzweil claimed to have overcome the disease, lost 40 pounds, and got off insulin through nutrition, stress management, and exercise.

Kurzweil's business pursuits did not stop during these creative years. In 1994 he received Carnegie Mellon University's Dixon Prize. He created Kurzweil Technologies, Inc. in 1995, and a year later he founded Kurzweil Educational Systems, Inc. In 1999 he created FAT KAT, Inc.

Unveiled "Virtual Person"

In 1999 Kurzweil expanded upon *The Age of Intelligent Machines.* in *The Age of Spiritual Machines,* in which he argued that the development of artificial intelligence is inevitable. He painted technological evolution with the same brush as human evolution. By modeling technological innovation with the computational speed per unit cost, he came to the conclusion that not only is technology changing, but the rate of change is also increasing. The human brain may have massive computational power, but it evolves slowly, while computational technology is evolving quickly enough that Kurzweil claimed that by 2029 there will be thoughtful artificial intelligence, and bodiless beings by 2099.

In that same year, he received the National Medal of Technology and Innovation, the United States' highest honor in technology. One year later he founded Kurzweil Cyber Art Technologies. On April 25, 2001, he received the Lemelson-Massachusetts Institute of Technology Award, the world's largest prize for invention and innovation at $500,000. That year he also debuted "Ramona" at the New York Music and Internet Expo. Ramona, a virtual person, used 3D computer animation, voice-to-text (in the form of questions), text-to-voice (in the form of answers), and a knowledge base to interpret questions. Ramona could answer simple questions put forth by Kurzweil during his keynote address. The most impressive example of this technology previously was a computer program, ELIZA, developed by MIT professor Joseph Weizenbaum in 1965.

In 2002 Kurzweil was inducted into the National Inventor Hall of Fame. In 2003 he created K-NFB Reading Technology.

Released Two More Books

In 2004 Kurzweil released his next book: *Fantastic Voyage: Live Long Enough to Live Forever.* This book discussed the use of technology to create immortality. He even listed a three-page list of supplements to take, in order to live long enough to see technological immortality.

One year later he released *The Singularity Is Near, When Humans Transcend Biology.* A singularity is a term used by astrophysicists to describe the area of a black hole that has infinite density. Kurzweil saw this singularity as the point where technology becomes more complex than human consciousness, which evolves more slowly. Once technology becomes fast enough and small enough, he argued, it will be able to process more than humans can. At this point we will lose the ability to control our technology, as its progress reaches to infinity.

In 2006 Kurzweil created the first pocket-sized print-to-speech reading machine. That same year he received the IEEE Alfred N. Goldsmith Award for Distinguished Contributions to Engineering Communication. He has continued to work in the fields of virtual reality and longevity.

Books

Doctorow, Cory, *Content,* Tachyon Publications, 2008.

Dooling, Richard, *Rapture for the Geeks: When AI Outsmarts IQ,* Harmony Books, 2009.

Henderson, Harry, *Encyclopedia of Computer Science and Technology,* Facts on File, 2008.

Kurzweil, Ray, *The Age of Intelligent Machines,* MIT Press, 1990.

Kurzweil, Ray, *The Age of Spiritual Machines: When Computers Exceed Human Intelligence,* Viking, 1999.

Kurzweil, Ray, *The Singularity Is Near: When Humans Transcend Biology,* Viking, 2005.

Kurzweil, Ray, and Terry Grossman, *Fantastic Voyage: Live Long Enough to Live Forever,* Rodale, 2004.

Notable Scientists: From 1900 to the Present, edited by Brigham Narins, Gale, 2008.

Williams, Sam, *Arguing A.I.: The Battle for Twenty-first-Century Science,* Random House, 2002.

Periodicals

Business Week, May 2, 2001.

Electronic Design, Vol. 54, Issue 23, 2006.□

L

Carl Laemmle

American film producer Carl Laemmle Sr. (1867–1943) was one of Hollywood's first movie moguls. The German immigrant founded Universal Pictures and was profiled as early as 1912 in the *New York Times* as "the man who introduced the motion picture drama to the public." A few years later, Laemmle purchased a large parcel of farmland in Los Angeles County to build a state-of-the-art studio and production facility for his company, a decisive moment in the entertainment industry's shift from New York to California.

A German Jew, Laemmle was a native of Laupheim, a town in the state of Württemberg. Born in 1867 as the tenth of 13 children, only five of whom survived childhood, he left school at age 13 to begin an apprenticeship with a stationery dealer in Ichenhausen, a nearby town. At 17, after the death of their mother, Laemmle followed his older brother Josef to the United States. He arrived in 1884 with $50 he had saved, and found a job in a New York City drugstore before joining his brother in Chicago. Over the next decade he worked in a variety of bookkeeping and clerk jobs in retail establishments, though he also worked in the hellish Chicago stockyards at one point. In 1894 he moved to Oshkosh, Wisconsin, to take a position as bookkeeper for the Continental Clothing Company, an apparel business. By then he had become a naturalized American citizen.

Saved $3,000 Nest Egg

In 1898 Laemmle married Recha Stern, the niece of his employer and a German-Jewish émigré like himself. When Continental's owners declined to make him a partner in the business a few years later, he returned to Chicago to seek new opportunities. A friend there, Robert H. Cochrane, urged him to start his own company. Laemmle considered opening a five-and-dime store similar to the Woolworth's chain, but while looking at commercial properties he saw the steady stream of patrons attending one of the city's first two movie theaters, called nickelodeons because the admission price was five cents. These venues showed the novel "moving pictures"—rudimentary short films, some just footage of news events, and most under 30 minutes—that had become a sensation with the public, especially new urban immigrant populations seeking an inexpensive form of entertainment in an era before radio stations existed.

Laemmle leased a storefront at 909 N. Milwaukee Avenue—later the site of the Dan Ryan (Interstate 94) Expressway overpass—painted it white, rented folding chairs from a nearby funeral home, found projection equipment and a film distributor, hired a pianist, and opened for business as the White Front Theatre on February 24, 1906. With several 20-minute showings, the theater began taking in as much as $200 a day. Laemmle opened a second theater on South Halstead Street near Van Buren several weeks later, and by the end of the year had started his own distribution company, the Laemmle Film Service, which supplied films for the growing number of nickelodeon theaters across the United States.

Battled Thomas Edison

Competition in the nascent film industry was fierce, and often cutthroat. Laemmle's distribution business soon ran up against a new collective formed by Thomas A. Edison, who had patented his movie camera in 1897, and the Biography Company, a former competitor of Edison's

company that also won an important patent for a projector that could play longer films. When those two entities merged in 1909 as the Motion Picture Patents Company, they also formed a consortium of movie producers and exhibitors who signed contracts to use that equipment. Edison pursued an aggressive battle in the courts over copyright infringement for those who opted out. Laemmle signed on, but within a few months broke away from the organization with a few other "independent" film distributors. Needing the support of theater owners, who depended on a constant supply of new movies, Laemmle dismissed the idea of renting expensive foreign reels from Europe and instead founded his own movie studio and moved his family to New York City.

Laemmle called his first production studio "Yankee Films," though the name was later changed to the Independent Motion Pictures Company of America, or IMP. Its first release was *Hiawatha,* a pantomime of the famous Henry Wadsworth Longfellow poem, released on October 25, 1909. It was shot at a building on Eleventh Avenue and in Fort Lee, New Jersey. Over the next three years, Laemmle's company teamed with two other independent production companies to become the Motion Picture Distributing and Sales Company, and began churning out nearly a dozen films each month. In 1910 he signed the woman who would become America's first movie star, Mary Pickford, whom he lured from Biography by nearly doubling her salary to $175 a week and offering her top billing with her full name. He also spent heavily on legal

battles with Edison's Motion Picture Patents Company, finally winning a landmark 1912 decision from the U.S. Department of Justice that ruled that the Edison consortium was indeed a "trust" and thus in violation of the 1890 Sherman Antitrust Act.

In June of 1912, Laemmle's IMP merged with several other filmmaking enterprises into the Universal Motion Picture Manufacturing Company. One of its first films was a "feature"-length project about a sex-trafficking ring, *Traffic in Souls,* released in 1913. With a 74-minute running time, it took up five reels and cost $5,700 to make. It earned almost eight times that amount at the box office and disproved critics who asserted that audiences would never sit in a theater to watch something over an hour's length.

Bought Barren Tract of Land

One of IMP's first movie directors was Tom Ince, who left Laemmle's company to relocate to southern California, where he could utilize its varied landscape in the first successful Westerns. Ince set up a studio in the Pacific Palisades area in 1912. Laemmle, too, opened an office in Los Angeles and began scouting properties. He found a 235-acre parcel on the other side of the Hollywood Hills that included a chicken ranch, and bought it in 1914 for $165,000, an exorbitant sum at the time for what was essentially scrubland. He dubbed it "Universal City," and began building the most modern movie-production facility in California. The first film shot there was Universal's *Damon and Pythias.*

Over the next few years Universal City expanded into a massive array of buildings, even including a zoo to house animals used on-screen and a fully staffed hospital for the inevitable injuries to actors. Other studios followed suit, including Famous Players-Lasky, which became Paramount Pictures, and Warner Brothers. All of the companies had been founded by Jewish émigrés who, like Laemmle, began in the nickelodeon and film distribution business and realized that the public's appetite for films was seemingly limitless. New York City and New Jersey declined as centers of production after a brutal 1918 winter that brought an influenza epidemic and the freezing of the Hudson River, which made getting to locations in the Fort Lee area impossible. The rest of the industry decamped to California that winter, and stayed.

In 1919, Laemmle agreed to give an Austrian immigrant actor and screenwriting hopeful, Erich von Stroheim, his first chance at directing. The picture was *Blind Husbands,* and Stroheim went on to become one of the most acclaimed directors in cinema history, and helped Laemmle's company set another first in 1922 with his project *Foolish Wives,* which exceeded its quarter-million dollar budget to become the first movie to cost more than $1 million to make. At Universal City, Stroheim replicated the French Riviera city of Monte Carlo for the plot's setting, and turned in a finished print that was eight hours in length.

Promoted Thalberg, Hollywood's "Boy Wonder"

Laemmle's success in the movie business came from his shrewd business decisions, but he also owed a debt to

Cochrane, the advertising executive from Chicago who was an early investor in the Laemmle Film Service and went on to become a vice president at Universal. Cochrane was a skilled copywriter who was instrumental in creating new ad campaigns and marketing strategies for IMP and then Universal. Laemmle also recognized filmmaking talent: in addition to Stroheim, other notable figures who started their careers at Universal included director John Ford and Irving Thalberg, who was Laemmle's 20-year-old personal assistant when Laemmle sailed for Europe and left Thalberg in charge of all major decisions for several months. Thalberg scored a terrific hit with one of Universal's greatest films of the 1920s, *The Hunchback of Notre Dame,* and went on to become a top executive with Metro-Goldwyn-Mayer.

By the early 1920s Laemmle had bought out his original partners in the Universal Motion Picture Manufacturing Company. The company became "Universal Pictures" in 1925 when it became a publicly traded company on the New York Stock Exchange. Like other studio moguls of the era, Laemmle retained total control and exercised it fully, though he was known as less of a tyrant than many of his rivals. His most ill-advised decision, however, was to place his son, Carl Jr., as head of all film production at the company after just a few years on the job. The younger Laemmle produced a string of notable flops, and Universal became the home of the campy horror film, although these productions later became the studio's most enduring classics. They included *Dracula* with Béla Lugosi and *Frankenstein,* played by Boris Karloff, both from 1931; Karloff's turn in *The Mummy* a year later; 1933's *The Invisible Man*; and *Bride of Frankenstein* from 1935.

One of the last great motion pictures Universal Studios produced under Laemmle's tenure was *All Quiet on the Western Front* in 1930, which won the third Academy Award for Best Picture in the early years of the industry fete. One of the final projects his son oversaw was *Show Boat,* a 1936 big-budget musical based on the Broadway original, that became both a box office hit and a critical success.

Stepped Down in March of 1936

By the time *Show Boat* reached theaters in May of 1936, Laemmle had already retired. The company's fortunes had plummeted in the Great Depression, and Laemmle sold the company to a group of outside investors for $5.5 million. His son was soon forced out, and never reentered the movie business. Laemmle spent his remaining years at Dias Dorados, the palatial Benedict Canyon estate built by Ince just before his mysterious 1924 death that was reported to have occurred there, but may instead have happened aboard newspaper tycoon William Randolph Hearst's yacht.

A widower since 1918, Laemmle was involved in thoroughbred racing and was active in the effort to help Jews in his native Germany emigrate after the Nazi Party came to power in 1933 and began implementing their infamous anti-Semitic policies. He died at the age of 72 on September 24, 1943, at his home after a heart attack, the third he suffered that day. He was survived by his son

and a daughter, Rosabelle Bergerman, along with two grandchildren. Laemmle also gave scores of extended family members their start in the movie business. His niece, Carla Laemmle, had a brief role in *Dracula,* and is credited with delivering the first line of dialogue in a horror film from the talking era. His second cousins, Kurt and Max, founded the Laemmle Theatres in Los Angeles in 1938, which was still run by Laemmle descendants 70 years later.

Laemmle's Universal Pictures fared even worse under its new owners after its 1936 sale. In 1959 it was acquired by the Music Corporation of America, or MCA, and finally regained its supremacy as a Hollywood player in 1975 with another horror classic, *Jaws,* by director Steven Spielberg. The company went through a series of owners and eventually became part of a media group called NBC Universal. The Universal City ranch Laemmle bought in 1914 remains a fully operating studio, and includes a popular theme park, Universal Studios Hollywood.

Books

Dick, Bernard F., *City of Dreams: The Making and Remaking of Universal Pictures,* University Press of Kentucky, 1997.

Dictionary of American Biography, Supplements 1-2: To 1940, American Council of Learned Societies, 1944-1958.

Drinkwater, John, *The Life and Adventures of Carl Laemmle,* Ayer Publishing, 1978.

International Dictionary of Films and Filmmakers, Volume 4, *Writers and Production Artists,* fourth edition, St. James Press, 2000.

Periodicals

Daily News (Los Angeles, CA), May 18, 1999.

New York Times, December 1, 1912; September 25, 1939.□

Stieg Larsson

Swedish author Stieg Larsson (1954–2004) became one of the best-selling and most acclaimed writers of the 2000s decade with his so-called Millennium Trilogy of mysteries, all of them posthumously published after Larsson's sudden death.

Larsson's three books rode a wave of popular Scandinavian crime fiction. He and other contemporary mystery writers from the region created compelling downbeat works that explored the social problems and stresses lurking beneath the region's prosperous lifestyles. What propelled Larsson's works to international fame was his compelling pair of investigators, journalist Mikael Blomkvist and, above all, the tattooed, angry young computer hacker Lisbeth Salander. "Reviewers have described Salander as the most original character in crime fiction since Patricia Highsmith's Ripley—a mixture of Lara Croft and Buffy the Vampire Slayer," noted the London *Sunday Times.*

active member of the Communist-oriented Swedish left, editing a magazine oriented toward the ideas of Soviet Communist theorist Leon Trotsky and continuing to oppose American involvement in Vietnam. Later he began tracking Swedish far-right groups, compiling his findings into a book, *Right-Wing Extremism,* written with Anna-Lena Lodenius and published in 1991. The book increased the volume of threats against Larsson, and one neo-Nazi newspaper in 1993 published Larsson and Lodenius's home addresses and phone numbers, asking its readers (according to Larsson's web site, whether "he [Larsson] should be allowed to continue his work, or if something should be done."

Unintimidated by these threats, Larsson pursued legal action that led to the publisher's imprisonment for four months. The threat of violence against him did affect his life in several ways, however, For one, he and Gabrielsson, although they had lived together for many years in a Stockholm apartment, never formally married (although, from 1983 on, they did wear rings engraved with their names), the reason being that according to Swedish law the address of a married couple is part of the public record. Furthermore, he naturally suffered from generally high levels of stress. Larsson smoked, according to various reports, "60 roll-up cigarettes a day" (*Economist*) or "20 Marlboro Lights a day" (Hoyle). His family had a history of heart problems, and he subsisted largely on takeout pizza or fried chicken.

Founded Anti-Nazi Magazine

Larsson's stress level increased when he added a second full-time job to his schedule. In 1995 he founded the magazine *Expo,* modeled on the British anti-Nazi magazine *Searchlight,* and served as its editor. In 1997 he quit his job at TT, but still faced numerous demands on his time. Looking to a future with more financial security, he began working late nights on mystery novels, planning a series of ten related books. He was well acquainted with genre fiction; he had served in 1978 and 1979 as president of the Scandinavian Science Fiction Association, and both he and Gabrielsson, an architectural historian, were enthusiastic readers with wide-ranging tastes. Too, his investigations into neo-fascist organizations had given him insights into the darker aspects of Swedish life. In 1999 the neo-Nazi murderer of a Swedish labor leader was found to have information on Larsson and Gabrielsson in his apartment. In 2000 Larsson wrote a guide for journalists on how to avoid violent attacks.

Beginning in about 2001, Larsson worked in earnest on his mystery novels. "Stieg would be up all night writing, and when I woke up he would say, 'You wouldn't believe what Salander just did!' It was like a menage a trois," Gabrielsson told Levine. Gabrielsson explained that she gave him substantial input and encouraged him to submit the first book, *Mäan som hatar kvinnor* (Men Who Hate Women), to the Norstedts publishing house. The publisher reacted enthusiastically, looking back on several decades of internationally successful Scandinavian crime fiction by the likes of Denmark's Peter Hoeg (author of *Smilla's Sense*

Inspired by Grandfather

Stieg Larsson was born in the small town of Skelleftehamn in northern Sweden on August 15, 1954. His teenage parents, both store clerks, felt unequipped to raise him and turned him over to his maternal grandparents. Larsson's grandfather, Severin Boström, became an important role model. As either "a diehard Stalinist" (according to Joshua Levine of *Newsweek International*) or merely a "staunch democrat" (in the words of Antonia Hoyle of Britain's *Mail on Sunday*), he resisted Nazi influence in Sweden during World War II and was put in a labor camp. Larsson grew up wanting, in the words of his web site biography, "to protect equal rights and fight for democracy and freedom of speech in order to prevent history, and what happened to his grandfather, from repeating itself." After his grandfather's death, Larsson went to live with his parents, who gave him a typewriter when he was 12.

From that point on, Larsson had the habit of writing late into the night, regardless of how his work might affect people who lived with him. Those soon included Eva Gabrielsson, whom Larsson met at an anti—Vietnam War rally when he was 18. Larsson served in the Swedish military and traveled to Africa, running out of money there and taking a job as a dishwasher in order to make his way back to Europe. In 1977 he took a job as a graphic designer with the Swedish news agency TT and worked in that position for many years.

Larsson's efforts in his free time were closer to his heart than his full-time job was. In the 1970s he was an of Snow) and the Swedish team of Maj Sjowall and Per Wahloo. Larsson was given a three-book contract and a large advance, very rare treatment for a first-time novelist from a small country. The works of Larsson's Scandinavian predecessors had a distinctively hard-bitten, cynical tone, with anti-heroic central figures who solve crimes almost despite their disillusionment with society.

Larsson topped them all with his 24-year-old central character, Lisbeth Salander. "Fearless, supremely self-confident, sexually voracious (when in the mood), she seems to walk off the pages into the room," noted the *Economist*. Pierced, heavily tattooed, and an expert computer hacker, Lisbeth suffered from a background of abuse that Larsson gradually revealed over the course of his three completed novels, and she displayed traits of autism or Asperger's syndrome. The theme of male violence against women was central to Larsson's thinking. "Above all he was a feminist," Gabrielsson pointed out to Hoyle. *The Girl with the Dragon Tattoo* dealt with the disappearance of an heiress who may have fallen victim to a serial killer. The title was changed from *Men Who Hate Women* to *The Girl with the Dragon Tattoo*, which was thought to be more commercially viable. Lisbeth's collaborator and opposite number was journalist Mikael Blomkvist, thought to be modeled partly on Larsson himself.

Left Invalid Will

Larsson did not live long enough to get even an inkling of the spectacular success his novels would attain. In November of 2004 he suffered a massive heart attack after climbing seven flights of stairs to his office when he found the elevator out of order. He died in Stockholm on November 9, 2004. Because of his anti-Nazi activities, there was some speculation that he had been the victim of foul play, but friends pointed to his poor health habits and generally accepted the idea that his death was due to natural causes. He died without a legitimate will, although in 1977 he had written out instructions that his estate should be given to the Communist Workers Party. That will, which was never legally witnessed, was ruled invalid.

The Girl with the Dragon Tattoo earned positive reviews internationally, and its successor, *The Girl Who Played with Fire*, was even more successful. The second novel, which focused more closely on Lisbeth Salander (originally Larsson envisioned Salander and Blomkvist as equal partners), dealt with international sex trafficking. The books were translated into English and other languages, becoming popular in countries as various as Albania and Vietnam (publishers in 40 countries had acquired the rights as of 2009), and most Swedes had read at least one. The apartment building at which Salander was supposed to have lived, on the island of Sodermalm in Stockholm, became a tourist attraction with a staff of 15 guides. In 2008 Larsson was the second-best-selling fiction author in the world, trailing only Afghan writer Khaled Hosseini, and, with the third book of the series, *The Girl Who Kicked the Hornet's Nest*, still slated to appear in the United States in 2010, Larsson's sales were not likely to slow down. The

three complete Larsson novels became known as the Millennium Trilogy.

The third novel dealt with a subject Larsson knew well: the presence of right-wing elements in Swedish law enforcement agencies. Much of the intrigue surrounding Larsson's books in the years after his death, however, involved not their political content but the circumstances of his own life, as an acrimonious struggle developed over his estate after his death. The participants were Gabrielsson on one hand and Larsson's father, Erland, and brother, Joakim, on the other. Swedish law granted no rights to common-law spouses, so in the absence of a valid will, Larsson's possessions belonged to his father and brother. The status of the apartment Larsson shared with Gabrielsson, however, was ambiguous, and Gabrielsson held a trump card: a computer containing a partially completed manuscript of a fourth Larsson novel, plus notes for a fifth and sixth. As of late 2009 negotiations between the parties were at a standstill, with Gabrielsson rejecting an offer of two million Euros and insisting that she was motivated not by financial gain but by the belief that she was the person best qualified to manage Larsson's literary legacy. By early 2010, that legacy involved worldwide sales of 23 million books.

Periodicals

Economist, October 31, 2009.
Macleans, July 27, 2009.
Mail on Sunday (London, England), January 3, 2010.
Newsweek International, July 20, 2009.
Sunday Times (London, England), September 27, 2009.

Online

"Biography," *Stieg Larsson Official Web site*, http://www.stieglarsson.com/Life-and-work (December 20, 2009).
"Global top 20 book bestsellers (fiction) 2008," *AbeBooks.com*, http://www.abebooks.com/blog/index.php/2009/01/15/bestselling-fiction-authors-in-the-world-for-2008/ (December 20, 2009).
"Stieg Larsson," *Contemporary Authors Online*, Gale, 2009. Reproduced in Biography Resource Center. http://www.galenet.galegroup.com/servlet/BioRC (December 20, 2009). □

Stan Lee

American writer and editor Stan Lee (born 1922) redefined the world of the comic book with realistic characters that combined typical human emotions and traits with their super powers. Lee created or co-created most of the characters that populated the comics published by the Marvel firm in the 1960s.

Those characters, including the Incredible Hulk, the Fantastic Four, and Spider-Man, spawned several television series and then, in the early 2000s, an impressive series of hit feature films. Lee's creations were

prominent in the American imagination, and not only among the young people whose preferences Lee read so clearly as a writer and editor. In a *Boys' Life* interview with Scott S. Smith, Lee explained his method succinctly. "Our fantasy characters are rather realistic, which sounds like a contradiction," he said. "The reader or viewer must suspend disbelief as far as crawling on walls or shooting a web or turning into a green monster. But everything else about the character we try to make realistic, so the audience could imagine 'that could be me.'"

Worked as Obituary Writer

Stan Lee was born Stanley Martin Lieber in New York City on December 28, 1922. His parents were Romanian-born Jews; his father, Jack, was a tailor of women's clothes, his mother, Celia, a homemaker. The family prospered during the Roaring Twenties, but business slowed during the Depression years, and they moved to a small apartment on Manhattan's Upper West Side. Attending DeWitt Clinton High School in the Bronx, Lee worked at a variety of part-time jobs as a teen, including theater usher, newspaper subscription salesman, pharmacy delivery boy, and obituary writer. But all these took second place to the adventure stories he liked to read: the Hardy Boys, the books of Tarzan creator Edgar Rice Burroughs, and the more obscure adventure stories of Leo Edwards, among many others. The literary craft of these writers rubbed off on Lee, and he began to write stories himself. He won a

New York Herald Tribune high school writing contest for three weeks in a row.

Graduating early from high school in 1939, Lee was hired as an office assistant by the comics and pulp fiction publishing firm Timely, whose owner, Martin Goodman, was related to Lee by marriage. When editors at Timely became aware of Lee's linguistic abilities, he was promoted to proofreader and then given the chance to make writing contributions to the firm's hit new superhero comic, *Captain America,* created by editor Joe Simon and artist Jack Kirby. The secret of the 17-year-old's rapid rise to writer, Lee told Tom Sinclair of *Entertainment Weekly,* was that "I knew the difference between a declarative sentence and a baseball bat." Lee's rise to the top of the company's creative hierarchy was completed just a year later, when Simon and Kirby departed; Lee was named interim editor, and the arrangement was quickly made permanent.

When he began writing for Timely, Lee used shortened or altered versions of his name such as S.T. Anley in his comics because he still hoped to publish a serious novel under his real name. One of those pseudonyms, Stan Lee, began to stick, and he later adopted it legally. Lee enlisted in the U.S. Army in 1942 and reached the rank of sergeant. He was only one of nine members of the army whose job title was "playwright"—he worked in the United States in the Signal Corps, writing manuals and scripts for training films. After leaving the military in 1945 Lee returned to his editor's post and soon faced a series of changes in the comics world: superhero comics fell out of fashion, replaced temporarily by western-themed and romance comics, and in the 1950s the industry-created Comics Code, adopted in response to political pressure, restricted violence and other controversial elements in comics story lines.

Planned to Quit Comic Business

Lee married English hat model and writer Joan Boocock in 1947, and the couple raised a daughter, also named Joan (born in 1950). Lee himself admitted to Sinclair that much of his work in the 1950s was done "by the book." "I wrote whatever they told me to write the way they told me to write it. It didn't matter: War stories, crime, Westerns, horror, humor; I wrote everything." By the early 1960s Lee was burned out on comics and facing middle age. He told his wife that he wanted to quit his job and start fresh. She agreed, but suggested that if he were leaving anyhow, he should do one last comic book exactly as he wanted to, constrained only by his own imagination.

Lee responded in late 1961 with the Fantastic Four, a superhero quartet bound together by family and romantic relationships as well as by their super powers. Lee brought in Jack Kirby, with whom he had worked two decades before at Timely (which later evolved into Atlas Comics). *The Fantastic Four* became an immediate success and set the pattern for the publications of the company that was soon, at Lee's suggestion, renamed Marvel Comics. *The Fantastic Four* revolutionized comics. Lee's new breed of superheroes had, in the words of *Comic Book DB,* "a flawed humanity, a change from the ideal archetypes that were typically written for pre-teens. His heroes could display bad tempers, melancholy fits, vanity, greed, etc. They bickered amongst themselves, worried about paying their bills and impressing girlfriends, and even were sometimes physically ill." Before Lee, superheroes were ideal figures; beginning with the Fantastic Four, they were, except for their super powers, quite real.

With the success of the Fantastic Four, Lee and the world of comics in general found a new energy. Lee said several times that it was as though he could do no wrong in the early and middle 1960s, as one unforgettable character after another—Thor, Iron Man, Daredevil, Doctor Strange, the Silver Surfer, the Incredible Hulk, and Spider-Man, among others, took shape in Marvel's studios. Even with Lee's new success, executives at Marvel questioned his pitch for a story about a socially maladjusted high school student, Peter Parker, who could instantly spin webs and use them to climb walls or cross gaps like a spider. The first *Spider-Man* comic, in a 1962 collection called *Amazing Fantasy*, blew by sales expectations, and Lee's instincts were vindicated anew.

As Marvel's popularity grew to a point where its creative team was turning out 12 titles a month, Lee created a unique assembly-line process for the creation of new material he called the Marvel Method. He worked closely with his illustrators, including Kirby and, for several years, illustrator Steve Ditko. Often Lee would supply only a synopsis to the artist, who would add artwork and fill out the story with more detail. Then the comic would be returned to Lee, who would write dialogue and add a humorous editorial presence that was an integral part of the comics' appeal. The question of the relative creative contributions of Lee and Kirby, especially, has been a subject of considerable debate among comics fans and scholars, and even led to disagreements among the creators themselves. Ditko left Marvel in 1966, and Kirby followed several years later, although he later returned. Lee often served as the public face of Marvel and, well in advance of the general appreciation of comics as a serious art form, he received visits and acclaim from top creative figures of the day such as Italian filmmaker Federico Fellini.

Emphasized Vocabulary

Lee's editorial method permitted and even encouraged the use of vocabulary words normally beyond the knowledge of his primarily youthful readership. "If a kid has to go to a dictionary, that's not the worst thing that could happen," he mused, according to *Comic Book DB*. In contrast to the common perspective among educators that comics were an impediment to learning, Lee maintained to Smith that they "are a great aid in teaching young people to read. When you enjoy what you're reading, it helps you get into the habit. At Marvel, we got a lot of mail from parents saying their son was getting bad grades and then started reading comics, and the next thing they knew, his marks in English started improving."

Lee and his wife moved to Los Angeles in 1980 and began to cultivate the relationship between Marvel and Hollywood that would eventually give his work a lasting cultural influence. The process was a slow one for some years. Cartoons based on *Spider-Man* and *The Incredible Hulk* appeared in the early 1980s, followed in 1992 by an *X-Men* series on the Fox network. Lee plunged forward into the Internet age with the formation of Stan Lee Media in 1998; the firm went bankrupt in 2000 after questionable investments by a business partner, but the octogenarian Lee remained alert to the possibilities of new media. In 2002 he formed POW! (Purveyors of Wonder!) Entertainment and developed a new adult-oriented animation series, *Stan Lee's Stripperella*, for the Spike TV cable television network. In 2007 POW! inaugurated a new series of "Stan Lee Presents" animated films marketed direct to digital video disc, leading to a new partnership with Walt Disney Studios. The following year he began developing a new series based on a gay superhero. Like Kirby, Lee wrangled in court with Marvel, but unlike his former partners he never cut his ties with the company.

Perhaps the most dramatic measure of Lee's cultural legacy, however, lay in the series of feature films based on Marvel characters that began with *Blade* in 1998. That film was followed by *X-Men* (2000), *Spider-Man* (2002), *Daredevil, X-Men United,* and *Hulk* (all 2003), *The Punisher* and *Spider-Man 2* (both 2004), *Fantastic Four* (2005), *Rise of the Silver Surfer* and *Spider-Man 3* (both 2007), and *The Incredible Hulk* (2008), among others. "Virtually every major character that I created at Marvel is being turned into movies," Lee told William Keck of *USA Today*. "When I go to the theater to see these, I'm able to just sit there and enjoy the movies without thinking, 'Hey, I created that.'" The fact that all these characters originated in the fertile mind of Stan Lee was not, however, lost on many viewers.

Books

Authors and Artists for Young Adults, volume 39, Gale, 2003.

Lee, Stan, and George Mair, *Excelsior!: The Amazing Life of Stan Lee,* Simon & Schuster, 2002.

Raphael, Jordan, and Tom Spurgeon, *Stan Lee and the Rise and Fall of the American Comic Book,* Chicago Review Press, 2003.

Stan Lee Conversations, edited by Jeff McLaughlin, University Press of Mississippi, 2007.

Periodicals

Boys' Life, May 2007.

Entertainment Weekly, June 20, 2003.

Forbes, March 22, 2009.

New York Times, March 25, 2005.

USA Today, May 5, 2008.

Variety, July 19, 2004; November 17, 2008.

Online

"Stan Lee," *Comic Book DB,* http://www.comicbookdb.com/creator.php?ID=98 (January 31, 2010). □

Karl Richard Lepsius

German Egyptologist Karl Richard Lepsius (1810–1884), also frequently called Carl Richard Lepsius or simply Richard Lepsius, is widely acknowledged today as one of the most important figures in the foundation of the field of Egyptian archeology. His expedition to Egypt of the mid-1840s led to the acquisition of some of the first artifacts of the Berlin Museum's famed collection of ancient Egyptian works, and provided information that contributed greatly to the young field of Egyptology. Lepsius collected the expedition's findings in the massive *Denkmäler aus Ägypten und Äthiopien* (Monuments from Egypt and Ethiopia) a twelve-volume tome filled with inscriptions, plates, and commentary that was a standard work for many decades. Later in his career, Lepsius served as professor of Egyptology at Berlin University, co-director of the Egyptian Museum in Berlin, head of the German Archeological Institute in Rome, and director of the Royal Library at Berlin as well as publishing works on Egyptology and African languages.

L epsius was born in the Saxon town of Naumburg an der Saale on December 23, 1810, to regional government official Charles Peter Lepsius and his wife, Friederike Gläser. Writing in *Richard Lepsius: A Biography,* Georg Ebers argued that the elder Lepsius was "represented as a strict and methodical official, of distinguished bearing, as well as an indefatigable worker; and precisely these qualities fell as a paternal inheritance to his son, and afterwards constituted the conditions of his greatness." The elder Lepsius also had a personal interest in ancient history and founded a local archeological club, the Thuringian-Saxon Archaeological Society. His son enjoyed an upbringing that was financially comfortable, and Lepsius' earliest education was at the hands of private tutors. In 1823 he won admission to a *gymnasium,* or German secondary school, located near Naumburg. He seems to have begun early studies in languages, and after completing his degree in 1829 enrolled at the University of Leipzig to study Greek and Roman archeology. Lepsius completed only two terms at Leipzig before transferring to the university at Göttingen in May of 1830. There, he knew the Brothers Grimm of fairy tale fame and continued his studies in linguistics, which included work in Greek, Latin, and even Sanskrit. Political turmoil rocked the campus, however, so in 1832 Lepsius again transferred, this time to Berlin. He completed his formal education there the following spring, and soon after set out for Paris.

Began Study of Egyptian Language

In the French capital, Lepsius visited museums and libraries, attended lectures, learned the technique of copper engraving, and even composed a few musical pieces.

He was intrigued by the study of Egyptology as had recently been put forth by French scholars Jean-François Champollion, who had been the first to decipher the Rosetta Stone, and his academic follower Jean Letronne. The recent graduate at first confined himself to the linguistics branch of the field, however. He relied heavily on the works of Champollion to master that ancient form, studying the by-then deceased scholar's posthumous *Grammar* with great intensity. By 1835 he had begun a comparative study of Egyptian Coptic grammar, later followed by investigations into older hieroglyphic forms. The following year Lepsius left Paris for Italy. In Pisa, he became acquainted with Ippolito Rosellini, a scholar who had previously accompanied Champollion to Egypt. Lepsius next continued to Rome, and there he began work on his first scholarly paper on Egyptology, *Professeur I. Rosellini sur l'alphabet hiéglyphique Lettre à M. le Professeur I. Rosellini etc.* (Professor I. Rosellini on the hieroglyphic alphabet, Letter to Professor I. Rosellini etc.). Couched in the form of a letter, the paper synthesized information that Lepsius had garnered from his conversation with the Italian scholar "in which he expanded on Champollion's explanation of the use of alphabetical signs in hieroglyphic writing," according to William H. Peck in the *Oxford Encyclopedia of Ancient Egypt.* "If [Lepsius] was not the sole individual who recognized the principal on which the ancient language was organized," Peck continued, "he certainly contributed one of the most helpful additions to the original theory." His next treatise, describing the relationship between Egyptian and Greek columns, appeared in 1838.

Later that same year, Lepsius left Rome and spent a period of time furthering his studies in England. By November of 1839, he had returned to Germany and was splitting his time between his native Naumburg and Berlin. He dedicated much of his time to editing an edition of the Egyptian funerary text the *Book of the Dead;* Lepsius himself gave the manuscript the title, which had not been used by the ancient Egyptians, and instituted a system of chapter numbering for the work that has been in use to the present day. In January of 1842, Lepsius was appointed professor of Egyptology at Berlin, although he at first performed few teaching duties. Instead, the scholar continued his work on the *Book of the Dead* and undertook preparations for a large-scale archeological expedition that had been commissioned by King Frederic William IV of Prussia—a country that preceded Germany and covered much of that present day country's northern regions—at the suggestion of government minister Johann Eichhorn and scholars Alexander von Humboldt and Robert Wilhelm Bunsen. With the support of Humboldt and Bunsen, Lepsius was named leader of the planned expedition.

Led Major Egyptian Exhibition

In September of 1842, Lepsius' team of experts, termed the "best equipped and qualified of any scholarly group" for some forty years by Peck, gathered in the Egyptian seaport of Alexandria. Comprising both German and English members, the expedition group included two architects charged with surveying the land and drawing maps and other topographical sketches; two copyists and a plaster molder responsible for duplicating symbols and inscriptions; two painters tasked with depicting buildings and landscapes; a sculptor and expert on Egyptian art; and a chaplain. The expedition spent only a brief time at the later archeological sites located at Giza, Abusir, Saqqara, and Dahshur before traveling south through Middle Egypt and into the area of Ethiopia that had encompassed the ancient civilization of Nubia; Lepsius' team is considered the first to have made a serious investigation of the region. They made lengthy stops at Beni Hasan, Tell el-Amarna, and Karnak, among others, and became the first group to measure the Valley of the Kings, home to the tomb of famed pharaoh Tutankhamen. At each stop along its route, the expedition conducted thorough archeological excavations, unearthing and recording details of temples, tombs, monuments, inscriptions, and other relevant findings. Painstaking attention to detail and a meticulous scientific approach characterized the group's work, enabling them to copy, draw, map, and model with remarkable degrees of accuracy. Laws regarding archeological artifacts were at the time quite loose, and Lepsius' expedition removed some 15,000 ancient artifacts from the country that he later installed at Berlin's Archeological Museum; although this practice was legal at the time, modern Egyptian authorities have since begun to request the return of some of the pieces removed by numerous European expeditions, albeit with varying degrees of success.

Back in Germany in 1846, Lepsius resumed his professorship at Berlin University and set to work organizing the vast amounts of information collected by his expedition. The fruits of these labors appeared in the 12-volume *Denkmäler aus Ägypten und Äthiopien.* Initially published in 1849, the work contained approximately 900 plates depicting inscriptions and monuments, along with drawings and maps of tombs and their surroundings. The work immediately made available a massive quantity of new information on Egyptian archeology, and has remained a vital resource to the present day due to both the quality of its contents and the reproduction of monuments either no longer in existence or inaccessible due to shifting sands. Subsequent editions contained descriptive information culled from the exhibition leader's notes, but these did not appear until after Lepsius' death. The same year as the first volume of this work appeared, Lepsius also published his *Chronologie der Ägypter* (Chronology of Egypt), which did much to establish the logical, chronological study of ancient Egypt in use today.

Held Prestigious Posts in Later Years

In 1855, Lepsius became the curator and co-director of the Egyptology department of the Berlin Museum. Under his tenure, the museum greatly developed its collection into one that is widely considered among the best in the world. At about this time Lepsius also developed a phonetic alphabet that he used to transliterate dozens of languages; this system found a ready audience among Christian missionaries, who used it broadly until an improved system superseded it during the 1930s. Lepsius returned to Egypt in 1866, and on this trip unearthed the Decree of Canopus, a multi-lingual inscription that confirmed Champollion's earlier interpretation of the Rosetta Stone. The following year, he became the president of board of directors for the German Archeological Institute of Rome, a position that he held until 1880. By the late 1860s, Lepsius had become the editor of the influential scholarly publication *Zeitschrift für Ägyptische Sprache und Altertumskunde* (Journal of the Egyptian Language and Archeology). In 1869, he was made a knight of the Bavarian order of Maximilian and made his third and final visit to Egypt, where he witnessed the opening of the Suez Canal. Ebers commented that "His hasty trip to Upper Egypt could yield little fruit to science, but it served to give him great pleasure, and in his letters to his wife he could not sufficiently praise the amiability of the Crown Prince, to whom . . . he showed the monuments." Four years later, Lepsius was named director of the Royal Library in Berlin. He embraced the opportunity to reform some of that institution's administrative practices and grow the library's collection so as to provide its patrons with an improved quantity and quality of research materials.

Remaining active in his later years, Lepsius conducted research into Nubian people and linguistics that he published in 1880 as *Nubische Grammatik, mit einer Anleitung über die Völker und Sprachen Afrikas* (Nubian Grammar, with an Introduction on the People and Languages of Africa). The book featured an over-125 page introduction that touched on diverse aspects of the continent's many nations. Writing in the *Encyclopedia of Language and Linguistics,* S. Pugach summarized Lepsius' efforts by saying that he "attempted to classify the people and languages of the continent, and argued that the languages of Nubia were formed from a mixture of Bantu and Hamitic languages. . . . Lepsius declared that the oldest languages in Africa were first spoken by peoples living south of the equator." Nubian also formed the basis of Lepsius' last major work, a translation of the Gospel of Saint Mark into that language.

Despite steadily declining health, Lepsius continued his scholarly efforts until scant days before his death on July 10, 1884, in Berlin. He had attained the age of 73. Lepsius' legacy lies not only in the wealth of information that he published as a result of his Egyptian expedition but also in his philological contributions, curatorial talents, and historical research. According to Peck, "Following the early progress of Champollion, [Lepsius] ranks as one of the fathers of the modern study of Egyptology and one of the early giants in the development of the discipline, essentially laying the groundwork for the chronological study of Egyptian history." Many scholars credit Lepsius with not only the creation of the modern scientific field of not only Egyptology but also the broader discipline of archeology itself, and he is generally regarded as the instigator of the "German School" of Egyptological study.

Books

Anderson, Anne, Graeme Hirst, and Jim Miller, eds., *Encyclopedia of Language and Linguistics,* Elsevier, 2005.

Ebers, Georg, *Richard Lepsius: A Biography,* William S. Gottsberger, 1887.

Redford, Donald B., ed. *The Oxford Encyclopedia of Ancient Egypt,* Oxford University Press, 2001.

Periodicals

New York Times, June 24, 1888; October 8, 2008.

Online

"Book of the Dead," University College London, http://www.digitalegypt.ucl.ac.uk/literature/religious/bdquestions.html (January 11, 2010).

"Richard Lepsius," Encyclopedia Britannica Online, http://www.britannica.com/EBchecked/topic/336885/Richard-Lepsius (January 11, 2010).

"Valley of the Kings," Travel Egypt, http://www.travelegypt.com/siteinfo/valleyofkings.htm (January 11, 2010). □

Sylvain Lévi

Sylvain Lévi (1863–1935) was France's foremost scholar of Asian culture and languages during his lifetime. His parsing of ancient Sanskrit texts helped uncover evidence that the Indian subcontinent had contact with the civilizations of ancient Greece and Mesopotamia as far back as the third millennium B.C.E. Lévi was also active in Judaic studies and the human rights organization Alliance Israélite Universelle (Universal Israelite Alliance), which worked to eradicate anti-Semitism in European society.

Lévi was born in Paris on March 28, 1863, into a family of Alsatian Jews. France had a long and problematic history with its Jewish citizens, who had been technically banned from the country for nearly four centuries,

from 1394 until 1790. Alsatian Jews came from a border region between France and Germany that was, until 1871, a part of France but boasted a strong German character. In the wake of the French Revolution in 1789, France implemented sweeping reforms that attempted to make the country a more welcoming home for Jews. During Lévi's childhood, however, a new influx of Jewish refugees from Eastern Europe and Prussia began pouring into France and other nations, fleeing pogroms and anti-Semitic decrees. These were impoverished Jews who had lived in close-knit village communities called *shtetls* for centuries, and their arrival reignited anti-Semitic hostilities in Western Europe.

Learned Sanskrit

A gifted student, Lévi entered the École Pratique des Hautes Études (Practical School for Higher Studies, known by its French-language acronym EPHE) in 1882 at the age of 19. This was one of the new elite academies established after the Revolution to make France a center of inquiry and advancement in the sciences and humanities. One of his teachers was an early Christian history scholar, Ernst Renan, who suggested that Lévi audit a Sanskrit class. This classical language of India was once dominant across the subcontinent and used in the sacred texts of Hinduism and Buddhism. Like Latin, Sanskrit provided the basis for more vernacular languages in the area and then fell into disuse. In the late eighteenth century European scholars discovered it and began comparing it to both Latin and ancient Greek, recognizing similarities in certain key terms that pointed to a common history at some long-ago point. This finding spurred the modern study of Indo-European languages.

France's leading Sanskrit linguist was Abel Bergaigne, who taught at the EPHE, and Lévi studied under him for the next three years. Lévi proved so adept at learning the ancient language and script that by 1885 he had become the school's second teacher of Sanskrit. A year later, the EPHE established its groundbreaking *Sciences Religieuses* (religious sciences) department, designed to foment a more scholarly, comparative approach to all the world's religions. Lévi became a lecturer there, and in 1889 took over the directorship of Sanskrit instruction at EPHE.

Sanskrit was the first of many languages Lévi learned over his lifetime to aid his career. He became fluent in Chinese, Japanese, Tibetan, and also mastered the Tocharian dialects, a now-defunct branch of the Indo-European languages group. As a scholar, he was intrigued by the earliest points of contact between the so-called East and the West. He believed that ancient Greek traders ventured eastward through Turkey, Iran, Afghanistan, and then to the Indian subcontinent long before Alexander the Great conquered India in 325 BCE.

Visited Nepal, India, Japan

Lévi's first published work was his dissertation, a study of Indian drama and theater published in 1890. Four years later, he left EPHE when another prestigious institute of higher learning in Paris, the Collège de France, offered him the post of professor of Sanskrit, which he accepted and held for the next 41 years until his death. In 1897 the

French Ministry of Public Instruction sent him on a mission to India and Japan, and he would return to these places, and many other parts of Asia, several more times over the course of his career. Nepal, the mysterious Himalayan kingdom that was supposedly the birthplace of Gautama Buddha, the founder of Buddhism, held a particular fascination for him. He spent three years there, welcomed by the Nepalese royal family, and produced a three-volume opus on the monarchy and its divine status in Nepal's branch of the Hindu belief system.

After 1904 Lévi served as founding director of the Institut de Civilisation Indienne, or Institute of Indian Studies, at the Sorbonne, part of the University of Paris system. He was a close friend of the famous poet and scholar Rabindranath Tagore, who led a renaissance in Bengali literature during the early twentieth century and founded a school in the Bengali city of Santiniketan, where Lévi taught courses for a time. The school later became Visva Bharati University. In between his travel and teaching assignments, Lévi produced scores of books and articles for scholarly journals. He wrote the 1926 classic *L'Inde et le monde* and contributed to the esteemed *Journal Asiatique*.

At the time, there was little knowledge about Nepal and its Himalayan neighbor, Tibet, which were remote and difficult to reach and had also decisively rebuffed foreign intrusions over the past few hundred years. In a lecture Lévi gave at the India Society of London in 1925, for example, he described the monumental wooden structures in Nepal that showed long-ago Chinese influences as well as the ancient Buddhist concepts that had disappeared in much of India. Even temples built in the remotest parts of mountainous Nepal displayed stunning artisanship, he declared.

L'Occident's Leading Orientalist

During his lifetime Lévi was considered France's chief expert on Asian culture and religions, and was well known in British academic circles, too. He was made an honorary member of the Royal Asiatic Society and served on the advisory committee that recommended guidelines for the School of Oriental Studies, founded as part of the University of London system in 1916. A decade later, he moved to Tokyo to establish the Maison Franco-Japonaise, or French-Japanese Institute, and in the Vietnamese capital of Hanoi set up France's École Française d'Extrême Orient, or French School of the Far East. Back in Paris, he was active in events and programs of the Musée national des Arts asiatiques-Guimet, or Musée Guimet, which held a trove of Asian art.

Lévi was also deeply involved in French and international Jewish organizations. He belonged to the Société d'Études Juives (Society of Jewish Studies), which worked to reverse some of the anti-Semitic tendencies inside French academia. At the end of World War I in 1918, in response to calls for the creation of a Jewish homeland in the Middle East, the British government established the Zionist Commission, named after the movement founded by Chaim Weizmann, the future first president of Israel. The Commission traveled to Palestine, which was then under British control, to judge the feasibility of the idea of a Jewish state. Lévi headed the French delegation on the trip, a placement that was said to have been the fruit of his longtime friendship with another of Europe's most influential Jewish figures, the banker Baron Edmond de Rothschild. The Baron had already funded the establishment of a few Jewish settlements in Palestine, but disagreed strongly with Weizmann's leadership style.

Broke with Zionists

According to David Andelman's 2008 book *A Shattered Peace: Versailles 1919 and the Price We Pay Today*, "Lévi turned on the Zionists" at the Paris Peace Talks, which were convened to hammer out the terms of the Treaty of Versailles after World War I. One item on the agenda was the possibility of a Jewish state in the Middle East. Lévi told the peace conference attendees that the area in question "was an impoverished territory with 600,000 Arabs. Immigrant Jews with a higher standard of living were already dispossessing the native Moslem population," Andelman quoted him as saying. According to Andelman, Lévi observed that the vast bulk of those Jews who were arriving in increasing numbers were mainly Russian Jews of 'explosive' temperament who could touch off serious trouble in a pressure cooker that would become effectively a concentration camp." Weizmann was reportedly so angry with Lévi that he refused to shake hands with him at the close of the conference. In the end, however, Weizmann and his supporters prevailed: France's main representative to the Versailles talks was André Tardieu, who a few hours later issued a statement that the French government would not oppose the establishment of a Jewish state in Palestine under British trusteeship.

Lévi was active in France's Alliance Israélite Universelle, or Universal Israelite Alliance (AIU), which worked to end anti-Semitism and eradicate centuries-old prejudices and biases against Jews in Europe. Lévi served as president of the Central Committee of the AIU after 1920 until his death in Paris on October 30, 1935. An obituary that ran in the *Times* of London described him as "singularly free from littleness of mind, [with] not a trace of an exclusive nationalism." The same article listed his surviving relatives as Desirée Bloch, a fellow scholar, and their two sons.

Books

Andelman, David, *A Shattered Peace: Versailles 1919 and the Price We Pay Today,* John Wiley and Sons, 2008, pp. 101–03.

"France, Practice of Judaism in, from Napoleon to De Gaulle," in *Encyclopedia of Judaism,* edited by Jacob Neusner, Alan Avery-Peck, and William Green, second edition, Volume 2, Brill Academic Publishers, 2005, pp. 824–837.

McCrindle, John Watson, et al., *The Invasion of India by Alexander the Great as described by Arrian, Q. Curtius, Diodoros, Plutarch and Justin: Being Translations of Such Portions of the Works of These and Other Classical Authors as Describe Alexander's Campaigns in Afghanistan, the Punjab, Sindh, Gedrosia and Karmania,* A. Constable and Co., 1896, p. 411.

Welbon, G., "Lévi, Sylvain," in *Encyclopedia of Religion,* edited by Lindsay Jones, second edition, Volume 8, Macmillan Reference USA, 2005, pp. 5418–5419.

Periodicals

New York Times, November 1, 1935.
Times (London, England), April 22, 1925; November 2, 1935. □

Helen Levitt

American photographer Helen Levitt (1913–2009) spent decades capturing everyday life on the streets of New York City. Some of her best known photographs immortalize the innocence of a bygone era, with kids darting around parked cars or clambering around various structures on improvised, perilous playscapes of cement and brick. The woman often called the artistic successor to French photography legend Henri Cartier-Bresson was largely unknown for decades, but began to gain formal recognition in the late 1970s after what was then a four-decade-long career. Levitt, wrote Owen Edwards in a 1980 *New York Times Magazine* article, "has long had a reputation among photography enthusiasts as a highly disciplined individualist in a form nearly overwhelmed by clichés."

L evitt was born on August 31, 1913, in Brooklyn, New York, the daughter of a knitwear wholesaler. Sam, her Russian Jewish father, had married May, a bookkeeper, and the couple settled in the Bensonhurst section of the borough. Levitt attended New Utrecht High School in Brooklyn, but left before graduating. She was drawn to the arts, and considered a career as a painter, but realized she was hopeless at drawing. For a time, she also explored dance as a possible future direction, but found her calling when she began working as an assistant at J. Florian Mitchell, a photography portrait studio in the Bronx owned by a friend of the family. For a salary of $6 a week, she learned all aspects of the art form, from setting up lighting to darkroom printing.

Tutored by Walker Evans

In the spring of 1935, Levitt heard about a group photography exhibition at the Julien Levy Gallery. It featured works from Manuel Álvarez Bravo of Mexico along with those of Walker Evans and Henri Cartier-Bresson. Evans was already using his camera to document the effects of the Great Depression in the United States, while Cartier-Bresson was instrumental in elevating the street photograph into an art form. Levitt befriended Cartier-Bresson, who was staying in New York at the time, and once accompanied him on a trek to the Brooklyn waterfront to take photographs. Not long afterward, she bought her first camera, a used Leica, the brand Cartier-Bresson favored, along with a Leica accessory called a *winkelsucher,* or "angle-finder." This allowed her to photograph sideways on the street, thus unnoticed by her subjects.

Levitt also befriended Evans and began informally studying with him around 1938. She had been greatly influenced by Evans's images for a 1933 book by investigative journalist Carleton Beals titled *The Crime of Cuba,* which exposed the unsavory ties between U.S. business interests and a corrupt Cuban regime. She found Evans in the phone directory and asked if she could show him her portfolio. When she stopped by, the journalist James Agee was there, too. In 1936 Evans and Agee had spent the summer in Alabama, living with impoverished tenant farmers there. *Fortune* magazine had sent them on that assignment, but the story never ran. In 1941, two years after Agee left the magazine, their collaborative effort came to light in the groundbreaking illustrated book *Let Us Now Praise Famous Men.*

Evans gave Levitt suggestions that helped erase some of the sentimentality in her work, and both Evans and Agee's contacts served to launch her freelance career. Her first published image was in *Fortune* magazine's July 1939 issue devoted to New York City. A few months later, she shot a trio of kids emerging from a city apartment building to go trick-or-treating on Halloween, which would later be included in a group show at the Museum of Modern Art (MOMA)'s new photography section. Margarett Loke wrote of the image in the *New York Times,* "Standing on the stoop outside their house, they are in almost metaphorical stages of readiness. The girl on the top step is putting on her mask; a boy near her, his mask in place, takes a graceful step down, while another boy, also masked, lounges on a lower step, coolly surveying the world."

Nominated for Academy Award

Levitt's contact with MOMA led to a job with renegade Spanish filmmaker Luis Buñuel, who was hired by MOMA to edit some film compilation projects. Levitt recalled being slightly intimidated when she first began working under the Spanish émigré, whose two short films from 1929 and 1930, *L'Âge d'Or* (The Golden Age) and *Un Chien Andalou* (An Andalusian Dog) are considered masterpieces of Surrealist film. "I didn't dare talk to him," she told Sarah Boxer in a *New York Times* interview. Nevertheless, the job was an enjoyable one. "I was a great splicer. Very fast. That was nice work, very satisfying work. It was like eating peanuts or something. Simple and easy, and you could think about other things."

Levitt's first solo museum show was held at the MOMA space in the spring of 1943. *Helen Levitt: Photographs of Children* featured images taken on New York City streets and in Mexico, but it was the New York scenes that would establish her reputation as an artist. Her work immortalized an era "before the advent of television and air conditioning in New York, a world where people lived and worked on the pavements, which became their living rooms," wrote London *Independent* writer Marcus Williamson. "It was this world of the underprivileged on the Lower East Side of Manhattan, Yorkville and Harlem that she sought to document."

During this period Levitt also worked with Agee, who was the film critic for *Time* and other magazines as well as a respected essayist, poet, and novelist. They collaborated on *A Way of Seeing,* a book that was finished in 1946 but not published until nearly 20 years later. Levitt's work at MOMA also drew her into filmmaking for a time, and she made two with Agee and Janice Loeb, a painter who for a time was married to Levitt's brother. One of these was *The Quiet One*, about a ten-year-old boy from Harlem with an unhappy home life who runs away but finds solace at the Wiltwyck School for Boys in upstate New York. The work was originally shot in 16-millimeter film by director Sidney Meyers, with Levitt aiding the cinematography and some of the screenwriting. They financed it themselves, and then worked overtime in an unheated Manhattan apartment to edit and transfer it to 35-millimeter format for theatrical release. Levitt, Loeb, and Meyers were nominated for an Academy Award in the screenwriting category, and *The Quiet One* was also nominated for best documentary film of 1949.

Career Languished

A year later, Levitt's work was included with that of Dorothea Lange, Margaret Bourke-White, and other notable names in a MOMA show organized by the pioneering photographer Edward Steichen, called *Sixty Prints by Six Woman Photographers*. Through the 1950s and 1960s Levitt continued to capture candid scenes with her Leica and winkelsucher apparatus on the streets of New York. Her images were also included in Steichen's enormously popular *Family of Man* show at the Museum of Modern Art. In 1959 she won a Guggenheim Foundation fellowship to start working in color photography. Many of these images were not seen until years later, for Levitt found the color printing process difficult to master and simply stored the negatives. She assumed the bulk of them had disappeared when her Greenwich Village apartment was burgled in the late 1960s or early 1970s, but they later turned up in Levitt's somewhat haphazard filing system, and appeared in book form. One of her best-known images is from this period, showing *Spider Girl,* a child crouching curbside under an avocado green muscle car.

Levitt's first published book was the Agee collaboration from the 1940s, *A Way of Seeing,* which Viking Press issued in 1965. This featured Levitt's images of children at play and Agee's well-crafted sentences accompanying them. Agee wrote in the foreword, "The overall preoccupation in the photographs is, it seems to me, with innocence—not as the word has come to be misunderstood and debased, but in its full, original wildness, fierceness, and instinct for grace and form."

Despite her auspicious start in the 1940s, Levitt moved to the margins of artistic obscurity for a number of years. Her name was resurrected in the late 1970s, and was rediscovered by a new generation of photography curators and gallerists. Finally, in late 1991 the San Francisco Museum of Modern Art honored her with a retrospective that also came to New York's Metropolitan Museum in early 1992 and went on to several more cities over the next two years. Writing in the *New York Times*, Charles Hagen lamented the fact that Levitt's early promise failed to evolve into a larger body of photographic work, but praised her images of children on the streets of New York City taken five decades before. "Made with a perfectly limpid style, these pictures capture the anarchic energy and exuberant mix of fantasy and reality that the children bring to their enterprise," Hagen wrote. "In her most powerful pictures, adults are nowhere to be seen. The city seems to belong solely to the children, who gleefully play on its stoops, engage in titanic battles in rubble-covered lots or dress up in ritualistic costumes made of rags and sticks."

Lamented Lost Era

Levitt was slowed by age, and sciatica made the requisite hours of standing in a darkroom physically difficult for her. She also suffered from Ménière's disease, an inner-ear disorder that affects balance. Furthermore, there seemed to be fewer children outside, even in a more populous city. Years before, "The streets were crowded with all kinds of things going on, not just children," she told Boxer. "Everything was going on in the street in the summertime. They didn't have air-conditioning. Everybody was out on the stoops, sitting outside, on chairs."

Levitt grew increasingly reclusive in her later years. The publisher Powerhouse Books began issuing collections of her lifetime of work, including *Here and There, Slide Show,* and *Helen Levitt.* When Boxer met her in 2004, Levitt was 90 years old and still living in a fifth-floor walk-up apartment in Greenwich Village. She died in her sleep there on March 29, 2009, at the age of 95. Her brother William survived her, and a single image of her, wearing a hat, taken in the early 1960s, was issued to accompany the posthumous articles in the press. She was famously curt with interviewers, preferring to let a body of work speak for her. Scores of tributes commended her ability to capture what Cartier-Bresson famously called the "decisive moment," but Agee—a gifted writer who was posthumously awarded a Pulitzer Prize for fiction—called her images "the record of an ancient, primitive, transient and immortal civilization, incomparably superior to our own," in *A Way of Seeing.* "Levitt is one of a handful who have to be described as good artists, not loosely, or arrogantly, or promotively, but simply because no other description will do."

Books

Levitt, Helen, with James Agee, *A Way of Seeing,* Viking Press, 1965.

Periodicals

Guardian (London, England), April 3, 2009.

Independent (London, England), April 18, 2009.*New York Times,* January 9, 1949; January 2, 1966; April 3, 1992; April 8, 2004; March 30, 2009.

New York Times Magazine, May 4, 1980.

Smithsonian, April 2003.

Times (London, England), April 18, 2009.☐

Jerry Lewis

The American actor Jerry Lewis (born 1926) has gained international acclaim for his career as a film comedian, and for his longstanding humanitarian efforts as host of the annual Muscular Dystrophy Telethon.

ewis's career has been notable for its sheer longevity. He began performing with his family in the so-called Borscht Belt of Jewish-oriented resorts and nightclubs north of New York City in the 1930s, and as of 2010 he was still active as an actor and entertainer. Lewis's career passed through several phases, including a ten-year period of slapstick comedy in which he was partnered with actor and singer Dean Martin; a period of more conceptually oriented comic films, some of which he directed himself, that gained more acclaim abroad than in the United States; and finally several decades in which, not content to rest on his laurels as an elder statesman of comedy, he explored a variety of new projects despite physical challenges. Asked by Graham Fuller in *Interview* for the secret of his long-lasting success, Lewis responded: "I would have been gone from the theatrical horizon many years ago if I was just a visual comic, period. But I've grown up with this country, and this country's grown up with me. And in the last fifty years, it's felt responsible for where I've gone and what I've become."

Born into Show Business

Born Joseph Levitch in Newark, New Jersey on March 16, 1926, Lewis grew up in a family of performers. His father, Daniel, performed as Danny Lewis, and his mother, Rachel (Rae), was active as a pianist on New York radio in the 1920s. Lewis's own stage debut came when he

donned a miniature tuxedo and took to the stage at a resort in the Catskills mountains, singing "Brother, Can You Spare a Dime?" "It's not like a decision was made: It was preordained," he explained to Fuller. "When your father's on the stage doing a show at three o'clock in the afternoon, and your mother is watching him, and then at eleven o'clock that night you're born, and he's trying to finish his last show to get to the hospital, and then you have your first breast-feeding in their dressing room—when you start like that, that's what's called getting it in the bones."

Lewis frequently traveled around with his parents and never flourished as a student. He was expelled from Irvington High School in Irvington, New Jersey, in 1941. By that time he had already become an entertainer on his own, developing an act in which he mouthed the lyrics of popular songs and accompanied them with mime and physical comedy. His career got off to a slow start, and he worked as an usher and a "soda jerk," or server at a diner counter, on the side. He thought of dropping out of show business but was encouraged to continue by comedian Irving Kaye. In 1942 Lewis was booked to perform at Brooklyn's Pitman Theatre, and he performed at other theaters around New York during the World War II years. He tried to join the military but was turned down because of a perforated eardrum and a congenital heart defect.

In 1944 or 1945 Lewis shared a bill at New York's Glass Hat club with singer Dean Martin. That same year he married singer Patti Palmer; the couple had six children, one of them adopted. One son, Gary Lewis, achieved stardom as a rock singer in the 1960s. In 1946 Lewis suggested Martin as a stand-in for another singer while he was performing at Atlantic City, New Jersey's 500 Club. The two scripted a duo act, which bombed. Threatened with being fired, they decided to try once more with a totally improvised act featuring Martin as a singer and Lewis as a comically inept busboy. The audience roared, and the duo took off to clubs along the northeastern seaboard with their classic handsome-straight-man-plus-physical-comedian act. Within 18 weeks, their asking price had reached $5,000.

Producers in the non-live media of radio, early television, and movies quickly caught on to the duo's appeal. *The Martin and Lewis Show* made its debut on the NBC radio network in 1949, with their first film appearance in supporting roles in *My Friend Irma* coming the same year. Between 1950 and 1955 they made frequent appearances on television's *Colgate Comedy Hour*. The first film with the team of Martin and Lewis as co-stars was *At War with the Army* in 1951, and by the mid-1950s they had 17 mostly very successful comedies to their credit. By 1955 they had enough clout that they could command the services of A-list Hollywood director Frank Tashlin for their well-regarded *Artists and Models*.

Feuded with Martin

That was also about the time the Martin-Lewis relationship began to go sour. Martin, his own career as a vocalist flourishing, began to resent press coverage that favored the more flamboyant Lewis, and things came to a head when Martin was completely cropped out of a *Look* magazine cover for which the two had been photographed. Lewis later freely conceded that his own egotistical behavior had contributed to the split. After making *Hollywood or Bust,* Martin and Lewis parted ways with a farewell performance at New York's Copacabana club on July 25, 1956, the tenth anniversary of their debut. Lewis continued solo with *The Delicate Delinquent;* planned as a Martin and Lewis film, it starred Darren McGavin in the police-officer role originally intended for Martin.

Working consistently with Tashlin, Lewis scored a series of film hits in the late 1950s with such releases as *Rock-a-Bye Baby* and *The Geisha Boy* (both 1958). Lewis made some recordings as a vocalist, scoring a hit with a cover of the Al Jolson standard "Rock-a-Bye Your Baby with a Dixie Melody," and even being featured in a comic book series, *The Adventures of Jerry Lewis.* In 1959 Lewis and his new company, Jerry Lewis Productions, signed a deal with Paramount Studios, promising Lewis a $10 million payment, 60 percent of the profits from his films, and creative control. During the filming of 1960's *Cinderfella,* Lewis was hospitalized for four days after bounding up a hotel staircase in seven seconds so that a shot could be completed in a single take.

Indeed, long before Chinese martial arts comedian Jackie Chan won acclaim for his physically daring brand of screen stuntwork, Lewis was fearless in his devotion to comic art. In 2002, in conversation with Mike Clark of *USA Today,* he looked back on nearly a lifetime of physical pain: "From 1936 on, I have taken more falls than any other 20 comedians put together. From the time I was 21, I've taken them on everything from clay courts to cement to wood floors, coming off pianos, going out a two-story window, landing on Dean, falling into the rough. You do that and you're gonna have problems. I had pain during the last eight films; I've had pain in 37 straight telethons. I've never had a day without pain since March 20, 1965."

In 1960, owing to Paramount's need for a quick summer release, Lewis got his first chance to direct a film, and quickly produced *The Bellboy,* a spare, spontaneous, almost plotless series of hotel-related sight gags with very little dialogue. The idea came to Lewis while he was performing at the Fontainebleau Hotel in Miami Beach, Florida, and he completed it in three weeks on a daytime-only shooting schedule. The film inaugurated a period in which, although he continued to experience commercial success, Lewis's films generally received a split critical reception. In the United States they were panned as simplistic slapstick, but in France Lewis found both lasting popularity and critical acclaim. There he became known as *Le Roi du Crazy,* or The King of Crazy, and was hailed as a cinematic great by the intellectual film magazine *Cahiers du Cinéma.*

Gained International Popularity

The general fascination with Lewis in France, where he was inducted into the Legion of Honor, and where years later the single name "Jerry" on a theater marquee was still sufficient to draw a crowd, has sometimes been greeted with bemusement by American film fans. But it had certain antecedents. The French admiration for the physical style of American silent film comedy dated back to the days of Charlie Chaplin and Buster Keaton, and French film comedian Jacques Tati had experimented with silent/sound hybrid films structured similarly to *The Bellboy.* And it was not only in France where Lewis was popular abroad. The French, he pointed out to Clark, "do not rank first as Jerry Lewis appreciators, by any means. Australia is No. 1, and Japan is 2, Italy and Germany 3 and 4. The Netherlands is 5, Belgium is 6, Spain is 7 and France is 8. We get that demographic through our mail every week. It's always been Australia first, Japan second."

Furthermore, Lewis was increasingly what French critics (and later those worldwide) called an auteur—a cinematic figure who exercised total control over all aspects of a film. Lewis is even credited with the development of the video assist, a group of cameras and monitors that enable a director to play back a segment of film immediately after it has been shot. The procedure is now in common use. American audiences concurred with those in France, flocking to films such as *The Ladies Man* (1961) and especially *The Nutty Professor* (1963), which became one of Lewis's most famous films. But in the late 1960s Lewis's popularity declined. *Which Way to the Front?* (1970) was his last film until the early 1980s.

During this period, Lewis was better known for his partnership with the Muscular Dystrophy Association (MDA), which he had helped to establish in 1952. As of 2009 he remained the only national chairman the organization had ever had. In 1966 the MDA began an annual fundraising telethon over the Labor Day holiday, with Lewis as host remaining on the air for almost 24 hours at a stretch even during periods of ill health, when he had to have oxygen on hand on the set. In 2007, when the telethon raised $63.7 million, Lewis was named the celebrity most effective in spreading the word about a charitable cause, in an assessment by the Nationwide Insurance firm. In 1977 he was nominated by Wisconsin U.S. Representative Les Aspin for the Nobel Peace Prize. Lewis took some criticism, however, from disability-rights activists who believed that the attitude exemplified by the "Jerry's Kids" motif in his presentation of the telethon was demeaning to the disabled.

In 1982 Lewis suffered a serious heart attack and was at one point deemed clinically dead. He survived, however, and awoke to hear his cardiologist and friend, renowned heart surgeon Michael DeBakey, telling him he had eight lives left. He bounced back to make a documentary film, *Smorgasbord,* about the experience and to play a talk-show host in director Martin Scorsese's dark star-stalker story *The King of Comedy* the following year, winning critical acclaim. In 1983 he married SanDee Pitnick; they adopted a daughter, Danielle, in 1992. In 1984 Lewis wrote an autobiography, *Jerry Lewis in Person.* Lewis made various television appearances in the late 1980s, including one multi-episode stint in the crime series *Wiseguy.* In 1995 he returned to the stage in the Broadway musical *Damn Yankees.* He served as executive producer for both comedian Eddie Murphy's remake of *The Nutty Professor* (1996) and its 2000 sequel.

Lewis continued to suffer from health problems, including prostate cancer, a second heart attack, and pulmonary fibrosis. A steroid prescribed for that condition left him struggling with addiction, and caused his weight to balloon to over 260 pounds. Lewis suffered additional negative publicity when he told *Entertainment Weekly* in 2000 that "I don't like any female comedians. A woman doing comedy doesn't offend me, but . . . I think of her as a producing machine that brings babies in the world." Lewis remained active, however, and was seemingly indestructible. By 2009, when he received the Jean Hersholt Humanitarian Award at the Academy Awards ceremony, he had raised an estimated $1.46 billion for the Muscular Dystrophy Association, and that year he was cast in the lead role of a new film, *Max Rose*.

Books

Levin, Shawn, *King of Comedy,* St. Martin's, 1996.

Lewis, Jerry, and Herb Gluck, *Jerry Lewis in Person,* Atheneum, 1982.

St. James Encyclopedia of Popular Culture, Gale, 2000.

Periodicals

Entertainment Weekly, February 25, 2000; January 30, 2009.

Esquire, January 2006.

Interview, April 1995.

Nation, September 14, 1992.

Variety, May 18, 2009.

WWD, September 2006.

Online

Clark, Mike, "Jerry Lewis Tells It Like It Is—and Was, *USA Today,* August 29, 2002, http://www.usatoday.com/life/2002-08-29-jerry_x.htm (February 3, 2010).

"Jerry Lewis," *All Movie Guide,* http://www.allmovie.com (February 3, 2010).

"Jerry Lewis," *Turner Classic Movies,* http://www.tcmdb.com/participant.jsp?participantId=113314 (February 3, 2010).

"Jerry Lewis Biography," *Jerry Lewis Official Web site,* http://www.jerrylewiscomedy.com (February 3, 2010). □

Judith Leyster

Dutch artist Judith Leyster (1609–1660) is a rare example of a woman painter from the pre-modern age. She was active in the 1620s and 1630s in her native city of Haarlem, where she earned a hard-won admittance to that city's guild of professional artists. A self-portrait, thought to have been the submission piece for her application to the Guild of St. Luke, shows the artist "with all the poise and appurtenances of an established professional artist," asserted *Art in America* writer Debra Bricker Balken. "She gazes at the viewer with a knowing smile. Her stylish dress conveys prosperity. The 20-some paintbrushes she balances beneath her palette symbolize her control of her craft. The image reflects both aplomb and a certain posturing in the wish to be linked with the artistic establishment of the time."

Leyster was born in Haarlem, a city about ten miles east of Amsterdam, and was baptized at Haarlem's famed Bavokerk, or St. Bavo's Church, on July 28, 1609. In the century past, Haarlem had suffered several political and social upheavals, including a Spanish occupation, massive fire, and influx of refugees from other cities due to regional conflicts. After the 1200s the city began to thrive as a hub for Holland's beer brewing, cloth bleaching, and tulip growing industries, then emerged as a textile production center of Northern Europe in the generation just before Leyster's birth. Her city was one of the most prosperous urban areas of what became known as the Dutch Golden Age, and that fiscal boom created a taste for status symbols formerly available only to royals, aristocrats, and landed gentry, such as original art.

Exposed to Utrecht Caravaggisti

Leyster's father was Jan Willemsz, a beer brewer who ventured into the clothmaking business. The "Leyster" name was taken from a piece of property he acquired around 1601 that was called De Leystar, which he used for his brewing business and then added to the family name with a slightly altered spelling. In the Dutch language, "Leystar" means lodestar, a name once used for the North Star, or Polaris, which guided mariners at sea.

Textile enterprises faced tough competition in the city, however, and Leyster's father also seemed to have made unwise investments in real estate. He declared bankruptcy in either 1624 or 1628, and the family moved to Vreeland, a town near the Dutch city of Utrecht. At some point in her teens Leyster began working to help support the family of nine children, and may have begun as an apprentice embroiderer. It was common for women to learn various needlework finishing techniques for the cloth trade, but quite rare for them to pick up a piece of charcoal or a paintbrush with the intention of pursuing art as a career. The handful of female artists on record from this period of Western art were usually the daughters of successful painters or sculptors, and thus trained in their fathers' workshops.

During Leyster's teen years Utrecht was home to a number of painters called the Caravaggisti, because they were followers of the groundbreaking Italian artist Caravaggio, who died in 1610. Caravaggio was one of Rome's most exalted painters in the decade before his death and had mastered a trick of capturing shadows and light that gave his works a distinctive realism and ushered in the transition period of European art from Renaissance to Baroque. A few young painters from Utrecht had visited Rome to see Caravaggio's famed paintings for the Contarelli Chapel. These Utrecht Caravaggisti—Hendrick ter Brugghen and Gerrit von Honthorst among them—introduced the dramatic *chiaroscuro* (contrast between light and dark tones) into Dutch painting in the 1620s, and Leyster's artistic output shows this influence.

Admitted to Professional Guild

Leyster may have started her career as a painter while living in Vreeland, the town near Utrecht, and art historians have surmised that she may have studied under Frans Hals at some point after she returned to Haarlem. Known for his portraiture, Hals was the city's most famous artist, and had come to Haarlem from Antwerp as a child when the latter city fell to the Spanish. He was listed as a member of the Guild of St. Luke by 1610, and as such could sell his works on the open market and hire and train apprentices. Leyster may have studied under him or under a less well known master painter for a number of years before she applied to join the Guild herself. Admitted to its rolls in 1633, she was one of just two women admitted to the Haarlem chapter during the entire seventeenth century.

The earliest known paintings from Leyster's hand predate this milestone. One of them is *Serenade* from 1629, finished when she was just 20 years old. The oil on panel shows a young man in extravagant dress playing a lute, looking slightly up and toward his right. The left side of the image is bathed in a light, toward which he seems to gaze, while his other hand, holding the neck of the guitar-like instrument, is barely visible in the shadows.

Leyster specialized in these and other "genre" paintings. In art history parlance, genre paintings are images of ordinary folk—that is, not a portrait commissioned by a person of rank, nor a religious icon, nor a figure from literature or mythology. Instead genre paintings depicted unnamed citizens from all ranks of society carrying on their daily business or, in many cases, taking part in some celebratory event. They were popularized in part by Flemish artists of the Baroque period like Pieter Brueghel the Elder, whose *Wedding Dance* from 1566 remains the hallmark of the style. By Leyster's era they had become interior scenes, often focusing on tavern revelries or musical pursuits.

Created Her Most Famous Work

Following this style, Leyster painted *A Game of Tric Trac* around 1630 or 1631. This shows three figures seated at a table engaged in a game of backgammon, a popular pastime in seventeenth-century Holland. The woman holds a drink and is offering a clay pipe to one of the men, who has turned around to gaze at the viewer. A second man slumps over, his head resting on his hand, seemingly dejected over the game or the interpersonal drama. *The Last Drop,* likely dating from the same time period, is one of her better known works. This is a typical genre painting, showing a pair of men who are obviously intoxicated, and is "one of her more acerbic morality tales," according to Balken. The man in red holds an upside-down beer stein, while his drinking companion gulps from a flask. The pair "remain oblivious to the intrusion of a skeleton which holds both a skull and an hourglass, symbolic references to the outcome of such overindulgence," Balken wrote.

Musical instruments feature prominently in many of Leyster's other works, such as *The Concert,* which shows a trio of richly dressed figures. A work thought to be painted near the end of her relatively brief career is *Young Flute Player,* which belongs to Sweden's Nationalmuseum in Stockholm but was loaned out for an important 2009 exhibition in honor of the 400th anniversary of Leyster's birthday. In a review of the paintings on display in *Judith Leyster: 1609–1660* at Washington, D.C.'s National Gallery of Art for the *Wall Street Journal,* critic Karen Wilkin called this particular work "a knockout. A robustly structured composition in nuanced browns, taupes and grays, sparked by deep red, it sets the standard by which she should be judged. The boy musician, arms angled to support his slender instrument, is seen from a low viewpoint and bathed in cool light; the generous space and the play of sharp diagonals, suave curves and tellingly placed shadows are irresistible."

Leyster seems to have abandoned her career just a few short years after being admitted to the Guild of St. Luke. This coincides with her 1636 marriage to Jan Miense Molenaer, a fellow artist. Haarlem historical records show that a year earlier she entered into a legal dispute with Frans Hals, who managed to hire away one of her new apprentices just a few days after the teen came to her workshop. The common arrangement at the time was for a young boy or teen to live at the home of a certified master of a profession, where he would receive training as well as room and board for a specified number of years. Leyster sued Hals for damages, and was awarded four guilders— which the teen's mother paid, not Hals—and Hals was allowed to keep the apprentice.

Managed Husband's Career

Leyster and Molenaer had five children, but three of them died before reaching adulthood. Historical records show she managed both their household and her husband's business, and Molenaer apparently even granted her power of attorney so that she could enter into contracts on his behalf. After their marriage they lived in Amsterdam for about a decade, then settled in Heemstede, a town on the outskirts of Haarlem. Molenaer painted what art historians believe is their 1636 marriage portrait, which shows the couple in an interior scene. Both are extravagantly dressed and hold stringed musical instruments, with a wall map of Italy behind them. Writing in the *New Yorker,* art critic Peter Schjeldahl called this work "irritating," after dismissing Molenaer as a "starkly inferior artist." Schjeldahl described the marriage portrait as a work that "virtually displays Leyster as one item in an array of his possessions, along with a sleek dog and a luxuriantly set dinner table."

Leyster may have painted alongside her husband in the studio, for a record of the inventory of his estate lists some still life works by her which have been lost to time. That document dates from 1668, eight years after Leyster's death on February 10, 1660. She was just 50 years old. Her career was largely forgotten, and because her style was so similar to that of Hals, her paintings were actually sold as his well into the nineteenth century. Leyster signed her works with a distinctive monogram of her initials, "JL," bisected by a miniature shooting star. Dealers even altered this, but finally curators at the Louvre Museum in Paris, thinking they were acquiring a costly Hals portrait, actually discovered they had bought her *Carousing Couple,* showing a man and woman seated at a table. The woman pours a drink and gazes at her companion, who is playing a violin.

Schjeldahl theorized that Leyster painted the popular drinking scenes because these were what sold in Haarlem and Holland in the 1630s. He singled out two examples from the National Gallery exhibition as better examples of her gifts. One was the aforementioned *Young Flute Player,* on loan from Stockholm's Nationalmuseum. "The work's finely modulated browns and grays are breathtaking," he wrote. "They affect like essences of the flute's sound—you practically hear them." Schjeldahl also cited *The Proposition,* which shows a woman seated and bent over in concentration at her sewing. At her left is an oil lamp and its glow, and behind it a man bearing a bag of coins. Schjeldahl called it "inexhaustibly interesting and disturbing.... She stolidly ignores the man, though one of his hands is draped on her right arm and the other, with the coins, is inches from her toiling fingers. Her intelligent face is painted with a crystalline precision that subtly cracks the convention of the picture's then-common genre, in which women were usually shown as more than receptive to temptation."

Periodicals

Art in America, May 1994.
Financial Times, June 25, 2009.
New Yorker, June 29, 2009.
New York Times, July 23, 2009.
Wall Street Journal, July 21, 2009.

Online

"Judith Leyster's 400th Birthday to be Celebrated with Exhibition at the National Gallery of Art," National Gallery of Art, June 3, 2009, http://www.nga.gov/press/exh/3037/index.shtm (January 11, 2010).□

Myra Adele Logan

African-American physician and surgeon Myra Adele Logan (1908–1977) was the first woman to perform open heart surgery. She also conducted important research related to antibiotics, developed an innovative breast imaging procedure, and championed civil rights.

During an illustrious medical career, Myra Adele Logan achieved significant accomplishments and proved to be a pioneer. She was not out to attain glory, however, nor was monetary reward a major concern. She simply wanted to perform a humanitarian service that would benefit patients and her community. This extended from her medical practice and into the civic responsibilities she willingly assumed.

Even so, the socially conscious Logan achieved substantial medical milestones related to gender, race and patient care: She is now recognized as the first African-American woman elected as a Fellow of the American College of Surgeons and the first woman, black or white, to perform open heart surgery. She also advanced research and treatment related to breast cancer, in the process saving the lives of many women.

Raised in Supportive Environment

Myra A. Logan was born in 1908 in Tuskegee, Alabama, but the month and date are unknown. But this much is indeed known: She was the eighth child of Warren and Adella Hunt Logan, and she enjoyed a privileged childhood. Her father was a trustee and treasurer of the Tuskegee Institute, the prestigious higher education facility. Her suffragette mother was a well-known social activist in the areas of health care and women's rights. Further, her preeminent parents fostered a home environment that placed great value on education, personal achievement and, in particular, health care. Like her mother, Logan's aunt and sister were involved in health-related activities. In addition, Logan's brother and brother-in-law were physicians. In 1973, the Knickerbocker Hospital in New York was renamed the Arthur R. Logan Memorial Hospital in honor of her brother.

Obtained Higher Education Degrees

With her advantages, Logan achieved much beyond high school. She attended Atlanta University in Georgia. She graduated in 1927 with a bachelor's of arts degree, and she was her class valedictorian. Following graduation, she went to New York City to do graduate work at Columbia University, where she earned her master's degree in psychology.

Afterward, she joined the Young Women's Christian Association (YWCA) staff in Connecticut. There, she decided to study medicine. Pursuing the ambition, she sought and received a Walter Gray Crump Scholarship for Young Women from the YWCA, which provided her with a four-year, $10,000 scholarship to New York Medical College, located in Valhalla, New York. Walter Gray Crump (1869–1945), a physician whose father, Samuel Crump, was an abolitionist, established the scholarship to assist African Americans who wanted to study medicine. Logan was the first recipient of the scholarship award.

Logan graduated from New York Medical College with her medical degree in 1933. She then performed an internship and served her residency at Harlem Hospital in New York City. Her mentor was the famous Louis T. Wright (1891–1952), a noted physician and researcher. Wright also championed civil rights and served as national chairman of the board of directors of the National Association for the Advancement of Colored People. He once said that "what the Negro physician needs is equal opportunity for training and practice–no more, nor less," (as quoted by the North by South web site). He also became the first black Fellow of the American College of Surgeons, an elite association of surgeons committed to improving surgical education and techniques.

During her internship at Harlem Hospital, Logan worked in the emergency room and rode on the ambulance. Many times, she delivered babies while in transit to the hospital. She also administered treatment to patients who had been stabbed in the heart during street fights. This emergency medical experience prepared her for a future surgical career. She later became associate surgeon at Harlem Hospital, and she also served as a visiting surgeon at Sydenham Hospital in New York City, a facility that provided much needed and convenient medical services for members of the Harlem community.

Accomplishes Two Important "Firsts"

In 1943, Logan became the first woman to perform open-heart surgery. At the time, she accomplished what was only the ninth open-heart surgical procedure performed in the world. Later, she followed her mentor Dr. Louis Wright into the American College of Surgeons, becoming the first African American woman to be elected as a Fellow in the organization.

Logan also became interested in the emerging area of antibiotic drugs. Results of her research on aureomycin (a tetracycline used to treat infections) and other antibiotics were published in two important medical publications, *Archives of Surgery* and the *Journal of American Medical Surgery*.

In the 1960s, Logan's medical interests shifted toward breast cancer. She developed an innovative, slow-speed X-ray process that enabled clinicians to better treat the disease. Specifically, the process allowed them to more accurately view differences in the density of breast tissue, which led to earlier tumor detection and subsequent treatment.

Logan also established a private medical practice, but she also became a charter member of the Upper Manhattan Medical Group of the Health Insurance Plan, one of the first group practices in the United States. Later, many medical specialists would come together to form many group medical practices to advance patient care. Logan was a founding partner of the Upper Manhattan Medical Group and served as the organization's treasurer for several years. Until 1970, she maintained a medical office at the Group's headquarters, located at Amsterdam Avenue and West 152nd Street in Manhattan. That same year, she joined the Physical Disability Program of the New York State Workman's Compensation Board. She would serve the program until her untimely death in 1977.

Committed to Social Causes

Throughout her professional life Logan also demonstrated a strong personal commitment to social issues. She became a member of the New York State Committee on Discrimination early in her career. In 1944, however, she resigned in protest when Thomas Dewey (1902–1971), who was then governor of New York, chose to ignore the anti-discrimination legislation that the Committee had designed. Dewey added insult to injury when he asked the New York legislature to establish a new panel to study discrimination, essentially removing the issue from the Committee's hands. Seven other angry Committee members joined Logan in resigning. Despite this negative experience, Logan remained active with many civic and professional groups throughout her career.

Married Charles Alston

In the area of her personal life, Logan enjoyed a long and happy marriage to Charles Alston. The couple wed in 1943. Alston, who was born on November 28, 1907 in Charlotte, North Carolina, was an accomplished African American artist and teacher who moved to New York City and became part of the "Harlem Renaissance," an artistic movement that flourished in the 1920s and 1930s and included black writers, painters, and intellectuals.

Like his future wife, Alston attended Columbia University, graduating in 1929. In 1931, he earned his master's degree from Columbia's Teachers College. Later, in New York, Alston directed art programs and operated community centers, including the Harlem Workshop. One of his students was Jacob Lawrence (1917–2000), the famous African American "cubist" painter.

Depicted in Famous Mural

In 1935 and 1936, Alston directed thirty-five young, aspiring African American artists in creating murals for the Federal Arts Project. These murals were displayed at medical facilities such as the Harlem Hospital, where Logan worked. The Works Progress Administration created the Federal Arts Project in 1935 to support and employ artists. The Harlem Hospital murals represented the first time that the United States government awarded a commission to African American artists.

Alston painted two of the murals himself. These were entitled "Modern Medicine" and "Magic in Medicine." The first depicted famous figures in western medicine, and it includes the image of a surgeon who was modeled after Louis Wright, Logan's mentor and Alston's friend. This inclusion honored Wright's commitment to integrating the Harlem Hospital staff. Commenting on the mural in 1940 (as recounted on the Columbia University web site), Alston said that he wanted to "show the different races working together on the same basis with an absolute lack of discrimination, illustrating the sheer objectivity of science."

Alston also painted his future wife into the "Modern Medicine" mural. Logan can be seen in the lower portion, depicted as a nurse holding a baby.

A talented, accomplished artist, Alston created other works that were published in major U.S. magazines such as *The New Yorker, Fortune,* and *Collier's.* In 1950, he sold one of his paintings to the Metropolitan Museum of Art in New York City, and he also became the first African American instructor at the Art Students League. In addition, he received numerous awards for his work. In 1975, he was the first recipient of Columbia University's Distinguished Alumni Award. His most famous paintings are "Family" and "Walking." The former was exhibited at the Whitney Museum in New York City, while the latter became part of a private collection.

Logan and Alston had no children, as they devoted their time to professional pursuits and outside interests. Along with her busy medical career, Logan was an active member in civic organizations such as Planned Parenthood, the National Health Committee of the NAACP, and the National Cancer Committee. After she retired from medical practice in 1970, she served on the New York State Workmen's Compensation Board. Alston later taught at the Museum of Modern Art and City College of New York.

Like her husband, Logan immersed herself in the fine arts. Reportedly, she loved music and was a trained and talented classical pianist. She also derived great pleasure from books and the theater.

Died of Cancer

Later in her life, Logan suffered lung cancer. She succumbed to the disease on January 13, 1977, at Mount Sinai Hospital in New York City. She was sixty-eight years old. She was survived by her sister and two brothers, as well as her husband. But Charles Alston died only a few months after his wife passed away. He, too, died of cancer on April 27, 1977.

Throughout her life and career, Logan gained the love and respect of her colleagues and community, both as a skilled and innovative medical practitioner and committed humanitarian. Described as urbane and modest, she willingly shouldered enormous civic responsibilities. In personal interactions, she was supportive and encouraging, and she helped chart the course for aspiring medical professionals. She became considered a pioneer of rights for African Americans and women, and she always believed in a world that would rise above and beyond mere gender and race.

Books

"Myra A. Logan," *Almanac of Famous People* Ninth Edition, Thomson Gale, 2007.
"Myra A. Logan," *World of Health,* Thomson Gale, 2006.

Periodicals

Journal of the National Medical Association, July 1977.

Online

"African American Pioneers in Health Care," *The Office of Minority Health,* http://minorityhealth.hhs.gov/templates/content.aspx?ID=4020 (December 22, 2009).
"African American Registry," *Aaregistry.com,,* http://www.aaregistry.com/african_american_history/1308/Painter_and_teacher_Charles_Alston (December 22, 2009).
"Louis T. Wright, MD," *North by South,* http://northbysouth.kenyon.edu/1998/health/wright.htm (December 22, 2009).
"Myra Adele Logan," *Thinkquest.org* http://library.thinkquest.org/20117/logan.html (December 22, 2009).
"The Murals: Modern Medicine," *Columbia University,* http://www.columbia.edu/cu/iraas/wpa/murals/modernmeds.html (December 22, 2009). □

Nancy Lopez

American professional golfer Nancy Lopez (born 1957) was the biggest star in women's golf in the late 1970s and 1980s, and her popularity was a key factor in elevating the general popularity of the women's game.

L opez's dominance of the game began almost as soon as she joined the Ladies' Professional Golf Association (LPGA) tour. In her first full year on the tour, she won a still-unmatched five tournaments in a row. As her face became well known to golf fans in person and on television, Lopez held onto her new fans with her magnetic personality, and in so doing brought women's golf to new levels of exposure. "So much is said about sex appeal and charisma being what the LPGA needs," golf pro Jane Blaylock told Ken Robison of the *Fresno Bee.* "All the LPGA ever needed was for Nancy Lopez to sink a putt and smile. That just sent shockwaves." Atypically for the game of golf, Lopez came to a golf career from modest circumstances.

Won Tournament by 110 Strokes

Nancy Lopez was born on January 6, 1957 in Torrance, California, near Los Angeles. The family moved to Roswell, New Mexico when she was young. Lopez's father, Domingo, was a Mexican immigrant who operated an auto repair shop; her mother, Marina, was a homemaker. Both parents enjoyed playing golf, and when their daughter was eight they gave her a set of clubs—used, with cut-off shafts to accommodate Nancy's small size. Soon they realized that they had a monster talent on their hands. Lopez entered her first tournament at age nine, winning by a staggering 110 strokes. The family began to make sacrifices in order to save money and help her develop her talent.

Instead of playing at the local country club in Roswell, Lopez had to take to the links in Albuquerque, a 200-mile drive away, in order to play on a top-flight course. "When you're young, you don't notice those things. I thought we weren't members of the country club because we couldn't afford it," Lopez recalled to Mercedes Marrero of the Latino Legends in Sports web site. "Now I think it was discrimination." But there was no stopping Lopez once she began to devote herself to the game. She won her first of three New Mexico Women's Amateur Championships when she was 12. The pressure of competition was always difficult for Lopez, who suffered from performance anxiety so severe that it made her nauseous, and at its worst forced her to bring a trash can with her on the course. Lopez's father remained supportive, telling her (as she recalled to Marrero), "Don't cry, because if I cried I couldn't see the golf ball."

In 1975 Lopez took home $7,040 for placing second at the U.S. Women's Open—a mark she would never exceed at that tournament. She won a golf scholarship to the University of Tulsa and enrolled that year, planning to study engineering. "But I was always off on the golf course," she recalled to Joseph Durso of the *New York Times*. "And I needed tutors to get through calculus, algebra and trig. I got a C average. Then I switched to business education. That was a lot easier; you could read it from a book." She continued to excel on the links, winning All-America honors, the national women's intercollegiate championship, and Tulsa's Female Athlete of the Year award during her freshman year. In 1976 she represented the United States in the Curtis Cup, contested every year by the U.S. and a British-Irish team.

Turned Pro After Sophomore Year

Lopez's coach at Tulsa, Dale McNamara, told her that she had the skills to turn professional, and in 1977 she did just that. McNamara saw her judgment vindicated when Lopez finished second in each of her first three tournaments as an official professional. With only a partial season, Lopez broke earnings records for a first-year golfer of either gender. But she was shaken by the sudden death of her mother in September of that year from a heart attack. Believing that by so doing she would honor her mother's memory, Lopez redoubled her efforts on the practice course.

Those efforts paid off in 1978 with one of the most remarkable performance streaks in the history of golf. In her first full year on the tour, Lopez won five tournaments in a row, including the nationally televised LPGA Championship in Kings Island, Ohio. Her earnings of more than $200,000 a year easily set a new LPGA record as she won a total of nine tournaments and took home the Vare Trophy for the lowest average score on the tour as well as LPGA Rookie of the Year honors (1978 was considered her official debut year). The streak drew nationwide attention, and when Lopez approached a tight finish at the Bankers Trust Classic in Rochester, New York, the NBC television network even interrupted its weekly baseball coverage in order to show her victory.

At first, Lopez's tension and intense concentration on the course sometimes put fellow players and viewers off,

but her natural charisma soon asserted itself. Lopez began drawing large crowds in person to LPGA events. LPGA commissioner Ty Votaw, as quoted by Robison, pointed to "five points of celebrity: Performance, relevance, joy and passion, appearance, approachability. Nancy Lopez certainly had all five." Among those who noticed was sportscaster Tim Melton, whom Lopez married in 1979.

Lopez was hardly less dominant in 1980, winning eight of 19 tournaments she entered and once again earning the Vare Trophy and LPGA Player of the Year honors. But her emotional state was deteriorating, and her physical condition and her golf game declined along with it. The cause was the failure of Lopez's marriage to withstand the high pressure of dual careers. Her tournament wins declined to three per year in 1981, and then two per year in 1982 and 1983, although her 1982 season was partially redeemed by a hole-in-one at the Peter Jackson Classic. That spring, Lopez divorced Melton and married professional baseball player Ray Knight. The two had become friends as they each worked through high-profile celebrity divorces. In 1984 their first child, daughter Ashley, was born, and Lopez later had two more children, Erinn and Torri.

Became Youngest Hall of Fame Qualifier

The marriage mirrored Lopez's traditional upbringing. "I was raised in a south Georgia home," Knight told Durso. "My mother was very submissive, and Nancy's that way, too." But the couple was supportive of each other's careers, and Lopez began to devote herself to golf with the intensity she had shown as a rookie. By 1985 she was back on top of the game, winning five tournaments and taking home her third Vare Trophy with an all-time LPGA low average score of 70.73. By the end of the 1987 season her total of 35 tournaments won qualified her for the LPGA Hall of Fame, making her the youngest qualifier in history. She was inducted into the Hall in 1989.

Lopez benefited from a rise in women's tournament purses that her own popularity had in large part helped to stimulate. For her first tournament win, at the LPGA Championship in 1978, she earned $22,500; 20 years later the winning purse had risen to $195,000. Lopez herself crossed the $2 million career-earnings mark in 1988, racked up $487,153 in purses during the 1989 season, and by 1997 had earned more than $5 million playing golf. She remained in the top ranks of the LPGA through the 1990s, winning several tournaments amidst growing family responsibilities. She hoped to reach the milestone of 50 tournament wins but has won only 48, the last of which was the Chick-Fil-A Charity Championship in 1997. Like Sam Snead, another golfer from a financially modest background, she never won the U.S. Open, despite a record-setting performance in 1997 in which she became the first woman to record scores in the 60s in all four rounds in that tournament.

After undergoing gall bladder surgery, Lopez announced her retirement from golf in 2002. Her decision was short-lived, however, as she continued to enter tournaments through most of the decade and served as captain of the U.S. Solheim Cup team in 2005, leading the team to a victory over a European team. She and Knight toured in support of "Back in Full Swing," a heart disease awareness program, after Knight suffered a heart attack in 2001. In 2007 she announced that she wanted to return to competition at the highest level, telling Steve DiMeglio of *USA Today* that "I want to be able to play with all those young players, to see if my body and game will allow me to." Her book *The Complete Golfer,* published in 1987, was reissued in 2000. She and Knight made their home near Albany, Georgia.

Books

Hahn, James and Lynn, *Nancy Lopez: Golfing Pioneer,* EMC, 1979.
Lopez, Nancy, with Peter Schwed, *The Education of the Woman Golfer,* Simon & Schuster, 1979.
Nickerson, Elinor, *Golf: A Women's History,* McFarland, 1987.
Notable Sports Figures, Gale, 2004.

Periodicals

Florida Times Union, April 30, 1998.

Fresno Bee, October 9, 2002.

New York Times, March 31, 1985.

USA Today, August 5, 2004; February 14, 2007.

Online

"Nancy Lopez," *Ladies Professional Golf Association,* http://www.lpga.com (January 1, 2010).

"Nancy López," *Latino Legends in Sports,* http://www.latinosportslegends.com/Lopez_Nancy-bio.htm (January 1, 2010).

"Nancy Lopez," *New Georgia Encyclopedia,* http://www.georgiaencyclopedia.org/nge/Article.jsp?path=/Sports Recreation/ (January 1, 2010).□

William Moulton Marston

American psychologist, inventor, and cartoonist William Moulton Marston (1893–1947) held the dual distinctions of being the creator of the lie detector test and, under the pseudonym Charles Moulton, the iconic comic book character Wonder Woman. His invention of the systolic blood pressure lie detector in 1913 made his name well-known in his lifetime. As a consulting psychologist, Marston wrote several popular books and articles for a general audience which revealed his philosophy of adherence to what he called the "three Ls:" live, love, and laugh. His career took him from universities to Hollywood to advertising to, in his later years, the desk at which Marston created the Amazonian superhero Wonder Woman. Although Marston is little known today, the legacy of his creations has informed American criminal science and popular culture over the decades since his death.

Born on March 9, 1893, in Cliftondale, Massachusetts, to Frederick W. Marston and Annie Dalton Moulton Marston, the future psychologist grew up outside of Boston and attended Cambridge, Massachusetts's renowned Harvard College. In 1915, Marston completed his bachelor's degree and married Mount Holyoke graduate Elizabeth Holloway; later, the couple had four children. He then continued his education at Harvard Law School. As early as 1913, however, Marston had begun developing what Geoffrey C. Bunn quoted Marston as terming "the so-called Marston Deception Test, better known as the Lie Detector," in *History of Human Sciences.* Conducting experiments at the Harvard Psychological Laboratory under the auspices of the somewhat flamboyant scientist Hugo Münsterberg, who was interested in such esoteric psychological topics as the occult alongside more traditional topics, Marston began working on the deception research that Münsterberg had originated some time before. Marston tested the theory that a person telling a lie would undergo a significant swing in his or her systolic blood pressure, and that identifying this shift could thus serve as an indication of the truthfulness of that person's statements.

Developed Lie Detector

Combining a number of already-extant scientific devices used to read blood pressure such as the sphygmomanometer—the common blood pressure testing cuff that was already in use by that time—Marston hit upon a process that enabled him to precisely identify changes in a speaker's blood pressure. According to his *New York Times* obituary, Marston insisted throughout his life "that there were no quasi-magical machines, simply various combinations of long-familiar scientific apparatus, and that these, to give results of value, must be operated by experts." The lie detector established the young psychologist's reputation, and soon earned him a post in the United States Army's psychological division. Meanwhile, Marston also continued his legal studies, completing his law degree at Harvard in 1918. That same year, he won admission to the bar although serving as a second lieutenant as the result of his Army affiliation at the time of his passage. With the close of World War I, Marston's tour of duty ended and he returned to Massachusetts, where he worked for a time as an attorney for the Boston Legal Aid Society.

Yet, the lie detector test remained one of his primary interests, and he quickly disregarded the practice of law in favor of continued scientific experimentation to refine that device. He conducted a great deal of research into the correlations between deception and systolic blood pressures, regularly publishing his findings in academic sources such as the *Journal of Experimental Psychology* and the *Journal of Criminal Law and Criminology* during the early 1920s. In time, Marston became particularly interested in what he believed to be the practical applications of the device ranging from criminal investigation to the resolution of martial disputes. Despite his efforts to win acceptance for the lie detector as admissible evidence in criminal trials, the 1923 court decision *Frye v. U.S.* rejected it on the grounds that the majority of the scientific community had not yet granted it validity. Although Marston's systolic lie detection device and its successor, the polygraph test, remained barred from most courtrooms, the Frye standard—that of the general acknowledgement of a scientific device's validity by the relevant community of experts—became a measure against which admissible evidence was weighed for some 70 years.

Marston's further experiments investigated the nature of emotions and their relationship to physical and environmental factors; in 1924, Marston tested some of these theories on the incarcerated populations of Texas's state penitentiary system. The following year, Marston established himself as a consulting psychologist, a position that Bunn quoted the *Harvard Class of 1915 25th Anniversary Report* as characterizing as "a new sort of creature who seems to combine the advisory functions of the old-time pastor and country doctor." During 1925 and 1926, he additionally served on the psychology and philosophy faculty at Boston's Tufts University; after leaving Tufts, he moved to New York City, where he taught psychology at both Columbia and New York University. By the latter half of the decade, the psychologist was ready to analyze his findings to produce a number of theories on human emotion that he put forth in his first book, 1928's *Emotions of Normal People.*

Became Popular Psychologist

That same year, Marston, who always had a certain level of showmanship about him, staged an experiment at New York City's Embassy Theatre that emblemized his growing psychological theories. Before an audience crowded with publicity agents and curiosity seekers, Marston measured the blood pressure and respiratory shifts of six chorus girls—three blondes and three brunettes—using his lie detector device and a breath meter while they watched dramatic scenes from contemporary films that Marston judged to be provocative in some way: *The Flesh and the Devil* and *Love,* a version of the classic Tolstoy novel *Anna Karenina.* According to the *New York Times,* the "experiments more or less proved, [Marston] said, that brunettes enjoyed the thrill of pursuit, while blondes preferred the more passive enjoyment of being kissed." Although some were skeptical of this experiment—one attendee reportedly inquired as to how Marston could even be sure that the apparent blondes had come by that hair color naturally—as well as of the usefulness of its results, Marston himself

believed firmly in the correlations between hair color and personality, conducting further investigation into the matter and publishing articles about it in popular magazines as late as 1939.

The Embassy Theatre experiment attracted the attention of executives at the Hollywood's Universal Pictures. At the end of the year, Marston accepted a position with the studio Public Service Bureau, and relocated to California to undertake observations of film audiences to determine their emotional reactions to the movies they viewed. He continued to maintain an academic presence, as well, lecturing on psychology at Los Angeles's University of Southern California. By 1931, Marston was back in New York State as a visiting professor of psychology at Long Island University. That year, he published *Integrative Psychology: A Study of Unit Response,* a lengthy scientific tome co-written by his wife and psychologist/fiction writer C. D. King. In this work, the three argued that psychology rested upon four essential traits: Dominance, Compliance, Submission, and Inducement. Today, the DISC Personality Test is based on this four-pronged approach to psychology. He also served as a vice-president of the Hampton, Weeks, and Marston advertising agency, and published a 1932 historical novel on the life of Gaius Julius Caesar entitled *Venus with Us: A Tale of the Caesar.* During the 1933–1934 academic year, Marston taught psychology at the New School of Social Science and the Rand School of Social Science, both in New York City.

Once his positions at these universities came to an end, Marston left the academic world altogether and devoted himself increasingly to popular psychology. He wrote several articles that were published in such magazines as *Look* and *Reader's Digest,* and became the consulting psychologist for *Family Circle.* He also wrote books for the lay audience including *You Can Be Popular,* (1936) *Try Living* (1937), and *The Lie Detector Test* (1938). His psychology at this time was based on the three Ls—live, love, and laugh. A *New York Times* article quoted him as explaining in 1937, "To be successful in the worldly sense, you don't have to get up in the morning with that 'go-getter' look in the eye and all the [hocus-pocus] that inspirational writers have been telling us about for years." Instead, he argued, a person must pursue what he or she most enjoyed. He also began to increasingly promote his theories on the inherent psychological and moral strength of women, arguing that the long-held traditional sex roles were guaranteed to begin to collapse within the coming century, and a complete matriarchal society would be in place within the next millennium.

Created Character of *Wonder Woman*

A full expression of these ideas on feminine strength came to fruition in 1941, when Marston created the character of Wonder Woman. Fully believing in the psychological power of the comics, Marston may have hoped to kick start his predicted shift to matriarchy through the influence of his strong, female protagonist; in her later year, his widow suggested the character may have been devised at her suggestion. The first female superhero, Wonder Women claimed lineage as an Amazonian princess and had a collection of tools that Bunn argued on *American National Biography Online* "personified Marston's knowledge of psychology. She carried a lie detector—a 'Golden Lasso of Truth'—and wore 'Bracelets of Submission.'" However, Marston—a psychologist rather than an artist—did not directly create the image of the character, instead hiring experienced cartoonist Harry Peter to actually draw the cartoons he conceived.

The first Wonder Woman saga appeared under the byline of Charles Moulton in issue eight of All American's *All Star Comics,* in what Les Daniels noted in *Wonder Woman: The Complete History* was "for all its vaunted feminism…a piece of flag-waving propaganda, perfectly timed to coincide with the attack on Pearl Harbor that brought Americans into World War II." In the story, Wonder Woman cares for a injured American pilot who lands on her native Paradise Island, and then returns with him to the United States to take up a secret identity as nurse Diana Prince. The characters and her adventures quickly became popular, and she was the cover star on the debut issue of *Sensation Comics* in January of 1942. Wonder Woman became a regular *Sensation Comics* feature before graduating to her own titular comic book that summer. Marston continually expanded her appearances, hoping to spread his feminist message to as many readers as possible, and Wonder Woman even had a short run as a daily comic strip during 1944 and 1945.

Her creator, however, began to suffer from declining health. In 1944, Marston contracted polio, which caused him to suffer from partial paralysis and forced him to use a wheelchair. He soldiered on, continuing to produce Wonder Woman stories but frustrated by his physical infirmity. Slow recovery efforts occurred and by 1947 he was beginning to walk, but his condition was further compounded by a diagnosis of lung cancer early that year. He died on May 2, 1947, at his home in Rye, New York, as a result of this illness. Despite being only in his mid-fifties at the time of his death, Marston had built up a considerable body of work that has proved to be an enduring legacy. As Bunn argued in *History of Human Sciences,* "Throughout his career, Marston consistently disregarded the apparent boundaries between academic and popular psychology, between science and values, and between the legitimate and illegitimate." He believed his lie detector to have both scientific and personal application, and his cartoon heroine to carry great powers of psychological persuasion. Although Marston's name has largely dropped from the public consciousness, these two creations live on; lie detection remains almost as controversial in the twenty-first century as it was at the time of its inception, and Wonder Woman has enjoyed a lengthy run not only in print but also on television and film.

Books

Daniels, Les. *Wonder Woman: The Complete History,* DC Comics, 2000.

Periodicals

History of the Human Sciences, February 1997.
New York Times, January 31, 1928; November 11, 1937; May 3, 1947; February 18, 1992.

Online

"William Moulton Marston," DiscProfile.com, http://www.discprofile.com/williammoultonmarston.htm (January 9, 2010).
"William Moulton Marston," *American National Biography Online,* http://www.anb.org/articles/ (January 9, 2010).□

Curtis Mayfield

The African-American singer and songwriter Curtis Mayfield (1942–1999) made major contributions to popular music in the second half of the twentieth century, recording songs closely associated with the civil rights movement and adding a powerful political dimension to the soul and funk genres.

Mayfield lived and worked in Chicago for much of his career, and his early recordings with the Impressions were central to the development of soul music in that city. His soundtrack music for the 1972 film *Super Fly* elevated the gritty themes of the screenplay and became more famous than the film itself. The soundtrack touched off a new period of detailed social commentary in Mayfield's music, and he was also important as a songwriter for other artists, as a producer and as an early example of an artist who created independent music-business entities rather than working within the world of major labels and large production studios. Mayfield continued working in music even after suffering a catastrophic accident that left him paralyzed from the neck down.

Inspired by Dr. Seuss

Born in Chicago on June 3, 1942, Curtis Lee Mayfield grew up poor; he and his mother moved from place to place around the city and eventually settled in the Cabrini-Green housing project on the North Side. A grandmother who preached at the Traveling Souls Spiritualist Church was an early influence, and Curtis began singing and writing gospel music as a preteen. The use of falsetto in his singing and the ecstatic tone of his music showed a gospel influence throughout his career. Mayfield cited a less commonly acknowledged influence in an interview with Jas Obrecht of *Guitar Player.* "I think my first teacher for writing was Dr. Seuss," he said. "I used to love limericks, and that helped too. They help teach you how to put your words in order and then close them out. You'd be surprised how much those simple things lay the foundation for writing." His guitar was his constant companion, to a point where he sometimes slept with it.

The Impressions came together in the mid-1950s when Mayfield's friend, Chicago vocalist Jerry Butler, met the members of a Tennessee vocal harmony group called the Roosters, was signed on as lead vocalist, and invited Mayfield to join. The Roosters made several recordings for Chicago's pioneering black-oriented record label Vee Jay, and then changed their name to the Impressions and began

to develop Butler as a solo artist. The group broke up temporarily as Butler's career grew in the late 1950s, and Mayfield continued to play guitar for Butler. He penned Butler's 1960 hit "He Will Break Your Heart." Mayfield brought the Impressions back together, with himself as lead vocalist, in 1961. Signed to the ABC-Paramount label, the Impressions had some success with the single "Gypsy Woman" and then, in 1963, topped rhythm-and-blues charts and crossed over to pop success with "It's All Right."

That song's feel-good lyric contained hints ("Clap your hands, give yourself a chance") of the emerging African-American consciousness of the era, and that consciousness came to the fore in hit Impressions singles (and Mayfield compositions) such as "Keep On Pushing" (1964), which became an unofficial anthem of the civil rights movement in the mid-1960s, and especially "People Get Ready" (1965), a popular music standard that later inspired covers by artists as diverse as reggae star Bob Marley and R&B chanteuse Alicia Keys. Mayfield wrote the song in 1964, inspired by the vast March on Washington for civil rights the previous year. The Impressions declined in popularity somewhat in the late 1960s, partly because the thoughtful message Mayfield offered in such songs as "Mighty Mighty (Spade and Whitey)" ("Your black and white power / Is gonna be a crumbling tower") was overshadowed by the more flamboyant lyrics, rhythms, and stage presentation of soul singer James Brown, whom Mayfield likely influenced. After the Impressions were dropped by ABC/Paramount, Mayfield set out as a solo artist.

Founded Own Label

Mayfield had founded his own publishing company, Curtom, in 1960, and in 1968, at a time when few artists aside from megastars like the Beatles had attempted the move, he expanded it into a record label of his own. He released his solo debut, *Curtis,* in 1970, and announced a new direction in his music with socially conscious songs up to ten minutes in length. But it was the *Super Fly* soundtrack in 1972 that made Mayfield a household name with the title track (spelled "Superfly" as a single record), "Pusherman," and the tragic "Freddie's Dead." Mayfield tried to ennoble the film's theme of drug dealing. "When he got the [*Super Fly*] script, he said it read well," Mayfield's widow Altheida told Margena A. Christian of *Jet.* "But when they did the film, they didn't put any money in it. It looked like a commercial for cocaine. He didn't think it was right. He tried to turn it around and make something positive with the music." Mayfield went on to score the music-business film *Sparkle,* with vocals by Aretha Franklin, as well as several other films.

The *Super Fly* music, as well as other Mayfield albums of the 1970s, such as the heavily political *There's No Place Like America Today,* did not succeed purely on the strength of their lyrics and Mayfield's soulful high vocals. Mayfield's own percussive guitar style, with its agile funk rhythms, also played an important role. He used a unique guitar tuning that he had devised himself when he was young, teaching himself the instrument. "I used to play boogie-woogie on the piano, and not ever having had lessons I subconsciously retuned the guitar to the key of F sharp [F sharp-A sharp-C sharp-F sharp-A sharp-F sharp]," he explained to Obrecht (the tuning corresponds to the black keys on the piano, used in boogie-woogie). An all-around musical talent, Mayfield was also active as a producer on albums by Franklin, the Staple Singers, and Gladys Knight & the Pips.

The disco environment of the late 1970s was less favorable for Mayfield's style, and in 1980 he moved Curtom's operations from Chicago to Atlanta. His 1982 album *Honesty,* which included country-flavored material, was well reviewed, and the Impressions reunited for a 1983 tour. Although Mayfield made no more new albums over the balance of the decade he built a new following through European tours and made contacts with musicians active in Atlanta's budding rap scene. By the end of the 1980s, hip-hop musicians were beginning to make frequent use of Mayfield's classic recordings via digital sampling.

Injured in On-Stage Accident

On August 13, 1990, a lighting tower fell on Mayfield during a concert in Brooklyn, New York, during a heavy storm. The singer was left a quadriplegic, and awards organizations wrote what they thought was the concluding chapter to his career. The Impressions were inducted into the Rock and Roll Hall of Fame in 1991, and Mayfield was given a Lifetime Achievement Grammy Award in

1995. In 1993 Butler and others recorded *People Get Ready,* one of several tribute albums featuring Mayfield's music, and three separate Mayfield box sets were issued. Mayfield did not give up on music, however. He entered physical therapy and established a research fund dedicated to finding a cure for paralysis. "I just mourned my guitar," Mayfield told *Jet.* "It was like a human being. It was like another brother for me. I used to sleep with my guitar."

Remarkably, Mayfield was able to make and release a final album, *New World Order,* in 1996. He recorded the music from a prone position so that gravity would put pressure on his lungs and increase their capacity. The Atlanta production team Organized Noize had to splice together the brief segments he could sing at a single stretch, but Mayfield's songwriting was still sharp, and the final album showed few traces of these problems. In Obrecht's words, "His sweet, hard-wrought vocals are achingly beautiful, and his lyrics stay true to his lifelong message of love." The album earned Mayfield the last of his four Grammy nominations. Mayfield that year also released a book of lyrics, *Poetic License: In Poem and Song.*

In 1999 Mayfield received another honor when he was inducted into the Rock and Roll Hall of Fame a second time, this time as a solo artist. He continued to suffer health problems as a result of his accident, however, and he died in Roswell, Georgia, on December 26, 1999.

His manager, Marv Heiman, according to BBC News, said that Mayfield "wanted people to think about themselves and the world around them, making this a better place for everyone to live." Mayfield was married twice and had ten children. His musical influence was evident in the hundreds of cover versions of his compositions, in the traces of his falsetto vocals in the work of artists such as Prince, and in the seriousness and social purpose of his music. Aretha Franklin, quoted on the web site of the Rock and Roll Hall of Fame, asserted that "Curtis Mayfield is to soul music what Bach was to the classics and Gershwin and Irving Berlin were to pop music." A documentary film, *Movin' On Up: The Music and Message of Curtis Mayfield and the Impressions,* was released in 2008.

Books

Burns, Peter, *Curtis Mayfield,* Sanctuary, 2003.
Contemporary Musicians, volume 8, Gale, 1992.

Periodicals

Atlanta Journal-Constitution, December 27, 1999.
Guardian (London, England), December 28, 1999.
Guitar Player, December 1996.
Independent (London, England), December 28, 1999.
Jet, April 28, 2008.
New York Times, December 27, 1999.
People Get Ready: The Curtis Mayfield Story, Rhino Records (box set with booklet), 1996.

Online

"Curtis Mayfield (1942–1999)," *New Georgia Encyclopedia,* http://www.georgiaencyclopedia.org/nge/Article.jsp?id=h-1659 (January 12, 2010).
"Curtis Mayfield," *Rock and Roll Hall of Fame,* http://www.rockhall.com/inductee/curtis-mayfield (January 12, 2010).
"'People Get Ready': Song Inspired by March on Washington Carries Enduring Message," *National Public Radio,* http://www.npr.org/news/specials/march40th/people.html (January 12, 2010).
"Soul Icon Curtis Mayfield Dies," *BBC News,* http://www.news.bbc.co.uk/2/hi/entertainment/579113.stm (January 12, 2010).□

Dmitry Medvedev

In 2008, Russian political leader Dmitry Medvedev (born 1965) was elected president of the Russian Federation. He was the third president of Russia after its reconstitution following the fall of the Soviet Union in 1991.

The presidency was Medvedev's first elective office. He rose to the top of the Russian government not through a sequence of official positions but through capable work for powerful patrons, most significantly his predecessor, Vladimir Putin. Yet Medvedev, younger than Putin and among the first Russian leaders who had not emerged from the Soviet Union's Communist government, proved to be something of an enigma when he assumed power—not a puppet for Putin, yet not an entirely independent figure, either. A technocrat and a promoter of efficiency in the notoriously sluggish bureaucracies of the geographically vast Russian state, Medvedev represented a new face in Russian politics.

Child of Educators

An only child, Dmitry Anatolyevich Medvedev was born in Leningrad in the Soviet Union, now St. Petersburg, Russia, on September 14, 1965. His father taught at a technical school, and his mother was a Russian language lecturer and later a museum guide. Their combined salaries were enough to buy them a small apartment on the city's outskirts, a typically spartan example of Soviet housing. "It wasn't much, to be honest, but I lived there for almost 30 years and even managed to write a Ph.D. there and didn't feel depressed or embarrassed," Medvedev was quoted as saying by Mark Franchetti of the London *Sunday Times.* "Our means were average. We didn't starve, though we had little money."

Medvedev helped out at an auto repair shop to get extra money to buy ice cream or movie tickets for his future wife, Svetlana, whom he met when he was seven. Medvedev enjoyed poetry and children's books, but luxury items like Western jeans or the heavy metal albums he loved—and continued to listen to as an adult—were out of the question. Medvedev focused on his schooling, hoping to become a judge. He earned a law degree from Leningrad

State University in 1987 (joining the Russian Orthodox church the same year), and a doctorate in law from the same institution in 1990, writing a Ph.D. thesis on the legal issues facing state enterprises and teaching civil law courses as a graduate student. In 1990 he joined the school's law faculty as an associate professor, a position he held until 1999. He became the co-author of a three-volume textbook on civil law.

More significant for his future career, however, was his decision to volunteer for the reformist mayoral and chamber-of-deputies campaigns of Anatoly Sobchak, who was elected mayor of Leningrad in 1991 and rode out the transition to non-Communist rule and the restoration of the city's original name of Petrograd or St. Petersburg. Sobchak named Putin, a former agent in the Soviet Union's KGB intelligence service, as a deputy and appointed Medvedev as Putin's legal advisor. The two men met in 1991 and grew closer as Putin observed Medvedev's methodical work in handling allegations that Putin had improperly steered export licenses to personal friends; Putin was eventually exonerated of the charges. Medvedev and his wife, Svetlana, had a son, Ilya, born in 1996. When Putin moved to Moscow in 1999, Medvedev followed.

Headed State Energy Company

Putin's election to the Russian presidency the following year vindicated that decision, for Medvedev received powerful posts: deputy prime minister, and, even more significant, head of Gazprom, the Russian state oil and

natural gas monopoly. That put Medvedev in the middle of disputes between Russia and its former satellites, still connected to Russia's energy infrastructure. But Medvedev, with a combination of negotiation and muscle, solved problems smoothly and brought some 30 percent of Russia's natural resources under control of the central government housed at the Kremlin in Moscow. "There's this chemistry, a personal trust between us," Putin was quoted as saying by Franchetti. "Not once did he let me down." Medvedev managed Putin's 2000 campaign and was named deputy head of the presidential administration, rising to head of the presidential administration in 2003.

Medvedev was able to move into a walled compound in Moscow and to indulge a childhood dream by booking the British heavy metal band Deep Purple to play at a Gazprom anniversary party. His chief rival within Putin's administration was defense minister Sergei Ivanov. As Putin's constitutionally limited two terms as president neared their end, Kremlin watchers tabbed Medvedev and Ivanov as possible anointed successors to the immensely popular president. It was also unclear whether Putin would actually relinquish the office as he was required to do. With Medvedev at the helm of plans to improve housing, health care, education, and agricultural production in Russia, he was given the nod by Putin as the candidate of his United Russia party in Russia's 2008 presidential election.

That election was not regarded as entirely free and fair; several high-profile candidates, including former world chess champion Garry Kasparov, were banned or squeezed out of the race, and Medvedev benefited from favorable coverage in the Russian media. Still, the more than 70 percent of the vote he amassed in the election on March 2, 2008, against opposition from both a Communist candidate and one from the nationalist right, was impressive. Medvedev emphasized reform in a general way and featured such innovations (for Russia) as a campaign web site. He promised independence from Putin, but it was also widely expected that he would nominate Putin to the position of prime minister, the second most powerful position in the Russian government, and he did in fact do so after he took office.

Asserted Independence from Putin

Even for the Russian people, to say nothing of the West, Medvedev was something of an unknown quantity. Shorter in stature even than Putin, but with a telegenic boyish face, he seemed to represent the interests of Russia's growing middle classes. He pledged to deregulate state-controlled industries and to increase the independence of Russia's judiciary. Both he and Putin insisted on his independence, but the degree to which the Russian public was persuaded that such independence actually existed was unclear; a poll taken in mid-2009 found that 50 percent of Russians believed that the two men shared power equally, 34 percent believed that Putin really held the reins, and 12 percent thought Medvedev was in fact the real leader.

Beyond public perceptions, the record offered mixed evidence as to the relative contributions of the two leaders. Medvedev, apparently on his own, announced ambitious goals of modernizing and diversifying Russia's economy, reducing its dependence on the raw materials that had long been its backbone. "The nation's prestige and welfare can't depend forever on the achievements of the past," he wrote in an article quoted by Charles Clover in London's *Financial Times.* "All that has kept the country afloat, but it is rapidly aging." Medvedev waded into an issue that had proved perilous for some of his predecessors: he announced new regulations on the sale of vodka and other alcoholic beverages, striving to lower Russia's per capita consumption of 32 pints of pure alcohol per year, a prime contributor to the country's low life expectancy and demographically hazardous loss in population. Medvedev himself, like Putin, exercised daily and projected an athletic image.

In the realm of foreign policy, Medvedev issued statements that supported European and American attempts to slow the nuclear program of Russia's onetime ally, Iran. At other times, it seemed as though Putin was the one in control. When armed conflict flared between Russia and its southern neighbor Georgia over the disputed regions of South Ossetia and Abkhazia in 2008, it was Putin, not Medvedev, who appeared on television issuing orders to the Russian military. The major question mark by 2010 was the 2012 presidential election, in which Putin was eligible to run again, but one in which he might find himself with a new competitor in his faithful right-hand man, who was quoted by the London *Independent* as saying, "We are well aware that no non-democratic state has ever become truly prosperous."

Periodicals

Daily Telegraph (London, England), September 15, 2009.

Financial Times (London, England), March 29, 2008; November 13, 2009.

Independent (London, England), March 1, 2008.

International Herald Tribune, February 5, 2009.

Sunday Times (London, England), March 2, 2008.

Xinhua News Agency, February 25, 2010.

Online

"Dmitry Medvedev," *Pravda* (December 12, 2007), http://www.english.pravda.ru/russia/kremlin/12-12-2007/102708-Dmitry_Medvedev-0 (February 10, 2010).

"Who Is Dmitry Medvedev?," *Russia Today,* http://www.rt.com/Top_News/2008-03-04/Who_is_Dmitry_Medvedev.html (February 10, 2010). □

Marvin Miller

American baseball executive and union leader Marvin Miller (born 1917) was one of the most influential twentieth-century American sports figures. During his tenure as the Major League Players Association's executive director, which lasted from 1966 to 1983, he overturned baseball's constrictive reserve clause and, in turn, ushered in the era of free agency, which enabled athletes to share the wealth with team owners.

Prior to Marvin Julian Miller's entrance into Major League Baseball as a forceful labor negotiator, athletes were subjected to an outdated but persistent labor arrangement that essentially made them enslaved chattel. Miller changed all of that, however, when he accepted the position as the Major League Baseball Players Association's (MLBPA) executive director. During his tenure, which lasted less than two decades (1966–1983), Miller irrevocably transformed the landscape of baseball. By challenging a restrictive reserve clause, he ushered an era of free agency and, in turn, moved baseball into the modern era, enabling talented athletes to quote their price according to their demonstrated skills. It all came down to exploitation: If a ballplayer could draw crowds by winning 20 games a season, or launching 35 home runs a year, or by compiling a .330 batting average, why shouldn't he share the hefty revenues that owners amassed? After all, no baseball fan ever paid a ticket in hopes of seeing a team owner's smiling face.

While Miller never played baseball, he became one of the sport's most influential figures. In the sixteen years that he served as the executive director of the MLBPA, Miller turned a weak organization into one of the United States' most powerful and effective labor unions.

Interested in Baseball and Economics

A child of Eastern European immigrants, Miller was born on April 14, 1917 in the Bronx, the northernmost section of New York City, but he grew up in Brooklyn, where he became a self-described "diehard" baseball fan. Miller naturally followed the Brooklyn Dodgers. The future head of the MLBPA typically purchased a thrifty ticket that afforded him a remote "bleacher bum" seat in the awkwardly dimensioned Flatbush baseball park, the team's home field. "Ebbets Field was not far from where my family lived," related Miller in a 2003 interview with book author and journalist David Davis (as quoted on The Baseball Reliquary web site). "[Pitcher] Dazzy Vance was probably my favorite player."

Miller graduated from Brooklyn's P.S. 153 elementary school in 1929. He then attended James Madison High School, where an economics teacher instilled in him a strong interest in the subject. This early fascination informed his subsequent career and later transformation of America's "national pastime."

Meanwhile, Miller grew up in a pro-union home. His father, Alexander Miller, a retailer who sold women's apparel on the Lower East Side, belonged to the wholesale clothing workers union. His mother, Gertrude (Wald) Miller, an elementary school teacher in New York's public school system, became one of the city's first members of the teachers' union.

After graduating from high school, Miller attended Miami University in Oxford, Ohio, entertaining ambitions of becoming an economics instructor. After his junior year, he transferred to New York University and graduated in 1938 with a bachelor's of science degree in economics.

Worked for Government Agencies and Unions

After college, Miller clerked at the United States Department of the Treasury in Washington, D.C. In 1940, he returned to New York City, where he became an investigator in the Department of Welfare. During World War II, he worked with the National War Labor Relations Board as a labor economist. True to his familial heritage and educational direction, Miller helped settle labor disputes.

Following government service, he assumed positions with the International Association of Machinists and the United Auto Workers union. In 1950, he became staff economist for the United Steelworkers of America union. By 1966, he became the chief staff economist, assistant to the president and the union's top negotiator. That same year, he shifted his career direction to sports.

Became Baseball Player Representative

On March 5, 1966, baseball player representatives elected Miller as executive director of the MLBPA. This came about after a difficult preliminary meeting with Major League pitchers Robin Roberts and Jim Bunning (two future MLB Hall of Famers) and infielder/outfielder Harvey Kuenn. The three men, who were members of the union's search committee, suggested that Miller work with Richard M. Nixon. At the time, Nixon was in career transition: He had lost the California Governor election in 1962 and was preparing a campaign for the U.S. presidency (he was elected in 1968).

Miller balked at the idea of working with the former United States Vice President. He described the circumstances for Davis: "I met with [Roberts, Bunning and Kuenn] in December of 1965 in Cleveland. We were about three hours

into the meeting before that bombshell was dropped [about Nixon serving as Miller's general counsel].... [But] it was a good-faith effort on Roberts' part."

Roberts's reasoning seemed sound enough: He understood that Miller would have to be voted on by all players, and that many existing major league players had no experience with or were hostile to unionization, against their better interests. Many players were conservative—coming from the south and other rural areas, as well as Orange County, California. Roberts, Miller related, felt that the conservative Nixon's presence in the proposed union package would engender a balancing effect. "They let me know that Nixon had accepted the idea [and] that he and his law firm would serve as general counsel," Miller recalled. "I swallowed twice and said it would not work, and [tried to] explain why."

Essentially, Miller explained that it would be counter-productive to hire two diametrically opposed individuals working within a relatively small organization. He wanted to focus on the most important player issue: a viable pension plan. Realizing that he was not compatible with Nixon throughout the many meetings and interviews they had, he made his position clear. Further, Miller recognized that Nixon wouldn't be fully committed, as it was well-known that Nixon was focusing on another presidential bid.

During the meeting, after Miller expressed his concerns to Roberts, Bunning and Kuenn, a significant silence ensued. Miller figured he lost the job, and on his way out of the door, he delivered a parting shot: "I'm going to offer you some advice," he related to his three interviewers. "Whoever gets elected executive director, let him pick the general counsel. It's got to be someone he's totally compatible with. Otherwise you're going to create chaos and undermine your situation."

Despondent, Miller returned to Pittsburgh, Pennsylvania, where he lived with his wife, Terry, and his children, sure that he had lost his chance to be involved. In the meantime, however, Roberts, Bunning and Kuenn considered Miller's ideas. After careful deliberation, they decided to offer Miller the job.

A Whole New Ballgame

Miller proved an appropriate choice, and baseball would never be the same. With his previous governmental and unionist activities, he would bring considerable insight and experience to his new position. Moreover, Miller wasn't an outside interloper: He truly understood and appreciated baseball. "I wasn't just a fan," he told Davis. "I knew all of the statistics and batting stances and pitching motions of every player."

But he was more than just a sport aficionado. He perceived the larger picture. As he stated to Davis, "labor relations are labor relations" no matter the industry and its product, and with his encyclopedic knowledge of statistics, he understood the full value of baseball players' worth. But, at the time, players didn't fully grasp this essential wisdom. "What really was new and different [within baseball] was that I was coming into a situation where there was no union nor a history of union activism," Miller said in the same interview.

Previously, ballplayers had been content to let the owners call the shots. True, players had a labor organization, but it was dominated by owner control. The players' union didn't even have its own headquarters, Miller realized to his dismay.

Obviously, he had a lot of work ahead of him. Club owners ruled the roost with an iron fist forged within baseballs' century-old existence. But times were not only changing, they needed to change, and Miller—now appointed as the MLBPA executive director—moved the sport from an eighteenth century mindset and into twentieth-century reality

Previously, players were chained to employers and teams by the manacle of the "reserve clause" concept, a form of bondage that best served owners by limiting salary and career choice. Essentially, players were tied to a club and subjected to a salary structure that best benefited team owners. In his effort to initiate change, Miller integrated outside concepts (e.g., fairness doctrines) into the sports world.

Bringing to his position a potent chemistry of charisma, union experience and vision, Miller won over the initially dubious players and convinced them that solidarity and collective bargaining would empower them. As a result, he transformed an amorphous association into one of the strongest unions in the United States. In the process, he revolutionized professional baseball's labor relations and economics and, in turn, he created a new template that would embolden other professional sports to increase labor union power.

Targeted Players' Contracts

Once installed, Miller first sought to renegotiate the basic player contract, which he considered one of the worst labor documents ever developed. Of course, team owners erected difficult hurdles in his path. First, they refused to provide a realistic representation of players' existing salaries. In response, Miller assigned union members from each team to provide accurate salary reports. In this way, he helped increase minimum salaries from $6,000 to $10,000 after the first collective bargaining agreement in professional sports' history. The raise was still a paltry sum, considering what the players contributed to the owners' bottom line and what would later come through the next two decades (with the changes that Miller would engineer).

Remaining obstinate, team owners refused a union request to hold union business meetings in ballpark locker rooms. Miller simply moved these meeting outside of the sports facilities.

Eventually, Miller negotiated a pension plan that become one of the best packages in the United States, no matter the industry. Also, in 1973, he gained for players the right to resolve grievances through arbitration. Looking back, Miller considered this the most significant player union advancement, as the impartial arbitration process fostered the most significant gains that players would enjoy in ensuing decades. It also brought in the era of free agency.

Overturned Reserve Clause

In 1975, Miller gained from management an agreement that allowed players to sign with other teams once their old contracts were up. This would end team owners' control over players' careers and provide established players with greater job security. Miller managed to accomplish this through a language flaw he recognized in player contracts. The flaw resided in Section 10A of the contract, or the "reserve" clause that bound players to teams and allowed owners to renew a player's contract in perpetuity.

The first major challenge to the reserve clause occurred in 1975 and involved Los Angeles Dodger pitcher Andy Messersmith. In this test case, Messersmith became baseball's first free agent after arbitrator Peter Seitz ruled in his favor on December 23. 1975. The Federal Court accepted Miller's argument and upheld the ruling. Seitz's arbitration ruling also made a free agent of pitcher Dave McNally. Both Messersmith and McNally had played out the option year of their contracts. McNally was so adamant that he even chose to retire from the sport in June 1975 rather than sign a one-year contract with the Montreal Expos. He sacrificed much in his principled stance: The Expos had offered him $125,000 to sign, but he refused. He and Messersmith filed a grievance with the MLB Players Union. Messersmith's and McNally's position, Miller's support, and Seitz's ruling overturned baseball's century-old reserve clause. As a result, the union and team owners created a labor deal that would allow players to become free agents after six years in the major leagues. This put teams in competition to sign baseball's best players. The average player salary rose from $44,000 in 1975 to $2.38 million in 2002.

Led Baseball Strikes

A tough negotiator, Miller didn't always endear himself to the sport's fans. They felt that he had transformed ballplayers into businessmen. Also, he led the baseball union into two labor strikes that interrupted baseball seasons, denying fans their spring-summer baseball fix. The first began on April 1, 1972. While it only lasted 13 day, the strike delayed the start of a new baseball season. The second and more substantial strike occurred in the middle of the 1981 baseball season and lasted fifty days. Reaction to that prolonged stoppage was profound. Fans went into a baseball withdrawal, and television outlets that broadcasted major league games tried to fill the void by televising minor league baseball games. But, for instance, Philadelphia Phillies fans (who celebrated a world championship in 1980) were less than satisfied with the alternative. Thus, they viewed Miller's mustachioed countenance as a villainous visage.

Still, Miller, while perceived as intractable, always proved willing to concede necessary compromises with owners throughout his tenure as head of the baseball players' union. He officially retired in 1984, after achieving significant progress on the players' behalf. Besides opening the door to free agency, during five collective bargaining agreements, he raised the average salary and ensured that players received a fair share of licensing and broadcasting revenues. He also advocated for player safety and successfully bargained for improved seasonal scheduling, padded outfield walls, well-defined outfield warning tracks and safer locker-room environments. Indeed, never once did Miller apply his efforts to his own benefit.

Left out of Hall of Fame

Despite the enormous impact he had on the game, Miller was continually denied entrance into MLB's Hall of Fame. This seemed to bother Miller's supporters more than Miller himself. After the Hall's Veteran Committee denied him induction yet again in 2009, Miller wrote a letter to the Hall asking that he not be considered for election on the 2010 ballot. Apparently, such an honor was meaningless.

But others chose to disagree. Those advocating Miller's induction included journalists Red Barber and Studs Terkel and retired players such as Jim Bunning and Jim Bouton, the former Yankees pitcher who wrote the controversial *Ball Four*. Sports broadcaster Bob Costas said no other non-player is more deserving of Hall of Fame induction. Terkel described Miller as the most effective union organizer since John L. Lewis, and Barber likened him to the great Babe Ruth and Jackie Robinson in terms of historical significance.

Placing Miller's impact in context, in 2000, *The Sporting News* ranked Miller fifth on its list of the "100 Most Powerful People in Sports for the 20th Century."

But a far more profound occurrence placed everything in its proper perspective. On October 27, 2009, Miller's wife Terry died. She was ninety years old. Marvin and Terry met in 1936, when Terry was a seventeen-year-old student at Brooklyn. Besides her husband, Terry Miller was survived by the couple's two children, daughter Susan and son Peter.

Preserving the Record

Miller related his career and accomplishments in *A Whole Different Ball Game: The Sport and Business of Baseball*. In the book, which was published in 1991, Miller describes how he turned the MLB Players Association into a powerful union. Miller also wrote the foreword for the novel *Man on Spikes*, written by baseball historian Eliot Asinof and published in 1998. In *Lords of the Realm: The Real History of Baseball* (1994), author John Helyar described Miller's years as the player union's leader.

In 2003, Miller donated his papers to the Tamiment Library at his alma mater, New York University. The contribution included 400,000 documents that included correspondence, contracts, and press clippings. The collection encompassed Miller's entire professional career, from his work with organizations such the International Association of Machinists, the United Automobile Workers, the United Steelworkers of America and up to his tenure as head of the MLB Players Association.

Books

"Miller, Marvin Julian," *Encyclopaedia Judaica*, Macmillan Reference USA, 2007.

"Miller, Marvin Julian," *The Scribner Encyclopedia of American Lives Thematic Series: Sport Figures*, Charles Scribner's Sons, 2002.

Online

"Dave McNally 1942-2002," *Sports Encyclopedia.com*, (December 31, 2009).

"Marvin Miller," *Baseball Library.com*,, http://www. baseball library.com/ballplayers/player.php?name=Marvin_Miller (December 31, 2009).

"Marvin Miller," *Spiritus-Temporis.com*,, http://www.spiritus-temporis.com/marvin-miller (December 31, 2009).

"Marvin Miller—Interviewed by David Davis July 2003," *The Baseball Reliquary Inc.com*, http://www.baseballreliquary. org/MarvinMillerInterview.htm (December 31, 2009).

"The Shame of Marvin Miller," *Baseball: Past and Present.com*,, http://baseballpastandpresent.com/2009/12/07/the-shame-of-marvin-miller/ (December 31, 2009).

"Terry Miller, Wife of Former MLBPA Exec. Dir. Marvin Miller, Passes Away at 90," *The Biz of Baseball.com*, http://www. bizofbaseball.com/index (December 31, 2009).

"Time for Miller's call from the Hall," *ESPN.com*,,http://sports. espn.go.com/mlb/columns/story?columnist=crasnick_jerry& id=4700428 (December 31, 2009).□

Henry Gwyn Jeffreys Moseley

English physicist Henry Gwyn Jeffreys Moseley (1887–1915) conducted experiments involving X-ray spectra that led to Moseley's Law and the establishment of the atomic number. His research not only engendered better understanding of the atomic structure but also provided the foundation for later scientific research. His promising career was cut short when he was killed in World War I.

The career of Henry Gwyn Jeffreys Moseley was a metaphoric supernova that exploded brilliantly during a short four-year period (1910–1914). In that brief span, Moseley made substantial contributions to science. He is not only remembered for his accomplishments, however. Today, his name serves as a painful reminder of how war robs humankind of its most precious intellectual resources. During his too-brief career, Moseley conducted experiments that subsequently led to the accurate ordering of elements and, in turn, a significant revision in the period table, which forever changed the course of physics and chemistry. Young and innately curious, Moseley appeared poised to make additional and equally substantial discoveries. But the scientific community can only speculate on his potential accomplishments and the impact that his prospective discoveries would have had on the world in which he lived: Moseley was killed in battle during World War I. His death is now regarded as a tragedy that transcends national boundaries, and his abbreviated legacy remains powerful, as his successful experiments provided the foundation for later scientific discoveries.

Inherited Strong Science Legacy

Better known as Harry throughout his life, Henry Gwyn Jeffreys Moseley was born November 23, 1887 and raised in Weymouth, England in a family that included two sisters.

His family boasted a strong scientific heritage. His father, Henry Nottidge Moseley, was a professor of anatomy and physiology at the University of Oxford. His mother, Amabel, was the daughter of John Gwyn Jeffreys, a British conchologist (a studier of mollusk shells). Moseley's paternal grandfather was the first professor of natural philosophy at King's College, in London, England. His paternal great grandfather was an expert on tropical diseases. Moseley's father also was a member of the famous HMS Challenger sea expedition that studied the world's oceans from 1872 to 1876. Unsurprisingly, the young Harry exhibited a strong interest in science, which was cultivated by his mother and further encouraged by friends. This early interest led to an enduring attraction toward natural history and natural science as well as his later research career.

Embraced a Scientific Curriculum

When his father died in 1891, Moseley moved with his mother and two sisters to Chilworth, a small town located in Surrey, England. There, he began his formal education. When he was nine years old, Moseley enrolled at Summer Fields, a school that prepared students for entrance into the prestigious Eton College, a boarding school for teenage

boys founded in 1440 by King Henry VI. In 1901, he obtained a scholarship at Eton, where he studied under T.C. Porter, one of the first English scientists that conducted research into X-rays. From that point, Moseley remained fascinated with X-rays. This new interest would culminate in his significant scientific discoveries.

Moseley graduated from Eton in 1906 and, thanks to another scholarship, continued his education at Trinity College at the University of Oxford. He earned a degree in physics in 1910 and garnered letters of recommendation that enabled him to become an instructor at the University of Manchester.

Worked in Rutherford's Laboratory

At Manchester, along with his teaching duties, Moseley worked with Ernest Rutherford, a pioneering nuclear physicist. At the time, Rutherford was investigating phenomena related to natural radioactivity. Moseley assisted Rutherford with his research, but later became more interested in the diffraction of X-rays, which had recently been discovered by German physicist Max von Laue (1879–1960), who received a Nobel Prize in 1914 for his discovery. Moseley convinced Rutherford to let him explore this area.

By the end of his first year at Manchester, Moseley was relieved of his heavy teaching schedule so that he could focus all of his energies on research. For several months, Moseley collaborated with mathematical physicist Charles Galton Darwin (1887–1962), the grandson of the famous naturalist Charles Darwin. Moseley and Darwin studied general characteristics of X-ray diffraction.

Studied X-ray Spectra

Then, in 1913, Moseley began using X-ray spectroscopy to determine the X-ray spectra of elements. Previously, William Henry Bragg (1862–1942) and his son, William Lawrence Bragg (1890–1971), performed a good deal of research on X-ray spectroscopy. The Braggs had discovered that when excited, elements emit an X-ray that consists of a continuous background spectrum as well as a small number of bright lines that proved characteristic for each element. Moseley studied with William Lawrence Bragg for a short period. For his own research activities in this area, Moseley developed a system that enabled him to study the X-ray diffraction patterns for elements. He eventually uncovered the co-relationship existing between emitted wavelength and atomic number, a discovery that became termed as Moseley's Law.

Specifically, by focusing on the nature of the spectra produced by scattered X-rays, Moseley saw that X-rays directed at certain crystalline materials diffracted by atoms within the crystals, which formed a continuous spectrum superimposed with a series of bright lines. Further, the number and locations of the lines proved to be characteristic of the element or elements under observation. In this way, Moseley observed that the frequencies of one set of spectral lines (called the K lines) changed from element to element in consistent and neat fashion. When elements were arranged in ascending order according to their atomic weight, the frequency of the K lines changed by a factor of one. Based on his results, he decided that some property existed within the atomic structure that produced these observed changes. Moseley then endeavored to better understand this property.

Developed Atomic Number Concept

Independent research conducted by Dutch amateur physicist Antonius Johannes van den Broek (1870–1926) helped Moseley realize the nature of this property. Van den Broek suggested it had to do with nuclear charge, specifically that the charge links itself to atomic weight in linear fashion. Moseley determined that the inherent property was, indeed, the charge of the nucleus. Also, when Moseley was working with Rutherford, he met Niels Bohr (1885–1962), who would later receive a Nobel Prize for research related to atomic structure and quantum mechanics. Bohr had advanced the idea that atomic number, rather than atomic weight, should govern the ordering of elements in the periodic table. With his deployment of X-ray crystallography in his experiments, Moseley would prove that Bohr was right.

During the course of his research, Moseley observed a significant correspondence: Elements arranged is ascending order according to atomic weight are also arranged in ascending order according to nuclear charge. Also, he pointed out that while there is a variation in atomic weights between adjacent elements that is never consistent, the variation in nuclear charge remains consistent and precise. Moseley attached the term "atomic number" to this property, because it proved a clearly defining characteristic of atoms and elements.

Moseley's discovery had enormous impact, as it provided a new basis for the periodic table. Previously, Russian chemist Dmitri Ivanovich Mendeleev (1834–1907) had proposed arranging elements according to their atomic weight. While this approach worked well, it proved flawed. But Moseley found that arrangement according to atomic numbers eliminated the flaws in Mendeleev's proposed approach. As such, Moseley concluded that atomic number was a more fundamental property of atoms and elements than atomic weight.

Pathfinder for New Elements

Moseley's work also helped establish the probable maximum number of elements, and it provided direction for researchers attempting to find new elements. As each element could be tagged with a unique atomic number, any missing numbers strongly suggested that a new element would be discovered and fit into the table in a precise position. Moseley's research enabled him to predict the number and location of elements missing from the periodic table. For instance, Moseley correctly predicted that an undiscovered element (#43) resided between molybdenum (#42) and ruthenium (#44). He also predicated that another element (#61) would turn up between neodymium (#60) and samarium (#62). In addition, he correctly predicted the expected spectral pattern to be expected for each missing element. This provided a valuable tool for researchers seeking the undiscovered elements.

Essentially, the atomic number related to the number of electrons an element possesses. The periodic table's structure came to reflect the particular electron arrangement in each type of atom. Later, researchers developing quantum mechanics in the 1920s determined exactly how electrons were arranged to provide a specific element its unique properties.

Moseley reported his findings in two papers that were published in *Philosophical Magazine*: "The Reflexion of X Rays" (1913) and "The High-Frequency Spectra of the Elements" (1914).

Enlisted in Army During World War I

In 1914, after publishing his groundbreaking papers, and as he was finishing his initial work on X-ray spectra, Moseley resigned from Manchester to return to Oxford, to continue his experiments and obtain a position as professor of experimental physics. At Oxford, he conducted ongoing research on X-ray spectra, particularly focusing on lanthanides, a little known group of elements. By this time, he was viewed as a young scientist positioned on the threshold of other important discoveries; however, world events interceded. In June of that year, Moseley boarded a ship headed to Australia, where he planned to attend a meeting of the British Association for the Advancement of Science. During the voyage, World War I started. Hearing the news, Moseley decided to immediately return to England to enlist in the army. He became a brigade signal officer with the rank of second lieutenant. Rutherford, Moseley's former mentor, fearing for the young researcher's safety, tried to have Moseley assigned to scientific duties.

Died in Battle

Rutherford's stratagem didn't work. Moseley underwent an eight-month training period and was sent into battle in Turkey, where the Allied armed forces—including soldiers from the British, Australian and New Zealand armies—tried to oust Turks from the Gallipoli Peninsula. It proved a fruitless and harrowing endeavor. Both sides suffered significant losses. Gallipoli came to symbolize the futility and irrational waste of war. Winston Churchill, at the time Britain's First Lord of the Admiralty, developed the disastrous plan and suffered public censure as well as a demotion. Moseley was one of the casualties. On August 10, 1915, during the campaign's battle of Sulva Bay, he was killed. Reportedly, a sniper's bullet pierced his fine brain.

Moseley was only twenty-seven years old when struck down. He never had an opportunity to marry, nor did he have a chance to receive the honors he so well deserved for his enormous contributions to science (later advances in physics and chemistry arose from his research). Many people believed that Moseley would have eventually received a Nobel Prize if he had lived. After all, his research led to fundamental understanding of the atom and greatly influenced later scientists.

Honored Long After Death

While Moseley never received important honors while alive, the Royal Society of Chemistry and the University of Oxford commemorated his achievements in September 2007, in a ceremony that not only acknowledged his substantial impact but also recognized the terrible toll that war takes on valuable human resources. To underscore the world's loss, the University and the Society quoted writer and science professor Isaac Asimov (as quoted on the NNDB web site): "In view of what he might have accomplished...his death might well have been the most costly single death of the war to mankind generally."

Moseley's death, it has been suggested, led to a tacit understanding that young scientists should be discouraged from engaging in battle at a war's front lines. The unofficial suggestion went unheeded.

For the occasion, the Royal Society and Oxford University succinctly summarized Moseley's importance as recorded on their web site: "[Moseley] made many important contributions to science, including demonstrating that atomic numbers were not arbitrary but had a physical basis that could be measured. This breakthrough (Moseley's Law) would enable the elements in the periodic table to be put in their correct order and the existence of as-yet-unknown elements to be accurately predicted. His work also provided one of the first experimental tests of quantum theory."

Books

"Henry Gwyn Jeffreys Moseley," *Notable Scientists: From 1900 to the Present,* Gale Group, 2008.

"Henry Gwyn Jeffreys Moseley," *World of Scientific Discovery,* Thomson Gale, 2006.

Online

"Biography," *Chemcool.com,,* http://www.chemcool.com/biography/moseley.htm (November 30, 2009)

"Henry Gwyn Jeffreys Moseley," *NNDB.com,*http://www.nndb.com/people/104/000099804/ (November 30, 2009)

"Henry Moseley," *Economicexpert.com,* http://www.economicexpert.com/a/Henry:Moseley.htm (November 30, 2009).

"Henry Moseley X-Ray Imaging Facility," *Materials. Manchester. ac.uk.,*http://www.materials.manchester.ac.uk/research/facilities/moseley/biography/ (November 30, 2009).

"Niels Bohr and H.G. Moseley," *ManhattanRareBook Company. com,,* http://www.manhattanrarebooks-science.com/bohr_moseley.htm (November 30, 2009).

"Scientists in History," *AmericanLaboratory.com,,* http://www.americanlaboratory.com/ME2/ (November 30, 2009).

"Tribute at Oxford RSC Landmark event for First World War's Lost Scientist," *RSC.org,,* http://www.rsc.org/AboutUs/News/Press Releases/2007/Moseley.asp (November 30, 2009).□

Mother Marianne

Mother Marianne Cope (1838–1918) was a Sister of St. Francis in Syracuse, New York, best known for her work with individuals with Hansen's disease, or leprosy, in Hawaii. She was proclaimed as Blessed Marianne Cope by the Roman Catholic Church in 2005.

Mother Marianne Cope was born Barbara Koob in Heppenheim, in the grand duchy of Hessen-Darmstadt, Germany, on January 23, 1838. Born to Peter Koob and Barbara Witzenbacher Koob, Cope immigrated to the United States with her family when she was one year old. Once in the United States, her family moved to Utica, New York, where their name became Americanized to Cope.

She felt called to enter the religious life at the age of 15, but due to family obligations, she was unable to comply until nine years later. During those nine years she worked in a factory, probably the Utica Steam Woolen Mills factory. She graduated from the eighth grade and immediately went to work to help her family, adding extra wages for the caring of her brothers and sisters. In July of 1862 Cope's father died, and she finally requested entrance into the St. Francis Convent in Syracuse, New York.

Entered Religious Life

Cope took the habit on November 19, 1862, and was given her new name, Sister Mary Anna Cope. Her name, colloquially, had several variations including Sister Marianna and Sister Marianne. In her early religious life, she adopted different versions in turn, but over time, she became almost exclusively known as Mother Marianne. She made her religious vows one year later on November 19, 1863.

After taking her vows, Cope worked for several elementary schools as both a teacher and a principal in New York state. She was made the temporary Superior for the Immaculate Conception Convent in Rome, New York, in 1866. She was later the Superior of St. Theresa's and the principal of St. Peter's School in Oswego, New York. In 1870, as a part of her Order's governing board, she helped to found two hospitals in central New York State. In 1870 she became the chief nurse and administrator of St. Joseph's Hospital, where she would remain for seven years. It was the only hospital in Syracuse with a unique charter to admit individuals regardless of race or creed. She was known for taking in rejected cases, such as alcoholics, and was spoken of as kind, wise, and practical. In December of 1877 she became the Provincial Superior of the Sisters of the Order of St. Francis; becoming Mother Marianne Cope.

Heeded the Call

In June of 1883, Cope received a letter from a priest assigned as a missionary to the Kingdom of Hawaii, Fr. Leonor Fouesnel. Fr. Fouesnel's letter asked Cope to bring

Sisters to the Sandwich Islands. He was sparse on details in his initial letter, only mentioning that the Sisters were to run hospitals and schools. She was immediately both intrigued and reticent. The Sisters were already spread thin, and their Rev. Father Superior was away in Europe. Something, though, continued to pull at her heart, and eventually she found the means and permission necessary to send the Sisters. Her biography on the *Vatican News Services* web site quoted her as saying, "I am hungry for the work and I wish with all my heart to be one of the chosen ones, whose privilege it will be to sacrifice themselves for the salvation of the souls of the poor Islanders.... I am not afraid of any disease, hence it would be my greatest delight even to minister to the abandoned 'lepers.'" In taking on this duty, Mother Marianne Cope would be establishing the first mission for Franciscans in Hawaii and the first American-founded mission outside of the United States.

Arrived on Oahu

Cope went to Hawaii to establish the convent there. She and six other sisters arrived aboard the *Mariposa* on November 8, 1883, along with Dr. Eduard Arning, who was brought to do research on Hansen's disease. Mother Marianne Cope was accompanied by Sisters Mary Bonaventure Caraher, Mary Crescentia Eilers, Mary Renata Nash, Mary Rosalia McLaughlin, Mary Ludovica Gibbons, and Mary Antonella Murphy.

The Sisters soon found themselves touring the grounds of Kakaako, a receiving station for patients, used to determine if patients had Hansen's disease. The conditions were deplorable. There was little concern for cleanliness, privacy, or medical care for these individuals who were thought to be dying as a result of the disease. The dining hall and kitchen were filthy and the living quarters were bare, straw mattresses on the floor, each with a dirty blanket. They were even shown where patients went to die: three cubicles used for patients who were, according to hospital steward J. H. Van Giesen, beyond hope. In the first cubicle, patients were left to die. In the second, doctors examined the corpses. The third was used to store bodies until burial. During their initial tour, there was a young man lying on the floor of the first cubicle, unattended, dehydrated and under a thin blanket. Walter Murray Gibson, the president of the Board of Health who had accompanied them on their introduction to Kakaako, ordered Van Giesen to send the patient back to his room and have nurses attend to him, where he subsequently recovered. Eventually Van Giesen would be removed, and the Sisters would be given full charge of the hospital.

Worked at Kakaako

The board built a convent on the grounds of Kakaako for the Sisters, to which they moved on January 3, 1884. The convent included living quarters, a chapel, and a visiting parlor. The Sisters appeared content. They employed a native woman as portress, and Sister Ludovica Gibbons stayed at the convent to act as housekeeper and cook. At the time, leprosy was believed to be contracted by mouth, and it was important to have someone with no contact with the lepers prepare meals. In addition, the patients at Kakaako were welcome to come to the chapel for Mass, though they entered through a door that opened into the hospital compound and the Sisters and the priest entered through the convent.

The Sisters went to work at Kakaako Hospital, cleaning first the kitchen and dining halls and then the living quarters. They quickly learned to adapt and care for the ill and to convince those who were ambulatory to take better care of themselves. They made many additional improvements in care and quality of life at the hospital over the next few years. In 1885 Cope helped to establish a home for the healthy daughters of patients with Hansen's disease. She worked closely with Hawaiian King Kalakaua and Queen Kapiolani to create the home, on the grounds of Kakaako, near the convent, but separated from the sick. Cope and her Sisters were the only people on the island who wanted to care for these children, and in autumn the home opened to much enthusiasm, named in honor of the Queen as the Kapiolani Home for Girls, the Offspring of Leper Patients.

It was while Mother Marianne was stationed at Kakaako that she first had occasion to meet Fr. Damien de Veuster, who was later accorded sainthood by the Catholic Church. Then Fr. Damien was a member of the same order as Fr. Fouesnel. She first met Fr. Damien in 1884, when he was not evidently ill. Fr. Damien and Mother Marianne continued to meet throughout the next few years as he pleaded with her to send Sisters to the leper settlement on the Kalaupapa peninsula on Moloka'i.

Moved to Moloka'i

In 1887, changes by the Board of Health led to all those with Hansen's disease being quarantined, and those at Kakaako were sent to Moloka'i. The government had slowly been buying up land on the peninsula in order to better segregate the lepers there. In 1888, Mother Marianne Cope brought two of her Sisters, Leopoldina Burns and Vincentia McCormick, with her to Moloka'i, arriving several months before Fr. Damien's death.

One of her first tasks was to form the Bishop Home for Girls, which the Sisters took charge of in 1888. This was a dormitory for orphan girls on the island. They also came to manage the Home for Boys that had earlier been established by Fr. Damien.

During their time on Moloka'i, Cope and her Sisters were visited by the author Robert Louis Stevenson during a trip to Kalaupapa. Though he was suffering from tuberculosis, he interacted with the girls at the Bishop Home with vigor and kindness. He bought them a croquet set and taught them to play. After his visit to Moloka'i, he even sent the girls a piano. He addressed a poem to Cope about the hopelessness on Moloka'i, and how the Sisters helped to overcome it. The last two lines of the poem, found in his *Complete Works,* read: "He marks the sisters on the mournful shores; / And even a fool is silent and adores." Throughout her time on Moloka'i, Mother Marianne was said to be a model for the other Sisters, optimistic and always willing to give. According to the *Vatican News Services* biography, she was recorded as telling them that their duty was "to make life as pleasant and as comfortable as possible for those of our fellow creatures whom God has chosen to afflict with this terrible disease."

Death and Beatification

Cope fell ill when she was in her late seventies, and died on August 9, 1918. She had spent 30 years on Moloka'i and 35 years in Hawaii. She was originally buried in the settlement on the grounds of the Bishop Home for Girls.

She was declared to have led a life of "heroic virtue" and was named Venerable in April of 2004. In order to be declared blessed by the Catholic Church, individuals need to have a miracle attributed to their intercession after their death. Mother Marianne Cope found hers in the healing of a girl with multiple organ failure. Pope Benedict XVI beatified her, declaring her Blessed Marianne Cope on May 14, 2005.

Books

Dictionary of Women Worldwide: 25,000 Women Through the Ages, Volume 1, edited by Anne Commire and Deborah Klezmer, Yorkin Publications, 2007.

Gallick, Sarah, *The Big Book of Women Saints,* Harper Collins, 2007.

Hanley, Sister Mary Laurence, and O. A. Bushnell, *A Song of Pilgrimage and Exile: The Life and Spirit of Mother Marianne of Molokai,* Franciscan Herald Press, 1980.

New Catholic Encyclopedia, Volume 4, 2nd Edition, Gale, 2003.

Stevenson, Robert Louis, *Complete Poems,* Charles Scribner's Sons, 1923.

Periodicals

Honolulu Star-Bulletin, May 15, 2005.

Online

"Bl. Marianne Cope (1838–1918)," *Vatican News Services,* http://www.vatican.va/news_services/liturgy/saints/ns_lit_doc_20050514_molokai_en.html (September 14, 2009).

"Blessed Marianne Cope," *Patron Saints Index,* http://www.saints.sqpn.com/saintmc4.htm (September 12, 2009). □

Harry Murray

Harry Murray (1880–1966) was the most decorated Australian soldier in World War I. He fought in Turkey, France, and Belgium, rising from the rank of private to become a lieutenant colonel in command of a battalion of 64 machine-gunners.

"He was known to the men as 'Mad Harry,' but there was considerable method to his madness," wrote J.M.A. Durrant in a history of Murray's 13th battalion (as quoted by George Franki and Clyde Slatyer in their biography *Mad Harry*). "No officer took more care to avoid losing men, and he took astonishing risks while personally reconnoit[e]ring, with the sole object of saving his men. A quick thinker in times of danger, he displayed extraordinary energy, resolution and courage."

A Bushman

Henry William (Harry) Murray was born December 1, 1880, near Launceston, Tasmania. He learned to fire a rifle around the age of 10 by shooting possums on the family's farm. From 1902 to 1908, he served part-time in a local militia, the Launceston Volunteer Artillery Corps. He became a skilled rifleman. "I knew the man I got a fair shot at was not likely to trouble me further," he later wrote (according to Franki and Slatyer's *Mad Harry*).

In 1908, Murray moved to Western Australia and worked as a courier for a gold-mining company, carrying gold and mail by bicycle and on horseback. For a while, he served as an armed security escort for a mining company. In 1914, when World War I began, Murray was supervising timber cutters in a forest in southwest Australia, supplying lumber for railways. When he enlisted in the armed forces in September, a month after the war began, he listed his occupation as "bushman," roughly the Australian equivalent of an American cowboy. Murray's brigade set sail from Melbourne, Australia in late December of 1914 and arrived in Alexandria, Egypt in February of 1915.

Bravery at Gallipoli

Australia was still part of the British Empire in World War I, and Murray fought in many of the major battles in Britain and France's war against Germany. In April of 1915, Murray took part in the invasion of the Gallipoli Peninsula in Turkey. Gallipoli stood on the Mediterranean Sea at the mouth of the Dardanelles, the strait that led to the Black Sea. The invasion, championed by future British prime minister Winston Churchill, aimed to seize control of the Dardanelles so that the British fleet could send supplies directly to its ally, Russia.

Murray landed on Gallipoli on April 25 as a member of a machine gun crew. Though wounded early in the invasion, he stayed on the front lines and proved his skill at observing Turkish soldiers' movements and firing his gun from concealed positions. He won the Distinguished Conduct Medal for bravery that May and was promoted to lance corporal. Shot in his right knee on May 30, he was evacuated to Alexandria, Egypt, declared physically unfit for military service, and booked on a hospital ship returning to Australia.

But Murray wanted to keep fighting. In July, he went to the wharf in Alexandria and boarded a troop transport for Gallipoli, where he returned to combat. In one incident, after charging into a Turkish trench, he killed a Turkish soldier with his bayonet. He was promoted to second lieutenant while at Gallipoli. Murray was evacuated again in September because he was suffering from dysentery, but he rejoined the battle in December, two weeks before the Australians withdrew from Gallipoli.

Fighting on the Western Front

After spending the first part of 1916 resting in Egypt, Murray's battalion was redeployed to France in June. The western front of World War I, which stretched 500 miles across Belgium and France, had settled into a bloody stalemate. The line was marked by endless mazes of trenches and a bombed-out, fire-gutted no-man's land. Thousands of soldiers died in attacks intended to seize a few miles or even a few hundred yards of territory. In this tragic and monotonous series of battles, Murray stood out for his bravery, his survival instincts, and his ability to inspire his men.

The Australians took part in a major offensive near the Somme River in July and August of 1916. In the first phase of the attack, 100,000 British troops were killed or wounded in 16 days, while failing to produce a breakthrough into German territory. The Australians, who attacked in the second phase, sustained 23,000 casualties in a month and a half and also failed to hold their objective, an area near the town of Pozières known as Mouquet Farm. Murray, promoted earlier in the year to captain, led an attack on a German trench system on August 13. He captured and cleared the trench system, but realized his men were in danger of being outflanked and had to order a retreat. As the wounded were evacuated, Murray and others used a dwindling supply of grenades to hold off the German troops pursuing them through the trenches.

In an example of the futility of the western front's trench warfare, Murray's battalion was again ordered to attack Mouquet Farm on August 29. Murray led the attack, and again, his men seized the farm while incurring heavy losses. Again, they could not hold their position. After 30 hours, they had to retreat. Murray won the Distinguished Service Order for his part in the August 29 attack, an award rarely given to officers below the rank of lieutenant colonel. "Although twice wounded, he commanded his company with the greatest courage and initiative, beating off four enemy counter attacks," read his commendation (as quoted by the web site The AIF Project). "Later, when an enemy bullet started a man's equipment explo[d]ing, he tore the man's equipment off at great personal risk." Murray was evacuated to a London hospital, but he returned to his battalion in October.

By February of 1917, Murray's battalion was stationed near the French village of Gueudecourt. Murray was ordered to attack a German position known as Stormy Trench. Before the attack, Murray and his scouts crawled across the area where the attack would take place. "He was never the man to leave anything undone that would help save his men or make victory surer," read the history of his battalion (quoted in Franki and Slatyer's *Mad Harry*). "Before dawn on the 3rd [of] February, he was familiar with every shell-hole and strand of wire in No Man's Land, and every possible route back to Battalion Headquarters."

Although he had a severe case of influenza and a 103-degree fever, Murray led a nighttime attack on Stormy Trench on February 4. His company captured the position as ordered, but a fierce 24-hour battle followed in which the Australians fended off three enemy counterattacks. During the fighting, 230 members of Murray's battalion were killed. Murray himself killed three Germans and single-handedly took three more as prisoners. The Australians held onto Stormy Trench, and Murray won the rarely awarded Victoria Cross for his leadership in the battle.

"Throughout the night his company suffered heavy casualties through concentrated enemy shell fire," read his Victoria Cross commendation (as quoted by The AIF Project). Murray "made his presence felt throughout the line, encouraging his men, heading bombing parties, leading bayonet charges, and carrying wounded to places of safety."

Two months later, Murray took part in a failed attack on German lines near the town of Bullecourt. After witnessing many fellow soldiers dying in the first wave of the attack, Murray took part in the second wave, leading his company two-thirds of a mile through shell and machine-gun fire. Though three out of four attacking Australians were killed or wounded, the survivors captured the trench they had aimed for. Murray sent a message back to headquarters asking for more rifles, grenades, and small-arms ammunition and said he could hold the position with artillery support. The senior officers never ordered the artillery to fire, however, despite the flares Murray and others sent that signaled for a barrage. Murray and his men finally retreated under heavy machine-gun fire, suffering heavy losses. Two thousand Australian soldiers were killed, wounded, or captured in the attack. Murray won a second Distinguished Service Order for his leadership in the battle.

In an article he wrote in 1936, Murray recalled watching several surviving officers who led the attack walk past the general and colonels who had ordered it. "Behind those burning eyes, and stern set lips, one could sense the dammed-back floods of denunciation which might break forth at any moment, but no word issued from those iron men," Murray wrote (as quoted in Franki and Slatyer's *Mad Harry*). "They seemed to epitomize in their stern silence all the tragic horror and heroic futility of Bullecourt—bitter grief and stern indignation at the recollection of their men, torn, dismembered, and blown to shreds on that fatal barrier [a barbed-wire fence]; then the hand-to-hand fighting, the temporary advantage, and finally the grim hanging-on and waiting for the barrage and munitions that never came."

On June 2, 1917, Murray received his Victoria Cross and two Distinguished Service Orders from King George V during a large public ceremony at Hyde Park in London. Though 351 decorations were awarded that day, Murray was the most prominent of the decorated soldiers. He was one of only 11 men to receive a Victoria Cross. He was then promoted to major in July.

Murray served in the bloody, muddy battle of Passchendaele in Belgium in October of 1917, then spent three weeks in Paris on leave in early 1918. In March, he was promoted to lieutenant colonel and given command of a machine-gun battalion. That month, the German army staged a successful offensive, and Australian troops, including Murray's battalion, formed part of the defensive line that stopped their advance, protecting the city of Amiens. Murray also took part in the planning of a successful counteroffensive known as the Battle of Hamel. In late September and early October, Murray aided a division of American troops, who had recently joined the war, in an attack on German lines. That month, he was awarded the French Croix de Guerre for his work in March and April.

Returned Home

After the war ended in November of 1918, Murray toured England, studying farming methods. He returned to Australia in December of 1919, showing a strong disregard for public celebrations of his heroism. He officially left the military in March of 1920 and bought a sheep-grazing property near Muckadilla, Queensland. He married Constance Cameron in 1921, but they proved incompatible. He wanted to avoid public attention by living a quiet, rural life, but she did not enjoy life on a remote sheep farm. They separated in 1925, and Murray traveled to New Zealand.

In 1927, an Australian court granted Constance a divorce from Harry. Nine days later, in New Zealand, he married Ellen Cameron, his first wife's niece. Despite a 24-year difference in their ages, the couple remained happily married for the rest of his life. Murray returned to Queensland with her in 1928, and they bought another sheep-grazing property near the town of Richmond. They had two children, a son, Douglas, and a daughter, Clem. Between 1929 and 1939, Murray wrote several articles about his wartime experiences for a veterans' magazine, *Reveille.*

As World War II approached, Murray enlisted in the Australian military once again. He was appointed commander of the 26th Battalion in north Queensland. In August of 1942, when he was 61, Murray was reassigned to command a Volunteer Defense Corps home-guard unit. His military appointment was terminated in February of 1944, and he returned to raising sheep after the war. He died in Miles, Queensland, of a heart attack after a car accident on January 7, 1966. He was 85.

Books

Franki, George, and Clyde Slater, *Mad Harry: Australia's Most Decorated Soldier,* Kangaroo Press, 2003.

Online

"Henry William Murray," The AIF Project, http://www.aif.adfa.edu.au:8080/showPerson?key=MURRAY/HW/31 (January 1, 2010).

"Lieutenant Colonel Henry William (Harry) Murray, VC, CMG, DSO & Bar, DCM," *Who's Who in Australian Military History,* http://www.awm.gov.au/people/863.asp (January 1, 2010).

"Mad Harry Murray," Australian War Memorial, http://www.awm.gov.au/exhibitions/fiftyaustralians/35.asp (January 1, 2010).□

N

Scott Nearing

The American writer and activist Scott Nearing (1883–1983) became best known later in life for his back-to-the-land lifestyle.

Nearing was one of the leaders of the American political left in the 1910s and 1920s. Due to his committed pacifism and his economic radicalism, he found it impossible to make a living in the academic world. At a dead end during the Great Depression, Nearing and his second wife, Helen, moved to a farm in Vermont and began to work it themselves, largely without the benefit of power tools or machines. They wrote prolifically about their experiences. Their 1954 book *Living the Good Life* was a central document of the student counterculture that flowered over the following decades, and Nearing remained a famous figure for the rest of his long life.

Studied Economics

Scott Nearing was born into a middle class family in Morris Run, Pennsylvania, on August 6, 1883. His father, Louis Nearing, was a prosperous store owner. Nearing was groomed for a career in business or law, but he took more after his grandfather, an engineer who was a gardening and carpentry enthusiast. Nearing enrolled in a pre-law program at the University of Pennsylvania in 1901 but quickly switched to economics, also studying oratory at nearby Temple University. Nearing received a B.S. degree at Pennsylvania in 1905 and went on for a Ph.D. while working on the side for the Pennsylvania Child Labor Commission. He received a Ph.D. in economics in 1909.

Nearing co-authored an economics textbook in 1908, but soon his writings began to reflect his activist concerns. In 1911 he authored *The Solution of the Child Labor Problem.* His work in this area was not greeted with enthusiasm by some members of the board of trustees at the University of Pennsylvania, where he served as an instructor from 1906 to 1914 and as an assistant professor of economics in 1914 and 1915. After that year, because of his denunciations of child labor and his emerging opposition to capitalism in general, he was dismissed from the Pennsylvania faculty. Nearing's firing was controversial, with many supporters arguing that his academic freedom had been violated, and he was hired in 1915 as a professor of social science and dean of the College of Arts and Sciences by the University of Toledo in Ohio. He also lectured at the socialist-oriented Rand School of Social Science in 1916.

Nearing showed absolutely no inclination to compromise, denouncing both World War I and the widely supported American involvement in the war that began in 1917. As a result he was arrested and tried for sedition. He was acquitted, but he was fired once again by the University of Toledo. In the years after the war, Nearing ran unsuccessfully for the U.S. House of Representatives and, along with other socialists, continued to experience government harassment. He was cited as an inspiration by Socialist Party presidential candidate Eugene V. Debs. Nearing issued numerous books and pamphlets in the 1920s, affiliating himself first with the weakening Socialist Party and then with the more radical Communists, who later expelled him over doctrinal disagreements. In the 1970s, according to Glenn Fowler of the *New York Times,* Nearing stated, "I have been a Socialist for a long time, but I am not a Marxist. Just a tough U.S.A. radical." Nearing married Nellie Seeds in 1908, and the two raised a son, John Scott, who lived in the Soviet Union for a time. Scott Nearing visited both the Soviet Union and Communist China.

Purchased Vermont Farm

By the early 1930s, Nearing was running out of money and ideas. In 1932 he and the aspiring concert violinist Helen Knothe purchased a failing farm in rural Vermont, for an amount variously reported as $1,100 and $2,500. The two married in 1947 after the death of Nearing's first wife. Helen Nearing had grown up in the suburbs and had no experience of farming; her husband had a smattering of skills learned from his grandfather. Nevertheless, their experiment in self-reliant living was a success. They learned masonry skills, built stone structures, and organically grew most of the vegetables they needed. And they found that they had time for other pursuits, generally dividing each day into equal thirds of "bread work," "head work," and service to the world community, as Nearing put it in his 1972 autobiography, *The Making of a Radical*. The Nearings were vegans, and they did not use tobacco, alcohol, caffeine, or refined food products such as white flour or sugar.

"Head work" continued to involve a good deal of writing, and beginning in 1950 the Nearings began a long series of jointly written books in which they documented their way of life and offered guidance to the similarly inclined. The first of their seven books (some of which continued to espouse leftist political positions) was *The Maple Sugar Book* (1950), but the most popular was *Living the Good Life: Being a Plain, Practical Account of a Twenty-Year Project on a Self-Subsistent Homestead in Vermont, Together with Remarks on How to Live Sanely and Simply in a Troubled World.* It was reissued in 1970 with the simpler title *Living the Good Life: How to Live Sanely and Simply in a Troubled World,*

and followed by a 1979 sequel, *Continuing the Good Life: Half a Century of Homesteading.*

By the time *Living the Good Life* was first published, Nearing and his wife had moved (in 1952) from Vermont to another farm near Harborside, Maine, on Penobscot Bay. They left Vermont because of the construction of the Stratton Mountain ski resort near their former farm. Although Scott Nearing was nearly 70 years old, they continued to work their new farm, at one point constructing a two-story stone house. The Nearings avoided the use of draft animals and had no phone, radio, or television, but they did own a car and a pickup truck—increasingly necessary, for as young people of the 1960s counterculture began to discover Nearing's back-to-the-soil ethos, he found himself in demand on the college lecture circuit and traveled frequently.

Condemned Materialist Influences

Nearing in his later years was not so much socialist or environmentalist as anti-consumerist. He was restored to professor emeritus status by the University of Pennsylvania in 1973, and charged in his remarks at a ceremony marking the occasion, according to Wayne King of the *New York Times,* that the American press was "being used to sell things that people don't want and don't need—trash gewgaws and gimcracks made from limited resources pandered in those sheets they call newspapers." Of the energy crisis that ensued after an oil embargo put in place by Arab countries during the Arab-Israeli war that year, he said, "I don't think the real problem in America today is the energy crisis. I think it's television."

Nearing became something of a celebrity as a result of his books and speeches, and his Maine farm attracted, through appointments made by letter, some 2,500 visitors a year, many of whom were put to work constructing a pond that required the manual removal of more than 15,000 wheelbarrow loads of dirt. The Nearings rarely if ever visited physicians, and both lived to great old ages. Scott Nearing remained in good health and fully active on the farm well into his tenth decade of life. At age 98, according to Helen Nearing, writing in the journal *In Context,* he mused, "Well, at least I can still split and carry in the wood." Helen also quoted him as saying that "work helps prevent one from getting old. My work is my life. I cannot think of one without the other. The man who works and is never bored, is never old."

Nearing drew a large crowd of admirers to celebrate his 100th birthday on August 6, 1983. He died, as he lived for much of his life, independently and unassisted by larger institutions. A month or so before his death he intentionally stopped eating solid food, then phased out fruit juices and subsisted on water for the last ten days of his life. On the morning of August 24, 1983, he died quietly—"gone out of his body," Helen wrote, "as easily as a leaf drops from the tree in autumn, slowly twisting and falling to the ground." Helen Nearing established the Good Life Center in the last house she and Scott had built together, and it continued to operate as of 2010. Helen Nearing died in 1995 when a car she was driving crashed into a tree.

Books

Nearing, Scott, *The Making of a Radical: A Political Autobiography,* Chelsea Green, 2000.

Nearing, Scott, with Helen K. Nearing, *Living the Good Life: How to Live Simply and Sanely in a Troubled World,* Schocken, 1970.

Periodicals

Christian Science Monitor, January 4, 1996.

New York Times, April 30, 1973; May 7, 1975; May 6, 1979; August 25, 1983; September 19, 1995.

Time, September 5, 1983.

Online

Contemporary Authors Online, Gale, 2010, reproduced in *Biography Resource Center,*http://www.galenet.galegroup.com/servlet/BioRC (February 12, 2010).

"At the End of a Good Life," *In Context* (Summer 1990), http://www.context.org/ICLIB/IC26/Nearing.htm (February 12, 2010).□

O

John Ogilby

Scottish cartographer John Ogilby (1600–1676) compiled the *Britannia Atlas*, the first comprehensive road map for England and Wales. The 1675 tome remains a marvel to modern mapmakers for the remarkable accuracy of Ogilby's measurements. The *Britannia Atlas*'s use of the mile as a standard of measurement, with 1,760 yards equaling one mile, served to establish that unit as the accepted form for distance measurement in modern atlas-making.

Some reports say that Ogilby came from Edinburgh, but he was born in Kellemeune, a town near the Scottish port city of Dundee, in November of 1600, and at some point the family moved to London. He claimed that during his childhood his father was jailed for debt, and Ogilby raised funds by selling needles and other small items as a street vendor. He also bought a ticket issued by the Virginia Company, a venture attempting to raise money for an English settlement at Jamestown, Virginia. His ticket number was one of the ones drawn for a parcel of property, and the proceeds from its sale were used to settle the elder Ogilby's debts and secure his release.

Founded Theater in Dublin

In London, Ogilby bought an apprenticeship, a commonplace method for learning a profession at the time. He became the assistant to a dance teacher named John Draper on Grayes Inn Lane, and eventually established his own school on London's Spread Eagle Court. His success brought increasingly important clients, one of whom was the Duke of Buckingham, George Villiers. The Duke was, for a time in the 1620s, one of the most influential figures at the court of King Charles I, who ascended to the English throne in 1625. Ogilby participated in one of the lavish court masques, which featured Charles and his queen, Henrietta Maria, as masked players in various allegorical tales that served to demonstrate the House of Stuart's political goals and policies.

Buckingham was assassinated in 1628, but Ogilby had befriended the children of another prominent figure, Thomas Wentworth, later to become the first Earl of Strafford. In 1632 the king appointed Wentworth to serve as the new Lord Deputy of Ireland, and Ogilby went along with the household as dancing master to the Wentworth children. Wentworth's tenure lasted seven somewhat notorious years, during which time the lord instituted near-autocratic rule with the goal of forcing the Irish to adopt English ways, and he was eventually recalled by the king. During this period, however, Wentworth had appointed Ogilby to serve as deputy Master of the Revels at his court, which involved the staging of all plays and other court spectacles.

In this capacity, Ogilby played a pivotal role in the establishment of the first purposefully built theater in Dublin. This was the New Street Theatre on Werburgh Street, and was erected at some point before 1637. After that year, Ogilby's friend, the playwright James Shirley, staged several important works of pre-Restoration English drama that were some of the first in the genre to premier outside of London. The theater was closed and destroyed after the *Éirí Amach*, or Irish Rebellion, of 1641. Wentworth, who had become the Earl of Strafford, ran afoul of the increasingly irate Members of Parliament and was executed in London in May of 1641.

Launched Publishing Career

That year also marked the start of the ten-year-long English Civil War. The conflict pitted Charles I against the Parliamentarians,

who were called "Roundheads" for the close-cropped hair-styles of the men, considered a statement of Puritan allegiance in contrast to the extravagant ringlets favored by the king and his courtiers. A number of significant issues were at stake, including the authority of the crown, the rights of parliament and landholders, and religious freedom in all the British Isles. In the end, the Parliamentarians controlling London prevailed against Charles's forces—known as the Cavaliers—and the king was beheaded in 1649. A republican government known as the Commonwealth of England was established, but four years later a leader of the Parliamentarians, Oliver Cromwell, declared himself Lord Protector and began to assume various privileges of monarchist rule.

Ogilby was said to have lost his fortune by the time he fled Ireland in 1644 on board a vessel that was shipwrecked. With Shirley's help he settled in London and immersed himself in the study of Greek and Latin languages by hiring tutors from Cambridge University. Once he regained his financial footing, he acquired a house on Shoe Lane, just off Fleet Street in the district known as the City of London. There he set up a printing press and began issuing works by great classical authors translated into English. Among these were an edition of the poems of Virgil and a collection of *Aesop's Fables*. He spent much of the 1650s in London as a publisher in business with William Morgan, who was the husband of his step-granddaughter from Ogilby's 1650 marriage to Christian Hunsdon, a widow.

The English monarchy was restored in a lavish coronation of Charles II, the son of the beheaded king, in April of 1661.

Ogilby was one of the planners for the king's official Coronation Procession, composing speeches, songs, and other elements for the pageantry. He also designed a series of three arches that symbolized the restored House of Stuart's power and authority as centered in London, a city of symbolic import that the first Charles had been forced to flee at the onset of the Civil War. With the "Restoration," as the new era was dubbed, theaters were reopened, and Ogilby returned as Master of the Revels in Ireland. He opened the Theatre Royal of Dublin, also called the Smock Alley Theatre, on Essex Street West in 1662.

Lost Assets in Great Fire

Back in London, Ogilby's publishing company on Shoe Lane continued operation and by 1665 had profited handsomely from the sale of various illustrated volumes. An outbreak of the bubonic plague in London decimated his business, however, and he again lost all of his property in the Great Fire of London that raged for four days in September of 1666. More than 13,000 houses were destroyed, along with 87 churches, including the old St. Paul's Cathedral, a Gothic landmark dating back to 1087. The heaviest losses were in the square mile district known as the City of London.

Once again, Ogilby's influential patrons helped him rebound from financial ruin. London's Lord Mayor appointed him and Morgan as "sworn viewers" or surveyors for London. Their duty was to research and establish the pre-fire property boundaries to settle the numerous disputes that began to consume the courts as London began the grand rebuilding process. Ogilby also resurrected the printing business, issuing volumes of engravings picturing the wonders of India, Japan, and other parts of Asia. These were primarily translations of reports along with illustrations made by explorers and other associates of the Dutch East India Company.

According to Ralph Hyde, a historian and curator of maps at the renowned Guildhall Library of London, Ogilby planned a massive international atlas project. In a 1980 article in *The Map Collector,* Hyde wrote that Ogilby "issued proposals for an international English Atlas in five volumes. . . . As the project developed, so it was modified and adjusted. In June 1670 Ogilby announced that priority would be given to Great Britain. In November 1671 he promised that this section of the atlas—which he referred to as 'Britannia'—would contain road maps and maps of the counties."

Published *Britannia Atlas*

This was the starting point for Ogilby's great *Britannia Atlas,* the first major printed guide to the main roads of England and Wales. Ogilby did not conduct the surveying himself, but hired teams of surveyors who walked and measured the main coach routes to and from London and other major cities. *Britannia Volume the First, or an Illustration of the Kingdom of England and Dominion of Wales* was issued in 1675 and dedicated to Charles II. Its frontispiece and other elements were the work of Wenceslaus Hollar, a renowned German artist originally from Prague who spent much of his life in England.

Ogilby's atlas consisted of one hundred double-page strip road maps showing the various routes. The roads were shown in continuous strips, in several panels across a double-page spread, with the starting point at the bottom lower left corner marked by a cross, and continuing up and down across the two pages. Ogilby used the mile standard of measurement, with 1,760 yards equaling one mile, as defined by an Act of Parliament of 1592. In the *Britannia* maps, one inch equaled one mile, which made it the first published atlas to use this standard that became the prevailing scale for the industry.

The *Britannia Atlas* routes included London to Islip, a town north of Oxford; London to Chichester; York to Chester-le-Street outside Newcastle; Bristol to Banbury; Nottingham to Grimsby; and Plymouth to Land's End, the westernmost point in England. All of these were long-used thoroughfares, most of them built during the Roman Empire's four-century occupation of Britain, which lasted until 410 A.D. The plates depicted rivers and bridges, elevations, cathedral towns, and other practical details for the traveler.

Affirmed Charles II's Authority

Historians and contemporary geographers have noted that Ogilby's most famous published title was also a sly piece of propaganda that displayed his strong pro-monarchist sentiments. Charles II had named him "His Majesty's Cosmographer and Geographic Printer" in 1674, and there are some references to towns that suffered greatly during the Civil War for their Cavalier sentiments. In other places, Ogilby mentions sites where some of the more notorious assaults on Roundhead leaders occurred. Furthermore, London was given primary importance as the heart of the realm. "*Britannia* was designed to give a 'prospect' of a nation," wrote Robert John Mayhew's *Enlightenment Geography: The Political Languages of British Geography, 1650-1850,* "which allowed for efficient governance, the route lines radiating as lines of information into London and Charles."

Ogilby was still working on the definitive map of London when he died on September 4, 1676, exactly ten years to the week after the Great Fire. He was buried in the churchyard of St. Bride's in the City of London district. At the time, the Anglican house of worship on Fleet Street was unfinished, but had been designed by Sir Christopher Wren, the architect of the new St. Paul's Cathedral, which became the symbol of London's transformation after the fire and an iconic landmark in the centuries since.

There were several more revised editions of the *Britannia Atlas* and volumes of the planned world atlas issued in parts, but the final work credited to Ogilby was published posthumously by Morgan, his business partner and step-grandson. This was *London Survey'd,* the great map of the City of London that detailed the rebuilding in the decade since the Great Fire. Morgan unveiled it to the Court of Aldermen just a few weeks after Ogilby's death, and it was published in January of 1677. "So detailed is Ogilby that it is hard to believe that only ten years earlier...two thirds of the city [had] perished," noted Felix Barker in *History Today* about a new edition of the map published by the London Topographical Society in 1993. "With virtually every street, house and garden depicted, Ogilby pays a

fitting tribute to the undertaking. Showing the new city on a scale of 100 feet to the inch, he produced a map which for detail remained incomparable until the Ordnance Survey two centuries later."

Books

Aubrey, John, Oliver Lawson Dick, and Edmund Wilson, *Aubrey's Brief Lives,* David R. Godine, 1999 (reprint), pp. 219-221.

Bell, Walter George, *Fleet Street in Seven Centuries: Being a History of the Growth of London Beyond the Walls into the Western Liberty, and of Fleet Street to Our Time,* Sir I. Pitman & Sons, Ltd., 1912, pp. 358–359.

Mayhew, Robert John, *Enlightenment Geography: The Political Languages of British Geography, 1650-1850,* Palgrave Macmillan, 2000, pp. 79, 82,.

Periodicals

History Today, December 1993.
The Map Collector, June 1, 1980.
Times (London, England), January 23, 1965.
Western Mail (Cardiff, Wales), May 12, 2008.

Online

"All About John Ogilby," AntiqueMaps.com, http://www.antiquemaps.com/uk/roads/ogilhist.htm (November 20, 2009). □

Walter Francis O'Malley

American baseball executive Walter Francis O'Malley (1903-1979) owned the National League Dodgers franchise from 1950 to 1979. In 1957, he moved the team from Brooklyn to Los Angeles. The move expanded Major League Baseball's national boundaries. He was posthumously inducted into the sport's Hall of Fame in 1979.

Baseball team owner Walter Francis O'Malley has a mixed legacy. He developed a well-earned reputation as one of baseball's smartest business executives and most influential pioneers. When he moved the Brooklyn Dodgers to Los Angeles, he brought baseball to the West Coast and nationalized the sport, which increased baseball's popularity and financial success. In the process, however, he became, in the eyes of many, one of baseball's biggest villains. Brooklyn Dodgers fans, long suffering and totally devoted to their team, perceived O'Malley as a mercenary who stole their team to make a buck.

Through the years, however, O'Malley gained a large degree of vindication, in large part due to well-researched books such as *The Last Good Season* (2003) by Michael Shapiro and *Forever Blue* (2009) by Michael D'Antonio. Reportedly, O'Malley wanted to keep the Dodgers in Brooklyn, but for the team to remain profitable it needed a new stadium. O'Malley tried for ten years to build a

replacement for the aging and awkward Ebbets Field, but he met continual roadblocks from New York City officials. Some baseball historians blame the Dodgers' move on Robert Moses, the New York Park Commissioner. ''Had Moses been agreeable, the world would have never been turned on its head and the Dodgers would not have left [Brooklyn],'' Shapiro wrote in *Forever Blue.*

Born in the Bronx

Walter Francis O'Malley was born on October 9, 1903 in the Bronx section of New York City. He was the only child of Edwin J. and Alma Feltner O'Malley. His father was a successful dry goods merchant and became New York City Commissioner of Public Markets. His parents eventually moved from the Bronx to Long Island, where he attended public school. An outdoor enthusiast and Boy Scout, O'Malley's early interests included boating, fishing, hunting and swimming. Ironically, while growing up, he was a fan of the New York Giants baseball team, the National League rival of the Brooklyn Dodgers, the team that he would head as an adult.

O'Malley's parents later enrolled him at Culver Military Academy in Culver, Indiana. There, O'Malley became a sports journalist and associate editor for the Academy's newspaper. He tried playing baseball, but his academic sports career came to an end when he suffered a face injury (a baseball struck him full force on the nose).

Later, he entered the University of Pennsylvania, graduating with an engineering degree in 1926. At Penn, he distinguished himself by becoming class president in his junior and senior years. He also served on the council of athletics (overseeing baseball) and became the senior class salutatorian.

Entered Law School

After graduation, he enrolled at Fordham University in New York City to study law. When his father went bankrupt during the 1929 stock market crash, O'Malley financed his continuing education by taking on two jobs (a junior engineer and surveyor for New York City) and starting his own business. Meanwhile, he continued his law studies at night. He finally earned his law degree in October 1930.

Nearly a year later, on September 5, 1931, O'Malley wed Kay Hanson, his childhood sweetheart. The couple had two children, daughter Terry (born 1933) and son Peter (born 1937). While O'Malley was establishing himself in business, he made a home for his family in a Saint Marks Avenue apartment in Brooklyn. To entertain his children, as well as his growing number of business clients, O'Malley purchased season tickets at Ebbets Field, the Brooklyn neighborhood ballpark that served as the home field for the Brooklyn Dodgers.

At the time, O'Malley was operating a successful New York legal practice. This was during the Great Depression, and his company specialized in bankruptcies and company reorganization. As such, and despite existing national economic circumstances, O'Malley's business thrived. Further, by engineering savvy business investments, he became a multi-millionaire. He became owner of the New York Subways Advertising Company, co-owner of a building supply company and a building block company, and he put money into a railroad and a brewery.

Became Involved in Professional Baseball

O'Malley's association with Major League baseball began in 1941, when the Brooklyn Trust Company, a major creditor of the nearly bankrupt Brooklyn Dodgers, asked him to oversee the baseball club's legal and business affairs. Already a baseball fan, O'Malley gave up his successful law practice to serve as president and general counsel of the financially troubled enterprise. Soon, he focused all of his energies toward reviving the team.

By 1945, O'Malley owned a healthy share of the team's stock after two transactions. In November 1944, he joined then-Dodger President Branch Rickey and New York insurance executive Andrew Schmitz in purchasing twenty-five percent of the team. In August 1945, O'Malley, Rickey, and Pfizer Chemical executive John L. Smith purchased fifty percent of the stock from the estate of Charles Ebbets. When Schmitz sold his share, O'Malley, Rickey and Smith then owned seventy-five percent. Dearie McKeever Mulvey, daughter of the late Dodger President Steve McKeever, owned the remaining portion.

In the meantime, O'Malley was already envisioning plans for a new Brooklyn ballpark. He solicited architectural ideas from Emil Praeger, the former Navy captain who later helped renovate the White House and engineer several United Nations buildings (Praeger also helped design Dodger Stadium in Los Angeles, after the team moved from Brooklyn to the West Coast). Also, O'Malley became a pioneering force when he signed Jackie Robinson to a minor league contract with a Dodgers' farm system team, the Montreal Royals. This eventually led to Robinson's historic entrance into Major League Baseball, which breached the previously tacit "color" barrier.

By 1950, O'Malley was the Dodgers' principal owner, and Rickey had become a business rival. But O'Malley compelled Rickey to sell his club interest for $1.05 million and resign as club president. Installed as the new president, O'Malley now had two priorities: to bolster the minor league system, which would feed the major league team with talent, and to address the Ebbets Field issue.

Tried to Build a New Stadium

Ebbets Field, which was built in 1913, was an aging edifice that, even as far back as 1950, possessed an inadequate infrastructure, in terms of seating, parking and accessibility. O'Malley sought to find a new location and build a new stadium. He didn't want to remove the team from its neighborhood, though. To that end, he set his sights on the intersection of Atlantic and Flatbush avenues in Brooklyn. This location included a Long Island Rail Road terminal as well as access to all New York City subway lines. O'Malley planned to enhance existing accessibility by redeveloping the surrounding congested area and even provide ample car parking space.

O'Malley faced formidable opposition, however. Robert Moses, the powerful New York Parks Commissioner, had other plans for the area. While Moses expressed interest in O'Malley's vision, he was not willing to invest the city's money into necessary infrastructure improvements, as he felt it would cost jobs and clash with the automobile highway-and-bridge system he sought to advance. O'Malley's ideas, which included an innovative domed stadium (more than a decade before Houston's famed Astrodome, which opened in 1965) would have enabled the Brooklyn Dodgers to remain firmly ensconced in its familiar and comfortable Flatbush setting.

While O'Malley wrestled with the architectural details and the business problems, the Brooklyn Dodgers became one of the most beloved teams in baseball. It also became one of the most successful, in terms of profit and play. Throughout the 1950s, the Dodgers accounted for forty-four percent of the National League's gross profits and attracted more than a million baseball fans. The team itself was one of the most dominant during the decade, becoming perennial National League contenders. In 1951, the club entered into an end-of-season playoff with the rival New York Giants, only to see its World Series hopes dashed by the legendary Bobby Thomson home run. The Dodgers responded by winning National League pennants in 1952 and 1953, but the "Bums" couldn't capitalize by winning the gold ring: a World Series championship. Instead, they were vanquished by the New York Yankees, their American League cross-town rival. In 1955, the Brooklyn Dodgers achieved vindication by defeating the Yankees in the World Series. It was one of the most exciting October Classics, as it went the full seven

games, and featured extraordinary mound performances from young pitcher Johnny Podres. Other team stars in the decade included Robinson, who became Major League baseball's first black player and one of its best second basemen; catcher Roy Campanella; pitchers Don Newcombe, Carl Erskine, and Ralph Branca; infielders Gil Hodges and "Pee Wee" Reese, and outfielders Duke Snider and Carl Furillo.

Received Overtures from the West Coast

Meanwhile, behind the scenes, Los Angeles began courting ball clubs to move west. On September 23, 1954, City Clerk Walter C. Peterson sent letters to team owners that expressed the City Council's hope to bring Major League baseball to Los Angeles. In September 1955, right before the World Series, O'Malley received a follow-up letter from Los Angeles City Councilwoman Rosalind Wyman. She requested a meeting with him to discuss the Brooklyn Dodger's possible relocation. But O'Malley was still focused on working out a solution in New York, and he turned Wyman down.

Circumstances would make him reconsider, though. As successful as the Dodgers had become, in terms of winning and drawing crowds, the team's attendance still lagged behind other Major League franchises. In fact, relocated teams like the Milwaukee Braves (a National League Club that moved from Boston) were drawing more than two million annual customers. Conversely, Brooklyn still only drew one million a year to the anachronistic Ebbets Field.

Obviously, O'Malley, who wanted his team to remain competitive, both in the standings and at the gate, was concerned. He perceived the answer to his problem as a family friendly stadium that would include more seats and increased parking facilities. The post-World War II suburban growth, with residents' dependence on the automobile, proved a strong consideration.

Try as he might to keep the Dodgers in Brooklyn, O'Malley was constantly rebuffed. He was willing to find a new site, pay for the land and even build a new stadium with private money. But he confronted a continued roadblock with Moses. Running out of options, O'Malley looked westward.

Moved Team to California

In 1957, he arranged a tentative agreement with the City of Los Angeles that included a potential site as well as territorial rights. The city council would provide 300 acres for a stadium and put $4.75 million into the project, while O'Malley would pay $350,000 a year in property taxes. A year later, the deal was approved through public referendum.

O'Malley made the move appear even more viable when he convinced Horace Stoneham, owner of National League rival New York Giants, to move to California. Stoneham was considering plans to move his team to Saint Paul, Minnesota. Like Ebbets Field, the Giants' ballpark, the Polo Grounds, was falling apart at the seams, and attendance suffered. By moving to California, as O'Malley suggested, the National League would have two teams on the West Coast, which would reduce traveling expenses. Stoneham—like O'Malley, an astute businessman—perceived the wisdom of the advice. San Francisco, like Los Angeles, courted Major League teams. O'Malley arranged a meeting between San Francisco Mayor

George Christopher and Stoneham. By 1957, the Giants and the Dodgers were ready to relocate.

O'Malley then obtained permission from the National League. On May 28, 1957, at a meeting in Chicago, league officials gave the Dodgers and Giants permission to move. O'Malley also successfully defended the relocation before a U.S. Congress subcommittee.

The moves would change professional baseball, turning what was essentially a regional sport into a national one, but it provoked public outcry, especially in Brooklyn. The faithful Dodgers fans didn't want to lose their home team, and they considered O'Malley the villain in the Brooklyn-to-Los Angeles scenario.

The move became official on October 7, 1957, when the Los Angeles City County passed a motion to welcome the Dodgers into its city. The formal contract required O'Malley to privately fund and build a 50,000-seat stadium. On October 8, the team released a statement (as quoted in a *New York Times* article from 2007): "In view of the action of the Los Angeles City Council yesterday and in accordance with the resolution of the National League made October first, the stockholders and directors of the Brooklyn Baseball Club have today met and unanimously agreed that the necessary steps be taken to draft the Los Angeles territory."

That settled it: O'Malley's team would play its next season on the West Coast as the Los Angeles Dodgers. However, the new stadium still needed to be built, so the team played its next four seasons at the Memorial Coliseum, which previously had been a football stadium. It proved an awkward venue, yet the city's new team attracted more than a million fans in its inaugural 1958 season. But on the playing field, the uprooted team was less than successful. In 1959, however, the Dodgers won the National League pennant and beat the Chicago White Sox in the World Series.

Opened New Stadium

Just before the 1959 World Series, on September 17, 1959, groundbreaking ceremonies for the new Dodger Stadium construction were held. O'Malley would finally realize his vision of building a new ballpark. He had hoped the stadium would be completed by 1960, but complications delayed its opening. Meanwhile, the city fell in love with its baseball team.

The $20 million dollar stadium, designed and bankrolled by O'Malley, opened on April 10, 1962. For the occasion, O'Malley's wife Kay threw out the ceremonial first pitch to new Dodgers catcher John Roseboro. Dodger Stadium scored a home run with both fans and the press. At the time, it represented a state-of-the-art professional ballpark, and first-season attendance (2.7 million) set a new Major League attendance record. Also, the Dodger team continued its winning ways. In 1963, it won yet another National League pennant and beat the Yankees in the World Series in four straight games, bolstered by pitching performances by Podres, Don Drysdale, and Sandy Koufax.

O'Malley helped draw fans to the ball park by offering the league's lowest ticket prices and offering an attractive product: a team of new star players that included Koufax, Drysdale, Roseboro, the Davis brothers (Tommy and Willie),

Maury Wills, Ron Fairly, and Phil Regan, among others. In addition, Dodger Stadium was an attractive venue, as O'Malley spent $1.5 million on landscaping (including gardens and trees) and seating provided customers with stunning views of the San Gabriel Mountains and downtown Los Angeles. Further, the stadium proved family friendly, safe and comfortable, which underscored the fact that O'Malley considered fans his top priority.

Handed Successful Team over to Son

O'Malley remained team president until 1969. From 1963 to 1969, the Dodgers won three National League Pennants (1963, 1965, and 1966) and two World Series (1963 and 1965). Average annual attendance at Dodger Stadium topped two million. On March 17, 1969, O'Malley named his son, Peter, the new Dodger president. Peter O'Malley headed the team for the next twenty-eight years.

Walter O'Malley remained active in the sport, however, and from 1970 to 1979, he served as the Dodgers' chairman of the board. He also retained his seat on Major League Baseball's Executive Council. He served the Council from 1951 to 1978, the longest of any baseball executive.

In 1975 he received the first Busch Award for "meritorious service to baseball," a well deserved honor, as O'Malley remained an influential figure in baseball's new era, confronting an increasingly complex range of issues that include television contracts, antitrust exemptions, player pension plans and global expansion.

On July 12, 1979, his wife passed away. O'Malley died 28 days later, on August 9, in Rochester, Minnesota, from heart disease. He was seventy-five years old. *Los Angeles Times* columnist Jim Murray wrote that "O'Malley belongs in the Hall of Fame as surely as Babe Ruth, Ty Cobb and certainly Judge [Kenesaw Mountain] Landis ... Ted Williams had the vision to see a ball curving 60 feet ahead, but Walter O'Malley had the vision to see three decades ahead ... He built a Taj Mahal of a ballpark, setting the tone for subsequent edifices. He brought the game kicking and screaming into the 20th Century."

O'Malley eventually was inducted into Major League Baseball's Hall of Fame, posthumously, on December 3, 2007. His plaque reads (as quoted on the Dodgers' website): "An influential and visionary owner who inspired baseball's move west in 1957. Relocated Dodgers from Brooklyn to Los Angeles and opened new markets for the major league game. Served as president and principal owner when his clubs won four World Series championships (1955, 1959, 1963 and 1965) and 11 pennants. Maintained affordable ticket prices while generating record attendance. Driving force behind design, construction and financing of Dodger Stadium, a benchmark for a new generation of modern ballparks."

In December 1999, *The Sporting News* named him the eleventh most power person in sports during the course of the twentieth century, and ABC Sports placed him in its Top 10 Most Influential People "Off the Field" in sports history (as voted by the Sports Century panel).

Despite later vindication, some still were not willing to either forgive or forget. One of these included *New York Times* sports columnist Dave Anderson. In his September 30, 2007 "Sports of the Times" column he wrote, "Fifty years later, historical revisionists have all but beatified Walter O'Malley for absconding to Los Angeles with the Brooklyn Dodgers after the 1957 season. O'Malley didn't do it, book authors and television shows insist. The villain was Robert Moses . . . [b]ut to anyone who was around the Dodgers and Ebbets Field in those years, as I and a few other survivors were, O'Malley has always been the villain. And always will be.''

Anderson indicated that he believed that O'Malley was more of a businessman than a baseball man and that he knew that Moses would never agree to a new stadium. Further, according to Anderson, O'Malley knew that moving his team to a new market would create a ''financial bonanza.'' Moses did not move the Dodgers, he emphasized, O'Malley did.'' Still, by moving his team to the West Coast and, in turn, expanding baseball's national boundaries, O'Malley only initiated the inevitable.

Books

''Walter Francis O'Malley,'' *Almanac of Famous People, 9th Edition,* Thomson Gale, 2007.

''Walter Francis O'Malley,'' *Dictionary of American Biography, Supplement 10: 1976-1980,* Charles Scribner's Sons, 1995.

Periodicals

Los Angeles Times, March 18, 2009.

The New York Times, September 30, 2007.

Online

''The Misunderstood Bum,'' *Second Pass,,* http://thesecondpass. com/?p=846 (November 26, 2009).

''Walter O'Malley,'' *Baseball Library.com,* http://www.baseballli brary.com/ballplayers/player.php?name=   Walter_OMalley_ 1903 (November 26, 2009).

''Walter O'Malley Biography,'' *WalterOMalley.com,,* http://www. walteromalley.com/new_biography.php (November 26, 2009).

''Who Framed Walter O'Malley,'' *Forbes.com,* http://www.forbes. com/2009/04/14/brooklyn-dodgers-stadium-lifestyle-sports-baseball-stadiums.html (November 26, 2009).

''Visionary Dodger Owner Walter O'Malley Enshrined in National Baseball Hall of Fame Ceremony,'' *Dodgers.com,,* http:// losangeles.dodgers.mlb.com/la/history/walter_omalley.jsp (November 26, 2009). □

P

Pier Paolo Pasolini

Poet, journalist, playwright, iconoclastic filmmaker, and one of Italy's most prominent intellectuals, Pier Paolo Pasolini (1922–1975) remains one of the most controversial cultural figures of the twentieth century, decades after his 1975 murder. Pasolini often used his talents to taunt Italian government censors, the Roman Catholic Church, and the increasingly bourgeois consumerist society of post-World War II Italy. His films ranged from a depiction of the final days of the life of Christ to a disturbing adaptation of the 1785 novel *The 120 Days of Sodom* by French writer Marquis de Sade. "Pasolini remains, perhaps above all, a subject for furious argument," asserted *New York Times* film critic A. O. Scott, 32 years after the filmmaker's death. "In an era when Italy produced a bumper crop of difficult, passionate artists, especially in the cinema, he may have been the most difficult of all, and arguably the most prodigiously talented."

Pasolini was born in the northern Italian city of Bologna on March 5, 1922, the son of an army officer and a mother who was a schoolteacher. Seven months later, Benito Mussolini and his National Fascist Party marched on Rome, and Italy's King Victor Emmanuel III handed over power to the right wing extremists. The Mussolini regime endured until 1943, when Allied armies invaded the Italian peninsula during World War II and the nation's ruinous alliance with Nazi Germany was ended by force.

As a young man Pasolini entered the University of Bologna, and published a volume of poetry, *Poesie a Casarsa,* in 1942. These poems were written in the Friulian dialect of northeastern Italy, where he had relatives and had spent summers since his childhood. In 1943 he was drafted into the Italian armed forces, but in the chaos surrounding Italy's surrender to U.S. and British troops Pasolini's regiment was seized by the Germans. He managed to escape and was sheltered by a family in Casarsa, where he took up his mother's profession and became a schoolteacher. He also joined the local branch of Italy's Communist Party.

Fired from Teaching Job

Pasolini was fired from his teaching job in 1949 after he was accused of sexual misconduct involving four teenage boys. The incident took place during an annual festival day, and the youths had apparently willingly sneaked away to a remote field to engage in sexual acts with the handsome but reckless 27-year-old teacher. Pasolini fought the case and was exonerated, but was ejected from the Communist Party and deemed unfit to teach. In January of 1950, he left Casarsa for Rome.

In Rome, Pasolini was able to find a teaching job at a private school, and also began writing newspaper articles to earn money. He also immersed himself in the relative anonymity of the sprawling urban landscape, for there were certain streets and Tiber River embankments in the ancient city that had been sites for "cruising," or initiating casual single-sex encounters among men, for centuries by then.

Pasolini's 1955 novel, *Ragazzi di vita* (The Boys of Life; alternately translated as "Real Life Kids"), brought a fresh round of trouble. This time he wrote about the teens who grew up impoverished in the mass housing built

during Mussolini's era, and the petty crime and sense of hopelessness that dominates their lives. Italian authorities charged him with obscenity, but when the case went to trial, the panel of judges disagreed with prosecutors and deemed it had some literary merit. It actually ended up on the short list for the Strega Prize, Italy's most prestigious literary award.

Worked with Neorealist Filmmakers

In Rome, Pasolini was drawn into Italy's emerging postwar film industry. Mussolini had built a massive studio complex called Cinecittà (Cinema City) to make propagandistic entertainment, and the site became the home to a new generation of young, disaffected, often left-leaning film-makers. Like Pasolini, they were disillusioned with the Roman Catholic Church's tight grip on Italian culture and society, and sought to expose the reality of life for the most impoverished and oppressed Italians through the lens of a film camera. Pasolini's first writing credit on a film came as one of several who penned *La Donna del Fiume* (The Woman of the River), a Sophia Loren vehicle about a poor field worker betrayed by the smuggler she loves.

Pasolini's career in film was cemented with his screenplay for *Le notti di Cabiria* (The Nights of Cabiria), about a prostitute in Rome that starred Giulietta Masina, the wife of its director, Federico Fellini. The film was greeted with both opprobrium and acclaim in Italy, but won the Academy Award for Best Foreign Language Film of 1957. Pasolini also worked on Fellini's 1960 masterpiece *La Dolce Vita*

(The Sweet Life), and Fellini agreed to produce Pasolini's first attempt at directing, but then backed out of the *Accattone* project. Pasolini found another producer to finance the story of a pimp, played by Franco Citti, whose main source of income is jailed, which forces him to try finding an honest job. *Accattone* debuted at the 1961 Venice Film Festival and reignited the ire of Italian censors and conservative critics in Italy. "Although the film is without any humor, or power, or bitterness," wrote *New York Times* critic Renata Adler, "Pasolini's direction has a certain squalid lyricism."

Pasolini's second film as a writer-director was *Mamma Roma,* which debuted at the Venice Film Festival of 1962. He lured one of Italian cinema's top stars, Anna Magnani, out of retirement to play the title role of a middle-aged Roman prostitute who achieves her goal of saving enough money for a decent apartment and a fruit stand so that she can bring her young son to live with her. The teenager, after years in the rural countryside, is quickly seduced by the aimless lifestyle of the *ragazzi,* or street kids.

Works Deemed Sacrilegious

In 1963 Pasolini was arrested and prosecuted again, this time on charges of vilifying the Roman Catholic Church in Italy, for his contribution to a work by French filmmaker Jean-Luc Godard, *Ro.Go.Pa.G.* The title is taken from the names of the four directors who contributed segments— Roberto Rossellini, Godard, Pasolini, and Ugo Gregoretti. Pasolini's segment was a film-within-a-film setting, with Orson Welles as a famous director attempting to make a film about the crucifixion of Christ who inadvertently starves one of his lead actors. The failure of organized religion to prevent the suffering of those who lack even the most basic human needs was the strong undercurrent in the film, but Pasolini's next work would further inflame the Vatican, Italian censors, and religious conservatives.

Despite the death threats Pasolini received at the debut of *Il vangelo secondo Matteo* (The Gospel According to Matthew), the film won two prizes at the 1964 Venice Film Festival. Italian film critics rallied behind it, too, giving the black-and-white movie several honors. Its climactic scene was considered scandalous at the time for graphically depicting Christ's death on the cross; other filmmakers had done this, but none with Pasolini's brutal realism and perceived lack of reverence. Finally, a prominent French cleric, Maurice Cardinal Feltin, defended the work. The Archbishop of Paris asserted that "no other religious film resembles this one—in which Christ is restored in all his humanity, in all his divinity," *New York Times* journalist Melton S. Davis quoted Feltin as saying.

The Gospel According to Matthew earned a great deal of international attention, and articles about Italy's most controversial director usually noted that he was an avowed Communist—though, incidentally, the Italian Communist Party regularly condemned his films, too. In interviews, Pasolini said that the story of Christ and his apostles was deeply inspirational and not at all at odds with his political convictions. "Someone who walks up to a couple of people and says, 'follow me' is a total revolutionary," he quipped, according to John Mage in the *Monthly Review.*

A mysterious, compelling stranger was also the focus of Pasolini's 1968 film *Teorema* (Theorem). This starred British actor Terence Stamp as a handsome visitor who turns up at an affluent family's villa seeking shelter, but then seduces every member of the household. Pasolini then began working on a trilogy of films based on the early masterpieces of Western literature, which he called the Trilogy of Life. The first was *Il decameron* (The Decameron) in 1971, followed by *I racconti di Canterbury* (The Canterbury Tales) a year later and finally *Il fiore delle mille e una notte* (A Thousand and One Nights) in 1974. All three featured nudity, sexual content, and even scatological humor. Mage praised the three works, calling them "achingly lyrical films" that were "filled with a nostalgia for noncommodified human relations."

Brutal Film, Brutal End

Pasolini's last work, however, endured as his most infamously risqué. This was the 1975 release *Salò o le 120 giornate di Sodome* (Salò—The 120 Days of Sodom), an adaptation of an extremely pornographic tale by de Sade, the eighteenth-century libertine. Salò was an actual town in northern Italy where Mussolini hid out in his final months as he clung to power. Pasolini set the story at a private school that has been taken over by a quartet of authority figures that de Sade also skewered—a political leader, an aristocrat, a church official, and a banker. De Sade's novel was an attempt to portray the basest impulses and cruelties of human nature through acts of excessive sexual perversion and physical violence. "The film opens with the rounding up, one by one, of young people by fascist soldiers—rather as though they were capturing partisans," wrote Joan Bakewall, a critic for the *New Statesman*. "But this is worse than warfare—where, after a fashion, certain rules apply. Instead, they are taken to an ancient Italian palace where rules of any kind are abandoned, and they are progressively abused and tortured for the remaining 90 minutes of the film."

Bakewall and other critics usually admitted the discomfort they experienced sitting through what is one of twentieth-century cinema's most shocking works. Vincent Canby saw it at the 1977 New York Film Festival and gave it a scathing review in the *New York Times*, asserting it was "a perfect example of the kind of material that, theoretically, anyway, can be acceptable on paper but becomes so repugnant when visualized on screen that it further dehumanizes the human spirit, which is supposed to be the artist's concern."

Salò—The 120 Days of Sodom remains one of the few films unable to be broadcast on television, even by pay television providers, because of its extreme content. Pasolini planned it as the first installment in his Trilogy of Death series, but he himself perished under dreadful circumstances three weeks before its premier at the Paris Film Festival on November 2, 1975. On the night of November 2, the filmmaker had dined with friends, then allegedly picked up a young man from Termini, Rome's main railway station. He bought the 17-year-old Giuseppe "Pino" Pelosi a spaghetti dinner at a trattoria, then drove them to Ostia, a beach area outside of Rome. Pelosi claimed that Pasolini had made unwanted sexual advances to him, and then in fear Pelosi bludgeoned him into unconsciousness and drove off in the silver Alfa Romeo. He may have accidentally struck Pasolini with the car, Pelosi added. Police arrested him for speeding shortly afterward.

Pelosi was a known male prostitute who served several years in prison for Pasolini's murder, but later recanted his confession. The salacious circumstances surrounding the death of one of Italy's most controversial cultural figures prompted decades of speculation, conspiracy theories, a book, and even a 1995 docudrama, *Who Killed Pasolini?*. The initial police report noted that Pelosi's clothes and evidence showed barely any hint that he had just beaten someone to a pulp with a wood plank, and there were other odd details about the night and its aftermath. One theory tied thugs from Movimento Sociale Italiano (MSI), a neo-Fascist party, to the murder.

Inspired Mel Gibson

In 2004 the Australian-American actor and director Mel Gibson made a religious movie about the final days in the life of Jesus, *The Passion of the Christ*. Gibson reportedly watched Pasolini's *Gospel According to Matthew* many times over while filming on location in Matera, a town in southern Italy. Pasolini, who produced volumes of well-received verse as well as opinion journalism during his career, had once written a series of articles on the poverty of this region. "What I was interested in was creating an equivalent of the simple people among whom Christ lived," Pasolini explained to Davis, about why he chose the town of Matera for his 1964 classic. "It seemed to me that Southern Italians were the closest."

Books

D'Arpino, Tony, "Pasolini, Pier Paolo," in *International Dictionary of Films and Filmmakers*, edited by Sara Pendergast and Tom Pendergast, fourth edition, *Volume 2: Directors*, St. James Press, 2001, pp. 750–753.

Rhodes, John David, *Stupendous, Miserable City: Pasolini's Rome*, University of Minnesota Press, 2007.

Periodicals

Independent (London, England), April 9, 2004.

Monthly Review, November 1995.

New Statesman, December 4, 2000.

New York Times, April 10, 1966; April 5, 1968; November 3, 1975; October 1, 1977; January 18, 1995; November 23, 2007. □

Claire Phillips

The story of the freelance American spy Claire Phillips (c.1908–1960), known as High Pockets, was one of the most colorful of World War II, even though it was bound up with one of the war's grimmest episodes— the mass internment of American soldiers at the Cabanatuan Prison camp in the Philippines.

The ruse Phillips created may be unique in the history of espionage. She opened a Manila nightspot, Club Tsubaki, which catered to Japanese officers and, using the twin intoxicants of alcohol and sexual temptation on the part of Phillips and sympathetic employees, attempted to glean information of military value by getting them to talk freely. The second phase of Phillips's operation was even more dangerous: she led a smuggling operation that provided money, medical equipment, badly needed food and beverages, letters and other means of communication, and clothes to prisoners at Cabanatuan. The nickname High Pockets came from Phillips's habit of carrying secret documents in her brassiere.

Conflicting Birth Dates Given

As befits a skilled practitioner of espionage, Claire Phillips remains a shadowy figure whose early background is uncertain. Her 1947 autobiography, *Manila Espionage,* discusses only her activities during the war years. A relative of Claire's second husband, John Phillips, told China National Aviation Corporation historian Tom Moore, who has maintained a website devoted to Phillips, that Phillips herself claimed to have been born on December 2, 1908. Phillips's Filipina biographer, Edna Bautista Binkowski, apparently relying on FBI files pertaining to Phillips's activities, stated that Phillips was born Mabel Claire Dela Taste in Michigan on December 2, 1915, to parents George Dela Taste and Mabel Cole. According to Binkowski she had two sisters, Neil Jean and Carol Eve. After George Dela Taste's death, Phillips's mother married Lloyd Snyder.

Claire grew up wanting to become a performer, and when she was 15 she ran away from home and signed on with a circus as a snake charmer. In the 1920s and 1930s she traveled around the United States as a vaudeville performer and singer, altering her personality and even her name according to the requirements of the places where she performed. She used the names Claire Dela Taste, Mabel C. Evette, Mabel Clara Dela Taste, and Claire Mabel Snyder. In 1938 she decided to try her luck in Honolulu, but work there was scarce. She bought a one-way ticket to Manila, then under American control as part of the colonial Philippines, and after her arrival she was hired by an American musical-theater company as a chorus girl at the Metropolitan Theatre and then booked to perform at the Alcazar club. She soon met and, on August 15 of 1938 married, a well-off Spanish-Filipino coffee plantation owner, Manuel L. Fuentes.

The marriage did not work out. Claire Fuentes did not speak Spanish, and her husband often left her alone as he traveled on business. Even the adoption (or natural birth; see below) of a Filipina baby girl, whom they named Dian, did not improve the couple's relationship. Claire's request for a divorce was met with complete refusal by the Catholic Fuentes, so Claire snatched Dian while Fuentes was away on an extended trip and fled to the U.S., financing the voyage with money gained from a fraudulent sale of the couple's house. But life back home did not satisfy her, either. Having had a taste of Manila's exotic nightlife, and having found her talents in demand there, she booked

passage on a Swedish freighter and arrived back in the Philippines in September of 1941—just as many other foreign nationals were leaving Manila amid rumors of war in the Pacific. This account of Phillips's first marriage and return to Manila is based on Binkowski's biography, where it is unsourced but much more detailed than Phillips's own account in *Manila Espionage.* That book placed the marriage in America but gave no names or locations.

Met and Married U.S. Officer

Accounts of Claire's life begin to coincide in December of 1941, when she met Sergeant John W. Phillips (born in 1918 and known as Phil), a radio operator with the 31st U.S. Infantry. Their first meeting occurred after he watched her singing "I Don't Want to Set the World on Fire." The two fell for each other hard and planned to marry, but the Japanese attack on Pearl Harbor, quickly followed by an invasion of the Philippines, resulted in John Phillips's transfer to the battlefront. Claire left Manila and stayed with Filipino friends in the Bataan region (something that supports Binkowski's claims that her acquaintance with the country was longer than that depicted in *Manila Espionage*). On December 24, 1941, the pair was married by a Catholic priest. The marriage, however, lacked legal standing since Claire had never been formally divorced.

John Phillips immediately returned to duty and soon disappeared as the Japanese overran American forces. Living like a Philippine guerrilla for several months, she searched for her husband but could not locate him. She later learned of his death at the Cabanatuan camp on July 27, 1942. During this period Phillips met John Boone, a renegade American soldier who had refused to participate in the American surrender to the Japanese in April of 1942 and had begun to organize local resistance to the occupation. Boone recruited Phillips as a spy, and after witnessing a forced march of desperately ill American soldiers, likely the Bataan Death March, she accepted. At Boone's suggestion she spent time over several weeks lying in a cane field to darken her skin enough that she could pass as Filipina. Photos of Phillips taken after the war show a light-skinned woman.

Phillips's actual mission, however, was apparently her own idea. She had help in carrying it out from a Filipina dancer, Fely Corcuera, and the financing of her posh new Club Tsubaki (named for the Japanese word meaning camellia) may have been aided by a sympathetic Chinese restaurateur in Manila. In October of 1942 the club opened at the corner of San Luis and Mabini streets and was talked up by the Japanese-controlled press. It soon began to attract a well-heeled clientele of Japanese military officers, business executives, ship captains, and others who could afford the club's high prices. "It is necessary to pay to be exclusive," Phillips told her customers (according to Hampton Sides in his book *Ghost Soldiers*). By this time Phillips had acquired yet another new identity: thanks to a friend who worked at the Italian embassy in Manila, she had papers identifying her as Dorothy Clara Fuentes, an Italian national and thus a citizen of a nation friendly to Japan. Neither Dorothy nor Fuentes was an Italian name, but most of her clientele was unaware of that, even if they were surprised when they quizzed her one time about Italian popular songs and found that she did not know them.

The club's stage shows, with elaborate fan dances suggesting female nudity, were top-notch, and "Dorothy Fuentes" or one of her trusted assistants delivered personal service, pouring drinks, lighting cigarettes, and cuddling up to her highly placed customers while engaging them in conversation about their plans. They gained advance knowledge of Japanese troop movements by asking how long an officer might be in Manila, or of force sizes by asking an officer how many men were under his command. The information they acquired was written down and transmitted by Filipino runners and delivered to Boone or another American guerrilla; some of it was then sent via shortwave radio to the American Pacific command.

Smuggled Supplies to U.S. Prisoners

Phillips's undercover involvement deepened still further when a waiter at the club told her of a camp he called Park Avenue, where prisoners were forced to march nine miles a day. The camp was the notorious Cabanatuan. Phillips left Manila to observe one of these marches and, distressed by the condition of the Americans she saw, decided to devote profits from Club Tsubaki to helping them. Mobilizing her network of Filipino couriers, she set out to infiltrate the camp and deliver supplies. For a time she and a local friend set up a food booth on the prisoners' route, bribing guards to look the other way while they dispensed free food or calamansi orange juice—desperately needed because scurvy, caused by a lack of vitamin C, was rampant among the prisoners. Sometimes the two buried supplies in gravel and got word to the prisoners telling them where to look.

Couriers carried other items, such as anti-malaria quinine tablets, directly into the camp, or radios that could sometimes receive signals from the U.S. West Coast. Among the deliveries from High Pockets most prized by prisoners were letters, bringing news of the outside. Some of the letters were written by Phillips herself, and responses from the prisoners have survived. "Hello High Pockets," one wrote (as quoted by Sides). "When I got your letter I came to life again....You deserve more gold medals than all of us in here together. You've done more for the boys' morale in here than you'll ever know. Some of them are flat on their backs and I wish you could have seen the looks of gratitude. In answer to your question about John's grave...don't worry, Pal. When it's all over you and I will come back here and get John."

Phillips's undercover activities lasted from October of 1942 until May 23, 1944, when she was arrested by agents of the Japanese *Kempei Tai* military police and accused of spying. Phillips was imprisoned at Fort Santiago, a dungeon built early in the Spanish occupation of the Philippines, and/or at the Bilibid penitentiary (sources do not agree). She was sentenced to death, but the sentence was reduced to a 12-year term of hard labor. In *Manila Espionage* she described torture she underwent at the hands of the Japanese.

Questioned by FBI

On February 10, 1945, Phillips was liberated by American troops. As she and Dian sailed for home, a trunk carrying her personal papers disappeared as the ship approached Honolulu. Partly as a result, she faced close questioning from FBI agents when she applied for the death benefits of $10,000 that were due to her as the wife of John Phillips. Her marriage was legally dubious, and the circumstances under which it occurred made formal documentation impossible. On the other hand, Phillips soon accumulated testimonials from Cabanatuan chaplain Robert Taylor and other detainees. On January 23, 1948 she was awarded the Medal of Freedom by General Mark Clark.

Phillips and her daughter moved to Portland, Oregon, where she married former Cabanatuan POW Robert R. Clavier; he had known of High Pockets but never met her until she visited him at a hospital in Vancouver, Washington. They divorced after two years and sold their small home, splitting the profits. In 1947 a small Portland publisher, Binfords & Mort, issued *Manila Espionage,* which Phillips co-wrote with Myron B. Goldsmith; Boone wrote the foreword. In 1951 the book was filmed as *I Was an American Spy,* with actress Ann Dvorak in the role of Phillips, who was dubbed an American Mata Hari. Phillips was active in veterans' groups in Portland, and in later life she worked as a branch manager of the National Laundry Company. She continued to pursue financial claims against the U.S. government, and a 1956 newspaper report located by Binkowski revealed that she had been awarded an unspecified sum. Dian was given a scholarship to Lewis and Clark College at Phillips's Medal of Freedom ceremony, but she did not complete her degree, and the mother and daughter drifted out of touch. A daughter, Wendy Johnson, whom Dian put up for adoption, has surfaced with the claim that Dian herself was not adopted but was the natural daughter of Phillips and Fuentes. With her health damaged by her imprisonment in Manila, Phillips died prematurely on May 22, 1960, at the Portland Sanitarium. The cause of death was listed as pneumococcal meningitis.

Books

Binkowski, Edna Bautista, *Code Name: High Pockets,* Valour Publishing (Limay, Bataan, Philippines), 2006.

Phillips, Claire, and Myron B. Goldsmith, *Manila Espionage,* Binfords & Mort, 1947.

Sides, Hampton, *Ghost Soldiers: The Forgotten Epic Story of World War II's Most Dramatic Mission,* Doubleday, 2001.

Periodicals

Investor's Business Daily, March 5, 2009.

Online

"Adoptee's Grandmother Was 'An American Spy,'" *Albany (OR) Democrat Herald* (September 2, 2009), http://www.democratherald.com/news/local/ (January 5, 2010).

"Claire Phillips, aka 'High Pockets,'" *China National Aviation Corporation,* http://www.cnac.org/emilscott/phillips01.htm (January 5, 2010).

"People & Events: Claire Phillips," *Public Broadcasting System: Bataan Rescue,* http://www.pbs.org/wgbh/amex/bataan/peopleevents/p_phillips.html (January 5, 20100. ☐

Ilya Piatetski-Shapiro

The Russian-born mathematician Ilya Piatetski-Shapiro (1929–2009), who emigrated to Israel in later life, gained international renown for his record of mathematical accomplishments, his struggle against anti-Semitism and government repression in the Soviet Union, and his persistence in continuing his work in the face of serious degenerative disease.

Piatetski-Shapiro was born in Moscow on March 30, 1929, to parents from families that followed traditional Jewish practices. His father, a chemical engineer, came from the once mostly Jewish town of Berdichev in what is now Ukraine; the near-total decimation of its Jewish population and institutions, begun under Ukrainian and Soviet forces, was completed by Germany during World War II. Piatetski-Shapiro's mother also came from a mostly Jewish town, Gomel, now in Belarus. When he was ten, his father introduced him to the concept of negative numbers, and according to Kenneth Chang of the *New York Times,* he was impressed "by the charm and unusual beauty" of the idea. After the war, Piatetski-Shapiro enrolled at Moscow University and majored in mathematics, graduating in 1951.

In 1952, after writing a paper covering the uniqueness of trigonometric series, he won the Moscow Mathematical Society Prize for a Young Musician. The prize was announced a week before the death of dictator Joseph Stalin, during a time when officially approved anti-Semitism was at a high point, and Piatetski-Shapiro remembered being surprised that he had been chosen for the award. He applied to the university's graduate program in mathematics, but his admission was blackballed by the university's Communist Party organ even though it had been strongly endorsed by the professor and party member Alexander Gelfond, whose father had been a friend of Vladimir Lenin, the leader of the Russian Revolution and the Soviet Union's first head of state.

Piatetski-Shapiro, with Gelfond's help, was admitted to the Moscow Pedagogical Institute. The Soviet government tried to transfer him to a teaching position at a remote high school in Kazakhstan, but he showed the first sign of his tendency toward resistance when he refused the assignment. After a year during which his parents, fearing that he might disappear into the Soviet prison gulag, urged him to back down, the assignment was canceled. Piatetski-Shapiro was deeply involved in research for his Ph.D. thesis at the institute, which granted him that degree in 1954 and, after he attended advanced seminars at Moscow's Steklov Mathematical Institute in the mid-1950s, the degree of Doctor of Sciences in 1958.

Declined Party Membership on Work Grounds

One fruit of Piatetski-Shapiro's studies at the Steklov Institute was a working relationship with Igor Shafarevich, a professor there. The two wrote an influential joint paper on algebraic surfaces. Their friendship even survived the anti-Semitic essays Shafarevich published—perhaps because it was mathematics, and mathematical discussions, that mattered to Piatetski-Shapiro most. Piatetski-Shapiro became a professor of mathematics at the Moscow Institute of Applied Mathematics in 1958, and in 1965 he gained a prestigious second position when he joined the faculty at Moscow State University. But when it was suggested that it would be advantageous for him to join the Communist Party, he gave the widely quoted reply (in a memorial essay appearing on the Yale University web site, among other places): "Membership in the Communist Party will distract me from my work."

The refusal cost him, for by the early 1960s his work was becoming internationally known, and he was being invited to present it in the West. The first of these invitations came in 1962, when Piatetski-Shapiro was asked to appear at the International Mathematical Congress in Stockholm, Sweden. But he was refused permission to attend that conference, or to leave the country at all except for one short trip to Communist Hungary. Piatetski-Shapiro did address the 1966 Moscow meeting of the International Mathematical Congress.

In the late 1960s, Piatetski-Shapiro began a path of more active resistance to the Soviet regime. He signed a petition in support of a dissident colleague in 1968, losing his Moscow State post as a result.

In the early 1970s, the Soviet Union permitted increasing numbers of Jewish citizens to emigrate to Israel. Piatetski-Shapiro's first wife, from whom he was divorced, and his 16-year-old son decided to leave, and Piatetski-Shapiro, increasingly discouraged about his son's ability to maintain a Jewish identity in the Soviet Union, supported their decision. At first, having begun to teach some of the great mathematicians of the next generation, he did not want to leave the country himself, but in 1974 he too applied for an exit visa to Israel.

That decision, since Piatetski-Shapiro was a dissident with international connections, unleashed the worst paranoid tendencies of the Soviet security bureaucracy. He lost his Institute of Applied Mathematics job, and soon even his permission to use mathematical libraries. Piatetski-Shapiro found himself being shadowed by a car and believed that his apartment was under audio surveillance. Sometimes he would carry on discussions of his situation with friends by writing on a plastic board. This treatment of a respected scholar did nothing but stir up international outrage, and in 1976 Piatetski-Shapiro was given a visa that allowed him to emigrate.

Received Israel Prize

Piatetski-Shapiro began teaching at Tel Aviv University in Israel in 1977 and became a member of the Israel Academy of Sciences the following year. He also began a long association with Yale University, for many years dividing his time between the two institutions. Piatetski-Shapiro received the Israel Prize, the state of Israel's highest honor, in 1981. One of the accomplishments for which he became best known was his proof of the Converse Theorem, which pertained to certain relationships between the branches of mathematics. He began to issue publications describing his proof in the mid-1970s, and they helped lay the groundwork for the proof, in 1994, of the centuries-old Fermat's Last Theorem, announced by American mathematician Andrew Wiles. Piatetski-Shapiro's interests extended beyond pure mathematics to applied science, and his work made contributions to fields including cell biology, geophysics, and digital computing.

By the early 1990s, Piatetski-Shapiro was showing serious symptoms of Parkinson's disease. He had had to give up his beloved hobby of hiking, which he often combined with visits to mathematical conferences, and then, in 1992, he stopped visiting the conferences themselves. Soon, however, he resumed his attendance, finding that he missed his discussions with fellow mathematicians and reasoning that he did not feel worse while traveling than he did trapped at home.

Most unusual was the fact that Piatetski-Shapiro did not simply maintain contacts but continued to carry out original research, even while hobbled by a degenerative disease and reaching an age that usually sidelined even healthy mathematicians from the cutting edge of the field. Princeton University professor Peter Sarnak told Chang that Piatetski-Shapiro, then in his 70s, was still "knocking off well-known, longstanding problems." Eventually he almost lost the ability to speak; only his third wife, Edith, and one of his longtime students, James Cogsdell, could still understand his half-mumbled whisper, and he communicated with the outside world with those two as interpreters.

Even with those handicaps, Piatetski-Shapiro was invited to address the International Mathematical Congress in 2002. He was active almost to the end of his life, which came in Tel Aviv on February 24, 2009. Piatetski-Shapiro was survived by three children, Gregory, Niki, and Shelley (Shlomit), and a stepdaughter, Vera Lipkin.

Periodicals

New York Times, March 5, 2009; March 18, 2009.

Online

"In Memoriam: Ilya Piatetski-Shapiro," *Yale University,* http://www.math.yale.edu/public_html/PS.html (February 12, 2010).

"1990 Wolf Foundation Prize in Mathematics," *Wolf Foundation* (Israel), http://www.wolffund.org.il/ (February 12, 2010).

"On the Life and Work of Ilya Piatetski-Shapiro," *Tel Aviv University,* http://www.math.tau.ac.il/people/memoriam/Piatetski-Shapiro-eng.pdf (February 12, 2010).□

Patriarch Pimen I

Sergei Mikhailovich Izvekov (1910–1990) was better known as Patriarch Pimen I of Moscow, the head of the Russian Orthodox Church. Pimen's tenure in the 1970s and 1980s coincided with the final years of the Cold War and the Soviet Union. In 1988 he presided over the Russian Orthodox Church's spectacle-rich 1,000-year anniversary marking the conversion of Vladimir I, Prince of Kiev, to Christianity in 988.

Pimen came from an affluent family in Bogorodsk, a city near Moscow that would later be renamed Noginsk. Born in 1910, he moved to Moscow at age 15 to enter a monastery there, taking the monk's name of Platon. Much had changed in Russia in his short life by then: a strong left wing element had taken advantage of imperial Russia's disastrous performance in World War I to depose Tsar Nicholas II in March of 1917, and later that year a Marxist wing fomented a second takeover, known as the Bolshevik Revolution, and ordered the executions of Nicholas and his family.

Studied for Priesthood in Secrecy

For centuries the Russian Orthodox Church had been a staunch supporter of the monarchy and a bastion of conservative ideology. Its privileged status not only vanished with the Romanov dynasty, but the new Soviet state became the first in history to announce that the elimination of religion was one of its policy goals. The Marxists who spearheaded the revolution believed strongly in the words of Karl Marx, who famously wrote that religion was "the opiate of the masses," and that "the abolition of religion as the illusory happiness of the people is the demand for their real happiness."

The new Soviet leadership acted accordingly. Scores of churches and monasteries were closed and their sacred icons and other artwork confiscated, while bishops, priests, monks, and nuns were harassed along with worshippers. Religious education, once mandatory in Russian schools, was outlawed, along with religious publications. The seminaries were closed, too, which meant that newcomers like Pimen studied for the priesthood on their own. During the Russian Civil War that followed the Bolshevik Revolution, Russian Orthodox Church leaders supported the monarchist side, which brought epic reprisals later in the 1920s. Thousands of priests and monks were arrested, sent to labor camps and subjected to "reeducation" efforts. Many died in custody. In short, it was a terrible time to enter the Russian Orthodox priesthood.

Pimen underwent his second tonsure, or ritualistic cutting of the hair, in October of 1927. In Christian churches of the Byzantine, or Eastern Rite, priests and monks never cut their hair or shave their beards from this point onward as a sign of devotion to a religious lifestyle. He took the name Pimen, after Pimen the Greek, a fourteenth-century Metropolitan of Moscow. With priestly duties drastically restricted, he became a choirmaster at Moscow's Cathedral of St. Pimen the Great. In July of 1931 he was ordained hierodeacon, one of the many levels of hierarchy in churches of Christianity's Eastern Rite, and six months later was ordained hieromonk, the next designation. Later in 1932 he took his vows as a priest.

Interned in Labor Camp

Details about Pimen's life in the 1930s and 1940s are unclear. He reportedly served in the Red Army during World War II but had not divulged his status as a cleric. His ruse was uncovered and he spent time in prison camps. "Information about the 'missing' years in Pimen's life came to light in an extract from official reports by the Council for Religious Affairs to the Central Committee of the Communist Party of the Soviet Union, which were 'leaked' to the West," noted his *Times* of London obituary. "This extract claimed that during these years Pimen served in the army (twice), was imprisoned (twice) and in between worked in Uzbekistan."

In the late 1940s Pimen served as the abbot of the Ilyinski Monastery in Odessa, and later moved on to the Pskovo-Pechersky Monastery in present-day Estonia, where he also served as abbot. This also coincided with a period of surprising renewal for the Russian Orthodox faith in the Soviet Union, with many of the government restrictions lifted during World War II. At the time, the Soviets were engaged in a calamitous war against Nazi Germany, and Communist Party leader Josef Stalin made concessions to the faithful as a way to bolster public support.

In 1950 Pimen was made archimandrite, or supervisor of abbots and monasteries, and four years later became the director of Troitse-Sergiyeva Lavra, a monastery dating back to 1345 that is considered the spiritual home of the Russian Orthodox Church. In 1957 he was consecrated a bishop and elevated to archbishop three years later. Early in the 1960s he served as Metropolitan, or archbishop, of Leningrad and Ladoga, and then was made Metropolitan of Krutitsy and Kolomna.

Followers of Pimen's faith were targeted once again during Nikita Khrushchev's era, when there was another official crackdown on religious participation in all forms. A person who attended church services would have a difficult time obtaining Communist Party membership, for example, which was a necessity for any professional or managerial career post. A number of priests formed a loose dissident movement in the mid-1960s and were jailed for their self-published calls for the government to end its control of the Russian Orthodox Church through the Council for Religious Affairs, which usurped the former authority of archbishops like Pimen during the Soviet era.

Elected Patriarch

It was as Metropolitan of Krutitsy and Kolomna that Pimen's name first appeared in the Western press. In 1964 the Soviet news agency TASS released an interview with Pimen over its English language radio service in which he asserted "the faith of our church members is strong," according to a *New York Times* report, and that Russian

Orthodox adherents were taking part "in the building of a new society" that would offer "no room for religious inventions about supernatural forces."

In the spring of 1970, the head of the Russian Orthodox Church, Patriarch Aleksii I, died at the age of 92. Aleksii had been the Patriarch of Moscow and All Rus since 1945. In 1971 a Special Council of the Russian Orthodox Church met at the Troitse-Sergiyeva Lavra Monastery to elect a new Patriarch from amongst themselves. Pimen was elected, but was already considered the favorite to win. His previous stints in the army and in labor camps likely played a role, noted Nathaniel Davis in Pimen's *Encyclopedia of Russian History* entry, who wrote that "his political vulnerability was said to have figured in the Soviet authorities' decision that he could be controlled as patriarch."

Targeted by Solzhenitsyn

Pimen was installed as Patriarch of Moscow and All Rus on June 2, 1971. He was the fourteenth cleric to head the Russian Orthodox Church, but the first to have grown up during the Soviet era. Not unexpectedly, he emerged as a strong supporter of official doctrine: he spoke out often on the follies of the Cold War and the perils of nuclear stockpiling, and participated in international peace conferences. After less than a year on the job, he became the target of Aleksandr Solzhenitsyn, the Soviet Union's most famous dissident writer. At the time, Solzhenitsyn was still living in the Soviet Union under the intense scrutiny of the secret police. The novelist had earned international acclaim for his literary documentation of life in the prison camps, which was originally published during a brief period of artistic, economic, and political liberalization in the 1950s. He was awarded the Nobel Prize for Literature in 1970, and was finally expelled from the Soviet Union in 1974. In the interim came Solzhenitsyn's famous "Lenten Letter" of 1972, his first full-on critique of the Russian Orthodox Church.

The Lenten Letter was addressed directly to Pimen, opening with the salutation "Most Holy Master!," according to the *New York Times,* which published a copy of it in April of 1972. In it, Solzhenitsyn called for Pimen and other church leaders to take a more active role in leading their flock, and to reject government interference. He found the authority of the Council for Religious Affairs particularly troubling, and remarked that "a church dictatorially ruled by atheists is a sight not seen in two thousand years." Solzhenitsyn appealed to Russians' deeply held sense of nationalism, and asserted that "we are losing the last traces and signs of a Christian people—is it possible that this should not be the main concern of the Russian Patriarch?"

Solzhenitsyn and others objected to official pronouncements from Pimen, which closely followed Politburo goals and initiatives. Typical of these was the Patriarch's Easter message of 1981, which was quoted by the *New York Times.* In it, Pimen "urged people of good will to oppose the 'revival of the Cold War, which kills the soul,' and to condemn 'the madness of the notion about the possibility of preserving peace by way of increasingly multiplying nuclear arms,'" according to the newspaper. In June of 1982, Pimen visited the United States—the first by a Patriarch of Moscow—and spoke before a special United Nations meeting on disarmament.

Presided over Millennial Celebrations

Pimen was an official participant in the funerals of several Soviet leaders, beginning with Leonid I. Brezhnev in November of 1982. He eulogized Brezhnev's successor, Yuri V. Andropov, 15 months later, and then Konstantin U. Chernenko in March of 1985. The next general secretary of the Communist Party was Mikhail Gorbachev, who began implementing unprecedented reforms at many levels of Soviet society. The new era of *glasnost,* or "openness," as decreed by Gorbachev, ushered in a wave of new critical appraisals of Pimen as the head of an estimated 40 million Russian Orthodox adherents. Some even called for him to step down as Patriarch, as *New York Times* correspondent Serge Schmemann reported in June of 1988. "For the Patriarch and the old metropolitans, survival during years of oppression meant a life of accommodation and obedience, a readiness to press Soviet peace propaganda abroad and to surrender all internal functions save ritual and ceremony," Schmemann wrote. "Now they face challenges from above, from a state trying to thrust more freedom on them, and from below, from believers clamoring for leadership, action and enlightenment."

Schmemann's article was actually devoted to the thousand-year anniversary celebration of Russia's conversion to Christianity. The fact that the millennial celebration took place at all, and with a noticeable amount of government support, heralded a new era for Pimen and his church. Pimen and the leading metropolitans had even met with Gorbachev at the Kremlin, the first time a Soviet leader had met with the Patriarch of Moscow since 1943. In addition to the large crowds that assembled in Kiev to re-create the mass baptisms under Vladimir I of Kiev in 988, the millennial festivities also included open-air services at the historic Danilov Monastery in Moscow, the official headquarters of the Russian Orthodox Church and residence of the Patriarch of Moscow. This had been turned into a detention facility back during Stalin's era but was restored to the Patriarchate in anticipation of the thousand-year celebration. Other important monasteries and churches were returned to the Patriarchate, along with hundreds of icons and sacred artworks that had been in museum custody for decades. Outside of Moscow, about 800 new parishes opened, along with new convents and seminaries.

Though aged and in poor health from diabetes and arthritis, Pimen took part in the millennial celebrations, and in 1989 won a seat in the 2,250-member Congress of Peoples' Deputies, the first legislative body to be elected in free, competitive elections. His was part of a third of the seats assigned to representatives of public institutions. Pimen died in office on May 3, 1990, at the age of 79. He was succeeded as Patriarch of Moscow by Metropolitan Aleksii II of Leningrad.

Books

Davis, Nathaniel, "Pimen, Patriarch," in *Encyclopedia of Russian History,* edited by James R. Millar, four volumes, Macmillan Reference USA, 2004.
Marx, Karl, *Early Writings,* Penguin Classics, 1992, p. 244.
Shubin, Daniel H., *History of Russian Christianity: Tsar Nicholas II to Gorbachev's Edict on the Freedom of Conscience,* (Volume 4 of *A History of Russian Christianity,*) Algora Publishing, 2006.

Periodicals

Guardian (London, England), May 8, 1990).
New York Times, March 22, 1964; March 23, 1972; April 9, 1972; April 27, 1981; February 13, 1984; June 13, 1988; May 4, 1990.
Times (London, England), May 4, 1990; June 9, 1990.
UNESCO Courier, January 1989.□

Tito Puente

American musician Tito Puente (1923–2000) has become widely recognized as the most successful and influential Latin jazz artist of the twentieth century. Known as the "King of Mambo" or "El Rey," the multi-talented Puente was a bandleader and composer as well as a skilled performer on several instruments, including the vibraphone, saxophone, piano, and timbales. From its first stirrings in New York City in the late 1930s, his career spanned several decades, spawning over 120 records and earning numerous accolades, including six Grammy Awards, a star on the Hollywood Walk of Fame, and even the keys to the cities of New York and Miami. By the time of his death in 2000, the musician had logged some 10,000 live shows, performing a series of concerts in Puerto Rico even in his last days.

B orn Ernesto Antonio Puente on April 20, 1923, in New York City's Spanish Harlem neighborhood, Puente was the eldest of the three children of Puerto Rican immigrants Ernesto and Ercilla Puente. His mother gave the young Ernesto the nickname of "Ernestito" ("Little Ernest"), which in turn was shortened to his lifelong moniker of "Tito." Growing up in El Barrio, the future musician—who enjoyed making a racket with pots and pans so much that his neighbors convinced the family to send him to music lessons—attended local public schools and Central Commercial High School. With piano training and a natural flair for percussion instruments, the schoolboy began performing professionally as a song and dance artist alongside his younger sister, Anna. Beginning in 1935, the Puente children took part in a local performance troupe known as the Stars of the Future, and Puente was recognized for his exceptional dance skills on four separate occasions before an ankle injury sidelined his physical abilities. Tragedy

also marred the boy's life, however, as both of his siblings died at young ages, his brother from a fall at the age of four and his sister from spinal meningitis as a teenager.

Started Off in New York City Orchestras

In 1939, Puente dropped out of high school to tour the United States as one of Cuban bandleader José Curbelo's performers; Curbelo served as a mentor for the budding musician, showing him the ropes of the business side of the music industry. The influence of bandleader Frank Grillo—popularly known as Machito—also informed the young musician's style. Beginning to play with Machito and His Afro-Cubans in 1940, Puente honed his skills on the timbales while soaking up Machito's blend of Caribbean and jazz beats. The musician played with Machito and others such as Johnny Rodriguez and Anselmo Sacassas, developing his style and meeting other important Latin artists, until he was drafted into the U.S. Navy in 1942, not long after the United States' entry into World War II. Between 1942 and 1945, Puente was stationed on the USS *Santee,* and he played in the *Santee's* band when not performing his military duties; a ship comrade who had worked as a big band arranger taught Puente the basics of that craft during his tour of duty. During this period, he also met and wed Mirta Sanchez, with whom he had a son before the marriage ended in divorce in 1947.

Back in New York City after the end of World War II, Puente passed on the opportunity to take back up his percussion slot with Machito's band, instead enrolling at the city's prestigious Juilliard School of Music on the GI Bill and playing with various bandleaders, including Curbelo, Pupi Campos, and Fernando Alvarez. By 1949, Puente's skills had sufficiently grown to permit him to form his own act, which made its debut in Atlantic Beach, New Jersey, in July of that year. Originally a nine-piece outfit called the Picadilly Boys, the band soon adopted the moniker of Tito Puente and His Orchestra and added sufficient members to justify that grander name. After Puente and his musicians won a battle of the bands at New York City's Manhattan Center, he gained what would be a lifelong title, the "King of Latin Music" or simply "El Rey." The outfit scored two popular hits in the late 1940s, "Abaniquito" and "Ran Kan Kan."

Shot to Fame in 1950s

During the early 1950s, Puente's fame continued to grow as he released albums on small labels Seeco and Tico. In 1952, he appeared as the only non-Cuban artist at the Cuban government's "50 Years of Cuban Music" celebration in Havana, an indication of his widespread popularity and esteem. After signing to RCA Victor, the artist helped kick start the decade's mambo craze with such recordings as *Cuban Carnival, which* Alex Henderson of *Allmusic Guide,* described as "outstanding from start to finish" and became Puente's first hit for RCA. 1957's *Dance Mania,* however, proved to be his true smash of the decade, selling over half a million copies and spawning two dance hits, "Cuyuco" and "Hong Kong Mambo." As the new genre of Latin jazz became fashionable, the bandleader began incorporating Latin rhythms into traditional jazz arrangements to create his own distinctive sound exhibited on the era's *Puente Goes Jazz.* Perhaps the most innovative of his many recordings of the 1950s, however, was *Puente in Percussion,* one of the first recordings to exclusively highlight drums and other percussion instruments. "We didn't even rehearse," Puente later recalled to Jesse Varela of *Jazz Times.* "We just put a bottle of rum in the center and stared at each other and when the breaks came they just fell in. It was great mental telepathy and the vibrations were right. Everybody was experienced and played at the same level. If we would have had a weak fellow on the session, one shot extra would have ruined it."

As Cuban emigrants flocked to New York City during the early 1960s in the wake of that country's political revolution, Puente began recording and performing with a more diverse group of artists. Among these were famed Cuban singers Celia Cruz and La Lupe, the latter of whom appeared frequently with Puente's band throughout the decade. In 1961, he released *Dance Mania, Volume 2,* a well-received sequel to his 1957 hit. He introduced his Afro-Caribbean-influenced jazz sounds to Japan the following year, but steadily released new albums that explored bossa nova, cha-cha, and even Broadway-style compositions on *My Fair Lady Goes Latin.* The Metropolitan Opera invited him to perform in 1967. The following year, Puente hosted his own program on Spanish-language television, *El Mundo del Tito Puente* (The World of Tito Puente) and served as Grand Marshall of New York City's Puerto Rican Day Parade. He received the key to New York City in 1969, a mark of his great cultural presence and influence within his hometown.

With the dawn of the 1970s, the Latin artist won over a new generation of listeners thanks to guitarist Carlos Santana's highly successful covers of Puente's "Oye Como Va" and "Pa' Los Rumberos." In 1977, the two Hispanic American stars performed together at New York City's Roseland Ballroom. The following year, Puente at last received his first Grammy Award for *Homenaje a Beny More*. To recognize his achievement, Latin music figures gathered to ceremonially roast Puente in a friendly evening of jibing and jokes. Performed before a live audience, this event helped raise funds for Puente to found the Tito Puente Scholarship, which provided funds for young musicians to pursue formal musical studies. By the end of the decade, Puente had also married longtime partner Margie Asencion, with whom he previously had two children.

Won Accolades in Later Years

Recording for the Tropijazz label, Puente continued to release numerous albums during the following decade that highlighted his distinctive combination of jazz and Latin rhythms. In fact, Puente's eclectic blends of sounds have caused him to be categorized under cha-cha, jazz, bossa nova, salsa, and several other genres. Puente, however, had strong feelings about at least one of these designations; in the *Scribner Encyclopedia of American Lives,* Steven Loza quoted Puente as observing that in Spanish, *salsa* means *sauce,* and declaring, "My problem is that we don't play sauce, we play music." Labels aside, the bandleader had a string of successes, picking up his second Grammy in 1983 for *On Broadway,* a feat he repeated in 1985 for *Mambo Diablo*. During the middle of the decade, Puente made his mainstream television debut with cameo roles on popular television program *The Cosby Show*—additionally filming a Coca Cola commercial with star Bill Cosby—and in comedy flick *Armed and Dangerous*. In 1987, he returned to the big screen in the Woody Allen nostalgia piece *Radio Days*. That same year, the National Academy of Recording Arts and Sciences granted him a Eubie Award.

Puente's storied career remained strong during the 1990s, kicking off with the bandleader winning a Grammy for "Lambada Timbales" in 1990 and later in the year receiving a star on the Hollywood Walk of Fame. In 2001, he released a remarkable one hundredth album, *The Mambo King: 100th LP*. The following year, he appeared in and wrote the music for the film *The Mambo Kings,* set in the Latin nightclub circuit of the 1950s that Puente had once dominated. As the decade progressed, the musician played at well over 100 jazz festivals around the world and even gave a high-profile performance at the 1996 Summer Olympic Games in Atlanta, Georgia. A retrospective box set, *50 Years of Swing,* hit the shelves in 1997. That same year, President Bill Clinton presented Puente with the National Medal of the Arts, the highest honor granted to artists by the United States federal government in recognition of what Jane Alexander, Chairperson of the National

Endowment For The Arts, described as "[enlightening] us with their vision...[uplifting] us with their art...and [strengthening] America with their extraordinary contributions to our culture," as quoted by the *Jazz Times*. Soon after, Puente won induction to the International Jazz Hall of Fame. Another Grammy nod for 1999's *Mambo Birdland,* a big band style album that recalled his mid-century high points, rounded out the millennium for the successful artist.

Forgoing retirement, Puente continued to maintain a busy schedule of some 200 to 300 performances each year until practically the moment of his death; he had a show on the books for the very day that he entered New York University Medical Center for open heart surgery. Puente died in New York City at the age of 77 on May 31, 2000, due to complications resulting from that procedure, scant weeks after winning the designation of "Living Legend" from the U.S. Library of Congress. Friends, family, and fans alike gathered to mourn the musician not only for his artistic significance, but for his cultural meaning. "'He was a superstar, but he was part of the [Puerto Rican] community," commented Bob Gotay to Juan Forero of the *New York Times*. "You knew that every time you saw him, that for one more day the culture was safe and in good hands." In fact, Puente's status as an ambassador for Puerto Rican culture was so great that the island territory declared three days of official mourning in his honor. In his hometown of New York City, hundreds attended the artist's two public wakes at Manhattan's Riverside Memorial Chapel before Puente was formally interred on June 6, 2000, at St. Anthony's Church Cemetery in Nanuet, New York. The following year, he won a posthumous Grammy Award for his 2000 recording with Eddie Palmieri, *Masterpiece/Obra Maestra,* a fitting epilogue to a career inarguably filled with many masterpieces.

Books

Contemporary Musicians, Gale, 1995.

Contemporary Hispanic Biography, Gale, 2002.

Dictionary of Hispanic Biography, Gale, 1996.

Jackson, Kenneth T., Karen Markoe, and Arnold Markoe, eds., *The Scribner Encyclopedia of American Lives,* Charles Scribner's Sons, 2004.

Loza, Steven, *Tito Puente and the Making of Latin Music,* University of Illinois Press, 1999.

Periodicals

Jazz Times, May 2000.

New York Times, June 2, 2000; June 3, 2000.

Online

"Puente, Tito," American National Biography Online, http://www.anb.org/articles/ (January 7, 2010).

"Tito Puente," Allmusic Guide, http://www.allmusic.com (January 7, 2010).

"Tito Puente," World Music Central, http://worldmusiccentral.org/artists/artist_page.php?id=970 (January 7, 2010). □

R

Marcantonio Raimondi

Marcantonio Raimondi (c. 1480–c. 1534) was an Italian engraver who created some of the first widely disseminated copies of Renaissance masterpieces from Raphael, Titian, and other Old Masters. These were not original works from him, but rather faithful and highly detailed reproductions of famous religious or allegorical paintings made by copperplate etching. "Thanks to Marcantonio's great technical skill, the suitability of engraving for reproducing designs was decisively demonstrated," wrote Antony Griffiths in *Prints and Printmaking: An Introduction to the History and Techniques,* "and it is the combination of designer, engraver and publisher that dominates the future history of the medium."

Little is known about Raimondi's life. Nearly two decades after his death, art historian Giorgio Vasari profiled him for the 1550 opus *Lives of the Most Excellent Italian Painters, Sculptors, and Architects, from Cimabue to Our Times.* Later scholars have disputed some of Vasari's details, however. Raimondi is believed to have been born around 1480 in Argine, a town midway between Bologna and Piacenza in the Emilia-Romagna region of northern Italy. In his teens, he learned goldsmithing as an apprentice to Francesco Raibolini in Bologna, who was called "Francesco Francia" professionally; similarly, Raimondi would use the name "Marcantonio" as his professional signature.

May Have Mastered Niello

Francia was an artist, but as a goldsmith was skilled in the art of *niello.* These were metal-relief engravings in which details were dramatically highlighted by carving out a background with a sharp tool called a burin, and then filling in that background with black-tinted alloy compound, most often lead. Vasari claimed that Raimondi emerged as a formidable contender to his master's prowess, particularly in the fashioning of niello-style waist buckles for clothing.

The first print that Raimondi produced is thought to be a reproduction of one of Francia's paintings. This was a portrait of a well-known philosopher from Bologna, Giovanni Philoteo Achillini, playing the guitar. The original work by Francia is lost to history. The first dated engraving Raimondi made is from 1505 and titled *Pyramus and Thisbe,* a tale from Roman mythology that later became the basis for William Shakespeare's tragic romance *Romeo and Juliet.*

Printmaking had existed in primitive forms for centuries around the world wherever paper or similar transfer mediums were available. The skilled Italian goldsmiths of Francia's time, however, began to use their sharp tools to create highly detailed images on copper plates. Ink would then be smeared over the plate's surface, then wiped off before the plate was pressed against a sheet of paper. The resulting engraved image was incredibly detailed and, at the time, was unlike anything known to humankind in the era before photographic reproduction. It was also a profitable form of art, too, for hundreds of prints could be stamped out from the same copper plate.

Copied Dürer Series

Raimondi is thought to have lived and worked in Venice roughly between 1506 and 1510. Venice had become the

center of the nascent publishing industry for nearly a quarter-century by then, partly as a result of laws enacted by the powerful city-state that protected the "privilege" of certain named persons or companies. A privilege assigned authorship rights for a specific period of time to publish a certain text or image, and these Venetian statutes were the forerunner of modern-day copyright laws.

In one of his most egregious errors, Vasari asserted that the famous German printmaker, Albrecht Dürer, actually traveled all the way to Venice when he learned Raimondi was copying his best-known works. Dürer was a well-known woodcut artist with a Nuremberg workshop, but he had been influenced by earlier travels through Italy and his printmaking served to introduce some of the early Renaissance techniques to the countries of northern Europe. Vasari claimed that Dürer went to Venice for the purpose of halting the practice, but the German artist was actually living in Italy at the time, including a stint in Venice, between 1505 and 1507. Dürer apparently even visited Bologna in 1506 to study the art of perspective, which Italian Renaissance artists in that city had re-mastered after it was lost for centuries following the end of the classical period of art, and he may have met Raimondi there.

The details of the timeline notwithstanding, Raimondi appears to have made copies of a well-known series by Dürer called *Life of the Virgin,* which even included the German artist's well-known monogram mark of his initials, "AD." Vasari claimed that unsuspecting art buyers purchased the folios, thinking they were the work of Dürer, and that Dürer

traveled to Venice to halt the fraudulent practice by petitioning his case before the Serenissima Signoria, or Senate. The entire incident—twinned with Raimondi's later highly fruitful collaboration with Raphael—was the focus of a 2004 book by art historian Lisa Pon. "It is less clear that Marcantonio was acting as an 'envious thief,' to use the term from Dürer's warning," Pon explained in *Raphael, Dürer, and Marcantonio Raimondi: Copying and the Italian Renaissance Print.* "For these copies were produced in an ambience that did not always understand pictures as an artist's property, as 'works of ours' that could be stolen."

Employed by Raphael

Raimondi is thought to have spent time in Florence before he settled in Rome, probably around 1510. In the Tuscan city he apparently encountered the cartoons, or full-sized drawings, of Michelangelo's planned *Battle of Cascina,* which had been commissioned for the Palazzo Vecchio, or Florentine city hall. The never-completed fresco was to depict a surprise attack on Florentine troops by forces of Pisa in 1364, and showed soldiers bathing nude in a river and surprised by the enemy raid. Only copies made by Raimondi and others from Michelangelo's cartoon, which was destroyed, survived the ages.

In Rome, Raimondi began working closely with the painter and architect known as Raphael, who was born Raffaello Sanzio da Urbino. Raphael was one of the leading artists of the Italian Renaissance and supervised a thriving workshop in the city, which had experienced a dramatic revitalization in recent years both artistically and politically. Raimondi first gained attention with his skilled copy of Raphael's famous *Lucretia* portrait. This was a dramatic image borrowed from a thousand-year-old incident in Roman history, when a noblewoman who endured a sexual assault by the emperor's son committed suicide. Lucretia's death was said to have been the impetus behind the overthrow of the monarchy and the establishment of the Roman Republic in 509 B.C.E.

Over the next decade Raimondi worked closely with Raphael to create engraved images of the esteemed painter's new works. These included 1511's *Parnassus* as well as *Galatea* and *The Judgment of Paris,* both from around 1515. The third work, named after a figure from Greek mythology, would become one of Raimondi's most acclaimed prints. It depicted the warrior Paris confronted by three naked goddesses—Athena, Aphrodite, and Hera—who were competing for his favor. The scene has been a favorite of artists for centuries, but Raimondi's version showed a multitude of peripheral characters from the tale, including a grouping of three off to the right that later inspired nineteenth-century French painter Édouard Manet's most famous work, *Le déjeuner sur l'herbe* (The Luncheon on the Grass).

Appears in *The Expulsion of Heliodorus*

Raphael's thriving workshop included a school where Raimondi trained a younger generation of Renaissance engravers. These included Marco Dente (Marco da Ravenna), Giovanni Jacopo Caraglio, and Agostino de Musi (Agostino

Veneziano). Raphael died in 1520, but by then his fame had spread throughout much of Europe, thanks to the engravings made by Raimondi. Raphael usually gave him a drawing to work with, but Raimondi's engraved plates often produced a result that differed from—but was not judged inferior to— Raphael's finished painting.

Few details are known about Raimondi's private life. The bulk of information comes from the unreliable Vasari or through records of business transactions related to his collaboration with Raphael. The Old Master is believed to have depicted Raimondi in his famous frescoes commissioned by Pope Julius II for the four rooms known as the *Stanze di Raffaello* (Raphael's Rooms) at the Palace of the Vatican. Raimondi is thought to be one of the figures next to the painter, who in *The Expulsion of Heliodorus* carries the pope on a throne. The contemporary Renaissance persona are observing an event chronicled in the Old Testament in which God's wrath is provoked by theft from a temple.

Arrested on Pornography Charge

After Raphael's death there was even less information about Raimondi, save for the fact that he was jailed on pornography charges in 1524 by the reigning pope, who was also the Bishop of Rome. This was the Pope Clement VII, a scion of the powerful Medici clan, who objected to a secret series of 16 erotic engravings of Europe's best-known courtesans and their wealthy lovers. *I Modi* (The Ways) depicted various sexual positions and were based in part on the paintings of one of Raphael's top acolytes, Giulio Romano, for the Duke of Mantua's palace. The print series of *I Modi* is considered the first mass-produced erotic art in Western history, but it brought a swift rebuke from Clement, who ordered that all copies be burned and Raimondi arrested and jailed. Two prominent figures—a Medici cardinal and a painter— interceded on his behalf and the artist was freed, but the plates apparently were not destroyed, for a famous figure from this era, Pietro Aretino, managed to publish a 1527 second edition accompanied by his sonnets.

Aretino—also known as Peter of Arezzo—may have been one of the world's first self-created celebrities. Of humble origins, he was a prolific letter writer to the famous and soon found his way into circles that included philosophers, monarchs, artists, and writers. Aretino lived in Venice and dubbed himself, among other titles, "Secretary of the World." He composed the prefatory letter to the 1527 edition of *I Modi*, and the work is believed to be the first time that erotic images and text were combined for publication.

The artist who interceded to secure Raimondi's release was Baccio Bandinelli, whom Vasari claimed was a jealous rival of Michelangelo. It was Bandinelli, supposedly, who destroyed the original cartoon of *Battle of Cascina*. Bandinelli's *The Martyrdom of St. Lawrence* was the last image that Raimondi was known to have engraved and published.

In 1527 Clement's attempt to influence the European political landscape resulted in a massive debacle known as the Sack of Rome in May of that year. Unpaid and unhappy troops of the Holy Roman Emperor pillaged, looted, and burned parts of the Eternal City, including its richest ecclesiastical treasures. Raimondi was taken prisoner by a Spanish contingent, who demanded a ransom that left him financially ruined. Vasari claimed that Raimondi spent the remaining years of his life in Bologna, where he died around 1534.

Books

DeLisle, Luci, "Raimondi, Marcantonio (c. 1480–c. 1534)," in *Renaissance and Reformation, 1500-1620: A Biographical Dictionary*, edited by Jo Carney, Greenwood Press, 2001, pp. 290–291.

Griffiths, Antony, *Prints and Printmaking: An Introduction to the History and Techniques*, University of California Press, second edition, 1996.

Pon, Lisa, *Raphael, Dürer, and Marcantonio Raimondi: Copying and the Italian Renaissance Print*, Yale University Press, 2004.

Periodicals

New York Times, January 9, 2000; September 23, 2005.
Renaissance Quarterly, Spring 2005.□

S

Meghnad Saha

In 1920 Indian astrophysicist Meghnad N. Saha (1893–1956) published a paper that changed the way scientists the world over studied the stars. A mathematical equation now known as the Saha equation connected the appearance of stars with their chemical composition, making it possible to judge the life stage of a star by visual observation. Throughout his life, Saha made many important contributions, not only to science but also to the society, education system, and government of India.

Meghnad N. Saha did not start out with privilege. Born to a shopkeeper and his wife on October 6, 1893, Saha grew up in the impoverished village of Seoratali in northern India. Raised with four older siblings in a society with a rigid class system, the probability that Saha might receive a full education was low. Neither of his older brothers received an education beyond primary school. The eldest went to work in a jute company and the second left school to help their father with the shop. Perhaps because his two elder brothers began working so early, Saha was able to complete primary school. From the beginning, Saha performed well in school and showed great promise, but even with two brothers working, his family did not have the resources to send him on to middle school. Their village had only a primary school, and the cost to transport and then house him in another town where a middle school existed was too high.

Fortunately for Saha, his eldest brother Jainath intervened. Jainath worked out an arrangement with a doctor, Ananta Kumar Das, in a neighboring town. In exchange for doing household chores and tending the cow, Saha would receive room and board during the week while he attended school there. Saha eagerly accepted this arrangement, and finished middle school at the top of the class for the entire district. His hard work also earned him a scholarship to the Government Collegiate School in Dhaka, where he went in 1905. Saha studied in Dhaka for several years, until political unrest rocked the district. At that time, the British government, which ruled India, decided to split the Bengali region of India, and many students rallied to protest the visit of the British regional governor. Sources differ as to whether Saha actually participated in these demonstrations, but he was suspended and lost his scholarship, reportedly for demonstrating against the government.

Saha quickly won another scholarship to another institution. In 1909 he passed the entrance exams for a private college, Kishori Lal Jubilee School, and began studies there with a full scholarship and a stipend. There, he devoted much of his time to math and history. In 1911 he went on to further his studies at the Presidency College at Kolkata, now known as Calcutta. By 1913 he had earned his bachelor of science degree in mathematics, and he completed a master's degree in applied mathematics two years later. He was ready now to put his knowledge to work outside of school.

From Student to Teacher

On earning his degrees, Saha had hoped to serve in civil administration. He took the exam to join the Financial Civil Service, but his application was denied on the grounds that he had close ties to revolutionaries who were a threat to British rule. During his time at the Presidency College, Saha had formed a friendship with a known revolutionary, Bagha Jatin. Though Saha was a friend to Jatin, no evidence suggests that he participated in the revolutionary movement. With the doors of government closed to him, he was forced to pursue other professional opportunities.

With two degrees in mathematics, Saha returned to the university environment, where he began lecturing at the University College of Science in Calcutta in 1916. The university had limited resources, and Saha was compelled to lecture in fields to which he had not previously devoted great time, so he found himself learning new forms of science and conducting new research as well. Two of the subjects he taught (and learned)—thermodynamics and spectroscopy—would lead to his groundbreaking contributions to the scientific field.

Thermodynamics is the study of heat, specifically variations in heat or temperature relative to certain forces. Spectroscopy is the study of visible light, which stretches across a spectrum of observable light waves, or colors. He applied both of these fields to the study of stars, which led to the thesis that earned him a doctorate in science from the University of Calcutta in 1919, as well as to world renown for the publication of his paper and equation in 1920. Saha's thesis put forth an equation that made the connection between visible observations of distant stars and their life stages. By applying principles of spectroscopy and thermodynamics, of light and heat, Saha recognized the differences in the spectrum (range of colors) of light emitted by stars, their temperature, and their chemical composition, which could be used to determine the place of a star along its life cycle. This revolutionized the field of stellar astrophysics. Titled "Origin of Lines in Stellar Spectra," Saha's thesis also earned him the esteemed Griffith Memorial Prize from Calcutta University that same year.

That same year, Saha also published another major title; he and his colleague, S.N. Bose, wrote the first published English translation of Albert Einstein's famous papers on the theory of relativity. This book was titled *The Principles of Relativity.* During his time at the University of Calcutta, Saha published numerous other articles on a variety of scientific topics. These articles appeared in *Philosophical Magazine, Journal of the Asiatic Society,* and *Astrophysical Journal.*

Saha used the monies from the Griffith Prize and from the Premchand Roychand Scholarship, which he won in 1919, to continue his studies and research in Europe. He spent the next two years living and working in London, England, and in Berlin, Germany. In London he conducted research at Alfred Fowler's Laboratory, and in Berlin he studied at Walther Nernst's Laboratory. On completing his research there, he returned to the University of Calcutta, this time as the chair, or head, of the school's new department of physics. However, limited resources compelled him to make another move in two years. Despite criticism from many of his fellows at Calcutta, Saha moved to the University of Allahabad in 1923. There, he also headed the department of physics, where he would stay for many years. At Allahabad, Saha was able to obtain the funding he needed to continue his research and to pursue other goals.

Beyond Classroom and Laboratory

Saha believed not only in the study and application of science for purely scientific purposes but also in the relationship of science to other aspects of life, including its role in civil society, environmental management, and economics.

He wanted to expand scientific education throughout India, and to raise the status of Indian educators and scientists in the world. He felt that science and scientific education was critical to the progress of India and the Indian people. At Allahabad more than anywhere else, Saha was able to begin doing this.

During his time at Allahabad, Saha formed the United Province Academy of Sciences, and co-authored and published three important textbooks: *Treatise on Heat, Junior Textbook on Heat,* and *Treatise on Modern Physics.* He went on to found the Indian Physical Society in Calcutta in 1933, and to spur the foundation of the National Institute of Sciences of India, which in 1935 became the Indian National Academy of Sciences. That same year, Saha formed the Indian Science News Association to expand public access to scientific information. The association published a journal, *Science and Culture,* for which Saha himself wrote more than 200 articles and served as editor until his death two decades later. The journal has continued to serve as an important vehicle for scientific discussion in India and in the world today. His work also earned him a nomination for the Nobel Prize in Physics that year.

In 1938, already having accomplished so much, Saha left Allahabad and went back to Calcutta. He had maintained close ties with the city and the university despite his place in Allahabad. On his return, he again became head of the department of physics and continued to teach, conduct research, and publish. His studies and interests had constantly been expanding over the course of his career, and his attention now focused on nuclear physics and quantum mechanics, two fields of keen interest to the global scientific community in the 1940s and beyond. Saha published papers on both topics in 1940.

During his tenure at the University of Calcutta, Saha continued institution-building activities. He helped form three new departments—radio physics, electronics, and applied physics. In 1950 he established the Institute of Nuclear Physics. He also participated in the Indian Association for the Cultivation of Science, first as honorary secretary in 1944 and then as president of the organization from 1946 to 1950. During the 1940s, Saha also saw progress on another front of concern to him, that of environmental management. Since his early studies in Dhaka, Saha had been concerned with river flooding and control in India. Significant flooding in 1923 had led him to do relief work, and his experiences had left him determined to find scientific remedies to combat the regular flooding. He regularly wrote and spoke about the topic, and increasingly urged private institutions and the government to study the problem. In 1943 the government responded by forming the Damodar Valley Enquiry Committee to research the severity of the flooding. Five years later, the government responded to the committee's findings by establishing the Damodar Valley Corporation (DVC), modeled after the Tennessee Valley Authority of the United States. The organization worked to provide river flood control as well as irrigation systems, dams, and other water resource management solutions.

From 1945-50 Saha was president of the Indian Association for the Cultivation of Science, and he left the university in 1952 to become the Association 's full-time director of laboratories. He would remain in that post for the rest of his life, working to renovate and build new laboratories and expand scientific learning and the association's outreach. Earlier, in the 1940s, Saha had participated in the Conference of Scientific Workers in Britain, which culminated in the formation of the World Federation of Scientific Workers (disbanded in 1994). The group sought to apply science to modern life for the benefit of the common welfare, and Saha carried these principles back to India with him. In the final years of his life, Saha was increasingly involved in public service.

Final Acts of Service

Saha ran for the Indian Parliament as an Independent candidate for North-West Calcutta in 1952 and won. India had won independence from Britain in 1944, and now Saha was part of that government, where he had wanted to be so many years before. That same year he chaired the Calendar Reform Committee, tasked with reconciling the many Indian calendars which derived from a variety of religions and traditions. Before as author and teacher, now as a legislator, Saha pushed for greater economic and environmental planning. He successfully persuaded the president of the Indian National Congress to establish a National Planning Committee to steer the Indian economy toward industrialization, which he believed would elevate Indian society. He also pushed for the use of nuclear energy as an alternative power source, and first introduced the matter to Parliament in 1954. As a member of Parliament, Saha continued his work with the DVC and prepared the organization's first plan of action, which called for the construction of a series of river dams.

Saha continued to serve in Parliament until 1956. On February 16 of that year, he suffered a massive heart attack and died on his way to a meeting. Today, many of the institutions that Saha founded or helped to put in place have continued to function, including the journal *Science and Culture* and the DVC. His scientific achievements have driven the field of astrophysics for decades and have helped further studies in the fields of physics and mathematics. Perhaps most significantly, Saha helped bring home the importance of scientific education, research, and progress to the people and government of his home, India.

In an article on the Vigyan Prasar Science Portal web site, Dr. Subodh Mahanti quoted D.S. Kothari from a 1970 article in *Biographical Memoirs of Fellows of the National Institute of Sciences of India, Vol. 2,* who said, "Outwardly, [Saha] sometimes gave an impression of being remote, matter of fact, and even harsh, but once the outer shell was broken, one invariably found in him a person of extreme warmth, deep humanity, sympathy and understanding; and though almost altogether unmindful of his own personal comforts, he was extremely solicitous in the case of others. . . . He was a man of undaunted spirit, resolute determination, untiring energy and dedication."

Saha spent much of his life applying not only his great knowledge but also his spirit, determination, and energy to the expansion of scientific understanding and the betterment of humanity.

Books

Arnold, David, *Science, Technology and Medicine in Colonial India,* Cambridge University Press, 2000.
Bowman, John S., *Columbia Chronologies of Asian History and Culture,* Columbia University Press, 2000.

Periodicals

Current Science, vol. 64, no. 7, April 10, 1993.
Publications of the Astronomical Society of the Pacific, vol. 68, no. 402, 1956.

Online

"About Us," Dr. Meghnad Saha College, http://www.drmsc.net/page2.htm (December 14, 2009).
"Meghnad N. Saha," *Encyclopedia Britannica,* http://www.britannica.com/EBchecked/topic/516342/Meghnad-N-Saha (December 14, 2009).
"Meghnad N. Saha: A Pioneer in Astrophysics," Vigyan Prasar Science Portal, http://www.vigyanprasar.gov.in/scientists/saha/sahanew.htm (December 14, 2009).
"Meghnad Saha Memorial Lecture," Digital Library of India, http://www.new.dli.ernet.in/rawdataupload/upload/insa/INSA_1/20005ac6_111.pdf (November 10, 2009).
"Meghnad Saha—Scientist," BBC: h2g2, http://www.bbc.co.uk/dna/h2g2/A24055607 (December 14, 209).
"Saha equation," *Encyclopedia Britannica,* http://www.britannica.com/EBchecked/topic/591438/Saha-equation (December 14, 2009).□

St. Scholastica

St. Scholastica (c. 480–547) belongs to the Roman Catholic pantheon of saints and is best remembered as the twin sister of the Italian monk Benedict, founder of the Benedictine order. Her brother established his famous monastery near Monte Cassino, Italy, around 529, and Scholastica founded her own convent for religious women nearby. Both houses adhered to what later became known as the Rule of Benedict, a set of guidelines for men and women living in monastic communities that profoundly influenced religious life in Europe for the next millennium.

"Very little is known of St. Scholastica," noted Peter Lechner in the book *The Life and Times of St. Benedict: Patriarch of the Monks of the West.* "It is said that she and her nuns lived a very austere life—*valde austera*—and that they were full of the sweet odour of sanctity." Nearly all of the extant information about Benedict and Scholastica comes from the writings of Pope Gregory I, also known as Gregory the Great, who left an extensive collection of writings behind when he died in 604. One of the works was *Dialogues,* which recounted various miracles attributed to holy men and women of the Christian church and featured a biography of Benedict. This was written around 593, more than 40 years after Benedict's death, but Gregory probably learned about Benedict from monks who had known him personally. The English historian Bede, who died in 735, wrote extensively about this era of the Church and corroborated some of Gregory's details about the lives of these siblings.

Came from Aristocratic Origins

The twins were probably born around 480 in Nursia, later called Norcia, a town in Italy's modern-day province of Perugia in the region of Umbria. "Scholastica" was not her given name; it is a Latin term for "she who has leisure to devote to study." Gregory called their family among the "liberiori genere," or "of good birth." Their father was Anicius Eutropius, whose name links the family to an old Roman aristocratic family, the Anicii, who produced a long line of emperors, military leaders, and other illustrious figures. Their mother was Claudia Abundantia, an only child from a well-to-do Norcian family who inherited her family's fortune but died either in childbirth or shortly after the twins' birth. The Church of St. Benedict, according to Norcian legend, is said to have been erected atop the site of the former family home where Benedict and Scholastica were born.

Scholastica and her brother arrived during a turbulent period of Italian history. The peninsula had been overrun by a pagan Germanic tribe called the Heruli, who may have wandered down from their original home in Denmark over several centuries. In 476, a Heruli general named Odoacer led troops into Rome and proclaimed himself *rex Italiae,* or king of Italy, and deposed the Roman emperor. Odoacer became the first non-Italian to rule on the peninsula in the newly declared Kingdom of the Ostrogoths. The parents of Scholastica and Benedict had likely been forced to cede a third of their property and assets to the Heruli, as was the custom in the conquered Roman states.

Brother Sent to Rome

Gregory reported that Benedict was sent to Rome for his education and brought his caregiver-nurse with him, both of which were customary for wealthy families. Historians believe this occurred around the year 500. By then, the city had had lost much of the majestic splendor it once offered as capital of the world's largest empire. Rome was still the seat of the Christian church, but this, too, had fallen into disarray. At the time of Benedict's arrival, there were two popes vying for title of head of the church, Symmacus and the antipope Lawrence. Even the city itself erupted into warfare for nearly three years over the dispute. Benedict fled this chaos with his nurse to live in the mountains at a town widely believed to be present-day Affile.

The practice of living apart from society was not a new one, nor was it exclusive to Christianity. Aside from a small community of monks in the area, most were *anchoritic,* or living solo in prayer and contemplation. A few communities of *cenobites,* or groups of monks under the guidance of an abbot, were formed. St. Pachomius, an Egyptian monk who died in 348, is considered the founder of cenobitic monasticism. There were some of these communities in Italy by the time of Benedict and Scholastica's time.

After Affile, Benedict went to a cave in nearby Subiaco, remaining there in isolation for three years. A nearby community of monks—probably one at Vicovaro—lost their leader, and asked Benedict to become their abbot. He agreed, but the community fell into discord, and he was the victim of an attempted poisoning. He fled, and settled at the lakefront site of former Emperor Nero's summer home in Subiaco. Other monks came to join him.

Both Settled at Monte Cassino

Benedict and the monks were harassed by Subiaco residents, and he withdrew to Monte Cassino, a mountain hideaway midway between Rome and Naples, around 529. It was there he drew upon an existing text, called the *Regula magistri,* or Rule of the Master, to formulate guidelines for Christian religious communities. This evolved into the Rule of St. Benedict, which scholars have noted was also based on the writings of St. Basil, John Cassian, and Augustine of Hippo.

Scholastica was said to have pleaded with her father to be allowed to join her brother in his religious vocation, and he agreed. Benedict helped his sister establish her own community of devout women about five miles from Monte Cassino. This was called St. Mary's of Plombariola, and it followed the same rules as his community, rules that eventually spread to twelve other monasteries in the area. According to the Rule, the abbess was to be elected by the community and would enjoy absolute authority, but she in turn was responsible for the salvation of the souls under her care. The Rule set forth guidelines for those who could join the community, and the process by which one was allowed to leave it. It forbid private ownership of property, and indicated that the two plain meals a day were to be conducted in silence except for a designated reader from a holy text, and prescribed silence after the final religious service in the evening, which was called the Compline.

Devotion Incited Thunder

The only story that survives about Scholastica is Gregory's recounting of the circumstances preceding her death. Because members of the opposite sex were forbidden to enter either religious community, once a year she and Benedict met at a house where they prayed together and discussed spiritual and monastic matters. In 547, they met in early February, but after their evening meal, she said, "I pray you, brother, remain with me this night and let us continue till morning to speak of the joys of heaven," according to Lechner. One of the Rules prohibited monks from spending the night outside the monastery, and he said no. At that, she began weeping, and praying. "Hitherto the sky had been so clear that no cloud was to be seen; but scarcely had she raised her head from her hands than a terrific clap of thunder rent the air, accompanied by such torrents of rain that it was absolutely impossible for any one to venture out," according to Lechner's account.

At that, Benedict railed at Scholastica, "God forgive you, sister, what have you done?" To which she replied, "I asked you and you would not hear me; I asked my Lord and He has deigned to grant my petition; now, therefore, if you can depart, in God's name return to your monastery and leave me here alone." Benedict was forced to remain at the hut, and they waited until morning for the storm to pass. Three days later, Benedict had a vision of his sister's spirit ascending to heaven in which she had been transformed into a white dove, and learned soon thereafter that she had indeed died.

With that the story of Scholastica ends. Benedict is believed to have died several weeks later. During the Lombard invasion of the Italian peninsula in the 560s, Scholastica's convent house at Plombariola was sacked, along with that of Monte Cassino. Benedict's monks had already disseminated the principles of his Rule elsewhere, and new Benedictine houses began to flourish throughout Western Europe over the next century. The monasteries established schools and *scriptoria* where manuscripts were laboriously copied by hand. Outside of the borders of learned Islamic Spain, these were the sole educational institutions in many parts of Europe for the next five centuries. Notable Benedictine missionaries included St. Boniface, known as the apostle to the Germans, and St. Wilfrid, the early English bishop.

A Lombard king known as Ratchis, who held the title of Duke of Friuli in the 740s, entered the ruins at Monte Cassino to take up the monastic life after a failed war with a neighboring duchy. His wife, Tasia, and daughter, Ratrudis, allegedly rebuilt Plombariola and lived in isolation there as women religious.

Scholastica's feast day is February 10, the date of her death in 547. Nine hundred years later, she was painted by Italian Renaissance artist Andrea Mantegna in the fabled San Luca Altarpiece. She is commonly portrayed as holding a crozier, or staff, and crucifix; in other images a dove flies out of her mouth. St. Scholastica is the patron saint of nuns and convulsive children.

Books

Lechner, Peter, *The Life and Times of St. Benedict: Patriarch of the Monks of the West,* Burns and Oates Ltd., 1900.

Rippinger, J., "Benedict, St.," in *New Catholic Encyclopedia,* volume 2, second edition, Gale, 2003, pp. 236–238. □

Jane Johnston Schoolcraft

Jane Johnston Schoolcraft (1800–1842), also known by her Ojibwe name of Bamewawagezhikaquay, was the first Native American known to write poetry, and the first to write literary texts of any kind. She wrote in both English and the Ojibwe language.

Schoolcraft was also the first to write down Native American tales, as opposed to transcribing oral versions of them, and some of her writings formed a source for the Henry Wadsworth Longfellow classic *The Song of Hiawatha.* Schoolcraft's literary production was sizable, and her life illustrates important traits of the métis or mixed-race culture that flourished across much of the American frontier until the widespread destruction of Native American cultures later in the nineteenth century. Yet her work and her remarkable story, which went essentially unpublished, were largely forgotten until the end of the twentieth century. Her writings were held in libraries, among the papers of her famous husband, explorer and government official Henry Rowe Schoolcraft, and in other places. But until recently, readers have generally thought of European and Native American cultures as separate, not mixed, and few scholars thought to look for writings by a literate Native American woman—it did not occur to them that such a person, who quoted Shakespeare and wrote in the most current forms of English poetry, yet remained vitally engaged with her Ojibwe roots, would have existed.

Born into Biracial Family

Schoolcraft was born in 1800, in what is now Sault Ste. Marie, Michigan, into a biracial family that had prospered on both sides from the fur trade in the region. Her father, John Johnston, was a trader from northern Ireland, of Scots-Irish Protestant background, who came to North America in 1790 and traveled up the Great Lakes system by canoe. When he met Ozhaguscodaywayquay, the daughter of a powerful Ojibwe leader, he was smitten and asked the Ojibwe chief, Waubojeeg, for her hand in marriage. Waubojeeg told Johnston to return to Montreal, but that if he came back to the Lake Superior region the following spring he would agree to the marriage. Johnston made the trip of over a thousand miles each way, by canoe, and despite initial reluctance on Ozhaguscodaywayquay's part, the couple prospered and built a large house in the strategically important Sault area, where Lake Superior narrows to the St. Mary's River. Part of the home still stands today. Jane Johnston was the third of eight children, all of whom were apparently given both English and Ojibwe names.

Jane's Ojibwe name, Bamewawagezhikaquay, meant Woman of the Sound the Stars Make Rushing Through the Sky. Marriages between white men and Native American women, although later outlawed, were not uncommon at the time, and Jane's upbringing was not unusual for the time in its mixture of cultures, except in that she was English on her father's side, while most of the European traders in the area were still French. Where Jane's childhood stood out from the norm was in the emphasis her father placed on education. He taught Jane to read, assigning her the classics of Shakespeare, Milton, and the writers of ancient Rome in translation, and, although she was already suffering health problems that plagued her for most of her life, took her on a trip to England and Ireland.

Although her writing was long mentioned in connection with Henry Schoolcraft's literary production, if it was mentioned at all, she began writing poetry some years before she met him. Perhaps one of her earliest poems, written in Ojibwe, referred to seeing pine trees on her return from the British Isles, an event that occurred in 1810. She was able to draw on Johnston's unusually large collection of books as she pursued her education. "I was surprised," noted a traveler quoted by Schoolcraft biographer and editor Robert Dale Parker, "at the value and extent of this gentleman's library: a thousand well-bound and well-selected volumes, French and English, evidently in much use, in winter especially."

From her mother, a highly regarded figure in her own right in both the Ojibwe and European communities, she absorbed Ojibwe lore, but she was raised with the idea that she would marry a successful European as her mother had done.

Married Henry Rowe Schoolcraft

When Henry Rowe Schoolcraft came to Sault Ste. Marie, as a so-called Indian Agent of the U.S. government, Jane Johnston must have seemed an ideal match. She was well-educated, and visitors often commented on her refinement. And she was ideally suited to help him realize his own interests, which extended beyond administration. The first European to see the headwaters of the Mississippi River, Henry Schoolcraft had become interested in the Native American cultures of the upper Midwest. Probably he understood what was going to happen to the tribes he visited, and he wanted to record details of their cultures and lifestyles. He was, in many ways, an early anthropologist. Henry Rowe Schoolcraft and Jane Johnston married in 1823 and moved into a newly built wing of the Johnston family home.

At the beginning, the couple's marriage was as happy as that of Jane's parents had been. They traveled to New York, where Jane's accomplishments impressed the prominent figures they met there. She wrote love notes to her husband, who was learning Ojibwe, using a mixture of Shakespearean and Ojibwe imagery, and the couple helped themselves and their friends pass the long Upper Peninsula winters by circulating, over several issues in 1826 and 1827, their own magazine, handwritten and copied, that they called *The Literary Voyager*. Surviving copies of these, which were first collated and published in 1962, form one major source for Jane Johnston Schoolcraft's writings, which number some 50 surviving poems plus several dozen stories modeled on traditional Ojibwe tales, as well as transcriptions of stories told directly to her and her husband.

The materials written by Jane Johnston Schoolcraft in *The Literary Voyager* were compelling, both in terms of their skill and in the way she negotiated European and Native American cultures. Schoolcraft adopted two different pen names in the magazine, Rosa and Leelinau. The pieces written under the name of Rosa were poems, many of them about nature. They were astonishingly adept in their emulations of European forms and rhyme schemes. The Leelinau pieces, on the other hand, had Native American subject matter. Henry Rowe Schoolcraft later used the name Leelinau, re-spelled Leelanau, as one of the fanciful Native American names he devised for counties in the new state of Michigan in the late 1830s.

Yet it would be too simple to say that Rosa represented Schoolcraft's purely European side and Leelinau her Ojibwe side. Michigan scholar and poet Margaret Noori, an Ojibwe speaker, has identified the presence of Ojibwe motifs in some of Schoolcraft's nature poetry, arguing, for example, that the couplet "Come, sisters, come! The shower's past / The garden walks are drying fast" refers to a set of four sisters in Ojibwe stories whose essence is connected with the passage of time. Likewise, by transferring Ojibwe stories to the written medium, Schoolcraft was aiding her husband in his endeavors. Henry Rowe Schoolcraft's attitude toward his wife's writing has been a matter of debate among observers. He never forbade her to write, and it is largely through his efforts that we know about her writings at all. Yet, especially in the Ojibwe stories, he felt free to make changes to her work.

Wrote Serious Poems in Ojibwe Language

The Schoolcrafts had four children. The first, William, died in early childhood, and a second child was stillborn. Two others, Jane (born in 1827) and John (born in 1829), survived. After Henry Schoolcraft experienced a religious conversion on a trip to Detroit in 1830, the upbringing of the couple's children began to cause cracks to show in their marriage. Jane was an active Christian, and she was in favor of the family's move to the Straits of Mackinac area in the early 1830s so that the children could attend a Presbyterian school. But Henry Schoolcraft grew less respectful of his wife's background, writing in a letter (quoted by Jeremy Mumford in the *Michigan Historical Review*) that she had grown up "without a mother in many things." Jane's poems were mostly written in English, but some from this period are in Ojibwe and have a personal and darker tone. In one she defends her father's legacy, and in one 1839 poem she laments the removal of her children to a government-run boarding school.

Schoolcraft's last years were not happy. She suffered from a variety of ailments, probably including what would today be called depression. In 1835 she was given laudanum, a derivative of opium, to combat a case of whooping cough, as was common practice at the time. The family's fortunes worsened as Henry Schoolcraft lost much of their savings in the collapse of a Michigan real estate bubble in 1837, and his government post was lost as well when the Whig Party administration of William Henry Harrison and then John Tyler took over the presidency in 1841. More broadly, she saw that the relatively harmonious relationship between Native and white Americans that had prevailed over two centuries of the fur trade was coming to an end. Schoolcraft died suddenly on a visit to a relative in Dundas in what is now Ontario, Canada, on May 22, 1842.

Even after the publication of *The Literary Voyager* in 1962, students of literature were slow to rediscover Schoolcraft. Her family on the Johnston side was the subject of books and even an opera, but studies of her writing mostly appeared in small Midwestern journals, and even though the Leelinau stories were known to have been consulted by Longfellow, only a few of Schoolcraft's works were published in anthologies. In the 1990s and 2000s, interest in her works increased, and Parker's *The Sound the Stars Make Rushing Through the Sky* (2007) combined a biography with an annotated presentation of her complete known writings.

Books

Bremer, Richard, *Indian Agent and Wilderness Scholar: The Life of Henry Rowe Schoolcraft,* Clarke Historical Library (Mount Pleasant, MI), 1987.

The Sound the Stars Make Rushing Through the Sky: The Writings of Jane Johnston Schoolcraft, edited by Robert Dale Parker, University of Pennsylvania Press, 2007.

Periodicals

Michigan Historical Review, March 22, 1999.

Online

"Bicultural Before There Was a Word for It," *Wellesley Centers for Women,* http://www.wcwonline.org/content/view/1670/38/ (January 18, 2010).

"Introduction to Jane Johnston Schoolcraft," *University of Illinois Urbana-Champaign,* https://www.netfiles.uiuc.edu/rparker1/www/JJS/ (January 18, 2010).

"Jane Johnston Schoolcraft," *Michigan Women's Hall of Fame,* http://www.hall.michiganwomenshalloffame.org (January 18, 2010).□

Thelma Schoonmaker

American film editor Thelma Schoonmaker (born 1940) has long served as the invisible hand guiding the finished product of renowned director Martin Scorsese's vision. Working with Scorcese on all of his movies since the production of acclaimed boxing biopic *Raging Bull* (1980), the editor has developed a creative partnership with the director considered one of the strongest in the industry. Following the death of her husband, British filmmaker Michael Powell, in 1990, Schoonmaker also dedicated part of her energies to promoting his work through film festivals and public events. Schoonmaker's skills have earned her six nomination and three wins at the Academy Awards for Best Film Editing—one trophy for *Raging Bull* in 1980, a second for *The Aviator* in 2004, and a third for *The Departed* in 2006—along with several other award nominations.

S choonmaker was born on January 3, 1940, in the North African capital of Algiers, Algeria, to American parents who had lived abroad for many years due to her father's work for the Standard Oil Company. After growing up largely on the Caribbean island of Aruba, the teenaged Schoonmaker came to the United States as a resident rather than a visitor for the first time in the mid-1950s. Recalling her culture shock upon her family's move to New Jersey to Jonathan Marlow of GreenCine, Schoonmaker explained, "I was just stunned when I came to America. I didn't know anything about rock music or football, and I felt very out of it... America was like a foreign country to me at first." Not until two years later when the future film editor enrolled at Ithaca, New York's Cornell University to study political science and Russian did she begin to feel at ease among her peers. Initially, Schoonmaker planned to parlay her international background into a career with the United States diplomatic service after she graduated in 1961, but her application ultimately did not succeed due at least in part to her outspokenness about her political views.

Edited First Films for Television and Theaters

Back in New York City, Schoonmaker worked for a time with the Peace Corps and enrolled in a graduate course in primitive art at New York City's Columbia University. When she fatefully saw an advertisement for a film editing position in the *New York Times* in 1962, however, Schoonmaker inadvertently set herself on the path to her lifelong career in the movies. Although at the time the young student had no experience in the film industry, she landed the job at Astor Films and began assisting a man who edited foreign pictures for the late night television market. While the position carried few creative opportunities, it did provide Schoonmaker with some of the basic technical skills used for film editing, such as negative cutting and subtitling, and incited her to enroll in a summer filmmaking course at the city's New York University. There, she met fellow film student Martin Scorsese when, in an unusually premonitory move, an instructor asked the barely experienced film editor to help the budding director correct some botched frames from his short film *What's A Nice Girl Like You Doing in a Place Like This?* (1963). She went on to help Scorsese complete the film. "If that hadn't happened, if someone hadn't cut the negative wrong, who knows what would've happened to me?" Schoonmaker later wondered to Marlow, admitting that if not for this chance meeting with Scorsese she may have left the film industry altogether.

The partnership proved an immediate creative success, however. Schoonmaker joined Scorsese as the editor on his feature debut, 1967's *Who's That Knocking at My Door?* (originally known as *I Call First*), and later assisted Scorsese with the editorial work on a series of New York University student films called *Street Scenes* (1970). While the director turned to other projects and eventually left for Hollywood, Schoonmaker built her craft by working as editor on the 1970 film *Woodstock*. A documentary depicting the famed musical festival held at Woodstock, New York, during the summer of 1969, *Woodstock* gave Schoonmaker her first taste of weaving together a coherent motion picture from masses of unscripted footage. Although others—including Scorsese—assisted with the concert film's editing, Schoonmaker received the lion's share of the credit as the supervising editor, picking up her first Academy Award nomination for Best Film Editing. More documentaries followed, including several about the American Revolution for Pittsburgh television and a short film on a Paul McCartney world tour.

Formed Long-Running Partnership with Scorsese

By the end of the decade, Scorsese showed that he had not forgotten his first editor, however, despite a decade-long interval since their last collaboration. During the 1970s, film union regulations prevented Schoonmaker, who had not completed the requisite Hollywood apprenticeships to become a union member and did not wish to step backwards in her career to do so, from working with her former classmate Scorsese on his movies despite his repeated requests for her services. Soon before the director began production on *Raging Bull*, however, he somehow won Schoonmaker admission to the union, although the editor claimed not to know how the feat was accomplished some 20 years later. Entrance into the union allowed the editor to join Scorsese on the project, and she did so, commencing work on what would become the first of a long string of partnerships with the director. *Raging Bull* displayed many of Schoonmaker's signature editing techniques, including quick cuts, montages, and other sharply modern visual devices. Bolstered by the intensity of Schoonmaker's editing, the film became a massive critical success, garnering a second Academy Award nomination and first win for Best Editing for Schoonmaker, as well as earning her nods from the British Academy of Film and Television Arts (BAFTA) and the American Cinema Editors guild.

Scorsese introduced the editor to British director Michael Powell—best known for his 1955 ballet film *The Red Shoes*—at about the time that the two were working on *Raging Bull*. Despite an age difference of some thirty years, Schoonmaker and Powell developed a lasting romantic bond, formalizing their relationship with a wedding on May 17, 1984. They remained married until the 84-year-old Powell passed away in 1990 following a battle with prostate cancer. His widow soon began working to share his film legacy with a broader audience. She appeared at film festivals and public screenings from the 1990s onward in an effort to bring Powell's at times controversial, but widely considered classic, movies to new audiences. In spite of this outreach, "I'm afraid most people still don't know who Michael Powell is," she sighed to Marlow in 2006.

With her union card and Academy Award under her belt, Schoonmaker entered the 1980s by Scorsese's side,

cutting his first feature of the decade, 1983's *The King of Comedy*. Although the movie generated much less notice than had *Raging Bull*, its opening sequence featured an early appearance of one of the editor's characteristic techniques, the freeze frame. Next up were two Scorsese films: the lighthearted *After Hours* (1985) and the sequel to 1961 classic *The Hustler, The Color of Money*, (1986) featuring Paul Newman and Tom Cruise. Reaching deep into history, Schoonmaker and Scorsese brought a controversial adaptation of Nikos Kazantzaki's novel *The Last Temptation of Christ* to the screen in 1988. In questioning the traditional interpretation of the Biblical story of Jesus Christ's life and death, the film angered many fundamentalist religious groups but earned strong critical notices. Back in the twentieth century for *Goodfellas* (1990), the film version of the story of real-life mobster and informant Henry Hill, Schoonmaker found herself reaching back to her documentary editing experiences to weave together often improvised exchanges between the film's stars. Widely acknowledged as one of Scorsese's finest efforts, *Goodfellas* swept the Academy Award nominations—including a nod to Schoonmaker—but won only the trophy for Best Supporting Actor.

During the 1990s, Schoonmaker explored different cinematic styles alongside Scorsese. For thriller *Cape Fear* (1991), Schoonmaker employed hectic imagery and quick jump cuts to heighten suspense and lend additional visual meaning. In sharp contrast was Scorsese's 1993 adaptation of classic Edith Wharton novel *The Age of Innocence*, a social commentary set largely in nineteenth-century New York City, which found the editor forsaking some of her more postmodern techniques in favor of dissolves and irises, a visual highlighting style dating from the early days of cinema. She traveled with Scorsese back to the world of organized crime with 1995's *Casino* before cutting her first movie with another director in two decades, the 1996 Allison Anders-helmed and Scorsese-executive produced *Grace of My Heart*. Dalai Lama biopic *Kundun* (1997) and Nicolas Cage vehicle *Bringing Out the Dead* (1999) followed, the latter reuniting editor and director with *Raging Bull* scriptwriter Paul Schrader.

Won Two Oscars During the 2000s

As Scorsese enjoyed a creative renaissance in the new millennium, Schoonmaker also reached new professional heights. Again joining the director on his 2002 historical epic *Gangs of New York*, Schoonmaker combined her well-worn documentary editing skills to manage large battle scenes with her postmodern interpretative lens to create a film "very fractured and abstract," as she characterized Scorsese's vision to Daniel Restuccio of *Post*. These deft editing touches earned her a fourth Academy Award nomination and a second Eddie from the American Cinema Editors guild. The Academy did grant Schoonmaker her second trophy for her work on Scorsese's next film, Howard Hughes biopic *The Aviator* (2004). The following year, the editor herself became the subject of a documentary when she was profiled in *Edge Codes.com: The Art of Motion Picture Editing*, a feature exploring the world of film editing.

Schoonmaker and Scorsese returned in 2006 with *The Departed*, starring frequent Scorsese collaborator

Leonardo DiCaprio alongside Matt Damon and Jack Nicholson. A multi-layered story of organized crime, Irish-American identity, and institutional corruption in a gritty modern Boston, *The Departed* was a great success with both moviegoers and critics. The film also brought a new personal triumph for Schoonmaker's longtime professional partner when Scorsese at last picked up an Oscar for Best Director on his sixth nominated effort. "It's really wonderful that Marty won at long last. We were praying for that. . . . It would have been pretty devastating if he hadn't won. I don't think I could have taken it, frankly," the editor—who had picked up her own third Academy Award for Best Editing for her work on the film—told the *Independent on Sunday* soon after the ceremony.

Despite coming into the field in a somewhat haphazard manner, Schoonmaker has made great personal achievements and found much personal satisfaction in her work. "Getting a film right is sometimes like a woman trying to fit into a tight dress. You edit it down to where it begins to have just the right shape and starts to shimmer. It's just an incredibly creative, wonderful job," she explained to Lisa Hirsch of *Daily Variety* in 2004. Her film technique has set her apart from her peers as a unique storytelling voice. As Schoonmaker's entry in *Women Filmmakers & Their Films* argued, "perhaps more than any other contemporary Hollywood editor, her distinct editorial signature positions her as an auteur. Working exclusively with Scorsese certainly supports this claim and demonstrates not only that editing must be viewed as an art but how film can function as a collaborative act of creativity." Indeed, that Schoonmaker's contributions to Scorsese's body of work have informed those pictures' style and form is widely acknowledged, with the film community long granting her recognition and respect for her efforts. With Schoonmaker attached to edit the director's projects into the 2010s, this fruitful partnership seems set to assure her continued creative challenges and rewards in the years to come.

Books

Women Filmmakers & Their Films, St. James Press, 1998.

Periodicals

Daily Variety, November 16, 2004; August 22, 2005.
Independent on Sunday, March 25, 2007.
Post, April 2003; March 2007.
Videography, December 1, 2004.

Online

"Thelma Schoonmaker," Internet Movie Database, http://www.imdb.com/name/nm0774817/ (January 5, 2010).
"Thelma Schoonmaker: A Personal Journey with Scorsese and Powell," GreenCine, http://www.greencine.com/ (January 5, 2010).
"Thelma Schoonmaker Biography," InBaseline, http://www.inbaseline.com/ (January 5, 2010).
"Thelma Schoonmaker, Martin Scorsese's Favorite Editor," *NPR,* http://www.npr.org/ (January 5, 2010).□

John Thomas Scopes

In 1925, American high school teacher John T. Scopes (1900–1970) gained notoriety as the defendant in the infamous Scopes Monkey Trial. The trial challenged the legitimacy of the Butler Act, which prohibited teaching evolution in Tennessee schools. The case drew national attention and was seen across the nation as a challenge against fundamentalist Christianity.

John Thomas Scopes was born in Paducah, Kentucky, on August 3, 1900, to railroad worker Thomas Scopes and homemaker Mary Alva Brown. The last of five children, he was the only boy born to his parents. The family spent the first 13 years of Scopes's life in Paducah before moving to Danville, Illinois, for his father's job. Living in Danville, with a population 30,000, broadened Scopes's perspective in regard to contemporary issues such as racial integration. In 1915 the family moved again, this time to Salem, Illinois, hometown of William Jennings Bryan. As Salem's favorite son, Bryan was a successful trial lawyer, had been secretary of state under Woodrow Wilson and was a three-time candidate for president of the United States. Growing up, Scopes often listened to Bryan's impassioned speeches at the town's annual homecoming.

Scopes remained in Salem until he graduated from high school in 1919. That fall he enrolled in college at the University of Illinois at Urbana. The next year he transferred to the University of Kentucky after a serious bout with bronchitis. While there, his illness returned so severely he was forced to drop out. When he returned in the fall of 1921, he was determined to make the most of his time in school, and began taking courses in every subject in which he held even the mildest of interest. He chose his classes based on the professors' teaching, preferring those who were the most personable and ignoring the requirements for obtaining an actual degree. When he became a senior he realized that his haphazard course selection had left him without a major. He decided to focus on obtaining a law degree simply because he had the most credits in that subject. He also managed to obtain minors in child psychology, education and geology.

The Making of a Law

In the spring of 1924, Scopes applied for teacher placement with the intention of saving enough money to attend law school. That fall he took a teaching position at Rhea County Central High School in Dayton, Tennessee, teaching algebra, chemistry, and physics. Scopes entered the teaching profession at a time of intense controversy, when an ongoing debate raged between the country's Christian Fundamentalists and the Modernists as to whether the science of evolution had a place in a public education curriculum. The heart of this battle was being waged in Kentucky. In his memoir, *Center of the Storm,* Scopes recalled Bryan's argument before the Kentucky legislature: "They have barred the Bible from schools—now all I ask is to have this heresy, this anti-Bible teaching, thrown out, too." Soon after, bills were introduced in the Kentucky House of Representatives and Senate that

would have banned the teaching of any and all theories of evolution in relation to humans. Opposition to these bills was swift. Professors from the University of Kentucky, many of whom Scopes had taken classes from, lobbied against passing them. Both bills were narrowly defeated.

Despite the loss in Kentucky, the Fundamentalists did not give up. Thus, just three short years later, the Tennessee legislature was considering its own anti-evolution bill. It was called the Butler Act, named after John Washington Butler, the state representative who wrote it. With virtually no organized opposition, the House of Representatives passed it almost unanimously. Bryan made a hasty trip to Nashville to ensure a similar outcome in the state senate. He was successful, with only six out of 30 senators voting against it. According to L. Sprague de Camp, in his book *The Great Monkey Trial,* the law stated: "That it shall be unlawful for any teacher in any of the Universities, Normals and all other public schools of the State which are supported in whole or in part by the public school funds of the State, to teach any theory that denies the story of the Divine Creation of man as taught in the Bible, and to teach instead that man has descended from a lower order of animals." In his autobiography, Scopes noted then-Tennessee Governor Austin Peay's statement when he signed the bill into law on March 21, 1925: "Probably the law will never be applied. It may not be sufficiently definite to permit of any specific application or enforcement. Nobody believes that it is going to be an active statute." It would take less than four months for him to be proven wrong.

Despite wholeheartedly supporting academic freedom, Scopes gave little thought to the Butler Act when it was passed. He was not a biology teacher and therefore had no cause to teach evolution to his students. According to Doug Linder, in an article on John Scopes published on the web site *Famous Trials in American History,* Scopes finished his first year of teaching without incident and made plans to return to Paducah for the summer. However, he delayed his trip home by a few days in order to attend a church supper in Dayton. His reason for staying was not as much religious as an opportunity to ask out an attractive blonde who would also be attending the event.

During that week, Scopes spent his time leisurely enjoying the warm weather. One day he was summoned to the local drug store by a local businessman, and when he arrived found a group of Dayton's leading citizens engaged in a debate over whether one could teach biology without teaching evolution. A copy of the state approved biology text book, which included a chapter on evolution, was open on the counter. Prominent Dayton businessman George Rappelyea asked whether Scopes had ever taught from the text book, and Scopes admitted that he had used the text once when substituting for the high school's regular biology teacher during an illness.

Upon this admission, the businessmen showed Scopes a recent newspaper advertisement in which the American Civil Liberties Union (ACLU) offered to fund any legitimate test case of the constitutionality of the Butler Act. According to Scopes's autobiography, when asked if was willing to serve as a defendant in such a case, he replied, "If you can prove that I've taught evolution, and that I can qualify as a defendant, then I'll be willing to stand trial." He explained later in the autobiography, "To tell the truth, I wasn't sure I had taught evolution." This detail did not concern the gathered businessmen, who saw the trial as an opportunity to garner publicity, and thus revenue, for their small town.

Soon after Scopes agreed to stand trial, Bryan was named special prosecutor for the case. In response to that announcement, Scopes's lawyer, John Randolph Neal, an accomplished constitutional attorney from Tennessee, was contacted by Clarence Darrow and Dudley Field Malone. Darrow was the most well- known defense attorney of the time, having worked a variety of intensely publicized cases, while Malone was also considered a major player in the courtroom. Both were added to the defense team despite the initial opposition of the ACLU which, according to Scopes biographer Linder, felt the sensationalism detracted from the issue at hand. It was Scopes himself who pushed to include them, arguing that Bryan's notoriety had already created a circus-like atmosphere around the trial.

Trial of the Century

Jury selection for The State of Tennessee vs. John T. Scopes began on July 10, 1925, and the media descended on Dayton. In hindsight, the first several days of the trial were of little consequence despite the uproar their events caused at the time. There was no question that Scopes was guilty, only whether the law itself was constitutional. The prosecution called only four witnesses. On July 20, having so far been unable to prove the validity of teaching evolution, the defense turned to disproving the validity of the Bible. Toward that end, they took the unprecedented step of calling Bryan, lawyer for the prosecution and Christian Fundamentalist, to the stand. The *New York Times* reported, "At last it has happened. After days of ineffective argument and legal quibbling...William Jennings Bryan, Fundamentalist, and Clarence Darrow, agnostic and pleader of unpopular causes, locked horns today under the most remarkable circumstances ever known to American court procedure....Mr. Bryan was put on the stand by the defense to prove that the Bible need not be taken literally."

According to most scholars, Darrow was the winner of day, questioning Bryan on multiple stories told in the Bible and asking if they should be taken literally. In an article on Darrow also published on the "Famous Trials" web site, Linder wrote, "The press reported the confrontation between Bryan and Darrow as a defeat for Bryan.... The problem, on close examination of the transcript, lay not so much with his own poor mind—Bryan was no blithering idiot—but with a faith that defied logic. It left him trapped, like 'a dumb animal.'"

Darrow cut the trial unexpectedly short the following day when, knowing the case would go to appeal regardless of the decision, he requested the jury find Scopes guilty. By doing so he denied Bryan the opportunity to make a closing argument. The 12 men of the jury complied, and issued a guilty verdict after deliberating less than nine minutes. Two years later, the appeals court ruled that the Scopes Trial was unjust because the judge and not the jury had determined the $100 fine. Thus, no decision was made regarding the constitutionality of the Butler Act.

Scopes never returned to teaching after the trial, although for the rest of his life he maintained that it was the job of the teacher, not the courts, to decide what to teach in a classroom. He went on to pursue a master's degree in geology at the University of Chicago, and worked for Gulf Oil Company and later United Gas Corporation. In 1930 he married Mildred Walker, and fathered two children. He died in 1970 of natural causes.

Books

DeCamp, L. Sprague, *The Great Monkey Trial,* Doubleday & Company, Inc., 1968.

Dictionary of American Biography, Supplement 8: 1966-1970, edited by Donald R. McCoy, American Council of Learned Societies, 1988

Ginger, Ray, *Six Days or Forever?,* Signet, 1958.

Ipsen, I.C., *Eye of the Whirlwind,* Addison-Wesley, 1973.

Scopes, John T., and James Presley, *Center of the Storm,* Holt, Reinhart and Winston, 1967.

Periodicals

Chattanooga News, July 20, 1925.
New York Times, July 21, 1925.

Online

"John Scopes," *Famous Trials in American History,* http://www.law.umkc.edu/faculty/projects/ftrials/scopes.htm (December 7, 2009).

"Clarence Darrow (1857-1938)," *Famous Trials in American History,* http://www.law.umkc.edu/faculty/projects/ftrials/scopes/darrowcl.htm (December 7, 2009).□

W. G. Sebald

The German author W.G. Sebald (1944–2001) combined serious themes of war and cultural decline with virtuoso literary experimentation in a series of novels that gained an international readership at the end of the twentieth century.

Sebald gained recognition for two separate but related literary accomplishments. He devoted much of his writing to recovering German memories of the devastation wrought by World War II, maintaining that Germans had repressed their own memories of what the war had led to. And he employed unusual narrative techniques to do so. Sebald's four major fictional works were often categorized as novels, but he himself rejected the label. They combined elements of the traditional novel with autobiography, travel narrative, oral history, journalistic research, and even photography. "I must admit a suspicion of most novels, in which the narrator claims omniscience but tells us nothing of who he is or where he's from," Sebald told Susan Salter Reynolds of the *Los Angeles Times.* "Why should we believe him?"

Isolated from War at First

Winfried Georg Sebald (ZAY-bahlt) was born in the small town of Wertach im Allgäu, in the German state of Bavaria, on May 18, 1944. He published his writings as W.G. Sebald, and some of them also involve a character by that name. In the English-speaking world, however, tired of being addressed with the similar but feminine name of Winifred, he used the first name Max. Sebald was too young to experience the carpet bombing of German cities of which he later wrote. His home town, high in the Bavarian Alps, was remote, largely cut off from the outside world by snow for several months of the year. As a child he was fascinated by photography and would sneak away from class to hide in the school darkroom to watch photographs as they appeared from their chemical bath. Some of his earliest memories were of the total destruction of the landscape around him. He told Reynolds that "wherever I went as a small child in Germany, there was usually rubble. In some small towns, 80 to 90 percent of the buildings were destroyed and took a long time to be built up again."

Contributing to Sebald's sense of dislocation, which would be lifelong, was his father's absence during his early childhood. A member of the German army, his father was taken prisoner by Allied forces and did not return home for several years. Sebald identified more closely with a grandfather who died when he was 12. For college, he left Germany, never to return as a permanent resident. He received his undergraduate degree from the University of Fribourg,

Switzerland, majoring in German literature. Sebald then moved to England in 1966 to take a job at Manchester University as a foreign languages lecturer. The following year he married his wife, Ute, who was from Austria, and the pair raised a daughter, Anna.

At Manchester Sebald completed a master's degree, writing a thesis on German expressionist playwright Carl Sternheim. He landed a teaching job at the newly built University of East Anglia and in 1970 decided to settle in Britain permanently. For some years he lived quietly in England with his family, lecturing and writing articles about Austrian literature. In 1987 Sebald was made Professor of European Languages at the university, but, perhaps because of the budget cutbacks that began to affect the British university system in the 1980s, he found that he needed extra money and began contributing articles to a local newspaper. Some of them were about Holocaust survivors.

Took to Writing Immediately

Sebald had never given any thought to becoming a writer, but he found unexpectedly that the act of writing connected him with deeper issues in his life. Aside from several collections of academic articles, his first book was *Nach der Natur* (From Nature), a long prose poem published in 1988. It contained recollections of Sebald's early life, including one in which he asked his school religion teacher why God would have allowed bombs to destroy, not a nearby army barracks or Hitler Youth headquarters, but instead a parish church and hospital chapel, with massive

civilian loss of life. At that time, writings about wartime in economically booming West Germany were still by no means common.

In 1990 Sebald published his first full-scale fictional work, *Schwindel, Gefühle* (Dizziness, Feelings), which was translated into English by Michael Hulse as *Vertigo* in 1999. Sebald, who spoke fluent English but wrote all his books in German, assisted with the translation. The book featured a narrator, also named W. G. Sebald, who resembled the author in some respects. The book's unusual storytelling style entailed frequent references to other wandering authors and their books, and Sebald also included complete or cut-up photos in the running text—not a completely unprecedented technique, but very unusual in the context of Sebald's heavily detailed descriptions of places and ideas. The book's final image depicts the towers of a city collapsing in flames.

Sebald returned to wartime themes in his 1993 book *Die Ausgewanderten* (The Emigrants), which appeared in English in 1996. The book dealt with the lives of four Germans who fled the Holocaust, and it again mixed fiction, nonfiction, and photographic images. That book and its 1995 successor, *Die Ringe des Saturns* (The Rings of Saturn), inaugurated a period in which Sebald won major European literary prizes such as the Berlin Literature Prize. *The Rings of Saturn,* a deep meditation on historical decay disguised as a traveler's account of a walk across parts of southern England, attracted further critical attention for its author's ability to weave together reflections and research on a large and varied group of historical, geographical, and economic subjects. *The Rings of Saturn* dwelt on subjects as diverse as casualties among the British air corps that bombed Germany during World War II, the Taiping Rebellion in nineteenth-century China, problems in European silkworm cultivation and herring fisheries, and the melancholy life of poet Edward FitzGerald.

Mentioned as Nobel Candidate

By the time *Austerlitz* appeared in 2001, Reynolds could write that Sebald's novels ''challenge traditional forms of fiction and nonfiction. Particular and profound all at once, they are very much about detail, very much about history and very much in vogue.'' *Austerlitz* mingled the story of a Czech Jewish child sent to England to evade the Holocaust with dense descriptions of British scenes. The cumulative effect of Sebald's books was a complex depiction of vast historical forces tending inevitably toward chaos, decay, and violence. By the time *Austerlitz* appeared, Sebald's books had been translated into 16 languages in 19 countries, and he was often being mentioned as a candidate for the Nobel Prize in Literature.

On December 14, 2001, Sebald lost control of his car near Norwich, England, where he lived, and ran into an oncoming truck. No cause for the accident was established; in *Austerlitz,* which had just appeared, the protagonist expressed fears that he would die of a heart attack. Sebald was killed, and his daughter, Anna, was severely injured. Early in 2002, Sebald was posthumously given the National Book Award for *Austerlitz*. Praise and tributes among English-speaking readers came from both sides of the Atlantic Ocean; Sebald's admirers in Britain included novelists Anita Brookner and A.S. Byatt, and among his American champions were novelist Jonathan Franzen and the influential critic Susan Sontag.

Sebald's reputation was extended by *On the Natural History of Destruction*, a book that appeared after his death. It was not a novel but a set of lectures Sebald gave in Zurich, Switzerland, in 1997. Driven by the belief that events not brought fully to light may be reenacted, Sebald described in detail the so-called carpet bombing of German cities by Allied planes, most notoriously the Gomorrah raid on Hamburg in the early morning of July 27, 1943, leveling nearly the entire city and killing tens of thousands of people. Sebald's tone was precise as he described a woman in shock who carried the mummified remains of her child in a suitcase through the burning city. Sebald "is a profoundly—and excitingly— unsettling writer," wrote Hamish Hamilton in the London *Independent.* "Believing that human history is a record of ever-intensifying disasters, he impersonates the coolly objective Messenger in classical tragedy, driven to tell you what no one wants to hear."

Sebald enjoyed nearly universal critical acclaim. The essentially serious nature of his books was leavened by his tendency to embark on diversions involving what Peter Heinegg of *Cross Currents* called his "vivid, loving use of his Nabokovian-Borgesian encyclopedic lore (is there anything, one wonders, that he doesn't know?)." Heinegg and others also pointed out that Sebald's books, while they featured different characters and settings, were similar in structure and tone: "Despite his vast frame of reference, his staggering vocabulary, his polyglot virtuosity," wrote Heinegg, "Sebald can't avoid a certain obsessive sameness, a fact he implicitly acknowledges with his metaphor of the rings of Saturn." Still, toward the end of his life, Sebald received a tribute different from all the positive reviews he could read in newspapers: he and his writing were subjected to parody by the popular British magazine *Private Eye.* It was an indication of how far his dark and difficult writing had penetrated into the literary world.

Books

Long, J.J., *W.G. Sebald: Image, Archive, Modernity,* Columbia University Press, 2008.

Long, J.J., and Anne Whitehead, *W.G. Sebald: A Critical Companion,* Edinburgh University Press, 2006.

Periodicals

Albany Times Union (Albany, NY), March 12, 2002.

Cross Currents, Spring 2002.

Daily Telegraph (London, England), December 17, 2001.

Independent (London, England), December 17, 2001. February 22, 2003.

Observer (London, England), February 23, 2003.

Online

"W(infried) G(eorg) Sebald," *Contemporary Authors Online,* Gale, 2010. http://www.galenet.galegroup.com/servlet/BioRC (January 25, 2010).

"A Writer Who Challenges Traditional Storytelling Style," *Los Angeles Times* (October 24, 2001), http://www.articles.latimes.com/2001/oct/24/news/cl-60893 (January 25, 2010). □

Mary Ann Shadd Cary

American and Canadian journalist, teacher, lawyer and abolitionist Mary Ann Shadd Cary (1823–1893) was the first black woman in North America to found and edit a weekly newspaper. She left the United States for Canada in the 1850s and published the *Provincial Freeman,* which encouraged fugitive American slaves to move to Canada and encouraged their efforts to build new lives there. After the American Civil War, Shadd Cary returned to the United States to teach and became one of the nation's first black female lawyers.

S hadd Cary was born Mary Ann Camburton Shadd in Wilmington, Delaware, on October 9, 1823, to Abraham Shadd, a shoemaker, and his wife, Harriet Shadd. The family moved to West Chester, Pennsylvania in 1833, where the Shadds enrolled their daughter in schools taught by Quakers, a religious group who were early believers in social activism and racial equality. Abraham Shadd was active in the movements for abolishing slavery and educating free blacks. In the early 1830s, he argued against the idea that blacks should move from the United States to Liberia in Africa, but he entertained the idea that they might move to Canada to gain equality. Abraham Shadd convinced his daughter, from an early age, to use her education to benefit African-Americans less fortunate than her. Starting in 1839, she spent 12 years teaching at schools for black students in Delaware, New Jersey, Pennsylvania, and New York.

Became a Social Activist

In her mid-20s, Shadd Cary emerged as a sharp social critic. In 1849, she wrote a letter to the *North Star,* a newspaper published by leading abolitionist Frederick Douglass. In addition to then-common arguments that free blacks should pursue education and buy and operate farms, Shadd Cary argued provocatively that many black clergy were not working to uplift the race. She criticized ministers who told their congregations that justice would come in the afterlife, instead of encouraging them to become more assertive in the present. She felt such ministers were motivated by money, because less educated congregations would be more dependent on them. "The influence of a corrupt clergy among us . . . sap[s] our every means, inculcating ignorance as a duty, superstition as true religion," she argued (as quoted by Kathy L. Glass in the book *Courting Communities*).

Emigrated to Canada

Shadd Cary's political conscience led her to leave the United States as its racial laws worsened. In 1850, the U.S. Congress passed the Fugitive Slave Act, which legally required black

Became First Black Female Publisher

In the *Provincial Freeman,* Shadd Cary argued bluntly that black Americans should leave the United States for Canada. "Cease to uphold the United States government, if it will, and while it does uphold human slavery," she argued in an 1856 editorial (quoted by Rhodes in *Mary Ann Shadd Cary*). She suggested blacks should pay attention to the nation's actions, not its ideals: "Cease to grapple after the shadow while you disregard the substance."

Shadd Cary argued that free blacks should strive for self-sufficiency by owning property and farming it or learning a trade. Though her own writing did not take on gender issues, she often printed articles by women journalists who argued for a woman's right to a prominent place in business and public affairs. One front-page article argued that girls, like boys, should receive educations that prepared them to run businesses and participate in trades and manual labor.

In 1855, Shadd Cary traveled to the Colored National Convention in Philadelphia to argue for emigration to Canada. Odds were against her argument winning a good reception, since most of the delegates were against emigration. Further, she was the only Canadian delegate and one of only two women. Her speech on the convention floor, however, captivated the audience.

"The House was crowded and breathless in its attention to her masterly exposition of our present condition, and the advantages Canada opens to colored men of enterprise," wrote newspaper correspondent William J. Watkins, a Brooklyn abolitionist (as quoted by Rhodes in *Mary Ann Shadd Cary*). Watkins did not agree with Shadd Cary about moving to Canada, but admired her oratory. "Miss Shadd's eyes are small and penetrating, and fairly flash when she is speaking," Watkins wrote. "Her ideas seem to flow so fast that she, at times, hesitates for words; yet she overcomes any apparent imperfection in her speaking by the earnestness of her manner, and the quality of her thoughts."

Broke with Early Mentors

By 1856, Frederick Douglass himself praised Shadd Cary's work in his newspaper. "We do not know her equal among the colored ladies of the United States," he wrote (as quoted by Rhodes in *Mary Ann Shadd Cary*). Douglass praised her "unceasing industry," her "unconquerable zeal and commendable ability," but he felt compelled to add a criticism. "The tone of her paper has been at times harsh and complaining," he wrote.

Though Shadd Cary often argued for unity among blacks, she was frequently critical of establishment black institutions. Before starting the newspaper, she had already broken with two of her early Canadian mentors, Henry and Mary Bibb, over an ideological disagreement. While the Bibbs' organization, the Refugee Home Society, tended to build all-black institutions that gave preference to former slaves, Shadd Cary felt black immigrants to Canada should integrate into Canadian society. The disagreement turned into a long feud.

"Shadd Cary was neither a saint nor a heroine in any romantic sense," Rhodes noted in *Mary Ann Shadd Cary*. "She could be headstrong, cantankerous, and abrasive. . . .

slaves who escaped from southern states to be returned to their owners and created penalties for anyone who did not cooperate. That meant that fugitive slaves were not safe from recapture unless they moved to Canada.

The following year, Shadd Cary attended the Great North American Anti-Slavery Convention in Toronto. The convention's mostly Canadian delegates argued that African-Americans should move to Canada, where slavery was abolished. Shadd Cary, then 28 years old, found their argument convincing. "I have been here more than a week, and I like Canada," she wrote in a letter to her younger brother, Isaac (quoted by Jane Rhodes in her biography, *Mary Ann Shadd Cary: The Black Press and Protest in the Nineteenth Century*). "[I] do not feel prejudice." Shadd Cary encouraged her brother to join her.

Shadd Cary was convinced enough, in fact, that she moved to Windsor, Ontario, where she opened a school for black exiles and former slaves. In 1853, she co-founded the *Provincial Freeman,* a newspaper for blacks in Canada and the United States. Though it often struggled financially, it was published for seven years, making it one of the longest-lasting abolitionist newspapers in the years before the Civil War. Before long, most of her family followed her to southwest Ontario. Her father, Abraham Shadd, bought a farm in Raleigh Township, near Chatham, Ontario. He later became the first black person to hold elected office in Canada, winning election to the town council in 1859.

She was motivated by both altruism and self-aggrandizement, by political philosophy and a quick temper. She enjoyed the sports of debate and repartee, and rarely hesitated to strike back at rivals and enemies. These qualities, while often admired in a man, were scorned in a woman.''

Shadd Cary married Thomas F. Cary, a barber from Toronto, in 1856. Their first child, Sarah, was born in 1857. Shadd Cary also raised her three stepchildren from her husband's previous marriage. The couple's relationship was unconventional, even by today's standards: She lived and worked in Windsor and Chatham, Ontario, while her husband worked in Toronto and visited her and their children when he could. Thomas Cary died on November 29, 1860 at age 35, while his wife was pregnant with their second child. Their son, Linton, was born the next year.

Returned to America

Widowed, Shadd Cary lived mostly on aid from family members who lived near her in Ontario and on income from the Chatham Mission School. Shadd Cary managed the school with her sister-in-law, Amelia Freeman Shadd; it mostly educated the children of fugitive slaves. Shadd Cary became a Canadian citizen in 1862, but the American Civil War soon drew her back to the country she had left.

After Abraham Lincoln's Emancipation Proclamation in early 1863, black abolitionists decided that black men could win respect and equality for their race by joining the Union Army. Abolitionist Martin Delaney, hired by the state of Connecticut to recruit black troops, invited Shadd Cary to join him as an army recruiter. Her persuasive speaking skills and contacts among American abolitionists made her well-qualified for the job. Shadd Cary traveled the United States, probably to Pennsylvania and several Midwestern states, signing up blacks as soldiers.

After the Union won the Civil War in 1865, Shadd Cary returned to Ontario, but she found the black enclave she had helped found disintegrating. While the war had liberated American blacks, racial prejudice was worsening in Canada, so many blacks left to return to their old homes and reunite with relatives. After she and her sister-in-law closed the Mission School for lack of funds, Shadd Cary decided that political conditions in the United States had improved enough for her to return.

Shadd Cary moved across the border to Detroit in 1867, where she worked as a public school teacher, then to Washington, D.C. in 1869. At the Colored National Labor Union meeting in Washington that year, she chaired the Committee on Female Suffrage and successfully pushed the group to oppose discrimination against working women. Hired as a teacher in Washington's public school system for black students, she was soon named principal of a night school for adults, then of a grammar school. She spent the summers of 1871 and 1872 as a traveling subscription agent for Douglass' latest newspaper, the *New National Era.*

Was a Groundbreaking Law Student

In September 1869, Shadd Cary enrolled in the first law school class at Howard University, the new, biracial school in Washington, D.C. That made her the first African-American woman ever admitted to a law school and one of the first female American law students of any race. She worked as a principal by day and studied law by night, while also raising her children. She was not part of Howard's first law school graduating class in 1871, however. The school may have denied her a diploma because of widespread opposition to women practicing law, or her financial hardships may have kept her from finishing. Meanwhile, she joined the movement for women's suffrage, attempting unsuccessfully to register to vote in Washington in 1871 and writing about a meeting of the National Women's Suffrage Association for the *New National Era* in 1874.

During the 1870s and 1880s, Shadd Cary gave regular lectures on racial uplift, women's rights, and temperance. Like many former abolitionists, she argued that forgoing alcohol was a major ingredient in black self-sufficiency and self-improvement. In 1883, at age 60, she finally received her law degree. By the mid-1880s, she had retired from teaching to practice law and continue lecturing. She could not make a living as an attorney, though, probably because the white legal establishment discriminated severely against black attorneys and because few blacks could afford lawyers.

In the 1880s, Shadd Cary often lived with her son, who worked as a federal government employee, and her daughter, Sarah a teacher and dressmaker. Shadd Cary died on June 5, 1893, at age 70, of stomach cancer. Her funeral was held at one of Washington's oldest black churches, Israel Metropolitan A.M.E. Church. She is buried in Harmony Cemetery in Washington D.C.

Books

Glass, Kathy L., *Courting Communities: Black Female Nationalism and "Syncre-Nationalism" in the Nineteenth-Century North*, Taylor &Francis Group, 2006, p. 57-75.
Rhodes, Jane, *Mary Ann Shadd Cary: The Black Press and Protest in the Nineteenth Century*, Indiana University Press, 1998.□

Shaw Brothers

The cinema executive brothers Runme (1901–1985) and Run Run (born 1907) Shaw were central figures in the development of Hong Kong's internationally successful film industry.

The marriage of film and martial arts came to seem commonplace in the late twentieth century, but it was the Shaw Brothers who pioneered it. They were successful in marketing that film genre internationally, but they had begun to think in big terms well before they ventured into kung fu films. The Shaw Brothers empire, which originated partly in Singapore and partly in Shanghai before its period of growth in Hong Kong, was adept at bringing its films to the linguistically and culturally diverse Chinese communities all over Southeast Asia. Their entertainment empire came to include amusement parks and other real estate as well as huge chains of movie theaters, and at the peak of the brothers' influence it was estimated that 1.5 million people saw a Shaw Brothers film every week. Many of the film-makers who made Hong Kong cinema popular in the West in the last decades of the twentieth century, including action-film director John Woo, got started in the industry as part of the Shaw Brothers empire.

Traced Family to Ming Dynasty

Runme (born in 1901 in Zhejian Province, China) and Run Run (born on October 14, 1907, in Shanghai) Shaw were born into an old family in eastern China that could trace its lineage 14 generations back to the early Ming Dynasty in the 1300s. Their father, Yuh Hsuen Shaw, worked his way up from the floor of a fabric dye factory to part ownership of a prosperous textile firm and import-export business of his own. He donated generously to public works (an example his sons would follow), and he invested in a Chinese opera house, the Laughter Theatre, in Shanghai. Yuh Hsuen Shaw hoped that his sons would follow him into the family business and tried to discourage them from going into the entertainment world. Run Run Shaw worked for his father as a sales manager for a time, but an older brother, Runje, whose education included the works of Chinese classical literature, soon showed talent as a playwright and director. Yuh Hsuen Shaw hired him at the opera house as director and chief playwright.

Runje Shaw saw that the world of entertainment was changing, and established a silent film studio called Unique Film Production Company. He was joined by Runme in this business, and Run Run, still attending school at the Young Men's Association, was impressed by the crowds that came to see such Unique productions as *The Man from Shensi*. In 1923 Runme and Run Run traveled to Singapore to market the firm's films to theaters serving the large Chinese population there. They decided to stay on in Singapore, which at the time was part of the British colony of Malaya, and they founded a new company, the Shaw Organization. At first they had little success, for movie theater syndicates controlled by members of the various Chinese ethnic groups in Singapore—Hokkien, Cantonese, and others—refused to show the Shaws' films.

The Shaw brothers realized that they could combat this cartel with a vertically integrated business structure, and in 1927 they opened their own theater, the Empire, in Singapore's Tanjong Pajar neighborhood, taking over a venue that had previously shown American silent films. The Empire was a spartan affair where patrons had the choice of benches or wooden chairs for seating, and were asked to bring cushions if they wanted them. A cloth hung from the ceiling served as a screen. But the theater soon drew crowds, and the brothers could count on a variety of strong products coming from the Unique studio, which by 1925 was releasing a film a month, and before long they received films from other Chinese film-makers who wanted in on the action.

Reputedly Hid Wealth During War

Plowing their profits back into the business and often working until 3 a.m. at the Shaw offices at 116 Robinson Road, the brothers expanded their distribution empire to include other theaters in Singapore and around what was then British Malaya—present-day Malaysia. By the mid-1930s they had taken over several nearby buildings and had a staff of 30, with all operations from film shipping to administration handled on site. By 1939 they controlled 139 movie houses in Singapore and Malaya. Before the outbreak of World War II the brothers also invested in a trio of Singapore amusement parks. After the Japanese expelled the British from Malaya, they arrested Runme Shaw and forced the brothers to show Japanese propaganda films at their theaters. Reportedly the brothers had seen the invasion coming and had converted their already considerable holdings to cash, gold, and jewelry, which they buried in a backyard garden at their home.

After the war's end, the brothers resumed where they had left off, and the region boomed. They rebuilt their theater chains, and their amusement park holdings grew to nine. Runme Shaw remained in Singapore for the rest of his life and became one of the city-state's leading citizens, serving on numerous charitable boards and in 1958 establishing the Shaw Foundation, which donated millions of dollars to charitable causes. He was given many awards in later life, not only in Singapore but also abroad; these included induction into the French Legion of Honor and, by Pope Paul VI, into the Order of the Holy Sepulchre. He and his wife, Peggy, had two sons and four daughters. Runme Shaw died in Singapore on March 2, 1985, after spending two and a half years in a coma following a fall.

The second phase of the Shaw family's career began when Sir Run Run Shaw (having been knighted by Queen Elizabeth) moved from Singapore to Hong Kong in 1957. He founded a new studio, Shaw Brothers (Hong Kong) Ltd., and in 1961 opened a state-of-the art new production complex, Clearwater Bay. It rested on 850,000 square feet of land—an impressive accomplishment in land-poor Hong Kong—and boasted a staff of 1,500. In the mid-1960s the Shaw Brothers studio reached a production schedule in which a new film was begun every nine days. Films were subtitled in Chinese characters—which are similar in all dialects of Chinese—and in English, so that Chinese audiences anywhere could enjoy them. International distribution was assured through the use of a team of dubbing specialists who worked on one of the complex's 12 sound stages and readied versions of a film in other Asian languages for release simultaneously with the original.

Beginning with *The Kingdom and the Beauty* (1958), the Shaw Brothers studio enjoyed a series of blockbuster hits. They drew on the major genres of Chinese-language films at the time—historical dramas, gangster sagas, ghost stories, adaptations of Chinese opera, and, increasingly often, action films, for which the studio was willing to import top directorial talent from Japan or South Korea if that meant a probable hit. *The One Armed Swordsman* (1967) became the first Hong Kong film to earn one million Hong Kong dollars at the box office. That film was directed by Chang Cheh, who delivered a series of hits for the Shaw Brothers in the late 1960s.

Pioneered Martial Arts Film

A 1970 Chang Cheh film, *Vengeance,* marked a new direction for the studio: preceding Chinese-American actor Bruce Lee's films by one to two years, it is often considered the first true kung fu film. Chang Cheh's martial arts heroes, grouped as "The Five Venoms," gained an international cult following. Among the Shaw Brothers films that were most successful in the United States was *The Five Fingers of Death* (1977), whose original title was *King Boxer*. Martial arts choreographer Lau Kar Leung gave the Shaw Brothers films their classic style in the 1970s, and eventually emerged as a leading director himself. Another Shaw Brothers staffer during this period was John Woo, who later extended Chang Cheh's often ultra-violent style in such cinephile cult favorites as *The Killer* and went on to a successful directorial career in Hollywood. The influences of the classic Shaw Brothers style in American director Quentin Tarantino's *Kill Bill* are so numerous that the film may be considered an homage.

The Shaw studio's fortunes finally began to decline in the late 1970s and 1980s when a martial arts star of a new breed, the superbly talented but also affably comic Jackie Chan, signed with the rival Golden Harvest studio. A new arthouse-oriented group of young directors, known as the Hong Kong New Wave, resisted the Shaw Brothers assembly-line approach, and the growth of an independent film industry in the People's Republic of China also helped break the studio's dominance. Shaw Brothers production slowed, and the studio began to devote most of its energy to its new television station, TVB. The studio never stopped making films altogether, and in 1995 it launched the career of director Stephen Chow, whose films parodied many of the studio's own earlier releases.

Run Run Shaw remained at the helm of the studio's operations and became enormously wealthy. In 1990 he endowed a new Institute of Chinese Studies at England's Oxford University with a gift of ten million pounds, and he invested in real estate around the world, including, at one point, the Macy's department store chain in the United States. A Run Run Shaw Theatre opened in London, with programming not restricted to China-related material, and many places in Hong Kong also bore the Shaw name. Run Run Shaw, with second wife Mona Fong as a trusted deputy, remained at the helm of Shaw Brothers through the Asian financial crisis and the transfer of Hong Kong from Britain to China in 1999, and presided over a major reissue of the studio's classic material in 2003. For his chauffeured ride to work he could choose from among a fleet of Rolls-Royce automobiles. As of January 1, 2010, at the age of 101, he had resigned his position as executive chairman at Shaw Brothers but remained a member of the executive committee of the company's board of directors.

Books

Contemporary Theatre, Film, and Television, volume 8, Gale, 1990.
Glaessner, Verina, *Kung Fu: Cinema of Vengeance,* Bounty, 1974.

Periodicals

Guardian (London, England), March 8, 1990.
Variety, July 21, 2003; December 16, 2008.
Xinhua News Agency, October 16, 2009.
WWD, December 21, 1990.

Online

"About Shaw," *Shaw Online* (Singapore), http://www.shaw.sg (January 24, 2010).

"Runme Shaw," *Singapore Infopedia,* http://www.infopedia.nl.sg/articles/SIP_477_2004-12-24.html (January 24, 2010).
"Run Run Shaw," *Internet Movie Database,* http://www.imdb.com/name/nm0788411/bio (January 24, 2010).
"Shaw Brothers Introduction," *Hong Kong Cinema,* http://www.hkcinema.co.uk/Articles/shawbronews.html (January 24, 2010).
"Shaw Scope: A History of the Shaw Bros. Studio," *Harvard Film Archive,* http://www.hcl.harvard.edu/hfa/films/2008mayjune/shaw.html (January 24, 2010). □

Ryotaro Shiba

The Japanese novelist, historian, and journalist Ryotaro Shiba (1923–1996) was among the most popular writers in Japan in the second half of the twentieth century.

In few other cases has the difference in a writer's status between his or her home country and the international scene been so pronounced as it is with Shiba. Ryotaro Shiba, in the words of Frank Gibney, writing in the introduction to Shiba's book *The Last Shogun,* was "justly acclaimed as Japan's national writer." A Kyoto Sangyo University web site on Shiba described him as "one of the greatest writers in Japan." Further, the genre of many of Shiba's books was unique; they occupied a hard-to-classify and characteristically Japanese space between fiction and history. There is even a Japanese term, *Shiba-shikan,* signifying Shiba's view of history. Yet few of his works have been translated into English, and major critical surveys of his work are lacking. With the translation of Shiba's *The Last Shogun* in 1998, he began to attract an English-speaking readership.

Studied Mongolian Language

Ryotaro Shiba (or, in the Japanese system in which the surname is placed first, Shiba Ryotaro) was born Teiichi Fukuda in Osaka, Japan, on August 7, 1923. He grew up during the long years of Japanese expansionism in the 1930s and 1940s, and at the end of World War II he was a naval officer trainee. The experience of the wartime years shaped his outlook for the rest of his life; he viewed Japan's military actions during the entire period as tragic mistakes, and he believed that Japanese nationalism was harmful. Shiba had a lifelong interest in other cultures, and after the war he entered the Osaka University of Foreign Languages and studied Mongolian. Later he became interested in the Basque culture of the Iberian peninsula—not only because several of the important early Westerners to visit Japan were Basque, but also because the Basque culture had survived in a distinctive form without ever becoming a nation.

Shiba went into journalism after graduating and landed with the newspaper publisher Sankei, where he worked as a reporter. He began writing historical novels on the side, and his first book, *Fukuro no Shiro* (The Castle of an Owl), won Japan's Naoki Prize in 1959, netting a large cash prize and recognition for the best work of popular literature by a rising young author. The prize money enabled Shiba to leave his

journalism job for good in 1962 and work at developing a new style of historical novel.

Donald Keene, in *Five Modern Japanese Novelists,* described Shiba's working method this way: "He first amassed a large collection of source materials that he carefully read over until he was thoroughly familiar with the facts behind the story he was about to relate; but once he actually began writing, he did not hesitate when necessary to intuit what the characters in his stories had thought or said on a particular occasion." A famous example was *The Last Shogun,* which first appeared as *Saigo no shogun* in 1967. The book read like a novel and hardly resembled straight academic history as it told the story of Tokugawa Yoshinobu, the last member of the Tokugawa shogunate to rule Japan before the Meiji Restoration of the late 19th century returned power to Japan's emperor and opened the country to Western influences.

Explored Zone Between Fiction and History

Yet *The Last Shogun* was not fiction—it closely followed actual events in great detail. The work might be called a nonfiction novel, and it has been compared with the writings of American Civil War historian Shelby Foote. Gibney noted that "if Shiba had lived in the United States, his book would be regarded as straight history, in an era when Americans seem to have lost the distinction between fact and fiction. The Japanese are more meticulous in these matters. . . . In [the book's] accuracy, however, it is a faithful depiction of events

in that now-far-off time, and can safely be called history for all practical purposes."

The Last Shogun was filled with invented dialogue but hewed closely to the events that precipitated the fall of the Tokugawa Shogunate in 1868. Shiba seemed to have become so deeply immersed in the subject that his ability to tell stories about it exceeded the time and space he had available. The book was intended to appear in the magazine *Bungei Shunju,* but, Shiba wrote in an afterword, "after finishing the first one hundred and twenty pages of manuscript I found I could not stop there, and ended up writing over one hundred more for the next issue as well. Even that was not enough; not until I had added on another two hundred pages in the next issue was I finished."

Shiba wrote some conventional novels, with characters and situations he invented himself, but many of his 57 books fit this description. Motivated by a desire to understand how modern Japan had taken shape and had gone down the path to nationalism and militarism, he was especially interested in the Meiji period, but his works touched all phases of Japanese history and brought them alive for ordinary Japanese readers. His book *Kukai the Universal: Scenes from His Life,* translated into English in 2003, concerned a ninth-century monk and educator who devised the *katakana* writing system for Japanese and is considered the founder of Japanese culture. Another Shiba book that touched on the end of the feudal shogun system was *Sakamoro Ryoma and the Meiji Restoration,* which became one of his best sellers. Shiba also wrote nonfiction works such as *Meiji to Iu Kokka* (A Nation Called Meiji).

Wrote Popular Travel Articles

A measure of Shiba's popularity was his series of travel articles, covering both Japan and points beyond, that appeared in the magazine *Shukan Asahi.* The series grew to include 1,146 articles and in turn reinforced sales of Shiba's more complex writings. Gibney noted that Shiba's "name on a book virtually guarantees a wide readership."

The complexity of Shiba's storytelling, which poses less of a challenge for a Japanese readership than for non-Japanese, is one factor that has restricted the popularity of his books outside Japan. Another is the difficulty of rendering his style in translation, and yet another has been the long-standing admiration of Japanese readers for Shiba the man. "His novels often contain digressions, labeled as such; but even though they interrupt the narration, they are welcome to readers because they tell the reader something about Shiba himself, or at least about the associations that a particular event aroused in his memory," wrote Keene. "He is very much a participant in his writings. For most foreign readers, however, Shiba's personality is not of such great interest, and the digressions may not seem justified."

As of early 2010, the only books by Shiba available in English were *The Last Shogun, Kukai the Universal, The Tatar Whirlwind: A Novel of Seventeenth-Century East Asia,* and the samurai novella collection *Drunk as a Lord.* He was much less well known among international readers than writers such as Nobel Prize winner Yasunari Kawabata, who presented a more exotic view of Japan. Yet at home Shiba received a variety of literary awards, including the

Japanese government's Order of Culture in 1993. He was also involved with the establishment of the Yamagata Banto Prize, awarded by Osaka's regional government to foreign scholars who have devoted their lives to the study of Japan.

Shiba died in Osaka on May 12, 1996, after suffering an internal hemorrhage and falling into a coma. His wife, Midori Fukuda, formed the Shiba Ryotaro Memorial Foundation to supervise his literary legacy. The foundation established prizes and fellowships named for Shiba, and in 2001 opened the Shiba Ryotaro Museum in a building designed by the internationally known Japanese architect Tadao Anda. Keene wrote in 2003 that many Japanese bookstores maintained a special section devoted to Shiba's writings.

Books

Keene, Donald, *Five Modern Japanese Novelists,* Columbia University Press, 2003.

Shiba, Ryotaro, *The Last Shogun,* introduction by Frank Gibney, Kodansha America, 1998.

Periodicals

New York Times, February 16, 1996.

Online

"Kukai the Universal, by Shiba Ryotaro," *Asian Studies Book Services,* http://www.asianstudiesbooks.com/4925080474.htm (January 6, 2010).

"Shiba Ryotaro," Kyoto Sanyo University, http://www.cc.kyoto-su.ac.jp/information/famous/shibar.html (January 6, 2010).

"Shiba Ryotaro & Shiba Ryotaro Memorial Foundation," *Ryotaro Shiba Memorial Museum,* http://www.shibazaidan.or.jp/00info/english2.html (January 6, 2010).□

Shigetaro Shimada

Japanese naval officer Shigetaro Shimada (1883–1976) served as an admiral in the Imperial Navy during World War II. He also served as Navy Minister and approved the surprise attack on Pearl Harbor in 1941. After Japan surrendered, he was tried as a war criminal and sentenced to life imprisonment.

On December 7, 1941, Japan staged a surprise attack on U.S. military operations in Pearl Harbor, located on the Hawaiian island of O'ahu. Results of the highly coordinated air raid—which started at 7:55 in the morning and lasted until about 10:00 a.m.—were devastating. The Japanese sank or damaged eighteen U.S. ships and destroyed or damaged more than 250 American planes. The Navy and Marine Corps suffered a total of 2,896 casualties (including 2,117 deaths). The Army suffered 228 deaths and 459 injuries.

Beyond its immediate carnage, the attack's impact was profound: The next day, almost immediately following U.S. President Franklin Delano Roosevelt's historic "day of infamy" speech, Congress declared war on Japan. Three days later, Germany and Italy declared war on the United States. The world was at war.

The Pearl Harbor attack was planned by Admiral Isoroku Yamamoto (1884–1943), who was then the commander of the Japanese Combined Fleet. Vice Admiral Chuichi Nagumo (1887–1944) oversaw the attack. Admiral Shigetaro Shimada, who was the Minister of the Navy at the time, knew of the attack plans and approved the mission. For the parts they played in World War II, Yamamoto and Shimada were tried as war criminals (Nagumo had committed suicide during the war). Yamamoto was executed. Shimada was imprisoned.

Shimada would seem an unlikely candidate to play such an infamous role in history's rich narrative. He was less than an awe-inspiring figure. In fact, colleagues regarded him as a "toady," a self-serving sycophant. He was a naval figure who loathed to rock the boat, demonstrating an absolute loyalty and submissiveness to authority that bordered on being obsequious. This quality earned him an insulting nickname within the Japanese navy: "Droopy Drawers." Behind his back, colleagues also called him Tojo's "tea servant"—in reference to Hideki Tojo, who served as Japan's fortieth prime minister, from October 1941 to July 1944.

Indeed, he was recognized as being a bit too deferential. As such, Keisuke Okada (1868–1952), an admiral in the Japanese Navy and a former Japanese prime minister (from 1934 to 1936), even called for Shimada's resignation. Shimada, Okada pointed out, had lost the respect of many

Japanese naval officers because of his overly extreme loyalty to Tojo.

Nevertheless, in collaborating with Tojo, Shimada played an important role in the coordination of Japanese Army and Navy operations in the Pacific theater in the early years of World War II. Also, his military career represented a steady rise through the Japanese naval ranks, an ascent that led to his admiralship.

Born in Tokyo

Shimada has been described as a very religious man with no noticeable vices: He did not smoke and he hardly ever drank. Further, he was devoted to his mother. He was born on September 24, 1883 in Tokyo, Japan. In 1904, he graduated from the Imperial Japanese Naval Academy located on Eta Jima, an island near Hiroshima. He placed twenty-seventh in a class of 192 cadets.

Following graduation, he was assigned as a midshipman to the Karasaki Maru, and the Izumi, a cruiser ship. He saw combat in the Russo-Japanese War in 1904 and 1905. In 1909, he became a sub-lieutenant and served on battleships.

Served in World War I

Shimada later attended Naval War College and graduated with high honors in 1913. By 1915, he was promoted to lieutenant. During World War I, he served as a naval attaché in Rome, Italy.

Following the war, he assumed various positions in the Imperial Japanese Navy. In 1922, he became executive officer of a battleship. A year later, he became an instructor at the Naval War College. In December 1924, he achieved the rank of captain. He continued rising up in the military and, in 1929, he became a rear admiral. Later, he was given the assignment of chief of staff to the Imperial Japanese Navy Second Fleet. In 1932, he became commander of the Third Fleet. The following year, Shimada became vice chief of the Naval General Staff. He was promoted to vice admiral in 1934.

Installed as War Cabinet Member

In October 1941, Shimada became the minister of the navy in Tojo's war cabinet. As a cabinet member, he learned of the planned attack on the U.S. military base at Pearl Harbor, and as the naval minister, he gave his approval.

A day after the Dec. 7, 1941 sneak attack, Shimada spoke with Vice Admiral Tomiji Koyanagi about observing how he witnessed Japanese legislators rejoicing. Shimada's own reaction was a bit more subdued. "It's going to get difficult from now on," he reportedly told Koyanagi as quoted in the *Mainichi Daily News*. "I felt like I was carrying a heavy load on my shoulders, and something was caught in my throat."

Gained and Lost High Positions

In 1944, during World War II, after Japan had suffered major losses to the Allied forces, Emperor Hirohito (1901–1989) became displeased with the performance of the chiefs of staff of his country's Army and Navy. As a result, Tojo dismissed Chief of the Army General Staff Hajime Sugiyama and Chief of the Naval General Staff Osami Nagano. Tojo himself replaced Sugiyama, while Shimada became naval chief. As Shimada was also the Naval Minister, his new assignment essentially made him the supreme commander of Japan's navy.

But his increased power only increased his prevailing unpopularity. With the new position came new enemies within the naval general staff and within Hirohito's court. Eventually, these rivals tried to convince Hirohito to dismiss Shimada, as the Japanese navy lost a number of significant battles under his command. After Saipan fell to the Allied forces, Hirohito expressed his dissatisfaction with Shimada to Prime Minister Tojo, who then asked Shimada to resign as the Naval Minister. Shimada complied with the request and was appointed Chief of the General Navy Staff. He would not retain that position for very long. As *Time* magazine reported in July 1944: "Admiral Shigetaro Shimada, the chubby, cherry-lipped little man who had steered Japan's Navy through its worst defeats, was sacked again. Already out of the Cabinet (Navy Minister), he was dropped from his No. 2 job: Chief of Naval Staff. His successor: Admiral Koshiro Oikawa, wealthy aristocrat and former mentor of the Emperor (1915–22)." After the dismissals, Shimada decided to retire from the military, on January 20, 1945.

Arrested by Allies after the War

The Japanese ultimately surrendered to the Allied forces in August 1945, two months after Germany surrendered in May. That same year, the Allies arrested Shimada for war crimes. He would later be tried by the International Military Tribunal for the Far East (IMTFE), who had issued a statement that some of the worst massacres and murders of prisoners were committed by members of the Japanese Navy in the Pacific islands. High-ranking officers in the Navy were held accountable, including admirals.

The International Military tribunal, which was also known as the Tokyo Trial or the Tokyo War Crimes Tribunal, lasted from May 3, 1946 to November 12, 1948. Japanese leaders were charged with war crimes committed between 1937 and 1945. The trial's legal basis was established by the Charter of the IMTFE. General Douglas MacArthur, Supreme Commander of the Allied Powers, made the proclamation on January 19, 1946.

The tribunal's trials were held at the Ichigaya Court, former headquarters of the Japanese Army, in Tokyo, Japan. Sir William Webb of Australia served as the tribunal president. Judges included John P. Higgins and Major General Myron C. Cramer from the United States, as well as Edward Stuart McDougall (Canada), Major General Mei Ju-ao (China), Henri Bernard (France), Radhabinod Pal (India), Professor Bert Röling (Netherlands), Harvey Northcroft (New Zealand), Colonel Delfin Jaranilla (Philippines), Honorable Lord Patrick (United Kingdom), and Major General I. M. Zarayanov (Soviet Union).

Joseph Keenan of the United States was appointed as the tribunal's chief prosecutor. Other prosecutors came from Australia, Canada, China, France, India, The Netherlands, New Zealand, the Philippines, the Soviet Union, and the United Kingdom. Twenty-eight Japanese leaders were charged with Class A crimes, or crimes against peace. More than 5,700 leaders were charged as Class B (crimes of war) and Class C (crimes against humanity) criminals.

Before the tribunal began, General MacArthur granted immunity to Emperor Hirohito and members of Japan's imperial family. This action generated a great deal of criticism. But that wasn't the only point of contention. The tribunal was also criticized for its apparent American bias during the proceedings. In addition, Radhabinod Pal, a judge from India, gave a dissenting opinion. He questioned why western imperialism and America's use of atomic bombs on Hiroshima and Nagasaki were excluded from the proceedings, while Japanese imperialism and Japan's use of chemical and biological weapons were included.

Leaders Convicted and Sentenced

Two Class A war criminals, Matsuoka Yosuke and Nagano Osami, died of natural causes during the trial. Seven more were found guilty and sentenced to death. Along with Tojo, these included General Kenji Doihara, Baron Koki Hirota, General Seishiro Itagaki, General Heitaro Kimura, General Iwane Matsui, and General Akira Muto. They were executed at Tokyo's Sugamo Prison on December 23, 1948.

Sixteen other Class A war criminals were sentenced to life imprisonment. Of the Class B and Class C war criminals, 984 were sentenced to death; however, some later received pardons. Among the rest, 475 were sentenced to life imprisonment, 2,944 received limited imprisonment sentences, 1,018 were acquitted, and 279 were not brought to trial or not sentenced.

The allies initially charged Shimada with fifty-five counts of Class A war crimes. The IMTFE decided, however, that there was insufficient evidence to convict him of ordering, authorizing or permitting the worst war crimes. Further, the IMTFE decided that Shimada didn't know war crimes were being committed and, as such, could not be convicted of failing to take adequate preventative measures. Instead, Shimada was only charged with crimes against peace: five counts related to the planning and waging an aggressive war against the United States, the United Kingdom, China and The Netherlands. (International law defines aggressive war as military conflicts waged beyond the need for self defense.)

Sentenced to Life

Shimada was tried and convicted. Specifically, of the fifty-charges initially leveled at Shimada, the IMTFE found him guilty only under Count 1 (conspiracy to wage wars of aggression against any country or countries, between January 1,1938 and September 2, 1945) and under counts 27, 29, 31 and 32 (waging aggressive wars). The tribunal sentenced him to life imprisonment on November 12, 1948.

Shimada only served seven years of his sentence, however. In 1955, by the time the American occupation of Japan had ended, Shimada was suffering poor health, and Japanese Prime Minister Ichiro Hatoyama granted him parole.

Shimada lived another twenty-one years. He died on June 7, 1976 in the city where he was born and later stood trial: Tokyo. He was ninety-two years old.

Periodicals

The Mainichi Daily News, December 7, 2009.

Time, July 24, 1944.

Online

"Father of Kamikaze," *Animeigo,* http://www.animeigo.com/OtherLiner/KAMIKAZELINER.t (December 21, 2009).

"Pearl Harbor," *World War II History,* http://www.worldwar2history.info/Pearl-Harbor (December 21, 2009).

"Shigetaro Shimada," *carstock.ru,* http://carstock.ru/Dictionary/Shimada_Shigetaro (December 21, 2009).

"Shimada Shigetaro (1883-1976)," *The Pacific War Online Encyclopedia,* http://pwencycl.kgbudge.com/S/h/Shimada_Shigetaro.htm (December 21, 2009).

"Shigetaro Shimada," *Trial Watch,* http://www.trial-ch.org/en/trial-watch/profile/db/legal-procedures/shigetaro_shimada_547.html (December 21, 2009).

"The Tokyo Trial and Other Trials Against Japan," *World War II Database,* http://ww2db.com/battle_spec.php?battle_id=221 (December 21, 2009). □

Viktor Shklovsky

The Russian critic Viktor Shklovsky (1893–1984), although not well known in the West, was a central figure in the fertile literary culture of the Soviet Union in the 1920s.

Shklovsky was influential both as a critic and as a writer of original material of his own, material that was difficult to classify as to genre. He was one of the originators of Russian Formalism, a school of literary criticism that held that art operated according to principles of its own. His ideas shaped the development of literary criticism in the West, but at home, where his adherence to Marxism was grudging at best, he suffered condemnation from academics who toed the Communist Party line. Nevertheless, Shklovsky survived the crises of twentieth-century life in Russia and produced a large body of critical and biographical writing.

Read Paper at Literary Cabaret

Of Jewish background, Viktor Borisovich Shklovsky was born in St. Petersburg, Russia, on January 24, 1893, and lived in the city for much of his life. His father, Boris Shklovsky, was a teacher. Shklovsky entered the University of St. Petersburg in 1913, shortly before the outbreak of World War I, and he quickly came under the spell of avant-garde European cultural ideas that were circulating on campus. Shklovsky enjoyed attending a sort of intellectual cabaret called The Stray Dog. There he encountered the ideas of the group of Italian writers known as Futurists, who believed in technology as a redemptive power that would remake human society. At the Stray Dog he read a paper of his own, titled "The Place of Futurism in the History of Language," that anticipated some of his later ideas. He and some other students formed a group called Opoyaz, which took its name from the Russian acronym for "Society for the Study of Poetic Language."

The war temporarily sidelined Shklovsky's growing literary career. He enlisted in the Russian army in the summer of 1914, was trained as a mechanic, and served in Ukraine and the Galicia region of what is now Poland. Sent back to St. Petersburg in 1916 and given a post as an instructor of armored-car personnel, he was able to rees-tablish contact with some of his literary friends and to issue new publications. Shklovsky's life after the fall of the tsar in Russia's February Revolution of 1917 was chaotic. He backed the democratic-oriented Provisional Government, which appointed him commissar attached to the Russian army. But when the Provisional Government lost ground to hardline Bolshevik Communist forces in the summer of that year, he asked for and received a transfer to Russian-occu-pied Persia (now Iran) in the last days of the war. There he noted a refreshing lack of anti-Semitic sentiment as com-pared with his homeland.

Back in St. Petersburg in 1918, Shklovsky joined an underground group that was plotting to restore democratic institutions in Russia. The failure of that group forced Shklovsky to flee to Ukraine. Upon his return, he and other members of the original Futurist group worked to develop a theory of the arts that did not subordinate them to social thought. In an essay in a small journal, Shklovsky wrote, as quoted by Richard Sheldon in his introduction to Shklov-sky's book *Third Factory,* "Art has always been free of life; its flag has never reflected the color of the flag flying over the city fortress." The statement was not only a credo of what would become known as Russian Formalism, but also a critique of some of Shklovsky's friends who were ingrati-ating themselves with the Communist regime.

Fled Russia for Germany

In the early 1920s, Shklovsky summarized some of his more technical literary ideas in a book called *The Unfolding of the Plot.* He was close to various young Russian writers, including Yevgeny Zamyatin, the author of the innovative science fiction novel *We.* By 1922, however, some of Shklovsky's friends had left Russia, while others were facing police harassment. In February of that year Shklovsky him-self fled to Finland and then settled in the large Russian literary community in Berlin, Germany.

Shklovsky's time in Berlin was creatively fertile. He fell in love with the young Russian Jewish writer Elsa Kagan, who would soon rename herself Elsa Triolet and go on to a suc-cessful literary career in France. She did not reciprocate his affection, but agreed to read his letters to her as long as they did not mention love. Shklovsky did not waste the resulting outpouring of letters—sometimes as many as two or three per day—but published them in Berlin (with a few of Triolet's answers included) as *Zoo, or Letters Not About Love.* The letters covered a wide range of subjects, from literary topics to Shklovsky's own wartime experiences, and in them his own style of creative prose began to emerge—poetic, quiz-zical, compact, and often using internal contradiction to make a larger point.

Another Shklovsky book largely written in Berlin, *A Sentimental Journey,* was even more innovative. The book, which took its name from one by eighteenth-century English novelist Laurence Sterne, a Shklovsky favorite, was ostensibly Shklovsky's autobiography. But Sheldon noted in the intro-duction to his 1970 translation of the book (its first

appearance in English) that in parts of the book Shklovsky "launches a massive assault on formal cohesiveness in which he violates the norms of literary language and composition systematically. Abrupt and frequent shifts in language levels and compositional planes break the narrative into a series of loosely strung, nearly autonomous segments." Despite the book's nonfiction material, sympathetic critics pointed to it as the possible beginning of a new trend in the Russian novel.

On the literary-critical front, Shklovsky introduced the concept of *ostranenie,* variously translated as estrangement or defamiliarization, in his book *Theory of Prose* in 1925. According to this idea, art does not reflect reality but remakes it, as those who experience artworks see the world on the terms of those works, with fresh eyes. Shklovsky's thesis, expanded upon in studies of Sterne and other writers, influ-enced many subsequent theorists as well as German play-wright Bertolt Brecht's use of the *Verfremdungseffekt* or defamiliarization effect, in which the action of a play would stop and give way to commentary or other extraneous material.

Diverted Criticism with Unorthodox Memoir

Shklovsky's lack of interest in socialist approaches, mean-while, was causing him to fall into disfavor with a literary apparatus increasingly controlled by the Soviet state. Critical attacks on his writings multiplied, and Shklovsky responded with another unorthodox memoir, *Third Factory,* that seemed to acknowledge the criticism. The title referred to three stages of Shklovsky's life, which he referred to as factories in the book's major sections. The first was his childhood, the sec-ond the Opoyaz period, and the third the Communist era. The book's style is as innovative and elliptical as that in Shklovsky's earlier books, and scholars have disagreed as to whether it really signaled a capitulation to government pres-sure or instead went through the motions while offering alternative viewpoints to careful readers. The book contained an open letter to literary critic Roman Jakobson in which Shklovsky wrote: "Roman, I am studying the unfreedom of the writer. I am studying unfreedom as though it were a set of gymnastic equipment. But the streets here are full of people, so what if I do leak like a rusty pipe? The land in which I leak is my own."

Shklovsky never quite got back into the Soviet regi-me's good graces, but he was skilled at staying a step ahead of government censors with cryptic writings that revealed their true nature only over time, and he was able to con-tinue living and working in St. Petersburg. Beginning with a study of Vladimir Mayakovsky, an early Soviet poet whom Shklovsky had known for many years, he wrote a series of books about famous Russian writers. He survived the dev-astation of Russia during World War II, and his 1963 biog-raphy of novelist Leo Tolstoy was translated abroad and earned him the Order of the Red Banner of Labor at home. His books were available in the Soviet Union, but mostly in heavily censored editions.

Shklovsky's major writings of the 1920s were all but unknown in the West until a series of translations by Sheldon and others began to appear in the 1960s and 1970s. He was awarded an honorary doctorate by Oxford University in Eng-land in 1972. Shklovsky remained active until the end of his life. In 1981, just under 90 years old, he issued a new book, translated into English in 2007 as *Energy of Delusion: A Book on Plot.* Christopher Byrd of the London *Guardian* called it "an extraordinary product of old age" in which Shklovsky examined how writers such as Tolstoy and Alexander Pushkin strove to "re-engineer stories from the past to reveal startling frontiers of literary representation." Shklovsky died in St. Petersburg on December 6, 1984. In the early 2000s, many existing translations of his books, along with other works newly translated into English, were reissued by the small Illinois publishing company Dalkey Archive Press.

Books

Robinson, Douglas, *Estrangement and the Somatics of Literature: Tolstoy, Shklovsky, Brecht,* Johns Hopkins, 2008.

Shklovsky, Viktor, *A Sentimental Journey,* trans. and with introduction by Richard Sheldon, Cornell, 1970.

Shklovsky, Viktor, *Third Factory,* trans. and with introduction by Richard Sheldon, Ardis, 1977.

Periodicals

Harvard Review, December 2006.

Online

Review of *Energy of Delusion: A Book on Plot, Guardian* (November 6, 2007), http://www.guardian.co.uk/books/2007/nov/06/featuresreviews.guardianreview/print (January 14, 2010).

"The Formalist's Formalist: On Viktor Shklovsky," *The Forward* (November 23, 2007), http://www.forward.com/articles/12055 (January 14, 2010).

Contemporary Authors Online, Gale, 2010. Farmington Hills, Mich.: Gale, 2010. http://www.galenet.galegroup.com/servlet/BioRC (January 14, 2010). □

Walter Wellesley "Red" Smith

During his fifty-four year writing career, American sports journalist Walter Wellesley "Red" Smith (1905–1982) became the most syndicated sports columnist in the United States. His work was both entertaining and highly literate, and his observations both witty and insightful. He received a Pulitzer Prize in 1976.

Ironically, sports writing legend Walter Wellesley "Red" Smith never really wanted to write about sports. Rather, the Pulitzer Prize-winning journalist envisioned for himself a career as a news reporter. But circumstances beyond his control—as well as a demonstrated natural ability to produced skillful, highly literate sports copy—directed his career course.

During his half-century-long career, Smith became regarded as one of the county's greatest sports columnist. He was appreciated not only by sports fans but also by other writers–and great writers, too. Nobel novelist Ernest

Hemingway even made reference to Smith in one of his books (*Across the River and Into the Trees* [1950]).

Smith was born in Green Bay, Wisconsin on September 25, 1905. His father, Walter Philip Smith, owned and operated a wholesale produce and retail grocery store, a business he inherited from his grandfather. Smith's mother, Ida (Richardson) Smith, was a homemaker.

Smith was the middle child in a family of three children. He and his older brother, Arthur, were named after Arthur Wellesley, the Duke of Wellington. Smith's mother claimed she was a descendent of Wellesley, who had defeated Napoleon Bonaparte at Waterloo. Smith's younger sister Catherine later died of tuberculosis when Smith was in college.

The young Smith's most distinctive physical characteristic was his red hair, a coloring that compelled his father to nickname him "Brick." In later years, people simply called him "Red," a nickname he integrated into his subsequently famous newspaper byline.

Beyond the physical, Smith distinguished himself with a precocity that enabled him to read by the time he was five years old and determine his career path when he was a teenager. He wanted to become a writer, an ambition that ultimately made him one of the nation's most famous and widely read sports journalists. Interestingly, his early sports involvement proved marginal: As a youth, he displayed limited on-field skills and his interests in professional sports did not extend far beyond following professional baseball.

He proved sure-footed in pursuing his career path, however, and engaged in educational extra-curricular activities, both in high school and in college, which involved publication production. While attending Green Bay's East High School, the aspiring scribe earned his first-ever writing award (he would collect many during his professional writing career) by writing a humorous essay about his alma mater's debating team. His prize was a free copy of East High's yearbook.

Accepted into Notre Dame University

In 1922, Smith graduated with a B average, which was good enough to gain him acceptance into Notre Dame University, where he wanted to take up journalism. He had to delay his entrance for a year, however, as his father's grocery business fell on hard times. Smith needed to work in a local hardware store to help fund his higher education.

Smith finally entered Notre Dame in 1923. As a freshman journalism major, Smith wrote for the student newspaper. In his junior year, he edited the university's yearbook, *The Dome*. He graduated cum laude with a bachelor of arts degree on June 5, 1927.

Soon after graduation, Smith secured his first newspaper job, working as a general assignment reporter for the *Milwaukee Sentinel* in Wisconsin, earning twenty-four dollars a week. Seeking higher pay, Smith left the paper after ten months to take a copy editor position with the *St. Louis Star*, in 1928. For forty-dollars a week, he wrote headlines and edited stories written by staff reporters.

Assigned to the Sports Desk

It was then that fate stepped in. The *Star's* managing editor fired half of the paper's sports department for taking bribes from a local professional wrestling promoter. To bolster the depleted staff, he transferred Smith to the sports desk.

The move unsettled Smith, as he didn't consider himself a sports expert, but he soon discovered that he enjoyed the creativity that sports writing afforded (in his first assignment, he reported on a night football practice at Washington University but, deploying his fertile imagination, he wrote from the perspective of a glow worm).

The position also allowed him to indulge in a strong youthful interest: baseball. The young reporter covered St. Louis's two Major League teams, the Browns and the Cardinals. The access and opportunity didn't immediately transform Smith into a dedicated sportswriter, however. Other sports bored him, particularly winter sports. Of basketball, he wryly commented in a *Time* interview, "[S]ome big goon throws the ball up and it either goes in or it doesn't." Baseball, though, engendered readily apparent drama and, thus, wrote itself, he observed: "It's two outs and the bases are loaded and—well, you've got the situation right there." Still, not completely sold on sports, he requested a reassignment to general reporting.

Hard-working Family Man

In the meantime, he met Catherine "Kay" Cody, who he married on February 11, 1933. Despite his busy work schedule (which kept him on the road) and his active social life (he made friends with baseball players and other sportswriters including the famed Grantland Rice), Smith proved a caring and responsible husband and family man. His main concern was supporting his wife and their two children. Never overindulgent, despite his profession and associates, Smith embraced a stable lifestyle, regularly attending Roman Catholic services and enjoying the peaceful pastime of fishing.

Moreover, he was always concerned about making enough money to meet his family obligations, especially during the Great Depression. By this time, his weekly salary had increased to fifty dollars, but he felt it wasn't enough. Still, he didn't want to leave the newspaper profession.

Moved to Philadelphia

His steadfastness was rewarded with a higher-salaried job offer from the *Philadelphia Record*, and he moved his family to Pennsylvania. Despite his preference for general assignment reporting, Smith would remain a sports writer. At this point, he settled into that role and eventually became one of the most widely read and best-known sports columnists. He also became known as "Red Smith." His first article for the *Record* was published on June 20, 1939 with the byline "Walt Smith," but he didn't like how it looked. He and his wife liked "Red Smith" better, and the new byline never changed in a career that endured through nearly fifty more years. In the next thirty years, Smith wrote as many as seven sports columns a week. In later years, the number decreased, but he could still be considered prolific. By the end of his career, Smith had written approximately 10,000 columns by his estimation.

Through the years, Smith would write about all sports, not just baseball, and his wit, knowledge, and entertaining style were clearly evident whether he was covering auto racing, basketball, boxing, fishing, football or Olympic events. He even memorably covered dog shows. It was the sport of baseball, however, that he enjoyed best. During his career, he covered forty-five World Series, and this allowed him to witness and write about the sport's tremendous capacity for drama. For instance, early in his career, in 1932, he covered the Chicago Cubs-New York Yankees series where Babe Ruth allegedly accomplished his highly disputed "called home run." Later in his career, in 1977, he wrote about the Yankees-Los Angeles Dodgers World Series highlighted by a Game Six, three-home-run power performance by Reggie Jackson. His baseball enthusiasm was always reflected in his writing. For instance, his lead for the October 4, 1951 column about Bobby Thomson's legendary, last-game-of-the-season home run that gave the New York Giants the National League Pennant over the Brooklyn Dodgers is considered classic sports writing. "Now it is done," he wrote about the dramatic finish (according to *The Scribner Encyclopedia of American Lives Thematic Series.*) "Now the story ends. And there is no way to tell it. The art of fiction is dead. Reality has strangled invention. Only the utterly impossible, the inexpressibly fantastic, can ever be plausible again."

Prolific but Pained Prose Stylist

Smith seemed to compose such prose effortlessly. After all, he was a necessarily prolific writer, as he was subjected to daily journalism's relentless deadlines, and he always hit it out of the park every time. Yet, for Smith, each column was a horror story composed in his own personal "torture chamber" (the term he used to describe his office). For him, no sight was more frightening than a blank page of typing paper, because he always dug deep within himself to produce what he considered a readable story. While he applied the journalistic method of integrating the essential facts into schematic narrative structure, he never took a short cut. He demanded much from himself, as he strived to entertain readers with each and every column, no matter the subject. He described writing as opening a vein, with a story coming out "with little drops of blood."

During this period, he also moved beyond newspaper writing. In 1944, he wrote the first of his many magazine articles, "Don't Send my Boys to Halas," which appeared in *The Saturday Evening Post*. He would also publish articles in other leading national magazines including *American Heritage*, *Collier's*, *Harper's Bazaar*, *Holiday*, *Liberty*, *New York Times Magazine* and *Reader's Digest*. In 1945, he published his first book, *Terry and Bunky Play Football*, co-written with Dick Fishel for young readers.

Wrote for New York City Papers

In August of that year, Smith took a job with the *New York Herald Tribune*, achieving an early career goal of writing for a New York daily newspaper. Four months later, he was writing his own column, "Views of Sport." First appearing in the paper's December 5, 1945 edition, the column was subsequently syndicated to newspapers throughout the country. The next year, the column earned Smith the National Headliners Club Award for excellence in newspaper writing. "Views of Sport" would appear six times a week until the *Tribune* folded in 1965. The column made Smith one of the best-known sportswriters and, by 1954, he emerged as the nation's most widely syndicated columnist.

After the *Tribune* ceased publication, Smith wrote for the *New York World Journal Tribune*. In May 1967, that paper also folded, and Smith's writing was then published by the Publishers-Hall Syndicate.

That same year, Smith lost his wife. Kay Smith died of liver cancer on February 19. She was survived by her two children, Catherine (Smith) Halloran and Terence Fitzgerald, who had followed his father's footsteps and became a sportswriter. Smith remarried in November 1968, to Phyllis Warner Weiss, a widowed artist with five children.

Hired by *The New York Times*

In 1971, Smith was offered the opportunity to write a column for the nation's best-known and most highly regarded newspaper, *The New York Times*. His new "Sports of the Times" column, which first appeared on November 15, 1971, was published four times a week. Smith wrote for the *Times* for the rest of his career. He filed his final column on January 11, 1982, four days before he died. By that time, his column was syndicated in 275 U.S. newspapers and 225 international newspapers.

In addition to his journalistic chores, Smith published numerous books throughout his career. Some of the most popular included *Out of the Red* (1950); *Views of Sport* (1954); *Red Smith's Sports Annual* (1961); *The Best of Red Smith* (1963); *Red Smith on Fishing Around the World* (1963); *Strawberries in Wintertime: The Sporting World of Red Smith* (1974); *Press Box: Red Smith's Favorite Sports Stories* (1976), and *The Red Smith Reader* and *To Absent Friends from Red Smith* (both 1982). Additionally, *Red Smith on Baseball: The Game's Greatest Writer on the Game's Greatest Years* was published in 2000, eighteen years after his death. Many of these books were collections of his best and most popular sports columns.

Noted for Outspoken Commentary

Smith wrote about more than just sports, though, and his commentary also addressed politics and world affairs. In 1937, he traveled to Mexico, to interview the exiled Russian revolutionary Leon Trotsky. Later in his career, he covered U.S. presidential conventions in 1956 and 1968. Sometimes he even expressed his political viewpoints in his sports columns. He could be quite outspoken, particularly when it came to the Olympic games. He denounced the International Olympic Committee (IOC) as a hypocritical organization, and he was outraged when the 1972 games held in Munich, Germany continued after five terrorists murdered eleven Israeli athletes.

In 1980, Smith became the first sports columnist to advocate a boycott of the 1980 Olympics in Moscow as a protest of the Soviet Union's invasion of Afghanistan. Reportedly, then-U.S. President Jimmy Carter adopted an official boycott after reading Smith's column.

Within sports, Smith's favorite targets for criticism included Major League Baseball Commissioner Bowie Kuhn, and team owners such as George Steinbrenner.

Died of Heart Failure

In the late 1970s, Smith was diagnosed with cancer, but he continued working. By 1981, however, he reduced his output from four to three columns each week. Smith filed his last column on January 11, 1982, four days before he died of congestive heart failure at Stamford Hospital in Connecticut. He was cremated, and his ashes were buried at Long Ridge Cemetery, also in Stamford.

His death generated widespread mourning as well as praise, as he influenced his contemporaries as well as a new generation of sports writers. Shirley Povich, a Washington Post sports columnist and member of the National Sportswriters Hall of Fame, said of Smith (as quoted by Leonard Shapiro in the *Washington Post*), "He raised the sports writing trade to a literacy and elegance it had not known before." Colleague John Leonard honored Smith in an article in the *New York Times* saying, "[Smith] was to sports what Homer was to war."

Smith won numerous awards during his career. In 1976, he received a Pulitzer Prize for "distinguished commentary." The awarding committee said, "In an area heavy with tradition and routine, Mr. Smith is unique in the erudition, the literary quality, the vitality and freshness of viewpoint he brings to his work and in the sustained quality of his columns'' (as quoted in the *Dictionary of Literary Biography*).

Other major awards that Smith received included the 1956 Grantland Rice Memorial Award from the Sportsmanship Brotherhood of New York and the 1976 J.G. Taylor Spink Award, which honors baseball writers ''for meritorious contributions to baseball writing.''

In 1986, Ira Berkow, a fellow *New York Times* sports columnist published *Red: A Biography of Red Smith*, which is considered the definitive assessment of Smith's life and distinguished career.

Books

''Red Smith,'' *Dictionary of Literary Biography, Volume 171: Twentieth-Century American Sportswriters*, The Gale Group, 1996.
''Smith, Walter Wellesley (''Red''), *The Scribner Encyclopedia of American Lives Thematic Series: Sports Figures*, Charles Scribner's Sons, 2002.
''Walter W(ellesley) Smith, *Contemporary Authors Online*, Gale, 2003.
''Walter Wellesley Smith,'' *The Scribner Encyclopedia of American Lives, Volume 1: 1981-1985*, Charles Scribner's Sons, 1998.

Periodicals

Gelf Magazine, February 5, 2008.
New York Times, July 15, 1982.
Time, May 15, 1950.
Washington Post, June 5, 1998.

Online

''J.G. Taylor Spink Award Honorees,'' *National Baseball Hall of Fame and Museum*, http://web.baseballhalloffame.org/hofers/spink.jsp (October 31, 2009).
''Red Smith,'' *Baseball Library.com*, http://www.baseballlibrary.com/ballplayers/player.php?name=Red_Smith (October 31, 2009).□

Robert Holbrook Smith M.D

With William G. Wilson, American physician Robert Holbrook Smith co-founded Alcoholics Anonymous. An alcoholic for most of his adult life, Holbrook helped Wilson develop the organization's pioneering twelve-step program. By the time he died in 1950, he had personally helped nearly 5,000 fellow alcoholics.

Fondly remembered as ''Dr. Bob,'' Robert Holbrook Smith, M.D., was tormented by an alcohol addiction that he described as a ''nightmare.'' With the loving support of his wife and his close friend, William G. Wilson,

however, Smith survived his decades-long ordeal and applied his experience to helping fellow alcoholics. Along with Wilson, he created Alcoholics Anonymous, an association that now has chapters throughout the world.

Rebellious Only Child

Smith was born on August 8, 1879 in Saint Johnsbury, Vermont. He described his birthplace as a liquor-free community populated by the religiously devout. ''Men who had liquor shipped in from Boston or New York by express were looked upon with great distrust and disfavor by most of the good townspeople,'' he recalled in the autobiographical section he wrote for the book *Alcoholics Anonymous*, the organization's so-called ''Big Book.''

His parents were Walter Perrin Smith, who served as a judge, and Susan A. Holbrook. Both were active in the community's civil, social, and religious affairs. ''Unfortunately for me I was the only child, which perhaps engendered the selfishness which played such an important part in bringing on my alcoholism,'' Smith observed in his ''Big Book'' autobiography.

Smith was not only strongly self-focused but also rebellious, defying parental authority whenever and however possible. Further, he disdained church services and the structured school environment. Still, the young Smith was a good student whose innate intelligence was reflected in his good grades, and his ambitions were precocious: When he was only nine years old, he knew he wanted to become a doctor. While his mother objected to this ambition, Smith defiantly proceeded undaunted on this career path.

Learned to Drink in College

Smith attended Dartmouth College, graduating in 1902. The college environment introduced him to an activity that would predominate his adult life: drinking. As with most alcoholics, he didn't suffer the same ''morning after'' consequences of casual imbibers, and this reinforced his habit. ''I seemed to be able to snap back the next morning better than most of my fellow drinkers, who were cursed, or perhaps blessed, with a great deal of morning-after nausea,'' recalled Smith in *Alcoholics Anonymous*. ''Never once in my life have I had a headache [which led me to believe] that I was an alcoholic from the start.''

Three years later, and pursuing his medical ambitions, Smith enrolled in the University of Michigan as a premed student, where his drinking activities increased. Indeed, it became such a problem that, during his sophomore year, he left school, fearing that he could not complete his course work.

He took a respite on a New England farm, where he realized that leaving school was a foolish decision. He soon returned to the university and decided to buckle down, but quickly recognized that he was not free from his personal demon. ''[My] drinking became so much worse that the boys in the fraternity house where I lived felt forced to send for my father, who made a long journey in the vain endeavor to get me straightened around,'' recounted Smith.

His father's intervention only had a short, temporary impact. Smith soon went back to drinking, imbibing greater quantities of even harder liquor. Amazingly enough, Smith managed to pass his exams. In 1910, after receiving additional medical training at Rush Memorial College in Chicago, he earned his medical degree and then interned at City Hospital in Akron, Ohio. The two-year internship was a short-lived period of sobriety.

Opened Medical Practice in Ohio

By 1912, he began his medical career, opening an office in Akron, where he remained until his retirement in 1948. Soon after starting his practice, he surreptitiously resumed his drinking habits. Like many fellow alcoholics, he remained functional and was able to hide his problem.

His alcoholism soon became unmanageable, however. Drinking began to take a physical and professional toll. Comprehending the severity of his situation, Smith resorted to voluntary incarceration, but this became a revolving-door scenario: Smith admitted himself into local sanitariums as many as a dozen times, according to his own count. By this time, he was subject to the physical entrapment that locks alcoholics into their habit. "If I did not drink, my stomach tortured me," he remembered in his autobiography, "and if I did, my nerves did the same thing."

This went on for three years before Smith had to be hospitalized for health problems. Even then, he would not and could not stop drinking. "I would get my friends to smuggle me a quart, or I would steal the alcohol about the building, so that I got rapidly worse," he wrote.

Wife Offered Help

At this point, the only thing that kept him from a street-level existence or even death was the loving support from his father and his wife. "My father had to send a doctor out from my hometown, who managed to get me back there some way," Smith said. "I was in bed about two months before I could venture out of the house."

His wife, too, supported him through his ordeals. Smith first met Anne Ripley in 1898 when they attended Saint Johnsbury Academy. He finally married her in 1915, when he was thirty-five years old and had set up medical practice.

Increased Drinking During Prohibition

The couple did enjoy several happy years when Smith attempted to confront his disease, but his problems increased in 1919. Ironically, the contributing factor was that year's ratification of the Eighteenth Amendment, which prohibited the sale of alcohol. Before prohibition went into full force, Smith decided he would have one last fling before alcohol became unavailable.

There was just one problem, however. Throughout the United States' so-called "dry years," alcohol was plentiful and readily available to those who sought it. As such, prohibition posed no barrier to the unquenchable Smith. As his alcoholism subsequently increased, he fell into a regular drinking pattern, which was provoked by fears shared by many, if not all, clinically diagnosed alcoholics: Loss of their liquor source and the physical terrors that would accompany a sudden withdrawal. "I developed two distinct phobias," recalled Smith. "One was the fear of not sleeping, and the

other was the fear of running out of liquor. . . . I knew that if I did not stay sober enough to earn money, I would run out of liquor. Most of the time, therefore, I did not take the morning drink . . . but instead would fill up on large doses of sedatives to quiet the jitters, which distressed me terribly."

Further, these fears compelled Smith, like fellow alcoholics, to weave a web of deception that eventually strangulates the weaver. Occasionally, Smith succumbed to his morning craving, with the risk of making himself unfit to perform surgery. "This would lessen my chances of smuggling some home that evening, which in turn would mean a night of futile tossing around in bed followed by a morning of unbearable jitters," he said.

This went on for fifteen years. During this period, Smith would sneak liquor into his house and hide this secret supply in the coal bin, clothes chute, over beams in the cellar and even with the cracks in the cellar tile. In addition, his prohibition bootlegger hid alcohol in his back steps. The disease alienated Smith and his wife from their friends. The couple dared not socialize or invite people into their home, for fear that Smith would get drunk. Meanwhile, to quell his sleep phobia, Smith became intoxicated every night. He often made promises to his wife, two children and friends that he would stop drinking, but these were pledges that he could not keep. He described his existence as a "nightmare."

Still, he continued searching for the solution to his problem. Ever supportive, his wife encouraged him to attend the meetings of the Oxford Group, a Christian evangelical fellowship established in 1919 by Dr. Frank N. D. Buchman (1878–1961). Now considered an antecedent to Alcoholics Anonymous, the group stressed self-examination, recognition and acceptance of personality imperfections, reliance on a higher spiritual power, restitution to those harmed by one's alcoholism, and willingness to reach out to the similarly afflicted. Smith's association with the group initiated his healing, but it was only a beginning. He continued drinking.

Met William Wilson

Smith's permanent sobriety, and the eventual formation of Alcoholics Anonymous, resulted from his May 1935 meeting with William Griffith Wilson (1895–1971), the organization's co-founder. Wilson was a prominent New York stockbroker from Brooklyn, but his own alcoholism almost destroyed his successful career. He found that he was able to reduce his alcohol cravings by helping other drinkers deal with their own problem.

In 1935, Wilson traveled to Akron to settle a business deal. When the deal fell through, though, he found himself on the street and tempted to get drunk. Fortunately, he then met up with Smith at a Christian Group meeting. Smith shared his problems, and Wilson moved in with him to help him get sober. The two men became close, supportive friends. Together, they read the Bible and discussed the Oxford Group ideas, which would form the basis of Alcoholics Anonymous' influential twelve-step recovery program.

Further, Smith and Wilson promised to help keep each other sober. When either experienced the urge to drink, they would go out together to try and find another drinker to help. In this way, they helped themselves and a number of chronic drinkers. This supportive method expanded into the Alcoholics Anonymous program. Wilson developed the fundamental principles that became the organization's famous twelve steps. These included:

We admitted we were powerless over alcohol—that our lives had become unmanageable.

Came to believe that a Power greater than ourselves could restore us to sanity.

Made a decision to turn our will and our lives over to the care of God as we understood Him.

Made a searching and fearless moral inventory of ourselves.

Admitted to God, to ourselves and to another human being the exact nature of our wrongs.

Were entirely ready to have God remove all these defects of character.

Humbly asked Him to remove our shortcomings.

Made a list of all persons we had harmed, and became willing to make amends to them all.

Made direct amends to such people wherever possible, except when to do so would injure them or others.

Continued to take personal inventory and when we were wrong promptly admitted it.

Sought through prayer and meditation to improve our conscious contact with God, as we understood Him, praying only for knowledge of His will for us and the power to carry that out.

Having had a spiritual awakening as the result of these steps, we tried to carry this message to alcoholics, and to practice these principles in all our affairs.

Drank One Last Bottle of Beer

But Smith had one more relapse to endure. It occurred in 1935, during a trip to Atlantic City, New Jersey, where he attended a medical meeting. The binge was quite harrowing. Smith drank scotch during the train ride to New Jersey. Once in Atlantic City, he purchased several quarts of scotch to take to his hotel. He stayed sober the next day until after dinner. From there, things got worse: "I drank all I dared in the bar, and then went to my room to finish the job. Tuesday I started in the morning, getting well organized by noon. I did not want to disgrace myself, so I then checked out. I bought some more liquor on the way to the depot. I had to wait some time for the train. I remember nothing from then on until I woke up at a friend's house, in a town near home," recalled Smith.

The friend contacted Smith's wife, who sent Wilson to attend to her husband. Wilson took Smith home, gave him a few drinks and the put him to bed. The next morning, Smith was due in surgery, but he had the "morning after" shakes. Wilson gave him a bottle of beer to settle him down. Smith then successfully performed the operation. The bottle of beer proved to be the last time he ever tasted liquor. The date was June 10, 1935.

Died of Cancer

Smith remained sober until he died of cancer, on November 16, 1950 at City Hospital in Akron. His wife had passed away a year earlier. According to witnesses, right before he died, Smith raised his hand to the light and said to a nurse, "I think this is it."

Smith was survived by his two children, Susan and Robert. Recalling his father, Robert said (as quoted on the Saddleback Valley Fellowship Center website), "He had tremendous drive, great physical stamina. He was reserved and formal on first acquaintance, but as you came to know him, he was just the opposite: friendly, generous, full of fun."

During the last fifteen years of his life, Smith applied that drive and stamina to helping others. It is estimated that he provided one-on-one help for as many as five thousand fellow alcoholics in the Akron area. Appropriate to his humble nature, he wanted no large monument to commemorate his life. Instead, only a small plaque in the alcoholic ward of Akron's Saint Thomas Hospital, where Smith performed a great deal of his compassionate service, honors his work.

Following Smith's death, Alcoholics Anonymous grew to become an international organization. Its innovative twelve-step recovery program served as a model for other recovery groups, including Narcotics Anonymous and Al-Anon/Alateen. Further, it continues to enjoy the endorsement of members of the medical, psychiatric and spiritual communities.

In his last public pronouncement shortly before his death, presented at the first International Alcoholics Anonymous Conference, Smith described what he felt the organization stood for: "Our [twelve steps], when simmered down to the last, resolve themselves into the words of love and service," as the Barefootsworld website reported.

Books

Alcoholics Anonymous, Alcoholics Anonymous World Services, Inc., 1976.

"Robert H. Smith." *Almanac of Famous People, 9 Ed.,* Thomson Gale, 2007.

Periodicals

American Weekly, March 11, 1951.

Time, March 31, 2003.

Online

"Dr. Bob's Last Message," *Barefootsworld.net,* http://www.barefootsworld.net/lastmess.html (October 29, 2009).

"Robert Holbrook Smith and Alcoholics Anonymous," *dd.lib.brown.edu,* http://dl.lib.brown.edu/bamco/ (October 29, 2009).

"Robert Holbrook Smith, M.D.," *svfc.net,* http://www.svfc.net/Dr_Bobs_Story.htm (October 29, 2009).

"The Twelve Steps of Alcoholics Anonymous," *AA.org.,* http://www.aa.org/en_pdfs/smf-121_en.pdf (October 29, 2009)□

Georg Solti

The Hungarian-born orchestral conductor Georg Solti (1912–1997) excelled in both symphonic music and opera. With an unusually long career that stretched from the period between the world wars to the era of

cable television and the Internet, he was among the most celebrated classical musicians of the 20th century.

S olti was born György Stern in Budapest on October 21, 1912, when the city was still part of the Austro-Hungarian Empire. His father, Móricz Stern, was a small businessman. The family fled Budapest during World War I but returned at the war's end. As their lives stabilized, Solti's mother, Teréz Rosenbaum Stern, noticed that her son had unusual musical talent. He quickly progressed from piano lessons to a small music school to the Franz Liszt Academy, Hungary's top musical institute. Among his teachers were the country's leading composers, Zoltán Kodály, Ernst von Dohnányi, and Béla Bartók. The name Solti came from a small Hungarian town; it was given both to Georg and to his older sister, Lilly, by Móricz Stern because it sounded more Hungarian than Stern did.

Solti's degrees were in piano and composition, and he could likely have pursued a career in either of those fields. But he was fascinated by conducting and looked for jobs in that field after receiving his degree from the academy. As a Jew, his opportunities were increasingly limited as Hungary swung to the right in the 1930s in order to avoid antagonizing increasingly belligerent Nazi Germany. His best apprenticeships came at the Salzburg Festival in Austria, where he worked as an assistant to the anti-Fascist Italian conductor Arturo Toscanini. On March 11, 1938, he was hired to conduct a performance of Mozart's *The Marriage*

of Figaro at the Budapest State Opera. On the same evening, word reached Budapest that German troops had overrun Vienna. A Jewish baritone whispered the news to Solti on the podium. Soon afterward, after losing his job as a ballet conductor at the Budapest State Opera because of new anti-Jewish regulations, he fled Budapest for Switzerland. His mother later died in a concentration camp.

Switzerland was not entirely hospitable territory for Solti, either, but he managed to attract piano students after winning the 1942 Geneva International Piano Competition and waited out the war on neutral territory. After the war's end, American troops occupying Germany were intent on rebuilding the country's cultural institutions along non-Fascist lines. With the help of a Hungarian-American musician friend and United States Army officer, Edward Kilenyi, Solti landed a post as conductor at the Bavarian State Opera in Munich in 1946. In devastated Munich, Solti and his wife had to live in a single room in a building that had been bombed; audience members—who might under more fortunate circumstances have given him flowers—gave him coal to heat the room instead. Although wary of anti-Semitism in German-speaking lands for decades afterward, he helped to rebuild Germany's musical life.

Conducted Wagner Cycle

In the late 1940s and early 1950s, Solti continued to work in Germany while beginning a long relationship with English audiences, conducting the London Philharmonic and leading it on tours as far away as South America. As he entered middle age, Solti was one of a number of rising young conductors in Europe but was still not really well known. He worked very hard through the 1950s, adding operatic performances in Chicago, San Francisco, and New York to his schedule and in general seeming to be attempting to make up for lost time. Finally the opportunity that made Solti a star in the classical music firmament came: the Decca record label chose him to lead the first complete recording of Richard Wagner's group of four operas known as the Ring cycle—a massive undertaking that took seven years to complete. The recordings, with Solti conducting the Vienna Philharmonic Orchestra and some of the top Wagnerian singers in the operatic world, have never gone out of print and remain standards of the recorded Wagner repertory.

Soon Solti found himself comparing major job offers. He was wooed by the Los Angeles Philharmonic Orchestra but, on the advice of the aging Austrian conductor Bruno Walter, he decided to remain in Europe for the time being and in 1961 accepted the post of music director of the Royal Opera at Covent Garden in London. Solti's strict Central European training sometimes clashed at first with the idiosyncratic British musical world. Scheduling a choral rehearsal on a Saturday, he was pulled aside and told that the rehearsal conflicted with a major rugby match. He also clashed with England's scrappy music critics, and orchestral musicians sometimes dubbed him the 'Screaming Skull' for his imperious ways in rehearsal. But in time, his ten-year reign at Covent Garden was seen as a golden age for the company. His repertory centered on Wagner and other German-language operas, but he also ventured freely into French, Russian, and Italian works.

Solti married a Swiss woman, Hedwig Oechsli, in 1946, but the marriage ended in divorce in 1966. The following year he met BBC journalist Valerie Pitts when she interviewed him at London's Savoy Hotel. They married and raised two daughters, Claudia (an actress) and Gabrielle (an educator). In 1971 Solti was knighted, and in 1972 he became a British citizen. In English-speaking countries he used the conventional "George" pronunciation for his first name, although he kept its original spelling. He built up the stamina for his jet-setting conducting schedule by playing tennis for an hour each day.

By that time, Solti had taken on the post for which he became best known: in 1969 he became music director of the Chicago Symphony Orchestra. Over his 22 years in that position, Solti built the orchestra into what was widely regarded as the top symphonic ensemble in the United States. The orchestra toured internationally and made a series of recordings that brought Solti a long string of awards. At his death he had received the most Grammy awards of any musician in history—his 32 awards included one for lifetime achievement, and his record still stood as of 2010. One of those awards came in 1988 for a performance in which Solti was at the piano rather than on the podium: a recording of Bartók's Sonata for Two Pianos and Percussion, a work for whose premiere performance a young Solti had served as page-turner.

Stabbed Own Forehead with Baton

Solti conducted works from the 18th century to the present day but focused on the heart of the Central European repertory of the Romantic era. "For me as a conductor, modern music stops around 1950, with late Stravinsky, Schoenberg and Bartók," he said (as quoted by Kozinn). "I don't go much farther. I leave it to the next generation to explore after 1950." In Chicago Solti was a celebrity, and the Chicago Symphony often sold out its entire season before the orchestra took the stage for its first concert. He preferred, however, to make his principal homes in Europe, one of them an Italian villa. An often-repeated story told to illustrate his intensity in action concerned a performance of *The Marriage of Figaro* at the Paris Opera on September 8, 1976: Solti accidentally stabbed himself in the forehead with his baton while conducting, and blood began to roll down his face. Signaling the players to continue, he left the podium to wash it off and soon afterward returned, not missing a beat.

The sound of the Chicago Symphony under Solti, with its burnished strings and powerful, perfectly synchronized brass instruments, was instantly recognizable to classical music enthusiasts, and his talent for drilling an orchestra and bringing it together in a complex score was unmatched. Solti was not exempt from criticism as a conductor, however. "Drama and power were more his thing than lightness or subtlety, and his Mozart was often criticized," noted the *Economist*. Philip Kennicott of the *St. Louis Post-Dispatch* summarized Solti's impact this way: "One went to Solti's concerts for the Solti experience. It was brassy, almost painfully so. He could extend phrases to ridiculous lengths, yet keep them tense

and demanding. He never scrimped on the fireworks of a finale and the chase always left one breathless. It was a mix of explosive bluster and lyrical persuasion; it was unique to Sir Georg Solti."

By the early 1990s, Solti was the last survivor of a large group of Central European conductors who had dominated musical life in much of Europe and the U.S. On stage he had a distinctive profile: bald since his 40s, with large, protruding ears, he was a familiar and much-loved figure. After stepping down as music director in Chicago in 1991, he maintained his busy schedule, releasing a new series of Mozart opera recordings in a lighter, airier style than he had offered previously. In 1997 his calendar was full. "They are going to work me hard, but I can't wait," the nearly 85-year-old conductor told Anthony Tommasini of the *New York Times*. Solti went to Antibes, France with his wife and daughter Claudia for a brief vacation; there he suffered a heart attack and died on September 5, 1997, having just completed his memoirs. Solti ended his career with a legacy of more than 300 recordings to his credit. Some of the best were collected on a five-CD box set, *Solti: A Passion for Music,* issued by Decca in 2007.

Books

Furlong, William Barry, *Season with Solti,* Macmillan, 1974.

Solti, Georg, *Memoirs,* Knopf, 1997.

Periodicals

Daily Mail (London, England), September 8, 1997.

Economist, September 13, 1997.

Investor's Business Daily, December 24, 2009.

Mail on Sunday (London, England), September 23, 2007.

New York Times, September 6, 1997; September 21, 1997.

St. Louis Post-Dispatch, September 14, 1997.

Times, September 8, 1997.

Online

"Georg Solti," *All Music Guide,* http://www.allmusic.com (January 3, 2010). □

Annika Sorenstam

Swedish professional athlete Annika Sorenstam (born 1970) dominated the game of women's golf in the 1990s and early 2000s.

S orenstam became something of a reluctant gender pioneer in 2003 when she entered the Colonial tournament on the men's Professional Golfers' Association (PGA) of America tour. But her most significant legacy when she retired from competitive golf at the end of the 2008 season was her crushing record of tournament victories—she won 89 tournaments, 72 of them LPGA (Ladies' Professional Golf Association) events, notched the lowest score ever in a round of LPGA tournament play, and

set numerous other records. Sometimes compared with Tiger Woods on the men's side of the game, Sorenstam impressed golf fans with sheer technical perfection. "Sorenstam hits a golf ball as if she were possessed, as well as blessed," wrote Andy Brumer in *Sport*, "conjuring up memories of the legendary Ben Hogan, who dazzled with a swing of such machine-like precision that the golf world thought it wouldn't see anything quite like it again."

Admired Tennis Star Borg

Sorenstam's orientation toward sports began early as she grew up in an athletic household in Stockholm, Sweden, where she was born Annika Sörenstam on October 9, 1970. Her younger sister, Charlotta, also became a professional golfer. Annika grew up admiring Swedish tennis star Bjorn Borg, and her quiet, methodical personality on the links came to resemble Borg's. At first, in fact, she took up tennis, not golf, and she made the top 15 in Sweden's junior rankings in that sport. Sorenstam's father, Tom, was a marketing executive with computer maker IBM, and the family spent three years in England after he was given an assignment there. Annika's excellent command of English dated to this period. She was sent to computer camps as a child, but her mind was always on athletics first and foremost.

When Sorenstam was 16, however, she announced that she was giving up tennis. She was burned out on the game, and perhaps she realized that it would be difficult for her to ascend to the game's top levels. Sorenstam's parents, both

avid golfers, encouraged her decision to switch to golf, a sport in which she had already taken lessons. Golf was a rarer sport in Sweden, with its long stretches of winter weather, but it appealed to Sorenstam—its requirement for long, solo practice sessions fit her focused, loner personality. Sometimes she practiced in the snow, using an orange golf ball. When she started playing in youth tournaments, she was so shy that she would sometimes miss putts intentionally to avoid winning and thus having to speak in public. But by her late teens, Sorenstam was a protegée of Pia Nilsson, one of the few Swedish female golfers who had played on the LPGA tour. Sorenstam played on Sweden's national golf team from 1987 to 1992, and her methodical work ethic grew stronger. "I've learned that if I was to get from here to success I have to do it," she explained to Ron Sirak of *Golf World*. "You've just got to dig in. And I think when you reach a certain place it's sweet knowing you did it on your own. As I get closer to what I want, it keeps me going."

Nilsson had played golf at Arizona State University, and no Swedish university had an intercollegiate golf team. So, in 1990 Sorenstam headed for the University of Arizona on a scholarship Nilsson had helped arrange. She fell in love with the American West, and her game developed rapidly in Arizona's year-round sunshine (and even Arizona's rare thunderstorms often found her on the course). In 1991 she led Arizona to the National Collegiate Athletic Association (NCAA) championship, and she earned All-America honors in both 1991 and 1992. She won seven national collegiate titles over her two years at Arizona, which came to an end after she got a taste of LPGA play: she qualified for the U.S. Open in the summer of 1992. Though she finished far back in the pack, she decided to turn pro.

Dividing her season between the European and LPGA tours in 1993, Sorenstam notched four second-place finishes in European tournaments and twice cracked the top ten in LPGA events. Sorenstam also met golf equipment salesman David Esch that year (on a golf course); the two married in 1997 after a long engagement. In 1994 Sorenstam joined the LPGA as a full-time member. She finished second in the British Open that year behind another Swede, Liselotte Neumann, and ended the year with a run of high finishes in LPGA tournaments and was named the LPGA Rookie of the Year.

Spent Week in Bed After Win

The year 1995 marked Sorenstam's breakthrough. Her first LPGA victory came in the U.S. Open at the difficult, high-altitude Broadmoor Golf Course in Colorado Springs, Colorado, as she edged Meg Mallon by one stroke and became the fifth-youngest Open champion in history. Suddenly Sorenstam was a sports star, and the world got its first glimpse of how her game depended on an inner equilibrium that allowed her to exercise her formidable powers of concentration. The sudden rush of media attention and product endorsement offers left Sorenstam tired and disoriented. She withdrew from several tournaments and at one point spent a week in bed. Already known as a loner on the tour, Sorenstam took some criticism for staying out of the spotlight.

Her instincts about her inner resources and capabilities, however, proved absolutely correct. When she returned to the course later in 1995 she finished second at the British Open for the second consecutive year and won the GHP Heartland Classic by ten strokes. Sorenstam ended the year with another major victory at the World Championship of Women's Golf and received Sweden's top sports award, Athlete of the Year. Coming into 1996, Sorenstam was ready to begin one of her stretches of total dominance over the women's game. She won the U.S. Open, held at the Pine Needles Lodge & Golf Club in North Carolina, for a second straight year with a record score of eight under par and an eight-stroke margin over her nearest competitor. Sorenstam's 1997 season began with another group of tournament victories, and the golf industry reaped benefits as sports fans wondered whether she could become the first woman ever to win three U.S. Open championships in a row.

Instead, Sorenstam missed the cut (was eliminated from the competition after two rounds) for the first time in several dozen tournaments. Characteristically, she blamed the debacle on her mental state and looked for ways to improve it. "When I teed off on the first hole at the '97 Open, it was like, 'I'm going to win this,' and I never played thinking that way before," she explained to Brumer. "Normally I go up there and say, 'I'm going to hit this shot in the fairway, I'm going to hit this shot on the green.' That's how I normally play: one shot at a time." Sorenstam bounced back with several more championships and an LPGA record year's earnings of $1,236,789.

Through the late 1990s Sorenstam continued to score several tournament wins each year, with annual earnings in the neighborhood of a million dollars. She and Esch took up residence in a spectacular modern mansion near Orlando, Florida. A largely media-fueled rivalry with Australian golfer Karrie Webb (the two players were friends) enhanced golf viewership. But Sorenstam's performance seemed to be slipping. She once again failed to make the U.S. Open cut in 1999, and by 2000 it had been five years since she had won any of the annual tournaments designated as "majors"—the U.S. Open, the women's British Open, and other tournaments that shifted over the course of Sorenstam's career.

Trained with 750 Daily Sit-Ups

Sorenstam responded by returning to the kind of concentrated training regimen that had propelled her to the top in the first place. She took lessons from PGA pro Dave Stockton Sr., and in early 2001 worked with a personal trainer who mandated running, cycling, swimming, kickboxing, and 750 sit-ups a day, all aimed at developing core strength. Sorenstam saw dramatic results that spring, shooting an all-time women's professional record of 59 in one round of the Standard Register Ping tournament in Arizona. She rolled on the next week with a victory at the LPGA Nabisco Championship—a major—and with that win became only the fourth female player in history to win three consecutive tournaments. Sorenstam began appearing in television advertisements for Michelob Light beer.

Those victories inaugurated another stretch in which Sorenstam ruled women's golf. She won more than $2.8 million in 2002, winning a staggering 13 championships in 25 events, and her average round score of 68.70 was the lowest in women's golf history. In 2003 she was inducted into the LPGA Hall of Fame. But all these accomplishments were eclipsed by her decision that year to enter the men's PGA event at the Colonial Country Club in Fort Worth, Texas. From the start, the decision stirred controversy. The club refused to issue Sorenstam an invitation but was pressured by tournament sponsors into doing so. PGA tour member Vijay Singh announced that if he were paired with Sorenstam in the tournament's first rounds, he would withdraw.

Yet no one could accuse Sorenstam of seeking publicity—although she had modified her solitary ways somewhat, she still shied away from public appearances. Instead, it was generally accepted that, as the *Scotsman* put it, "her decision can be read as a desire to enhance her performance without recourse to drugs." The results when Sorenstam stepped onto the green were mixed. With scores of 71 and 74 over two rounds, Sorenstam came close to making the cut but faltered on the tournament's second day as the pressure increased. However, Sorenstam attributed a subsequent improvement in her short game (play close to the green) to experience she gained in the tournament. The following year, at the Office Depot Championship in Tarzana, California, Sorenstam passed the 50-win mark in LPGA tournament victories, and her eight wins in 2004 brought her to a total of 56. Between 2001 and 2005 Sorenstam entered 104 LPGA tournaments, won 43 of them and finished in the top ten 86 times. In 2005 she published a book, *Golf Annika's Way*.

Observers wondered whether Sorenstam's divorce from Esch early in 2005 might affect her game, but with five consecutive tournament wins that year she seemed unstoppable. A new relationship with marketing executive Mike McGee, who became involved with a range of ANNIKA products ranging from perfume to wine, perhaps took the edge off of any emotional fallout from her divorce. The couple married in February of 2009, and later that year Sorenstam had a daughter, Ava.

Sorenstam was finally slowed by medical problems. In 2007 she was diagnosed with ruptured and bulging discs in her back, and though she recovered to start the 2008 season with three victories, she announced her retirement at the end of that year. "I was getting to the point in golf that there was nothing that motivated me anymore," she told Don Yaeger of *Success*. "I was looking more at my watch than ever. For many years, when I was going to be practicing, the sun was my watch. If it was light, I was out there, and when it was dark I went home." Since her retirement she has been involved with golf course design and has led the Annika Sorenstam Foundation, a nonprofit group that provides help to young female athletes.

Books

Newsmakers, issue 1, Gale, 2001.

Periodicals

Golf World, June 14, 2002.

New York Times, May 18, 2003; October 18, 2009.

Scotsman (Edinburgh, Scotland), May 24, 2003.

Sport, June 1998.

Success, July 200962.

Online

"About Annika," *Annika Sorenstam Official Website,* http://www.annikasorenstam.com (January 5, 2009).

"Annika Sorenstam," *JockBio.com,* http://www.jockbio.com/Bios/Sorenstam/Sorenstam_bio.html (January 5, 2009).

"Biography—Annika Sorenstam," *Ladies' European Tour,* http://www.ladieseuropeantour.info/profiles/010792.htm (January 5, 2009). □

Carl W. Stalling

The American composer Carl Stalling (c. 1891–1974) created a distinctive musical style to accompany the animated cartoons released by the Warner Brothers film studio from the 1930s through the 1950s.

Madcap and inventively eclectic at the same time, Stalling's scores used music from many genres, giving energy to the films in Warner Brothers' *Looney Tunes and Merrie Melodies* series. Stalling was a master at quoting popular songs and classical compositions in such a way as to provide a subtle illustration of the action on screen. In his early years at Walt Disney Studios, Stalling was a key innovator in the field of animated films; he composed some of the earliest animated film scores of the sound film era, and he devised the click track technique that was used for decades to synchronize the playing of soundtrack musicians with the breakneck pace of the action on screen. Only sparsely recognized during his lifetime, Stalling later inspired avant-garde musicians who experimented with styles based on genre mixture and musical quotation.

Found Movie House Work as Teen

Stalling's career has not been fully documented. A native of Lexington, Missouri, he was born around 1891. The year 1888 has also been given, but Stalling was apparently performing at the piano in silent film venues by his early teens; in 1901 and 1902 full-scale theatrical presentations of films were in their infancy. Stalling took lessons on a toy piano repaired and given to him by his carpenter father, and he began playing the organ in church as a child. He remembered being inspired by the film *The Great Train Robbery,* but his recollection of seeing the film at age five must be erroneous; the film did not appear until 1903. Stalling moved to the Kansas City area, and as the film industry grew he found work playing the piano at silent film venues while still in his teens.

The experience of accompanying silent films, a difficult art with few surviving practitioners, was fundamental to Stalling's later accomplishments. Working from a few basic musical themes or preexisting ideas, he had to improvise music for an entire film—and as Stalling continued to work in theaters, films grew from a few minutes in length to as much as four hours. A full-scale movie palace in the 1920s might feature more than just Stalling playing the piano or a theater organ—a full orchestra would be on hand to play pre-composed music for a major production, and in the 1920s Stalling served as music director in Kansas City theaters and conducted their orchestras. It was at Kansas City's Isis Theatre that Stalling happened to meet Walt Disney. The two corresponded, and Disney asked Stalling to come to Hollywood to help him realize films involving a new character created by animator Ub Iwerks: Mickey Mouse.

Two silent Mickey Mouse cartoons had been released without much success by the time Stalling arrived, but the third, *Steamboat Willie* (a parody of the Buster Keaton silent comedy *Steamboat Bill Jr.*), was the first one with Stalling's music and sound. Although it was not the first cartoon with a musical score, *Steamboat Willie* was a landmark in the history of animation. Stalling's music for the film, unlike earlier experiments, was closely synchronized with the action. The synchronization process was long and difficult at first; an initial recording session with conductor Carl Edouarde, simply watching the film on the screen, was a disaster. But Disney was sufficiently convinced that he was on the right track that he sold his expensive Moon Motor Car in order to finance an expensive second session, this time with a bouncing ball in a corner of the screen to help the musicians keep time.

Developed Click Track

When *Steamboat Willie* opened as a curtain-raiser for the now-forgotten crime drama *Gang War* in November of 1928, it became a major hit. Synchronization was difficult to maintain, and as a solution Stalling and others devised the click track, a set of rhythmic cues that studio musicians would hear (at first by means of a telephone hookup, later as a separate recording track) as they played. Stalling later stated that the click track was his idea; it has also been credited to other composers involved with music for early sound films, but Stalling was certainly closely involved with the creation of the technique. It has remained in use for both animated and live-action soundtracks, only partially superseded many decades later by digital recording techniques.

In the early 1930s, as cartoon animation developed rapidly, Stalling was lured away from Disney and worked for several different animators, mostly as an arranger. He joined Iwerks's new studio for its *Flip the Frog* series, and returned to Disney as an arranger on a freelance basis for *The Three Little Pigs.* That film was part of a *Silly Symphonies* series that had begun, at Stalling's suggestion, with *Skeleton Dance* in 1929, and it inspired the enormously successful *Looney Tunes and Merrie Melodies* series at Disney's competitor Warner Brothers. The *Looney Tunes* had been in existence since 1930, but they got a large boost when Stalling, after the closing of Iwerks's studio, came on board in 1936, just as Warner Brothers was assembling its team of pioneering animators such as Tex Avery, Chuck Jones, and others.

Stalling remained with Warner Brothers until his retirement in 1958, and his music accompanied many of the cartoons featuring Bugs Bunny, Daffy Duck, the Road Runner, and other animated figures that continue to delight audiences of all ages. His style as it developed was aided by the fact that Warner Brothers was also a major music publisher, meaning that he had at his disposal a selection of thousands of songs and instrumental compositions that he could draw on in his musical allusions. Stalling's scores, which he turned out at rates as fast as one per week, made liberal use of musical quotations—the viewer of a Road Runner chase in a cloverleaf pattern would suddenly hear the melody of "I'm Looking Over a Four-Leaf Clover," for example. In Stalling's scores, jazz, classical, and popular music bumped up against each other in a way that matched the action onscreen but that was conceptually unusual for the middle of the twentieth century. Stalling was well acquainted with the classical repertory, and it was his longtime arranger, Milt Franklyn, who created the score for a famous meeting of animation and classical music, the Bugs Bunny short *What's Opera, Doc?*

Perfected Musical Techniques in Cartoons

Not all of Stalling's musical innovations involved genre mixture and quotation. Over his 22 years at Warner Brothers, noted Andy Gill in the London *Independent,* "he invented a complete style that we take for granted today." Stalling enlarged the animation studio orchestra in his scores, and his instinct for using it to generate suspense or heighten a film's excitement level put him in a league with serious film composers. "He created the musical language that we associate with animation today," his successor Richard Stone pointed out to Gill. "Devices such as having the music be in sync with people walking; doing eye-blinks on a xylophone; doing a piano glissando when something falls; and using musical puns such as 'The Lady in Red' when a character is wearing a red dress—it's all really his doing."

The jazz element became more important in the high-energy cartoons of the late 1940s and 1950s, and Stalling frequently drew on the music of bandleader and *Your Hit Parade* music director Raymond Scott (Harry Warnow)—so much so that Scott's music has continued to be identified with animated cartoons even though he never composed original music intended for animation. Stalling's production remained strong through much of the 1950s, turning out dozens of scores for cartoons by Jones, Friz Freleng, and other directors each year. After scoring *To Itch His Own* (1957), he retired the following year.

For several decades Stalling, like the other efforts of the animation studios in general, received little recognition, and his name has rarely appeared in musical reference books. He deplored television cartoons, which emphasized dialogue over music. But he lived long enough to see his influence cited by the influential avant-garde composer John Zorn (whose own style has been cinematically oriented in part), who acknowledged Stalling as a primary influence. Zorn explained, as quoted by August Kleinzahler in the online magazine *Slate,* that "in following the visual logic of screen action rather than the traditional rules of musical form (development, theme, variation, etc.), Stalling created a radical compositional arc unprecedented in the history of music.... All the basic musical elements are there—but they are broken into shards, a constantly changing kaleidoscope of styles, forms, melodies, quotations." Stalling died in the Los Angeles area on November 25, 1974.

Books

Contemporary Musicians, volume 50, Gale, 2004.
Goldmark, Daniel, *Tunes for 'Toons: Music and the Hollywood Cartoon,* University of California Press, 2005.
International Dictionary of Films and Filmmakers, Volume 4: Writers and Production Artists, 4th ed., St. James,, 2000.

Periodicals

Austin American-Statesman, November 13, 2003.
Film Comment, September–October 1992.
Independent (London, England), February 16, 1996.

Online

"And Then Came the Jazz Singer and Walt Disney Saw the Future," *The Encyclopedia of Disney Animated Shorts,* http://www.disneyshorts.org/years/1928/steamboatwillie.html (January 4, 2010).
"Carl Stalling," *All Music Guide,* http://www.allmusic.com (January 4, 2010).
"Carl Stalling and Humor in Cartoons," *Animation World Magazine* (April 1997), http://www.awn.com/mag/issue2.1/articles/goldmark2.1.html (January 4, 2010).
Kleinzahler, August, "The Mickey Mouse Genius: The Brilliant Composer Behind Looney Tunes," *Slate,* http://www.slate.msn.com/id/2092021 (January 4, 2010).
"Warner Bros. Cartoons," *Toonopedia,* http://www.toonopedia.com/warner.htm (January 4, 2010).□

William Steinway

German-born American manufacturer William Steinway (1835–1896) built the piano-making firm of Steinway & Sons into a leader in its industry—a position it retains today.

The manufacture and marketing of pianos in the United States in the late nineteenth century in some ways represented the beginnings of the modern consumer economy. The piano, much like the entertainment devices found in middle-class homes of today, was a status symbol worth a major investment for those who could afford it, and it was Steinway who devised ways of convincing buyers that they needed to own the premium products his company offered. As a key figure in this important industry, Steinway exerted an influence on American life that extended far beyond music, and the city of New York, where he spent most of his life, still bears many marks of his presence.

Musically Oriented as Child

William Steinway was born Wilhelm Steinweg in Seesen, in Germany's musically rich Lower Saxony region, on March 5, 1835. His father, Heinrich Steinweg, was a piano maker. Wilhelm attended the Jacobsohn Schule, a mixed Jewish-Christian trade school in Seesen, but he did not have the technical orientation of most of his six siblings. His interests ran to music—he was a fine pianist and a strong enough tenor that some of his friends hoped he would try to become an opera singer. He was athletic, and he also had verbal gifts, mastering both French and English by the time most of the family, fleeing the upheavals begun by the Revolutions of 1848, left Germany for the United States. They arrived in 1850 or 1851, whereupon Heinrich Steinweg anglicized his name to Henry, and Wilhelm became William. Their American surname, Steinway, was partly translated from its German original; "Weg" meant "way" in German.

At first Steinway and his older brother Charles worked as apprentices for the firm of William Nunns & Company. Charles's salary, for work that involved moving pianos on a frequent basis, was recorded at three dollars a week, and William hardly fared better: he had to invest some of his salary in a kind of company bank known as the truck system. When the company went bankrupt, Steinway, owed $300, was among its debtors. Showing a generous streak that persisted through a lifetime frequently marked by litigation, however, he forgave the debt after his own company began to prosper, and even made monthly contributions to a retirement account for Nunns.

A Steinweg piano firm had already existed in Germany, but its American descendant took shape only gradually in the early 1850s as father and sons made pianos for various buyers and honed their skills. The founding of the Steinway & Sons firm dates to March 5, 1853. The company imported European pianos as well as making its own, and despite stiff competition from the Boston firm of Chickering as well as other new American builders, it benefited from a growing market for pianos. William began his career with the company on the shop floor, but it soon became evident that his talents lay in management and marketing rather than in the exacting Steinway manufacturing process, which concluded with the application of six coats of varnish by a skilled workforce dedicated to the task. After some early marketing triumphs that included the placement of a Steinway piano on one of the carriages in a parade celebrating the Union's victory in the Civil War, Steinway took over the business operations of Steinway & Sons in 1865, after the deaths of two of his brothers. Another brother, Theodore (Theodor), managed the manufacturing process.

Promoted Classical Music to Boost Sales

Steinway realized that he could broaden the market for his pianos by promoting classical music in the U.S., and to that end he shepherded the construction of the Steinway Hall on West 14th Street in New York. That venue, attached to Steinway & Sons showroom space, was financed by Henry Steinway, but the younger Steinway continued with the project after Henry's death in 1871, building a new Steinway Hall in London. Similar buildings are now associated with Steinway operations in various European and Asian cities. Steinway also bankrolled tours by visiting European artists, patronized New York's growing opera companies, served for 14 years as president of an organization called *Der deutscher Liederkranz* (The German Song Circle), and backed up all these efforts with print advertising campaigns, something unheard of in an industry that until quite recently had been associated exclusively with the genteel world of European nobility. Steinway understood the value of celebrity endorsements, publicizing the names of artists who played Steinway pianos, and he embarked on an extended behind-the-scenes campaign to influence the judges who rated pianos at the giant Centennial Exposition fair held in Philadelphia in 1876.

These measures propelled Steinway & Sons to the forefront of the industry, rivaled only by Chickering, and the company's workers, many of them skilled craftspeople who had moved from Germany and brought the ideals of trade unionism with them, noticed the company's profits (Steinway himself was worth more than $700,000 by 1872 and soon became a millionaire) and their own advantageous bargaining position: in 1871 the company had been able to fill less than half its orders despite a streamlined operation capable of turning out one piano per hour. The average Steinway worker's wage was less than $900 a year. The natural outcome of this situation was a series of strikes, which plagued Steinway & Sons through the 1870s, with one union action ending violently as police clubbed a group of strikers.

Steinway's response did not rely exclusively on law enforcement, however. Hoping to forestall labor unrest by improving workers' quality of life, he built an entire small community adjacent to the vast new Steinway factory complex in Long Island's Astoria region, now part of the borough of Queens. This company town, which preceded Chicago's Pullman district and other similar projects by several years, consisted of attractive row houses, many of which still exist, and it included amenities such as a church and a public kindergarten. The neighborhood, still occasionally known by its original name of Steinway but now more frequently called Ditmars, was capped by a hilltop mansion on 41st Street, built for Steinway himself; it too still stands.

Envisioned Subway System

As Steinway became one of New York's leading industrialists, his activities began to shape the city's infrastructure. Steinway was the initial developer of the area that became LaGuardia Airport, originally a resort. His Steinway Railway Company brought trolleys and trains to the Steinway factory and served the workers who lived nearby. In the 1890s Steinway wanted to connect his growing Long Island trolley system to that serving Manhattan. He became involved in the planning for the first sections of New York's subway system. He did not live to see the subway completed, but a pair of tunnels under the East River are still known as the Steinway Tunnels.

Steinway was even involved with early American automobile manufacturing and laid the groundwork for what was perhaps the first instance of multinational automaking. His association with autos grew from a meeting at the Centennial Exposition between German automotive designer Wilhelm Maybach and a Steinway employee. In 1888 Steinway and Gottlieb Daimler of the German Daimler-Benz partnership signed an agreement establishing the Daimler Motor Company in the U.S. Steinway contracted with the National Machine Company of Hartford, Connecticut for the building of Daimler engines, which were at first installed in boats at the Steinway factory on Long Island. Shortly before Daimler's death the company produced its first automobiles in the U.S.

Steinway's personal life was less smooth than his professional career, and recent biographies have examined it in often intimate detail; much of it was recorded in the archives of extensive court actions. Steinway married Regina Roos in 1861. The couple raised a son and a daughter but the marriage dissolved after acrimonious accusations of infidelity on Regina's part, corroborated by court testimony. After the death of his brother Henry, Steinway launched an unsuccessful effort to win custody of her three children from his wife, who had immediately remarried. Steinway married Elizabeth Raupt in 1880; they had a daughter and two sons.

In 1892 Steinway was named official piano manufacturer to the imperial German court; closer to home, a succession of Steinway pianos has served the inhabitants of the White House in Washington. Many of the Steinway children remained involved with the operation of the company as its name maintained a long association with the high end of the piano market. Steinway died in New York after a weeks-long struggle with typhoid fever on November 30, 1896. Widely perceived as a multi-millionaire, and worth $13,000,000 by his own estimation, he apparently overextended himself with investments and died, it gradually emerged, in a state of insolvency.

Books

Fostle, D.W., *The Steinway Saga: An American Dynasty,* Scribner, 1995.

Lieberman, Richard K., *Steinway & Sons,* Yale University Press, 1995.

Loesser, Arthur, *Men, Women, and Pianos: A Social History,* Dover, 1990.

Ratcliffe, Ronald V., *Steinway,* Chronicle, 2002.

Online

"A Piano as Bold and Original as the Man It Honors," *Steinway & Sons,* http://www.steinway.com/steinway/limited_edition/wes.shtml (January 2 2010).

"The Men Who Built the Subway," *Forbes* (October 18, 2004), http://www.forbes.com/2004/10/18/cx_sr_1018transitside3_2.html (January 2, 2010).

"Mr. Steinway, Meet Mr. Kreischer," *Forgotten Street Scenes NY,* http://www.forgotten-ny.com/STREET%20SCENES/Steinway/steinway.html (January 2, 2010).

"Steinway and Daimler-Benz," *German-American History and Heritage,* http://www.germanheritage.com/Essays/steinwaydaimler.html (January 2, 2010).□

George Gabriel Stokes

British mathematician and physicist Sir George Gabriel Stokes (1819–1903) made numerous and significant contributions to science in the areas of fluid dynamics, mathematical physics and optics. Among his many achievements, he developed the law of viscosity and developed Stokes' law and Stokes' theorem. He was knighted in 1889.

S ir George Gabriel Stokes, who achieved knighthood in 1889 in recognition for his substantial and numerous scientific contributions, helped advance the fields of hydrodynamics and optics. Most significantly, through his research into viscous fluids, he was instrumental in establishing the foundation for the hydrodynamics science. The equations he developed with French engineer and physicist Claude Navier (1785–1836), which became known as the Navier-Stokes equations, explained the motion of viscous fluids.

Stokes also performed important research related to wave theory of light, pioneered spectrum analysis and discovered the nature of fluorescence. In addition, Stokes became known as the founder of geodesy (the branch of science that deals with the curvature, shape, and dimensions of the earth) through his research into variations of gravity.

Stokes was born August 13, 1819 in Skreen, Ireland in County Sligo. As County Sligo is located close to the sea, people later speculated Stokes' birthplace sparked his later interest in water that, in turn, led to his research on fluid flow.

Stokes was the youngest of six children who grew up in a strong religious home. His father, Gabriel Stokes, was a rector, and his mother, Elizabeth Haughton Stokes, was the daughter of another rector. His three older brothers studied to become priests. Stokes' early education included home tutoring from his father and a church clerk. He began his formal education when he was thirteen years old, when he attended a school in Dublin, Ireland.

A year after his father died (1835), Stokes moved to England where he enrolled in Bristol College, where he studied for two years to prepare for entrance into the University of Cambridge, one of Europe's leading academic institutions. His mother helped finance his tuition.

In 1837, Stokes entered Cambridge as an undergraduate in the university's Pembroke College, where he studied mathematics. After graduating in 1841 with academic honors, he was awarded a Cambridge fellowship. He remained at the university for the rest of his life.

Became a Prolific Researcher

With the security and stability provided by the Cambridge fellowship, Stokes entered into a remarkably productive twenty-year period (1842-1862) that witnessed his most important contributions to science. During this period, he developed the theory of the motion of viscous liquids, conducted research into optics (in particular, investigations on the wave theory of light), developed Stokes' Law (related to hydrodynamics), pioneered spectrum analysis, discovered fluorescence, conducted experiments on the ultraviolet spectrum, and studied variations of gravity (which advanced the field of geodesy).

His first important scientific paper was "On Some Cases of Fluid Motion" (1843), which, as the title implied, involved cases of fluid motion, as well as the steady motion of incompressible fluids. Stokes followed this publication two years later with another equally significant paper that dealt with friction of fluids in motion and the equilibrium and motion of elastic solids. In this 1845 paper, Stokes also improved on Claude Navier's research and his equations of incompressible fluid motion. Stokes' contribution in this area—a new explanation for the internal friction of fluids—resulted in the "Navier-Stokes equation," which revealed that fluid flow is determined by external and internal forces effecting the fluid.

In 1849, Stokes became Lucasian Professor at Cambridge and lectured on hydrostatics and optics. The same year, he published yet another important paper ("The Dynamical Theory of Diffraction"), which involved the effect of internal friction and pendulum motion. Specifically, this major work on hydrodynamics described Stokes' Law, which included Stokes' calculation of the terminal velocity of an object falling through a liquid. Stokes tested his calculations with the action of pendulums.

During this active period, Stokes also studied the principles of sound, analyzing how sound was produced and how its intensity was impacted by wind. Stokes' observations, supplemented by experiments conducted by fellow researchers, fostered greater understanding of previously puzzling natural phenomena, such as the formation of clouds in the sky and the motion of water waves and ripples. Further, his discoveries led to practical applications related to flow of water in rivers and the impact on ships. As a result of his conclusions, and his experiments involving surface gravity, Stokes earned the reputation as a leading authority on the then-emerging science of geodesy, a scientific discipline that focuses on the earth's gravitational field.

Stokes also researched the wave theory of light, publishing his first papers on the aberration of light in 1845 and 1846. In 1848, he published a paper that dealt with theories related to the spectrum. A year later, he produced a paper on the dynamical theory of diffraction, demonstrating that the plane of polarization is perpendicular to propagation direction. In addition, in 1852, he developed a mathematical formula, called Stokes' parameters, which described the characteristics and behavior of polarized light. His work in this area had impact on other research: In 1849, he designed instruments to measure astigmatism in the human eye, and in 1851 he invented a device that analyzed polarized light.

Discovered Fluorescence

Stokes also conducted experiments involving fluorescence, which he first described in his 1852 paper on the wavelength of light. His discovery came about through his earlier experiments with filtered light, which involved passing sunlight through a blue-tinted glass and shining the beam through a yellow-colored quinone solution, which ultimately created a strong yellow illumination. Stokes called this color-changing effect fluorescence. Stokes used fluorescence to study ultraviolet spectra, and he eventually determined that dark spectral lines, which had been discovered by German optician Joseph von Fraunhofer (1787–1826), were lines of elements that absorbed light from the outer crust of the sun. Stokes also conducted research on the theory of spectroscopy, conduction of heat in crystals and X-rays.

In 1862, Stokes published his last major paper (a mathematical study on the dynamical theory double refraction), which he prepared for the British Association for the Advancement of Science.

Influenced Other Researchers

As a university fellow, Stokes proved to be an enormous influence on later Cambridge physics researchers, through his own work and his wide-ranging knowledge of current research that was being conducted outside of Britain. Also, along with Scottish theoretical physicist and mathematician James Clerk Maxwell (1831–1879) and mathematical physicist William Thomson (1824–1907), who is better known as Lord Kelvin, Stokes made Cambridge's school of mathematical physics a major mid-nineteenth century research institution. Stokes worked closely with Lord Kelvin. After Kelvin discovered a little-known work by fellow mathematical physicist George Green (1793-1841), Stokes expanded Green's theorems on invector calculus and subsequently published Stokes' Theorem, a three-dimensional generalization of Green's theorem.

Married Life Reduced Research Activities

In 1857, Stokes married Mary Susannah Robinson, who was the daughter of a well-known astronomer, Thomas Romney Robinson. The marriage would have a significant effect on Stokes' research activities. First, in order to marry, Stokes had to give up his Cambridge fellowship. (At the time, the university had a rule that barred its fellows from marrying. In 1862, however, it rescinded the rule and Stokes was allowed to take up his fellowship again.) Second, Stokes became concerned that his research activities would negatively affect his marriage. Before he wed, he wrote to Robinson expressing in great detail his worries that his work habits wouldn't be conducive to married life. (During his life, Stokes earned a reputation as a prolific letter writer. Reportedly, one of his correspondences ran fifty-five pages.) He appeared more inclined to sacrifice his research, however, instead of his wedding. As he explained to Robinson, he wanted to expand his life experience beyond academic institutions and research laboratories.

After Stokes and Robinson married, they moved to Lensfield Cottage in Cambridge, where they would live for the rest of their lives. There, Stokes set up a small, makeshift laboratory at the cottage. Subsequently, Stokes' career shifted away from intense mathematical research.

At the university, Stokes became much more involved in administrative tasks. His new activities consumed much of his time and seriously curtailed his research output for the remainder of his life and career. In addition, he served as a secretary for the Royal Society of London for the Improvement of Natural Knowledge. As secretary of the Society, Stokes advised researchers on their scientific papers and related work, often suggesting improvements. His dedication to this role was complete, and a fellow Society council member commented (as quoted on the Center for Modelling with Differential Equations website), "One of the distinguishing characteristic qualities of Sir George was the generous way in which he was always ready to lay aside at once, for the moment, his own scientific work, and give his whole attention and full sympathy to any point of scientific theory or experiment about which his correspondent had sought his council."

But close colleagues strongly suggested to Stokes that he find a position that would entail far less administrative functions and allow him more time for research. Stokes ignored the criticisms and continued his administrative work as well as his teaching duties. Still, Stokes was always ready to help other physicists with their own research. This led to an enormous amount of letter writing to people like Green, Lord Kelvin, James Challis, and William Crookes.

Later Career

Stokes' later activities also included lecturing. From 1883 to 1885, he delivered a series of lectures on light at the University of Aberdeen in Aberdeen, Scotland. He also lectured on theology, delivering a series of lectures at the University of Edinburgh, also in Scotland (1891–1893). Appropriate to his upbringing, Stokes remained a religious man throughout his life. In 1886, he became president of the Victoria Institute, an organization that defended religious doctrine against latest scientific discoveries. It was established in response to the publication of Charles Darwin's On the Origin of the Species. Stokes sided with other scientists, including Lord Kelvin, who were skeptical of Darwin's theory of evolution. Stokes remained the Institute's president until he died.

During this later period, Stokes also served as president of the Royal Society (1885–1890). Active in a number of scientific and academic societies, Stokes also served as president of the Cambridge Philosophical Society, from 1859 to 1861. In 1887, he became a member of Parliament, serving as a representative of the University of Cambridge until 1891. In 1889, Queen Victoria knighted him for his scientific contributions.

Died at Cambridge

Stokes died at his Cambridge cottage on February 1, 1903. His wife passed away in 1899. The couple had three daughters and two sons, but their family life was marked by tragedy. Their first two daughters died in infancy. Their second son, William George, who studied to be a doctor, died in 1893 from an accidental overdose of morphine during medical training. Their oldest son, Arthur Romney, however, graduated from King's College at the University of London and later became a master at Shrewsbury School, a renowned public school for boys located in Shrewsbury, Shropshire, England. Their oldest daughter, Isabella Lucy, married a physician and the couple lived with Stokes at Lensfield Cottage after his wife died.

Besides his knighthood, Stokes received many distinguished honors throughout his career. The most important included the Rumford Medal, which he received in 1852 for work related to the wavelength of light, and the Copley Medal (1893). His academic awards included honorary degrees from many universities.

In 1887, his Aberdeen lectures were published as On Light: delivered at Aberdeen University; Burnett Lectures. His other major publications included Mathematical and Physical Papers (five volumes published between 1880 and 1905); Natural Theology (which included the Gifford Lectures delivered at the University of Edinburgh, published in two volumes in 1891 and 1893); Roentgen Rays; Memoirs by Roentgen (1899), and Memoir and Scientific Correspondence of the Late Sir George Gabriel Stokes (1907).

Books

"George Gabriel Stokes," Notable Scientists: From 1900 to the Present, Gale Group, 2008.

"George Gabriel Stokes, Sir," Almanac of Famous People (ninth edition), Thomson Gale, 2007.

"Stokes, Sir George Gabriel. 1st Baronet Stokes," Merriam-Webster's Biographical Dictionary, Merriam-Webster Incorporated, 1995.

Online

"George Gabriel Stokes," Gap-System.org, http://www.gap-system.org/~history/Biographies/Stokes.html (November 23, 2009).

"George Gabriel Stokes," GiffordLectures.org, http://www.giffordlectures.org/Author.asp?AuthorID=160 (November 23, 2009).

"George Gabriel Stokes," Molecular Expressions,, http://micro.magnet.fsu.edu/optics/timeline/people/stokes.html (November 23, 2009).

"George Gabriel Stokes," New World Encyclopedia, http://www.newworldencyclopedia.org/entry/George_Gabriel_Stokes (November 23, 2009).

"George Gabriel Stokes," NNDB.com, http://www.nndb.com/people/131/000097837/ (November 23, 2009).

"George Gabriel Stokes (1819–1903)," Corrosion Doctors,, http://corrosion-doctors.org/Biographies/StokesBio.htm (November 23, 2009).

"George Gabriel Stokes 1819–1903: An Irish Mathematical Physicist," Center for Modelling with Differential Equations, http://www.cmde.dcu.ie/Stokes/GGStokes.html (November 23, 2009).□

James Stuart

English architect, artist, and archeologist James Stuart (1713–1788)—also known as "Athenian" Stuart—contributed greatly to the resurgence of classical architecture and design that pervaded the Western world during the eighteenth century. A somewhat dashing figure who emerged from an untutored background to explore the ruins of Athens and Rome, Stuart worked in practically every field relating to the design of homes, their interiors, and their grounds. The architect's achievements won him numerous honors in his lifetime, including fellowships with the Royal Society and Society of Antiquaries of London, and membership in the drinking club-cum-intellectual group Society of the Dilettanti. His *Antiquities of Athens* was the definitive work of Stuart's career, with new volumes appearing some decades after his death. His inherently indolent nature hampered the depth of his achievements, however, with many scholars speculating that his accomplishments could have been considerably greater if not for Stuart's disinclination to work.

Born in 1713 in the Ludgate Hill area of central London, England, Stuart was the son of a lower-class mariner who died while the future classicist was still a child, leaving his wife and four children completely impoverished. The Stuart family was probably of Scottish descent and practicing Catholics, a religion that had been largely criminalized in sixteenth-century England, with Catholic religious services banned and its adherents barred from a number of public and private positions. Combined with the family's penury and low social standing, this likely kept Stuart from acquiring much beyond the most basic of education in reading and writing; certainly, he lacked knowledge of Latin early in his adult career, a subject typically taught in the schools of the era. Rather than pursuing academia, Stuart signed on as an apprentice to Lewis Goupy, a fan maker and decorator working in London's Soho district. Through this employment, Stuart improved his copying, drawing, and painting skills, producing his first known work, a charcoal self-portrait, sometime between 1730 and 1735.

Traveled to Rome and Athens

At about this time, Stuart seems to have studied Latin and Greek on this own, and employed these skills along with his fan painting expertise to support himself on a trip to Rome in the early 1740s. Writing in *James "Athenian" Stuart: The Rediscovery of Antiquity,* Catherine Arbuthnott noted "that Stuart decided to make the trip indicates he had ambitions beyond simply earning a reasonable living as a copyist and fan painter," due to the possibility of high-profile connections and social expectations that such a voyage entailed. The young artist traveled on foot,

stopping first for a time in Paris to earn some money before continuing through the south of France into Italy; some have speculated that Stuart may have served in the army of Maria Theresa, Queen of Hungary, then engaged in a lengthy conflict over succession to the Austrian throne, as an engineer or other service member. Regardless of this possible delay, Stuart arrived in Rome perhaps as early as 1742 and certainly by 1744, when records attest that he was living in the Salita di San Giuseppe. If Stuart had not already mastered Latin and Greek, during this period he certainly did so, and probably studied painting as well.

Although continuing to make a living largely as a fan painter, Stuart began giving tours to visiting Britons making the Grand Tour and helping them locate quality artworks available for purchase. He seems to have remained constantly in Rome until 1748, when he traveled south to Naples with fellow Englishmen Matthew Brettingham, Gavin Hamilton, and Nicholas Revett on a painting tour. The ruins of Pompeii had at that time been only recently discovered, and the combination of art and archeology was irresistible to the traveling companions. Legend recounts that a trip to Athens was alternately proposed by Stuart, Revett, or Hamilton, and initially all four planned to make the voyage. In 1750, however, only Stuart and Revett—financed by the members of the Society of Dilettanti, which also soon nominated the pair for membership—set out by way of Venice for the ancient Greek capital, then a part of the Ottoman Empire, on what proved to be a dramatic trip. Disease, pirates, and foul weather plagued the journey, but Stuart and Revett arrived in Athens intact in March of 1751.

The events of Stuart's stay in Athens, a somewhat dangerous locale at the time, inspired Jonathan Glancey of the *Guardian* to proclaim Stuart "the Indiana Jones of his day, dodging murderers to pull off astounding architectural coups" in 2007. Amidst the day-to-day work of Revett drawing classical Greek temples and other buildings and Stuart capturing vistas of the countryside and surroundings, the pair's diligent efforts to precisely measure and record every detail of the buildings they observed won them the unpleasant attentions of local officials, who believed them to be spies. The apparently intrepid Stuart also faced down death at least once on an adventure-filled trip from Athens to Constantinople (present-day Istanbul) in 1753, narrowly escaping the intention of his Athenian guide to murder him on the trip by fleeing from a guarded overnight stopping point and pretending to be insane as he came bursting into the next village. Despite these exploits, Stuart successfully reached Constantinople, and from there he and Revett began their journey home to England in 1754.

Began Work on the *Antiquities of Athens*

Stuart arrived back in England later that year or early in 1755, nearly fifteen years after originally setting out for Italy. By this time, his remaining immediate family seems to have all passed away, freeing the artist from the financial responsibility of looking after their welfare but also forcing him to seek lodging, which he took with a James Dawkins. He and Revett turned their attention to finalizing their Athenian drawings, and spent several years perfecting a series of works depicting the city's smaller, less grand edifices. Tireless self-promotion and word of mouth publicity put about by Stuart's and Revett's friends and colleagues drummed up considerable interest in the project, and Arbuthnott observed that "as a result of this publicity, Stuart's reputation in London was made long before a single volume of *Antiquities of Athens* appeared." The Royal Society and Society of Antiquaries granted him membership in 1758, and he became the Surveyor to Greenwich Hospital thanks to the support of Thomas Anson that same year. In 1759, the reading room of the British Museum offered him temporary privileges. Nevertheless, the lengthy manuscript production process of *Antiquities of Athens* irritated those awaiting their promised—and paid for—copies, and has been cited as an example of Stuart's perceived indolent nature.

His return to England also marked the beginning of Stuart's architectural career. Although Stuart had practically no previous experience as an architect, his reputation as a connoisseur of fine art and expert of classical décor apparently qualified him for the job in the minds of the England aristocracy. His first commission, a small job involving the design of a hallway and decorative panels at the country estate Wentworth Woodhouse in Yorkshire, seems to have occurred in the fall of 1755. Stuart's next architectural undertakings, a series of garden structures at Hagley in Worcestershire and the country house Shugborough in Staffordshire, are widely considered the introduction of true Greek Revivalist orders, or column styles. He

also designed for London's Spencer House—the ancestral home of the family of the late Princess Diana Spencer—and decorated the interior of London's Holdernesse House beginning in about 1760.

After several years spent perfecting the text and illustrations for *Antiquities of Athens,* the long-awaited first volume was at last published in 1762. Any grumbles of its delay were swallowed by the immediate outpouring of critical and popular enthusiasm for the work, which was recognized as a seminal piece of scholarship on the art and architecture of classical times. The publication bolstered Stuart's already impressive reputation as an architectural expert, despite the fact that Revett had been the primary creator of the architectural drawings. By the time of the volume's appearance, however, Stuart had bought Revett out of their partnership and—although Revett's name appeared prominently in the opus's full title, *The Antiquities of Athens Measured and Delineated by James Stuart, F.R.S. and F.S.A., and Nicholas Revett, Painters and Architects*—it was Stuart who publicly assumed both the risks of error and the rewards of recognition for the piece. Among these rewards was a sinecure position with the Society of the Dilettanti, which designated him the group's official Painter in 1763; Stuart was later released from this position after years of neglect of his portraiture duties, but not before receiving thousands of pounds in payment from the Society.

As early as the 1760s, Stuart began a lengthy battle with gout, a disease affecting the joints that has been traditionally associated with heavy consumption of meat, fatty foods, and alcohol. Accusations that Stuart was an alcoholic began to surface at about this time, with some also condemning his late-in-life marriage to the sixteen-year-old Elizabeth Blacland as evidence of "Epicureanism," or over-indulgence. The couple seemed genuinely happy, however, remaining married until Stuart's death and having five children together. The architect's professional life faltered, however, as distracted by illness and drink, the naturally somewhat lazy Stuart lagged on the completion of projects and sometimes failed to finish them at all. During the 1770s, society hostess Elizabeth Montagu commissioned Stuart to oversee the design and construction of a new home in Mayfair; she fired him with the house still unfinished in 1780, Stuart having famously taken some five years to decorate one of the house's bedrooms. His final project, the Chapel at Greenwich Hospital, occupied the last eight years of his life. By the time of his death on February 2, 1788, Stuart's gout had probably caused him to suffer from arthritis and other painful complications, contributing to his predilection to the numbing effects of alcohol and further dampening his already limited productivity.

Even after his death, however, the architect had great influence over the physical landscape of London and its environs. The year after his demise, Blacland and former Stuart assistant William Newtown completed the second volume of *Antiquities of Athens*, and a third volume edited by Willey Reveley was published in 1795. In 1816, the fourth version of *Antiquities of Athens* went to press, with a final tome edited by Josiah Taylor rounding out the work's lengthy publication history in 1830. This volume held great sway over the tastes and practices of architects and designers throughout the century and beyond as the Neoclassical style rose to the forefront, and Stuart's own buildings, such as London's Spencer House, standing as prototypical examples of Greek Revivalist architecture. His entry in the *International Dictionary of Architects and Architecture* argued that "Stuart's place in the history of European taste is secure, for he, more than anybody, revealed the glories, dignity and qualities of antique Greek architecture to the world; his influence has been immense, from Russia to America, and from Scandinavia to the Mediterranean Sea." Indeed, art historians and architects continue to recognize Stuart's lasting importance, with London's Victoria and Albert Museum mounting a major retrospective of his artistic and architectural work in 2007.

Books

Campbell, Gordon, ed., *Grove Encyclopedia of Decorative Arts,* Oxford University Press, 2006.

Curl, James Stevens, *A Dictionary of Architecture and Landscape Architecture,* Oxford University Press, 2006.

International Dictionary of Architects and Architecture, St. James Press, 1993.

Soros, Susan Weber, ed., *James "Athenian" Stuart: The Rediscovery of Antiquity,* Yale University Press, 2006.

Watkin, David. *Athenian Stuart: Pioneer of the Greek Revival,* George Allen and Unwin, 1982.

Periodicals

The Guardian, March 23, 2007.

Online

"James 'Athenian' Stuart, 1713–1788," Victoria & Albert Museum, http://www.vam.ac.uk/collections/architecture/past/james_athenian_stuart/index.html (January 4, 2010).□

Pat Summitt

American college basketball coach Pat Summitt (born 1952), during her long career as coach of the University of Tennessee women's basketball team, has amassed more wins than any other coach in college basketball, male or female.

A resumé of Summitt's accomplishments might begin with her 1,000th win, which she notched on February 5, 2009, when her Tennessee Lady Volunteers stomped Georgia by a score of 73–43. But each multiple of 100 wins before that had been a milestone as well: Summitt was the youngest women's basketball coach to win 300, 400, 500, 600, 700, 800, and 900 games. Summitt's teams have won eight National Collegiate Athletic Association (NCAA) championships, and she has made Tennessee into a virtual fixture of the Final Four teams in the NCAA's season-ending annual tournament; incredibly, no University of Tennessee women's player who has entered the program since 1976 has missed playing in at least one Final Four game. And Summitt's coaching accomplishments have come without sacrificing academic accomplishment; the graduation rate for women players who have completed their period of eligibility at Tennessee under Summitt has been 100 percent.

Lived in Log Cabin

Born Patricia Head on June 14, 1952, in Clarksville, Tennessee, Summitt grew up on farms—at first in a log cabin—between Clarksville and Nashville. She was called Tricia or Trish when she was young; the nickname Pat was given to her by supervisors early in her career, when she did not yet have the confidence to correct them. Summitt, the fourth of five children and the first girl, grew up poor at first, as the family lived from crop to crop. Her father, Richard Head, was a strict and physically violent disciplinarian, and she feared him but also credited him with instilling drive and competitiveness in his children. "My father played my nephew in checkers," Summitt recalled to Dick Patrick of *USA Today,* "and Derek would cry because Dad was always beating him. I said, 'Dad, why don't you let him win?' He goes, 'I'm never going to let him win. He's going to have to learn how to beat me.' That's how I grew up. We had to learn to be successful."

One way in which Richard Head was supportive was in his encouragement of his daughter's obvious basketball talent, honed at first on an impromptu court on the top level of a hayloft in competition with her three older brothers, Tommy, Charles, and Kenneth, and younger sister Linda. Summitt, who did not miss a day of school in 12 years of primary education, was a starter for all four years, 1967 to 1970, in which she attended Cheatham County in Ashland City, Tennessee. At the University of Tennessee at Martin she became the school's all-time leading scorer with 1,045 points over four seasons. She was a member of several U.S. national teams, including the silver medal-winning U.S. World University Games team in 1973, the gold medal winners of the 1975 Pan American Games team, and, after graduating, the silver medal-winning 1976 U.S. Olympic team, of which she was co-captain. Summitt received a bachelor's degree in physical education from UT–Martin in 1974 and earned a master's degree in the same subject at Tennessee's Knoxville campus the following year.

By that time, Summitt's coaching career had already begun. Her career on the court had been hampered by a knee injury in her senior year of college, although she battled back from that injury to make the Olympic squad. Hired as an assistant coach and graduate assistant at UT–Knoxville, she was offered the position of head coach by physical education department chair Helen B. Watson after the previous head coach unexpectedly decided to go on leave. Hardly older than her players, and pressured by multiple responsibilities, Summitt led the team to a 16–8 record in her first season (1974–1975) and a 16–11 record the following year. In 1977 she coached the U.S. Junior National Team and led it to two gold medals in international competition.

Won Olympic Gold

After being named assistant U.S. Olympic coach for the 1980 Olympic team (which did not participate in the games due to the U.S. boycott that year), Summitt emerged as head coach in 1984 and led the United States to a gold medal. Meanwhile, her Tennessee teams were racking up winning seasons. In 1982 Tennessee made the NCAA quarterfinals, the so-called Sweet 16, a circle from which they would not depart until 2009. Tennessee went all the way to the Final Four that year, the first of 22 appearances there as of 2010. In 1987 Summitt's Lady Volunteers won the first of the eight NCAA titles they would earn under her leadership.

Head married bank executive R.B. Summitt in 1980; he was the son of the first female pilot in Tennessee's Monroe County. The couple had one son, Ross Tyler Summitt, born on September 21, 1990. The story of his birth is often told as an illustration of Summitt's determination to make a plan and follow through with it. When her water broke, she was on a recruiting trip in Pennsylvania, headed for the home of future Tennessee player Michelle Marciniak. Summitt not only completed her recruiting pitch but boarded her private plane for home, insisting that it not stop until it reached Tennessee airspace. Pat Summitt filed for divorce from her husband in 2007, after an 18-month separation.

As the Lady Volunteers racked up NCAA titles in 1989, 1991, 1996, 1997, and 1998, Summitt's fame grew. The 1996–1998 run marked the first time any women's NCAA team had won back-to-back championships, let alone three in a row. Perhaps the high point of Summitt's career in sheer numerical terms was the 1997–1998 season, when Tennessee did not lose a single game. That season itself became the subject of a book, *Raise the Roof*, that Summitt co-wrote with Sally Jenkins. The same year, the two penned a more general

leadership and management volume, *Reach for the Summit: The Definite Dozen System for Succeeding at Whatever You Do,* in which Summitt also recounted the childhood roots, positive and negative, of her future success. Summitt is also the author of two technical books, *Basketball* and *Basketball: Fundamentals and Team Play,* both written with Debby Jennings.

Inducted into Hall of Fame

The players Summitt coached became stars of women's basketball themselves. Twelve have participated in the Olympics, and 43 have gone on to careers in professional basketball, some of them overseas. Since Summitt became coach, Tennessee has won 27 Southeastern Conference championships in either the regular season or the league's postseason tournament, and 71 players have been named to the All-SEC team. Perhaps the greatest Summitt product of all was Washington Mystics star Chamique Holdsclaw, who was a four-time All-America player at Tennessee and in 2000 was named Naismith Player of the Century. That year Summitt won two important honors of her own: she was named Naismith Coach of the Century and was inducted into the Basketball Hall of Fame.

Summitt achieved all this without distorting her players' priorities. Players spoke of "the stare," but she was never the sort of coach who screamed or threw tantrums, and team cohesion was always a big part of Tennessee's success. "In my four years at Tennessee, I grew as a player, but I grew more as a person," wrote Candace Parker in *Sports Illustrated.* "What I remember most are the times when just she and I were in the office talking. Her door was always open. Coach always remembers birthdays, cares about feelings, and wants her athletes to succeed. . . . Everything she did was to make me a better individual." The Lady Volunteers' perfect graduation record stood in sharp contrast to player graduation rates for most other basketball programs. Friends who interacted with Summitt at her seaside home on the Florida panhandle described her as an individual who was unpressured away from the court. "She doesn't scowl at the beach," University of Mississippi coach Carol Ross told Keith Niebuhr of Florida's *St. Petersburg Times.* "I get to see a different side. I've seen her relax and just be a person."

In the first decade of the new millennium, Summitt ascended to legendary status as she passed one all-time milestone after another. Her 104 victories, out of 124 NCAA tournament games, is an all-time record unlikely to be surpassed among coaches of either women's or men's teams. On March 22, 2005, with a 75–54 victory over Purdue, Summitt notched her 880th victory and became the winningest coach in college basketball, surpassing the record held by University of North Carolina men's coach Dean Smith. Summitt did not slow down in the least after that accomplishment; Tennessee won back-to-back NCAA titles again in 2007 and 2008. Summitt coached her 1,000th victory on February 5, 2009, as the Volunteers beat Georgia 73–43. She told Patrick that she loved the college game and had no desire to coach in a professional league.

That season marked a rebuilding year for Summitt and the Lady Volunteers, as all five starters from the 2008 championship team graduated. In the 2009 NCAA tournament,

Tennessee lost in the first round to Ball State, missing the Sweet 16 round for the first time since 1981. But few doubted that Summitt and the Tennessee squad would be back. Indeed, as of mid-February of 2010, they had lost only two games. The only record left for Summitt to exceed was University of California at Los Angeles coach John Wooden's mark of ten NCAA championships, and, with some years left before retirement, she seemed a strong candidate to do just that. "I love what I do and look forward to going to work," she told Patrick. "I just love it. One thing that motivates me is the competition. It's greater than it's ever been. So is the desire to help this program stay at the top. It's harder now to stay at the top. That challenge inspires me as a coach."

Books

Notable Sports Figures, 4 vols., Gale, 2004.

Summitt, Pat, with Sally Jenkins, *Reach for the Summit: The Definite Dozen System for Succeeding at Whatever You Do,* Broadway, 1998.

Periodicals

St. Petersburg Times (FL), April 4, 2004.

Sports Illustrated, March 2, 1998; February 16, 2009; March 30, 2009.

USA Today, March 15, 2005.

Online

"Head Coach Pat Summitt," *Pat Summitt Official Website,* http://www.coachsummitt.com (January 27, 2010).

"Pat Head Summitt," *Naismith Memorial Basketball Hall of Fame,* http://www.hoophall.com/hall-of-famers/tag/pat-head-summitt (January 27, 2010). □

Marina Svetlova

The French-born, Russian-trained dancer Marina Svetlova (1922–2009), who spent much of her life in the United States, bridged the world of classic ballet and that of American dance education.

S vetlova emerged from her training in the Soviet Union as a teenage dance star. She gained rapturous notices from critics and drew enormous crowds on three continents. In the U.S., where she took up a post as prima ballerina of the Metropolitan Opera Ballet in New York in 1943, she was a noted dancer. But what interested her most about her adopted country was not its existing dance institutions but its potential. In the words of Luca Peragallo, writing in the Bloomington, Indiana *Herald Times,* "She believed in American possibilities, but she gave more than she took. After retiring from the stage, Svetlova enjoyed a long and varied career as a dance educator."

Child of Russian Emigrés

Marina Svetlova was a stage name, taken in emulation of one of the dancer's Russian teachers. Svetlova was born, according to differing reports, Yvette von Hartmann or Tamara-Yvette Hartmann in Paris, France on May 3, 1922. "Born in France," Peragallo wrote, "she was purely a Russian phenomenon in upbringing, character and training." She was the daughter of Max von Hartmann and his wife, Tamara, both of Russian background; part of the White Russian faction that opposed the Bolshevik Communist takeover in Russia, they fled their homeland after the 1917 revolution. When Svetlova was six, she was taken to see a Christmas pantomime and announced afterward that she wanted to be a dancer. The rigorous work required of a top-notch child ballerina was not always agreeable; sometimes she had to be bribed with vanilla ice cream given on the completion of her lessons, and she went through a phase in which she dreamed of becoming an aviatrix. An indication of her determination was that she pursued that dream as well; she took flying lessons starting at age eight and made a solo flight at 12.

Svetlova made her ballet debut in 1931, in *Amphion,* an experimental ballet choreographed by Léonide Massine and mounted by the troupe of Ida Rubinstein. For the most part, however, Svetlova's parents turned down offers from ballet companies that wanted to feature her while she was still a child. She studied in Paris at the Brevet Superieur with Russian ballerinas who had emigrated to France—Vera Trefiloa, Lubov Egorova, and one more whom she memorialized in a 1972 letter to the *New York Times* as a teacher and friend: Mathilde Kchessinska, who had been the mistress of the Russian czar. Svetlova kept in contact with Kchessinska for her entire life, visiting her 97-year-old teacher in Paris and finding her there playing poker. As a teen Svetlova won the International Championship of Dance in Paris for an unprecedented three years in a row.

When Svetlova was 17, she left France for a ten-month tour of Australia with the Original Ballet Russe troupe of the impresario Colonel de Basil, a descendant of the Ballets Russes that had introduced Russian modern dance to Paris in the years before World War I. Although trained in classical ballet, Svetlova had, in the words of an essay by Olia Philippoff included in an American souvenir booklet, "alongside the classical bases, an understanding of modern rhythm and dance." During her Australian tour she was featured in a comic ballet called *Graduation Ball* that later became a favorite in the U.S.; she played a student facing two balding professors, one holding a compass and the other a butterfly net.

Netted Estimated Audience of Two Million

During the first months of World War II, while travel was still relatively unimpeded, Svetlova toured extensively in Australia, Europe, and the Americas, making stops in Mexico City as well as a variety of U.S. and Canadian locations. The souvenir booklet mentioned above, printed in the 1940s, estimated her total miles traveled as 145,000 by steamship, 55,000 by train, and 28,000 by plane, asserting that she had performed for more than two million people. In 1941 she appeared in New York with the Original Ballet

Russe in a ballet by choreographer George Balanchine, *Balustrade,* set to music by Igor Stravinsky. She landed a role as a guest artist with the Ballet Theater (now the American Ballet Theater) and soon after that an ongoing position as prima ballerina (leading female dancer) at the Metropolitan Opera Ballet.

She remained at the Metropolitan Opera until 1950, but almost from the start she had the ambition to perform beyond the island of European culture present in New York City. She formed a small dance troupe of her own and took it on tour, appearing in high school auditoriums or wherever else she could find a stage, in the middle of World War II when disposable income was scarce. Svetlova's parents tried to talk her out of the tour, and the famed Russian dancer Rudolf Nureyev, when he met her, exclaimed (according to Peragallo), "Ah, you're the ballerina who tours the continent in a station wagon!" Svetlova danced with the New York City Opera in 1951 and 1952, took on guest ballerina appearances in the U.S. and Europe, and did some choreography of her own. She also continued to tour with her own small company.

In the 1950s and 1960s Svetlova was associated with various ballet companies. In 1964, as prima ballerina and director of the Dallas Civic Opera and Ballet, she organized a "Tribute in Dance" in memory of President John F. Kennedy, who had been assassinated in the city just over a year before. In 1969 or 1970 she took a teaching job at the University of Indiana, staying on to become professor and, as of the fall of 1970, chairman of the school's dance department. Although she sometimes said that a dancer counts the minutes after turning 22, she appeared in a pair of ballet productions at the school in 1971, when she was almost 50 years old.

Promoted College Education for Dancers

In her role as something of an ambassador for European dance culture in the U.S., Svetlova contributed a number of articles to the *New York Times, Dance Magazine,* and other publications. In a long article called "If Your Daughter Wants to Be a Dancer," published in the *New York Times* in 1972, she contrasted the importance placed on a college degree in the U.S. with the impressive results obtained by early specialization in the Russian and then the Soviet system of training dancers. Although the American emphasis on college "long seemed to me the height of foolishness," she wrote, but "I

have come finally to think it may not be such a bad idea. Just as the experiences of a long and varied life seemed to add depth and understanding to the performances of dancers in my youth, so at least some knowledge of a variety of disciplines (art, science, history, etc.) does seem to speed maturity and consequent insight and breadth of artistry in the young."

Svetlova stayed on as chairman at Indiana until 1976, doubling enrollment in the dance department and arguing in favor of student scholarships. She continued to teach at Indiana until 1992, when she retired and was given the title of Professor Emeritus. Even the heavy teaching demands of a large state university did not exhaust her energy. After having taught at the Southern Vermont Art Center in Manchester, Vermont from 1959 to 1964, she established her own summer dance program, the Svetlova Dance Center, in the town of Dorset, Vermont the following year, continuing as its director until 1995. In addition to classical ballet, the school offered classes in jazz, flamenco, modern dance, and water ballet. Student Jackie Bell-Sargood, speaking to Patrick McArdle of the *Rutland Herald,* recalled Svetlova's "Russian temper. It would flare up but then just as quickly it would be completely gone." Svetlova died at her home in Bloomington, Indiana on February 11, 2009; Peragallo was at work on her biography.

Periodicals

Dance Magazine, May 2009.

New York Times, November 26, 1964; March 26, 1972; August 27, 1972; February 18, 2009.

Online

"About Marina Svetlova," *IU News Room (Indiana University),* http://newsinfo.iu.edu/web/page/normal/10134.html (January 2, 2010).

"Marina Svetlova" (souvenir booklet, New York, 1940s), *National Library of Australia,* http://nla.gov/au/nla.gen-vn3660968 (January 2, 2010).

"Princess of the Dance, Tsarina of the Will," *Herald Times* (Bloomington, IN), http://www.music.indiana.edu/publicity/press/ArticlesPreviews&Reviews/articles/ (January 2, 2010).

"Residents Recall Dancer Svetlova," *Rutland Herald* (Rutland, VT), February 21, 2009, http://www.rutlandherald.com/article/20090221/NEWS02/902210349/1003/NEWS02 (January 2, 2010). □

T

Carl Tausig

The Polish pianist Carl Tausig (1841–1871) was one of the greatest classical musicians of the nineteenth century.

As a pianist, Tausig was rivaled only by his teacher Franz Liszt and by the Russian virtuoso Anton Rubinstein in his own time, and some chroniclers felt that his skills even exceeded those of the more flamboyant Liszt. Tausig at his peak was famous for never letting the audience see him sweat, with only a small wrinkle of tension at the corner of his mouth showing the tremendous physical effort he put forth in virtuoso passages. Tausig is less well known today than those other pianists primarily because he died young, leaving few compositions that might have suggested the nature of his skills; modern historians must rely on verbal descriptions of his playing. Yet the sheer volume of the descriptions that have come down to us, including some from musicians not much given to praising their peers, suggests that those skills were considerable. Tausig has not been well served by English-language biographers; a full-length study of his life would be useful, for his career intersected with those of many of the most famous musicians of the century.

Sneaked Up to Liszt's Piano

Born on November 4, 1841, Carl (or, in Polish, Karol) Tausig was of Polish Jewish background. His father, Aloys Tausig, was a pianist and composer who had studied with the piano virtuoso Sigismund Thalberg. In 1855 Tausig's father took him to the German city of Weimar, hoping to enroll him for lessons with Liszt. The famed pianist, known all over Europe, answered that he had no interest in teaching child prodigies, but Tausig's father did not give up, and managed to get his son seated at a piano in Liszt's rooms. Tausig launched into the "Polonaise in A flat major" by Fryderyk Chopin—one of his specialties, he claimed, because his left hand was oddly shaped in a way that allowed him to play the piece's difficult parallel octaves with ease. Liszt agreed to take him on for a year or two of lessons in Weimar.

At first, Tausig was known for his wild personality, just as Liszt himself had been known as a younger man. The composer and critic Louis Ehlert, as quoted by Harold C. Schonberg in *The Great Pianists,* wrote that his personality combined "gypsy wildness, repulsive rudeness, and prejudice." But no one doubted his talent, and in 1858 he made his formal debut as a touring pianist in Berlin, Germany. Tausig as a 16- or 17-year-old was undisciplined, arrogant, and technically brilliant. Liszt had him visit and play for the greatest German opera composer of the day, Richard Wagner, and Tausig ate his way through Wagner's cheese and candy, complaining that the much older composer was forcing him to go on too long a walk.

Yet Wagner (according to Schonberg) was also bowled over by Tausig's talent, writing back to Liszt: "He is a terrible youth; now I am amazed at his eminently developed intelligence, now at his mad nature." With praise coming his way and training from the two great radicals of central European composition under his belt, Tausig had big plans. He moved from Berlin to Dresden to Vienna, where he decided to establish his own concert series featuring the most musically advanced compositions of the day. The conservative Viennese public was notably unimpressed, and the young pianist faced his first setback. He married pianist Seraphine von Vrabely in 1864, but the marriage did not last.

Took Several Years Off

For several years Tausig stayed off the road, remaking his technique and, if contemporary observers are to be believed,

his personality. When he returned to performing, he had reached the peak of his talents. Gone were the flamboyant gestures, replaced by a seemingly effortless grace that conveyed the impression of total involvement in the music. As the German critic Wilhelm von Lenz put it in his *The Great Pianists of Our Time,* written in the early 1870s, "His distinguishing characteristic was, that he never played for *effect,* but was always absorbed in the piece itself and its artistic interpretation. This objectivity the general public never understood; whenever serpents are strangled, it always wants to know just how big and dangerous they are, and judges of this by the performer's behavior. The general public thinks that whatever *appears* easily surmounted, is not really difficult, and that son or daughter at home might do it just as well! But it was this outward calm, this perfect steadiness of Tausig's attitude, which crowned his virtuosity."

Tausig amassed a considerable reputation over his short life. He toured all the major German cities and visited Russia. A driven man whose hair had begun turning gray by the time he was 27, Tausig practiced for most of the day, pausing only to give lessons and, occasionally, to smoke a cigar or to play chess, a game in which he had a reputation as one of the best players in Berlin. One of Liszt's other pupils, Eugen d'Albert, compared Tausig's piano skills with those of Liszt himself. Reputedly Tausig had memorized the entire repertoire for the piano as it was known at that time and could produce any piece of music for the instrument if asked to, and if he so desired.

Such subjective comments may be difficult to evaluate, but it is significant that Tausig's admirers included not only musicians from the radical side of the European musical divide of the middle nineteenth century, but also those identified with traditional forms and a more conservative outlook. According to Schonberg, Johannes Brahms in Vienna called him "a remarkable little fellow, and a very exceptional pianist, who, incidentally, as far as it is possible for a man to do, is constantly changing for the better." The Viennese critic Eduard Hanslick, who championed Brahms and became Wagner's nemesis, at first criticized Tausig but was later forced to revise his opinion.

Opened School

In 1865 Tausig opened the Schule des höheren Klavierspiels (School for Advanced Piano Playing) in Berlin. As a teacher he could be intimidating. He would often sit down at the keyboard himself and demonstrate how he thought a piece should be played, which made the young American pianist Amy Fay feel, according to Schonberg, "as if some one wished me to copy a streak of forked lightning with the end of a wetted match." Tausig remained in close contact with Wagner and helped to raise money to build the opera house at Bayreuth, Germany, that was (and remains) dedicated to the performance of Wagner's works. Tausig prepared a piano version of Wagner's five-hour opera *Die Meistersinger.* After Tausig's death, however, the anti-Semitic Wagner and his wife, Cosima, appeared to have ambivalent reactions. They professed themselves indifferent to the event, but an epitaph from Wagner appeared on Tausig's gravestone.

Many of Tausig's existing compositions were arrangements of other works, among them the "Toccata and Fugue

in D minor for organ" by Johann Sebastian Bach. That piece remained a standard of the concert repertory for decades after Tausig's death. He composed concert paraphrases, which were elaborate medleys of tunes from popular operas and other works. He also wrote a set of finger exercises for the piano that are still in use among piano students today. A specialist in the piano works of Beethoven, he also arranged six of Beethoven's string quartets for piano. Sergei Rachmaninoff, Tausig's equal at the keyboard, made a recording of Tausig's arrangement of the Johann Strauss II waltz "Man lebt nur einmal" (You Only Live Once).

Shortly before his death, Tausig published two concert etudes that showed a new depth and sophistication. Whether they presaged a significant new direction in his music will never be known; Tausig died of typhus in Leipzig, Germany, on July 17, 1871. His music fell out of fashion along with most of the other showpiece works of the Romantic era, but Schonberg was just one of a number of critics who hoped for its rediscovery.

Books

Baker's Biographical Dictionary of Musicians, ed. emeritus, Nicolas Slonimsky, centennial ed., Schirmer, 2001.

Schonberg, Harold C., *The Great Pianists,* Fireside, 1987.

Von Lenz, Wilhelm, *The Great Pianists of Our Time from Personal Acquaintance: Liszt, Chopin, Tausig, Henselt,* Schirmer, 1899.

Online

"Carl Tausig," *All Music Guide,* http://www.allmusic.com (February 4, 2010).

"Tausig, Carl," *The Jewish Encyclopedia,* http://www.jewish encyclopedia.com/ (February 4, 2010).□

Osamu Tezuka

In his native Japan comics artist Osamu Tezuka (1928–1989) is known as the father of manga or even as the god of manga.

Tezuka did not invent manga, or Japanese comics, but he developed an entirely new style for them. His drawings, which he and others described as cinematic, contributed to the intense, kinetic quality that have made Japanese comics internationally successful. In fact, Tezuka created the first manga character that became widely known outside of Japan: the young robot Astro Boy, known in Japan as Mighty Atom, was featured in an American television series in the early 1960s and has since been transferred to other media including anime, Western animated film, digital download, and even (in 1957) a puppet show. Tezuka also contributed to the broad thematic range that has characterized the manga genre, creating, among other serious volumes, a manga version of Fyodor Dostoevsky's novel *Crime and Punishment* and a manga biography of the Buddha.

Created Martian Trading Cards as Fifth-Grader

Osamu Tezuka (or, in the Japanese naming system, Tezuka Osamu) was born on November 3, 1928, in Osaka, Japan. He came from a family of professionals who generally had an interest in the arts, and once he showed an interest in drawing, his parents gave him a fresh sketchbook each day. He drew his first comic in the third grade, and became an avid reader of the newspaper comics of Tagawa Hosui. By the fifth grade he was creating trading cards with Martian characters for his friends and circulating a mimeographed comics bulletin. His teachers noticed the unusual detail and complexity of his long comic ''A Night in China.''

When he was 11, Tezuka read a picture book about insects and gained a lifelong fascination with them. He incorporated a Japanese character meaning ''insect'' into his pen name. During the World War II years he drew comics about insects and formed a group called the Rikuryo Insect Study Society. In 1944 he contracted a severe case of the skin disease ringworm and was told that he would have to have both of his arms amputated, but he avoided this fate after successful treatment by a specialist. The following year, he was in Osaka when it was firebombed. He drew one war-oriented comic called ''Until the Day of Victory.'' In the summer of 1945 he was admitted to the medical program at Osaka University.

Tezuka conscientiously pursued his medical studies, even though he may have been slowed down by his growing interest in manga. He graduated from the program in

Osaka in 1951, was licensed as a physician, and even completed a doctorate in medicine at Nara University in 1961, writing a dissertation on the spermatozoa of the mud snail. But as early as 1947 he was making waves as a manga artist with his *New Treasure Island* comic, which sold some 400,000 copies. *New Treasure Island* introduced a dramatically new style to the manga world, exemplified by a scene in which a car arrives at a dock and the protagonist must rush to board a ship: Tezuka devoted eight pages to this scene, breaking it down to a succession of frames that resembled those of movie film.

Attempted Cinematic Style

''I felt that existing comics were limiting,'' Tezuka once said, as quoted in an article by Teddy Jamieson of the Glasgow, Scotland, *Sunday Herald.* ''Most were drawn as if seated in an audience viewing from a stage.... This made it impossible to create dramatic or psychological effects, so I began to use cinematic techniques.... I experimented with close-ups and different angles and instead of using only one frame for an action scene or the climax (as was customary), I made a point of depicting a movement or facial expression with many frames, even many pages.'' Tezuka's comic books might be hundreds of pages long.

Even considering that he worked with a staff of assistants—whom he was able to hire as his estimated annual income rose to 2.17 million yen (a little over $6,000) in 1954 and 9.145 million yen in 1961—Tezuka was impressively prolific. By the time he died he had created about 170,000 pages of comics, 700 separate manga series, and 200,000 anime storyboards and scripts. According to Jamieson, his last words were ''I'm begging you—let me work.'' Yet it took Tezuka a long time to become a household name. In 1954 the magazine *Shukan Asahi* noted his high income but described him as an unknown.

By that time, however, Tezuka had created the character that would bring him international renown. Astro Boy, who was the first manga character to make the leap to animated film, first appeared in a comic series Tezuka penned in 1951. The series continued for 16 years, and Astro Boy gradually became ubiquitous in the various versions of the character that appeared in Japanese media. Yoshihiro Shimuzu, general manager of the Tezuka Production Company that was created to administer the artist's growing empire, pointed out to James Brooke of the *New York Times* that when Tezuka created Astro Boy, ''there were still ruins in Japan. People made efforts to create a bright future and better Japan. Astro Boy became the symbol of their dream.

Astro Boy made his debut on television in the United States in 1963 and then in the United Kingdom, France, West Germany, Australia, Taiwan, Hong Kong, Thailand, the Philippines, and other countries as well. Set in 2003, the animated series introduced viewers to the title character, a young robot with human characteristics. Astro Boy not only carried out such typical superhero tasks as fighting crime but also sought to find a peaceful way out of conflicts between robots and their human overlords, hated by Astro Boy's rogue robot brother, Atlas. The series took place in the year 2003, thought in the early 1960s to be a time in which robots would be commonplace. An *Astro Boy* feature film, produced by an American-Japanese-Chinese consortium, was released in 2010.

Deployed Characters in Multiple Stories

Part of Tezuka's appeal was the variety in his work, which was by no means restricted to science fiction. In a country with strong gender divisions in the orientation of comics, Tezuka's work appealed to both boys and girls. He devised hundreds of characters and incorporated them into multiple stories that developed their characters, a process he called his "star system." One of his most popular lead characters was the orphaned white lion, Kimba, who was called Leo in the Japanese version that Tezuka created in 1950. Like *Astro Boy*, the Kimba series, both in print and on television (broadcast as *Kimba the White Lion* in the United States), has enjoyed international distribution and ongoing popularity. The Japanese anime television series based on Kimba's character was the first animated series in Japan to be made in color. The appearance of the animated film *The Lion King* in 1994 caused some viewers to note its resemblances with Tezuka's series, but the film's maker, Disney Studios, denied any direct inspiration.

Treatments of classic Japanese literature were rather common in manga, but Tezuka was notable for his adaptations of Western novels and biographical treatments of Western figures. He released a manga version of *Crime and Punishment* as early as 1953, and in the 1970s and 1980s he created biographical manga representing the lives of Adolf Hitler, Joseph Stalin, and the Buddha. The last of these began to appear in Japan in 1972 and ran to eight volumes; it was issued in English in the United States in 2004 and in Britain in 2006. He also drew an animated version of the Middle Eastern classic *1001 Nights*. These books and films were generally not intended for children. At his death, Tezuka was at work on a manga version of the Bible.

Tezuka married Okada Etsuko on October 4, 1959, and the couple had three children, Makoto, Rumiko, and Chiiko. Beginning in the mid-1960s his influence was frequently recognized in Japan with awards, although outside of his homeland he remained little known until the widespread discovery of manga and anime in the 1990s. Adaptation of Tezuka's manga into Western languages was difficult because the Japanese language is written from right to left, necessitating some rearrangement of the artwork. Tezuka's death from stomach cancer in Tokyo on February 9, 1989, was marked with only brief notices in the Western press, but a large literature on Tezuka and other creators of manga began to appear just a few years later. A full-length treatment of Tezuka's work, *The Art of Osamu Tezuka: God of Manga*, by Helen McCarthy, appeared in the United Kingdom at the end of 2009.

Books

Authors and Artists for Young Adults, Vol. 56, Gale, 2004.

McCarthy, Helen, *The Art of Osamu Tezuka,* Ilex, 2009.

Periodicals

Daily Telegraph (London, England), April 15, 2006.

Globe & Mail (Toronto, Ontario, Canada), February 10, 1989.

New York Times, April 7, 2003; March 13, 2008.

Publishers Weekly, December 22, 2003.

Sunday Herald (Glasgow, Scotland), November 8, 2009.

Online

"Osamu Tezuka," *Comiclopedia,* http://www.lambiek.net/artists/t/tezuka.htm (February 1, 2010).

"Profile," *Osamu Tezuka Official Web site,* (February 1, 2010). □

Vladislav Tretiak

Vladislav Tretiak (born 1952), goaltender for the Soviet Union's national hockey team in the 1970s and early 1980s, is considered one of the best goaltenders in the history of hockey. A three-time Olympic gold medal winner, Tretiak participated in historic exhibition matches against North American professional hockey players that electrified crowds in Canada and the Soviet Union and broke down Cold War barriers in international sports.

Tretiak was born April 25, 1952, in Russia, which was then part of the Communist-era Soviet Union. He grew up in Dmitrovo, a small town near Moscow. He became a hockey player at age 11 after accompanying his mother to the Central Army Sports Club, where she was a gym teacher, and saw other kids in hockey uniforms and wanted to join them. He participated in a tryout the next day, and his natural athleticism won him a spot on the team. He switched from forward to goalie in a deal with the coach: He wanted a uniform, but the team had a shortage of them, so the coach agreed to give him one if he would play in goal.

"In my sports club I grew up among legendary aces of Soviet hockey," Tretiak wrote in his autobiography, *Tretiak: The Legend.* "If I had to count all of my mentors, I would have to name almost all [of the] staff at the Red Army Club at the end of the '60s." By age 19, Tretiak was the top goaltender on the Soviets' Red Army team.

Tretiak first became internationally known in 1972, when he started in goal for the Soviet national hockey team in the Olympics in Sapporo, Japan. The Soviets won the Olympic gold medal. The Summit Series between the Canadian and Soviet national teams later in 1972 was the true turning point in Tretiak's career, though. Before the series, Canadian scouts had dismissed Tretiak as inconsistent and reported that shooters could score on him easily by shooting toward his glove hand. The scouts happened to have based their opinions on one of Tretiak's worst performances, however: an exhibition game in Moscow that year in which he let in nine goals.

The Soviet team surprised North American hockey fans by beating Canada 7-3 in the first game at the Montreal Forum. The extremely hard-fought series, made up of

four games in Canada and four in Moscow, ended dramatically, with Canada scoring the winning goal with less than a minute left in the final game to win the series, four games to three (with one tie). The series established the Soviet national team as equals to North American players. "Those days in the fall of 1972 were the most memorable of my life," Tretiak wrote in his autobiography. "I still get goosebumps whenever I think about it."

Often, Tretiak played best in exhibitions against North American professional players. Some hockey fans consider Tretiak's goaltending in a December 31, 1975 game against the Montreal Canadiens the greatest performance by a goalie ever. Though the Canadiens outshot the Soviets, 38-13, Tretiak made 35 saves to preserve a 3-3 tie. "The Montreal game made a lasting impression on us," Tretiak recalled in his autobiography. "This is what the game of hockey is all about; fast, full of combinations, rough (but not rude), with an exciting plot. I would love [to] play it over again."

Setback in Lake Placid

The 1980 Olympics in Lake Placid, New York, remembered in the United States as the "miracle on ice," represented a low point in Tretiak's career. The Soviets went into the Olympics heavily favored to win a third straight gold medal. In the semi-finals, they faced a United States team made up of young amateur players, not professionals. Tretiak started the game, but as the first period ended, he made a mistake, leaving a rebound in front of the goal after a shot

from center ice. U.S. player Mark Johnson skated in and shot the puck past Tretiak to tie the game at 2-2. Coach Viktor Tikhonov replaced Tretiak with backup goalie Vladimir Myshkin, who faced eight shots and gave up two goals, allowing the U.S. to eliminate the Soviets, 4-3.

The memory still upset Tretiak when *Sports Illustrated* writer E.M. Swift asked him about it in 1983. "I felt fine," Tretiak told Swift. " I was playing well but not spectacularly. The coach panicked. If I had been able to stay on, who knows what the outcome would have been? . . . I will remember this the rest of my life. For me, this was a catastrophe."

After the Olympics, Tretiak considered quitting hockey, but after taking a vacation in a Russian forest to fish and think, he decided to return. In 1981, Tretiak led the Soviets to their first victory in the Canada Cup tournament and was named the series' most valuable player. In 1982, he joined the Soviet All-Stars tour of North America. When Tretiak shut out the Canadiens in Montreal, he was named the game's first star and received a four-minute standing ovation.

Goaltending Secrets

"Technically, what sets Tretiak apart from other goalies is his skating ability," Swift wrote in *Sports Illustrated*. "He flows about the crease seamlessly. . . . Tretiak's superior skating enables him to cut down angles a fraction more quickly, to set himself for a rebound the moment the first shot is stopped. And when he does leave his feet, Tretiak recovers almost instantaneously." Beyond physical skill, Swift added, "Tretiak has a sort of genius for his position, a love of the game, an unwillingness to fail and the absolute conviction that he is a better man than the shooter he is facing."

Tretiak revealed some secrets of his goaltending skills in his autobiography. "Each player has his own distinguishing characteristics on the ice," he wrote. "You only have to understand and remember the mechanics of his movements and then choose the right position in the net. . . . Coming out on the ice, I always had a mental file on the rivals who were most dangerous." When two forwards attacked, Tretiak noted, he watched the eyes of the one with the puck. "If, at the last moment, he looked first at me, and then at the puck, I knew he would shoot," Tretiak wrote. "But if he looked for a moment at his teammate, and then at the puck, I knew he would pass to his partner and I was ready for it."

In 1983, the Montreal Canadiens drafted Tretiak, acquiring the rights to sign him to an NHL contract. Under the Communist system, however, Soviet players, who were also members of the army, needed permission from the Soviet Ice Hockey Federation to play for foreign teams. When Swift of *Sports Illustrated* asked Tretiak in 1983 whether he would play for Montreal, Tretiak grew upset. "I told you," Tretiak said. "I cannot dispose of myself as I wish."

Tretiak never played in the NHL. The Soviet ice federation refused to give him permission. Hockey was the national sport in the Soviet Union, a source of national pride. Soviet premier Leonid Brezhnev often sat on the Red Army team bench during games. "In Russia there were three important things: ballet, cosmonauts and hockey," Tretiak later told Scott MacGregor and Larry Wigge of *The Sporting News*. "The government liked hockey the best. They pushed too hard."

A Final Triumph

By 1984, Tretiak was focused on one final career goal: making up for the loss in Lake Placid by earning another gold medal at the 1984 Olympics in Sarajevo, Yugoslavia. "We waited for the Olympics to come, and trained with no regard for our own health," Tretiak wrote in his autobiography. "Our coaches tried to consider all possible circumstances to prepare the team to fight to the last drop of strength." Tretiak led the Soviet team to a third Olympic gold medal, shutting out Canada 4-0 and Czechoslovakia 2-0 in the final two games. "He was seldom tested, but when the opponents did get a scoring chance, Tretiak never looked better," Swift of *Sports Illustrated* reported.

Tretiak announced his retirement at the end of 1984. He later attributed his decision to the government's insistence on barring him from playing in the NHL and Tikhonov, the coach, refusing his request to spend more time at home with his family instead of living with the team during hockey season. Tretiak finished his career with an appearance in the Izvestia tournament in December of 1984 and an All-Star game of Soviet and European players who had appeared in past Izvestia tournaments.

From 1972 to 1984, Tretiak played 98 international games for the Soviet national team, compiling a goals-against average of only 1.78. With Tretiak as their main goaltender, the Soviets won three Olympic gold medals, 10 world championships, and nine European titles. Within the Soviet hockey league, Tretiak was the first-team all-star goalie for 14 years straight. His Central Red Army team won 13 league titles, and he was named the league's most valuable player five times. He was awarded the Order of Lenin for service to the Soviet Union in 1978. In the early 1980s, he won the Golden Hockey Stick award for most outstanding player in Europe three years straight.

Looking to North America

In 1989, Tretiak was inducted into the Hockey Hall of Fame in Toronto, Canada. He was the first Russian and first non-NHL player to receive the honor. The following year, the NHL's Chicago Blackhawks signed Tretiak as a goaltending coach. Tretiak also set up the Vladislav Tretiak Elite School of Goaltending, which holds annual camps in Canada, with Tretiak providing personal instruction. He was part of a trend: in the early 1990s, as Soviet Communism lost power and the Soviet Union broke up, many Russian players signed with NHL teams. Years later, a Montreal journalist and former member of the Canadian Security Intelligence Service wrote that the CSIS suspected Tretiak of recruiting intelligence informants for Russia in Canada during his visits in the 1990s.

By 1996, however, Tretiak told MacGregor and Wigge of *The Sporting News,* he had grown to love the American national anthem because of Chicago hockey fans' tradition of cheering when it is played before home games. "I like [the] Russian anthem, but [the] American anthem is precious to me," he told them. "The people are so excited. It's unbelievable." Though Tretiak still spent most of his time in Russia, he visited Chicago five times a year during hockey season and was putting all his professional energy into the NHL. "I have

no interest in Russian hockey now," he told MacGregor and Wigge. "The best players are here."

That made Tretiak's return to Russian hockey all the more dramatic. In the late 2000s, Tretiak was named president of the Russian ice hockey federation, the successor to the organization that had once barred him from joining the NHL. In late 2009, Tretiak was named general manager of Russia's 2010 Olympic hockey team. Expectations for the national team were higher than they had been since the 1980s, since the Russians had won the world championships two years straight, and seeing Tretiak as their manager reminded hockey fans of his glory years.

Books

Tretiak, Vladislav, *Tretiak: The Legend,* Plains Publishing, 1987.

Periodicals

Sporting News, December 30, 1996.

*Sports Illustrated,*November 14, 1983; February 27, 1984.

Online

"Q&A with Vladislav Tretiak," SI.com, http://sportsillustrated.cnn.com/hockey/news/2002/09/27/tretiak_interview/ (January 1, 2010).

"Russian rises again on world stage," SI.com, http://sportsillustrated.cnn.com/2009/writers/darren_eliot/10/13/russian.hockey/index.html (January 1, 2010).

"Tretiak's Olympic intrigue, best first-passers, more notes," SI.com, http://sportsillustrated.cnn.com/2009/writers/michael_farber/10/13/tretiak.defensemen.leafs/index.html (January 1, 2010).

"Vladislav Tretiak," Vladislav Tretiak Elite School of Goaltending, http://www.goaltending.net (January 1, 2010). □

Tasha Tudor

The American illustrator and writer Tasha Tudor (1915–2008) gained fame with her books for children as well as for her own lifestyle, which inspired many who sought a more spartan, modest existence.

Tudor lived her entire life in the 20th century, but she often insisted she was the reincarnation of a sea captain's wife who lived from 1800 to 1842. Her watercolors and elegant pen-and-ink drawings recalled the pastoral simplicity of early nineteenth-century America. In *Major Authors and Illustrators for Children and Young Adults,* Ilse L. Hontz wrote that Tudor "brings another world of peacefulness into our consciousness." Her illustrations were an extension of a deep-rooted longing for what she called her former life, and she expressed this longing authentically in the way she lived. Tudor spent her adulthood in rural settings, living and working in farmhouses often with no electricity or running water. She woke early, milked her cows and goats, gathered eggs from her chickens, and harvested fabric from her flaxseed field to spin into clothing. And along the way, she created a durable body of children's literature.

Nickname came from *War and Peace*

Tudor's ardent enthusiasm for a virtually extinct world began when she was around nine years old. Born in Boston as Starling Burgess on August 28, 1915, to well-connected socialites Rosamond Tudor and William Starling Burgess, she spent her early childhood nurtured by nannies and engrossed in dance lessons. The artists John Singer Sargent and Maxfield Parrish were among the family's friends. Tasha's mother was a portrait painter, and her father was a nautical engineer who called her Natasha after Leo Tolstoy's heroine in *War and Peace*. After her parents' divorce in 1924, she took to using her mother's last name, and eventually had her name legally changed to Tasha Tudor. The divorce brought on even greater changes. After the separation, Rosamond Tudor moved to Greenwich Village to establish herself as an artist. Reluctant to raise her daughter amidst the Jazz Age lifestyle of 1920s New York, she sent Tasha to live with family friends at a large farm in Redding, Connecticut, where she visited her daughter on weekends.

Tasha's new Connecticut family lived a life far removed from her Boston upbringing. Rules were decidedly lax, and the guardian she called Aunt Gwen wrote plays for Tasha and the neighborhood children to act out, often dressing them in old-fashioned costumes. Tasha took to those, going to auctions as early as age ten to buy old clothes of her own. The atmosphere in which Tudor grew up was, by her own recollection, unconventional, creative, and free from discipline. On weekends, she often returned to New York to be with her mother.

The atmosphere in Connecticut inspired some of Tudor's earliest drawings, which depicted old-fashioned rural living, cozy farmhouse hearths, and some of the animals she cared for and adopted as pets. Tudor grew up reading books illustrated by Beatrix Potter, Edmund Dulac, Randolph Caldecott, and Walter Crane, all of whom would later have an influence on her own illustration style. As a teenager she read the eighteenth-century novel *The Vicar of Wakefield* in an edition illustrated by Hugh Thompson, and suddenly decided she wanted to be an illustrator. She also knew the illustrations of *Peter Rabbit* author Beatrix Potter as a child and was likely influenced by them. For a year Tudor attended the School of the Museum of Fine Arts in Boston, but she always credited her mother with teaching her the finer points of painting and drawing. Over a span of 70 years she would illustrate nearly 100 books and lend her talent to thousands of Christmas cards, calendars, posters, and valentines.

Sent Hand-Bound Volumes to Publishers

In 1938 Tudor married fellow Redding resident Thomas Leighton McCready, Jr. in a small ceremony. She wore her great-grandmother's dress and walked down the aisle to a fiddler's rendition of the wedding march. They raised two sons, Seth and Thomas, and two daughters, Bethany and Efner. Tudor's new husband encouraged her to put together a portfolio of drawings to send to publishers. She was turned down many times before her first book was accepted by

Oxford University Press. *Pumpkin Moonshine* (1938) was a story inspired by and written for her young niece Sylvie Ann. The version sent to publishers was hand-bound by Tudor in a calico fabric. Oxford issued several of Tudor's books with a similar-looking binding; these are known today as Tudor's "calico books." Tudor's first few publications established her signature drawing style, which was carefully detailed and delicate. Her *New York Times* obituary quoted a 1941 article, also from the *Times*, that described her drawings as having "the same fragile beauty of early spring evenings."

Early on in Tudor's career, both she and McCready (and later their daughter Efner) wrote the books that served as vehicles for her illustrations. Some were about family pets, such as *Linsey Woolsey* (1946), *Thistly B* (1949) and later *The Christmas Cat* (1976). In addition, Tudor drew new illustrations for classics such as Frances Hodgson Burnett's *The Secret Garden*. Her version of *Mother Goose* (1944), which was successful enough to finance the family's move to a New Hampshire farm, was named a Caldecott Honor Book, as was the learn-to-count guide *1 Is One* (1956), which she wrote as well as illustrated. By that time she was popular enough that *Life* magazine reported on the wedding of two of her dolls. Tudor received many honors as a writer and illustrator, including the Catholic Library Association's Regina Medal, but she never kept track of these accolades herself.

Tudor was divorced from McCready while their four children were still young, and she raised them on her own at their rustic New Hampshire farmhouse. There was no electricity, and water was obtained from a pump in the barn. According to a visitor, nothing in the house whatsoever was made of plastic. Tudor lived as self-sufficiently as possible, teaching her children from an early age to help her around the farm. Together the family grew their own food, and Tasha spun thread and wove or sewed most of their clothing. She made homemade cheese with antique presses. Tudor continued to use the world around her as inspiration for her work, often dressing her children in Victorian garb and having them sit for sketching sessions. Tudor's daughter Bethany recalled having the sense of living in one of the tales her mother illustrated, and many of the stories Tudor wrote were taken directly from real goings-on around her home. *Becky's Birthday* (1960) was a retelling of one of Bethany's birthday parties, and *A Time to Keep* (1977) detailed the family tradition of decorating an egg tree each Easter. Tudor's personal favorite of all her books was *Corgiville Fair* (1971), which depicted the world through the eyes of her 13 beloved Welsh Corgi dogs. That and several other Corgiville books were written by Tudor herself. A second marriage, to Allan John Woods, also ended in divorce.

In 1972 Tudor purchased 250 acres in Marlboro, Vermont, near her son Seth's home. Seth, a carpenter, built his mother a nineteenth-century-inspired farmhouse to her specifications. The home included the comfort of electricity, but still had no running water. Tudor continued to write and draw her stories in the same way she always had, at her kitchen table with the work balanced in her lap. She applied her gardening prowess to the new home, planting elaborate flower and vegetable gardens that themselves reflected her delicate artistic style. Her homespun ways included folklike maxims, such as her contention that it was best to sleep in a feather bed with one's nose pointing north. Tudor was skilled in handling both a dulcimer and a gun.

In 1989 Tudor became a partner with Mrs. David Mathers in the small Indiana-based publishing house Jenny Wren Press. She regularly appeared at book signings and talks all over the United States, establishing cottage industries around her books and varied other talents, which also included basket weaving, soapmaking, and handmade crafts, costumes, and illustrations. Tudor's artwork has been shown at the Norman Rockwell Museum in Massachusetts, the Henry Ford Museum in Michigan, and in Japan, where she has been popular. Beginning in the late 1990s she spent less time in the public eye, with the exception of a tradition started with friends at Adams Farm in Wilmington, Vermont: a tea party was held each year on her birthday and 85 guests from all over the world would pay to come and have tea with Tudor. Tudor published her last book, *Corgiville Christmas,* in 2002.

Tasha Tudor maintained her dedication to farm life, with help from her family, until her death at the age of 92. She regularly credited her long life to goat's milk, gardening, and the maintenance of a positive outlook. Tudor passed away peacefully at her Marlboro home on June 18, 2008. "Einstein said that time is like a river," she was quoted as saying on the web site Legacy.com. "It flows in bends. If we could only step back around the turns, we could travel in either direction. I'm sure it's possible. When I die, I'm going right back to the 1830s. I'm not even afraid of dying. I think it must be quite exciting."

Books

Major Authors and Illustrators for Children and Young Adults, 2nd ed., Gale, 2002.

Tudor, Bethany, *Drawn from New England: Tasha Tudor, a Portrait in Words and Pictures,* Collins, 1979.

Periodicals

Albany Times Union (Albany, NY), August 31, 2003.

Christian Science Monitor, July 25, 2008.

New York Times, June 20, 2008.

USA Today Magazine, January 2006.

Online

"Tasha Tudor," *Memorial Websites,* http://www.memorial websites.legacy.com/tashatudor/homepage.aspx (January 22, 2010).

"Who Is Tasha Tudor?," *Tasha Tudor and Family,* http://www. tashatudorandfamily.com/who-is-tasha-tudor.html (January 22, 2010).□

V

Bill Veeck

American baseball team owner Bill Veeck (1914–1986) was the most eccentric, colorful, and innovative executive in his sport. He was often called the Barnum of Baseball, after circus promoter P.T. Barnum, because of his outrageous showman's stunts to promote the game.

William L. Veeck, Jr. was born on February 9, 1914, in Hinsdale, Illinois. His father, former sportswriter William Veeck, became president of the Chicago Cubs when his son was three years old. The younger Bill worked at the stadium starting at age 11, filling mail orders for tickets and selling soft drinks in the stands during games. He helped launch a baseball tradition before he was even an adult: he planted the ivy that still covers the brick walls of Wrigley Field, the Cubs' stadium.

When his father died in 1933, Veeck left college to make a living working for the Cubs. He became an office assistant with the team, making $15 a week. Meanwhile, he took night classes in business law and accounting. Veeck worked his way up in the Cubs organization and became treasurer of the Cubs in November of 1940, when he was only 26. The following year, he purchased the Milwaukee Brewers, then a minor-league team in the American Association, for $100,000. The team improved under his leadership, winning three league championships in a row.

Talking to an interviewer in 1941, Veeck succinctly explained his ownership philosophy. "To be successful in baseball, you must have more than a winner," he said (as quoted by George Sweda of the *Plain Dealer* in Cleveland). "You have to sell baseball to the customer other than from the field of play. Once you get the customer into your park, you have to show him you still are interested in him after he has paid to get in."

In December of 1943, Veeck enlisted in the U.S. Marine Corps. He spent nine months serving in the Pacific during World War II. While Veeck was serving on the island of Bougainville in Papua New Guinea, the recoil of an antiaircraft gun crushed his right foot. He was given an honorable discharge after his injury. Over the years, he underwent several surgeries and eventually had to have his right foot and his leg below the knee amputated.

Bought Cleveland Team

In 1946, when he was 32, Veeck and several partners bought the Cleveland Indians baseball team. That made him the youngest person who had ever been top executive of a major-league baseball team. Veeck made his mark quickly. His fun, down-to-earth personality impressed Clevelanders. He sat in the stands with them, instead of in a private box. Once, he helped the grounds crew roll up the tarpaulin from the infield after rain. Veeck displayed his knack for showmanship: he set up an Indian tepee in center field and had an orchestra and strolling musical bands play at each game. He added fireworks and vaudeville shows to night games and gave away free nylon stockings on Ladies' Days. He moved the team out of Cleveland's small League Park, where they had been playing on weekdays, and installed them full-time in the enormous Municipal Stadium downtown, on the shore of Lake Erie.

Veeck played a major role in ending organized racism in baseball. Soon after Jackie Robinson became the first black player in major-league baseball in 1947 by joining the National League's Brooklyn Dodgers, Veeck broke down the racial barrier in the American League by signing Larry Doby to

the Indians. The next year, Veeck signed Satchel Paige, a black pitcher who had spent most of his career in baseball's Negro leagues. Veeck received 20,000 protest letters from racists who objected to the signing of Doby. In his autobiography, *Veeck—As In Wreck,* he said he responded to them all. "Any man should be judged on his personal merit and allowed to exploit his talents to the fullest, whether he happened to be black, green, or blue with pink dots," he wrote. The 1948 Indians, with Doby in the starting lineup and Paige a star pitcher, won the American League pennant for the first time in 28 years and went on to win the World Series. That season, 2.6 million fans visited Municipal Stadium, making the Indians the first major-league team with a season-long home attendance of more than two million.

Veeck's flair for pageantry helped keep the team's home attendance above the two million mark in 1949, even though the Indians did not return to the World Series. The day the Indians were mathematically eliminated from the pennant race, Veeck held a funeral for the team in center field, complete with a horse-drawn hearse, and buried the pennant from the previous year. "I cast myself as the mortician, a role for which I was undoubtedly fitted," Veeck wrote in *Veeck—As In Wreck.* "I was resplendent in a high silk hat and a low sense of humor. To the accompaniment of a funeral dirge, the flag was lowered and folded sadly into a pine coffin."

Veeck sold the Indians in late 1949 to help pay for his divorce from his first wife, Eleanor Raymond, a former elephant trainer for Ringling Bros. Circus. (He married Mary Frances Ackerman, whom he met while she was working as a publicist for an ice show, in 1950. They had eight children together.) Though he owned the Indians for less than four years, Veeck probably remains the most beloved owner in the history of Cleveland sports.

Hired Pinch-Hitting Midget

In the summer of 1951, Veeck and most of his partners from the Indians bought the St. Louis Browns, a perennial losing team that was struggling financially. Veeck decided the Browns needed an entertaining stunt to attract attention and excitement. So in August of 1951, Veeck signed Eddie Gaedel, a 26-year-old midget from Chicago, and had him pinch-hit in a game. He had Gaedel pop out of a giant cake created to celebrate the American League's 50th anniversary. Then, the three-foot-seven-inch Gaedel, wearing a uniform with the number 1/8, strode to home plate and walked on four straight pitches, mostly because his strike zone was only a few inches tall. Critics called the stunt vulgar and exploitative. The next day, American League president Will Harridge banned Gaedel from baseball. Veeck, mock-outraged, declared Harridge was discriminating against little people.

"Eddie gave the Browns their only distinction," Veeck wrote in *Veeck—As In Wreck.* "He was, by golly, the best darn midget who ever played big-league ball. He was also the only one."

The stunt did not help the Browns' dire economic situation or Veeck's low standing with other baseball team owners. Veeck and his partners concluded that the Browns could not compete with St. Louis' other team, the Cardinals, and sought permission to move his team to Baltimore. After much disagreement, the American League approved the move in 1953, but only after Veeck and his partners agreed to sell the team.

Chicago Tribune columnist Bob Verdi explained Veeck's poor relations with other owners this way: "Veeck disliked presence and formality, and if you wore a necktie, especially on a hot afternoon, you automatically were down to your last strike with him." That went over poorly with the other owners, "the grim and officious pinstriped gang he made sport of" (as Verdi put it). "If they viewed him and his . . . designated midget as props of an unbalanced mind, he nailed them on three counts of being utterly gloomy."

Two Stints with the White Sox

Veeck returned to Chicago baseball by buying the city's White Sox in 1959. The team had a strong lineup—it had played well toward the end of the 1958 season—so Veeck did not make major changes, except for an intangible one. "Veeck created a mood," baseball writer Bill Gleason told Gerald Eskenazi, author of *Bill Veeck: A Baseball Legend.* "Veeck came in and he just excited the entire city. There was a feeling that never was here before — that this man wanted to win."

The 1959 White Sox won the American League pennant, though they lost the World Series to the Los Angeles Dodgers. Before the next season, Veeck traded away several of the team's young players, and the White Sox performed poorly the next year. Yet Veeck's innovative showmanship was as sharp as ever. He created a new baseball tradition by putting White Sox players' names on the backs of their uniforms (at first, just on their road uniforms, not the ones they wore at home). In 1960, he debuted Comiskey Park's famous 130-foot-tall ''exploding scoreboard,'' which lit up like a pinball machine and set off fireworks when a White Sox player hit a home run.

Veeck sold the White Sox in June of 1961 on the advice of his doctors. He was suffering from several illnesses and had been advised to slow down and recover. Veeck spent the next several years in early retirement in a converted farmhouse in Easton, Maryland. He bought the Suffolk Downs racetrack near Boston and owned and operated it until 1971. A bold supporter of social causes, Veeck walked in the famous civil-rights march in Selma, Alabama in 1965, insisting on walking on his peg leg without a crutch. He declared that he had voted for the late Socialist candidate for president, Norman Thomas, in 1968 and 1972. ''I'd rather vote for a dead man with class than a live bum,'' he explained (according to Sweda of the *Plain Dealer*).

After hearing in 1975 that the White Sox were near bankruptcy and that the owners were on the verge of moving the team from Chicago to Seattle, Veeck stepped in. In about 10 days, he and his friend Andrew McKenna, with the help of Chicago Mayor Richard J. Daley, raised $11 million to buy the team. On the team's opening day at Comiskey Park, Veeck celebrated his return, and the 200th anniversary of the United States' Declaration of Independence, by reenacting an iconic painting from the American Revolutionary War, the ''Spirit of '76'' march, with Veeck as a fife player, his friend and fellow White Sox executive Rudie Schaffer as drummer, and manager Paul Richards as flag-bearer.

But another trip to the playoffs was not to be. The White Sox finished in last place in 1976 and, though they surged into first place for part of 1977, they fell to third place by the end of the season. As ever, Veeck enlivened Comiskey Park with his promotions: belly dancers, circus acts, actors performing scenes from Shakespeare plays, and ethnic nights to celebrate the diverse heritage of Chicagoans.

One promotion, Disco Demolition Night in 1979, is known as one of the worst (yet most legendary) stunts in baseball history. A Chicago disc jockey who hated disco music promised to blow up a huge boxful of disco records in center field between games of a White Sox doubleheader. After the explosion, crowds of young music fans rushed the field, pulled down the batting practice cage, set fires, and tore up clumps of sod. Veeck himself grabbed a microphone and repeatedly asked the youths to leave. Police eventually had to clear the field, arresting 37 people.

Under Veeck, the White Sox struggled to compete in the new era of free agency, which placed teams in bidding wars for players and drove their salaries toward the millions. ''It's not the high price of stardom that bothers me,'' Veeck quipped (according to Verdi of the *Chicago Tribune*), ''it's the high price of mediocrity.'' Veeck sold the team in 1981, but he remained a fan. In 1985, a photographer took a picture of Veeck sitting in the bleachers in Comiskey Park, shirtless and shoeless, enjoying a White Sox game and the summer sun.

Veeck died of cancer on January 2, 1986. He was 71. He was inducted into the National Baseball Hall of Fame in 1991.

Books

Eskenazi, Gerald, *Bill Veeck: A Baseball Legend,* McGraw-Hill, 1988.

Lewis, Franklin, *The Cleveland Indians,* Kent State University Press, 2006, p. 231-276.

Veeck, Bill, and Ed Linn, *Veeck—As In Wreck: The Autobiography of Bill Veeck,* The University of Chicago Press, 1962.

Periodicals

Chicago Tribune, January 3, 1986; January 3, 2008.

Plain Dealer (Cleveland), January 3, 1986.

Online

''Veeck, Bill.'' World Book Advanced. http://www.worldbookon line.com (January 1, 2010).□

Lars von Trier

The Danish filmmaker Lars von Trier (born 1956) became one of the most controversial figures in European cinema in the late twentieth and early twenty-first centuries, with extreme films that were completely original in conception, yet filled with dark imagery, usually involving women, that humiliated even the performers in his films.

V on Trier won awards and received scathing criticism, sometimes from the same critics or at the same events. He has been, in the words of Lucia Bozzola of the *All Movie Guide,* ''unapologetically confident in his artistry and an unabashed provocateur''; he has shown an ability to create shocking images and to keep his work in the headlines of cinema writing for an extended period of time. Yet the critical focus has been on von Trier's work rather than on the director himself. A sufferer from agoraphobia and plagued by an extreme fear of flying, von Trier has spent most of his life in the Danish capital of Copenhagen where he was born. ''Basically, I'm afraid of everything in life, except filmmaking,'' he was quoted as saying by Jason Burke of the London *Guardian.* Von Trier has been anything but a publicity hound, and this has forced critics and fans of experimental film to try to come to terms with his movies themselves.

Given Super 8 Camera

Von Trier was born Lars Trier in Copenhagen on April 30, 1956. He added the ''von'' while in film school as a tribute to the Austrian silent filmmaker Erich von Stroheim (whose own real name likewise lacked that noble prefix). Von Trier grew up in a permissive environment even by the standards

writers of the epidemic story themselves contract the disease. Von Trier first showed hints of his future inclination toward dark stories involving women with a 1988 production and re-envisioning of the Greek tragedy *Medea,* made for Danish television. Von Trier released the final film in his trilogy, *Europa,* in 1991. That film was retitled *Zentropa* for its release in the United States, and von Trier also used that name for the Copenhagen studio he established the following year on the site of a disused U.S. army base, complete with a tank that rested for years just outside his office. In 1991 von Trier also began work on *Dimensions,* for which he planned to film three minutes per year for 30 years, aiming at a premiere on April 30, 2024.

Zentropa, a surrealistic film set in Germany just after World War II, impressed critics with its virtuoso use of technical experiments such as superimposition of images and shifts between black-and-white and color film, and it began to bring von Trier international renown. Over the next several years he made the Danish television series *The Kingdom,* which may have been inspired by the U.S. series *Twin Peaks.* Von Trier suffered a personal crisis in 1995 when his mother died, revealing on her deathbed that von Trier's biological father was not the man who had helped raise him.

Von Trier's response to this event took several forms, which combined to lead the director into deeper rebellion against conventional modes of filmmaking. He converted to Roman Catholicism. He joined a group of other film-makers in signing a manifesto known as Dogma 95 (or, in Danish, Dogme 95), which held that filmmakers should tell contemporary stories in a simple, naturalistic style marked by the use of natural light and sound, handheld cameras, and on-location filming. And his storytelling turned toward female figures who suffer some kind of tragic event and then are drawn into humiliation or degradation.

These new directions were all evident in *Breaking the Waves* (1996), which remains perhaps the director's best-regarded film. Shakespearean actress Emily Watson starred as Bess, a woman in a seaside village in Scotland whose husband is paralyzed in an accident. Since physical inti-macy is no longer possible for the couple, her husband asks her to have affairs with other men so that he can experience sex with her vicariously, and the situation spirals down toward a grim conclusion. Von Trier's knack for creating a bleak atmosphere was effectively deployed in *Breaking the Waves,* which earned him a Best Director award from the New York Film Critics Circle.

Von Trier also continued with a somewhat more main-stream parallel career directing or producing films for Dan-ish television, including *The Kingdom II* and the romance *Morten Korch,* based on a series of paperback books that were pooh-poohed by literary critics but to which he had cannily acquired the rights. His own films, however, grew steadily darker. *The Idiots* (1999) stirred controversy with its depiction of a group of commune members who "spaz" (using the film's word) to disturb those around them. The full-scale critical division that greeted many of von Trier's later films first appeared in the reaction to *Dancer in the Dark* (2000), an extremely unorthodox film musical in which the heroine, played by the experimental Icelandic musician

of one of Europe's freest societies. His parents were fol-lowers of both Communism and nudism who disdained ideas of discipline, and he has said, according to Jessica Winter of *Slate,* that the only things that were prohibited to him as a child were "feelings, religion, and enjoyment." He began making films with a Super 8 camera he was given at age 11, and in 1968 he appeared in a Scandinavian tele-vision series called *Clandestine Summer.*

The director-to-be, mostly homeschooled, spent much of his twenties partying, but he also educated himself thor-oughly in the history of European cinema. He knew the canon of film classics well by the time he enrolled at the Danish Film School in Copenhagen in 1979, and he was especially influenced by a director from his own country, Carl Theodor Dreyer, whose silent film classic *The Passion of Joan of Arc* (1928) combined technical experimentation with an excruciating portrayal of female martyrdom. Von Trier's student films inspired excitement as well as unease, and after he graduated in 1983 he was able to find financing and begin his career with *The Element of Crime* in 1984. Like some of von Trier's other films, *The Element of Crime* was in English.

The film, telling the story of a detective brought down by his own methodical nature, was the first of a trilogy of dark thrillers that painted a bleak picture of contemporary Europe; its successor, *Epidemic* (1987), involved a film-within-a-film story of a doctor who tries to cure a deadly disease, not real-izing that he himself is spreading it. The border between film and a layer closer to reality is blurred when the screenplay

Björk, goes blind and is later robbed, compelled to commit a murder, and eventually hanged. The film won von Trier his long-sought Golden Palm award at the prestigious Cannes Film Festival in France, but its grim subject matter disturbed many viewers, and according to Winter, a disillusioned Björk accused von Trier of emotional pornography.

Recruited Nicole Kidman for Film

Dancer in the Dark was the first of several von Trier films set in the United States, a place von Trier had never visited. His 2003 film *Dogville* featured a cast of American stars capped with a performance by Australian-American star actress Nicole Kidman in the lead role of a woman named Grace, set in the small town named in the title. Dogville, as in the classic Thornton Wilder play *Our Town,* is minimally defined through the use of a few painted lines depicting different buildings. "Grace," in the words of *Time*'s Richard Corliss, "is the beneficiary of the townspeople's Christian charity, then the victim of their envy, malice, lies and sadism. She stoically endures a spate of abuse nearly as long and relentless as Jesus' in the Mel Gibson gospel [*The Passion of the Christ*]. Her resurrection, though, takes a different, darker turn."

After the production of *Dogville* and its 2005 sequel, *Manderlay,* von Trier was accused of anti-Americanism. He offered some justification and a partial guilty plea in an interview with Geoffrey Macnab of the London *Guardian*: "I must say I am as anti-Danish as I am anti-American, but it's OK. I don't mind being called anti-American. There's a big part of America I like—but then there is a part that I am not so crazy about." Von Trier planned to complete his American trilogy with a film called *Washington,* but interrupted it to work on other projects. Von Trier was sidelined in 2007 by a period of hospitalization for depression.

The Boss of It All, a satirical film set in an office, was something of a change of pace for von Trier, but his commitment to technical experimentation was undiminished. He made the film using a computerized process he called Automavision, in which a computer took over the function of shot selection from the director. Von Trier returned to his usual preoccupations in 2009 with *Antichrist,* which became his most controversial film up to that time. Combining elements of psychological drama, marital saga, and horror, *Antichrist* told the story of a couple (designated only as He and She) whose toddler falls to his death through an open window while they are having sex. After a period in which they seem to come to terms with their grief, they descend into a nightmare of violence and mutilation.

Antichrist heightened the polarization of critics and cinema lovers into firmly pro- and anti-von Trier camps. Lead actress Charlotte Gainsbourg won the Best Actress award at the Cannes Film Festival for her performance in the film, but von Trier was given a special ad hoc award for misogyny at the same festival, and charges of misogyny were leveled at the director from various quarters. Winter defended the director in her *Slate* essay, conceding that von Trier "has got hang-ups, no question. But his saving grace is that he couldn't give an actress a standard 'wife' or 'girlfriend' role if his life depended on it." One of the few critics to occupy the middle ground was Anthony Lane of the *New Yorker,* who wrote, " I

see no reason to ally oneself wholeheartedly either with those who despise von Trier for his horrific silliness or with those who revere his ambition. Both have a point, and the problem is that von Trier, even at his most objectionable, can summon a wealth of images that defy explanation." By the end of the twenty-first century's first decade, von Trier's reputation as a fearless original, whether one to be welcomed or criticized, was fully secure.

Books

International Dictionary of Films and Filmmakers, Volume 2: Directors, 4th ed., St. James, 2000.
Stevenson, Jack, *Lars von Trier,* British Film Institute, 2008.

Periodicals

Entertainment Weekly, October 30, 2009.
Guardian (London, England), May 13, 2007.
New Yorker, October 26, 2009.
Newsweek, December 9, 1996.
Time, October 11, 1999, p. 84; April 12, 2004.

Online

"I'm a Control Freak—But I Was Not in Control," *Guardian* (London, England), http://www.guardian.co.uk/film/2006/sep/22/londonfilmfestival2006.londonfilmfestival (January 22, 2010).
"Is Lars von Trier a Misogynist?," *Slate,* http://www.slate.com/id/2233158 (January 22, 2010).
"Lars von Trier," *All Movie Guide,* http://www.allmovie.com (January 22, 2010).
"Lars von Trier," *Senses of Cinema,* http://www.archive.sensesofcinema.com/contents/directors/02/vontrier.html (January 22, 2010).
"Lars von Trier Interview," *Time Out London* (July 28, 2005), http://www.timeout.com/film/news/553/lars-von-trier-interview.html (January 22, 2010).□

Diana Vreeland

American style icon Diana Vreeland (1903–1989) dominated fashion journalism for the better part of the twentieth century. Born in Paris, Vreeland grew up in Manhattan, and as a young woman spent some formative years in Europe that served to hone her innate elegance, eccentric beauty, and keen intuition for fashion and style. She began at *Harper's Bazaar* in the 1930s and spent nearly three decades there before becoming editor in chief of the U.S. edition of *Vogue.* Her editorial vision was pivotal in the transformation of women's fashion magazines from moribund chronicles about the lives of socialites to publications that discovered and promoted the latest trends. "Ravishing personalities are the most riveting things in the world," she once explained, according to Eleanor Dwight's 2002 biography *Diana Vreeland.*

"**Conversation, people's interests, the atmosphere that they create round them—these are the things that I feel are the only things worth putting in any issue.**"

Vreeland penned a volume of memoirs, *D.V.,* that was published just after her eightieth birthday in 1984. There are some factual errors, but Dwight, her biographer, did establish that Vreeland was indeed born in Paris on July 29, 1903. Her father, Frederick Dalziel, was from a respectable Scottish family that had few financial assets left by that point. Emily Hoffman Dalziel, her mother, came from a more substantial American fortune. When Vreeland was still an infant the family returned to New York City, where her younger sister, Alexandra, was born. During her childhood and teen years the eldest daughter had a complicated relationship with her gallivanting, tempestuous mother, who once reportedly told her, "It's too bad that you have such a beautiful sister and that you are so extremely ugly and so terribly jealous of her," Vreeland recalled in *D.V.* "This, of course, is why you are so impossible to deal with."

Married Banker Reed Vreeland

Vreeland was slim and elegant, but had a rather pronounced nose in an era before rhinoplasty became commonplace. Nevertheless, she was a popular teenager in Manhattan's rarified world of elite private schools and society events. Her formal education was nominal and included a stint at the Brearley School and private ballet classes. At the age of 19 she was "presented" at her debutante ball, which took place at the Ritz-Carlton Hotel and was attended by 800 guests. A few months later, she met Reed Vreeland, a recent graduate of Yale University who was just starting a career in banking. They wed on March 1, 1924, just a few days after a scandalous story broke in the New York newspapers involving Vreeland's peripatetic mother. Emily Dalziel was named as a correspondent in a divorce case filed by the wife of Sir Charles Lockhart Ross, the inventor of the Ross rifle and a man with whom Emily had spent time in Africa on big game hunts. Vreeland's planned society wedding was severely curtailed, and her mother died just three years later at the age of 50.

As newlyweds, the Vreelands lived in Albany, New York, where her husband's bank job took them, and they soon became parents to two sons, Thomas (called "Tim") and Frederick (known as "Frecky"). In 1929 Reed was transferred to London, and in the space of a little over a year the Vreelands' names could be found on the "Court Circular" pages of the *Times* of London, which lists the social events attended by England's royals. They lived in grand style in a house at 17 Hanover Terrace, for Vreeland had inherited some money, but financial worries would plague the couple for much of their otherwise harmonious married life; her husband earned only a modest salary, and both spent lavishly. "When I was living in London, if you were sufficiently well-born and well known, you could mount bills *forever,*" Vreeland recalled years later in an interview with Jesse Kornbluth in *New York* magazine. For a time, she had a lingerie boutique off Berkeley Square patronized by affluent women. She sourced the fabrics in Paris and hired Spanish nuns to sew the garments.

Hired by *Harper's Bazaar*

Vreeland and her husband returned to New York City in late 1935. Not long afterward, she was spotted dancing at the Hotel St. Regis—wearing a white lace Chanel dress paired with a bolero jacket and red roses in her hair—by Carmel Snow, at the time the editor of *Harper's Bazaar.* Snow was entranced by Vreeland's chic look and invited her in for a meeting; Vreeland later asserted that her visit to the magazine was the first time she had ever been inside an actual office. Snow hired Vreeland to write a column for the monthly magazine called "Why Don't You?" It first appeared in August of 1936 and featured such outré suggestions as "Why don't you ... Turn your child into an Infanta for a fancy-dress party? Remember that little girls of eleven to thirteen look divine in black taffeta with crimson sashes," according to Dwight's biography. The outlandish suggestions, borrowed heavily from Vreeland's experiences abroad among a declining European elite, were at once widely discussed and quickly parodied by satirical journalists of the day.

Vreeland became a fashion editor on staff at *Harper's Bazaar,* working with art director Alexey Brodovitch to create elegant, creative editorial spreads. When she started working full time, she was exhausted at the end of the first week and said she might quit. In the interview with Kornbluth, she described telling her managing editor, "'I can't go from eight o'clock breakfast to 8:30 dinner with nothing to eat.' [The managing editor] said, 'Why don't you have *lunch?*' It's true—*absolutely* true—and it rather changed my life."

Before Vreeland's boys entered boarding school, they were looked after by a German governess who spoke French to them. The family lived at 400 Park Avenue, but also had a country house on an estate belonging to Reed's family in Brewster, New York. Its two-story living room was painted shocking pink. During World War II, her husband moved to Montreal for his job, and Vreeland worked on finding new fashion trends for American readers in light of drastic wartime shortages. Leather was scarce, for example, so Vreeland pushed ballet flats as alternative footwear; heating oil was rationed, and *Harper's Bazaar* featured turtleneck sweaters, like the swan-necked Vreeland herself favored.

Moved to *Vogue*

Vreeland had long been favored with free clothes from top designers in both Paris and London, but kept her own look streamlined. She had a penchant for a uniform of sorts, habitually wearing a simple black sweater and black wrap skirt to the office, accessorized with t-strap heels whose soles her maid supposedly polished religiously. Red remained her favorite color for interiors, however. "Red is the great clarifier—bright and revealing. It makes all other colors beautiful," she said, according to Dwight. "I can't imagine becoming bored with red—it would be like becoming bored with the person you love."

After more than 20 years with *Harper's Bazaar,* Vreeland was widely expected to become editor in chief upon Carmel Snow's retirement, but was bypassed in favor of Snow's niece in 1958. Vreeland remained on the job as fashion editor for the next four years, and began taking photo shoots to even more exotic locales with the advent of the Jet Age that drastically reduced transoceanic flight times. In 1962 she was hired by *Harper's Bazaar's* longtime competitor, *Vogue,* as its fashion editor. The title and other Condé Nast publications had recently been acquired by Samuel I. Newhouse Sr., who promised Vreeland a generous salary and unlimited budget for editorial shoots. Vreeland quickly ran afoul of *Vogue's* editor in chief, Jessica Daves, who quit a few months later. Vreeland succeeded her in the job.

Became Iconic New Yorker

Vogue under Vreeland reached further than any mainstream American fashion magazine had ever done. Though she was nearly 60, she recognized that a decisive new era of fashion was emerging in what would become known as the "Youthquake." She hired a slew of young, college-educated assistants and subeditors, who energized the copy and overall content. Known for her famously arcane pronouncements, Vreeland was also a fastidious manager who trained staffers to keep track of details via the various yellow legal pads she wielded. The walls of her office were painted in a deep red lacquer, offset by leopard-print carpet.

The imperious editor in chief played by Meryl Streep in the 2006 screen adaptation of the novel *The Devil Wears Prada* actually dated back all the way to Vreeland's era. Though she generally arrived at the office after the noon hour, Vreeland kept her aides busy all morning taking dictation over the phone. Her maid would phone to alert staffers of her arrival. Felicity Clark, her assistant, told Dwight that when that call came in, the premium Rigaud candles the editor favored for her office would be lit. "I think most of her staff, when they started to smell the candles, knew that she was either in or on her way," Clark recalled. "She would then make this sort of royal progress down the passage." Unlike the film's fearsomely chilly boss, however, Vreeland treated staffers to a ride home in her own town car if she asked them to work late at the office.

Always devoted to the exotic, Vreeland sent teams of models, stylists, and photographers to Turkey, Morocco, India, Thailand, and even the mountains of Japan and the Syrian desert for *Vogue* photo shoots. She launched the careers of some of the era's top-earning models—Veruschka, Penelope Tree, Marisa Berenson, and Lauren Hutton among them—and encouraged creative ideas from her staffers, some of whom would go on to head *Vogue, Harper's Bazaar,* and other magazines.

Vreeland's tenure at *Vogue* ended with the onset of an economic recession in 1969–70. The president of Condé Nast, Perry Ruston, began to question her extravagant expenses, especially when she went to view the Paris collections. Vreeland habitually favored European designers in the magazine, and advertising revenues began to drop. Several major advertisers associated with Seventh Avenue, the center of the U.S. fashion design and manufacturing industry, petitioned Ruston and Newhouse for a change. In the January 1, 1972, issue—*Vogue* was a bimonthly at that point—Vreeland was listed as a consultant editor, and her "retirement" was announced the following August.

Revitalized the Met's Costume Institute

Vreeland had been widowed six years earlier, and though she was a doting grandmother to several children of her two sons, she wanted—and needed—to keep working. She landed at the newly reopened Costume Institute of the Metropolitan Museum of Art. Because its permanent collection was of a fragile nature, its board decided to create an annual exhibition centered around a particular theme, and Vreeland was appointed consultant for these. Her visionary ideas were a perfect fit for the Costume Institute, and her long list of friends and associates contributed generously to the kickoff fundraising galas. Her first show was a tribute to the Spanish couturier Cristóbal Balenciaga in early 1973, followed by tributes to Russian peasant design, late imperial China, and the equestrian life. In her final years, her health began to fail. She suffered from macular degeneration and, thanks to a lifelong cigarette habit, emphysema. In the last two years before her death, only a few close friends, among them Jacqueline Kennedy Onassis and *Vogue's* André Leon Talley, were permitted to visit her Park Avenue abode. She died on the way to New York City's Lenox Hill Hospital on August 22, 1989, at the age of 86.

A memorial service was held for Vreeland at the Metropolitan Museum several weeks later. True to form, she was extravagant until the very end. The programs for the service were emblazoned with "D.V." in the exuberant way she signed her memos and correspondence. "She always said she loved 'D.V.,'" writer George Plimpton told Georgia Dullea of the *New York Times,* who wrote that the term was "also shorthand for *Deo volente* ('by the grace of God')" in Latin. "That," explained Plimpton, "was how Popes signed their papal bulls."

Books

Dwight, Eleanor, *Diana Vreeland,* HarperCollins, 2002.
Vreeland, Diana, *D.V.,* Alfred A. Knopf, 1984.

Periodicals

New York Magazine, November 29, 1982.
New York Times, February 27, 1924; March 28, 1962; November 7, 1989.□

Bill W.

The American organization leader William Griffith Wilson (1895–1971), known for much of his life simply as Bill W., was the co-founder and primary coordinator of Alcoholics Anonymous.

Wilson's identity was publicly revealed only after his death, but the British novelist Aldous Huxley famously called him "the greatest social architect of our century." Wilson established an entirely new way of treating alcoholism in the United States, with, by most accounts, dramatically better results than those obtained by the methods used before Alcoholics Anonymous (AA) was founded. He named the group, devised its basic decentralized structure, shepherded it through its early years, and created a vocabulary of 12-step programs, admissions of powerlessness, and vows to make amends that became familiar in the United States and worldwide.

Raised in Single-Parent Home

William Griffith Wilson was born on November 26, 1895, in East Dorset, Vermont. His paternal grandfather operated a tavern (where Wilson was born), and his father, who was an alcoholic, was a quarry supervisor until he left the family and looked for work in Canada. Wilson was raised by his mother, Emily. He compensated for his insecurity and slight stature by working hard at whatever he did, and he rose to become captain of the baseball team and conductor of the school orchestra at Burr and Burton Academy, a private high school. Shaken by the sudden death of a girlfriend, he did not graduate, but instead enrolled at Norwich University, a Vermont military college, and majored in engineering. With

the entry of the United States into World War I in 1917 he enlisted in the army, attended officers' training school, and was commissioned as a second lieutenant and stationed at New Bedford, Massachusetts.

At a party there, Wilson accepted his first drink, widely reported as a Bronx cocktail. In Vermont he had met Lois Burnham, a member of an old New York family, while she was on vacation, and the two married in 1918. He was sent to France days later and returned, according to an account in his *New York Times* obituary, "with a hangover." The couple moved into Burnham's parents' house in New York, where Wilson worked as an insurance company investigator and took law school classes at night. When the stock market began its great upward run in the 1920s, Wilson abandoned his law school plans and took off on a tour of the Northeast on a motorcycle, with his wife riding in a sidecar, searching out promising small companies. He mailed confidential reports back to brokerage houses, which profited handsomely and rewarded him well.

The trip was accompanied by heavy alcohol consumption. "I was drinking to dream great dreams of greater power," Wilson later recalled, as quoted in his *Times* obituary. He shrugged off his wife's concerns by saying that great men often came up with their best ideas while drunk. The stock market crash of 1929 did not dent Wilson's self-confidence but did initiate his slide toward rock bottom. Convinced of his own genius, he thought he could turn his household's deteriorating finances around. That attitude was fueled by still greater alcohol intake, and in 1933 Wilson began the first of four stays at New York's Towns Hospital. There he was subjected to the largely ineffective alcohol cures of the day, one of which involved treatment with the poison belladonna and was popularly called, according to Susan Cheever, writing in *Time* magazine, "purge and puke."

Read Philosophical Works

Alcoholics Anonymous, so different from any approach to addiction that had existed previously, may seem to have emerged out of nowhere, but, as Jack Alexander of the *Saturday Evening Post* put it early in the program's existence, it was in some ways a "synthesis of old ideas rather than a new discovery." Wilson had plenty of time for reading in his hospital bed, and he turned to philosophy to try to understand his problems. He absorbed writings by Austrian psychiatrist Carl Jung, who had explored how profound spiritual awakenings could sometimes combat alcoholism, and he read *The Varieties of Religious Experience* by the American philosopher William James. One of his doctors told him of his then-rare belief that alcoholism was a disease, not a moral failing, and Wilson later worked to promote that attitude. Another seed of the future organization came in November of 1934, when Wilson was visited by his friend Ebby Thacher, a member of a loosely evangelical British organization called the Oxford Group, which emphasized personal moral responsibility and specific restitution to those an individual has wronged. Thacher suggested that Wilson should admit he was beaten by alcohol and pray to whatever God he might believe in. Wilson would later call Thacher his sponsor.

Even then, Wilson did not stop drinking, but soon—sources give various dates in late 1934—he experienced a supernatural event. In his book *Alcoholics Anonymous Comes of Age* he described it this way: "All at once I found myself crying out, 'If there is a God, let Him show himself! I am ready to do anything, anything!' Suddenly the room lit up with a great white light. I was caught up in an ecstasy which there are no words to describe. It seemed to me in my mind's eye, that I was on a mountain and that a wind not of air but of spirit was blowing. And then it burst upon me that I was a free man." His doctor, according to the *Times* obituary, said, "Something has happened to you that I don't understand. But you had better hang onto it. Anything is better than the way you were." Wilson never took another drink, and he began to attend Oxford Group meetings and to attempt, zealously but usually unsuccessfully, to convert other alcoholics to his way of thinking.

He continued to experience the temptation to drink, after he returned to his brokerage work and found it no more successful than before. During a fruitless trip to Akron, Ohio, Wilson paced in front of the Mayflower Hotel, trying to talk himself out of going in and ordering a drink. Panicking, he entered the hotel and called a local minister. Through a chain of several other phone calls involving Oxford Group members, Wilson was led to Dr. Robert H. Smith, a surgeon who had struggled unsuccessfully with alcoholism. As the two talked, Wilson's own desire for a drink disappeared. Smith himself quit drinking on June 10, 1935, and the two would recognize that day as the birthdate of Alcoholics Anonymous. Both realized that helping other alcoholics was a crucial part of their own cures. Wilson later wrote, as quoted by Cheever, that "because of our kinship in suffering, our channels of contact have always been charged with the language of the heart."

Asked Rockefeller for Support

As Wilson and Smith began to meet with other alcoholics, they came to believe that it was important to leave their social backgrounds behind and assume a temporary anonymity. Wilson became Bill W., and Smith became Dr. Bob. Wilson held meetings at his wife's home on Clinton Street in New York City, and it was at this point, according to Cheever, that he began to use the now-familiar introduction: "My name is Bill W., and I'm an alcoholic." Wilson by now had no full-time means of support, but he had characteristically big plans for a chain of alcoholism treatment centers. At one point he appealed to financier John D. Rockefeller for support, but the tycoon advised him that his ideas were of the sort that large amounts of money would ruin, and gave him only a modest sum. By 1939 Wilson and his wife had lost their house to foreclosure; they were forced to depend for some years on the hospitality of friends, and for a time they lived in a room above the New York headquarters of Alcoholics Anonymous. The organization got its name from a book Wilson published that year.

Alexander's 1941 *Saturday Evening Post* profile of Wilson and his organization marked a major step in AA's public acceptance, citing physician and judiciary approval of the group's techniques. The article repeated AA's claims of a 50 percent immediate success rate, plus another 25 percent whose cures were interrupted by one or two relapses, as opposed to an estimated cure rate of just two or three percent for traditional approaches. The group's membership ballooned from 2,000 to 8,000 after the article appeared. As AA grew, Wilson began to stress the concept of anonymity; he began to use the name Bill W. exclusively and left instructions that his identity be revealed only after his death. He said, according to the *Times* obituary, that "anonymity isn't just something to save us from alcoholic shame and stigma; its deeper purpose is to keep those fool egos of ours from running hog wild after money and fame at AA's expense." He was widely recognized when he visited AA meetings, however. Wilson was responsible for AA's modest scope as a corporate body; individual chapters of the group collected their own dues and elected delegates to a General Services Board that Wilson promoted and which, in 1954, took over the leadership of AA from its two founders. Individuals who wished to contribute to AA were limited to a gift of $1,000.

Wilson devoted himself partly to writing, as the organization he created grew into a ubiquitous feature of American life (and eventually became worldwide in scope, although it has been strongest in North America). The 12-step formulation embraced by AA members was codified in the 1953 book *Twelve Steps and Twelve Traditions*. *Alcoholics Anonymous Comes of Age* (1957) was a history of the organization, and was at first unattributed on the cover. Wilson wrote numerous articles, some of which were collected into the book *The AA Way of Life as Bill Sees It*. Wilson declined a request from *Time* to feature him on the magazine's cover, even with his back turned. His wife, Lois, founded the auxiliary Al-Anon and Alateen groups, aimed at family members of problem drinkers.

After retiring from formal involvement with AA in 1962, Wilson continued to speak at AA gatherings. Wilson personally, along with AA in general, took some criticisms as the organization grew; one was that Wilson remained addicted to tobacco use, which may have caused the emphysema that plagued him in the 1960s and forced him to make his final annual address to AA members from a wheelchair. He died on January 24, 1971, in Miami Beach, Florida, while he was under treatment for emphysema and pneumonia.

In the years since his death, Wilson's trials and accomplishments have received increased exposure in various media. Actor James Woods won an Emmy Award for his portrayal of Bill W. in the 1989 Hallmark Hall of Fame television production "My Name is Bill W." In 1999 *Time* named Bill W. to its list of 100 top heroes and icons of the twentieth century. Full-length biographies of Wilson by Robert Thomsen (1975) and Francis Hartigan (2000) were published, and the play *Bill W. and Dr. Bob* was successfully performed Off-Broadway in 2007.

Books

Contemporary Heroes and Heroines, Book II, Gale, 1992.

Hartigan, Francis, *Bill W.: A Biography of Alcoholics Anonymous Cofounder Bill Wilson,* St. Martin's, 2000.

Thomsen, Robert, *Bill W.,* Harper & Row, 1975.

Wilson, William G., *Alcoholics Anonymous Comes of Age,* Alcoholics Anonymous World Service, 1957.

Periodicals

New York Times, January 26, 1971.

Time, June 14, 1999.

Online

"Bill W.: Co-Founder of Alcoholics Anonymous," *Alcoholics Anonymous,* http://www.alcoholicsanonymous.9f.com/bill.htm (January 13, 2010).□

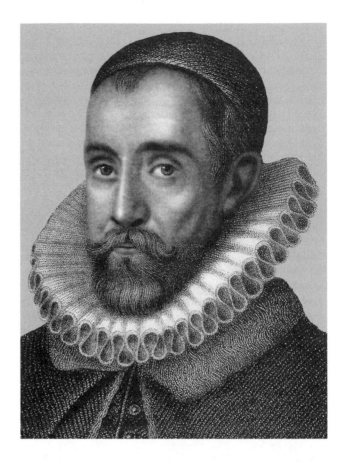

Francis Walsingham

English courtier Sir Francis Walsingham (c. 1532–1590) served as secretary of state for Queen Elizabeth I and foiled several credible plots to either assassinate the queen or remove her from the throne during a particularly tenuous period of English history. Trained in the law and fluent in several languages, Walsingham established a network of paid informants in the British Isles and Continental Europe that is considered the first modern espionage agency operated by a government. For this, Walsingham is often called England's first "spymaster," or chief of intelligence services.

Walsingham was probably born around 1532 at Scadbury Park, a manor home near Chislehurst, Kent. His father was William, a lawyer and sheriff who died when Walsingham was two years old. His mother Joyce, whose brother Anthony served as "Groom of the Stool," or toilet attendant to King Henry VIII, married Sir John Carey a few years later.

The England of Walsingham's childhood was a kingdom in uneasy transition. Its king, Henry VIII, sought a divorce from his Spanish-born wife, with whom he had just one daughter, in order to wed Anne Boleyn. When the Pope in Rome refused to grant Henry a special dispensation, Henry repudiated Rome's authority and formed the Church of England, naming himself its supreme head. All subjects were compelled to reject Roman Catholicism entirely and adopt the Protestant reforms Henry enacted. The king went on to marry four other women, and finally sired a long-awaited heir to the throne, Edward, who became Edward VI at the age of nine upon his father's death in 1547.

Fled Religious Strife

Walsingham's family were among the new class of staunch Church of England adherents, known as Protestants. He was probably about 16 when he entered the Protestant stronghold of King's College at Cambridge University in 1548, to study Greek and Latin. Around 1550 he made a tour of Europe, becoming fluent in Italian and French—a proficiency that would later serve him well as spymaster—and was back in London by 1552 to formally begin law studies at Gray's Inn, one of the four Inns of Court where lawyers and barristers received their professional training and certification.

Edward VI was just 15 years old when he died of a suspected respiratory ailment or infection. The Princess Mary, his half-sister from his father's first marriage, was declared heir to the throne after an intense period of diplomatic maneuvering with France and Spain, England's nearest threats to its sovereignty. Queen Mary I, crowned in 1553, was known as "Mary Tudor" and was a devout Roman Catholic. She began to restore the Roman Catholic faith in England, and some Protestants faced charges of heresy and were burned at the stake.

To avoid this fate, the young Walsingham returned to Europe. He took law courses at the University of Padua and lived in Switzerland between 1556 and 1558. Mary Tudor died in November of 1558 at the age of 42. Her marriage to Philip II of Spain, also a Catholic, produced no children. The late Henry VIII's only surviving legitimate child, the Princess Elizabeth, became Queen Elizabeth I.

Elected to House of Commons

Elizabeth was the product of her father's marriage to Anne Boleyn, who came from a family of staunch Protestants with ties by marriage to the Careys, the family of Walsingham's stepfather. Elizabeth's ascendancy marked the return of Protestant rule in England, and Walsingham returned from the Continent. Some sources say he was elected to the House of Commons for Parliament's 107th term, which met for about five months in early 1559. He represented the district of Banbury in Oxfordshire. He was known for certain to have sat in the next parliament, which met from 1563 to 1567, as the House of Commons member for Lyme Regis in Dorset.

Walsingham was admitted to the bar in 1562 and married twice in that decade. His first wife was Ann Carteill, a widow with a son. She died in 1564, and two years later he married another widow, Ursula St. Barbe Worseley. Worseley had two young sons from her first marriage who died in a gunpowder accident that occurred on Worseley family property on the Isle of Wight later around 1566 of 1567. In the fall of 1567 Walsingham's first child, a daughter named Frances, was born.

Elizabeth's closest advisor was the powerful William Cecil, also known as Lord Burghley. Cecil served as the queen's secretary of state after 1558, and it was Cecil who gave Walsingham his first important espionage-related task around 1570. With rumors of a plot to assassinate Elizabeth and place her cousin, the Scottish queen Mary Stuart, on the English throne, Cecil sent Walsingham to ferret out information about the plan in London. Walsingham made contact with agents of foreign governments in London, and helped foil the Ridolfi Plot, named after one of its key figures, a Florentine banker and ardent Catholic named Roberto di Ridolfi.

Family Under Siege

Elizabeth appointed Walsingham as her ambassador to France. In that capacity he negotiated the 1572 Treaty of Blois between England and France, which united them against a common enemy, Spain. Several months later, a revolt erupted in Spanish-held provinces in the Netherlands. Walsingham secured a promise from Charles IX, the Catholic king of France, regarding the protection of France's Protestant population, known as the Huguenots, who supported the anti-Spanish uprising. Spanish forces quelled the revolt, however, and then the French king's sister, Marguerite de Valois, was married to a Protestant prince, Henry of Navarre. The marriage took place in August of 1572, and scores of prominent Huguenot families came to Paris for the occasion. A leading Huguenot military figure was assassinated, and the city erupted in anti-Protestant violence in what became known as the St. Bartholomew's Day Massacre. About 3,000 French Protestants died in the violence.

Walsingham's ambassadorial quarters on the Quai des Bernardins, where he lived with his wife and four-year-old daughter, became the hideout for dozens of English Protestants fearful for their lives. The terrifying four days of carnage further amplified Walsingham's anti-Catholic bias. Elizabeth finally recalled him to England, and in December of 1573 he was appointed to the queen's Privy Council and she also named him the new joint Secretary of State after Cecil, who had become Lord High Treasurer. Walsingham initially shared the post with Sir Thomas Smith, another advisor, who retired in 1576. After that, Walsingham served as Elizabeth's "principal secretary," as the post was called, until his death in 1590.

Religious turmoil and plots to remove England's famous "Virgin Queen" continued. Adherents of the Roman Catholic faith did not consider Elizabeth a legitimate heir. She had been the product of Henry VIII's controversial marriage to Anne Boleyn, which had prompted the historic split with Rome. Therefore, the second marriage was not recognized as valid under Catholic doctrine, and thus any children born during it were considered illegitimate. The Catholic Mary Stuart was deemed the closest living legitimate descendant of Elizabeth's father, for her grandmother had been Henry VIII's older sister, Margaret Tudor. Mary had ties to France on her mother's side and had served for a brief time as Queen of France when her husband, Francis II, became king in 1559. He died and she married again after returning to Scotland; that spouse died under mysterious circumstances and she fled Scotland after marrying the earl suspected of killing her second husband. In the wake of this scandal, Mary was forced to abdicate her throne in favor of her young son, and decamped to England, where she believed Elizabeth could protect her. This was in 1568. Instead, Elizabeth, realizing the threat a Catholic monarch posed in her lands, ordered Mary Stuart to be placed under guard at various castles whose lords were known as staunch loyalists to the Protestant cause. English Protestants like Walsingham knew that if the Catholic religion was once again restored in England, it might provoke a wave of retaliatory bloodshed similar to the St. Bartholomew's Day Massacre. According to Stephen Budiansky in his book *Her Majesty's Spymaster: Elizabeth I, Sir Francis Walsingham, and the Birth of Modern Espionage*, Walsingham wrote to Cecil that "so long as that devilish woman lives," referring to the Queen of Scots, neither would Elizabeth "continue in quiet possession of the crown, nor her faithful subjects assure themselves of the safety of their lives."

Became England's First Spymaster

As secretary of state, Walsingham was responsible for apprising threats to Elizabeth's rule. He established a network of paid informants throughout England, Scotland, and the rest of Europe, often paying them for information out of his own earnings. In the mid-1570s, he discovered secret communications that Mary Stuart was conducting with her supporters. Like other confidential correspondence, these missives employed coded writing or forms of invisible ink, and Walsingham's office remained ahead of the latest ruses with the help of talented cryptographers, or code-breakers, like Thomas Phelippes.

Walsingham's network was credited with uncovering the Throckmorton plot of 1583, which involved a bid by English Catholics abroad to convince France's new king, Henry III, to send an invasionary force to aid a Catholic rebellion after the assassination of Elizabeth. Mary Stuart would then be freed and crowned Queen of England. Walsingham ordered the main conspirator, Sir Francis Throckmorton, to be questioned under torture after incriminating documents were found in his home. Throckmorton maintained that those papers, which included notes about parts of England's coastline that were not well guarded, were planted by Walsingham's agents, but gave a full confession after a second day of excruciating torture on the infamous rack. This frame used a system of ropes and pulleys to slowly separate a detainee's four limbs. Throckmorton was executed for treason in July of 1584. The sentence ordered that he be hanged, drawn, and quartered—a particularly heinous way to die. The body was still alive when removed from the noose and then disemboweled; executioners then chopped off the limbs and finally the head.

Walsingham also uncovered an even more sinister plot arranged by Sir Anthony Babington, a well-born courtier whose family were Recusants, or secret Catholics, in 1586. Babington was corresponding with the still-confined Mary Stuart and in contact with English conspirators abroad. The Babington Plot, as it was called, was cleverly foiled by Walsingham and his team: they deployed an informant named Gilbert Gifford to infiltrate the Babington circle. Gifford volunteered to help arrange more secure communication for Mary Stuart, who was under guard at Chartley Castle in Staffordshire. Her official gaoler was Sir Amias Paulet, the Governor of Jersey and a zealous Protestant. As directed by Walsingham, Gifford paid the local brewer, who delivered barrels of beer to Chartley, to secrete letters in the stoppers of the full and empty barrels. Paulet then approached the brewer and paid him to gain access to the letters.

Foiled Nefarious Plot

In this way, Walsingham was able to read every single letter between Mary Stuart and the Babington plotters. When one of them mentioned the assassination of Elizabeth, the culprits were arrested. Babington and 13 others were convicted of treason and executed in September of 1586. Mary Stuart was also tried, and executed on February 8, 1587, but her son would later rule England as King James I in the early 1600s.

Walsingham was devoted to his Queen, but was not entirely trusted by Elizabeth, though she knighted him in 1577 and a year later bestowed another honor, this one as chancellor of the Order of the Garter. The queen also called Walsingham the "dark Moor," perhaps because of the dark clothing he favored or his olive-skinned complexion. The final years of his tenure as secretary of state were marked by planning for a coming war with Spain and its mighty Armada, or fleet of warships. Walsingham ensured that the

men who served aboard Royal Navy vessels had better food rations, and set up local militia outfits.

Walsingham had a second daughter with his wife Ursula, but little Mary died at the age of seven. His older daughter Frances lost her husband in the war with Spain. She remarried Robert Devereux, the 2nd Earl of Essex, who was executed for treason in 1601 in yet another plot against Elizabeth. By then Walsingham had died, most likely from testicular cancer, on April 6, 1590. His home in London, Papey House, was a former friary situated in what is now the City of London district. He also had a country estate, Barn Elms, in Surrey, where he enjoyed the sport of falconry. Among Catholics, Walsingham was so detested a figure that following the news of his death vicious rumors circulated that urine had poured out of his mouth and nose in his final moments.

Books

Budiansky, Stephen, *Her Majesty's Spymaster: Elizabeth I, Sir Francis Walsingham, and the Birth of Modern Espionage*, Viking, 2005, p. 81.

"Walsingham, Francis," in *Elizabethan World Reference Library*, edited by Sonia Benson, Volume 2, UXL, 2007, pp. 235–242.

Periodicals

Guardian (London, England), May 6, 2006. □

Ida B. Wells

The African-American journalist and activist Ida B. Wells (1862–1931) crusaded against the rampant practice of lynching in the American South.

Wells began her career as a teacher and journalist in the city of Memphis, Tennessee, attacking the injustices that African Americans faced during the Reconstruction era in the South. After three of her friends were murdered, she began to focus on the issue of lynching (extra-judicial mob hanging) and the complex of social and sexual issues with which it was involved. As a result, she was driven out of Memphis by terrorist acts and spent the rest of her life in the northern states as a writer, speaker, and organizer. Wells pioneered techniques of direct action, including the boycott, that would become common only much later in the history of the civil rights movement she did much to inspire.

Parents Died in Epidemic

Ida B. Wells was born into slavery in Holly Springs, Mississippi, on July 16, 1862. Both of her parents, atypically among slaves, could read. Her father was a carpenter, her mother a cook. After emancipation and the end of the Civil War, they looked to a better life for their seven children and emphasized education. Ida's father, James, served on the board of trustees of Rust College, a small school (also known as Shaw University) that had been established by missionaries. Ida was educated there, reading the Bible, the plays of Shakespeare, and other classics. But her education was cut short by the yellow fever epidemic of 1878, which took the lives of both her parents and one of her siblings.

Left to support the other five children, Wells told the superintendent of a small country school that she was 18, and got a job there as a teacher. In 1882, as her brothers found work, she moved to Memphis, became certified as a teacher, and began working in the city's segregated school system. She also took courses at Nashville's Fisk University, riding the train between Memphis and Nashville. One early event that encouraged her militant attitude occurred on that train in 1884: a conductor told her to leave the first-class car for which she had purchased a ticket and move into segregated seating. Wells refused, and physically resisted the efforts of railway personnel to move her from the car and then throw her off the train. Wells filed suit against the Chesapeake and Ohio Railroad and won a $500 judgment in a circuit court, but the ruling was overturned by the Tennessee Supreme Court.

Writing articles for African American–oriented Memphis newspapers about these events, Wells began to realize the potential power of the mass media. She began contributing articles to the *Memphis Free Speech and Headlight,* using the pen name "Iola," and pointedly attacking the unequal treatment of African Americans that she saw all around her. Soon she invested in the paper and began to intensify her campaign. An exposé of the miserable conditions of Memphis's black schools antagonized the Shelby County School Board, and, with her authorship of the Iola articles an open secret, she was fired from her teaching job. By 1887 her articles were being syndicated among other black newspapers as far away as New York and Detroit, and she was named the nation's most prominent correspondent at a meeting of the National Afro-American Press Convention.

Promoted Boycott

Wells's newspaper, its name shortened to *Free Speech,* gained circulation as Wells refused to shy away from controversial topics. Things came to a head in Memphis after three African-American men, all Wells's friends, were lynched in May of 1892, in a dispute springing out of the rivalry between black-owned and white-owned grocery stores. Wells responded to the killings by stepping up her anti-lynching campaign and broadening it across other parts of the South. In Memphis, she urged blacks to boycott white-owned businesses and even to consider moving to the territory of Oklahoma. Business at downtown stores was hurt, and the enmity of the white power structure toward Wells increased. Wells took to carrying a gun, and she urged gun ownership for black families everywhere.

Allegations of rape often served as a pretext for white terrorist violence in Memphis and elsewhere, and a Wells editorial in 1892, drawing on her research into various lynching incidents, made reference to this when she wrote, as quoted by P. Gabrielle Foreman in the *African American Review:* "Nobody in this section believes that old threadbare lie that Negro men assault white women. If Southern white men are not careful they will overreach themselves and a conclusion will be reached which will be very damaging to the moral reputation of their women." The reaction was swift. It was fortunate that Wells was on her way to New York City when a mob broke into the *Free Speech* offices and set its printing press on fire. Wells's business partner, J.L. Fleming, barely escaped. Friends warned Wells not to return to Memphis, and gunmen were spotted when trains from the North arrived there.

Wells began writing for the *New York Age* and its editor, T. Thomas Fortune. She published a major lynching exposé showing that mob violence was not confined to lower-class Southern whites but sometimes involved highly placed members of society. In order to broaden awareness of her activities among whites, she undertook a speaking tour of Europe in 1893. Attacks on her by conservative newspapers on her return further helped her to achieve her goal. Wells moved to Chicago and began writing for the black-owned *Conservator* newspaper.

Soon after her arrival in Chicago, Wells waded into controversy. The Columbian Exposition world's fair held in Chicago in 1893 banned African Americans from the corps of exhibitors, and Wells, along with abolitionist pioneer Frederick Douglass and *Conservator* editor Ferdinand Barnett, produced a pamphlet protesting this injustice, and circulated 10,000 copies of it among fairgoers. Barnett and Wells married in 1895, after which Wells used the name Ida B. Wells-Barnett. They raised four children. Wells's diaries, first published in 1995, contained numerous reflections on the conflict she felt between her professional career and her desire for domestic stability, and she retired from her *Conservator* post after the birth of her second child.

Wrote Book with Jane Addams

Wells continued to speak out against discrimination, at one point joining with social reformer Jane Addams in a protest over segregation. She co-authored a book with Addams, *Lynching and Rape: An Exchange of Views.* In 1898 Wells led an anti-lynching protest at the White House. Wells published several books, including *Mob Rule in New Orleans* (1900). An autobiography, *Crusade for Justice,* remained unpublished until it was issued by her daughter, Alfreda Duster, in 1970. Wells supported the establishment of various organizations set up to assist Southern African-American migrants as they settled in Chicago, and she searched for a civil rights organization whose outlook matched her own. She joined in the founding of the National Association for the Advancement of Colored People, which was initially formed in response to a race riot in Springfield, Illinois, but she later left the group, frustrated by the predominance of whites in leadership positions and what she saw as its overly cautious approach.

In 1913 Wells founded the first African-American women's suffrage organization in Illinois, the Alpha Suffrage House. During a Washington, D.C., protest organized to coincide with the inauguration of President Woodrow Wilson, Wells refused to march in a designated space at the back of the group but insisted on joining the Illinois delegation under its banner. There was tension at the actual moment when she stepped out from the crowd and joined the group, but she was protected by sympathetic white marchers. The incident was later noted as a milestone in the integration of the woman suffrage movement.

In 1916 Wells addressed a meeting of Marcus Garvey's Universal Negro Improvement Association, and as a result she was banned by the U.S. government from attending the Versailles Peace Conference at the end of World War I.

Wells remained active in the cause of civil rights almost until the end of her life. She ran unsuccessfully for the U.S. Congress in 1930. On March 25, 1931, she died in Chicago after suffering from kidney problems. Wells's work at the junction of civil rights and gender issues has received attention from scholars, but she remains less well known among general readers than her male counterparts in the civil rights movement. A large collection of her personal papers, including draft copies of her autobiography, is held at the University of Chicago Library.

Books

Contemporary Heroes and Heroines, Book III, edited by Terrie M. Rooney, Gale, 1998.
Crusade for Justice: The Autobiography of Ida B. Wells, edited by Alfreda M. Duster, University of Chicago Press, 1970.
Giddings, P.J., *Ida: A Sword Among Lions,* HarperCollins, 2008.
The Memphis Diary of Ida B. Wells, edited by Maria DeCosta-Willis, Beacon, 1995.

Periodicals

African American Review, Summer 1997.

Online

"Biography: Ida B. Wells-Barnett," *Library of Congress,* http://www.lcweb2.loc.gov/ammem/aap/idawells.html (January 27, 2010).
"Her Biography and Time Line of Important Dates," *Ida B. Wells Official Web site,* http://www.idabwells.org (January 27, 2010).
"Ida B. Wells, 1862–1931," *Tennessee Newspaper Hall of Fame,* http://www.cci.utk.edu/~jem/TNHF/Wells.html (January 27, 2010).
"Ida B. Wells," *Voices from the Gaps: University of Minnesota,* http://www.voices.cla.umn.edu/artistpages/wellsIda.php (January 27, 2010).
"Ida B. Wells Barnett," *Lakewood (OH) Public Library,* http://www.lkwdpl.org/wihohio/barn-ida.htm (January 27, 2010).□

Frank Anthony Wilczek

American theoretical physicist Frank Anthony Wilczek (born 1951) is co-recipient of the 2004 Nobel Prize in Physics. With fellow physicists David Gross and H. David Politzer, he helped to discover the concept of asymptotic freedom and to develop the theory of quantum chromodynamics.

Frank Anthony Wilczek is one of the world's best-known and accomplished theoretical physicists. He was only twenty-two years old when his collaboration with fellow physicist David Gross helped explain the mysterious behavior behind matter's smallest components: quarks. His

research helped increase knowledge about one of the universe's most important operational forces. The Royal Swedish Academy of Sciences, which awarded Wilczek a share of the 2004 Nobel Prize in Physics, considers the impact of his research to be profound.

Wilczek was born on May 15, 1951 in the Queens borough of New York to Frank John and Mary Rose (Cona) Wilczek. His grandparents, on both the paternal and maternal side, emigrated from Europe after World War I. His father's parents came from Poland and his mother's from Italy.

His parents grew up in Long Island, New York, where their respective families struggled with the deprivations of the Great Depression. The experience shaped their attitudes, particularly about aspirations for their offspring, and they continually pushed Wilczek to do well in school.

Education and Environment Shaped Young Mind

Wilczek's parents perceived substantial academic success for their highly intelligent and analytical son, who enjoyed solving puzzles and mastering games. Thus, they envisioned for him a career in medicine or engineering. The expansive Queens public school system bolstered their hopes, as the large schools provided specialized and advanced classes for students like Wilczek.

While attending Martin Van Buren High School, Wilczek was among the select group of accelerated students. Time and place further aroused his innate intellectual curiosity. His father worked in electronics, and the family's apartment was always filled with radios and early television models as well as the technical books his father studied. Also, as Wilczek grew up in the Cold War era, he relished the excitement of new space exploration and experienced the shared fears related to nuclear weaponry, including frequent air raid drills.

All of this combined to imbue the impressionable and precociously intelligent Wilczek with new vistas of understanding. "I got the idea that there was secret knowledge that, when mastered, would allow mind to control matter in seemingly magical ways," he said (as quoted on the Nobel Prize website).

Religious education in the Catholic faith in which he was raised bolstered this pivotal revelation that later informed his career direction and personal focus. Affected by his increasing scientific knowledge and influenced by the writings of logician and philosopher Bertrand Russell (1872-1970), however, Wilczek lost faith in conventional religion. "A big part of my later quest has been trying to regain some of the sense of purpose and meaning that was lost. I'm still trying," he revealed in 2004 on the Nobel Prize website.

Studied Math but Attracted to Physics

His early questing began in earnest when he entered the University of Chicago in 1967. He was only sixteen years old but had self-described "large but amorphous ambitions."

Eventually, he focused his intellectual interests specifically toward mathematics after indulging his curiosity in brain science. Brain research greatly interested him, but he soon perceived that the field's most important questions were not yet ready for mathematical treatment. He also discovered that he lacked the patience for laboratory work. "I wound up majoring in mathematics, largely because [it] gave me the most freedom," he recalled according to the Nobel Prize website.

As his time at the university drew to a close, he developed an interest in physics. In his last semester, he took a course that involved the use of symmetry and group theory in physics. His teacher was Peter Freund (born 1936), an esteemed professor of theoretical physics, one who inspired and enthused Wilczek to pursue the material.

After earning his Bachelor of Science degree in mathematics in 1970, Wilczek proceeded to Princeton University in New Jersey, where he earned a master's degree in mathematics in 1972. As a graduate student involved in mathematics, he also closely watched developments in physics, and recognized its relation to his own field. "I became aware that deep ideas involving mathematical symmetry were turning up at the frontiers of physics," he related (as quoted on the Nobel Prize website interview), "specifically, the gauge theory of electroweak interactions, and the scaling symmetry in [Nobel laureate Kenneth] Wilson's theory of phase transitions."

Helped Develop New Theories

These personal observations initiated conversations with a young Princeton professor named David Jonathan Gross (born 1941), and his career as a physicist began thereafter. His association with Gross, which began in 1973, led to what Wilczek would later describe as the "great event" of his early career: Together, they discovered the phenomenon called "asymptotic freedom" and, in turn, helped develop the basic theory of quantum chromodynamics (QCD), or the strong force.

The strong force, also called the "color force," is the dominant force in the atomic nucleus and acts as a binding force between the quarks inside the proton and the neutron. The strong force is one of the four basic universal forces, along with gravity (the force that pulls particles together), electromagnetism (which acts between charged particles), and the weak nuclear force (which is important for the sun's energy production). But the strong force was also the least understood of the four forces. Gross and Wilczek would help unlock its mysteries, demonstrating how the strong force bound quarks within the nucleus.

Gross and Wilczek discovered something that initially appeared contradictory: The closer that quarks are to each other, the weaker the "color change." Further, when quarks are extremely close to each other, the force is so weak that the quarks almost behave as free particles. This phenomenon is called "asymptotic freedom." Conversely, when quarks move farther apart, the attractive force becomes stronger. This property has been compared to a rubber band: the farther the band is stretched, the stronger the force.

Received Nobel Prize

Working independently, H. David Politzer, a graduate student at Harvard University in Cambridge, Massachusetts, essentially made the same discovery. The related research led to the new QCD theory.

In 2004, the three men received a Nobel Prize for their work, specifically for the discovery of asymptotic freedom in the theory of the strong interaction, according to the Royal Swedish Academy of Sciences. By this time, Wilczek was at Massachusetts Institute of Technology (MIT), in Cambridge; Gross was at the Kavli Institute for Theoretical Physics at the University of California, in Santa Barbara; and Politzer was at the California Institute of Technology (Caltech), in Pasadena.

In bestowing the honor, the Royal Swedish Academy of Sciences acknowledged that the three men addressed fundamental questions that had occupied physicists throughout the twentieth century and still challenged both theoreticians and experimentalists working with major particle accelerators: What are the smallest building blocks in nature? How do these particles build up everything we see around us? What forces act in nature and how do they actually function?

Further, the Academy indicated that the QCD theory was an important contribution to the Standard Model, the theory that describes all physics connected with the electromagnetic force and the weak force and the strong force. "With the aid of QCD physicists can at last explain why quarks only behave as free particles at extremely high energies," the Academy pointed out in its Nobel Prize announcement as quoted on their website.

The independent but related discoveries of Wilczek, Gross, and Politzer was expressed in "an elegant mathematical framework" that led to the new QCD theory, the Academy added.

Research Led to Important Academic Positions

After his graduate work with Gross, Wilczek remained at Princeton University and obtained his Ph.D in physics in 1974. For the next seven years, he taught at Princeton, first as an instructor, then as an assistant professor (1974-1978), an associate professor (1978-1980), and finally as a full professor, a position he attained in 1980.

In 1981, he transferred to the Institute for Theoretical Physics at University of California at Santa Barbara. Until 1988, Wilczek was the institute's Chancellor Robert Huttenback Professor of Physics. In addition, during the decade, he became the first permanent member of the National Science Foundation's Institute for Theoretical Physics. He also served as a visiting professor at Harvard University (1987-88).

In 1997, he returned to Princeton, serving as the J. Robert Oppenheimer Professor within the Institute for Advanced Study. In the fall of 2000, he left the Institute to join the Massachusetts Institute of Technology, where he became the Herman Feshbach Professor of Physics at the Center for Theoretical Physics. Two years later, he became an adjunct professor in the Centro de Estudios Cient ficos of Valdivia, in Chile.

Recognized for Many Contributions

Along with his Nobel Prize, Wilczek collected numerous awards. He received the American Physical Society's J.J. Sakurai Prize in 1986 and UNESCO's Dirac Medal in 1994. In 2002, he received the Lorentz Medal, a prize established in 1925 by the Royal Netherlands Academy of Arts and Sciences. Awarded every four years, the Medal recognizes important contributions to theoretical physics. The same year, Wilczek also received the Michelson-Morley Prize from Case Western Reserve University.

In 2003, he received the Julius Edgar Lilienfeld Prize from the American Physical Society in recognition for outstanding contributions to physics. Specifically, the Society recognized Wilczek's writing contributions to publications such as *Physics Today* and *Nature*. His articles helped explain complex physics-related topics to a broader scientific readership. In 2003 and 2005, two of his articles were published in annual *Best American Science Writing* anthologies. Also in 2003, he received the Faculty of Mathematics and Physics Commemorative Medal from Charles University in Prague, and he was the co-recipient (along with Gross and Politzer) of the High Energy and Particle Physics Prize of the European Physical Society. The three men were honored for their fundamental contributions to the QCD theory.

In 2005, Wilczek was a co-recipient of the King Faisal International Prize for Science. He shared the prize with Federico Capasso of the United States and Anton Zeilinger of Austria. The three men were honored for their "distinguished contributions in their respective specializations in the field of physics."

Along with his educational and research activities, Wilczek has been an A.P. Sloan Foundation Fellow, a MacArthur Foundation Fellow, a Regent's Fellow of the Smithsonian Astrophysical Observatory, a trustee of the University of Chicago, and a member of the National Academy of Sciences, the Netherlands Academy of Sciences, and the American Academy of Arts and Sciences.

Publications Drew Further Praise

Wilczek also wrote several well-received books. In 1988, Wilczek co-wrote *Longing for Harmonies: Themes and Variations from Modern Physics* with Betsy Devine, who he married on July 3, 1973 (the couple have two children, Amity and Mira). His other books include *Geometric Phases in Physics* (1989), *Fractional Statistics and Anyon Superconductivity* (1990), and *Fantastic Realities* (2006).

He has also served as editor-in-chief for *Annals of Physics* (2001) and editorial advisor for *Daedalus* (2002). In addition, he published articles in many scientific journals about his ongoing interests. According to Wilczek, these interests have included "pure" particle physics, especially involving connections between ambitious theoretical ideas and concrete observable phenomena (e.g. applications of asymptotic freedom); behavior of matter at ultra-high temperature and/or density (e.g. phase structure of QCD, application to cosmology, neutron stars and stellar explosions); application of insights from particle physics to cosmology (e.g. axions as dark matter candidates); application of field theory techniques to condensed matter physics; and the quantum theory of black holes.

When awarding the 2004 Nobel Prize, the Royal Swedish Academy of Sciences noted (according to the press release on their website): "Thanks to their discovery [Gross, Politzer and Wilczek] have brought physics one step closer to fulfilling a grand dream, to formulate a unified theory comprising gravity as well—a theory for everything."

Books

"Wilczek, Frank Anthony," *American Men & Women of Science,* Gale, 2008.

Online

"Frank Wilczek," *Amazines,,* http://www.amazines.com/Frank_Wilczek_related.html (November 6, 2009).

"Frank Wilczek," *MSN Encarta,* http://encarta.msn.com/encyclopedia_701711813/frank_wilczek.html (November 6, 2009).

"Frank Wilczek, Herman Feshbach Professor of Physics;2004 Nobel Laureate," *Physics@MIT,,* http://web.mit.edu/physics/facultyandstaff/faculty/frank_wilczek.html (November 6, 2009).

"Frank Wilczek, The Nobel Prize in Physics 2004, Autobiography," *Nobelprize.org,,* http://nobelprize.org/nobel_prizes/physics/laureates/ 2004/wilczek- autobio.html (November 6, 2009).

"The Nobel Prize in Physics 2004," *Nobelprize.org,* http://nobelprize.org/nobel_prizes/physics/laureates/2004/press.html (November 6, 2009). □

Esther Williams

American actress and swimmer Esther Williams (born 1922) rose to become a Hollywood star in the 1940s by appearing in a series of popular films for MGM that

greatly affected the family and proved a formative event for the eight-year-old Williams. "That little girl," she later wrote in *The Million Dollar Mermaid,* "who already had learned that to find her place in the sun would...have to give what was wanted...[and] now also had to take Stanton's place and become *strong.* Personally and professionally, those two competing strains in my character—strength and giving—were to shape my life."

With her parents hoping that their youngest daughter could replace her deceased's brother contributions to the household's finances, Williams began her professional swimming career with the opening of a nearby pool. Her early, tentative efforts quickly grew into confident strokes, and before long she was winning local swimming competitions. In 1937, the teenager joined the Los Angeles Athletic Club swimming team, and soon after won three gold medals at the 1939 national swimming championship in Des Moines, Iowa, one for each event that she entered. Although Williams earned a spot on the 1940 United States Olympic team, she did not have the chance to participate in the games when World War II forced their cancellation. Instead of traveling to Scandinavia for the planned sporting events, the young swimmer returned to Los Angeles, where she was recruited to join Billy Rose's San Francisco-based water show, Aquacade. Appearing alongside Johnny Weissmuller, a swimmer who had appeared in the *Tarzan* films, Williams found her star unexpectedly on the rise as a showgirl rather than as a swimmer. That same year, the seventeen-year-old married her first husband, medical student Leonard Kovner.

Signed with MGM Studios

When the Aquacade closed in late 1940, Williams returned to Los Angeles and worked for a time as a department store model. MGM Studios soon approached the young female star, however, with an invitation to film a screen test with famed actor Clark Gable. Williams succeeded, and MGM offered her a contract. "I suddenly realized...that I didn't know anything about being in a front of a camera," she later recalled to Pat Perry of the *Saturday Evening Post.* "I asked if I could take on a couple of little roles before I starred in a big one." The first of these modest roles came in the *Andy Hardy* comedy *Double Life* (1942) alongside Mickey Rooney, which was quickly followed by a second small appearance in *A Guy Named Joe* (1943) alongside such luminaries as Spencer Tracy and Irene Dunn. After cutting her teeth in these supporting slots, Williams graduated to a title role with 1944's *Bathing Beauty.* A musical that featured the actress's swimming abilities in what has been considered the first on-screen synchronized swimming performance, the film set the stage for Williams' increasing popularity; in fact, her debut starring performance was so striking that the film's test audience reaction led to its renaming as *Bathing Beauty* rather than the intended *Mr. Coed,* meant to highlight the work of Williams' co-star Red Skelton. This rise in films was also accompanied by a shifting personal life; the budding actress had split from Kovner over her decision to sign with MGM, and married performer Ben Gage in 1945.

combined music, comedy, and aquatics. Renowned for her synchronized swimming skills, the actress had competed as a professional athlete before making the dive into motion pictures. Her career peaked with the 1952 musical *Million Dollar Mermaid,* but Williams continued to act throughout the decade and staged two major televised aquatic shows. After a long hiatus from public life, she returned in the 1980s as an Olympic commentator and swimwear designer. In 1999, Williams published a tell-all autobiography, *The Million Dollar Mermaid,* that explored her often difficult personal life alongside her professional persona.

The youngest of the five children of Louis Stanton Williams and Bula Myrtle (Gilpin) Williams, the future swimming sensation was born Esther Jane Williams on August 8, 1922, in Los Angeles, California. At the time of Williams' birth, her family had only recently relocated to Los Angeles from Salt Lake City, Utah, to enable the eldest Williams son, Stanton, to pursue a career in the nascent motion picture industry. Although he experienced some success as a child actor, appearing in silent films produced by the Equity movie studio, the youthful actor had his career cut short when he died unexpectedly as the result of a ruptured colon at the age of 16. His death

A number of similarly light-hearted successes followed on the heels of *Bathing Beauty,* including *Thrill of a Romance* (1945), *Easy to Wed* (1946), and *Fiesta* (1947). Soon, Williams was one of MGM's top box office draws, although some critics dismissed her acting abilities. Towards the end of filming *Neptune's Daughter* (1949), the actress discovered that she was pregnant. A previous miscarriage and the studio's desire to keep unflattering photos of its normally svelte swimming star out of the gossip magazines led to Williams' keeping a low profile until giving birth to son Benjamin Stanton Gage in 1949. Returning to work, the actress filmed *The Duchess of Idaho* (1950) and had begun work on *Pagan Love Song* (1950) in Hawaii before discovering that she was again pregnant, leading to some creative shooting choices to hide her growing bump. In October of 1950, she gave birth to second son Kimball Austin Gage.

Career Peaked with *Million Dollar Mermaid*

Roles in *Texas Carnival* (1951) and *Skirts Ahoy!* (1952) preceded Williams' starring turn in what is widely considered her signature MGM film, *Million Dollar Mermaid.* The actress—who had repeatedly been called a mermaid herself throughout the first decade of her career—portrayed real-life Australian professional swimmer and actress Annette Kellerman, who had risen to fame in the early twentieth century. Replete with lavish costumes, theatrical aquatic productions, and a dashing romance, the film allowed Williams to play to her strengths both in and out of the water. *Million Dollar Mermaid* did not come without its share of perils, however. During one aquatic shoot, Williams began to feel tired from the high levels of carbon dioxide in her bloodstream and nearly fell asleep on a piece of the underwater set. A scene requiring her to take a swan dive from a height of some 50 feet resulting in the actress breaking three vertebrae in her neck when her head, topped with an aluminum crown, snapped back upon hitting the surface of the water. Williams wore a neck-to-knee cast for several months after the shoot, but ultimately made a more or less full recovery. When *Million Dollar Mermaid* opened in December of 1952, it became an immediate hit and won Williams the Henrietta award from the Hollywood Foreign Press Association, the forerunner of today's Golden Globe Awards.

Despite these successes, Williams faced personal and financial problems that she attributed to Gage's drinking and gambling. Amidst these marital problems, she met South American actor Fernando Lamas on the set of her MGM *Million Dollar Mermaid* follow-up, *Dangerous When Wet* (1953). Although the two did not pursue a romantic relationship at the time, Williams acknowledged an early attraction to the man who later became her husband. She and Gage briefly rekindled their marriage in 1953, however, and the actress became pregnant with her third child just before commencing filming for *Easy to Love* (1953) at Florida's Cypress Gardens theme park. On October 1 of that year, Williams gave birth to daughter Susan Tenney Gage.

Upon her return to work, the actress began to feel betrayed by MGM. A role that she had anticipated receiving in the movie *Athena* went to another performer, and with her ego bruised Williams began filming her last role for MGM, *Jupiter's Darling* (1955). After its release, Williams left MGM

Studios, an action that proved damaging to her acting career. The simplistic romantic comedies and musicals that had made Williams a star gave way to a couple of more serious films for Universal, including *The Unguarded Moment* (1956) and *Raw Wind in Eden* (1958), that failed to appeal to the actress's longtime audience. Financial woes caused by Gage's heavy spending compounded the difficult period, and Williams and Gage split for good in 1957. Williams appeared in a handful of television specials late in the decade, and one of these—*Esther Williams at Cypress Gardens*—led to her reunion with Lamas. The couple became embroiled in a romance and after two more films, *The Big Show* (1961) and *The Magic Fountain* (1963), Williams decided to retire from motion pictures to dedicate herself to her relationship with the Argentinean actor. After the Spain-based production of *The Magic Fountain* wrapped, the couple remained in Madrid for a time, living as man and wife although not formally married until 1969. In 1962, they returned to Los Angeles, and Williams began a long period of dedicating herself to her partner. Domesticity led to weight gain, which combined with Lamas' discouragement kept the former star from returning to the big screen. She faded from the public eye and endured, at times, private anguish over the life with a demanding husband that she had chosen.

Diversified in Later Career

Lamas' death in 1982 ended Williams' third marriage after over essentially two decades and the actress—who had for so long served as her husband's caretaker—found herself at loose ends, noting in *The Million Dollar Mermaid* that "marriage to a difficult man means that when he dies, you are out of a job." Seeking to reclaim her independent identity, Williams turned to rebuilding her career, commencing work on a water safety instructional video for children and granting a high-profile interview to Barbara Walters. Soon after, NBC tapped the former athlete as a color commentator for the swimming events at the 1984 Los Angeles Summer Olympics. This event also led to Williams' meeting with former French literature professor Edward Bell, who became her fourth husband and business partner.

Along with Bell, Williams launched a line of swimwear bearing her name in 1988. Speaking to Todd S. Purdum of the *New York Times* about her label in 1999, the star-turned-businessperson explained bluntly, "Women worldwide are fighting a thing called gravity . . . I say to women when I talk to them, 'You girls of 18 have until about 25, 30 at the most, and then you have to report to me.' . . . I have very definite ideas about what a swimsuit should be: it should be swimmable." Drawing inspiration from the classic swimwear styles worn by Williams during her aquatic heyday, the line has endured for over two decades. The former actress also devoted part of her later days to writing an autobiography, *The Million Dollar Mermaid,* that was published in 1999. Packed with tales of Williams' professional and personal peaks and valleys, the memoir was dubbed "tremendously entertaining" by *Publisher's Weekly.* In the new millennium, she lent her production and costume expertise to a proposed $30 million Las Vegas aquatic spectacle, *Aquaria,* based on the classical Greek myth of Persephone. The show did not reach the stage as planned, however. Nevertheless, Williams remains an iconic American figure, with her performances kept alive through classic movie channels and her contributions to the sport and art of swimming winning her notoriety long after her heyday.

Books

Notable Sports Figures, Gale, 2004.

Williams, Esther with Digby Diehl, *The Million Dollar Mermaid,* Simon & Schuster, 1999.

Periodicals

Interview, February 1998.

New York Times, September 2, 1999.

Publishers' Weekly, August 23, 1999.

Saturday Evening Post, January–February 1998.

Online

"Esther Williams," Internet Movie Database, http://www.imdb.com/name/nm0930565/ (January 3, 2010).

"Esther Williams," Turner Classic Movies, http://www.tcm.com/thismonth/article/?cid=253038 (January 3, 2010).□

Natalie Wood

The American actress Natalie Wood (1938–1981) was an iconic figure in American cinema in the mid-twentieth century.

As the strands of youth rebellion in the 1950s grew into the sexual revolution of the 1960s, Wood several times played key female film roles that defined changing attitudes and mores. Wood died young, but starting as a child star, she had a film career that lasted almost 40 years. She remains best known for her starring roles in *Rebel Without a Cause* (1955) and *West Side Story* (1961), with several other ambitious dramas close behind. Wood was a troubled figure whose life had mysterious aspects at both its beginning and its end. For much of her career, though, Wood's inner demons added intensity to her performances. According to Wood biographer Gavin Lambert, writing in the London *Guardian,* actor George Segal said that "nobody could lose control on screen like Natalie," and her on-screen persona radiated a unique combination of suppressed inner emotion and sexuality.

Born to Russian Refugees

Born on July 20, 1938, in San Francisco, California, Natalie Wood was the product of a volatile marriage between two Russians who had fled the Bolshevik revolution of 1917 in their homeland and had made their separate ways to California. Her father, Nicholas Zacharenko, used the name Nick Gurdin in the United States. Wood's name at birth has appeared in various forms, but according to California state records examined by Lambert and appearing on the Family Tree Legends website, it was Natalie Zacharenko. Both Wood herself and observers familiar with Russian theatrical traditions pointed to a Russian aspect in her personality and performances.

As a girl she was called Natalie or Natasha Gurdin, but as soon as she entered the world of film very early in her life, she became Natalie Wood. Natalie's mother, Maria, wanted from the start to make her daughter into a child star. Natalie was enrolled in ballet lessons as a young child, and when director Irving Pichel was looking for extras for his 1943 film *Happy Land,* Maria signed Natalie up for a screen test. She failed the first time, after which Maria doubled the pressure and reminded Natalie of the time she had watched her German Shepherd puppy get hit by a truck. Unsurprisingly, Wood's second screen test impressed the assembled studio executives with its emotional force. Two of them, David Lewis and William Goetz, decided on the name Wood for their new child actress because they wanted to wish good luck to a friend, director Sam Wood.

In *Happy Land,* all Wood had to do was drop an ice cream cone and cry, but she soon graduated to bigger child roles. She appeared in a tearjerker role as the daughter of Orson Welles's character in Pichel's 1946 melodrama *Tomorrow Is Forever,* and her most famous performance as a child came the following year in the family Christmas classic *Miracle on 34th Street.* By that time her salary had risen to a reported $1,000 per week, and the family had moved from an economically difficult life in the town of Santa Rosa, California, to the Los Angeles suburb of Van Nuys, where Natalie attended high school. A stint in the television situation comedy *Pride of the Family* in 1953 helped her make the transition to adult roles in the public eye.

When Wood did emerge full-grown into the world of Hollywood, she did so in unforgettable fashion. In 1955 Wood was cast as Judy opposite loner James Dean in *Rebel Without a Cause,* winning the role despite the Warner studio's desire that a more established star be engaged for the role. At age 16 when filming began, Wood was just the age of her character, and teen roles were more often played by actors several years older. The film also set another pattern for Wood personally; she reportedly became romantically involved with both director Nicholas Ray and supporting actor Dennis Hopper during filming. Her performance earned a Best Actress Academy Award nomination and set the pattern for the next several years of her career, where she played serious roles featuring teen girls in conflict. An exception was the John Wayne Western *The Searchers,* but Wood felt that she was miscast in the role of Wayne's abducted niece Deborah. That film introduced Wood's younger sister Lana (born Svetlana), who played the same character at a younger stage.

Showed Dancing Skills in Famed Musical

Wood married actor Robert Wagner in 1957, but the couple divorced in 1962. By that time she was hitting her creative peak as an actress. Her childhood dance lessons served her well in the musical *West Side Story,* in which she played the lead role of Maria. Her singing voice was dubbed by Broadway vocalist Marni Nixon. Wood won another Academy Award nomination for *Splendor in the Grass* (1961), a small-town Kansas tale of sexual repression and its consequences, written by playwright William Inge. The changing sexual attitudes of the 1960s seemed to be bubbling under the surface of each new Wood performance, and for the comedy-drama *Love with the Proper Stranger,* which touched on themes of premarital pregnancy and abortion, Wood earned a third Academy Award nomination. Wood's performance opposite male lead Steve McQueen in that film was widely considered one of her best.

Meanwhile, Wood's personal life was deteriorating. A series of unsuccessful romances followed her divorce from Wagner, and in 1966, after almost ten years of psychotherapy, she attempted suicide by taking an overdose of pills. The previous year, in *Inside Daisy Clover* (based on a novel by Lambert), Wood had portrayed a young woman who attempted suicide in response to pressures from her mother, who pushed her to become a Hollywood star. Wood survived her suicide attempt and took time off to regain her mental health. The years 1967 and 1968 were the first since 1946 in which no film with Wood in the cast had appeared. In 1969 she resurfaced in the couples-therapy comedy *Bob and Carol and Ted and Alice,* another film that broke new ground in its treatment of sexuality.

As with the majority of other Hollywood actresses, Wood found film roles scarcer as she grew older. Much of her work in the 1970s was in television films and miniseries. In 1976 she appeared opposite Wagner in a

television adaptation of the Tennessee Williams play *Cat on a Hot Tin Roof.* Among her best-received television performances was the 1979 miniseries *From Here to Eternity,* in which Wood played the role of Karen Holmes, the commanding officer's wife played by Deborah Kerr in the original 1953 film. Wood won a Golden Globe award for her performance in the role.

Married Wagner for Second Time

In 1969 Wood married British theatrical agent Richard Gregson in a Russian Orthodox church, with actor Robert Redford as best man. The couple had a daughter, who became a successful actress now known as Natasha Gregson Wagner. But the marriage dissolved in 1972 amid Wood's accusations of infidelity on Gregson's part. She remarried Robert Wagner in 1972, and the couple had a second daughter, Courtney. Wagner also adopted Natasha Gregson. Wood was no longer the household name she had been in the 1960s, but she remained a powerful and popular figure in Hollywood.

On November 27, 1981, as filming concluded on what would be Wood's last feature, *Brainstorm,* Wood, Wagner, Wood's co-star Christopher Walken, and the yacht's captain, Dennis Davern, boarded Wood and Wagner's yacht, *Splendour,* sailed to Santa Catalina Island off the Southern California coast, and moored the boat near the island. The group went to the El Galleon bar and began drinking margaritas with beer chasers. They then returned to the yacht. What happened next has remained a matter of debate, partly because the memories of the surviving participants were clouded by alcohol; the following is based on Lambert's account, derived from firsthand sources.

Wood, Wagner, and Walken argued, and Wood became so angry that she asked Davern to take her to the island's main town, Avalon, in the yacht's motorized dinghy. According to a phone message Wood left with playwright Mart Crowley, she booked a room for the two of them at the Pavilion Lodge because she was afraid of sleeping alone; Davern, she said, slept on the floor. The following day they returned to the yacht. In the afternoon Wood and Walken went together to the island, followed by the others, and the group spent several hours drinking. Walken at one point threw his glass to the floor, breaking it; Wood did the same, explaining that this was an old Russian custom. When the group returned to the yacht once again, tensions exploded anew—whether because Wood and Walken were flirting, or for some other reason, cannot be definitively established.

Wagner told Lambert that he had grown angry after asking Walken to stay out of a discussion about the direction of Wood's career, but he was rebuffed and then broke a bottle of wine on the yacht saloon's floor. Wood then left the saloon, presumably to go to bed. After several hours, Wagner went to check on Wood in their stateroom and found both her and the yacht's dinghy missing. In the early morning of November 29 he called for help, and as dawn broke, searchers found Wood's body in a cove on the island, with the dinghy found some distance away. An autopsy revealed that Wood had had considerably more than the seven to eight drinks found in her system (she would have lived for several hours after her last drink), and she had taken both the painkiller Darvon and a powerful anti-seasickness drug called cyclizine. Los Angeles County coroner Thomas Noguchi concluded that Wood, drunk and disoriented, had fallen accidentally into the water, bruising her cheek as she went overboard. Wagner, in interviews with Lambert and in a later autobiography, asserted his belief that she had untied the dinghy in order to move it to a location where it would not make noise knocking against the side of the yacht, and Lambert's detailed review of the events of that evening found "strong circumstantial support" for Wagner's belief.

Books

Finstad, Suzanne, *Natasha: The Biography of Natalie Wood,* Century, 2001.
Lambert, Gavin, *Natalie Wood: A Life,* Knopf, 2004.

Periodicals

Daily Mail (London, England), February 10, 2000; June 2, 2001.
Guardian (London, England), June 25, 2004.
Interview, February 2004.
Maclean's, September 1, 2008.
People, May 21, 1984.
Time, December 14, 1981.

Online

"California Births and Deaths, 1905–1995," *Family Tree Legends,* http://www.familytreelegends.com/records/ (January 26, 2010).
"Natalie Wood," *All Movie Guide,* http://www.allmovie.com (January 26, 2010).□

Z

Shneur Zalman

Russian rabbi Shneur Zalman of Liadi (1745–1813) founded the Chabad branch of Hasidism during a troubled period for Jews living under the harsh laws of imperial Russia. Chabadim are also known as Lubavitchers, and remained a persecuted group in Russia for generations until a successor to the "Alter Rebbe," as Zalman was called, emigrated to the United States. This particular sect of Orthodox Jews claims 200,000 followers around the world, but is based in the Crown Heights section of Brooklyn, New York.

The "Shneur" in Zalman's name is thought to have linguistic links to the Spanish "Señor," which places his family's roots in the Iberian peninsula before the kingdom of Spain expelled all Jews by the Alhambra Decree of 1492. He came from a long line of rabbis who moved eastward from Prague into the Polish city of Poznań, then to Vitebsk, where Zalman's father, Baruch, was born. Baruch was also a rabbi and moved the family to nearby Liozna. It was here that Zalman was born in 1745. At the time, the larger Vitebsk Province belonged to the Polish-Lithuanian Commonwealth that existed between 1569 and 1795.

Married at 15

As a child, Zalman proved a quick learner of Hebrew and the Talmud. He studied under Rabbi Issachar Ber in Lyubavichi, a Russian village that would later provide the Lubavitcher sect with its name. He was called "Rav," a form of "rabbi," after his bar mitzvah. In 1760 he wed Sterna Segal, whose father was a successful merchant in Vitebsk. His newly affluent status permitted him a pair of private tutors who came from the Czech Republic, and from them he learned about the Kabbalah, an ancient school of thought that focused on the abstract mystical attributes of Judaism. At the time, Jews in the Polish-Lithuanian Commonwealth were divided over Kabbalah study, with more conservative elders opposing it as a possibly heretical movement fomented by spiritual leaders who rapidly gained messianic followings in their respective regions.

Desiring to learn more about these trends, Zalman walked several hundred miles from Vitebsk to Mezhirich, a town in Ukraine, to study under the famed Rabbi Dov Ber of Mezhirich. Ber was the second leader of a new branch of Orthodox Judaism that came to be called Hasidism. Its founder was Rabbi Israel ben Eliezer, also called *Baal Shem Tov* (Master [of the] Good Name), who settled in Ukraine in the 1740s and began to gather followers of his teachings, which stressed mysticism over strict observance of Jewish law. Ber became the leader of the movement after Eliezer's death in 1760. Zalman was one of several disciples who studied under Ber and went on to lead the Hasidic movement to a position of tremendous influence in this part of the world in the late eighteenth and nineteenth centuries.

Revised Code of Jewish Law

Zalman arrived in Mezhirich in 1764 and would spend several years there under the guidance of Ber, known as the *Maggid,* or preacher. He learned the wisdom of the Kabbalah from Ber's son, Avraham HaMalach, or Abraham the Angel. Ber appointed Zalman as the Maggid of Liozna, his hometown, in 1767, and a few years later asked him to revise the *Shulchan Arukh,* or Code of Jewish Law. His version is called the *Shulchan Arukh Ha-Rav,* or "From the Rabbi," to distinguish it from other versions either written during this era or after his death. Zalman spent several years updating the Code, which deals with matters of prayer, keeping of the Sabbath and holy days, dietary law, marriage and divorce, conversion to Judaism, and community ethics. Some portions were published during his lifetime but a large section was lost in a fire. The surviving chapters were collated for 1814 publication and the work remains an important text for Lubavitcher and Hasidic Jews.

Rabbi Ber died in 1772, with Zalman succeeding him as leader of the Hasidim. In this part of Eastern Europe where Hasidism originated, there were several geopolitical areas, once united but later emerging as the independent republics of Lithuania, Poland, Russia, Ukraine, and Belarus. During Zalman's lifetime, there were major cultural differences among all of them, and Jewish life also varied significantly. In Ukraine, for example, Hasidic Judaism under Ber had flourished, but in urban centers like Vilnius—a major center of rabbinical Jewish scholarship and influence that would later become Lithuania's capital—opposition was fierce. Hasidic tenets appealed to poorer Jews in the *shtetls,* or predominantly Jewish villages of the region.

Opponents of Hasidism were known by the Hebrew term *Misnagdim.* Zalman and another influential Hasidic leader and follower of Ber, Menachem Mendel of Vitebsk, tried to quell a growing division between the Hasidim and the Misnagdim. The latter movement was spearheaded by Elijah ben Solomon, also known as the Gaon ("genius") of Vilnius, or Vilna as it was called then. The Vilna Gaon was a famous Talmudic scholar known throughout Eastern Europe, and he issued an excommunication order against the Hasidim and a ban on marriage between Hasidic and non-Hasidic Jews. In 1774, Zalman and Mendel went to Vilnius in an attempt to meet with the Vilna Gaon, who refused to see them. Three years later, Mendel emigrated with around 300 Hasidim to Safed, Israel.

Shtetl Life Imperiled

The movement led by Zalman also faced a major threat as a trio of superpowers—imperial Russia, the Austrian Hapsburg empire, and the kingdom of Prussia—battled to control the Polish-Lithuanian Commonwealth. The land grab began in 1772 with the first of three diplomatically arranged Partitions, and by the time of the Third Partition of 1795, those living in Lithuania, Poland, Ukraine, and Belarus had been subsumed into the realms of their larger, more powerful neighbors.

After the First Partition, thousands of Jews found themselves living under the Tsarina Catherine the Great. An even greater number came after 1793, the year of the Second Partition. Catherine decreed a Jews-only area, known as the *Cherta Osedlosti,* or "Reserved Zone" in Russian, that is more commonly known as the Pale of Settlement. With few exceptions, Jews were forbidden from living anywhere else in Imperial Russia unless they obtained a special residence permit.

Wrote Chabad's Founding Text

The clash between the Hasidim and Misnagdim escalated after 1797, when Zalman's book *Likkutei Amarim* ("Collected Sayings") was published anonymously. More commonly known as the *Tanya,* this became the core text of the Chabad Hasidic movement. It was in this tract that the term "Chabad" first appeared. Zalman invented it out of three Hebrew

words: *chokmah* (wisdom), *binah* (intelligence), and *Da'at* (knowledge). "From its beginning, Lubavitch teaching . . . had a strong anti-elitist, outward impulse expressed in the writings of its founder," wrote Peter Steinfels in the *New York Times* generations later. The rabbi, Steinfels continued, "wanted to make even the mystical dimension of Jewish observance accessible to the average Jews."

As the Hasidim began to gain followers in the relatively important city of Pinsk in imperial Russia (now in Belarus), Pinsk's rabbi, Avigdor ben Hayim, retaliated by accusing Zalman of treason. Hayim claimed that Zalman and the Hasidim were aiding a renegade sect in the Ottoman Empire founded more than a century earlier by Sabbatai Zevi, who claimed to be the Jewish messiah but then converted to Islam. The Sabbateans, as Zevi's followers were known, had established other messianic sects in places under Ottoman rule, and Hayim asserted that the Hasidim were sending money to Eretz Yisrael, or Palestine, which under tsarist law was a treasonous act, for Palestine was under the control of the Ottoman Empire, Russia's historic rival for supremacy across a wide swath of Eurasia.

Zalman was arrested and taken to St. Petersburg for his trial. It was likely a secret trial heard by a panel of judges appointed to adjudicate political crimes, and because he did not speak Russian, his responses had to be translated from the Yiddish language. He was held in the prison of the famed Peter and Paul Fortress for more than seven weeks until Tsar Paul I ordered him to be freed. The date of his release, December 8, 1798, was the 19th day in the Hebrew calendar month of Kislev. It remains a major holiday for Lubavitcher Jews, celebrated as the Holiday of Deliverance and symbolic moment when the Hasidic movement was legitimized.

Died During Napoleon's Invasion

Zalman was arrested a second time, on similar charges, and Paul's successor, Tsar Alexander I, also declined to prosecute. After this Zalman settled in Liadi, near Vitebsk, and continued to write, teach, and even compose music. In Western Europe, Napoleon I of France had began an aggressive military campaign that drew in all of the major powers on the continent, including Britain and Sweden. Tenuous alliances between the nations shattered, and in 1812 the French army invaded imperial Russia. Zalman opposed the French, fearing that France's Enlightenment-era ideals would erase Jewish life forever. Napoleon's Russian campaign was only briefly successful, but Alexander's armies were forced from the Vitebsk area and Zalman fled with them. He planned to settle in Ukraine, but died on December 15, 1813, in Piena in the Kursk district. He was entombed in Hadiach, a Ukrainian city.

Zalman's son Rabbi Dov Ber Schneuri succeeded him as leader of the Chabad branch of Hasidism and moved to the shtetl of Lyubavichi. This became the epicenter of Chabad Hasidism over the next century. The persecution of Jews in tsarist Russia escalated, however, which prompted Schneuri to encourage his followers to move to Palestine. A group of them settled in Hebron around 1820. After Schneuri died in 1827, the Chabad of Lyubavichi were led by Zalman's grandson, Menachem Mendel Schneersohn, until 1866. Zalman's great-grandson Shmuel Schneersohn was the Lubavitcher Rebbe until 1882, followed by Sholom Dov Ber Schneersohn, the fifth to lead the sect. That rabbi's son, Yosef Yitzchok Schneersohn, took over just a few years after the Bolshevik Revolution of 1917, and was forced into exile. It was this descendant of Zalman's who relocated the Lubavitcher to the Crown Heights section of Brooklyn, New York, in the 1940s. The émigré rabbi's son-in-law, Menachem Mendel Schneerson, led the Lubavitcher sect until his death in 1994.

Books

The Jewish Religion: A Companion, edited by Louis Jacobs, Oxford University Press, 1995, pp. 463– 464.

Stroll, Avrum, "Shneur Zalman of (Liozna-) Lyady," in *Encyclopaedia Judaica,* edited by Michael Berenbaum and Fred Skolnik, Volume 18, second edition, Macmillan Reference USA, 2007, pp. 501-505.

Periodicals

New York Times, January 22, 2000.

Online

"Rabbi Shneur Zalman of Liadi," Chabad.org, http://www.chabad.org/library/article_cdo/aid/110437/jewish/The-Alter-Rebbe.htm (October 3, 2009). □

Stefan Zweig

The Austrian writer Stefan Zweig (1881–1942) was renowned during his own lifetime for his psychologically penetrating novellas, short stories, and biographical studies.

Zweig was an idealist who believed in the possibility of a united Europe, and he was disillusioned by World War I and devastated by the rise of Nazism and the outbreak of World War II. For a time, his ardent pacifism dented his popularity. But in the 1980s and 1990s Zweig's literary reputation began to rise once again as his stories of psychological obsession were hailed for their compulsive readability. "If all Zweig's fiction feels peculiarly intense and feverish, here the effect is quite hypnagogic," wrote David Sexton of the London *Evening Standard* in a review of Zweig's novel *The Post Office Girl.* "It's as though you're not so much reading as inside a dream of your own."

Met Wife after Fan Letters

Born on November 28, 1881 in Vienna, Austria, Zweig grew up in a secular Jewish household. His father, Moritz Zweig, was a well-off textile manufacturer, and his mother, Ida Brettauer Zweig, also came from a wealthy background. His family's circle included Jewish intellectuals and creative artists such as composers Gustav Mahler and Arnold Schoenberg, and playwright Arthur Schnitzler. Zweig, whose later life was fundamentally shaped by anti-Semitism, had little sympathy for Jewish nationalism. His education was cosmopolitan, involving travel to Germany and France, where one of his

intellectual mentors was the idealistic writer Romain Rolland. In 1904 Zweig earned a doctoral degree from the University of Vienna. After a period of travel as far as India and Russia, Zweig settled in Salzburg in 1913 and married Friderike Maria Burger von Winternitz the following year. Divorced and with two daughters of her own, she made Zweig's acquaintance by sending him fan mail.

By that time Zweig was already an established author. At first he focused on drama and poetry, genres that interested him less later on in his career. His first published work, *Silberne Saiten* (Silver Strings, 1901), was a volume of poems. Among his early plays was one, *Das Hause am Meer* (The House by the Sea, 1912), that dealt with the American Revolutionary War. With the outbreak of World War I he took a job as an archivist with the Austrian War Office, but was dismayed by the carnage that filled news reports as hundreds of thousands of Austro-Hungarian soldiers lost their lives. In 1917 he wrote an antiwar play, *Jeremiah,* that ran afoul of Austrian officialdom to a point where he was forced to move temporarily to Zurich, Switzerland (where the play was eventually produced).

Back in Salzburg after the war, Zweig grew disgusted by the libertine atmosphere of the big German-speaking cities— prostitutes were a common sight on the streets of both Vienna and Berlin—and rented a house on a hill outside Salzburg, overlooking the mountain retreat of Adolf Hitler in Berchtesgaden, Germany. Zweig wrote a biography of his first major influence, Romain Rolland, in 1921, but was also coming under the influence of psychoanalysis pioneer Sigmund Freud.

Sexually charged Zweig novellas such as *Amok* (1922) and *Verwirrung der Gefühle* (Confusion of Feelings, translated as *Twenty-Four Hours in the Life of a Woman* and later filmed no fewer than six times) became highly popular.

Pruned Writing Ruthlessly

Zweig modeled his prose style on that of French short story writer Guy de Maupassant, who specialized in short, shocking stories that cut away the veils of illusion surrounding human relationships. He strove for a concentrated style in his writing, ruthlessly pruning what he considered unnecessary material. He might take a manuscript of 100,000 words and halve its length. "I can't think of a writer who is more successful at depicting *amour fou*—what one critic describes as 'sex and madness breaking through the lacquered screen of upper-bourgeois society,'" wrote Julie Kavanagh in *Intelligent Life*.

Among European readers in the 1920s and 1930s Zweig was equally well known for his nonfiction writings, especially biographies. Some of these showed Freud's influence as well. Zweig was fluent in several languages, and translated or adapted various foreign works, including the Ben Jonson play *Volpone* (1926), for German audiences. He liked to write triple biographies tracing the development of an idea or psychological impulse in the works of three different writers. Zweig issued four books with this structure: *Drei Meister: Balzac, Dickens, Dostojewski* (1920, translated as *Three Masters*), *Der Kampf mit dem Dämon: Hölderlin, Kleist, Nietzsche* (1925, translated as *The Struggle with the Demon*), *Drei Dichter ihres Lebens: Casanova, Stendhal, Tolstoi* (1928, translated as *Adepts in Self-Portraiture*), and *Die Heilung durch den Geist: Franz Anton Mesmer, Mary Baker Eddy, Sigmund Freud* (1931, translated as *Mental Healing*). Zweig also wrote popular biographies of Marie Antoinette and the Dutch theologian Desiderius Erasmus. In the latter book he presciently contrasted Erasmus's humanism with what he called a demonic spirit that lurked in Germany's national character.

By the time that volume appeared in 1934, Zweig was increasingly worried about the growing influence of fascism in all phases of German and increasingly Austrian life. Agreeing to write the libretto for an opera, *Die schweigsame Frau* (The Silent Woman), with music by Richard Strauss, he found that the work came under close scrutiny from Nazi cultural authorities. At first Strauss, who was serving as president of the Reich music chamber, defended his Jewish librettist, and the opera was staged, but it was closed down after four performances. Later in 1934, as violent clashes erupted in Austria between leftists and pro-fascist forces, Zweig's home was searched by police looking for leftist materials. Zweig fled to England, telling authorities that he was doing research for a biography of Mary, Queen of Scots. He left his wife in Austria to settle their affairs.

This decision touched off a personally unsettled but creatively fertile period in Zweig's life. In England, Zweig met the much younger refugee Lotte Altmann, hired her as his secretary, fell in love with her, and married her in 1939. Perhaps as a way of dealing with his guilt over the episode, Zweig turned to writing with fresh vigor. In 1939 his novel *Ungeduld des Herzens* (Impatience of the Heart) was published in Stockholm, Sweden (by this time he had been completely blacklisted in

Germany and Austria), and immediately translated into English as *Beware of Pity*.

Spoke at Freud's Funeral

That book was long thought to be Zweig's only full-length novel. It was a grim tale of emotional blackmail, with a plot involving a disabled girl who draws an Austro-Hungarian officer into her life. The novel's latter-day admirers have included singer Neil Tennant and actor Colin Firth, who told Kavanagh that reading it brought him "the thrill of feeling you have this forgotten masterpiece in your hand that no one else has discovered. I was riveted by it—the way the strange pathology of the story takes the lid off what might just look like romantic love." *Beware of Pity* took shape as Zweig entered psychoanalysis in London with the aging Freud, who had also been forced to leave Austria. Freud died in 1939, and Zweig spoke at his funeral.

Another novel, *Rausch der Verwandlung* (The Thrill of Transformation), was found among Zweig's papers after his death; it ends somewhat abruptly, and it is unknown whether Zweig was still working on it, or was trying to decide whether to publish it. The book was finally published in 1982 and was translated into English as *The Post Office Girl*. The book dealt with a penniless young woman who works in a rural post office and gets a taste of urban glamour. She becomes involved with a man in similar circumstances, and as their lives deteriorate they contemplate suicide. The book again seemed to have parallels with Zweig's own life, which was increasingly despairing. He and Lotte continued to travel, trying at some level to escape memories of the life they had left behind. They went to the United States in 1940, and then to Brazil, where Zweig promptly turned out a book about the country, *Brazil, Land der Zukunft* (translated as *Brazil: Land of the Future*). On February 22 (or 23), 1942, in Petropolis, Brazil, Zweig and Lotte together took massive doses of barbiturates and were found dead, lying hand in hand, with a suicide note saying that Zweig hoped that his friends would live to see the end of the horrors into which the world had descended.

The day before his death, Zweig sent a new book, *Die Welt von Gestern* (The World of Yesterday), to a publisher. The book was part autobiography and part memoir of the Vienna of Zweig's youth, with its vibrant intellectual life and sometimes sensual atmosphere. "When I attempt to find a simple formula for the period in which I grew up, prior to the First World War, I hope that I convey its fullness by calling it the Golden Age of Security. Everything in our almost thousand-year-old Austrian monarchy seemed based on permanency, and the State itself was the chief guarantor of this stability," Zweig wrote at the beginning of the book. He alluded to Freud's belief that civilization was fragile and could easily dissolve under the pressures of darker human impulses. Zweig left other writings unfinished at his death, including another novel, *Clarissa,* and perhaps this was because his life during his last years was chaotic and unsatisfied. Always popular with German-speaking readers, Zweig's works gained new attention in England and the United States as well, after many of them appeared in new editions published by England's Pushkin Press.

Books

Zweig, Stefan, *The World of Yesterday,* Herperides, 2008.

Periodicals

Daily Telegraph (London, England), February 7, 2009; January 9, 2010.
Evening Standard (London, England), January 26, 2009.
Guardian (London, England), March 16, 1992.
New Statesman, March 9, 2009.

Online

''Stefan Zweig,'' *Books and Writers,* http://www.kirjasto.sci.fi/szweig.htm (January 10, 2010).

Stefan Zweig, Contemporary Authors Online (reproduced in Biography Resource Center), http://www.galenet.galegroup.com/servlet/BioRC (January 10, 2010).

''Stefan Zweig: The Secret Superstar,'' *Intelligent Life (Spring 2009),* http://www.moreintelligentlife.com/story/stefan-zweig-secret-superstar (January 10, 2010).□

HOW TO USE THE *SUPPLEMENT* INDEX

The *Encyclopedia of World Biography Supplement (EWB)* Index is designed to serve several purposes. First, it is a cumulative listing of biographies included in the entire second edition of *EWB* and its supplements (volumes 1-30). Second, it locates information on specific topics mentioned in volume 30 of the encyclopedia—persons, places, events, organizations, institutions, ideas, titles of works, inventions, as well as artistic schools, styles, and movements. Third, it classifies the subjects of *Supplement* articles according to shared characteristics. Vocational categories are the most numerous—for example, artists, authors, military leaders, philosophers, scientists, statesmen. Other groupings bring together disparate people who share a common characteristic.

The structure of the *Supplement* Index is quite simple. The biographical entries are cumulative and often provide enough information to meet immediate reference needs. Thus, people mentioned in the *Supplement* Index are identified and their life dates, when known, are given. Because this is an index to a *biographical* encyclopedia, every reference includes the *name* of the article to which the reader is directed as well as the volume and page numbers. Below are a few points that will make the *Supplement* Index easy to use.

Typography. All main entries are set in boldface type. Entries that are also the titles of articles in *EWB* are set entirely in capitals; other main entries are set in initial capitals and lowercase letters. Where a main entry is followed by a great many references, these are organized by subentries in alphabetical sequence. In certain cases—for example, the names of countries for which there are many references—a special class of subentries, set in small capitals and preceded by boldface dots, is used to mark significant divisions.

Alphabetization. The Index is alphabetized word by word. For example, all entries beginning with *New* as a separate word *(New Jersey, New York)* come before

Newark. Commas in inverted entries are treated as full stops *(Berlin; Berlin, Congress of; Berlin, University of; Berlin Academy of Sciences)*. Other commas are ignored in filing. When words are identical, persons come first and subsequent entries are alphabetized by their parenthetical qualifiers (such as *book, city, painting*).

Titled persons may be alphabetized by family name or by title. The more familiar form is used—for example, *Disraeli, Benjamin* rather than *Beaconsfield, Earl of.* Cross-references are provided from alternative forms and spellings of names. Identical names of the same nationality are filed chronologically.

Titles of books, plays, poems, paintings, and other works of art beginning with an article are filed on the following word *(Bard, The)*. Titles beginning with a preposition are filed on the preposition *(In Autumn)*. In subentries, however, prepositions are ignored; thus *influenced by* would precede the subentry *in* literature.

Literary characters are filed on the last name. Acronyms, such as UNESCO, are treated as single words. Abbreviations, such as *Mr., Mrs.,* and *St.,* are alphabetized as though they were spelled out.

Occupational categories are alphabetical by national qualifier. Thus, *Authors, Scottish* comes before *Authors, Spanish,* and the reader interested in Spanish poets will find the subentry *poets* under *Authors, Spanish.*

Cross-references. The term *see* is used in references throughout the *Supplement* Index. The *see* references appear both as main entries and as subentries. They most often direct the reader from an alternative name spelling or form to the main entry listing.

This introduction to the *Supplement* Index is necessarily brief. The reader will soon find, however, that the *Supplement* Index provides ready reference to both highly specific subjects and broad areas of information contained in volume 30 and a cumulative listing of those included in the entire set.

INDEX

A

"A"
see Arnold, Matthew

"A.B."
see Pinto, Isaac

AALTO, HUGO ALVAR HENRIK
(born 1898), Finnish architect, designer, and town planner **1** 1-2

AARON, HENRY LOUIS (Hank; born 1934), American baseball player **1** 2-3

ABAKANOWICZ, MAGDALENA (Marta Abakanowicz-Kosmowski; born 1930), Polish sculptor **25** 1-3

Abarbanel
see Abravanel

ABBA ARIKA (c. 175-c. 247), Babylonian rabbi **1** 3-4

ABBAS I (1571-1629), Safavid shah of Persia 1588-1629 **1** 4-6

ABBAS, FERHAT (born 1899), Algerian statesman **1** 6-7

ABBAS, MAHMOUD (Abu Masen; born 1935), Palestinian statesman **27** 1-3

Abbas the Great
see Abbas I

Abbé Sieyès
see Sieyès, Comte Emmanuel Joseph

ABBEY, EDWARD (Edward Paul Abbey; 1927-1989), American author and environmental activist **27** 3-5
    Crumb, R. **30** 130-132

ABBOTT, BERENICE (1898-1991), American artist and photographer **1** 7-9

ABBOTT, DIANE JULIE (born 1953), British politician and journalist **26** 1-3

ABBOTT, EDITH (1876-1957), American social reformer, educator, and author **26** 3-5

ABBOTT, GRACE (1878-1939), American social worker and agency administrator **1** 9-10

ABBOTT, LYMAN (1835-1922), American Congregationalist clergyman, author, and editor **1** 10-11

ABBOUD, EL FERIK IBRAHIM (1900-1983), Sudanese general, prime minister, 1958-1964 **1** 11-12

ABC
see American Broadcasting Company (United States)

ABD AL-MALIK (646-705), Umayyad caliph 685-705 **1** 12-13

ABD AL-MUMIN (c. 1094-1163), Almohad caliph 1133-63 **1** 13

ABD AL-RAHMAN I (731-788), Umayyad emir in Spain 756-88 **1** 13-14

Abd al-Rahman ibn Khaldun
see Ibn Khaldun, Abd al-Rahman ibn Muhammad

ABD AL-RAHMAN III (891-961), Umayyad caliph of Spain **1** 14

ABD AL-WAHHAB, MUHAMMAD IBN (Muhammad Ibn Abd al-Wahab; 1702- 1703-1791-1792), Saudi religious leader **27** 5-7

ABD EL-KADIR (1807-1883), Algerian political and religious leader **1** 15

ABD EL-KRIM EL-KHATABI, MOHAMED BEN (c. 1882-1963), Moroccan Berber leader **1** 15-16

Abdallah ben Yassin
see Abdullah ibn Yasin

ABDELLAH, FAYE GLENN (born 1919), American nurse **24** 1-3

ABDUH IBN HASAN KHAYR ALLAH, MUHAMMAD (1849-1905), Egyptian nationalist and theologian **1** 16-17

Abdu-I-Malik
see Abd al-Malik

ABDUL RAHMAN, TUNKU (1903-1990), Former prime minister of Malaysia **18** 340-341

ABDUL-BAHA (Abbas Effendi; 1844-1921), Persian leader of the Baha'i Muslim sect **22** 3-5

ABDUL-HAMID II (1842-1918), Ottoman sultan 1876-1909 **1** 17-18

ABDULLAH II (Abdullah bin al Hussein II; born 1962), king of Jordan **22** 5-7

'ABDULLAH AL-SALIM AL-SABAH, SHAYKH (1895-1965), Amir of Kuwait (1950-1965) **1** 18-19

ABDULLAH IBN HUSEIN (1882-1951), king of Jordan 1949-1951, of Transjordan 1946-49 **1** 19-20

ABDULLAH IBN YASIN (died 1059), North African founder of the Almoravid movement **1** 20

ABDULLAH, MOHAMMAD (Lion of Kashmir; 1905-1982), Indian political leader who worked for an independent Kashmir **22** 7-9

Abdul the Damned
see Abdul-Hamid II

ABE, KOBO (born Kimifusa Abe; also transliterated as Abe Kobo; 1924-1993), Japanese writer, theater director, photographer **1** 20-22

ABE, SHINZO (born 1954), Japanese prime minister **28** 1-3

ABEL, IORWITH WILBER (1908-1987), United States labor organizer **1** 22-23

ABEL, NIELS (1802-1829), Norwegian mathematician **20** 1-2

ABELARD, PETER (1079-1142), French philosopher and theologian **1** 23-25

ABERCROMBY, RALPH (1734-1801), British military leader **20** 2-4

ABERDEEN, 4TH EARL OF (George Hamilton Gordon; 1784-1860), British statesman, prime minister 1852-55 **1** 25-26

393

ADENAUER, KONRAD (1876-1967), German statesman, chancellor of the Federal Republic 1949-63 **1** 59-61

ADLER, ALFRED (1870-1937), Austrian psychiatrist **1** 61-63

ADLER, FELIX (1851-1933), American educator and Ethical Culture leader **1** 63-64

ADLER, LARRY (Lawrence Cecil Adler; 1914-2001), American harmonica player **26** 5-7

ADLER, MORTIMER JEROME (1902-2001), American philosopher and educator **22** 9-11

ADLER, RENATA (born 1938), American author **26** 8-9

Adolphe I
see Thiers, Adolphe

ADONIS ('Ali Ahmad Said; born 1930), Lebanese poet **1** 64-65

ADORNO, THEODOR W. (1903-1969), German philosopher and leader of the Frankfurt School **1** 65-67

ADRIAN, EDGAR DOUGLAS (1st Baron Adrian of Cambridge; 1889-1977), English neurophysiologist **1** 67-69

Adventures of Pinocchio, The (book)
Lorenzini, Carlo **30** 118-120

ADZHUBEI, ALEKSEI IVANOVICH (1924-1993), Russian journalist and editor **18** 9-11

AELFRIC (955-c. 1012), Anglo-Saxon monk, scholar, and writer **1** 69-70

AEROSMITH (began 1969), American rock band **24** 4-7

AESCHYLUS (524-456 B.C.), Greek playwright **1** 70-72

AESOP (c. 620 B.C.E.-c. 560 B.C.E.), Greek fabulist **24** 7-8

AFFONSO I (1460?-1545), king of Kongo **1** 72

AFINOGENOV, ALEKSANDR NIKOLAEVICH (1904-1941), Russian dramatist **1** 72-73

'AFLAQ, MICHEL (born 1910), Syrian founder and spiritual leader of the Ba'th party **1** 73-74

African American art
see African American history (United States)

African American history (United States)
POLITICIANS
members of Congress
De Priest, Oscar **30** 142-144
RECONSTRUCTION-1896
education
Brown, Hallie Quinn **30** 83-85
equal protection denied
Wells-Barnett, Ida B. **30** 376-378

''SEPARATE BUT EQUAL'' (1896-1954)
civil rights leaders
Wells-Barnett, Ida B. **30** 376-378
segregation unconstitutional (Brown v. Board of Education of Topeka; 1954)
Clark, Mamie Phipps **30** 115-118
SOCIETY and CULTURE
cultural influence
Anderson, Regina M. **30** 5-7
education
Brown, Hallie Quinn **30** 83-85
Clark, Mamie Phipps **30** 115-118
journalism
Wells-Barnett, Ida B. **30** 376-378
literature (20th century)
Johnson, Georgia Douglas **30** 230-232
medicine
Logan, Myra Adele **30** 266-268
motivational and public speakers
Brown, Hallie Quinn **30** 83-85
music
Dixon, Willie **30** 148-150
Ertegun, Ahmet **30** 162-164
Mayfield, Curtis **30** 273-275
sports
Doby, Larry **30** 150-152
Jackson, Nell **30** 216-218
THROUGH CIVIL WAR
abolitionists
Shadd Cary, Mary Ann **30** 324-326

African Americans
see African American history (United States)

African Methodist Episcopal Church (United States)
Brown, Hallie Quinn **30** 83-85

AGA KHAN (title), chief commander of Moslem Nizari Ismailis **1** 74-76

AGAOGLU, ADALET (Adalet Agoglu; born 1929), Turkish playwright, author, and human rights activist **22** 11-13

Agassi, Andre, (born 1970), American tennis player
Graf, Steffi **30** 184-186

AGASSIZ, JEAN LOUIS RODOLPHE (1807-1873), Swiss-American naturalist and anatomist **1** 76-78

AGEE, JAMES (1909-1955), American poet, journalist, novelist, and screenwriter **1** 78-79
Levitt, Helen **30** 260-261

AGESILAUS II (c. 444-360 B.C.), king of Sparta circa 399-360 B.C. **1** 79-80

AGHA MOHAMMAD KHAN (c. 1742-1797), shah of Persia **1** 80-81

AGIS IV (c. 262-241 B.C.), king of Sparta **1** 81-82

AGNELLI, GIOVANNI (1920-2003), Italian industrialist **1** 82-83

AGNES (c. 292-c. 304), Italian Christian martyr **24** 8-10

AGNESI, MARIA (1718-1799), Italian mathematician, physicist, and philosopher **20** 4-5

AGNEW, DAVID HAYES (1818-1892), American physician **28** 3-5

AGNEW, SPIRO THEODORE (1918-1996), Republican United States vice president under Richard Nixon **1** 83-85

AGNODICE (born ca. 300 BC), Greek physician **20** 5-5

AGNON, SHMUEL YOSEPH (1888-1970), author **1** 85-86

AGOSTINO (1557-1602), Italian painter **1** 86

AGOSTINO DI DUCCIO (1418-c. 1481), Italian sculptor **1** 86

Agricola
see Crèvecoeur, St. J.

AGRICOLA, GEORGIUS (1494-1555), German mineralogist and writer **1** 86-87

AGRIPPINA THE YOUNGER (Julia Agrippina; 15-59), wife of Claudius I, Emperor of Rome, and mother of Nero **20** 5-8

AGUINALDO, EMILIO (1869-1964), Philippine revolutionary leader **1** 88

Agustin I
see Iturbide, Augustin de

AHAD HAAM (pseudonym of Asher T. Ginsberg, 1856-1927), Russian-born author **1** 88-89

AHERN, BERTIE (Bartholomew Ahern; born 1951), Irish Prime Minister **18** 11-13

AHIDJO, AHMADOU (1924-1989), first president of the Federal Republic of Cameroon **1** 89-90

AHMADINEJAD, MAHMOUD (Mahmoud Ahmadi Nejad; born 1956), Iranian politician **27** 7-10

AIDOO, AMA ATA (Christina Ama Aidoo; born 1942), Ghanaian writer and educator **20** 8-10

AIKEN, CONRAD (1889-1973), American poet, essayist, novelist, and critic **1** 90-91

AIKEN, HOWARD (1900-1973), American physicist, computer scientist, and inventor **20** 10-12

AILEY, ALVIN (1931-1989), African American dancer and choreographer **1** 91-94

AILLY, PIERRE D' (1350-1420), French scholar and cardinal **1** 94

AITKEN, WILLIAM MAXWELL (Lord Beaverbrook; 1879-1964), Canadian businessman and politician **1** 94-96

AKBAR, JALAL-UD-DIN MOHAMMED (1542-1605), Mogul emperor of India 1556-1605 **1** 96

AKHENATEN (Amenhotep IV; c. 1385-c. 1350 B.C.), Egyptian pharaoh and religious leader **25** 5-7

AKHMATOVA, ANNA (pseudonym of Anna A. Gorenko, 1889-1966), Russian poet **1** 96-97

AKIBA BEN JOSEPH (c. 50-c. 135), Palestinian founder of rabbinic Judaism **1** 97-98

AKIHITO (born 1933), 125th emperor of Japan **1** 98-99

AKIYOSHI, TOSHIKO (born 1929), Japanese musician **24** 10-12

AKUTAGAWA, RYUNOSUKE (Ryunosuke Niihara; 1892-1927), Japanese author **22** 13-14

AL-ABDULLAH, RANIA (Rania al-Yasin; born 1970), Queen Rania of Jordan **25** 8-10

ALAMÁN, LUCAS (1792-1853), Mexican statesman **1** 99-100

Alamein, 1st Viscount Montgomery of
see Montgomery, Bernard Law

Alamo, battle of the (1836)
Bowie, James **30** 71-73

ALARCÓN, PEDRO ANTONIO DE (1833-1891), Spanish writer and politician **1** 100-101

ALARCÓN Y MENDOZA, JUAN RUIZ DE (1581?-1639), Spanish playwright **1** 101

ALARIC (c. 370-410), Visigothic leader **1** 101-102

Alau
see Hulagu Khan

ALA-UD-DIN (died 1316), Khalji sultan of Delhi **1** 102-103

ALAUNGPAYA (1715-1760), king of Burma 1752-1760 **1** 103

AL AQQAD, ABBAS MAHMOUD (Abbas Mahmud al Aqqad; 1889-1964), Egyptian author **24** 25-27

ALBA, DUKE OF (Fernando Álvarez de Toledo; 1507-1582), Spanish general and statesman **1** 103-104

AL-BANNA, HASSAN (1906-1949), Egyptian religious leader and founder of the Muslim Brotherhood **1** 104-106

Albategnius
see Battani, al-

AL-BATTANI (Abu abdallah Muhammad ibn Jabir ibn Sinan al-Raqqi al Harrani al-Sabi al-Battani; c. 858-929), Arab astronomer and mathematician **25** 10-12

ALBEE, EDWARD FRANKLIN, III (born 1928), American playwright **1** 106-108

Albemarle, Dukes of
see Monck, George

ALBÉNIZ, ISAAC (1860-1909), Spanish composer and pianist **1** 108-109

ALBERDI, JUAN BAUTISTA (1810-1884), Argentine political theorist **1** 109-110

ALBERS, JOSEPH (1888-1976), American artist and art and design teacher **1** 110

ALBERT (1819-1861), Prince Consort of Great Britain **1** 110-112

ALBERT I (1875-1934), king of the Belgians 1909-1934 **1** 112

ALBERT II (born 1934), sixth king of the Belgians **1** 112-113

Albert the Great
see Albertus Magnus, St.

ALBERTI, LEON BATTISTA (1404-1472), Italian writer, humanist, and architect **1** 113-115

ALBERTI, RAFAEL (born 1902), Spanish poet and painter **18** 13-15

ALBERTUS MAGNUS, ST. (c. 1193-1280), German philosopher and theologian **1** 115-116

ALBRIGHT, MADELEINE KORBEL (born 1937), United States secretary of state **1** 116-118

ALBRIGHT, TENLEY EMMA (born 1935), American figure skater **23** 3-6

ALBRIGHT, WILLIAM (1891-1971), American archaeologist **21** 1-3

ALBUQUERQUE, AFONSO DE (c. 1460-1515), Portuguese viceroy to India **1** 118-119

Alcántara, Pedro de
see Pedro II

ALCIBIADES (c. 450-404 B.C.), Athenian general and politician **1** 119-120

Alcoholics Anonymous
Smith, Robert Holbrook **30** 337-339
W., Bill **30** 372-374

ALCORN, JAMES LUSK (1816-1894), American lawyer and politician **1** 120-121

ALCOTT, AMOS BRONSON (1799-1888), American educator **1** 121

ALCOTT, LOUISA MAY (1832-1888), American author and reformer **1** 122

ALCUIN OF YORK (c. 730-804), English educator, statesman, and liturgist **1** 122-123

ALDRICH, NELSON WILMARTH (1841-1915), American statesman and financier **1** 123-124

Aldrin, Buzz
see Aldrin, Edwin Eugene, Jr.

ALDRIN, EDWIN EUGENE, JR. (Buzz Aldrin; born 1930), American astronaut **18** 15-17

ALDUS MANUTIUS (Teobaldo Manuzio; c. 1450-1515), Italian scholar and printer **21** 3-5

ALEICHEM, SHOLOM (Sholom Rabinowitz; 1859-1916), writer of literature relating to Russian Jews **1** 124-125

ALEIJADINHO, O (Antônio Francisco Lisbôa; 1738-1814), Brazilian architect and sculptor **1** 125-126

ALEMÁN, MATEO (1547-c. 1615), Spanish novelist **1** 126

ALEMÁN VALDÉS, MIGUEL (1902-1983), Mexican statesman, president 1946-1952 **1** 126-127

ALEMBERT, JEAN LE ROND D' (1717-1783), French mathematician and physicist **1** 127-128

ALESSANDRI PALMA, ARTURO (1868-1950), Chilean statesman, president 1920-1925 and 1932-1938 **1** 128-129

ALESSANDRI RODRIGUEZ, JORGE (born 1896), Chilean statesman, president 1958-1964 **1** 129-130

ALEXANDER I (1777-1825), czar of Russia 1801-1825 **1** 130-132

Alexander I, king of Yugoslavia
see Alexander of Yugoslavia

ALEXANDER II (1818-1881), czar of Russia 1855-1881 **1** 132-133

ALEXANDER III (1845-1894), emperor of Russia 1881-1894 **1** 133-134

ALEXANDER III (Orlando Bandinelli; c. 1100-1181), Italian pope 1159-1181 **24** 12-14

Alexander III, king of Macedon
see Alexander the Great (literary work)

ALEXANDER VI (Rodrigo Borgia; 1431-1503), pope 1492-1503 **1** 134-135

ALEXANDER VII (Fabio Chigi; 1599-1667), Roman Catholic pope **25** 12-13

ALEXANDER, JANE (nee Jane Quigley; born 1939), American actress **26** 9-12

Anatomy (science)
circulatory
Fabrici, Girolamo **30** 167-169
educators
Eustachi, Bartolomeo **30** 164-166
Fabrici, Girolamo **30** 167-169
founders
Fabrici, Girolamo **30** 167-169
pulmonary
Colombo, Realdo **30** 120-122

ANAXAGORAS (c. 500-c. 428 B.C.), Greek philosopher **1** 208-209

ANAXIMANDER (c. 610-c. 546 B.C.), Greek philosopher and astronomer **1** 209-210

ANAXIMENES (flourished 546 B.C.), Greek philosopher **1** 210

ANAYA, RUDOLFO ALFONSO (born 1937), Chicano American author **27** 17-19

ANCHIETA, JOSÉ DE (1534-1597), Portuguese Jesuit missionary **1** 210-211

Andahazi, Federico, (born 1963), Argentinian author
Colombo, Realdo **30** 120-122

ANDERSEN, DOROTHY (1901-1963), American physician and pathologist **1** 212

ANDERSEN, HANS CHRISTIAN (1805-1875), Danish author **1** 212-214

ANDERSON, CARL DAVID (1905-1991), American physicist **1** 214-215

ANDERSON, IVIE MARIE (Ivy Marie Anderson; 1905-1949), African-American singer **28** 10-12

ANDERSON, JUDITH (1898-1992), American stage and film actress **1** 215-216

ANDERSON, JUNE (born 1953), American opera singer **1** 216-218

ANDERSON, MARIAN (1902-1993), African American singer **1** 218-219

ANDERSON, MAXWELL (1888-1959), American playwright **1** 219-220

ANDERSON, REGINA M. (1901-1993), Librarian and playwright **30** 5-7

ANDERSON, SHERWOOD (1876-1941), American writer **1** 220-221

ANDO, TADAO (born 1941), Japanese architect **18** 17-19

ANDRADA E SILVA, JOSÉ BONIFÁCIO DE (1763-1838), Brazilian-born statesman and scientist **1** 221-222

ANDRÁSSY, COUNT JULIUS (1823-1890), Hungarian statesman, prime minister 1867-1871 **1** 222-223

Andrea da Pontedera
see Andrea Pisano

ANDREA DEL CASTAGNO (1421-1457), Italian painter **1** 223-224

ANDREA DEL SARTO (1486-1530), Italian painter **1** 224-225

ANDREA PISANO (c. 1290-1348), Italian sculptor and architect **1** 225-226

ANDREAS-SALOMÉ, LOU (Louise Salomé; 1861-1937), Russian-born German author and feminist **28** 12-14

ANDRÉE, SALOMON AUGUST (1854-1897), Swedish engineer and Arctic balloonist **1** 226

ANDREESSEN, MARC (born 1972), American computer programmer who developed Netscape Navigator **19** 3-5

Andreino
see Andrea del Sarto

ANDREOTTI, GIULIO (born 1919), leader of Italy's Christian Democratic party **1** 226-228

ANDRETTI, MARIO (born 1940), Italian/American race car driver **1** 228-230

ANDREW, JOHN ALBION (1818-1867), American politician **1** 230-231

ANDREWS, BENNY (1930-2006), African American artists **25** 23-25

ANDREWS, CHARLES MCLEAN (1863-1943), American historian **1** 231

ANDREWS, FANNIE FERN PHILLIPS (1867-1950), American educator, reformer, pacifist **1** 231-232

ANDREWS, JULIE (Julie Edwards; born 1935), British singer, actress, and author **25** 25-28

ANDREWS, ROY CHAPMAN (1884-1960), American naturalist and explorer **1** 232-233

ANDREYEV, LEONID NIKOLAYEVICH (1871-1919), Russian author **29** 11-13

ANDRIĆ, IVO (1892-1975), Yugoslav author **24** 21-24

Andromeda Nebula (astronomy)
Baade, Walter **30** 24-26

ANDRONIKOS ii PALAIOLOGOS (1260-1332), Byzantine emperor **30** 7-9

ANDROPOV, IURY VLADIMIROVICH (1914-1984), head of the Soviet secret police and ruler of the Soviet Union (1982-1984) **1** 233-234

ANDROS, SIR EDMUND (1637-1714), English colonial governor in America **1** 234-235

ANDRUS, ETHEL (1884-1976), American educator and founder of the American Association of Retired Persons **19** 5-7

Angel of the Crimea
see Nightingale, Florence

ANGELICO, FRA (c. 1400-1455), Italian painter **1** 235-236

ANGELL, JAMES ROWLAND (1869-1949), psychologist and leader in higher education **1** 236-237

Angelo de Cosimo
see Bronzino

ANGELOU, MAYA (Marguerite Johnson; born 1928), American author, poet, playwright, stage and screen performer, and director **1** 238-239

Anglican King's College
see Toronto, University of (Canada)

ANGUISSOLA, SOFONISBA (Sofonisba Anguisciola; c. 1535-1625), Italian artist **22** 22-24

Anna Comnena
see Comnena, Anna

ANNA IVANOVNA (1693-1740), empress of Russia 1730-1740 **1** 240-241

ANNAN, KOFI (born 1938), Ghanaian secretary-general of the United Nations **18** 19-21

Annapurna I (mountain, Nepal)
Blum, Arlene **30** 61-63

ANNE (1665-1714), queen of England 1702-1714 and of Great Britain 1707-1714 **1** 241-242

ANNE OF BRITTANY (1477-1514), queen of France 1491-1498 and 1499-1514 **29** 13-15

ANNE OF CLEVES (1515-1557), German princess and fourth wife of Henry VIII **27** 19-21

ANNENBERG, WALTER HUBERT (1908-2002), American publisher and philanthropist **26** 16-18

ANNING, MARY (1799-1847), British fossil collector **20** 14-16

Annunzio, Gabriele d'
see D'Annunzio, Gabriel

ANOKYE, OKOMFO (Kwame Frimpon Anokye; flourished late 17th century), Ashanti priest and statesman **1** 242-243

ANOUILH, JEAN (1910-1987), French playwright **1** 243-244

Anschluss (1938)
Gruen, Victor **30** 192-194

ANSELM OF CANTERBURY, ST. (1033-1109), Italian archbishop and theologian **1** 244-245

ANSERMET, ERNEST (1883-1969), Swiss orchestral conductor **30** 9-11

Anson, Charles Edward
see Markham, Edwin

ASAM, COSMAS DAMIAN (1686-1739), German artist **1** 323-324

ASAM, EGID QUIRIN (1692-1750), German artist **1** 323-324

ASBURY, FRANCIS (1745-1816), English-born American Methodist bishop **1** 324-325

ASCH, SHALOM (1880-1957), Polish-born playwright and novelist **1** 325-326

Asclepiades
see Hippocrates

ASH, MARY KAY WAGNER (born c. 1916), cosmetics tycoon **1** 326-327

ASHARI, ABU AL- HASAN ALI AL- (873/883-935), Moslem theologian **1** 327-328

ASHCROFT, JOHN (born 1942), American statesman and attorney general **23** 18-21

ASHE, ARTHUR ROBERT, JR. (1943-1993), world champion athlete, social activist, teacher, and charity worker **1** 328-330

ASHFORD, EVELYN (born 1957), American athlete **24** 29-32

ASHIKAGA TAKAUJI (1305-1358), Japanese shogun **1** 330-332

ASHKENAZY, VLADIMIR (born 1937), Russian musician **22** 24-26

Ashley, 1st Baron
see Shaftesbury, 1st Earl of

ASHLEY, LAURA (Mountney; 1925-1985), British designer of women's clothes and home furnishings **1** 332-333

Ashley, Lord
see Shaftesbury, 7th Earl of

ASHLEY, WILLIAM HENRY (c. 1778-1838), American businessman, fur trader, and explorer **1** 333-334

ASHMORE, HARRY SCOTT (1916-1998), American journalist **1** 334-335

ASHMUN, JEHUDI (1794-1828), American governor of Liberia Colony **1** 335-336

ASHRAWI, HANAN MIKHAIL (born 1946), Palestinian spokesperson **1** 336-338

ASHTON, FREDERICK (Frederick William Ashton; 1904-1988), British choreographer **26** 22-24

ASHURBANIPAL (died c. 630 B.C.), Assyrian king 669-ca. 630 **1** 338

ASIMOV, ISAAC (1920-1992), American author **1** 338-341

Askia the Great
see Muhammad Ture, Askia

ASOKA (ruled c. 273-232 B.C.), Indian emperor of the Maurya dynasty **1** 341-342

ASPASIA (ca. 470-410 BC), Milesian courtesan and rhetorician **22** 26-28

ASPIN, LES (1938-1995), United States congressman and secretary of defense **1** 342-344

ASPLUND, ERIC GUNNAR (1885-1945), Swedish architect **1** 344

ASQUITH, HERBERT HENRY (1st Earl of Oxford and Asquith; 1852-1928), English statesman, prime minister 1908-1916 **1** 344-346

ASSAD, HAFIZ (born 1930), president of Syria **1** 346-348

ASTAIRE, FRED (Frederick Austerlitz; 1899-1987), dancer and choreographer **1** 348-350

ASTELL, MARY (Tom Single, Mr. Wooton; 1666-1731), English author **24** 32-34

ASTON, FRANCIS WILLIAM (1877-1945), English chemist and physicist **1** 350-351

ASTOR, JOHN JACOB (1763-1848), American fur trader, merchant, and capitalist **1** 351-352

ASTOR, NANCY LANGHORNE (1879-1964), first woman to serve as a member of the British Parliament (1919-1945) **1** 352-354

Astor Place Theater (New York City)
Buntline, Ned **30** 88-90

Astrea
see Behn, Aphra

Astro Boy (cartoon character)
Tezuka, Osamu **30** 357-359

Astronomy
observatories
Brisbane, Thomas Makdougall **30** 79-81

Astronomy (science)
galaxies
Baade, Walter **30** 24-26
photography
Baade, Walter **30** 24-26
photometry
Baade, Walter **30** 24-26
stellar evolution
Baade, Walter **30** 24-26

Astrophysics
Saha, Meghnad N. **30** 312-314

ASTURIAS, MIGUEL ANGEL (1899-1974), Guatemalan novelist and poet **1** 354-355

Asymptotic freedom (physics)
Wilczek, Frank Anthony **30** 378-380

ATAHUALPA (c. 1502-1533), Inca emperor of Peru 1532-1533 **1** 355-356

Emigrants, The (novel)
Sebald, W.G. **30** 322-324

ATANASOFF, JOHN (1903-1995), American physicist **20** 21-22

ATATÜRK, GHAZI MUSTAPHA KEMAL (1881-1938), Turkish nationalist, president 1923-1938 **1** 356-357

ATCHISON, DAVID RICE (1807-1886), American lawyer and politician **1** 357-358

ATHANASIUS, ST. (c. 296-373), Christian theologian, bishop of Alexandria **1** 358-359

ATHERTON, GERTRUDE (Gertrude Franklin Horn Atherton; 1857-1948), American author **23** 21-23

Athletes
Canadian
Jenkins, Ferguson **30** 225-227
French
Autissier, Isabelle **30** 21-23
German
Graf, Steffi **30** 184-186
Peruvian
Cintrón, Conchita **30** 114-115
Russian
Tretiak, Vladislav **30** 359-361
Swedish
Sorenstam, Annika **30** 341-344

BACH, CARL PHILIPP EMANUEL (1714-1788), German composer **1** 414-415

BACH, JOHANN CHRISTIAN (1735-1782), German composer **1** 415-416

BACH, JOHANN SEBASTIAN (1685-1750), German composer and organist **1** 416-419

BACHARACH, BURT (born 1928), American composer **22** 38-39

BACHE, ALEXANDER DALLAS (1806-1867), American educator and scientist **1** 420

Baciccio
see Gaulli, Giovanni Battista

BACKUS, ISAAC (1724-1806), American Baptist leader **1** 420-421

BACON, SIR FRANCIS (1561-1626), English philosopher, statesman, and author **1** 422-424

BACON, FRANCIS (1909-1992), English artist **1** 421-422

BACON, NATHANIEL (1647-1676), American colonial leader **1** 424-425

BACON, PEGGY (Margaret Francis Bacon; 1895-1987), American artist and author **25** 29-31

BACON, ROGER (c. 1214-1294), English philosopher **1** 425-427

Bad Hand
see Fitzpatrick, Thomas

BAD HEART BULL, AMOS (1869-1913), Oglala Lakota Sioux tribal historian and artist **1** 427-428

BADEN-POWELL, ROBERT (1857-1941), English military officer and founder of the Boy Scout Association **21** 16-18

BADINGS, HENK (Hendrik Herman Badings; 1907-1987), Dutch composer **23** 26-28

BADOGLIO, PIETRO (1871-1956), Italian general and statesman **1** 428-429

BAECK, LEO (1873-1956), rabbi, teacher, hero of the concentration camps, and Jewish leader **1** 429-430

BAEKELAND, LEO HENDRIK (1863-1944), American chemist **1** 430-431

BAER, GEORGE FREDERICK (1842-1914), American businessman **22** 39-41

BAER, KARL ERNST VON (1792-1876), Estonian anatomist and embryologist **1** 431-432

BAEZ, BUENAVENTURA (1812-1884), Dominican statesman, five time president **1** 432-433

BAEZ, JOAN (born 1941), American folk singer and human rights activist **1** 433-435

BAFFIN, WILLIAM (c. 1584-1622), English navigator and explorer **1** 435-436

BAGEHOT, WALTER (1826-1877), English economist **1** 436-437

BAGLEY, WILLIAM CHANDLER (1874-1946), educator and theorist of educational "essentialism" **1** 437-438

BAHÁ'U'LLÁH (Husayn-'Ali', Bahá'u'lláh Mírzá; 1817-1982), Iranian religious leader **28** 21-23

BAHR, EGON (born 1922), West German politician **1** 438-440

BAIKIE, WILLIAM BALFOUR (1825-1864), Scottish explorer and scientist **1** 440

BAILEY, F. LEE (born 1933), American defense attorney and author **1** 441-443

BAILEY, FLORENCE MERRIAM (1863-1948), American ornithologist and author **1** 443-444

BAILEY, GAMALIEL (1807-1859), American editor and politician **1** 444-445

BAILEY, JAMES A. (1847-1906), American circus owner **30** 26-28

BAILEY, MILDRED (Mildred Rinker, 1907-1951), American jazz singer **23** 28-30

BAILLIE, D(ONALD) M(ACPHERSON) (1887-1954), Scottish theologian **1** 445

BAILLIE, ISOBEL (Isabella Baillie; 1895-1983), British singer **26** 27-29

BAILLIE, JOANNA (1762-1851), Scottish playwright and poet **28** 23-25

BAILLIE, JOHN (1886-1960), Scottish theologian and ecumenical churchman **1** 445-447

BAIUS, MICHAEL (1513-1589), Belgian theologian **29** 31-33

BAKER, ELLA JOSEPHINE (1903-1986), African American human and civil rights activist **18** 26-28

BAKER, GEORGE PIERCE (1866-1935), American educator **29** 33-35

BAKER, HOWARD HENRY, JR. (born 1925), U.S. senator and White House chief of staff **18** 28-30

BAKER, JAMES ADDISON III (born 1930), Republican party campaign leader **1** 447-448

BAKER, JOSEPHINE (1906-1975), Parisian dancer and singer from America **1** 448-451

BAKER, NEWTON DIEHL (1871-1937), American statesman **1** 451

BAKER, RAY STANNARD (1870-1946), American author **1** 451-452

BAKER, RUSSELL (born 1925), American writer of personal-political essays **1** 452-454

BAKER, SIR SAMUEL WHITE (1821-1893), English explorer and administrator **1** 454-455

BAKER, SARA JOSEPHINE (1873-1945), American physician **1** 455-456

BAKHTIN, MIKHAIL MIKHAILOVICH (1895-1975), Russian philosopher and literary critic **1** 456-458

BAKST, LEON (1866-1924), Russian painter **29** 35-37

BAKUNIN, MIKHAIL ALEKSANDROVICH (1814-1876), Russian anarchist **1** 458-460

BALAGUER Y RICARDO, JOAQUÍN (1907-2002), Dominican statesman **1** 460-461

BALANCHINE, GEORGE (1904-1983), Russian-born American choreographer **1** 461-462

Balanchivadze, Georgi Melitonovitch
see Balanchine, George

BALBO, ITALO (1896-1940), Italian air marshal **29** 37-39

BALBOA, VASCO NÚÑEZ DE (c. 1475-1519), Spanish explorer **1** 462-463

BALBULUS, NOTKER (c. 840-912), Swiss poet-musician and monk **11** 434-435

BALCH, EMILY GREENE (1867-1961), American pacifist and social reformer **1** 463-464

BALDOMIR, ALFREDO (884-1948), Uruguayan president 1938-1943 **29** 39-41

BALDWIN I (1058-1118), Norman king of Jerusalem 1100-1118 **1** 464-465

BALDWIN, JAMES ARTHUR (1924-1987), African American author, poet, and dramatist **1** 465-466

BALDWIN, ROBERT (1804-1858), Canadian politician **1** 466-468

BALDWIN, ROGER NASH (1884-1981), American civil libertarian and social worker **25** 31-33

BALDWIN, STANLEY (1st Earl Baldwin of Bewdley; 1867-1947), English statesman, three times prime minister **1** 468-469

Baldwin of Bewdley, 1st Earl
see Baldwin, Stanley

Baldwin of Boulogne
see Baldwin I, king

BALENCIAGA, CRISTÓBAL (1895-1972), Spanish fashion designer **30** 28-30

BALFOUR, ARTHUR JAMES (1st Earl of Balfour; 1848-1930), British statesman and philosopher **1** 469-470

Baline, Israel
see Berlin, Irving

BALL, GEORGE (1909-1994), American politician and supporter of an economically united Europe **1** 470-471

BALL, LUCILLE (Lucille Desiree Hunt; 1911-1989), American comedienne **1** 472-473

BALLA, GIACOMO (1871-1958), Italian painter **1** 473-474

BALLADUR, EDOUARD (born 1929), premier of the French Government **1** 474-475

BALLANCE, JOHN (1839-1893), New Zealand journalist and statesman **29** 42-44

BALLARD, J. G. (1930-2009), British author **30** 30-32

BALLARD, LOUIS WAYNE (born 1913), Native American musician **26** 29-31

BALLARD, ROBERT (born 1942), American oceanographer **19** 10-12

Ballet (dance)
Grisi, Carlotta **30** 190-192
Svetlova, Marina **30** 354-355

Ballets Russes de Sergei Diaghilev (dance company)
Ansermet, Ernest **30** 9-11
Auric, Georges **30** 16-18

BALLIVIÁN, JOSÉ (1805-1852), Bolivian president 1841-1847 **1** 475

BALMACEDA FERNÁNDEZ, JOSÉ MANUEL (1840-1891), Chilean president 1886-1891 **1** 475-476

BALTHUS (Balthasar Klossowski; born 1908), European painter and stage designer **1** 476-477

BALTIMORE, DAVID (born 1938), American virologist **1** 477-478

BALZAC, HONORÉ DE (1799-1850), French novelist **1** 478-480

BAMBA, AMADOU (1850-1927), Senegalese religious leader **1** 481-482

BAMBARA, TONI CADE (1939-1995), African American writer and editor **1** 482-483

Bamewawagezhikaquay
see Schoolcraft, Jane Johnston

BAN KI-MOON (born 1944), South Korean diplomat **27** 29-31

BAN ZHAO (Pan Chao, Ban Hui-ji, Cao Dagu; c. 45-51-c. 114-120), Chinese author and historian **24** 38-40

BANCROFT, ANN (born 1955), American explorer **30** 32-34

BANCROFT, ANNE (nee Anna Maria Louisa Italino; 1931-2005), American actress **26** 31-33

BANCROFT, GEORGE (1800-1891), American historian and statesman **1** 483-484

BANCROFT, HUBERT HOWE (1832-1918), American historian **1** 484-485

BANCROFT, MARY (Mary Bancroft Badger; 1903-1997), American author and intelligence analyst **27** 31-33

BANDA, HASTINGS KAMUZU (1905-1997), Malawi statesman **1** 485-486

BANDARANAIKE, SIRIMAVO (ALSO SIRIMA) RATWATTE DIAS (born 1916), first woman prime minister in the world as head of the Sri Lankan Freedom party government (1960-1965, 1970-1976) **1** 486-488

Bandinelli, Bartolommeo "Baccio", (1493-1560), Italian sculptor
Ammanati, Bartolomeo **30** 3-5
Raimondi, Marcantonio **30** 309-311

Bandinelli, Orlando
see Alexander III, pope

BANERJEE, SURENDRANATH (1848-1925), Indian nationalist **1** 488

BANKS, DENNIS J. (born 1932), Native American leader, teacher, activist, and author **1** 488-489

BANKS, SIR JOSEPH (1743-1820), English naturalist **1** 489-490

BANNEKER, BENJAMIN (1731-1806), African American mathematician **1** 490-491

BANNISTER, EDWARD MITCHELL (1828-1901), African American landscape painter **1** 491-493

BANNISTER, ROGER (born 1929), English runner **21** 18-20

BANTING, FREDERICK GRANT (1891-1941), Canadian physiolgist **1** 493-494

BAÑUELOS, ROMANA ACOSTA (born 1925), Mexican businesswoman and American government official **24** 40-42

BANZER SUÁREZ, HUGO (1926-2002), Bolivian president (1971-1979) **1** 494-496

BAO DAI (born 1913), emperor of Vietnam 1932-1945 and 1949-1955 **1** 496-497

BAR KOCHBA, SIMEON (died 135), Jewish commander of revolt against Romans **2** 5

BARAGA, FREDERIC (Irenej Frederic Baraga; 1797-1868), Austrian missionary and linguist **27** 33-35

BARAK, EHUD (born 1942), Israeli prime minister **1** 497-498

BARAKA, IMAMU AMIRI (Everett LeRoi Jones; born 1934), African American poet and playwright **1** 498-499

BARANOV, ALEKSANDR ANDREIEVICH (1747-1819), Russian explorer **1** 499-500

BARBARA, AGATHA (1923-2002), Maltese politician **27** 36-38

Barbarossa, Frederick
see Frederick I, (1657-1713)

BARBAULD, ANNA (MRS.) (nee Anna Laetitia Aiken; 1743-1825), British author **27** 38-40

BARBEAU, MARIUS (1883-1969), Canadian ethnographer, anthropologist, and author **24** 42-44

BARBER, SAMUEL (1910-1981), American composer **1** 500-501

Barbera, Joseph
see Hanna and Barbera

Barberini, Maffeo
see Urban VIII

BARBIE, KLAUS (Klaus Altmann; 1913-1991), Nazi leader in Vichy France **1** 501-503

Barbieri, Giovanni Francesco
see Guercino

BARBIROLLI, JOHN (Giovanni Battista Barbirolli; 1899-1970), British conductor **24** 44-46

Barbo, Pietro
see Paul II, pope

BARBONCITO (1820-1871), Native American leader of the Navajos **20** 25-27

BARBOSA, RUY (1849-1923), Brazilian journalist and politician **1** 503-504

BARCLAY, EDWIN (1882-1955), Liberian statesman, twice president **29** 44-45

BARDEEN, JOHN (1908-1991), American Nobel physicist **2** 1-3

Bardi, Donato di Niccolò
see Donatello

BARENBOIM, DANIEL (born 1942), Israeli pianist and conductor **2** 3-4

BARENTS, WILLEM (died 1597), Dutch navigator and explorer **2** 4-5

Baring, Evelyn
see Cromer, 1st Earl of

BARING, FRANCIS (1740-1810), English banker **21** 20-22

BARKLA, CHARLES GLOVER (1877-1944), English physicist **29** 46-48

BARLACH, ERNST (1870-1938), German sculptor **2** 5-6

BARLOW, JOEL (1754-1812), American poet **2** 6-7

Barnabetta (novel)
de Forest, Marian **30** 138-139

BARNARD, CHRISTIAAN N. (1922-2001), South African heart transplant surgeon **2** 7-8

BARNARD, EDWARD EMERSON (1857-1923), American astronomer **2** 8-9

BARNARD, FREDERICK AUGUSTUS PORTER (1809-1889), American educator and mathematician **2** 9-10

BARNARD, HENRY (1811-1900), American educator **2** 10

BARNES, DJUNA (Lydia Steptoe; 1892-1982), American author **2** 11-13

BARNETT, ETTA MOTEN (1901-2004), African American actress and singer **25** 34-36

BARNETT, MARGUERITE ROSS (1942-1992), American educator **21** 22-24

BARNUM, PHINEAS TAYLOR (1810-1891), American showman **2** 13-15
Bailey, James A. **30** 26-28

Barocchio, Giacomo
see Vignola, Giacomo da

BAROJA Y NESSI, PÍO (1872-1956), Spanish novelist **2** 15-16

BARON, SALO WITTMAYER (1895-1989), Austrian-American educator and Jewish historian **2** 16-17

BARONESS ORCZY (Emma Magdalena Rosalia Maria Josefa Orczy; 1865-1947), Hungarian-British author **28** 25-27

Barozzi, Giacomo
see Vignola, Giacomo da

BARRAGÁN, LUIS (1902-1988), Mexican architect and landscape architect **2** 17-19

BARRAS, VICOMTE DE (Paul François Jean Nicolas; 1755-1829), French statesman and revolutionist **2** 19

BARRE, RAYMOND (1924-1981), prime minister of France (1976-1981) **2** 19-20

BARRÈS, AUGUSTE MAURICE (1862-1923), French writer and politician **2** 20-21

Barrett, Elizabeth
see Browning, Elizabeth Barrett

BARRIE, SIR JAMES MATTHEW (1860-1937), British dramatist and novelist **2** 21-22

BARRIENTOS ORTUÑO, RENÉ (1919-1969), populist Bolivian president (1966-1969) **2** 22-23

BARRIOS, AGUSTIN PÌO (1885-1944), Paraguayan musician and composer **28** 27-29

BARRIOS, JUSTO RUFINO (1835-1885), Guatemalan general, president 1873-1885 **2** 23-24

Barristers
see Jurists, English

Barrow, Joe Louis
see Louis, Joe

BARROWS, ISABEL CHAPIN (1845-1913), American missionary, stenographer, and physician **30** 34-36

Barrows, Samuel June, (1845-1909), American politician, minister, and journalist
Barrows, Isabel Chapin **30** 34-36

BARRY, ELIZABETH (1658-1713), English actress **30** 36-38
Bracegirdle, Anne **30** 73-75

BARRY, JAMES (Miranda Stuart Barry; 1795-1865), First British female physician **27** 40-41

BARRY, JOHN (1745-1803), American naval officer **2** 24-25

BARRY, MARION SHEPILOV, JR. (born 1936), African American mayor and civil rights activist **2** 25-28

BARRYMORES, American theatrical dynasty **2** 28-30

BARTH, HEINRICH (1821-1865), German explorer **2** 30-31

BARTH, KARL (1886-1968), Swiss Protestant theologian **2** 31-32

BARTHÉ, RICHMOND (1901-1989), African American sculptor **2** 33-34

BARTHOLDI, FRÉDÉRIC-AUGUSTE (1834-1904), French sculptor **28** 29-31

BARTHOLOMAEUS ANGLICUS (Bartholomew the Englishman; Bartholomew de Glanville; flourished 1220-1240), English theologian and encyclopedist **21** 24-25

BARTLETT, SIR FREDERIC CHARLES (1886-1969), British psychologist **2** 34-35

BARTÓK, BÉLA (1881-1945), Hungarian composer and pianist **2** 35-36

BARTON, BRUCE (1886-1967), American advertising business executive and congressman **2** 36-37

BARTON, CLARA (1821-1912), American humanitarian **2** 37-39

BARTON, SIR EDMUND (1849-1920), Australian statesman and jurist **2** 39-40

BARTRAM, JOHN (1699-1777), American botanist **2** 40-41
Garden, Alexander **30** 176-178

BARTRAM, WILLIAM (1739-1823), American naturalist **2** 41-42

BARUCH, BERNARD MANNES (1870-1965), American statesman and financier **2** 42-43

BARYSHNIKOV, MIKHAIL (born 1948), ballet dancer **2** 43-44

BARZIZZA, GASPARINO (1360-c. 1430), Italian humanist **30** 38-40

BARZUN, JACQUES (born 1907), American writer **30** 40-42

BASCOM, FLORENCE (1862-1945), American geologist **22** 42-43

Baseball Hall of Fame (Cooperstown, New York State)
Doby, Larry **30** 150-152
Harwell, Ernie **30** 202-204
Hulbert, William Ambrose **30** 210-213
Jenkins, Ferguson **30** 225-227
Johnson, Ban **30** 227-230
O'Malley, Walter Francis **30** 293-297

Baseball players
see Athletes

BASEDOW, JOHANN BERNHARD (1724-1790), German educator and reformer **2** 44-45

BASHO, MATSUO (1644-1694), Japanese poet **2** 45-48

BASIE, COUNT (William Basie; 1904-1984), pianist and jazz band leader **2** 48-49

BASIL I (c. 812-886), Byzantine emperor 867-886 **2** 49-50

BASIL II (c. 958-1025), Byzantine emperor 963-1025 **2** 50-51

BASIL THE GREAT, ST. (329-379), theologian and bishop of Caesarea **2** 51-52

Basil the Macedonian
see Basil I

Basketball (United States)
see Athletes

Basketball Hall of Fame
Summitt, Pat **30** 352-354

BASKIN, LEONARD (1922-2000), American artist and publisher **22** 43-46

BASS, SAUL (1920-1996), American designer of film advertising **21** 25-27

BASSANI, GIORGIO (1916-2000), Italian author **30** 42-44

BASSI, LAURA (1711-1778), Italian physicist **20** 27-29

Bassianus
see Caracalla

BASTIAN, ADOLF (1826-1905), German ethnologist **30** 44-46

BATES, DAISY MAE (née O'Dwyer; 1861-1951), Irish-born Australian social worker **2** 52-53

BATES, HENRY WALTER (1825-1892), English explorer and naturalist **2** 53-54

BATES, KATHARINE LEE (1859-1929), American poet and educator **2** 54-55

BATESON, WILLIAM (1861-1926), English biologist concerned with evolution **2** 55-57

BATISTA Y ZALDÍVAR, FULGENCIO (1901-1973), Cuban political and military leader **2** 57-58

BATLLE Y ORDÓÑEZ, JOSÉ (1856-1929), Uruguayan statesman and journalist **2** 58-59

BATTEN, JEAN (1909-1982), New Zealander aviatrix **26** 33-35

Battiferri, Laura, (c. 1524-1589)
Ammanati, Bartolomeo **30** 3-5

BATTLE, KATHLEEN (born 1948), American opera and concert singer **2** 59-60

BATU KHAN (died 1255), Mongol leader **2** 60-61

BAUDELAIRE, CHARLES PIERRE (1821-1867), French poet and art critic **2** 61-63

BAUER, EDDIE (1899-1986), American businessman **19** 13-14

Bauer, Georg
see Agricola, Georgius

BAULIEU, ÉTIENNE-ÉMILE (Étienne Blum; born 1926), French physician and biochemist who developed RU 486 **2** 63-66

BAUM, ELEANOR (born 1940), American engineer **30** 47-48

BAUM, HERBERT (1912-1942), German human/civil rights activist **2** 66-73

BAUM, L. FRANK (1856-1919), author of the Wizard of Oz books **2** 73-74

Baumfree, Isabella
see Truth, Sojourner

BAUR, FERDINAND CHRISTIAN (1792-1860), German theologian **2** 74-75

BAUSCH, PINA (born 1940), a controversial German dancer/choreographer **2** 75-76

BAXTER, RICHARD (1615-1691), English theologian **2** 76-77

Bay of Pigs invasion (1961)
Dulles, Allen Welsh **30** 152-154

BAYLE, PIERRE (1647-1706), French philosopher **2** 77-78

Bayley, Elizabeth
see Seton, Elizabeth Ann Bayley

BAYNTON, BARBARA (1857-1929), Australian author **22** 46-48

BAZIN, ANDRÉ (1918-1958), French film critic **28** 32-33

BEA, AUGUSTINUS (1881-1968), German cardinal **2** 79

BEACH, AMY (born Amy Marcy Cheney; 1867-1944), American musician **23** 30-32

BEACH, MOSES YALE (1800-1868), American inventor and newspaperman **2** 79-80

Beaconsfield, Earl of
see Disraeli, Benjamin

BEADLE, GEORGE WELLS (1903-1989), American scientist, educator, and administrator **2** 80-81

BEALE, DOROTHEA (1831-1906), British educator **2** 81-83

BEAN, ALAN (born 1932), American astronaut and artist **22** 48-50

BEAN, LEON LEONWOOD (L.L. Bean; 1872-1967), American businessman **19** 14-16

BEARD, CHARLES AUSTIN (1874-1948), American historian **2** 84

BEARD, MARY RITTER (1876-1958), American author and activist **2** 85-86

BEARDEN, ROMARE HOWARD (1914-1988), African American painter-collagist **2** 86-88

BEARDSLEY, AUBREY VINCENT (1872-1898), English illustrator **2** 88-89

BEATLES, THE (1957-1971), British rock and roll band **2** 89-92

BEATRIX, WILHELMINA VON AMSBERG, QUEEN (born 1938), queen of Netherlands (1980-) **2** 92-93

BEAUCHAMPS, PIERRE (1636-1705), French dancer and choreographer **21** 27-29

BEAUFORT, MARGARET (1443-1509), queen dowager of England **20** 29-31

BEAUJOYEULX, BALTHASAR DE (Balthasar de Beaujoyeux; Baldassare de Belgiojoso; 1535-1587), Italian choreographer and composer **21** 29-30

BEAUMARCHAIS, PIERRE AUGUST CARON DE (1732-1799), French playwright **2** 93-94

BEAUMONT, FRANCIS (1584/1585-1616), English playwright **2** 95

BEAUMONT, WILLIAM (1785-1853), American surgeon **2** 95-96

BEAUREGARD, PIERRE GUSTAVE TOUTANT (1818-1893), Confederate general **2** 96-97

Beaverbrook, Lord
see Aitken, William Maxwell

BECARRIA, MARCHESE DI (1738-1794), Italian jurist and economist **2** 97-98

BECHET, SIDNEY (1897-1959), American jazz musician **22** 50-52
Ansermet, Ernest **30** 9-11

BECHTEL, STEPHEN DAVISON (1900-1989), American construction engineer and business executive **2** 98-99

BECK, JÓZEF (1894-1944), Polish statesman **29** 48-50

BECK, LUDWIG AUGUST THEODOR (1880-1944), German general **2** 99-100

BECKER, CARL LOTUS (1873-1945), American historian **2** 100-101

BECKET, ST. THOMAS (1128?-1170), English prelate **2** 101-102

BECKETT, SAMUEL (1906-1989), Irish novelist, playwright, and poet **2** 102-104

BECKHAM, DAVID (David Robert Joseph Beckham; born 1975), British soccer player **26** 36-38

BECKMANN, MAX (1884-1950), German painter **2** 104-105

BECKNELL, WILLIAM (c. 1797-1865), American soldier and politician **2** 105-106

BECKWOURTH, JIM (James P. Beckwourth; c. 1800-1866), African American fur trapper and explorer **2** 106-107

BÉCQUER, GUSTAVO ADOLFO DOMINGUEZ (1836-1870), Spanish lyric poet **2** 107-108

BECQUEREL, ANTOINE HENRI (1852-1908), French physicist **2** 108-109

BEDE, ST. (672/673-735), English theologian **2** 109-110

BOSOMWORTH, MARY MUSGROVE
(Cousaponokeesa;1700-1765), Native
American/American interpreter,
diplomat, and businessperson **20** 54-56

Bossism (United States politics)
see Political machines (United States)

BOSSUET, JACQUES BÉNIGNE (1627-1704),
French bishop and author **2** 431-432

Boston Strong Boy
see Sullivan, John Lawrence

BOSWELL, JAMES (1740-1795), Scottish
biographer and diarist **2** 432-434

Botany (science)
collections (18th century)
Garden, Alexander **30** 176-178

BOTERO, FERNANDO (born 1932),
Colombian artist **24** 59-61

BOTHA, LOUIS (1862-1919), South
African soldier and statesman **2** 434-436

BOTHA, PIETER WILLEM (1916-2006),
prime minister (1978-1984) and first
executive state president of the Republic
of South Africa **2** 436-438

BOTHE, WALTHER (1891-1957), German
physicist **2** 438-439

Boto, Eza
see Beti, Mongo

BOTTICELLI, SANDRO (1444-1510),
Italian painter **2** 439-440

Bou Kharouba, Mohammed Ben Brahim
see Boumediene, Houari

BOUCHER, FRANÇOIS (1703-1770),
French painter **2** 440-442

BOUCICAULT, DION (1820-1890),
Irish-American playwright and actor **2**
442-443

BOUDICCA (Boadicea; died 61 A.D.),
Iceni queen **18** 56-58

BOUDINOT, ELIAS (Buck Watie;
Galagina; 1803-1839), Cherokee leader
and author **21** 52-54

BOUGAINVILLE, LOUIS ANTOINE DE
(1729-1811), French soldier and
explorer **2** 443-444

Boulanger, N.A. (pseudonym)
see Holbach, Baron d'

BOULANGER, NADIA (1887-1979),
French pianist and music teacher **20**
56-58

BOULEZ, PIERRE (born 1925), French
composer, conductor, and teacher **2**
444-445

BOULT, ADRIAN CEDRIC (1889-1983),
English conductor **24** 61-64

BOUMEDIENE, HOUARI (born 1932),
Algerian revolutionary, military leader,
and president **2** 445-446

BOURASSA, JOSEPH-HENRI-NAPOLEON
(1868-1952), French-Canadian
nationalist and editor **2** 446-447

BOURASSA, ROBERT (born 1933), premier
of the province of Quebec (1970-1976
and 1985-) **2** 447-449

Bourcicault, Dion
see Boucicault, Dion

BOURDELLE, EMILE-ANTOINE
(1861-1929), French sculptor **2** 449-450

BOURGEOIS, LÉON (1851-1925), French
premier 1895-1896 **2** 450-451

BOURGEOIS, LOUISE (born 1911),
American sculptor **2** 451-452

BOURGEOIS, LOUYSE (Louise Bourgeois;
c. 1563-1636), French midwife **25** 58-60

BOURGEOYS, BLESSED MARGUERITE
(1620-1700), French educator and
religious founder **2** 452-453

Bourgogne, Jean de
see Mandeville, Sir John

BOURGUIBA, HABIB (1903-2000),
Tunisian statesman **2** 453-455

BOURIGNON, ANTOINETTE
(1616-1680), Flemish mystic **29** 80-83

BOURKE-WHITE, MARGARET
(1904-1971), American photographer
and photojournalist **2** 455-456

BOURNE, RANDOLPH SILLIMAN
(1886-1918), American pacifist and
cultural critic **2** 456-457

Boursiquot, Dionysius Lardner
see Boucicault, Dion

BOUTMY, ÉMILE (1835-1906), French
educator **29** 83-84

BOUTROS-GHALI, BOUTROS (born
1922), Egyptian diplomat and sixth secretary-general of the United Nations
(1991-) **2** 457-458

BOUTS, DIRK (1415/20-1475), Dutch
painter **2** 458-459

Bouvier, Jacqueline Lee
see Kennedy, Jacqueline

BOVERI, THEODOR HEINRICH
(1862-1915), German biologist **25** 60-62

BOWDITCH, HENRY INGERSOLL
(1808-1892), American physician **2**
459-460

BOWDITCH, NATHANIEL (1773-1838),
American navigator and mathematician
2 460-461

BOWDOIN, JAMES (1726-1790),
American merchant and politician **2**
461-462

BOWEN, EDWARD GEORGE
(1911-1991), Welsh physicist **29** 84-86

BOWEN, ELIZABETH (1899-1973), British
novelist **2** 462-463

BOWERS, CLAUDE GERNADE
(1878-1958), American journalist,
historian, and diplomat **2** 463

BOWIE, DAVID (David Robert Jones; born
1947), English singer, songwriter, and
actor **18** 58-60

BOWIE, JAMES (1796-1836), American
soldier **30** 71-73

BOWLES, PAUL (1910-1999), American
author, musical composer, and
translator **19** 31-34

BOWLES, SAMUEL (1826-1878), American
newspaper publisher **2** 464

BOWMAN, ISAIAH (1878-1950),
American geographer **2** 464-465

BOXER, BARBARA (born 1940), U.S.
Senator from California **2** 465-468

Boxers
see Athletes–boxers

Boy bachelor
see Wolsey, Thomas

Boycott
see Civil rights movement (United
States); Labor unions (United States)

BOYD, LOUISE ARNER (1887-1972),
American explorer **22** 73-74

Boyd, Nancy
see Millay, Edna St. Vincent

Boyd Orr, John
see Orr, John Boyd

BOYER, JEAN PIERRE (1776-1850),
Haitian president 1818-1845 **2** 468-469

BOYER, PAUL DELOS (born 1918),
American biochemist **25** 62-65

BOYLE, ROBERT (1627-1691), British
chemist and physicist **2** 469-471

BOYLSTON, ZABDIEL (1679-1766),
American physician **2** 471

Boz
see Dickens, Charles

BOZEMAN, JOHN M. (1837-1867),
American pioneer **2** 471-472

Bozzie
see Boswell, James

BRACEGIRDLE, ANNE (c. 1663-1748),
English actress **30** 73-75
Barry, Elizabeth **30** 36-38

BRACKENRIDGE, HUGH HENRY
(1749-1816), American lawyer and
writer **2** 472-473

BRACTON, HENRY (Henry of Bratton;
c. 1210-1268), English jurist **21** 54-55

BRADBURY, RAY (born 1920), American fantasy and science fiction writer **2** 473-474

Bradby, Lucy Barbara
see Hammond, John and Lucy

BRADDOCK, EDWARD (1695-1755), British commander in North America **2** 474-475

BRADFORD, WILLIAM (1590-1657), leader of Plymouth Colony **2** 475-476

BRADFORD, WILLIAM (1663-1752), American printer **2** 476-477

BRADFORD, WILLIAM (1722-1791), American journalist **2** 477

BRADLAUGH, CHARLES (1833-1891), English freethinker and political agitator **2** 478

BRADLEY, ED (1941-2006), African American broadcast journalist **2** 478-481

BRADLEY, FRANCIS HERBERT (1846-1924), English philosopher **2** 481-482

BRADLEY, JAMES (1693-1762), English astronomer **2** 482-483

BRADLEY, JOSEPH P. (1813-1892), American Supreme Court justice **22** 74-77

BRADLEY, LYDIA MOSS (1816-1908), American businesswoman and philanthropist **30** 75-77

BRADLEY, MARION ZIMMER (born 1930), American author **18** 60-62

BRADLEY, OMAR NELSON (1893-1981), American general **2** 483-484

BRADLEY, TOM (1917-1998), first African American mayor of Los Angeles **2** 484-485

Bradley Polytechnic Institute
Bradley, Lydia Moss **30** 75-77

BRADMAN, SIR DONALD GEORGE (born 1908), Australian cricketer **2** 485-486

BRADSTREET, ANNE DUDLEY (c. 1612-1672), English-born American poet **2** 486-487

BRADWELL, MYRA (Myra Colby; 1831-1894), American lawyer and publisher **24** 64-66

BRADY, MATHEW B. (c. 1823-1896), American photographer **2** 487-488

BRAGG, SIR WILLIAM HENRY (1862-1942), English physicist **2** 488-489
Moseley, Henry Gwyn Jeffreys **30** 280-283

Bragg, William L., (1890-1971), English physicist
Moseley, Henry Gwyn Jeffreys **30** 280-283

BRAHE, TYCHO (1546-1601), Danish astronomer **2** 489-490

BRAHMAGUPTA (c. 598-c. 670), Indian mathematician and astronomer **26** 44-46

BRAHMS, JOHANNES (1833-1897), German composer **2** 490-492
associates
Tausig, Carl **30** 356-357

BRAILLE, LOUIS (1809-1852), French teacher and creator of braille system **2** 492-493

Brain (dog)
Jackson, John Hughlings **30** 214-216

Brain (human)
Jackson, John Hughlings **30** 214-216

BRAINARD, BERTHA (Bertha Brainard Peterson; died 1946), American radio executive **28** 47-48

BRAMAH, JOSEPH (Joe Bremmer; 1749-1814), English engineer and inventor **20** 58-59

BRAMANTE, DONATO (1444-1514), Italian architect and painter **2** 493-494

BRANCUSI, CONSTANTIN (1876-1957), Romanian sculptor in France **2** 494-496

BRANDEIS, LOUIS DEMBITZ (1856-1941), American jurist **2** 496-497

BRANDES, GEORG (Georg Morris Cohen Brandes; 1842-1927), Danish literary critic **23** 45-47

BRANDO, MARLON (born 1924), American actor **2** 497-499

BRANDT, WILLY (Herbert Frahm Brandt; 1913-1992), German statesman, chancellor of West Germany **2** 499-500

BRANSON, RICHARD (born 1950), British entrepreneur **19** 34-36

BRANT, JOSEPH (1742-1807), Mohawk Indian chief **2** 500-501

BRANT, MARY (1736-1796), Native American who guided the Iroquois to a British alliance **2** 501-503

BRANT, SEBASTIAN (1457-1521), German author **2** 503-504

BRAQUE, GEORGES (1882-1967), French painter **2** 504-505

Braschi, Gianangelo
see Pius VI

BRATTAIN, WALTER H. (1902-1987), American physicist and co-inventor of the transistor **2** 505-507

Bratton, Henry de
see Bracton, Henry de

BRAUDEL, FERNAND (1902-1985), leading exponent of the *Annales* school of history **2** 507-508

BRAUN, FERDINAND (1850-1918), German recipient of the Nobel Prize in Physics for work on wireless telegraphy **2** 508-509

BRAY, JOHN RANDOLPH (1879-1978), American animator and cartoonist **21** 55-57

Brazilian literature
Boal, Augusto **30** 63-65

BRAZZA, PIERRE PAUL FRANÇOIS CAMILLE SAVORGNAN DE (1852-1905), Italian-born French explorer **2** 509-510

Breaking the Waves (film)
Von Trier, Lars **30** 366-368

BREASTED, JAMES HENRY (1865-1935), American Egyptologist and archeologist **2** 510-511

BRÉBEUF, JEAN DE (1593-1649), French Jesuit missionary **2** 511-512

BRECHT, BERTOLT (1898-1956), German playwright **2** 512-514

BRECKINRIDGE, JOHN CABELL (1821-1875), American statesman and military leader **22** 77-79

Brède, Baron de la
see Montesquieu, Baron de

BREGUET, ABRAHAM-LOUIS (1747-1823), French instrument maker **29** 86-88

BREMER, FREDRIKA (1801-1865), Swedish author **26** 46-48

BRENDAN, SAINT (Brenainn; Brandon; Brendan of Clonfert; c. 486- c. 578), Irish Abbott and explorer **22** 79-80

BRENNAN, WILLIAM J., JR. (born 1906), United States Supreme Court justice **2** 514-515

Brent of Bin Bin
see Franklin, Miles

BRENTANO, CLEMENS (1778-1842), German poet and novelist **2** 515-516

BRENTANO, FRANZ CLEMENS (1838-1917), German philosopher **2** 516-517

BRESHKOVSKY, CATHERINE (1844-1934), Russian revolutionary **2** 517-519
Barrows, Isabel Chapin **30** 34-36

BRESSON, ROBERT (1901-1999), French filmmaker **25** 65-67

BRETON, ANDRÉ (1896-1966), French author **2** 519-520

Bretton, Henry de
see Bracton, Henry de

BUCHANAN, PATRICK JOSEPH (born 1938), commentator, journalist, and presidential candidate 3 90-91

BUCHWALD, ART (Arthur Buchwald; 1925-2007), American journalist 27 55-57

BUCK, JACK (John Francis Buck; 1924-2002), American sportscaster 27 57-59

BUCK, PEARL SYDENSTRICKER (1892-1973), American novelist 3 91-93

BUCKINGHAM, 1ST DUKE OF (George Villiers; 1592-1628), English courtier and military leader 3 93-94
Ogilby, John 30 291-293

BUCKINGHAM, 2D DUKE OF (George Villiers; 1628-1687), English statesman 3 94-95

BUCKLE, HENRY THOMAS (1821-1862), English historian 3 95-96

BUCKLEY, WILLIAM F., JR. (1925-2008), conservative American author, editor, and political activist 3 96-97

BUDDHA (c. 560-480 B.C.), Indian founder of Buddhism 3 97-101

BUDDHADĀSA BHIKKHU (Nguam Phanich; born 1906), founder of Wat Suan Mokkhabalārama in southern Thailand and interpreter of Theravāda Buddhism 3 101-102

BUDÉ, GUILLAUME (1467-1540), French humanist 3 102-103

BUDGE, DON (J. Donald Budge; born 1915), American tennis player 21 57-59

BUECHNER, FREDERICK (born 1926), American novelist and theologian 3 103-105

BUEL, JESSE (1778-1839), American agriculturalist and journalist 3 105

Buell, Sarah Josepha
see Hale, Sarah Josepha

Buffalo (animal)
Garrett, Patrick Floyd 30 180-182

Buffalo (city, New York State)
de Forest, Marian 30 138-139

BUFFALO BILL (William Frederick Cody; 1846-1917), American scout and publicist 3 105-106
Bailey, James A. 30 26-28
Buntline, Ned 30 88-90

Buffalo Express (newspaper)
de Forest, Marian 30 138-139

BUFFETT, WARREN (born 1930), American investment salesman 3 106-109

BUFFON, COMTE DE (Georges Louis Leclerc; 1707-1788), French naturalist 3 109-111

BUGEAUD DE LA PICONNERIE, THOMAS ROBERT (1784-1849), Duke of Isly and marshal of France 3 111

BUICK, DAVID (1854-1929), American inventor and businessman 19 44-45

BUKHARI, MUHAMMAD IBN ISMAIL AL- (810-870), Arab scholar and Moslem saint 3 111-112

BUKHARIN, NIKOLAI IVANOVICH (1858-1938), Russian politician 3 112-113

BUKOWSKI, CHARLES (1920-1994), American writer and poet 3 113-115

BULATOVIC, MOMIR (born 1956), president of Montenegro (1990-1992) and of the new Federal Republic of Yugoslavia (1992-) 3 115-116

BULFINCH, CHARLES (1763-1844), American colonial architect 3 116-117

BULGAKOV, MIKHAIL AFANASIEVICH (1891-1940), Russian novelist and playwright 3 117

BULGANIN, NIKOLAI (1885-1975), chairman of the Soviet Council of Ministers (1955-1958) 3 118-119

Bulgaroctonus (Bulgar-Slayer)
see Basil II, (1415-1462)

BULL, OLE (Ole Bornemann Bull; 1810-1880), Norwegian violinist and composer 28 54-56

Bullfighting (sport)
Cintrón, Conchita 30 114-115

BULOSAN, CARLOS (1911-1956), American author and poet 21 59-61

BULTMANN, RUDOLF KARL (1884-1976), German theologian 3 119-120

BULWER-LYTTON, EDWARD (1st Baron Lytton of Knebworth; 1803-1873), English novelist 22 87-88

BUNAU-VARILLA, PHILIPPE JEAN (1859-1940), French engineer and soldier 3 120-121

BUNCHE, RALPH JOHNSON (1904-1971), African American diplomat 3 121-122

BUNDY, MCGEORGE (born 1919), national security adviser to two presidents 3 122-124

BUNIN, IVAN ALEKSEEVICH (1870-1953), Russian poet and novelist 3 124

BUNSEN, ROBERT WILHELM (1811-1899), German chemist and physicist 3 124-125

BUNSHAFT, GORDON (1909-1990), American architect 3 125-127

BUNTING-SMITH, MARY INGRAHAM (Polly Bunting; 1910-1998), American educator 27 59-61

BUNTLINE, NED (c. 1821-1886), American writer and publisher 30 88-90

BUÑUEL, LUIS (1900-1983), Spanish film director 3 127-128
Levitt, Helen 30 260-261

BUNYAN, JOHN (1628-1688), English author and Baptist preacher 3 128-129

BURBAGE, RICHARD (c. 1567-1619), British actor 24 70-72

BURBANK, LUTHER (1849-1926), American plant breeder 3 129-131

BURBIDGE, E. MARGARET (Eleanor Margaret Burbidge; born 1919), British-American astronomer and physicist 26 48-50

BURCHFIELD, CHARLES (1893-1967), American painter 3 131-132

BURCKHARDT, JACOB CHRISTOPH (1818-1897), Swiss historian 3 132-133

BURCKHARDT, JOHANN LUDWIG (1784-1817), Swiss-born explorer 3 133

Bureau of Investigation
see Federal Bureau of Investigation (FBI)

BURGER, WARREN E. (1907-1986), Chief Justice of the United States Supreme Court (1969-1986) 3 133-136

BURGESS, ANTHONY (John Anthony Burgess Wilson; 1917-1993), English author 3 136-137

Burghley, Lord, (Sir William Cecil; 1520-1598), English statesman
Walsingham, Sir Francis 30 374-376

BURGOYNE, JOHN (1723-1792), British general and statesman 3 137-138

BURKE, EDMUND (1729-1797), British statesman, political theorist, and philosopher 3 138-141

BURKE, JOHN BERNARD (1814-1892), British genealogist and publisher 30 90-91

BURKE, KENNETH (born 1897), American literary theorist and critic 3 141-142

BURKE, ROBERT O'HARA (1820-1861), Irish-born Australian policeman and explorer 3 142-143

BURKE, SELMA (1900-1995), African American sculptor 3 143-144

Burke's Peerage (genealogical guide)
Burke, John Bernard 30 90-91

BURLIN, NATALIE CURTIS (Natalie Curtis; 1875-1921), American ethnomusicologist 23 50-52

BURLINGAME, ANSON (1820-1870), American diplomat 3 144-145

BYRD, WILLIAM II (1674-1744), American diarist and government official **3** 189-190

BYRNE, JANE (born 1934), first woman mayor of Chicago **3** 190-191

BYRNES, JAMES FRANCIS (1879-1972), American public official **3** 191-192

BYRON, GEORGE GORDON NOEL (6th Baron Byron; 1788-1824), English poet **3** 193-194

Byzantine Church
see Orthodox Eastern Church

Byzantine Empire (395-1453; Eastern Roman Empire 395-474)
and Bulgaria
Andronikos II Palaiologos **30** 7-9
decline and fall
Andronikos II Palaiologos **30** 7-9

Byzantium
see Byzantine Empire (395-1453; Eastern Roman Empire 395-474)

C

Cabanatuan prison camp (Philippines)
Phillips, Claire **30** 300-303

CABELL, JAMES BRANCH (1879-1958), American essayist and novelist **3** 195-196

CABET, ÉTIENNE (1788-1856), French political radical **3** 196

CABEZA DE VACA, ÁLVAR NÚÑEZ (c. 1490-c. 1557), Spanish explorer **3** 197

CABEZÓN, ANTONIO (1510-1566), Spanish composer **3** 197-198

CABLE, GEORGE WASHINGTON (1844-1925), American novelist **3** 198-199

CABOT, JOHN (flourished 1471-1498), Italian explorer in English service **3** 199-200

CABOT, RICHARD CLARKE (1868-1939), American physician **3** 200

CABOT, SEBASTIAN (c. 1482-1557), Italian-born explorer for England and Spain **3** 200-201

Caboto, Giovanni
see Cabot, John

CABRAL, AMÍLCAR LOPES (1924-1973), father of modern African nationalism in Guinea-Bissau and the Cape Verde Islands **3** 202-203

CABRAL, PEDRO ÁLVARES (c. 1467-1520), Portuguese navigator **3** 203-204

Cabrera, Manuel Estrada
see Estrada Cabrera, Manuel

CABRILLO, JUAN RODRÍGUEZ (died 1543), Portuguese explorer for Spain **3** 204-205

CABRINI, ST. FRANCES XAVIER (1850-1917), Italian-born founder of the Missionary Sisters of the Sacred Heart **3** 205

CACCINI, GIULIO (c. 1545-1618), Italian singer and composer **3** 205-206

CACHAO (1918-2008), Cuban musician **29** 104-106

CADAMOSTO, ALVISE DA (c. 1428-1483), Italian explorer **3** 206-207

CAEDMON (650-c.680), English Christian poet **20** 66-67

CADILLAC, ANTOINE DE LAMOTHE (1658-1730), French explorer and colonial administrator **18** 69-71

CADMUS, PAUL (1904-1999), American painter **27** 64-66

CAESAR, (GAIUS) JULIUS (100-44 B.C.), Roman general and statesman **3** 207-210

CAESAR, SHIRLEY (born 1938), African American singer **3** 210-211

Caetani, Benedetto
see Boniface VIII

CAGE, JOHN (1912-1992), American composer **3** 211-214

CAGNEY, JAMES (1899-1986), American actor **21** 68-71
Day, Doris **30** 135-137

CAHAN, ABRAHAM (1860-1951), Lithuanian-American Jewish author **3** 214

Cahier d'un retour au pays natal (autobiography)
Césaire, Aimé **30** 108-110

CAILLIÉ, AUGUSTE RENÉ (1799-1838), French explorer **3** 214-215

CAIN, JAMES (1892-1977), American journalist and author **19** 50-52

CAJETAN, ST. (1480-1547), Italian reformer; cofounder of the Theatines **3** 215-216

Calabria, Duke of
see Guiscard, Robert

CALAMITY JANE (Martha Jane Cannary; 1852-1903), American frontier woman **3** 216

CALATRAVA, SANTIAGO (born 1951), Spanish/Swiss architect **27** 66-68

Calcutta, University of (India)
Saha, Meghnad N. **30** 312-314

CALDECOTT, RANDOLPH (1846-1886), English artist and illustrator **19** 52-55

CALDER, ALEXANDER (1898-1976), American sculptor **3** 216-218

CALDERA RODRÍGUEZ, RAFAEL (born 1916), president of Venezuela (1969-1974) **3** 218-219

CALDERÓN, ALBERTO P. (1920-1998), Hispanic American mathematician **3** 219-220

CALDERÓN, FELIPE (Felipe de Jesús Calderon Hinojosa; born 1962), Mexican politician **27** 68-70

CALDERÓN, PEDRO (1600-1681), Spanish poet and playwright **3** 221-222

CALDERÓN FOURNIER, RAFAEL (born 1949), president of Costa Rica (1990-) **3** 222-223

CALDERONE, MARY STEICHEN (1904-1998), American public health educator **30** 94-96

CALDICOTT, HELEN BROINOWSKI (born 1938), Australian physician and activist **18** 71-73

CALDWELL, ERSKINE (1903-1987), American novelist **3** 223-224

CALDWELL, SARAH (1924-2006), long-time artistic director, conductor, and founder of the Opera Company of Boston **3** 224-226

Caletti-Bruni, Pietro Francesco
see Cavalli, Pietro Francesco

CALHOUN, JOHN CALDWELL (1782-1850), American statesman **3** 226-228

Caliari, Paolo
see Veronese, Paolo

CALIGULA (12-41), Roman emperor 37-41 **3** 228-229

CALISHER, HORTENSE (1911-2009), American writer **30** 96-98

CALLAGHAN, EDWARD MORLEY (1903-1990), Canadian novelist **3** 229-230

CALLAGHAN, LEONARD JAMES (born 1912), Labor member of the British Parliament and prime minister, 1976-1979 **3** 230-231

CALLAHAN, DANIEL (born 1930), American philosopher who focused on biomedical ethics **3** 231-233

CALLAHAN, HARRY (1912-1999), American photographer **20** 67-69

CALLAS, MARIA (Cecilia Sophia Anna Maria Kalogeropoulos; 1923-1977), American opera soprano **18** 73-75

CALLEJAS ROMERO, RAFAEL LEONARDO (born 1943), president of Honduras (1990-) **3** 233-234

CALLENDER, CLIVE ORVILLE (born 1936), African American surgeon **18** 75-77

Caravaggisti (Utrecht art group)
Leyster, Judith **30** 264-266

CARAWAY, HATTIE WYATT (1878-1950), first woman elected to the United States Senate in her own right **3** 284-285

CARDANO, GERONIMO (1501-1576), Italian mathematician, astronomer, and physician **3** 285-286

CARDENAL, ERNESTO (born 1925), Nicaraguan priest, poet, and revolutionary **19** 57-59

Cárdenas, Bartolomé de
see Bermejo, Bartolomé

CÁRDENAS, LÁZARO (1895-1970), Mexican revolutionary president 1934-1940 **3** 286-287

CÁRDENAS SOLORZANO, CUAUHTÉMOC (born 1934), Mexican politician **3** 287-288

CARDIN, PIERRE (born 1922), French fashion designer **18** 79-81

CARDOSO, FERNANDO HENRIQUE (born 1931), sociologist and president of Brazil **18** 81-83

CARDOZO, BENJAMIN NATHAN (1870-1938), American jurist and legal philosopher **3** 288-290

CARDUCCI, GIOSUÈ (1835-1907), Italian poet **3** 290-291

CAREW, ROD (born 1945), Panamanian baseball player **3** 291-292

CAREY, GEORGE LEONARD (born 1935), archbishop of Canterbury **3** 293-294

CAREY, HENRY CHARLES (1793-1879), American writer on economics **3** 294-295

CAREY, PETER (born 1943), Australian author **3** 295-297

CAREY, WILLIAM (1761-1834), English Baptist missionary **3** 297

CAREY THOMAS, MARTHA (1857-1935), American educator **3** 297-298

CARÍAS ANDINO, TIBURCIO (1876-1969), Honduran dictator (1932-1949) **3** 298-299

CARISSIMI, GIACOMO (1605-1674), Italian composer **3** 299-300

CARLETON, GUY (1st Baron Dorchester; 1724-1808), British general and statesman **3** 300-301

CARLIN, GEORGE (born 1937), American comedian **3** 301-303

CARLOTTA (1840-1927), empress of Mexico 1864-1867 **29** 108-110

CARLSON, CHESTER F. (1906-1968), American inventor of the process of xerography **3** 303-304

Carlstadt
see Karlstadt

CARLYLE, THOMAS (1795-1881), Scottish essayist and historian **3** 304-305

CARMICHAEL, HOAGY (Hoagland Howard Carmichael; 1899-1981), American songwriter **26** 57-60

CARMICHAEL, STOKELY (1941-1998), African American civil rights activist **3** 305-308

CARNAP, RUDOLF (1891-1970), German-American philosopher **3** 308-309

CARNÉ, MARCEL ALBERT (1909-1996), French film director and screenwriter **26** 60-62

CARNEADES (c. 213-c. 128 B.C.), Greek philosopher **3** 309

CARNEGIE, ANDREW (1835-1919), American industrialist and philanthropist **3** 309-312

CARNEGIE, HATTIE (born Henrietta Kanengeiser; 1889-1956), American fashion designer **3** 313

CARNOT, LAZARE NICOLAS MARGUERITE (1753-1823), French engineer, general, and statesman **3** 313-314

CARNOT, NICHOLAS LÉONARD SADI (1796-1832), French physicist **3** 315

CARO, ANTHONY (born 1924), English sculptor **3** 316

CARO, JOSEPH BEN EPHRAIM (1488-1575), Jewish Talmudic scholar **3** 316-317

Caron, Pierre August
see Beaumarchais, Pierre August Caron de

CAROTHERS, WALLACE HUME (1896-1937), American chemist **3** 317-318

CARPEAUX, JEAN BAPTISTE (1827-1875), French sculptor and painter **3** 318-319

CARR, EMILY (1871-1945), Canadian painter and writer **3** 319

CARR, EMMA PERRY (1880-1972), American chemist and educator **22** 89-91

CARR-SAUNDERS, SIR ALEXANDER MORRIS (1886-1966), English demographer and sociologist **3** 333-334

CARRANZA, VENUSTIANO (1859-1920), Mexican revolutionary, president 1914-1920 **3** 321-322

CARREL, ALEXIS (1873-1944), French-American surgeon **3** 322-323

CARRERA, JOSÉ MIGUEL (1785-1821), Chilean revolutionary **3** 323-324

CARRERA, JOSÉ RAFAEL (1814-1865), Guatemalan statesman, president 1851-1865 **3** 324-325

CARRERA, JUAN JOSÉ (1782-1818), Chilean revolutionary **29** 110-112

CARRERAS, JOSE MARIA (born 1946), Spanish opera singer **22** 91-93

Carrick, Earl of
see Robert III

CARRIER, WILLS (1876-1950), American inventer who was the "father of air conditioning" **3** 325-326

CARRILLO, BRAULIO (1800-1845), Costa Rican jurist and president **29** 112-113

CARRINGTON, BARON (born 1919), British politician and secretary-general of the North Atlantic Treaty Organization (1984-1988) **3** 326-327

CARROLL, ANNA ELLA (1815-1893), American political writer and presidential aide **3** 327-331

Carroll, Edward Zane
see Buntline, Ned

CARROLL, JOHN (1735-1815), American Catholic bishop **3** 331-332

CARROLL, LEWIS (pseudonym of Charles Lutwidge Dodgson; 1832-1898), English cleric and author **3** 332-333

Carrucci, Jacopo
see Pontormo

CARSON, BEN (born 1951), African American surgeon **18** 83-85

CARSON, CHRISTOPHER "KIT" (1809-1868), American frontiersman **3** 334-335

CARSON, JOHNNY (1925-2005), American television host and comedian **3** 335-337

CARSON, RACHEL LOUISE (1907-1964), American biologist and author **3** 337-338

CARTE, RICHARD D'OYLY (1844-1901), English impressario **30** 101-103

CARTER, BENNY (Benny Carter, 1907-2003), African American musician **24** 73-75

CARTER, BETTY (Lillie Mae Jones; 1930-1998), American jazz singer **25** 75-77

CARTER, ELLIOTT COOK, JR. (born 1908), American composer **3** 338-339

CARTER, HOWARD (1874-1939), English archaeologist and artist **20** 74-76

CARTER, JAMES EARL ("Jimmy" Carter; born 1924), United States president (1977-1981) **3** 339-342
Carter, Rosalynn **30** 103-105

DOUGLAS, MARY TEW (1921-2007), British anthropologist and social thinker **5** 79-80

DOUGLAS, STEPHEN ARNOLD (1813-1861), American politician **5** 80-82

Douglas, Thomas
see Selkirk, 5th Earl of

DOUGLAS, THOMAS CLEMENT (1904-1986), Canadian clergyman and politician, premier of Saskatchewan (1944-1961), and member of Parliament (1962-1979) **5** 82-83

DOUGLAS, WILLIAM ORVILLE (1898-1980), American jurist **5** 83-85

DOUGLAS-HOME, ALEC (Alexander Frederick Home; 1903-1995), Scottish politician **20** 117-119

DOUGLASS, FREDERICK (c. 1817-1895), African American leader and abolitionist **5** 85-86
associates
    Brown, Hallie Quinn **30** 83-85
    Shadd Cary, Mary Ann **30** 324-326

DOUHET, GIULIO (1869-1930), Italian military leader **22** 151-152

DOVE, ARTHUR GARFIELD (1880-1946), American painter **5** 86-87

DOVE, RITA FRANCES (born 1952), United States poet laureate **5** 87-89

DOVZHENKO, ALEXANDER (Oleksandr Dovzhenko; 1894-1956), Ukrainian film director and screenwriter **25** 120-122

DOW, CHARLES (1851-1902), American journalist **19** 95-97

DOW, HERBERT H. (Herbert Henry Dow; 1866-1930), American chemist and businessman **28** 100-102

DOW, NEAL (1804-1897), American temperance reformer **5** 89-90

DOWLAND, JOHN (1562-1626), British composer and lutenist **5** 90

DOWNING, ANDREW JACKSON (1815-1852), American horticulturist and landscape architect **5** 90-91

DOYLE, SIR ARTHUR CONAN (1859-1930), British author **5** 91-92

D'Oyly Carte
see Carte, Richard D'Oyly

D'Oyly Carte Opera Company
    Carte, Richard D'Oyly **30** 101-103

Dracula (novel and film)
    Laemmle, Carl, Sr. **30** 249-251

DRAGO, LUIS MARÍA (1859-1921), Argentine international jurist and diplomat **5** 92-93

DRAKE, DANIEL (1785-1852), American physician **5** 93-94

DRAKE, EDWIN (1819-1880), American oil well driller and speculator **21** 108-110

DRAKE, SIR FRANCIS (c. 1541-1596), English navigator **5** 94-96
    Cortés de Albacar, Martín **30** 129-130

DRAPER, JOHN WILLIAM (1811-1882), Anglo-American scientist and historian **5** 96-97

Drapier, M.B.
see Swift, Jonathan

DRAYTON, MICHAEL (1563-1631), English poet **5** 97-98

DREBBEL, CORNELIUS (Jacobszoon Drebbel; Cornelius Van Drebbel; 1572-1633), Dutch inventor and engineer **28** 102-104

DREISER, (HERMAN) THEODORE (1871-1945), American novelist **5** 98-100

DREW, CHARLES RICHARD (1904-1950), African American surgeon **5** 100-101

DREW, DANIEL (1797-1879), American stock manipulator **5** 101-102

DREXEL, KATHERINE (1858-1955), founded a Catholic order, the Sisters of the Blessed Sacrament **5** 102-103

DREXLER, KIM ERIC (born 1955), American scientist and author **20** 119-121

DREYER, CARL THEODOR (1889-1968), Danish film director **22** 152-155
    Von Trier, Lars **30** 366-368

DREYFUS, ALFRED (1859-1935), French army officer **5** 103-105

DRIESCH, HANS ADOLF EDUARD (1867-1941), German biologist and philosopher **5** 105

DRUCKER, PETER (1909-2005), American author and business consultant **21** 110-112

Drummond, James Eric
see Perth, 16th Earl of

Drury Lane Theatre (London)
    Bracegirdle, Anne **30** 73-75

DRUSUS, MARCUS LIVIUS (c. 124-91 B.C.), Roman statesman **5** 105-106

DRYDEN, JOHN (1631-1700), English poet, critic, and dramatist **5** 106-107
associates
    Bracegirdle, Anne **30** 73-75

DRYSDALE, SIR GEORGE RUSSELL (1912-1981), Australian painter **5** 107-109

DU SABLE, JEAN BAPTISTE POINTE (Jean Baptiste Point Desable; c. 1745-1818), African-American explorer and founder of Chicago, IL **28** 104-106

DUANE, WILLIAM (1760-1835), American journalist **5** 109

DUARTE, JOSÉ NAPOLEÓN (1926-1990), civilian reformer elected president of El Salvador in 1984 **5** 109-111

DUBČEK, ALEXANDER (1921-1992), Czechoslovak politician **5** 112-113

DUBE, JOHN LANGALIBALELE (1870-1949), South African writer and Zulu propagandist **5** 113

DU BELLAY, JOACHIM (c. 1522-1560), French poet **5** 113-114

DUBINSKY, DAVID (1892-1982), American trade union official **5** 114-115

DUBNOV, SIMON (1860-1941), Jewish historian, journalist, and political activist **5** 115-116

DUBOIS, EUGÈNE (Marie Eugène Dubois; 1858-1940), Dutch anatomist and pale-oanthopologist **28** 106-108

DU BOIS, WILLIAM EDWARD BURGHARDT (1868-1963), African American educator, pan-Africanist, and protest leader **5** 116-118
associates
    Anderson, Regina M. **30** 5-7

DU BOIS-REYMOND, EMIL (1818-1896), German physiologist **5** 118-119

DUBOS, RENÉ JULES (1901-1982), French-born American microbiologist **5** 119

DUBUFFET, JEAN PHILLIPE ARTHUR (born 1901), French painter **5** 119-120

DUCCIO DI BUONINSEGNA (1255/60-1318/19), Italian painter **5** 121-122

Duce, II
see Mussolini, Benito

DUCHAMP, MARCEL (1887-1968), French painter **5** 122-123

DUCHAMP-VILLON, RAYMOND (1876-1918), French sculptor **5** 123

Dudevant, Amandine Aurore Lucie Dupin
see Sand, George

Dudley, Anne
see Bradstreet, Anne Dudley

DUDLEY, BARBARA (born 1947), American director of Greenpeace **5** 123-124

Dudley, John
see Northumberland, Duke of

Dudley, Robert
see Leicester, Earl of

E

EADS, JAMES BUCHANAN (1820-1887), American engineer and inventor **5** 175-176

EAKINS, THOMAS (1844-1916), American painter **5** 176-177

Ear (anatomy)
Eustachi, Bartolomeo **30** 164-166

EARHART, AMELIA MARY (1897-1937), American aviator **5** 177-179

EARL, RALPH (1751-1801), American painter **5** 179

EARLE, SYLVIA A. (Born Sylvia Alice Reade; born 1935), American marine biologist and oceanographer **5** 180-181

EARNHARDT, DALE (1951-2001), American race car driver **22** 156-158

EARP, WYATT BARRY STEPP (1848-1929), gun-fighting marshal of the American West **5** 181-182

EAST, EDWARD MURRAY (1879-1938), American plant geneticist **5** 182-183

Eastern Catholic Church
see Orthodox Eastern Church

Eastern Orthodox Church
see Orthodox Eastern Church

Eastern Roman Empire
see Byzantine Empire (395-1453; Eastern Roman Empire 395-474)

EASTMAN, CHARLES A. (1858-1939), Native American author **5** 183-185

EASTMAN, GEORGE (1854-1932), American inventor and industrialist **5** 186

EASTMAN, MAX (Max Forrester Eastman; 1883-1969), American poet, radical editor, translator, and author **5** 187-188

EASTWOOD, ALICE (1859-1953), American botanist **22** 158-160

EASTWOOD, CLINT (born 1930), American movie star and director **5** 188-190

EATON, DORMAN BRIDGMAN (1823-1899), American lawyer and author **5** 190-191

EBADI, SHIRIN (born 1947), Iranian author and human rights activist **25** 124-126

EBAN, ABBA (Abba Solomon Eban; 1915-2002), Israeli statesman, diplomat, and scholar **5** 191-192

EBB, FRED (1935-2004), American lyricist **21** 113-115

EBBERS, BERNIE (born 1941), American businessman **20** 122-124

Ebbets Field (sports stadium)
O'Malley, Walter Francis **30** 293-297

EBBINGHAUS, HERMANN (1850-1909), German psychologist **5** 192-193

EBERT, FRIEDRICH (1871-1925), German president 1919-1925 **5** 193-194

EBOUÉ, ADOLPHE FELIX SYLVESTRE (1885-1944), African statesman, governor of French Equatorial Africa **5** 194

EÇA DE QUEIRÓS, JOSÉ MARIA (1845-1900), Portuguese writer **30** 158-160

ECCLES, MARRINER STODDARD (1890-1977), American banker **22** 160-162

ECCLES, SIR JOHN CAREW (1903-1997), Australian neurophysiologist **5** 195-196

ECEVIT, BÜLENT (1925-2006), Turkish statesman and prime minister **5** 196-197

Echaurren, Roberto Matta
see Matta Echaurren, Roberto Sebastian Antonio

ECHEVERRÍA, JOSÉ ESTÉBAN (1805-1851), Argentine author and political theorist **5** 197-198

ECHEVERRIA ALVAREZ, LUIS (born 1922), president of Mexico (1970-1976) **5** 198-200

ECK, JOHANN MAIER VON (1486-1543), German theologian **5** 200

ECKERT, JOHN PRESPER (1919-1995), American computer engineer **20** 124-126

ECKHART, (JOHANN) MEISTER (c. 1260-c. 1327), German Dominican theologian **5** 200-201

ECO, UMBERTO (born 1932), Italian scholar and novelist **18** 128-130

École Pratique des Hautes Études (Paris)
Lévi, Sylvain **30** 258-260

EDDINGTON, SIR ARTHUR STANLEY (1882-1944), English astronomer **5** 201-202

EDDY, MARY BAKER (1821-1910), American founder of the Christian Science Church **5** 202

EDELMAN, GERALD MAURICE (born 1929), American neuroscientist **27** 106-108

EDELMAN, MARIAN WRIGHT (born 1939), lobbyist, lawyer, civil rights activist, and founder of the Children's Defense Fund **5** 202-204

EDEN, ANTHONY (1897-1977), English statesman, prime minister 1955-1957 **5** 204-205

EDERLE, GERTRUDE (born 1906), American swimmer **19** 98-100

EDGERTON, HAROLD EUGENE (1903-1990), American inventor **28** 109-111

EDGEWORTH, MARIA (1767-1849), British author **5** 205-206

EDINGER, TILLY (Johanna Gabriella Ottelie Edinger; 1897-1967), American paleontologist **22** 163-164

EDISON, THOMAS ALVA (1847-1931), American inventor **5** 206-208
movie industry
Laemmle, Carl, Sr. **30** 249-251

Editors
Canadian
Shadd Cary, Mary Ann **30** 324-326

Editors, American
film editors
Schoonmaker, Thelma **30** 318-320
magazines and journals (20th century)
Vreeland, Diana **30** 368-371
newspapers (19th century)
Shadd Cary, Mary Ann **30** 324-326

EDMISTON, ALTHEA MARIA (Althea Maria Brown; 1874-1937), African American missionary **27** 108-111

Education (Europe)
Italy
Barzizza, Gasparino **30** 38-40

Education (United States)
curriculum
Barzun, Jacques **30** 40-42
dance
Svetlova, Marina **30** 354-355
health
Calderone, Mary Steichen **30** 94-96
of African Americans
Wells-Barnett, Ida B. **30** 376-378
of women
Baum, Eleanor **30** 47-48
science
Baum, Eleanor **30** 47-48
sexual
Calderone, Mary Steichen **30** 94-96

Education Amendments of 1972 (United States)
de Varona, Donna **30** 144-146
Hamm, Mia **30** 197-199

EDWARD I (1239-1307), king of England 1272-1307 **5** 208-210

EDWARD II (Edward of Carnarvon; 1284-1327), king of England 1307-27 **5** 210

EDWARD III (1312-1377), king of England 1327-77 **5** 211-212

Edward IV (1330-1376)
see Edward the Black Prince

EDWARD IV (1442-1483), king of England 1461-70 **5** 212-213

EDWARD VI (1537-1553), king of England and Ireland 1547-53 **5** 213-214

GARNIER, JEAN LOUIS CHARLES (1825-1898), French architect **6** 221-222

GARRETT, JOHN WORK (1820-1884), American railroad magnate **6** 225

GARRETT, PATRICK FLOYD (1850-1908), American sheriff **30** 180-182

GARRETT, THOMAS (1789-1871), American abolitionist **6** 225-226

GARRETT (ANDERSON), ELIZABETH (1836-1917), English physician and women's rights advocate **6** 222-225

GARRISON, WILLIAM LLOYD (1805-1879), American editor and abolitionist **6** 226-228

GARVEY, MARCUS MOSIAH (1887-1940), Jamaican leader and African nationalist **6** 228-229

GARY, ELBERT HENRY (1846-1927), American lawyer and industrialist **6** 229-230

GASCA, PEDRO DE LA (c. 1496-1567), Spanish priest and statesman **6** 230-231

Gascoyne-Cecil, Robert Arthur Talbot see Salisbury, 3rd Marquess of

GASKELL, ELIZABETH (1810-1865), English novelist **6** 231-232

Gaspé, Philippe Aubert de see Aubert de Gaspé, Philippe

GATES, HORATIO (c. 1728-1806), Revolutionary War general **29** 169-172

GATES, WILLIAM HENRY, III ("Bill"; born 1955), computer software company co-founder and executive **6** 232-234

GATLING, RICHARD JORDAN (1818-1903), American inventor of multiple-firing guns **6** 234-235

GAUDÍ I CORNET, ANTONI (1852-1926), Catalan architect and designer **6** 235-236

GAUGUIN, PAUL (1848-1903), French painter and sculptor **6** 236-238

GAULLI, GIOVANNI BATTISTA (1639-1709), Italian painter **6** 238-239

GAULTIER, JEAN PAUL (born 1952), French avant-garde designer **6** 239-240

GAUSS, KARL FRIEDRICH (1777-1855), German mathematician and astronomer **6** 240-242

Gautama, Prince see Buddha (play)

Gautier, Théophile, (1811-1872), French writer
Grisi, Carlotta **30** 190-192

GAVIRIA TRUJILLO, CESAR AUGUSTO (born 1947), president of Colombia **6** 242-243

GAY, JOHN (1685-1732), English playwright and poet **6** 243-244

GAYE, MARVIN (Marvin Pentz Gay; 1939-1984), American musician **26** 119-123

GAYLE, HELENE DORIS (born 1955), African American epidemiologist and pediatrician **6** 244-245

GAY-LUSSAC, JOSEPH LOUIS (1778-1850), French chemist and physicist **6** 245-246

Gazprom (Russian state energy company) Medvedev, Dmitry **30** 275-277

Geber see Jabir ibn Hayyan

GEDDES, SIR PATRICK (1854-1932), Scottish sociologist and biologist **6** 246-247

GEERTGEN TOT SINT JANS (Geertgen van Haarlem; c. 1460/65-1490/95), Netherlandish painter **6** 248

GEERTZ, CLIFFORD (1926-2006), American cultural anthropologist **6** 248-249

GEFFEN, DAVID LAWRENCE (born 1943), American record and film producer **23** 119-122

GEHRIG, LOU (Henry Louis Gehrig; 1903-1941), American baseball player **19** 119-121

GEHRY, FRANK O. (née Goldberg; born 1929), American architect **6** 250-251

GEIGER, HANS (born Johannes Wilhelm Geiger; 1882-1945), German physicist **6** 251-253

GEISEL, ERNESTO (1908-1996), Brazilian army general, president of Brazil's national oil company (Petrobras), and president of the republic (1974-1979) **6** 253-255

GEISEL, THEODOR (a.k.a. Dr. Seuss; 1904-1991), American author of children's books **6** 255-256

Geiseric see Gaiseric

Gellée, Claude see Claude Lorrain

GELLER, MARGARET JOAN (born 1947), American astronomer **6** 256-257

GELLHORN, MARTHA ELLIS (1908-1998), American journalist and author **27** 141-143

GELL-MANN, MURRAY (born 1929), American physicist **6** 257-258

GEMAYEL, AMIN (born 1942), Lebanese nationalist and Christian political leader; president of the Republic of Lebanon (1982-1988) **6** 258-259

GEMAYEL, BASHIR (1947-1982), Lebanese political and military leader **28** 136-138

GEMAYEL, PIERRE (1905-1984), leader of the Lebanese Phalangist Party **6** 259-261

GEMINIANI, FRANCESCO SAVERIO (Francesco Xaviero Geminiani; 1687-1762), Italian violinist and composer **26** 123-125

Genealogists Burke, John Bernard **30** 90-91

Genesis (Old Testament book) Crumb, R. **30** 130-132

GENET, EDMOND CHARLES (1763-1834), French diplomat **6** 261-262

GENET, JEAN (1910-1986), French novelist and playwright **6** 262-263

Genga, Annibale Francesco della see Leo XII

GENGHIS KHAN (1167-1227), Mongol chief, creator of the Mongol empire **6** 263-265

GENSCHER, HANS-DIETRICH (born 1927), leader of West Germany's liberal party (the FDP) and foreign minister **6** 265-266

Genseric see Gaiseric

GENTILE, GIOVANNI (1875-1944), Italian philosopher and politician **6** 267

GENTILE DA FABRIANO (Gentile di Niccolò di Giovanni di Massio; c. 1370-1427), Italian painter **6** 266-267

GENTILESCHI, ARTEMISIA (1593-1652), Italian painter **22** 195-196

Geocentric theory (astronomy) see Universe, systems of–geocentric

Geodesy (science) Stokes, Sir George Gabriel **30** 347-349

GEOFFREY OF MONMOUTH (c. 1100-1155), English pseudohistorian **6** 268

GEORGE I (1660-1727), king of Great Britain and Ireland 1714-1727 **6** 268-269

GEORGE II (1683-1760), king of Great Britain and Ireland and elector of Hanover 1727-1760 **6** 269-270

GEORGE III (1738-1820), king of Great Britain and Ireland 1760-1820 **6** 270-272

GEORGE IV (1762-1830), king of Great Britain and Ireland 1820-1830 **6** 272-273

GEORGE V (1865-1936), king of Great Britain and Northern Ireland and emperor of India 1910-1936 **6** 273-275

Gordon, George Hamilton
see Aberdeen, 4th Earl of

GORDON, JOHN BROWN (1832-1904), American businessman and politician **6** 449-450

GORDON, PAMELA (born 1955), Bermudan politician **18** 166-167

GORDY, BERRY, JR. (born 1929), founder of the Motown Sound **6** 450-451

GORE, ALBERT, JR. (born 1948), Democratic U.S. representative, senator, and 45th vice president of the United States **6** 452-453

Gorenko, Anna Andreyevna
see Akhmatova, Anna

GORGAS, JOSIAH (1818-1883), American soldier and educator **6** 453-454

GORGAS, WILLIAM CRAWFORD (1854-1920), American general and sanitarian **6** 454-455

GORGES, SIR FERDINANDO (1568-1647), English colonizer and soldier **6** 455-456

GORGIAS (c. 480-c. 376 B.C.), Greek sophist philosopher and rhetorician **6** 456

GÖRING, HERMANN WILHELM (1893-1946), German politician and air force commander **6** 457-458

GORKY, ARSHILE (1905-1948), American painter **6** 458

GORKY, MAXIM (1868-1936), Russian author **6** 458-460

GORMAN, R.C. (Rudolph Carl Gorman; 1931-2005), Native American artist **23** 128-130

GORRIE, JOHN (1803-1855), American physician and inventor **21** 172-174

GORTON, SAMUELL (c. 1592-1677), English colonizer **6** 460

GOSHIRAKAWA (1127-1192), Japanese emperor **6** 460-461

GOSHO, HEINOSUKE (1902-1981), Japanese filmmaker **22** 199-200

Gösta
see Gustavus II

Got, Bertrand de
see Clement V

Gothart, Mathis Neithart
see Grünewald, Matthias

GOTTFRIED VON STRASSBURG (c. 1165-c. 1215), German poet and romancer **6** 461-462

GOTTLIEB, ADOLPH (1903-1974), American Abstract Expressionist painter **6** 462-463

Gottrecht, Friedman
see Beissel, Johann Conrad

GOTTSCHALK, LOUIS MOREAU (1829-1869), American composer **6** 463-464

GOTTWALD, KLEMENT (1896-1953), first Communist president of Czechoslovakia (1948-1953) **6** 464-466

GOUDIMEL, CLAUDE (c. 1514-1572), French composer **6** 466

GOUJON, JEAN (c. 1510-1568), French sculptor **6** 466-467

GOULART, JOÃO (1918-1976), Brazilian statesman **6** 467-469

GOULD, GLENN (1932-1982), Canadian musician **6** 469-470

GOULD, JAY (1836-1892), American financier and railroad builder **6** 470-472

GOULD, STEPHEN JAY (1941-2002), American paleontologist **6** 472-473

Goulden, Emmeline
see Pankhurst, Emmeline

GOUNOD, CHARLES FRANÇOIS (1818-1893), French composer **6** 473-474

GOURLAY, ROBERT (1778-1863), British reformer in Canada **6** 474

GOURMONT, REMY DE (1858-1915), French author, critic, and essayist **6** 475

GOWER, JOHN (c. 1330-1408), English poet **6** 475-476

GOYA Y LUCIENTES, FRANCISCO DE PAULA JOSÉ DE (1746-1828), Spanish painter and printmaker **6** 476-478

Goyakla
see Geronimo

GOYEN, JAN VAN (1596-1656), Dutch painter **6** 478-479

GRACCHUS, GAIUS SEMPRONIUS (ca. 154-121 B.C.), member of a Roman plebeian family referred to as the Gracchi **6** 479-480

GRACCHUS, TIBERIUS SEMPRONIUS (ca. 163-133 B.C.), member of a Roman plebeian family referred to as the Gracchi **6** 479-480

GRACE, WILLIAM RUSSELL (1832-1904), Irish-born American entrepreneur and politician **6** 480-481

GRACIÁN Y MORALES, BALTASAR JERÓNIMO (1601-1658), Spanish writer **6** 481-482

GRADY, HENRY WOODFIN (1850-1889), American editor and orator **6** 482-483

GRAETZ, HEINRICH HIRSCH (1817-1891), German historian and biblical exegete **6** 483

GRAF, STEFFI (born 1969), German tennis player **30** 184-186

Graham, John
see Phillips, David Graham

GRAHAM, KATHARINE MEYER (1917-2001), publisher who managed *The Washington Post* **6** 483-485

GRAHAM, MARTHA (1894-1991), American dancer and choreographer **6** 485-486

GRAHAM, OTTO (born 1921), American football player and coach **21** 174-176

GRAHAM, SHEILAH (1904-1988), English-born American columnist **29** 174-176

GRAHAM, SYLVESTER (1794-1851), American reformer and temperance minister **6** 486-487

GRAHAM, WILLIAM FRANKLIN, JR. ("Billy"; born 1918), American evangelist **6** 487-488

GRAHAME, KENNETH (1859-1932), British author **28** 138-140

GRAINGER, PERCY (Percy Aldridge Grainger; George Percy Grainger; 1882-1961), Australian American musician **25** 160-161

GRAMSCI, ANTONIO (1891-1937), Italian writer and Communist leader **6** 488-489

GRANADOS, ENRIQUE (1867-1916), Spanish composer and pianist **6** 489-490

GRAND DUCHESS OLGA NIKOLAEVNA (Grand Duchess Olga Nikolaevna; 1895-1918), Russian grand duchess **28** 141-143

GRANDA, CHABUCA (Isabel Granda Larco; 1920-1983), Peruvian singer and songwriter **28** 143-144

GRANDVILLE, J.J. (Jean-Ignace-Isidore Gérard; 1803-1847), French artist and cartoonist **28** 144-146

GRANGE, RED (Harold Edward Grange; 1903-1991), American football player **19** 128-130

GRANT, CARY (born Archibald Alexander Leach; 1904-1986), English actor **6** 490-492

GRANT, ULYSSES SIMPSON (1822-1885), American general, president 1869-1877 **6** 492-494

GRANVILLE, CHRISTINE (Krystyna Skarbek; c. 1915-1952), Polish secret agent **27** 153-154

GRANVILLE, EVELYN BOYD (born 1924), African American mathematician **6** 494-496

GUISEWITE, CATHY (born 1950), American cartoonist and author **18** 176-177

Guitar (music)
Jamerson, James **30** 218-220
Mayfield, Curtis **30** 273-275

GUIZOT, FRANÇOIS PIERRE GUILLAUME (1787-1874), French statesman and historian **7** 40-41

GUMPLOWICZ, LUDWIG (1838-1909), Polish-Austrian sociologist and political theorist **7** 41

GUNN, THOM (born 1929), English poet **18** 177-178

Guns
see Weapons and explosives

GÜNTHER, IGNAZ (1725-1775), German sculptor **7** 41-42

Gustafsson, Greta Lovisa
see Garbo, Greta

GUSTAVUS I (Gustavus Eriksson; 1496-1560), king of Sweden 1523-1560 **7** 42-43

GUSTAVUS II (Gustavus Adolphus; 1594-1632), king of Sweden 1611-1632 **7** 43-45

GUSTAVUS III (1746-1792), king of Sweden 1771-1792 **7** 45-46

GUSTON, PHILIP (1913-1980), American painter and a key member of the New York School **7** 47-48

GUTENBERG, JOHANN (c. 1398-1468), German inventor and printer **7** 48-49

GUTHRIE, EDWIN RAY (1886-1959), American psychologist **7** 49-50

GUTHRIE, JANET (born 1938), American race car driver **29** 178-181

GUTHRIE, TYRONE (1900-1971), English theater director **7** 50-51

GUTHRIE, WOODROW WILSON ("Woody"; 1912-1967), writer and performer of folk songs **7** 51-52

GUTIÉRRÉZ, GUSTAVO (born 1928), Peruvian who was the father of liberation theology **7** 52-53

GUY-BLACHÉ, ALICE (Alice Blaché; 1873-1968), French filmmaker **26** 133-135

GUY DE CHAULIAC (c. 1295-1368), French surgeon **7** 54

Guzmán Blanco, Antonio
see Blanco, Antonio Guzmán

GUZY, CAROL (Born 1956), American photographer **25** 173-175

GYGAX, GARY (1938-2008), American game designer **30** 194-196

H

H.D.
see Doolittle, Hilda

H.H.
see Jackson, Helen Hunt

H.M.S. Pinafore (operetta)
Carte, Richard D'Oyly **30** 101-103

Haarlem school (art)
Leyster, Judith **30** 264-266

HABASH, GEORGE (1926-2008), founder of the Arab Nationalists' Movement (1952) and of the Popular Front for the Liberation of Palestine (PFLP; 1967) **7** 55-56

HABER, FRITZ (1868-1934), German chemist **7** 56-58
Bergius, Friedrich Karl Rudolph **30** 51-53

Haber-Bosch Process
Bergius, Friedrich Karl Rudolph **30** 51-53

HABERMAS, JÜRGEN (born 1929), German philosopher and sociologist **7** 58-60

HABIBIE, BACHARUDDIN JUSUF (born 1936), president of Indonesia **19** 134-136

HADID, ZAHA (Zaha M. Hadid; born 1950), Iraqi-born British architect **27** 155-157

HADRIAN (76-138), Roman emperor 117-138 **7** 60-61

HAECKEL, ERNST HEINRICH PHILIPP AUGUST (1834-1919), German biologist and natural philosopher **7** 61-62

HAEFLIGER, ERNST (Ernst Häflinger; 1919-2007), Swiss singer **28** 152-154

HAFIZ, SHAMS AL-DIN (c. 1320-1390), Persian mystical poet and Koranic exegete **7** 63

HAGEN, UTA THYRA (born 1919), American actress **18** 179-180

HAGEN, WALTER (1892-1969), American golfer **21** 188-190

HAGENS, GUNTHER VON (Guinther Gerhard Liebchen; born 1945), German anatomist **27** 157-159

HAGUE, FRANK (1876-1956), American politician **7** 63-64

HAHN, OTTO (1879-1968), German chemist **7** 64-65

HAHNEMANN, SAMUEL (Christian Friedrich Samuel Hahnemann; 1755-1843), German physician and chemist **21** 190-193

HAIDAR ALI (c. 1721-1782), Indian prince, ruler of Mysore 1759-1782 **7** 65-66

HAIG, ALEXANDER M., JR. (1924-2010), American military leader, diplomat, secretary of state, and presidential adviser **7** 66-67

HAIG, DOUGLAS (1st Earl Haig; 1861-1928), British field marshal **7** 67-68

HAIGNERE, CLAUDIE ANDRE-DESHAYS (born 1957), French astronaut and government official **25** 176-178

HAILE SELASSIE (1892-1975), emperor of Ethiopia **7** 68-70

Haiti, Republic of (nation; West Indies)
Canadian diplomacy
Jean, Michaëlle **30** 223-225
struggle for democracy
Jean, Michaëlle **30** 223-225

HAKLUYT, RICHARD (1552/53-1616), English geographer and author **7** 70

HALBERSTAM, DAVID (1934-2007), American journalist, author and social historian **18** 180-183

HALDANE, JOHN BURDON SANDERSON (1892-1964), English biologist **7** 70-71

HALE, CLARA (nee Clara McBride; 1905-1992), American humanitarian and social reformer **20** 166-168

HALE, EDWARD EVERETT (1822-1909), American Unitarian minister and author **7** 71-72

HALE, GEORGE ELLERY (1868-1938), American astronomer **7** 72-74

HALE, SARAH JOSEPHA (née Buell; 1788-1879), American editor **7** 74-75

HALES, STEPHEN (1677-1761), English scientist and clergyman **7** 75

HALÉVY, ÉLIE (1870-1937), French philosopher and historian **7** 76

HALEY, ALEX (1921-1992), African American journalist and author **7** 76-78

HALEY, MARGARET A. (1861-1939), American educator and labor activist **7** 78-79

HALFFTER, CHRISTÓBAL (born 1930), Spanish composer **7** 79-80

HALIBURTON, THOMAS CHANDLER (1796-1865), Canadian judge and author **7** 80

HALIDE EDIP ADIVAR (1884-1964), Turkish woman writer, scholar, and public figure **7** 80-82

Halifax, 3rd Viscount
see Halifax, 1st Earl of

HALIFAX, 1ST EARL OF (Edward Frederick Lindley Wood; 1881-1959), English statesman **7** 82-83

HALL, ASAPH (1829-1907), American astronomer **7** 83-84

HARSHA (Harshavardhana; c. 590-647), king of Northern India 606-612 **7** 181-182

Hart, Emma
see Hamilton, Lady; Willard, Emma Hart

HART, GARY W. (born 1936), American political campaign organizer, U.S. senator, and presidential candidate **7** 182-184

HART, HERBERT LIONEL ADOLPHUS (1907-1992), British legal philosopher **22** 218-219

HART, LORENZ (1895-1943), American lyricist **29** 184-186

HARTE, FRANCIS BRET (1837-1902), American poet and fiction writer **7** 184-185

HARTLEY, DAVID (1705-1757), British physician and philosopher **7** 185

HARTLEY, MARSDEN (1877-1943), American painter **7** 186

HARTSHORNE, CHARLES (born 1897), American theologian **7** 186-187

HARUN AL-RASHID (766-809), Abbasid caliph of Baghdad 786-809 **7** 188

HARUNOBU, SUZUKI (ca. 1725-1770), Japanese painter and printmaker **7** 188-189

HARVARD, JOHN (1607-1638), English philanthropist **21** 195-197

HARVEY, WILLIAM (1578-1657), English physician **7** 189-190
Colombo, Realdo **30** 120-122
Fabrici, Girolamo **30** 167-169

HARWELL, ERNIE (William Earnest Harwell; 1918-2010), American sports broadcaster **30** 202-204

HARWOOD, GWEN (nee Gwendoline Nessie Foster; 1920-1995), Australian poet **26** 144-146

HASAN, IBN AL-HAYTHAM (ca. 966-1039), Arab physicist, astronomer, and mathematician **7** 190-191

Hasan, Mansur ben
see Firdausi

Hasan Ali Shah
see Aga Khan

Hasan ibn-Hani, al-
see Abu Nuwas

Hasidism (Jewish religious movement)
Zalman, Shneur **30** 386-388

HASKINS, CHARLES HOMER (1870-1937), American historian **7** 191-192

Hasong, Prince
see Sonjo

HASSAM, FREDERICK CHILDE (1859-1935), American impressionist painter **7** 192

HASSAN, MOULEY (King Hassan II; 1929-1999), inherited the throne of Morocco in 1961 **7** 194-195

HASSAN, MUHAMMAD ABDILLE (1864-1920), Somali politico-religious leader and poet **7** 194-195

HASTINGS, PATRICK GARDINER (1880-1952), British lawyer and politician **22** 219-221

HASTINGS, WARREN (1732-1818), English statesman **7** 195-196

HATCH, WILLIAM HENRY (1833-1896), American reformer and politician **7** 196

Hathorne, Nathaniel
see Hawthorne, Nathaniel

HATSHEPSUT (ruled 1503-1482 B.C.), Egyptian queen **7** 196-197

HATTA, MOHAMMAD (1902-1980), a leader of the Indonesian nationalist movement (1920s-1945) and a champion of non-alignment and of socialism grounded in Islam **7** 197-199

HAUPTMAN, HERBERT AARON (born 1917), American mathematician **24** 165-167

HAUPTMANN, GERHART JOHANN ROBERT (1862-1946), German dramatist and novelist **7** 199-201

HAUSHOFER, KARL (1869-1946), German general and geopolitician **7** 201

HAUSSMANN, BARON GEORGES EUGÈNE (1809-1891), French prefect of the Seine **7** 201-202

Haute couture
Balenciaga, Cristóbal **30** 28-30

Hauteclocque, Philippe Marie de
see Leclerc, Jacques Philippe

HAVEL, VACLAV (born 1936), playwright and human rights activist who became the president of Czechoslovakia **7** 202-205

HAVEMEYER, HENRY OSBORNE (1847-1907), American businessman **22** 222-224

HAVILAND, LAURA SMITH (1808-1898), American anti-slavery activist **27** 161-163

HAWES, HARRIET ANN BOYD (1871-1945), American archeologist **22** 224-225

HAWKE, ROBERT JAMES LEE (born 1929), Australian Labor prime minister **7** 205-206

Hawkesbury, Baron
see Liverpool, 2nd Earl of

HAWKING, STEPHEN WILLIAM (born 1942), British physicist and mathematician **7** 206-208

HAWKINS, COLEMAN (1904-1969), American jazz musician **7** 208-210

HAWKINS, SIR JOHN (1532-1595), English naval commander **7** 210-211

HAWKS, HOWARD WINCHESTER (1896-1977), American film director **22** 225-226

HAWKSMOOR, NICHOLAS (1661-1736), English architect **7** 211-212

HAWTHORNE, NATHANIEL (1804-1864), American novelist **7** 212-215

HAY, JOHN (1838-1905), American statesman **7** 215-216

HAYA DE LA TORRE, VICTOR RAUL (born 1895), Peruvian political leader and theorist **7** 216-217

HAYDEN, FERDINAND VANDIVEER (1829-1887), American geologist and explorer **22** 227-229

HAYDEN, ROBERT EARL (1913-1980), African American poet **22** 229-231

HAYDEN, THOMAS EMMET (born 1939), American writer and political activist **7** 217-219

HAYDN, FRANZ JOSEPH (1732-1809), Austrian composer **7** 219-221

HAYEK, FRIEDRICH A. VON (1899-1992), Austrian-born British free market economist, social philosopher, and Nobel Laureate **7** 221-223

HAYES, HELEN (1900-1993), American actress **7** 223-224

HAYES, LUCY WEBB (Lucy Ware Webb Hayes; 1831-1889), American Fist Lady **28** 163-166

HAYES, CARDINAL PATRICK JOSEPH (1867-1938), American cardinal **7** 224-225

HAYES, ROLAND (1887-1977), African American classical singer **7** 225-227

HAYES, RUTHERFORD BIRCHARD (1822-1893), American statesman, president 1877-1881 **7** 227-228

HAYFORD, J. E. CASELY (1866-1903), Gold Coast politician, journalist, and educator **7** 228-230

HAYKAL, MUHAMMAD HUSAIN (born 1923), Egyptian journalist and editor of *al-Ahram* (1957-1974) **7** 230-231

HAYNE, ROBERT YOUNG (1791-1839), American politician **7** 231-232

HAYNES, ELWOOD (1857-1925), American inventor and businessman **22** 231-234

HERRERA, JUAN DE (c. 1530-1597), Spanish architect **7** 335

HERRERA LANE, FELIPE (1922-1996), Chilean banker and economist **7** 336

HERRICK, ROBERT (1591-1674), English poet and Anglican parson **7** 336-339

HERRIOT, ÉDOUARD (1872-1957), French statesman and author **7** 339-340

HERRMANN, BERNARD (Benny Herrmann; 1911-1975), American composer **21** 199-202

Herrmann, Garry, (1859-1931), American baseball executive
Johnson, Ban **30** 227-230

HERSCHEL, CAROLINE (1750-1848), German/English astronomer and mathematician **20** 175-176

HERSCHEL, SIR JOHN FREDERICK WILLIAM (1792-1871), English astronomer **7** 340-341

HERSCHEL, SIR WILLIAM (1738-1822), German-born English astronomer **7** 341-343

HERSHEY, ALFRED DAY (1908-1997), American microbiologist **7** 343-345

HERSHEY, MILTON (1857-1945), American businessman and philanthropist **19** 142-144

HERSKOVITS, MELVILLE JEAN (1895-1963), American anthropologist **7** 345

Hertford, 1st Earl of
see Somerset, Duke of

HERTZ, GUSTAV (1887-1975), German physicist **25** 192-194

HERTZ, HEINRICH RUDOLF (1857-1894), German physicist **7** 346-347

HERTZOG, JAMES BARRY MUNNIK (1866-1942), South African prime minister 1924-39 **7** 347-348

HERUY WÄLDÄ-SELLASÉ (1878-1938), Ethiopian writer and government press director **7** 348-349

HERZBERG, GERHARD (born 1904), German-born Canadian chemist/physicist **7** 349-350

HERZEN, ALEKSANDR IVANOVICH (1812-1870), Russian author and political agitator **7** 351-352

HERZL, THEODOR (1860-1904), Hungarian-born Austrian Zionist author **7** 352-354

HERZOG, CHAIM (1918-1997), president of the State of Israel **7** 354-355

HERZOG, ROMAN (born 1934), president of the German Federal Constitutional Court (1987-1994) and president of Germany **7** 355-357

HERZOG, WERNER (Werner Stipetic; born 1942), German film director and producer **25** 194-197

HESBURGH, THEODORE MARTIN (born 1917), activist American Catholic priest who was president of Notre Dame (1952-1987) **7** 357-358

HESCHEL, ABRAHAM JOSHUA (1907-1972), Polish-American Jewish theologian **7** 358-359

HESELTINE, MICHAEL (born 1933), British Conservative politician **7** 359-361

HESIOD (flourished c. 700 B.C.), Greek poet **7** 361-362

HESS, MYRA (1890-1965), British pianist **27** 169-171

HESS, VICTOR FRANCIS (1883-1964), Austrian-American physicist **7** 362-363

HESS, WALTER RICHARD RUDOLF (1894-1987), deputy reichsführer for Adolf Hitler (1933-1941) **7** 363-365

HESS, WALTER RUDOLF (1881-1973), Swiss neurophysiologist **7** 365

HESSE, EVA (1936-1970), American sculptor **7** 365-367

HESSE, HERMANN (1877-1962), German novelist **7** 367-369

HESSE, MARY B. (born 1924), British philosopher **7** 369-371

HEVESY, GEORGE CHARLES DE (1885-1966), Hungarian chemist **7** 371

HEWITT, ABRAM STEVENS (1822-1903), American politician and manufacturer **7** 371-372

HEYDRICH, REINHARD (1904-1942), German architect of the Holocaust **20** 176-178

HEYERDAHL, THOR (1914-2002), Norwegian explorer, anthropologist and author **18** 194-196

HEYSE, PAUL JOHANN LUDWIG (1830-1914), German author **7** 372-373

HEYWOOD, THOMAS (1573/1574-1641), English playwright **7** 373-374

HIAWATHA (c. 1450), Native American Leader **23** 143-145

HICKOK, JAMES BUTLER ("Wild Bill"; 1837-1876), American gunfighter, scout, and spy **7** 374-375

HICKS, EDWARD (1780-1849), American folk painter **7** 375

HIDALGO Y COSTILLA, MIGUEL (1753-1811), Mexican revolutionary priest **7** 375-377

HIDAYAT, SADIQ (1903-1951), Persian author **7** 377-378

Hideyoshi
see Toyotomi Hideyoshi

Hieroglyph (Egyptian writing)
Lepsius, Karl Richard **30** 256-258

Higgins, Margaret
see Sanger, Margaret

HIGGINS, MARGUERITE (1920-1966), American journalist **7** 378-380

HIGGINSON, THOMAS WENTWORTH (1823-1911), American reformer and editor **7** 380

HIGHTOWER, ROSELLA (born 1920), Native American dancer **26** 154-156

Hildebrand
see Gregory VII, Pope

HILDEBRANDT, JOHANN LUCAS VON (1663-1745), Austrian architect **7** 380-381

HILDRETH, RICHARD (1807-1865), American historian and political theorist **7** 382

HILFIGER, TOMMY (born 1952), American fashion designer **19** 144-146

HILL, ANITA (born 1956), African American lawyer and professor **7** 382-385

HILL, ARCHIBALD VIVIAN (1886-1977), English physiologist **7** 385-386

HILL, BENJAMIN HARVEY (1823-1882), American politician **7** 386-387

HILL, HERBERT (1924-2004), American scholar and civil rights activist **7** 387-388

HILL, BENNY (Alfred Hawthorn Hill; 1924-1992), English comedian **28** 170-172

HILL, JAMES JEROME (1838-1916), American railroad builder **7** 388-389

HILL, ROWLAND (1795-1879), British educator, postal reformer, and administrator **21** 202-204

HILLARY, EDMUND (1919-2008), New Zealander explorer and mountaineer **7** 389-390

Hillel Hazaken
see Hillel I

HILLEL I (c. 60 B.C. -c. 10 A.D.), Jewish scholar and teacher **7** 390-391

HILLEMAN, MAURICE RALPH (1919-2005), American microbiologist **26** 156-158

HILLIARD, NICHOLAS (c. 1547-1619), English painter **7** 391-392

HILLMAN, SIDNEY (1887-1946), Lithuanian-born American labor leader **7** 392-393

HILLQUIT, MORRIS (1869-1933), Russian-born American lawyer and author **7** 393-394

HILLS, CARLA ANDERSON (born 1934), Republican who served three presidents as lawyer, cabinet member, and U.S. trade representative **7** 394-396

HILTON, BARRON (William Barron Hilton; born 1927), American businessman **19** 146-148

HILTON, CONRAD (1887-1979), American hotelier **20** 178-180

HIMES, CHESTER BOMAR (1909-1984), American author **22** 242-244

HIMMELFARB, GERTRUDE (born 1922), American professor, writer, and scholar **7** 396-398

HIMMLER, HEINRICH (1900-1945), German Nazi leader **7** 398-399

HINDEMITH, PAUL (1895-1963), German composer **7** 399-400

HINDENBURG, PAUL LUDWIG HANS VON BENECKENDORFF UND VON (1847-1934), German field marshal, president 1925-1934 **7** 400-401

Hinduism (religion)
theologians
Chinmayananda, Swami **30** 112-114

HINE, LEWIS WICKES (1874-1940), American photographer **28** 172-174

Hiner, Cincinnatus
see Miller, Joaquin

HINES, GREGORY OLIVER (born 1946), American dancer and actor **7** 401-403

HINOJOSA, ROLANDO (born 1929), Hispanic-American author **7** 403-405

HINSHELWOOD, SIR CYRIL NORMAN (1897-1967), English chemist **7** 405-406

HINTON, SUSAN ELOISE (born 1950), American novelist and screenwriter **7** 406-407

HIPPARCHUS (flourished 162-126 B.C.), Greek astronomer **7** 407-408

HIPPOCRATES (c. 460-c. 377 B.C.), Greek physician **7** 408-410

HIROHITO (1901-1989), emperor of Japan **7** 410-412
Shimada, Shigetaro **30** 330-332

HIROSHIGE, ANDO (1797-1858), Japanese painter and printmaker **7** 412-413

HIRSCHFELD, AL (Albert Hirschfeld; 1903-2003), American caricaturist **25** 197-199

HISS, ALGER (1904-1996), U.S. State Department official convicted of having provided classified documents to an admitted Communist **7** 413-415

Historical linguistics
see Linguistics (science)

HITCHCOCK, ALFRED (1899-1980), English-born film director **7** 415-416

HITCHCOCK, GILBERT MONELL (1859-1934), American publisher and politician **7** 416-417

HITLER, ADOLF (1889-1945), German dictator, chancellor-president 1933-1945 **7** 417-420
propagandists for
Joyce, William **30** 234-237

HO, DAVID DA-I (born 1952), American AIDS researcher **23** 145-148

HO CHI MINH (1890-1969), Vietnamese revolutionary and statesman **7** 426-428

HO, XUAN HUONG (c. late 18th-c. early 19th century), Vietnamese poet and feminist **28** 174-176

HOBART, JOHN HENRY (1775-1830), American Episcopal bishop **7** 420-421

HOBBES, THOMAS (1588-1679), English philosopher and political theorist **7** 421-423

HOBBY, OVETA CULP (1905-1995), American government official and businesswoman **7** 423-425

HOBHOUSE, LEONARD TRELAWNY (1864-1929), English sociologist and philosopher **7** 425-426

Hobrecht, Jacob
see Obrecht, Jacob

HOBSON, WILLIAM (1793-1842), British naval commander and colonial governor **7** 426

Hobun
see Yamashita, Tomoyuki

Hockey (sport)
Brooks, Herb **30** 81-83
Tretiak, Vladislav **30** 359-361

Hockey Hall of Fame (Toronto, Canada)
Tretiak, Vladislav **30** 359-361

HOCKING, WILLIAM ERNEST (1873-1966), American philosopher **7** 428-429

HOCKNEY, DAVID (born 1937), English photographer and artist **7** 429-431

HODGKIN, ALAN LLOYD (born 1914), English physiologist **7** 431-432

HODGKIN, DOROTHY CROWFOOT (1910-1964), English chemist **7** 432-434

HODLER, FERDINAND (1853-1918), Swiss painter **7** 434-435

HOE, RICHARD MARCH (1812-1886), American inventor and manufacturer **7** 435-436

HOFF, TED (Marcian Edward Hoff, Jr.; born 1937), American inventor **28** 176-178

HOFFA, JAMES R. ("JIMMY") (1913-1975), American union leader **7** 436-437

HOFFMAN, ABBIE (1936-1989), American writer, activist, and leader of the Youth International Party **7** 437-439

HOFFMANN, ERNST THEODOR AMADEUS (1776-1822), German author, composer, and artist **7** 439-440

HOFFMANN, FELIX (1868-1946), German chemist and inventor **28** 179-180

HOFFMANN, JOSEF (1870-1956), Austrian architect and decorator **7** 440-441

HOFFMAN, MALVINA CORNELL (1885-1966), American sculptor **23** 148-150

HOFHAIMER, PAUL (1459-1537), Austrian composer, and organist **7** 441

HOFMANN, ALBERT (1906-2008), Swiss chemist **30** 206-208

HOFMANN, AUGUST WILHELM VON (1818-1892), German organic chemist **7** 441-442

HOFMANN, HANS (1880-1966), German-American painter **7** 442-443

HOFMANNSTHAL, HUGO VON (1874-1929), Austrian poet and dramatist **7** 443-444

HOFSTADTER, RICHARD (1916-1970), American historian **7** 444-445

HOFSTADTER, ROBERT (1915-1990), American physicist **25** 199-202

HOGAN, BEN (1912-1997), American golfer **19** 148-150

HOGARTH, WILLIAM (1697-1764), English painter and engraver **7** 446-447

HOGG, HELEN BATTLES SAWYER (1905-1993), Canadian astronomer **22** 244-247

Hohenheim, Theophrastus Bombastus von
see Paracelsus, Philippus Aureolus

HOKINSON, HELEN ELNA (1893-1949), American cartoonist **23** 150-152

HOKUSAI, KATSUSHIKA (1760-1849), Japanese painter and printmaker **7** 447-448

HUGHES, WILLIAM MORRIS
(1864-1952), Australian prime minister
1915-1923 **8** 21-22

HUGO, VICOMTE VICTOR MARIE
(1802-1885), French author **8** 22-25

HUI-TSUNG (1082-1135), Chinese
emperor and artist **8** 25

HUI-YÜAN (334-416), Chinese Buddhist
monk **8** 25-26

HUIZINGA, JOHAN (1872-1945), Dutch
historian **8** 26-27

HULAGU KHAN (Hüle'ü; c. 1216-1265),
Mongol ruler in Persia **8** 27-28

HULBERT, WILLIAM AMBROSE
(1832-1882), American baseball
executive **30** 210-213

HULL, BOBBY (Robert Marvin Hull; born
1939), Canadian hockey player **20**
181-183

HULL, CLARK LEONARD (1884-1952),
American psychologist **8** 28

HULL, CORDELL (1871-1955), American
statesman **8** 28-29

HULL, WILLIAM (1753-1825), American
military commander **8** 29-30

Human experimentation (medicine)
Hofmann, Albert **30** 206-208

Humanism (cultural movement)
MIDDLE AGES and RENAISSANCE
literature: Italian
Barzizza, Gasparino **30** 38-40

HUMAYUN (1508-1556), Mogul emperor
1530-1556 **20** 183-185

**HUMBOLDT, BARON FRIEDRICH
HEINRICH ALEXANDER VON**
(1769-1859), German naturalist and
explorer **8** 30-31
scientific expeditions
Garden, Alexander **30** 176-178

HUMBOLDT, BARON WILHELM VON
(1767-1835), German statesman and
philologist **8** 31

HUME, BASIL CARDINAL (George
Haliburton Hume; 1923-1999), English
clergyman and theologian **22** 249-250

HUME, DAVID (1711-1776), Scottish
philosopher **8** 31-34

HUMMEL, JOHANN NEPOMUK
(1778-1837), Austrian pianist and
composer **25** 204-206

HUMPHREY, DORIS (Doris Batcheller
Humphrey; 1895-1959), American
dancer and choreographer **23** 157-159

HUMPHREY, HUBERT HORATIO, JR.
(1911-1978), mayor of Minneapolis,
U.S. senator from Minnesota, and
vice-president of the U.S. **8** 34-36

HUN SEN (born 1951), Cambodian prime
minister **8** 39-42

HUNDERTWASSER, FRIEDENSREICH
(Friedrich Stowasser; 1928-2000),
Austrian-born visionary painter and
spiritualist **8** 36-37

HUNG HSIU-CH'ÜAN (1814-1864),
Chinese religious leader, founder of
Taiping sect **8** 37-38

Hung-li
see Qianlong

Hungson, Prince
see Taewon'gun, Hungson

HUNG-WU (1328-1398), Chinese Ming
emperor 1368-98 **8** 38-39

HUNT, H. L. (1889-1974), American entrepreneur **8** 42-44

HUNT, RICHARD MORRIS (1827-1895),
American architect **8** 44

HUNT, WALTER (1796-1859), American
inventor **21** 210-212

HUNT, WILLIAM HOLMAN (1827-1910),
English painter **8** 44-45

HUNTER, ALBERTA (1895-1984), African
American blues singer **23** 160-162

HUNTER, FLOYD (born 1912), American
social worker and administrator,
community worker, professor, and
author **8** 45-46

HUNTER, JOHN (1728-1793), Scottish
surgeon **29** 202-204
Garden, Alexander **30** 176-178

HUNTER, MADELINE CHEEK
(1916-1994), American educator **8**
47-48

HUNTER, WILLIAM (1718-1783), Scottish
anatomist **8** 48-49

HUNTINGTON, ANNA HYATT (Anna
Vaughn Hyatt; 1876-1973), American
sculptor and philanthropist **23** 162-164

HUNTINGTON, COLLIS POTTER
(1821-1900), American railroad builder
8 49

HUNTLEY AND BRINKLEY (1956-1970),
American journalists and radio and
television news team **8** 49-51

**Huntley, Chester Robert, (Chet;
1911-1974)**
see Huntley and Brinkley

HUNYADI, JOHN (1385-1456),
Hungarian military leader, regent
1446-1452 **8** 51-52

HURD, DOUGLAS (born 1930), English
Conservative Party politician and foreign
secretary **8** 52-55

HURSTON, ZORA NEALE (1903-1960),
African American folklorist and novelist
8 55-56

HUS, JAN (a.k.a. John Hus; ca.1369-1415),
Bohemian religious reformer **8** 56-59

HUSÁK, GUSTÁV (1913-1991), president
of the Czechoslovak Socialist Republic **8**
59-61

HUSAYN, TAHA (1889-1973), Egyptian
author, educator, and statesman **8** 61-62

HUSAYNI, AL-HAJJ AMIN AL- (1895-1974),
Moslem scholar/leader and mufti of
Jerusalem (1922-1948) **8** 62-63

HUSEIN IBN ALI (c. 1854-1931), Arab
nationalist, king of Hejaz 1916-1924
8 63

Huss, John
see Hus, Jan

HUSSAIN, ZAKIR (born 1951), Indian
singer and musician **29** 204-206

HUSSEIN IBN TALAL (1935-1999), king of
the Hashemite Kingdom of Jordan
(1953-80s) **8** 65-67

HUSSEIN, SADDAM (1937-2006), socialist
president of the Iraqi Republic and
strongman of the ruling Ba'th regime **13**
415-416

HUSSEINI, FAISAL (1940-2001),
Palestinian political leader **19** 160-162

HUSSERL, EDMUND (1859-1938),
German philosopher **8** 67-68

HUSTON, JOHN MARCELLUS
(1906-1987), American film director,
scriptwriter, and actor **22** 250-252

HUTCHINS, ROBERT MAYNARD
(1899-1977), American educator **8**
68-69

HUTCHINSON, ANNE MARBURY
(1591-1643), English-born American
religious leader **8** 69-71

HUTCHINSON, THOMAS (1711-1780),
American colonial governor **8** 71-72

Hu-t'ou
see Ku K'ai-chih

HUTT, WILLIAM (William Ian DeWitt
Hutt; 1920-2007), Canadian actor and
director **27** 171-173

HUTTEN, ULRICH VON (1488-1523),
German humanist **8** 72-73

HUTTON, JAMES (1726-1797), Scottish
geologist **8** 73-74

HUXLEY, ALDOUS LEONARD
(1894-1963), English novelist and
essayist **8** 74-75

HUXLEY, JULIAN (1887-1975), English
biologist and author **8** 75-77

KAWAWA, RASHIDI MFAUME (born 1929), Tanzanian political leader **8** 464-465

KAYE, DANNY (David Daniel Kaminsky; 1913-1987), American film and stage actor **25** 231-234

KAZAN, ELIA (born 1909), American film and stage director **8** 465-466

KAZANTZAKIS, NIKOS (1883-1957), Greek author, journalist, and statesman **8** 466-468

KEAN, EDMUND (1789-1833), English actor **21** 237-239

KEARNEY, DENIS (1847-1907), Irish-born American labor agitator **8** 468

KEARNY, STEPHEN WATTS (1794-1848), American general **8** 468-469

KEATING, PAUL JOHN (born 1944), federal treasurer of Australia (1983-1991) **8** 469-470

KEATON, BUSTER (Joseph Frank Keaton; 1895-1966), American comedian **20** 199-201

KEATS, JOHN (1795-1821), English poet **8** 470-472

KEENAN, BRIAN (1940-2008), Irish peace activist **29** 223-225

KEFAUVER, CAREY ESTES (1903-1963), U.S. senator and influential Tennessee Democrat **8** 472-474

KEILLOR, GARRISON (Gary Edward Keillor, born 1942), American humorist, radio host, and author **22** 271-273

KEITA, MODIBO (1915-1977), Malian statesman **8** 474-475

KEITEL, WILHELM (1882-1946), German general **18** 224-226

KECKLEY, ELIZABETH HOBBS (Elizabeth Hobbs Keckly; 1818-1907), African American seamstress and author **28** 196-199

KEITH, SIR ARTHUR (1866-1955), British anatomist and physical anthropologist **8** 475-476

KEITH, MINOR COOPER (1848-1929), American entrepreneur **8** 476-477

KEKKONEN, URHO KALEVA (1900-1986), Finnish athlete and politician **23** 189-191

KEKULÉ, FRIEDRICH AUGUST (1829-1896), German chemist **8** 477-478

KELLER, ELIZABETH BEACH (Elizabeth Waterbury Beach; 1918-1997), American biochemist **25** 234-235

KELLER, GOTTFRIED (1819-1890), Swiss short-story writer, novelist, and poet **8** 478-479

KELLER, HELEN ADAMS (1880-1968), American lecturer and author **8** 479-480

KELLEY, FLORENCE (1859-1932), American social worker and reformer **8** 483-484

KELLEY, HALL JACKSON (1790-1874), American promoter **8** 480

KELLEY, OLIVER HUDSON (1826-1913), American agriculturalist **8** 480-481

KELLOGG, FRANK BILLINGS (1856-1937), American statesman **8** 481

KELLOGG, JOHN HARVEY (1852-1943), American health propagandist and cereal manufacturer **21** 239-242

KELLOGG, W. K. (Will Keith Kellogg; 1860-1951), American cereal manufacturer and philanthropist **28** 199-201

KELLOR, FRANCES (1873-1952), American activist and politician **8** 481-482

KELLY, ELLSWORTH (born 1923), American artist **8** 482-483

KELLY, GENE (born Eugene Curran Kelly; 1912-1996), American actor, dancer, and choreographer **8** 484-486

KELLY, GRACE (Grace, Princess; 1929-1982), princess of Monaco **19** 174-176

KELLY, NED (1854-1880), Australian horse thief, bank robber, and murderer **29** 226-228

KELLY, PATRICK (1954-1990), African American fashion designer **22** 273-275

KELLY, PETRA (born 1947), West German pacifist and politician **8** 486-487

KELLY, WALT (Walter Crawford Kelly; 1913-1973), American Cartoonist **22** 275-278

KELLY, WILLIAM (1811-1888), American iron manufacturer **8** 487-488

KELSEY, HENRY (c. 1667-1724), English-born Canadian explorer **8** 488

KELVIN OF LARGS, BARON (William Thomson; 1824-1907), Scottish physicist **8** 488-489
    Stokes, Sir George Gabriel **30** 347-349

Kemal, Mustapha (Kemal Atatürk)
    see Atatürk, Ghazi Mustapha Kemal

KEMAL, YASHAR (born 1922), Turkish novelist **8** 489-491

KEMBLE, FRANCES ANNE (Fanny Kemble; 1809-1893), English actress **8** 491

KEMP, JACK FRENCH, JR. (1935-2009), Republican congressman from New York and secretary of housing and urban development **8** 491-493

KEMPE, MARGERY (1373-1440), English religious writer **29** 228-230

KEMPIS, THOMAS À (c. 1380-1471), German monk and spiritual writer **8** 493-494

KENDALL, AMOS (1789-1869), American journalist **8** 494

KENDALL, EDWARD CALVIN (1886-1972), American biochemist **8** 495

KENDALL, THOMAS HENRY (Henry Clarence Kendall; 1839-1882), Australian poet **23** 191-194

Kendrake, Carleton
    see Gardner, Erle Stanley

KENDREW, JOHN C. (1917-1997), English chemist and Nobel Prize winner **8** 495-496

KENEALLY, THOMAS MICHAEL (born 1935), Australian author **18** 226-228

KENNAN, GEORGE F. (1904-2005), American diplomat, author, and scholar **8** 496-498

Kennedy, Aimee
    see McPherson, Aimee Semple

KENNEDY, ANTHONY M. (born 1936), United States Supreme Court justice **8** 498-500

KENNEDY, EDWARD M. (Ted, 1932-2009), U.S. senator from Massachusetts **8** 500-502

KENNEDY, FLORYNCE RAE (1916-2000), African American Activist and Lawyer **27** 199-201

Kennedy, Jacqueline Lee Bouvier
    see Onassis, Jacqueline Lee Bouvier Kennedy

KENNEDY, JOHN FITZGERALD (1917-1963), American statesman, president 1960-1963 **8** 502-506
    media coverage
        Capa, Cornell **30** 98-101

KENNEDY, JOHN FITZGERALD, JR. (1960-1999), American icon and publisher **25** 235-238

KENNEDY, JOHN PENDLETON (1795-1870), American author and politician **8** 506-507

KENNEDY, JOHN STEWART (1830-1909), American financier and philanthropist **8** 507-508

KENNEDY, JOSEPH (1888-1969), American financier, ambassador, and movie producer **19** 176-178

L

Lane, Carrie
see Catt, Carrie Chapman

LANE, DICK (Richard Lane; Dick "Night Train" Lane; 1928-2002), American football player **27** 227-229

LANE, FITZ HUGH (1804-1865), American marine painter **9** 189

LANFRANC (c. 1010-1089), Italian theologian, archbishop of Canterbury **9** 189-190

LANG, FRITZ (1890-1976), German film director **9** 190-192

LANG, JOHN THOMAS (1876-1975), Australian politician **9** 192-193

LANGDELL, CHRISTOPHER COLUMBUS (1826-1906), American lawyer **23** 204-206

LANGE, DOROTHEA (1895-1965), American photographer **9** 193-194

LANGER, SUSANNE (nee Susanne Katherina Knauth; 1895-1985), American philosopher **26** 218-220

LANGLAND, WILLIAM (c. 1330-1400), English poet **9** 194-195

LANGLEY, SAMUEL PIERPONT (1834-1906), American scientist **9** 195-196

LANGMUIR, IRVING (1881-1957), American chemist **9** 196-197

LANGSTON, JOHN MERCER (1829-1897), American educator and diplomat **9** 197

LANGTON, STEPHEN (c. 1155-1228), English prelate and signer of the Magna Carta **21** 249-251

LANIER, JARON (born ca. 1961), American computer engineer **9** 198-199

LANIER, SIDNEY (1842-1881), American poet, critic, and musician **9** 199-200

LANSING, ROBERT (1864-1928), American lawyer and statesman **9** 200

Lao Lai Tzu
see Lao Tzu

LAO SHÊ (1899-1966), Chinese novelist **9** 200-201

LAO TZU (flourished 6th century B.C.), Chinese philosopher **9** 201-202

LAPLACE, MARQUIS DE (Pierre Simon; 1749-1827), French mathematician **9** 202-204

Larco, Isabel Granda
see Granda, Chabuca

LARDNER, RINGGOLD WILMER (1885-1933), American author **9** 204-205

LAREDO, RUTH (nee Ruth Meckler; 1937-2005), American pianist **26** 220-222

LARIONOV, MIKHAIL (1881-1964), Russian artist **9** 205-206

LARKIN, PHILIP (1922-1986), English poet **9** 206-207

LARKIN, THOMAS OLIVER (1802-1858), American merchant and diplomat **9** 208

LARROCHA, ALICIA DE (Alicia de Larrocha y de la Calle; born 1923), Spanish painist **27** 230-231

LARSEN, NELLA (1893-1963), Harlem Renaissance writer **9** 209-210

LARSON, JONATHAN (1961-1996), American playwright, composer, and lyricist **18** 243-145

LARSSON, STIEG (1954-2004), Swedish author **30** 251-253

LAS CASAS, BARTOLOMÉ DE (1474-1566), Spanish Dominican missionary and historian **9** 211-212

Lasal, Ferdinand
see Lassalle, Ferdinand

LASCH, CHRISTOPHER (1932-1994), American historian and social critic **9** 212-214

LASHLEY, KARL SPENCER (1890-1958), American neuropsychologist **9** 214-215

LASKER, ALBERT (1880-1952), American advertising executive **21** 251-254

LASKER, EMANUEL (1868-1941), German chess grandmaster **20** 218-220

LASKI, HAROLD J. (1893-1950), English political scientist and Labour party leader **9** 215-216

LASKY, JESSE (1880-1958), American film producer **21** 254-256

LASSALLE, FERDINAND (1825-1864), German socialist leader **9** 216

Lasso, Orlando di
see Lassus, Roland de

LASSUS, ROLAND DE (1532-1594), Franco-Flemish composer **9** 216-218

LASSWELL, HAROLD DWIGHT (born 1902), American political scientist **9** 218-219

Last Command, The (film)
Jannings, Emil **30** 220-222

Last Shogun, The (nonfiction novel)
Shiba, Ryotaro **30** 328-330

LÁSZLÓ I, KING OF HUNGARY (ca. 1040-1095), king of Hungary and saint **9** 219-221

LATIMER, HUGH (c. 1492-1555), English Protestant bishop, reformer, and martyr **9** 221

LATIMER, LEWIS (1848-1928), American inventor and electrical engineer **19** 191-193

Latin American music
United States
Puente, Tito **30** 306-308

Latitude (geography)
Cortés de Albacar, Martín **30** 129-130

LATROBE, BENJAMIN HENRY (1764-1820), English-born American architect **9** 222-224

LATYNINA, LARISA (Larissa Semyonovna Latynina; born 1934), Russian gymnast **26** 222-224

LAUD, WILLIAM (1573-1645), English archbishop of Canterbury **9** 224-225

LAUDER, ESTEE (née Josephine Esthe Menzer, born ca. 1908), founder of an international cosmetics empire **9** 225-226

Laue, Max von
see von Laue, Max

Lauenburg, Duke of
see Bismarck, Otto Edward Leopold von

LAUREL, SALVADOR H. (Doy; born 1928), member of the Philippine Congress and vice-president **9** 226-227

LAUREN, RALPH (Ralph Lipschitz; born 1939), American fashion designer **9** 228-229

LAURENCE, MARGARET (Jean Margaret Wemyss; 1926-1987), Canadian writer **9** 229-230

LAURENS, HENRI (1885-1954), French sculptor **9** 230-231

LAURENS, HENRY (1724-1792), American merchant and Revolutionary statesman **9** 232

LAURIER, SIR WILFRID (1841-1919), Canadian statesman, prime minister 1896-1911 **9** 232-234

LAURO, ACHILLE (1887-1984), Italian business and political leader **9** 234-235

LAUTARO (c. 1535-1557), Araucanian Indian chieftain in Chile **9** 235

LAVAL, FRANCOIS XAVIER DE (1623-1708), French bishop in Canada **9** 235-236

LAVAL, PIERRE (1883-1945), French politician, chief Vichy minister **9** 237-238

LAVALLEJA, JUAN ANTONIO (1778-1853), Uruguayan independence leader **9** 238-239

LAVER, ROD (Rodney George Laver; born 1938), Australian tennis player **25** 257-259

LAVERAN, ALPHONSE (Charles Louis Alphonse Laveran; 1845-1922), French medical researcher **28** 207-209

LAVIGERIE, CHARLES MARTEL ALLEMAND (1825-1892), French cardinal **9** 240

LAVISSE, ERNEST (1842-1922), French historian **9** 241

LAVOISIER, ANTOINE LAURENT (1743-1794), French chemist **9** 241-244

LAVOISIER, MARIE PAULZE (1758-1836), French chemist **22** 292-294

LAW, JOHN (1671-1729), Scottish monetary theorist and banker **9** 244-245

LAW, WILLIAM (1686-1761), English devotional writer **9** 245-246

Law enforcement
Garrett, Patrick Floyd **30** 180-182

Lawman
see Layamon

LAWRENCE, ABBOTT (1792-1855), American manufacturer and diplomat **9** 246

LAWRENCE, DAVID HERBERT (1885-1930), English novelist, poet, and essayist **9** 247-248

LAWRENCE, ERNEST ORLANDO (1901-1958), American physicist **9** 248-250

LAWRENCE, FLORENCE (Florence Annie Bridgwood; 1886-1938), Canadian-born American actress **28** 209-211

LAWRENCE, JACOB (born 1917), African American painter **9** 250-251

LAWRENCE, JAMES (1781-1813), American naval officer **9** 251-252

LAWRENCE, SIR THOMAS (1769-1830), English portrait painter **9** 252-253

LAWRENCE, THOMAS EDWARD (1888-1935), British soldier and author **9** 253-254
Bolt, Robert **30** 69-71

Lawrence of Arabia
see Lawrence, Thomas Edward

Lawrence of Arabia (film)
Bolt, Robert **30** 69-71

LAWSON, HENRY (1867-1922), Australian poet and short-story writer **9** 254-255

LAWSON, THOMAS WILLIAM (1857-1925), American entrepreneur and reformer **9** 255-256

Lawyers
see Jurists

LAYAMON (flourished c. 1200), English poet **9** 256-257

LAYBOURNE, GERALDINE (born 1947), American businesswoman **26** 224-226

LAYE, CAMARA (1928-1980), Guinean novelist **9** 257-259

LAZARSFELD, PAUL F. (1901-1976), American sociologist **9** 259-260

LAZARUS, EMMA (1849-1887), American poet and playwright **9** 260-261

LAZARUS, SHELLY (Rochelle Braff; born 1947), American businesswoman **27** 231-233

LE BON, GUSTAVE (1841-1931), French social scientist and philosopher **9** 268-269

LE BRUN, CHARLES (1619-1690), French painter, decorator, and draftsman **9** 269-270

LE CARRE, JOHN (born David Cornwell, 1931), British spy novelist **9** 270-271

LECLERCQ, TANAQUIL (Tanny; 1929-2000), French American dancer **27** 234-235

LE CORBUSIER (Charles Édouard Jeanneret-Gris; 1887-1965), Swiss architect, city planner, and painter **9** 274-275

LE DUAN (1908-1986), North Vietnamese leader and later head of the government of all Vietnam **29** 150-153

LE FANU, JOSEPH SHERIDAN (1814-1873), Irish author **23** 206-208

LE GUIN, URSULA KROEBER (born 1929), American author **18** 249-251

LE JEUNE, CLAUDE (c. 1530-1600), Flemish composer **9** 314-315

Le Moyne, Pierre
see Iberville, Sieur d'

LE NAIN BROTHERS, 17TH-CENTURY FRENCH PAINTERS 9 321-322

LE NÔTRE, ANDRÉ (or Le Nostre; 1613-1700), French landscape architect **9** 328-329

LE PEN, JEAN MARIE (born 1928), French political activist of the radical right **9** 348-350

LE PLAY, GUILLAUME FRÉDÉRIC (1806-1882), French sociologist and economist **9** 350-351

Le Prestre, Sébastien
see Vauban, Marquis de

LE VAU, LOUIS (1612-1670), French architect **9** 360-361

LEA, HENRY CHARLES (1825-1909), American historian **9** 261-262

LEADBELLY (Huddie William Leadbetter; 1885-1949), African American folk singer **23** 208-211

LEAKEY, LOUIS SEYMOUR BAZETT (1903-1972), British anthropologist **9** 262

LEAKEY, MARY DOUGLAS (1913-1996), English archaeologist **9** 263-264

LEAKEY, RICHARD ERSKINE FRERE (born 1944), Kenyan researcher in human prehistory and wildlife conservationist **9** 264-265

LEAN, DAVID (1908-1991), English film director and producer **29** 239-241
Bolt, Robert **30** 69-71

LEAR, EDWARD (1812-1888), English writer and artist **9** 265-266

LEAR, NORMAN (born 1922), American author and television director and producer **19** 193-195

LEARY, TIMOTHY (1920-1996), American psychologist, author, lecturer, and cult figure **9** 266-267
Hofmann, Albert **30** 206-208

LEASE, MARY ELIZABETH CLYENS (1853-1933), American writer and politician **9** 268

LEAVITT, HENRIETTA SWAN (1868-1921), American astronomer **23** 211-213

LEBED, ALEXANDER IVANOVICH (1950-2002), Russian general and politician **18** 245-247

LEBLANC, NICOLAS (1742-1806), French industrial chemist **21** 256-258

LECKY, WILLIAM EDWARD HARTPOLE (1838-1903), Anglotrish historian and essayist **9** 271-272

Leclerc, Georges Louis
see Buffon, Comte de

LECLERC, JACQUES PHILIPPE (1902-1947), French general **9** 272-273

LECONTE DE LISLE, CHARLES MARIE RENÉ (1818-1894), French poet **9** 273-274

LECUONA, ERNESTO (Ernesto Sixto de la Asuncion Lecuona y Casado; 1896-1963), Cuban musician **23** 213-216

LED ZEPPELIN (1968-1980), British "Heavy Metal" band **23** 216-218

LEDERBERG, JOSHUA (1925-2008), Nobel Prize winning geneticist **9** 275-277

LEDERER, ESTHER PAULINE (Ann Landers; 1918-2002), American Columnist **25** 255-257

MARRIOTT, J. WILLARD (Bill Marriott; 1900-1985), American hotel and restaurant chain executive **28** 232-234

MARSALIS, WYNTON (born 1961), American trumpeter and bandleader **19** 224-226

MARSH, GEORGE PERKINS (1801-1882), American diplomat, philologist, and conservationist **21** 275-277

MARSH, NGAIO (Edith Ngaio Marsh; 1899-1982), New Zealander author and playwright **19** 226-228

MARSH, OTHNIEL CHARLES (1831-1899), American paleontologist **10** 275-276

MARSH, REGINALD (1898-1954), American painter and printmaker **10** 276-277

MARSHALL, ALFRED (1842-1924), English economist **10** 277-278

MARSHALL, GEORGE CATLETT (1880-1959), American soldier and statesman **10** 278-279

MARSHALL, JOHN (1755-1835), American jurist, chief justice of United States. Supreme Court 1801-1835 **10** 279-281

MARSHALL, PAULE BURKE (born 1929), American author **10** 281-282

MARSHALL, THURGOOD (1908-1993), African American jurist **10** 282-284

MARSILIUS OF PADUA (1275/80-1342), Italian political philosopher **10** 284

MARSTON, WILLIAM MOULTON (1893-1947), American psychologist, inventor, and cartoonist **30** 271-273

MARTEL, CHARLES (c. 690-741), Frankish ruler **10** 285

MARTÍ, JOSÉ (1853-1895), Cuban revolutionary, poet, and journalist **10** 285-286

MARTIAL (Marcus Valerias Martialis; c. 38/41-c. 104), Roman epigrammatist **10** 286-287

Martial arts
Shaw Brothers **30** 326-328

MARTIN V (Oddone Colonna; 1368-1431), pope 1417-1431 **10** 287-288

MARTIN, AGNES (1912-2004), American painter **10** 288-289

MARTIN, DEAN (Dino Paul Crocetti; 1917-1995), American entertainer **26** 245-247
Lewis, Jerry **30** 261-264

MARTIN, GLENN L. (1886-1955), American aircraft manufacturer and aviator **29** 265-267

MARTIN, GREGORY (c. 1540-1582), British Bible translator and scholar **21** 277-279

MARTIN, LUTHER (1748-1826), American lawyer and Revolutionary patriot **10** 289-290

MARTIN, LYNN MORLEY (born 1939), Republican representative from Illinois and secretary of labor under George Bush **10** 290-292

MARTIN, MARY (1913-1990), popular stage actress, singer, and dancer and a television and film star **10** 292-293

Martin, Violet
see Somerville, E.

MARTIN, WILLIAM MCCHESNEY, JR. (1906-1998), American business executive and federal government official **10** 293-295

MARTIN DU GARD, ROGER (1881-1958), French author **10** 295-296

MARTINEAU, HARRIET (1802-1876), English writer and philosopher **10** 296-297

MARTINEZ, MARIANNE (Marianne von Martinez; Anna Katherina Martinez; 1744- 1812), Austrian musician **27** 256-258

MARTINEZ, MARIA MONTOYA (Maria Antonia Montoya; Marie Poveka; Pond Lily; 1881?-1980), Pueblo potter **24** 241-243

MARTÍNEZ, MAXIMILIANO HERNÁNDEZ (1882-1966), president of El Salvador (1931-1944) **10** 297-298

MARTINEZ, VILMA SOCORRO (born 1943), Hispanic American attorney and activist **18** 276-279

Martinez Ruíz, José
see Ruíz, José Martinez

MARTINI, SIMONE (flourished 1315-1344), Italian painter **10** 298-299

Martinique (island; West Indies)
Césaire, Aimé **30** 108-110

MARTINU, BOHUSLAV (1890-1959), Czech composer **10** 299-300

MARTY, MARTIN E. (born 1928), Lutheran pastor, historian of American religion, and commentator **10** 300-301

Marvel Comics
Kirby, Jack **30** 240-242
Lee, Stan **30** 253-255

MARVELL, ANDREW (1621-1678), English poet and politician **10** 301-303

MARX, KARL (1818-1883), German political philosopher **10** 304-308

MARX BROTHERS, 20th-Century American Stage and Film Comedians **10** 303-304

Marxism (philosophy)
Russia
Pimen I, Patriarch of Moscow **30** 304-306

MARY, QUEEN OF SCOTS (1542-1587), queen of France and Scotland **10** 308-309
opponents
Walsingham, Sir Francis **30** 374-376

MARY, SAINT (Blessed Virgin Mary; late 1st century B.C.-1st century A.D.), New Testament figure, mother of Jesus **10** 308-309

MARY I (1516-1558), queen of England 1553-1558 **10** 308-309

MARY II (1662-1694), queen of England, Scotland, and Ireland 1689-1694 **10** 309-310

MARY MAGDALENE (Mary of Magdala), Catholic saint and biblical figure **24** 243-246

MASACCIO (1401-1428), Italian painter **10** 312-313

Masafuji
see Mabuchi, Kamo

Masahito
see Goshirakawa

Masanobu
see Mabuchi, Kamo

MASARYK, JAN (1886-1948), Czech foreign minister **20** 243-246

MASARYK, TOMÁŠ GARRIGUE (1850-1937), Czech philosopher and statesman, president 1919-1935 **10** 314-315

MASINA, GIULIETTA (1921-1994), Italian actress **29** 268-270

MASINISSA, KING OF NUMIDIA (240 B.C. - 148 B.C.), prince of the Massylians who consolidated the Numidian tribes to form a North African kingdom **10** 315-317

MASIRE, QUETT KETUMILE (born 1925), a leader of the fight for independence and president of Botswana **10** 318-319

MASON, BRIDGET (Biddy Mason; 1818-1891), African American nurse, midwife, and entrepreneur **22** 312-314

MASON, GEORGE (1725-1792), American statesman **10** 319-320

MASON, JAMES MURRAY (1796-1871), American politician and Confederate diplomat **10** 320-321

MASON, LOWELL (1792-1872), American composer and music educator **10** 321-322

Mason, Perry (fictional character)
Ehrlich, Jake W. **30** 160-162

MAYER, JEAN (born 1920), nutritionist, researcher, consultant to government and international organizations, and president of Tufts University **10** 365-366

MAYER, LOUIS BURT (Eliezer Mayer; 1885-1957), American motion picture producer **19** 234-235

MAYFIELD, CURTIS (1942-1999), American musician **30** 273-275

MAYNARD, ROBERT CLYVE (1937-1993), African American journalist and publisher **10** 366-367

MAYO, WILLIAM J. AND CHARLES H. (1861-1939; 1865-1939), American physicians **10** 367-369

MAYOR ZARAGOSA, FEDERICO (born 1934), Spanish biochemist who was director-general of UNESCO (United Nations Educational, Scientific, and Cultural Organization) **10** 369-371

MAYO-SMITH, RICHMOND (1854-1901), American statistician and sociologist **10** 371-372

MAYR, ERNST (1904-2005), American evolutionary biologist **10** 372-374

MAYS, BENJAMIN E. (1894-1984), African American educator and civil rights activist **10** 374-376

MAYS, WILLIE (William Howard Mays, Jr.; born 1931), African American baseball player **10** 376-379

Mayson, Isabella Mary
see Beeton, Isabella Mary

MAZARIN, JULES (1602-1661), French cardinal and statesman **10** 379-380

MAZEPA, IVAN STEPANOVICH (c. 1644-1709), Ukrainian Cossack leader **10** 381

Mazzarini, Giulio
see Mazarin, Jules

MAZZINI, GIUSEPPE (1805-1872), Italian patriot **10** 381-383

Mazzola, Francesco
see Parmigianino

M'BOW, AMADOU-MAHTAR (born 1921), director general of UNESCO (United Nations Educational, Scientific, and Cultural Organization) **10** 383-384

MBOYA, THOMAS JOSEPH (1930-1969), Kenyan political leader **10** 384-385

MCADOO, WILLIAM GIBBS (1863-1941), American statesman **10** 385-386

MCAULIFFE, ANTHONY (1898-1975), American army officer **19** 236-239

MCAULIFFE, CHRISTA (nee Sharon Christa Corrigan; 1948-1986), American teacher **20** 254-257

MCCAIN, JOHN SIDNEY, III (born 1936), American politician **25** 285-287

MCCANDLESS, BRUCE (born 1937), American astronaut **23** 243-246

MCCARTHY, EUGENE JOSEPH (1916-2005), American statesman **10** 386-388

MCCARTHY, JOSEPH RAYMOND (1908-1957), American politician **10** 388-389

MCCARTHY, MARY T. (born 1912), American writer **10** 389-391

MCCARTHY, NOBU (nee Nobu Atsumi; 1934-2002), Japanese actress and model **26** 250-252

MCCARTNEY, PAUL (James Paul McCartney; born 1942), British musician **24** 250-253

MCCAY, WINSOR (Zenas Winsor McKay; c. 1871-1934), American cartoonist and animator **21** 288-291

MCCLELLAN, GEORGE BRINTON (1826-1885), American general **10** 391-392

MCCLELLAN, JOHN LITTLE (1896-1977), U.S. senator from Arkansas **10** 392-393

MCCLINTOCK, BARBARA (1902-1992), geneticist and winner of the Nobel Prize in physiology **10** 393-394

MCCLINTOCK, SIR FRANCIS LEOPOLD (1819-1907), British admiral and Arctic explorer **10** 394-395

MCCLOSKEY, JOHN (1810-1885), American cardinal **10** 395

MCCLUNG, NELLIE LETITIA (1873-1951), Canadian suffragist, social reformer, legislator, and author **10** 396-397

MCCLURE, SIR ROBERT (1807-1873), English explorer and navy officer **10** 398-399

MCCLURE, SAMUEL SIDNEY (1857-1949), American editor and publisher **10** 398-399

McClure's Magazine (periodical; 1893-1929)
Knight, Charles R. **30** 242-244

MCCORMACK, JOHN WILLIAM (1891-1980), U.S. congressman and Speaker of the House **10** 399-400

MCCORMICK, CYRUS HALL (1809-1884), American inventor, manufacturer, and philanthropist **10** 400-401

MCCORMICK, ROBERT RUTHERFORD (1880-1955), American publisher **10** 401-402

MCCOSH, JAMES (1811-1894), Scottish-American minister, philosopher, and college president **10** 402-403

MCCOY, ELIJAH (1843-1929), American engineer and inventor **19** 239-241

MCCOY, ISAAC (1784-1846), American Indian agent and missionary **10** 403

MCCOY, JOSEPH GEITING (1837-1915), American cattleman **10** 403-404

MCCULLERS, CARSON (Lula Carson Smith; 1917-1967), American novelist and playwright **18** 281-283

MCCULLOCH, HUGH (1808-1895), American banker and lawyer **10** 404-405

MCDANIEL, HATTIE (1898-1952), African American actress **10** 405-408

MCDUFFIE, GEORGE (1790-1851), American statesman **10** 408

MCENROE, JOHN PATRICK, JR. (born 1959), American tennis player **10** 408-411

MCGILL, RALPH EMERSON (1898-1969), American journalist **10** 411-412

MCGILLIVRAY, ALEXANDER (c. 1759-1793), American Creek Indian chief **10** 412

MCGOVERN, GEORGE STANLEY (born 1922), American statesman **10** 412-414

MCGUFFEY, WILLIAM HOLMES (1800-1873), American educator **10** 414-415

MCHENRY, EARLE WILLARD (1899-1961), Canadian biochemist **29** 277-279

MCINTIRE, SAMUEL (1757-1811), American builder and furniture maker **10** 415

MCKAY, CLAUDE (1890-1948), African American poet and novelist **10** 416

MCKAY, DONALD (1810-1880), American ship builder **10** 416-417

MCKELLEN, IAN MURRAY (born 1939), English actor **28** 234-237

MCKIM, CHARLES FOLLEN (1847-1909), American architect **10** 417-418

MCKINLEY, WILLIAM (1843-1901), American statesman, president 1897-1901 **10** 418-420

MCKISSICK, FLOYD B., (1922-1991), African American civil rights leader **10** 420-422

MCLAREN, NORMAN (1914-1987), Canadian filmmaker **25** 287-289

MCLEAN, JOHN (1785-1861), American jurist and politician **10** 422-423

McLeod, Mary
see Bethune, Mary McLeod

METACOM (a.k.a. King Philip; 1640-1676), Wampanoag cheiftain **10** 529-531

METCALFE, CHARLES THEOPHILUS (1st Baron Metcalfe; 1785-1846), British colonial administrator **10** 531-532

METCHNIKOFF, ÉLIE (1845-1916), Russian physiologist and bacteriologist **10** 532-533

Method acting (theater) Duse, Eleonora **30** 154-157

METHODIUS, SAINT (825-885), Greek missionary and bishop **4** 362-363

Metro-Goldwyn-Mayer (film studio) Williams, Esther **30** 380-383

Metropolitan Museum of Art (New York City) Vreeland, Diana **30** 368-371

Metropolitan Opera Company (New York City) Svetlova, Marina **30** 354-355

Metsys, Quentin see Massys, Quentin

METTERNICH, KLEMENS VON (1773-1859), Austrian politician and diplomat **10** 533-536

Meun, Jean de see Jean de Meun

Mexican art Del Rio, Dolores **30** 146-148

MEYERBEER, GIACOMO (1791-1864), German composer **10** 536-537

MEYERHOF, OTTO FRITZ (1884-1951), German biochemist **10** 537-539

MEYERHOLD, VSEVOLOD EMILIEVICH (1874-1942?), Russian director **10** 539

MFUME, KWEISI (born Frizzell Gray; born 1948), African American civil rights activist and congressman **10** 539-542

MGM see Metro-Goldwyn-Mayer (film studio)

MI FEI (1051-1107), Chinese painter, calligrapher, and critic **11** 12-13

MICAH (flourished 8th century B.C.), prophet of ancient Israel **10** 542-543

MICHAEL VIII (Palaeologus; 1224/ 25-1282), Byzantine emperor 1259-1282 **11** 1-2 Andronikos II Palaiologos **30** 7-9

Michel, Claude see Clodion

MICHELANGELO BUONARROTI (1475-1564), Italian sculptor, painter, and architect **11** 2-5 associates Ammanati, Bartolomeo **30** 3-5 Colombo, Realdo **30** 120-122

MICHELET, JULES (1798-1874), French historian **11** 5-6

MICHELOZZO (c. 1396-1472), Italian architect and sculptor **11** 6-7

MICHELSON, ALBERT ABRAHAM (1852-1931), American physicist **11** 7-8

MICHENER, JAMES (1907-1997), American author **19** 245-247

MICKIEWICZ, ADAM BERNARD (1798-1855), Polish poet **27** 263-265

MIDDLETON, THOMAS (1580-1627), English playwright **11** 8-9

MIDGELY, MARY BURTON (born 1919), British philosopher who focused on the philosophy of human motivation and ethics **11** 9-10

MIES VAN DER ROHE, LUDWIG (1886-1969), German-born American architect **11** 10-12

Migration (United States) De Priest, Oscar **30** 142-144

Mikado, The (operetta) Carte, Richard D'Oyly **30** 101-103

MIKAN, GEORGE (1924-2005), American basketball player **21** 297-299

MIKULSKI, BARBARA (born 1936), United States senator from Maryland **11** 13-15

MILÁN, LUIS (c. 1500-after 1561), Spanish composer **11** 15-16

MILES, NELSON APPLETON (1839-1925), American general **11** 16-17

MILHAUD, DARIUS (born 1892), French composer and teacher **11** 17-18

Military leaders, Argentine ArÁmburu, Pedro Eugenio **30** 14-16

Military leaders, British ARMY majors Brisbane, Thomas Makdougall **30** 79-81

Military leaders, Byzantine Andronikos II Palaiologos **30** 7-9

Military leaders, Japanese admirals Shimada, Shigetaro **30** 330-332

Military leaders, Russian marshals Blücher, Vasily Konstantinovich **30** 59-61 military commissars Blücher, Vasily Konstantinovich **30** 59-61

MILIUKOV, PAVEL NIKOLAYEVICH (1859-1943), Russian historian and statesman **11** 18-19

MILK, HARVEY BERNARD (1930-1978), American politician and gay rights activist **11** 19-21

MILKEN, MICHAEL (born 1946), American businessman **19** 247-249

MILL, JAMES (1773-1836), Scottish philosopher and historian **11** 21

MILL, JOHN STUART (1806-1873), English philosopher and economist **11** 21-23

MILLAIS, SIR JOHN EVERETT (1829-1896), English painter **11** 23-24

MILLAY, EDNA ST. VINCENT (1892-1950), American lyric poet **11** 24-25

MILLER, ARTHUR (1915-2005), American playwright, novelist, and film writer **11** 25-26

MILLER, GLENN (Alton Glenn Miller; 1904-1944), American musician **19** 250-251

MILLER, HENRY (1891-1980), American author **11** 26-27

MILLER, JOAQUIN (1837-1913), American writer **11** 27-28

MILLER, MARVIN (born 1917), American baseball executive and union leader **30** 277-280

MILLER, PERRY (1905-1963), American historian **11** 28-29

MILLER, SAMUEL FREEMAN (1816-1890), American jurist **11** 29-30

MILLER, WILLIAM (1782-1849), American clergyman **11** 30-31

MILLES, CARL WILHEIM EMIL (1875-1955), Swedish sculptor **24** 260-263

MILLET, JEAN FRANÇOIS (1814-1875), French painter **11** 31

MILLET, KATE (born 1934), American feminist author and sculptor **11** 31

MILLIKAN, ROBERT ANDREWS (1868-1953), American physicist **11** 33-35

Million Dollar Mermaid (film) Williams, Esther **30** 380-383

MILLS, BILLY (Makata Taka Hela; born 1938), Native American runner and businessman **19** 251-253

MILLS, C. WRIGHT (1916-1962), American sociologist and political polemicist **11** 35-36

MILLS, ROBERT (1781-1855), American architect **11** 36-37

MILNE, ALAN ALEXANDER (A.A. Milne; 1882-1956), British author **19** 253-254

MILNE, DAVID BROWN (1882-1953), Canadian painter and etcher **11** 37-38

MILNE, JOHN (1850-1913), English seismologist **28** 245-247

MILNER, ALFRED (1st Viscount Milner; 1854-1925), British statesman **11** 38-39

MILOSEVIC, SLOBODAN (1941-2006), president of Serbia **11** 39-40

MILOSZ, CZESLAW (1911-2004), Nobel Prize winning Polish author and poet **11** 40-42

MILTIADES (c. 549-488 B.C.), Athenian military strategist and statesman **11** 42-43

MILTON, JOHN (1608-1674), English poet and controversialist **11** 43-46

MIN (1851-1895), Korean queen **11** 46-47

MINDON MIN (ruled 1852-1878), Burmese king **11** 47

MINDSZENTY, CARDINAL JÓZSEF (1892-1975), Roman Catholic primate of Hungary **11** 47-49

MINETA, NORMAN YOSHIO (born 1931), Asian American government official **25** 293-295

MINGUS, CHARLES, JR. (1922-1979), African American jazz musician **26** 254-256

Minh, Duong Van
see Duong Van Minh

MINK, PATSY TAKEMOTO (1927-2003), Asian American congresswoman **18** 287-289

MINNELLI, LIZA (born 1946), American entertainer **26** 256-259

MINNELLI, VINCENTE (Lester Anthony Minnelli; 1903-1986), American film director **29** 281-283

Minnesota, University
of (Minneapolis-Saint Paul)
Brooks, Herb **30** 81-83

MINTZ, BEATRICE (born 1921), American embryologist **11** 49-50

MINUIT, PETER (1580-1638), Dutch colonizer **11** 50

MIRABAI (Meera Bai; 1498-1547), Indian poet and mystic **24** 263-265

MIRABEAU, COMTE DE (Honoré Gabriel Victor de Riqueti; 1749-1791), French statesman and author **11** 51-52

MIRANDA, CARMEN (Maria do Carmo Miranda da Cunha; 1909-1955), Brazilian singer and actress **26** 259-261

MIRANDA, FRANCISCO DE (1750-1816), Latin American patriot **11** 52-53

Mirandola, Pico della
see Pico della Mirandola

MIRÓ, JOAN (1893-1983), Spanish painter **11** 53-54

MIRREN, HELEN (Ilyene Lydia Mironoff; born 1945), British actress **28** 247-249

Mirza Malkam Khan
see Malkam Khan, Mirza

Mises, Dr.
see Fechner, Gustav Theodor

MISHIMA, YUKIO (1925-1970), Japanese novelist and playwright **11** 54-55

Mrs. Belloc Lowndes
see Belloc Lowndes, Marie Adelaide

Mr. Tsungli Yaman
see Wen-hsiang

MISTRAL, FREDERIC (1830-1914), French author and philologist **25** 295-297

MISTRAL, GABRIELA (1889-1957), Chilean poet and educator **11** 55-56

MITCHELL, BILLY (1879-1936), American military officer and aviator **20** 269-272

MITCHELL, EDGAR DEAN (born 1930), American astronaut **22** 318-320

MITCHELL, GEORGE JOHN (born 1933), Maine Democrat and majority leader in the United States Senate **11** 56-58

Mitchell, Helen Porter
see Melba, Nellie

MITCHELL, JOHN (1870-1919), American labor leader **11** 58-59

MITCHELL, JONI (Roberta Joan Anderson; born 1943), Canadian American singer **23** 246-248

MITCHELL, MARGARET (Munnerlyn; 1900-1949), American author of Gone With the Wind **11** 59-60

MITCHELL, MARIA (1818-1889), American astronomer and educator **11** 61

MITCHELL, WESLEY CLAIR (1874-1948), American economist **11** 61-62

MITRE, BARTOLOMÉ (1821-1906), Argentine historian and statesman, president 1862-1868 **11** 62-63

MITTERRAND, FRANÇOIS (born 1916), French politician and statesman and president (1981-1990) **11** 63-66

MIYAKE, ISSEY (born 1938), Japanese fashion designer **25** 297-299

MIYAZAKI HAYAO (born 1941), Japanese filmmaker and artist **28** 249-252

MIZOGUCHI, KENJI (1898-1956), Japanese film director **23** 248-250

MIZRAHI, ISAAC (born 1961), American designer **11** 66-67

MLADIC, RATKO (born 1943), Bosnian Serb military leader **11** 68-69

MOBUTU SESE SEKO (Joseph Désiré Mobuto; 1930-1997), Congolese president **11** 69-71

Mo-chieh
see Wang Wei

MODEL, LISETTE (nee Lisette Seyberg; c. 1906-1983), American photographer and educator **19** 254-256

Modernism (architecture)
Europe
Berlage, Hendrick Petrus **30** 53-55
Gruen, Victor **30** 192-194

MODERSOHN-BECKER, PAULA (1876-1907), German painter **11** 71-72

MODIGLIANI, AMEDEO (1884-1920), Italian painter and sculptor **11** 72-73

MODIGLIANI, FRANCO (1918-2003), Italian American economist **24** 265-267

MOFFETT, WILLIAM ADGER (1869-1933), American naval officer **21** 299-301

MOFOLO, THOMAS (1876-1948), Lesothoan author **11** 74

MOGILA, PETER (1596/1597-1646), Russian Orthodox churchman and theologian **11** 74-75

Mogul empire
see India—1000-1600

MOHAMMAD REZA SHAH PAHLAVI (1919-1980), king of Iran **11** 75-76
Dulles, Allen Welsh **30** 152-154

MOHAMMED (c. 570-632), founder of Islam **11** 76-78

Mohammed II (1432-1481)
see Mehmed the Conqueror

MOHAMMED V (Mohammed Ben Youssef; 1911-1961), king of Morocco **11** 79-81

Mohammed Ahmed
see Mahdi, The

MOHAMMED ALI (1769-1849), Ottoman pasha of Egypt 1805-1848 **11** 81-82

Mohammed Ben Youssef
see Mohammed V

MOHOLY-NAGY, LÁSZLÓ (1895-1946), Hungarian painter and designer **11** 82-83

Mohr
see Marx, Karl

MOI, DANIEL ARAP (born Daniel Toroitich arap Moi; born 1924), president of Kenya **11** 83-86

MONTREUIL, PIERRE DE (flourished c. 1231-1266/67), French architect **11** 139

MONTT TORRES, MANUEL (1809-1880), Chilean statesman, president 1851-1861 **11** 139-140

MOODIE, SUSANNA (1803-1885), Canadian poet, novelist, and essayist **11** 140-141

MOODY, DWIGHT L. (1837-1899), American evangelist **11** 141-142

MOODY, PAUL (1779-1831), American inventor **29** 283-284

MOOG, ROBERT (1934-2005), American inventor **26** 265-267

MOON, SUN MYUNG (born 1920), founder of the Unification Church **11** 142-143

Moor, the
see Sforza, Ludovico

Moore, Carry Amelia
see Nation, Carry Amelia Moore

MOORE, CHARLES WILLARD (1925-1993), American architect and educator **11** 143-145

MOORE, CHARLOTTE E. (1898-1990), American astrophysicist **11** 145-146

MOORE, GEORGE EDWARD (1873-1958), English philosopher **11** 146

MOORE, HENRY (1898-1986), English sculptor **11** 146-148

MOORE, MARIANNE (1887-1972), American poet and translator **11** 148-149

MOORE, MICHAEL (born 1954), American author and filmmaker **25** 299-302

MOORE, THOMAS (1779-1852), Irish Poet, essayist, and composer **28** 254-256

MORAES, VINICIUS DE (Marcus Vinicius da Cruz de Mello Moraes; 1913-1980), Brazilian songwriter and author **26** 268-269

MORALES, LUIS DE (c. 1519-1586), Spanish painter **11** 150

MORALES-BERMÚDEZ CERRUTI, FRANCISCO (born 1921), president of Peru (1975-1980) **11** 150-151

MORAN, THOMAS (1837-1926), American painter and graphic artist **11** 151-152

MORANDI, GIORGIO (1890-1964), Italian painter of still lifes **11** 152-153

MORAVIA, ALBERTO (1907-1990), Italian author **11** 153-155

MORAZÁN, JOSÉ FRANCISCO (1792-1842), Central American general and statesman **11** 155

MORE, SIR THOMAS (1478-1535), English humanist and statesman **11** 156-157

MOREAU, GUSTAVE (1826-1898), French artist and professor **22** 324-326

MORELOS, JOSÉ MARÍA (1765-1815), Mexican priest and revolutionary leader **11** 157-158

Moreno, Gabriel García
see García Moreno, Gabriel

MORENO, MARIANO (1778-1811), Argentine revolutionary **20** 274-275

MORGAGNI, GIOVANNI BATTISTA (1682-1771), Italian anatomist **11** 158-159

MORGAN, ANN HAVEN (Anna Haven Morgan; 1882-1966), American ecologist and teacher **24** 270-271

MORGAN, CONWAY LLOYD (1852-1936), English psychologist **11** 159-160

MORGAN, DANIEL (c. 1735-1802), American soldier and tactician **11** 160-161

MORGAN, GARRETT A. (1877-1963), African American inventor and publisher **11** 161-162

MORGAN, SIR HENRY (1635-1688), British buccaneer **29** 284-287

MORGAN, JOHN (1735-1789), American physician **11** 162-163

MORGAN, JOHN PIERPONT (1837-1913), American banker **11** 163-165
arts funding
Knight, Charles R. **30** 242-244

MORGAN, JOHN PIERPONT, II (1867-1943), American banker **11** 165

MORGAN, JULIA (1872-1957), American architect **11** 165-166

MORGAN, JUNIUS SPENCER (1813-1890), American banker **11** 166-167

MORGAN, LEWIS HENRY (1818-1881), American anthropologist **11** 167-168

MORGAN, ROBIN (born 1941), feminist writer, editor, poet, and political activist **11** 168-170

MORGAN, THOMAS HUNT (1866-1945), American zoologist and geneticist **11** 170-171

MORGENTHAU, HANS J. (1904-1979), American political scientist **11** 171-172

MORGENTHAU, HENRY, JR. (1891-1967), American statesman **11** 172-173

MORIN, PAUL (1889-1963), French-Canadian poet **11** 174

MORÍNIGO, HIGINIO (1897-1985), Paraguayan statesman **11** 174-175

MORISON, SAMUEL ELIOT (1887-1976), American historian and biographer **11** 175-176

MORISOT, BERTHE (1841-1895), French painter **21** 303-305

MORITA, AKIO (born 1921), Japanese industrial leader **11** 176-178

MORLEY, JOHN (Viscount Morley of Blackburn; 1838-1923), English statesman and author **11** 178-179

MORLEY, THOMAS (c. 1557-c. 1602), English composer and organist **11** 179-180

Morning Star (Northern Cheyenne tribal leader)
see Dull Knife

MORO, ALDO (1916-1978), leader of Italy's Christian Democratic Party **11** 180-181

MORODER, GIORGIO (born 1940), Italian producer and songwriter **29** 288-290

MORRICE, JAMES WILSON (1865-1924), Canadian painter **11** 181-182

MORRILL, JUSTIN SMITH (1810-1898), American legislator **11** 182

MORRIS, GOUVERNEUR (1752-1816), American statesman and diplomat **11** 182-183

MORRIS, LEWIS (1671-1746), American colonial official **11** 183-184

MORRIS, MARK (born 1956), American choreographer **11** 184-185

MORRIS, ROBERT (1734-1806), American financer and statesman **11** 185-187

MORRIS, WILLIAM (1834-1896), English man of letters, artist, and politician **11** 187-188

MORRISON, JIM (James Douglas Morrison; 1943-1971), American singer and songwriter **18** 293-295

MORRISON, TONI (Chloe Anthony Wofford; born 1931), African American novelist **11** 188-190

Morrow, Anne Spencer
see Lindbergh, Anne Morrow

MORROW, DWIGHT WHITNEY (1873-1931), American banker and diplomat **11** 190-191

NIEBUHR, HELMUT RICHARD
(1894-1962), American Protestant
theologian **11** 386-387

NIEBUHR, REINHOLD (1892-1971),
American Protestant theologian **11** 387-388

NIELSEN, CARL AUGUST (1865-1931),
Danish composer **11** 388-389

NIEMEYER SOARES FILHO, OSCAR (born
1907), Brazilian architect **11** 389-390

NIETZSCHE, FRIEDRICH (1844-1900),
German philosopher and poet **11** 390-392

NIGHTINGALE, FLORENCE (1820-1910),
English nurse **11** 392-393

NIJINSKY, VASLAV (1890-1950), Russian
ballet dancer **11** 393-395

NIKON, NIKITA MINOV (1605-1681),
patriarch of the Russian Orthodox
Church 1652-1666 **11** 395

NIMITZ, CHESTER WILLIAM (1885-1966),
American admiral **11** 395-396

NIN, ANAIS (1903-1977), American
author **11** 397-398

NIN-CULMELL, JOAQUÍN MARÍA (born
1908), American composer, pianist, and
conductor **11** 398

19th Amendment
see Constitution of the United
States–Amendments

NIRENBERG, MARSHALL WARREN (born
1927), American biochemist **11** 399-400

Nirvani, Carma
see Kazantzakis, Nikos

NIWANO, NIKKYO (Shikazo Niwano;
born 1906), Buddhist Japanese religious
leader **11** 400-401

NIXON, RICHARD MILHOUS
(1913-1994), president of the United
States (1969-1974) **11** 401-404
law work
Miller, Marvin **30** 277-280
Watergate scandal
Felt, W. Mark **30** 169-171

Niza, Marcos de
see Marcos de Niza, Friar

NIZAMI, KHALIQ AHMAD (born 1925),
Indian historian, religious scholar, and
diplomat **11** 405

NKOMO, JOSHUA MQABUKO
(1917-1999), leading African nationalist
in former colony of Rhodesia and
president of the Zimbabwe African
People's Union **11** 405-407

NKOSI, LEWIS (born 1936), South African
author and literary critic **11** 407-408

NKRUMAH, KWAME (Francis Nwa
Nkrumah; 1909-1972), Ghanaian
statesman, president 1960-1966 **11**
408-410

No drama
see Japanese literature–No drama

NOBEL, ALFRED BERNHARD (1833-1896),
Swedish chemist **11** 410-411

Nobel Prize winners
chemistry
Bergius, Friedrich Karl Rudolph **30**
51-53
physics
Wilczek, Frank Anthony **30** 378-380

NOBILE, UMBERTO (1885-1978), Italian
explorer and airship designer **11** 411-412

NOBUNAGA, ODA (1534-1582), Japanese
general and statesman **11** 413-414

Noech'on
see Kim Pusik

NOETHER, EMMY (born Amalie Emmy
Noether; 1882-1935), German
American mathematician **11** 414-416

NOGUCHI, ISAMU (1904-1988), American
sculptor and designer **11** 416-418

Nol, Lon
see Lon Nol, (1913-1985)

NOLAN, SIDNEY ROBERT (1917-1992),
Australian expressionist painter **11** 418

NOLAND, KENNETH (born 1924),
American color-field painter **11** 418-419

NOLDE, EMIL (1867-1956), German
expressionist painter **11** 419-420

NONO, LUIGI (1924-1990), Italian
composer **11** 420-421

NOONUCCAL, OODGEROO (Kath
Wlaker; Kathleen Jean Mary Ruska;
1920- 1993), Australian Aboriginal poet
27 272-274

NOOYI, INDRA KRISHNAMURTHY (born
1955), Indian-American business
woman **27** 274-276

**NORDENSKJÖLD, BARON NILS ADOLF
ERIK** (1832-1901), Finnish-Swedish polar
explorer and mineralogist **11** 421-422

NORDENSKOLD, NILS OTTO GUSTAF
(1869-1928), Swedish polar explorer
and geologist **11** 422-423

NORDSTROM, JOHN (Johan W. Nordstrom;
1871-1963), American shoe retailer **19**
270-272

NORFOLK, 3D DUKE OF (Thomas
Howard; 1473-1554), English soldier
and councilor **11** 423

NØRGÅRD, PER (born 1932), Danish
composer **23** 265-267

NORIEGA, MANUEL A. (born 1934),
strongman of Panama (1980s) forced out
in 1989 by the United States **11** 423-425

NORMAN, JESSYE (born 1945), American
singer **11** 425-427

Normandy, Duke of
see Charles V(king of France)

NORRIS, BENJAMIN FRANKLIN, JR.
(1870-1902), American novelist and
critic **11** 427-428

NORRIS, GEORGE WILLIAM (1861-1944),
American statesman **11** 428-429

NORTH, FREDERICK (2nd Earl of Guilford;
1732-1792), English statesman **11** 429-430

NORTH, MARIANNE (1830-1890), English
naturalist and painter **23** 268-270

North Pole
see Arctic exploration

NORTHROP, JOHN HOWARD
(1891-1987), American biological
chemist **11** 430-431

Northside Center for Child Development
Clark, Mamie Phipps **30** 115-118

NORTHUMBERLAND, DUKE OF (John
Dudley; c. 1502-1553), English soldier
and statesman **11** 431-432

NORTON, ANDRE (Alice Mary Norton;
1912-2005), American science fiction
and fantasy writer **28** 257-259

NOSTRADAMUS (born Michel de
Notredame; 1503-1566), French physician,
astrologist, and author **11** 432-434

Notker Balbulus
see Balbulus, Notker

Novak, Joseph
see Kosinsky, Jerzy

NOVALIS (1772-1801), German poet and
author **11** 435

Novanglus
see Adams, John

NOVELLO, ANTONIA (Antonia Coello;
born 1944), Puerto Rican American
pediatrician **18** 308-310

NOVOTNÝ, ANTONÍN (1904-1975),
Czechoslovak politician **29** 291-293

NOYCE, ROBERT (1927-1990), American
physicist and inventor **11** 436-437

NOYES, JOHN HUMPHREY (1811-1886),
American founder of the Oneida
Community **11** 437-438

NOZICK, ROBERT (1938-2002), American
philosopher and polemical advocate of
radical libertarianism **11** 438-439

N'si Yisrael
see Bar Kochba, Simeon

NU, U (1907-1995), Burmese statesman **11**
439-441

NUJOMA, SHAFIIHUNA ("Sam"; born
1929), first president of independent
Namibia **11** 441-443

OYONO, FERDINAND LEOPOLD (born 1929), Cameroonian author and diplomat **24** 290-292

OZ, AMOS (born 1939), Israeli author **12** 45-47

OZAL, TURGUT (born 1927), Turkish prime minister and president **12** 47-49

OZAWA, SEIJI (born 1935), Japanese musician and conductor **12** 49-51

OZU, YASUJIRO (1903-1963), Japanese film director **23** 279-281

P

PA CHIN (pen name of Li Fei-kan; 1904-2005), Chinese novelist **12** 53-54

PAAR, JACK HAROLD (1918-2004), American comedian and radio personality **26** 284-286

PABST, G. W. (Georg Wilhelm Pabst; 1885-1967), Austrian film director **23** 282-284

Pacelli, Eugenio Maria Giuseppe
see Pius XII

Pacheco y Padilla, Juan Vicente Güemes
see Revillagigedo, Conde de

PACHELBEL, JOHANN (1653-1706), German composer and organist **12** 52

PACHER, MICHAEL (c. 1435-1498), Austro-German painter and wood carver **12** 53

PACINO, AL (Alfredo James Pacino; born 1940), American actor and film director **23** 284-286

PACKARD, DAVID (1912-1996), cofounder of Hewlett-Packard Company and deputy secretary of defense under President Nixon **12** 54-56

PADEREWSKI, IGNACE JAN (1860-1941), Polish pianist, composer, and statesman **12** 56-57

PADMORE, GEORGE (1902/03-1959), Trinidadian leftist political activist **12** 57-58

Padua, University of (Italy)
Barzizza, Gasparino **30** 38-40
Colombo, Realdo **30** 120-122
Fabrici, Girolamo **30** 167-169

PÁEZ, JOSÉ ANTONIO (1790-1873), Venezuelan general and president 1831-46 **12** 58

PAGANINI, NICCOLO (1782-1840), Italian violinist and composer **12** 58-59

PAGE, THOMAS NELSON (1853-1922), American author and diplomat **12** 59-60

PAGE, WALTER HINES (1855-1918), American journalist and diplomat **12** 60-61

PAGELS, ELAINE HIESEY (born 1943), historian of religion **12** 61-62

PAGLIA, CAMILLE (born 1947), American author and social critic **23** 286-288

PAIGE, SATCHEL (Leroy Robert Paige; 1906-1982), African American baseball player **12** 62-65
Veeck, Bill **30** 364-366

PAINE, JOHN KNOWLES (1839-1905), American composer **12** 65

PAINE, THOMAS (1737-1809), English-born American journalist and Revolutionary propagandist **12** 66-67

PAISLEY, IAN K. (born 1926), political leader and minister of religion in Northern Ireland **12** 67-69

Pak Chong-hŭi
see Park, Chung Hee

PALACKÝ, FRANTIŠEK (1798-1876), Czech historian and statesman **12** 69-70

Palaeologan dynasty (Byzantine Empire; ruled 1261-1453)
Andronikos II Palaiologos **30** 7-9

Palaiologian dynasty
see Palaeologan dynasty (Byzantine Empire; ruled 1261-1453)

PALAMAS, KOSTES (1859-1943), Greek poet **12** 70

Paleontology (science)
illustration
Knight, Charles R. **30** 242-244

PALESTRINA, GIOVANNI PIERLUIGI DA (c. 1525-1594), Italian composer **12** 70-72

PALEY, GRACE (1922-2007), American author and activist **22** 348-350

PALEY, WILLIAM (1743-1805), English theologian and moral philosopher **12** 72

PALEY, WILLIAM S. (1901-1990), founder and chairman of the Columbia Broadcasting System **12** 72-75

PALLADIO, ANDREA (1508-1580), Italian architect **12** 75-77

PALMA, RICARDO (1833-1919), Peruvian poet, essayist, and short-story writer **12** 77

PALME, OLOF (Sven Olof Joachim Palme; 1927-1986), Swedish prime minister (1969-1973; 1982-1986) **28** 267-269

PALMER, ALEXANDER MITCHELL (1872-1936), American politician and jurist **12** 77-78

PALMER, ARNOLD DANIEL (born 1929), American golfer **12** 78-80

PALMER, NATHANIEL BROWN (1799-1877), American sea captain **12** 80-81

PALMER, PHOEBE WORRALL (1807-1847), American evangelist **23** 288-290

PALMERSTON, 3D VISCOUNT (Henry John Temple; 1784-1865), English prime minister 1855-65 **12** 81-83

Pamfili, Giovanni Batista
see Innocent X

PAMUK, ORHAN (born 1952), Turkish novelist and Nobel Prize Winner **28** 269-272

PAN KU (32-92), Chinese historian and man of letters **12** 86-87

Pan-American Exposition (1900; Buffalo, New York State)
de Forest, Marian **30** 138-139

PANDIT, VIJAYA LAKSHMI (1900-1990), Indian diplomat and politician **12** 83-84

PANETTA, LEON E. (born 1938), Democratic congressman from California and chief of staff to President Clinton **12** 84-85

PANINI (fl. c. 5th century BCE), Indian grammarian **24** 293-295

PANKHURST, CHRISTABEL HARRIETTE (1880-1948), English reformer and suffragette **22** 350-352

PANKHURST, EMMELINE (1858-1928), English reformer **12** 85-86

PANKHURST, SYLVIA (1882-1960), English reformer **29** 309-311

PANNENBERG, WOLFHART (born 1928), German Protestant theologian **12** 87-88

PANUFNIK, ANDRZEJ (1914-1991), Polish/British composer and conductor **24** 295-298

PAPANDREOU, ANDREAS (1919-1996), Greek scholar and statesman and prime minister **12** 88-91

PAPINEAU, LOUIS-JOSEPH (1786-1871), French-Canadian radical political leader **12** 91

PARACELSUS, PHILIPPUS AUREOLUS (1493-1541), Swiss physician and alchemist **12** 91-93

PARBO, ARVI (born 1926), Australian industrial giant **12** 93-94

PARÉ, AMBROISE (1510-1590), French military surgeon **12** 94-95

PARETO, VILFREDO (1848-1923), Italian sociologist, political theorist, and economist **12** 95-96

PARHAM, CHARLES FOX (1873-1929), American evangelist **23** 291-293

Paris, Matthew
see Matthew Paris

Canadian
Shadd Cary, Mary Ann **30** 324-326

Publishers, American

magazines
Buntline, Ned **30** 88-90
Heldman, Gladys **30** 204-206
newspapers
Shadd Cary, Mary Ann **30** 324-326

Publius Aelius Hadrianus
see Hadrian

PUCCINI, GIACOMO (1858-1924), Italian composer **12** 474-476

PUDOVKIN, V. I. (Vsevolod Illiarionovich Pudovkin; 1893-1953), Russian film director **24** 316-318

PUENTE, TITO (Ernesto Antonio Puente, 1920-2000), Hispanic American band leader, musician, and composer **12** 476-477 **30** 306-308

PUFENDORF, BARON SAMUEL VON (1632-1694), German jurist and historian **12** 477-478

PUGACHEV, EMELYAN IVANOVICH (1742-1775), Russian Cossack soldier **12** 478-479

PUGIN, AUGUSTUS WELBY NORTHMORE (1812-1852), English architect **12** 479-480

PULASKI, CASIMIR (1747/48-79), Polish patriot **12** 480-481

PULCI, LUIGI (1432-1484), Italian poet **12** 481

PULITZER, JOSEPH (1847-1911), American editor and publisher **12** 481-482

Pulitzer Prize winners
Foote, Horton **30** 171-173
Smith, Red **30** 334-337

PULLMAN, GEORGE MORTIMER (1831-1897), American industrial innovator **12** 482-483

Pulse theory (light)
see Light–wave theory

PUPIN, MICHAEL IDVORSKY (1858-1935), Serbo-American physicist and inventor **12** 483-484

Purge trials (Soviet history)
see Great Purge (1936-38; Union of Soviet Socialist Republics)

PURVIS, ROBERT (1810-1898), African American abolitionist **12** 485-486

PURYEAR, MARTIN (born 1941), African American artist **12** 486-487

PUSEY, EDWARD BOUVERIE (1800-1882), English clergyman and scholar **12** 488-489

PUSHKIN, ALEKSANDR SERGEEVICH (1799-1837), Russian poet and prose writer **12** 489-491

PUTIN, VLADIMIR (born 1952), Russian president **21** 355-358
Medvedev, Dmitry **30** 275-277

PUTNAM, ISRAEL (1718-1790), American Revolutionary War general **12** 491-492

Putnam, Mary Corinna
see Jacobi, Mary Putnam

Putsches
see Coups d'état–Germany

PUVIS DE CHAVANNES, PIERRE (1824-1898), French painter **12** 492-493

PYLE, ERNIE (Earnest Taylor Pyle; 1900-1945), American war correspondent during World War II **12** 493-494

PYM, FRANCIS (Francis Leslie Pym; 1922-2008), British statesman **12** 494-495

PYM, JOHN (1584-1643), English statesman **12** 495-496

PYNCHON, THOMAS (Thomas Ruggles Pynchon, Jr.; born 1937), American writer **12** 496-498

PYTHAGORAS (c. 575-c. 495 B.C.), Greek philosopher, scientist, and religious teacher **12** 498-499

PYTHEAS (c. 380 B.C.-c. 300 B.C.), Greek explorer **12** 499-500

Q

QABOOS IBN SA'ID (born 1940), ruler of the Sultanate of Oman **12** 501-502

QIANLONG (Ch'ien-lung and Hung-li; 1711-1799), Chinese emperor **12** 502-505

Quaid-i-Azam
see Jinnah, Mohammad Ali

QUANT, MARY (born 1934), British fashion designer and businesswoman **19** 303-305

Quantum theory (physics)
quantum chromodynamics
Wilczek, Frank Anthony **30** 378-380
quantum mechanics
Moseley, Henry Gwyn Jeffreys **30** 280-283

Quaregna e di Cerreto, Conti di
see Avogadro, Lorenzo Romano Amedeo Carlo

Quark (hypothetical particle)
Wilczek, Frank Anthony **30** 378-380

Quarton, Enguerrand
see Charonton, Enguerrand

QUASIMODO, SALVATORE (1901-1968), Italian poet, translator, and critic **12** 506

QUAY, MATTHEW STANLEY (1833-1904), American politician **12** 507

QUAYLE, J(AMES) DANFORTH (born 1947), vice president under George Bush **12** 507-509

QUELER, EVE RABIN (born 1936), American pianist and conductor **26** 309-311

QUERCIA, JACOPO DELLA (1374?-1438), Italian sculptor and architect **12** 509

Quesada, Gonzalo Jiménez de
see Jiménez de Quesada, Gonzalo

QUESTEL, MAE (Maq Kwestel; 1908-1998), American actress and voice-over professional **27** 299-301

QUÉTELET, LAMBERT ADOLPHE JACQUES (1796-1874), Belgian statistician and astronomer **12** 510-511

QUEVEDO Y VILLEGAS, FRANCISCO GÓMEZ DE (1580-1645), Spanish poet, satirist, and novelist **12** 511

QUEZON, MANUEL LUIS (1878-1944), Philippine statesman **12** 511-513

QUIMBY, HARRIET (1875-1912), American aviator **28** 285-287

QUINE, WILLARD VAN ORMAN (born 1908), American philosopher **12** 514-515

QUINN, ANTHONY (Antonio Rudolph Oaxaca Quinn; born 1915), Hispanic American actor and artist **20** 302-304

QUINTILIAN (c. 35-c. 99), Roman rhetorician and literary critic **12** 518-519

QUIRINO, ELPIDIO (1890-1956), Philippine statesman **12** 519-520

QUIROGA, HORACIO (1878-1937), Uruguayan writer **12** 520-521

QUIROGA, JUAN FACUNDO (1788/1790-1835), Argentine caudillo **12** 521-522

QUISLING, VIDKIN (1887-1945), Norwegian traitor **20** 304-306

R

Rabbenu Gershom
see Gershom ben Judah

Rabbis
see Religious leaders, Jewish

RABEARIVELO, JEAN JOSEPH (1901-1937), Malagasy poet **12** 523-524

RABELAIS, FRANÇOIS (c. 1494-c. 1553), French humanist, doctor, and writer **12** 524-526

RABI, ISIDOR ISAAC (1898-1988), American physicist **12** 526-527

RABIN, YITZCHAK (1922-1995), Israeli statesman **12** 527-529

Rabindranath
see Tagore, Rabindranath

Rabinowitz, Sholem
see Sholem Aleichem

RACHMANINOV, SERGEI VASILIEVICH (1873-1943), Russian composer, pianist, and conductor **12** 531-532

RACINE, JEAN BAPTISTE (1639-1699), French dramatist **12** 532-535

RADCLIFFE, ANN (Ann Ward Radcliffe; 1764-1823), English author and poet **28** 288-290

RADCLIFFE, TED (Theodore Roosevelt Radcliffe; 1902-2005), African American baseball player **26** 312-314

RADCLIFFE-BROWN, A(LFRED) R(EGINALD) (1881-1955), English anthropologist **12** 535-536

RADEK, KARL BERNARDOVICH (1885-1939), Russian Communist leader **12** 536-537

RADHAKRISHNAN, SARVEPALLI (1888-1995), Indian philosopher and statesman **12** 537-538

RADIN, PAUL (1883-1959), American anthropologist and ethnographer **12** 538-539

Radio Hall of Fame
Harwell, Ernie **30** 202-204

RADISSON, PIERRE-ESPRIT (c. 1636-1710), French explorer **12** 539-540

Radomyslsky, Grigori Evseevich
see Zinoviev, Grigori Evseevich

RAFFLES, SIR THOMAS STAMFORD (1781-1826), English colonial administrator **13** 1-2

RAFINESQUE, CONSTANTINE SAMUEL (1783-1840), French naturalist **21** 359-361

RAFSANJANI, AKBAR HASHEMI (born 1934), president of Iran **13** 3-4

Raging Bull (film)
Schoonmaker, Thelma **30** 318-320

RAHNER, KARL (1904-1984), German Catholic theologian **13** 4-5

RAI, LALA LAJPAT (1865-1928), Indian nationalist leader **13** 5-6

RAIMONDI, MARCANTONIO (c. 1480-c. 1534), Italian engraver **30** 309-311

RAIN IN THE FACE (Itonagaju; c. 1835-1905), Native American warrior **26** 314-316

RAINEY, MA (Gertrude Pridgett; 1886-1939), American singer **19** 306-308

RAINIER III, PRINCE OF MONACO (1923-2005), ruler of the principality of Monaco **18** 335-337

RAJAGOPALACHARI, CHAKRAVARTI (1879-1972), Indian nationalist leader **13** 6-7

RAJARAJA I (985-1014), Indian statesman **13** 7

RAJNEESH, BHAGWAN SHREE (Rahneesh Chandra Mohan; 1931-1990), Indian religious leader **13** 7-9

RALEIGH, SIR WALTER (or Ralegh; c. 1552-1618), English statesman, soldier, courtier, explorer, and poet **13** 9-11

Rama IV
see Mongkut

Rama V
see Chulalongkorn

RAMA KHAMHAENG (c. 1239-c. 1299), king of Sukhothai in Thailand **13** 11

RAMAKRISHNA, SRI (1833-1886), Indian mystic, reformer, and saint **13** 11-13

RAMAN, SIR CHANDRASEKHAR VENKATA (1888-1970), Indian physicist **13** 13-14

RAMANUJA (Ramanujacarya; c. 1017-1137), Indian theologian and philosopher **21** 361-362

RAMANUJAN AIYANGAR, SRINIVASA (1887-1920), India mathematician **13** 14-15

RAMAPHOSA, MATEMELA CYRIL (born 1952), general secretary of the National Union of Mineworkers (NUM) in South Africa and secretary general of the African National Congress **13** 15-16

RAMAZZINI, BERNARDINO (1633-1714), Italian physician **21** 362-364

Ramboldini, Vittorino
see Feltre, Vittorino da

RAMEAU, JEAN PHILIPPE (1683-1764), French music theorist and composer **13** 17-18

RAMGOOLAM, SEEWOOSAGUR (1900-1985), president of Mauritius **24** 319-321

RAMON, ILAN (Ilan Wolferman; 1954-2003), Israeli astronaut **25** 345-347

RAMOS, FIDEL VALDEZ (born 1928), president of the Philippines (1992-) **13** 18-19

RAMPAL, JEAN-PIERRE LOUIS (1922-2000), French flutist **22** 362-364

RAMPHAL, SHRIDATH SURENDRANATH (born 1928), Guyanese barrister, politician, and international civil servant **13** 19-20

RAMSAY, DAVID (1749-1815), American historian **13** 21

Ramsay, James Andrew Broun
see Dalhousie, 1st Marquess of

RAMSAY, SIR WILLIAM (1852-1916), British chemist and educator **13** 21-22

RAMSES II (ruled 1304-1237 B.C.), pharaoh of Egypt **13** 22-23

RAMSEY, ARTHUR MICHAEL (1904-1988), archbishop of Canterbury and president of the World Council of Churches **13** 23-25

RAMSEY, FRANK PLUMPTON (1903-1930), English mathematician and philosopher **13** 25

RAMSEY, NORMAN FOSTER, JR. (born 1915), American physicist **13** 25-27

RAMUS, PETRUS (1515-1572), French humanist, logician and mathematician **13** 27-28

RANAVALONA I (c. 1788-1861), Queen of Madagascar **27** 302-304

RAND, AYN (1905-1982), American author and philosoher **20** 307-309

RANDOLPH, A. PHILIP (1889-1979), African American labor and civil rights leader **13** 28-29

RANDOLPH, EDMUND (1753-1813), American statesman **13** 29-30

RANDOLPH, JOHN (1773-1833), American statesman **13** 30

RANDOLPH, PEYTON (1721-1775), American statesman **18** 337-339

RANDS, BERNARD (born 1934), American musician **23** 324-326

RANGEL, CHARLES B. (born 1930), Democratic U.S. representative from New York City **13** 31-32

RANJIT SINGH (1780-1839), ruler of the Punjab **13** 32-33

RANK, OTTO (1884-1939), Austrian psychotherapist **13** 33

RANKE, LEOPOLD VON (1795-1886), German historian **13** 33-35

RANKIN, JEANNETTE PICKERING (1880-1973), first woman elected to the U.S. Congress **13** 35-37

RANNARIDH, PRINCE NORODOM (born 1944), first prime minister of Cambodia **13** 37-39

SCHECHTER, SOLOMON (1849-1915), Romanian-American Jewish scholar and religious leader **13** 524

SCHEELE, KARL WILHELM (1742-1786), Swedish pharmacist and chemist **13** 525-526

SCHELLING, FRIEDRICH WILHELM JOSEPH VON (1775-1854), German philosopher **13** 526-527

SCHIELE, EGON (1890-1918), Austrian Expressionist painter and draftsman **14** 1-2

SCHIESS, BETTY BONE (born 1923), American Episcopalian priest **18** 360-362

SCHIFF, JACOB HENRY (1847-1920), German-American banker **14** 2-3

SCHILLEBEECKX, EDWARD (born 1914), Belgian Roman Catholic theologian **14** 3-4

SCHILLER, JOHANN CHRISTOPH FRIEDRICH VON (1759-1805), German dramatist, poet, and historian **14** 4-7

SCHINDLER, ALEXANDER MOSHE (1925-2000), American Jewish leader **23** 360-362

SCHINDLER, OSKAR (1908-1974), German businessman and humanitarian **18** 362-365

SCHINDLER, SOLOMON (1842-1915), German-American rabbi and social theorist **14** 7-8

SCHINKEL, KARL FRIEDRICH (1781-1841), German architect, painter and designer **14** 8

SCHLAFLY, PHYLLIS (born 1924), American political activist and author **14** 9-10

SCHLEGEL, FRIEDRICH VON (1772-1829), German critic and author **14** 10-11

SCHLEIERMACHER, FRIEDRICH ERNST DANIEL (1768-1834), German theologian and philosopher **14** 11-12

SCHLEMMER, OSKAR (1888-1943), German painter, sculptor, and stage designer **14** 12-13

SCHLESINGER, ARTHUR MEIER (1888-1965), American historian **14** 13

SCHLESINGER, ARTHUR MEIER, JR. (1917-2007), American historian and Democratic party activist **14** 13-15

SCHLESINGER, JAMES RODNEY (born 1929), American government official **14** 15-16

SCHLICK, FRIEDRICH ALBERT MORITZ (1882-1936), German physicist and philosopher **14** 16-17

SCHLIEMANN, HEINRICH (1822-1890), German merchant and archeologist **14** 17-18

SCHLÜTER, ANDREAS (c. 1660-1714), German sculptor and architect **14** 18-19

SCHMELING, MAX (1905-2005), German boxer **29** 337-339

SCHMIDT, HELMUT (born 1918), Social Democrat and chancellor of the Federal Republic of Germany (the former West Germany), 1974-82 **14** 19-21

Schmidt, Johann Caspar
see Stirner, Max

SCHMITT, JACK (Harrison Hagan Schmitt; born 1935), American astronaut and geologist **22** 385-386

Schmitz, Ettore
see Svevo, Italo

SCHMOLLER, GUSTAV FRIEDRICH VON (1838-1917), German economist **14** 21

SCHNABEL, ARTUR (1882-1951), Austrian American pianist **27** 319-321

SCHNEERSON, MENACHEM MENDEL (The Rebbe; 1902-1994), Russian-American Hassidic Jewish leader **22** 386-388

SCHNEIDER, ROMY (Rosemarie Magdalena Albach-Retty; 1938-1982), Austrian actress **24** 350-352

SCHNEIDERMAN, ROSE (1882-1972), labor organizer and activist for the improvement of working conditions for women **14** 22-23

SCHNITZLER, ARTHUR (1862-1931), Austrian dramatist and novelist **14** 23-24

SCHOENBERG, ARNOLD (1874-1951), Austrian composer **14** 24-26

SCHOLASTICA, SAINT (c. 480-547), Italian abbess **30** 314-316

SCHOLEM, GERSHOM (1897-1982), Jewish scholar **14** 26

SCHONGAUER, MARTIN (c. 1435-91), German engraver and painter **14** 26-28

SCHÖNHUBER, FRANZ XAVER (1923-2005), German right-wing political leader **14** 28-29

SCHOOLCRAFT, HENRY ROWE (1793-1864), American explorer and ethnologist **14** 29
Schoolcraft, Jane Johnston **30** 316-318

SCHOOLCRAFT, JANE JOHNSTON (1800-1842), Native American poet **30** 316-318

SCHOONMAKER, THELMA (born 1940), American film editor **30** 318-320

SCHOPENHAUER, ARTHUR (1788-1860), German philosopher **14** 29-31

SCHOUTEN, WILLIAM CORNELIUS (c. 1580-1625), Dutch explorer and navigator **14** 31

SCHRAMM, TEXAS ERNEST ("Tex"; 1920-2003), American football team owner **24** 352-355

SCHREINER, OLIVE (Olive Emilie Albertina Schreiner; Ralph Iron; 1855-1920), South African author **23** 362-364

SCHREMPP, JUERGEN (born 1944), German automobile industry executive **20** 331-332

SCHRODER, GERHARD (born 1944), German chancellor **19** 325-327

SCHRÖDINGER, ERWIN (1887-1961), Austrian physicist **14** 31-33

SCHROEDER, PATRICIA SCOTT (born 1940), first U.S. congresswoman from Colorado **14** 33-35

SCHUBERT, FRANZ PETER (1797-1828), Austrian composer **14** 35-37

SCHULLER, GUNTHER (born 1925), American musician **14** 37-38

SCHULZ, CHARLES M. (1922-2000), American cartoonist and creator of "Peanuts" **14** 38-39

SCHUMACHER, KURT (1895-1952), German socialist statesman **14** 40-41

SCHUMAN, ROBERT (1886-1963), French statesman **14** 41

SCHUMAN, WILLIAM HOWARD (1910-1992), American composer and educator **22** 388-391

SCHUMANN, CLARA (Clara Josephine Wieck Schumann; 1819-1896), German pianist and composer **26** 338-340

SCHUMANN, ROBERT ALEXANDER (1810-1856), German composer and critic **14** 41-43

SCHUMPETER, JOSEPH ALOIS (1883-1950), Austrian economist **14** 43-44

SCHURZ, CARL (1829-1906), American soldier, statesman, and journalist **14** 44-45

SCHUSCHNIGG, KURT VON (1897-1977), Austrian statesman, chancellor of Austria 1934-38 **14** 45-46

SCHÜSSLER FIORENZA, ELIZABETH (born 1938), biblical scholar and theologian **14** 46-48

SCHÜTZ, HEINRICH (1585-1672), German composer **14** 48-49

SHAYS, DANIEL (c. 1747-1825), American Revolutionary War Captain **14** 168

SHCHARANSKY, ANATOLY BORISOVICH (born 1948), prominent figure of the Helsinki Watch Group **14** 168-170

SHEARER, NORMA (1902-1982), Canadian actress **29** 343-345

SHEBA (Makeda; Bilqis; c. 1075 BCE-c. 955 BCE), queen of Sheba **24** 365-367

SHEELER, CHARLES (1883-1965), American painter **14** 170-171

SHEEN, FULTON J. (1895-1979), American Roman Catholic bishop and television host **14** 171-172

Shehu
see Uthman don Fodio

Sheikh Ibrahim
see Burkhardt, Johann Ludwig

SHELDON, CHARLES M. (1857-1946), American social reformer who also wrote *In His Steps* **14** 172-174

SHELDON, SIDNEY (1917-2007), American author **28** 323-325

SHELLEY, MARY WOLLSTONECRAFT (1797-1851), English author **14** 174-176

SHELLEY, PERCY BYSSHE (1792-1822), English romantic poet **14** 176-178

Shelomoh Yitzhaki
see Rashi

SHEPARD, ALAN (1923-1998), American astronaut **14** 178-180

SHEPARD, SAM (Samuel Shepard Rogers VII; born 1943), American playwright, rock performer, and film actor **14** 180-181

SHEPPARD, WILLIAM HENRY (1865-1927), African American missionary to Africa **27** 325-327

SHERATON, THOMAS (1751-1806), English furniture designer **14** 181-182

SHERIDAN, PHILIP HENRY (1831-1888), American general **14** 182-183

SHERIDAN, RICHARD BRINSLEY (1751-1816), British playwright and orator **14** 183-184

SHERMAN, CINDY (Cynthia Morris Sherman; born 1954), American photographer **19** 335-337

SHERMAN, JOHN (1823-1900), American politician **14** 184-185

SHERMAN, ROGER (1721-1793), American patriot **14** 185-186

SHERMAN, WILLIAM TECUMSEH (1820-1891), American general **14** 186-187

SHERRINGTON, SIR CHARLES SCOTT (1857-1952), English physiologist **14** 187-189

SHERWOOD, ROBERT EMMET (1896-1955), American playwright **14** 189-190

SHESTOV, LEV (Lev Isaakovich Schwarzmann; 1866-1938), Russian Jewish thinker and literary critic **14** 190-191

SHEVARDNADZE, EDUARD AMVROSEVICH (born 1928), foreign minister of the U.S.S.R. (1985-1990) **14** 191-193

SHEVCHENKO, TARAS GRIGORYEVICH (1814-1861), Ukrainian poet **24** 367-369

SHIBA, RYOTARO (1923-1996), Japanese novelist, historian, and journalist **30** 328-330

SHIH KO-FA (died 1644), Chinese scholar-soldier **14** 194-195

SHIH LE (274-333), Chinese emperor 330-333 **14** 195

SHIHAB, FU'AD (1903-1973), Father of the Lebanese Army and president of Lebanon (1958-1964) **14** 193-194

Shih-heng
see Lu Chi

SHILS, EDWARD ALBERT (born 1911), American sociologist **14** 195-197

SHIMADA, SHIGETARO (1883-1976), Japanese naval admiral **30** 330-332

SHINRAN (1173-1262), Japanese Buddhist monk **14** 197

SHIPPEN, EDWARD (1728-1806), American jurist **14** 197-198

SHIRER, WILLIAM L. (born 1904), American journalist and historian who wrote on the history of Nazi Germany **14** 198-199

SHIVAJI
see Śivajī

SHKLOVSKY, VIKTOR (1893-1984), Russian critic **30** 332-334

SHOCKLEY, WILLIAM (1910-1989), American physicist **14** 200-202

SHOEMAKER, GENE (Eugene Merle Shoemaker; 1928-1997), American geologist and planetary scientist **20** 335-338

SHOEMAKER, WILLIE (Billy Lee Shoemaker; born 1931), American jockey and horse trainer **21** 381-383

SHOLEM ALEICHEM (Sholem Rabinowitz; 1859-1916), Russian-born American author **14** 202-203

SHOLES, CHRISTOPHER LATHAM (1819-1890), American publisher, inventor, and social reformer **21** 383-385

SHOLOKHOV, MIKHAIL ALEKSANDROVICH (1905-1984), Russian novelist **14** 203-204

SHORT, WALTER (1880-1949), American army officer **19** 337-339

Shorthand writing
Barrows, Isabel Chapin **30** 34-36

SHOSTAKOVICH, DMITRI DMITRIEVICH (1906-1975), Russian composer **14** 204-205

SHOTOKU TAISHI (573-621), Japanese regent, statesman, and scholar **14** 205-207

Showa Tenno
see Hirohito

SHREVE, HENRY MILLER (1785-1851), American steamboat designer and builder **14** 207

SHRIVER, EUNICE KENNEDY (born 1921), American activist **19** 339-341

Shu Ch'ing-ch'un
see Lao Shê

Shu Maung
see Ne Win

SHUB, ESTHER (Esfir Ilyanichna Shub; 1894-1959), Ukrainian filmmaker **24** 369-371

SHUBERT BROTHERS (1883-1963), theatrical managers **14** 207-209

SHULTZ, GEORGE PRATT (born 1920), labor and economics specialist, educator, businessman, and international negotiator **14** 209-211

Shunro
see Hokusai, Katsushika

Shuta
see Liang Wu-ti

SIBELIUS, JEAN JULIUS CHRISTIAN (1865-1957), Finnish composer **14** 211-212

Sicily, Duke of
see Guiscard Robert

SICKERT, WALTER RICHARD (1860-1942), English painter **14** 212-213

SICKLES, DANIEL EDGAR (1819-1914), American politician and diplomat **21** 385-388

SIDGWICK, HENRY (1838-1900), English philosopher and moralist **14** 213

SIDNEY, SIR PHILIP (1554-1586), English poet, courtier, diplomat, and soldier **14** 214-215

SISLEY, ALFRED (1839-1899), English-born French artist **26** 342-344

SISMONDI, JEAN CHARLES LÉONARD SIMONDE DE (1773-1842), Swiss-born historian and political economist **14** 258-259

SISULU, NONTSIKELELO ALBERTINA (1918-2003), leader of the anti-apartheid movement in South Africa **14** 259-261

SISULU, WALTER MAX ULYATE (born 1912), leader of the African National Congress (ANC) of South Africa **14** 261-262

SITHOLE, NDABANINGI (born 1920), African nationalist **14** 262-264

SITTING BULL (c. 1834-1890), American Indian leader and medicine man **14** 264-265

SITWELL, DAME EDITH (1887-1964), English poet and critic **14** 265-266

ŚIVAJT (1627-1680), Indian warrior and leader of a Hindu nation **14** 266-267

Six, The (Les Six; French composers)
Auric, Georges **30** 16-18

SIXTUS V (Felice Perreti; 1520-90), pope 1585-90 **14** 267-268

SIZA, ALVARO (Alvaro Joaquim Melo Siza Vieria; born 1933), Portugese architect **18** 375-376

SKELTON, JOHN (c. 1460-1529), English poet and humanist **14** 268-269

Skiagraphos
see Apollodorus

SKINNER, BURRHUS FREDERIC (1904-1990), American experimental psychologist **14** 269-270

SKINNER, CORNELIA OTIS (1901-1979), American actress and author **19** 346-348

Sklodowska, Marie
see Curie, Marie Sklodowska

SKOBLIKOVA, LYDIA PAVLOVNA (born 1939), Russian ice skater **26** 344-346

SKRAM, AMALIE (Berthe Amalie Alver; Amalie Mueller; 1846-1905), Norwegian author **28** 331-333

SLÁNSKÝ, RUDOLF SALZMANN (1901-1952), founding member of the Czechoslovak Communist Party and vice-premier of the former Czechoslovakia **14** 270-271

Slapstick (comedy technique)
Lewis, Jerry **30** 261-264

SLATER, SAMUEL (1768-1835), English-born American manufacturer **14** 272-273

Slave trade, African
late (18th-19th century)
Bowie, James **30** 71-73

Slee, Margaret
see Sanger, Margaret

SLIDELL, JOHN (1793-1871), American politician **14** 273

SLIM, WILLIAM JOSEPH (a.k.a. Anthony Mills; 1891-1970), English general and governor-general of Australia **18** 377-378

SLOAN, ALFRED PRITCHARD, JR. (1875-1966), American automobile executive **14** 274

SLOAN, JOHN (1871-1951), American painter **14** 274-275

SLOCUM, JOSHUA (Joshua Slocombe; 1844-1909), Canadian mariner, adventurer, and author **28** 333-335

SLUTER, CLAUS (c. 1350-1405/1406), Dutch-Burgundian sculptor **14** 275-276

SLYE, MAUD (1879-1954), American pathologist **14** 276-277

SMALL, ALBION WOODBURY (1854-1926), American sociologist and educator **14** 277

SMALLS, ROBERT (1839-1916), African American statesman **14** 277-278

SMEAL, ELEANOR (Eleanor Marie Cutri Smeal; born 1939), American women's rights activist and president of the National Organization for Women **14** 278-280

SMEATON, JOHN (1724-1792), English civil engineer **14** 280-281

SMETANA, BEDŘICH (1824-1884), Czech composer **14** 281-282

SMIBERT, JOHN (1688-1751), Scottish-born American painter **14** 282

SMITH, ADAM (1723-1790), Scottish economist and moral philosopher **14** 283-284

SMITH, ALFRED EMMANUEL (1873-1944), American politician **14** 284-285

SMITH, BESSIE (1894-1937), African American blues singer **14** 285-287

SMITH, DAVID (1906-1965), American sculptor **14** 287-288

SMITH, DEAN EDWARDS (born 1931), American college basketball coach **18** 378-380

SMITH, DONALD ALEXANDER (1st Baron Strathcona and Mount Royal; 1820-1914), Canadian politician and philanthropist **14** 288-289

SMITH, DORA VALENTINE (1893-1985), American educator **14** 289-290

SMITH, GERRIT (1797-1874), American philanthropist and reformer **14** 290-291

SMITH, IAN DOUGLAS (1919-2007), African prime minister **14** 291-293

SMITH, JAMES MCCUNE (1813-1865), African American physician and author **14** 293-294

SMITH, JEDEDIAH S. (1799-1831), American trapper, fur trader, and explorer **14** 294-295

SMITH, JESSIE CARNEY (Jessie M. Carney; born 1930), African American librarian and educator **24** 374-376

SMITH, JOHN (c. 1580-1631), English colonist in America **14** 295-297

SMITH, JOSEPH (1805-1844), American Mormon leader **14** 297-298

SMITH, LILLIAN EUGENIA (1897-1966), Southern writer and critic of white supremacy and segregation **14** 298-299

SMITH, MARGARET CHASE (1897-1995), first woman elected to both houses of Congress **14** 299-300

SMITH, PAULINE (Pauline Janet Urmson Smith; Janet Tamson; 1882-1959), South African author **23** 372-373

SMITH, RED (Walter Wellesley Smith, 1905-1982), American sportswriter **30** 334-337

SMITH, ROBERT HOLBROOK (1879-1950), American physician **30** 337-339
W., Bill **30** 372-374

Smith, Robert Barnwell
see Rhett, Robert Barnwell

Smith, Walter Bedell
see Bedell Smith, Walter

SMITH, WILLIAM (1727-1803), American educator and churchman **14** 301

SMITH, WILLIAM EUGENE (1918-1978), American photojournalist **19** 348-350

SMITH COURT, MARGARET JEAN (born 1942), Australian tennis player **24** 376-378

SMITHSON, ROBERT (1938-1973), American sculptor, essayist, and filmmaker **14** 301-303

Smithsonian Institution (Washington, D.C.)
Knight, Charles R. **30** 242-244

SMOHALLA (1815-1895), Native American warrior, medicine man, and spiritual leader **14** 303-305

SMOLLETT, TOBIAS GEORGE (1721-1771), English novelist and satirist **14** 305-307

SMUIN, MICHAEL (1938-2007), American dancer-choreographer-director **14** 307-309

STOUT, JUANITA KIDD (1919-1998), African American judge 23 382-384

STOVALL, LUTHER MCKINLEY (born 1937), American silkscreen artist 14 483-484

STOWE, HARRIET ELIZABETH BEECHER (1811-1896), American writer 14 484-485

STRABO (c. 64 B.C.-c. A.D. 23), Greek geographer and historian 14 485-486

STRACHAN, JOHN (1778-1867), Canadian Anglican bishop 14 486-487

STRACHEY, GILES LYTTON (1880-1932), English biographer and critic known for his satire of the Victorian era 14 487-488

STRACHEY, JOHN (Evelyn John St. Loe Strachey; 1901-1963), British author and politician 20 352-354

STRADIVARI, ANTONIO (c. 1644-1737), Italian violin maker 14 488-490

STRAFFORD, 1ST EARL OF (Thomas Wentworth; 1593-1641), English statesman 14 490-491
Ogilby, John 30 291-293

STRAND, MARK (born 1934), fourth Poet Laureate of the United States 14 491-493

STRAND, PAUL (1890-1976), American photographer 19 369-371

STRANG, RUTH MAY (1895-1971), American educator 14 493-494

STRASBERG, LEE (Israel Strasberg; 1901-82), American acting instructor, director, and founding member of the Group Theatre 14 494-495

Strathcona and Mount Royal, 1st Baron
see Smith, Donald Alexander

STRAUS, ISIDOR (1845-1912), American merchant 14 496

STRAUSS, DAVID FRIEDRICH (1808-1874), German historian and Protestant theologian 14 496-497

STRAUSS, FRANZ JOSEF (1915-1988), West German politician 14 497-498

STRAUSS, JOHANN, JR. (1825-1899), Austrian composer 14 498-499

STRAUSS, LEO (1899-1973), German Jewish Socratic political philosopher 14 499-500

STRAUSS, LEVI (Loeb Strauss; 1829-1902), American businessman 20 354-356

STRAUSS, RICHARD (1864-1949), German composer and conductor 14 500-501

STRAUSS, ROBERT SCHWARZ (born 1918), Democratic fundraiser and strategist 14 501-502

STRAVINSKY, IGOR FEDOROVICH (1882-1971), Russian-born composer 14 502-506
contemporaries
Ansermet, Ernest 30 9-11

STRAWSON, SIR PETER FREDRICK (1919-2006), English philosopher 14 506-507

STREEP, MERYL LOUISE (born 1949), American actress 23 384-387

STREETON, SIR ARTHUR ERNEST (1867-1943), Australian landscape painter 14 507-508

STREISAND, BARBRA (Barbara Joan Streisand; born 1942), American entertainer 18 386-388

STRESEMANN, GUSTAV (1878-1929), German statesman and diplomat 14 508-509

Strickland, Susanna
see Moodie, Susanna

STRINDBERG, AUGUST (1849-1912), Swedish author 14 509-511

STRINGER, HOWARD (born 1942), Welsh-American businessman 28 338-340

STROESSNER, ALFREDO (1912-2006), Paraguayan statesman 14 511-512

STRONG, JOSIAH (1847-1916), American clergyman and social activist 14 512-513

STROZZI, BARBARA (Barbara Valle; 1619-1677), Italian composer and singer 26 350-351

STRUSS, KARL (1886-1981), American photographer and cinematographer 21 398-399

Strutt, John William
see Rayleigh, 3d Baron

STRUVE, FRIEDRICH GEORG WILHELM VON (1793-1864), German-born Russian astronomer and geodesist 14 513

Stuart, Athenian
see Stuart, James

Stuart, Charles
see Charles I and II (king of England)

Stuart, Charles Edward Louis Philip Casimir
see Charles Edward Louis Philip Casimir Stuart

STUART, GILBERT (1755-1828), American painter 14 513-515

Stuart, House of
see Great Britain–1603-1714; Scotland

STUART, JAMES (1713-1788), English architect, artist, and archeologist 30 350-352

STUART, JAMES EWELL BROWN (Jeb; 1833-64), Confederate cavalry officer 14 515-516

Stuart, John
see Bute, 3d Earl of; Cugoano, Ottobah

Stuart Restoration
see Restoration, The (England; 1660)

STUDENT, KURT (1890-1978), German general 20 356-358

STUDI, WES (born Wesley Studie; born c. 1944), Native American actor 15 1-2

STUHLINGER, ERNST (1913-2008), German rocket scientist 29 349-351

STURGES, PRESTON (Edmund Preston Biden; 1898-1959), American playwright, screenwriter, director, and businessman 19 371-374

STURLUSON, SNORRI (1179-1241), Icelandic statesman and historian 14 310-311

STURT, CHARLES (1795-1869), British officer, explorer, and colonial administrator 15 2-3

STURTEVANT, A. H. (Alfred Henry Sturtevan t; 1891-1970), American geneticist 15 3-5

STUYVESANT, PETER (c. 1610-72), Dutch colonial administrator 15 5-6

STYRON, WILLIAM (1925-2006), American southern writer of novels and articles 15 6-8

SUÁREZ, FRANCISCO (1548-1617), Spanish philosopher and theologian 15 8

Suárez de Figueroa, Gòmez
see Garcilaso de la Vega, Inca

SUAZO CÓRDOVA, ROBERTO (born 1927), physician and president of Honduras (1982-1986) 15 8-10

SUCKLING, SIR JOHN (1609-1642), English poet and playwright 15 10-11

SUCRE, ANTONIO JOSÉ DE (1795-1830), Venezuelan general, Bolivian president 1826-28 15 11-12

SUDERMANN, HERMANN (1857-1928), German dramatist and novelist 15 12-13

SUETONIUS TRANQUILLUS, GAIUS (c. 70-c. 135), Roman administrator and writer 15 13

Sugar
scientific research
Bergius, Friedrich Karl Rudolph 30 51-53

SUHARTO (1921-2008), second president after Indonesia's independence 15 14-15

SUI WEN-TI (541-604), Chinese emperor 15 16-18

WAJDA, ANDRZEJ (Andrzej Wajda; born 1926), Polish film director and screenwriter **25** 432-434

WAKEFIELD, EDWARD GIBBON (1796-1862), British colonial reformer and promoter **16** 48-49

WAKSMAN, SELMAN ABRAHAM (1888-1973), American microbiologist **16** 49-50

WALCOTT, DEREK ALTON (born 1930), West Indian poet and dramatist **16** 50-51

WALCOTT, MARY VAUX (Mary Morris Vaux; 1860-1940), American artist and naturalist **25** 434-437

WALD, FLORENCE S. (Florence Sophie Schorske; born 1917), American founder of the hospice movement **24** 436-437

WALD, GEORGE (born 1906), American biochemist interested in vision **16** 51-53

WALD, LILLIAN (1867-1940), American social worker and reformer **16** 53-54

WALDEMAR IV (Wlademar Atterdag; 1320-1375), King of Denmark, 1340-1375 **20** 395-397

WALDHEIM, KURT (1918-2007), Austrian statesman and president **16** 54-55

WALDO, PETER (flourished 1170-84), French religious leader **16** 55-56

WALDSEEMÜLLER, MARTIN (c. 1470-c. 1518), German geographer and cartographer **16** 56

WALESA, LECH (born 1943), Polish Solidarity leader and former president **16** 57-59

Walken, Christopher, (born 1943), American actor
Wood, Natalie **30** 383-385

WALKER, ALICE MALSENIOR (born 1944), African American novelist, poet, and short story writer **16** 59-61

WALKER, MADAME C. J. (Sarah Breedlove; 1867-1919), African American entrepreneur **16** 61-62

WALKER, DAVID (1785-1830), African American pamphleteer and activist **16** 62-63

WALKER, JOSEPH REDDEFORD (1798-1876), American fur trader **16** 63-64

WALKER, LEROY TASHREAU (born 1918), U.S. sports official, university chancellor, educator, and track coach **16** 64-65

WALKER, MAGGIE LENA (1867-1934), American entrepreneur and civic leader **16** 65-66

WALKER, MARGARET (born 1915), American novelist, poet, scholar, and teacher **16** 67

WALKER, MARY EDWARDS (1832-1919), American physician and feminist **23** 432-434

WALKER, ROBERT JOHN (1801-1869), American politician **16** 67-68

WALKER, WILLIAM (1824-1860), American adventurer and filibuster **16** 68-69

WALL, JEFF (born 1946), Canadian photographer and artist **23** 434-436

WALLACE, ALFRED RUSSEL (1823-1913), English naturalist and traveler **16** 69-70

WALLACE, DEWITT (1889-1981), American publisher and founder of *Reader's Digest* **16** 70-71

WALLACE, GEORGE CORLEY (1919-1998), American political leader **16** 71-72

WALLACE, HENRY (1836-1916), American agricultural publicist and editor **16** 73

WALLACE, HENRY AGARD (1888-1965), American statesman, vice-president 1940-44 **16** 73-74

WALLACE, LEWIS (1827-1905), American general and author **16** 74-75

WALLACE, LURLEEN BURNS (1926-1968), American governor of Alabama **29** 370-372

WALLACE, SIPPIE (Beulah Belle Thomas; 1898-1986), African American singer **24** 437-440

WALLACE, SIR WILLIAM (c. 1270-1305), Scottish soldier **16** 75-76

WALLACE-JOHNSON, ISAAC THEOPHILUS AKUNNA (1895-1965), West African political leader and pan-Africanist **16** 76-77

Wallach, Meyer
see Litvinov, Maxim Maximovich

WALLAS, GRAHAM (1858-1932), English sociologist and political scientist **16** 77-78

WALLENBERG, RAOUL (1912-c. 1947), Swedish diplomat **16** 78-80

WALLENSTEIN, ALBRECHT WENZEL EUSEBIUS VON (1583-1634), Bohemian soldier of fortune **16** 80-81

WALLER, THOMAS WRIGHT (Fats; 1904-43), American jazz singer, pianist, organist, bandleader, and composer **16** 81-82

WALPOLE, ROBERT (1st Earl of Oxford; 1676-1745), English statesman **16** 82-84

WALRAS, MARIE ESPRIT LÉON (1834-1910), French economist **16** 84-85

WALSH, BILL (William Ernest Walsh; American football coach), 1931-2007 **28** 370-372

WALSH, STELLA (Stanislawa Walasiewiczowna; 1911-1980), Polish American athlete **19** 404-406

WALSH, THOMAS JAMES (1859-1933), American statesman **16** 85-86

WALSINGHAM, SIR FRANCIS (c. 1532-1590), Secretary of State to Elizabeth I **30** 374-376

WALTER, JOHANN (1496-1570), German composer **16** 86

WALTERS, BARBARA (born 1931), American network newscast anchor **16** 86-88

WALTON, ERNEST (1903-1995), Irish physicist **16** 88-90

WALTON, IZAAK (1593-1683), English writer and biographer **16** 90-91

WALTON, SAM MOORE (1918-1992), American businessman who co-founded Wal-Mart **16** 91-92

WALTON, SIR WILLIAM TURNER (1902-1983), English composer **16** 91-92

WANAMAKER, JOHN (1838-1922), American merchant **29** 372-375

WANG, AN (1920-1990), Chinese-American inventor, electronics expert, and businessman **16** 93-95

WANG AN-SHIH (1021-1086), Chinese reformer, poet, and scholar **16** 95-97

WANG CHING-WEI (1883-1944), Chinese revolutionary leader **16** 98

WANG CH'UNG (27-c. 100), Chinese philosopher **16** 98-99

WANG FU-CHIH (1619-1692), Chinese philosopher **16** 99-101

WANG GUANGMEI (1921-2006), Chinese first lady **27** 357-358

WANG KON (877-943), Korean king **16** 101

WANG MANG (45 B.C.-A.D. 23), Chinese statesman, emperor 9-23 **16** 101-103

WANG MING (Chen Shaoyu; 1904-74), leader of the "Internationalist" group within the Chinese Communist Party **16** 103-104

WANG PI (226-249), Chinese philosopher **16** 104-105

WANG T'AO (1828-1897), Chinese reformer and scholar **16** 105-106

WIDNALL, SHEILA E. (born 1938), American aeronautical engineer **16** 258-259

WIELAND, CHRISTOPH MARTIN (1733-1813), German poet and author **16** 260-261

WIEMAN, HENRY NELSON (1884-1975), American philosopher and theologian **16** 261-262

WIENER, NORBERT (1894-1964), American mathematician **16** 262-263

WIESEL, ELIE (born 1928), writer, orator, teacher, and chairman of the United States Holocaust Memorial Council **16** 263-264

WIESENTHAL, SIMON (1908-2005), Ukrainian Jew who tracked down Nazi war criminals **16** 264-266

WIGGLESWORTH, MICHAEL (1631-1705), American Puritan poet and minister **16** 266-267

WIGMAN, MARY (Marie Wiegmann; 1886-1973), German dancer, choreographer, and teacher **16** 267-268

WIGNER, EUGENE PAUL (1902-1995), Hungarian-born American physicist **16** 268-269

Wilberforce College
Brown, Hallie Quinn **30** 83-85

WILBERFORCE, WILLIAM (1759-1833), English statesman and humanitarian **16** 269-270

WILBUR, RICHARD PURDY (born 1921), translator and poet laureate of the United States (1987-1988) **16** 271-272

WILCZEK, FRANK ANTHONY (born 1951), American theoretical physicist **30** 378-380

Wild West shows
Bailey, James A. **30** 26-28

WILDE, OSCAR FINGALL O'FLAHERTIE WILLS (1854-1900), British author **16** 272-273

WILDER, AMOS NIVEN (1895-1993), American New Testament scholar, poet, minister, and literary critic **16** 273-274

WILDER, BILLY (Samuel Wilder; 1906-2002), American film director, screenwriter, and producer **21** 430-432

WILDER, LAURA INGALLS (1867-1957), American author and pioneer **18** 413-414

WILDER, LAWRENCE DOUGLAS (born 1931), first African American elected governor in the United States **16** 274-276

WILDER, THORNTON NIVEN (1897-1975), American novelist and playwright **16** 276-277

WILES, ANDREW J. (born 1953), English mathematician **23** 442-444
Piatetski-Shapiro, Ilya **30** 303-304

WILEY, HARVEY WASHINGTON (1844-1930), American chemist **16** 277-278

Wilhelm II
see William II (emperor of Germany)

WILHELMINA (1880-1962), queen of the Netherlands 1890-1948 **16** 278-279

WILKES, CHARLES (1798-1877), American naval officer **16** 279-280

WILKES, JOHN (1727-1797), English politician **16** 280-281

WILKINS, SIR GEORGE HUBERT (1888-1958), Australian explorer, scientist, and adventurer **16** 281-282

WILKINS, MAURICE HUGH FREDERICK (1916-2005), English biophysicist **18** 415-416

WILKINS, ROY (1901-1981), African American civil rights leader **16** 282-283

WILKINSON, ELLEN (1891-1947), British Labour politician and crusader for the unemployed **16** 283-284

WILKINSON, JAMES (1757-1825), American army general and frontier adventurer **16** 284-286

WILL, GEORGE FREDERICK (born 1941), syndicated columnist and television commentator **16** 286-287

WILLAERT, ADRIAN (c. 1480-1562), Franco-Flemish composer active in Italy **16** 287-288

WILLARD, EMMA HART (1787-1870), American educator and author **16** 288-289

WILLARD, FRANCES ELIZABETH CAROLINE (1839-1898), American temperance and women's suffrage leader **16** 289-290

William (duke of Normandy)
see William I (king of England)

William I (prince of Orange)
see William the Silent

WILLIAM I (the Conqueror; 1027/ 28-1087), king of England 1066-1087 **16** 290-291

WILLIAM I (1772-1843), king of the Netherlands 1815-40 **16** 291-292

WILLIAM I (1797-1888), emperor of Germany 1871-88 and king of Prussia 1861-88 **16** 292-293

WILLIAM II (William Rufus; c. 1058-1100), king of England 1087-1100 **16** 293-294

WILLIAM II (1859-1941), emperor of Germany and king of Prussia 1888-1918 **16** 294-295

William III (prince of Orange)
see William III (king of England)

WILLIAM III (1650-1702), king of England, Scotland, and Ireland 1689-1702 **16** 295-296

WILLIAM IV (1765-1837), king of Great Britain and Ireland 1830-37 **16** 296-297

WILLIAM OF MALMESBURY (c. 1090-c. 1142), English historian **16** 297-298

WILLIAM OF OCKHAM (c. 1284-1347), English philosopher and theologian **16** 298-299

WILLIAM OF SENS (Guillaume de Sens; died 1180), French architect **21** 432-434

WILLIAM OF TYRE (c. 1130-84/85), French archbishop, chancellor of the Latin Kingdom of Jerusalem **16** 299-300

William the Conqueror
see William I (king of England)

WILLIAM THE SILENT (1533-1584), prince of Orange and stadholder of the Netherlands **16** 300-302

WILLIAMS, BERT (Egbert Austin Williams; 1874-1922), African American comedian and songwriter **27** 368-370

Williams, Betty
see CORRIGAN and WILLIAMS

WILLIAMS, DANIEL HALE (1856-1931), African American surgical pioneer **16** 302-303

WILLIAMS, EDWARD BENNETT (1920-1988), American lawyer and sports club owner **22** 422-424

WILLIAMS, ESTHER (born 1922), American swimmer and actress **30** 380-383

WILLIAMS, HANK (Hiram King Williams; 1923-1953), American singer and songwriter **20** 402-404

WILLIAMS, HENRY SYLVESTER (1869-1911), Trinidadian lawyer and pan-African leader **16** 303-304

WILLIAMS, JODY (born 1950), American political activist **25** 441-443

WILLIAMS, JOE (Joseph Goreed; 1918-1999), American singer **20** 404-407

WILLIAMS, MARY LOU (Mary Lou Burley; Mary Elfrieda Scruggs; Mary Elfreda Winn; 1910-1981), African American musician **23** 444-446

Williams, Ralph Vaughan
see Vaughan Williams, Ralph